Psychology

ELEVENTH EDITION

Psychology
MODULES FOR ACTIVE LEARNING

DENNIS COON

JOHN O. MITTERER
Brock University

THOMSON
WADSWORTH

Australia • Brazil • Canada • Mexico • Singapore • Spain
United Kingdom • United States

Psychology: Modules for Active Learning, Eleventh Edition
Dennis Coon / John O. Mitterer

Psychology Editor: Jaime Perkins
Development Editor: Jeremy Judson
Assistant Editor: Magnolia Molcan
Editorial Assistant: Wilson Co
Technology Project Manager: Bessie Weiss
Marketing Manager: Sara Swangard
Marketing Assistant: Melanie Cregger
Marketing Communications Manager: Linda Yip
Project Manager, Editorial Production: Jerilyn Emori
Creative Director: Rob Hugel

Art Director: Vernon Boes
Print Buyer: Karen Hunt
Permissions Editor: Bob Kauser
Production Service: Carol O'Connell, Graphic World Inc.
Text Designer: Diane Beasley
Photo Researcher: Kathleen Olson
Cover Designer: Larry Didona
Cover Image: ©Panoramic Images/Getty Images
Compositor: Graphic World Inc.

© 2009, 2006 Thomson Wadsworth, a part of The Thomson Corporation. Thomson, the Star logo, and Wadsworth are trademarks used herein under license.

ALL RIGHTS RESERVED. No part of this work covered by the copyright hereon may be reproduced or used in any form or by any means—graphic, electronic, or mechanical, including photocopying, recording, taping, Web distribution, information storage and retrieval systems, or in any other manner—without the written permission of the publisher.

Printed in the United States of America
1 2 3 4 5 6 7 11 10 09 08 07

For more information about our products, contact us at:
Thomson Learning Academic Resource Center
1-800-423-0563
For permission to use material from this text or product, submit a request online at **http://www.thomsonrights.com**.
Any additional questions about permissions can be submitted by e-mail to **thomsonrights@thomson.com**.

© 2009 Thomson Learning, Inc. All Rights Reserved. Thomson Learning WebTutor™ is a trademark of Thomson Learning, Inc.

Thomson Higher Education
10 Davis Drive
Belmont, CA 94002-3098
USA

Library of Congress Control Number: 2007933445
Student Edition:
ISBN-13: 978-0-495-55338-0
ISBN-10: 0-495-55338-7
Cloth Edition:
ISBN-13: 978-0-495-50496-2
ISBN-10: 0-495-50496-3
Loose-leaf Edition:
ISBN-13: 978-0-495-50453-5
ISBN-10: 0-495-50453-X

*This edition is dedicated to
our students, who are our future.*

Brief Contents

INTRODUCTION The Psychology of Studying 1

1. Introducing Psychology and Research Methods 12
2. Brain and Behavior 56
3. Human Development 96
4. Sensation and Perception 148
5. States of Consciousness 202
6. Conditioning and Learning 246
7. Memory 286
8. Intelligence, Cognition, Language, and Creativity 326
9. Motivation and Emotion 370
10. Personality 412
11. Health, Stress, and Coping 456
12. Psychological Disorders 496
13. Therapies 540
14. Gender and Sexuality 582
15. Social Behavior 620
16. Applied Psychology 668

APPENDIX Behavioral Statistics 708

Contents

Introduction   The Psychology of Studying   1

The SQ4R Method—How To Tame a Textbook   1
   How to Use Psychology: Modules for Active Learning   2
The LISAN Method—How To Tame a Lecture   3
   Using and Reviewing Your Notes   4
Study Strategies—Making a Habit of Success   4
Self-Regulated Learning—Academic All-Stars   5
Procrastination—Avoiding the Last-Minute Blues   6
   Time Management   6
   Goal Setting   6
   Make Learning an Adventure   7

Taking Tests—Are You "Test Wise"?   7
   General Test-Taking Skills   7
Using Digital Media—Netting New Knowledge   8
   Digital Journeys   8
   The Book Companion Website   8
   ThomsonNOW   9
   Psych Sites   9
Knowledge Builder   10
   A Final Word   11

1   Introducing Psychology and Research Methods   12

MODULE 1.1 The Sciency of Psychology   14
Psychology—Spotlight on Behavior   14
   Defining Psychology   14
   Empiricism   14
Critical Thinking *Testing Commonsense Beliefs*   15
   Psychological Research   15
   Psychology's Goals   17
Module 1.1: Summary   18
Knowledge Builder   19

MODULE 1.2 Critical Thinking and the Scientific Method in Psychology   20
Critical Thinking—Take It With a Grain of Salt   20
   Thinking about Behavior   20
Pseudopsychologies—Palms, Planets, and Personality   21
   Problems in the Stars   22
Scientific Research—How to Think Like a Psychologist   23
   The Scientific Method   23
Module 1.2: Summary   26
Knowledge Builder   26

MODULE 1.3 History and Contemporary Perspectives   20
A Brief History of Psychology—Psychology's Family Album   27
   Structuralism   27
   Functionalism   27

   Behaviorism   28
   Gestalt Psychology   29
   Psychoanalytic Psychology   30
   Humanistic Psychology   30
   The Role of Women in Psychology's Early Days   31
Psychology Today—Three Complementary Perspectives on Behavior   32
   The Biological Perspective   32
   The Psychological Perspective   33
   The Sociocultural Perspective   33
Module 1.3: Summary   34
Knowledge Builder   35

MODULE 1.4 Psychologists and Their Specialties   36
Psychologists—Guaranteed Not to Shrink   36
   Other Mental Health Professionals   36
Discovering Psychology *Is a Career in Psychology Right for You?*   38
   The Profession of Psychology   38
   Specialties in Psychology   38
Module 1.4: Summary   39
Knowledge Builder   40

MODULE 1.5 The Psychology Experiment   41
The Psychology Experiment—Where Effect Meets Cause   41
   Variables and Groups   41

viii CONTENTS

Placebo Effects, Sugar Pills, and Saltwater 42
Critical Thinking *That's Interesting, But Is It Ethical?* 43
  The Experimenter Effect 44
Module 1.5: Summary 44
Knowledge Builder 45

MODULE 1.6 Nonexperimental Research Methods 46
Psychological Research—Different Strokes 46
Naturalistic Observation—Psychology Steps Out! 46
  Limitations 46
  Recording Observations 47
Correlational Studies—In Search of the Perfect Relationship 47
  Correlation Coefficients 47

The Clinical Method—Data by the Case 48
Survey Method—Here, Have a Sample 49
Module 1.6: Summary 51
Knowledge Builder 52

MODULE 1.7 Psychology in Action: Psychology in the Media 53
Psychology in the Media—Separating Fact from Fiction 53
Knowledge Builder 55
Module 1.7: Psychology in Action Summary 55
Interactive Learning 55

2 Brain and Behavior 56

MODULE 2.1 Neurons and the Nervous System 58
Neurons—Building a "Biocomputer" 58
  Parts of a Neuron 58
  The Nerve Impulse 59
  Synapses and Neurotransmitters 60
Discovering Psychology *Dollars, Drag Racing, and the Nervous System* 61
  Neural Networks 62
The Nervous System—Wired for Action 63
  Neurons and Nerves 63
  Subparts of the Nervous System 64
Module 2.1: Summary 66
Knowledge Builder 67

MODULE 2.2 Brain Research 68
Mapping Brain Structure—Parts of the Puzzle 68
  CT Scan 68
  MRI Scan 68
Mapping Brain Function—Figuring Out What the Parts Do 68
  EEG 69
  PET Scan 70
  fMRI 70
Module 2.2: Summary 71
Knowledge Builder 72

MODULE 2.2 Hemispheres and Lobes of the Cerebral Cortex 73
The Cerebral Cortex—My, What a Big Brain You Have! 73
  Cerebral Hemispheres 73
  Hemispheric Specialization 74

The Clinical File *A Stroke of Bad Luck* 75
  Lobes of the Cerebral Cortex 76
Human Diversity *His and Her Brains?* 79
Module 2.3: Summary 80
Knowledge Builder 81

MODULE 2.4 Subcortex and Endocrine System 82
The Subcortex—At the Core of the (Brain) Matter 82
  The Hindbrain 82
  The Forebrain 83
  The Magnificent Brain 84
Critical Thinking *If You Change Your Mind, Do You Change Your Brain?* 85
The Endocrine System—My Hormones Made Me Do It 85
Module 2.4: Summary 88
Knowledge Builder 89

MODULE 2.5 Psychology in Action: Handedness—Are You Dexterous or Sinister? 90
Are You Right- or Left-Handed? 90
Module 2.5: Psychology in Action Summary 93
Knowledge Builder 94
Interactive Learning 94

3 Human Development 96

MODULE 3.1 The Interplay of Heredity and Environment 98
Nature and Nurture—It Takes Two to Tango 98
   Heredity 98
   Environment 99
   Deprivation and Enrichment 102
   Reaction Range 102
Module 3.1: Summary 103
Knowledge Builder 104

MODULE 3.2 The Neonate and Early Maturation 105
The Newborn—Baby, You're So Smart 105
   The World of the Neonate 105
Early Maturation—Grow Baby Grow 107
   Motor Development 107
   Emotional Development 108
Module 3.2: Summary 109
Knowledge Builder 110

MODULE 3.3 Social Development in Childhood 111
Social Development—Baby, I'm Stuck on You 111
   Attachment 111
   Day Care 112
   Attachment and Affectional Needs 112
Discovering Psychology *What's Your Attachment Style?* 113
Parental Influences—Life with Mom and Dad 113
   Parenting Styles 113
   Maternal and Paternal Influences 114
   Ethnic Differences: Four Flavors of Parenting 115
Module 3.3: Summary 116
Knowledge Builder 117

MODULE 3.4 Language Development in Childhood 118
Language Development—Fast-Talking Babies 118
   Language and the Terrible Twos 118
   The Roots of Language 118
Module 3.4: Summary 120
Knowledge Builder 121

MODULE 3.5 Cognitive Development in Childhood 122
Cognitive Development—How Do Children Learn to Think? 122
   Piaget's Theory of Cognitive Development 122
   Piaget Today 124
   Vygotsky's Sociocultural Theory 126

Module 3.5: Summary 127
Knowledge Builder 128

MODULE 3.6 Adolescence, Young Adulthood, and Moral Development 129
Adolescence and Young Adulthood—The Best of Times, the Worst of Times 129
   Puberty 129
   The Search for Identity 129
Human Diversity *Ethnic Diversity and Identity* 130
   The Transition to Adulthood 130
Critical Thinking *The Twixters* 131
Moral Development—Growing a Conscience 131
   Levels of Moral Development 132
Module 3.6: Summary 133
Knowledge Builder 134

MODULE 3.7 Challenges Across the Lifespan 135
The Story of a Lifetime—Rocky Road or Garden Path? 135
   Erikson's Psychosocial Theory 135
Later Adulthood: Will You Still Need Me When I'm 64? 137
   A Midlife Crisis? 137
   Old Age 138
Death and Dying—The Final Challenge 139
   Reactions to Impending Death 140
Module 3.7: Summary 141
Knowledge Builder 142

MODULE 3.8 Psychology in Action: Effective Parenting—Raising Healthy Children 143
   Effective Discipline 143
   Communicating Effectively with Children 145
Module 3.8: Psychology in Action Summary 146
Knowledge Builder 146
Interactive Learning 147

4 Sensation and Perception 148

MODULE 4.1 Sensory Systems and Selective Attention 150
A World of Sensation—Too Much of a Good Thing? 150
- *Selection* 150
- *Sensory Adaptation* 150
- *Analysis* 150
- *Sensory Coding* 151

Selective Attention—Tuning In and Tuning Out 152
Module 4.1: Summary 153
Knowledge Builder 154

MODULE 4.2 Vision 155
Vision—Catching Some Rays 155
- *Structure of the Eye* 155
- *Rods and Cones* 156
- *Color Vision* 157
- *Adapting to Dim Light* 159

Discovering Psychology *Are You Color-Blind?* 160
Module 4.2: Summary 161
Knowledge Builder 162

MODULE 4.3 Hearing, the Chemical Senses, and the Somesthetic Senses 163
Hearing—Good Vibrations 163
- *How We Hear Sounds* 163

The Chemical Senses—The Nose Knows When the Tongue Can't Tell 166
- *The Sense of Smell* 166
- *Taste and Flavors* 167

The Somesthetic Senses—Flying by the Seat of Your Pants 168
- *The Skin Senses* 168
- *Pain* 168

Brainwaves *The Matrix: Do Phantoms Live Here?* 170
- *The Vestibular System* 171

Module 4.3: Summary 171
Knowledge Builder 172

MODULE 4.4 Perceptual Constancies and Perceptual Grouping 173
Perceptual Constancies—Taming an Unruly World 173
Perceptual Organization—Getting It All Together 174
Module 4.4: Summary 177
Knowledge Builder 178

MODULE 4.5 Depth Perception 179
Depth Perception—What If the World Were Flat? 179
- *Binocular Depth Cues* 180
- *Monocular Depth Cues* 181

Module 4.5: Summary 184
Knowledge Builder 185

MODULE 4.6 Perception and Objectivity 186
Perception and Objectivity—Believing Is Seeing 186
- *Perceptual Expectancies* 186

Critical Thinking *The Boiled Frog Syndrome* 187
- *Motives, Emotions, and Perception* 188
- *Perceptual Learning* 188

The Clinical File *Staying in Touch with Reality* 191
Module 4.6: Summary 192
Knowledge Builder 193

MODULE 4.7 Extrasensory Perception 194
Extrasensory Perception—Do You Believe in Magic? 194
- *An Appraisal of ESP* 194
- *Stage ESP* 196

Module 4.7: Summary 197
Knowledge Builder 197

MODULE 4.8 Psychology in Action: Becoming a Better Eyewitness to Life 198
Positive Psychology: Perceptual Awareness 198
How to Become a Better "Eyewitness" to Life 200
Module 4.8: Psychology in Action Summary 200
Knowledge Builder 201
Interactive Learning 201

5 States of Consciousness 202

MODULE 5.1 Altered States and Sleep 204
States of Consciousness—The Many Faces of Awareness 204
- *Altered States of Consciousness* 204

Sleep—A Nice Place to Visit 204
Critical Thinking *What Is It Like to Be a Bat?* 205
- *The Need for Sleep* 205

Human Diversity *Consciousness and Culture* 206
- *Sleep Patterns* 206

The Clinical File *Teenage Sleep Zombies* 207
Stages of Sleep—The Nightly Roller-Coaster Ride 208
- *Stages of Sleep* 209
- *Two Basic Kinds of Sleep* 209

Critical Thinking *Abducted by Space Aliens?* 210

Module 5.1: Summary 211
Knowledge Builder 212

MODULE 5.2 Sleep Disturbances and Dreaming 213
Sleep Disturbances—Showing Nightly: Sleep Wars! 213
   Insomnia 213
   Sleepwalking, Sleeptalking, and Sleepsex 214
   Nightmares and Night Terrors 215
   Narcolepsy 215
   Sleep Apnea 215
Dreams—A Separate Reality? 216
   REM Sleep Revisited 216
   Dream Worlds 216
   Dream Theories 217
Module 5.2: Summary 218
Knowledge Builder 219

MODULE 5.3 Hypnosis, Meditation, and Sensory Deprivation 220
Hypnosis—Look into My Eyes 220
   Theories of Hypnosis 220
   Stage Hypnosis 220
Discovering Psychology *Swinging Suggestions* 221
   The Reality of Hypnosis 222
Meditation—Chilling, the Healthy Way 223
   Meditation 223
   Sensory Deprivation 224
   Positive Psychology: Mindfulness and Well-Being 225
Module 5.3: Summary 225
Knowledge Builder 226

MODULE 5.4 Psychoactive Drugs 227
Drug-Altered Consciousness—The High and Low of It 227
   Dependence 227
Brainwaves *How Addictive Drugs Affect the Brain* 230
Uppers—Amphetamines, Cocaine, MDMA, Caffeine, Nicotine 230
   Amphetamines 230
   Cocaine 231
   MDMA ("Ecstasy") 232
   Caffeine 232
   Nicotine 233
Downers—Sedatives, Tranquilizers, and Alcohol 234
   Barbiturates 234
   GHB 234
   Tranquilizers 235
   Alcohol 235
Hallucinogens—Tripping the Light Fantastic 238
   LSD and PCP 238
   Marijuana 238
   Summary 239
   A Look Ahead 240
Module 5.4: Summary 240
Knowledge Builder 241

MODULE 5.5 Psychology in Action: Exploring and Using Dreams 242
   Dream Work 242
   Using Your Dreams 243
   Dreams and Creativity 244
Knowledge Builder 245
Module 5.5: Psychology in Action Summary 245
Interactive Learning 245

6 Conditioning and Learning 246

MODULE 6.1 Learning and Classical Conditioning 248
What Is Learning—Does Practice Make Perfect? 248
   Classical Conditioning 248
   Operant Conditioning 248
Classical Conditioning—Does the Name Pavlov Ring a Bell? 249
   Pavlov's Experiment 249
Principles of Classical Conditioning—The Boy and the Bell 250
   Acquisition 250
The Clinical File *Coping with Chemo* 251
   Expectancies 251
   Extinction and Spontaneous Recovery 252
   Generalization 252
   Discrimination 252
Classical Conditioning in Humans—An Emotional Topic 253
   Conditioned Emotional Responses 253
   Vicarious, or Secondhand, Conditioning 253
Module 6.1: Summary 254
Knowledge Builder 255

MODULE 6.2 Operant Conditioning 256
Operant Conditioning—Can Pigeons Play Ping-Pong? 256
   Positive Reinforcement 256
   Acquiring an Operant Response 257

The Timing of Reinforcement 258
Shaping 258
Operant Extinction 259
Negative Reinforcement 259
Punishment 260
Operant Reinforcers—What's Your Pleasure? 260
Primary Reinforcers 260
Secondary Reinforcers 260
Brainwaves *Tickling Your Own Fancy* 261
Feedback 262
Discovering Psychology *Conditioning and Conservation* 263
Learning Aids 263
Module 6.2: Summary 264
Knowledge Builder 265

MODULE 6.3 Partial Reinforcement and Stimulus Control 266
Partial Reinforcement—Las Vegas, a Human Skinner Box? 266
Schedules of Partial Reinforcement 266
Critical Thinking *Are Animals Stuck in Time?* 268
Stimulus Control—Red Light, Green Light 268
Module 6.3: Summary 270
Knowledge Builder 271

MODULE 6.4 Punishment 272
Punishment—Putting the Brakes on Behavior 272
Variables Affecting Punishment 272
Side Effects of Punishment 273
Using Punishment Wisely 273
Module 6.4: Summary 275
Knowledge Builder 275

MODULE 6.5 Cognitive Learning and Imitation 276
Cognitive Learning—Beyond Conditioning 276
Cognitive Maps 276
Latent Learning 276
Modeling—Do as I Do, Not as I Say 278
Observational Learning 278
Modeling and the Media 279
Critical Thinking *You Mean Video Games Might Be Bad for Me?* 280
Module 6.5: Summary 280
Knowledge Builder 281

MODULE 6.6 Psychology in Action: Behavioral Self-Management—A Rewarding Project 282
Self-Managed Behavior 282
Self-Recording 283
Good Ways to Break Bad Habits 283
Alternate Responses 283
Extinction 283
Response Chains 283
Cues and Antecedents 283
Contracting 283
Getting Help 284
Where to Obtain More Information 284
Module 6.6: Psychology in Action Summary 284
Knowledge Builder 285
Interactive Learning 285

7 Memory 286

MODULE 7.1 Memory Systems 288
Stages of Memory—Do You Have a Mind Like a Steel Trap? or a Sieve? 288
Sensory Memory 288
Short-Term Memory 288
Long-Term Memory 289
Human Diversity *Cows, Memories, and Culture* 290
Module 7.1: Summary 290
Knowledge Builder 291

MODULE 7.2 STM and LTM 292
Short-Term Memory—Do You Know the Magic Number? 292
Chunking 292
Rehearsing Information 292
Long-Term Memory—Where the Past Lives 293
Constructing Memories 293
Critical Thinking *Do You Like Jam With Your Memory?* 294
Critical Thinking *Telling Wrong from Right in Forensic Memory* 295
Organizing Memories 296
Skill Memory and Fact Memory 297
Module 7.2: Summary 298
Knowledge Builder 299

MODULE 7.3 Measuring Memory 300
Measuring Memory—The Answer Is on the Tip of My Tongue 300
Recalling Information 300
Recognizing Information 300
Relearning Information 301
Implicit and Explicit Memories 302
Module 7.3: Summary 302
Knowledge Builder 303

MODULE 7.4 Forgetting 304
Forgetting—Why We, Uh, Let's See; Why We, Uh . . . Forget! 304
    When Encoding Fails 304
Discovering Psychology *Card Magic!* 305
    Memory Decay 306
    Cue-Dependent Forgetting 306
    Interference 307
    Repression and Suppression of Memories 309
    Flashbulb Memories 309
The Clinical File *The Recovered Memory/False Memory Debate* 310
Memory and the Brain—Some "Shocking" Findings 311
    Consolidation 311
    The Brain and Long-Term Memory 312
Module 7.4: Summary 312
Critical Thinking *The Long-Term Potential of a Memory Pill* 313
Knowledge Builder 314

MODULE 7.5 Exceptional Memory and Improving Memory 315
Exceptional Memory—Wizards of Recall 315
    Eidetic Imagery 315
    A Case of Photographic Memory 316
    Strategies for Remembering 316
    Memory Champions 317
Improving Memory—Keys to the Memory Bank 317
    Memory Strategies 317
Module 7.5: Summary 320
Knowledge Builder 321

MODULE 7.6 Psychology in Action: Mnemonics— Memory Magic 322
Module 7.6: Psychology in Action Summary 324
Knowledge Builder 325
Interactive Learning 325

8 Intelligence, Cognition, Language, and Creativity 326

MODULE 8.1 Intelligence 328
Human Intelligence—The IQ and You 328
    Defining Intelligence 328
Human Diversity *Intelligence—How Would a Fool Do It?* 329
    Intelligence Tests 329
    Intelligence Quotients 330
    The Wechsler Tests 331
    Group Tests 331
Variations in Intelligence—Curved like a Bell 332
    The Mentally Gifted 332
    Intellectual Disability 333
Questioning Intelligence—How Intelligent Are Intelligence Tests? 334
    Multiple Intelligences 334
    Artificial Intelligence: I Compute, Therefore I Am 335
    Heredity, Environment, and Intelligence 336
Critical Thinking *You Mean Video Games Might Be Good for Me?* 337
Module 8.1: Summary 338
Knowledge Builder 339

MODULE 8.2 Imagery, Concepts, and Language 340
What Is Thinking?—It's All in Your Head! 340
    Some Basic Units of Thought 340
Mental Imagery—Does a Frog Have Lips? 340
    The Nature of Mental Images 340

Concepts—I'm Positive, It's a Whatchamacallit 342
    Forming Concepts 342
    Types of Concepts 343
Language—Don't Leave Home without It 344
    The Structure of Language 345
Human Diversity *Bilingualism—Si o No, Oui ou Non, Yes or No?* 346
    The Animal Language Debate 347
Module 8.2: Summary 349
Knowledge Builder 350

MODULE 8.3 Problem Solving 351
Problem Solving—Getting an Answer in Sight 351
    Mechanical Solutions 351
    Solutions by Understanding 351
    Heuristics 352
    Insightful Solutions 352
Human Diversity *How to Weigh an Elephant* 354
    Common Barriers to Problem Solving 355
Module 8.3: Summary 356
Knowledge Builder 356

MODULE 8.4 Creative Thinking and Intuition 357
Creative Thinking—Down Roads Less Traveled 357
    Tests of Creativity 357
    Stages of Creative Thought 359
    Positive Psychology: The Creative Personality 360
    Living More Creatively 360

Intuitive Thought—Mental Shortcut? Or Dangerous Detour? 360
Critical Thinking *Have You Ever Thin Sliced Your Teacher?* 361
    Intuition 361
    Framing 362
    Wisdom 363
Module 8.4: Summary 363
Knowledge Builder 364

MODULE 8.5 Psychology in Action: Culture, Race, IQ, and You 365
    Culture-Fair Testing 357
The Politics of Race, Culture, and IQ 366
Thinking Beyond the Numbers Game 367
    High-Stakes Testing 367
    Conclusion 367
Module 8.5: Psychology in Action Summary 367
Knowledge Builder 368
Interactive Learning 368

9 Motivation and Emotion 370

MODULE 9.1 Overview of Motivation 372
Motivation—Forces that Push and Pull 372
    A Model of Motivation 372
    Primary Motives and Homeostasis 373
    Circadian Rhythms 374
Module 9.1: Summary 375
Knowledge Builder 375

MODULE 9.2 Hunger, Thirst, Pain, and Sex 376
Hunger—Pardon Me, My Hypothalamus Is Growling 376
    Internal Factors in Hunger 376
    Brain Mechanisms 376
Brainwaves *Your Brain's "Fat Point"* 378
    External Factors in Hunger and Obesity 378
    Dieting 379
    Eating Disorders 380
Discovering Psychology *Behavioral Dieting* 381
Primary Motives Revisited—Thirst, Pain, and Sex 383
    Thirst 383
    Pain 383
    The Sex Drive 383
Module 9.2: Summary 384
Knowledge Builder 385

MODULE 9.3 Arousal, Achievement, and Growth Needs 386
Stimulus Drives—Skydiving, Horror Movies, and the Fun Zone 386
    Arousal Theory 386
Human Diversity *Xtreme!* 387
    Levels of Arousal 387
    Coping with Test Anxiety 388
Social Motives—In Pursuit of Excellence 388
    The Need for Achievement 388
    The Key to Success 389
Motives in Perspective—A View from the Pyramid 390
    Intrinsic and Extrinsic Motivation 391
    Turning Play into Work 391
Module 9.3: Summary 392
Knowledge Builder 393

MODULE 9.4 Emotion and Physiological Arousal 394
Inside an Emotion—How Do You Feel? 394
    Primary Emotions 394
    The Brain and Emotion 395
Physiology and Emotion—Arousal, Sudden Death, and Lying 395
    Fight or Flight 396
    Lie Detectors 397
Critical Thinking *To Catch a Terrorist* 398
Module 9.4: Summary 398
Knowledge Builder 399

MODULE 9.5 Emotional Expression and Theories of Emotion 400
Expressing Emotions—Making Faces and Talking Bodies 400
    Facial Expressions 400
    Cultural Differences in Emotion 401
    Body Language 401
Theories of Emotion—Several Ways to Fear a Bear 402
    The James-Lange Theory 402
    The Cannon-Bard Theory 402
    Schachter's Cognitive Theory of Emotion 402
    The Facial Feedback Hypothesis 404
    Emotional Appraisal 404
The Clinical File *Suppressing Emotion—Don't Turn Off the Music* 405
    A Contemporary Model of Emotion 405
Module 9.5: Summary 406
Knowledge Builder 407

MODULE 9.6 Psychology in Action: Emotional Intelligence—The Fine Art of Self-Control 408
Emotional Flexibility 409
Positive Psychology and Positive Emotions 409
Becoming Emotionally Smart 409
Module 9.6: Psychology in Action Summary 409
Knowledge Builder 410
Interactive Learning 410

10 Personality 412

MODULE 10.1 Overview of Personality 414
The Psychology of Personality—Do You Have Personality? 414
   Traits 414
Critical Thinking *The Amazing Twins* 415
   Do We Inherit Personality? 416
   Types 416
   Self-Concept 417
   Personality Theories 417
Human Diversity *Self-Esteem and Culture—Hotshot or Team Player?* 418
Module 10.1: Summary 419
Knowledge Builder 420

MODULE 10.2 Trait Theories 421
The Trait Approach—Describe Yourself in 18,000 Words or Less 421
   Predicting Behavior 421
   Describing People 421
   Classifying Traits 421
Discovering Psychology *What's Your Musical Personality?* 422
   The Big Five 423
The Clinical File *Perfectly Miserable* 424
   Traits, Consistency, and Situations 425
Module 10.2: Summary 425
Knowledge Builder 426

MODULE 10.3 Psychoanalytic Theory 427
Psychoanalytic Theory—Id Came to Me in a Dream 427
   The Structure of Personality 427
   The Dynamics of Personality 428
   Personality Development 429
Module 10.3: Summary 431
Knowledge Builder 431

MODULE 10.4 Behavioral and Social Learning Theories 432
Learning Theories of Personality—Habit I Seen You Before? 432
   Personality = Behavior 433
   Social Learning Theory 433
   Behavioristic View of Development 434

Module 10.4: Summary 436
Knowledge Builder 437

MODULE 10.5 Humanistic Theories 438
Humanistic Theory—Peak Experiences and Personal Growth 438
   Maslow and Self-Actualization 438
   Positive Psychology: Positive Personality Traits 440
   Carl Rogers' Self Theory 440
The Clinical File *Telling Stories about Ourselves* 441
   Humanistic View of Development 442
Module 10.5: Summary 442
Knowledge Builder 443

MODULE 10.6 Personality Assessment 444
Personality Assessment—Psychological Yardsticks 444
   The Interview 444
   Direct Observation and Rating Scales 445
   Personality Questionnaires 446
Critical Thinking *Honesty Tests—Do They Tell the Truth?* 448
Projective Tests of Personality—Inkblots and Hidden Plots 448
   The Rorschach Inkblot Test 448
   The Thematic Apperception Test 448
Sudden Murderers—A Research Example 450
Module 10.6: Summary 450
Knowledge Builder 451

MODULE 10.7 Psychology in Action: Barriers and Bridges—Understanding Shyness 452
Elements of Shyness 452
Dynamics of the Shy Personality 452
Shy Beliefs 453
Social Skills 453
   Conversation 453
Module 10.7: Psychology in Action Summary 454
Knowledge Builder 454
Interactive Learning 455

11 Health, Stress, and Coping 456

MODULE 11.1 Health Psychology 458
Health Psychology—Here's to Your Good Health 458
   Behavioral Risk Factors 458
   Health-Promoting Behaviors 459
   Early Prevention 460
   Community Health 460
   Positive Psychology: Wellness 461
Module 11.1: Summary 461
Knowledge Builder 462

MODULE 11.2 Stress, Frustration, and Conflict 463
Stress—Thrill or Threat? 463
   General Adaptation Syndrome 463
   Stress, Illness, and Your Immune System 464
   When Is Stress a Strain? 464
   Appraising Stressors 465
The Clinical File *Burnout—The High Cost of Caring* 466
The Clinical File *Coping with Traumatic Stress* 467
   Coping with Threat 468
Frustration—Blind Alleys and Lead Balloons 468
   Reactions to Frustration 469
   Coping with Frustration 470
Conflict—Yes, No, Yes, No, Yes, No, Well, Maybe 470
   Managing Conflicts 472
Module 11.2: Summary 472
Knowledge Builder 474

MODULE 11.3 Defenses, Helplessness, and Depression 475
Psychological Defense—Mental Karate? 475
Learned Helplessness—Is There Hope? 477
   Depression 478
   Depression: Why Students Get the Blues 479
   Coping with Depression 479

Module 11.3: Summary 480
Knowledge Builder 481

MODULE 11.4 Stress and Health 482
Stress and Health—Unmasking a Hidden Killer 482
   Life Events and Stress 482
Human Diversity *Acculturative Stress—Stranger in a Strange Land* 484
   Psychosomatic Disorders 484
   Biofeedback 485
Critical Thinking *It's All in Your Mind* 486
   The Cardiac Personality 486
   Hardy Personality 488
   Positive Psychology: Hardiness, Optimism, and Happiness 488
   The Value of Social Support 488
Discovering Psychology *Feeling Stressed? You've Got a Friend* 489
Module 11.4: Summary 489
Knowledge Builder 490

MODULE 11.5 Psychology in Action: Stress Management 491
Managing Bodily Reactions 491
Modifying Ineffective Behavior 493
Avoiding Upsetting Thoughts 494
Module 11.5: Psychology in Action Summary 494
Knowledge Builder 495
Interactive Learning 495

12 Psychological Disorders 496

MODULE 12.1 Normality and Psychopathology 498
Normality—What Is Normal? 498
Discovering Psychology *Crazy for a Day* 499
   Core Features of Disordered Behavior 499
Human Diversity *A Disease Called Freedom* 500
Classifying Mental Disorders—Problems by the Book 500
   An Overview of Psychological Disorders 502
Human Diversity *Running Amok with Cultural Maladies* 504
   General Risk Factors 504
   Insanity 504

Module 12.1: Summary 505
Knowledge Builder 506

MODULE 12.2 Personality Disorders and Anxiety-Based Disorders 507
Personality Disorders—Blueprints for Maladjustment 507
   Maladaptive Personality Patterns 507
   Antisocial Personality 507
Anxiety-Based Disorders—When Anxiety Rules 509
   Adjustment Disorders 509
   Anxiety Disorders 509

Stress Disorders 512
Dissociative Disorders 512
The Clinical File *Sick of Being Sick* 513
Somatoform Disorders 513
Anxiety and Disorder—Four Pathways to Trouble 514
Psychodynamic Approach 515
Humanistic-Existential Approaches 515
Behavioral Approach 515
Cognitive Approach 516
Module 12.2: Summary 516
Knowledge Builder 517

MODULE 12.3 Psychosis, Delusional Disorders, and Schizophrenia 518
Psychotic Disorders—Life in the Shadow of Madness 518
The Nature of Psychosis 518
Delusional Disorders—An Enemy Behind Every Tree 520
Paranoid Psychosis 520
Schizophrenia—Shattered Reality 521
Disorganized Schizophrenia 521
Catatonic Schizophrenia 522
Paranoid Schizophrenia 522
Critical Thinking *Are the Mentally Ill Prone to Violence?* 523
Undifferentiated Schizophrenia 524
The Causes of Schizophrenia 524

Brainwaves *The Schizophrenic Brain* 526
Implications 527
Module 12.3: Summary 527
Knowledge Builder 528

MODULE 12.4 Mood Disorders 529
Mood Disorders—Peaks and Valleys 529
Major Mood Disorders 529
What Causes Mood Disorders? 530
Disorders in Perspective—
Psychiatric Labeling 532
Social Stigma 532
Module 12.4: Summary 533
Knowledge Builder 534

MODULE 12.5 Psychology in Action: Suicide—Lives on the Brink 535
Immediate Causes of Suicide 536
Preventing Suicide 536
How to Help 536
Crisis Intervention 537
Module 12.5: Psychology in Action Summary 537
Knowledge Builder 538
Interactive Learning 538

13 Therapies 540

MODULE 13.1 Psychotherapy and Psychoanalysis 542
Psychotherapy—Getting Better by the Hour 542
Dimensions of Therapy 542
Origins of Therapy—Bored Skulls and Hysteria on the Couch 542
Psychoanalysis—Expedition into the Unconscious 544
Psychoanalysis Today 545
Module 13.1: Summary 546
Knowledge Builder 547

MODULE 13.2 Insight Therapies 548
Humanistic Therapies—Restoring Human Potential 548
Client-Centered Therapy 548
Existential Therapy 548
Gestalt Therapy 549
Therapy at a Distance—Psych Jockeys and Cybertherapy 550
Media Psychologists 550
Telephone Therapists 550
Internet Therapy 550
Module 13.2: Summary 551
Knowledge Builder 552

MODULE 13.3 Behavior Therapy 553
Behavior Therapy—Healing by Learning 553
Aversion Therapy 553
Desensitization 554
Discovering Psychology *Feeling a Little Tense? Relax!* 555
Module 13.3: Summary 556
Knowledge Builder 557

MODULE 13.4 Operant Therapies and Cognitive Therapies 558
Operant Therapies—All the World Is a Skinner Box? 558
Nonreinforcement and Extinction 558
Reinforcement and Token Economies 559
Cognitive Therapy—Think Positive! 560
Cognitive Therapy for Depression 560
Discovering Psychology *Ten Irrational Beliefs—Which Do You Hold?* 561
Rational-Emotive Behavior Therapy 561
The Clinical File *Overcoming the Gambler's Fallacy* 562
Module 13.4: Summary 562
Knowledge Builder 563

MODULE 13.5 Group Therapy, Therapy Skills, and Medical Therapies 564

Group Therapy—People Who Need People 564
  Psychodrama 564
  Family Therapy 564
  Group Awareness Training 565
Psychotherapy—An Overview 565
Critical Thinking *How Do We Know Therapy Actually Works?* 566
  Core Features of Psychotherapy 566
  The Future of Psychotherapy 567
  Basic Counseling Skills 567
Human Diversity *Therapy and Culture—A Bad Case of "Ifufunyane"* 569
Medical Therapies—Psychiatric Care 569
  Drug Therapies 570
  Electroshock 570
  Psychosurgery 571
  Hospitalization 571
  Community Mental Health Programs 573
Module 13.5: Summary 573
Knowledge Builder 574

MODULE 13.6 Psychology in Action: Self-Management and Seeking Professional Help 575

Self-Directed Desensitization—Overcoming Common Fears 576
Seeking Professional Help—When, Where, and How? 577
  Locating a Therapist 577
Module 13.6: Psychology in Action Summary 579
Knowledge Builder 580
Interactive Learning 580

14 Gender and Sexuality 582

MODULE 14.1 Sex, Gender, and Androgyny 584

Sexual Development—Circle One: *XX* or *XY*? 584
  Female or Male? 584
  Prenatal Sexual Development 585
  Gender Identity 586
The Clinical File *Bruce or Brenda—Can Sex Be Assigned?* 587
  Origins of Male-Female Differences 587
  Gender Roles 588
Discovering Psychology *Man's Work* 589
  Gender Role Socialization 589
Androgyny—Are You Masculine, Feminine, or Androgynous? 590
  Psychological Androgyny 591
Module 14.1: Summary 592
Knowledge Builder 593

MODULE 14.2 Sexual Behavior and Sexual Orientation 594

Sexual Behavior—Mapping the Erogenous Zone 594
  Sexual Arousal 594
Brainwaves *Genes, the Brain, and Sexual Orientation* 597
Sexual Orientation—Who Do You Love? 597
  Homosexuality 598
Module 14.2: Summary 598
Knowledge Builder 599

MODULE 14.3 Sexual Response, Attitudes, and Behavior 600

Human Sexual Response—Sexual Interactions 600
  Comparing Male and Female Responses 601
Atypical Sexual Behavior—Trench Coats, Whips, Leathers, and Lace 602
  Paraphilias 602
Attitudes and Sexual Behavior—The Changing Sexual Landscape 603
  Is the Revolution Over? 604
Critical Thinking *Are We Oversexualizing Young Girls?* 605
Critical Thinking *Gender Role Stereotyping and Rape* 606
  The Crime of Rape 606
STDs and Safer Sex—Choice, Risk, and Responsibility 607
  HIV/AIDS 607
  Behavioral Risk Factors 608
  Risk and Responsibility 610
Module 14.3: Summary 610
Knowledge Builder 611

MODULE 14.4 Psychology in Action: Sexual Problems—When Pleasure Fades 612

Desire Disorders 612
Arousal Disorders 612
Orgasm Disorders 614
Sexual Pain Disorders 615
Relationships and Sexual Adjustment 615
Intimacy and Communication 616
Module 14.4: Psychology in Action Summary 617
Knowledge Builder 618
Interactive Learning 618

15 Social Behavior 620

MODULE 15.1 Affiliation, Friendship, and Love 622
Affiliation and Attraction—Come Together 622
   Social Comparison Theory 622
   Interpersonal Attraction 623
   Self-Disclosure 624
Loving and Liking—Dating, Rating, Mating 625
   Sex, Evolution, and Mate Selection 626
Module 15.1: Summary 627
Knowledge Builder 627

MODULE 15.2 Groups, Social Influence, and Conformity 628
Life in Groups—People, People, Everywhere 628
   Group Structure, Cohesion, and Norms 628
   Making Attributions 629
Social Influence—Follow the Leader 630
   Conformity 631
Critical Thinking *Groupthink—Agreement at Any Cost* 632
Module 15.2: Summary 632
Knowledge Builder 633

MODULE 15.3 Compliance, Obedience, and Self-Assertion 634
Compliance—A Foot in the Door 634
Discovering Psychology *How to Drive a Hard Bargain* 635
Obedience—Would You Electrocute a Stranger? 635
   Milgram's Obedience Studies 636
Discovering Psychology *Quack Like a Duck* 637
Assertiveness Training—Standing Up for Your Rights 638
Module 15.3: Summary 639
Knowledge Builder 640

MODULE 15.4 Attitudes and Persuasion 641
Attitudes—Doomsday for the Seekers 641
   Belief + Emotion + Action 641
   Forming Attitudes 641
   Attitudes and Behavior 642
Attitude Change—Why the "Seekers" Went Public 643
   Persuasion 643
   Cognitive Dissonance Theory 644

Forced Attitude Change—Brainwashing and Cults 645
   Brainwashing 645
   Cults 645
Module 15.4: Summary 647
Knowledge Builder 647

MODULE 15.5 Prejudice and Intergroup Conflict 648
Prejudice—Attitudes That Injure 648
   Becoming Prejudiced 648
   The Prejudiced Personality 648
Intergroup Conflict—The Roots of Prejudice 649
Critical Thinking *Terrorists, Enemies, and Infidels* 651
   Experiments in Prejudice 651
Critical Thinking *Is America Purple?* 652
Module 15.5: Summary 654
Knowledge Builder 655

MODULE 15.6 Aggression and Prosocial Behavior 656
Aggression—The World's Most Dangerous Animal 656
   Instincts 656
   Biology 656
   Frustration 657
   Social Learning 658
   Preventing Aggression 659
Prosocial Behavior—Helping Others 660
   Bystander Intervention 660
   Who Will Help Whom? 661
   Positive Psychology: Everyday Heroes 662
Module 15.6: Summary 662
Knowledge Builder 663

MODULE 15.7 Psychology in Action: Multiculturalism—Living with Diversity 664
Breaking the Prejudice Habit 664
Tolerance and Cultural Awareness 665
Module 15.7: Psychology in Action Summary 666
Knowledge Builder 667
Interactive Learning 667

16 Applied Psychology 668

MODULE 16.1 Industrial/Organizational Psychology 670
Industrial/Organizational Psychology—
Psychology at Work 670
   Theories of Leadership 670
   Theory X and Theory Y Leadership 670
Critical Thinking *Beyond the Glass Ceiling: Enter the Labyrinth* 671
   Job Satisfaction 673
Critical Thinking *Flexible Work* 674
   Job Enrichment 674
   Organizational Culture 674
The Clinical File *Desk Rage and Healthy Organizations* 675
   Personnel Psychology 675
   Job Analysis 675
   Selection Procedures 676
Discovering Psychology *Surviving Your Job Interview* 677
Communication at Work—Getting the Message Across 678
   Effective Communication 678
   Being a Good Listener 679
Module 16.1: Summary 680
Knowledge Builder 681

MODULE 16.2 Environmental Psychology 682
Environmental Psychology—Life in the Big City 682
   Personal Space 683
   Spatial Norms 683
   Environmental Influences 684
   Stressful Environments 685
   Toxic Environments 687
Discovering Psychology *Planet in Peril?* 688
   Sustainable Lifestyles 688
   Social Dilemmas 689
Discovering Psychology *Reduce, Reuse, Recycle* 690
   Environmental Problem Solving 691
   Conclusion 692
Module 16.2: Summary 692
Knowledge Builder 693

MODULE 16.3 The Psychology of Law and Sports 694
Psychology and Law—Judging Juries 694
   Jury Behavior 694
Critical Thinking *Death-Qualified Juries* 695
   Jury Selection 695
Sports Psychology—The Athletic Mind 696
   Positive Psychology: Peak Performance 698
Module 16.3: Summary 699
Knowledge Builder 700

MODULE 16.4 Psychology in Action: Human Factors Psychology—Who's the Boss Here? 701
Designing for Human Use 701
Human–Computer Interaction 702
Using Tools Effectively 703
Space Habitats 703
Module 16.4: Psychology in Action Summary 704
Knowledge Builder 705
Interactive Learning 706
The Journey Continues: Psychology and You 706

Preface

To the Student—An Invitation to Psychology

Psychology is an exciting field. It is at once familiar, exotic, surprising, and challenging. Most of all, psychology is ever changing. Indeed, this book is just a "snapshot" of a colorful passing scene. Yet, change makes psychology especially fascinating: What, really, could be more intriguing than our evolving knowledge of human behavior?

Psychology is about each of us. It asks us to adopt a reflective attitude as we ask, "How can we step outside of ourselves to look objectively at how we live, think, feel, and act?" Psychologists believe the answer is through careful thought, observation, and inquiry. Although that may seem simple, thoughtful reflection takes practice to develop. It is the guiding light for all that follows in this text.

Each chapter of this book will take you into a different realm of psychology, such as personality, abnormal behavior, memory, consciousness, and child development. Each realm is complex and fascinating in its own right, with many pathways, landmarks, and interesting detours to discover. *Psychology: Modules for Active Learning* is your passport to an adventure in learning. It is, in a very real sense, written about you, for you, and to you. Like any journey of discovery, your "tour" of psychology will help you better understand yourself, others, and the world around you. It's definitely a trip worth taking. In the pages that follow, we have done all that we could imagine to make your journey through psychology enjoyable and worthwhile.

Getting Started

None of us likes to start out a new adventure by reading the manual. We just want to get right into our new computer game, step off the plane and begin our vacation, or just start using our new camera or cell phone. You might be similarly tempted to just start reading this textbook.

Please be patient. Learning psychology depends on how you study this book, as well as how you read it. *Psychology: Modules for Active Learning* is your passport to an active adventure in learning, and not just passive reading. To help you get off to a good start, we strongly encourage you to read our short Introduction, which precedes Chapter 1. The Introduction describes study skills, including the SQ4R method, which you can use to get the most out of this text and your psychology course. It also tells how you can explore psychology through the Internet, electronic databases, and interactive CDs.

To the Instructor—A Concise Survey of Psychology

Psychology: Modules for Active Learning was written to provide a concise, but complete, first course in psychology. It is organized in modules, which are grouped into 16 chapters, to allow flexibility in assigning topics for your course. Throughout this text, we have tried to select only the very "best" material from the many topics that could be presented. Nevertheless, *Psychology* covers not only the heart of psychology, but also many topics at the cutting edge of current knowledge. New information, anecdotes, perspectives, and narratives appear throughout the Eleventh Edition. The result is a concise text that is readable, manageable, informative, and motivating.

Marcel Proust wrote, "The real voyage of discovery consists not in seeing new landscapes but in having new eyes." It is in this spirit that this book is designed to help you promote an interest in human behavior, including an appreciation of the practical applications of psychology, the richness of human diversity, the relationship between brain and behavior, and the field of positive psychology.

In this edition we have also updated the SQ4R method. The steps are now Survey, Question, Read, Recite, Reflect, Review. This update has allowed us to expand the Reflect step to strengthen the relationship between learning and doing the kinds of active, elaborative processing and critical thinking that characterize the reflective student (Gadzella, 1995). The end result is a more effective promotion of active learning, better long-term retention of ideas, and a reflective attitude that lies at the heart of critical thinking. Without such skills, students cannot easily go, as Jerome Bruner put it, "beyond the information given" (Bruner, 1973).

Readability and Narrative Emphasis

Selecting a textbook is half the battle in teaching a successful course. A good text does much of the work of imparting information to your students. This frees class time for discussions, extra topics, or media presentations. It also leaves students asking for more. When a book overwhelms students or cools their interest, teaching and learning suffer.

Many introductory psychology students are reluctant readers. No matter how interesting a text may be, its value is lost if students fail to read it. That's why we've worked hard to make this a clear, readable, and engaging text. We want students to read this book with genuine interest and enthusiasm, not merely as an obligation.

To encourage students to read, we made a special effort to weave narrative threads through every chapter. Everyone loves a good story, and the story of psychology is among the most compelling to be told. Throughout *Psychology,* we have used intriguing anecdotes and examples to propel reading and sustain interest. As students explore concepts, they are asked to think about ideas and relate them to their own experiences.

Practical Applications

Psychology: Modules for Active Learning is designed to give students a clear grasp of major concepts, without burying them in details. At the same time, it offers a broad overview that reflects psychology's rich heritage of ideas. We think students will find this book informative and intellectually stimulating. Moreover, we have emphasized the many ways that psychology relates to practical problems in daily life.

A major feature of this book is the *Psychology in Action* modules found at the end of each chapter. These high-interest discussions bridge the gap between theory and practical applications. We believe it is fair for students to ask, "Does this mean anything to me? Can I use it? Why should I learn it if I can't?" The Psychology in Action modules show students how to solve practical problems and manage their own behavior. This allows them to see the benefits of adopting new ideas, and it breathes life into psychology's concepts.

Modular Approach and Integrated Study Guide

The chapters of this text are divided into short, self-contained modules. Each module concludes with a summary and a feature called a *Knowledge Builder*. These "mini-study guides" challenge students to quiz themselves, relate concepts to their own experiences, and think critically about the principles they are learning. For this edition, we have reorganized the Knowledge Builders into *Recite* and *Reflect* sections, to better mirror the SQ4R method. Recite questions are similar in difficulty to in-class test questions, and they provide immediate feedback to students. If students would like more feedback and practice, an excellent new printed supplement, *Concept Modules with Note-Taking and Practice Exams,* is bundled with this text. Also, a traditional *Study Guide* is available.

Electronic Resources

To encourage further reflection, students will find a section called *Links* in each Knowledge Builder. The websites described there invite students to go beyond the text to explore a wealth of interesting information on topics related to psychology. In addition, the *Interactive Learning* section at the end of each chapter directs students to *ThomsonNOW,* a powerful online study tool that provides students with a rich assortment of interactive learning experiences, animations, and simulations.

ThomsonNOW is a Web-based, personalized study system that provides a pre-test and a post-test for each chapter and can also create personalized study plans that point students to areas in the text, as well as additional learning materials that will help them master course content.

On the Internet, students can visit this text's *Book Companion Website,* where they will find quizzes, a final exam, chapter-by-chapter Web links, flash cards, a glossary, and more (http://academic.cengage.com/psychology/coon).

At www.iChapters.com, students can select from over 10,000 print and digital study tools, inlcuding the option to buy individual e-chapters and e-books. The first e-chapter is free!

Human Diversity

Today's students reflect the multicultural, multifaceted nature of contemporary society. In *Psychology,* students will find numerous discussions of human diversity, including differences in race, ethnicity, culture, gender, abilities, sexual orientation, and age. Too often, such differences needlessly divide people into opposing groups. Our aim throughout this text is to discourage stereotyping, prejudice, discrimination, and intolerance. We've tried to make this book gender neutral and sensitive to diversity issues. All pronouns and examples involving females and males are equally divided by gender. In artwork, photographs, and examples, we have tried to portray the rich diversity of humanity. In addition, *Human Diversity* highlights appear throughout the book, providing students with examples of how to be more reflective about human diversity. Many topics and examples in this book encourage students to appreciate social, physical, and cultural differences and to accept them as a natural part of being human.

Positive Psychology

Over the past 100 years, psychologists have paid ample attention to the negative side of human behavior. This is easy to understand because we urgently need to find remedies for human problems. However, Martin Seligman and Mihaly Csikszentmihalyi have urged us to also study positive psychology. What do we know, for instance, about love, happiness, creativity, well-being, self-confidence, and achievement? Throughout this book, we have attempted to answer such questions for students. Our hope is that students who read this book will gain an appreciation for the potential we all have for optimal functioning. Also, of course, we hope that they will leave introductory psychology with emotional and intellectual tools they can use to enhance their lives.

How Module Features Support the SQ4R Method

Psychology: Modules for Active Learning uses an SQ4R, active-learning format to make studying psychology a rewarding experience. Notice how the steps of the SQ4R method—*survey, question, read, recite, reflect,* and *review*—are incorporated into the modular design.

Survey At the front of each chapter, several features help students build cognitive maps of upcoming topics. A short vignette arouses interest, provides a preview of the main topic of the chapter, and focuses attention. Next, a list of *Modules* and *Survey Questions* provides an overview of the chapter. To help students structure their learning, the same Survey Questions appear again in the modules, where they are used to introduce major topics. The Survey Questions also appear in the *Study Guide* to give students a consistent framework for learning.

Question Throughout each chapter, italicized *Guide Questions* serve as advance organizers that prompt students to look for important ideas as they read. These questions also establish a dialogue in which the concerns and reactions of students are anticipated. This ongoing dialogue clarifies difficult points—in a lively give-and-take between questions and responses.

Read We've made every effort to make this a clear, readable text. To further aid comprehension, we've used a full array of traditional learning aids. These include: boldface terms (with phonetic pronunciations), bullet summaries, a robust illustration program, summary tables, a name index, a subject index, and a detailed glossary. As an additional aid, figure and table references in the text are marked with small geometric shapes. These "placeholders" make it easier for students to return to reading after they have paused to view a table or figure.

An integrated Glossary aids reading comprehension by providing precise definitions directly in context. When important terms first appear, they are immediately defined. In this way, students get clear definitions when and where they need them—in the general text itself. In addition, a parallel Running Glossary defines key terms in the margins of pages.

The Running Glossary makes it easier for students to find, study, and review important terms.

In each chapter, several boxed highlights discuss high-interest topics related to human diversity, using psychology, and critical thinking. In addition, new *Discovering Psychology* highlights get students involved through in-text demonstrations and self-assessment exercises. Highlights are stimulating but nonintrusive supplements to the main text. They enrich the presentation and encourage students to think about the ideas they are learning.

Recite At the end of each module, the Knowledge Builder gives students a chance to test their understanding and recall of preceding topics. Knowledge Builders include an opportunity to *Recite* (a short, noncomprehensive quiz) in order to enhance learning. They also help students actively process information and assess their progress. Students who miss any items are asked to backtrack and clarify their understanding before reading more.

Reflect Cognitive psychology tells us that elaboration, the reflective processing of new information, is one of the best ways to actively foster understanding and form lasting memories (Gadzella, 1995). The more elaborated that processing, the richer the understanding and the better the resulting memory. To help students reflect, each Knowledge Builder includes a series of Reflect exercises.

Self-reference, a particularly powerful form of elaboration, makes new information more meaningful by relating it to what is already known (Klein & Kihlstrom, 1986). To help students elaborate their new understanding, each Knowledge Builder includes a series of *Relate* questions. These questions encourage students to associate new concepts with personal experiences and prior knowledge. New in this edition are the *Discovering Psychology* boxes. These "try-it" demonstrations allow students to observe interesting facets of their own behavior or do self-assessment exercises, thus linking new chapter information to the student's concrete experience.

A course in psychology naturally contributes to critical thinking abilities. To further facilitate critical thinking, each Knowledge Builder also includes one or more *Critical Thinking* questions. These stimulating questions challenge students to think critically and analytically about psychology. Each is followed by a brief answer with which students can compare their own thoughts. Many of these answers cite research findings and are informative in their own right.

In addition, several boxed highlights encourage other forms of reflective thought. The *Critical Thinking* features model a reflective approach to critical thinking in psychology. In addition, *Human Diversity* features encourage reflection on the variability of the human experience, *The Clinical File* features encourage reflection on the clinical applications of psychology, and *Brainwaves* features encourage reflection on the role of the brain in understanding psychological phenomena.

Review To help students consolidate their learning, each module concludes with a bulleted summary of major ideas presented in the unit. As noted previously, chapter-ending Psychology in Action modules show students how psychological concepts relate to practical problems, including problems in their own lives. The information found in the Psychology in Action modules helps reinforce learning by illustrating psychology's practicality. Also, as noted previously, all important terms appear in a Running Glossary throughout the book, which aids review.

Critical Thinking

The active, questioning nature of the SQ4R method is, in itself, an inducement to think critically. Many of the guide questions that introduce topics in the text serve as examples of critical thinking. Further, Chapter 1 contains a discussion of critical thinking skills and a rational appraisal of pseudo-psychologies. In addition, the discussion of research methods in Chapter 1 is actually a short course on how to think clearly about behavior. It is augmented by suggestions about how to critically evaluate claims in the popular media. Chapter 8, "Intelligence, Cognition, Language, and Creativity," includes many topics that focus on thinking skills. Throughout the text, many boxed highlights promote critical thinking about specific topics that students should approach with healthy skepticism. As mentioned earlier, every Knowledge Builder includes Critical Thinking questions. Taken together, these features will help students gain thinking skills of lasting value.

Psychology: Modules for Active Learning—What's New?

Thanks to psychology's vitality, this text is improved in many ways. The title has been changed to reflect our enhanced focus on active processing, reflection, and critical thinking. The two human development chapters of the previous edition have been combined, resulting in a 16-chapter book. Another notable change is the enhanced modular format of the Eleventh Edition. As mentioned earlier, topics are still grouped by chapters. However, modules are now more clearly defined within chapters. Many chapters have also been reorganized so that modules are more, well, modular.

Specifically, each numbered module begins on a separate page and concludes with a point-by-point summary and a Knowledge Builder, with Recite and Reflect exercises. Entire chapters or individual modules can be assigned with equal ease, and reading assignments can be closely integrated with your course syllabus.

The Eleventh Edition of *Psychology: Modules for Active Learning* features some of the most recent and interesting information in psychology, supported with many new and recent references. The following annotations highlight some of the new topics and features that appear in this edition.

Introduction: The Psychology of Studying

The Introduction shows students how to read effectively, study more efficiently, take good notes, prepare for tests, perform well on various types of tests, create study schedules, and avoid procrastination. The advice to students in this edition has been adapted to match the modular format of the text.

Chapter 1: Introducing Psychology and Research Methods

- This chapter has been extensively reorganized.
- A module is now specifically dedicated to critical thinking and the scientific method.
- Experimental and nonexperimental methods are now treated in thier own modules.
- A new highlight, *Testing Common-Sense Beliefs,* indicates why psychology's reliance on empirical methods is superior to a reliance on unreflective common sense.
- Three major modern perspectives are now outlined (biological, psychological, and sociocultural) and referred to throughout the remainder of the book.
- Brief research updates improve discussions of current trends in psychology, prescription privileges, mechanisms of the placebo effect, and self-fulfilling prophecies.

Chapter 2: Brain and Behavior

- This chapter has been lengthened and updated to reflect the growing importance of neuroscience to psychology today.
- This new focus on neuroscience is extended throughout the book, including *Brainwaves* features, which appear in various modules and highlight the growing importance of the biological perspective.
- Two new features have been added to this chapter, *A Stroke of Bad Luck* and *If You Change Your Mind, Do You Change Your Brain?*
- An old module has been split into two separate modules, *Neurons and the Nervous System* and *Brain Research,* resulting in a clearer organization of topics.

- The module *Hemispheres and Lobes of the Cerebral Cortex* has been extensively updated to better highlight differences between the primary areas and association areas. Mirror neurons are now discussed, as is the relationship between the prefrontal area and the sense of self.
- Many updates have been included in the chapter, including new material on neural networks, sidedness (along with handedness), and recent research on use of the fMRI as a lie detector.

Chapter 3: Human Development
- Chapters 3 and 4 of the previous edition have been combined and rewritten to create a single chapter that is organized chronologically.
- The opening module on heredity and environment has been rewritten and expanded to include a discussion of the concept of reaction range. It also eschews simple either/or discussions of the relationship between nature and nurture.
- Material on effective parenting is now collected in the chapter-closing Psychology in Action module.
- A new feature, *The Twixters,* introduces the phenomenon of delayed adulthood.

Chapter 4: Sensation and Perception
- This chapter has been reorganized so that the opening module, *Sensory Systems and Selective Attention,* now draws together in one place information about the general functioning of sensory systems. Vision is now treated in its own module, as is material on the other senses.
- A new Brainwaves feature, *The Matrix: Do Phantoms Live Here?* introduces students to the neuromatrix theory of phantom limb pain.
- Another new feature, *The Boiled Frog Syndrome,* explores the dangers to humankind of failing to encode life-threatening sensory information.
- The highlight, *Staying in Touch with Reality,* updates a previous highlight to explain the concept of reality testing, to better explain when hallucinations can be regarded as a symptom of mental disorders, and to describe how "sane hallucinations" can occur.

Chapter 5: States of Consciousness
- A new Brainwaves feature, *How Addictive Drugs Affect the Brain,* better explains synaptic mechanisms underlying drug effects.
- A new feature, *What Is It Like to Be a Bat?* invites students to reflect on the difference between subjective and objective perspectives on consciousness.
- A new feature, *Abducted by Space Aliens?* explores hypnopompic imagery.
- References and statistics (drug abuse rates, accidents due to sleepiness or drug use, and so forth) have been updated throughout the chapter.
- Several sections have been updated, including *Sleep Patterns, Types and Causes of Insomnia,* and a number of subsections about drugs.
- The treatment of hypnosis now includes coverage of Hilgard's dissociation theory and the hidden observer.
- The new section, *Hypnosis, Meditation, and Sensory Deprivation,* combines information on sensory deprivation with a discussion of meditation and gives both topics a fuller treatment, rather than implying that they are only helpful for relaxation.
- The College Alcohol Problems Scale is used to help students recognize problem drinking.
- More recent work suggesting that marijuana can produce physical dependence is now included.
- The questions in the Probing Dreams section now reflect the Hall–Van de Castle system of dream content analysis.

Chapter 6: Conditioning and Learning
- The *Classical Conditioning* module has been reorganized to clarify the basic classical conditioning model.
- A new highlight, *Are Animals Stuck In Time?* explores a method for studying time perception by animals.
- A new highlight, *Coping with Chemo,* discusses the role of classical conditioning in conditioned nausea during chemotherapy.
- A new highlight, *You Mean Video Games Might Be Bad for Me?* is part of a reworked treatment of the role of media in fostering aggressive behavior.

Chapter 7: Memory
- Material on exceptional memory has been combined with a discussion about how to improve memory, resulting in a new module, *Exceptional Memory and Improving Memory.* Methods of measuring memory are now treated in their own module.
- Mnemonic memory strategies are more clearly distinguished from meaning-based memory improvement.
- A new highlight, *Telling Wrong from Right in Forensic Memory,* combines information on the use of hypnosis and the cognitive interview to clarify the impor-

tance of reducing false memories in eye-witness testimony.
- A new highlight, *Do You Like Jam With Your Memory?* explores the memory-jamming theory of advertising.

Chapter 8: Intelligence, Cognition, Language, and Creativity
- The chapter title has been changed to reflect both an extensive reorganization and a recognition of the importance of human language.
- The chapter-opening vignette focuses on the autistic savant Kim Peek.
- The opening module is now *Intelligence*.
- The distinction between intelligence as "g" and multiple intelligences is given more prominence, and the section on multiple intelligences has been lengthened.
- Artificial intelligence is now given a different emphasis and is included in the *Intelligence* module. The material on expertise is now in the section on problem solving.
- A new highlight on bilingualism introduces the benefits of additive bilingualism.
- A new highlight, *Have You Ever Thin Sliced Your Teacher?* discusses the potential importance of rapid cognition and impressions gained from minimal information.
- A new highlight, *Intelligence—How Would a Fool Do It?* focuses on cross-cultural definitions of intelligence.
- A new highlight, *You Mean Video Games Might Be Good for Me?* offers a counterpoint as it explores the possibility that popular culture is raising IQs.
- The Psychology in Action module now focuses on race, intelligence, and IQ.

Chapter 9: Motivation and Emotion
- An engaging new vignette on alexythymia opens this chapter, to promote interest in the modules that follow.
- The material on circadian rhythms was moved to the opening section of the book. The discussion of *Stimulus Drives* was restructured as a result.
- The section on hunger was restructured into major sections on internal and external factors, and the section on eating disorders now includes information about eating disorders among men.
- A new highlight, *Xtreme!* upgrades the discussion of sensation seeking.
- Material on fat set points is now treated as a Brainwaves highlight.
- A new highlight, *To Catch a Terrorist,* presents some new approaches to lie detection.

Chapter 10: Personality
- The opening module now offers an overview of personality, the role of heredity, and theories of personality, while the second module focuses exclusively on trait theories.
- A new highlight, *Telling Stories about Ourselves,* discusses narrative psychology and personality change.
- The highlight on identical twins has been updated.
- Direct and indirect aggression has been differentiated in the section on personality and gender, highlighting the rising rate of female aggression.

Chapter 11: Health, Stress, and Coping
- The module on stress, frustration, and conflict now includes the general adaptation syndrome. The module on stress and health has been rewritten accordingly.
- An updated table now lists the most common sources of stress at work.
- A new highlight, *Acculturative Stress—Stranger in a Strange Land,* focuses on the stresses of immigrants.
- A new highlight, *It's All in Your Mind,* distinguishes between the medical model and the biopsychosocial model.
- The discussion of burnout has been highlighted.

Chapter 12: Psychological Disorders
- Mental health statistics have been updated throughout the chapter, as have many case study examples.
- A new Brainwaves highlight, *The Schizophrenic Brain,* stresses the role of neuroscience in understanding psychological disorders.
- A new highlight, *Sick of Being Sick,* introduces the interesting topic of Munchausen syndrome by proxy.
- The discussion of culturally defined maladies and the politics of mental illness has been updated.

Chapter 13: Therapies
- A new section on interpersonal psychotherapy has been added.
- The section on cybertherapy has been rewritten.

- A new highlight, *Ten Irrational Beliefs—Which Do You Hold?* concretely connects students with key ideas in rational-emotive therapy.
- A new highlight on gambling addiction has been added.
- The treatment of cultural issues in therapy has been updated.

Chapter 14: Gender and Sexuality
- In view of the controversy surrounding John Money's research on gender assignment, the entire discussion of intersexual infants has been revised.
- The updated highlight, *Bruce or Brenda—Can Sex Be Assigned?* discusses one of the most famous, yet failed, cases of sex reassignment.
- Statistics on sexuality and sexually transmitted diseases have been updated.
- A new highlight asks if we are oversexualizing young girls.
- Material on the role of genetics, the brain, and sexual orientation has been upgraded into a Brainwaves feature.
- Information about HIV and AIDS reflects the latest findings.

Chapter 15: Social Behavior
- The chapter has been reorganized so that social influence topics are treated in increasing order of directness from conformity to compliance to obedience.
- Material on self-assertiveness now follows the presentation of the three major forms of social influence.
- The explanation of the role of chance conditioning in forming attitudes has been integrated with the concept of direct contact.
- A new highlight box, *Is America Purple?* describes how oversimplification contributes to stereotyping and prejudice.
- The material on media violence has been rewritten and updated.

Chapter 16: Applied Psychology
- The module on industrial/organizational psychology has been extensively rewritten. Leadership is now the lead-off topic.
- A new highlight on women as corporate leaders has been added.
- The treatment of flextime has been expanded into a discussion of flexible work in general.
- A new highlight offers practical tips about how to prepare for a job interview.
- The module on evironmental psychology has been updated and reorganized.
- The concepts of ecological footprints and carbon footprints are now discussed and characterized as important souces of feedback for fostering environmentally friendly behaviors.
- The Psychology in Action module is new and now focuses on human factors psychology, including the design of human-computer interfaces and the role of human factors in space psychology.

A Complete Course—Teaching and Learning Supplements

A rich array of supplements accompanies *Psychology: Modules for Active Learning,* including several that make use of the latest technologies. These supplements are designed to make teaching and learning more effective. Many are available free to professors or students. Others can be packaged with this text at a discount. For more information on any of the listed resources, please call the Thomson Learning™ Academic Resource Center at 800-423-0563.

Student Support Materials

Introductory students must learn a multitude of abstract concepts, which can make a first course in psychology difficult. The materials listed here will greatly improve students' chances for success.

Concept Modules with Note Taking and Practice Exams Created by Claudia Cochran of El Paso Community College and Shawn Talbot of Kellogg Community College, this booklet includes key concepts in each chapter, a place to take notes, and a practice exam of 20 multiple-choice questions. (ISBN: 0-495-50709-1)

Study Guide with Language Development Guide The *Study Guide,* prepared by Steven Hoekstra of Kansas Wesleyan University, is an invaluable student resource. It contains a variety of study tools, including: Chapter Overviews, Recite and Review (fill-in-the-blank), Connections (matching), Check your Memory (true-false), Final Survey and Review (fill-in-the-blank), and Mastery Test. A language development section clarifies idioms, special phrases, cultural and historical allusions, and difficult vocabulary. New to this edition is a Critical Thinking feature. Study Guide content is keyed to Learning Objectives to help students master important concepts. (ISBN: 0-495-50711-3)

Careers in Psychology: Opportunities in a Changing World This informative booklet, written by Tara L. Kuther and Robert D. Morgan, is a Wadsworth exclusive. The pamphlet describes the field of psychology, as well as how to prepare for a career in psychology. Career options and resources are also discussed. *Careers in Psychology* can be packaged with this text at no additional cost to students. (ISBN 0-495-09078-6)

Multimedia CD-ROMs

Interactive CD-ROMs make it possible for students to directly experience some of the phenomena they are studying. The following CDs from Wadsworth provide a wealth of engaging modules and exercises.

Sniffy™ the Virtual Rat, Lite Version 2.0 There's no better way to master the basic principles of learning than working with a real laboratory rat. However, this is usually impractical in introductory psychology courses. *Sniffy the Virtual Rat* offers a fun, interactive alternative to working with lab animals. This innovative and entertaining software teaches students about operant and classical conditioning by allowing them to condition a virtual rat. Users begin by training Sniffy to press a bar to obtain food. Then they progress to studying the effects of reinforcement schedules and simple classical conditioning. In addition, special "Mind Windows" enable students to visualize how Sniffy's experiences in the Skinner Box produce learning. The Sniffy CD-ROM includes a Lab Manual that shows students how to set up various operant and classical conditioning experiments. *Sniffy™ the Virtual Rat, Lite Version 2.0* may be packaged with this text for a discount. (ISBN: 0-534-63357-9)

Internet Resources

The Internet is providing new ways to exchange information and enhance education. In psychology, Wadsworth is at the forefront in making use of this exciting technology.

Book Companion Website As users of this text, you and your students will have access to the companion site for *Psychology: Modules for Active Learning* (http://academic.cengage.com/psychology/coon). Access is free and no pincode is required. This outstanding site features Learning Objectives, Tutorial Quizzes, Essay Questions, Glossary, Web Links, Flash Cards, Crossword Puzzles, and more!

ThomsonNow™ This Web-based program helps your students discover the areas of text where they need to focus their efforts through a series of diagnostic pre-tests and post-tests (written by Christopher Mayhorn of North Carolina State University), personalized study plans with learning modules that parallel the modules in the book, eBook files, and other integrated media elements. While students can use ThomsonNow™ without any instructor setup or involvement, an Instructor Gradebook is available for you to monitor student progress.
Printed Access Card: 0-495-59502-0
Instant Access Card: 0-495-59503-9

Psychology Resource Center The new Psychology Resource Center features powerful teaching and learning tools, bringing psychology to life with a full library of original and classic video clips plus interactive learning modules tied to all of the topics covered in an Introductory Psychology course. Organized by topic, the Resource Center is easy to navigate by students to find learning resources, and instructors will also find it an amazing lecture resource to easily stream multimedia into their classrooms. For more information, please contact your representative.

InfoTrac® College Edition *InfoTrac College Edition* is a powerful online learning resource, consisting of thousands of full-text articles from hundreds of journals and periodicals. Students using *Psychology: Modules for Active Learning* receive four months of free access to the *InfoTrac College Edition*. This fully searchable database offers over 20 years' worth of full-text articles from thousands of scholarly and popular sources—updated daily, and available 24 hours a day from any computer with Internet access. By doing a simple keyword search, students can quickly generate a list of relevant articles from thousands of possibilities. Then they can select full-text articles to read, explore, and print for reference or further study. *InfoTrac College Edition's* collection of articles can be useful for doing reading and writing assignments that reach beyond the pages of this text. Students also have access to *InfoWrite*, which provides extensive resources for writing papers, including suggested topics, APA guidelines, and more. (*InfoTrac College Edition* is at http://www.infotrac-college.com.)

WebTutor™ WebTutor™ course cartridges provide an easy, fast, and reliable way to integrate and customize rich text-specific content into your on-campus course management system. For students, *WebTutor* offers real-time access to a full array of study tools, including flash cards, practice quizzes and tests, online tutorials, exercises, asynchronous discussion, a whiteboard, and an integrated e-mail system. Students will also have integrated access to *InfoTrac College Edition*, the online library.

Professors can use *WebTutor* to offer virtual office hours, to post syllabi, to set up threaded discussions, to track student progress on quizzes, and more. You can customize the content of *WebTutor* in any way you choose, including uploading images and other resources, adding Web links, and creating course-specific practice materials. (*Web Tutor* on *WebCT,* ISBN: 0-495-59563-2; on *Blackboard,* ISBN: 0-495-59564-0)

Thomson Audio Study Tools Audio Study Tools provides audio reinforcement of key concepts that students can listen to from their personal computer or MP3 player. Created specifically for *Psychology: Modules for Active Learning,* Audio Study Tools provides approximately 10 minutes of audio content for each chapter, giving students a quick and convenient way to master key concepts. Audio content allows students to test their knowledge with quiz questions, listen to a brief overview reflecting the major themes of each chapter, and review key terminology. Order Audio Study Tools directly at www.ichapters.com.

Essential Teaching Resources

As every professor knows, teaching an introductory psychology course is a tremendous amount of work. Not only should the supplements listed here make life easier for you, they should also make it possible for you to concentrate on the more creative and rewarding facets of teaching.

Instructor's Resource Manual The *Instructor's Manual,* by Susan Weldon of Henry Ford Community College, contains resources designed to streamline and maximize the effectiveness of your course preparation. In a three-ring binder, this IRM is a treasure trove—from the introduction section, which includes grading rubrics, a sample syllabus, and a Resource Integration Guide, to a full array of chapter resources. Each chapter includes learning objectives, discussion questions, lecture enhancements, role-playing scenarios, "one-minute motivators," broadening our cultural horizons exercises, journal questions, suggestions for further reading, media suggestions, Web links, and more. (ISBN 0-495-50707-5)

Test Bank The *Test Bank* was prepared by Jeannette Murphey of Meridian Community College. It includes over 5,000 questions. The multiple-choice questions are correlated to learning objectives and are labeled with question-type, difficulty, and main text page reference. Essay questions and true-false questions are also included. All questions new to this edition are marked with an asterisk. (ISBN: 0-495-50708-3)

PowerLecture CD-ROM (with JoinIn™ on TurningPoint® and ExamView®) This one-stop lecture and class preparation tool, prepared by Corinne McNamara of Kennesaw State University, contains ready-to-use Microsoft® PowerPoint® slides and allows you to assemble, edit, publish, and present custom lectures for your course. PowerLecture lets you bring together text-specific lecture outlines and art from Coon's text, along with videos or your own materials-culminating in a powerful, personalized, media-enhanced presentation. The CD-ROM also includes TurningPoint® software that lets you pose book-specific questions and display students' answers seamlessly within the Microsoft PowerPoint slides of your own lecture, in conjunction with the "clicker" hardware of your choice, as well as the ExamView® assessment and tutorial system, which guides you step by step through the process of creating tests. (ISBN: 0-495-50777-6)

Videotapes and Films

Wadsworth offers a variety of videotapes and films to enhance classroom presentations. Many video segments in the Wadsworth collection pertain directly to major topics in this text, making them excellent lecture supplements.

Wadsworth Film and Video Library for Introductory Psychology Adopters can select from a variety of continually updated film and video options. The Wadsworth Film and Video Library includes selections from the *Discovering Psychology* series, the *Annenberg* series, and *Films for Humanities.* It also includes the exclusive ABC offerings described below. Contact your local sales representative or Wadsworth Marketing at 877-999-2350 for details.

ABC® Videos for Introductory Psychology These one- to four-minute video clips, a Wadsworth exclusive, allow you to integrate the newsgathering and programming power of ABC into the classroom to show students the relevance of psychology to daily life. Organized by course topics, these compelling clips are ideal for launching lectures and encouraging discussion. Adopters receive one new, updated video each year. A Wadsworth/Thomson Learning Exclusive!

Topics covered in the videos include:

- **New Brain Scan** A new brain scan using adapted MRI technology gives doctors a more detailed look at the brain, enabling them to treat brain injuries more effectively.
- **Artificial Eye** New artificial eye technology enables spatial recognition and navigation in the blind.
- **Curing Insomnia** An alternative treatment to prescription sleep drugs for insomnia patients using cognitive behavioral therapy to retrain the body and induce sleep.
- **Weight Loss Hypnosis** Hypnosis helps one woman find the motivation to eat healthier and exercise. A look at the scientific side of hypnosis, how it can help, and its limitations.

- **Gay Teens** Gay teens talk about coming out to their families and friends, and the difficulties they encountered along the way.
- **Rules of Attraction** Dating criteria are evaluated through a test to determine the level of shallowness in the dating pool.
- **Suicide Bomber Profile** An in-depth look at the background of the suicide bomber who killed a group of civilians at an Israeli night club.

Contact your sales representative to order.

Wadsworth Psychology: Research in Action Videos The Wadsworth Psychology: Research in Action Videos offer students a look at cutting-edge research in psychology, illustrating real-life applications of concepts they're learning in their textbook and classroom. Authored and produced by Roger Klein, Associate Professor of Educational Psychology at the University of Pittsburgh, the videos feature established and up-and-coming researchers from leading research institutions around the country. Volume I (0-495-59520-9, available for Spring 2008) presents 25 segments, and Volume II (available for Fall 2008) presents 23; together, the volumes comprise more than 2½ hours of stimulating research video. For more information, please contact your representative.

Wadsworth Media Guide for Introductory Psychology This essential instructor resource, edited by Russell J. Watson, contains hundreds of video and feature film recommendations for all major topics in Introductory Psychology. (ISBN: 0-534-17585-6)

Supplementary Books

No text can cover all of the topics that might be included in an introductory psychology course. If you would like to enrich your course, or make it more challenging, the Wadsworth titles listed here may be of interest.

Challenging Your Preconceptions: Thinking Critically about Psychology, Second Edition This paperbound book (ISBN: 0-534-26739-4), written by Randolph Smith, helps students strengthen their critical thinking skills. Psychological issues such as hypnosis and repressed memory, statistical seduction, the validity of pop psychology, and other topics are used to illustrate the principles of critical thinking.

Writing Papers in Psychology: A Student Guide The Seventh Edition of *Writing Papers in Psychology* (ISBN: 0-534-53331-0), by Ralph L. Rosnow and Mimi Rosnow, is a valuable "how-to" manual for writing term papers and research reports. This edition has been updated to reflect the latest APA guidelines. The book covers each task with examples, hints, and two complete writing samples. Citation ethics, how to locate information, and new research technologies are also covered.

Cross-Cultural Perspectives in Psychology How well do the concepts of psychology apply to various cultures? What can we learn about human behavior from cultures different from our own? These questions lie behind a collection of original articles written by William F. Price and Rich Crapo. The Fourth Edition of *Cross-Cultural Perspectives in Psychology* (ISBN: 0-534-54653-6) contains articles on North American ethnic groups as well as cultures from around the world.

Culture and Psychology, Fourth Edition David Matsumoto and Linda Juang's unique book (ISBN: 0-495-09787-X) discusses similarities and differences in research findings in the United States and other cultures. By doing so, it helps students see psychology and their own behavior from a broader, more culturally aware perspective.

Summary

We sincerely hope that teachers and students will consider this book and its supporting materials a refreshing change from the ordinary. Creating it has been quite an adventure. In the pages that follow, we think students will find an attractive blend of the theoretical and the practical, plus many of the most exciting ideas in psychology. Most of all, we hope that students using this book will discover that reading a college textbook can be entertaining and enjoyable.

Acknowledgments

Psychology is a cooperative effort requiring the talents and energies of a large community of scholars, teachers, researchers, and students. Like most endeavors in psychology, this book reflects the efforts of many people. We deeply appreciate the contributions of the following professors, whose sage advice helped improve the Eleventh Edition of *Psychology: Modules for Active Learning*:

Kimberly Glackin, Blue River Community College
Gene Indenbaum, SUNY–Farmingdale
Patricia Lanzon, Henry Ford Community College
Andrea Macari, Suffolk County Community College
J. Mark McKellop, Juniata College
Dan Patanella, John Jay College of Criminal Justice
Pete Peterson, Johnson County Community College
Thomas Weatherly, Georgia Perimeter College
Tammi Wynn, Rowan-Cabarrus Community College

We would like to thank the following reviewers of the previous editions: Judith Balcerzak, Ventura College; Bakhtawar Bhadha, Glendale College; LeAnn Binger, Richard Bland College; John Dilworth, Kellogg Community College; Patricia Donat, Mississippi University for Women; Cindy Lehar, York County Community College; Katherine McNellis, Lakeshore Technical College; Bill Roe, Phoenix College; James Scepansky, Cedar Crest College; Dawn Strongin, California State University at Stanislaus; Shawn Talbot, Kellogg Community College; Lisa Wood, Ouchita Technical College; Brian R. Bate, Cuyahoga Community College; James R. Bean, Lock Haven University; Gary A. Biel, Schreiner University; Martin Bourgeois, University of Wyoming; T. L. Brink, Crafton Hills Community College; Lucy Capuano-Brewer, Ventura College; Roy Cohen, Mesa Community College; Robert S. Coombs, Southern Adventist University; Beatrice M. de Oca, Western New Mexico University; Linda DiDesidero, Capitol College; David N. Entwistle, Malone College; Christopher J. Frost, Southwest Texas State University; Adrienne Garro, Kean University; Gordon Hammerle, Adrian College; Mark L. Harmon, Reedley College–North Centers; Robert A. Hayes, Westfield State College; Diedra T. Hayman, Virginia Western Community College; William R. Holt, University of Massachusetts–Dartmouth; Lawrence Jesky, Seton Hill College; Diana Jimeno, University of Illinois–Urbana/Champaign; James J. Johnson, Illinois State University; William G. LaChappelle, Brevard Community College; Fred Leavitt, California State University at Hayward; John F. Lindsay, Jr., Georgia College and State University; Britton L. Mace, Southern Utah University; Denise McClung, West Virginia University–Parkersburg; Michael McVay, Colby Community College; Sandra Merryman, Southwest Texas State University; Robert L. Moore, Marshalltown Community College; Colleen Moran, Gloucester County College; Donna Webster Nelson, Winthrop University; Caroline Olko, Nassau Community College–SUNY; Randall E. Osborne, Southwest Texas State University; Michelle L. Pilati, Rio Hondo College; Kathy Pillow-Price, Arkansas State University–Beebe; Beth Robinson, Lubbock Christian University; Cynthia Ross, Las Positas College; Edward Samulewicz, Rosemont College; Karen K. Saules, Eastern Michigan University; Donna Love Seagle, Chattanooga State Technical Community College; Barbara Biondo Sloan, Marshalltown Community College; Steven M. Specht, Utica College; Martha S. Spiker, University of Charleston; Elizabeth Swenson, John Carroll University; Inger Thompson, Glendale Community College; Robert J. Wood, Las Positas College.

Producing *Psychology: Modules for Active Learning* and its supplements was a formidable task. We are especially indebted to each of the following individuals, for supporting this book:

Susan Badger

Sean Wakely

Eve Howard and Michele Sordi

We also wish to thank the individuals at Wadsworth who so generously shared their knowledge and talents over the past year. These are the people who made it happen: Vernon Boes, Chris Caldeira, Jerilyn Emori, Jeremy Judson, Magnolia Molcan, Rachel Guzman, Wilson Co, Sara Swangard, and Margaret Parks.

It has been a pleasure to work with such a gifted group of professionals and many others at Wadsworth. We are grateful to Jaime Perkins for his wisdom, creativity, humor, and unflagging support. We especially want to thank Jeremy Judson for his unstintingly invaluable editorial assistance.

Up in St. Catharines, Barbara Kushmier, Kayleigh Hagerman, and Heather Mitterer pitched in to lend a hand. Last of all, we would like to thank our wives, Sevren and Heather, for making the journey worthwhile.

The Psychology of Studying

Introduction

You're actually reading this! As your authors, we're impressed. Too often, students just jump in and read a textbook from the first assigned chapter to the last one. As far as we're concerned, that's a shame because a textbook needs to be studied, not just read. Think about it: How much do you typically remember after you've read straight through a whole textbook chapter? If the answer is "Nada," "Zilch," or simply "Not enough," it may be because reading a chapter is not really the same as studying it. Even if you're an excellent student, you may be able to improve your study skills. Students who get good grades tend to work *smarter*, not just longer or harder (Santrock & Halonen, 2007). To help you get a good start, let's look at several ways to improve studying.

The SQ4R Method—How To Tame a Textbook

What's the difference between reading a textbook and studying it? You have probably spent the occasional evening just vegging out in front of the TV set. According to psychologist Donald Norman (1993), you were engaging in *experiential cognition*, more or less passively letting the experience happen to you. There is nothing at all wrong with merely experiencing entertainment. But have you ever noticed that the morning after one of those evenings you often have trouble remembering just exactly what you watched the night before?

In contrast, suppose one of those programs was about, say, global warming and it really got you thinking. You might have wondered how global warming will affect your own future plans. You might have questioned some of the program's more dire projections for the future. You might have thought back to another program on global warming and remembered some different perspectives. Now you are "going beyond the information given" (Bruner, 1973). For Norman (1993), this is *reflective cognition*: not just experiencing something, but also actively thinking *about* what you have just experienced. The next morning you may well forget most of what you watched the night before, but the odds are you will remember the program on global warming. To use Norman's terms, then, studying a textbook involves not just experiencing it; it also involves actively reflecting on what you have just read.

One way to be more reflective while reading a textbook is to use the **SQ4R method.** SQ4R stands for *survey, question, read, recite, reflect,* and *review*. These six steps can help you learn as you read and reflect, remember more, and review effectively:

- **S** = *Survey*. Skim through a chapter before you begin reading it. Start by looking at topic headings, figure captions, and summaries. Try to get an overall picture of what lies ahead. Because this textbook is organized into short modules, you can survey just one module at a time if you prefer.
- **Q** = *Question*. As you read, turn each topic heading into one or more questions. For example, when you read the heading "Stages of Sleep" you might ask: "Is there more than one stage of sleep?" "What are the stages of sleep?" "How do they differ?" Asking questions helps you read with a purpose.
- **R1** = *Read*. The first R in SQ4R stands for *read*. As you read, look for answers to the questions you asked. Read in short "bites," from one topic heading to the next, then stop. For difficult material you may want to read only a paragraph or two at a time.

SQ4R method An active study-reading technique based on these steps: survey, question, read, recite, reflect, and review.

Rubberball/Jupiterimages

R2 = *Recite*. After reading a small amount, you should pause and recite or rehearse. That is, try to mentally answer your questions. Better yet, summarize what you just read in brief notes. Making notes will show you what you know and don't know, so you can fill gaps in your knowledge (Peverly et al., 2003).

If you can't summarize the main ideas, skim over each section again. Until you can remember what you just read, there's little point to reading more. After you've studied a short "bite" of text, turn the next topic heading into questions. Then read to the following heading. Remember to look for answers as you read and to recite or take notes before moving on. Ask yourself repeatedly, "What is the main idea here?"

Repeat the question-read-recite cycle until you've finished an entire chapter (or just one module if you want to read shorter units).

R3 = *Reflect*. As you read, try to reflect on what you are reading. One powerful way to do this is to relate new facts, terms, and concepts to information you already know well or to your own experiences. You've probably noticed that it is especially easy to remember ideas that are personally meaningful, so try to relate the ideas you encountered to your own life. This may be the most important step in the SQ4R method. The more genuine interest you can bring to your reading, the more you will learn (Hartlep & Forsyth, 2000).

R4 = *Review*. When you're done reading, skim back over a module or the entire chapter, or read your notes. Then check your memory by reciting and quizzing yourself again. Try to make frequent, active review a standard part of your study habits (See ● Fig. I.1.)

Does this really work? Yes. Using a reflective reading strategy improves learning and course grades (Taraban, Rynearson, & Kerr, 2000). Simply reading straight through a chapter can give you "intellectual indigestion." That's why it's better to stop often to think, question, recite, reflect, review, and "digest" information as you read.

How to Use *Psychology: Modules for Active Learning*

You can apply the SQ4R method to any textbook. However, we have specifically designed this textbook to help you actively learn psychology.

Survey Each chapter opens with a chapter survey that includes a *Preview* as well as a list of *Modules* and *Survey Questions* that will be covered. You can use these features to identify important ideas as you begin reading. The Preview should help you get interested in the topics you will be reading about, and the Survey Questions are a good guide to the kinds of information to look for as you read. After you've studied these features, take a few minutes to do your own survey of the chapter. Doing so will help you build a "mental map" of upcoming topics.

Question *How can I use the SQ4R method to make reading more interesting and effective?* One of the key steps is to ask yourself lots of questions while you read. The Survey Questions are repeated throughout each chapter to help you recognize key topics. In addition, questions like the one that began this paragraph appear throughout each module. They will help you focus on seeking information as you read. However, be sure to ask your own questions, too. Try to actively interact with your textbooks as you read.

Read As an aid to reading, important terms are printed in **boldface type** and defined where they first appear. (Some are followed by pronunciations—capital letters show which syllables are accented.) You'll also find a *running glossary* on the page you are reading, so you never have to guess about the meaning of technical terms. If you need to look up a term from lecture or another module, check the main *Glossary*. This "mini-dictionary" is located near the end of the book. Perhaps you should take a moment to find it now.

Recite and Reflect To help you study in smaller "bites," each module in this textbook ends with a study guide called a *Knowledge Builder*. Knowledge Builders provide opportuni-

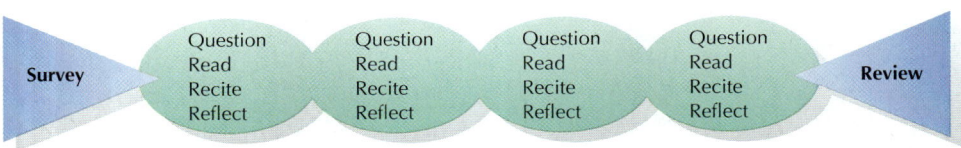

● **FIGURE I.1** The SQ4R method promotes active learning and information processing. You should begin with a survey of the chapter or module, depending on how much you plan to read. Then you should proceed through cycles of questioning, reading, reflecting, and relating, and conclude with a review of the module or the entire chapter.

ties to check your memory for what you just read. They also invite you to think more deeply by presenting critical thinking questions as well as questions designed to help you relate material to your own life and web links leading to more information on topics of particular interest. (Don't forget to also take notes or recite and reflect on your own.)

This book also provides other opportunities for you to reflect more deeply about what you are reading. Each chapter ends with a *Psychology in Action* module. These discussions are filled with practical ideas you can relate to your own life. *Discovering Psychology* boxes also invite you to relate psychology to your own life. The *Critical Thinking* boxes will help you reflect on intriguing questions and apply critical thinking skills to psychology. In addition, *Human Diversity* boxes encourage you to reflect on the rich variability of human experience, *Brainwaves* boxes invite you to reflect on how the brain relates to psychology, and *The Clinical File* encourages you to reflect on ways that psychology can be applied to treat clinical problems.

Review Each module concludes with a point-by-point *Summary* to help you identify important ideas to remember. These summaries are organized around the same Survey Questions you read at the beginning of the module. You can also return to the glossary items throughout each module for further review.

● Table I.1 summarizes how this text helps you apply the SQ4R method. Even with all this help, there is still much more you can do on your own.

TABLE I.1 Using the SQ4R Method

Survey
- Preview
- List of Modules
- Survey Questions
- Figure Captions
- Module Summaries

Question
- Topic Headings
- Survey Questions
- In-Text Dialogue Questions

Read
- Topic Headings
- Boldface Terms
- Running Glossary (in margins)
- Figures and Tables

Recite
- Recite Questions (in Knowledge Builders)
- Practice Quizzes (online)
- Notes (make them while reading)

Reflect
- Reflect Questions and Web Links (in Knowledge Builders)
- Boxed Features (throughout the text)

Review
- Modules Summaries
- Boldface Terms
- Running Glossary (in margins)
- Tables
- Practice Quizzes (online)
- Study Guide

The LISAN Method—How To Tame a Lecture

Reading strategies may be good for studying, but what about taking notes in class? Sometimes it's hard to know what's important. Just as studying a textbook is best done reflectively, so too is attending class (Norman, 1993). Like effective reading, good notes come from actively seeking information. People who are **active listeners** avoid distractions and skillfully gather ideas. Here's a listening/note-taking plan that works for many students. The letters LISAN, pronounced like the word *listen*, will help you remember the steps.

L = *Lead. Don't follow.* Try to anticipate what your teacher will say by asking yourself questions. If your teacher provides course notes or PowerPoint overheads before lecture, review them before coming to class. Reflective questions can come from those materials or from study guides, reading assignments, or your own curiosity.

I = *Ideas.* Every lecture is based on a core of ideas. Usually, an idea is followed by examples or explanations. Ask yourself often, "What is the main idea now? What ideas support it?"

S = *Signal words.* Listen for words that tell you what direction the instructor is taking. For instance, here are some signal words:

There are three reasons why . . .   Here come ideas
Most important is . . .   Main idea
On the contrary . . .   Opposite idea
As an example . . .   Support for main idea
Therefore . . .   Conclusion

Active listener A person who knows how to maintain attention, avoid distractions, and actively gather information from lectures.

A = *Actively listen.* Sit where you can get involved and ask questions. Bring questions you want answered from the last lecture or from your text. Raise your hand at the beginning of class or approach your professor before the lecture. Do anything that helps you stay active, alert, and engaged.

N = *Note taking.* Students who take accurate lecture notes tend to do well on tests (Williams & Eggert, 2002). However, don't try to be a tape recorder. Listen to everything, but be selective and write down only key points. If you are too busy writing, you may not grasp what your professor is saying. When you're taking notes, it might help to think of yourself as a reporter who is trying to get a good story (Ryan, 2001).

Actually, most students take reasonably good notes—and then don't use them! Many students wait until just before exams to review. By then, their notes have lost much of their meaning. If you don't want your notes to seem like "chicken scratches," it pays to review them every day (Rowe, 2007).

Using and Reviewing Your Notes

When you review, you will learn more if you take the extra steps listed here (Knaus & Ellis, 2002; Rowe, 2007; Santrock & Halonen, 2007).

- As soon as you can, reflect on and improve your notes by filling in gaps, completing thoughts, and looking for connections among ideas.
- Remember to link new ideas to what you already know.
- Summarize your notes. Boil them down and *organize* them.
- After each class session, write down at least seven major ideas, definitions, or details that are likely to become test questions. Then, make up questions from your notes and be sure you can answer them.

Summary The letters LISAN are a guide to active listening, but listening and good note taking are not enough. You must also review, organize, reflect, extend, and think about new ideas. Use active listening to get involved in your classes and you will undoubtedly learn more (Rowe, 2007).

Study Strategies—Making a Habit of Success

Grades depend on effort. However, don't forget that good students work more *efficiently*, not just harder. Many study practices are notoriously poor, such as recopying lecture notes, studying class notes but not the textbook (or the textbook but not class notes), outlining chapters, answering study questions with the book open, and "group study" (which often becomes a party). The best students emphasize *quality:* They study their books and notes in depth and attend classes regularly. It's a mistake to blame poor grades on events "beyond your control." Students who are motivated to succeed usually get better grades (Perry et al., 2001). Let's consider a few more things you can do to improve your study habits.

Study in a Specific Place Ideally, you should study in a quiet, well-lighted area free of distractions. If possible, you should also have at least one place where you *only study.* Do nothing else at that spot: Keep magazines, MP3 players, friends, cell phones, pets, posters, video games, puzzles, food, lovers, sports cars, elephants, pianos, televisions, YouTube, and other distractions out of the area. In this way, the habit of studying will become strongly linked with one specific place. Then, rather than trying to force yourself to study, all you have to do is go to your study area. Once there, you'll find it is relatively easy to get started.

Use Spaced Study Sessions It is reasonable to review intensely before an exam. However, you're taking a big risk if you are only "cramming" (learning new information at the last minute). Spaced practice is much more efficient (Anderson, 2005). **Spaced practice** consists of a large number of relatively short study sessions. Long, uninterrupted study sessions are called **massed practice.** (If you "massed up" your studying, you probably messed it up too.)

Cramming places a big burden on memory. Usually, you shouldn't try to learn anything new about a subject during the last day before a test. It is far better to learn small amounts every day and review frequently (Anderson, 2005).

Try Mnemonics Learning has to start somewhere, and memorizing is often the first step. Let's consider just one technique here.

A **mnemonic** (nee-MON-ik) is a memory aid. Most mnemonics link new information to ideas or images that are easy to remember. For example, what if you want to remember that the Spanish word for duck is *pato* (pronounced POT-oh)? To use a mnemonic, you could picture a duck in a pot or a duck wearing a pot for a hat. Likewise, to remember that the cerebellum controls coordination, you might picture someone named "Sarah Bellum" who is very coordinated. For best results, make your mnemonic images exaggerated or bizarre, vivid, and interactive (Macklin & McDaniel, 2005). There are many ways to create mnemonics. If you would like to learn more about memory strategies, see Chapter 7, especially Modules 7.5 and 7.6.

Mnemonics make new information more familiar and memorable. Forming an image of a duck wearing a pot for a hat might help you remember that *pato* is the Spanish word for duck.

Test Yourself A great way to improve grades is to take practice tests before the real one in class. In other words, studying should include **self-testing,** in which you pose questions to yourself. You can use flash cards, "Learning Check" questions, online quizzes, a study guide, or other means. As you study, ask many questions and be sure you can answer them. Studying without self-testing is like practicing for a basketball game without shooting any baskets.

For more convenient self-testing, your professor may make a *Study Guide* or a separate booklet of *Practice Quizzes* available. You can use either to review for tests. Practice quizzes are also available on the *Book Companion Website*, as described later. However, don't use practice quizzes as a substitute for studying your textbook and lecture notes. Trying to learn from quizzes alone will probably *lower* your grades. It is best to use quizzes to find out what topics you need to study more (Brothen & Wambach, 2001).

Overlearn Many students *underprepare* for exams, and most *overestimate* how well they will do. A solution to both problems is **overlearning,** in which you continue studying beyond your initial mastery of a topic. In other words, plan to do extra study and review *after* you think you are prepared for a test. One way to overlearn is approach all tests as if they will be essays. That way, you will learn more completely, so you really "know your stuff."

Self-Regulated Learning— Academic All-Stars

Think of a topic you are highly interested in, such as music, sports, fashion, cars, cooking, politics, or movies. Whatever the topic, you have probably learned a lot about it—painlessly. How could you make your college work more like voluntary learning? An approach called self-regulated learning might be a good start. **Self-regulated learning** is deliberately reflective and active self-guided study (Hofer & Yu, 2003). Here's how you can change passive studying into reflective, goal-oriented learning.

1. *Set specific, objective learning goals.* Try to begin each learning session with specific goals in mind. What knowledge or skills are you trying to master? What do you hope to accomplish (Knaus & Ellis, 2002)?

2. *Plan a learning strategy.* How will you accomplish your goals? Make daily, weekly, and monthly plans for learning. Then put them into action.

3. *Be your own teacher.* Effective learners silently give themselves guidance and ask themselves questions. For example, as you are learning, you might ask yourself, "What are the important ideas here? What do I remember? What don't I understand? What do I need to review? What should I do next?"

4. *Monitor your progress.* Self-regulated learning depends on self-monitoring. Exceptional learners keep records of their progress toward learning goals (pages read, hours of studying, assignments completed, and so forth). They quiz themselves, use study guides, make sure they follow the SQ4R system, and find other ways to check their understanding while learning.

5. *Reward yourself.* When you meet your daily, weekly, or monthly goals, reward your efforts in some way, such as going to a movie or downloading some new music. Be aware that self-praise also rewards learning. Being able to say "Hey, I did it!" or "Good work!" and knowing that you deserve it can be very rewarding. In the long run, success, self-improvement, and personal satisfaction are the real payoffs for learning.

6. *Evaluate your progress and goals.* It is a good idea to frequently evaluate your performance records and goals. Are there specific areas of your work that need improvement? If you are not making good progress toward long-range goals, do you need to revise your short-term targets?

7. *Take corrective action.* If you fall short of your goals, you may need to adjust how you budget your time.

Spaced practice Practice spread over many relatively short study sessions.
Massed practice Practice done in a long, uninterrupted study session.
Mnemonic A memory aid or strategy.
Self-testing Evaluating learning by posing questions to yourself.
Overlearning Continuing to study and learn after you think you've mastered a topic.
Self-regulated learning Deliberately reflective and active self-guided study.

You may also need to change your learning environment, to deal with distractions such as watching TV, daydreaming, talking to friends, or testing the structural integrity of the walls with your stereo system.

If you discover that you lack necessary knowledge or skills, ask for help, take advantage of tutoring programs, or look for information beyond your courses and textbooks. Knowing how to regulate and control learning can be a key to lifelong enrichment and personal empowerment.

Procrastination—Avoiding the Last-Minute Blues

All these study techniques are fine. But what can I do about procrastination? A tendency to procrastinate is almost universal. (When campus workshops on procrastination are offered, many students never get around to signing up!) Even when procrastination doesn't lead to failure, it can cause much suffering. Procrastinators work only under pressure, skip classes, give false reasons for late work, and feel ashamed of their last-minute efforts. They also tend to feel frustrated, bored, and guilty more often (Blunt & Pychyl, 2005).

Why do so many students procrastinate? Many students equate grades with their *personal worth*. That is, they act as if grades tell whether they are good, smart people who will succeed in life. By procrastinating they can blame poor work on a late start, rather than a lack of ability (Beck, Koons, & Milgrim, 2000). After all, it wasn't their best effort, was it?

Perfectionism is a related problem. If you expect the impossible, it's hard to start an assignment. Students with high standards often end up with all-or-nothing work habits (Onwuegbuzie, 2000).

Time Management

Most procrastinators must eventually face the self-worth issue. Nevertheless, most can improve by learning study skills and better time management. We have already discussed general study skills, so let's consider time management in a little more detail.

A **weekly time schedule** is a written plan that allocates time for study, work, and leisure activities. To prepare your schedule, make a chart showing all the hours in each day of the week. Then fill in times that are already committed: sleep, meals, classes, work, team practices, lessons, appointments, and so forth. Next, fill in times when you will study for various classes. Finally, label the remaining hours as open or free times.

Each day, you can use your schedule as a checklist. That way you'll know at a glance which tasks are done and which still need attention (Knaus & Ellis, 2002).

You may also find it valuable to make a **term schedule** that lists the dates of all quizzes, tests, reports, papers, and other major assignments for each class.

The beauty of sticking to a schedule is that you know you are making an honest effort. It will also help you avoid feeling bored while you are working or guilty when you play.

Be sure to treat your study times as serious commitments, but respect your free times, too. And remember, students who study hard and practice time management *do* get better grades (Rau & Durand, 2000).

Goal Setting

As mentioned earlier, students who are active learners set **specific goals** for studying. Such goals should be clear-cut and measurable (Knaus & Ellis, 2002). If you find it hard to stay motivated, try setting goals for the semester, the week, the day, and even for single study sessions. Also, be aware that more effort early in a course can greatly reduce the "pain" and stress you will experience later. If your professors don't give frequent assignments, set your own day-by-day goals. That way, you can turn big assignments into a series of smaller tasks that you can actually complete (Ariely & Wertenbroch, 2002). An example would be reading, studying, and reviewing 8 pages a day to complete a 40-page chapter in 5 days. For this textbook, reading one module a day might be a good pace. Remember, many small steps can add up to an impressive journey. (See ● Fig. I.2 for a summary of study skills.)

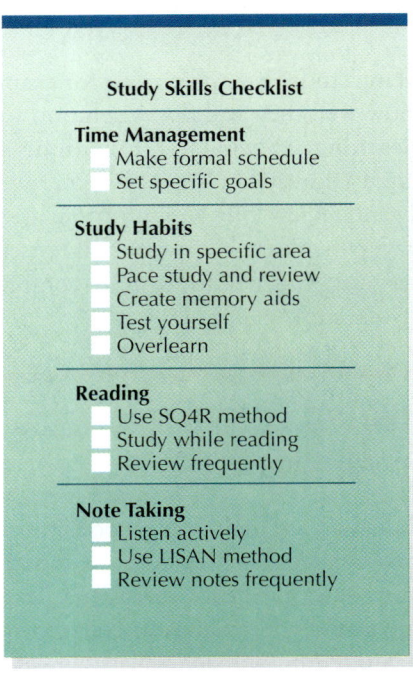

● **FIGURE I.2** Study skills checklist.

Make Learning an Adventure

A final point to remember is that you are most likely to procrastinate if you think a task will be unpleasant (Pychyl et al., 2000). Learning can be hard work. Nevertheless, many students find ways to make schoolwork interesting and enjoyable. Try to approach your schoolwork as if it were a game, a sport, an adventure, or simply a way to become a better person. The best educational experiences are challenging, yet fun (Ferrari & Scher, 2000).

Virtually every topic is interesting to someone, somewhere. You may not be particularly interested in the sex life of South American tree frogs. However, a biologist might be fascinated. (Another tree frog might be, too.) If you wait for teachers to "make" their courses interesting, you are missing the point. Interest is a matter of *your attitude*.

Taking Tests—Are You "Test Wise"?

If I read and study effectively, is there anything else I can do to improve my grades? You must also be able to show what you know on tests. Here are some suggestions for improving your test-taking skills.

General Test-Taking Skills

You'll do better on all types of tests if you observe the following guidelines (Wood & Willoughby, 1995).

1. Read all directions and questions carefully. They may give you good advice or clues.
2. Quickly survey the test before you begin.
3. Answer easy questions before spending time on more difficult ones.
4. Be sure to answer all questions.
5. Use your time wisely.
6. Ask for clarification when necessary.

Objective Tests Several additional strategies can help you do better on objective tests. Objective tests (multiple-choice and true-false items) require you to recognize a correct answer among wrong ones or a true statement versus a false one. Here are some strategies for taking objective tests.

1. First, relate the question to what you know about the topic. Then, read the alternatives. Does one match the answer you expected to find? If none match, reexamine the choices and look for a *partial* match.
2. Read *all* the choices for each question before you make a decision. Here's why: If you immediately think that *a* is correct and stop reading, you might miss seeing a better answer like "both *a* and *d*."
3. Read rapidly and skip items you are unsure about. You may find "free information" in later questions that will help you answer difficult items.
4. Eliminate certain alternatives. With a four-choice multiple-choice test, you have one chance in four of guessing right. If you can eliminate two alternatives, your guessing odds improve to 50-50.
5. Unless there is a penalty for guessing, be sure to answer any skipped items. Even if you are not sure of the answer, you may be right. If you leave a question blank, it is automatically wrong. When you are forced to guess, don't choose the longest answer or the letter you've used the least. Both strategies lower scores more than random guessing does.
6. There is a bit of folk wisdom that says "Don't change your answers on a multiple-choice test. Your first choice is usually right." This is *false*. If you change answers, you are more likely to gain points than to lose them. This is especially true if you are uncertain of your first choice or it was a hunch, and if your second choice is more reflective (Higham & Gerrard, 2005).
7. Remember, you are searching for the one *best* answer to each question. Some answers may be partly true, yet flawed in some way. If you are uncertain, try rating each multiple-choice alternative on a 1-to-10 scale. The answer with the highest rating is the one you are looking for.
8. Few circumstances are *always* or *never* present. Answers that include superlatives such as *most, least, best, worst, largest,* or *smallest* are often false.

Essay Tests Essay questions are a weak spot for students who lack organization, don't support their ideas, or don't directly answer the question (Rowe, 2007). When you take an essay exam, try the following:

1. Read the question carefully. Be sure to note key words, such as *compare, contrast, discuss, evaluate, analyze,* and *describe*. These words all demand a certain emphasis in your answer.
2. Answer the question. If the question asks for a definition and an example, make sure you provide both. Providing just a definition or just an example will

Weekly time schedule A written plan that allocates time for study, work, and leisure activities during a 1-week period.

Term schedule A written plan that lists the dates of all major assignments for each of your classes for an entire semester or quarter.

Specific goal A goal with a clearly defined and measurable outcome.

get you half marks. Giving three examples instead of the one asked for will not earn you any extra marks.

3. Think about your answer for a few minutes and list the main points you want to make. Just write them as they come to mind. Then rearrange the ideas in a logical order and begin writing. Elaborate plans or outlines are not necessary.
4. Don't beat around the bush or pad your answer. Be direct. Make a point and support it. Get your list of ideas into words.
5. Look over your essay for errors in spelling and grammar. Save this for last. Your *ideas* are of first importance. You can work on spelling and grammar separately if they affect your grades.

Short-Answer Tests Tests that ask you to fill in a blank, define a term, or list specific items can be difficult. Usually, the questions themselves contain little information. If you don't know the answer, you won't get much help from the questions.

The best way to prepare for short-answer tests is to overlearn the details of the course. As you study, pay special attention to lists of related terms.

Again, it is best to start with the questions you're sure you know. Follow that by completing items you think you probably know. Questions you have no idea about can be left blank.

Again, for your convenience, Figure I.2 provides a checklist summary of the main study skills we have covered.

Using Digital Media—Netting New Knowledge

Google any psychological term ranging from *amnesia* to *zoophobia* and you will find a vast library of information, from serious websites like that maintained by the American Psychological Association to Wikipedia entries to personal blogs. Even if you don't own a computer, you can usually use one on campus to learn more about psychology. However, be aware that information on the Internet is not always accurate. It is wise to approach all websites with a healthy dose of skepticism.

Digital Journeys

The **Internet** is a network of interlinked computers. An important subpart of the Internet is the **World Wide Web (WWW)** or just plain "web," an interlinked system of information "sites" or "pages." If you know the URL, the "address" of a website, you can view the information it contains. Almost all web pages also have links to other websites. These **links** let you "jump" from one site to the next to find more information.

Google It To find psychological information on the Internet you'll need a computer and an Internet connection. If you don't own a computer, you can usually use one on campus. Various software browsers make it easier to navigate around the web. A **browser** allows you to see text, images, sounds, and video clips stored on other computers. Browsers also keep lists of your favorite URLs so that you can return to them.

The Book Companion Website

How would I find information about psychology on the Internet? Your first stop on the Internet should be the *Book Companion Website*. Here's what you'll find there:

- **Online Quizzes.** You can use these chapter-by-chapter multiple choice quizzes to practice for tests and check your understanding.
- **Interactive Activities.** The demonstrations and mini-experiments in this feature allow you to directly experience various psychological principles.
- **Internet Resources.** This area is a "launching pad" that will take you to other psychology-related sites on the Internet. If a site sounds interesting, a click of the mouse will link you to it.
- **Online Flash Cards.** These online flash cards allow you to practice terms and concepts interactively.
- **Psych in the News.** This section features a news item or current event that is explored from a psychological perspective. After you've thought about a topic, you can share your opinions with others in an online discussion.
- **Discussion Forum.** In the Discussion Forum you'll have a chance to share your ideas with those of psychology students from all over the country.
- **Research and Teaching Showcase.** Here you'll find regularly updated summaries of presentations, articles, or other teaching and research materials.
- **Archives.** Using the Archives, you can quickly search for current and past articles from Psych in the News and the Research and Teaching Showcase.
- **Meet the Author.** Meet the author of your text in an interactive, multimedia presentation.

The Book Companion Website is located at **www.thomsonedu.com/psychology/coon.** Be sure to visit this site for valuable information about how to improve your grades and enhance your appreciation of psychology.

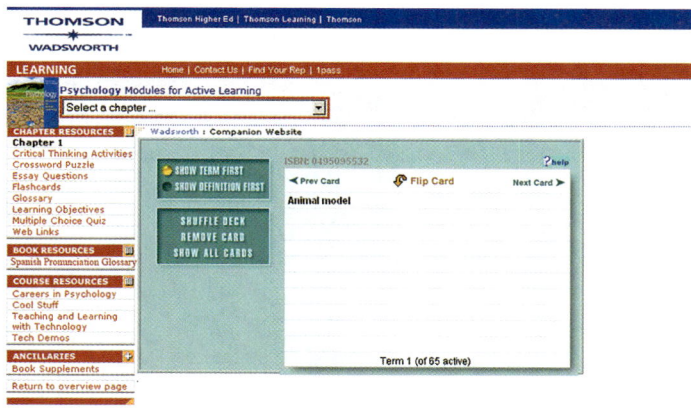

The *Book Companion Website* gives you online access to a variety of valuable learning aids and interesting materials.

ThomsonNOW

Students can also make use of *ThomsonNOW for Coon/Mitterer's Psychology: Modules for Active Learning 11e,* a web-based, personalized study system that provides a pre-test and a post-test for each chapter and separate chapter quizzes. *ThomsonNOW,* located at **www.thomsonedu.com**, can also create personalized study plans—which include rich media such as videos, animations, and learning modules—that point students to areas in the text that will help them master course content (● Fig. I.3). An additional set of integrative questions helps students pull all the material together.

Psych Sites

You'll find a list of interesting websites you may want to explore at the end of each module in this book, including this one. The best way to reach these sites is through the Book Companion Website. We have not included website addresses in the book because they often change or may become inactive. At the website you'll find up-to-date links for websites listed in this book. The sites we've listed are generally of high quality. However, be aware that information on the Internet is not always accurate. It is wise to approach all Websites with a healthy dose of skepticism.

PsycINFO Psychological knowledge can also be found through specialized online databases. One of the best is PsycINFO, offered by the American Psychological Association. **PsycINFO** provides summaries of the scientific and scholarly literature in psychology. Each record in PsycINFO consists of an abstract (short summary), plus notes about the author, title, source, and other details (● Fig. I.4). All entries are indexed using key terms. Thus, you can search for various topics by entering words such as *drug abuse, postpartum depression,* or *creativity.*

You can gain access to PsycINFO in several ways. Almost every college and university subscribes to PsycINFO. If this is the case, you can usually search PsycINFO from a terminal in your college library or computer center—for free. PsycINFO can also be directly accessed (for a fee) through the Internet via APA's PsycINFO Direct service. For more information on how to gain access to PsycINFO, check this website: **www.apa.org/psycinfo.**

The APA Website The APA also maintains an online library of general interest articles on aging, anger, children and families, depression, divorce, emotional health, kids and the media, sexuality, stress, testing issues, women and men, and other topics. They are well worth consulting when you have questions about psychological issues. You'll find them at **www.apa.org.** For links to recent articles in newspapers and magazines, be sure to check the APA's PsycPORT page at **www.psycport.com.**

Please do take some of the "digital journeys" described here. You might be surprised by the fascinating information that awaits you. Investigating psychology on your own is one of the best ways to enrich an already valuable course.

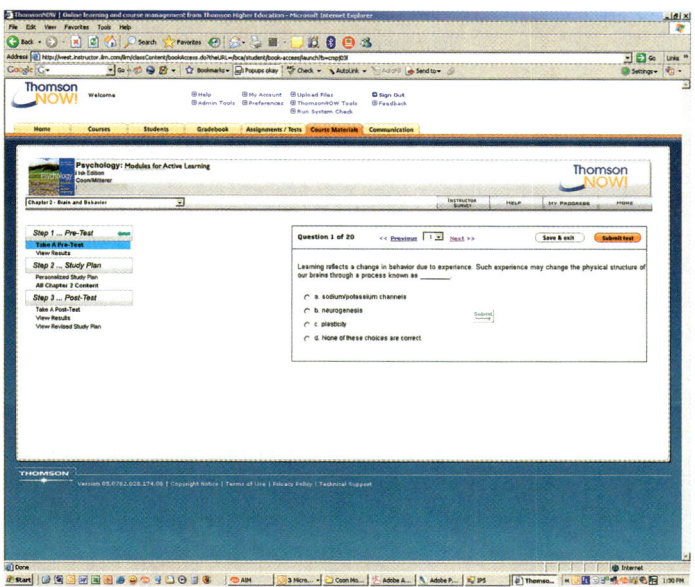

● **FIGURE I.3** A sample screen from *ThomsonNOW.*

> **Internet** An electronic network of interlinked computers.
> **World Wide Web (WWW)** A system of information "sites" accessible through the Internet.
> **Links** Connections built into Internet sites that let you "jump" from one site to the next.
> **Browser** Software that facilitates access to text, images, sounds, video, and other information stored in formats used on the Internet.
> **PsycINFO** A searchable, online database that provides brief summaries of the scientific and scholarly literature in psychology.

● **FIGURE I.4** This is a sample abstract from the PsycINFO database. If you search for the term *study skills*, you will find this article and many more in PsycINFO. (This record is reprinted with permission of the American Psychological Association, publisher of the PsycINFO Database, all rights reserved. May not be reproduced without prior permission.)

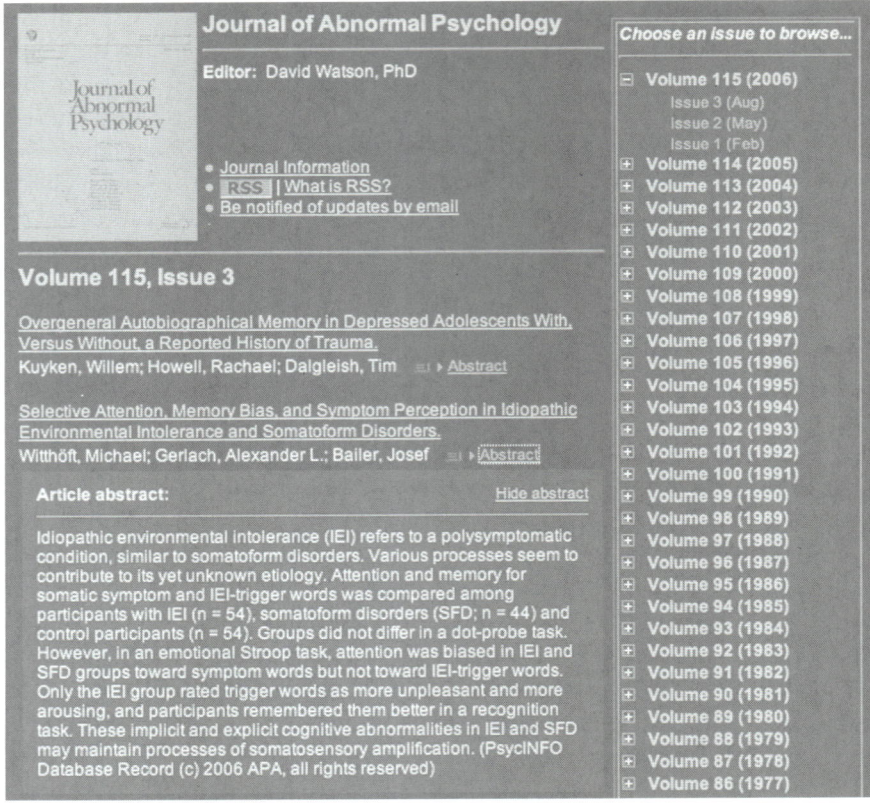

KNOWLEDGE BUILDER

Study Skills

Recite

1. The four R's in SQ4R stand for "read, recite, reflect, and review." T or F?
2. When using the LISAN method, students try to write down as much of a lecture as possible so that their notes are complete. T or F?
3. Spaced study sessions are usually superior to massed practice. T or F?
4. According to research, you should almost always stick with your first answer on multiple-choice tests. T or F?
5. To use the technique known as overlearning, you should continue to study after you feel you have begun to master a topic. T or F?
6. Setting learning goals and monitoring your progress are important parts of _____ _____ learning.
7. Procrastination is related to seeking perfection and equating self-worth with grades. T or F?

Reflect
Critical Thinking

8. How are the SQ4R method and the LISAN method related?

Reflect

Which study skills do you think would help you the most? Which techniques do you already use? Which do you think you should try? To what extent do you already engage in self-regulated learning? What additional steps could you take to become a more active, goal-oriented learner?

Link

Internet addresses frequently change. To find the sites listed here, visit **http://www.thomsonedu.com/psychology/coon** for an updated list of Internet addresses and direct links to relevant sites.

- **How to Succeed as a Student** Advice on how to be a college student. Topics from studying to housing to preparation for work are included.
- **Library Research in Psychology** Hints on how to do library research in psychology.
- **Psychology Glossary** You can use this glossary to get additional definitions for common psychological terms.
- **Study Skills** More information on SQ4R, taking tests, note taking, and time management.

ANSWERS

1. T 2. F 3. T 4. F 5. T 6. self-regulated 7. T 8. Both encourage people to be reflective and to actively seek information as a way of learning more effectively.

A Final Word

There is a distinction in Zen between "live words" and "dead words." Live words come from personal experience; dead words are "about" a subject. This book can only be a collection of dead words unless you accept the challenge of making an intellectual journey. You will find many helpful, useful, and exciting ideas in the pages that follow. To make them yours, you must set out to *actively* learn as much as you can. The ideas presented here should get you off to a good start. Good luck!

For more information, consult any of the following books.

Hettich, P. I. (2005). *Connect college to career: Student guide to work and life transition.* Belmont, CA: Wadsworth.

Knaus, W. J., & Ellis, A. (2002). *The procrastination workbook: Your personalized program for breaking free from the patterns that hold you back.* Oakland, CA: New Harbinger Press.

Rosnow, R. L. (2006). *Writing papers in psychology: A student guide to research papers, essays, proposals, posters, and handouts* (7th Ed.). Belmont, CA: Wadsworth.

Rowe, B. (2007). *College awareness guide: What students need to know to succeed in college.* Upper Saddle River, NJ: Prentice Hall.

Santrock, J. W., & Halonen, J. S. (2007). *Connections to college success.* Belmont, CA: Wadsworth.

1 Introducing Psychology and Research Methods

MODULE 1.1 The Science of Psychology
SURVEY QUESTIONS: What is psychology? What are its goals?

MODULE 1.2 Critical Thinking and the Scientific Method in Psychology
SURVEY QUESTION: What is critical thinking?
SURVEY QUESTION: How does psychology differ from false explanations of behavior?
SURVEY QUESTION: Why is the scientific method important to psychologists?

MODULE 1.3 History and Contemporary Perspectives
SURVEY QUESTION: How did the field of psychology emerge?
SURVEY QUESTION: What are the contemporary perspectives in psychology?

MODULE 1.4 Psychologists and Their Specialties
SURVEY QUESTION: What are the major specialties in psychology?

MODULE 1.5 The Psychology Experiment
SURVEY QUESTION: How is an experiment performed?

MODULE 1.6 Nonexperimental Research Methods
SURVEY QUESTION: What other research methods do psychologists use?

MODULE 1.7 Psychology in Action: Psychology in the Media
SURVEY QUESTION: How good is psychological information found in the popular media?

The Mysteries of Human Behavior

Your authors are often asked, "Why did you become a psychologist?" Because we are just getting acquainted, let us answer this way:

> You are a universe, a collection of worlds within worlds. Your brain is arguably the most complicated system in existence. Through its action you are capable of love, science, art, music, philosophy, hatred, and charity. You are the most challenging riddle ever written, a mystery even to yourself at times. Your thoughts, emotions, and actions—and those of your family and friends—are the most fascinating subject we can imagine. We chose to study psychology because almost everything of interest and importance in the world is ultimately related to human behavior.

Look around you: The Internet, television, newspapers, radio, and magazines are brimming with psychological topics. Psychology is an ever-changing panorama of people and ideas. You really can't call yourself educated without knowing something about it. And, although we might envy those who have walked on the moon or explored the ocean's depths, the ultimate frontier lies much closer to home. Psychology can help you better understand yourself and others. This book is a guided tour of human behavior. We hope you enjoy the adventure.

Corbis Images/Jupiterimages

MODULE 1.1 The Science of Psychology

PSYCHOLOGY touches our lives in many ways. Psychology is about memory, stress, therapy, love, persuasion, hypnosis, perception, death, conformity, creativity, learning, personality, aging, intelligence, sexuality, emotion, happiness, wisdom, and much more. Psychologists use critical thinking and scientific investigation to achieve the goals of describing, understanding, predicting, and controlling human behavior.

Psychology—Spotlight on Behavior

SURVEY QUESTIONS: *What is psychology? What are its goals?*

Psychology is both a *science* and a *profession.* As scientists, some psychologists do research to discover new knowledge. Others are teachers who pass this knowledge on to students. Still others apply psychology to solve problems in mental health, education, business, sports, law, and medicine. Later we will return to the profession of psychology. For now, let's focus on how knowledge is created. Whether they work in a lab, a classroom, or a clinic, all psychologists rely on critical thinking and information gained from scientific research.

Defining Psychology

The word *psychology* comes from the roots *psyche,* which means "mind," and *logos,* meaning "knowledge or study." However, when did you last see or touch a "mind"? Because the mind can't be studied directly, **psychology** is now defined as the scientific study of behavior and mental processes.

Psychologists are highly trained professionals. In addition to the psychological knowledge they possess, psychologists learn specialized skills in counseling and therapy, measurement and testing, research and experimentation, statistics, diagnosis, treatment, and many other areas.

What does behavior *refer to in the definition of psychology?* Anything you do—eating, emailing, sleeping, talking, or sneezing—is a behavior. So are snowboarding, gambling, watching television, picking your nose, learning Spanish, and reading this book. Naturally, we are interested in *overt behaviors* (directly observable actions and responses). But psychologists also study *covert behaviors.* These are private, internal activities, such as thinking, dreaming, remembering, and other mental events (Jackson, 2008).

Empiricism

Many people regard themselves as expert "people watchers." "Common-sense" theories abound. However, you may be surprised to learn how often self-appointed authorities and common-sense beliefs about human behavior are wrong. Take a moment and read "Testing Commonsense Beliefs" for more information.

Because of the limitations of common sense, psychologists have a special respect for *empirical evidence* (information gained from direct observation), especially when it is collected systematically. We study behavior directly and collect data (observed facts) so that we can draw valid conclusions. Would you say it's true, for instance, that "You can't teach an old dog new tricks"? Why argue about it? As psychologists, we would simply get some "old" dogs and some "new" dogs (and some "borrowed" dogs and some "blue" dogs?) and then try to teach them all a new trick to find out!

Basically, the empirical approach says, "Let's take a look" (Stanovich, 2007). Have you ever wondered if people become more hostile when it's blazing hot outside? John Simister and Cary Cooper (2005) decided to find out. They obtained data on temperatures and criminal activity in Los Angeles over a 4-year period. When air temperature and the frequency of aggravated assaults was graphed, a clear relationship emerged. (See ● Fig. 1.1.) Temperatures and crime rates rise and fall more or less in parallel (so there may be something to the phrase "hot under the collar").

Isn't the outcome of this study fairly predictable? Sometimes the results of studies are consistent with common knowledge, and sometimes they come as a surprise. In this instance, you may have guessed the outcome. However, hostile actions that require more extreme physical exertion, such as fistfights, become *less* likely at very high temperatures. Without systematically gathering data, we wouldn't know for sure if overheated Angelenos become more lethargic or more aggressive. Thus, the study tells us something interesting about frustration, discomfort, and aggression.

CRITICAL THINKING

Testing Commonsense Beliefs

It may appear that psychological research "discovers" what we already know from everyday experience. Why waste time and money confirming the obvious? Actually, commonsense beliefs are often wrong. See if you can tell which of the following commonsense beliefs are true and which are false (Landau & Bavaria, 2003).

- Babies love their mothers because mothers fulfill their babies' physiological need for food. True or False?
- Most humans use only 10 percent of their potential brainpower. True or False?
- Blind people have unusually sensitive organs of touch. True or False?
- The more motivated you are, the better you will do at solving a complex problem. True or False?
- The weight of evidence suggests the major cause of forgetting is that memory traces decay as time passes. True or False?
- Psychotherapy has its greatest success in the treatment of psychotic patients who have lost touch with reality. True or False?
- Personality tests reveal your basic motives, including those you may not be aware of. True or False?
- To change people's behavior toward members of ethnic minority groups, we must first change their attitudes. True or False?

It turns out that research has shown that *all* these commonsense beliefs are false. Yet in a survey, *all* the beliefs were accepted as true by a large number of college students (Landau & Bavaria, 2003). How did you do?

We can all benefit from being more reflective in evaluating our beliefs. It's valuable to apply your critical thinking skills by asking whether a belief makes logical sense. Can it be explained by any of the concepts in this book? Can you imagine what sort of study you could do that might yield evidence to get you closer to the truth? *Critical Thinking* boxes like this one will help you be more reflective and think critically about human behavior.

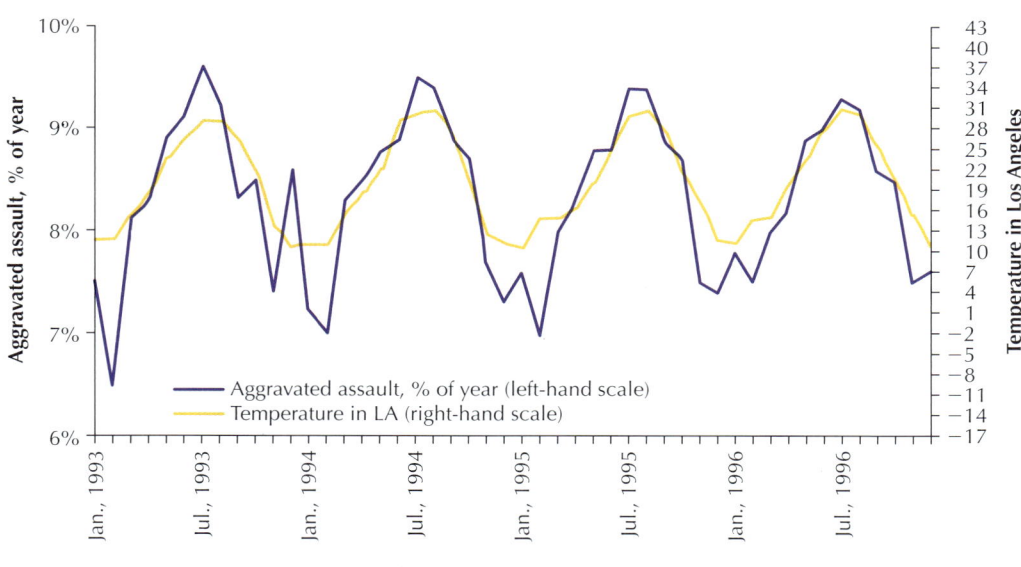

● **FIGURE 1.1** Results of an empirical study. The graph shows that aggravated assaults in Los Angeles become more likely as air temperature increases. This suggests that physical discomfort is associated with interpersonal hostility. (Data from Simister & Cooper, 2005.)

Psychological Research

Many fields, such as history, law, art, and business, are interested in human behavior. How is psychology different? Psychology's great strength is that it uses **scientific observation** to systematically answer questions about behavior (Stanovich, 2007).

Of course, some topics can't be studied because of ethical or practical concerns. More often, questions go unanswered for lack of a suitable **research method** (a systematic process for answering scientific questions). In the past, for example, we had to take the word of people who say they never dream. Then the EEG (electroencephalograph, or brain-wave machine) was invented. Certain EEG patterns, and the presence of eye movements, can reveal that a person is dreaming. People who "never dream," it turns out, dream frequently. If they are awakened during a dream, they vividly remember it. Thus, the EEG helped make the study of dreaming more scientific.

Psychology The scientific study of behavior and mental processes.
Scientific observation An empirical investigation that is structured so that it answers questions about the world.
Research method A systematic approach to answering scientific questions.

Research Specialties *What kinds of topics do psychologists study?* Here's a sample of what various psychologists might say about their work.

"In general, *developmental psychologists* study the course of human growth and development, from conception until death. I'm especially interested in the transition from the teenage years to early adulthood."

"Like other *learning theorists,* I study how and why learning occurs in humans and animals. Right now I'm investigating how patterns of punishment affect learning."

"I'm a *personality theorist.* I study personality traits, motivation, and individual differences. I am especially interested in the personality profiles of highly creative college students."

"As a *sensation and perception psychologist,* I investigate how we discern the world through our senses. I am using a perceptual theory to study how we are able to recognize faces in a crowd."

"*Comparative psychologists* study and compare the behavior of different species, especially animals. Personally, I'm fascinated by the communication abilities of porpoises."

"*Biopsychologists* are interested in how behavior relates to biological processes, especially activities in the nervous system. I've been doing some exciting research on how the brain controls hunger."

"*Cognitive psychologists* are primarily interested in thinking. I want to know how reasoning, problem solving, memory, and other mental processes relate to computer game playing."

"*Gender psychologists* study differences between females and males. I want to understand how gender differences are influenced by biology, child rearing, education, and stereotypes."

"*Social psychologists* explore human social behavior, such as attitudes, persuasion, riots, conformity, leadership, racism, and friendship. My own interest is interpersonal attraction. I place two strangers in a room and analyze how strongly they are attracted to each other."

"*Cultural psychologists* study the ways in which culture affects human behavior. The language you speak, the foods you eat, how your parents disciplined you, what laws you obey, who you regard as 'family,' whether you eat with a spoon or your fingers—these and countless other details of behavior are strongly influenced by culture."

"*Evolutionary psychologists* are interested in how our behavior is guided by patterns that evolved during the long history of humankind. I am studying some interesting trends in male and female mating choices that don't seem to be merely learned or based on culture."

"*Forensic psychologists* apply psychological principles to legal issues. I am interested in improving the reliability of eyewitness testimony during trials."

This small sample should give you an idea of the diversity of psychological research. It also hints at some of the kinds of information we will explore in this book.

Animals and Psychology *Research involving animals was mentioned in some of the preceding examples. Why is that?*

The scientific study of dreaming was made possible by use of the EEG, a device that records the tiny electrical signals generated by the brain as a person sleeps. The EEG converts these electrical signals to a written record of brain activity. Certain shifts in brain activity, coupled with the presence of rapid eye movements, are strongly related to dreaming. (See Module 5.1 for more information.)

Some of the most interesting research with animals has focused on attempts to teach primates to communicate with sign language. Psychologist Penny Patterson has spent 25 years teaching Koko more than 1,000 signs. One of Koko's favorite signs ("stink") is shown here. (For more, google The Gorilla Foundation.) Such research has led to better methods for teaching language to aphasic children (children with serious language impairment).

The variety and complexity of human behavior make psychological investigation challenging. How would you explain the behaviors shown here?

You may be surprised to learn that psychologists are interested in the behavior of *any* living creature—from flatworms to humans. Indeed, some comparative psychologists spend their entire careers studying rats, cats, dogs, turtles, or chimpanzees.

Although only a small percentage of psychological studies involve animals, they include many different types of research (Ord et al., 2005). Some psychologists use **animal models** to discover principles that apply to humans. For instance, animal studies have helped us understand stress, learning, obesity, aging, sleep, and many other topics. Psychology also benefits animals. For example, caring for domestic animals, as well as endangered species in zoos, relies on behavioral studies.

Psychology's Goals

What do psychology's goals mean in practice? Imagine that we would like to answer questions such as these: What happens when the right side of the brain is injured? Why are some people risk seekers while others avoid risk at all costs? Do autistic children react abnormally to their parents?

Description Answering psychological questions requires a careful description of behavior. **Description,** or naming and classifying, is typically based on making a detailed record of behavioral observations.

But a description doesn't explain anything, does it? Right. Useful knowledge begins with accurate description, but descriptions fail to answer the important "why" questions. *Why* do more women attempt suicide, and *why* do more men complete it? *Why* are people more aggressive when they are uncomfortable? *Why* are bystanders often unwilling to help in an emergency?

Understanding We have met psychology's second goal when we can explain an event. That is, **understanding** usually

> **Animal model** In research, an animal whose behavior is used to derive principles that may apply to human behavior.
> **Description** In scientific research, the process of naming and classifying.
> **Understanding** In psychology, understanding is achieved when the causes of a behavior can be stated.

means we can state the causes of a behavior. Take our last "why" question as an example: Research on "bystander apathy" reveals that people often fail to help when *other* possible helpers are nearby. Why? Because a "diffusion of responsibility" occurs. Basically, no one feels personally obligated to pitch in. As a result, the more potential helpers there are, the less likely it is that anyone will help (Darley, 2000; Darley & Latané, 1968). Now we can explain a perplexing problem.

Prediction Psychology's third goal, **prediction,** is the ability to forecast behavior accurately. Notice that our explanation of bystander apathy makes a prediction about the chances of getting help. If you've ever been stranded on a busy freeway with car trouble, you'll recognize the accuracy of this prediction: Having many potential helpers nearby is no guarantee that anyone will stop to help.

Control *Description, explanation, and prediction seem reasonable, but is control a valid goal?* Control may seem like a threat to personal freedom. However, to a psychologist, **control** simply refers to altering conditions that affect behavior. If you suggest changes in a classroom that help children learn better, you have exerted control. If a clinical psychologist helps a person overcome a terrible fear of heights, control is involved. Control is also involved in designing airplanes to keep pilots from making fatal errors. Clearly, psychological control must be used wisely and humanely.

In summary, psychology's goals are a natural outgrowth of our desire to understand behavior. Basically, they boil down to asking the following questions:

What is the nature of this behavior? (description)
Why does it occur? (understanding and explanation)
Can we forecast when it will occur? (prediction)
What conditions affect it? (control)

Some psychologists specialize in administering, scoring, and interpreting psychological tests, such as tests of intelligence, creativity, personality, or aptitude. This specialty, which is called psychometrics, is an example of using psychology to predict future behavior.

MODULE 1.1 Summary

What is psychology? What are its goals?

- Psychology is the scientific study of behavior and mental processes.
- Psychologists engage in critical thinking as they gather and analyze empirical evidence to answer questions about behavior.
- Some major areas of research in psychology are comparative psychology, learning, sensation, perception, personality, biopsychology, motivation and emotion, social psychology, cognitive psychology, developmental psychology, the psychology of gender, cultural psychology, evolutionary psychology, and forensic psychology.
- Some psychologists are directly interested in animal behavior. Others study animals as models of human behavior.
- As a science, psychology's goals are to describe, understand, predict, and control behavior.

KNOWLEDGE BUILDER

The Science of Psychology

Recite

To check your memory, see if you can answer these questions. If you miss any, skim over the preceding material before continuing, to make sure you understand what you just read.

1. Psychology is the _____ study of _____ and _____ processes.
2. Information gained through direct observation and measurement is called _____ evidence.
3. In psychological research, animal _____ may be used to discover principles that apply to human behavior.
4. Which of the following questions relates most directly to the goal of *understanding* behavior?
   a. Do the scores of men and women differ on tests of thinking abilities?
   b. Why does a blow to the head cause memory loss?
   c. Will productivity in a business office increase if room temperature is raised or lowered?
   d. What percentage of college students suffer from test anxiety?

Match the following research areas with the topics they cover.

____ 5. Developmental psychology
____ 6. Learning
____ 7. Personality
____ 8. Sensation and perception
____ 9. Biopsychology
____ 10. Social psychology
____ 11. Comparative psychology

A. Attitudes, groups, leadership
B. Conditioning, memory
C. The psychology of law
D. Brain and nervous system
E. Child psychology
F. Individual differences, motivation
G. Animal behavior
H. Processing sensory information

Reflect

Critical Thinking

12. All sciences are interested in controlling the phenomena they study. True or false?

Relate

At first, many students think that psychology is primarily about abnormal behavior and psychotherapy. Did you? How would you describe the field now?

Link

Internet addresses frequently change. To find the sites listed here, visit **http://www.thomsonedu.com/psychology/coon** for an updated list of Internet addresses and direct links to relevant sites.

- **Definition of "Psychology"** Provides definitions of *psychology* and *psychologist*.
- **Self-Quiz on Psychology and Science** A 10-item online test (with answers) about psychology and science.
- **What Is Psychology?** Discusses psychology as a science, with links to other articles about various branches of psychology.

ANSWERS

1. scientific, behavior, mental 2. empirical 3. models 4. b 5. E 6. B 7. F 8. H 9. D 10. A 11. G 12. False. Astronomy and archaeology are examples of sciences that do not share psychology's fourth goal.

Prediction An ability to accurately forecast behavior.
Control Altering conditions that influence behavior.

MODULE 1.2 Critical Thinking and the Scientific Method in Psychology

TO ACHIEVE THEIR GOALS of describing, understanding, predicting, and controlling behavior, psychologists rely on critical thinking and the scientific method. As critical thinkers, psychologists actively evaluate ideas about human behavior. Critical thinking in psychology most often takes the form of collecting empirical evidence, as guided by the scientific method. It would be impossible to answer most questions about human behavior without the aid of scientific research methods.

Critical Thinking—Take It With a Grain of Salt

SURVEY QUESTION: *What is critical thinking?*

How does critical thinking play a role in psychology? Most of us would be skeptical when buying a used car. But all too often, we may be tempted to "buy" outrageous claims about the occult, UFOs, Tarot cards, healing crystals, some herbal remedies, psychics "channeling" dead people, and so forth. Likewise, most of us easily accept our ignorance of sub-atomic physics. But because we deal with human behavior every day, we tend to think that we already know what is true in psychology.

For these and many more reasons, learning to think critically is one of the lasting benefits of a college education. **Critical thinking** refers to an ability to evaluate, compare, analyze, critique, synthesize, and reflect on information. Critical thinkers are willing to ask the hard questions and challenge conventional wisdom. For example, many people believe that punishment (a spanking) is a good way to reinforce learning in children. Actually, nothing could be further from the truth (Gershoff, 2002). That's why a critical thinker would immediately ask: "Does punishment work? If so, when? Under what conditions does it not work? What are its drawbacks? Are there better ways to guide learning?"

Thinking about Behavior

The core of critical thinking is a willingness to actively *evaluate* ideas. Critical thinkers analyze the evidence supporting their beliefs and probe for weaknesses in their reasoning. They question assumptions and look for alternate conclusions. True knowledge, they recognize, comes from constantly revising our understanding of the world. As Susan Blackmore (2001) said when her studies caused her to abandon some long-held beliefs, "Admitting you are wrong is always hard—even though it's a skill that every psychologist has to learn."

Critical thinking is built upon a few basic principles (Elder, 2006; Kida, 2006):

1. *Few "truths" transcend the need for empirical testing.* While religious beliefs and personal values may be held as matters of faith without supporting evidence, most other ideas can be evaluated by applying the rules of logic, evidence, and the scientific method.

2. *Judging the quality of evidence is crucial.* Imagine that you are a juror in a courtroom, judging claims made by two battling lawyers. To decide correctly, you can't just weigh the amount of evidence. You must also critically evaluate the *quality* of the evidence. Then you can give greater weight to the most credible facts.

3. *Authority or claimed expertise does not automatically make an idea true.* Just because a teacher, guru, celebrity, or authority is convinced or sincere doesn't mean you should automatically believe them. It is unscientific and self-demeaning to just take the word of an "expert" without asking, "What evidence convinced her or him? How good is it? Is there a better explanation?"

4. *Critical thinking requires an open mind.* Be prepared to consider daring departures and go wherever the evidence leads. However, don't become so "open-minded" that you are simply gullible. As Carl Sagan once noted, "It seems to me that what is called for is an exquisite balance between two conflicting needs: the most skeptical scrutiny of all hypotheses that are served up to us and at the same time a great openness to new ideas" (Kida, 2006, p51).

To put these principles into action, here are some questions to ask over and over again as you evaluate new information (Browne & Keeley, 2007; Elder, 2006):

1. What claims are being made?
2. What test (if any) of these claims has been made?
3. Who did the test? How good is the evidence?
4. What was the nature and quality of the tests? Are they credible? Can they be repeated?
5. How reliable and trustworthy were the investigators? Do they have conflicts of interest? Do their findings

appear to be objective? Has any other independent researcher duplicated the findings?

6. Finally, how much credibility can the claim be given? High, medium, low, provisional?

A course in psychology naturally enriches thinking skills. To add to the process, all upcoming modules include Critical Thinking questions like the ones you have seen here. Tackling these questions will sharpen your thinking abilities and make learning more lively. For an immediate thinking challenge, let's take a critical look at several nonscientific systems that claim to explain behavior.

Pseudopsychologies—Palms, Planets, and Personality

SURVEY QUESTION: *How does psychology differ from false explanations of behavior?*

A **pseudopsychology** (SUE-doe-psychology) is any unfounded system that resembles psychology. Many pseudopsychologies give the appearance of science but are actually false. (*Pseudo* means "false.") Pseudopsychologies change little over time because their followers seek evidence that appears to confirm their beliefs and avoid evidence that contradicts their beliefs. Scientists, in contrast, actively look for contradictions as a way to advance knowledge. They are skeptical critics of their own theories (Schick & Vaughn, 2004).

Can you give some examples of false psychologies? One early pseudopsychology, *phrenology,* was popularized in the nineteenth century by Franz Gall, a German anatomy teacher. Phrenology claimed that personality traits are revealed by the shape of the skull. Modern research has long since shown that bumps on the head have nothing to do with talents or abilities. In fact, the phrenologists were so far off that they listed the part of the brain that controls hearing as a center for "combativeness"! *Palmistry* is a similar false system that claims lines on the hand reveal personality traits and predict the future. Despite the overwhelming evidence against this, palmists can still be found separating the gullible from their money in many cities.

At first glance, a pseudopsychology called *graphology* might seem more reasonable. Graphologists claim that personality traits are revealed by handwriting. Based on such claims, some companies use graphologists to select job candidates. This is troubling because graphologists score close to zero on tests of accuracy in rating personality (Furnham, Chamorro-Premuzic, & Callahan, 2003). In fact, graphologists do no better than untrained college students in rating personality and job performance (Neter & Ben-Shakhar, 1989). Even a graphological society recently concluded that handwriting analysis should not be used to select people for jobs (Simner & Goffin, 2003). (By the way, graphology's failure at revealing personality should be separated from its value for detecting forgeries.)

Graphology might seem harmless enough. However, this false system has been used to determine who is hired, given bank credit, or selected for juries. In these and similar situations, pseudopsychologies do, in fact, harm people.

If pseudopsychologies have no scientific basis, how do they survive and why are they popular? There are several reasons, all of which can be illustrated by a critique of astrology.

Phrenology was an attempt to assess personality characteristics by examining various areas of the skull. Phrenologists used charts such as the one shown here as guides. Like other pseudopsychologists, phrenologists made no attempt to empirically verify their concepts.

Would you hire this man? Here's a sample of your author's handwriting. What do you think it reveals? Your interpretations are likely to be as accurate (or inaccurate) as those of a graphologist.

Critical thinking An ability to evaluate, compare, analyze, critique, synthesize, and reflect on information.

Pseudopsychology Any false and unscientific system of beliefs and practices that is offered as an explanation of behavior.

Problems in the Stars

Astrology is probably the most popular pseudopsychology. Astrology holds that the positions of the stars and planets at the time of one's birth determine personality traits and affect behavior. Like other pseudopsychologies, astrology has repeatedly been shown to have no scientific validity (Hartmann, Reuter, & Nyborg, 2006; Kelly, 1999). The objections to astrology are numerous and devastating:

1. The zodiac has shifted in the sky by one full constellation since astrology was first set up. However, most astrologers simply ignore this shift. (In other words, if astrology calls you a Scorpio you are really a Libra, and so forth.)
2. Astrologers have failed to explain why the moment of birth should be more important than, say, the moment of conception.
3. There is no connection between the "compatibility" of couples' astrological signs and their marriage and divorce rates or between astrological signs and leadership, physical characteristics, career choices, or personality traits.
4. A study of more than 3,000 predictions by famous astrologers found that only a small percentage were fulfilled. These "successful" predictions tended to be vague ("There will be a tragedy somewhere in the east in the spring") or easily guessed from current events.
5. If astrologers are asked to match people with their horoscopes, they do no better than would be expected by chance (Kelly, 1999).
6. A few astrologers have tried to test astrology. Their results have been just as negative as those obtained by critics. (Hartmann, Reuter, & Nyborg, 2006; Kelly, 1999; Martens & Trachet, 1998.)

In short, astrology doesn't work.

Then why does astrology often seem to work? The following discussion explains why.

Uncritical Acceptance

If you have ever had your astrological chart done, you may have been impressed with its apparent accuracy. However, such perceptions are typically based on **uncritical acceptance** (the tendency to believe positive or flattering descriptions of yourself). Many astrological charts are made up of mostly flattering traits. Naturally, when your personality is described in *desirable* terms, it is hard to deny that the description has the "ring of truth." How much acceptance would astrology receive if a birth sign read like this:

> **Virgo:** You are the logical type and hate disorder. Your nitpicking is unbearable to your friends. You are cold, unemotional, and usually fall asleep while making love. Virgos make good doorstops.

Positive Instances

Even when an astrological description contains a mixture of good and bad traits it may seem accurate. To find out why, read the following personality description.

> **YOUR PERSONALITY PROFILE**
> You have a strong need for other people to like you and for them to admire you. You have a tendency to be critical of yourself. You have a great deal of unused energy which you have not turned to your advantage. While you have some personality weaknesses, you are generally able to compensate for them. Your sexual adjustment has presented some problems for you. Disciplined and controlled on the outside, you tend to be worrisome and insecure inside. At times you have serious doubts as to whether you have made the right decision or done the right thing. You prefer a certain amount of change and variety and become dissatisfied when hemmed in by restrictions and limitations. You pride yourself on being an independent thinker and do not accept other opinions without satisfactory proof. You have found it unwise to be too frank in revealing yourself to others. At times you are extroverted, affable, sociable, while at other times you are introverted, wary, and reserved. Some of your aspirations tend to be pretty unrealistic.*

Does this describe your personality? A psychologist read this summary individually to college students who had taken a personality test. Only 5 students out of 79 felt that the description was inaccurate. Another classic study found that people rated this "personality profile" as more accurate than their actual horoscopes (French et al., 1991).

Reread the description and you will see that it contains both sides of several personality dimensions ("At times you are extroverted . . . while at other times you are introverted"). Its apparent accuracy is an illusion based on the **fallacy of positive instances,** in which we remember or notice things that confirm our expectations and forget the rest. The pseudopsychologies thrive on this effect. For example, you can always find "Aquarius characteristics" in an Aquarius. If you looked, however, you could also find "Gemini characteristics," "Scorpio characteristics," or whatever.

The fallacy of positive instances is used by various "psychic mediums" who pretend to communicate with the deceased friends and relatives of audience members. An analysis

---

*R. E. Ulrich, T. J. Stachnik, and N. R. Stainton, "Student acceptance of generalized personality interpretations," *Psychological Reports,* 13, 1963, 831–834.

shows that the number of "hits" (correct statements) made by these fakes tends to be very low. Nevertheless, many viewers are impressed because of the natural tendency to remember apparent hits and ignore misses. Also, embarrassing misses are often edited out before the shows appear on television (Nickell, 2001).

The Barnum Effect Pseudopsychologies also take advantage of the **Barnum effect,** which is a tendency to consider personal descriptions accurate if they are stated in general terms (Kida, 2006). P. T. Barnum, the famed circus showman, had a formula for success: "Always have a little something for everybody." Like the all-purpose personality profile, palm readings, fortunes, horoscopes, and other products of pseudopsychology are stated in such general terms that they can hardly miss. There is always "a little something for everybody." To observe the Barnum effect, read *all 12* of the daily horoscopes found in newspapers for several days. You will find that predictions for other signs fit events as well as those for your own sign do. You can also give a friend the wrong horoscope for his or her sign. Your friend may still be quite impressed with the "accuracy" of the horoscope.

Astrology's popularity shows that many people have difficulty separating valid psychology from systems that seem valid but are not. The goal of this discussion, then, has been to make you a more critical observer of human behavior and to clarify what is, and what is not, psychology. Here is what the "stars" say about your future:

> Emphasis now on education and personal improvement. A learning experience of lasting value awaits you. Take care of scholastic responsibilities before engaging in recreation. The word *psychology* figures prominently in your future.

Pseudopsychologies may seem like no more than a nuisance, but they can do harm. For instance, people seeking treatment for psychological disorders may become the victims of self-appointed "experts" who offer ineffective, pseudoscientific "therapies" (Kida, 2006; Lilienfeld et al., 2005). Valid psychological principles are based on observation and evidence, not fads, opinions, or wishful thinking.

say when he loses interest and quits? "Well, you can't teach an old dog new tricks." Let's examine another *commonsense statement*. It is frequently said that "absence makes the heart grow fonder." Those of us separated from friends and lovers can take comfort in this knowledge—until we remember "Out of sight, out of mind"! Much of what passes for common sense is equally vague and inconsistent. Notice also that most of these B. S. statements work best after the fact. (B. S., of course, stands for *Before Science*.)

Carefully recording facts and events is the heart of all sciences. To be *scientific*, our observations must be *systematic*, so that they reveal something about behavior (Stanovich, 2007). To use an earlier example, if you are interested in heat and aggression, you will learn little by driving around and making haphazard observations of aggressive behavior. To be of value, your observations must be planned and systematic.

The Scientific Method

The **scientific method** is a form of critical thinking based on careful collection of evidence, accurate description and measurement, precise definition, controlled observation, and repeatable results (Jackson, 2008). In its ideal form the scientific method has six elements:

1. Making observations
2. Defining a problem
3. Proposing a hypothesis
4. Gathering evidence/testing the hypothesis
5. Publishing results
6. Theory building

Scientific Research—How to Think Like a Psychologist

SURVEY QUESTION: *Why is the scientific method important to psychologists?*

Suppose that your grandfather goes back to college. What do people say? "Ah . . . never too old to learn." And what do they

Uncritical acceptance The tendency to believe generally positive or flattering descriptions of oneself.

Fallacy of positive instances The tendency to remember or notice information that fits one's expectations, while forgetting discrepancies.

Barnum effect The tendency to consider a personal description accurate if it is stated in very general terms.

Scientific method A form of critical thinking based on careful measurement and controlled observation.

Applying the scientific method to the study of behavior requires careful observation. Here, a psychologist videotapes a session in which a child's thinking abilities are being tested.

● **FIGURE 1.2** Operational definitions are used to link concepts with concrete observations. Do you think the examples given are reasonable operational definitions of frustration and aggression? Operational definitions vary in how well they represent concepts. For this reason, many different experiments may be necessary to draw clear conclusions about hypothesized relationships in psychology.

Let's take a closer look at some elements of the scientific method.

Hypothesis Testing *Yes, what exactly is a hypothesis?* A **hypothesis** (hi-POTH-eh-sis) is a tentative explanation of an event or relationship. In common terms, a hypothesis is a *testable* hunch or educated guess about behavior. For example, you might hypothesize that "Frustration encourages aggression." How could you test this hypothesis? First you would have to decide how you are going to frustrate people. (This part might be fun.) Then you will need to find a way to measure whether or not they become more aggressive. (Not so much fun if you plan to be nearby.) Your observations would then provide evidence to confirm or disconfirm the hypothesis.

Operational Definitions Because we cannot see or touch frustration, it must be defined operationally. An **operational definition** states the exact procedures used to represent a concept. Operational definitions allow unobservable ideas, such as covert behaviors, to be tested in real-world terms. (See ● Fig. 1.2.) For example, since you can't measure an abstract covert behavior like "frustration" directly, you might define frustration as "interrupting an adult before he or she can finish a puzzle and win an iPhone." And aggression might be defined as "the number of times a frustrated individual insults the person who prevented work on the puzzle." In other words, covert behaviors are operationally defined in terms of overt behavior so they can be studied scientifically.

Clever Hans Several steps of the scientific method can be illustrated with the story of Clever Hans, a horse who became famous in Germany 100 years ago (Rosenthal, 1965). Clever Hans seemed to solve math problems, which he answered by tapping his hoof. If you asked Hans, "What is 12 times 2, minus 18," Hans would tap his hoof six times. This was so astonishing that one skeptical scientist decided to find out if Hans really could do arithmetic. Assume that you are the scientist and that you are just itching to discover how Hans *really* does his trick.

CAN A HORSE ADD NUMBERS?
Your investigation of Hans's math skills would probably begin with careful *observation* of both the horse and his owner. Assume that these observations fail to reveal any obvious cheating. Then the *problem* becomes more clearly *defined*: What signals Hans to start and stop tapping his hoof? Your first *hypothesis* might be that the owner is giving Hans a signal. Your proposed *test* would be to make the owner leave the room. Then someone else could ask Hans questions. Your test would either confirm or deny the owner's role. This *evidence* would support or eliminate the cheating hypothesis. By changing the conditions under which you observe Hans, you have *controlled* the situation to gain more information from your observations.

Incidentally, Hans could still answer when his owner was out of the room. But a brilliant series of controlled observations revealed Hans's secret. If Hans couldn't see the questioner, he couldn't answer. It seems that questioners always *lowered their heads* (to look at Hans's hoof) after asking a question. This was Hans's cue to start tapping. When Hans had tapped the correct number, a questioner would always *look up* to see if Hans was going to stop. This was Hans's cue to stop tapping!

Theories *What about theory building?* Since Clever Hans's ability to do math was an isolated case, no theorizing was involved. However, in actual research, a **theory** acts as a map of knowledge. Good theories summarize observations, explain them, and guide further research (● Fig. 1.3). Without theories of forgetting, personality, stress, mental illness, and the like, psychologists would drown in a sea of disconnected facts (Stanovich, 2007).

Publication Scientific information must always be *publicly available*. The results of psychological studies are usually published in professional journals. (See ■ Table 1.1.) That way, anyone willing to make appropriate observations can see whether or not a claim is true (Jackson, 2008).

Summary Now let's summarize more realistically. All the basic elements of the scientific method are found in the example that follows.

> **Observation:** Isidora, a psychologist, observes that some computer game designers seem to experience less work-related stress than others.

■ TABLE 1.1 Outline of a Research Report

- **Abstract** Research reports begin with a very brief summary of the study and its findings. The abstract allows you to get an overview without reading the entire article.
- **Introduction** The introduction describes the question to be investigated. It also provides background information by reviewing prior studies on the same or related topics.
- **Method** This section tells how and why observations were made. It also describes the specific procedures used to gather data. That way, other researchers can repeat the study to see if they get the same results.
- **Results** The outcome of the investigation is presented. Data may be graphed, summarized in tables, or statistically analyzed.
- **Discussion** The results of the study are discussed in relation to the original question. Implications of the study are explored and further studies may be proposed.

> **Defining a Problem:** Isidora's problem is to identify the ways in which high-stress and low-stress game designers are different.
>
> **Observation:** Isidora carefully questions game designers about how much stress they experience. These additional observations suggest that low-stress game designers feel they have more control over their work.
>
> **Proposing a Hypothesis:** Isidora hypothesizes that having control over difficult tasks reduces stress.
>
> **Gathering Evidence/Testing the Hypothesis:** Isidora designs an experiment in which people must solve a series of very difficult problems. In one group, people solve the problems at a forced pace, dictated by Isidora. In another group, they are allowed to set the pace themselves. While working, the second group reports lower stress levels than the first did. This suggests that Isidora's hypothesis is correct.
>
> **Publishing Results:** In a scholarly article, Isidora carefully describes the question she investigated, the methods she used, and the results of her experiment. The article is published in the *Journal of Clinical Psychology*.
>
> **Theory Building:** Drawing on the results of similar experiments, Isidora and other psychologists create a theory to explain why having control over a task helps reduce stress.

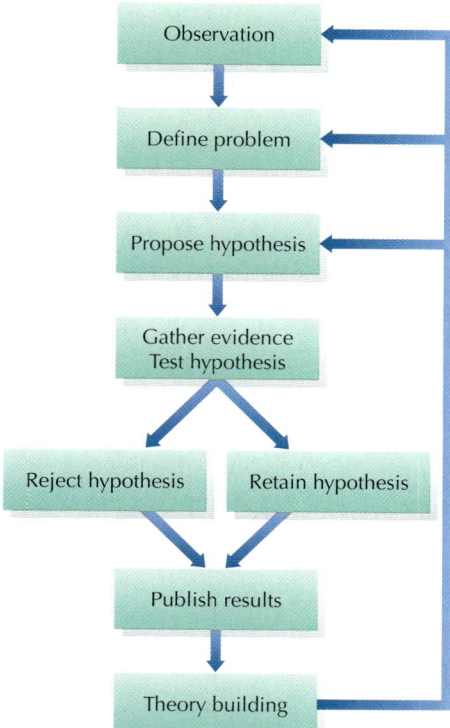

● **FIGURE 1.3** Psychologists use the logic of science to answer questions about behavior. Specific hypotheses can be tested in a variety of ways, including naturalistic observation, correlational studies, controlled experiments, clinical studies, and the survey method. Psychologists revise their theories to reflect the evidence they gather. New or revised theories then lead to new observations, problems, and hypotheses.

Hypothesis The predicted outcome of an experiment or an educated guess about the relationship between variables.

Operational definition Defining a scientific concept by stating the specific actions or procedures used to measure it. For example, "hunger" might be defined as "the number of hours of food deprivation."

Theory A system of ideas designed to interrelate concepts and facts in a way that summarizes existing data and predicts future observations.

MODULE 1.2 Summary

What is critical thinking?
- Critical thinking is the ability to actively evaluate, compare, analyze, critique, synthesize, and reflect on information.
- To judge the validity of a claim, it is important to gather evidence for and against the claim and to evaluate the *quality* of the evidence.

How does psychology differ from false explanations of behavior?
- Numerous pseudopsychologies exist. These false systems are frequently confused with valid psychology. Belief in pseudopsychologies is based in part on uncritical acceptance, the fallacy of positive instances, and the Barnum effect.

Why is the scientific method important to psychologists?
- In the scientific method, systematic observation is used to test hypotheses about behavior and mental events.
- Important elements of a scientific investigation include observing, defining a problem, proposing a hypothesis, gathering evidence/testing the hypothesis, publishing results, and forming a theory.
- Concepts must be defined operationally before they can be studied empirically.

KNOWLEDGE BUILDER

Critical Thinking and the Scientific Method in Psychology

Recite

1. The fallacy of positive instances refers to graphology's accepted value for the detection of forgeries. T or F?
2. Personality descriptions provided by pseudopsychologies are stated in general terms, which provide "a little something for everybody." This fact is the basis of the
   a. palmist's fallacy b. uncritical acceptance pattern c. fallacy of positive instances d. Barnum effect
3. Most of psychology can rightfully be called common sense because psychologists prefer informal observation to systematic observation. T or F?
4. A psychologist does a study to see if exercising increases sense of well-being. In the study she will be testing an
   a. experimental hypothesis b. operational definition c. empirical definition d. anthropomorphic theory
5. _____ behaviors are operationally defined in terms of _____ behavior
   a. overt, covert b. observable, overt c. covert, overt d. covert, abstract

Reflect
Critical Thinking

6. Can you think of some "commonsense" statements that contradict each other?
7. Try constructing a few "Barnum statements," personality statements that are so general that virtually everyone will think they apply to themselves. Can you string them together to make a "Barnum personality profile"? Can you adapt the same statements to construct a "Barnum horoscope"?

Relate

How might you scientifically test the old saw that you can't teach an old dog new tricks? Follow the steps of the scientific method to propose a testable hypothesis and decide how you would gather evidence. (Well, OK, you don't have to publish your results.)

Link

Internet addresses frequently change. To find the sites listed here, visit **http://www.thomsonedu.com/psychology/coon** for an updated list of Internet addresses and direct links to relevant sites.

- **Critical Thinking in Everyday Life: 9 Strategies** Some useful critical thinking strategies, along with many other articles on aspects of critical thinking.
- **Logic in Everyday Life** A series of podcasts of everyday examples of how flawed logic is often used to justify arguments.
- **The Scientific Method** The scientific method in psychology.

ANSWERS

1. F 2. d 3. F 4. a 5. c 6. There are many examples. Here are a few more to add to the ones you thought of: "Where there's smoke there's fire." versus "You can't judge a book by its cover." "He (or she) who hesitates is lost." versus "Haste makes waste." "Birds of a feather flock together." versus "Opposites attract." 7. The term "Barnum statement" comes from Levy (2003), who offers the following examples: You are afraid of being hurt. You are trying to find a balance between autonomy and closeness. You don't like being overly dependent. You just want to be understood.

MODULE 1.3 History and Contemporary Perspectives

STARTING WITH PHILOSOPHY and continuing through psychology's history, various viewpoints have helped us understand and interpret human behavior. Today, three complementary perspectives guide research and theorizing in psychology. These are the biological perspective, the psychological perspective, and the sociocultural perspective.

A Brief History of Psychology— Psychology's Family Album

SURVEY QUESTION: *How did the field of psychology emerge?*

People have been informally observing about human behavior and speculating about it for thousands of years. In contrast, psychology's short history as a science dates back only about 130 years. Of course, to some students any history is "not short enough!" Nevertheless, to understand psychology today, we need to explore its past.

Psychology's history as a science began in 1879 in Leipzig, Germany. There, the "father of psychology," Wilhelm Wundt (VILL-helm Voont), set up the first psychological laboratory to study conscious experience. What happens, he wondered, when we have sensations, images, and feelings? To find out, Wundt systematically observed and measured stimuli of various kinds (lights, sounds, weights). A **stimulus** is any physical energy that affects a person and evokes a response (stimulus: singular; stimuli [STIM-you-lie]: plural). Wundt then used **introspection,** or "looking inward," and careful measurement to probe his reactions to various stimuli. (If you carefully examine your thoughts, feelings, and sensations for a moment, you will have done some introspecting.) Over the years, Wundt studied vision, hearing, taste, touch, memory, time perception, and many other topics. By insisting on systematic observation and measurement, he asked some interesting questions and got psychology off to a good start (Schultz & Schultz, 2008).

Structuralism

Wundt's ideas were carried to the United States by a man named Edward Titchener (TICH-in-er). Titchener called Wundt's ideas **structuralism** and tried to analyze the structure of mental life into basic "elements" or "building blocks."

How could they do that? You can't analyze experience like a chemical compound, can you? Perhaps not, but the structuralists tried, mostly by using introspection. For instance, an observer might heft an apple and decide that she had experienced the elements "hue" (color), "roundness," and "weight." Another example of a question that might have interested a structuralist is, What basic tastes mix together to create complex flavors as different as liver, lime, bacon, and burnt-almond fudge?

Introspection proved to be a poor way to answer most questions. Why? Because no matter how systematic the observations, the structuralists frequently *disagreed.* And when they did, there was no way to settle differences. Think about it. If you and a friend both introspect on your perceptions of an apple and end up listing different basic elements, who would be right? Despite such limitations, "looking inward" is still used in studies of hypnosis, meditation, problem solving, moods, and many other topics.

Functionalism

William James, an American scholar, broadened psychology to include animal behavior, religious experience, abnormal behavior, and other interesting topics. James's brilliant first book, *Principles of Psychology* (1890), helped establish the field as a separate discipline (Hergenhahn, 2005).

The term **functionalism** comes from James's interest in how the mind functions to help us adapt to the environment. James regarded consciousness as an ever-changing *stream* or

Wilhelm Wundt, 1832–1920. Wundt is credited with making psychology an independent science, separate from philosophy. Wundt's original training was in medicine, but he became deeply interested in psychology. In his laboratory, Wundt investigated how sensations, images, and feelings combine to make up personal experience.

Stimulus Any physical energy sensed by an organism.
Introspection To look within; to examine one's own thoughts, feelings, or sensations.
Structuralism The school of thought concerned with analyzing sensations and personal experience into basic elements.
Functionalism The school of psychology concerned with how behavior and mental abilities help people adapt to their environments.

William James, 1842-1910. William James was the son of philosopher Henry James, Sr., and the brother of novelist Henry James. During his long academic career, James taught anatomy, physiology, psychology, and philosophy at Harvard University. James believed strongly that ideas should be judged in terms of their practical consequences for human conduct.

flow of images and sensations—not a set of lifeless building blocks, as the structuralists claimed.

The functionalists admired Charles Darwin, who deduced that creatures evolve in ways that favor survival. According to Darwin's principle of **natural selection,** physical features that help animals adapt to their environments are retained in evolution. Similarly, the functionalists wanted to find out how the mind, perception, habits, and emotions help us adapt and survive.

What effect did functionalism have on modern psychology? Functionalism brought the study of animals into psychology. It also promoted *educational psychology* (the study of learning, teaching, classroom dynamics, and related topics). Learning makes us more adaptable, so the functionalists tried to find ways to improve education. For similar reasons, functionalism spurred the rise of *industrial psychology,* the study of people at work.

Behaviorism

Functionalism and structuralism were soon challenged by **behaviorism,** the study of observable behavior. Behaviorist John B. Watson objected strongly to the study of the "mind" or "conscious experience." He believed that introspection is unscientific because there is no way to settle disagreements between observers. Watson realized that he could study the overt behavior of animals even though he couldn't ask them questions, or know what they were thinking (Watson, 1913/1994). He simply observed the relationship between *stimuli* (events in the environment) and an animal's **responses** (any muscular action, glandular activity, or other identifiable behavior). These observations were objective because they did not involve introspecting on subjective experience. Why not, he asked, apply the same objectivity to human behavior?

Watson soon adopted Russian physiologist Ivan Pavlov's (ee-VAHN PAV-lahv) concept of *conditioning* to explain most behavior. (A *conditioned response* is a learned reaction to a particular stimulus.) Watson eagerly claimed, "Give me a dozen healthy infants, well-formed, and my own special world to bring them up in and I'll guarantee to take any one at random and train him to become any type of specialist I might select—doctor, lawyer, artist, merchant-chief, and yes, beggarman and thief" (Watson, 1913/1994).

Would most psychologists agree with Watson's claim? No, today it is regarded as an overstatement. Just the same, behaviorism helped make psychology a natural science, rather than a branch of philosophy (Benjafield, 2004).

One of the best-known behaviorists, B. F. Skinner (1904–1990), believed that our actions are controlled by rewards and punishments. To study learning, Skinner created his famous conditioning chamber, or "Skinner box." With it, he could present stimuli to animals and record their responses

John B. Watson, 1878-1958. Watson's intense interest in observable behavior began with his doctoral studies in biology and neurology. Watson became a psychology professor at Johns Hopkins University in 1908 and advanced his theory of behaviorism. He remained at Johns Hopkins until 1920 when he left for a career in the advertising industry!

B. F. Skinner, 1904-1990. Skinner studied simple behaviors under carefully controlled conditions. The "Skinner Box" you see here has been widely used to study learning in simplified animal experiments. In addition to advancing psychology, Skinner hoped that his radical brand of behaviorism would improve human life.

(see Module 6.2, "Operant Conditioning"). Many of Skinner's ideas about learning grew out of work with rats and pigeons. Nevertheless, he believed that the same laws of behavior apply to humans. As a "radical behaviorist," Skinner also believed that mental events, such as thinking, are not needed to explain behavior (Schultz & Schultz, 2008).

Skinner was convinced that a "designed culture" based on positive reinforcement could encourage desirable behavior. (Skinner disliked the use of punishment because it doesn't teach correct responses.) Too often, he believed, misguided rewards lead to destructive actions that create problems such as overpopulation, pollution, and war.

Cognitive Behaviorism Radical behaviorists have been criticized for ignoring the role that thinking plays in our lives. One critic even charged that Skinnerian psychology had "lost consciousness"! However, many criticisms have been answered by **cognitive behaviorism,** a view that combines cognition (thinking) and conditioning to explain behavior (Zentall, 2002). As an example, let's say you frequently visit a particular website because it offers free streaming videos. A behaviorist would say that you visit the site because you are rewarded by the pleasure of watching interesting videos each time you go there. A cognitive behaviorist would add that, in addition, you *expect* to find free videos at the site. This is the cognitive part of your behavior.

Behaviorists deserve credit for much of what we know about learning, conditioning, and the proper use of reward and punishment. Behaviorism is also the source of behavior therapy, which uses learning principles to change problem behaviors such as overeating, unrealistic fears, or temper tantrums. (See Modules 13.3 and 13.4 for more information.)

Gestalt Psychology

Imagine that you just played "Happy Birthday" on a low-pitched tuba. Next, you play it on a high-pitched clarinet. The clarinet duplicates none of the tuba's sounds. Yet, we notice something interesting: The melody is still recognizable—as long as the *relationship* between notes remains the same.

Now, what would happen if you played the notes of "Happy Birthday" in the correct order, but at a rate of one per hour? What would we have? Nothing! The separate notes would no longer be a melody. Perceptually, the melody is somehow more than the individual notes that define it.

It was observations like these that launched the Gestalt school of thought. The German word *Gestalt* means form, pattern, or whole. **Gestalt psychologists** studied thinking, learning, and perception as whole units, not by analyzing experiences into parts. Their slogan was, "The whole is greater than the sum of its parts." (See ● Fig. 1.4.)

● **FIGURE 1.4** The design you see here is entirely made up of broken circles. However, as the Gestalt psychologists discovered, our perceptions have a powerful tendency to form meaningful patterns. Because of this tendency, you will probably see a triangle in this design, even though it is only an illusion. Your whole perceptual experience exceeds the sum of its parts.

In Germany, Max Wertheimer (VERT-hi-mer) was the first psychologist to advance the Gestalt viewpoint. It is a mistake, he said, to analyze psychological events into pieces or "elements," as the structuralists did. Like a melody, many experiences cannot be broken into smaller units, as the Structuralists proposed. For this reason, studies of perception and personality have been especially influenced by the Gestalt viewpoint.

Max Wertheimer, 1880–1941. Wertheimer first proposed the Gestalt viewpoint to help explain perceptual illusions. He later promoted Gestalt psychology as a way to understand not only perception, problem solving, thinking, and social behavior, but also art, logic, philosophy, and politics.

Natural selection Darwin's theory that evolution favors those plants and animals best suited to their living conditions.
Behaviorism The school of psychology that emphasizes the study of overt, observable behavior.
Response Any muscular action, glandular activity, or other identifiable aspect of behavior.
Cognitive behaviorism An approach that combines behavioral principles with cognition (perception, thinking, anticipation) to explain behavior.
Gestalt psychology A school of psychology emphasizing the study of thinking, learning, and perception in whole units, not by analysis into parts.

Psychoanalytic Psychology

As American psychology grew more scientific, an Austrian doctor named Sigmund Freud was developing his own theories. Freud believed that mental life is like an iceberg: Only a small part is exposed to view. He called the area of the mind that lies outside of personal awareness the **unconscious.** According to Freud, our behavior is deeply influenced by unconscious thoughts, impulses, and desires—especially those concerning sex and aggression. Freud's ideas opened new horizons in art, literature, and history, as well as psychology (Jacobs, 2003).

Freud theorized that many unconscious thoughts are **repressed** (held out of awareness) because they are threatening. But sometimes, he said, they are revealed by dreams, emotions, or slips of the tongue. ("Freudian slips" are often humorous, as when a student who is tardy for class says, "I'm sorry I couldn't get here any later.")

Freud believed that all thoughts, emotions, and actions are *determined*. In other words, nothing is an accident: If we probe deeply enough we will find the causes of every thought or action. Freud was also among the first to appreciate that childhood affects adult personality ("The child is father to the man"). Most of all, perhaps, Freud is known for creating **psychoanalysis,** the first "talking cure." Freud's method of psychotherapy explores unconscious conflicts and emotional problems (see Module 13.1).

It wasn't very long before some of Freud's students began to promote their own theories. Several who modified Freud's ideas became known as neo-Freudians (*neo* means "new" or "recent"). **Neo-Freudians** accept much of Freud's theory but revise parts of it. Many, for instance, place less emphasis on sex and aggression and more on social motives and relationships. Some well-known neo-Freudians are Alfred Adler, Anna Freud (Freud's daughter), Karen Horney (HORN-eye), Carl Jung (yoong), Otto Rank (rahnk), and Erik Erikson. Today, Freud's ideas have been altered so much that few strictly psychoanalytic psychologists are left. However, his legacy is still evident in various **psychodynamic theories,** which continue to emphasize internal motives, conflicts, and unconscious forces (Gedo, 2002).

Humanistic Psychology

Humanism is a view that focuses on subjective human experience. Humanistic psychologists are interested in human problems, potentials, and ideals.

How is the humanistic approach different from others? Carl Rogers, Abraham Maslow, and other humanists rejected the Freudian idea that we are ruled by unconscious forces. They were also uncomfortable with the behaviorist emphasis on conditioning. Both views have a strong undercurrent of **determinism** (the idea that behavior is determined by forces beyond our control). Instead, the humanists stress **free will,** our ability to make voluntary choices. Of course, past experiences do affect us. Nevertheless, humanists believe that people can freely *choose* to live more creative, meaningful, and satisfying lives.

Humanists are interested in psychological needs for love, self-esteem, belonging, self-expression, creativity, and spirituality. Such needs, they believe, are as important as our biological urges for food and water. For example, newborn infants deprived of human love may die just as surely as they would if deprived of food.

How scientific is the humanistic approach? Initially, humanists were less interested in treating psychology as a science. They stressed more subjective factors, such as one's self-image, self-evaluation, and frame of reference. (*Self-image* is your perception of your own body, personality, and capabilities. *Self-evaluation* refers to appraising yourself as good or bad. A *frame of reference* is a mental perspective used to interpret events.) Today, humanists still seek to understand how we perceive ourselves and experience the world. However, most now do research to test their ideas, just as other psychologists do (Schneider, Bugental, & Pierson, 2001).

Maslow's concept of self-actualization is a special feature of humanism. **Self-actualization** refers to developing one's potential fully and becoming the best person possible. According to humanists, everyone has this potential. Humanists

Sigmund Freud, 1856-1939. For over 50 years, Freud probed the unconscious mind. In doing so, he altered modern views of human nature. His early experimentation with a "talking cure" for hysteria is regarded as the beginning of psychoanalysis. Through psychoanalysis, Freud added psychological treatment methods to psychiatry.

Abraham Maslow, 1908-1970. As a founder of humanistic psychology, Maslow was interested in studying people of exceptional mental health. Such self-actualized people, he believed, make full use of their talents and abilities. Maslow offered his positive view of human potential as an alternative to the schools of behaviorism and psychoanalysis.

TABLE 1.2 The Early Development of Psychology

PERSPECTIVE	DATE	NOTABLE EVENTS
Experimental psychology	1875	• First psychology course offered by William James
	1878	• First American Ph.D. in psychology awarded
	1879	• Wilhelm Wundt opens first psychology laboratory in Germany
	1883	• First American psychology lab founded at Johns Hopkins University
	1886	• First American psychology textbook written by John Dewey
Structuralism	1898	• Edward Titchener advances psychology based on introspection
Functionalism	1890	• William James publishes *Principles of Psychology*
	1892	• American Psychological Association founded
Psychodynamic psychology	1895	• Sigmund Freud publishes first studies
	1900	• Freud publishes *The Interpretation of Dreams*
Behaviorism	1906	• Ivan Pavlov reports his research on conditioned reflexes
	1913	• John Watson presents behavioristic view
Gestalt psychology	1912	• Max Wertheimer and others advance Gestalt viewpoint
Humanistic psychology	1942	• Carl Rogers publishes *Counseling and Psychotherapy*
	1943	• Abraham Maslow publishes "A Theory of Human Motivation"

seek ways to help it emerge. (See ■ Table 1.2 for a summary of psychology's early development.)

The Role of Women in Psychology's Early Days

Were all the early psychologists men? Even though most of the early psychologists were men, women have contributed to psychology from the beginning (Minton, 2000). By 1906, in America, about 1 psychologist in 10 was a woman. Who were these "foremothers" of psychology? Three who became well known are Mary Calkins, Christine Ladd-Franklin, and Margaret Washburn.

Mary Calkins did valuable research on memory. She was also the first woman president of the American Psychological Association, in 1905. Christine Ladd-Franklin studied color vision. In 1906 she was ranked among the 50 most important psychologists in America. In 1908 Margaret Washburn published an influential textbook on animal behavior, titled *The Animal Mind.*

The first woman to be awarded a Ph.D. in psychology was Margaret Washburn, in 1894. Over the next 15 years many more women followed her pioneering lead. Today, two out of three graduate students in psychology are women. And, in recent years, nearly 75 percent of all college graduates with a major in psychology have been women. Clearly, psychology has become fully open to both men and women (Hyde, 2004).

Christine Ladd-Franklin, 1847-1930.

Margaret Washburn, 1871-1939.

Mary Calkins, 1863-1930.

Unconscious Contents of the mind that are beyond awareness, especially impulses and desires not directly known to a person.

Repression The unconscious process by which memories, thoughts, or impulses are held out of awareness.

Psychoanalysis A Freudian approach to psychotherapy emphasizing the exploration of unconscious conflicts.

Neo-Freudian A psychologist who accepts the broad features of Freud's theory but has revised the theory to fit his or her own concepts.

Psychodynamic theory Any theory of behavior that emphasizes internal conflicts, motives, and unconscious forces.

Humanism An approach to psychology that focuses on human experience, problems, potentials, and ideals.

Determinism The idea that all behavior has prior causes that would completely explain one's choices and actions if all such causes were known.

Free will The idea that human beings are capable of freely making choices or decisions.

Self-actualization The ongoing process of fully developing one's personal potential.

Psychology Today—Three Complementary Perspectives on Behavior

SURVEY QUESTION: *What are the contemporary perspectives in psychology?*

At one time, loyalty to each school of thought was fierce, and clashes were common. Today, viewpoints such as functionalism and Gestalt psychology have blended into newer, broader perspectives. Also, some early systems, such as structuralism, have disappeared entirely while new ones have gained prominence. Certainly, loyalties and specialties still exist. But today, many psychologists are *eclectic* (ek-LEK-tik), because they realize that a single perspective is unlikely to fully explain complex human behavior. As a result, psychologists commonly draw insight from a variety of perspectives, insights from one complementing insights from the other. The three broad views that shape modern psychology are the *biological, psychological,* and *sociocultural* perspectives (■ Table 1.3).

The Biological Perspective

The **biological perspective** seeks to explain behavior in terms of biological principles such as brain processes, evolution, and genetics. By using new techniques, *biopsychologists* are producing exciting insights about how the brain relates to thinking, feelings, perception, abnormal behavior, and other topics. Biopsychologists and others who study the brain and nervous system, such as biologists and biochemists, are part

■ TABLE 1.3 Contemporary Ways to Look at Behavior

BIOLOGICAL PERSPECTIVE

Biopsychological View
Key Idea: *Human and animal behavior is the result of internal physical, chemical, and biological processes.*
Seeks to explain behavior through activity of the brain and nervous system, physiology, genetics, the endocrine system, and biochemistry; neutral, reductionistic, mechanistic view of human nature.

Evolutionary View
Key Idea: *Human and animal behavior is the result of the process of evolution.*
Seeks to explain behavior through evolutionary principles based on natural selection; neutral, reductionistic, mechanistic view of human nature.

PSYCHOLOGICAL PERSPECTIVE

Behavioristic View
Key Idea: *Behavior is shaped and controlled by one's environment.*
Emphasizes the study of observable behavior and the effects of learning; stresses the influence of external rewards and punishments; neutral, scientific, somewhat mechanistic view of human nature.

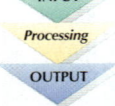

Cognitive View
Key Idea: *Much human behavior can be understood in terms of the mental processing of information.*
Concerned with thinking, knowing, perception, understanding, memory, decision making, and judgment; explains behavior in terms of information processing; neutral, somewhat computer-like view of human nature.

Psychodynamic View
Key Idea: *Behavior is directed by forces within one's personality that are often hidden or unconscious.*
Emphasizes internal impulses, desires, and conflicts—especially those that are unconscious; views behavior as the result of clashing forces within personality; somewhat negative, pessimistic view of human nature.

Humanistic View
Key Idea: *Behavior is guided by one's self-image, by subjective perceptions of the world, and by needs for personal growth.*
Focuses on subjective, conscious experience, human problems, potentials, and ideals; emphasizes self-image and self-actualization to explain behavior; positive, philosophical view of human nature.

SOCIOCULTURAL PERSPECTIVE

Sociocultural View
Key Idea: *Behavior is influenced by one's social and cultural context.*
Emphasizes that behavior is related to the social and cultural environment within which a person is born, grows up, and lives from day to day; neutral, interactionist view of human nature.

of the broader field of *neuroscience*. *Evolutionary psychologists* look at how human evolution and genetics might explain our current behavior.

The Psychological Perspective

The **psychological perspective** takes the view that behavior is shaped by psychological processes occurring within each person. While it continues the objective observation championed by the *behavioristic view*, the psychological perspective now includes cognitive behaviorism and cognitive psychology, which acknowledge that mental processes underlie much of our behavior.

Over the last 50 years, a "cognitive revolution" has taken place as *cognitive psychologists* have successfully applied objective observation to study covert mental behaviors, such as thinking, memory, language, perception, problem solving, consciousness, and creativity. Cognitive psychologists and other researchers interested in cognition, such as computer scientists and linguists, form the broader field of *cognitive science*. With a renewed interest in thinking, it can be said that psychology has finally "regained consciousness" (Robins, Gosling, & Craik, 1998).

Freudian psychoanalysis continues to evolve into the broader *psychodynamic view*. Although many of Freud's ideas have been challenged, psychodynamic psychologists continue to trace human behavior to unconscious processes. They also seek to develop therapies to help people lead happier, fuller lives. Humanistic psychologists do, too, although they stress subjective, conscious experience and the positive side of human nature, rather than unconscious processes.

Positive Psychology Psychologists have always paid attention to the negative side of human behavior. This is easy to understand because of the pressing need to solve human problems. However, inspired by the humanists, more and more psychologists have recently begun to ask, What do we know about love, happiness, creativity, well-being, self-confidence, and achievement? Together, such topics make up **positive psychology,** the study of human strengths, virtues, and optimal behavior (Compton, 2005; Seligman & Csikszentmihalyi, 2000). Many topics from positive psychology can be found in this book. Ideally, they will help make your own life more positive and fulfilling (Simonton & Baumeister, 2005).

The Sociocultural Perspective

As you can see, it is helpful to view human behavior from more than one perspective. This is also true in another sense. The **sociocultural perspective** stresses the impact that social and cultural contexts have on our behavior. We are rapidly becoming a multicultural society, made up of people from many different nations. How has this affected psychology? Let us introduce you to Jerry, who is Japanese American and is married to an Irish Catholic American. Here is what Jerry, his wife, and their children did one New Year's Day:

> We woke up in the morning and went to Mass at St. Brigid's, which has a black gospel choir.... Then we went to the Japanese-American Community Center for the Oshogatsu New Year's program and saw Buddhist archers shoot arrows to ward off evil spirits for the year. Next, we ate traditional rice cakes as part of the New Year's service and listened to a young Japanese-American storyteller. On the way home, we stopped in Chinatown and after that we ate Mexican food at a taco stand. (Njeri, 1991)

Jerry and his family reflect a new social reality: Cultural diversity is becoming the norm. About one third of the population in the United States is now African American, Hispanic, Asian American, Native American, or Pacific Islander. In some large cities "minority" groups are already the majority (Schmitt, 2001).

In the past, psychology was based mostly on the cultures of North America and Europe. Now, we must ask, Do the principles of Western psychology apply to people in all cultures? Are some psychological concepts invalid in other cultures? Are any universal? As psychologists have probed such

To fully understand human behavior, personal differences based on age, race, culture, ethnicity, gender, and sexual orientation must be taken into account.

Biological perspective The attempt to explain behavior in terms of underlying biological principles.

Psychological perspective The traditional view that behavior is shaped by psychological processes occurring at the level of the individual.

Positive psychology The study of human strengths, virtues, and effective functioning.

Sociocultural perspective The focus on the importance of social and cultural contexts in influencing the behavior of individuals.

questions, one thing has become clear: Most of what we think, feel, and do is influenced in one way or another by the social and cultural worlds in which we live (Lehman, Chiu, & Schaller, 2004).

Cultural Relativity Imagine that you are a psychologist. Your client, Linda, who is a Native American, tells you that spirits live in the trees near her home. Is Linda suffering from a delusion? Is she abnormal? Obviously, you will misjudge Linda's mental health if you fail to take her cultural beliefs into account. **Cultural relativity** (the idea that behavior must be judged relative to the values of the culture in which it occurs) can greatly affect the diagnosis and treatment of mental disorders (Draguns, Gielen, & Fish, 2004). Cases like Linda's teach us to be wary of using narrow standards when judging others or comparing groups.

A Broader View of Diversity In addition to cultural differences, age, ethnicity, gender, religion, disability, and sexual orientation all affect the **social norms** that guide behavior. Social norms are rules that define acceptable and expected behavior for members of various groups. All too often, the unstated standard for judging what is "average," "normal," or "correct" has been the behavior of white, middle-class males (Reid, 2002). To fully understand human behavior, psychologists need to know how people differ, as well as the ways in which we are all alike (APA, 2003). For the same reason, an appreciation of human diversity can enrich your life, as well as your understanding of psychology (Denmark, Rabinowitz, & Sechzer, 2005).

MODULE 1.3 Summary

How did the field of psychology emerge?
- Historically, psychology is an outgrowth of philosophy. Psychology first became a science when researchers began to directly study and observe psychological events.
- The first psychological laboratory was established in Germany by Wilhelm Wundt, who studied conscious experience.
- The first school of thought in psychology was structuralism, a kind of "mental chemistry" based on introspection.
- Structuralism was followed by functionalism, behaviorism, and Gestalt psychology.
- Psychodynamic approaches, such as Freud's psychoanalytic theory, emphasize the unconscious origins of behavior.
- Humanistic psychology accentuates subjective experience, human potentials, and personal growth.

What are the contemporary perspectives in psychology?
- Three complementary streams of thought in modern psychology are the biological perspective, including biopsychology and evolutionary psychology; the psychological perspective, including behaviorism, cognitive psychology, the psychodynamic approach, and humanism; and the sociocultural perspective.
- Psychologists have recently begun to formally study positive aspects of human behavior, or positive psychology.
- Most of what we think, feel, and do is influenced by the social and cultural worlds in which we live.

KNOWLEDGE BUILDER

History and Contemporary Perspectives

Recite

Match:

1. ____ Philosophy
2. ____ Wundt
3. ____ Structuralism
4. ____ Functionalism
5. ____ Behaviorism
6. ____ Gestalt
7. ____ Psychodynamic
8. ____ Humanistic
9. ____ Cognitive
10. ____ Washburn
11. ____ Biopsychology

A. Against analysis; studied whole experiences
B. "Mental chemistry" and introspection
C. Emphasizes self-actualization and personal growth
D. Interested in unconscious causes of behavior
E. Interested in how the mind aids survival
F. First woman Ph.D. in psychology
G. Studied stimuli and responses, conditioning
H. Part of psychology's "long past"
I. Concerned with thinking, language, problem solving
J. Used introspection and careful measurement
K. Relates behavior to the brain, physiology, and genetics
L. Also known as engineering psychology

12. Who among the following was not a historic woman psychologist?
    a. Calkins b. Ladd-Franklin c. Washburn d. Watson

13. A psychotherapist is working with a person from an ethnic group other than her own. She should be aware of how cultural relativity and _____ affect behavior.
    a. the anthropomorphic error b. operational definitions c. biased sampling d. social norms

Reflect
Critical Thinking

14. Modern sciences like psychology are built on observations that can be verified by two or more independent observers. Did structuralism meet this standard? Why or why not?

Relate

Which school of thought most closely matches your own view of behavior? Do you think any of the early schools offers a complete explanation of why we behave as we do? What about the three contemporary perspectives? Can you explain why so many psychologists are eclectic?

Link

Internet addresses frequently change. To find the sites listed here, visit http://www.thomsonedu.com/psychology/coon for an updated list of Internet addresses and direct links to relevant sites.

- **Today in the History of Psychology** Events in the history of psychology by the date, including podcasts.
- **Classics in the History of Psychology** Original articles by a wide range of psychologists from Allport to Yerkes, including Sigmund Freud, B. F. Skinner, and Carl Rogers.
- **Women's Intellectual Contributions to the Field of Psychology** Information about women's contributions to the field of psychology from a historical perspective.

ANSWERS

1. H 2. J 3. B 4. E 5. G 6. A 7. D 8. C 9. I 10. F 11. K 12. d 13. d 14. No, it did not. The downfall of structuralism was that each observer examined the contents of his or her own mind—which is something that no other person can observe.

Cultural relativity The idea that behavior must be judged relative to the values of the culture in which it occurs.

Social norms Rules that define acceptable and expected behavior for members of a group.

MODULE 1.4 Psychologists and Their Specialties

CONTRARY to common belief, clinical psychology is not the only specialty in the field. Only a little over half of all psychologists study mental disorders or do therapy. Others apply their expertise to problems in research, education, medicine, health, business, the environment, and other nonclinical areas. Also, clinical psychologists are not the only people who work in the field of mental health. Often they coordinate their efforts with other specially trained professionals.

Psychologists—Guaranteed Not to Shrink

SURVEY QUESTION: *What are the major specialties in psychology?*

Psychologists are all shrinks, right? Nope. "Shrinks" (a slang term derived from "head shrinkers") are *psychiatrists,* a different type of mental health professional. A **psychologist** is highly trained in the methods, knowledge, and theories of psychology. Psychologists usually have a master's degree or a doctorate. These degrees typically require several years of postgraduate training. Psychologists may teach, do research, give psychological tests, or serve as consultants to business, industry, government, or the military.

Psychologists are often inaccurately portrayed in the media. For example, in the comedy *Prime* a therapist listens to a patient describe intimate details of her relationship with a man but fails to tell the patient that the man is her son. Other films have featured psychologists who are more disturbed than their patients (such as Jack Nicholson's character in *Anger Management*) or psychologists who are bumbling buffoons (such as Billy Crystal's character in *Analyze This*). Such characters may be dramatic and entertaining, but they seriously distort public perceptions of responsible and hardworking psychologists (Schultz, 2004). Real psychologists follow an ethical code that stresses respect for people's privacy, dignity, confidentiality, and welfare (APA, 2002).

Even without media distortions, misconceptions about psychologists are common. For instance, most psychologists are not therapists in private practice. Instead, they are employed by schools, businesses, and social agencies. Likewise, only 16 percent work in clinics or hospitals.

One perception of psychologists is accurate: Most do help people in one way or another. Psychologists interested in emotional problems specialize in clinical or counseling psychology (■ Table 1.4). **Clinical psychologists** treat psychological problems or do research on therapies and mental disorders. In contrast, **counseling psychologists** tend to treat milder problems, such as poor adjustment at work or school. However, such differences are fading, and many counseling psychologists now work full time as therapists.

In the film *Prime*, Meryl Streep plays a therapist who listens to her patient, played by Uma Thurman, describe intimate details of her relationship with a man. However, the therapist neglects to tell her patient that the man is her son. Such premises are typical of the way psychologists and psychotherapy are misrepresented in the media.

To enter the profession of psychology, it is best to have a doctorate (Ph.D., Psy.D., or Ed.D.). Most clinical psychologists have a Ph.D. degree and follow a scientist-practitioner model. That is, they are trained to do either research or therapy. Many do both. Other clinicians earn the Psy.D. (Doctor of Psychology) degree, which emphasizes therapy skills rather than research.

Have you ever wondered what it takes to become a psychologist? See "Is a Career in Psychology Right for You?"

Other Mental Health Professionals

A **psychiatrist** is a medical doctor who treats mental disorders, usually by doing psychotherapy. Psychiatrists can also prescribe drugs, which is something a psychologist usually cannot do. This is changing, however. Psychologists in New Mexico and Louisiana can now legally prescribe drugs. It will be interesting to see whether other states grant similar privileges (Munsey, 2006).

To be a psychoanalyst, you must have a moustache and goatee, spectacles, a German accent, and a well-padded couch—or so the media stereotype goes. Actually, to become a **psychoanalyst,** you must have an M.D. or Ph.D. degree plus further training in Freudian psychoanalysis. In other words, either a physician or a psychologist may become an analyst by learning a specific type of psychotherapy.

TABLE 1.4 Kinds of Psychologists and What They Do

SPECIALTY		TYPICAL ACTIVITIES
Biopsychology	B*	Does research on the brain, nervous system, and other physical origins of behavior
Clinical	A	Does psychotherapy; investigates clinical problems; develops methods of treatment
Cognitive	B	Studies human thinking and information processing abilities
Community	A	Promotes community-wide mental health through research, prevention, education, and consultation
Comparative	B	Studies and compares the behavior of different species, especially animals
Consumer	A	Researches packaging, advertising, marketing methods, and characteristics of consumers
Counseling	A	Does psychotherapy and personal counseling; researches emotional disturbances and counseling methods
Cultural	B	Studies the ways in which culture, subculture, and ethnic group membership affect behavior
Developmental	A, B	Conducts research on infant, child, adolescent, and adult development; does clinical work with disturbed children; acts as consultant to parents and schools
Educational	A	Investigates classroom dynamics, teaching styles, and learning; develops educational tests, evaluates educational programs
Engineering	A	Does applied research on the design of machinery, computers, airlines, automobiles, and so on, for business, industry, and the military
Environmental	A, B	Studies the effects of urban noise, crowding, attitudes toward the environment, and human use of space; acts as a consultant on environmental issues
Forensic	A	Studies problems of crime and crime prevention, rehabilitation programs, prisons, courtroom dynamics; selects candidates for police work
Gender	B	Does research on differences between males and females, the acquisition of gender identity, and the role of gender throughout life
Health	A, B	Studies the relationship between behavior and health; uses psychological principles to promote health and prevent illness
Industrial-organizational	A	Selects job applicants; does skills analysis; evaluates on-the-job training; improves work environments and human relations in organizations and work settings
Learning	B	Studies how and why learning occurs; develops theories of learning
Medical	A	Applies psychology to manage medical problems, such as the emotional impact of illness, self-screening for cancer, compliance in taking medicine
Personality	B	Studies personality traits and dynamics; develops theories of personality and tests for assessing personality traits
School	A	Does psychological testing, referrals, emotional and vocational counseling of students; detects and treats learning disabilities; improves classroom learning
Sensation and perception	B	Studies the sense organs and the process of perception; investigates the mechanisms of sensation and develops theories about how perception occurs
Social	B	Investigates human social behavior, including attitudes, conformity, persuasion, prejudice, friendship, aggression, helping, and so forth

*Research in this area is typically applied (A), basic (B), or both (A, B).

Psychologist A person highly trained in the methods, factual knowledge, and theories of psychology.
Clinical psychologist A psychologist who specializes in the treatment of psychological and behavioral disturbances or who does research on such disturbances.
Counseling psychologist A psychologist who specializes in the treatment of milder emotional and behavioral disturbances.
Psychiatrist A medical doctor with additional training in the diagnosis and treatment of mental and emotional disorders.
Psychoanalyst A mental health professional (usually a medical doctor) trained to practice psychoanalysis.

DISCOVERING PSYCHOLOGY

Is a Career in Psychology Right for You?

As you read these modules we encourage you to frequently reflect on new ideas by relating them to your own life in order to better understand and remember them. "Discovering Psychology" boxes like this one are designed to help you be more reflective about how psychology relates to your own life. Answer the following questions to explore whether you would enjoy becoming a psychologist:

1. I have a strong interest in human behavior. True or False?
2. I am good at recognizing patterns, evaluating evidence, and drawing conclusions. True or False?
3. I am emotionally stable. True or False?
4. I have good communication skills. True or False?
5. I find theories and ideas challenging and stimulating. True or False?
6. My friends regard me as especially sensitive to the feelings of others. True or False?
7. I enjoy planning and carrying out complex projects and activities. True or False?
8. Programs and popular books about psychology interest me. True or False?
9. I enjoy working with other people. True or False?
10. Clear thinking, objectivity, and keen observation appeal to me. True or False?

If you answered "True" to most of these questions, a career in psychology might be a good choice. And remember that many psychology majors also succeed in occupations such as management, public affairs, social services, business, sales, and education.

In many states, counselors also do mental health work. A **counselor** is an adviser who helps solve problems with marriage, career, school, work, or the like. To be a licensed counselor (such as a marriage and family counselor, a child counselor, or a school counselor) typically requires a master's degree plus 1 or 2 years of full-time supervised counseling experience. Counselors learn practical helping skills and do not treat serious mental disorders.

Psychiatric social workers play an important role in many mental health programs. Psychiatric social workers apply social science principles to help patients in clinics and hospitals. Most hold an M.S.W. (Master of Social Work) degree. Often, they assist psychologists and psychiatrists as part of a team. Their typical duties include evaluating patients and families, conducting group therapy, or visiting a patient's home, school, or job to alleviate problems.

The Profession of Psychology

Does a person have to have a license to practice psychology? At one time, it was possible in many states for anyone to "hang out a shingle" as a "psychologist." Now, psychologists must meet rigorous educational and legal requirements. To work as a clinical or counseling psychologist, you must have a license issued by a state examining board. However, the law does not prevent you from calling yourself anything else you choose—therapist, rebirther, primal feeling facilitator, cosmic aura balancer, or Rolfer—or from selling your "services" to anyone willing to pay. Beware of people with self-proclaimed titles. Even if their intentions are honorable, they may have little training. A licensed psychologist who chooses to use a particular type of therapy is not the same as someone "trained" solely in that technique.

Ethics Most psychologists take pride in following a professional code that stresses (1) high levels of competence, integrity, and responsibility; (2) respect for people's rights to privacy, dignity, confidentiality, and personal freedom; and above all, (3) protection of the client's welfare. Psychologists are also expected to use their knowledge to contribute to society. Many do volunteer work in the communities in which they live (APA, 2002; Barnett et al., 2007).

Specialties in Psychology

Do all psychologists do therapy and treat abnormal behavior? No. Only about 58 percent are clinical and counseling psychologists. The rest are found in other specialties. At present, the American Psychological Association (APA) consists of more than 50 divisions, each reflecting special skills or areas of interest. Some of the major specialties are listed in Table 1.4. (Also see ● Fig. 1.5.) Nearly 30 percent of all psychologists are employed full-time at colleges or universities, where they teach and do research, consulting, or therapy. Some do *basic research,* in which they seek knowledge for its own sake. For example, a psychologist might study memory simply to understand how it works. Others do *applied research* to solve immediate practical problems, such as finding ways to improve athletic performance. Some do both types of research.

In the next module we'll take a closer look at how research is done. Before that, here's a chance to do a little research on how much you've learned.

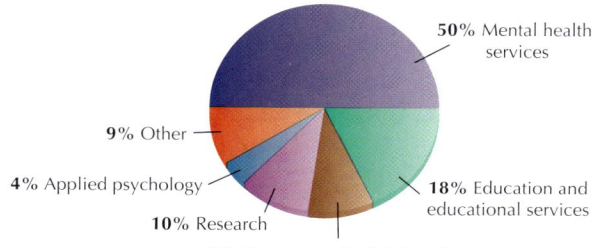

● **FIGURE 1.5** *(a)* Specialties in psychology (APA, 2005). Percentages are approximate. *(b)* Where psychologists work (APA, 2000). *(c)* This chart shows the main activities psychologists engage in at work (APA, 2000). Any particular psychologist might do several of these activities during a work week. As you can see, most psychologists specialize in applied areas and work in applied settings.

MODULE 1.4 Summary

What are the major specialties in psychology?

- Although psychologists, psychiatrists, psychoanalysts, and counselors all work in the field of mental health, their training and methods differ considerably.
- Clinical and counseling psychologists, who do psychotherapy, represent only two of dozens of specialties in psychology.
- Other representative areas of specialization are industrial, educational, consumer, school, developmental, engineering, medical, environmental, forensic, community, psychometric, and experimental psychology.
- Psychological research may be basic or applied.

Counselor A mental health professional who specializes in helping people with problems not involving serious mental disorder; for example, marriage counselors, career counselors, or school counselors.

Psychiatric social worker A mental health professional trained to apply social science principles to help patients in clinics and hospitals.

KNOWLEDGE BUILDER

Psychologists and Their Specialties

Recite

1. Which of the following is a medical doctor?
   a. a psychologist b. a psychiatrist c. a psychotherapist d. a counselor
2. A psychologist who specializes in treating human emotional difficulties is called a _____ psychologist.
3. Roughly 40 percent of psychologists specialize in counseling psychology. T or F?
4. Who among the following would most likely be involved in the detection of learning disabilities?
   a. a consumer psychologist b. a forensic psychologist c. an experimental psychologist d. a school psychologist

Reflect

Critical Thinking

5. If most psychologists work in applied settings, why is basic research still of great importance?

Relate

Which specialty in psychology is most interesting to you? What is it about that specialty that most attracts you?

Link

Internet addresses frequently change. To find the sites listed here, visit http://www.thomsonedu.com/psychology/coon for an updated list of Internet addresses and direct links to relevant sites.

- **Divisions of the American Psychological Association** The different specialties in psychology.
- **Careers in Psychology** Marky Lloyd's Careers in Psychology Page.
- **For Students of Psychology** Information for students interested in psychology from the American Psychological Association and the Association for Psychological Science.

ANSWERS

1. b 2. clinical or counseling 3. F 4. d 5. Because practitioners benefit from basic psychological research in the same way that physicians benefit from basic research in biology. Discoveries in basic science form the knowledge base that leads to useful applications.

MODULE 1.5 The Psychology Experiment

PSYCHOLOGISTS want to be able explain *why* we act the way we do. Many different research strategies may be used to investigate human behavior. However, we must usually do an experiment to discover the *causes* of behavior. Experiments bring cause-and-effect relationships into sharp focus.

The Psychology Experiment—Where Effect Meets Cause

SURVEY QUESTION: *How is an experiment performed?*

The most powerful scientific research tool is the **experiment** (a formal trial undertaken to confirm or disconfirm a hypothesis about the causes of behavior). Psychologists carefully control conditions in experiments to identify cause-and-effect relationships. To perform an experiment you would do the following:

1. Directly vary a condition you think might affect behavior.
2. Create two or more groups of subjects. These groups should be alike in all ways *except* the condition you are varying.
3. Record whether varying the condition has any effect on behavior.

Assume that you want to find out if hunger affects creativity. First, you would form two groups of people. Then you could give the members of one group a test of creativity while they are hungry. The second group would take the same test after eating a meal. By comparing average creativity scores for the two groups, you could tell if hunger affects creative thinking.

As you can see, the simplest psychological experiment is based on two groups of **experimental subjects** (animals or people whose behavior is investigated; human subjects are also commonly called **participants**). One group is called the *experimental group;* the other becomes the *control group.* The control group and the experimental group are treated exactly alike except for the condition you intentionally vary. This condition is called the *independent variable.*

Variables and Groups

A **variable** is any condition that can change and that might affect the outcome of the experiment. Identifying causes and effects in an experiment involves three types of variables:

1. **Independent variables** are conditions altered or varied by the experimenter, who sets their size, amount, or value. Independent variables are suspected *causes* for differences in behavior.
2. **Dependent variables** measure the results of the experiment. That is, they reveal the *effects* that independent variables have on *behavior.* Such effects are often revealed by measures of performance, such as test scores.
3. **Extraneous variables** are conditions that a researcher wishes to prevent from affecting the outcome of the experiment.

We can apply these terms to our hunger/creativity experiment in this way: Creativity is the independent variable—we want to know if hunger affects creativity. Creativity (defined by scores on the creativity test) is the dependent variable—we want to know if the ability to think creatively depends on how creative a person is. All other variables that could affect creativity scores are extraneous. Examples are the number of hours slept the night before the test, intelligence, or difficulty of the questions.

As you can see, an **experimental group** consists of participants exposed to the independent variable (creativity in the preceding example). Members of the **control group** are exposed to all conditions except the independent variable.

Let's examine another simple experiment. Suppose you notice that you seem to study better while listening to your iPod. This suggests the hypothesis that music improves learning. We could test this idea by forming an experimental

> **Experiment** A formal trial undertaken to confirm or disconfirm a hypothesis about cause and effect.
> **Experimental subjects** Humans (also referred to as **subjects** or **participants**) or animals whose behavior is investigated in an experiment.
> **Variable** Any condition that changes or can be made to change; a measure, event, or state that may vary.
> **Independent variable** In an experiment, the condition being investigated as a possible cause of some change in behavior. The values that this variable takes are chosen by the experimenter.
> **Dependent variable** In an experiment, the condition (usually a behavior) that is affected by the independent variable.
> **Extraneous variables** Conditions or factors excluded from influencing the outcome of an experiment.
> **Experimental group** In a controlled experiment, the group of subjects exposed to the independent variable or experimental condition.
> **Control group** In a controlled experiment, the group of subjects exposed to all experimental conditions or variables *except* the independent variable.

CONTROL GROUP   OUT OF CONTROL GROUP

group that studies with music. A control group would study without music. Then we could compare their scores on a test.

Is a control group really needed? Can't people just study while listening to their iPods to see if they do better? Without a control group it would be impossible to tell if music had any effect on learning. The control group provides a *point of reference* for comparison with the scores in the experimental group. If the average test score of the experimental group is higher than the average of the control group, we can conclude that music improves learning. If there is no difference, it's obvious that the independent variable had no effect on learning.

In this experiment, the amount learned (indicated by scores on the test) is the *dependent variable*. We are asking, Does the independent variable *affect* the dependent variable? (Does music affect, or influence, learning?)

Experimental Control *How do we know that the people in one group aren't more intelligent than those in the other group?* It's true that personal differences might affect the experiment. However, they can be controlled by randomly assigning people to groups. **Random assignment** means that a participant has an equal chance of being in either the experimental group or the control group. Randomization evenly balances personal differences in the two groups. In our musical experiment, this could be done by simply flipping a coin for each participant: Heads, and the participant is in the experimental group; tails, it's the control group. This would result in few average differences in the number of people in each group who are women or men, geniuses or dunces, hungry, hung over, tall, music lovers, or whatever.

Other *extraneous*, or outside, variables—such as the amount of study time, the temperature in the room, the time of day, the amount of light, and so forth—must also be prevented from affecting the outcome of an experiment. But how? Usually this is done by making all conditions (except the independent variable) *exactly* alike for both groups. When all conditions are the same for both groups—*except* the presence or absence of music—then a difference in the amount learned *must* be caused by the music (● Fig. 1.6). (Psychology

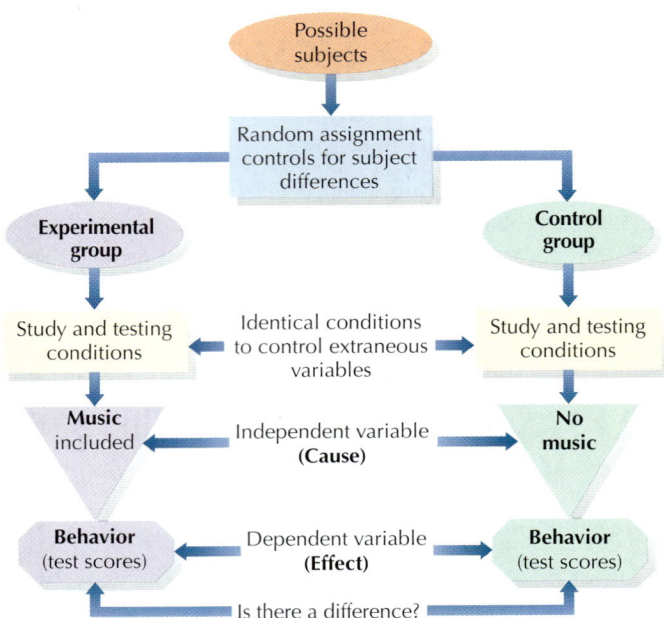

● **FIGURE 1.6** Elements of a simple psychological experiment to assess the effects of music during study on test scores.

experiments sometimes raise ethical questions. See "That's Interesting, But Is It Ethical" for more information.)

Cause and Effect Now let's summarize. In an experiment two or more groups of subjects are treated differently with respect to the independent variable. In all other ways they are treated the same. That is, extraneous variables are equalized for all groups. The effect of the independent variable (or variables) on some behavior (the dependent variable) is then measured. In a carefully controlled experiment, the independent variable is the only possible *cause* for any *effect* noted in the dependent variable. This allows clear cause-and-effect connections to be identified (● Fig. 1.7).

Placebo Effects, Sugar Pills, and Saltwater

Now let's do an experiment to see if the drug amphetamine (a stimulant) affects learning: Before studying, members of our experimental group take an amphetamine pill. Control group members get nothing. Later, we assess how much each participant learned. Does this experiment seem valid? Actually, it is seriously flawed.

Why? The experimental group took the drug and the control group didn't. Differences in the amount they learned must have been caused by the drug, right? No, because the drug wasn't the only difference between the groups. People in the experimental group swallowed a pill, and control participants did not. Without using a placebo (plah-SEE-bo), it is impossible to

CRITICAL THINKING

That's Interesting, But Is It Ethical?

Three areas of ethical concern in behavioral research are the use of *deception, invasion of privacy,* and the risk of *lasting harm.* Deception and potential harm are illustrated by a classic study of obedience. Participants were ordered to give what they thought were painful electric shocks to another person (no shocks were actually given) (Milgram, 1974). Believing that they had hurt someone, many people left the experiment shaken and upset. A few suffered guilt and distress for some time afterward.

Such experiments raise serious ethical questions. Did the information gained justify the emotional costs? Was deception really necessary? As a reply to such questions, American Psychological Association guidelines state that "Psychologists must carry out investigations with respect for the people who participate and with concern for their dignity and welfare." Similar guidelines apply to animals, where investigators are expected to "ensure the welfare of animals and treat them humanely" (APA, 2002). (See ■ Table 1.5.) To ensure this, most university psychology departments have ethics committees that oversee research. Nevertheless, no easy answers exist for the ethical questions raised by psychology, and debate about specific experiments is likely to continue.

■ **TABLE 1.5** Basic Ethical Guidelines for Psychological Researchers

Do no harm.

Accurately describe risks to potential participants.

Ensure that participation is voluntary.

Minimize any discomfort to participants.

Maintain confidentiality.

Do not unnecessarily invade privacy.

Use deception only when absolutely necessary.

Remove any misconceptions caused by deception (debrief).

Provide results and interpretations to participants.

Treat participants with dignity and respect.

- Extraneous Variables
- Independent Variable

● **FIGURE 1.7** Experimental control is achieved by balancing extraneous variables for the experimental group and the control group. For example, the average age (A), education (B), and intelligence (C) of group members could be made the same for both groups. Then we could apply the independent variable to the experimental group. If their behavior (the dependent variable) changes (in comparison with the control group), the change must be caused by the independent variable.

tell if the drug affects learning. It could be that those who swallowed a pill *expected* to do better. This alone might have affected their performance, even if the actual pill didn't.

What is a placebo? Why would it make a difference? A **placebo** is a fake drug. Inactive substances such as sugar pills and saline (saltwater) injections are commonly used as placebos. If a placebo has any effect, it must be based on suggestion, rather than chemistry (Thompson, 2005).

The **placebo effect** (changes in behavior caused by belief that one has taken a drug) can be powerful. For instance, a saline injection is 70 percent as effective as morphine in reducing pain. That's why doctors sometimes prescribe placebos—especially for complaints that seem to have no physical basis. Placebos have been shown to affect pain, anxiety, depression, alertness, tension, sexual arousal, cravings for alcohol, and many other processes (Wampold et al., 2005).

How could an inert substance have any effect? Placebos alter our expectations about our own emotional and physical reactions. Because we associate taking medicine with feeling better, we expect placebos to make us feel better, too (Stewart-Williams, 2004). After a person takes a placebo, there is a reduction in brain activity linked with pain, so the effect is not imaginary (Wager et al., 2004).

Random assignment The use of chance (for example, flipping a coin) to assign subjects to experimental and control groups.

Placebo An inactive substance given in the place of a drug in psychological research or by physicians who wish to treat a complaint by suggestion.

Placebo effect Changes in behavior due to expectations that a drug (or other treatment) will have some effect.

The placebo effect is a major factor in medical treatments. Would you also expect the placebo effect to occur in psychotherapy? (It does, which complicates studies on the effectiveness of new psychotherapies.)

Controlling Placebo Effects To control for placebo effects, we could use a **single-blind experiment.** In this case, participants do not know if they are receiving a real drug or a placebo. All subjects get a pill or injection. People in the experimental group get a real drug and the control group gets a placebo. Because participants are *blind* as to whether they received the drug or not, their expectations are the same. Any difference in their behavior must be caused by the drug. Even this is not enough because researchers themselves sometimes affect experiments by influencing the behavior of their participants. Let's see how this occurs.

The Experimenter Effect

How could a researcher influence participants? The **experimenter effect** (changes in behavior caused by the unintended influence of an experimenter) is a common problem in psychological research. In essence, experimenters run the risk of finding what they expect to find. This occurs because humans are very sensitive to hints about what is expected of them (Rosenthal, 1994).

The experimenter effect even applies outside the laboratory. Psychologist Robert Rosenthal (1973) reports a classic example of how expectations can influence people: At the U.S. Air Force Academy Preparatory School, 100 airmen were randomly assigned to five different math classes. Their teachers did not know about this random placement. Instead, each teacher was told that his or her students had unusually high or low ability. Students in the classes labeled "high ability" improved much more in math scores than those in "low-ability" classes. Yet, initially all the classes had students of equal ability.

Apparently, the teachers subtly communicated their expectations to students. Most likely, they did this through tone of voice, body language, and by giving encouragement or criticism. Their "hints," in turn, created a self-fulfilling prophecy that affected the students. A **self-fulfilling prophecy** is a prediction that prompts people to act in ways that make the prediction come true. In short, people sometimes become what we prophesy for them. It is wise to remember that others tend to live *up* or *down* to our expectations for them (Jussim & Harber, 2005).

Because of the experimenter effect, it is common to keep both participants and researchers "blind." In a **double-blind experiment** neither participants nor experimenters know who has received a drug and who has taken a placebo. This also keeps researchers from unconsciously influencing participants. Typically, someone else prepares the pills or injections so that experimenters don't know until after testing who got what.

Double-blind testing has shown that about 50 percent of the effectiveness of antidepressant drugs, such as the "wonder drug" Prozac, is due to the placebo effect (Kirsch & Sapirstein, 1998). It's very likely that much of the current popularity of herbal health remedies is also based on the placebo effect (Seidman, 2001). Some psychologists have even suggested replacing the term *placebo effect* with the term *meaning response*, to better reflect just how important people's beliefs are to influencing their behavior (Moerman, 2002).

MODULE 1.5 Summary

How is an experiment performed?

- Experiments involve two or more groups of subjects that differ only with regard to the independent variable.
- Effects on the dependent variable are then measured. All other conditions (extraneous variables) are held constant.
- Because experiments are set up so the independent variable is the only possible cause of a change in the dependent variable, clear cause-and-effect connections can be identified.
- The placebo effect is a problem in some studies, especially in experiments involving drugs, but double-blind testing allows us to draw valid conclusions. The placebo effect is also referred to as the *meaning response*.
- A related problem is the experimenter effect (a tendency for experimenters to unconsciously influence the outcome of an experiment). Researcher expectations can create a self-fulfilling prophecy, in which a participant changes in the direction of the expectation.
- Psychological research must be done ethically, in order to protect the rights, dignity, and welfare of participants.

KNOWLEDGE BUILDER

The Psychology Experiment

Recite

1. To understand cause and effect, a simple psychological experiment is based on creating two groups: the _____ group and the _____ group.

2. There are three types of variables to consider in an experiment: _____ variables (which are manipulated by the experimenter); _____ variables (which measure the outcome of the experiment); and _____ variables (factors to be excluded in a particular experiment).

3. A researcher performs an experiment to learn if room temperature affects the amount of aggression displayed by college students under crowded conditions in a simulated prison environment. In this experiment, the independent variable is which of the following?
   a. room temperature b. the amount of aggression c. crowding d. the simulated prison environment

4. A procedure used to control both the placebo effect and the experimenter effect in drug experiments is the
   a. correlation method b. extraneous prophecy c. double-blind technique d. random assignment of subjects

Reflect

Critical Thinking

5. There is a loophole in the statement, "I've been taking Echinacea tablets, and I haven't had a cold all year. Echinacea is great!" What is the loophole?

6. People who believe strongly in astrology have personality characteristics that actually match, to a degree, those predicted by their astrological signs. Can you explain why this occurs?

Relate

In a sense, we all conduct little experiments to detect cause-and-effect connections. If you are interested in gardening, for example, you might try adding plant food to one bed of flowers but not another. The question then becomes, Does the use of plant food (the independent variable) affect the size of the flowers (the dependent variable)? By comparing unfed plants (the control group) to those receiving plant food (the experimental group) you could find out if plant food is worth using.

Can you think of at least one informal experiment you've run in the last month? What were the variables? What was the outcome?

Link

Internet addresses frequently change. To find the sites listed here, visit **http://www.thomsonedu.com/psychology/coon** for an updated list of Internet addresses and direct links to relevant sites.

- **The Experimental Method** An introduction to experimental research methods.
- **The Simple Experiment** A description of a basic two-group experimental design.
- **Ethical Principles of Psychologists and Code of Conduct** The full text of the ethical principles that guide professional psychologists.

ANSWERS

1. experimental, control 2. independent, dependent, extraneous 3. a 4. c 5. The statement implies that Echinacea prevented colds. However, not getting a cold could just be a coincidence. A controlled experiment with a group given Echinacea and a control group not taking Echinacea would be needed to learn if Echinacea actually has any effect on susceptibility to colds. 6. Belief in astrology can create a self-fulfilling prophecy in which people alter their behaviors and self-concepts to match their astrological signs (van Rooij, 1994).

Single-blind experiment An arrangement in which participants remain unaware of whether they are in the experimental group or the control group.

Experimenter effect Changes in subjects' behavior caused by the unintended influence of an experimenter's actions.

Self-fulfilling prophecy A prediction that prompts people to act in ways that make the prediction come true.

Double-blind experiment An arrangement in which both participants and experimenters are unaware of whether participants are in the experimental group or the control group.

MODULE 1.6 Nonexperimental Research Methods

WHILE THE EXPERIMENT is frequently used by psychologists, many questions cannot be answered without the aid of nonexperimental methods. For example, psychologists who want to study behavior in natural settings use a technique called naturalistic observation. Psychologists who are looking for interesting relationships between events often rely on the correlational method. It can be difficult or impossible to study mental disorders, such as depression or psychosis, with the experimental method. In such cases, the clinical method may be used. Likewise, questions about the behavior of large groups of people are often best answered with the survey method.

Psychological Research—Different Strokes

SURVEY QUESTION: *What other research methods do psychologists use?*

Determining cause-and-effect relationships between variables lies at the heart of explaining not just *what* we do, but *why* we do it. For this reason, psychologists place a special emphasis on controlled experimentation (**experimental method**). However, because it is not always possible to conduct experiments, psychologists gather evidence and test hypotheses in many others ways: They observe behavior as it unfolds in natural settings (**naturalistic observation**); they make measurements to discover relationships between events (**correlational method**); they study psychological problems and therapies in clinical settings (**clinical method**); and they use questionnaires to poll large groups of people (**survey method**). Let's see how each of these is used to advance psychological knowledge.

Naturalistic Observation—Psychology Steps Out!

Psychologists sometimes actively observe behavior in a *natural setting* (the typical environment in which a person or animal lives). The work of Jane Goodall provides a good example. She and her staff have been observing chimpanzees in Tanzania since 1960. A quote from her book, *In the Shadow of Man*, captures the excitement of a scientific discovery:

> Quickly focusing my binoculars, I saw that it was a single chimpanzee, and just then he turned my direction.... He was squatting beside the red earth mound of a termite nest, and as I watched I saw him carefully push a long grass stem into a hole in the mound. After a moment he withdrew it and picked something from the end with his mouth. I was too far away to make out what he was eating, but it was obvious that he was actually using a grass stem as a tool (● Fig. 1.8). (Van Lawick-Goodall, 1971)

Notice that naturalistic observation only provides *descriptions* of behavior. In order to *explain* observations we may need information from other research methods. Just the same, Goodall's discovery showed that humans are not the only tool-making animals (Nakamichi, 2004).

Chimpanzees in zoos use objects as tools. Doesn't that demonstrate the same thing? Not necessarily. Naturalistic observation allows us to study behavior that hasn't been tampered with or altered by outside influences. Only by observing chimps in their natural environment can we tell if they use tools without human interference.

Limitations

Doesn't the presence of human observers affect the animals' behavior? Yes. The observer effect is a major problem. The **observer effect** refers to changes in a subject's behavior caused by an awareness of being observed. Naturalists must be very careful to keep their distance and avoid "making friends" with the animals they are watching. Likewise, if you are interested in why automobile drivers have traffic accidents, you can't simply get in people's cars and start taking notes. As a stranger, your presence would probably change the driver's behaviors. When possible, this problem can be minimized by concealing the observer. Another solution is to use hidden recorders. For example, a naturalistic study of traffic accidents was done with video cameras installed in 100 cars (Dingus et al., 2006). It turns out that most accidents are caused by failing to look at the traffic in front of the car (eyes forward!).

Observer bias is a related problem in which observers see what they expect to see or record only selected details. For instance, teachers in one study were told to watch normal elementary school children who had been labeled (for the study) as "learning disabled," "mentally retarded," "emotionally disturbed," or "normal." Sadly, teachers gave the children very different ratings, depending on the labels used (Foster & Ysseldyke, 1976). In some situations, observer bias can have serious consequences (Jackson, 2008). For example, psychotherapists tend to get better results with the type of therapy they favor (Lambert, 1999).

46

● **FIGURE 1.8** A special moment in Jane Goodall's naturalistic study of chimpanzees. A chimp uses a grass stem to extract a meal from a termite nest. Goodall's work also documented the importance of long-term emotional bonds between chimpanzee mothers and their offspring, as well as fascinating differences in the behavior and "personalities" of individual chimps (Goodall, 1990). (Photo by Baron Hugo van Lawick. © National Geographic Society.)

The Anthropomorphic Error A special mistake to avoid while observing animals is the **anthropomorphic** (AN-thro-po-MORE-fik) **error.** This is the error of attributing human thoughts, feelings, or motives to animals—especially as a way of explaining their behavior (Wynne, 2004). The temptation to assume that an animal is "angry," "jealous," "bored," or "guilty" can be strong. If you have pets at home, you probably already know how difficult it is to avoid anthropomorphizing. But it can lead to false conclusions. For example, if your dog growls at your girlfriend every time she visits, you might assume the dog doesn't like her. But maybe she wears a perfume that irritates the dog's nose.

Recording Observations

Psychologists doing naturalistic studies make a special effort to minimize bias by keeping an **observational record,** or detailed summary of data and observations. As suggested by the study of traffic accidents, video recording often provides the most objective record of all.

Despite its problems, naturalistic observation can supply a wealth of information and raise many interesting questions. In most scientific research it is an excellent starting point.

Correlational Studies—In Search of the Perfect Relationship

Let's say a psychologist notes an association between the IQs of parents and their children, or between beauty and social popularity, or between anxiety and test performance, or even between crime and the weather. In each case, two observations or events are **correlated** (linked together in an orderly way).

A **correlational study** finds the degree of relationship, or correlation, between two existing traits, behaviors, or events. First, two factors are measured. Then a statistical technique is used to find their degree of correlation. (See the Appendix near the end of this book for more information.) For example, we could find the correlation between the number of hours spent practicing and sports performance during competitions. If the correlation is large, knowing how much a person practices would allow us to predict his or her success in competition. Likewise, success in competition could be used to predict the amount of practice.

Correlation Coefficients

How is the degree of correlation expressed? The strength and direction of a relationship can be expressed as a **coefficient of correlation.** This is simply a number falling somewhere between +1.00 and −1.00. (See the Appendix.) If the number is zero or close to zero, the association between two measures is weak or nonexistent. For example, the correlation between shoe size and intelligence is zero. (Sorry, size 12 readers.) If the correlation is +1.00, a perfect positive relationship exists; if it is −1.00, a perfect negative relationship has been discovered.

Correlations in psychology are rarely perfect. But the closer the coefficient is to +1.00 or −1.00, the stronger the relationship. For example, identical twins tend to have almost

---

Experimental method Investigating causes of behavior through controlled experimentation.
Naturalistic observation Observing behavior as it unfolds in natural settings.
Correlational method Making measurements to discover relationships between events.
Clinical method Studying psychological problems and therapies in clinical settings.
Survey method Using questionnaires and surveys to poll large groups of people.
Observer effect Changes in a person's behavior brought about by an awareness of being observed.
Observer bias The tendency of an observer to distort observations or perceptions to match his or her expectations.
Anthropomorphic error The error of attributing human thoughts, feelings, or motives to animals, especially as a way of explaining their behavior.
Observational record A detailed summary of observed events or a videotape of observed behavior.
Correlation The existence of a consistent, systematic relationship between two events, measures, or variables.
Correlational study A nonexperimental study designed to measure the degree of relationship (if any) between two or more events, measures, or variables.
Coefficient of correlation A statistical index ranging from −1.00 to +1.00 that indicates the direction and degree of correlation.

identical IQs. In contrast, the IQs of parents and their children are only generally similar. The correlation between the IQs of parents and children is .35; between identical twins it's .86.

What do the terms "positive" and "negative" correlation mean? A **positive correlation** shows that increases in one measure are matched by increases in the other (or decreases correspond with decreases). For example, there is a positive correlation between high school grades and college grades; students who do well in high school tend to do well in college (and the reverse). In a **negative correlation,** increases in the first measure are associated with decreases in the second (● Fig. 1.9). We might observe, for instance, that students who play many hours of computer games get lower grades than those who play few hours. (This is the well-known computer-game-zombie effect.)

Wouldn't that show that playing computer games too much causes lower grades? It might seem so, but we cannot be sure without performing an experiment.

Correlation and Causation Correlational studies help us discover relationships and make predictions. However, correlation *does not* demonstrate **causation** (a cause-effect relationship) (Elder, 2006). It could be, for instance, that students who aren't interested in their classes have more time for computer games. If so, then their lack of study and lower grades would *both* result from disinterest, not from excess game playing. Just because one thing *appears* to be related to another does not mean that a cause-and-effect connection exists.

Here is another example of mistaking correlation for causation: What if a psychologist discovers that the blood of patients with schizophrenia contains a certain chemical not found in the general population? Does this show that the chemical *causes* schizophrenia? It may seem so, but schizophrenia could cause the chemical to form. Or, both schizophrenia and the chemical might be caused by some unknown third factor, such as the typical diet in mental hospitals. Just because one thing *appears* to cause another does not *confirm* that it does. The best way to be confident that a cause-and-effect relationship exists is to perform a controlled experiment.

The Clinical Method—Data by the Case

It can be difficult or impossible to use the experimental method to study mental disorders, such as depression or psychosis. Many experiments are impractical, unethical, or impossible to do. In such instances, a **case study** (an in-depth focus on a single subject) may be the best source of information. Clinical psychologists rely heavily on case studies, especially as a way to investigate rare or unusual problems.

Case studies may sometimes be thought of as **natural clinical tests** (accidents or other natural events that provide psychological data). Gunshot wounds, brain tumors, accidental poisonings, and similar disasters provide much information about the human brain. One remarkable case from the history of psychology is reported by Dr. J. M. Harlow (1868). Phineas Gage, a young foreman on a work crew, had a 13-pound steel rod blown through the front of his brain by a dynamite explosion (● Fig. 1.10). Amazingly, he survived the accident. Within 2 months Gage could walk, talk, and move normally. But the injury forever changed his personality. Instead of the honest and dependable worker he had been before, Gage became a surly, foul-mouthed liar. Dr. Harlow carefully recorded all details of what was perhaps the first in-depth case study of an accidental frontal lobotomy (the destruction of front brain matter).

● **FIGURE 1.9** The correlation coefficient tells how strongly two measures are related. These graphs show a range of relationships between two measures, A and B. If a correlation is negative, increases in one measure are associated with decreases in the other. (As B gets larger, A gets smaller.) In a positive correlation, increases in one measure are associated with increases in the other. (As B gets larger, A gets larger.) The center-left graph ("medium negative relationship") might result from comparing anxiety level (B) with test scores (A): Higher anxiety is associated with lower scores. The center graph ("no relationship") would result from plotting a person's shoe size (B) and his or her IQ (A). The center-right graph ("medium positive relationship") could be a plot of grades in high school (B) and grades in college (A) for a group of students: Higher grades in high school are associated with higher grades in college.

● **FIGURE 1.10** Some of the earliest information on the effects of damage to frontal areas of the brain came from a case study of the accidental injury of Phineas Gage.

When a Los Angeles carpenter named Michael Melnick suffered a similar injury, he recovered completely, with no sign of lasting ill effects. Melnick's very different reaction to a similar injury shows why psychologists prefer controlled experiments and often use lab animals for studies of the brain. Case studies lack formal control groups. This, of course, limits the conclusions that can be drawn from clinical observations. Nonetheless, case studies are especially valuable for studying rare events, such as unusual mental disorders, childhood "geniuses," or "rampage" school shootings (Harding, Fox, & Mehta, 2002). Also, case studies of psychotherapy have provided many useful ideas about how to treat emotional problems (Wedding & Corsini, 2005).

Case studies can provide special opportunities to answer interesting questions. For instance, a classic case study in psychology concerns four identical quadruplets, known as the Genain sisters. In addition to having identical genes, all four women became schizophrenic before age 25 (Rosenthal & Quinn, 1977). The Genains, who have been studied for more than 40 years, were in and out of mental hospitals most of their lives. The fact that they share identical genes suggests that mental disorders are influenced by heredity. The fact that some of the sisters are more disturbed than others suggests that environmental conditions also affect mental illness. Indeed, Myra, the least ill of the four, was the only sister who was able to avoid her father, an alcoholic who terrorized, spied on, and sexually molested the girls. (See Module 12.3 for more information about the causes of schizophrenia.)

The chances of four identical quads all becoming schizophrenic are about 1 in 1.5 billion. Thus, cases like theirs provide insights that can't be obtained by any other means (Mirsky et al., 2000).

Survey Method—Here, Have a Sample

Sometimes psychologists would like to ask everyone in the world a few well-chosen questions: "Do you drink alcoholic beverages? How often per week?" "What form of discipline did your parents use when you were a child?" "What is the most creative thing you've done?" Honest answers to such questions can reveal much about behavior. But because it is impossible to question everyone, doing a survey is often more practical.

In the **survey method,** public polling techniques are used to answer psychological questions (Tourangeau, 2004). Typically, people in a representative sample are asked a series of carefully worded questions. A **representative sample** is a small group that accurately reflects a larger population. A good sample must include the same proportion of men, women, young, old, professionals, blue-collar workers, Republicans, Democrats, whites, African Americans, Native Americans, Latinos, Asians, and so on, as found in the population as a whole.

A **population** is an entire group of animals or people belonging to a particular category (for example, all college students or all single women). Ultimately, we are interested in entire populations. But by selecting a smaller sample, we can draw conclusions about the larger group without polling each and every person. Representative samples are often ob-

Positive correlation A statistical relationship in which increases in one measure are matched by increases in the other (or decreases correspond with decreases).
Negative correlation A statistical relationship in which increases in one measure are matched by decreases in the other.
Causation The act of causing some effect.
Case study An in-depth focus on all aspects of a single person.
Natural clinical test An accident or other natural event that allows the gathering of data on a psychological phenomenon of interest.
Survey method The use of public polling techniques to answer psychological questions.
Representative sample A small, randomly selected part of a larger population that accurately reflects characteristics of the whole population.
Population An entire group of animals or people belonging to a particular category (for example, all college students or all married women).

tained by *randomly* selecting who will be included (● Fig. 1.11). (Notice that this is similar to randomly assigning participants to groups in an experiment.)

How accurate is the survey method? Modern surveys like the Gallup and Harris polls are quite accurate. The Gallup poll has erred in its election predictions by only 1.5 percent since 1954. However, if a survey is based on a biased sample, it may paint a false picture. A *biased sample* does not accurately reflect the population from which it was drawn. Surveys done by magazines, websites, and online information services can be quite biased. Surveys on the use of guns done by *O: The Oprah Magazine* and *Guns and Ammo* magazine would probably produce very different results—neither of which would represent the general population. That's why psychologists using the survey method go to great lengths to ensure that their samples are representative. Fortunately, people can often be polled by telephone, which makes it easier to obtain large samples. Even if one person out of three refuses to answer survey questions, the results are still likely to be valid (Hutchinson, 2004).

Internet Surveys Recently, psychologists have started doing surveys and experiments on the Internet. Web-based research has the advantage of low cost, and it can reach very large groups of people. Internet studies have provided interesting information about topics such as anger, decision-making, racial prejudice, what disgusts people, religion, sexual attitudes, and much more. Biased samples can limit web-based research (because it isn't easy to control who actually answers your online questionnaire), but psychologists are finding ways to gather valid information with it (Birnbaum, 2004; Whitaker, 2007).

Social Desirability Even well-designed surveys may be limited by another problem. If a psychologist were to ask you detailed questions about your sexual history and current sexual behavior, how accurate would your replies be? Would you exaggerate? Would you be embarrassed? Replies to survey questions are not always accurate or truthful. Many people show a distinct *courtesy bias* (a tendency to give "polite" or socially desirable answers). For example, answers to questions concerning sex, drinking or drug use, income, and church attendance tend to be less than truthful. Likewise, the week after an election, more people will say they voted than actually did (Hutchinson, 2004).

Summary Despite their limitations, surveys frequently produce valuable information. For instance, the survey method has been used to find out about the attitudes of Muslims in the Middle East toward U.S. policies in the region and to clarify the debate about Islam and violence that has arisen since the terrorist attacks of 9/11 (Haddad, 2003). To sum up, the survey method can be a powerful research tool. Like other methods, it has limitations, but new techniques and strategies are providing valuable information about our behavior (Kahneman et al., 2004). ■ Table 1.6 summarizes many of the important ideas we have covered.

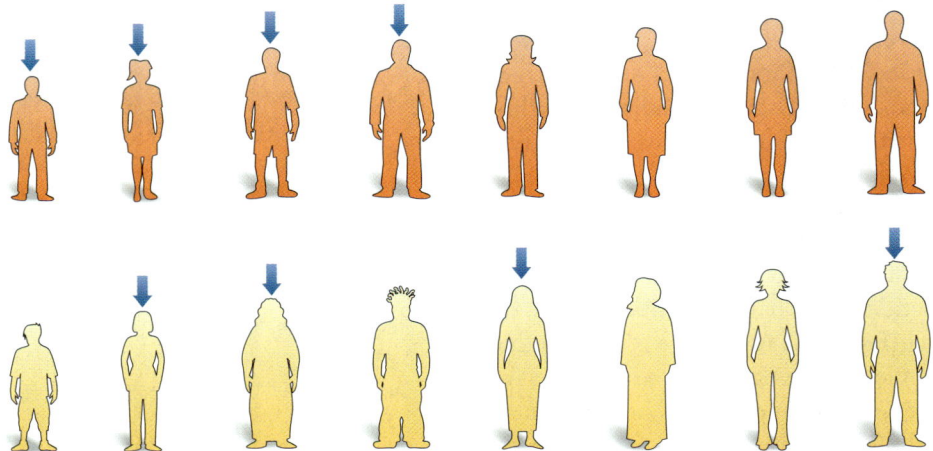

● **FIGURE 1.11** If you were conducting a survey in which a person's height might be an important variable, the upper, nonrandom sample would be very unrepresentative. The lower sample, selected using a table of random numbers, better represents the group as a whole.

TABLE 1.6 Comparison of Psychological Research Methods

	ADVANTAGES	DISADVANTAGES
Naturalistic Observation	Behavior is observed in a natural setting; much information is obtained, and hypotheses and questions for additional research are formed	Little or no control is possible; observed behavior may be altered by the presence of the observer; observations may be biased; causes cannot be conclusively identified
Correlational Method	Demonstrates the existence of relationships; allows prediction; can be used in lab, clinic, or natural setting	Little or no control is possible; relationships may be coincidental; cause-and-effect relationships cannot be confirmed
Experimental Method	Clear cause-and-effect relationships can be identified; powerful controlled observations can be staged; no need to wait for natural event	May be somewhat artificial; some natural behavior not easily studied in laboratory (field experiments may avoid these objections)
Clinical Method	Takes advantage of "natural clinical trials" and allows investigation of rare or unusual problems or events	Little or no control is possible; does not provide a control group for comparison, subjective interpretation is often necessary, a single case may be misleading or unrepresentative
Survey Method	Allows information about large numbers of people to be gathered; can address questions not answered by other approaches	Obtaining a representative sample is critical and can be difficult to do; answers may be inaccurate; people may not do what they say or say what they do

MODULE 1.6 Summary

What other research methods do psychologists use?

- Unlike controlled experiments, nonexperimental methods usually cannot demonstrate cause-and-effect relationships.
- Naturalistic observation is a starting place in many investigations.
- Two problems with naturalistic observation are the effects of the observer on the observed and observer bias.
- In the correlational method, relationships between two traits, responses, or events are measured.
- A correlation coefficient is computed to gauge the strength of the relationship. Correlations allow prediction but do not demonstrate cause-and-effect.
- Case studies and natural clinical tests provide insights into human behavior that can't be gained by other methods.
- In the survey method, people in a representative sample are asked a series of carefully worded questions.
- Obtaining a representative sample of people is crucial when the survey method is used to study large populations.

KNOWLEDGE BUILDER

Nonexperimental Research Methods

Recite

1. Two major problems in naturalistic observation are the effects of the observer and observer bias. T or F?
2. Correlation typically does not demonstrate causation. T or F?
3. Which correlation coefficient represents the strongest relationship?
   a. −0.86 b. +0.66 c. +0.10 d. +0.09
4. Case studies can often be thought of as natural tests and are frequently used by clinical psychologists. T or F?
5. For the survey method to be valid, a representative sample of people must be polled. T or F?
6. Amnesia would most likely be investigated by use of
   a. a representative sample b. field experiments c. the double-blind procedure d. case studies

Reflect
Critical Thinking

7. Adults who often ate Frosted Flakes cereal as children now have half the cancer rate seen in adults who never ate Frosted Flakes. What do you think explains this strange correlation?
8. A psychologist conducting a survey at a shopping mall (The Gallery of Wretched Excess) flips a coin before stopping passersby. If the coin shows heads, he interviews the person; if it shows tails, he skips that person. Has the psychologist obtained a random sample?
9. Attributing mischievous motives to a car that is not working properly is a thinking error similar to anthropomorphizing. T or F?

Relate

Have you ever been asked to complete a survey, either in person or via the telephone or the Internet? Did you do it or did you refuse? If you refused, do you think your refusal influenced the final results of the survey? What would it say about accuracy if lots of people refused to complete the survey? If you completed the survey, were you honest about your answers? What would it say about accuracy if lots of people refused to answer accurately?

Link

Internet addresses frequently change. To find the sites listed here, visit **http://www.thomsonedu.com/psychology/coon** for an updated list of Internet addresses and direct links to relevant sites.

- **Psychological Research on the Net** Find and complete a survey study.
- **The Jane Goodall Institute** Information about Goodall's work at Gombe, in Tanzania, where she has studied and protected wild chimpanzees for more than 40 years.
- **Research Methods and the Correlation** Explore different research methods in psychology.

ANSWERS

1. T 2. T 3. a 4. T 5. T 6. d 7. The correlation is related to an age bias in the group of people studied. Older adults have higher cancer rates than younger adults, and Frosted Flakes weren't available during the childhoods of older people. Thus, Frosted Flakes appear to be related to cancer, when age is the real connection (Tierny, 1987). 8. The psychologist's coin flips *might* produce a reasonably good sample of people *at the mall*. The real problem is that people who go to the mall may be mostly from one part of town, from upper income groups, or from some other nonrepresentative group. The psychologist's sample is likely to be seriously flawed. 9. True. It appears to be difficult for humans to resist thinking of other species and even machines in human terms.

MODULE 1.7 Psychology in Action: Psychology in the Media

TO HELP YOU get the most out of psychology, each section of this text includes a "Psychology in Action" module. Here you will find ideas you can actually use, now or in the future. To complete the topics we have been discussing, let's take a critical look at information reported in the popular press. You should find this an interesting way to conclude our opening tour of psychology and its methods.

Psychology in the Media—Separating Fact from Fiction

SURVEY QUESTION: *How good is psychological information found in the popular media?*

Psychology is a popular topic in contemporary media. Unfortunately, much of what you will encounter is based on entertainment value rather than critical thinking or science. Here are some suggestions for separating high-quality information from misleading fiction.

Suggestion 1: Be skeptical. Reports in the popular press tend to be made uncritically and with a definite bias toward reporting "astonishing" findings and telling interesting stories. Remember, saying, "That's incredible" means, "That's not believable"—which is usually true.

Example 1: The Internet is awash with rumors, hoaxes, half-truths, and urban legends like the one about giant alligators living in New York sewers. One of our all-time favorites was a story about the health department in Oregon seeking a Klingon interpreter for mental health patients who only speak in the fictional language used on the *Star Trek* TV series. This tale started when a newspaper reported that Klingon was on a list of languages that some psychiatric patients claimed they could speak. The article specifically noted that "in reality, no patient has yet tried to communicate in Klingon." Nevertheless, as the story spread around the Web, the idea that Oregon was looking for someone fluent in Klingon had become a "fact" (O'Neill, 2003).

Example 2: Back in the 1960s, news articles described an amazing new "sixth sense" called "dermo-optical perception." A few gifted people, the articles claimed, could use their fingertips to identify colors and read print while blindfolded.

In reality, such "abilities" are based on what stage magicians call a "nose peek." It is impossible to prepare a blindfold (without damaging the eyes) that does not leave a tiny space on each side of the nose. Were the people who claimed to have "X-ray eyes" taking nose peeks? Apparently they were, because "dermo-optical abilities" disappeared as soon as the opportunity to peek was controlled.

Amazingly, despite the complete refutation, 30 years later a Russian company began charging for courses to train people in "dermo-optical perception." This "outbreak" was once again debunked (Benski, 1998). You'll find similar misinformation and sensationalism throughout the popular media. Be on guard. It is just a matter of time before old, thoroughly discredited, and sensational claims are recycled. (Want to learn how to read with your nose with your eyes closed?)

Suggestion 2: Consider the source of information. It should come as no surprise that information used to sell a product often reflects a desire for profit rather than the objective truth. Here is a typical advertising claim: "Government tests prove that no sleep medicine is stronger or more effective than Coma." A statement like this usually means that there was *no difference* between Coma and the other products tested. No other sleep aid was stronger or more effective. But none was weaker either.

Keep the source in mind when reading the claims of makers of home biofeedback machines, sleep-learning devices, subliminal CDs, and the like. Remember that psychological services may be merchandised as well. Be wary of expensive courses that promise instant mental health and happiness, increased efficiency, memory, extrasensory perception (ESP) or psychic ability, control of the unconscious mind, an end to smoking, and so on. Usually they are promoted with a few testimonials and many unsupported claims (Lilienfeld, 2005).

Psychic claims should be viewed with special caution. Stage mentalists make a living by deceiving the public. Understandably, they are highly interested in promoting belief in their nonexistent powers. Psychic phenomena, when (and if) they do occur, are quite unpredictable. It would be impossible for a mentalist to do three shows a night, six nights a week, without consistently using deception. The same is true of the so-called psychic advisers promoted in TV commercials. These charlatans make use of the Barnum effect (the tendency to consider personal descriptions accurate if they are stated in general terms) to create an illusion that they know private information about the people who call them (Nickell, 2001). Google magician James Randi's Million Dollar Challenge. Randi is offering $1,000,000 to anyone demonstrating such abilities under controlled conditions. Are you surprised to learn that no one has even passed the preliminary tests yet?

Suggestion 3: Ask yourself if there was a control group. The key importance of a control group in any experiment is frequently overlooked by the unsophisticated—an error to which you are no longer susceptible! The popular press is full of reports of "experiments" performed without control groups: "Talking to

Plants Speeds Growth"; "Special Diet Controls Hyperactivity in Children"; "Food Shows Less Spoilage in Pyramid Chamber"; "Graduates of Firewalking Seminar Risk Their Soles."

Consider the last example for a moment. Expensive commercial courses have long been promoted to teach people to walk barefoot on hot coals. (Why anyone would want to do this is itself an interesting question.) Firewalkers supposedly protect their feet with a technique called "neurolinguistic programming." Many people have paid good money to learn the technique, and most do manage a quick walk on the coals. But is the technique necessary? And is anything remarkable happening? We need a comparison group!

Fortunately, physicist Bernard Leikind has provided one. Leikind showed with volunteers that anyone (with reasonably callused feet) can walk over a bed of coals without being burned. The reason is that the coals, which are light, fluffy carbon, transmit little heat when touched. The principle involved is similar to briefly putting your hand in a hot oven. If you touch a pan, you will be burned because metal transfers heat efficiently. But if your hand stays in the heated air you'll be fine because air transmits little heat (Kida, 2006; Mitchell, 1987). Mystery solved.

Suggestion 4: Look for errors in distinguishing between correlation and causation. As you now know, it is dangerous to presume that one thing *caused* another just because they are correlated. In spite of this, you will see many claims based on questionable correlations. Here's an example of mistaking correlation for causation: Jeanne Dixon, a well-known astrologer, once answered a group of prominent scientists—who had declared that there is no scientific foundation for astrology—by saying, "They would do well to check the records at their local police stations, where they will learn that the rate of violent crime rises and falls with lunar cycles." Dixon, of course, believes that the moon affects human behavior.

If it is true that violent crime is more frequent at certain times of the month, doesn't that prove her point? Far from it. Increased crime could be due to darker nights, the fact that many people expect others to act crazier, or any number of similar factors. Besides, direct studies of the alleged "lunar effect" have shown that it doesn't occur (Dowling, 2005). Moonstruck criminals, influenced by "a bad moon rising," are a fiction (Iosif & Ballon, 2005).

Suggestion 5: Be sure to distinguish between observation and inference. If you see a person *crying*, is it correct to assume that she or he is *sad*? Although it seems reasonable to make this assumption, it is actually quite risky. We can observe objectively that the person is crying, but to *infer* sadness may be in error. It could be that the individual has just peeled 5 pounds of onions. Or maybe he or she just won a million-dollar lottery or is trying contact lenses for the first time.

Psychologists, politicians, physicians, scientists, and other experts often go far beyond the available facts in their claims. This does not mean that their inferences, opinions, and interpretations have no value; the opinion of an expert on the causes of mental illness, criminal behavior, learning problems, or whatever can be revealing. But be careful to distinguish between fact and opinion.

Suggestion 6: Beware of oversimplifications, especially those motivated by monetary gain. Courses or programs that offer a "new personality in three sessions," "six steps to love and fulfillment in marriage," or some newly discovered "secret for unlocking the powers of the mind and the universe" should be immediately suspect.

An excellent example of oversimplification is provided by websites devoted to *The Secret*, a video that promises to reveal "the secret to unlimited joy, health, money, relationships, love, youth: everything you have ever wanted" According to *The Secret*, all you need to do is put your desires out to the universe and the universe must respond by granting your wishes. And all it will cost you is the price of ordering the video.

Suggestion 7: Remember, "for example" is no proof. After reading the preceding modules, you should be sensitive to the danger of selecting single examples. If you read, "Law student passes state bar exam using sleep-learning device," don't rush out to buy one. Systematic research showed long ago that these devices are of little or no value (Druckman & Bjork, 1994). A corollary to this suggestion is to ask, Are the reported observations important or widely applicable?

Examples, anecdotes, single cases, and testimonials are all potentially deceptive. According to numerous testimonials, believers in the power of *The Secret* have been showered with money, success, and happiness immediately after viewing the video. Unfortunately, such *individual cases* (or even several) tell nothing about what is true *in general* (Stanovich, 2007). For instance, studies of large groups of people show that smoking increases the likelihood of lung cancer. It doesn't matter if you know a lifelong heavy smoker who is 95 years old. The general finding is the one to remember.

Firewalking is based on simple physics, not on any form of supernatural psychological control. The temperature of the coals may be as high as 1,200° F. However, coals are like the air in a hot oven: They are very inefficient at transferring heat during brief contact.

KNOWLEDGE BUILDER

The Science of Psychology

Recite
1. Newspaper accounts of dermo-optical perception have generally reported only the results of carefully designed psychological experiments. T or F?
2. Stage mentalists and psychics often use deception in their acts. T or F?
3. Blaming the lunar cycle for variations in the rate of violent crime is an example of mistaking correlation for causation. T or F?
4. If a psychology student uses a sleep-learning device to pass a midterm exam, it proves that the device works. T or F?

Reflect
Critical Thinking

5. Many parents believe that children become "hyperactive" when they eat too much sugar, and some early studies seemed to confirm this connection. However, we now know that eating sugar rarely has any effect on children. Why do you think that sugar appears to cause hyperactivity?

Relate
Do you tend to assume that a statement must be true if it is in print, on television, or made by an authority? How actively do you evaluate and question claims found in the media? Could you be a more critical consumer of information? *Should* you be a more critical consumer of information?

Link
Internet addresses frequently change. To find the sites listed here, visit **http://www.thomsonedu.com/psychology/coon** for an updated list of Internet addresses and direct links to relevant sites.

- **That's Infotainment!** Article about sensationalism in the news media.
- **The Oregon UFO Wave That Wasn't** A discussion the role of media in a wave of UFO sightings in 1896-1897.
- **Psychology and the News Media: Reflections on a Ten Year Initiative** Article on the presentation of psychology in the news media.

ANSWERS
1. F 2. T 3. T 4. F 5. This is another case of mistaking correlation for causation. Children who are hyperactive may eat more sugar (and other foods) to fuel their frenetic activity levels.

Summary We are all bombarded daily with such a mass of new information that it is difficult to absorb it. The available knowledge, even in a limited area like psychology, biology, medicine, or contemporary hip-hop music, is so vast that no single person can completely know and comprehend it. With this situation in mind, it becomes increasingly important that you become a critical, selective, and informed consumer of information.

MODULE 1.7 Psychology in Action Summary

How good is psychological information found in the popular media?

- Information in the mass media varies greatly in quality and accuracy.
- It is wise to approach such information with skepticism and caution. Critical thinking and skepticism about media reports is often necessary to separate facts from fallacies.
- Problems in media reports are often related to biased or unreliable sources of information, uncontrolled observation, misleading correlations, false inferences, oversimplification, use of single examples, and unrepeatable results.

Interactive Learning

Psychology: Active Learning Modules Book Companion Website

Visit the book's companion website, **http://www.thomsonedu.com/psychology/coon**, where you will find flash cards, practice quizzes, Internet links, and more to help you study.

ThomsonNOW

Just What You Need to Know NOW!

http://psychology.wadsworth.com

Spend time on what you need to master rather than on information you already have learned. Take a pre-test for this chapter, and ThomsonNOW will generate a personalized study plan based on your results. The study plan will identify the topics you need to review and direct you to online resources to help you master those topics. You can then take a post-test to help you determine the concepts you have mastered and what you will need to work on. Try it out! Go to **www.thomsonedu.com/login** to sign in with an access code or to purchase access to this product.

2 Brain and Behavior

MODULE 2.1 Neurons and the Nervous System
SURVEY QUESTION: How do nerve cells operate and communicate?
SURVEY QUESTION: What are the functions of the major parts of the nervous system?

MODULE 2.2 Brain Research
SURVEY QUESTION: How are different parts of the brain identified?
SURVEY QUESTION: What do the different parts of the brain do?

MODULE 2.3 Hemispheres and Lobes of the Cerebral Cortex
SURVEY QUESTIONS: How do the left and right hemispheres differ? What are the different functions of the lobes of the cerebral cortex?

MODULE 2.4 Subcortex and Endocrine System
SURVEY QUESTION: What kinds of behaviors are controlled by the subcortex?
SURVEY QUESTION: Does the glandular system affect behavior?

MODULE 2.5 Psychology in Action: Handedness—Are You Dexterous or Sinister?
SURVEY QUESTION: In what ways do right- and left-handed individuals differ?

Finding Music in Tofu

When your authors watch gifted musicians, we often think about the brain (Really!). One of us recently saw Yo-Yo Ma, a master cellist, play a Bach suite with amazing skill. If Ma had been an athlete, you would say he was "in the zone." His performance was unforgettable. Of course, in everything from classical to jazz to hip-hop, musicians regularly make music that no machine could duplicate. A virtual Carlos Santana? A mechanical Nelly Furtado? We don't think so. That's why music is a good example of the central role the brain plays in all that is human.

Your brain is the size of a grapefruit. It weighs around 3 pounds and looks a lot like tofu. The next time you are in a market that sells beef brains, stop and have a look. What you will see is similar to your own brain, only smaller. How could such a squishy little blob of tissue allow us to make music of exquisite beauty? To seek a cure for cancer? To fall in love? Or read a book like this one?

Each of the billions of nerve cells in your brain is linked to as many as 15,000 others. The resulting network makes it possible to process immense amounts of information. In fact, there may be more *possible* pathways between the neurons in your brain than there are atoms in the entire universe! Undeniably, the human brain is the most amazing of all computers.

Scientists use the power of the brain to study the brain. Yet, even now we must wonder if the brain will ever completely understand itself. Nevertheless, answers to many age-old questions about the mind, consciousness, and knowledge lie buried within the brain. Let's visit this fascinating realm.

Arthur Toga, UCLA/Photo Researchers, Inc.

MODULE 2.1 Neurons and the Nervous System

ALL of your thoughts, feelings, and actions can be traced back to electrical impulses flashing through the spidery branches of nerve cells within your brain. Although they may seem far removed from daily life, everything you do begins with these tiny cells. Let's see how nerve cells operate and how the nervous system is "wired."

Neurons—Building a "Biocomputer"

SURVEY QUESTION: *How do nerve cells operate and communicate?*

The brain consists of some 100 billion **neurons** (NOOR-ons: individual nerve cells). Neurons carry information from the senses to the brain, where they process it. They also activate muscles and glands. A single neuron is not very smart—it would take many just to make you blink. Yet, when neurons form vast networks, they produce intelligence and consciousness. Neurons link to one another in tight clumps and long "chains." Each neuron receives messages from many others and sends its own message on. Millions of neurons must send messages at the same time to produce even the most fleeting thought (Kalat, 2007). When a musician such as Eric Clapton plays a guitar riff, literally billions of neurons may be involved.

Parts of a Neuron

What does a neuron look like? What are its main parts? No two neurons are exactly alike, but most have four basic parts (● Fig. 2.1). The **dendrites** (DEN-drytes), which look like tree roots, receive messages from other neurons. The **soma** (SOH-mah: cell body) does the same. In addition, the soma sends messages of its own (nerve impulses) down a thin fiber called the **axon** (AK-sahn).

Most axons end in **axon terminals.** These "branches" link up with the dendrites and somas of other neurons. This allows

● **FIGURE 2.1** A neuron, or nerve cell. In the right foreground you can see a nerve cell fiber in cross section. The upper left photo gives a more realistic picture of the shape of neurons. Nerve impulses usually travel from the dendrites and soma to the branching ends of the axon. The nerve cell shown here is a motor neuron. The axons of motor neurons stretch from the brain and spinal cord to muscles or glands of the body.

58

● **FIGURE 2.2** Electrical probes placed inside and outside an axon measure its activity. (The scale is exaggerated here. Such measurements require ultra-small electrodes, as described in Module 2.2.) The inside of an axon at rest is about −60 to −70 millivolts, compared with the outside. Electrochemical changes in a neuron generate an action potential. When sodium ions (Na^+) that have a positive charge rush into the cell, its interior briefly becomes positive. This is the action potential. After the action potential, positive potassium ions (K^+) flow out of the axon and restore its negative charge. (See Fig. 2.3 for further explanation.)

information to pass from neuron to neuron. Some axons are only 0.1 millimeter long. (That's about the width of a pencil line.) Others stretch up to a meter through the nervous system. (From the base of your spine to your big toe, for instance.) Like miniature cables, axons carry messages through the brain and nervous system. Altogether, your brain contains about 3 million miles of axons (Rosenzweig, Breedlove, & Watson, 2004).

Now let's summarize with a metaphor. Imagine that you are standing in a long line of people who are holding hands. A person on the far right end of the line wants to silently send a message to the person on the left end. She does this by pressing the hand of the person to her left, who presses the hand of the person to his left, and so on. The message arrives at your right hand (your dendrites). You decide whether to pass it on. (You are the soma.) The message goes out through your left arm (the axon). With your left hand (the axon terminals), you squeeze the hand of the person to your left, and the message moves on.

The Nerve Impulse

Electrically charged molecules called *ions* (EYE-ons) are found inside each neuron (● Fig. 2.2). Other ions lie outside the cell. Some ions have a positive electrical charge, and some are negative. When a neuron is inactive, more of these "plus" charges exist outside the neuron and more "minus" charges exist inside. As a result, the inside of each neuron in your brain has an electrical charge of about minus 70 millivolts. (A millivolt is one thousandth of a volt.) This charge allows each neuron in your brain to act like a tiny biological battery.

The electrical charge of an inactive neuron is called its **resting potential.** But neurons seldom get much rest: Messages arriving from other neurons raise and lower the resting potential. If the electrical charge rises to about minus 50 millivolts, the neuron will reach its *threshold,* or trigger point for firing. (See Fig. 2.2.) It's as if the neuron says "Ah ha! It's time to send a message to my neighbors." When a neuron reaches −50 millivolts, an **action potential,** or nerve impulse, sweeps down the axon at up to 200 miles per hour (● Fig. 2.3). That may seem fast, but it still takes at least a split second to react. That's one reason why hitting a 95-mile-per-hour major league fastball is so difficult. (See "Dollars, Drag Racing, and the Nervous System.")

What happens during an action potential? The axon membrane is pierced by tiny tunnels or "holes" called **ion channels.** Normally, these tiny openings are blocked by molecules that act like "gates" or "doors." During an action potential, the gates pop open. This allows sodium ions (Na^+) to rush

Neuron An individual nerve cell.
Dendrites Neuron fibers that receive incoming messages.
Soma The main body of a neuron or other cell.
Axon Fiber that carries information away from the cell body of a neuron.
Axon terminals Branching fibers at the ends of axons.
Resting potential The electrical charge of a neuron at rest.
Action potential The nerve impulse.
Ion channels Tiny openings through the axon membrane.

● **FIGURE 2.3** The inside of an axon normally has a negative electrical charge. The fluid surrounding an axon is normally positive. As an action potential passes along the axon, these charges reverse, so that the interior of the axon briefly becomes positive.

1. In its resting state, the axon has a negatively charged interior.

2. During an action potential, positively charged atoms (ions) rush into the axon. This briefly changes the electrical charge inside the axon from negative to positive. Simultaneously, the charge outside the axon becomes negative.

3. The action potential advances as positive and negative charges reverse in a moving zone of electrical activity that sweeps down the axon.

4. After an action potential passes, positive ions rapidly flow out of the axon to quickly restore its negative charge. An outward flow of additional positive ions returns the axon to its resting state.

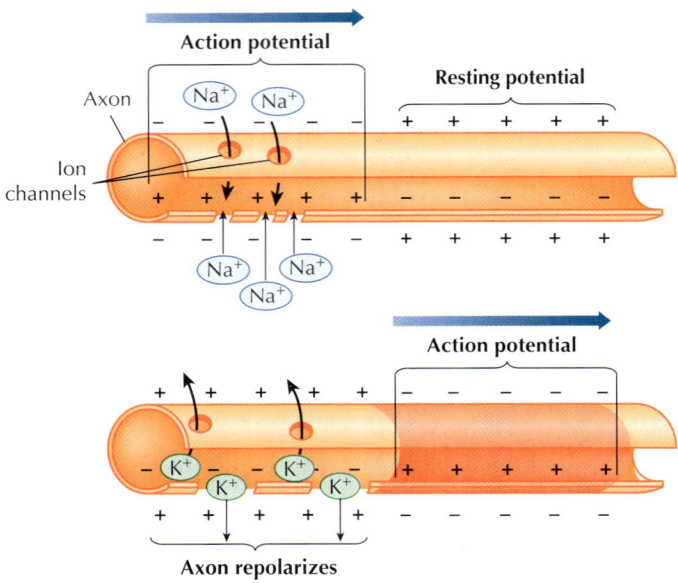

● **FIGURE 2.4** The interior of an axon. The right end of the top axon is at rest. Thus, it has a negative charge inside. An action potential begins when ion channels open and sodium ions (Na$^+$) rush into the axon. In this drawing, the action potential would travel from left to right along the axon. In the lower axon, the action potential has moved to the right. After it passes, potassium ions (K$^+$) flow out of the axon. This quickly renews the negative charge inside the axon, so that it can fire again. Sodium ions that enter the axon during an action potential are pumped out more slowly. Removing them restores the original resting potential.

into the axon (Carlson, 2007). The channels first open near the soma. Then, gate after gate opens down the length of the axon, as the action potential zips along (● Fig. 2.4).

Each action potential is an *all-or-nothing event* (a nerve impulse occurs completely or not at all). You might find it helpful to picture the axon as a row of dominoes set on end. Tipping over the dominoes is an all-or-nothing act. Once the first domino drops, a wave of falling blocks will zip rapidly to the end of the line. Similarly, when a nerve impulse is triggered near the soma, a wave of activity (the action potential) travels down the length of the axon. This is what happens in long chains of neurons as Yo-Yo Ma's brain tells his hands what to do next, note after note.

After each nerve impulse, the cell briefly dips below its resting level, and it becomes less willing to fire. This **negative after-potential** occurs because potassium ions (K$^+$) flow out of the neuron while the membrane gates are open. (See Fig. 2.4.) After a nerve impulse, ions flow both into and out of the axon, recharging it for more action. In our model, it takes an instant for the row of dominoes to be set up again. Soon, however, the axon is ready for another wave of activity.

Synapses and Neurotransmitters

How does information move from one neuron to another? The nerve impulse is primarily electrical. That's why electrically stimulating the brain affects behavior. To prove the point,

DISCOVERING PSYCHOLOGY

Dollars, Drag Racing, and the Nervous System

In the sport of drag racing, victory depends on a driver's reaction time. When a light signals the start of a race, the driver must react as quickly as possible, usually in less than a half second. To test your own reaction time, have a friend hold a dollar bill from the top, as shown in ● Figure 2.5. Spread your thumb and fingers about 2 inches apart and place them around the bill, near the middle of Washington's portrait. Watch the bill intently. Without warning, your friend should release the bill. When you see it begin to move, try to catch it by pressing your thumb and fingers together. Most likely, the bill will slip through your fingers. It takes a split second for you to see the bill's movement, process that information in your brain, and send signals to your hand, causing it to move. Because neural processing takes time, our experiences and reactions lag slightly behind events in the world. In fact, your sense of control over your actions is partly an illusion. For instance, if you decide to wiggle your finger, your brain will begin a series of events that leads to finger movement. This activity will start *before* you begin to feel that you are intentionally moving your finger (Obhi & Haggard, 2004)!

● **FIGURE 2.5**

researcher José Delgado once entered a bullring with a cape and a radio transmitter. The bull charged. Delgado retreated. At the last instant the speeding bull stopped short. Why? Because Delgado's radio-activated electrodes (metal wires) that were placed deep within the bull's brain. These, in turn, stimulated "control centers" that brought the bull to a halt (Horgan, 2005).

In contrast to the nerve impulse, communication between neurons is chemical. The microscopic space between two neurons, over which messages pass, is called a **synapse** (SIN-aps) (● Fig. 2.6). When an action potential reaches the tips of the axon terminals, **neurotransmitters** (NOOR-oh-TRANS-mit-ers) are released into the synaptic gap. Neurotransmitters are chemicals that alter activity in neurons.

Let's return to the people standing in a line. To be more accurate, you and the others shouldn't be holding hands. Instead, each person should have a squirt gun in his or her left hand. To pass along a message, you would squirt the right hand of the person to your left. When that person notices this "message," he or she would squirt the right hand of the person to the left, and so on.

When chemical molecules cross over a synapse, they attach to special receiving areas on the next neuron. (See Fig. 2.6.) These tiny **receptor sites** on the cell membrane are sensitive to neurotransmitters. The sites are found in large numbers on nerve cell bodies and on dendrites. Muscles and glands have receptor sites, too.

Do neurotransmitters always trigger an action potential in the next neuron? No, but they do change the likelihood of an action potential in the next neuron. Some neurotransmitters

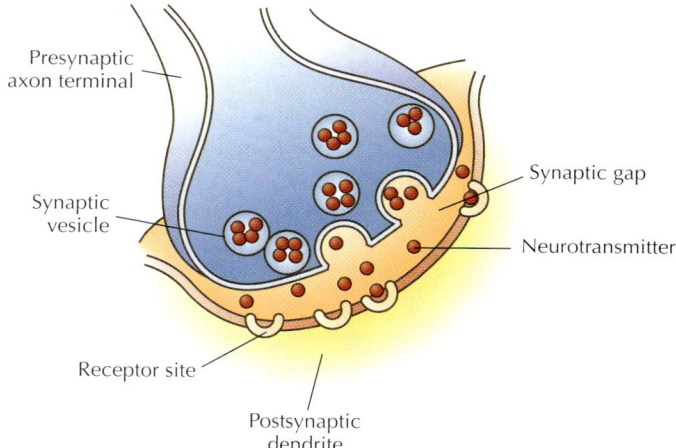

● **FIGURE 2.6** A highly magnified view of a synapse. Neurotransmitters are stored in tiny sacs called synaptic vesicles (VES-ih-kels). When a nerve impulse reaches the end of an axon, the vesicles move to the surface and release neurotransmitters. These molecules cross the synaptic gap to affect the next neuron. The size of the gap is exaggerated here; it is actually only about one millionth of an inch. Some transmitter molecules excite the next neuron and some inhibit its activity.

Negative after-potential A drop in electrical charge below the resting potential.

Synapse The microscopic space between two neurons, over which messages pass.

Neurotransmitter Any chemical released by a neuron that alters activity in other neurons.

Receptor sites Areas on the surface of neurons and other cells that are sensitive to neurotransmitters or hormones.

excite the next neuron (move it closer to firing). Others *inhibit* it (make firing less likely).

More than 100 transmitter chemicals are found in the brain. Some examples are acetylcholine, epinephrine, norepinephrine, serotonin, dopamine, histamine, and various amino acids. Disturbances of any of these substances can have serious consequences. For example, too little dopamine can cause the shaking and muscle tremors of Parkinson's disease. Too much dopamine may cause the severe mental disorder known as schizophrenia (Di Forti, Lappin, & Murray, 2007).

Many drugs imitate, duplicate, or block neurotransmitters. For example, *acetylcholine* (ah-SEET-ul-KOH-leen) normally activates muscles. Without acetylcholine, our musical friend Yo-Yo Ma couldn't even move, much less play Bach. That's exactly how the drug curare (cue-RAH-ree) causes paralysis. By attaching to receptor sites on muscles, curare competes with acetylcholine. This prevents acetylcholine from activating muscle cells. As a result, a person or animal given curare cannot move—a fact known to South American Indians of the Amazon River Basin, who use curare as an arrow poison for hunting.

Neural Regulators More subtle brain activities are affected by chemicals called **neuropeptides** (NOOR-oh-PEP-tides). Neuropeptides do not carry messages directly. Instead, they *regulate* the activity of other neurons. By doing so, they affect memory, pain, emotion, pleasure, moods, hunger, sexual behavior, and other basic processes. For example, when you touch something hot, you jerk your hand away. The messages for this action are carried by neurotransmitters. At the same time, pain may cause the brain to release *enkephalins* (en-KEF-ah-lins). These opiate-like neural regulators relieve pain and stress. Related chemicals called *endorphins* (en-DORF-ins) are released by the pituitary gland. Together, these chemicals reduce the pain so that it is not too disabling (Drolet et al., 2001).

Such discoveries help explain the painkilling effect of placebos (fake pills or injections), which raise endorphin levels (Stewart-Williams, 2004). A release of endorphins also seems to underlie "runner's high," masochism, acupuncture, and the euphoria sometimes associated with childbirth, painful initiation rites, and even sport parachuting (Janssen & Arntz, 2001). In each case, pain and stress cause the release of endorphins. These in turn induce feelings of pleasure or euphoria similar to being "high" on morphine. People who say they are "addicted" to running or eating hot chilies may be closer to the truth than they realize. And more important, we may at last know why some hardy souls take hot saunas followed by cold showers! Ultimately, brain regulators may help explain depression, schizophrenia, drug addiction, and other puzzling topics. For example, women who suffer from severe premenstrual pain and distress have unusually low endorphin levels (Straneva et al., 2002).

Neural Networks

Let's put together what we now know about the nerve impulse and synapses to see how *neural networks* process information in our brains. ● Figure 2.7 shows a small part of a neural network. Five neurons synapse with a single neuron that, in turn, connects with three more neurons. At the point in time depicted in the diagram, the single neuron is receiving two weaker and one stronger excitatory messages (+) as well as two inhibitory ones (−). Does it fire an impulse? It depends: If enough "exciting" messages arrive close in time, the neuron will fire—but only if it doesn't get too many "inhibiting" messages that push it *away* from its trigger point. In this way, messages are *combined* before a neuron "decides" to fire its all-or-nothing action potential.

Let's try another metaphor. You are out shopping for new blue jeans with five friends. Three of them think you should buy the jeans (your best friend is especially positive) and two think you shouldn't. Because, on balance, their input is positive, you go ahead and buy the jeans. Maybe you even tell some other friends they should buy those jeans as well. Similarly, any single neuron in a neural network "listens" to the neurons that synapse with it and combines that input into an output. At any instant, a single neuron may weigh hundreds or thousands of inputs to produce an output. After the neuron recovers from the resulting action potential, it again combines the inputs, which may well have changed in the meantime, into another output, and another, and another.

In this way, each neuron in your brain functions as a tiny computer. Compared with the average laptop computer, a neuron is terribly simple and slow. But multiply these events

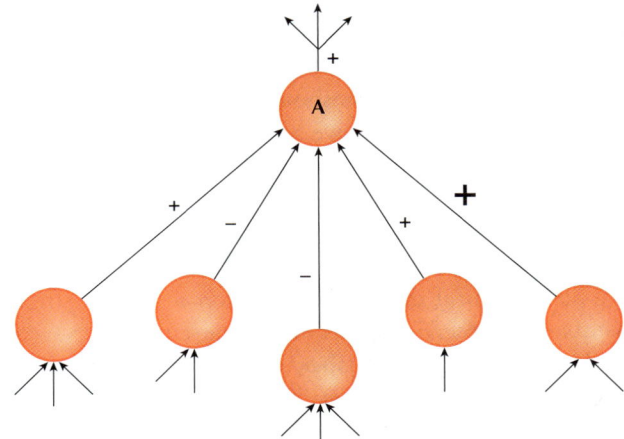

● **FIGURE 2.7** A small neural network. Neuron A receives inputs from two weaker and one stronger excitatory connections (+) and two inhibitory connections (−) and combines the inputs into a "decision" to launch an action potential, which may help trigger further synaptic transmissions in other neurons.

by 100 billion neurons and 100 trillion synapses, all operating at the same time, and you have an amazing computer—one that could easily fit inside a shoebox.

Plasticity The term **plasticity** refers to the capacity of our brains to change in response to experience. The neural networks in your brain constantly change. New synapses may form between neurons or they may grow stronger (Figure 2.7 shows one particularly strong synapse—the large +). Other synaptic connections weaken and might even die. Every new experience you have is reflected in changes in your brain. For example, rats raised in a complex environment have more synapses and longer dendrites in their brains than rats raised in a simpler environment (Kolb, Gibb, & Gorny, 2003).

Brain Repair Until only a few years ago, it was widely believed that we are born with all the brain cells we will ever have. This led to the depressing idea that we all slowly go downhill, as the brain loses thousands of neurons every day. However, we now know that a healthy 75-year-old brain has just as many neurons as it did when it was careening through life in the body of a 25-year-old. Although it is true that the brain loses cells daily, it simultaneously grows new neurons to replace them. This process is called **neurogenesis** (noor-oh-JEN-uh-sis: the production of new brain cells) (Kempermann, 2005). Each day, thousands of new cells originate deep within the brain, move to the surface, and link up with other neurons to become part of the brain's circuitry. This is stunning news to brain scientists, who must now figure out what the new cells do. Most likely they are involved in learning, memory, and our ability to adapt to changing circumstances (Gould & Gross, 2002).

The discovery of neurogenesis in adult brains has raised hope that some types of brain damage can be repaired. For example, doctors are testing new methods to treat strokes, which occur when an artery carrying blood to the brain becomes blocked, causing some brain tissue to die. Imagine that Bobby M. suffered a stroke that damaged his brain, causing partial paralysis in his left arm. What could be done to help him recover? In an approach called constraint-induced movement therapy, his good right arm would be immobilized. Doing this would force his impaired left arm to become more active, increasing the rate of neurogenesis in the damaged part of his brain and speeding his recovery (Taub, 2004). In another approach, drugs that speed up neurogenesis could be injected into the damaged area of Bobby's brain (Zhang, Zhang, & Chopp, 2005). Yet another remedy involves injecting immature nerve cells into Bobby's damaged brain areas. This would allow the new cells to link up with existing neurons in order to repair Bobby's stroke damage (Borlongan, Sanberg, & Freeman, 1999; Zhang, Zhang, & Chopp, 2005). Such techniques are beginning to offer new hope for people suffering from a variety of other disabilities, such as blindness and Parkinson's disease (Brinton & Wang, 2006).

But don't these treatments assume that Bobby's brain is still capable of neurogenesis? What if it isn't? Brilliant! Although a stroke most likely doesn't damage the brain's ability to repair itself, it is quite possible that other brain disorders do arise from impaired neurogenesis. That is exactly the theory proposed by neuroscientists Carla Toro and Bill Deakin to explain schizophrenia (Toro & Deakin, 2007). The brains of schizophrenic persons are usually smaller than normal, indicating that they have fewer neurons. Toro and Deakin's idea is that the schizophrenic brain may be unable to continually create new neurons to replace old ones that have died. If they are right, new therapies to promote neurogenesis may hold the key to treating schizophrenia, one of the most devastating mental illnesses.

The Nervous System—Wired for Action

SURVEY QUESTION: *What are the functions of the major parts of the nervous system?*

Jamal and Vicki are playing catch with a Frisbee. This may look fairly simple. However, to merely toss the Frisbee or catch it, a huge amount of information must be sensed, interpreted, and directed to countless muscle fibers. As they play, Jamal and Vicki's neural networks are ablaze with activity. Let's explore the "wiring diagram" that makes their Frisbee game possible.

Neurons and Nerves

Are neurons the same as nerves? No. Neurons are tiny cells. You would need a microscope to see one. **Nerves** are large bundles of axons. You can easily see nerves without magnification.

Many nerves are white because they contain axons coated with a fatty layer called **myelin** (MY-eh-lin). Small gaps in the myelin help nerve impulses move faster. Instead of passing down the entire length of the axon, the action potential leaps from gap to gap. Without the added speed this allows, it would probably be impossible to brake in time to avoid many automobile accidents. When the myelin layer is damaged, a person may suffer from numbness, weakness, or paralysis. That, in fact, is what happens in multiple sclerosis, a

> **Neuropeptides** Brain chemicals, such as enkephalins and endorphins, that regulate the activity of neurons.
> **Plasticity** The capacity of our brains to change in response to experience.
> **Neurogenesis** The production of new brain cells.
> **Nerve** A bundle of neuron fibers.
> **Myelin** A fatty layer coating some axons.

disease that occurs when the immune system attacks and destroys the myelin in a person's body.

A thin layer of cells called the **neurilemma** (NOOR-rih-LEM-ah) is also wrapped around most axons outside the brain and spinal cord. (Return to Fig. 2.1.) The neurilemma forms a "tunnel" that damaged fibers can follow as they repair themselves.

Subparts of the Nervous System

As you can see in ● Figure 2.8, the **central nervous system (CNS)** consists of the brain and spinal cord. The brain carries out most of the "computing" in the nervous system. Jamal must use his brain to anticipate when and where the Frisbee will arrive. Jamal's brain communicates with the rest of his body through a large "cable" called the spinal cord. From there, messages flow through the **peripheral nervous system (PNS).** This intricate network of nerves carries information to and from the CNS.

A serious injury to the brain or spinal cord is usually permanent. However, as we have just noted, scientists are starting to make progress in repairing damaged neurons in the CNS. For instance, they have partially repaired cut spinal cords in rats. First they close the gap with nerve fibers from outside the spinal cord. Then they biochemically coax the severed spinal nerve fibers to grow through the "tunnels" provided by the implanted fibers. Within months, rats treated this way regain some use of their hind legs (Cheng, Cao, & Olson, 1996). Similarly, medical researchers have already begun the first human trials in which nerve grafts will be used to repair damaged spinal cords (Féron et al., 2005). Imagine what that could mean to a person confined to a wheelchair. Although it is unwise to raise false hopes, solutions to such problems are beginning to emerge. Nevertheless, it is wise to take good care of your own CNS. That means using seat belts when you drive, wearing a helmet if you ride a motorcycle or bicycle, wearing protective gear for sports, and avoiding activities that pose a risk to your head or spinal cord.

Each year spinal cord injuries rob many thousands of people of the ability to move. Yet, there is growing hope that nerve grafting techniques may someday make it possible for some of these people to walk again.

The Peripheral Nervous System The peripheral system can be divided into two major parts. (See Fig. 2.8.) The **somatic nervous system (SNS)** carries messages to and from the sense organs and skeletal muscles. In general, it controls voluntary behavior, such as when Vicki tosses the Frisbee or Tiger Woods putts a golf ball. In contrast, the **autonomic nervous system (ANS)** serves the internal organs and glands. The word *autonomic* means "self-governing." Activities governed by the autonomic nervous system are mostly "vegetative" or automatic, such as heart rate, digestion, and perspiration. Thus, messages carried by the somatic system can make your hand move, but they cannot cause your eyes to dilate. Likewise, messages carried by the ANS can stimulate digestion, but they cannot help you carry out a voluntary ac-

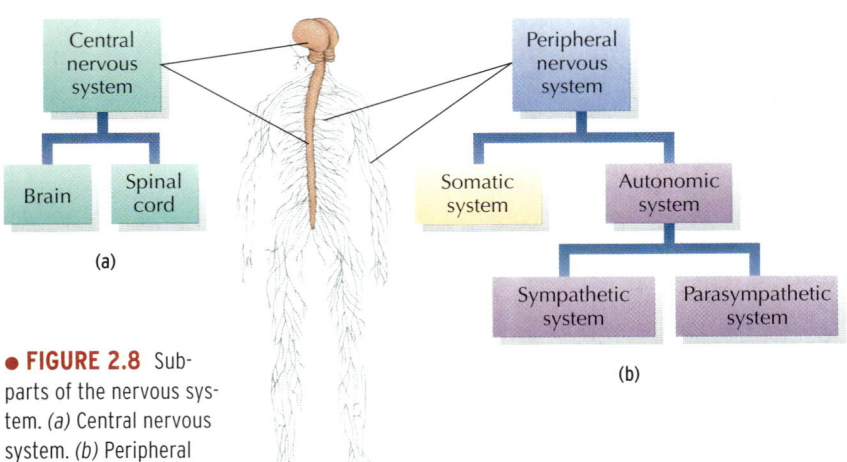

● **FIGURE 2.8** Subparts of the nervous system. *(a)* Central nervous system. *(b)* Peripheral nervous system.

tion, such as writing a letter. If Jamal feels a flash of anger when he misses a catch, a brief burst of activity will spread through his autonomic system.

The ANS and SNS work together to coordinate the body's internal reactions to events in the world outside. For example, if a snarling dog lunges at you, the somatic system will control your leg muscles so that you can run. At the same time, the autonomic system will raise your blood pressure, quicken your heart, and so forth. The ANS can be divided into the sympathetic and parasympathetic branches. Both are related to emotional responses, such as crying, sweating, heart rate, and other involuntary behavior (● Fig. 2.9).

How do the branches of the autonomic system differ? The **sympathetic branch** is an "emergency" system. It prepares the body for "fight or flight" during times of danger or high emotion. In essence, it arouses the body for action. (Yo-Yo Ma once left his $2 million cello in a taxi. No doubt his sympathetic nervous system became quite active when he first noticed his error.)

The **parasympathetic branch** quiets the body and returns it to a lower level of arousal. It is most active soon after an emotional event. The parasympathetic branch also helps keep vital processes such as heart rate, breathing, and digestion at moderate levels.

Of course, both branches of the ANS are always active. At any given moment, their combined activity determines if your body is more or less relaxed or aroused.

The Spinal Cord As mentioned earlier, the spinal cord connects the brain to other parts of the body. If you were to cut through this "cable," you would see columns of *white matter* (bundles of axons covered with myelin). This tissue is made up of axons that eventually leave the spinal cord to form nerves. Thirty-one **spinal nerves** carry sensory and motor messages to and from the spinal cord. In addition, 12 pairs of **cranial nerves** leave the brain directly. Together, these nerves keep your entire body in communication with your brain.

How is the spinal cord related to behavior? The simplest behavior pattern is a **reflex arc,** which occurs when a stimulus provokes an automatic response. Such reflexes occur within the spinal cord, without any help from the brain. (See ● Fig. 2.10.) Imagine that Vicki steps on a thorn. (Yes, they're still playing catch.) Pain is detected in her foot by a *sensory neuron* (a nerve cell that carries messages from the senses toward the CNS). Instantly, the sensory neuron fires off a message to Vicki's spinal cord.

Inside the spinal cord, the sensory neuron synapses with a *connector neuron* (a nerve cell that links two others). The connector neuron activates a *motor neuron* (a cell that carries commands from the CNS to muscles and glands). The muscle fibers are made up of *effector cells* (cells capable of producing a response). The muscle cells contract and cause Vicki's foot to withdraw. Note that no brain activity is required for a reflex arc to occur. Vicki's body will react automatically to protect itself.

In reality, even a simple reflex usually triggers more complex activity. For example, muscles of Vicki's other leg must contract to support her as she shifts her weight. Even this can be done by the spinal cord, but it involves many more cells and several spinal nerves. Also, the spinal cord normally informs the brain of its actions. As her foot pulls away from the

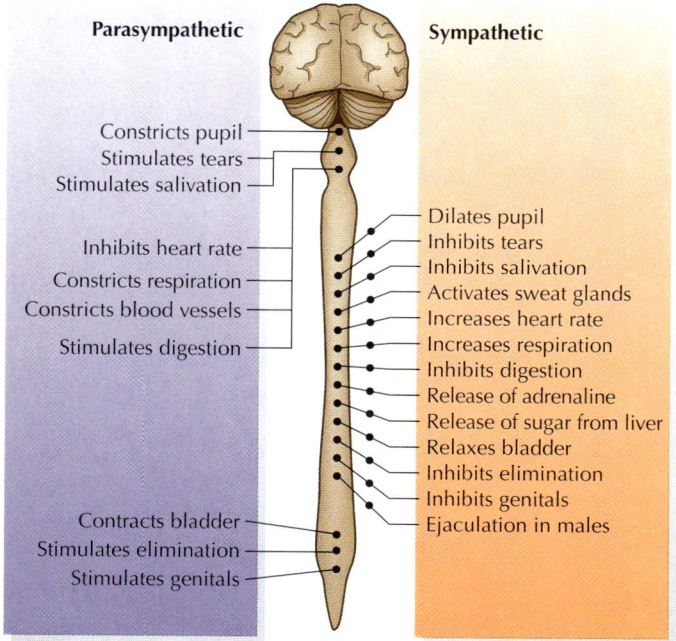

● **FIGURE 2.9** Sympathetic and parasympathetic branches of the autonomic nervous system. Both branches control involuntary actions. The sympathetic system generally activates the body. The parasympathetic system generally quiets it. The sympathetic branch relays its messages through clusters of nerve cells outside the spinal cord.

Neurilemma A layer of cells that encases many axons.
Central nervous system (CNS) The brain and spinal cord.
Peripheral nervous system (PNS) All parts of the nervous system outside the brain and spinal cord.
Somatic nervous system (SNS) The system of nerves linking the spinal cord with the body and sense organs.
Autonomic nervous system (ANS) The system of nerves carrying information to and from the internal organs and glands.
Sympathetic branch A branch of the ANS that arouses the body.
Parasympathetic branch A branch of the ANS that quiets the body.
Spinal nerves Major nerves that carry sensory and motor messages in and out of the spinal cord.
Cranial nerves Major nerves that leave the brain without passing through the spinal cord.
Reflex arc The simplest behavior, in which a stimulus provokes an automatic response.

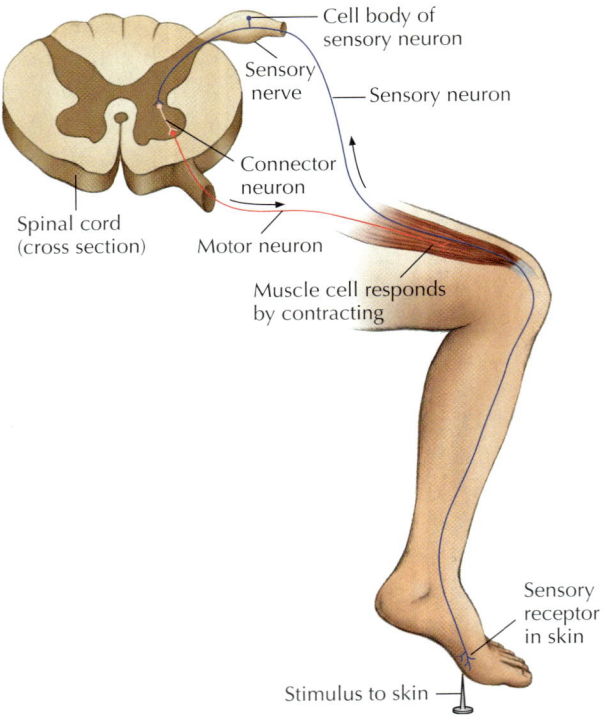

● **FIGURE 2.10** A sensory-motor arc, or reflex, is set in motion by a stimulus to the skin (or other part of the body). The nerve impulse travels to the spinal cord and then back out to a muscle, which contracts. Such reflexes provide an "automatic" protective device for the body.

thorn, Vicki will feel the pain and think "Ouch, what was that?"

Perhaps you have realized how adaptive it is to have a spinal cord capable of responding on its own. Such automatic responses leave the brains of our Frisbee aces free to deal with more important information—such as the location of trees, lampposts, and attractive onlookers—as they take turns making grandstand catches.

MODULE 2.1 Summary

How do nerve cells operate and communicate?
- All behavior can be traced to the activity of neurons, which carry information from one cell to another.
- The dendrite and soma of a neuron combine neural input and send it down the axon to the axon terminals for output to other neurons.
- The firing of an action potential (nerve impulse) is basically an electrical event.
- Communication between neurons is chemical: Neurotransmitters cross the synapse, attach to receptor sites, and excite or inhibit the receiving cell.
- Chemicals called neuropeptides regulate activity in the brain.

What are the functions of the major parts of the nervous system?
- The nervous system can be divided into the central nervous system and the peripheral nervous system, which includes the somatic (bodily) and autonomic (involuntary) nervous systems.
- The peripheral nervous system carries sensory information to the brain and motor commands to the body.
- "Vegetative" and automatic bodily processes are controlled by the autonomic nervous system, which has a sympathetic branch and a parasympathetic branch.

KNOWLEDGE BUILDER

Neurons and the Nervous System

Recite

1. The _____ and _____ are the receiving areas of a neuron where information from other neurons is accepted.
2. Nerve impulses are carried down the _____ to the _____ _____.
3. The _____ potential becomes a(n) _____ potential when a neuron passes the threshold for firing.
4. Neuropeptides are transmitter substances that help regulate the activity of neurons. T or F?
5. The somatic and autonomic systems are part of the _____ nervous system.
6. Sodium and potassium ions flow through ion channels in the synapse to trigger a nerve impulse in the receiving neuron. T or F?
7. The simplest behavior sequence is a _____ _____.
8. The parasympathetic nervous system is most active during times of high emotion. T or F?

Reflect
Critical Thinking

9. What effect would you expect a drug to have if it blocked passage of neurotransmitters across the synapse?

Relate

To cope with all the technical terms in this module, think of neurons as strange little creatures. How do they act? What excites them? How do they communicate? To remember the functions of major branches of the nervous system, think about what you *couldn't* do if each part were missing.

Link

Internet addresses frequently change. To find the sites listed here, visit **http://www.thomsonedu.com/psychology/coon** for an updated list of Internet addresses and direct links to relevant sites.

- **Neural Transmission** View a series of animations about neural transmission illustrating the action potential and the resting potential.
- **Synaptic Transmission** Read more detail about synaptic transmission or view an animation.
- **The Nervous System** Explore an overview of the major divisions of the nervous system.

ANSWERS

1. dendrites, soma 2. axon, axon terminals 3. resting, action 4. T 5. peripheral 6. F 7. reflex arc 8. F 9. Such a drug could have wide-ranging effects. If the drug blocked excitatory synapses, it would depress brain activity. If it blocked inhibitory messages, it would act as a powerful stimulant.

MODULE 2.2 Brain Research

BIOPSYCHOLOGY is the study of how biological processes, and especially those of the nervous system, relate to behavior. One major research strategy of biopsychologists is to relate specific brain structures to the control of particular psychological or behavioral functions, such as recognizing faces or moving your hands. That is, they try to learn where functions are localized in the brain. Many techniques have been developed to help identify structures of the brain and the functions they control.

Mapping Brain Structure—Parts of the Puzzle

SURVEY QUESTION: *How are different parts of the brain identified?*

Anatomists have learned much about brain structure by dissecting (cutting apart) autopsied human and animal brains and examining them under a microscope. Dissection reveals that the brain is made up of many anatomically distinct areas or "parts." Less intrusive newer methods, such as the CT scan and the MRI scan, can be used to map brain structures in living brains.

CT Scan

Computerized scanning equipment has revolutionized the study of brain structure and the identification of brain diseases and injuries. At best, conventional X-rays produce only shadowy images of the brain. **Computed tomographic (CT) scanning** is a specialized type of X-ray that does a much better job of making the brain visible. In a CT scan, X-rays taken from a number of different angles are collected by a computer and formed into an image of the brain. A CT scan can reveal the location of strokes, injuries, tumors, and other brain disorders.

MRI Scan

Magnetic resonance imaging (MRI) uses a very strong magnetic field, rather than X-rays, to produce an image of the body's interior. During an MRI scan, the body is placed inside a magnetic field. Processing by a computer then creates a three-dimensional model of the brain or body. Any two-dimensional plane, or slice, of the body can be selected and displayed as an image on a computer screen. MRI scans produce more detailed images than are possible with CT scans, allowing us to peer into the living brain almost as if it were transparent (● Fig. 2.11).

● **FIGURE 2.11** A colored MRI scan of the brain reveals many details. Can you identify any brain regions?

Mapping Brain Function—Figuring Out What the Parts Do

SURVEY QUESTION: *What do the different parts of the brain do?*

How does the brain allow us to think, feel, perceive, or act? To answer questions like these, biopsychologists must **localize function** by linking these psychological or behavioral capacities with particular brain structures. In many instances, this has been done through **clinical case studies.** Such studies examine changes in personality, behavior, or sensory capacity caused by brain diseases or injuries. If damage to a particular part of the brain consistently leads to a particular loss of function, then we say the function is localized in that structure. Presumably, that part of the brain controls the same function in all of us.

Consider, for example, the story of Kate Adamson (Adamson, 2004). At the age of 33, she had a stroke that caused catastrophic damage to her brainstem. This event left her with *locked-in syndrome:* One moment she was fine, and the next she was totally paralyzed, trapped in her own body and barely able to breathe. As you can see, this clinical case suggests that our brainstems play a role in the control of vital life functions, such as movement and breathing.

But what happened to Kate? Oh, yes. Unable to move a muscle, but still fully awake and aware, Kate thought she was going to die. Her doctors, who thought she was brain dead, did not administer painkillers as they inserted breathing and feeding tubes down her throat. However, in time Kate discovered that she could communicate by blinking her eyes. Ultimately, she appeared before the U.S. Congress, after a recovery that has been miraculous by any measure.

Instead of relying on clinical studies, much has been learned from **ablation** (ab-LAY-shun: surgical removal) of parts of the brain (● Fig. 2.12). When ablation causes changes in behavior or sensory capacity, we also gain insight into the purpose of the missing "part." An alternate approach is to use electrical stimulation to "turn on" brain structures. For example, the surface of the brain can be activated by touching it with a small electrified wire called an *electrode*. When this is done during brain surgery, the patient can describe what effect the stimulation had. (The brain has no pain receptors, so surgery can be done while a patient is awake. Only local painkillers are used for the scalp and skull.) (Any volunteers?)

Even structures below the surface of the brain can be activated or removed. In **deep lesioning** (LEE-zhun-ing), a thin wire electrode, insulated except at the tip, is lowered into a target area inside the brain. (See Fig. 2.12.) An electric current is then used to destroy a small amount of brain tissue. Again, changes in behavior give clues to the function of the affected area. Using a weaker current, it is also possible to *activate* target areas, rather than remove them. This is called **ESB,** for **electrical stimulation of the brain.** ESB can call forth behavior with astonishing power. Instantly, it can bring about aggression, alertness, escape, eating, drinking, sleeping, movement, euphoria, memories, speech, tears, and more. By using ablation and ESB, researchers are creating a three-dimensional brain map. This "atlas" shows the sensory, motor, and emotional responses that can be elicited from various parts of the brain. It promises to be a valuable guide for medical treatment, as well as for exploring the brain (Kalat, 2007; Yoshida, 1993).

Could ESB be used to control a person against his or her will? It might seem that ESB could be used to control a person like a robot. But the details of emotions and behaviors elicited by ESB are modified by personality and circumstances. Sci-fi movies to the contrary, it would be impossible for a ruthless dictator to enslave people by "radio controlling" their brains.

To find out what individual neurons are doing, we need to do a microelectrode recording. A *microelectrode* is an extremely thin glass tube filled with a salty fluid. The tip of a microelectrode is small enough to detect the electrical activity of a *single* neuron. Watching the action potentials of just one neuron provides a fascinating glimpse into the true origins of behavior. (The action potential shown in Figure 2.2 was recorded with a microelectrode.)

Are any less invasive techniques available for studying brain function? Yes, several techniques allow us to observe the activity of parts of the brain without doing any damage at all. These include the EEG, PET scan, and fMRI. Such techniques are allowing scientists to pinpoint areas in the brain responsible for thoughts, feelings, and actions.

EEG

Electroencephalography (ee-LEK-tro-in-SEF-ah-LOG-ruh-fee) measures the waves of electrical activity produced near the surface of the brain. Small disk-shaped metal plates are placed on a person's scalp. Electrical impulses from the brain are detected by these electrodes and sent to an **electroencephalograph (EEG).** The EEG amplifies these very weak signals (brain waves) and records them on a moving sheet of paper or a computer screen (● Fig. 2.13). Various brain-wave patterns can identify the presence of tumors, epilepsy, and other diseases. The EEG also reveals changes in brain activity during sleep, daydreaming, hypnosis, and other mental states.

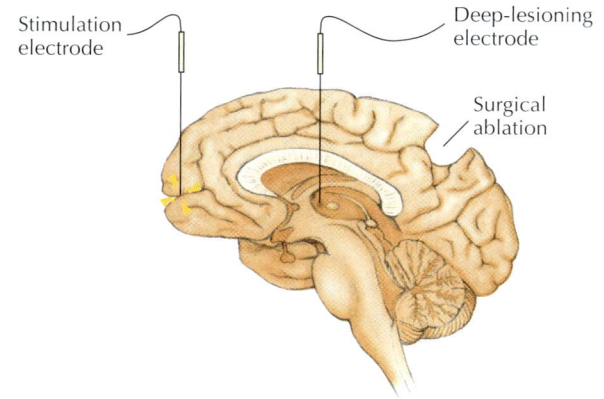

● **FIGURE 2.12** The functions of brain structures are explored by selectively activating or removing them. Brain research is often based on electrical stimulation, but chemical stimulation is also used at times.

> **Computed tomographic scan (CT scan)** Computed tomography scan; a computer-enhanced X-ray image of the brain or body.
>
> **Magnetic resonance imaging (MRI)** Magnetic resonance imaging; a three-dimensional image of the brain or body, based on its response to a magnetic field.
>
> **Localization of function** The research strategy of linking specific structures in the brain with specific psychological or behavioral functions.
>
> **Clinical case study** A detailed investigation of a single person, especially one suffering from some injury or disease.
>
> **Ablation** Surgical removal of tissue.
>
> **Deep lesioning** Removal of tissue within the brain by use of an electrode.
>
> **Electrical stimulation of the brain (ESB)** Direct electrical stimulation and activation of brain tissue.
>
> **Electroencephalograph (EEG)** A device that detects, amplifies, and records electrical activity in the brain.

● **FIGURE 2.13** An EEG recording.

PET Scan

A newer technology, called positron emission tomography (PET), provides much more detailed images of activity both *near* the surface and *below* the surface of the brain. A **PET scan** detects positrons (sub-atomic particles) emitted by weakly radioactive glucose (sugar) as it is consumed by the brain. Because the brain runs on glucose, a PET scan shows which areas are using more energy. Higher energy use corresponds with higher activity. Thus, by placing positron detectors around the head and sending data to a computer, it is possible to create a moving, color picture of changes in brain activity. As you can see in ● Figure 2.14, PET scans reveal that very specific brain areas are active when you see, hear, speak, or think.

More active brains are good, right? Surprisingly, although we might assume that smart brains are hardworking brains, the reverse appears to be true. Using PET scans, psychologist Richard Haier and his colleagues found that the brains of people who perform well on a difficult reasoning test consume less energy than those of poor performers (Haier et al., 1988) (● Fig. 2.15). Haier believes this shows that intelligence is related to brain efficiency: Less efficient brains work harder and still accomplish less (Haier, White, & Alkire, 2003). We've all had days like that!

Is it true that most people use only 10 percent of their brain capacity? This is one of the lasting myths about the brain. Brain scans show that all parts of the brain are active during waking hours. Obviously, some people make better use of their innate brainpower than others do. Nevertheless, there are no great hidden or untapped reserves of mental capacity in a normally functioning brain.

fMRI

A **functional MRI (fMRI)** uses MRI technology to make brain activity visible. Like PET scans, functional MRIs also provide images of activity throughout the brain. For example, if we scanned Carlos Santana while he played his guitar, areas of his brain that control his hands would be highlighted in an fMRI image.

Psychiatrist Daniel Langleben and his colleagues have even used fMRI images to tell if a person is lying (Langleben et al., 2005). As ● Figure 2.16 shows, the front of the brain is more active when a person is lying, rather than telling the truth. This may occur because it takes extra effort to lie and the resulting extra brain activity is detected with fMRI. Eventually, fMRI may help us distinguish between lies, false statements made with the intention to deceive, and *confabulations*, which are false claims believed to be true (Hirstein, 2005; Langleben, Dattilio, & Gutheil, 2006). Clearly, it is just a matter of time until even brighter beacons are flashed into the shadowy inner world of thought.

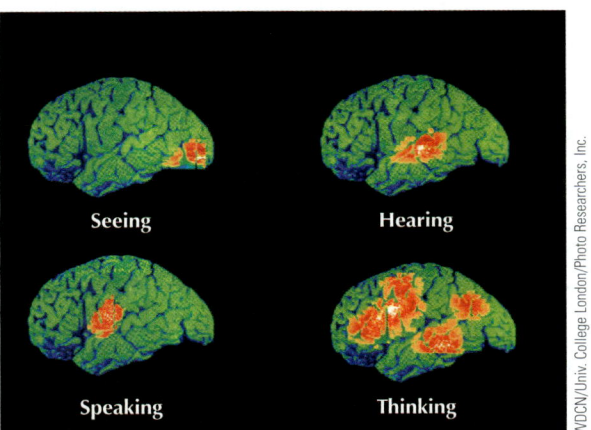

● **FIGURE 2.14** Colored PET scans reveal different patterns of brain activation when we engage in different tasks.

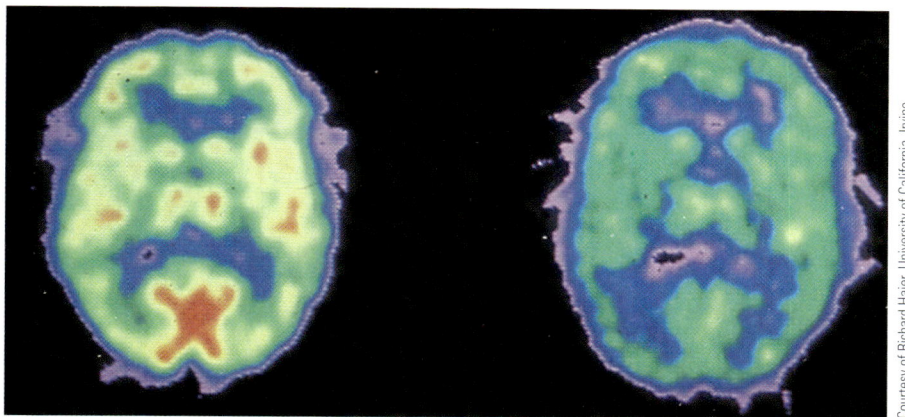

● **FIGURE 2.15** In the images you see here, red, orange, and yellow indicate high consumption of glucose; green, blue, and pink show areas of low glucose use. The PET scan of the brain on the left shows that a man who solved 11 out of 36 reasoning problems burned more glucose than the man on the right, who solved 33.

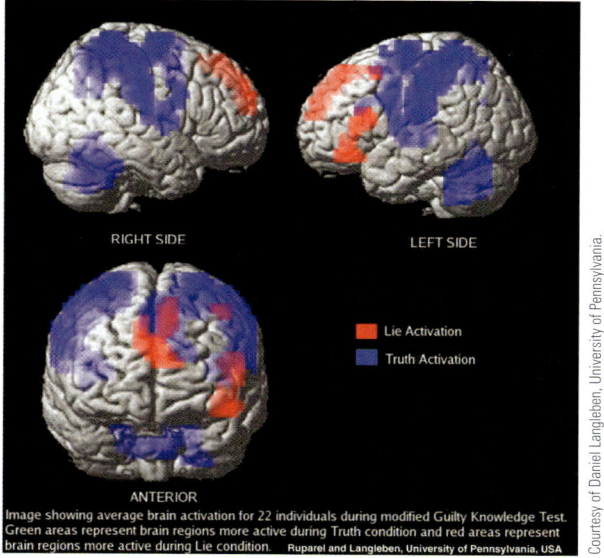

● **FIGURE 2.16** Participants were asked to tell the truth or to lie while fMRI images of their brains were taken. When compared with telling the truth (shown in blue), areas toward the front of the brain were active during lying (shown in red). (Adapted from Langleben et al., 2005.)

MODULE 2.2 Summary

How are different parts of the brain identified?
- A major brain research strategy involves localization of function to link specific structures in the brain with specific psychological or behavioral functions.
- Brain structure is investigated though dissection and less intrusive CT scans and MRI scans.

What do the different parts of the brain do?
- Brain function is investigated through clinical case studies, electrical stimulation, ablation, deep lesioning, electrical recording, and microelectrode recording, as well as less intrusive EEG recording, PET scans, and fMRI scans.

PET scan Positron emission tomography; a computer-generated image of brain activity, based on glucose consumption in the brain.

Functional MRI (fMRI) Functional magnetic resonance imaging that records brain activity.

KNOWLEDGE BUILDER

Brain Research

Recite

1. Which of the following research techniques has the most in common with clinical studies of the effects of brain injuries?

   a. EEG recording b. deep lesioning c. microelectrode recording d. PET scan

2. CT scans cannot determine which part of your brain plays a role in speech because CT scans

   a. use X-rays b. reveal brain structure, not brain activity c. reveal brain activity, not brain structure d. use magnetic fields

3. _____ links brain structures to brain functions.

4. People only use 10 percent of their brain capacity. T or F?

Reflect

Critical Thinking

5. Deep lesioning is used to ablate an area in the hypothalamus of a rat. After the operation, the rat seems to lose interest in food and eating. Why would it be a mistake to conclude that the ablated area is a "hunger center"?

Relate

You suspect that a certain part of the brain is related to risk-taking. How could you use clinical studies, ablation, deep lesioning, and ESB to study the structure? You are interested in finding out how single neurons in the optic nerve respond when the eye is exposed to light. What technique will you use? You want to know which areas of the brain's surface are most active when a person sees a face. What methods will you use?

Link

Internet addresses frequently change. To find the sites listed here, visit **http://www.thomsonedu.com/psychology/coon** for an updated list of Internet addresses and direct links to relevant sites.

- **The Whole Brain Atlas** View images of various parts of the brain.
- **The PET Scan** Read more about PET scans.
- **fMRI for Newbies** Learn about fMRI; includes fMRI images.

ANSWERS

1. b 2. b 3. Localization of function 4. F 5. Because other factors might explain the apparent loss of appetite. For example, the taste or smell of food might be affected, or the rat might simply have difficulty swallowing. It is also possible that hunger originates elsewhere in the brain and the ablated area merely relays messages that cause the rat to eat.

MODULE 2.3 Hemispheres and Lobes of the Cerebral Cortex

MANY parts of your brain are surprisingly similar to corresponding brain areas in lower animals, such as lizards. Superior human intelligence is related to the fact that our brains have a large cerebrum. The wrinkled surface of the cerebrum can be divided into two hemispheres and smaller areas known as lobes. Parts of various lobes are responsible for the ability to see, hear, move, think, and speak. Thus, a map of the cerebrum is in some ways like a map of human behavior, as we shall see.

The Cerebral Cortex—My, What a Big Brain You Have!

SURVEY QUESTIONS: *How do the left and right hemispheres differ? What are the different functions of the lobes of the cerebral cortex?*

In many ways we are pretty unimpressive creatures. Animals surpass humans in almost every category of strength, speed, and sensory sensitivity. The one area in which we excel is intelligence.

Don't humans have the largest brains? Surprisingly, no. Elephant brains weigh 13 pounds, and whale brains, 19 pounds. At 3 pounds, the human brain seems puny—until we compare brain weight to body weight. We then find that an elephant's brain is 1/1,000 of its weight; the ratio for sperm whales is 1 to 10,000. The ratio for humans is 1 to 60. If someone tells you that you have a "whale of a brain" be sure to find out if they mean size or ratio!

So having a larger brain doesn't necessarily make a person smarter? That's right. While a small positive correlation exists between intelligence and brain size, overall size alone does not determine human intelligence (Wickett, Vernon, & Lee, 2000; Witelson, Beresh, & Kigar, 2006). The *cerebrum* consists of the two large hemispheres that cover the upper part of the brain. Its outer layer is known as the **cerebral** (seh-REE-brel or ser-EH-brel) **cor-tex**, which looks a little like a giant, wrinkled walnut. It covers most of the brain with a mantle of *gray matter* (spongy tissue made up mostly of cell bodies). The cortex in lower animals is small and smooth. In humans it is twisted and folded, and it is the largest brain structure. (See ● Fig. 2.17.) The fact that humans are more intelligent than other animals is related to this **corticalization** (KORE-tih-kal-ih-ZAY-shun), or increase in the size and wrinkling of the cortex.

Although the cortex is only 3 millimeters thick (one tenth of an inch), it contains 70 percent of the neurons in the central nervous system. It is largely responsible for our ability to use language, make tools, acquire complex skills, and live in complex social groups (Gibson, 2002). Without the cortex, we humans wouldn't be much smarter than toads.

Cerebral Hemispheres

The cortex is composed of two sides, or *cerebral hemispheres* (half-globes). The two hemispheres are connected by a thick band of fibers called the *corpus callosum* (KORE-pus kah-LOH-sum) (● Fig. 2.18). The left side of the brain mainly

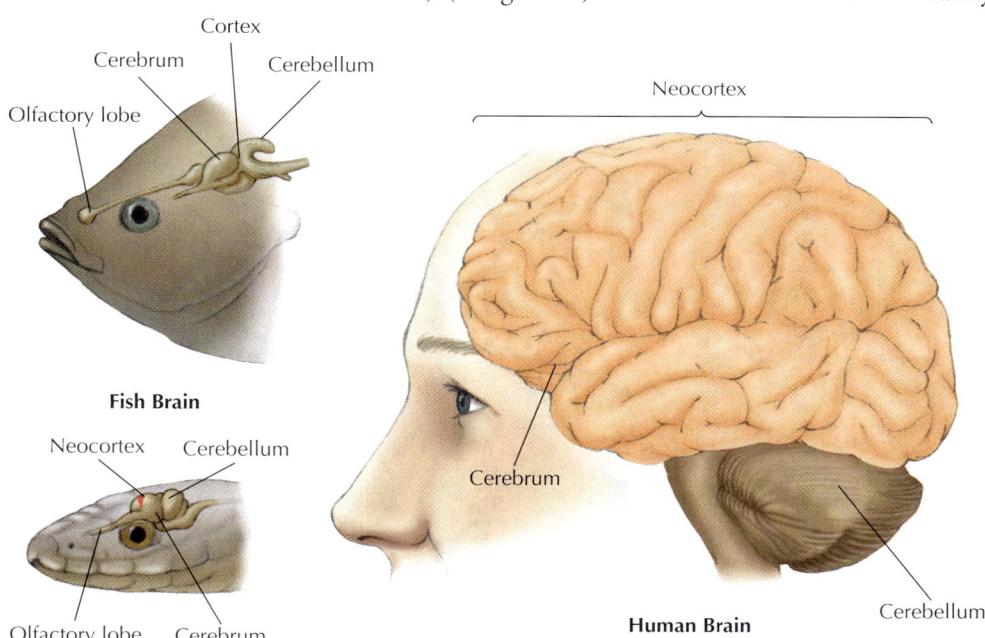

● **FIGURE 2.17**

Cerebral cortex The outer layer of the cerebrum.
Corticalization An increase in the relative size of the cerebral cortex.

● FIGURE 2.18

controls the right side of the body. Likewise, the right brain mainly controls left body areas. When our friend Marge had a stroke, her right hemisphere suffered damage. In Marge's case, the stroke caused some paralysis and loss of sensation on the left side of her body.

Damage to one hemisphere may also cause a curious problem called *spatial neglect*. A patient with right hemisphere damage may pay no attention to the left side of visual space. (See ● Fig. 2.19.) Often, the patient will not eat food on the left side of a plate. Some even refuse to acknowledge a paralyzed left arm as their own (Hirstein, 2005). If you point to the "alien" arm, the patient is likely to say, "Oh, that's not my arm. It must belong to someone else." (To learn more about strokes, see "A Stroke of Bad Luck.")

Hemispheric Specialization

In 1981, Roger Sperry (1914–1994) won a Nobel Prize for his remarkable discovery that the right and left brain hemispheres perform differently on tests of language, perception, music, and other capabilities.

How is it possible to test only one side of the brain? One way is to work with people who've had a **"split-brain" operation.** In this rare type of surgery, the corpus callosum is cut to control severe epilepsy. The result is essentially a person with two brains in one body (Gazzaniga, 2005). After the surgery, it is possible to send information to one hemisphere or the other. (See ● Fig. 2.20)

"Split Brains" After the right and left brain are separated, each hemisphere will have its own separate perceptions, concepts, and impulses to act.

How does a split-brain person act after the operation? Having two "brains" in one body can create some interesting dilemmas. When one split-brain patient dressed himself, he

● FIGURE 2.19 Spatial neglect. A patient with right-hemisphere damage was asked to copy three model drawings. Notice the obvious neglect of the left side in his drawings. Similar instances of neglect occur in many patients with right-hemisphere damage. From *Left Brain, Right Brain, Fifth Edition* by Sally P. Springer and Georg Deutsch. © 1981, 1985, 1989, 1993, 1998 by Sally P. Springer and Georg Deutsch. Used with permission of W. H. Freeman and Company.

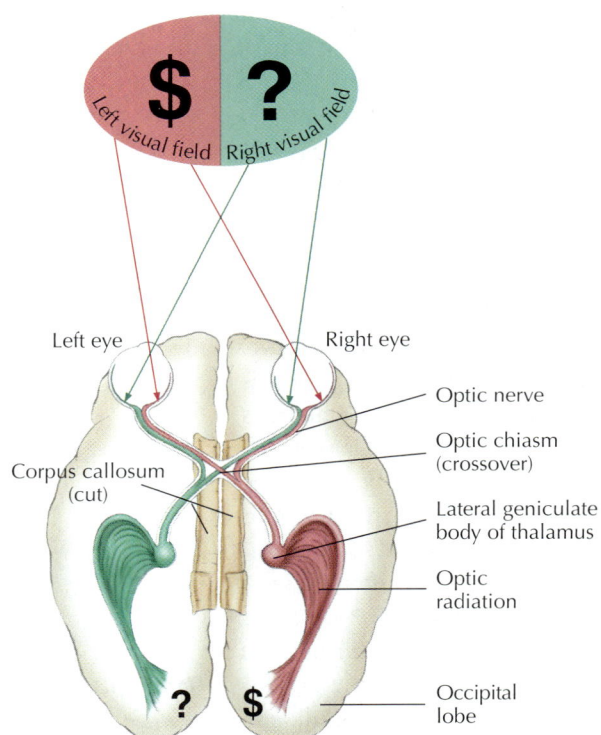

● FIGURE 2.20 Basic nerve pathways of vision. Notice that the left portion of each eye connects only to the left half of the brain; likewise, the right portion of each eye connects to the right brain. When the corpus callosum is cut, a "split brain" results. Then visual information can be sent to just one hemisphere by flashing it in the right or left visual field as the person stares straight ahead.

Module 2.3 • HEMISPHERES AND LOBES OF THE CEREBRAL CORTEX 75

THE CLINICAL FILE
A Stroke of Bad Luck

One morning Bryan Kolb lost his left hand. Up early to feed his cat, he could not see his hand, or anything else to his upper left side. Kolb, a Canadian neuroscientist, instantly realized that he had suffered a right hemisphere stroke. (Remember, a stroke occurs when an artery carrying blood to the brain becomes blocked, causing some brain tissue to die.) He drove to the hospital, where he argued with the doctors about his own diagnosis. (He was right, of course!) He eventually resumed his career and even wrote a fascinating account of his case (Kolb, 1990).

Strokes and other brain injuries can hit like a thunderbolt. Almost instantly, victims realize that something is wrong. You would, too, if you suddenly found that you couldn't move, or feel parts of your body, or see, or speak. However, some brain injuries are not so obvious. Many involve less dramatic, but equally disabling, changes in personality, thinking, judgment, or emotions (Banich, 2004; Borod et al., 2002). Although major brain injuries are easy enough to spot, psychologists also look for more subtle signs that the brain is not

working properly. Neurological soft signs, as they are called, include clumsiness, an awkward gait, poor hand-eye coordination, and other problems with perception or fine muscle control (Stuss & Levine, 2002). These telltale signs are "soft" in the sense that they aren't direct tests of the brain, like an EEG or CT scan. Bryan Kolb initially diagnosed himself entirely with soft signs. Likewise, soft signs help psychologists diagnose problems ranging from childhood learning disorders to full-blown psychosis (Ward, 2006).

sometimes pulled his pants up with one hand (*that* side of his brain wanted to get dressed . . .) and down with the other (. . . while *this* side didn't). Once, he grabbed his wife with his left hand and shook her violently. Gallantly, his right hand came to her aid and grabbed the aggressive left hand (Gazzaniga, 1970). However, such conflicts are actually rare. That's because both halves of the brain normally have about the same experience at the same time. Also, if a conflict arises, one hemisphere usually overrides the other.

Split-brain effects are easiest to see in specialized testing. For example, we could flash a dollar sign to the right brain and a question mark to the left brain of a patient named Tom. (Figure 2.20 shows how this is possible.) Next, Tom is asked to draw what he saw, using his left hand, out of sight. Tom's left hand draws a dollar sign. If Tom is then asked to point with his right hand to a picture of what his hidden left hand drew, he will point to a question mark (Sperry, 1968). In short, for the split-brain person, one hemisphere may not know what is happening in the other. This has to be the ultimate case of the "right hand not knowing what the left hand is doing"! ● Figure 2.21 provides another example of split-brain testing.

Left Brain
- Language
- Speech
- Writing
- Calculation
- Time sense
- Rhythm
- Ordering of complex movements

Right Brain
- Nonverbal
- Perceptual skills
- Visualization
- Recognition of patterns, faces, melodies
- Recognition and expression of emotion
- Spatial skills
- Simple language comprehension

Left Hemisphere

Right Hemisphere

● **FIGURE 2.21** A circle is flashed to the left brain of a split-brain patient and he is asked what he saw. He easily replies, "A circle." He can also pick out the circle by merely touching shapes with his right hand, out of sight behind a screen. However, his left hand can't identify the circle. If a triangle is flashed to the patient's right brain, he can't say what he saw (speech is controlled by the left hemisphere). He also can't identify the triangle by touch with the right hand. Now, however, the left hand has no difficulty picking out the triangle. In other tests, the hemispheres reveal distinct skills, as listed above the drawing.

Right Brain/Left Brain *Earlier it was stated that the hemispheres differ in abilities; in what ways are they different?* The

"Split-brain" operation Cutting the corpus callosum.

brain divides its work in interesting ways. Roughly 95 percent of us use our left brain for language (speaking, writing, and understanding). In addition, the left hemisphere is superior at math, judging time and rhythm, and coordinating the order of complex movements, such as those needed for speech.

In contrast, the right hemisphere can produce only the simplest language and numbers. Working with the right brain is like talking to a child who can say only a dozen words or so. To answer questions, the right hemisphere must use nonverbal responses, such as pointing at objects. (See Fig. 2.21.)

Although it is poor at producing language, the right brain is especially good at perceptual skills, such as recognizing patterns, faces, and melodies, putting together a puzzle, or drawing a picture. It also helps you express emotions and detect the emotions that other people are feeling (Borod et al., 2002; Stuss & Alexander, 2000).

Even though the right hemisphere is nearly "speechless," it is superior at some aspects of understanding language. If the right side of the brain is damaged, people lose their ability to understand jokes, irony, sarcasm, implications, and other nuances of language. Basically, the right hemisphere helps us see the overall context in which something is said (Beeman & Chiarello, 1998). For instance, let's say you tell a patient with right-brain damage the following joke:

"Dad," said Jason, "I'm late for soccer practice. Would you do my math homework for me?"

The boy's father answered, "Son, it just wouldn't be right."

"That's okay," replied Jason. "You could at least try, right?"

When asked what this story means, the patient might say, "The father doesn't want to do it, but the son is persistent." Without the right brain's ability to perceive context, the patient doesn't get the joke about the father's math abilities. The left hemisphere understands the words literally, one at a time, but it can't grasp the bigger picture.

One Brain, Two Styles In general, the left hemisphere is mainly involved with *analysis* (breaking information into parts). It also processes information *sequentially* (in order, one item after the next). The right hemisphere appears to process information *simultaneously* and *holistically* (all at once) (Springer & Deutsch, 1998).

To summarize further, you could say that the right hemisphere is better at assembling pieces of the world into a coherent picture; it sees overall patterns and general connections. The left brain focuses on small details. (See ● Fig. 2.22.) The right brain sees the wide-angle view; the left zooms in on specifics. The focus of the left brain is local, the right is global (Hübner & Volberg, 2005).

● **FIGURE 2.22** The left and right brain have different information processing styles. The right brain gets the big pattern; the left focuses on small details. (Photograph by R. C. James.)

Do people normally do puzzles or draw pictures with just the right hemisphere? Do they do other things with only the left? Numerous books have been written about how to use the right brain to manage, teach, draw, ride horses, learn, and even make love (Clark, Boutros, & Mendez, 2005). But such books drastically oversimplify right-brain and left-brain differences. People normally use both sides of the brain at all times. It's true that some tasks may make *more* use of one hemisphere or the other. But in most "real world" activities, the hemispheres share the work. Each does the parts it does best and shares information with the other side. Popular books and courses that claim to teach "right-brain thinking" ignore the fact that everyone already uses the right brain for thinking (Clark, Boutros, & Mendez, 2005). To do anything well requires the talents and processing abilities of both hemispheres. A smart brain is one that grasps both the details and the overall picture at the same time. For instance, during a concert Yo-Yo Ma will use his left brain to judge time and rhythm and coordinate the order of his hand movements. At the same time, he will use his right brain to recognize and organize melodies.

Lobes of the Cerebral Cortex

Each of the two hemispheres of the cerebral cortex can be divided into several smaller lobes. Some of the **lobes of the cerebral cortex** are defined by larger fissures on the surface of the cerebrum. Others are regarded as separate areas because their functions are quite different. (See ● Fig. 2.23.)

The Frontal Lobes The **frontal lobes** are associated with higher mental abilities and they play a role in your sense of self.

● **FIGURE 2.23**

This area is also responsible for the control of movement. Specifically, an arch of tissue at the rear of the frontal lobes, called the **primary motor area** (or **primary motor cortex**), directs the body's muscles. If this area is stimulated with an electrical current, various parts of the body will twitch or move. The drawing wrapped around the motor cortex in Figure 2.24 is out of proportion because it reflects the *dexterity* of body areas, not their size. The hands, for example, get more area than the feet. (See ● Fig. 2.24.) If you've ever wondered why your hands are more skilled or agile than your feet, it's partly because more motor cortex is devoted to the hands. Incidentally, learning and experience can alter these "motor maps." For instance, violin, viola, and cello players like Yo-Yo Ma have larger "hand maps" in the cortex (Hashimoto et al., 2004).

Motor cortex is one brain area that contains **mirror neurons**. These are neurons that become active when we perform an action *and* when we merely observe someone else carrying out the same action. Because they *mirror* the actions of others, such neurons may explain how we can intuitively understand the behavior of others. They may also underlie our ability to learn new skills by imitating others (Rizzolatti & Craighero, 2004).

The rest of the frontal lobes are often referred to as *frontal association areas*. Only a small portion of the cerebral cortex (the primary areas) directly controls the body or receives information from the senses. All the surrounding areas, which are called **association areas** (or **association cortex**), combine and process information. For example, if you see a rose, association areas will help you connect your primary sensory impressions with memories, so that you can recognize the rose and name it. Some association areas also contribute to higher mental abilities. For example, a person with damage to association areas in the left hemisphere may suffer **aphasia** (ah-FAZE-yah: an impaired ability to use language).

One type of aphasia is related to **Broca's** (BRO-cahs) **area,** a "speech center" that is part of the left frontal association area (for 5 percent of all people, the area is part of the right frontal association area). Damage to Broca's area causes *motor* (or *expressive*) *aphasia*, a great difficulty in speaking or writing (Ward, 2006). Generally, the person knows what she or he wants to say but can't seem to utter the words (Geschwind, 1979). Typically, a patient's grammar and pronunciation are poor and speech is slow and labored. For example, the person may say "bife" for bike, "seep" for sleep, or "zokaid" for zodiac.

The very front of the frontal association region is known as the **prefrontal area** (or **prefrontal cortex**). This part of the brain is related to more complex behaviors. If the frontal lobes are damaged, a patient's personality and emotional life may change dramatically. Remember Phineas Gage, the railroad foreman described in Module 1.6? It's likely that Phineas Gage's personality changed after he suffered brain damage because the prefrontal cortex generates our sense of self, including an awareness of our current emotional state (Moran et al., 2006; Kawasaki et al., 2005).

Reasoning or planning may also be affected (Goel & Dolan, 2004). Patients with damage to the frontal lobes often get "stuck" on mental tasks and repeat the same wrong answers over and over (Goel & Grafman, 1995; Stuss & Knight, 2002). PET scans suggest that much of what we call intelligence is related to increased activity in the frontal areas of the cortex (Duncan, 2005). Sadly, drug abuse can damage this important area of the brain (Liu et al., 1998).

The Parietal Lobes Bodily sensations register in the **parietal** (puh-RYE-ih-tal) **lobes,** located just above the occipital lobes. Touch, temperature, pressure, and other somatic sensa-

---

Lobes of the cerebral cortex Areas on the cortex bordered by major fissures or defined by their functions.
Frontal lobes A brain area associated with movement, the sense of self, and higher mental functions.
Primary motor area (primary motor cortex) A brain area associated with control of movement.
Mirror neuron A neuron that becomes active when a motor action is carried out *and* when another organism is observed carrying out the same action.
Association area (association cortex) All areas of the cerebral cortex that are not primarily sensory or motor in function.
Aphasia A speech disturbance resulting from brain damage.
Broca's area A language area related to grammar and pronunciation.
Prefrontal area (prefrontal cortex) The very front of the frontal lobes; involved in sense of self, reasoning, and planning.
Parietal lobes Area of the brain where body sensations register.

• **FIGURE 2.24** The lobes of the cerebral cortex and the primary sensory, motor, visual, and auditory areas on each. The top diagrams show (in cross section) the relative amounts of cortex "assigned" to the sensory and motor control of various parts of the body. (Each cross section, or "slice," of the cortex has been turned 90 degrees so that you see it as it would appear from the back of the brain.)

tions flow into the **primary somatosensory** (SO-mat-oh-SEN-so-ree) **area** (or **primary somatosensory cortex**) of the parietal lobes. Again we find that the map of bodily sensations is distorted. In the case of somatosensory cortex, the drawing in Figure 2.24 reflects the *sensitivity* of body areas, not their size. For example, the lips are large in the drawing because of their great sensitivity, whereas the back and trunk, which are less sensitive, are much smaller. Notice that the hands are also large in the map of body sensitivity—which is obviously an aid to musicians, typists, watchmakers, massage therapists, lovers, and brain surgeons.

The Temporal Lobes The **temporal lobes** are located on each side of the brain. Auditory information projects directly to the **primary auditory area,** making it the main site where hearing first registers. If we did a PET scan of your brain while you listened to your favorite MP3 tune, your primary auditory area would be the first to light up, followed by association areas in your temporal lobes. Likewise, if we could electrically stimulate the primary auditory area of your temporal lobe, you would "hear" a series of sound sensations.

An association area, called **Wernicke's** (VER-nick-ees; see Fig. 2.24) **area,** lies on the left temporal lobe (again, for 5 percent of all people, the area is on the right temporal lobe). Wernicke's area also functions as a language site. If it is damaged, the result is a *receptive (or fluent) aphasia*. Although the person can hear speech, he or she has difficulty understanding the meaning of words. Thus, when shown a picture of a chair, someone with Broca's aphasia might say "tssair." In contrast, a Wernicke's patient might say "truck" fluently, but incorrectly (Ward, 2006).

The Occipital Lobes At the back of the brain, we find the **occipital** (awk-SIP-ih-tal) **lobes,** the area of the cortex concerned with vision. Patients with tumors (cell growths that interfere with brain activity) in the **primary visual area,** the

HUMAN DIVERSITY

His and Her Brains?

As you read this book you may be curious about the many ways people can differ from each other. These "Human Diversity" boxes are designed to help you be more reflective about the rich variety of humanity.

Are men's and women's brains specialized in different ways? Yes, to some extent. Many physical differences between male and female brains have been found, although their significance remains debatable. In one series of studies, researchers observed brain activity while people did language tasks. Both men and women showed increased activity in Broca's area, on the left side of the brain, exactly as expected. Surprisingly, however, the left *and* the right brain were activated in more than half the women tested (Shaywitz & Gore, 1995; see ● Fig. 2.25).

Using both sides of the brain for language may be a big advantage. When Broca's area is damaged, some women can use the right side of their brains to compensate for the loss (Hochstenbach et al., 1998). Thus, when a man says, "I have half a mind to tell you what I think," he may be stating a curious truth. Despite this difference, the two sexes performed equally well on a task that involved sounding out words (Shaywitz et al., 1995). The researchers concluded that nature has given the brain different routes to the same ability.

● **FIGURE 2.25** Language tasks activate both sides of the brain in many women but only the left side in men.

In a study of men and women with similar IQ scores, brain images revealed major differences in brain areas involved in intelligence (Haier et al., 2004). In general, the men had more gray matter (neuron cell bodies), while the women had more white matter (axons coated in myelin). Further, the women had more gray and white matter concentrated in their frontal lobes than the men did. The men's gray matter was split between their frontal and parietal lobes, while their white matter was mostly in the temporal lobes. Whatever else these differences mean, they show that the human brain can be specialized in different ways to arrive at the same capabilities.

In summary, the bulk of our daily experience and all of our understanding of the world can be traced to the different areas of the cortex. The human brain is among the most advanced and sophisticated of the brain-bearing species on earth. This, of course, is no guarantee that this marvelous "biocomputer" will be put to full use. Still, we must stand in awe of the potential it represents.

---

part of cortex to first receive input from the eyes, experience blind spots in their vision.

Do the primary visual areas of the cortex correspond directly to what is seen? Images are mapped onto the cortex, but the map is greatly stretched and distorted (Carlson, 2007). That's why it is important to avoid thinking of the visual area as being like a little TV screen in the brain. Visual information creates complex patterns of activity in nerve cells; it does *not* make a TV-like image.

One of the most fascinating results of brain injury is **visual agnosia** (ag-KNOW-zyah), an inability to identify seen objects. Visual agnosia is often caused by damage to the association areas on the occipital lobes (Farah, 2004). This condition is sometimes referred to as "mindblindness." For

Primary somatosensory area (primary somatosensory cortex) A receiving area for body sensations.
Temporal lobes Areas on each side of the brain where hearing registers in the brain.
Primary auditory area Part of the temporal lobe where auditory information is first registered.
Wernicke's area A temporal lobe brain area related to language comprehension.
Occipital lobes Portion of the cerebral cortex where vision registers in the brain.
Primary visual area The part of occipital lobe that first receives input from the eyes
Visual agnosia Inability to identify seen objects.

example, if we show Alice, an agnosia patient, a candle, she can see it and can describe it as "a long narrow object that tapers at the top." Alice can even draw the candle accurately, but she cannot name it. However, if she is allowed to feel the candle, she will name it immediately. In short, Alice can still see color, size, and shape. She just can't form the associations necessary to perceive the meanings of objects.

Are agnosias limited to objects? No. A fascinating form of "mindblindness" is **facial agnosia,** an inability to perceive familiar faces (Farah, 2006). One patient with facial agnosia couldn't recognize her husband or mother when they visited her in the hospital, and she was unable to identify pictures of her children. However, as soon as a visitor spoke she knew them immediately by their voices.

Areas devoted to recognizing faces lie in association areas on the underside of the occipital lobes. These areas appear to have no other function. Why would part of the brain be set aside solely for identifying faces? From an evolutionary standpoint it is not really so surprising. After all, we are social animals, for whom facial recognition is very important. This specialization is just one example of what a marvelous organ of consciousness we possess.

How much do individual brains differ? Could we find different specializations from brain to brain? Perhaps. "His and Her Brains?" explains why.

MODULE 2.3 Summary

How do the left and right hemispheres differ?
- Sensations, thoughts, feelings, motives, actions, memories, and all other human capacities are associated with brain activities and structures.
- The human brain is marked by advanced corticalization, or enlargement of the cerebral cortex.
- The left cerebral hemisphere contains speech or language "centers" in most people. It also specializes in writing, calculating, judging time and rhythm, and ordering complex movements.
- The right hemisphere is largely nonverbal. It excels at spatial and perceptual skills, visualization, and recognition of patterns, faces, and melodies.
- The left hemisphere is good at analysis and it processes small details sequentially. The right hemisphere detects overall patterns; it processes information simultaneously and holistically.
- "Split brains" can been created by cutting the corpus callosum. The split-brain individual shows a remarkable degree of independence between the right and left hemispheres.

What are the different functions of the lobes of the cerebral cortex?
- Primary sensory and motor areas are found on the lobes of the cerebral cortex. Higher mental abilities are related to the association areas.
- The most basic functions of the lobes of the cerebral cortex are as follows: frontal lobes—motor control, speech, abstract thought, and sense of self; parietal lobes—bodily sensation; temporal lobes—hearing and language; occipital lobes—vision. Damage to any of these areas will impair the named functions.
- Association areas on the cortex are neither sensory nor motor in function. They are related to more complex skills such as language, memory, recognition, and problem solving.
- Damage to either Broca's area or Wernicke's area causes speech and language problems known as aphasias.

KNOWLEDGE BUILDER

Hemispheres and Lobes of the Cerebral Cortex

Recite

See if you can match the following.

1. ____ Corpus callosum
2. ____ Occipital lobes
3. ____ Parietal lobes
4. ____ Temporal lobes
5. ____ Frontal lobes
6. ____ Association cortex
7. ____ Aphasias
8. ____ Corticalization
9. ____ Left hemisphere
10. ____ Right hemisphere
11. ____ "Split brain"
12. ____ Agnosia

A. Visual area
B. Language, speech, writing
C. Motor cortex and abstract thinking
D. Spatial skills, visualization, pattern recognition
E. Speech disturbances
F. Causes sleep
G. Increased ratio of cortex in brain
H. Bodily sensations
I. Treatment for severe epilepsy
J. Inability to identify seen objects
K. Fibers connecting the cerebral hemispheres
L. Cortex that is not sensory or motor in function
M. Hearing

Reflect
Critical Thinking

13. If you wanted to increase the surface area of the cerebrum so that more cerebral cortex would fit within the skull, how would you do it?

14. What would be some of the possible advantages and disadvantages to having a "split brain"?

15. If your brain were removed, replaced by another, and moved to a new body, which would you consider to be yourself, your old body with the new brain, or your new body with the old brain?

Relate

Learning the functions of the brain lobes is like learning areas on a map. Try drawing a map of the cortex. Can you label all the different "countries" (lobes)? Can you name their functions? Where is the primary motor area? The primary somatosensory area? Broca's area? Keep redrawing the map until it becomes more detailed and you can do it easily.

Link

Internet addresses frequently change. To find the sites listed here, visit **http://www.thomsonedu.com/psychology/coon** for an updated list of Internet addresses and direct links to relevant sites.

- **Split Brain Consciousness** Explore the cerebral hemispheres and what happens when they are split.
- **Probe the Brain** Explore the motor homunculus of the brain interactively.
- **Brain Maps** Information on the functions of a healthy cortex and also some effects of brain injury.

ANSWERS

1. K 2. A 3. H 4. M 5. C 6. L 7. E 8. G 9. B 10. D 11. I 12. J 13. One solution would be to gather the surface of the cortex into folds, just as you might if you were trying to fit a large piece of cloth into a small box. This, in fact, is probably why the cortex is more convoluted (folded or wrinkled) in higher animals. 14. If information were properly routed to each brain hemisphere, it would be possible to have both hands working simultaneously on conflicting tasks. However, such possible benefits would apply only under highly controlled conditions. 15. Although there is no "correct" answer to this question, your personality, knowledge, personal memories, and self-concept all derive from brain activity—which makes a strong case for your old brain in a new body being more nearly the "real you."

Facial agnosia Inability to perceive familiar faces.

MODULE 2.4 Subcortex and Endocrine System

YOU could lose large portions of your cerebrum and still survive. Not so with the subcortex, the brain structures immediately below the cerebral cortex. Serious damage to the subcortex (lower brain) can be fatal. Hunger, thirst, sleep, attention, sex, breathing, and many other vital functions are controlled by parts of the subcortex.

Our behavior is not solely a product of the nervous system. The endocrine glands form a second communication system in the body. Hormones can affect everything from personality and emotions to hunger and reactions to stress.

The Subcortex—At the Core of the (Brain) Matter

SURVEY QUESTION: *What kinds of behaviors are controlled by the subcortex?*

The **subcortex** lies immediately below the cerebral hemispheres. This area can be divided into the brainstem (or hindbrain), the midbrain, and the forebrain. (The forebrain also includes the cerebral cortex, which we discussed separately in Module 2.3, because of its size and importance.) For our purposes the midbrain can be viewed as a link between the forebrain and the brainstem. Therefore, let's focus on the rest of the subcortex. (See ● Fig. 2.26.)

The Hindbrain

Why are the lower brain areas so important? As the spinal cord joins the brain, it widens into the brainstem. The **brainstem** consists mainly of the medulla (meh-DUL-ah) and the cerebellum (ser-ah-BEL-uhm). The **medulla** contains centers important for the reflex control of vital life functions, including heart rate, breathing, swallowing, and the like. Various drugs, diseases, and injuries can disrupt the medulla and end or endanger life. That's why a karate chop to the back of the neck can be extremely dangerous.

The **pons,** which looks like a small bump on the brainstem, acts as a bridge between the medulla and other brain areas. In addition to connecting with many other locations, including the cerebellum, the pons influences sleep and arousal.

The cerebellum, which looks like a miniature cerebral cortex, lies at the base of the brain. The **cerebellum** primarily regulates posture, muscle tone, and muscular coordination. The cerebellum also stores memories related to skills and

● **FIGURE 2.26** This simplified drawing shows the main structures of the human brain and describes some of their most important features. (You can use the color code in the foreground to identify which areas are part of the forebrain, midbrain, and hindbrain.)

82

habits (Christian & Thompson, 2005). Again we see that experience shapes the brain: Musicians, who practice special motor skills throughout their lives, have larger than average cerebellums (Hutchinson et al., 2003).

What happens if the cerebellum is injured? Without the cerebellum, tasks like walking, running, or playing catch become impossible. The first symptoms of a crippling disease called *spinocerebellar degeneration* are tremor, dizziness, and muscular weakness. Eventually, victims have difficulty merely standing, walking, or feeding themselves.

Reticular Formation A network of fibers and cell bodies called the **reticular** (reh-TICK-you-ler) **formation (RF)** lies inside the medulla and brainstem. As messages flow into the brain, the RF gives priority to some while turning others aside (Kalat, 2007). By doing so, the RF influences *attention*. The RF doesn't fully mature until adolescence, which may be why children have such short attention spans. The RF also modifies outgoing commands to the body. In this way the RF affects muscle tone, posture, and movements of the eyes, face, head, body, and limbs. At the same time, the RF controls reflexes involved in breathing, sneezing, coughing, and vomiting.

The RF also keeps us vigilant, alert, and awake. Incoming messages from the sense organs branch into a part of the RF called the **reticular activating system (RAS).** The RAS bombards the cortex with stimulation, keeping it active and alert. For instance, let's say a sleepy driver rounds a bend and sees a deer standing in the road. The driver snaps to attention and applies the brakes. She can thank her RAS for arousing the rest of her brain and averting an accident. If you're getting sleepy while reading this module, try pinching your ear—a little pain will cause the RAS to momentarily arouse your cortex.

The Forebrain

Like hidden gemstones, two of the most important parts of your body lie buried deep within your brain. The thalamus (THAL-uh-mus) and an area just below it called the hypothalamus (HI-po-THAL-uh-mus) are key parts of the forebrain. (See Fig. 2.26.)

How could these be any more important than other areas already described? The **thalamus** acts as a final "switching station" for sensory messages on their way to the cortex. Vision, hearing, taste, and touch all pass through this small, football-shaped structure. Thus, injury to even small areas of the thalamus can cause deafness, blindness, or loss of any other sense, except smell.

The human hypothalamus is about the size of a small grape. Small as it may be, the **hypothalamus** is a kind of master control center for emotion and many basic motives (Carlson, 2007). The hypothalamus affects behaviors as diverse as sex, rage, temperature control, hormone release, eating and drinking, sleep, waking, and emotion. The hypothalamus is basically a "crossroads" that connects many areas of the brain. It is also the final pathway for many kinds of behavior. That is, the hypothalamus is the last place where many behaviors are organized or "decided on" before messages leave the brain, causing the body to react.

The Limbic System As a group, the hypothalamus, parts of the thalamus, the amygdala, the hippocampus, and other structures make up the limbic system (● Fig. 2.27). The

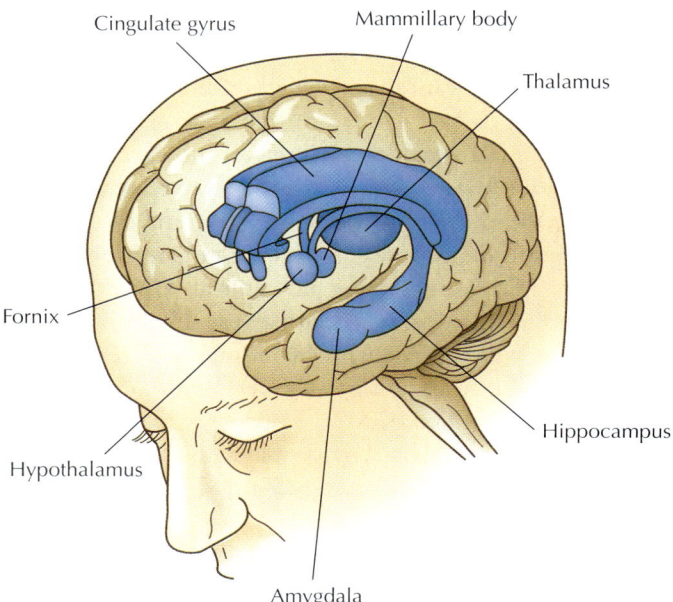

● **FIGURE 2.27** Parts of the limbic system. Although only one side is shown here, the hippocampus and the amygdala extend out into the temporal lobes at each side of the brain. The limbic system is a sort of "primitive core" of the brain strongly associated with emotion.

Subcortex All brain structures below the cerebral cortex.
Brainstem The lowest portions of the brain, including the cerebellum, medulla, pons, and reticular formation.
Medulla The structure that connects the brain with the spinal cord and controls vital life functions.
Pons An area on the brainstem that acts as a bridge between the medulla and other structures.
Cerebellum A brain structure that controls posture and coordination.
Reticular formation (RF) A network within the medulla and brainstem; associated with attention, alertness, and some reflexes.
Reticular activating system (RAS) A part of the reticular formation that activates the cerebral cortex.
Thalamus A brain structure that relays sensory information to the cerebral cortex.
Hypothalamus A small area of the brain that regulates emotional behaviors and motives.

limbic system has a major role in producing emotion and motivated behavior. Rage, fear, sexual response, and intense arousal can be localized to various points in the limbic system. Laughter, a delightful part of human social life, also has its origins in the limbic system (Cardoso, 2000).

During evolution, the limbic system was the earliest layer of the forebrain to develop. In lower animals, the limbic system helps organize basic survival responses: feeding, fleeing, fighting, or reproduction. In humans, a clear link to emotion remains. The **amygdala** (ah-MIG-dah-luh), in particular, is strongly related to fear. For example, during medical testing one woman reacted with a sudden outburst of fear and anger when the amygdala was stimulated, saying, "I feel like I want to get up from this chair! Please don't let me do it! I don't want to be mean! I want to get something and just tear it up!" (King, 1961).

The amygdala provides a primitive, "quick pathway" to the cortex. Like lower animals, we are able to react to dangerous stimuli before we fully know what is going on. In situations where true danger exists, such as in military combat, the amygdala's rapid response may aid survival. However, disorders of the brain's fear system can be very disruptive. An example is the war veteran who involuntarily dives into the bushes when he hears a car backfire (Fellous & LeDoux, 2005; LaBar & LeDoux, 2002). The role of the amygdala in emotion may also explain why people who suffer from phobias and disabling anxiety often feel afraid without knowing why (LeDoux, 1999).

People who suffer damage to the amygdala become "blind" to emotion. An armed robber could hold a gun to the person's head and the person wouldn't feel fear. Such people are also unable to "read" or understand other people's emotions. Many lose their ability to relate normally to friends, family, and co-workers (Goleman, 1995).

The limbic system is responsible for many of our emotional responses. The amygdala, in particular, produces rapid fear, which can help protect us from danger. If you unexpectedly saw a rattlesnake, it is likely that you would instantly jump back in fear, without having to first think about whether you were in danger.

Some parts of the limbic system have taken on additional, higher level functions. A part called the **hippocampus** (HIP-oh-CAMP-us) is important for forming lasting memories (Kumaran & Maguire, 2005). The hippocampus lies inside the temporal lobes, which is why stimulating the temporal lobes can produce memory-like or dream-like experiences. The hippocampus also helps us navigate through space. Your right hippocampus will become more active, for instance, if you mentally plan a drive across town (Maguire, Frackowiak, & Frith, 1997).

Psychologists have discovered that animals will learn to press a lever to deliver a dose of electrical stimulation to the limbic system. The animals act like the stimulation is satisfying or pleasurable. Indeed, several areas of the limbic system act as reward, or "pleasure," pathways. Many are found in the hypothalamus, where they overlap with areas that control thirst, sex, and hunger. Commonly abused drugs, such as cocaine, amphetamine, heroin, nicotine, marijuana, and alcohol, activate many of the same pleasure pathways. This appears to be part of the reason these drugs are so powerfully rewarding (Kandel, Schwartz, & Jessell, 2003).

You might also be interested to know that music you would describe as "thrilling" activates pleasure systems in your brain. This may explain some of the appeal of music that can send shivers down your spine (Blood & Zatorre, 2001). (It may also explain why people will pay so much for concert tickets!)

Punishment, or "aversive," areas have also been found in the limbic system. When these locations are activated, animals show discomfort and will work hard to turn off the stimulation. Because much of our behavior is based on seeking pleasure and avoiding pain, these discoveries continue to fascinate psychologists.

The Magnificent Brain

Given the amount of information covered in our journey through the brain, a short review is in order. We have seen that the human brain is an impressive assembly of billions of sensitive cells and nerve fibers. The brain controls vital bodily functions, keeps track of the external world, issues commands to the muscles and glands, responds to current needs, regulates its own behavior, and even creates the "mind" and the magic of consciousness—*all* at the same time. (See "If You Change Your Mind, Do You Change Your Brain?")

A final note of caution is now in order. For the sake of simplicity we have assigned functions to each "part" of the brain as if it were a computer. This is only a half-truth. In reality, the brain is a vast information-processing system. Incoming information scatters all over the brain and converges again as it goes out through the spinal cord, to muscles and glands. The overall system is much, much more complicated

CRITICAL THINKING

If You Change Your Mind, Do You Change Your Brain?

You can always change your mind. But does that have anything to do with your brain? The relationship of the mind to the brain (and the rest of the body) has been debated by philosophers for centuries. Biopsychologists argue that every mental event involves a brain event.

In one study, people suffering from spider phobias were treated with cognitive behavior therapy. (See Module 13.4.) After therapy, they could actually touch spiders (although they might not have been ready to appear on *Fear Factor*). Their fMRI brain images revealed reduced activity in the brain areas involved in the phobia (Paquette et al., 2003). Not only did they change their minds about spiders, they literally changed their brains.

In another study, stroke patients with left hemisphere damage were given language comprehension training to help them overcome aphasia. Not only did the training help improve the patients' language comprehension, but PET scans revealed that their undamaged right hemispheres became more active to compensate for their damaged left hemispheres (Musso et al., 1999). Again, a learning experience changed their brains.

Just think. As you study this psychology textbook you are changing your mind, and your brain, about psychology. There is even a fancy phrase to describe what you are doing: *self-directed neuroplasticity*. Every time you learn something, you are reshaping your living brain.

---

than our discussion of separate "parts" implies. In addition, the brain constantly revises its circuits in response to changing life experiences (Kolb & Whishaw, 2006).

We began our exploration of the brain with a virtuoso musician. Imagine the other extreme of being completely unable to move or speak. Even though you would remain alert and intelligent, you would be unable to communicate your simplest thoughts and feelings to others. Each year, this is the fate of thousands of people, like Kate Adamson, who are paralyzed by stroke, disease, or injury. In a very real sense, these people are *locked in*, prisoners in their own bodies (Smith & Delargy, 2005).

What if they could "will" a computer to speak for them? Right on! German researchers have developed a brain–computer interface that translates a patient's EEG recordings into commands that can be used to control a computer (Hinterberger et al., 2003) and even access the Internet (Karim et al., 2006).

The Endocrine System—My Hormones Made Me Do It

SURVEY QUESTION: *Does the glandular system affect behavior?*

Our behavior is not solely a product of the nervous system. The endocrine (EN-duh-krin) glands form an equally important parallel communication system in the body. The **endocrine system** is made up of glands that secrete chemicals directly into the bloodstream or lymph system. (See ● Fig. 2.28). These chemicals, called **hormones**, are carried throughout the body, where they affect both internal activities and visible behavior. Hormones are related to neurotransmitters. Like other transmitter chemicals, hormones activate cells in the body. To respond, the cells must have receptor sites for the hormone. Hormones affect puberty, personality, dwarfism, jet lag, and much more.

How do hormones affect behavior? Although we are seldom directly aware of them, hormones affect us in many ways. Here is a brief sample: Pregnancy and motherhood cause the release of hormones that lead to the dramatic changes involved in maternal behavior (Kingsley & Lambert, 2006). Hormone output from the adrenal glands rises during stressful situations; androgens ("male" hormones) are related to the sex drive in both males and females; hormones secreted during times of high emotion intensify memory formation; at least some of the emotional turmoil of adolescence is due to elevated hormone levels; different hormones prevail when you are angry, rather than fearful. In fact, something as routine as watching a movie can alter hormone levels. After watching violent scenes from *The Godfather,* men had higher levels of the male hormone testosterone. For both men and women, watching a romantic film boosted a hormone that's linked to relaxation and reproduction (Schultheiss, Wirth, & Stanton, 2004). Because these are just samples, let's consider some additional effects hormones have on the body and behavior.

Limbic system A system in the forebrain that is closely linked with emotional response.

Amygdala A part of the limbic system associated with fear responses.

Hippocampus A part of the limbic system associated with storing memories.

Endocrine system Glands whose secretions pass directly into the bloodstream or lymph system.

Hormone A glandular secretion that affects bodily functions or behavior.

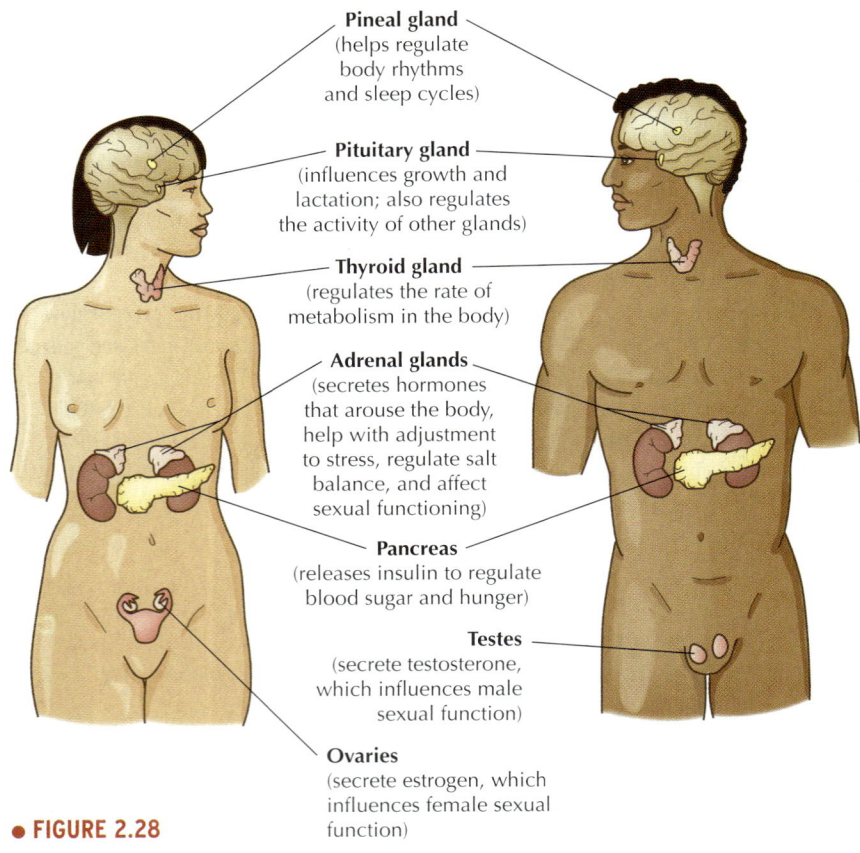

- **Pineal gland** (helps regulate body rhythms and sleep cycles)
- **Pituitary gland** (influences growth and lactation; also regulates the activity of other glands)
- **Thyroid gland** (regulates the rate of metabolism in the body)
- **Adrenal glands** (secretes hormones that arouse the body, help with adjustment to stress, regulate salt balance, and affect sexual functioning)
- **Pancreas** (releases insulin to regulate blood sugar and hunger)
- **Testes** (secrete testosterone, which influences male sexual function)
- **Ovaries** (secrete estrogen, which influences female sexual function)

● **FIGURE 2.28**

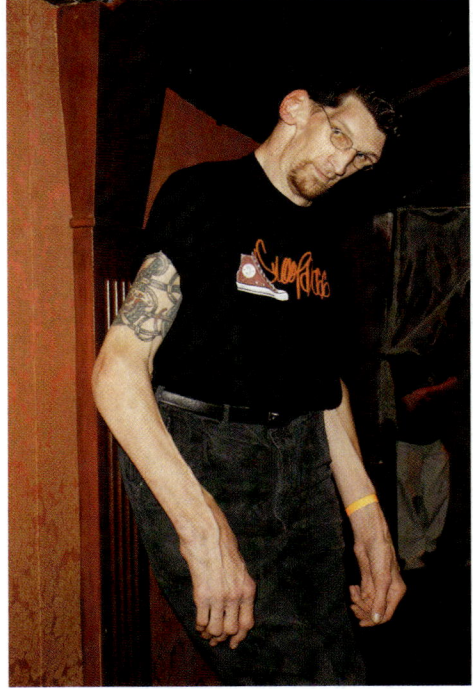

Underactivity of the pituitary gland may produce a dwarf. Verne Troyer, best known for playing Mini-Me in the *Austin Powers* movies, has enjoyed an impressive career as an actor. Overactivity of the pituitary gland may produce a giant. Until his premature death in 2005, actor Matthew McGrory was best known for his role of Karl the Giant in the 2003 movie *Big Fish*.

The pituitary is a pea-sized globe hanging from the base of the brain. (Return to Fig. 2.28.) One of the pituitary's more important roles is to regulate growth. During childhood, the pituitary secretes a hormone that speeds body development. If too little **growth hormone** is released, a person may remain far smaller than average. If this condition is not treated, a child may be 6 to 12 inches shorter than age-mates. As adults, some will have *hypopituitary* (HI-po-pih-TU-ih-ter-ee) *dwarfism*. Such individuals are perfectly proportioned, but tiny. Regular injections of growth hormone can raise a hypopituitary child's height by several inches, usually to the short side of average.

Too much growth hormone produces *gigantism* (excessive bodily growth). Secretion of too much growth hormone late in the growth period causes *acromegaly* (AK-row-MEG-uh-lee), a condition in which the arms, hands, feet, and facial bones become enlarged. Acromegaly produces prominent facial features, which some people have used as a basis for careers as character actors, wrestlers, and the like.

The pituitary also governs the functioning of other glands (especially the thyroid, adrenal glands, and ovaries or testes). These glands in turn regulate such bodily processes as metabolism, responses to stress, and reproduction. In women, the pituitary controls milk output during breast-feeding.

The **pituitary gland** is often called the "master gland" because it influences other endocrine glands. But the master has a master: The pituitary is directed by the hypothalamus, which lies directly above it. In this way, the hypothalamus can affect glands throughout the body. This, then, is the major link between the brain and hormones (Carlson, 2007).

The **pineal** (pin-EE-ul) **gland** was once considered a useless remnant of evolution. In certain fishes, frogs, and lizards, the gland is associated with a well-developed light-sensitive organ, or so-called "third eye." In humans, the function of the pineal gland is just now coming to light (so to speak). The pineal gland releases a hormone called **melatonin** (mel-ah-TONE-in) in response to daily variations in light. Melatonin levels in the bloodstream rise at dusk, peak around midnight, and fall again as morning approaches. As far as the brain is concerned, it's bedtime when melatonin levels rise (Kennaway & Wright, 2002).

The **thyroid gland,** located in the neck, regulates metabolism. As you may remember from a biology course, *metabolism* is the rate at which energy is produced and expended in the body. By altering metabolism, the thyroid can have a sizable effect on personality. A person suffering from *hyperthyroidism* (an overactive thyroid) tends to be thin, tense, excitable, and nervous. An underactive thyroid (*hypothyroidism*) in an adult can cause inactivity, sleepiness, slowness, and obesity. In infancy, hypothyroidism limits development of the nervous system, leading to severe mental retardation.

When you are frightened or angry, some important reactions prepare your body for action: Your heart rate and blood pressure rise; stored sugar is released into the bloodstream for quick energy; your muscles tense and receive more blood; and your blood is prepared to clot more quickly in case of injury. As we discussed earlier, these changes are controlled by the autonomic nervous system. Specifically, the sympathetic branch of the ANS causes the hormones *epinephrine* (ep-eh-NEF-rin) and *norepinephrine* to be released by the adrenal glands. (Epinephrine is also known as adrenaline, which may be more familiar to you.) **Epinephrine,** which is associated with fear, tends to arouse the body. **Norepinephrine** also tends to arouse the body, but it is linked with anger.

The **adrenal glands** are located just under the back of the rib cage, atop the kidneys. The *adrenal medulla,* or inner core of the adrenal glands, is the source of epinephrine and norepinephrine. The *adrenal cortex,* or outer "bark" of the adrenal glands, produces a set of hormones called corticoids (KOR-tih-coids). One of their jobs is to regulate salt balance in the body. A deficiency of certain corticoids can evoke a powerful craving for the taste of salt in humans. The corticoids also help the body adjust to stress, and they are a secondary source of sex hormones.

An oversecretion of the adrenal sex hormones can cause *virilism* (exaggerated male characteristics). For instance, a woman may grow a beard or a man's voice may become so low it is difficult to understand. Oversecretion early in life can cause *premature puberty* (full sexual development during childhood). One of the most remarkable cases on record is that of a 5-year-old Peruvian girl who gave birth to a son (Strange, 1965).

While we are on the topic of sex hormones, there is a related issue worth mentioning. One of the principal androgens, or "male" hormones, is testosterone, which is supplied in small amounts by the adrenal glands. (The testes are the main source of testosterone in males.) Perhaps you have heard about the use of anabolic steroids by athletes who want to "bulk up" or promote muscle growth. Most of these drugs are synthetic versions of testosterone.

Flight crews often suffer severe disruptions in their sleep cycles. For example, a crew that leaves Los Angeles at 4 P.M., bound for London, will arrive in 8 hours. Crew members' bodies, which are on California time, will act as if it is 12 A.M. Yet in London, it will be 8 A.M. Recent studies confirm that melatonin can help people adjust more rapidly to such time-zone changes.

Growth hormone A hormone, secreted by the pituitary gland, that promotes body growth.

Pituitary gland The "master gland" whose hormones influence other endocrine glands.

Pineal gland Gland in the brain that helps regulate body rhythms and sleep cycles.

Melatonin Hormone released by the pineal gland in response to daily cycles of light and dark.

Thyroid gland Endocrine gland that helps regulate the rate of metabolism.

Epinephrine An adrenal hormone that tends to arouse the body; epinephrine is associated with fear. (Also known as adrenaline.)

Norepinephrine An adrenal hormone that tends to arouse the body; norepinephrine is associated with anger. (Also known as noradrenaline.)

Adrenal glands Endocrine glands that arouse the body, regulate salt balance, adjust the body to stress, and affect sexual functioning.

Although there is some disagreement about whether steroids actually improve athletic performance, it is widely accepted that they may cause serious side effects. Problems include voice deepening or baldness in women and shrinkage of the testicles, sexual impotence, or breast enlargement in men (Millman & Ross, 2003). Dangerous increases in hostility and aggression ("roid rage") have also been linked with steroid use (Hartgens & Kuipers, 2004). Also common when steroids are used by younger adolescents are an increased risk of heart attack and stroke, liver damage, or stunted growth. Understandably, almost all major sports organizations ban the use of anabolic steroids.

In this brief discussion of the endocrine system we have considered only a few of the more important glands. Nevertheless, this should give you an appreciation of how completely behavior and personality are tied to the ebb and flow of hormones in the body.

Although Barry Bonds has passed Hank Aaron on the all-time home run list, his achievement has been overshadowed by allegations of steroid use. In response, major league baseball has begun to make steroids illegal. Many athletes in other sports have been disqualified, banned from competing, or stripped of medals for steroid use.

MODULE 2.4 Summary

What kinds of behaviors are controlled by the subcortex?

- The brain can be subdivided into the forebrain, midbrain, and hindbrain. The subcortex includes hindbrain and midbrain brain structures as well as the lower parts of the forebrain, below the cortex.
- The medulla contains centers essential for reflex control of heart rate, breathing, and other "vegetative" functions.
- The cerebellum maintains coordination, posture, and muscle tone.
- The reticular formation directs sensory and motor messages, and part of it, known as the RAS, acts as an activating system for the cerebral cortex.
- The thalamus carries sensory information to the cortex. The hypothalamus exerts powerful control over eating, drinking, sleep cycles, body temperature, and other basic motives and behaviors.
- The limbic system is strongly related to emotion. It also contains distinct reward and punishment areas and an area known as the hippocampus that is important for forming memories.

Does the glandular system affect behavior?

- Endocrine glands serve as a chemical communication system within the body. The ebb and flow of hormones from the endocrine glands entering the bloodstream affect behavior, moods, and personality.
- Many of the endocrine glands are influenced by the pituitary (the "master gland"), which is in turn influenced by the hypothalamus. Thus, the brain controls the body through both the fast nervous system and the slower endocrine system.

KNOWLEDGE BUILDER

Subcortex and Endocrine System

Recite

1. Three major divisions of the brain are the brainstem or _____, the _____, and the _____.
2. Reflex centers for heartbeat and respiration are found in the
   a. cerebellum b. thalamus c. medulla d. RF
3. A portion of the reticular formation, known as the RAS, serves as an _____ system in the brain.
   a. activating b. adrenal c. adjustment d. aversive
4. The _____ is a final relay, or "switching station," for sensory information on its way to the cortex.
5. "Reward" and "punishment" areas are found throughout the _____ system, which is also related to emotion.
6. Undersecretion from the thyroid can cause both
   a. dwarfism b. gigantism c. obesity d. mental retardation
7. The body's ability to resist stress is related to the action of the adrenal _____.

Reflect
Critical Thinking

8. Subcortical structures in humans are quite similar to corresponding lower brain areas in animals. Why would knowing this allow you to predict, in general terms, what functions are controlled by the subcortex?
9. Where in all the brain's "hardware" do you think the mind is found? What is the relationship between mind and brain?

Relate

If Mr. Medulla met Ms. Cerebellum at a party, what would they say their roles are in the brain? Would a marching band in a "reticular formation" look like a network? Would it get your attention? If you were standing in the final path for behavior leaving the brain, would you be in the thalamus? Or in the hy-**path**-alamus (please forgive the misspelling)? When you are emotional do you wave your limbs around (and does your limbic system become more active)?

Name as many of the endocrine glands as you can. Which did you leave out? Can you summarize the functions of each of the glands?

Link

Internet addresses frequently change. To find the sites listed here, visit **http://www.thomsonedu.com/psychology/coon** for an updated list of Internet addresses and direct links to relevant sites.

- **The Patient's Journey: Living With Locked-In Syndrome** Meet Nick, who lives with locked-in syndrome after suffering brainstem damage.
- **Endo 101: The Endocrine System** A description of the endocrine system and hormones.
- **Anabolic Steroid Abuse** An article on steroids and steroid abuse from the National Institute on Drug Abuse.

ANSWERS

1. hindbrain, midbrain, forebrain 2. c 3. a 4. thalamus 5. limbic 6. c, d (in infancy) 7. cortex 8. Because the subcortex must be related to basic functions common to all higher animals: motives, emotions, sleep, attention, and vegetative functions such as heartbeat, breathing, and temperature regulation. The subcortex also routes and processes incoming information from the senses and outgoing commands to the muscles. 9. This question, known as the mind-body problem, has challenged thinkers for centuries. One recent view is that mental states are "emergent properties" of brain activity. That is, brain activity forms complex patterns that are, in a sense, more than the sum of their parts. Or, to use a rough analogy, if the brain were a musical instrument, then mental life would be like music played on that instrument.

MODULE 2.5 Psychology in Action

Handedness—Are You Dexterous or Sinister?

SURVEY QUESTION: *In what ways do right- and left-handed individuals differ?*

Around the world, left-handedness has been frowned upon. "Lefties" have often been characterized as clumsy, awkward, unlucky, or insincere. The Latin word for left is actually *sinister*! In contrast, right-handedness is the paragon of virtue. The Latin word for right is *dexter* and "righties" are more likely to be referred to as dexterous, coordinated, skillful, and just. But is there any basis in fact for these attitudes?

What causes **handedness** (a preference for the right or left hand)? Why are there more right-handed than left-handed people? How do left-handed and right-handed people differ? Does being left-handed create any problems—or benefits? The answers to these questions lead us back to the brain, where handedness begins. Let's see what research has revealed about handedness, the brain, and you.

Assessing Handedness Write your name on a sheet of paper, first using your right hand and then your left. You were probably much more comfortable writing with your dominant hand. This is interesting because there's no real difference in the strength or dexterity of the hands themselves. The agility of your dominant hand is an outward expression of superior motor control on one side of the brain. If you are right-handed, there is literally more area on the left side of your brain devoted to controlling your right hand. If you are left-handed, the reverse applies.

The preceding exercise implies that you are either entirely right- or left-handed. But handedness is a matter of degree. To better assess your handedness, complete a few questions adapted from the Waterloo Handedness Questionnaire (Brown et al., 2006) by circling an answer for each questions. The more "Rights" you circle, the more right-handed you are.

Are You Right- or Left-Handed?

1. Which hand would you use to spin a top? — Right Left Either
2. With which hand would you hold a paintbrush to paint a wall? — Right Left Either
3. Which hand would you use to pick up a book? — Right Left Either
4. With which hand would you use a spoon to eat soup? — Right Left Either
5. Which hand would you use to flip pancakes? — Right Left Either
6. Which hand would you use to pick up a piece of paper? — Right Left Either
7. Which hand would you use to draw a picture? — Right Left Either
8. Which hand would you use to insert and turn a key in a lock? — Right Left Either
9. Which hand would you use to insert a plug into an electrical outlet? — Right Left Either
10. Which hand would you use to throw a ball? — Right Left Either

About 90 percent of all humans are right-handed; 10 percent are left-handed. Most people (about 75 percent) are strongly right- or left-handed. The rest show some inconsistency in hand preference. Which were you?

Is there such a thing as being left-footed? Excellent question. Do you have "two left feet"? **Sidedness** is often measured by assessing hand, foot, eye, *and* ear preference (Greenwood, et al. 2006). We also generally prefer breathing though one nostril over the other and even have a preference for which direction we lean our head when kissing (Barrett, Greenwood, & McCullagh, 2006). (Do you "kiss right"?) Nevertheless, handedness remains the single most important behavioral indicator of sidedness.

If a person is strongly left-handed, does that mean the right hemisphere is dominant? Not necessarily. It's true that the right hemisphere controls the left hand, but a left-handed person's language-producing, **dominant hemisphere** may be on the opposite side of the brain.

Brain Dominance About 97 percent of right-handers process speech in the left hemisphere and are left-brain dominant (● Fig. 2.29). A good 68 percent of left-handers produce speech from the left hemisphere, just as right-handed people do. About 19 percent of all lefties and 3 percent of righties use their right brain for language. Some left-handers (approximately 12 percent) use both sides of the brain for language processing. All told, 94 percent of the population uses the left brain for language (Coren, 1992).

Is there any way for a person to tell which of his or her hemispheres is dominant? One classic clue is the way you write. Right-handed individuals who write with a straight hand and lefties who write with a hooked hand are usually left-brain

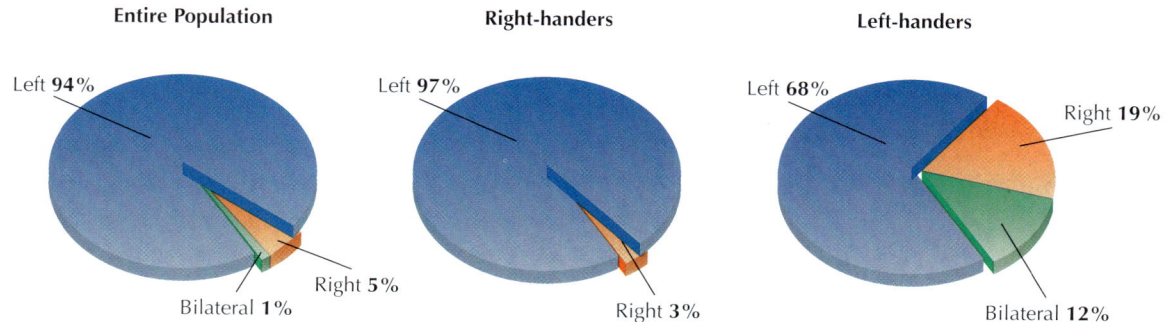

● **FIGURE 2.29** Language is controlled by the left side of the brain in the majority of right- and left-handers.

● **FIGURE 2.30** Research suggests that the hand position used in writing may indicate which brain hemisphere is used for language. (Redrawn from an illustration by M. E. Challinor.)

dominant for language. Left-handed people who write with their hand below the writing line and righties who use a hooked position are usually right-brain dominant (Levy & Reid, 1976). (See ● Fig. 2.30.) Another hint is provided by hand gestures. If you gesture mostly with your right hand as you talk, you probably process language in your left hemisphere. Gesturing with your left hand is associated with right-brain language processing (Hellige, 1993). Are your friends right brained or left brained?

Before you leap to any conclusions, be aware that writing position and gestures are not foolproof. The only sure way to check brain dominance is to do medical tests that involve assessing one cerebral hemisphere at a time (Kirveskari, Salmelin, & Hari, 2006).

Causes of Handedness *Is handedness inherited from parents?* Yes, at least partly. Clear hand preferences are apparent even before birth, as can be seen in a fetal ultrasound image (● Fig. 2.31). According to British psychologist Peter Hepper, prenatal handedness preferences persist for at least 10 years after birth (Hepper, McCartney, & Shannon, 1998; Hepper, Wells, & Lynch, 2005). This suggests that handedness can-

not be dictated. Parents should never try to force a left-handed child to use the right hand. To do so may create speech or reading problems.

Studies of twins show that hand preferences are not directly inherited like eye color or skin color (Ooki, 2005; Reiss et al., 1999). Yet, two left-handed parents are more likely to have a left-handed child than two right-handed parents are (McKeever, 2000). The best evidence to date shows that handedness is influenced by a single gene on the X (female) chromosome (Jones & Martin, 2001).

On the other hand, environmental factors such as learning, birth traumas, and social pressure to use the right hand can also affect which hand you end up favoring (Bailey & McKeever, 2004; McKeever et al., 2000). In the past, many left-handed children were forced to use their right hand for

Handedness A preference for the right or left hand in most activities.
Sidedness A combination of preference for hand, foot, eye, and ear.
Dominant hemisphere A term usually applied to the side of a person's brain that produces language.

● **FIGURE 2.31** In this ultrasound image, a 4-month-old fetus sucks her right thumb. A study by psychologist Peter Hepper suggests that she will continue to prefer her right hand after she is born and that she will be right-handed as an adult.

writing, eating, and other skills. This is especially true in collectivist cultures like India and Japan, where left-handedness is viewed as especially negative. Not surprisingly, the proportion of left-handers in these societies is only about half that found in individualist cultures such as the United States and Canada (Ida & Mandal, 2003).

Advantage Right *Are there any drawbacks to being left-handed?* A small minority of lefties owe their hand preference to birth traumas (such as prematurity, low birth weight, and breech birth). These individuals have higher rates of allergies, learning disorders, and other problems (Betancur et al., 1990). Similarly, people with inconsistent handedness (as opposed to consistent left-handers) may be at risk for more immune-related diseases (Bryden, Bruyn, & Fletcher, 2005).

Is it true that right-handed people live longer than left-handed people? It is true that there is a shortage of very old lefties. One possible explanation lies in the widespread finding that left-handers are more accident prone (Dutta & Mandal, 2005). However, the supposed clumsiness of lefties may well be a result of living in a right-handed world. One study showed that left-handed locomotive engineers have higher accident rates and suggested that the cause was due to the design of locomotive controls (Bhushan & Khan, 2006). If it can be gripped, turned, or pulled, it's probably designed for the right hand. Even toilet handles are on the right side.

On the other hand, the shortage of very old lefties may just reflect the fact that, in the past, more left-handed children were forced to become right-handed. That makes it look like many lefties don't survive to old age. In reality, they do, but many of them are masquerading as righties (Martin & Freitas, 2002)!

Advantage Left Actually, there are some clear advantages to being left-handed. Throughout history a notable number of artists have been lefties, from Leonardo da Vinci and Michelangelo to Pablo Picasso and M. C. Escher. Conceivably, because the right hemisphere is superior at imagery and visual abilities, there is some advantage to using the left hand for drawing or painting (Springer & Deutsch, 1998). At the least, lefties are definitely better at visualizing three-dimensional objects. This may be why there are more left-handed architects, artists, and chess players than would be expected (Coren, 1992).

Similarly, being right-handed does not guarantee sports superiority, as you can see in ■ Table 2.1.

By the way, chalk up a few more for the left-handers, who have also done well in handball (Dane & Erzurumluoglu, 2003) and professional tennis (Holtzen, 2000).

Lateralization refers to specialization in the abilities of the brain hemispheres. One striking feature of lefties is that they are generally less lateralized than the right-handed. In fact, even the physical size and shape of their cerebral hemispheres are more alike. If you are a lefty, you can take pride in the fact that your brain is less lopsided than most! In general, left-handers are more symmetrical on almost everything, including eye dominance, fingerprints—even foot size (Polemikos & Papaeliou, 2000).

In some situations, less lateralization may be a real advantage. For instance, individuals who are moderately left-handed or ambidextrous seem to have better than average pitch memory, which is a basic musical skill. Correspondingly, more musicians are ambidextrous than would normally be expected (Springer & Deutsch, 1998).

Math abilities may also benefit from fuller use of the right hemisphere. Students who are extremely gifted in math are much more likely to be left-handed or ambidextrous (Benbow, 1986). Even where ordinary arithmetic skills are

■ **TABLE 2.1 Sports and Handedness**

SPORT	HANDEDNESS ADVANTAGE
Baseball	No overall left or right advantage
Boxing	Left
Fencing	Left
Basketball	Mixed and ambidextrous
Ice hockey	Mixed and ambidextrous
Field hockey	Mixed and ambidextrous
Tennis	Strong left or strong right
Squash	Strong left or strong right
Badminton	Strong left or strong right

(Adapted from Coren, 1992.)

Left-handers have an advantage in sports such as fencing and boxing. Most likely, their movements are less familiar to opponents, who usually face right-handers (Coren, 1992).

MODULE 2.5 Psychology in Action Summary

In what ways do right- and left-handed individuals differ?

- Brain dominance and brain activity determine if you are right-handed, left-handed, or ambidextrous.
- Most people are strongly right-handed. A minority are strongly left-handed. A few have moderate or mixed hand preferences or they are ambidextrous. Thus, handedness is not a simple either/or trait.
- The vast majority of people are right-handed and therefore left-brain dominant for motor skills. Ninety-seven percent of right-handed persons and 68 percent of the left-handed also produce speech from the left hemisphere.
- Left-handed people tend to be less strongly lateralized than right-handed people (their brain hemispheres are not as specialized).

concerned, lefties seem to excel (Annett, 2002; Annett & Manning, 1990).

The clearest advantage of being left-handed shows up when there is a brain injury. Because of their milder lateralization, left-handed individuals typically experience less language loss after damage to either brain hemisphere, and they recover more easily (Geschwind, 1979). Maybe having "two left feet" isn't so bad after all.

Lateralization Differences between the two sides of the body; especially, differences in the abilities of the brain hemispheres.

KNOWLEDGE BUILDER

Handedness and Brain Lateralization

Recite

1. About 97 percent of left-handed people process language on the left side of the brain, the same as right-handed people do. T or F?
2. Left-handed individuals who write with their hand below the writing line are likely to be right-brain dominant. T or F?
3. People basically learn to be right- or left-handed. T or F?
4. In general, left-handed individuals show less lateralization in the brain and throughout the body. T or F?

Reflect
Critical Thinking

5. News reports that left-handed people tend to die younger have been flawed in an important way: The average age of people in the left-handed group was younger than that of subjects in the right-handed group. Why would this make a difference in the conclusions drawn?

Relate

Think for a moment about what you "knew" about handedness and left-handed people before you read this section. Which of your beliefs were correct? How has your knowledge about handedness changed?

Link

Internet addresses frequently change. To find the sites listed here, visit **http://www.thomsonedu.com/psychology/coon** for an updated list of Internet addresses and direct links to relevant sites.

- **What Is "Handedness"?** Information about handedness and brain laterality, including a list of famous left handers.
- **The Sinister Hand** Interview on handedness with Dr. Michael Corballis.
- **Left Brain, Right Brain** Article on popular conceptions of the differences between brain hemispheres.

ANSWERS

1. F 2. T 3. F 4. T 5. Because we can't tell if handedness or average age accounts for the difference in death rates. For example, if we start with a group of 20- to 30-year-old people, in which some die, the average age of death has to be between 20 and 30. If we start with a group of 30- to 40-year-old people, in which some die, the average age of death has to be between 30 and 40. Thus, the left-handed group might have an earlier average age at death simply because members of the group were younger to start with.

Interactive Learning

Psychology: Active Learning Modules Book Companion Website

http://www.thomsonedu.com/psychology/coon
Visit your Book Companion Website, where you will find flash cards, practice quizzes, Internet links, and more to help you study.

ThomsonNOW

Just what you need to know NOW!

Spend time on what you need to master rather than on information you already have learned. Take a pre-test for this chapter, and ThomsonNOW will generate a personalized study plan based on your results. The study plan will identify the topics you need to review and direct you to online resources to help you master those topics. You can then take a post-test to help you determine the concepts you have mastered and what you will need to work on. Try it out! Go to **www.thomsonedu.com/login** to sign in with an access code or to purchase access to this product.

3 Human Development

MODULE 3.1 The Interplay of Heredity and Environment
SURVEY QUESTION: How do heredity and environment affect development?

MODULE 3.2 The Neonate and Early Maturation
SURVEY QUESTION: What can newborn babies do?
SURVEY QUESTION: What influence does maturation have on early development?

MODULE 3.3 Social Development in Childhood
SURVEY QUESTION: Of what significance is a child's emotional bond with parents?
SURVEY QUESTION: How important are parenting styles?

MODULE 3.4 Language Development in Childhood
SURVEY QUESTION: How do children acquire language?

MODULE 3.5 Cognitive Development in Childhood
SURVEY QUESTION: How do children learn to think?

MODULE 3.6 Adolescence, Young Adulthood, and Moral Development
SURVEY QUESTION: Why is development during adolescence and young adulthood especially challenging?
SURVEY QUESTION: How do we develop morals and values?

MODULE 3.7 Challenges Across the Lifespan
SURVEY QUESTION: What are the typical tasks and dilemmas through the lifespan?
SURVEY QUESTION: What issues arise during later adulthood?
SURVEY QUESTION: How do people typically react to death?

MODULE 3.8 Psychology in Action: Effective Parenting—Raising Healthy Children
SURVEY QUESTION: How do effective parents discipline and communicate with their children?

A Star Is Born—Here's Amy!

Olivia has just given birth to her first child, Amy. Frankly, at the moment Amy looks something like a pink prune, with pudgy arms, stubby legs, and lots of wrinkles. She also has the face of an angel—at least in her parents' eyes. As Olivia and her husband Tom look at Amy they wonder, "How will her life unfold? What kind of a person will she be?"

What if we could skip ahead through Amy's life and observe her at various ages? What could we learn? Seeing the world through her eyes would be fascinating and instructive. For example, a child's viewpoint can make us more aware of things we take for granted. Younger children, in particular, are very literal in their use of language. When Amy was 3, she thought her bath was too hot and said to Tom, "Make it warmer, daddy." At first,

Tom was confused. The bath was already fairly hot. But then he realized that what she really meant was, "Bring the water closer to the temperature we call *warm*." It makes perfect sense if you look at it that way.

Tom and Olivia can only hope that by the time Amy is 83, she will have lived a full and satisfying life. Research done by developmental psychologists tells a fascinating story about human growth and development. Let's let Olivia, Tom, and Amy represent parents and children everywhere, as we see what psychology can tell us about the challenges of growing up, maturing, aging, and facing death. Tracing Amy's development might even help you answer two very important questions, How did I become the person I am today? and Who will I become tomorrow?

© Hank Morgan/Rainbow

MODULE 3.1
The Interplay of Heredity and Environment

HEREDITY influences development during the entire human growth sequence. Prenatal risks, sensitive periods, and conditions of deprivation or enrichment all show how the environment can influence development. Ultimately, the person you are today reflects a continuous interplay between the forces of nature and nurture. Even young infants have inborn differences in personality.

Nature and Nurture—It Takes Two to Tango

SURVEY QUESTION: *How do heredity and environment affect development?*

When we think of development we naturally think of children "growing up" into adults. But even as adults we never really stop changing. **Developmental psychology,** the study of progressive changes in behavior and abilities, involves every stage of life from conception to death (or "the womb to the tomb"). Heredity and environment also affect us throughout life. Some events, such as when Amy achieves sexual maturity, are mostly governed by heredity. Others, such as when Amy learns to swim, read, or drive a car, are primarily a matter of environment.

But which is more important, heredity or environment? Actually, neither. Biopsychologist D. O. Hebb (1904–1985) once offered a useful analogy: To define the area of a rectangle, what is more important, height or width? Of course, both dimensions are absolutely essential. If either is reduced to zero, there is no rectangle. Similarly, if Amy grows up to become a prominent civil rights lawyer, her success will be due to both heredity and environment.

While heredity gives each of us a variety of potentials and limitations, these are, in turn, affected by environmental influences, such as learning, nutrition, disease, and culture. Thus, the person you are today reflects a constant *interaction*, or interplay, between the forces of nature and nurture (Kalat, 2007). Let's look in more detail at this dance.

Heredity

Heredity ("nature") refers to the genetic transmission of physical and psychological characteristics from parents to their children. An incredible number of personal features are set at conception, when a sperm and an ovum (egg) unite.

How does heredity operate? The nucleus of every human cell contains **DNA,** deoxyribonucleic acid (dee-OX-see-RYE-bo-new-KLEE-ik). DNA is a long, ladder-like chain of pairs of chemical molecules (● Fig. 3.1). The order of these molecules, or organic bases, acts as a code for genetic information. The DNA in each cell contains a record of all the instructions needed to make a human—with room left over to spare. A major scientific milestone was reached with the completion in 2003 of the Human Genome Project, an effort to completely identify the sequence of all 3 billion chemical base pairs in human DNA (U.S. Department of Energy Office of Science, 2005).

● **FIGURE 3.1** *(Top left)* Linked molecules (organic bases) make up the "rungs" on DNA's twisted "molecular ladder." The order of these molecules serves as a code for genetic information. The code provides a genetic blueprint that is unique for each individual (except identical twins). The drawing shows only a small section of a DNA strand. An entire strand of DNA is composed of billions of smaller molecules. *(Bottom left)* The nucleus of each cell in the body contains chromosomes made up of tightly wound coils of DNA. (Don't be misled by the drawing: Chromosomes are microscopic, and the chemical molecules that make up DNA are even smaller.)

Human DNA is organized into 46 **chromosomes.** (The word *chromosome* means "colored body.") These thread-like structures hold the coded instructions of heredity (● Fig. 3.2). A notable exception is sperm cells and ova, which contain only 23 chromosomes. Thus, Amy received 23 chromosomes from Olivia and 23 from Tom. This is her genetic heritage.

Genes are small areas of DNA that affect a particular process or personal characteristic. Sometimes, a single gene is responsible for an inherited feature, such as Amy's eye color. Genes may be dominant or recessive. When a gene is **dominant,** the feature it controls will appear every time the gene is present. When a gene is **recessive,** it must be paired with a second recessive gene before its effect will be expressed. For example, if Amy got a blue-eye gene from Tom and a brown-eye gene from Olivia, Amy will be brown-eyed, because brown-eye genes are dominant.

If brown-eye genes are dominant, why do two brown-eyed parents sometimes have a blue-eyed child? If one or both parents have two brown-eye genes, the couple's children can only be brown-eyed. But what if each parent has one brown-eye gene and one blue-eye gene? In that case, both parents would have brown eyes. Yet there is 1 chance in 4 that their children will get two blue-eye genes and have blue eyes (● Fig. 3.3).

In actuality, few of our characteristics are controlled by single genes. Instead, most are **polygenic** (pol-ih-JEN-ik), or controlled by many genes working in combination. Through the expression of genes, heredity determines eye color, skin color, and susceptibility to some diseases. Also, genes can switch on (or off) at certain ages or developmental stages. In this way, heredity continues to exert a powerful influence throughout maturation, the unfolding of the *human growth sequence.* (See ■ Table 3.1.) To a degree, genetic instructions affect body size and shape, height, intelligence, athletic potential, personality traits, sexual orientation, and a host of other details (Cummings, 2006).

Environment

Our environment also exerts a profound influence on our development. For example, the brain of a newborn baby has fewer *dendrites* (nerve cell branches) and *synapses* (connections between nerve cells) than an adult brain (● Fig. 3.4).

● **FIGURE 3.2** This image, made with a scanning electron microscope, shows several pairs of human chromosomes. (Colors are artificial.)

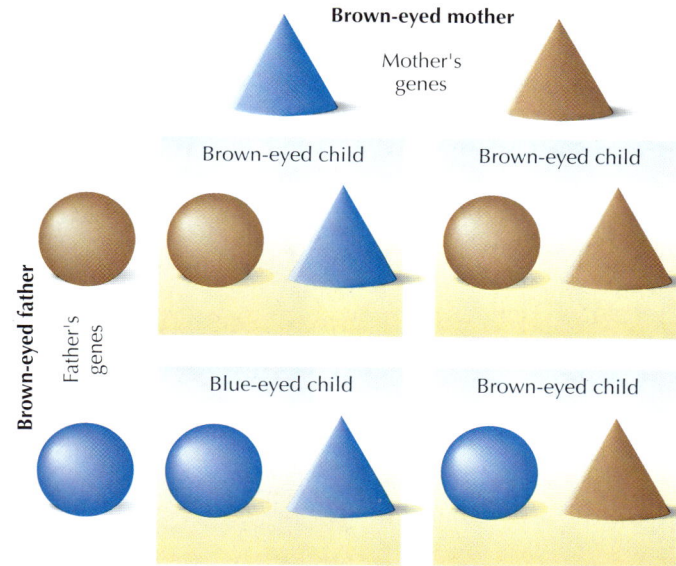

● **FIGURE 3.3** Gene patterns for children of brown-eyed parents, where each parent has one brown-eye gene and one blue-eye gene. Because the brown-eye gene is dominant, 1 child in 4 will be blue-eyed. Thus, there is a significant chance that two brown-eyed parents will have a blue-eyed child.

However, the newborn brain is highly *plastic* (capable of being altered by experience). During the first 3 years of life, millions of new connections form in the brain every day. At the same time, unused connections disappear. As a result, early learning environments literally shape the developing brain, through "blooming and pruning" of synapses (Nelson, 1999).

Environment ("nurture") refers to the sum of all external conditions that affect a person. The environments in which a child grows up can have a powerful impact on development. Humans today are genetically very similar to cave

---

Developmental psychology The study of progressive changes in behavior and abilities from conception to death.

Heredity ("nature") The transmission of physical and psychological characteristics from parents to offspring through genes.

DNA Deoxyribonucleic acid, a molecular structure that contains coded genetic information.

Chromosomes Thread-like "colored bodies" in the nucleus of each cell that are made up of DNA.

Genes Specific areas on a strand of DNA that carry hereditary information.

Dominant gene A gene whose influence will be expressed each time the gene is present.

Recessive gene A gene whose influence will be expressed only when it is paired with a second recessive gene.

Polygenic characteristics Personal traits or physical properties that are influenced by many genes working in combination.

Environment ("nurture") The sum of all external conditions affecting development, including especially the effects of learning.

dwellers who lived 30,000 years ago. Nevertheless, a bright baby born today could learn to become almost anything—a ballet dancer, an engineer, a gangsta rapper, or a biochemist who likes to paint in watercolors. But an Upper Paleolithic baby could have only become a hunter or food gatherer.

Prenatal Influences The interplay of nature and nurture actually starts before birth. Although the intrauterine environment (interior of the womb) is highly protected, environmental conditions can affect the developing child. For example, when Olivia was pregnant, Amy's fetal heart rate and movements increased when loud sounds or vibrations penetrated the womb (Kisilevsky et al., 2004).

If Olivia's health or nutrition had been poor, or if she had German measles, syphilis, or HIV, or used drugs, or was exposed to X-rays or atomic radiation, Amy's growth sequence might have been harmed. In such cases babies can suffer from **congenital problems,** or "birth defects." These environmental problems affect the developing fetus and become apparent at birth. In contrast, **genetic disorders** are inherited from parents. Examples are sickle-cell anemia, hemophilia, cystic fibrosis, muscular dystrophy, albinism, and some types of mental retardation.

Identical twins. Twins who share identical genes (identical twins) demonstrate the powerful influence of heredity. Even when they are reared apart, identical twins are strikingly alike in motor skills, physical development, and appearance. At the same time, twins are less alike as adults than they were as children, which shows environmental influences are at work (Larsson, Larsson, & Lichtenstein, 2004).

TABLE 3.1 Human Growth Sequence

PERIOD	DURATION	DESCRIPTIVE NAME
Prenatal Period	From conception to birth	
Germinal period	First 2 weeks after conception	Zygote
Embryonic period	2-8 weeks after conception	Embryo
Fetal period	From 8 weeks after conception to birth	Fetus
Neonatal Period	From birth to a few weeks after birth	Neonate
Infancy	From a few weeks after birth until child is walking securely; some children walk securely at less than a year, while others may not be able to until age 17-18 months	Infant
Early Childhood	From about 15-18 months until about 2-2½ years	Toddler
	From age 2-3 to about age 6	Preschool child
Middle Childhood	From about age 6 to age 12	School-age child
Pubescence	Period of about 2 years before puberty	
Puberty	Point of develoment at which biological changes of pubescence reach a climax marked by sexual maturity	
Adolescence	From the beginning of pubescence until full social maturity is reached (difficult to fix duration of this period)	Adolescent
Adulthood Young adulthood (19-25) Adulthood (26-40) Maturity (41 plus)	From adolescence to death; sometimes subdivided into other periods as shown at left	Adult
Senescence	No defined limit that would apply to all people; extremely variable; characterized by marked physiological and psychological deterioration	Adult (senile), "old age"

Note: There is no exact beginning or ending point for various growth periods. The ages are approximate, and each period may be thought of as blending into the next. (Table courtesy of Tom Bond.)

Neonate　　Six months　　Two years

● **FIGURE 3.4** A rapid increase in brain synapses continues until about age 4. At that point, children actually have more brain synapses than adults do. Then, after age 10, the number slowly declines, reaching adult levels at about age 16. (Reprinted by permission of the publisher from *The Postnatal Development of the Human Cerebral Cortex, Vols. I–III* by Jesse LeRoy Conel, Cambridge, Mass.: Harvard University Press, Copyright © 1935, 1975 by the President and Fellows of Harvard College.)

Because of the rapid growth of basic structures, the developing fetus is sensitive to a variety of diseases, drugs, and sources of radiation. This is especially true during the first trimester (3 months) of gestation (pregnancy).

Some of the typical features of children suffering from fetal alcohol syndrome (FAS) include a small nonsymmetrical head, a short nose, a flattened area between the eyes, oddly shaped eyes, and a thin upper lip. Many of these features become less noticeable by adolescence. However, mental retardation and other problems commonly follow the FAS child into adulthood. The child shown here represents a moderate example of FAS.

How is it possible for the embryo or the fetus to be harmed? No direct intermixing of blood takes place between a mother and her unborn child. Yet some substances—especially drugs—do reach the fetus. Anything capable of directly causing birth defects is called a **teratogen** (teh-RAT-uh-jen). Sometimes women are exposed to powerful teratogens, such as radiation, lead, pesticides, or polychlorinated biphenyls (PCBs), without knowing it. But pregnant women do have direct control over many teratogens. For example, a woman who takes cocaine runs a serious risk of injuring her fetus (Schuetze & Eiden, 2006). In short, when a pregnant woman takes drugs, her unborn child does too.

Unfortunately, in the United States this is one of the greatest risk factors facing unborn children (Coles & Black, 2006). If a mother is addicted to morphine, heroin, or methadone, her baby may be born with an addiction. Repeated heavy drinking during pregnancy causes *fetal alcohol syndrome (FAS)*. Affected infants have low birth weight, a small head, body defects, and facial malformations. Many also suffer from emotional, behavioral, and mental handicaps (Golden, 2005).

Tobacco is also harmful. Smoking during pregnancy greatly reduces oxygen to the fetus. Heavy smokers risk miscarrying or having premature, underweight babies who are more likely to die soon after birth. Children of smoking mothers score lower on tests of language and mental ability (Huijbregts et al., 2006). In other words, an unborn child's future can go "up in smoke." That goes for marijuana as well (Viveros et al., 2005).

Sensitive Periods Early experiences can have particularly lasting effects. For example, children who are abused may suffer lifelong emotional problems (Goodwin, Fergusson, & Horwood, 2005). At the same time, extra care can sometimes reverse the effects of a poor start in life (Bornstein & Tamis-LeMonda, 2001). In short, environmental forces guide human development, for better or worse, throughout life.

Congenital problems Problems or defects that originate during prenatal development in the womb.

Genetic disorders Problems caused by defects in the genes or by inherited characteristics.

Teratogen Radiation, a drug, or other substance capable of altering fetal development in nonheritable ways that cause birth defects.

Why do some experiences have more lasting effects than others? Part of the answer lies in **sensitive periods.** These are times when children are more susceptible to particular types of environmental influences. Events that occur during a sensitive period can permanently alter the course of development (Bruer, 2001). For example, forming a loving bond with a caregiver early in life seems to be crucial for optimal development. Likewise, babies who don't hear normal speech during their first year may have impaired language abilities (Thompson & Nelson, 2001).

Deprivation and Enrichment

Some environments can be described as *enriched* or *deprived*. **Deprivation** refers to a lack of normal nutrition, stimulation, comfort, or love. **Enrichment** exists when an environment is deliberately made more stimulating, loving, and so forth.

What happens when children suffer severe deprivation? Tragically, a few mistreated children have spent their first years in closets, attics, and other restricted environments. When first discovered, these children are usually mute, retarded, and emotionally damaged. Fortunately, such extreme deprivation is unusual.

Nevertheless, milder perceptual, intellectual, or emotional deprivation occurs in many families, especially those that must cope with poverty. Poverty can effect the development of children in at least two ways (Sobolewski & Amato, 2005). First, poor parents may not be able to give their children needed resources such as nutritious meals, health care, or learning materials (Bradley & Corwyn, 2002). As a result, impoverished children tend to be sick more often, their cognitive development lags, and they do poorly at school. Second, the stresses of poverty can also be hard on parents, leading to marriage problems, less positive parenting, and poorer parent-child relationships. The resulting emotional turmoil can damage a child's socioemotional development. In the extreme, it may increase the risk of mental illness and delinquent behavior (Bradley & Corwyn, 2002).

Adults who grew up in poverty often remain trapped in a vicious cycle of continued poverty. Because one in seven American families fall below the poverty line, this grim reality plays itself out in millions of American homes every day (Sobolewski & Amato, 2005).

Can an improved environment enhance development? To answer this question, psychologists have created *enriched environments* that are especially novel, complex, and stimulating. Enriched environments may be the "soil" from which brighter children grow. To illustrate, let's consider the effects of raising rats in a sort of "rat wonderland." The walls of their cages were decorated with colorful patterns, and each cage was filled with platforms, ladders, and cubbyholes. As adults, these rats were superior at learning mazes. In addition, they had larger, heavier brains, with a thicker cortex (Benloucif, Bennett, & Rosenzweig, 1995). Of course, it's a long leap from rats to people, but an actual increase in brain size is impressive. If extra stimulation can enhance the "intelligence" of a lowly rat, it's likely that human infants also benefit from enrichment. Many studies have shown that enriched environments improve abilities or enhance development. It would be wise for Tom and Olivia to make a point of nourishing Amy's mind, as well as her body (Beeber et al., 2007).

What can parents do to enrich a child's environment? They can encourage exploration and stimulating play by paying attention to what holds the baby's interest. It is better to "child-proof" a house than to strictly limit what a child can touch. There is also value in actively enriching sensory experiences. Infants are not vegetables. Babies should be surrounded by colors, music, people, and things to see, taste, smell, and touch. It makes perfect sense to take them outside, to hang mobiles over their cribs, to place mirrors nearby, to play music for them, or to rearrange their rooms now and then. Children progress most rapidly when they have responsive parents and stimulating play materials at home (Beeber et al., 2007). In light of this, it is wise to view all of childhood as a *relatively sensitive period* (Nelson, 1999).

Reaction Range

One way to visualize the interplay of heredity and environment is through the concept of **reaction range,** the limits that one's environment places on the effects of heredity (● Fig. 3.5). Let's suppose that Amy was born with genes for a normal level of intelligence. If Amy grows up in a deprived environment, she might well end up with lower than average adult intelligence. If Olivia and Tom provide her with an enriched environment, she will probably have normal, or even above normal, intelligence. While Amy might not be genetically capable of becoming a genius, the environment her parents provide for her will also determine her developmental path.

Children who grow up in poverty run a high risk of experiencing many forms of deprivation. There is evidence that lasting damage to social, emotional, and cognitive development occurs when children must cope with severe early deprivation.

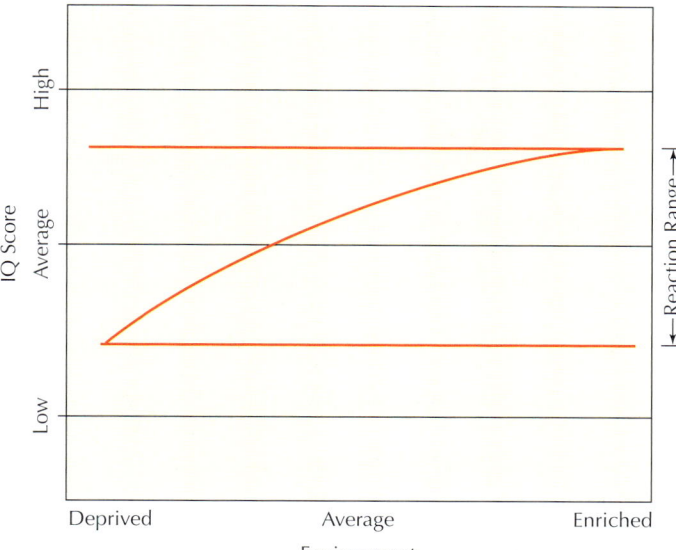

● **FIGURE 3.5** The effect of heredity on the development of human traits, such as intelligence, can often influenced by environmental circumstances. A child with average genes for intelligence growing up in an average environment might have an average IQ score as an adult. However, growing up in a deprived environment might result in a somewhat lower IQ score and growing up in an enriched environment might result in a somewhat higher IQ score. In this way, the environment sets a range within which our hereditary potential is actually expressed. This range is called the *reaction range*.

Reciprocal Influences Nurture often affects the expression of hereditary tendencies through ongoing reciprocal influences. A good example of such influences is the fact that growing infants influence their parents' behavior at the same time they are changed by it.

Newborn babies differ noticeably in **temperament.** This is the inherited, physical core of personality. It includes sensitivity, irritability, distractibility, and typical mood (Kagan, 2004). About 40 percent of all newborns are *easy children* who are relaxed and agreeable. Ten percent are *difficult children* who are moody, intense, and easily angered. *Slow-to-warm-up children* (about 15 percent) are restrained, unexpressive, or shy. The remaining children do not fit neatly into a single category (Chess & Thomas, 1986).

Because of differences in temperament, some babies are more likely than others to smile, cry, vocalize, reach out, or pay attention. As a result, babies rapidly become active participants in their own development. For example, Amy is an easy baby who smiles frequently and is easily fed. This encourages Olivia to touch, feed, and sing to Amy. Olivia's affection rewards Amy, causing her to smile more. Soon, a dynamic relationship blossoms between mother and child. Similarly, good parenting can reciprocally influence a very shy child who, in turn, becomes progressively less shy.

The reverse also occurs: Difficult children make parents unhappy and elicit more negative parenting (Parke, 2004).

Alternately, negative parenting can turn a moderately shy child into a very shy one. This suggests that inherited temperaments are dynamically modified by learning (Kagan, 2005).

A person's **developmental level** is his or her current state of physical, emotional, and intellectual development. To summarize, three factors combine to determine your developmental level at any stage of life. These are *heredity, environment,* and your *own behavior,* each tightly interwoven with the others.

MODULE 3.1 Summary

How do heredity and environment affect development?

- Heredity (nature) and environment (nurture) are interacting forces that are both necessary for human development. However, caregivers can only influence environment.
- Hereditary instructions are carried by the chromosomes and genes in each cell of the body. Most characteristics are polygenic and reflect the combined effects of dominant and recessive genes.
- Prenatal development is influenced by environmental factors, such as diseases, drugs, radiation, various teratogens, and the mother's diet, health, and emotions.
- During sensitive periods in development, infants are more sensitive to specific environmental influences.
- Early perceptual, intellectual, or emotional deprivation seriously retards development, whereas deliberate enrichment of the environment has a beneficial effect on infants.
- Temperament is hereditary. Most infants fall into one of three temperament categories: easy children, difficult children, and slow-to-warm-up children.
- A child's developmental level reflects heredity, environment, and the effects of the child's own behavior.

Sensitive period During development, a period of increased sensitivity to environmental influences. Also, a time during which certain events must take place for normal development to occur.
Deprivation In development, the loss or withholding of normal stimulation, nutrition, comfort, love, and so forth; a condition of lacking.
Enrichment In development, deliberately making an environment more stimulating, nutritional, comforting, loving, and so forth.
Reaction range The limits environment places on the effects of heredity.
Temperament The physical core of personality, including emotional and perceptual sensitivity, energy levels, typical mood, and so forth.
Developmental level An individual's current state of physical, emotional, and intellectual development.

KNOWLEDGE BUILDER

The Interplay of Heredity and Environment

Recite

1. Areas of the DNA molecule called genes are made up of dominant and recessive chromosomes. T or F?
2. Most inherited characteristics can be described as polygenic. T or F?
3. If one parent has a one dominant brown-eye gene and one recessive blue-eye gene and the other parent has two dominant brown-eye genes, what is the chance that their child will have blue eyes?
   a. 25 percent
   b. 50 percent
   c. 0 percent
   d. 75 percent
4. "Slow-to-warm-up" children can be described as restrained, unexpressive, or shy. T or F?
5. A _____ _____ is a time of increased reactivity to environmental influences.
6. As a child develops there is a continuous _____ between the forces of heredity and environment.

Reflect
Critical Thinking

7. Environmental influences can interact with hereditary programming in an exceedingly direct way. Can you guess what it is?

Relate

Can you think of clear examples of some ways in which heredity and environmental forces have combined to affect your development? What kind of temperament did you have as an infant? How did it affect your relationship with your parents or caregivers?

What advice would you give a friend who has just become pregnant? Be sure to consider the prenatal environment and sensitive periods.

Link

Internet addresses frequently change. To find the sites listed here, visit **http://www.thomsonedu.com/psychology/coon** for an updated list of Internet addresses and direct links to relevant sites.

- **Heredity Versus Environment** Read more about the interplay of nature and nurture.
- **Diving into the Gene Pool** From the Exploratorium, this site teaches about modern genetics.
- **Human Genome Project** Learn more about your human genetic heritage.

ANSWERS

1. F 2. T 3. c 4. T 5. sensitive period 6. interaction 7. Environmental conditions sometimes turn specific genes on or off, thus directly affecting the expression of genetic tendencies (Gottlieb, 1998).

MODULE 3.2 The Neonate and Early Maturation

CONTRARY TO COMMON BELIEF, newborn babies are not oblivious to their surroundings. Infants have mental capacities that continue to surprise researchers and delight parents. The emergence of many of these capacities, as well as a baby's physical abilities, is closely related to maturation of the brain, nervous system, and body. Likewise, a baby's early emotional life unfolds on a timetable that is largely controlled by maturation.

The Newborn—Baby, You're So Smart

SURVEY QUESTION: *What can newborn babies do?*

At birth the human *neonate* (NEE-oh-NATE: newborn infant) will die if not cared for by adults. Newborn babies cannot lift their heads, turn over, or feed themselves. Does this mean they are inert and unfeeling? Definitely not! Neonates like Amy can see, hear, smell, taste, and respond to pain and touch. Although their senses are less acute, babies are very responsive. Amy will follow a moving object with her eyes and will turn in the direction of sounds.

Amy also has a number of adaptive infant reflexes (Siegler, DeLoache, & Eisenberg, 2006). To elicit the *grasping reflex*, press an object in the neonate's palm and she will grasp it with surprising strength. Many infants, in fact, can hang from a raised bar, like little trapeze artists. The grasping reflex aids survival by helping infants avoid falling. You can observe the *rooting reflex* (reflexive head turning and nursing) by touching Amy's cheek. Immediately, she will turn toward your finger, as if searching for something.

How is such turning adaptive? The rooting reflex helps infants find a bottle or a breast. Then, when a nipple touches the infant's mouth, the *sucking reflex* (rhythmic nursing) helps her obtain needed food. Like other reflexes, this is a genetically programmed action. At the same time, food rewards nursing. Because of this, babies quickly learn to nurse more actively. Again, we see how the interplay of nature and nurture alters a baby's behavior.

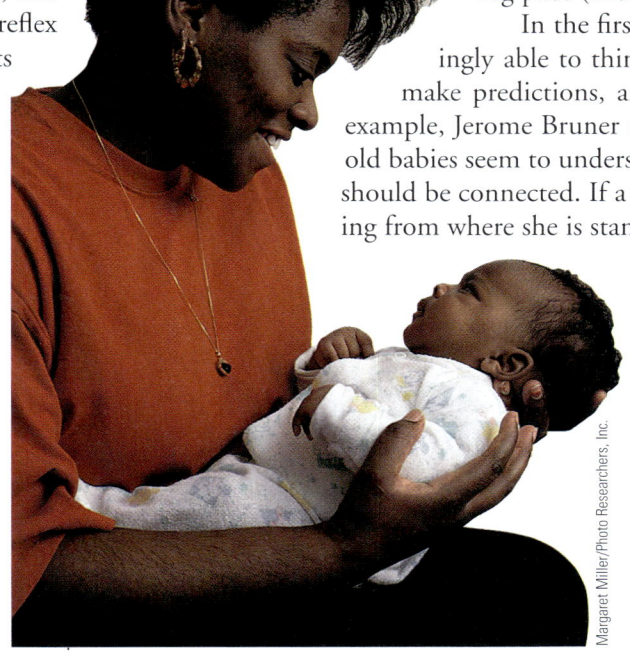
Newborn babies display a special interest in the human face. A preference for seeing their mother's face develops rapidly and encourages social interactions between mother and baby.

The *Moro reflex* is also interesting. If Amy's position is changed abruptly or if she is startled by a loud noise, she will make a hugging motion. This reaction has been compared to the movements baby monkeys use to cling to their mothers. (We leave it to the reader's imagination to decide if there is any connection.)

The World of the Neonate

Thirty years ago, many people thought of newborn babies as mere bundles of reflexes, like the ones just described. But infants are capable of much more. For example, psychologist Andrew Meltzoff has found that babies are born mimics (Meltzoff, 2005). ● Figure 3.6 shows Meltzoff as he sticks out his tongue, opens his mouth, and purses his lips at a 20-day-old girl. Will she imitate him? Videotapes of babies confirm that they imitate adult facial gestures. As early as 9 months of age, infants can imitate actions a day after seeing them (Heimann & Meltzoff, 1996). Such mimicry obviously aids rapid learning in infancy.

How intelligent are neonates? Babies are smarter than many people think. From the earliest days of life, babies are learning how the world works. They immediately begin to look, touch, taste, and otherwise explore their surroundings. From an evolutionary perspective, a baby's mind is designed to soak up information, which it does at an amazing pace (Meltzoff & Prinz, 2002).

In the first months of life, babies are increasingly able to think, to learn from what they see, to make predictions, and to search for explanations. For example, Jerome Bruner (1983) observed that 3- to 8-week-old babies seem to understand that a person's voice and body should be connected. If a baby hears his mother's voice coming from where she is standing, the baby will remain calm. If her voice comes from a loudspeaker several feet away, the baby will become agitated and begin to cry.

Another look into the private world of infants can be drawn from testing their vision. However, such testing is a challenge because infants cannot talk. Robert Fantz invented a device called a *looking chamber* to find out what infants can see and what holds their attention (● Fig. 3.7*a*). Imagine that Amy is placed on her back inside the chamber, fac-

● **FIGURE 3.6** Infant imitation. In the top row of photos, Andrew Meltzoff makes facial gestures at an infant. The bottom row records the infant's responses. Videotapes of Meltzoff and of tested infants helped ensure objectivity. (Photos courtesy of Andrew N. Meltzoff.)

ing a lighted area above. Next, two objects are placed in the chamber. By observing the movements of Amy's eyes and the images they reflect, we can tell what she is looking at. Such tests show that adult vision is about 30 times sharper, but babies can see large patterns, shapes, and edges.

Fantz found that 3-day-old babies prefer complex patterns, such as checkerboards and bull's-eyes, to simpler colored rectangles. Other researchers have learned that infants are excited by circles, curves, and bright lights (● Fig. 3.7b) (Brown, 1990). Immediately after birth, Amy will be aware of changes in the position of objects (Slater et al., 1991). When she is 6 months old, she will be able to recognize categories of objects that differ in shape or color. By 9 months of age she will be able to tell the difference between dogs and birds or other groups of animals (Mandler & McDonough, 1998). By 1 year of age, she will see as well as her parents (Sigelman & Rider, 2006). So, there really is a person inside that little body!

Neonates can most clearly see objects about a foot away from them. It is as if they are best prepared to see the people who love and care for them (Gopnik, Meltzoff, & Kuhl, 2000). Perhaps that's why babies have a special fascination with human faces. Just *hours* after they are born, babies begin to prefer seeing their mother's face, rather than a stranger's (Walton, Bower, & Bower, 1992). When babies are only 2 to 5 days old, they will pay more attention to a person who is gazing directly at them, rather than one who is looking away (Farroni et al., 2004) (● Fig. 3.7c).

In a looking chamber, most infants will spend more time looking at a human face pattern than a scrambled face or a

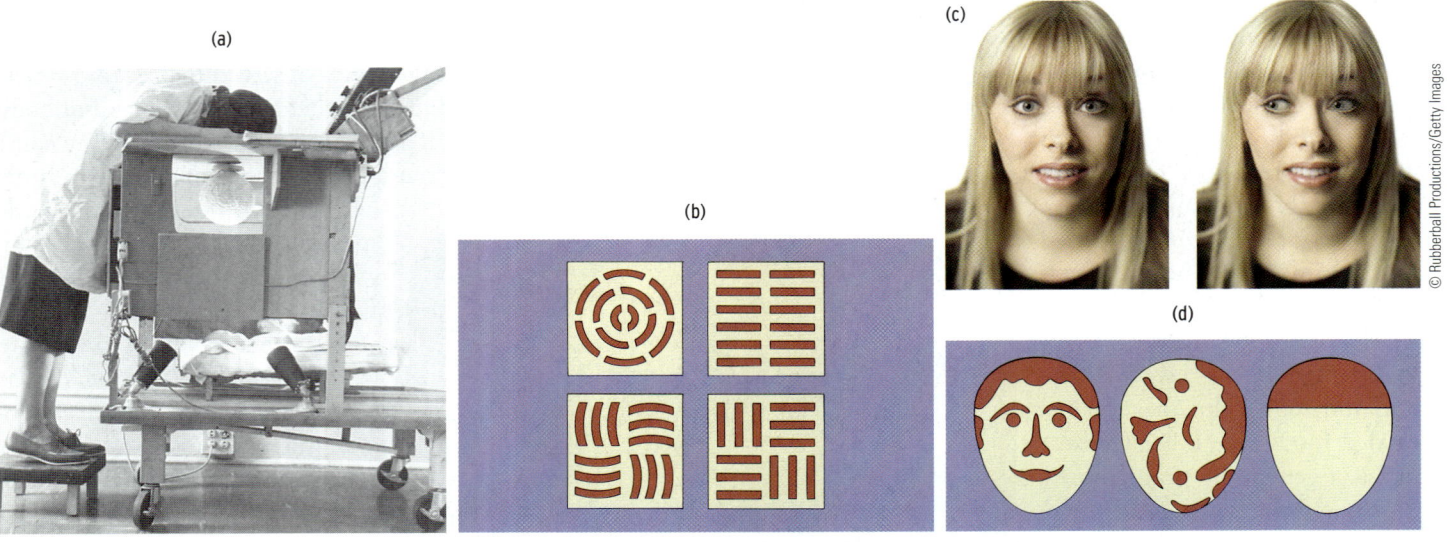

● **FIGURE 3.7** (a) Eye movements and fixation points of infants are observed in Fantz's "looking chamber." (b) Thirteen-week-old infants prefer concentric and curved patterns like those on the left to nonconcentric and straight-line patterns like those on the right. (c) Infants look at the normal face longer than at the scrambled face and at both faces longer than at the design on the right. (Photo *a* courtesy of David Linton. Drawing from "The Origin of Form Perception" by Robert L. Fantz, Copyright © 1961 by Scientific American, Inc. All rights reserved.)

● **FIGURE 3.8** Motor development. Most infants follow an orderly pattern of motor development. Although the order in which children progress is similar, there are large individual differences in the ages at which each ability appears. The ages listed are averages for American children. It is not unusual for many of the skills to appear 1 or 2 months earlier than average or several months later (Harris & Liebert, 1991). Parents should not be alarmed if a child's behavior differs some from the average.

colored oval (● Fig. 3.7*d*). When real human faces are used, infants prefer familiar faces to unfamiliar faces. However, this reverses at about age 2. At that time, unusual objects begin to interest the child. For instance, in a classic study Jerome Kagan (1971) showed face masks to 2-year-olds. Kagan found that the toddlers were fascinated by a face with eyes on the chin and a nose in the middle of the forehead. He believes the babies' interest came from a need to understand why the scrambled face differed from what they had come to expect. Such behavior is further evidence that babies actively try to make sense of their surroundings (Gopnik, Meltzoff, & Kuhl, 2000).

Early Maturation—Grow Baby Grow

SURVEY QUESTION: *What influence does maturation have on early development?*

The emergence of many basic abilities is closely tied to **maturation** (physical growth and development of the body, brain, and nervous system). Maturation will be evident, for example, as Amy learns motor skills, such as crawling and walking. Of course, the *rate* of maturation varies from child to child. Nevertheless, the *order* of maturation is almost universal. For instance, Amy will be able to sit without support from Tom before she has matured enough to crawl. Indeed,

infants around the world typically sit before they crawl, crawl before they stand, and stand before they walk (● Fig. 3.8).

What about my weird cousin Emo who never crawled? Like cousin Emo, a few children substitute rolling, creeping, or shuffling for crawling. A very few move directly from sitting to standing and walking. Even so, their motor development is orderly. In general, muscular control spreads in a pattern that is *cephalocaudal* (SEF-eh-lo-KOD-ul: from head to toe) and *proximodistal* (PROK-seh-moe-DIS-tul: from the center of the body to the extremities). Even if cousin Emo flunked Elementary Crawling, his motor development followed the standard top-down, center-outward pattern (Piek, 2006).

Motor Development

Although maturation has a big impact, motor skills don't simply "emerge." Amy must learn to control her actions. When babies are beginning to crawl or walk, they actively try new movements and select those that work. Amy's first efforts may be flawed—a wobbly crawl or some shaky first steps. However, with practice, babies "tune" their movements to be smoother and more effective. Such learning is evident from

> **Maturation** The physical growth and development of the body and nervous system.

the very first months of life (Piek, 2006; Thelen, 2000). (See ● Fig. 3.9.)

Readiness At what ages will Amy be ready to feed herself, to walk alone, or to say goodbye to diapers? Such milestones tend to be governed by a child's **readiness** for rapid learning. That is, minimum levels of maturation must occur before some skills can be learned. Parents are asking for failure when they try to force a child to learn skills too early (Schum et al., 2002). It is impossible, for instance, to teach children to walk or use a toilet before they have matured enough to control their bodies.

Consider the eager parents who toilet trained an 18-month-old child in 10 trying weeks of false alarms and "accidents." If they had waited until the child was 24 months old, they might have succeeded in just 3 weeks. Parents may control when toilet training starts, but maturation tends to dictate when it will be completed (Schum et al., 2002). The average age for *completed* toilet training is about 3 years (girls a little earlier, boys a little later) (Schum et al., 2001). So why fight nature? (The wet look is in.)

Emotional Development

Early emotional development also follows a pattern closely tied to maturation (Panksepp & Pasqualini, 2005). Even the basic emotions of *anger, fear,* and *joy*—which appear to be unlearned—take time to develop. General *excitement* is the only emotion newborn infants clearly express. However, as Tom and Olivia can tell you, a baby's emotional life blossoms rapidly. One researcher (Bridges, 1932) observed that all the basic human emotions appear before age 2. Bridges found that emotions appear in a consistent order and that the first basic split is between pleasant and unpleasant emotions (● Fig. 3.10).

Experts do not yet agree on how quickly emotions unfold (Oster, 2005). For example, psychologist Carroll Izard thinks that infants can express several basic emotions as early as 10 weeks of age. When Izard looks carefully at the faces of babies, he sees abundant signs of emotion. (See ● Fig. 3.11.) The most common infant expression, he found, is not excitement, but *interest*—followed by *joy, anger,* and *sadness* (Izard et al., 1995).

If Izard is right, then emotions are "hardwired" by heredity and related to evolution. Perhaps that's why smiling is one of a baby's most common reactions. Smiling probably helps babies survive by inviting parents to care for them (Izard et al., 1995).

At first, a baby's smiling is haphazard. By the age of 8 to 12 months, however, infants smile more frequently when another person is nearby (Jones & Hong, 2001). This **social smile** is especially rewarding to parents. Infants can even use their social smile to communicate interest in an object, like the time Amy smiled when her mother held up her favorite teddy bear (Venezia et al., 2004). On the other hand, when new parents see and hear a crying baby, they feel annoyed, irritated, disturbed, or unhappy. Babies the world over, it seems, rapidly become capable of letting others know what they like and dislike. (Prove this to yourself sometime by driving a baby buggy.)

● **FIGURE 3.9** Psychologist Carolyn Rovee-Collier has shown that babies as young as 3 months old can learn to control their movements. In her experiments, babies lie on their backs under a colorful crib mobile. A ribbon is tied around the baby's ankle and connected to the mobile. Whenever babies spontaneously kick their legs, the mobile jiggles and rattles. Within a few minutes, infants learn to kick faster. Their reward for kicking is a chance to see the mobile move (Hayne & Rovee-Collier, 1995).

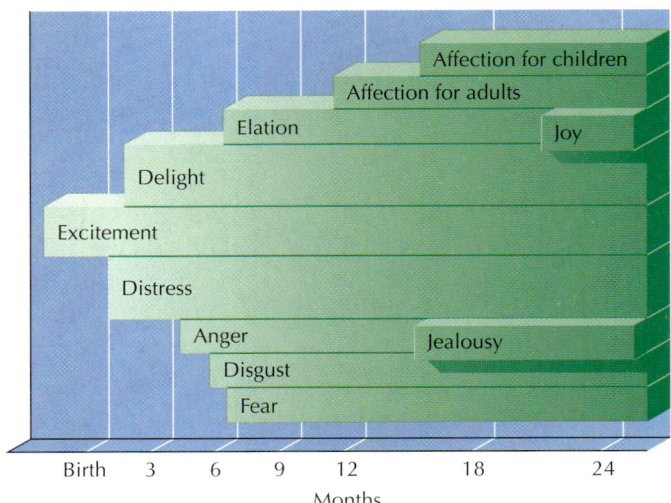

● **FIGURE 3.10** The traditional view of infancy holds that emotions are rapidly differentiated from an initial capacity for excitement. (After K. M. B. Bridges, 1932. Reprinted by permission of the Society for Research in Child Development, Inc.)

● **FIGURE 3.11** Infants display many of the same emotional expressions as adults do. Carroll Izard believes such expressions show that distinct emotions appear within the first months of life. Other theorists argue that specific emotions come into focus more gradually, as an infant's nervous system matures. Either way, parents can expect to see a full range of basic emotions by the end of a baby's first year.

With dazzling speed, human infants are transformed from helpless babies to independent persons. Early growth is extremely rapid. By her third year, Amy will have a unique personality and she will be able to stand, walk, talk, and explore. At no other time after birth does development proceed more rapidly. During the same period, Amy's relationships with other people will expand as well. Before we explore that topic, here's a chance to review what you've learned.

MODULE 3.2 Summary

What can newborn babies do?

- Infant development is strongly influenced by heredity. However, environmental factors such as nutrition, parenting, and learning are also important.
- The human neonate has a number of adaptive reflexes, including the grasping, rooting, sucking, and Moro reflexes. Neonates begin to learn immediately, and they appear to be aware of the effects of their actions.
- Tests in a looking chamber reveal a number of visual preferences in the newborn. The neonate is drawn to bright lights and circular or curved designs.
- Infants prefer human face patterns, especially familiar faces. In later infancy, interest in the unfamiliar emerges.

What influence does maturation have on early development?

- Maturation of the body and nervous system underlies the orderly development of motor skills, cognitive abilities, emotions, and language.
- The rate of maturation varies from person to person. Also, learning contributes greatly to the development of basic motor skills.
- Emotions develop in a consistent order, starting with generalized excitement in newborn babies. Three of the basic emotions—fear, anger, and joy—may be unlearned.
- Many early skills are subject to the principle of readiness.

Readiness A condition that exists when maturation has advanced enough to allow the rapid acquisition of a particular skill.
Social smile Smiling elicited by social stimuli, such as seeing a parent's face.

KNOWLEDGE BUILDER

The Neonate and Early Maturation

Recite

1. If an infant is startled, he or she will make movements similar to an embrace. This is known as the
   a. grasping reflex b. rooting reflex c. Moro reflex d. adaptive reflex
2. During infancy, a capacity for imitating others first becomes evident at about 9 months of age. T or F?
3. After age 2, infants tested in a looking chamber show a marked preference for familiar faces and simpler designs. T or F?
4. The orderly sequence observed in the unfolding of many basic responses can be attributed to _____.
5. General excitement or interest is the clearest emotional response present in newborn infants, but meaningful expressions of delight and distress appear soon after. T or F?
6. Neonates display a social smile as early as 10 days after birth. T or F?

Reflect

Critical Thinking

7. If you were going to test newborn infants to see if they prefer their own mother's face to that of a stranger, what precautions would you take?

Relate

What infant reflexes have you observed? How would maturation affect the chances of teaching an infant to eat with a spoon? Can you give an example of how heredity and environment interact during motor development?

To know what a baby is feeling would it be more helpful to be able to detect delight and distress (Bridges) or joy, anger, and sadness (Izard)?

Link

Internet addresses frequently change. To find the sites listed here, visit **http://www.thomsonedu.com/psychology/coon** for an updated list of Internet addresses and direct links to relevant sites.

- **The Parent's Page** Comprehensive site full of links for expectant couples and new parents.
- **Parenthood.com** A comprehensive site for parents.
- **Crack Babies** A photostory by Ken Kobre.

ANSWERS

1. c 2. F 3. F 4. maturation 5. T 6. F 7. In one study of the preferences of newborns, the hair color and complexion of strangers was matched to that of the mothers. Also, only the mother's or stranger's face was visible during testing. And finally, a scent was used to mask olfactory (smell) cues so that an infant's preference could not be based on the mother's familiar odor (Bushnell, Sai, & Mullin, 1989).

MODULE 3.3 Social Development in Childhood

INFANTS begin to develop self-awareness and to become aware of others at about the same time they first form an emotional bond with an adult. Each of these developments is an important step toward entering the social world. Parents are the most important influences in early social development. Later, playing with other children begins to extend a child's social life beyond the family.

Social Development—Baby, I'm Stuck on You

SURVEY QUESTION: *Of what significance is a child's emotional bond with parents?*

Like all humans, babies are social creatures. Their early **social development** lays a foundation for relationships with parents, siblings, friends, and relatives. A first basic step into the social world involves becoming aware of oneself as a person. When you look in a mirror, you recognize the image staring back as your own—except, perhaps, early on Monday mornings. Like many such events, initial self-awareness depends on maturation of the nervous system. In a typical test of self-recognition, infants are shown images of themselves on a TV. Most infants have to be 18 months old before they recognize themselves (Nielsen & Dissanayake, 2004).

A sense of self, or self-awareness, develops at about age 18 months. Before children develop self-awareness, they do not recognize their own image in a mirror. Typically, they think they are looking at another child. Some children hug the child in the mirror or go behind it looking for the child they see there (Lewis, 1995).

Attachment

The real core of social development is found in the **emotional attachment**, or close emotional bond, that babies form with their primary caregivers. There is a sensitive period (roughly the first year of life) during which this must occur for optimal development. Returning to Amy's story, we find that attachment keeps her close to Olivia, who provides safety, stimulation, and a secure "home base" from which Amy can go exploring.

Mothers usually begin to feel attached to their baby before birth. For their part, as babies mature, they become more and more capable of bonding with their mothers. For the first few months, babies respond more or less equally to everyone. By 2 or 3 months, most babies prefer their mothers to strangers. By around 7 months, babies generally become truly attached to their mothers, crawling after her if they can. Shortly thereafter they also begin to form attachments to other people as well, such as father, grandparents, or siblings (Sigelman & Rider, 2006).

A direct sign that an emotional bond has formed appears around 8 to 12 months of age. At that time Amy will display **separation anxiety** (crying and signs of fear) when she is left alone or with a stranger. Mild separation anxiety is normal. When it is more intense, it may reveal a problem. At some point in their lives, about 1 in 20 children suffer from *separation anxiety disorder* (Dick-Niederhauser & Silverman, 2006). These children are miserable when they are separated

Most parents are familiar with the storm of crying that sometimes occurs when babies are left alone at bedtime. Bedtime distress can be a mild form of separation anxiety. As many parents know, it is often eased by the presence of "security objects," such as a stuffed animal or favorite blanket (Donate-Bartfield & Passman, 2004).

Social development The development of self-awareness, attachment to parents or caregivers, and relationships with other children and adults.
Emotional attachment An especially close emotional bond that infants form with their parents, caregivers, or others.
Separation anxiety Distress displayed by infants when they are separated from their parents or principal caregivers.

from their parents, whom they cling to or constantly follow. Some fear that they will get lost and never see their parents again. Many refuse to go to school, which can be a serious handicap. Children tend to grow out of the disorder (Kearney et al., 2003), but if separation anxiety is intense or lasts for more than a month, parents should seek professional help for their child (Masi, Mucci, & Millepiedi, 2001).

Attachment Quality According to psychologist Mary Ainsworth (1913–1999), the quality of attachment is revealed by how babies act when their mothers return after a brief separation. Infants who are **securely attached** have a stable and positive emotional bond. They are upset by the mother's absence and seek to be near her when she returns. **Insecure-avoidant** infants have an anxious emotional bond. They tend to turn away from the mother when she returns. **Insecure-ambivalent** attachment is also an anxious emotional bond. In this case, babies have mixed feelings: They both seek to be near the returning mother and angrily resist contact with her. (See ● Fig. 3.12.)

Attachment can have lasting effects. Infants who are securely attached at the age of 1 year show more resiliency, curiosity, problem-solving ability, and social skill in preschool (Collins & Gunnar, 1990). In contrast, attachment failures can be quite damaging. Consider, for example, the plight of children raised in severely overcrowded Romanian orphanages. These children got almost no attention from adults for the first year or two of their lives. Some have now been adopted by American and Canadian families, but many are poorly attached to their new parents. Some, for instance, will wander off with strangers; they are anxious and remote, and they don't like to be touched or make eye contact with others (O'Conner et al., 2003). In short, for some children, a lack of affectionate care early in life leaves a lasting emotional impact well into adulthood. (See "What's Your Attachment Style?")

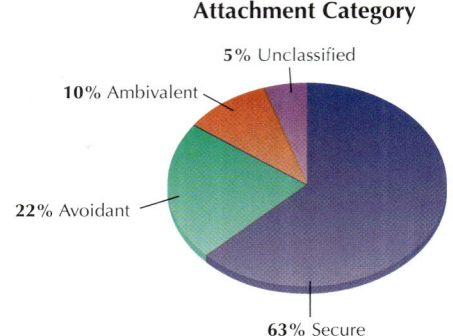

● **FIGURE 3.12** In the United States, about two thirds of all children from middle-class families are securely attached. About 1 child in 3 is insecurely attached. (Percentages are approximate. From Kaplan, 1998.)

Promoting Secure Attachment The key to secure attachment is a mother who is accepting and sensitive to her baby's signals and rhythms. Poor attachment occurs when a mother's actions are inappropriate, inadequate, intrusive, overstimulating, or rejecting. An example is the mother who tries to play with a drowsy infant or who ignores a baby who is looking at her and vocalizing. The link between sensitive caregiving and secure attachment appears to apply to all cultures (Posada et al., 2002).

What about attachment to fathers? Fathers of securely attached infants tend to be outgoing, agreeable, and happy in their marriage. In general, a warm family atmosphere—one that includes sensitive mothering *and* fathering—produces secure children (Belsky, 1996).

Day Care

Does commercial day care interfere with the quality of attachment? It depends on the quality of day care. Overall, *high-quality* day care does not adversely affect attachment to parents (National Institute of Child Health and Human Development, 1999). In fact, children in high-quality day care tend to have better relationships with their mothers and fewer behavior problems. They also have better cognitive skills and language abilities (Burchinal et al., 2000; Vandell, 2004). Thus, high-quality day care can actually improve children's social and mental skills (Mercer, 2006).

However, all the positive effects just noted are *reversed* for low-quality day care. Poor-quality day care can actually create behavior problems that didn't exist beforehand (Pierrehumbert et al., 2002). Parents are wise to carefully evaluate and monitor the quality of day care their children receive.

What should parents look for when they evaluate the quality of child care? Low-quality day care *is* risky and it *may* weaken attachment. Parents seeking quality should insist on *at least* the following: (1) a small number of children per caregiver, (2) small overall group size (12 to 15), (3) trained caregivers, (4) minimal staff turnover, and (5) stable, consistent care (Howes, 1997). (Also, avoid any child-care center with the words *zoo, menagerie,* or *stockade* in its name.)

Attachment and Affectional Needs

A baby's **affectional needs** (needs for love and affection) are every bit as important as more obvious needs for food, water, and physical care. All things considered, creating a bond of trust and affection between the infant and at least one other person is a key event during the first year of life. Parents are sometimes afraid of "spoiling" babies with too much attention, but for the first year or two this is nearly impossible. In fact, a later capacity to experience warm and loving relationships may depend on it.

DISCOVERING PSYCHOLOGY

What's Your Attachment Style?

Do our first attachments continue to affect us as adults? Some psychologists believe they do, by influencing how we relate to friends and lovers (Bridges, 2003; Sroufe et al., 2005). Read the following statements and see which best describes your adult relationships.

Secure Attachment Style

In general, I think most other people are well intentioned and trustworthy.
I find it relatively easy to get close to others.
I am comfortable relying on others and having others depend on me.
I don't worry much about being abandoned by others.
I am comfortable when other people want to get close to me emotionally.

Avoidant Attachment Style

I tend to pull back when things don't go well in a relationship.
I am somewhat skeptical about the idea of true love.
I have difficulty trusting my partner in a romantic relationship.
Other people tend to be too eager to seek commitment from me.
I get a little nervous if anyone gets too close emotionally.

Ambivalent Attachment Style

I have often felt misunderstood and unappreciated in my romantic relationships.
My friends and lovers have been somewhat unreliable.
I love my romantic partner but I worry that she or he doesn't really love me.
I would like to be closer to my romantic partner, but I'm not sure I trust her or him.

Do any of the preceding statements sound familiar? If so, they may describe your adult attachment style. Most adults have a secure attachment style that is marked by caring, supportiveness, and understanding. However, it's not unusual to have an avoidant attachment style that reflects a tendency to resist intimacy and commitment to others (Collins et al., 2002). An ambivalent attachment style is marked by mixed feelings about love and friendship (Tidwell, Reis, & Shaver, 1996). Do you see any similarities between your present relationships and your attachment experiences as a child?

Parental Influences—Life with Mom and Dad

SURVEY QUESTION: *How important are parenting styles?*

From the first few years of life, when caregivers are the center of a child's world, through to adulthood, the style and quality of mothering and fathering are very important.

Parenting Styles

Psychologist Diana Baumrind (1991, 2005) has studied the effects of three major **parental styles,** which are identifiable patterns of parental caretaking and interaction with children. See if you recognize the styles she describes.

Authoritarian parents enforce rigid rules and demand strict obedience to authority. Typically they view children as having few rights but adult-like responsibilities. The child is expected to stay out of trouble and to accept, without question, what parents regard as right or wrong. ("Do it because I say so.") The children of authoritarian parents are usually obedient and self-controlled. But they also tend to be emotionally stiff, withdrawn, apprehensive, and lacking in curiosity.

Overly permissive parents give little guidance, allow too much freedom, or don't hold children accountable for their actions. Typically, the child has rights similar to an adult's but few responsibilities. Rules are not enforced, and the child usually gets his or her way. ("Do whatever you want.") Permissive parents tend to produce dependent, immature children who misbehave frequently. Such children are aimless and likely to "run amok."

Baumrind describes **authoritative parents** as those who supply firm and consistent guidance, combined with love and affection. Such parents balance their own rights with those of their children. They control their children's behavior in a caring, responsive, nonauthoritarian way. ("Do it for this reason.") Effective parents are firm and consistent, not harsh or rigid. In general, they encourage the child to act responsibly, to think, and to make good decisions. This style produces

---

Secure attachment A stable and positive emotional bond.
Insecure-avoidant attachment An anxious emotional bond marked by a tendency to avoid reunion with a parent or caregiver.
Insecure-ambivalent attachment An anxious emotional bond marked by both a desire to be with a parent or caregiver and some resistance to being reunited.
Affectional needs Emotional needs for love and affection.
Parental styles Identifiable patterns of parental caretaking and interaction with children.
Authoritarian parents Parents who enforce rigid rules and demand strict obedience to authority.
Overly permissive parents Parents who give little guidance, allow too much freedom, or do not require the child to take responsibility.
Authoritative parents Parents who supply firm and consistent guidance combined with love and affection.

"All right now, give Mommy the super-glue."

children who are *resilient* (good at bouncing back after bad experiences) and develop the strengths they need to thrive even in difficult circumstances (Kim-Cohen et al., 2004; Masten, 2001). The children of authoritative parents are competent, self-controlled, independent, assertive, and inquiring. They know how to manage their emotions and use positive coping skills (Eisenberg et al., 2003; Lynch et al., 2004). To read more about effective parenting, see this chapter's "Psychology in Action" module.

Maternal and Paternal Influences

Don't mothers and fathers parent differently? Yes. Although **maternal influences** (all the effects a mother has on her child) generally have a greater impact, fathers do make a unique contribution to parenting (Santrock, 2007). Although fathers are spending more time with their children, mothers still do most of the nurturing and caretaking, especially of young children (Craig, 2006).

Studies of **paternal influences** (the sum of all effects a father has on his child) reveal that fathers are more likely to play with their children and tell them stories. In contrast, mothers are typically responsible for the physical and emotional care of their children (● Fig. 3.13).

It might seem that the father's role as a playmate makes him less important. Not so. Amy's playtime with Tom is actually very valuable. From birth onward, fathers pay more visual attention to children than mothers do. Fathers are much more tactile (lifting, tickling, and handling the baby), more physically arousing (engaging in rough-and-tumble play),

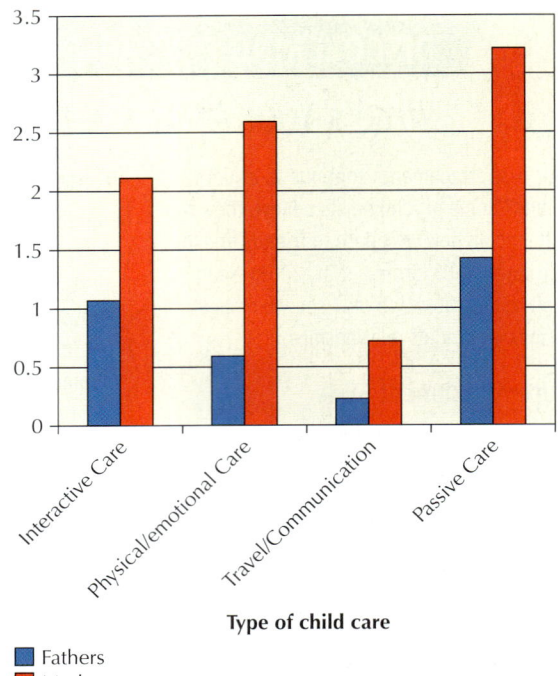

● **FIGURE 3.13** Mother-child and father-child interactions. This graph shows what occurred on routine days in a sample of more than 1,400 Australian homes. Mothers spend about twice as long each day on child care, compared with fathers. Further, mothers spend more time on physical and emotional care (e.g., feeding, bathing, soothing) than on interactive care (e.g., playing, reading, activities); fathers show the reverse pattern. Finally, mothers spend more time on travel (e.g., driving children to sports or music lessons), communication (e.g., talking to teachers about their children), and passive care (e.g., supervising children while they play). (Adapted from Craig, 2006.)

and more likely to engage in unusual play (imitating the baby, for example) (Crawley & Sherrod, 1984; Paquette et al., 2003). In comparison, mothers speak to infants more, play more conventional games (such as peekaboo), and, as noted, spend much more time in care giving. Young children

Fathering typically makes a contribution to early development that differs in emphasis from mothering.

who spend a lot of time playing with their fathers tend to be more competent in many ways (Tamis-LeMonda, et al., 2004).

Overall, fathers can be as affectionate, sensitive, and responsive as mothers are. Nevertheless, infants and children tend to get very different views of males and females. Females, who offer comfort, nurturance, and verbal stimulation, tend to be close at hand. Males come and go, and when they are present, action, exploration, and risk-taking prevail. It's no wonder, then, that the parental styles of mothers and fathers have a major impact on children's gender role development (Lindsay, Mize, & Pettit, 1997; Videon, 2005).

Ethnic Differences: Four Flavors of Parenting

Do ethnic differences in parenting affect children in distinctive ways? Diana Baumrind's work provides a good overall summary of the effects of parenting. However, her conclusions are probably most valid for families whose roots lie in Europe. Child-rearing in other ethnic groups often reflects different customs and beliefs. Cultural differences are especially apparent with respect to the meaning attached to a child's behavior. Is a particular behavior "good" or "bad"? Should it be encouraged or discouraged? The answer will depend greatly on parents' cultural values (Leyendecker et al., 2005).

Making generalizations about groups of people is always risky. Nevertheless, some typical differences in child-rearing patterns have been observed in North American ethnic communities (Kaplan, 1998; Parke, 2004).

African-American Families Traditional African-American values emphasize loyalty and interdependence among family members, security, developing a positive identity, and not giving up in the face of adversity. African-American parents typically stress obedience and respect for elders. Child discipline tends to be fairly strict (Parke, 2004), but many African-American parents see this as a necessity, especially if they live in urban areas where safety is a concern. Self-reliance, resourcefulness, and an ability to take care of oneself in difficult situations are also qualities that African-American parents seek to promote in their children.

Hispanic Families Like African-American parents, Hispanic parents tend to have relatively strict standards of discipline. They also place a high value on family values, family pride, and loyalty. Hispanic families are typically affectionate and indulgent toward younger children. However, as children grow older, they are expected to learn social skills and to be calm, obedient, courteous, and respectful. In fact, such social skills may be valued more than cognitive skills (Delgado & Ford, 1998). In addition, Hispanic parents tend to stress cooperation more than competition. Such values can put Hispanic children at a disadvantage in highly competitive, European-American culture.

Asian-American Families Asian cultures tend to be group oriented, and they emphasize interdependence among individuals. In contrast, Western cultures value individual effort and independence. This difference is often reflected in Asian-American child-rearing practices (Chao & Tseng, 2002). Asian-American children are taught that their behavior can bring either pride or shame to the family. Therefore, they are obliged to set aside their own desires when the greater good of the family is at stake (Parke, 2004). Parents tend to act as teachers who encourage hard work, moral behavior, and achievement. For the first few years, parenting is lenient and permissive. However, after about age 5, Asian-American parents begin to expect respect, obedience, self-control, and self-discipline from their children.

In other ethnic communities, norms for effective parenting often differ in subtle ways from parenting styles in Euro-American culture.

Maternal influences The aggregate of all psychological effects mothers have on their children.

Paternal influences The aggregate of all psychological effects fathers have on their children.

Arab-American Families In Middle Eastern cultures, children are expected to be polite, obedient, disciplined, and conforming. Punishment generally consists of spankings, teasing, or shaming in front of others. Arab-American fathers tend to be strong authority figures who demand obedience so that the family will not be shamed by a child's bad behavior. Success, generosity, and hospitality are highly valued in Arab-American culture. The pursuit of family honor encourages hard work, thrift, conservatism, and educational achievement. The welfare of the family is emphasized over individual identity. Thus, Arab-American children are raised to respect their parents, members of their extended family, and other adults as well (Erickson & Al-Timimi, 2001; Medhus, 2001).

Implications Child-rearing is done in a remarkable variety of ways around the world. In fact, many of the things we do in North America, such as forcing young children to sleep alone, would be considered odd or wrong in other cultures. In the final analysis, parenting can only be judged if we know what culture or ethnic community a child is being prepared to enter (Leyendecker et al., 2005).

MODULE 3.3 Summary

Of what significance is a child's emotional bond with parents?
- Opportunities for social interaction increase as infants develop self-awareness and they begin to actively seek guidance from adults.
- Emotional attachment of human infants is a critical early event.
- Infant attachment is reflected by separation anxiety. The quality of attachment can be classified as secure, insecure-avoidant, or insecure-ambivalent.
- Secure attachment is fostered by consistent care from parents who are sensitive to a baby's signals and rhythms.
- High-quality day care is not harmful and can even be helpful to preschool children. Low-quality care can be risky.
- Meeting a baby's affectional needs is as important as meeting needs for physical care.

How important are parenting styles?
- Studies suggest that parental styles have a substantial impact on emotional and intellectual development.
- Three major parental styles are authoritarian, permissive, and authoritative (effective). Authoritative parenting appears to benefit children the most.
- Whereas mothers typically emphasize care giving, fathers tend to function as playmates for infants. Both care-giving styles contribute to the competence of young children.
- The ultimate success of various parenting styles depends on what culture or ethnic community a child will enter.
- Parenting styles vary across cultures.

KNOWLEDGE BUILDER

Social Development in Childhood

Recite

1. Clear signs of self-awareness or self-recognition are evident in most infants by the time they reach 8 months of age. T or F?
2. The development of separation anxiety in an infant corresponds to the formation of an attachment to parents. T or F?
3. High-quality day care can actually improve children's social and mental skills. T or F?
4. Fathers are more likely to act as playmates for their children, rather than caregivers. T or F?
5. According to Diana Baumrind's research, effective parents are authoritarian in their approach to their children's behavior. T or F?
6. Asian-American parents tend to be more individually oriented than parents whose ethnic roots are European. T or F?

Reflect
Critical Thinking

7. Can you think of another way to tell if infants have self-awareness?
8. Can emotional bonding begin before birth?
9. If power assertion is a poor way to discipline children, why do so many parents use it?

Relate

Do you think that your experiences as a child, such as your early attachment pattern, really affect your life as an adult? Can you think of any examples from your own life?

Do you know any parents who have young children and who are authoritarian, permissive, or authoritative? What are their children like?

Do you think parenting depends on ethnicity? If so, why? If not, why not?

Link

Internet addresses frequently change. To find the sites listed here, visit http://www.thomsonedu.com/psychology/coon for an updated list of Internet addresses and direct links to relevant sites.

- **I'm Embarrassed!** Read more about the development of self-awareness in young children.
- **Attachment Theory** Read more on attachment styles.
- **How to Choose a Daycare That's Right for Your Child** An information resource about day care options.

ANSWERS

1. F 2. T 3. T 4. T 5. F 6. F 7. Another successful method is to secretly rub a spot of rouge on an infant's nose. The child is then placed in front of a mirror. The question is, Will the child touch the red spot, showing recognition of the mirror image as his or her own? The probability that a child will do so jumps dramatically during the second year. 8. It certainly can for parents. When a pregnant woman begins to feel fetal movements, she becomes aware that a baby is coming to life inside of her. Likewise, prospective parents who hear a fetal heartbeat at the doctor's office or see an ultrasound image of the fetus begin to become emotionally attached to the unborn child (Santrock, 2007). 9. Most parents discipline their children in the same ways that they themselves were disciplined. Parenting is a responsibility of tremendous importance, for which most people receive almost no training.

MODULE 3.4 Language Development in Childhood

THERE'S SOMETHING ALMOST MIRACULOUS about a baby's first words. As infants, how did we manage to leap into the world of language? Even a quick survey like this one reveals that both maturation (nature) and social development (nurture) provide a foundation for language learning. Let's begin with a quick survey of language development.

Language Development— Fast-Talking Babies

SURVEY QUESTION: *How do children acquire language?*

Language development is closely tied to maturation (Carroll, 2008; Gleason, 2005). As every parent knows, babies can cry from birth on. By 1 month of age they use crying to gain attention. Typically, parents can tell if an infant is hungry, angry, or in pain from the tone of the crying (Kaplan, 1998). Around 6 to 8 weeks of age, babies begin *cooing* (the repetition of vowel sounds such as "oo" and "ah").

By 7 months of age, Amy's nervous system will mature enough to allow her to grasp objects, smile, laugh, sit up, and *babble*. In the babbling stage, the consonants *b, d, m,* and *g* are combined with the vowel sounds to produce meaningless language sounds: *dadadadada* or *bababa*. At first, babbling is the same around the world. But soon, the language spoken by parents begins to have an influence. That is, Japanese babies start to babble in a way that sounds like Japanese, Mexican babies babble in Spanish-like sounds, and so forth (Gopnik, Meltzoff, & Kuhl, 2000; Kuhl, 2004).

At about 1 year of age, children respond to real words such as *no* or *hi*. Soon afterward, the first connection between words and objects forms, and children may address their parents as "Mama" or "Dada." By age 18 months to 2 years, Amy's vocabulary may include a hundred words or more. At first there is a *single-word stage*, during which children use one word at a time, such as "go," "juice," or "up." Soon after, words are arranged in simple two-word sentences called *telegraphic speech*: "Want-Teddy," "Mama-gone."

Language and the Terrible Twos

At about the same time that children begin to put two or three words together they become much more independent. Two-year-olds understand some of the commands parents make, but they are not always willing to carry them out. A child like Amy may assert her independence by saying "No drink," "Me do it," "My cup, my cup," and the like. It can be worse, of course. A 2-year-old may look at you intently, make eye contact, listen as you shout "No, no," and still pour her juice on the cat.

During their second year, children become increasingly capable of mischief and temper tantrums. Thus, calling this time "the terrible twos" is not entirely inappropriate. One-year-olds can do plenty of things parents don't want them to do. However, it's usually 2-year-olds who do things *because* you don't want them to (Gopnik, Meltzoff, & Kuhl, 2000).

Perhaps parents can take some comfort in knowing that a stubborn, negative 2-year-old is simply becoming more independent. When Amy is 2, Olivia and Tom would be wise to remember that "This, too, shall pass." After age 2, the child's comprehension and use of words takes a dramatic leap forward. From this point on, vocabulary and language skills grow at a phenomenal rate (Fernald, Perfors, & Marchman, 2006). By first grade, Amy will be able to understand around 8,000 words and use about 4,000. She will have truly entered the world of language.

The Roots of Language

What accounts for this explosion of language development? Linguist Noam Chomsky (1975, 1986) has long claimed that humans have a **biological predisposition** or hereditary readiness to develop language. According to Chomsky, language patterns are inborn, much like a child's ability to coordinate walking. If such inborn language recognition does exist, it may explain why children around the world use a limited number of patterns in their first sentences. Typical patterns include the following (Mussen et al., 1979):

Identification:	"See kitty."
Nonexistence:	"Allgone milk."
Possession:	"My doll."
Agent-Action:	"Mama give."
Negation:	"Not ball."
Question:	"Where doggie?"

Does Chomsky's theory explain why language develops so rapidly? It is certainly part of the story. But many psychologists feel that Chomsky underestimates the importance of learning (Tomasello, 2003) and the social contexts that shape language development (Hoff, 2006). *Psycholinguists* (specialists in the psychology of language) have shown that imitation of adults and rewards for correctly using words (as when a child asks for a cookie) are an important part of language learning. Also, babies actively participate in language learning by asking questions, such as "What dis?" (Domingo & Goldstein-Alpern, 1999).

When a child makes a language error, parents typically repeat the child's sentence, with needed corrections (Bohannon & Stanowicz, 1988; Hoff, 2006) or ask a clarifying question to draw the child's attention to the error (Saxton, Houston-Price, & Dawson, 2005). More important is the fact that parents and children begin to communicate long before the child can speak. A readiness to interact *socially* with parents may be as important as innate language recognition. The next section explains why.

Early Communication *How do parents communicate with infants before they can talk?* Parents go to a great deal of trouble to get babies to smile and vocalize (● Fig. 3.14). In doing so, they quickly learn to change their actions to keep the infant's attention, arousal, and activity at optimal levels. A familiar example is the "I'm-Going-to-Get-You Game." In it, the adult says, "I'm gonna getcha.... I'm gonna getcha.... I'm gonna getcha.... Gotcha!" Through such games, adults and babies come to share similar rhythms and expectations (Carroll, 2008). Soon a system of shared **signals** is created, including touching, vocalizing, gazing, and smiling. These help lay a foundation for later language use (Tamis-LeMonda, Bornstein, & Baumwell, 2001). Specifically, signals establish a pattern of "conversational" *turn-taking* (alternate sending and receiving of messages).

Olivia	*Amy*
	(smiles)
"Oh what a nice little smile!"	
"Yes, isn't that nice?"	
"There."	
"There's a nice little smile."	(burps)
"Well, pardon you!"	
"Yes, that's better, isn't it?"	
"Yes."	(vocalizes)
"Yes."	(smiles)
"What's so funny?"	

From the outside, such exchanges may look meaningless. In reality, they represent meaningful communication. Amy's vocalizations and attention provide a way of interacting emotionally with Olivia and Tom. Infants as young as 4 months engage in vocal turn-taking with adults (Jaffe et al., 2001). The more children interact with parents, the faster they learn to talk and the faster they learn thinking abilities (Dickinson & Tabors, 2001; Hoff & Tian, 2005). One study found that 6-week-old babies gaze at an adult's face in rhythm with the adult's speech (Crown et al., 2002). Unmistakably, social relationships contribute to early language learning (Hoff, 2006).

● **FIGURE 3.14** Infant engagement scale. These samples from a 90-point scale show various levels of infant engagement, or attention. Babies participate in prelanguage "conversations" with parents by giving and withholding attention and by smiling, gazing, or vocalizing. (From Beebe et al., 1982.)

85
Medium high positive

50
Neutral attention

20
Avert

Biological predisposition The presumed hereditary readiness of humans to learn certain skills, such as how to use language, or a readiness to behave in particular ways.

Signal In early language development, any behavior, such as touching, vocalizing, gazing, or smiling, that allows nonverbal interaction and turn-taking between parent and child.

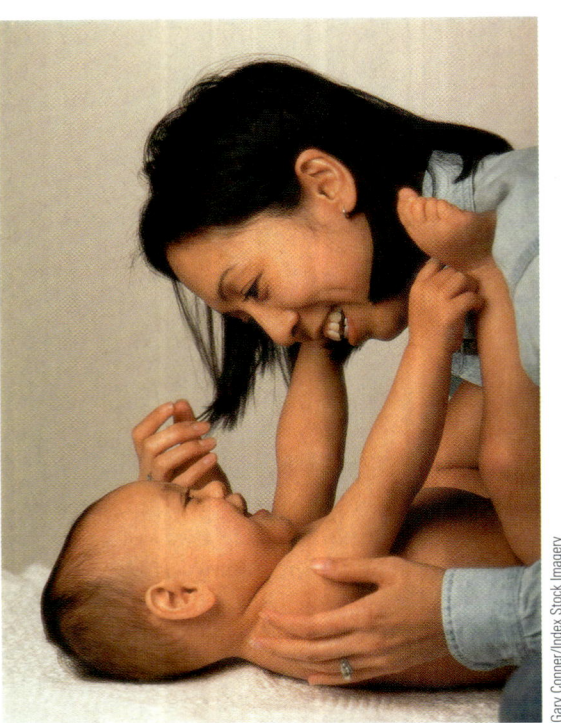

As with motherese, parents use a distinctive style when singing to an infant. Even people who speak another language can tell if a tape-recorded song was sung to an infant or an adult. Likewise, lullabies remain recognizable when electronic filtering removes words (Trehub et al., 1993a, 1993b).

Parentese When they talk to infants, parents use an exaggerated pattern of speaking called **motherese** or **parentese.** Typically, they raise their tone of voice, use short, simple sentences, repeat themselves more, and use frequent gestures (Gogate, Bahrick, & Watson, 2000). They also slow their rate of speaking and use exaggerated voice inflections: "Did Amy eat it A-L-L UP?"

What is the purpose of such changes? Parents are apparently trying to help their children learn language. When a baby is still babbling, parents tend to use long, adult-style sentences. But as soon as the baby says its first word they switch to parentese. By the time babies are 4 months old they prefer parentese over normal speech (Cooper et al., 1997).

In addition to being simpler, parentese has a distinct "musical" quality (Trainor & Desjardins, 2002). No matter what language mothers speak, the melodies, pauses, and inflections they use to comfort, praise, or give warning are universal. Psychologist Anne Fernald has found that mothers of all nations talk to their babies with similar changes in pitch. For instance, we praise babies with a rising, then falling pitch ("BRA-vo!" "GOOD girl!"). Warnings are delivered in a short, sharp rhythm ("Nein! Nein!" "Basta! Basta!" "Not! Dude!"). To give comfort, parents use low, smooth, drawn-out tones ("Oooh poor baaa-by." "Oooh pobrecito.") A high-pitched, rising melody is used to call attention to objects ("See the pretty BIRDIE?") (Fernald, 1989).

Parentese helps parents get babies' attention, communicate with them, and teach them language (Thiessen, Hill, & Saffran, 2005). Later, as a child's speaking improves, parents tend to adjust their speech to the child's language ability. Especially from 18 months to 4 years of age, parents seek to clarify what a child says and prompt the child to say more.

In summary, some elements of language are innate. Nevertheless, our inherited tendency to learn language does not determine if we will speak English or Vietnamese, Spanish or Russian. Environmental forces also influence whether a person develops simple or sophisticated language skills. The first 7 years of life are a sensitive period in language learning (Eliot, 1999). Clearly, a full flowering of speech requires careful cultivation.

MODULE 3.4 Summary

How do children acquire language?

- Learning to use language is a cornerstone of early intellectual development.
- Language development proceeds from crying to cooing, then babbling, the use of single words, and then to telegraphic speech.
- The underlying patterns of telegraphic speech suggest a biological predisposition to acquire language. This innate tendency is augmented by learning.
- Prelanguage communication between parent and child involves shared rhythms, nonverbal signals, and turn-taking.
- Motherese or parentese is a simplified, musical style of speaking that parents use to help their children learn language.

KNOWLEDGE BUILDER

Language Development in Childhood

Recite

1. The development of speech and language usually occurs in which order?
   a. crying, cooing, babbling, telegraphic speech
   b. cooing, crying, babbling, telegraphic speech
   c. babbling, crying, cooing, telegraphic speech
   d. crying, babbling, cooing, identification
2. Simple two-word sentences are characteristic of _____ speech.
3. Noam _____ has advanced the idea that language acquisition is built on innate patterns.
4. Prelanguage turn-taking and social interactions would be of special interest to a psycholinguist. T or F?
5. The style of speaking known as _____ is higher in pitch and has a musical quality.

Reflect
Critical Thinking

6. The children of professional parents hear more words per hour than the children of welfare parents, and they also tend to score higher on tests of mental abilities. How else could their higher scores be explained?

Relate

In order, see if you can name and imitate the language abilities you had as you progressed from birth to age 2 years. Now see if you can label and imitate some basic elements of parentese.

In your own words, state at least one argument for and against Chomsky's view of language acquisition.

You are going to spend a day with a person who speaks a different language than you do. Do you think you would be able to communicate with the other person? How does this relate to language acquisition?

Link

Internet addresses frequently change. To find the sites listed here, visit http://www.thomsonedu.com/psychology/coon for an updated list of Internet addresses and direct links to relevant sites.

- **Language Development In Children** Much more information about language development in children.
- **How Does Your Child Hear and Talk?** Discover a milestone chart for hearing and talking.
- **Speech & Language: Talk to Me** Explore the role parents play in early language development.

ANSWERS

1. a 2. telegraphic 3. Chomsky 4. T 5. Parentese or motherese 6. Children in professional homes receive many educational benefits that are less common in welfare homes. Yet, even when such differences are taken into account, brighter children tend to come from richer language environments (Hart & Risley, 1999).

Motherese (or parentese) A pattern of speech used when talking to infants, marked by a higher-pitched voice; short, simple sentences; repetition, slower speech; and exaggerated voice inflections.

MODULE 3.5 Cognitive Development in Childhood

JEAN PIAGET provided some of the first great insights into how children develop thinking abilities. Piaget proposed that children's cognitive skills progress through a series of maturational stages. Although Piaget's theory has been very valuable, psychologists continue to update his ideas. Also, many psychologists have become interested in how children learn the intellectual skills valued by their culture. Typically, children do this with guidance from skilled "tutors" (parents and others).

Cognitive Development—How Do Children Learn to Think?

SURVEY QUESTION: *How DO children learn to think?*

Now that we have Amy talking, let's move on to a broader view of intellectual development. Jean Piaget (Jahn pea-ah-ZHAY) provided some of the first great insights into how children develop thinking abilities.

How different is a child's understanding of the world from that of an adult? Generally speaking, their thinking is less abstract. Children use fewer generalizations, categories, and principles. They also tend to base their understanding on particular examples and objects they can see or touch.

Before the age of 6 or 7, thinking is very concrete. Younger children cannot make **transformations** in which they must mentally change the shape or form of a substance (such as clay or water). Let's visit Amy at age 5: If you show her a short, wide glass full of milk and a taller, narrow glass (also full), she will most likely tell you that the taller glass contains more milk (even if it doesn't). Amy will tell you this even if she watches you pour milk from the short glass into an empty, tall glass. She is not bothered by the fact that the milk appears to be transformed from a smaller to a larger amount. Instead, she responds only to the fact that *taller* seems to mean *more*. (See ● Fig. 3.15.) After about age 7, children are no longer fooled by this situation. Perhaps that's why 7 has been called the "age of reason." From age 7 on, we see a definite trend toward more logical, adult-like thought (Flavell, 1992).

Is there any pattern to the growth of intellect in childhood? According to the Swiss psychologist and philosopher Jean Piaget (1951, 1952), there is.

Piaget's Theory of Cognitive Development

Jean Piaget believed that all children mature through a series of distinct stages in intellectual development. Many of his ideas came from observing his own children as they solved

● **FIGURE 3.15** Children under age 7 intuitively assume that a volume of liquid increases when it is poured from a short, wide container into a taller, thinner one. This boy thinks the tall container holds more than the short one. Actually each holds the same amount of liquid. Children make such judgments based on the height of the liquid, not its volume.

various thought problems. (It is tempting to imagine that Piaget's illustrious career was launched one day when his wife said to him, "Watch the children for a while, will you, Jean?")

Mental Adaptations Piaget was convinced that intellect grows through processes he called assimilation and accommodation. **Assimilation** refers to using existing mental patterns in new situations. Let's say that a plastic hammer is the favorite toy of a boy named Benjamin, who pounds on blocks with it. For his birthday Benjamin gets an oversized toy wrench. If he uses the wrench for pounding, it has been assimilated to an existing knowledge structure.

Jean Piaget—philosopher, psychologist, and keen observer of children.

In **accommodation,** existing ideas are modified to fit new requirements. For instance, a younger child might think that a dime is worth less than a (larger) nickel. However, as children begin to spend money, they must alter their ideas about what "more" and "less" mean. Thus, new situations are

122

assimilated to existing ideas, and new ideas are created to accommodate new experiences.

Piaget's ideas have deeply affected our view of children (Feldman, 2004). The following is a brief summary of what he found.

The Sensorimotor Stage (0–2 Years) In the first 2 years of life, Amy's intellectual development will be largely nonverbal. She will be mainly concerned with learning to coordinate information from her senses with her motor movements. Also, **object permanence** (an understanding that objects continue to exist when they are out of sight) emerges at this time. Sometime during their first year, babies begin to actively pursue disappearing objects. By age 2, they can anticipate the movement of an object behind a screen. For example, when watching an electric train, Amy will look ahead to the end of a tunnel, rather than staring at the spot where the train disappeared.

In general, developments in this stage indicate that the child's conceptions are becoming more *stable.* Objects cease to appear and disappear magically, and a more orderly and predictable world replaces the confusing and disconnected sensations of infancy.

The Preoperational Stage (2–7 Years) During this period, children begin to think *symbolically* and use language. But the child's thinking is still very **intuitive** (it makes little use of reasoning and logic). (Do you remember thinking as a child that the sun and the moon followed you when you took a walk?) In addition, the child's use of language is not as sophisticated as it might seem. Children have a tendency to confuse words with the objects they represent. If Benjamin calls a toy block a "car" and you use it to make a "house," he may be upset. To children, the name of an object is as much a part of the object as its size, shape, and color. This seems to underlie a preoccupation with name calling. To the preoperational child, insulting words may really hurt. Consider one rather protected youngster who was angered by her older brother. Searching for a way to retaliate against her larger and stronger foe, she settled on, "You panty-girdle!" It was the worst thing she could think of saying.

During the preoperational stage, the child is also quite **egocentric** (unable to take the viewpoint of other people). The child's ego seems to stand at the center of his or her world. To illustrate, show Amy a two-sided mirror. Then hold it between you and her, so she can see herself in it. If you ask her what she thinks *you* can see, she imagines that you see *her* face reflected in the mirror, instead of your own. Such egocentrism explains why children can seem exasperatingly selfish or uncooperative at times. If Benjamin blocks your view by standing in front of the TV, he assumes that you can see it if he can. If you ask him to move so you can see better,

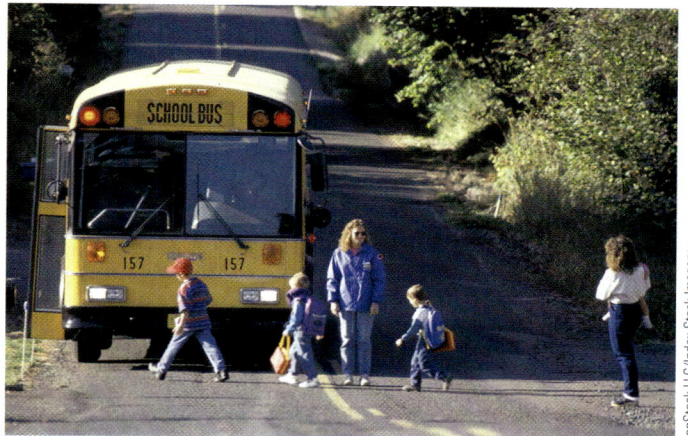

Crossing a busy street can be dangerous for the preoperational child. Because their thinking is still egocentric, younger children cannot understand why the driver of a car can't see them if they can see the car. Children under the age of 7 also cannot consistently judge speeds and distances of oncoming cars. Adults can easily overestimate the "street smarts" of younger children. It is advisable to teach children to cross with a light, in crosswalks, or with assistance.

he may move so that he can see better! Benjamin is not being selfish in the ordinary sense. He just doesn't realize that your view differs from his.

The Concrete Operational Stage (7–11 Years) An important development during this stage is mastery of **conservation** (the concept that mass, weight, and volume remain un-

---

Transformation The mental ability to change the shape or form of a substance (such as clay or water) and to perceive that its volume remains the same.

Assimilation In Piaget's theory, the application of existing mental patterns to new situations (that is, the new situation is assimilated to existing mental schemes).

Accommodation In Piaget's theory, the modification of existing mental patterns to fit new demands (that is, mental schemes are changed to accommodate new information or experiences).

Sensorimotor stage Stage of intellectual development during which sensory input and motor responses become coordinated.

Object permanence Concept, gained in infancy, that objects continue to exist even when they are hidden from view.

Preoperational stage Period of intellectual development during which children begin to use language and think symbolically, yet remain intuitive and egocentric in their thought.

Intuitive thought Thinking that makes little or no use of reasoning and logic.

Egocentric thought Thought that is self-centered and fails to consider the viewpoints of others.

Concrete operational stage Period of intellectual development during which children become able to use the concepts of time, space, volume, and number, but in ways that remain simplified and concrete, rather than abstract.

Conservation In Piaget's theory, mastery of the concept that the weight, mass, and volume of matter remains unchanged (is conserved) even when the shape or appearance of objects changes.

changed when the shape of objects changes). Children have learned conservation when they understand that rolling a ball of clay into a "snake" does not increase the amount of clay. Likewise, pouring liquid from a tall, narrow glass into a shallow dish does not reduce the amount of liquid. In each case the volume remains the same despite changes in shape or appearance. The original amount is *conserved*. (See Fig. 3.15.)

During the concrete operational stage, children begin to use concepts of time, space, and number. The child can think logically about very concrete objects or situations, categories, and principles. Such abilities explain why children stop believing in Santa Claus when they reach this stage. Because they can conserve volume, they realize that Santa's sack couldn't possibly hold enough toys for millions of girls and boys.

Another important development at this time is the ability to *reverse* thoughts or mental operations. A 4-year-old boy in the preoperational stage might have a conversation like this (showing what happens when a child's thinking *lacks* reversibility):

"Do you have a brother?"
"Yes."
"What's his name?"
"Sam."
"Does Sam have a brother?"
"No."

Reversibility of thought allows children in the concrete operational stage to recognize that if $4 \times 2 = 8$, then 2×4 does, too. Younger children must memorize each relationship separately. Thus, a preoperational child may know that $4 \times 9 = 36$, without being able to tell you what 9×4 equals.

The Formal Operations Stage (11 Years and Up) After about the age of 11, children begin to break away from concrete objects and specific examples. Thinking is based more on abstract principles, such as "democracy," "honor," or "correlation." Children who reach this stage can think about their thoughts, and they become less egocentric. Older children and young adolescents also gradually become able to consider hypothetical possibilities (suppositions, guesses, or projections). For example, if you ask a younger child, "What do you think would happen if it suddenly became possible for people to fly?" the child might respond, "People can't fly." Older children are able to consider such possibilities.

Full adult intellectual ability is attained during the stage of formal operations. Older adolescents are capable of inductive and deductive reasoning, and they can comprehend math, physics, philosophy, psychology, and other abstract systems. They can learn to test hypotheses in a scientific manner. Of course, not everyone reaches this level of thinking. Also, many adults can think formally about some topics, but their thinking becomes concrete when the topic is unfamiliar.

This implies that formal thinking may be more a result of culture and learning than maturation. In any case, after late adolescence, improvements in intellect are based on gaining specific knowledge, experience, and wisdom, rather than on any leaps in basic thinking capacity.

How can parents apply Piaget's ideas? Piaget's theory suggests that the ideal way to guide intellectual development is to provide experiences that are only slightly novel, unusual, or challenging. Remember, a child's intellect develops mainly through accommodation. It is usually best to follow a *one-step-ahead strategy*, in which your teaching efforts are aimed just beyond a child's current level of comprehension (Brainerd, 2003).

Parents should avoid *forced teaching*, or "hothousing," which is like trying to force plants to bloom prematurely. Forcing children to learn reading, math, gymnastics, swimming, or music at an accelerated pace can bore or oppress them. True intellectual enrichment respects the child's interests. It does not make the child feel pressured to perform (Alvino et al., 1996).

For your convenience, ■ Table 3.2 briefly summarizes each Piagetian stage. To help you remember Piaget's theory, the table describes what would happen at each stage if we played a game of *Monopoly* with the child. You'll also find brief suggestions about how to relate to children in each stage.

Piaget Today

Piaget's theory is a valuable "road map" for understanding how children think. However, many psychologists are convinced that Piaget gave too little credit to the effects of the learning environment. For example, children who grow up in villages where pottery is made can correctly answer questions about the conservation of clay at an earlier age than Piaget would have predicted.

According to learning theorists, children continuously gain specific knowledge; they do not undergo stage-like leaps in general mental ability (Siegler, 2004). On the other hand, the growth in connections between brain cells occurs in waves that parallel some of Piaget's stages. (See ● Fig. 3.16.) Thus, the truth may lie somewhere between Piaget's stage theory and modern learning theory.

On a broad scale, many of Piaget's *observations* have held up well. However, his *explanations* of childhood thinking abilities continue to be debated (Feldman, 2004). Where early infancy is concerned, even Piaget's observations may need updating. It looks like Piaget greatly underestimated the mental abilities of infants.

Infant Cognition *What evidence is there that Piaget underestimated infant abilities?* Piaget believed that infants under the age of 1 year cannot think. Babies, he said, have no memory

TABLE 3.2 Piaget—A Guide for Parents

PIAGET	MONOPOLY GAME	GUIDELINES FOR PARENTS
Sensorimotor Stage (0–2 Years) The stage during which sensory input and motor responses become coordinated.	The child puts houses, hotels, and dice in her mouth and plays with "Chance" cards.	Active play with a child is most effective at this stage. Encourage explorations in touching, smelling, and manipulating objects. Peekaboo is a good way to establish the permanence of objects.
Preoperational Stage (2–7 Years) The period of cognitive development when children begin to use language and think symbolically, yet remain intuitive and egocentric.	The child plays *Monopoly*, but makes up her own rules and cannot understand instructions.	Specific examples and touching or seeing things continues to be more useful than verbal explanations. Learning the concept of conservation may be aided by demonstrations with liquids, beads, clay, and other substances.
Concrete Operational Stage (7–11 Years) The period of cognitive development during which children begin to use concepts of time, space, volume, and number, but in ways that remain simplified and concrete.	The child understands basic instructions and will play by the rules but is not capable of hypothetical transactions dealing with mortgages, loans, and special pacts with other players.	Children are beginning to use generalizations, but they still require specific examples to grasp many ideas. Expect a degree of inconsistency in the child's ability to apply concepts of time, space, quantity, and volume to new situations.
Formal Operations Stage (11 Years and Up) The period of intellectual development marked by a capacity for abstract, theoretical, and hypothetical thinking.	The child no longer plays the game mechanically; complex and hypothetical transactions unique to each game are now possible.	It is now more effective to explain things verbally or symbolically and to help children master general rules and principles. Encourage the child to create hypotheses and to imagine how things could be.

3 to 6 years

7 to 15 years

16 to 20 years

Growth
Pruning

● **FIGURE 3.16** Between the ages of 3 and 6 a tremendous wave of growth occurs in connections among neurons in the frontal areas of the brain. This corresponds to the time when children make rapid progress in their ability to think symbolically. Between ages 7 and 15, peak synaptic growth shifts to the temporal and parietal lobes. During this period children become increasingly adept at using language, a specialty of the temporal lobes. In the late teens, the brain actively destroys unneeded connections, especially in the frontal lobes. This pruning of synapses sharpens the brain's capacity for abstract thinking (Restak, 2001).

of people and objects that are out of sight. Yet, we now know that infants begin forming representations of the world very early in life. For example, babies as young as 3 months of age appear to know that objects are solid and do not disappear when out of view (Baillargeon, 2004).

Why did Piaget fail to detect the thinking skills of infants? Most likely, he mistook babies' limited *physical* skills for *mental* incompetence. Piaget's tests required babies to search for objects or reach out and touch them. Newer, more sensitive methods are uncovering abilities Piaget missed. One such method takes advantage of the fact that babies, like adults, act surprised when they see something "impossible" or unexpected occur. To use this effect, psychologist Renee Baillargeon (1991, 2004) puts on little "magic shows" for infants. In her "theater," babies watch as possible and impossible events occur with toys or other objects. Some 3-month-old infants act surprised and gaze longer at impossible events. An example is seeing two solid objects appear to pass through each other. By the time they are 8 months old, babies can remember where objects are (or should be) for at least 1 minute (● Fig. 3.17).

Formal operations stage Period of intellectual development characterized by thinking that includes abstract, theoretical, and hypothetical ideas.

● **FIGURE 3.17** The panels on the left show a possible event, in which an infant watches as a toy is placed behind the right of two screens. After a delay of 70 seconds, the toy is brought into view from behind the right screen. In the two panels on the right, an impossible event occurs. The toy is placed behind the left screen and retrieved from behind the right. (A duplicate toy was hidden there before testing.) Eight-month-old infants react with surprise when they see the impossible event staged for them. Their reaction implies that they remember where the toy was hidden. Infants appear to have a capacity for memory and thinking that greatly exceeds what Piaget claimed is possible during the sensorimotor period. (Adapted from Baillargeon et al., 1989.)

Piaget believed that abilities like those described in Figure 3.17 emerge only after a long period of sensorimotor development. However, it's clear that babies quickly acquire the capacity to form concepts about the world (Eimas, Quinn, & Cowan, 1994). It looks as if further study is likely to refine and amend the ideas that grew from Piaget's fateful decision to "watch the children for a while."

Another criticism of Piaget is that he underestimated the impact of culture on mental development. The next section tells how Amy will master the intellectual tools valued by her culture.

Vygotsky's Sociocultural Theory

Whereas Piaget stressed the role of maturation in cognitive development, Russian scholar Lev Vygotsky (1896–1934) focused on the impact of sociocultural factors. Vygotsky's key insight is that children's thinking develops through dialogues with more capable persons (Vygotsky, 1962, 1978).

How does that relate to intellectual growth? So far, no one has ever published *A Child's Guide to Life on Earth.* Instead, children must learn about life from various "tutors," such as parents, teachers, and older siblings. Even if *A Child's Guide to Life on Earth* did exist, we would need a separate version for every culture. It is not enough for children to learn how to think. They must also learn specific intellectual skills valued by their culture.

Like Piaget, Vygotsky believed that children actively seek to discover new principles. However, Vygotsky emphasized that many of a child's most important "discoveries" are guided by skillful tutors. Psychologist David Shaffer (2002) offers the following example:

Annie, a 4-year-old, has just received her first jigsaw puzzle as a birthday present. She attempts to work the puzzle but gets nowhere until her father comes along, sits down beside her, and gives her some tips. He suggests that it would be a good idea to put together the corners first, points to the pink area at the edge of one corner piece and says, "Let's look for another pink piece." When Annie seems frustrated, he places two interlocking pieces near each other so that she will notice them, and when Annie succeeds, he offers words of encouragement. As Annie gradually gets the hang of it, he steps back and lets her work more and more independently. (p. 260.)

Interactions like this are most helpful when they take place within a child's **zone of proximal development.**

What did Vygotsky mean by that? The word *proximal* means close or nearby. Vygotsky realized that, at any given time, some tasks are just beyond a child's reach. The child is close to having the mental skills needed to do the task, but it is a little too complex to be mastered alone. However, children working within this zone can make rapid progress if they receive sensitive guidance from a skilled partner (LeBlanc & Bearison, 2004).

Vygotsky also emphasized a process he called **scaffolding.** A scaffold is a framework or temporary support. Vygotsky believed that adults help children learn how to think by "scaffolding," or supporting, their attempts to solve problems or discover principles (Daniels, 2005). To be most effective, scaffolding must be responsive to a child's needs. For example, as Annie's father helped her with the puzzle, he tailored his hints and guidance to match her evolving abilities. The two of them worked together, step by step, so that Annie could better understand how to assemble a puzzle. In a sense, Annie's father set up a series of temporary bridges that helped her move into new mental territory. As predicted by Vygotsky's theory, the reading skills of 8- to 10-year-old children are closely related to the amount of verbal scaffolding their mothers provided at ages 3 and 4 (Dieterich et al., 2006).

During their collaborations with others, children learn important cultural beliefs and values. For example, imagine that a boy wants to know how many baseball cards he has. His mother helps him stack and count the cards, moving each card to a new stack as they count it. She then shows him how to write the number on a slip of paper so he can remember it. This teaches the child not only about counting, but also that writing is valued in our culture. In other parts of the world, a child learning to count might be shown how to make notches on a stick or tie knots in a cord.

Implications Vygotsky saw that grown-ups play a crucial role in what children know. As they try to decipher the world, children rely on adults to help them understand how things work. Vygotsky further noticed that adults unconsciously adjust their behavior to give children the information they need to solve problems that interest the child. In this way, children use adults to learn about their culture and society (Gopnik, Meltzoff, & Kuhl, 2000; LeBlanc & Bearison, 2004).

MODULE 3.5 Summary

How do children learn to think?

- The intellect of a child is less abstract than that of an adult. Jean Piaget theorized that intellectual growth occurs through a combination of assimilation and accommodation.
- Piaget also held that children mature through a fixed series of cognitive stages. The stages and their approximate age ranges are sensorimotor (0–2), preoperational (2–7), concrete operational (7–11), and formal operations (11–adult).
- Caregivers should offer learning opportunities that are appropriate for a child's level of cognitive development.
- Learning principles provide an alternate explanation that assumes cognitive development is continuous; it does not occur in stages.
- Recent studies of infants under the age of 1 year suggest that they are capable of thought well beyond that observed by Piaget.
- Lev Vygotsky's sociocultural theory emphasizes that a child's mental abilities are advanced by interactions with more competent partners. Mental growth takes place in a child's zone of proximal development, where a more skillful person may scaffold the child's progress. As children rely on adults to help them discover new skills and principles, they learn cultural beliefs and values.

Zone of proximal development Refers to the range of tasks a child cannot yet master alone, but that she or he can accomplish with the guidance of a more capable partner.

Scaffolding The process of adjusting instruction so that it is responsive to a beginner's behavior and supports the beginner's efforts to understand a problem or gain a mental skill.

KNOWLEDGE BUILDER

Cognitive Development in Childhood

Recite

Match each item with one of the following stages.

A. Sensorimotor B. Preoperational C. Concrete operational D. Formal operations

1. ____ egocentric thought
2. ____ abstract or hypothetical
3. ____ purposeful movement
4. ____ intuitive thought
5. ____ conservation
6. ____ reversibility thought
7. ____ object permanence
8. ____ nonverbal development
9. *Assimilation* refers to applying existing thought patterns or knowledge to new situations. T or F?
10. Newer methods for testing infant thinking abilities frequently make note of whether an infant is _____ by seemingly _____ events.
11. Vygotsky called the process of providing a temporary framework of supports for learning new mental abilities _____.

Reflect

Critical Thinking

12. Using Piaget's theory as a guide, at what age would you expect a child to recognize that a Styrofoam cup has weight?

Relate

You are going to make cookies with children of various ages. See if you can name each of Piaget's stages and give an example of what a child in that stage might be expected to do.

You have been asked to help a child learn to use a pocket calculator to do simple addition. How would you go about identifying the child's zone of proximal development for this task? How would you scaffold the child's learning?

Link

Internet addresses frequently change. To find the sites listed here, visit **http://www.thomsonedu.com/psychology/coon** for an updated list of Internet addresses and direct links to relevant sites.

- **Jean Piaget Archives: Biography** The life of Jean Piaget, plus five photos from birth to old age.
- **Jean Piaget and Cognitive Development** Read a fuller account of Piaget's theory.
- **Scaffolding as a Teaching Strategy** Download a paper on the application of Vygotsky's idea of scaffolding to teaching.

ANSWERS

1. B 2. D 3. A 4. B 5. C 6. C 7. A 8. A 9. T 10. surprised, impossible 11. scaffolding 12. Seventy-five percent of 4- to 6-year-olds say that a Styrofoam cup has no weight after lifting it! Most children judge weight intuitively (by the way an object feels) until they begin to move into the concrete operational stage (Smith, Carey, & Wiser, 1985).

MODULE 3.6 Adolescence, Young Adulthood, and Moral Development

ADOLESCENCE and young adulthood is a time of change, exploration, exuberance, and youthful searching. It can also be a time of worry and problems, especially in today's world. It might even be fair to describe this period as "the best of times, the worst of times." During adolescence, a person's identity and moral values come into sharper focus even as the transition to adulthood is occurring at ever-later ages.

Adolescence and Young Adulthood— The Best of Times, the Worst of Times

SURVEY QUESTION: *Why is development during adolescence and young adulthood especially challenging?*

Adolescence is the culturally defined period between childhood and adulthood. Socially, the adolescent is no longer a child, yet not quite an adult. Almost all cultures recognize this transitional status. However, the length of adolescence varies greatly from culture to culture. For example, most 14-year-old girls in North America live at home and go to school. In contrast, many 14-year-old females in rural villages of many poorer countries are married and have children. In our culture, 14-year-olds are adolescents. In others, they may be adults.

Is marriage the primary criterion for adult status in North America? No, it's not even one of the top three criteria. Today, the most widely accepted standards are (1) taking responsibility for oneself, (2) making independent decisions, and (3) becoming financially independent. In practice, this typically means breaking away from parents by taking a job and setting up a separate residence (Arnett, 2001).

Puberty

Many people confuse adolescence with puberty. However, puberty is a *biological* event, not a social status. During **puberty,** hormonal changes promote rapid physical growth and sexual maturity. Biologically, most people reach reproductive maturity in the early teens. Social and intellectual maturity, however, may lie years ahead. Young adolescents often make decisions that affect their entire lives, even though they are immature mentally and socially. The tragically high rates of teenage pregnancy and drug abuse are prime examples. Despite such risks, most people do manage to weather adolescence without developing any serious psychological problems (Steinberg, 2001).

How much difference does the timing of puberty make? For boys, maturing early is generally beneficial. Typically, it enhances their self-image and gives them an advantage socially and athletically. Early-maturing boys tend to be more relaxed, dominant, self-assured, and popular. However, early puberty does carry some risks because early-maturing boys are also more likely to get into trouble with drugs, alcohol, and antisocial behavior (Steinberg, 2001).

For girls, the advantages of early maturation are less clear-cut. In elementary school, fast-maturing girls are *less* popular and have poorer self-images, perhaps because they are larger and heavier than their classmates (Alsaker, 1992). By junior high, however, early development includes sexual features. This leads to a more positive body image, *greater peer prestige*, and adult approval (Brooks-Gunn & Warren, 1988). Early-maturing girls tend to date sooner and are more independent and more active in school. However, like their male counterparts, they are also more often in trouble at school and more likely to engage in early sex (Flannery, Rowe, & Gulley, 1993).

As you can see, there are costs and benefits associated with early puberty. One added cost of early maturation is that it may force premature identity formation. When a teenager begins to look like an adult, she or he may be treated like an adult. Ideally, this change can encourage greater maturity and independence. However, if the search for identity ends too soon, it may leave the person with a distorted, poorly formed sense of self (● Fig. 3.18).

The Search for Identity

Identity formation is a key task of adolescence. Of course, problems of identity occur at other times too. But in a very real sense, puberty signals that it's time to begin forming a new, more mature self-image (Douvan, 1997). Many problems stem from unclear standards about the role adolescents should play within society. Are they adults or children? Should they be autonomous or dependent? Should they work or play? Such ambiguities make it difficult for young people to form clear images of themselves and of how they should act (Alsaker, 1995).

Adolescence The culturally defined period between childhood and adulthood.
Puberty The biologically defined period during which a person matures sexually and becomes capable of reproduction.

HUMAN DIVERSITY

Ethnic Diversity and Identity

For adolescents of ethnic descent, the question is often not just "Who am I?" Rather, it is "Who am I at home? Who am I at school? Who am I with friends from my neighborhood?"

Ethnic heritage can have a powerful influence on personal identity (Weisskirch, 2005). Yet, at a time when teens are trying to find their place in society, they may feel rejected or excluded because of their ethnic heritage. In America, popular culture is loaded with images that dismiss anyone who doesn't look like Scarlett Johansson or Orlando Bloom. Also, ethnic adolescents often face degrading stereotypes concerning their intelligence, sexuality, social status, manners, and so forth. The result can be lowered self-esteem and confusion about roles, values, and personal identity (de las Fuentes & Vasquez, 1999).

In forming an identity, adolescents of ethnic descent face the question of how they should think of themselves. Is Lori an American or a Chinese American or both? Is Jaime a Latino, a Chicano, or a Mexican American? The answer typically depends on how strongly adolescents identify with their family and ethnic community. Teens who take pride in their ethnic heritage have higher self-esteem, a better self-image, and a stronger sense of personal identity (Roberts et al., 1999; Tse, 1999). They are also less likely to engage in drug use (Marsiglia et al., 2004) or violent behavior (French, Kim, & Pillado, 2006).

Group pride, positive models, and a more tolerant society could do much to keep a broad range of options open to *all* adolescents.

● **FIGURE 3.18** Dramatic differences in physical size and maturity are found in adolescents of the same age. The girls pictured are all 13, the boys 16. Maturation that occurs earlier or later than average can affect the "search for identity." (Adapted from "Growing Up" by J. M. Tanner. Copyright © September 1973 by Scientific American, Inc. All rights reserved.)

Answering the question "Who am I?" is also spurred by cognitive development. After adolescents have attained the stage of formal operations, they are better able to ask questions about their place in the world and about morals, values, politics, and social relationships. Then too, being able to think about hypothetical possibilities allows the adolescent to contemplate the future and ask more realistically, "Who will I be?" (Suls, 1989). (See "Ethnic Diversity and Identity.")

The Transition to Adulthood

Today the challenge of identity formation is further complicated by the fact that more and more young people are deferring young adulthood, preferring to prolong identity explorations into their 20s before they commit to long-term choices in love and work (Arnett, 2000, 2004; Arnett & Tanner, 2006). According to sociologist James Côté, western industrialized societies, like the United States and Canada, are becoming increasingly tolerant of this period of extended adolescence (Côté, 2006). (See "The Twixters.")

CRITICAL THINKING

The Twixters

As you read these modules, we encourage you to reflect on new ideas and concepts by thinking critically about them. Consider, for example, the term *adulthood*. Is becoming an adult strictly a biological event? Meet 22-year old Kirsten:

"When our mothers were our age, they were engaged.... They at least had some idea what they were going to do with their lives.... I, on the other hand, will have a dual degree in majors that are ambiguous at best and impractical at worst (English and political science), no ring on my finger and no idea who I am, much less what I want to do.... I realize that having nothing ahead to count on means I now have to count on myself; that having no direction means forging one of my own." (Page, 1999).

Kirsten is a "twixter": twentysomething, still living at home, not yet married, with no children, and no settled career. In England, twixsters are called "kippers" (Kids In Parents' Pockets Eroding Retirement Savings). In Australia they are "boomerang kids" (they always come back home). And in Germany they are "Nesthocker" (nest squatters). Are twixters adolescents who are taking longer to find their identity? Or are they young adults avoiding their need to enter the adult world? Are they self-indulgent individuals trapped in a "maturity gap" (Galambos, Barker, & Tilton-Weaver, 2003)? Or are they part of a new social status that could be called "emerging adulthood" (Arnett & Tanner, 2006)?

According to psychologist Jeffrey Arnett, emerging adulthood is increasingly common in affluent Westernized cultures that allow young people to take longer to settle into their adult roles (Arnett, 2000, 2004). However, in less affluent countries, as in poorer parts of America, most adolescents continue to "become adults" at much younger ages (Arnett & Galambos, 2003). Thus, words like *adolescent* or *adulthood* cannot be defined solely in terms of physical maturation. Sociocultural factors also play a role in defining when we stop being children or become adults (Arnett, 2004).

Amy may live with Olivia and Tom until her mid-20s, delaying her transition to adulthood. Alternately, she may make the transition to young adulthood during the traditional 18-to-21 period. Regardless, she will eventually face the primary adult issues of marriage, children, and career. How she manages, especially in her core relationships, will determine whether she feels a sense of intimacy or feels isolated from others.

In many ways adolescence and young adulthood are more emotionally turbulent than midlife or old age. This is borne out by a national survey in which younger adults reported feeling more negative emotions than older adults did. Likewise, older adults are more likely than younger adults to say they often feel happy, truly alive, and peaceful (● Fig. 3.19). One important aspect of the emotional turbulence of adolescence and young adulthood is the struggle with right and wrong—in other words, the need to develop moral values.

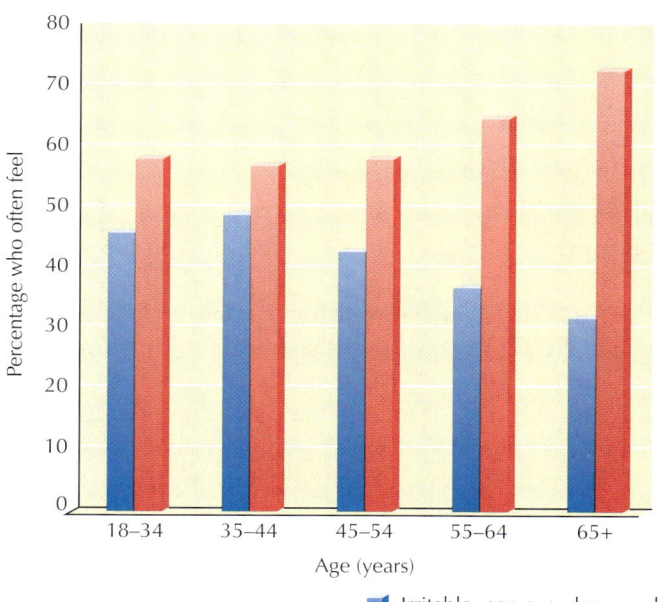

● **FIGURE 3.19** Negative emotions are more common before age 50 than after. The frequency of positive feelings tends to increase from midlife on into old age.

Moral Development— Growing a Conscience

SURVEY QUESTION: *How do we develop morals and values?*

A person with a terminal illness is in great pain. She is pleading for death. Should extraordinary medical efforts be made to keep her alive? A friend of yours desperately needs to pass a test and asks you to help him cheat. Will you do it? These are *moral* questions, or questions of conscience.

Moral development starts in childhood and continues into adulthood (Turiel, 2006). Through this process, we acquire values, beliefs, and thinking patterns that guide responsible behavior. Moral values are especially likely to come into sharper focus during adolescence and the transition to adulthood, as capacities for self-control and abstract thinking increase (Hart & Carlo, 2005). Let's take a brief look at this interesting aspect of personal development.

Levels of Moral Development

How are moral values acquired? In an influential account, psychologist Lawrence Kohlberg (1981) held that we learn moral values through thinking and reasoning. To study moral development, Kohlberg posed dilemmas to children of different ages. The following is one of the moral dilemmas he used (Kohlberg, 1969, adapted).

> A woman was near death from cancer, and there was only one drug that might save her. It was discovered by a druggist who was charging 10 times what it cost to make the drug. The sick woman's husband could only pay $1,000, but the druggist wanted $2,000. He asked the druggist to sell it cheaper or to let him pay later. The druggist said no. So the husband became desperate and broke into the store to steal the drug for his wife. Should he have done that? Was it wrong or right? Why?

Each child was asked what action the husband should take. Kohlberg classified the reasons given for each choice and identified three levels of moral development. Each is based not so much on the choices made, but on the reasoning used to arrive at a choice.

At the lowest, **preconventional level,** moral thinking is guided by the consequences of actions (punishment, reward, or an exchange of favors). For example, a person at this level might reason that "The man shouldn't steal the drug because he could get caught and sent to jail" (avoiding punishment) or "It won't do him any good to steal the drug because his wife will probably die before he gets out of jail" (self-interest).

At the second, or **conventional level,** reasoning is based on a desire to please others or to follow accepted authority, rules, and values. For example, a person at this intermediate level might say "He shouldn't steal the drug because others will think he is a thief. His wife would not want to be saved by thievery" (avoiding disapproval) or "Although his wife needs the drug, he should not break the law to get it. Everyone has to obey the law. His wife's condition does not justify stealing" (traditional morality of authority).

At the highest, or **postconventional level,** moral behavior is directed by self-chosen ethical principles that tend to be general, comprehensive, or universal. People at this level place high value on justice, dignity, and equality. For example, a highly principled person might say "He should steal the drug and then inform the authorities that he has done so. He will have to face a penalty, but he will have saved a human life" (self-chosen ethical principles).

Does everyone eventually reach the highest level? People advance at different rates, and many fail to reach the postconventional level of moral reasoning. In fact, many do not even reach the conventional level. For instance, one English survey revealed that 11 percent of men and 3 percent of women would commit murder for $1 million if they could be sure of getting away with the crime ("They'd kill," 1991).

The preconventional level is most characteristic of young children and delinquents (Forney, Forney, & Crutsinger, 2005). Conventional, group-oriented morals are typical of older children and most adults. Kohlberg estimated that only about 20 percent of the adult population achieves postconventional morality, representing self-direction and higher principles. (It would appear that few of these people enter politics!)

Developing a "moral compass" is an important part of growing up. Many of the choices we make every day involve fundamental questions of right and wrong. Being able to think clearly about such questions is essential to becoming a responsible adult.

Justice or Caring?

Carol Gilligan (1982) pointed out that Kohlberg's system is concerned mainly with *justice*. Based on studies of women who faced real-life dilemmas, Gilligan argued that there is also an ethic of *caring* about others. As one illustration, Gilligan presented the following story to 11- to 15-year-old American children.

> **THE PORCUPINE AND THE MOLES**
> Seeking refuge from the cold, a porcupine asked to share a cave for the winter with a family of moles. The moles agreed. But because the cave was small, they soon found they were being scratched each time the porcupine moved about. Finally, they asked the porcupine to leave. But the porcupine refused, saying, "If you moles are not satisfied, I suggest that you leave."

Boys who read this story tended to opt for justice in resolving the dilemma: "It's the moles' house. It's a deal. The porcupine leaves." In contrast, girls tended to look for solutions that would keep all parties happy and comfortable, such as "Cover the porcupine with a blanket."

Gilligan's point is that male psychologists have, for the most part, defined moral maturity in terms of justice and autonomy. From this perspective, a woman's concern with relationships can look like a weakness rather than a strength.

(A woman who is concerned about what pleases or helps others would be placed at the conventional level in Kohlberg's system.) But Gilligan believes that caring is also a major element of moral development, and she suggests that males may lag in achieving it (Botes, 2000; Gilligan & Attanucci, 1988).

Does the evidence support Gilligan's position? Several studies have found little or no difference in men's and women's overall moral reasoning abilities (Glover, 2001; Wilson, 1995). Indeed, both men and women may use caring *and* justice to make moral decisions. The moral yardstick they use appears to depend on the situation they face (Wark & Krebs, 1996). Just the same, Gilligan deserves credit for identifying a second major way in which moral choices are made. It can be argued that our best moral choices combine justice and caring, reason and emotion—which may be what we mean by wisdom (Pasupathi & Staudinger, 2001).

MODULE 3.6 Summary

Why is development during adolescence and young adulthood especially challenging?

- Transitioning from childhood to adulthood requires the formation of a personal identity; the major life task of adolescence. Identity formation is even more challenging for adolescents of ethnic descent.

- In western industrialized societies the transition into adulthood is further complicated as it is increasingly delayed well into the 20s.

How do we develop morals and values?

- Lawrence Kohlberg identified preconventional, conventional, and postconventional levels of moral reasoning.

- Most people function at the conventional level of morality, but some never get beyond the selfish, preconventional level. Only a minority of people attain the highest, or postconventional level, of moral reasoning.

Moral development The development of values, beliefs, and thinking abilities that act as a guide regarding what is acceptable behavior.

Preconventional moral reasoning Moral thinking based on the consequences of one's choices or actions (punishment, reward, or an exchange of favors).

Conventional moral reasoning Moral thinking based on a desire to please others or to follow accepted rules and values.

Postconventional moral reasoning Moral thinking based on carefully examined and self-chosen moral principles.

KNOWLEDGE BUILDER

Adolescence, Young Adulthood, and Moral Development

Recite

1. In North America the primary criterion for the transition from adolescence to adulthood is marriage. T or F?
2. Identify formation is spurred by _____ and _____ _____.
3. According to Jeffrey Arnett, the trend in affluent Westernized cultures towards allowing young people to take longer to settle into their adult roles is best referred to as
   a. emerging adulthood
   b. hurried childhood
   c. a maturity gap
   d. extended adolescence
4. According to Kohlberg, the conventional level of moral development is marked by a reliance on outside authority. T or F?
5. Self-interest and avoiding punishment are elements of postconventional morality. T or F?
6. About 80 percent of all adults function at the postconventional level of moral reasoning. T or F?
7. Gilligan regards gaining a sense of justice as the principal basis of moral development. T or F?

Reflect

Critical Thinking

8. Are labels like "adolescent" or "young adult" reflective of heredity or environment?

Relate

To what extent does the concept of identity formation apply to your own experience during adolescence?

Do you know any twixters? (Are you one?) Do you think twixters are adolescents taking longer to find their identity or young adults avoiding their need to establish themselves in the world of adults?

At what stage of moral development do you think most terrorists function?

Link

Internet addresses frequently change. To find the sites listed here, visit **http://www.thomsonedu.com/psychology/coon** for an updated list of Internet addresses and direct links to relevant sites.

- **A Positive Approach to Identity Formation of Biracial Children** Join the debate about multiethnicity and identity formation.
- **Delayed Adulthood** Read two articles about delayed adulthood.
- **Kohlberg Dilemmas** Try your hand at answering several moral dilemmas.

ANSWERS

1. F 2. puberty, cognitive development 3. a 4. T 5. F 6. F 7. F 8. Environment, rather than heredity, is the better answer. Even better, the meanings of terms like "adolescence" or "adult" vary considerably from culture to culture indicating that it is really a matter of definition (Côté, 2006).

MODULE 3.7 Challenges Across the Lifespan

ERIK ERIKSON'S psychosocial theory provides a good overview of the major psychological conflicts that occur during a "typical" life. In later adulthood we all face many additional challenges, including physical aging. Regardless, it is possible to age successfully. We also must face our own mortality and inevitable death.

The Story of a Lifetime— Rocky Road or Garden Path?

SURVEY QUESTION: *What are the typical tasks and dilemmas through the lifespan?*

Every life is marked by a number of developmental milestones. These are notable events, markers, or turning points in personal development. Some examples include graduating from school, voting for the first time, getting married, watching a child leave home (or move back!), the death of a parent, becoming a grandparent, retirement, and one's own death. Thus far, we have traced Amy's progress through childhood, adolescence, and young adulthood. What challenges lie ahead for her?

Erikson's Psychosocial Theory

Perhaps the best way to get a preview of Amy's life is to consider some of the major psychological challenges she is likely to encounter. Broad similarities can be found in the life stages of infancy, childhood, adolescence, young adulthood, middle adulthood, and old age. Each stage confronts a person with new **developmental tasks** that must be mastered for optimal development. Examples are learning to read in childhood, adjusting to sexual maturity in adolescence, and establishing a vocation as an adult.

In an influential book titled *Childhood and Society* (1963), personality theorist Erik Erikson (1903–1994) suggests that we face a specific *psychosocial dilemma*, or "crisis," at each stage of life. A **psychosocial dilemma** is a conflict between personal impulses and the social world. Resolving each dilemma creates a new balance between a person and society. A string of "successes" produces healthy development and a satisfying life. Unfavorable outcomes throw us off balance, making it harder to deal with later crises. Life becomes a "rocky road," and personal growth is stunted. ■ Table 3.3 lists Erikson's dilemmas.

What are the major developmental tasks and life crises? A brief description of each psychosocial dilemma follows.

Stage One, First Year of Life: Trust versus Mistrust
During the first year of life, children are completely dependent on

■ **TABLE 3.3** Erikson's Psychosocial Dilemmas

AGE	CHARACTERISTIC DILEMMA
Birth to 1 year	Trust versus mistrust
1 to 3 years	Autonomy versus shame and doubt
3 to 5 years	Initiative versus guilt
6 to 12 years	Industry versus inferiority
Adolescence	Identity versus role confusion
Young adulthood	Intimacy versus isolation
Middle adulthood	Generativity versus stagnation
Late adulthood	Integrity versus despair

Personality theorist Erik Erikson (1903–1994) is best known for his life-stage theory of human development.

Developmental task Any skill that must be mastered, or personal change that must take place, for optimal development.

Psychosocial dilemma A conflict between personal impulses and the social world.

others. Erikson believes that a basic attitude of trust or mistrust is formed at this time. **Trust** is established when babies are given warmth, touching, love, and physical care. **Mistrust** is caused by inadequate or unpredictable care and by parents who are cold, indifferent, or rejecting. Basic mistrust may later cause insecurity, suspiciousness, or an inability to relate to others. Notice that trust comes from the same conditions that help babies become securely attached to their parents.

Stage Two, 1–3 Years: Autonomy versus Shame and Doubt

In stage two, children express their growing self-control by climbing, touching, exploring, and trying to do things for themselves. Tom and Olivia fostered Amy's sense of **autonomy** by encouraging her to try new skills. However, her first efforts were sometimes crude, involving spilling, falling, wetting, and other "accidents." If Tom and Olivia had ridiculed or overprotected Amy, they might have caused her to **doubt** her abilities and feel **shameful** about her actions.

Stage Three, 3–5 Years: Initiative versus Guilt

In stage three, children move beyond simple self-control and begin to take initiative. Through play, children learn to make plans and carry out tasks. Parents reinforce **initiative** by giving children freedom to play, ask questions, use imagination, and choose activities. Feelings of **guilt** about initiating activities are formed if parents criticize severely, prevent play, or discourage a child's questions.

Stage Four, 6–12 Years: Industry versus Inferiority

Many events of middle childhood are symbolized by that fateful day when you first entered school. With dizzying speed your world expanded beyond your family, and you faced a whole series of new challenges.

The elementary school years are a child's "entrance into life." In school, children begin to learn skills valued by society, and success or failure can affect a child's feelings of adequacy. Children learn a sense of **industry** if they win praise for productive activities, such as building, painting, cooking, reading, and studying. If a child's efforts are regarded as messy, childish, or inadequate, feelings of **inferiority** result. For the first time, teachers, classmates, and adults outside the home become as important as parents in shaping attitudes toward oneself.

Stage Five, Adolescence: Identity versus Role Confusion

As we have noted, adolescence is often a turbulent time Erikson considers a need to answer the question "Who am I?" the primary task during this stage of life. As Amy matures mentally and physically, she will have new feelings, a new body, and new attitudes. Like other adolescents, she will need to build a consistent **identity** out of her talents, values, life history and relationships and the demands of her culture (Côté & Levine, 2002). Her conflicting experiences as a student, friend, athlete, worker, daughter, lover, and so forth must be integrated into a unified sense of self. Persons who fail to develop a sense of identity suffer from **role confusion,** an uncertainty about who they are and where they are going.

Stage Six, Young Adulthood: Intimacy versus Isolation

What does Erikson believe is the major conflict in early adulthood? In stage six, the individual feels a need for *intimacy* in his or her life. After establishing a stable identity, a person is prepared to share meaningful love or deep friendship with others. By **intimacy,** Erikson means an ability to care about others and to share experiences with them. In line with Erikson's view, 75 percent of college-age men and women rank a good marriage and family life as important adult goals (Bachman & Johnson, 1979). And yet, marriage or sexual involvement is no guarantee of intimacy: Many adult relationships remain shallow and unfulfilling. Failure to establish intimacy with others leads to a deep sense of **isolation** (feeling alone and uncared for in life). This often sets the stage for later difficulties.

Stage Seven, Middle Adulthood: Generativity versus Stagnation

According to Erikson, an interest in guiding the next generation provides emotional balance in mature adulthood. Erikson called this quality **generativity.** It is expressed by caring about oneself, one's children, and future generations. Generativity may be achieved by guiding one's own children or by helping other children (as a teacher or coach, for ex-

According to Erikson, an interest in future generations characterizes optimal adult development.

ample). Productive or creative work can also express generativity. In any case, a person's concerns and energies must broaden to include the welfare of others and society as a whole. Failure to do this is marked by a **stagnant** concern with one's own needs and comforts. Life loses meaning, and the person feels bitter, dreary, and trapped (Friedman, 2004).

Stage Eight, Late Adulthood: Integrity versus Despair *What does Erikson see as the conflicts of old age?* Old age is a time of reflection. According to Erikson, when Amy grows old it would be best if she were able to look back over her life with acceptance and satisfaction. People who have lived richly and responsibly develop a sense of **integrity** (self-respect). This allows them to face aging and death with dignity. If previous life events are viewed with regret, the elderly person experiences **despair** (heartache and remorse). In this case, life seems like a series of missed opportunities. The person feels like a failure and knows it's too late to reverse what has been done. Aging and the threat of death then become sources of fear and depression.

The Lifespan in Perspective To squeeze a lifetime into a few pages, we had to ignore countless details. Although much is lost, the result is a clearer picture of an entire life cycle. Is Erikson's description, then, an exact map of Amy's past and her future—or your own? Probably not. Still, psychosocial dilemmas are major events in many lives. Knowing about them may allow you to anticipate typical trouble spots in your own life. You may also be better prepared to understand the problems and feelings of friends and relatives at various points in the life cycle.

Later Adulthood: Will You Still Need Me When I'm 64?

SURVEY QUESTION: *What issues arise during later adulthood?*

Although Erikson's dilemmas extend into adulthood, they are not the only challenges adults face. Others are all too familiar: marital strife, divorce, career difficulties, unemployment, health problems, financial pressures, legal conflicts, and personal tragedies—to name but a few. How do people maintain a state of well-being as they run the gauntlet of modern life? Psychologist Carol Ryff (1995; Ryff, Singer, & Palmersheim, 2004) believes that well-being during adulthood has six elements:

1. Self-acceptance
2. Positive relations with others
3. Autonomy (personal freedom)
4. Environmental mastery
5. A purpose in life
6. Continued personal growth

Ryff found that for many older adults, age-related declines are offset by positive relationships and greater mastery of life's demands (Ryff & Keyes, 1995). Thus, sharing life's joys and sorrows with others, coupled with a better understanding of how the world works, can help carry people through midlife and into their later years (Ryff & Singer, 2000; Ryff, Singer, & Palmersheim, 2004). Despite the emphasis on youth in our culture, middle age and beyond can be a rich period of life in which people feel secure, happy, and self-confident (Rubenstein, 2002).

A Midlife Crisis?

But don't people face a "midlife crisis" at this point in their lives? Yes and no. Serious difficulties at the midpoint of life are certainly not universal. Most people thrive during middle adulthood and have no special problems. Only about a quarter of men and women believe they have experienced a midlife crisis (Wethington, Kessler, & Pixley, 2004).

Nevertheless, midlife does pose special challenges. According to Roger Gould (1975), a psychiatrist interested in adult personality, North American adults actually experience two "crisis" points in their development.

Crisis of Questions According to Gould, around the age of 30 many people experience a minor life crisis. The heart of this crisis is a serious questioning of what life is all about. People tend to ask themselves, "Is this it?" and confidence in previous choices and values can waver. Unsettled by these developments, the person actively searches for a style of living that will bring more meaning to life. Marriages are particularly vulnerable during this time of dissatisfaction. Extramarital affairs and divorces are common symptoms of the "crisis of questions."

Trust versus mistrust A conflict early in life about learning to trust others and the world.

Autonomy versus shame and doubt A conflict created when growing self-control (autonomy) is pitted against feelings of shame or doubt.

Initiative versus guilt A conflict between learning to take initiative and overcoming feelings of guilt about doing so.

Industry versus inferiority A conflict in middle childhood centered around lack of support for industrious behavior, which can result in feelings of inferiority.

Identity versus role confusion A conflict of adolescence, involving the need to establish a personal identity.

Intimacy versus isolation The challenge of overcoming a sense of isolation by establishing intimacy with others.

Generativity versus stagnation A conflict of middle adulthood in which self-interest is countered by an interest in guiding the next generation.

Integrity versus despair A conflict in old age between feelings of integrity and the despair of viewing previous life events with regret.

"Follow that dream!"

Crisis of Urgency People in their late 30s and 40s are typically beginning to become more aware of the reality of death. Having a limited number of years to live begins to exert pressure on the individual. Intensified attempts are made to succeed at a career or to achieve one's life goals. Generativity, in the form of nurturing, teaching, or serving others, helps alleviate many of the anxieties of this stage.

If a midlife crisis does occur, what does it look like? Psychologist Daniel Levinson carried out a classic in-depth study of adulthood and identified several periods when people typically make major transitions. A **transition period** ends one life pattern and opens the door to new possibilities (Levinson, 1986). At such times, people address concerns about their identity, their work, and their relationships to others.

Levinson's first study focused on men. As they approached the midlife transition (between the ages of 37 and 41), most men went through a period of instability, anxiety, and change. (Notice that this corresponds closely to Gould's crisis-of-urgency period.) In a later study, Levinson found that most of what he learned about men also applies to women (Levinson & Levinson, 1996).

Of the men Levinson studied, roughly half defined the midlife period as a "last chance" to achieve their goals. Such goals were often stated as a key event, such as reaching a certain income or becoming a supervisor, a full professor, a shop steward, and so forth. For these men the midlife period was stressful but manageable.

A smaller percentage of men experienced a serious midlife decline. Many of these men had to face the fact that they had chosen a dead-end job or lifestyle. Others had achieved financial success but felt that what they were doing was pointless.

In a third pattern, a few hardy individuals appeared to "break out" of a seriously flawed life structure. For them, a decision to "start over" was typically followed by 8 to 10 years of rebuilding.

In what ways does the midlife transition differ for women? Compared with men, women were less likely to enter adulthood with specific "goals." As a result, they were less likely to define "success" in terms of some key event. Rather than focusing on external goals, women tended to seek changes in personal identity at midlife. For example, a woman might become more self-reliant and independent—qualities she might have regarded as "masculine" earlier in life (Levinson & Levinson, 1996). But make no mistake, midlife can be challenging for women, too (Wethington, 2000). In another survey of middle-aged women, two thirds said they made major changes in their lives between ages 37 and 43 (Stewart & Vandewater, 1999).

Midcourse Corrections In summary, people tend to move through cycles of stability and transition in their adult lives (Ornstein & Isabella, 1990). However, it is more common to make a "midcourse correction" at midlife than it is to survive a "crisis" (Lachman, 2004). Ideally, the midlife transition involves reworking old identities, achieving valued goals, finding one's own truths, and preparing for old age. Taking stock may be especially valuable at midlife, but reviewing past choices to prepare for the future is helpful at any age (Lewchanin & Zubrod, 2001). For some people, difficult turning points in life can serve as "wake-up calls" that create opportunities for personal growth (Wethington, 2003).

Old Age

After the late 50s, personal development is complicated by physical aging. However, it is wrong to believe that most elderly people are sickly, infirm, or senile. (Nowadays, 60 is the new 40, an idea both of your authors whole-heartedly agree with!) Only about 5 percent of those older than 65 are in nursing homes. Mentally, many elderly persons are at least as capable as the average young adult. On intellectual tests, top scorers over the age of 65 match the average for men younger than 35. What sets these silver-haired stars apart? Typically they are people who have continued to work and remain intellectually active (Salthouse, 2004). Gerontologist Warner Schaie (1994, 2005) found that you are most likely to stay mentally sharp in old age if:

1. You remain healthy.
2. You live in a favorable environment. (You are educated and have a stimulating occupation, an above-average income, and an intact family.)

3. You are involved in intellectually stimulating activities (reading, travel, cultural events, continuing education, clubs, professional associations).
4. You have a flexible personality.
5. You are married to a smart spouse.
6. You maintain your perceptual processing speed.
7. You were satisfied with your accomplishments in midlife.

A shorter summary of this list is "Those who live by their wit die with their wits."

Successful Aging *What are the keys to successful aging?* They are not unlike the elements of well-being at midlife. Four psychological characteristics shared by the healthiest, happiest older people are (de Leon, 2005; Vaillant, 2002):

Optimism, hope, and an interest in the future

Gratitude and forgiveness; an ability to focus on what is good in life

Empathy; an ability to share the feelings of others and see the world through their eyes

Connection with others; an ability to reach out, to give and receive social support

Actually, these are excellent guidelines for well-being at any stage of adulthood.

In summary, enlightened views of aging call for an end to the forced obsolescence of the elderly. As a group, older people represent a valuable source of skill, knowledge, and energy that we can't afford to cast aside. As we face the challenges of this planet's uncertain future, we need all the help we can get!

At age 77, John Glenn became the oldest person to fly into space, in October 1998. Glenn was also the first American astronaut to orbit Earth, in 1962. As Glenn's space adventure shows, aging does not inevitably bring an end to engaging in challenging activities.

Aging and Ageism You have almost certainly encountered ageism in one way or another. **Ageism,** which refers to discrimination or prejudice based on age, can oppress the young as well as the old. For instance, a person applying for a job may just as well be told "You're too young" as "You're too old." In some societies ageism is expressed as respect for the elderly. In Japan, for instance, aging is seen as positive, and greater age brings more status and respect. In most Western nations, however, ageism tends to have a negative impact on older individuals (Ng, 2002).

Ageism is often expressed through patronizing language. Older people are frequently spoken to in an overly polite, slow, loud, and simple way implying that they are infirm, even when they are not (Nelson, 2005). Popular stereotypes of the "dirty old man," "meddling old woman," "senile old fool," and the like also help perpetuate myths about aging. But such stereotypes are clearly wrong: A tremendous diversity exists among the elderly—ranging from the infirm to aerobic-dancing grandmothers.

In many occupations, older workers perform well in jobs that require *both* speed and skill. Of course, people do experience a gradual loss of *fluid abilities* (those requiring speed or rapid learning) as they age but often this can be offset by many *crystallized abilities* (learned knowledge and skills), such as vocabulary and stored-up facts, which may actually improve—at least into the 60s (Schaie, 2005). Overall, very little loss of job performance occurs as workers grow older. In the professions, wisdom and expertise can usually more than compensate for any loss of mental quickness (Ericsson, 2000). Basing retirement solely on a person's age makes little sense.

Death and Dying—The Final Challenge

SURVEY QUESTION: *How do people typically react to death?*

DEAR ABBY: Do you think about dying much? *(signed)* CURIOUS

DEAR CURIOUS: No, it's the last thing I want to do.

"I'm not afraid of dying. I just don't want to be there when it happens." Woody Allen

"Why not? Why not?" LSD guru Timothy Leary (his last words before dying)

Transition period Time span during which a person leaves an existing life pattern behind and moves into a new pattern.

Ageism Discrimination or prejudice based on a person's age.

THE STATISTICS ON DEATH are very convincing: One out of one dies. In spite of this, most of us are poorly informed about a process that is as basic as birth. We have seen through the modules in this chapter that it is valuable to understand major trends in the course of development. With this in mind, let us now explore emotional responses to death, the inevitable conclusion of every life. For many people, to die well is no less an accomplishment than to live well.

It might seem that as people grow older they would fear death more. However, older persons actually have fewer death fears than younger people. Older people more often fear the *circumstances* of dying, such as pain or helplessness, rather than death itself (Thorson & Powell, 1990). These findings seem to show a general lack of death fears, but they may actually reflect a widespread denial of death. Notice how denial is apparent in the language used to talk about death: Often we speak of a dead person as having "passed away," "expired," "gone to God," or "breathed one's last."

Many people have little direct experience with death until they, themselves, are fairly old. The average person's exposure to death consists of the artificial and unrealistic portrayals of death on TV. By the time the average person is 17 years old, she or he will have witnessed thousands of TV deaths. With few exceptions these are *homicides*, not deaths due to illness or aging.

Reactions to Impending Death

A direct and highly influential account of emotional responses to death comes from the work of Elisabeth Kübler-Ross (1926–2004). Kübler-Ross was a **thanatologist** (THAN-ah-TOL-oh-jist: one who studies death). Over the years she spent hundreds of hours at the bedsides of the terminally ill, where she observed five basic emotional reactions to impending death (Kübler-Ross, 1975).

1. **Denial and isolation.** A typical first reaction is to deny death's reality and isolate oneself from information confirming that death is really going to occur. Initially the person may be sure that "It's all a mistake." "Surely," she or he thinks, "the lab reports have been mixed up or the doctor made an error." This sort of denial may proceed to attempts to avoid any reminder of the situation.

2. **Anger.** Many dying individuals feel anger and ask, "Why me?" As they face the ultimate threat of having life torn away, their anger may spill over into rage toward the living. Even good friends may temporarily evoke anger because their health is envied.

3. **Bargaining.** In another common reaction, the terminally ill bargain with themselves or with God. The dying person thinks, "Just let me live a little longer and I'll do anything to earn it." Individuals may bargain for time by trying to be "good" ("I'll never smoke again"), by righting past wrongs, or by praying that if they are granted more time they will dedicate themselves to their religion.

4. **Depression.** As death draws near and the person begins to recognize that it cannot be prevented, feelings of futility, exhaustion, and deep depression may set in. The person realizes she or he will be separated from friends, loved ones, and the familiar routines of life, and this causes a profound sadness.

5. **Acceptance.** If death is not sudden, many people manage to come to terms with dying and accept it calmly. The person who accepts death is neither happy nor sad, but at peace with the inevitable. Acceptance usually signals that the struggle with death has been resolved. The need to talk about death ends, and silent companionship from others is frequently all the person desires.

Death may be inevitable, but it can be faced with dignity and, sometimes, even humor. Mel Blanc's famous sign-off, "That's all folks," is engraved on a marble headstone over his grave. Blanc was the voice of Bugs Bunny, Porky Pig, and many other cartoon characters.

Not all terminally ill persons display all these reactions, nor do they always occur in this order. Individual styles of dying vary greatly. Generally, there does tend to be a movement from initial shock, denial, and anger toward eventual acceptance. However, some people who seem to have accepted death may die angry and raging against the inevitable. Conversely, the angry fighter may let go of the struggle and die peacefully. In general, one's approach to dying will mirror his or her style of living (Yedidia & MacGregor, 2001).

It is a mistake, then, to think that Kübler-Ross's list is a series of stages to go through in order or that there is something wrong if a person does not show all these emotions. Rather, the list describes typical reactions to impending death. Note, as well, that many of the same reactions accompany any major loss, be it divorce, loss of a home due to fire, death of a pet, or loss of a job.

Implications *How can I make use of this information?* First, it can help both the dying and survivors to recognize and cope with periods of depression, anger, denial, and bargaining. Second, it helps to realize that close friends or relatives may feel many of the same emotions before or after a person's death because they, too, are facing a loss.

Perhaps the most important thing to recognize is that the dying person needs to share feelings with others and to discuss death openly. Too often, dying persons feel isolated and separated from others. Adults tend to "freeze up" with someone who is dying. For such people, thanatologist Kirsti Dyer (2001) has this advice:

- Be yourself and relate person to person.
- Be ready to listen again and again.
- Be respectful.
- Be aware of feelings and nonverbal cues.
- Be comfortable with silence.
- Be genuine.
- Most of all, be there.

Understanding what the dying person is going through may make it easier for you to offer support at this important time. A simple willingness to be with the person and to honestly share his or her feelings can help bring dignity, acceptance, and meaning to death (Holstein, 1997).

MODULE 3.7 Summary

What are the typical tasks and dilemmas through the lifespan?
- Erik Erikson identified a series of challenges that occur across the lifespan. These range from a need to gain trust in infancy to the need to live with integrity in old age.

What issues arise during later adulthood?
- Well-being during adulthood consists of six elements: self-acceptance, positive relations with others, autonomy, environmental mastery, having a purpose in life, and continued personal growth.
- Only a minority of people have a midlife crisis, but midlife course corrections are more common.
- Even if no crisis occurs, people tend to move through repeated cycles of stability and transition throughout adulthood.
- Intellectual declines associated with aging are limited, at least through one's 70s. This is especially true of individuals who remain mentally active.
- *Ageism* refers to prejudice, discrimination, and stereotyping on the basis of age. It affects people of all ages but is especially damaging to older people. Most ageism is based on stereotypes, myths, and misinformation.

How do people typically react to death?
- Death is a natural part of life. There is value in understanding it and accepting it.
- Typical emotional reactions to impending death include denial, anger, bargaining, depression, and acceptance, but not necessarily in that order or in every case.

Thanatologist A specialist who studies emotional and behavioral reactions to death and dying.

KNOWLEDGE BUILDER

Challenges Across the Lifespan

Recite

As a way to improve your memory, you might find it helpful to summarize Erikson's eight life stages. Complete this do-it-yourself summary and compare your answers to those given below.

Stage	Crisis	Favorable Outcome
First year of life	1. _____ vs.	Faith in the environment and in others
	2. _____	
Ages 1–3	Autonomy vs.	Feelings of self-control and adequacy
	3. _____	
Ages 3–5	4. _____ vs. guilt	Ability to begin one's own activities
Ages 6–12	Industry vs.	Confidence in productive skills, learning how to work
	5. _____	
Adolescence	6. _____ vs. role confusion	An integrated image of oneself as a unique person
Young adulthood	Intimacy vs.	Ability to form bonds of love and friendship with others
	7. _____	
Middle adulthood	Generativity vs.	Concern for family, society, and future generations
	8. _____	
Late adulthood	9. _____ vs.	Sense of dignity and fulfillment, willingness to face death
	10. _____	

11. Nearly everyone experiences a midlife crisis sometime around age 40. T or F?
12. After age 65, a large proportion of older people show significant signs of mental disability and most require special care. T or F?
13. Job performance tends to decline rapidly in older workers. T or F?
14. In the reaction that Kübler-Ross describes as bargaining, the dying individual asks, "Why me?" T or F?

Reflect
Critical Thinking

15. Trying to make generalizations about development throughout life is complicated by at least one major factor. What do you think it is?

Relate

See if you can think of a person you know who is facing one of Erikson's psychosocial dilemmas. Now see if you can think of specific people who seem to be coping with each of the other dilemmas.

See if you can describe three instances of ageism you have witnessed.

Link

Internet addresses frequently change. To find the sites listed here, visit **http://www.thomsonedu.com/psychology/coon** for an updated list of Internet addresses and direct links to relevant sites.

- **Welcome to Middle Age** Home page of middleage.org.
- **The AARP** Home page of the American Association of Retired Persons.
- **Hospice** A website of information about death, bereavement, and hospices.

ANSWERS

1. Trust 2. mistrust 3. shame or doubt 4. Initiative 5. inferiority 6. Identity 7. isolation 8. stagnation 9. Integrity 10. despair 11. F 12. F 13. F 14. F 15. Different *cohorts* (groups of people born in the same year) live in different historical times. People born in various decades may have very different life experiences. This makes it difficult to identify universal patterns (Stewart & Ostrove, 1998).

MODULE **Psychology in Action**

3.8 Effective Parenting–Raising Healthy Children

SURVEY QUESTION: *How do effective parents discipline and communicate with their children?*

Authoritative parents help their children grow up with a capacity for love, joy, fulfillment, responsibility, and self-control through *positive parent-child interactions*. Positive interactions occur when parents spend enjoyable time encouraging their children in a loving and mutually respectful fashion (Dinkmeyer, McKay, & Dinkmeyer, 1997).

As any parent can tell you, it is all well and good to talk about positive interactions until little Johnny misbehaves (and he will, count on it!). As children mature and become more independent, parents must find ways to control their children's behavior. ("No, you may not smear banana pudding on daddy's face.") When parents fail to provide *discipline* (guidance regarding acceptable behavior), children become antisocial, aggressive, and insecure. And yet, it is not easy to have a positive interaction while disciplining your child. This is one reason why overly permissive parents avoid disciplining their children.

Effective discipline is created through communication that is fair but loving, authoritative yet sensitive. It socializes a child without destroying the bond of love and trust between parent and child. Children should feel free to express their deepest feelings. However, this does not mean they can do whatever they please. Rather, the child is allowed to move freely within consistent, well-defined boundaries for acceptable behavior.

Effective Discipline

Parents typically discipline children in one of three ways. **Power assertion** refers to physical punishment or a show of force, such as taking away toys or privileges. As an alternative, some parents use **withdrawal of love** (withholding affection) by refusing to speak to a child, threatening to leave, rejecting the child, or otherwise acting as if the child is temporarily unlovable. **Management techniques** combine praise, recognition, approval, rules, reasoning, and the like to encourage desirable behavior. Each of these approaches can control a child's behavior, but their side effects differ considerably.

What are the side effects? Power-oriented techniques—particularly harsh or severe physical punishment—are associated with fear, hatred of parents, and a lack of spontaneity

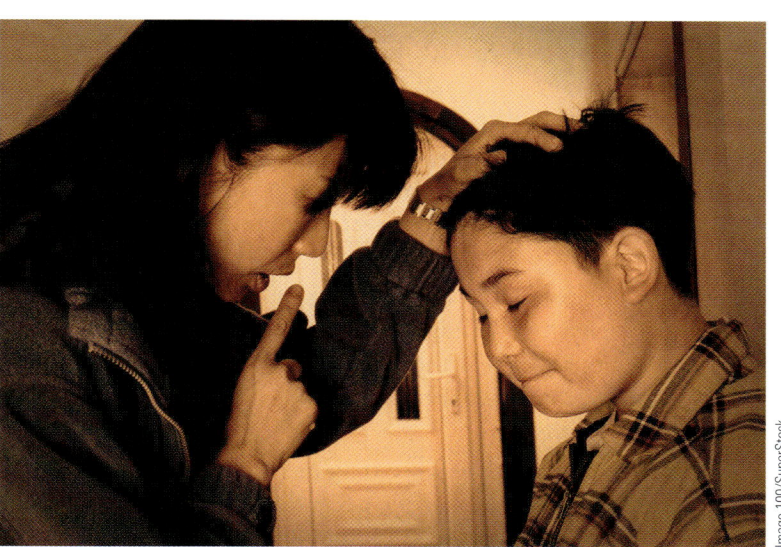

Power assertion The use of physical punishment or coercion to enforce child discipline.
Withdrawal of love Withholding affection to enforce child discipline.
Management techniques Combining praise, recognition, approval, rules, and reasoning to enforce child discipline.

and warmth. Most children show no signs of long-term damage from spanking—*if* spanking is backed up by supportive parenting (Baumrind, Larzelere, & Cowan, 2002). However, emotional damage does occur if spankings are severe, frequent, or coupled with harsh parenting. In addition, frequent spanking tends to increase aggression, and it leads to *more* problem behaviors, not fewer (McLoyd & Smith, 2002). After reviewing many studies, psychologist Elizabeth Gershoff concludes that parents should minimize spanking or avoid it entirely (Gershoff, 2002).

Withdrawal of love produces children who tend to be self-disciplined. You could say that such children have developed a good conscience. Often, they are described as "model" children or as unusually "good." But as a side effect, they are also frequently anxious, insecure, and dependent on adults for approval.

Management techniques also have limitations. Most important is the need to carefully adjust to a child's level of understanding. Younger children don't always see the connection between rules, explanations, and their own behavior. Nevertheless, management techniques receive a big plus in another area: There is a direct connection between discipline and a child's self-esteem.

How does discipline affect self-esteem? If you regard yourself as a worthwhile person, you have **self-esteem.** High self-esteem is essential for good emotional health. In elementary school, children with high self-esteem tend to be more popular, cooperative, and successful in class. Children with low self-esteem are more withdrawn and tend to perform below average (Amato & Fowler, 2002).

Low self-esteem is related to physical punishment and the withholding of love. And why not? What message do children receive if a parent beats them or tells them they are not worthy of love? Thus, it is best to minimize physical punishment and avoid withdrawal of love. In contrast, high self-esteem is promoted by management techniques. Children who feel that their parents support them emotionally tend to have high self-esteem (Amato & Fowler, 2002; Nielsen & Metha, 1994).

Consistent Discipline Individual parents choose limits on behavior that are more "strict" or less "strict." But this choice is less important than **consistency** (maintaining stable rules of conduct). Consistent discipline gives a child a sense of security and stability. Inconsistency makes the child's world seem insecure and unpredictable.

What does consistent discipline mean in practice? To illustrate the errors parents often make, let's consider a few examples of inconsistency (Fontenelle, 1989). The following are mistakes to avoid:

> Saying one thing and doing something else. You tell the child, "Bart, if you don't eat your brussels sprouts you can't have any dessert." Then you feel guilty and offer him some dessert.

> Making statements you don't mean. "If you don't quiet down, I'm going to stop the car and make you walk home."

> Changing *no* to *yes,* especially to quiet a nagging child. A good example is the parent who first refuses to buy the child a toy and later gives in and buys it.

> Responding differently to the same misbehavior. One day a child is sent to his room for fighting with his sister. The next day the fighting is overlooked.

Inconsistency makes children feel angry and confused because they cannot control the consequences of their own behavior. Inconsistency also gives children the message: "Don't believe what I say because I usually don't mean it."

Using Discipline Constructively At one time or another, most parents use power assertion, withdrawal of love, or management techniques to control their children. Each mode of discipline has its place. However, physical punishment and withdrawal of love should always be used with caution. Here are some guidelines.

1. Parents should separate disapproval of the act from disapproval of the child. Instead of saying, "I'm going to punish you because *you are bad,*" say, "I'm upset about *what you did.*"
2. State specifically what misbehavior you are punishing. Explain why you have set limits on this kind of conduct.
3. Punishment should never be harsh or injurious. Don't physically punish a child while you are angry. Also remember that the message "I don't love you right now" can be more painful and damaging than any spanking.
4. Punishment, such as a scolding or taking away privileges, is most effective when done immediately. This statement is especially true for younger children.
5. Spanking and other forms of physical punishment are not particularly effective for children younger than age 2. The child will only be confused and frightened. Spankings also become less effective after age 5 because they tend to humiliate the child and breed resentment.
6. As discussed earlier, many psychologists believe that children should never be spanked. If you do use physical punishment, reserve it for situations that pose an immediate danger to younger children; for example, when a child runs into the street.

7. Remember, too, that it is usually more effective to reward children when they are being good than it is to punish them for misbehavior.

After age 5, management techniques are the most effective form of discipline, especially techniques that emphasize communication and the relationship between parent and child.

Communicating Effectively with Children

Creative communication is another important ingredient of successful child management (Bath, 1996). Child expert Haim Ginott (1965) believed that making a distinction between feelings and behavior is the key to clear communication. Because children (and parents, too) do not choose how they feel, it is important to allow free expression of feelings.

Accepted Feelings The child who learns to regard some feelings as "bad," or unacceptable, is being asked to deny a very real part of his or her experience. Ginott encouraged parents to teach their children that all feelings are appropriate; it is only actions that are subject to disapproval. Consider this typical conversation excerpted from Ginott's classic book (1965):

Son: I am stupid, and I know it. Look at my grades in school.

Father: You just have to work harder.

Son: I already work harder and it doesn't help. I have no brains.

Father: You are smart, I know.

Son: I am stupid, I know.

Father: (loudly) You are not stupid!

Son: Yes, I am!

Father: You are not stupid. Stupid!

By debating with the child, the father misses the point that his son *feels* stupid. It would be far more helpful for the father to encourage the boy to talk about his feelings. For instance, he might say, "You really feel that you are not as smart as others, don't you? Do you feel this way often?" In this way, the child is given a chance to express his emotions and to feel understood. The father might conclude by saying, "Look, son, in my eyes you are a fine person. But I understand how you feel. Everyone feels stupid at times." He might also offer some encouragement: "You're improving. Look at the progress you've made."

I-Messages Child psychologist Thomas Gordon (2000) believes that parents should send *I-messages* to their children, rather than *you-messages*.

What's the difference? **You-messages** take the form of threats, name-calling, accusing, bossing, lecturing, or criticizing. Generally, you-messages tell children what's "wrong" with them. An **I-message** tells children what effect their behavior had on you. For example, after a hard day's work, Maria wants to sit down and rest awhile. She begins to relax with a newspaper when her 5-year-old daughter starts banging loudly on a toy drum. Many parents would respond with a you-message such as "You go play outside this instant." (bossing) or "Don't you ever make such a racket when someone is reading." (lecturing). Gordon suggests sending an I-message such as, "I am very tired, and I would like to read. I feel upset and can't read with so much noise." This forces the child to accept responsibility for the effects of her actions (Dinkmeyer, McKay, & Dinkmeyer, 1997).

Using Natural and Logical Consequences Sometimes events automatically discourage misbehavior. For example, a child who refuses to eat dinner will get uncomfortably hungry. A child who throws a temper tantrum may gain nothing but a sore throat and a headache if the tantrum is ignored (Fontenelle, 1989). In such instances, a child's actions have **natural consequences** (intrinsic effects). In situations that don't produce natural consequences, parents can set up **logical consequences** (rational and reasonable effects). For example, a parent might say, "We'll go to the zoo when you've picked up all those toys," or "You can play with your dolls as soon as you've taken your bath," or "You two can stop arguing or leave the table until you're ready to join us."

The concept of logical, parent-defined consequences can be combined with I-messages to handle many day-to-day instances of misbehavior. The key idea is to use an I-message to set up consequences and then give the child a choice to make: "Michelle, we're trying to watch TV. You can settle down and watch with us or go play elsewhere. You decide which you'd rather do" (Dinkmeyer, McKay, & Dinkmeyer, 1997).

Self-esteem Regarding oneself as a worthwhile person; a positive evaluation of oneself.

Consistency With respect to child discipline, the maintenance of stable rules of conduct.

You-message Threatening, accusing, bossing, lecturing, or criticizing another person.

I-message A message that states the effect someone else's behavior has on you.

Natural consequences The effects that naturally tend to follow a particular behavior.

Logical consequences Reasonable consequences that are defined by parents.

How could Maria have dealt with her 5-year-old—the one who was banging on a drum? A response that combines an I-message with logical consequences would be, "I would like for you to stop banging on that drum; otherwise, please take it outside." If the child continues to bang on the drum inside the house, then she has caused the toy to be put away. If she takes it outside, she has made a decision to play with the drum in a way that respects her mother's wishes. In this way, both parent and child have been allowed to maintain a sense of self-respect and a needless clash has been averted.

After you have stated consequences and let the child decide, be sure to respect the child's choice. If the child repeats the misbehavior, you can let the consequences remain in effect longer. But later, give the child another chance to cooperate.

With all child management techniques, remember to be firm, kind, consistent, respectful, and encouraging. And most of all, try every day to live the message you wish to communicate.

MODULE 3.8 Psychology in Action Summary

How do effective parents discipline and communicate with their children?

- Positive parent-child interactions occur when parents spend enjoyable time encouraging their children in a loving and mutually respectful fashion.
- Effective parental discipline tends to emphasize child management techniques (especially communication), rather than power assertion or withdrawal of love.
- Consistency is also an important aspect of effective parenting.
- Effective parents allow their children to express their feeling but place limits on their behavior.
- Much misbehavior can be managed by use of I-messages and the application of natural and logical consequences.

KNOWLEDGE BUILDER

Effective Parenting

Recite
1. Effective discipline gives children freedom within a structure of consistent and well-defined limits. T or F?
2. One good way to maintain consistency in child management is to overstate the consequences for misbehavior. T or F?
3. Spankings and other physical punishments are most effective for children under the age of 2. T or F?
4. Giving recognition for progress and attempts to improve is an example of parental _____.
5. I-messages are a gentle way of accusing a child of misbehavior. T or F?
6. In situations where natural consequences are unavailable or do not discourage misbehavior, parents should define logical consequences for a child. T or F?

Reflect
Critical Thinking
7. Several Scandinavian countries have made it illegal for parents to spank their own children. Does this infringe on the rights of parents?

Relate
What do you think are the best ways to discipline children? How would your approach be classified? What are its advantages and disadvantages?

Parents can probably never be completely consistent. Think of a time when your parents were inconsistent in disciplining you. How did it affect you?

Think of a you-message you have recently given a child, family member, roommate, or spouse. Can you change it into an I-message?

Link
Internet addresses frequently change. To find the sites listed here, visit **http://www.thomsonedu.com/psychology/coon** for an updated list of Internet addresses and direct links to relevant sites.

- **Nine Steps to More Effective Parenting** Read some more good advice on effective parenting.
- **Discipline: Logical & Natural Consequences** Read about ways to effectively structure discipline.
- **Ten Reasons Not to Hit Your Kids** Some reasons to avoid a heavy reliance on power-oriented discipline techniques.

ANSWERS
1. T 2. F 3. F 4. encouragement 5. F 6. T 7. Such laws are based on the view that it should be illegal to physically assault any person, regardless of their age. Although parents may believe they have a "right" to spank their children, it can be argued that children need special protection because they are small, powerless, and dependent (Durrant & Janson, 2005).

Interactive Learning

Psychology: Active Learning Modules Book Companion Website

Visit the book's companion website, **http://www.thomsonedu.com/psychology/coon**, where you will find flash cards, practice quizzes, Internet links, and more to help you study.

ThomsonNOW

Just What You Need to Know NOW!

http://psychology.wadsworth.com

Go to **www.thomsonedu.com** to link to ThomsonNOW, your online study tool. First take the **pre-test** for the modules making up this chapter to get your **personalized study plan,** which will identify topics you need to review and direct you to online resources. Then take the **post-test** to determine what concepts you have mastered and what you still need work on.

4 Sensation and Perception

MODULE 4.1 Sensory Systems and Selective Attention
SURVEY QUESTION: In general, how do sensory systems function?
SURVEY QUESTION: Why are we more aware of some sensations than others?

MODULE 4.2 Vision
SURVEY QUESTION: How is vision accomplished?

MODULE 4.3 Hearing, the Chemical Senses, and the Somesthetic Senses
SURVEY QUESTION: What are the mechanisms of hearing?
SURVEY QUESTION: How do the chemical senses operate?
SURVEY QUESTION: What are the somesthetic senses and why are they important?

MODULE 4.4 Perceptual Constancies and Perceptual Grouping
SURVEY QUESTION: How do perceptual constancies affect our perceptions?

SURVEY QUESTION: What basic principles do we use to group sensations into meaningful patterns?

MODULE 4.5 Depth Perception
SURVEY QUESTION: How is it possible to see depth and judge distance?

MODULE 4.6 Perception and Objectivity
SURVEY QUESTION: How is perception altered by expectations, motives, emotions, and learning?

MODULE 4.7 Extrasensory Perception
SURVEY QUESTION: Is extrasensory perception possible?

MODULE 4.8 Psychology in Action: Becoming a Better Eyewitness to Life
SURVEY QUESTION: How can I learn to perceive events more accurately?

Bats and Murder

At this very moment you are bathed in a swirling kaleidoscope of light, heat, pressure, vibrations, molecules, radiation, and mechanical forces. Without the senses, all of this would seem like nothing more than a void of darkness and silence. The next time you drink in the beauty of a sunset, a flower, or a friend, remember this: Sensation makes it all possible.

One of your authors was once in a supermarket when an 8-year-old girl suddenly came running around a corner. She looked back and screamed, "Stop! Stop! You're killing him! You're killing my father!" Here is your author's account of what followed:

"As a witness, I would have told a jury that I had seen one man strangling another and that there was blood everywhere on the floor. Yet, no murder ever took place that day at the supermarket. When the police arrived, they discovered that the 'guy on the bottom' had passed out and hit his head. That caused the cut (actually quite minor) that explained the 'blood everywhere.' The 'guy on top' saw the first man fall and was trying to loosen his collar. Obviously, the girl had misunderstood what was happening to her father. As a psychologist, I still find it fascinating that her words so dramatically influenced what I saw."

As our murder-in-the-supermarket story shows, sensing the world is really just a first step. Sensory information can be interpreted or *misinterpreted* in various ways. In this chapter we will begin with a look at how the senses operate. Then you will learn how we assemble sensations into a meaningful "picture" or model of the world. Our perceptions create faces, melodies, works of art, illusions, and, on occasion, "murders" out of the raw material of sensation. Let's see how this takes place.

© 2007 "Pintos" by Bev Doolittle®, courtesy of The Greenwich Workshop, Inc. www.greenwichworkshop.com

MODULE 4.1 Sensory Systems and Selective Attention

PHYSICAL ENERGY in the form of light or heat or sound strikes your senses. An instant later you notice a snowball whiz past your nose or the warmth of the sun on your face or a catchy tune on the radio. In that instant, a remarkable series of events will have transpired as you detect, analyze, and interpret sensory information. Before we examine specific senses in more detail, let's explore how the senses and selective attention reduce the amount of information the brain must process.

A World of Sensation—Too Much of a Good Thing?

SURVEY QUESTION: *In general, how do sensory systems function?*

Our eyes give us amazingly wide access to the world. In one instant you can view a star light-years away, and in the next, you can peer into the microscopic universe of a dewdrop. Yet, vision also narrows what it is possible to observe. Like the other senses, vision acts as a *data reduction system*. Your senses send only the most important data to your brain so that it is not overwhelmed by the sheer volume of sensory information (Sekuler & Blake, 2006).

Selection

How does data reduction take place? Some selection occurs because sensory receptors are *biological transducers,* devices that convert one kind of energy into another (Fain, 2003). For example, a guitar transduces string vibrations into sound waves. Pluck a string and the guitar will produce a sound. However, stimuli that don't cause the string to move will have no effect. For instance, if you shine a light on the string, or pour cold water on it, the guitar will remain silent. (The owner of the guitar, however, might get quite loud at this point!) Thus, the eye transduces electromagnetic radiation, the ear transduces sound waves, and so on. Many other types of stimuli cannot be sensed directly because we have no sense receptors to transduce their energy. For example, humans cannot sense fine vibrations in water (but sharks have special organs that can; do they *hear* the vibrations or *feel* them or what?).

In an approach called **psychophysics,** physical energy (such as sound waves or electromagnetic radiation) is measured and related to dimensions of the resulting sensations we experience (such as loudness or brightness). Psychophysical research has shown that sense receptors transduce only part of their target energy range (Fain, 2003). For example, your eyes transduce only the *visible spectrum*, which is just a tiny fraction of the entire range of electromagnetic energies. In contrast, the eyes of honeybees transduce parts of the electromagnetic spectrum invisible to humans. Bats use *echolocation*; their ears transduce sound waves that we humans cannot hear.

Similarly, energy below a certain minimum intensity is necessary for a sensation to occur. The necessary minimum defines the **absolute threshold** for a sensory system. For example, very soft sounds (which could be heard if they were just a little louder) fall below the absolute threshold for human hearing. Of course owls, who hunt at night, have much lower absolute thresholds for hearing. As you can see, our rich sensory experience is only a small part of what *could* be sensed and what some animals *can* sense.

Sensory Adaptation

Sensations are altered in another way. Think about walking into a house where fried fish, sauerkraut, and head cheese were prepared for dinner. (Some dinner!) You would probably pass out at the door, yet people who had been in the house for some time wouldn't be aware of the food odors. Why? Because sensory receptors respond less to unchanging stimuli, a process called **sensory adaptation.**

Fortunately, the olfactory (smell) receptors adapt quickly. When exposed to a constant odor, they send fewer and fewer nerve impulses to the brain until the odor is no longer noticed. Adaptation to pressure from a wristwatch, waistband, ring, or glasses is based on the same principle. Since there is usually little reason to keep reminding the brain that a sensory input is unchanged, sensory receptors generally respond best to *changes* in stimulation. No one wants or needs to be reminded 16 hours a day that his or her shoes are on.

Analysis

What we experience is further influenced by **sensory analysis.** As they process information, the senses divide the world into important **perceptual features** (basic stimulus patterns). The visual system, for example, has a set of *feature detectors* that are attuned to very specific stimuli, such as lines, shapes, edges, spots, colors, and other patterns (Hubel & Wiesel, 2005). Look at ● Figure 4.1 and notice how eye-catching the

● **FIGURE 4.1** Visual pop-out. Pop-out is so basic that babies as young as 3 months respond to it. (Adapted from Adler & Orprecio, 2006.)

single vertical line is among a group of slanted lines. This effect, which is called *pop-out,* occurs because your visual system is highly sensitive to perceptual features such as line orientation (Adler & Orprecio, 2006).

Similarly, frog eyes are highly sensitive to small, dark, moving spots. In other words, they are basically "tuned" to detect bugs flying nearby (Lettvin, 1961). But the insect (spot) must be moving, or the frog's "bug detectors" won't work. A frog could starve to death surrounded by dead flies.

Our sensitivity to perceptual features is an innate characteristic of the nervous system. Like other inborn capacities, this sensitivity is influenced by early experience. For instance, Colin Blakemore and Graham Cooper of Cambridge University raised kittens in a room with only vertical stripes on the walls. Another set of kittens saw only horizontal stripes. When returned to normal environments, the "horizontal" cats could easily jump onto a chair, but when walking on the floor, they bumped into chair legs. "Vertical" cats, on the other hand, easily avoided chair legs, but they missed when trying to jump to horizontal surfaces. The cats raised with vertical stripes were "blind" to horizontal lines, and the "horizontal" cats acted as if vertical lines were invisible (Blakemore & Cooper, 1970). Other experiments show that there is an actual decrease in brain cells tuned to the missing features (Grobstein & Chow, 1975).

Sensory Coding

As they select and analyze information, sensory systems *code* it. **Sensory coding** refers to converting important features of the world into neural messages understood by the brain (Hubel & Wiesel, 2005). For example, not every difference between two stimuli can be coded; instead the difference must be sufficiently large. Psychophysics also involves the study of **difference thresholds.** Here we are asking, "How different must two stimuli be before the difference becomes noticeable and, hence, codable?

To see coding at work, try closing your eyes for a moment. Then take your fingertips and press firmly on your eyelids. Apply enough pressure to "squash" your eyes slightly. Do this for about 30 seconds and observe what happens. (Readers with eye problems or contact lenses should not try this.)

Did you "see" stars, checkerboards, and flashes of color? These are called *phosphenes* (FOSS-feens: visual sensations caused by mechanical excitation of the retina). They occur because the eye's receptor cells, which normally respond to light, are also somewhat sensitive to pressure. Notice though, that the eye is only prepared to code stimulation—including pressure—into visual features. As a result, you experience light sensations, not pressure. Also important in producing this effect is *sensory localization* in the brain.

Sensory localization means that the type of sensation you experience depends on which brain area is activated. Some brain areas receive visual information; others receive auditory information, and still others receive taste or touch. (See Module 2.3.) Knowing which brain areas are active tells us, in general, what kinds of sensations you are feeling.

Sensory localization makes it possible to artificially restore sight, hearing, or other senses. For example, in July 2006, a woman named Cheri Robinson became the sixteenth person in the world with an implant that allows a miniature television camera to send electrical signals to her brain's visual cortex (● Fig. 4.2). She can now "see" 100 dots of light. Like a sports scoreboard, these lights can be used to form crude letters (Dobelle, 2000; Warren & Normann, 2005). Eventually, increasing the number of dots could make reading and "seeing" large objects, such as furniture and doorways, possible.

Psychophysics Study of the relationship between physical stimuli and the sensations they evoke in a human observer.
Absolute threshold The minimum amount of physical energy necessary to produce a sensation.
Sensory adaptation A decrease in sensory response to an unchanging stimulus.
Sensory analysis Separation of sensory information into important elements.
Perceptual features Basic elements of a stimulus, such as lines, shapes, edges, or colors.
Sensory coding Codes used by the sense organs to transmit information to the brain.
Difference threshold The minimum difference between two stimuli that is detectable to an observer.

● **FIGURE 4.2** An artificial visual system.

It is fascinating to realize that "seeing" and "hearing" take place in your brain, not in your eyes or ears. Information arriving from the sense organs creates **sensations.** When the brain organizes sensations into meaningful patterns, we speak of **perception,** which we will discuss later. For now, let's examine selective attention, another important process that influences what we can become aware of.

Selective Attention—Tuning In and Tuning Out

SURVEY QUESTION: *Why are we more aware of some sensations than others?*

Although the senses reduce a mixture of sights, sounds, odors, tastes, and touch sensations to more manageable amounts, they are still too much for the brain to handle. That's why sensory information must also be filtered by selective attention. For example, as you sit reading this page, receptors for touch and pressure in the seat of your pants are sending nerve impulses to your brain. Although these sensations have been present all along, you were probably not aware of them until just now. This "seat-of-the-pants phenomenon" is an example of **selective attention** (voluntarily focusing on a specific sensory input). Selective attention appears to be based on the ability of brain structures to select and divert incoming sensory messages (Freiwald & Kanwisher, 2004). We are able to "tune in on" a single sensory message while excluding others.

Another familiar example of this is the *cocktail party effect*. When you are in a group of people, surrounded by voices, you can still select and attend to the voice of the person you are facing. Or if that person gets dull, you can eavesdrop on conversations all over the room. (Be sure to smile and nod your head occasionally!) Actually, no matter how interesting your companion may be, your attention will probably shift away if you hear your own name spoken somewhere in the room (Conway, Cowan, & Bunting, 2001). We do find what others say about us to be very interesting, don't we?

At times, we can even suffer from *inattentional blindness* (Most et al., 2005). That is, we may not see something that is plainly before our eyes when our attention is narrowly focused (Mack, 2002). Inattentional blindness is vividly illustrated by the work of psychologists Daniel Simons and Christopher Chabris. In one study, Simons and Chabris showed people a film of two basketball teams, one wearing black shirts and the other wearing white. Observers were asked to watch the film closely and count how many times a basketball passed between members of one of the teams, while ignoring the other team. As observers watched and counted, a person wearing a gorilla suit walked into the middle of the basketball game, faced the camera, thumped its chest, and walked out of view. Half the observers failed to notice this rather striking event (Simons & Chabris, 1999). This effect probably explains why fans of opposing sports teams often act as if they had seen two completely different games. In a similar way, using a cell phone while driving can cause inattentional blindness. Instead of ignoring a gorilla, you might miss seeing another car, a motorcyclist, or a pedestrian while your attention is focused on the phone (Strayer, Drews, & Johnson, 2003).

You might find it helpful to think of selective attention as a *bottleneck,* or narrowing in the information channel linking the senses to perception. When one message enters the bottleneck, it seems to prevent others from passing through. (See ● Fig. 4.3.) Imagine, for instance, that you are a pilot preparing to land a jumbo jet. You need to be sure the flaps are down. Just as you are about to check them, your co-pilot says something to you. If you then fail to notice the flaps are still up, an air disaster is just seconds away.

Are some stimuli more attention getting than others? Yes. Very *intense* stimuli usually command attention. Stimuli that are brighter, louder, or larger tend to capture attention: A gunshot in a library would be hard to ignore. If a brightly

● **FIGURE 4.3** The attentional "spotlight" can be widened or narrowed. If you focus on local details in this drawing, you will see the letter *A* repeated 13 times. If you broaden your field of attention to encompass the overall pattern, you will see the letter *H*. (Adapted from Lamb & Yund, 1996.)

● **FIGURE 4.4** One of the drawings used by Loftus and Mackworth (1978) to investigate attention. Observers attend to unexpected objects longer than they do to expected objects. In this drawing, observers looked longer at the octopus than they did at a tractor placed in the same spot. What do you think would happen if a tractor were shown upside down or on the roof of the barn? (From "Cognitive Determinants of Fixation Location During Picture Viewing," by G. R. Loftus and N. H. MacWorth, *Journal of Experimental Psychology: Human Perception and Performance*, 4th ed., 1978, p. 565-572. Reprinted by permission of American Psychological Association.)

colored hot-air balloon ever lands at your college campus, it will almost certainly draw a crowd.

Repetitious stimuli, repetitious stimuli, repetitious stimuli, repetitious stimuli, repetitious stimuli, repetitious stimuli are also attention getting. A dripping faucet at night makes little noise by normal standards, but because of repetition, it may become as attention getting as a single sound many times louder. This effect is used repeatedly, so to speak, in television and radio commercials.

ATTENTION IS ALSO **FREQUENTLY** RELATED TO contrast OR *change* IN STIMULATION. The contrasting type styles in the preceding sentence draw attention because they are *unexpected*. Geoffrey Loftus and Norman Mackworth (1978) found that people who look at drawings like ● Figure 4.4 focus first and longest on unexpected objects (the octopus, in this case).

The senses supply raw data to the brain, but the information remains mostly meaningless until it is interpreted. It's as if the senses provide only the jumbled pieces of a complex puzzle. In the remaining modules of this chapter we will further explore the various senses and how we put the puzzle together.

MODULE 4.1 Summary

In general, how do sensory systems function?
- The senses act as data reduction systems in order to prevent the brain from being overwhelmed by sensory input.
- Sensation begins with transduction in a receptor organ; other data reduction processes are sensory adaptation, analysis, and coding.
- Sensory processing is localized in specific parts of the brain.

Why are we more aware of some sensations than others?
- Incoming sensations are affected by selective attention, a brain-based process that allows some sensory inputs to be selected for further processing while others are ignored.

Sensation A sensory impression; also, the process of detecting physical energies with the sensory organs.
Perception The mental process of organizing sensations into meaningful patterns.
Selective attention Giving priority to a particular incoming sensory message.

KNOWLEDGE BUILDER

Sensory Systems and Selective Attention

Recite

1. Sensory receptors are biological _____, or devices for converting one type of energy to another.
2. As time passes, nerve endings in the skin under your wristwatch send fewer signals to the brain and you become able to feel the watch. This process is called
   a. transduction *b.* difference threshold *c.* reverse attention *d.* sensory adaptation
3. Lettvin found that a frog's eyes are especially sensitive to phosphenes. T or F?
4. Important features of the environment are transmitted to the brain through a process known as
   a. phosphenation *b.* coding *c.* detection *d.* programming
5. The brain-centered ability to influence what sensations we will receive is called
   a. sensory adaptation *b.* psychophysics *c.* selective attention *d.* sensory biasing
6. Which of the following stimuli are more effective at getting attention:
   a. unexpected stimuli *b.* repetitious stimuli *c.* intense stimuli *d.* all of the above

Reflect
Critical Thinking

7. William James once said, "If a master surgeon were to cross the auditory and optic nerves, we would hear lightning and see thunder." Can you explain what James meant?

Relate

How does sensation affect what you are experiencing right now? Try to imagine how overwhelmed you would be if data reduction didn't occur?

What if, like some other animals, you could transduce other energies? What if your senses were tuned to detect different perceptual features? How would the sensory world you live in change?

As you sit reading this book, which sensory inputs have undergone adaptation? What new inputs can you become aware of by shifting your focus of attention? Can you attend to more than one sensory input at a time?

Link

Internet addresses frequently change. To find the sites listed here, visit **http://www.thomsonedu.com/psychology/coon** for an updated list of Internet addresses and direct links to relevant sites.

- **Psychophysics** Explore absolute and discrimination thresholds as well as other psychophysics phenomena.
- **Video of Units in Visual Cortex** Download and view a video of some of the original research, by David Hubel and Torsten Wiesel, on sensory coding in vision.
- **Selective Attention** Read about and experience dichotic listening.

ANSWERS

1. transducers 2. d 3. F 4. b 5. c 6. d 7. The explanation is based on sensory localization. Even if a lightning flash caused rerouted messages from the eyes to activate auditory areas of the brain, we would experience a thunderclap and sent impulses to the visual area, a sensation of light would occur. Amazingly, some people, called *synesthetes*, naturally experience sensory inputs in terms of other senses. For example, one synesthete experiences pain as the color orange, whereas for another the taste of spiced chicken is pointy (Dixon, Smilek, & Merikle, 2004).

MODULE 4.2 Vision

IN THE MORNING when you awaken and open your eyes you effortlessly become aware of the visual richness of the world around you. But the ease with which normally sighted people can *see* conceals incredible complexity. Vision is an impressive sensory system, worthy of a detailed discussion.

Vision—Catching Some Rays

SURVEY QUESTION: *How is vision accomplished?*

What are the basic dimensions of light and vision? Various wavelengths of light make up the *visible spectrum* (the narrow spread of electromagnetic energies to which the eyes respond). Visible light starts at "short" wavelengths of 400 *nanometers* (nan-OM-et-er: one billionth of a meter), which we sense as purple or violet. Longer light waves produce blue, green, yellow, orange, and red, which has a wavelength of 700 nanometers (● Fig. 4.5).

The term *hue* refers to the basic color categories of red, orange, yellow, green, blue, indigo, and violet. As just noted, various hues (or color sensations) correspond to the wavelength of the light that reaches our eyes (Sekuler & Blake, 2006). White light, in contrast, is a mixture of many wavelengths. Hues (colors) from a narrow band of wavelengths are very *saturated,* or "pure." (An intense "fire-engine" red is more saturated than a muddy "brick" red.) A third dimension of vision, *brightness,* corresponds roughly to the amplitude, or height of light waves. Waves of greater amplitude are "taller," carry more energy, and cause the colors we see to appear brighter or more intense. For example, the same "brick" red would look bright under intense, high-energy illumination and drab under dim light.

Structure of the Eye

Although the visual system is much more complex than any camera, both cameras and eyes have a *lens* to focus images on a light-sensitive layer at the back of a closed space. In a camera, this layer is the film. In the eye, it is a layer of *photoreceptors* (light-sensitive cells) in the **retina,** an area about the size and thickness of a postage stamp (● Fig. 4.6).

How does the eye focus? Most focusing is done at the front of the eye by the *cornea,* a clear membrane that bends light inward. The lens makes additional, smaller adjustments. Your eye's focal point changes when muscles attached to the lens alter its shape. This process is called **accommodation.** In cameras, focusing is done more simply—by changing the distance between the lens and the film.

Visual Problems Focusing is also affected by the shape of the eye. If your eye is too short, nearby objects will be blurred, but distant objects will be sharp. This is called **hyperopia** (HI-per-OPE-ee-ah: farsightedness). If your eyeball is too long, images fall short of the retina and you won't be able to focus distant objects. This results in **myopia** (my-OPE-ee-ah: nearsightedness). When the cornea or the lens is misshapen, part of vision will be focused and part will be fuzzy. In this case, the eye has more than one focal point, a problem called

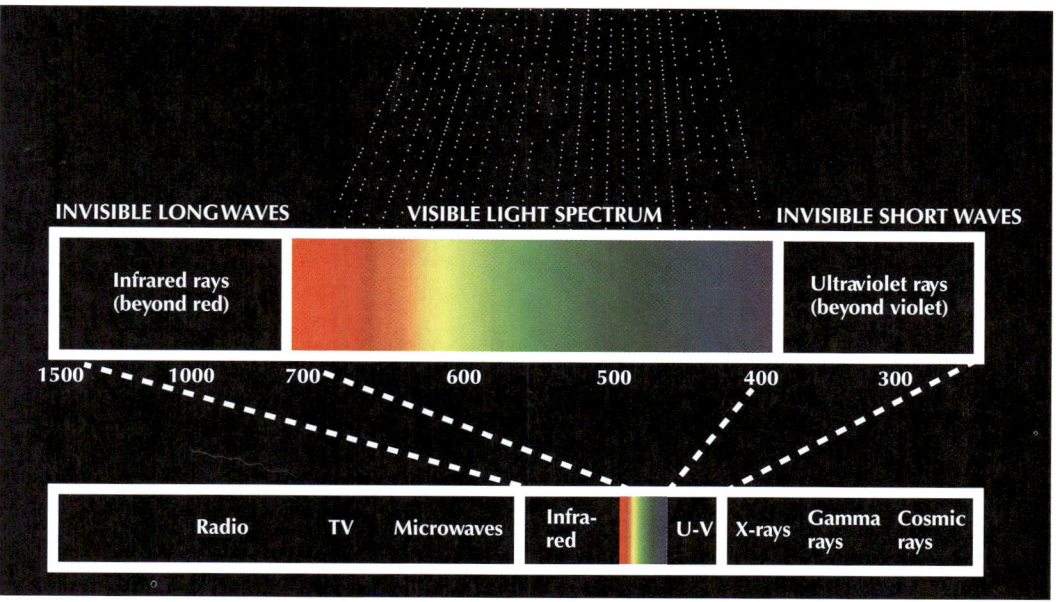

● **FIGURE 4.5** The visible spectrum.

Retina The light-sensitive layer of cells at the back of the eye.
Accommodation Changes in the shape of the lens of the eye.
Hyperopia Difficulty focusing nearby objects (farsightedness).
Myopia Difficulty focusing distant objects (nearsightedness).

155

156 Chapter 4 • SENSATION AND PERCEPTION

● **FIGURE 4.6** The human eye, a simplified view.

astigmatism (ah-STIG-mah-tiz-em). All three visual defects can be corrected by placing glasses (or contact lenses) in front of the eye to change the path of light (● Fig. 4.7).

As people age, the lens becomes less flexible and less able to accommodate. The result is **presbyopia** (prez-bee-OPE-ee-ah: old vision, or farsightedness due to aging). Perhaps you have seen a grandparent or older friend reading a newspaper at arm's length because of presbyopia. If you now wear glasses for nearsightedness, you may need bifocals as you age. (Just like your authors. Sigh.) Bifocal lenses correct near vision *and* distance vision.

Rods and Cones

The eye has two types of "film," consisting of receptor cells called *rods* and *cones* (Goldstein, 2007). The 5 million **cones** in each eye work best in bright light. They also produce color sensations and fine details. In contrast, the **rods,** numbering about 120 million, can't detect colors (● Fig. 4.8). Pure rod vision is black and white. However, the rods are much more sensitive to light than the cones are. The rods therefore allow us to see in very dim light.

Surprisingly, the retina has a "hole" in it: Each eye has a *blind spot* because there are no receptors where the optic nerve leaves the eye (● Fig. 4.9*a*). The blind spot shows that vision depends greatly on the brain. If you close one eye, part of what you see will fall on the blind spot of your open eye. Why isn't there a gap in your vision? The answer is that the visual cortex of the brain actively fills in the gap with patterns from surrounding areas (Fig. 4.9*b*). By closing one eye, you can visually "behead" other people by placing their images on your blind spot. (Just a hint for some classroom fun.) The brain can also "erase" distracting information. Roll your eyes all the way to the right and then close your right eye. You should clearly see your nose in your left eye's field of vision. Now, open your right eye again and your nose will nearly disappear as your brain disregards its presence.

Visual Acuity The rods and cones also affect **visual acuity**, or sharpness. The cones lie mainly at the center of the eye. In fact, the *fovea* (FOE-vee-ah: a small cup-shaped area in the middle of the retina) contains only cones—about 50,000 of them. Like a newspaper photograph made of many small dots, the tightly packed cones in the fovea produce the sharpest images. Normal acuity is designated as 20/20 vision: At 20 feet in distance, you can distinguish what the average person can see at 20 feet (● Fig. 4.10). If your vision is 20/40, you can only see at 20 feet what the average person can see at 40 feet. If your vision is 20/200, everything is a blur and you need glasses! Vision that is 20/12 would mean that you can see at 20 feet what the average person must be 8 feet nearer

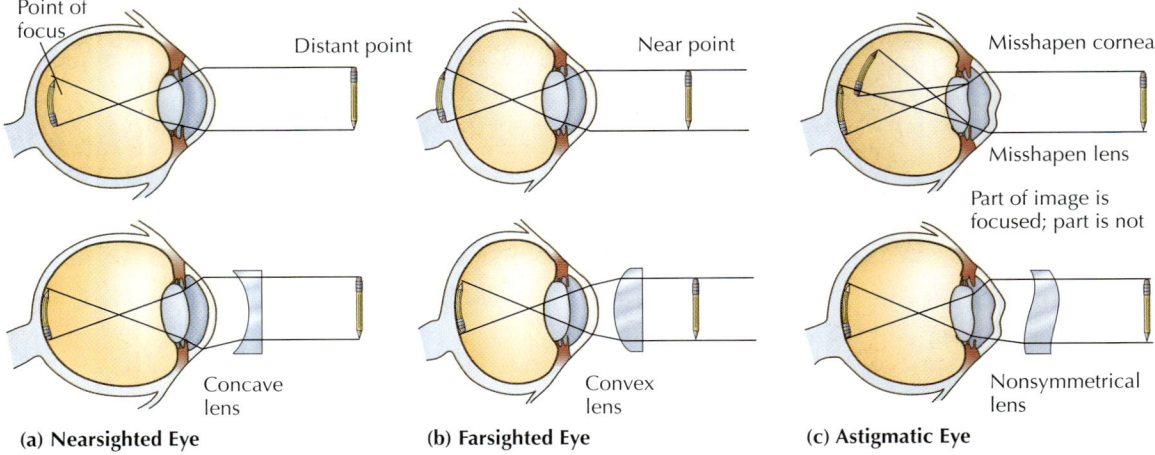

● **FIGURE 4.7** Visual defects and corrective lenses: *(a)* A myopic (longer than usual) eye. The concave lens spreads light rays just enough to increase the eye's focal length. *(b)* A hyperopic (shorter than usual) eye. The convex lens increases refraction (bending) to focus light on the retina. *(c)* An astigmatic (lens or cornea not symmetrical) eye. In astigmatism, parts of vision are sharp and parts are unfocused. Lenses that correct astigmatism are nonsymmetrical.

● **FIGURE 4.8** Anatomy of the retina. Note that light does not fall directly on the rods and cones. It must first pass through the cornea, the lens, the vitreous humor (a jelly-like substance that fills the eyeball), and the outer layers of the retina. Only about one half of the light at the front of the eye reaches the rods and cones—testimony to the retina's amazing sensitivity. The lower left photograph shows rods and cones as seen through an electron microscope. In the photograph the cones are colored green and the rods blue.

Color Vision

How do the cones produce color sensations? The **trichromatic theory** (TRY-kro-MAT-ik) of color vision holds that there are three types of cones, each most sensitive to either red, green, or blue. Other colors result from combinations of these three. Black and white sensations are produced by the rods.

A basic problem with the trichromatic theory is that four colors of light—red, green, blue, and yellow—seem to be primary (you can't get them by mixing other colors). Also, why is it impossible to have a reddish green or a yellowish blue? These problems led to the development of a second view, known as the **opponent-process theory,** which states that vision analyzes colors into "either-or" messages (Goldstein, 2007). That is, the visual system can produce messages for either red or green, yellow or blue, black or white. Coding one color in a pair (red, for instance) seems to block the opposite message (green) from coming through. As a result, a reddish green is impossible, but a yellowish red (orange) can occur.

to see, indicating better than average acuity. American astronaut Gordon Cooper, who claimed to see railroad lines in northern India from 100 miles above, had 20/12 vision.

Peripheral Vision *What is the purpose of the rest of the retina?* Areas outside the fovea also get light, creating a large region of **peripheral** (side) **vision.** The rods are most numerous about 20 degrees from the center of the retina, so much of our peripheral vision is rod vision. Although rod vision is not very sharp, the rods are quite sensitive to *movement* in peripheral vision. To experience this characteristic of the rods, look straight ahead and hold your hand beside your head, at about 90 degrees. Wiggle your finger and slowly move your hand forward until you can detect motion. You will become aware of the movement before you can actually "see" your finger.

The rods are also highly responsive to dim light. Because most rods are 20 degrees to each side of the fovea, the best night vision comes from looking *next to* an object you wish to see. Test this yourself some night by looking at, and next to, a very dim star.

Astigmatism Defects in the cornea, lens, or eye that cause some areas of vision to be out of focus.
Presbyopia Farsightedness caused by aging.
Cones Visual receptors for colors and daylight visual acuity.
Rods Visual receptors for dim light that produce only black and white sensations.
Visual acuity The sharpness of visual perception.
Peripheral vision Vision at the edges of the visual field.
Trichromatic theory Theory of color vision based on three cone types: red, green, and blue.
Opponent-process theory Theory of color vision based on three coding systems (red or green, yellow or blue, black or white).

● **FIGURE 4.9** Experiencing the blind spot. *(a)* With your right eye closed, stare at the upper right cross. Hold the book about 1 foot from your eye and slowly move it back and forth. You should be able to locate a position that makes the black spot disappear. When it does, it is on your blind spot. With a little practice you can learn to make people or objects you dislike disappear too! *(b)* Repeat the procedure described, but stare at the lower cross. When the white space falls on the blind spot, the black lines will appear to be continuous. This may help you understand why you do not usually notice a blind spot in your visual field.

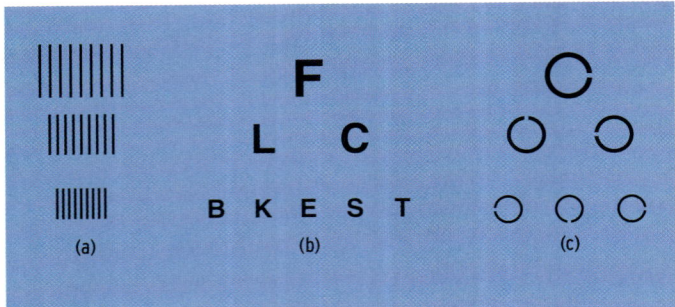

● **FIGURE 4.10** Tests of visual acuity. Here are some common tests of visual acuity. In *(a)*, sharpness is indicated by the smallest grating still seen as individual lines. The Snellen chart *(b)* requires that you read rows of letters of diminishing size until you can no longer distinguish them. The Landolt rings *(c)* require no familiarity with letters. All that is required is a report of which side has a break in it.

● **FIGURE 4.11** Negative afterimages. Stare at the dot near the middle of the flag for at least 30 seconds. Then look immediately at a plain sheet of white paper or a white wall. You will see the American flag in red, white, and blue. Reduced sensitivity to green, black, and yellow in the visual system, caused by prolonged staring, produces the complementary colors.

According to opponent-process theory, fatigue caused by making one response produces an afterimage of the opposite color as the system recovers. *Afterimages* are visual sensations that persist after a stimulus is removed—like seeing a spot after a flashbulb goes off. To see an afterimage of the type predicted by opponent-process theory, look at ● Figure 4.11 and follow the instructions there.

Which color theory is correct? Both! The three-color theory applies to the retina, where three different types of *visual pigments* (light-sensitive chemicals) have been found in cones. As predicted, each pigment is most sensitive to light in roughly the red, green, or blue region. The three types of cones fire nerve impulses at different rates to produce various color sensations (● Fig. 4.12).

In contrast, the opponent-process theory better explains what happens in optic pathways and the brain *after* information leaves the eye. For example, some nerve cells in the brain are excited by the color red and inhibited by the color green. So both theories are "correct." One explains what happens in the eye itself. The other explains how colors are analyzed after messages leave the eye (Gegenfurtner & Kiper, 2003).

Color Blindness Do you know anyone who regularly draws hoots of laughter by wearing clothes of wildly clashing colors? Or someone who sheepishly tries to avoid saying what color an object is? If so, you probably know someone who is color-blind.

What is it like to be color-blind? What causes color blindness? A person who is **color-blind** cannot perceive colors at all. It is as if the world is a black-and-white movie. The color-blind person either lacks cones or has cones that do not function normally (Deeb, 2004). Such total color blindness is rare. In **color weakness,** or partial color blindness, a person can't see certain colors. Approximately 8 percent of Caucasian males (but fewer Asian, African and Native American males and less than 1 percent of women) are red-green color-blind (Delpero et al., 2005). These people see reds and greens as the same color, usually a yellowish brown. (See ● Fig. 4.13.) Another form of color weakness, involving yellow and blue, is quite rare (Hsia & Graham, 1997). (See "Are You Color-Blind?")

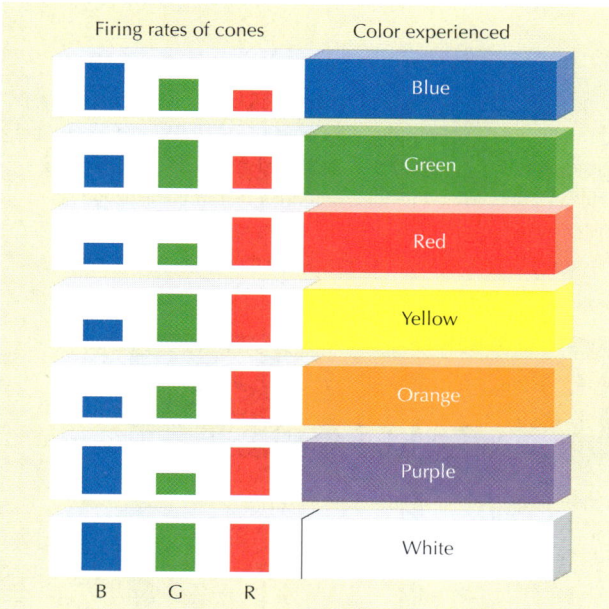

● **FIGURE 4.12** Firing rates of blue, green, and red cones in response to different colors. The taller the colored bar, the higher the firing rates for that type of cone. As you can see, colors are coded by differences in the activity of all three types of cones in the normal eye. (Adapted from Goldstein, 2007.)

How can color-blind individuals drive? Don't they have trouble with traffic lights? Red-green color-blind individuals have normal vision for yellow and blue, so the main problem is telling red lights from green. In practice, that's not difficult. The red light is always on top, and the green light is brighter than the red. Also, "red" traffic signals have yellow light mixed in with the red and a "green" light that is really blue-green.

Adapting to Dim Light

What happens when the eyes adjust to a dark room? **Dark adaptation** is the dramatic increase in retinal sensitivity to light that occurs after a person enters the dark (Goldstein, 2007). Consider walking into a theater. If you enter from a brightly lighted lobby, you practically need to be led to your seat. After a short time, however, you can see the entire room in detail (including the couple kissing over in the corner). It takes about 30 to 35 minutes of complete darkness to reach maximum visual sensitivity (● Fig. 4.15). At that point, your eye will be 100,000 times more sensitive to light.

What causes dark adaptation? Like the cones, the rods contain a light-sensitive visual pigment called *rhodopsin* (row-DOP-sin). When struck by light, visual pigments *bleach,* or break down chemically. The afterimages you have seen after looking at a flashbulb are a result of this bleaching. In fact, a few seconds of exposure to bright white light can completely wipe out dark adaptation. That's why you should be sure to

● **FIGURE 4.13** Color blindness and color weakness. *(a)* Photograph illustrates normal color vision. *(b)* Photograph is printed in blue and yellow and gives an impression of what a red-green color-blind person sees. *(c)* Photograph simulates total color blindness. If you are totally color-blind, all three photos will look nearly identical.

Color blindness A total inability to perceive colors.
Color weakness An inability to distinguish some colors.
Dark adaptation Increased retinal sensitivity to light.

DISCOVERING PSYCHOLOGY

Are You Color-Blind?

How can I tell if I am color-blind? Surprisingly, it is not as obvious as you might think; some people reach adulthood without knowing that some colors are missing (Gündogan et al., 2005). The *Ishihara test* is commonly used to measure color blindness and weakness. In the test, numbers and other designs made of dots are placed on a background also made of dots (Fig. 4.14). The background and the numbers are of different colors (red and green, for example). A person who is color-blind sees only a jumble of dots. If you have normal color vision you can detect the numbers or designs (Birch & McKeever, 1993; Coren, Ward, & Enns, 2004). The chart below Figure 4.14 lists what people with normal color vision, and those with color blindness, see. Because Figure 4.14 is just a replica, it is not a definitive test of color blindness. Nevertheless, if you can't see all of the embedded designs, you may be color-blind or color-weak.

FIGURE 4.14 A replica of the Ishihara test for color blindness.

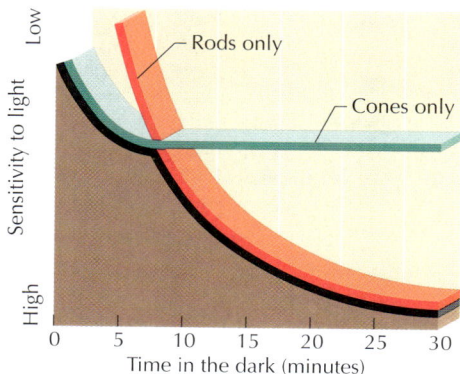

● **FIGURE 4.15** Typical course of dark adaptation. The black line shows how the threshold for vision lowers as a person spends time in the dark. (A lower threshold means that less light is needed for vision.) The green line shows that the cones adapt first, but they soon cease adding to light sensitivity. Rods, shown by the red line, adapt more slowly. However, they continue to improve night vision long after the cones are fully adapted.

Red light allows dark adaptation to occur because it provides little or no stimulation to the rods.

avoid looking at oncoming headlights when you are driving at night—especially the new bluish-white xenon lights. To restore light sensitivity, the visual pigments in the rods must recombine, which takes time.

Is there any way to speed up dark adaptation? The rods are *insensitive* to extremely red light. That's why submarines, airplane cockpits, and ready rooms for fighter pilots are illuminated with red light. In each case, people can move quickly into the dark without having to adapt. Because the red light doesn't stimulate the rods, it is as if they had already spent time in the dark.

MODULE 4.2 Summary

How is vision accomplished?

- The eye acts as an optical system to focus light on the retina.
- Four common visual defects are myopia, hyperopia, presbyopia, and astigmatism.
- The rods and cones are the eye's photoreceptors in the retina.
- The rods specialize in peripheral vision, night vision, seeing black and white, and detecting movement. The cones specialize in color vision, acuity, and daylight vision.
- Our ability to see colors is explained by the trichromatic theory (in the retina) and by the opponent-process theory (in the visual system beyond the eyes).
- Total color blindness is rare, but 8 percent of males and 1 percent of females are red-green color-blind or color-weak.
- Dark adaptation is caused mainly by an increase in the amount of rhodopsin in the rods.

KNOWLEDGE BUILDER

Vision

Recite

1. Match:
   - ____ Myopia
   - ____ Hyperopia
   - ____ Presbyopia
   - ____ Astigmatism

   A. Farsightedness
   B. Elongated eye
   C. Farsightedness due to aging
   D. Lack of cones in the fovea
   E. Misshapen cornea or lens

2. In dim light, vision depends mainly on the _____. In brighter light, color and fine detail are produced by the _____.

3. The greatest visual acuity is associated with the _____ and the _____.
   a. trichromat, rods
   b. vitreous humor, cones
   c. fovea, cones
   d. nanometer, cones

4. Colored afterimages are best explained by
   a. trichromatic theory
   b. the effects of astigmatism
   c. sensory localization
   d. opponent-process theory

5. Dark adaptation is directly related to an increase in
   a. rhodopsin
   b. astigmatism
   c. accommodation
   d. saturation

Reflect
Critical Thinking

6. Sensory transduction in the eye takes place first in the cornea, then in the lens, then in the retina. T or F?

Relate

Pretend you are a beam of light. What will happen to you at each step as you pass into the eye and land on the retina? What will happen if the eye is not perfectly shaped? How will the retina know you've arrived? How will it tell what color of light you are? What will it tell the brain about you?

Link

Internet addresses frequently change. To find the sites listed here, visit **http://www.thomsonedu.com/psychology/coon** for an updated list of Internet addresses and direct links to relevant sites.

- **Eye Anatomy and Information About Eye Conditions** A guide to the parts of the eyes and eye conditions.
- **Organization of the Retina and Visual System** A detailed description of the entire vertebrate visual system.
- **The Joy of Visual Perception** An online book about visual perception, including information on the eye.

ANSWERS

1. B, A, C, E 2. rods, cones 3. c 4. d 5. A 6. False. The cornea and lens bend and focus light rays, but they do not change light to another form of energy. No change in the *type* of energy takes place until the retina converts light to nerve impulses.

MODULE 4.3 Hearing, the Chemical Senses, and the Somesthetic Senses

WE DEPEND SO MUCH ON VISION that we sometimes neglect the other senses. But you only need to wear earplugs for a short time to appreciate how much we rely on hearing for communication, navigation, entertainment, and many other purposes. How are we able to sense invisible tremors in the air? Similarly, skilled novelists always include descriptions of odors and tastes in their writings. Perhaps they intuitively realize that a scene is incomplete without smells and tastes. Further, it would be very difficult to move, stay upright, or even stay alive without touch, pain, balance, and other bodily senses. Like the other senses, the bodily senses are also an essential part of our sensory world.

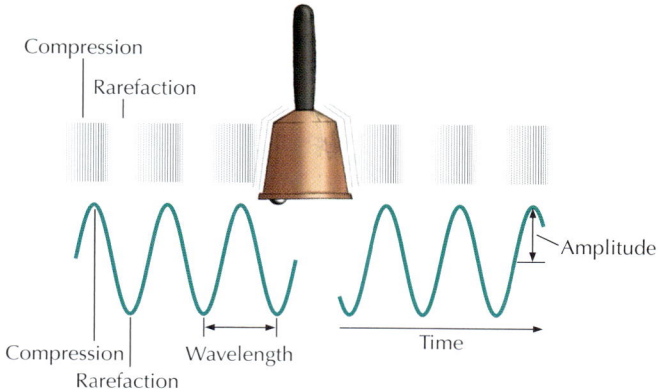

● **FIGURE 4.16** Waves of compression in the air, or vibrations, are the stimulus for hearing. The frequency of sound waves determines their pitch. The amplitude determines loudness.

Hearing—Good Vibrations

SURVEY QUESTION: *What are the mechanisms of hearing?*

Rock, classical, jazz, rap, country, electronic, hip-hop—whatever your musical taste, you have probably been moved by the riches of sound. Hearing also collects information from all around the body, such as detecting the approach of an unseen car (Yost, 2007). Vision, in all its glory, is limited to stimuli in front of the eyes (unless, of course, your "shades" have rearview mirrors attached).

What is the stimulus for hearing? If you throw a stone into a quiet pond, a circle of waves will spread in all directions. In much the same way, sound travels as a series of invisible waves of *compression* (peaks) and *rarefaction* (RARE-eh-fak-shun: valleys) in the air. Any vibrating object—a tuning fork, the string of a musical instrument, or the vocal cords—will produce sound waves (rhythmic movement of air molecules). Other materials, such as fluids or solids, can also carry sound. But sound does not travel in a vacuum or the airless realm of outer space. Movies that show characters reacting to the "roar" of alien starships or titanic battles in deep space are in error.

The *frequency* of sound waves (the number of waves per second) corresponds to the perceived *pitch* (higher or lower tone) of a sound. The *amplitude*, or physical "height," of a sound wave tells how much energy it contains. Psychologically, amplitude corresponds to sensed *loudness* (sound intensity) (● Fig. 4.16).

How We Hear Sounds

How are sounds converted to nerve impulses? Hearing begins with the *pinna* (PIN-ah: the visible, external part of the ear). In addition to being a good place to hang earrings or balance pencils, the pinna acts like a funnel to concentrate sounds. After they are guided into the ear canal, sound waves collide with the *tympanic membrane* (eardrum), setting it in motion. This, in turn, causes three small bones (the *auditory ossicles*) (OSS-ih-kuls) to vibrate (● Fig. 4.17). The ossicles are the malleus (MAL-ee-us), incus, and stapes (STAY-peas). Their common names are the hammer, anvil, and stirrup. The ossicles link the eardrum with the *cochlea* (KOCK-lee-ah: a snail-shaped organ that makes up the inner ear). The stapes is attached to a membrane on the cochlea called the *oval window*. As the oval window moves back and forth, it makes waves in a fluid inside the cochlea.

Inside the cochlea tiny **hair cells** detect waves in the fluid. The hair cells are part of the **organ of Corti** (KOR-tee), which makes up the center part of the cochlea (● Fig. 4.18). A set of *stereocilia* (STER-ee-oh-SIL-ih-ah), or "bristles," atop each hair cell brush against the tectorial membrane when waves ripple through fluid surrounding the organ of Corti. As the stereocilia are bent, nerve impulses are triggered, which then flow to the brain. (Are your ears "bristling" with sound?)

How are higher and lower sounds detected? The **frequency theory** of hearing states that as pitch rises, nerve impulses of

> **Hair cells** Receptor cells within the cochlea that transduce vibrations into nerve impulses.
> **Organ of Corti** Center part of the cochlea, containing hair cells, canals, and membranes.
> **Frequency theory** Holds that tones up to 4,000 hertz are converted to nerve impulses that match the frequency of each tone.

164 Chapter 4 • SENSATION AND PERCEPTION

● **FIGURE 4.17** Anatomy of the ear. The inset in the foreground (Cochlea "Unrolled") shows that as the stapes moves the oval window, the round window bulges outward, allowing waves to ripple through fluid in the cochlea. The waves move membranes near the hair cells, causing cilia, or "bristles," on the tips of the cells to bend. The hair cells then generate nerve impulses carried to the brain. (See an enlarged cross section of cochlea in Fig. 4.18.)

● **FIGURE 4.18** A closer view of the hair cells shows how movement of fluid in the cochlea causes the bristling "hairs," or cilia, to bend, generating a nerve impulse.

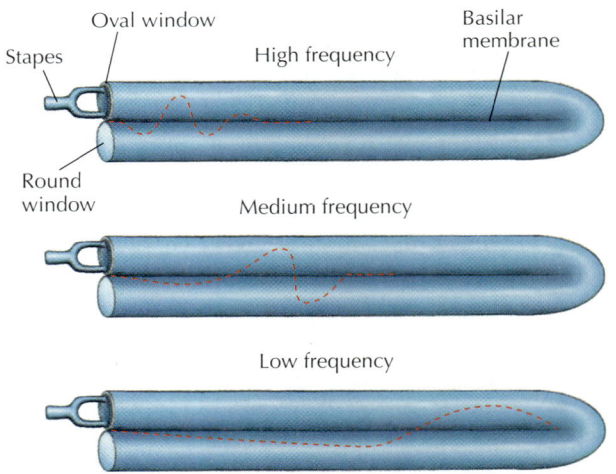

● **FIGURE 4.19** Here we see a simplified side view of the cochlea "unrolled." Remember that the basilar membrane is the elastic "roof" of the lower chamber of the cochlea. The organ of Corti, with its sensitive hair cells, rests atop the basilar membrane. The colored line shows where waves in the cochlear fluid cause the greatest deflection of the basilar membrane. (The amount of movement is exaggerated in the drawing.) The area of greatest movement helps identify sound frequency.

a corresponding frequency are fed into the auditory nerve. That is, an 800-hertz tone produces 800 nerve impulses per second. (*Hertz* refers to the number of vibrations per second.) This explains how sounds up to about 4,000 hertz reach the brain. But what about higher tones? **Place theory** states that higher and lower tones excite specific areas of the cochlea. High tones register most strongly at the base of the cochlea (near the oval window). Lower tones, on the other hand, mostly move hair cells near the narrow outer tip of the cochlea (● Fig. 4.19). Pitch is signaled by the area of the cochlea most strongly activated. Place theory also explains why hunters sometimes lose hearing in a narrow pitch range. "Hunter's notch," as it is called, occurs when hair cells are damaged in the area affected by the pitch of gunfire.

Hearing Loss *What causes other types of hearing loss?* There are two main types of hearing loss. **Conductive hearing loss** occurs when the transfer of vibrations from the outer ear to the inner ear is weak. For example, the eardrums or ossicles may be damaged or immobilized by disease or injury. In many cases, conductive hearing loss can be overcome with a hearing aid, which makes sounds louder and clearer.

Sensorineural hearing loss results from damage to the inner ear hair cells or auditory nerve. Many jobs, hobbies, and pastimes can cause **noise-induced hearing loss**, a common form of sensorineural hearing loss that occurs when very loud sounds damage hair cells (as in hunter's notch). The hair cells, which are about as thin as a cobweb, are very fragile (● Fig. 4.20). By the time you are 65, more than 40 percent of them will be gone, mainly those that transduce high pitches (Chisolm, Willott, & Lister, 2003). This explains why younger students are beginning to download very high-pitched ring tones for their cell phones: If their teacher has an aging ear, the

● **FIGURE 4.21** The loudness of sound is measured in decibels. Zero decibels is the faintest sound most people can hear. Sounds of 110 decibels are uncomfortably loud. Prolonged exposure to sounds above 85 decibels may damage the inner ear. Rock music, which may be 120 decibels, has caused hearing loss in musicians and may affect audiences as well. Sounds of 130 decibels pose an immediate danger to hearing.

students can hear the ring tone while their teacher cannot. (Your authors may have experienced this effect without knowing it!)

If you work in a noisy environment or enjoy loud music, motorcycling, snowmobiling, hunting, or similar pursuits, you are risking noise-induced hearing loss. Consider taking precautions because dead hair cells are never replaced: When you abuse them, you lose them.

How loud must a sound be to be hazardous? Daily exposure to 85 decibels or more may cause permanent hearing loss (Sekuler & Blake, 2006). *Decibels* are a measure of sound intensity. Every 20 decibels increases the sound pressure by a factor of 10. In other words, a rock concert at 120 decibels is 1,000 times stronger than a voice at 60 decibels. Even short

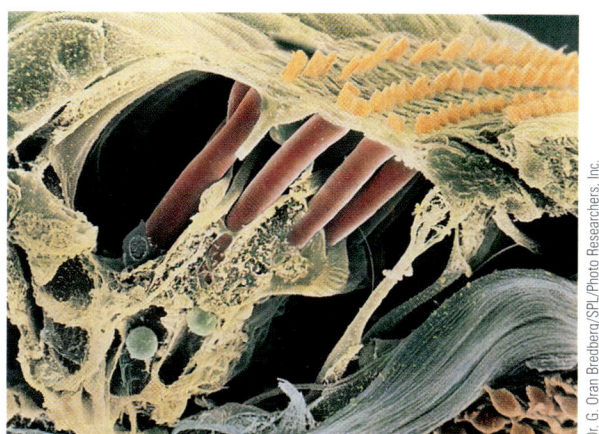

● **FIGURE 4.20** A highly magnified electron microscope photo of the cilia (orange bristles) on the top of human hair cells. (Colors are artificial.)

Place theory Theory that higher and lower tones excite specific areas of the cochlea.
Conductive hearing loss Poor transfer of sounds from the eardrum to the inner ear.
Sensorineural hearing loss Loss of hearing caused by damage to the inner ear hair cells or auditory nerve.
Noise-induced hearing loss Damage caused by exposing the hair cells to excessively loud sounds.

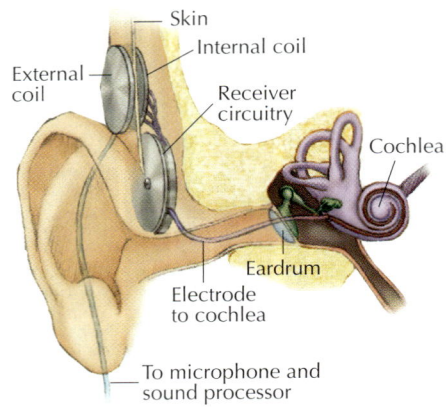

● **FIGURE 4.22** A cochlear implant, or "artificial ear."

periods at 120 decibels can cause temporary hearing loss. Brief exposure to 150 decibels (a jet airplane nearby) may cause permanent hearing loss. You might find it interesting to check the decibel ratings of some of your activities in ● Figure 4.21. Be aware that amplified musical concerts, iPod-style headphones, and "boom-box" car stereos can also damage your hearing.

Hearing aids are of no help in cases of sensorineural hearing loss because auditory messages are blocked from reaching the brain. However, artificial hearing systems are making it possible for some persons with this form of hearing loss to break through the wall of silence.

Artificial Hearing In many cases of sensorineural hearing loss, the auditory nerve is actually intact. This finding has spurred the development of cochlear implants that bypass hair cells and stimulate the auditory nerves directly (● Fig. 4.22). Wires from a microphone carry electrical signals to an external coil. A matching coil under the skin picks up the signals and carries them to one or more areas of the cochlea. The latest implants make use of place theory to separate higher and lower channels. This has allowed some formerly deaf persons to hear human voices, music, and other higher frequency sounds. About 60 percent of all multichannel implant patients can understand some spoken words and appreciate music (Leal et al., 2003; Tye-Murray, Spencer, & Woodworth, 1995). Some deaf children with implants learn to speak. Those who receive a cochlear implant before age 2 learn spoken language at a near normal rate (Dorman & Wilson, 2004). At present, artificial hearing remains crude. All but the most successful cochlear implant patients describe the sound as "like a radio that isn't quite tuned in." Nevertheless, it is hard to argue with enthusiasts like Kristen Cloud. Shortly after Kristen received an implant, she was able to hear a siren and avoid being struck by a speeding car. She says simply, "The implant saved my life."

The Chemical Senses—The Nose Knows When the Tongue Can't Tell

SURVEY QUESTION: *How do the chemical senses operate?*

Unless you are a wine taster, a perfume blender, a chef, or a gourmet, you may think of **olfaction** (smell) and **gustation** (taste) as minor senses. Certainly you could survive without these *chemical senses* (receptors that respond to chemical molecules). Just the same, smell and taste occasionally prevent poisonings and they certainly add pleasure to our lives (Wolfe et al., 2005). Let's see how they operate.

The Sense of Smell

Smell receptors respond to airborne molecules. As air enters the nose, it flows over roughly 5 million nerve fibers in the upper nasal passages (● Fig. 4.23). Receptor proteins on the surface of the fibers are sensitive to various airborne molecules. When a fiber is stimulated, it sends signals to the brain.

How are different odors produced? This is still an unfolding mystery. One hint comes from a problem called *anosmia* (an-OZE-me-ah: defective smell), a sort of "smell blindness" for a single odor. Anosmia suggests there are receptors for specific odors. Indeed, molecules having a particular odor are quite similar in shape. Specific shapes produce the following types of odors: floral (flower-like), camphoric (camphor-like), musky (have you ever smelled a sweaty musk ox?), minty (mint-like), and etherish (like ether or cleaning fluid). This does not mean, however, that there are just five different olfactory receptors. In humans, about 1,000 types of smell receptors are believed to exist (Bensafi et al., 2004).

Does the existence of 1,000 different types of receptors mean that we can sense only 1,000 different odors? No, molecules trigger activity in different *combinations* of odor receptors. Thus, humans can detect at least 10,000 different odors. Just as you can make many thousands of words from the 26 letters of the alphabet, many combinations of receptors are possible, resulting in many different odors. The brain uses the distinctive patterns of messages it gets from the olfactory receptors to recognize particular scents (Laurent et al., 2001).

It appears that different-shaped "holes," or "pockets," exist on the surface of olfactory receptors. Like a piece fits in a puzzle, chemicals produce odors when part of a molecule matches a hole of the same shape. This is the **lock and key theory.** Scents are also identified, in part, by the *location* of the receptors in the nose that are activated by a particular odor. And finally, the *number of activated receptors* tells the brain how strong an odor is (Bensafi et al., 2004).

What causes anosmia? Risks include infections, allergies, and blows to the head (which may tear the olfactory nerves). Exposure to chemicals such as ammonia, photo-developing

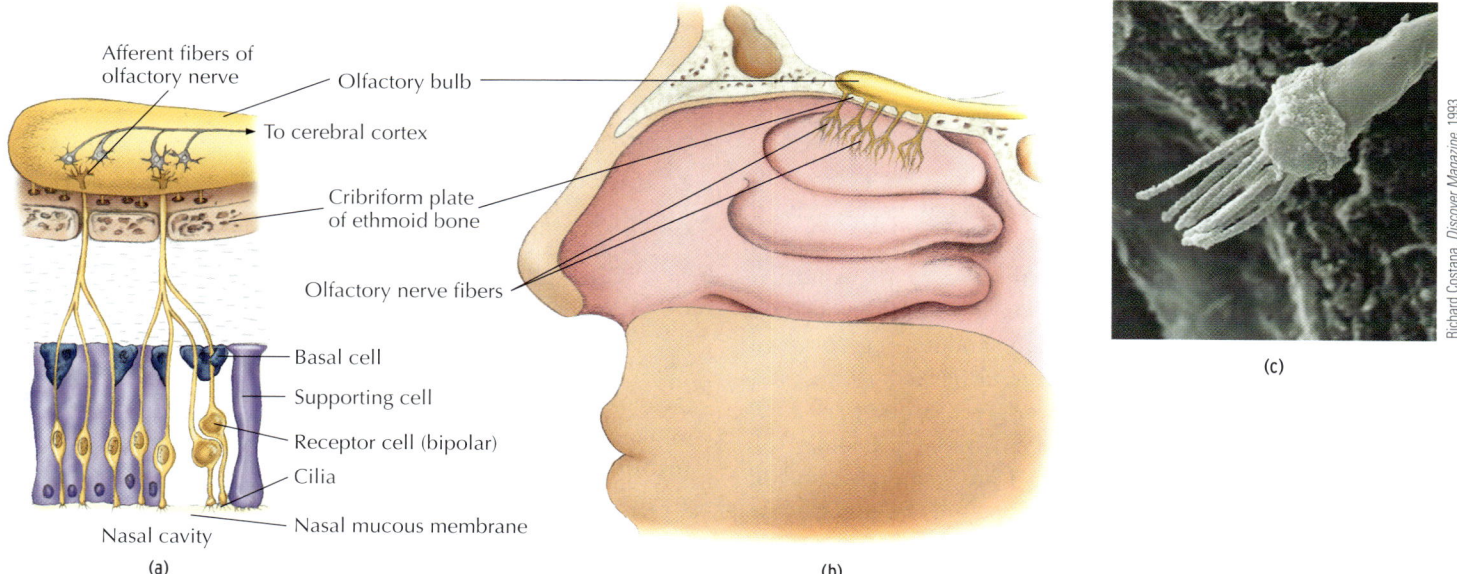

● **FIGURE 4.23** (a) Olfactory nerve fibers respond to gaseous molecules. Receptor cells are shown in cross section to the left. (b) Olfactory receptors are located in the upper nasal cavity. (c) On the right, an extreme close-up of an olfactory receptor shows fibers that sense gaseous molecules of various shapes.

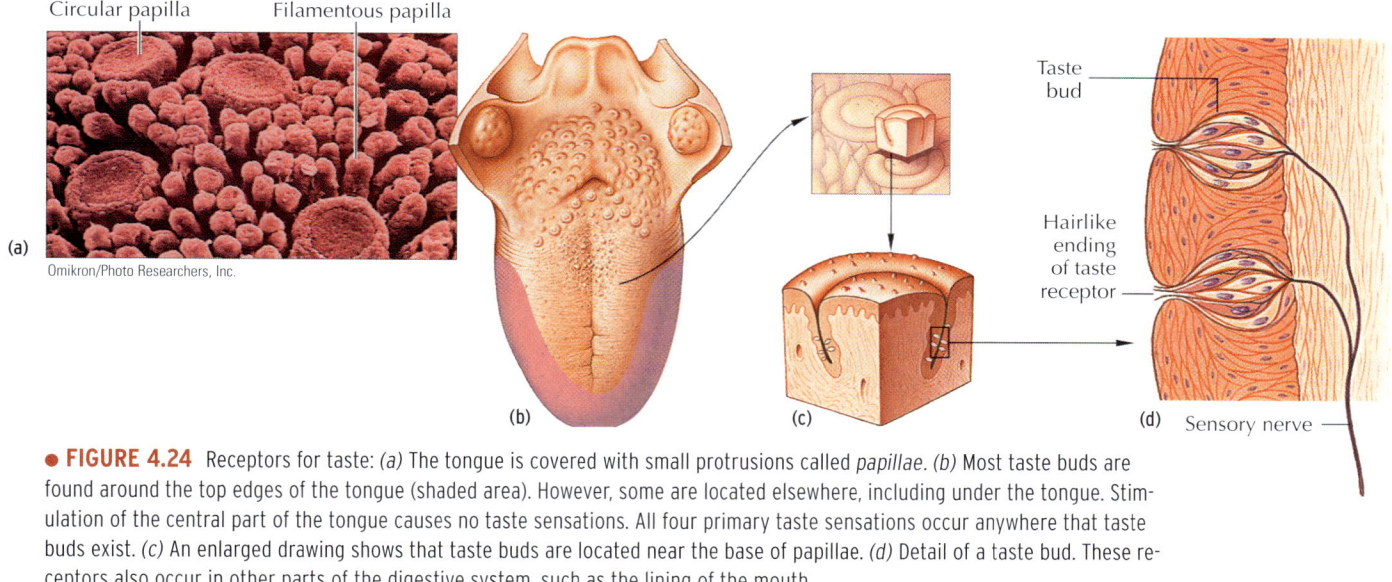

● **FIGURE 4.24** Receptors for taste: (a) The tongue is covered with small protrusions called *papillae*. (b) Most taste buds are found around the top edges of the tongue (shaded area). However, some are located elsewhere, including under the tongue. Stimulation of the central part of the tongue causes no taste sensations. All four primary taste sensations occur anywhere that taste buds exist. (c) An enlarged drawing shows that taste buds are located near the base of papillae. (d) Detail of a taste bud. These receptors also occur in other parts of the digestive system, such as the lining of the mouth.

chemicals, and hair-dressing potions can also cause anosmia. If you value your sense of smell, be careful what you breathe (Herz, 2001).

Taste and Flavors

There are at least four basic taste sensations: *sweet, salt, sour,* and *bitter*. We are most sensitive to bitter, less sensitive to sour, even less sensitive to salt, and least sensitive to sweet. This order may have helped prevent poisonings when most humans foraged for food, because bitter and sour foods are more likely to be inedible.

Many experts now believe that a fifth taste quality exists. The Japanese word *umami* (oo-MAH-me) describes a pleasant savory or "brothy" taste associated with certain amino acids in chicken soup, some meat extracts, kelp, tuna, human milk, cheese, and soybeans. The receptors for *umami* are sen-

Olfaction The sense of smell.
Gustation The sense of taste.
Lock and key theory Holds that odors are related to the shapes of chemical molecules.

sitive to glutamate, a substance found in monosodium glutamate (msG) (Sugimoto & Ninomiya, 2005). Perhaps MSG's reputation as a "flavor enhancer" is based on the pleasant *umami* taste (Lindemann, 2000). At the very least, we may finally know why chicken soup is such a "comfort food."

If there are only four or five tastes, how can there be so many different flavors? Flavors seem more varied because we tend to include sensations of texture, temperature, smell, and even pain ("hot" chili peppers) along with taste. Smell is particularly important in determining flavor. If you plug your nose and eat small bits of apple, potato, and onion, they will "taste" almost exactly alike. So do gourmet jelly beans! It is probably fair to say that subjective flavor is one half smell. That's why food loses its "taste" when you have a cold.

Taste buds (taste-receptor cells) are mainly located on the top side of the tongue, especially around the edges. However, a few are found elsewhere inside the mouth (● Fig. 4.24). As food is chewed, it dissolves and enters the taste buds, where it sets off nerve impulses to the brain (Northcutt, 2004). Much like smell, sweet and bitter tastes appear to be based on a lock-and-key match between molecules and intricately shaped receptors. Saltiness and sourness, however, are triggered by a direct flow of charged atoms into the tips of taste cells (Lindemann, 2001).

If smell and taste are seen as minor senses, then the somesthetic senses are the unnoticed senses. Let's turn our attention to the somesthetic senses and see why they merit our notice.

The Somesthetic Senses—Flying by the Seat of Your Pants

SURVEY QUESTION: *What are the somesthetic senses and why are they important?*

A gymnast "flying" through a routine on the uneven bars may rely as much on the **somesthetic senses** as on vision (*soma* means "body," *esthetic* means "feel"). Even the most routine activities, such as walking, running, or passing a sobriety test, would be impossible without the **skin senses** (touch), the **kinesthetic senses** (receptors in muscles and joints that detect body position and movement), and the **vestibular senses** (receptors in the inner ear for balance, gravity, and acceleration). Because of their importance, let's begin with the skin senses (● Fig. 4.25).

The Skin Senses

It's difficult to imagine what life would be like without the sense of touch, but the plight of Ian Waterman gives a hint. After an illness, Waterman permanently lost all feeling below his neck. Now, in order to know what position his body is in he has to be able to see it. If he moves with his eyes closed, he has no idea where he is moving. If the lights go out in a room, he's in big trouble (Cole, 1995).

Skin receptors produce at least five different sensations: *light touch, pressure, pain, cold,* and *warmth.* Receptors with particular shapes appear to specialize somewhat in various sensations. (See Fig. 4.25.) However, free nerve endings alone can produce all five sensations (Carlson, 2005). Altogether, the skin has about 200,000 nerve endings for temperature, 500,000 for touch and pressure, and 3 million for pain.

Does the number of receptors in an area of skin relate to its sensitivity? Yes. Your skin could be "mapped" by applying heat, cold, touch, pressure, or pain to points all over your body. Such testing would show that the number of skin receptors varies, and that sensitivity generally matches the number of receptors in a given area. Generally speaking, important areas such as the lips, tongue, face, hands, and genitals have a higher density of receptors.

● **FIGURE 4.25** The skin senses include touch, pressure, pain, cold, and warmth. This drawing shows different forms the skin receptors can take. The only clearly specialized receptor is the Pacinian corpuscle, which is highly sensitive to pressure. Free nerve endings are receptors for pain and any of the other sensations. For reasons that are not completely clear, cold is sensed near the surface of the skin, and warmth is sensed deeper (Carlson, 2005).

Pain

The number of pain receptors also varies, right? Yes, like the other skin senses, pain receptors vary in their distribution. About 230 pain points per square centimeter (about a half inch) are found behind the knee, 180 per centimeter on the buttocks, 60 on the pad of the thumb, and 40 on the tip of the nose. (Is it better, then, to be pinched on the nose or behind the knee? It depends on what you like!)

Pain carried by *large nerve fibers* is sharp, bright, fast, and seems to come from specific body areas (McMahon & Koltzenburg, 2005). This is the body's **warning system.** Give yourself a small jab with a pin and you will feel this type of pain. As you do this, notice that warning pain quickly disappears. Much as we may dislike warning pain, it is usually a signal that the body has been, or is about to be, damaged. Without warning pain, we would be unable to detect or prevent injury. Children who are born with a rare inherited insensitivity to pain repeatedly burn themselves, break bones, bite their tongues, and become ill without knowing it (Larner et al., 1994). As you might imagine, it's also hard for people with *congenital pain insensitivity* to have empathy for the pain of others (Danziger, Prkachin, & Willer, 2006).

A second type of somatic pain is carried by *small nerve fibers*. This type is slower, nagging, aching, widespread, and very unpleasant (McMahon & Koltzenburg, 2005). It gets worse if the pain stimulus is repeated. This is the body's **reminding system.** It reminds the brain that the body has been injured. For instance, lower back pain often has this quality. Sadly, the reminding system can cause agony long after an injury has healed, or in terminal illnesses, when the reminder is useless.

The Pain Gate You may have noticed that one type of pain will sometimes cancel another. **Gate control theory** suggests that pain messages from the different nerve fibers pass through the same neural "gate" in the spinal cord. If the gate is "closed" by one pain message, other messages may not be able to pass through (Melzack & Katz, 2004; Melzack & Wall, 1996).

How is the gate closed? Messages from small, slow fibers go through the pain gate and on to a "central biasing system" in the brain. Messages carried by large, fast nerve fibers take a different route and can close the spinal pain gate directly. Under some circumstances, the brain then sends a message back down the spinal cord, closing the pain gates. Doing so can prevent slower, "reminding system" pain from reaching the brain (● Fig. 4.26). Researchers Ronald Melzack and Patrick Wall believe that gate control theory also explains the painkilling effects of acupuncture (but see "The Matrix: Do Phantoms Live Here?").

Acupuncture is the Chinese medical art of relieving pain and illness by inserting thin needles into the body. As the acupuncturist's needles are twirled, heated, or electrified, they activate small pain fibers. These relay through the biasing system to close the gates to intense or chronic pain (Melzack

● **FIGURE 4.26** Diagram of a sensory gate for pain. A series of pain impulses going through the gate may prevent other pain messages from passing through. Or pain messages may relay through a "central biasing mechanism" that exerts control over the gate, closing it to other impulses.

 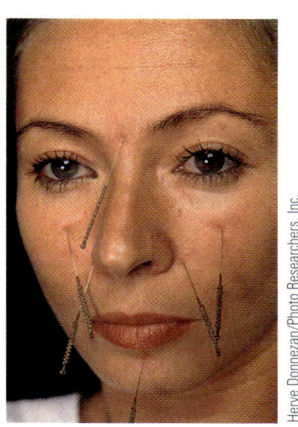

(Left) An acupuncturist's chart. *(Right)* Thin stainless steel needles are inserted into areas defined by the chart. Modern research has begun to explain the pain-killing effects of acupuncture (see text). Acupuncture's claimed ability to cure diseases is more debatable.

Taste bud The receptor organ for taste.
Somesthetic senses Sensations produced by the skin, muscles, joints, viscera, and organs of balance.
Skin senses The senses of touch, pressure, pain, heat, and cold.
Kinesthetic senses The senses of body movement and positioning.
Vestibular senses The senses of balance, position in space, and acceleration.
Warning system Pain based on large nerve fibers; warns that bodily damage may be occurring.
Reminding system Pain based on small nerve fibers; reminds the brain that the body has been injured.
Gate control theory Proposes that pain messages pass through neural "gates" in the spinal cord.

BRAINWAVES

The Matrix: Do Phantoms Live Here?

As you read this book, you may find yourself wondering why psychologists are so interested in the brain. "Brainwaves" boxes like this one are designed to help you think about how the biopsychological perspective contributes to a better understanding of human behavior.

In the popular *Matrix* films, Neo, as played by Keanu Reeves, discovers that machines have imprisoned humans in a phantom world called the Matrix, in order to steal human energy for their own use. Actually, the idea of a "matrix" is not totally farfetched. In fact, your own brain may be creating a *neuromatrix* that allows you to perceive your own body.

A person who suffers an amputation doesn't need to believe in the Matrix to encounter phantoms. Most amputees have phantom limb sensations, including pain, for months or years after losing a limb (Fraser, 2002; Halbert, Crotty, & Cameron, 2002). Because the phantom limb feels so "real," a patient with a recently amputated leg may inadvertently try to walk on it, risking further injury. Sometimes, phantom limbs feel like they are stuck in awkward positions. For instance, one man can't sleep on his back because his missing arm feels like it is twisted behind him.

What causes phantom limbs? Gate control theory cannot explain phantom limb pain (Hunter, Katz, & Davis, 2003). Because pain can't be coming from the missing limb, it cannot pass through pain gates to the brain (after all, it's missing!). Instead, according to Ronald Melzack (1999; Melzack & Katz, 2006), the brain creates a body image called the *neuromatrix*. This internal model of the body generates our sense of bodily self. Although amputation may remove a limb, as far as the neuromatrix in the brain is concerned, the limb still exists. Functional magnetic resonance imaging (MRI) confirms that sensory and motor areas of the brain are more active when a person feels a phantom limb (Rosen et al., 2001). Even though pain signals no longer come from the amputated limb, the neuromatrix evidently interprets other sensory experiences as pain from the missing limb.

Sometimes the brain gradually reorganizes to adjust for the sensory loss (Wu & Kaas, 2002). For example, a person who loses an arm may at first have a phantom arm and hand. After many years, the phantom may shrink, until only a hand is felt at the shoulder. Perhaps more vividly than others, people with phantom limbs are reminded that the sensory world we experience is constructed, moment by moment, not by some futuristic machines but by our very own neuromatrix in our brains.

& Wall, 1996). Studies have shown that acupuncture produces short-term pain relief for 50 percent to 80 percent of patients tested (Ernst, 1994; Murray, 1995). (However, its ability to cure illness is much more debatable.)

Pain Control Gate control theory helps explain *counterirritation*, one widely used pain control technique. Pain clinics use it by applying a mild electrical current to the skin. This causes only a mild tingling, but it can greatly reduce more agonizing pain (Köke et al., 2004). For more extreme pain, the electrical current can be applied directly to the spinal cord (Linderoth & Foreman, 2006).

You can use counterirritation to control your own pain. For instance, if you are having a tooth filled, try pinching yourself or digging a fingernail into a knuckle while the dentist is working. Focus your attention on the pain you are creating, and increase it anytime the dentist's work becomes more painful. This strategy may seem strange, but it works. Generations of children have used it to take the edge off a spanking.

In some cultures, people endure tattooing, stretching, cutting, and burning with little apparent pain. How do they do it? Very likely the answer lies in a reliance on psychological factors that anyone can use to reduce pain, such as anxiety reduction, control, and attention (Mailis-Gagnon & Israelson, 2005).

In general, unpleasant emotions such as fear and anxiety increase pain; pleasant emotions decrease it (Rainville, 2004). Anytime you can anticipate pain (such as a trip to the doctor, dentist, or tattoo parlor), you can lower anxiety by making sure you are *fully informed*. Be sure everything that will happen is explained. In general, the more control you *feel* you have over a painful stimulus, the less pain you will experience. To apply this principle, you should arrange a signal so your doctor, dentist, or body piercer will know when to start and stop a painful procedure. Finally, distraction also reduces pain. Instead of listening to the whirr of a dentist's drill, for example, you might imagine that you are lying in the sun at a beach, listening to the roar of the surf. Or, take an iPod along and crank up your favorite MP3s (Bushnell, Villemure, & Duncan, 2004).

Weightlessness presents astronauts with a real challenge in sensory adaptation.

The Vestibular System

Space flight might look like fun. But if you ever get a ride into space, it is about 70 percent likely that your first experience in orbit will be throwing up. Weightlessness and space flight affect the vestibular system, often causing severe motion sickness. Within the vestibular system, fluid-filled sacs called *otolith organs* (OH-toe-lith) are sensitive to movement, acceleration, and gravity (● Fig. 4.27). The otolith organs contain tiny crystals in a soft, gelatin-like mass. The tug of gravity or rapid head movements can cause the mass to shift. This, in turn, stimulates hair-like receptor cells, allowing us to sense gravity, acceleration, and movement through space (Lackner & DiZio, 2005).

Three fluid-filled tubes called the *semicircular canals* are the sensory organs for balance. If you could climb inside these tubes, you would find that head movements cause the fluid to swirl about. As the fluid moves, it bends a small "flap," or "float," called the *crista,* that detects movement in the semicircular canals. The bending of each crista again stimulates hair cells and signals head rotation.

What causes motion sickness? According to **sensory conflict theory,** dizziness and nausea occur when sensations from the vestibular system don't match sensations from the eyes and body (Flanagan, May, & Dobie, 2004). On solid ground, information from the vestibular system, vision, and kinesthesis usually matches. However, in a heaving, pitching boat, car, or airplane, a serious mismatch can occur—causing disorientation and heaving of another kind.

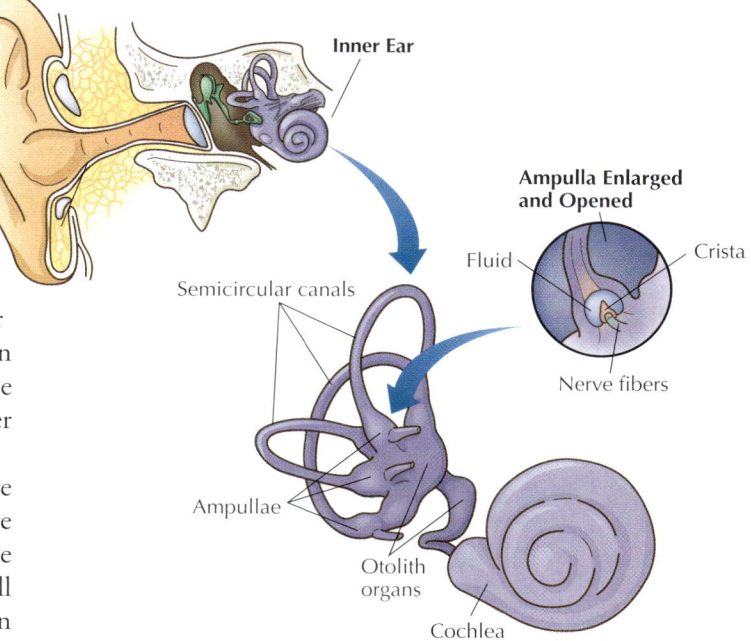

● **FIGURE 4.27** The vestibular system. (See text for explanation.)

Why would sensory conflict cause nausea? You can probably blame (or thank) evolution. Many poisons disturb the vestibular system, vision, and the body. Therefore, we may have evolved so that we react to sensory conflict by vomiting to expel poison. The value of this reaction, however, may be of little comfort to anyone who has ever been "green" and miserable with motion sickness. To minimize such conflicts, try to keep your head still, fix your vision on a distant immobile object, and lie down if you can.

MODULE 4.3 Summary

What are the mechanisms of hearing?
- Sound waves are the stimulus for hearing. They are transduced by the eardrum, auditory ossicles, oval window, cochlea, and ultimately the hair cells.
- Frequency theory explains how we hear tones up to 4,000 hertz; place theory explains tones above 4,000 hertz.
- Two basic types of hearing loss are conductive hearing loss and sensorineural hearing loss. Noise-induced hearing loss is a common form of sensorineural hearing loss caused by exposure to loud noise.

How do the chemical senses operate?
- Olfaction (smell) and gustation (taste) are chemical senses that respond to airborne or liquefied molecules.

Sensory conflict theory Explains motion sickness as the result of a mismatch among information from vision, the vestibular system, and kinesthesis.

Many people become nauseated the first time they experience virtual reality. Why? Because virtual reality also creates a sensory conflict: Computer-generated visual images change as if the viewer's body is in motion, but the vestibular system tells viewers that they are standing still. The result? The scenery may not be real but the nausea is.

- The lock and key theory partially explains smell. In addition, the location of the olfactory receptors in the nose helps identify various scents.
- Sweet and bitter tastes are based on a lock-and-key coding of molecule shapes. Salty and sour tastes are triggered by a direct flow of ions into taste receptors.

What are the somesthetic senses and why are they important?

- The somesthetic senses include the skin senses, kinesthesis, and the vestibular senses.
- The skin senses are touch, pressure, pain, cold, and warmth. Sensitivity to each is related to the number of receptors found in an area of skin.
- Distinctions can be made between warning pain and reminding pain.
- Selective gating of pain messages takes place in the spinal cord, as explained by gate control theory.
- Pain can be reduced through counterirritation and by controlling anxiety and attention.
- Various forms of motion sickness are related to messages received from the vestibular system, which detects gravity and movement.

KNOWLEDGE BUILDER

Hearing, the Chemical Senses, and the Somesthetic Senses

Recite

1. The frequency of a sound wave corresponds to how loud it is. T or F?
2. Which of the following is not a part of the cochlea?
   a. ossicles
   b. pinna
   c. tympanic membrane
   d. all of the above
3. Sensorineural hearing loss occurs when the auditory ossicles are damaged. T or F?
4. Daily exposure to sounds with a loudness of _____ decibels may cause permanent hearing loss.
5. Olfaction appears to be at least partially explained by the _____ _____ _____ theory of molecule shapes and receptor sites.
6. The term *umami* refers to
   a. smell blindness
   b. temporary damage to the hair cells
   c. secondary olfaction
   d. a taste quality
7. Which of the following is a somesthetic sense?
   a. gustation
   b. olfaction
   c. rarefaction
   d. kinesthesis
8. Warning pain is carried by _____ nerve fibers.
9. Head movements are detected primarily in the semicircular canals, gravity by the otolith organs. T or F?

Reflect

Critical Thinking

10. Why do you think your voice sounds so different when you hear a tape recording of your speech?
11. Smell and hearing differ from vision in a way that may aid survival. What is it?
12. What measures would you take to ensure that an experiment involving pain is ethical?
13. Drivers are less likely to become carsick than passengers are. Why do you think drivers and passengers differ in susceptibility to motion sickness?

Relate

Close your eyes and listen to the sounds around you. As you do, try to mentally trace the events necessary to convert vibrations in the air into the sounds you are hearing. Review the discussion of hearing if you leave out any steps.

What is your favorite food odor? What is your favorite taste? Can you explain how you are able to sense the aroma and taste of foods?

Stand on one foot with your eyes closed. Now touch the tip of your nose with your index finger. Which of the somesthetic senses did you use to perform this feat?

Can you think of any ways in which you have used counterirritation to lessen pain?

Imagine you are on a boat ride with a friend who starts to feel queasy. Can you explain to your friend what causes motion sickness and what she or he can do to prevent it?

Link

Internet addresses frequently change. To find the sites listed here, visit **http://www.thomsonedu.com/psychology/coon** for an updated list of Internet addresses and direct links to relevant sites.

- **Virtual Tour of the Ear** This site provides educational information about the ear and hearing and provides quick access to ear and hearing Web resources.
- **Taste and Smell Disorders** Read about various disorders of taste and smell and what can be done about them.
- **American Pain Foundation** Find out more about pain and its treatment.

ANSWERS

1. F 2. d 3. F 4. 85 5. lock and key 6. d 7. d 8. large 9. T 10. Other people hear your voice only as it is carried through the air. You hear not only that sound, but also vibrations conducted by the bones of your skull. 11. Both smell and hearing can detect stimuli (including signals of approaching danger) around corners, behind objects, and behind the head. 12. Experiments that cause pain must be handled with care and sensitivity. Participation must be voluntary; the source of pain must be noninjurious; and subjects must be allowed to quit at any time. 13. Drivers experience less sensory conflict because they control the car's motion. This allows them to anticipate the car's movements and to coordinate their head and eye movements with those of the car.

MODULE 4.4 Perceptual Constancies and Perceptual Grouping

WHILE DRIVING AT NIGHT, a woman slams on her brakes to avoid hitting a deer. As she skids to a stop, she realizes that the "deer" is actually a bush at roadside. Such misperceptions are common. The brain must continuously find patterns in a welter of sensations. How do we organize sensations into meaningful perceptions? Perceptual constancies and the principles of perceptual grouping help us make sense out of sensations.

Perceptual Constancies— Taming an Unruly World

SURVEY QUESTION: *How do perceptual constancies affect our perceptions?*

What would it be like to have your vision restored after a lifetime of blindness? Actually, a first look at the world can be disappointing because your newfound ability to *sense* the world does not guarantee that you can *perceive* it. Newly sighted persons must *learn* to identify objects, to read clocks, numbers, and letters, and to judge sizes and distances (Gregory, 2003). For instance, a cataract patient named Mr. S. B. had been blind since birth. After an operation restored his sight at age 52, Mr. S. B. struggled to use his vision. At first, he could only judge distance in familiar situations (Gregory, 1990). One day he was found crawling out of a hospital window to get a closer look at traffic on the street. It's easy to understand his curiosity, but he had to be restrained. His room was on the fourth floor!

Why would Mr. S. B. try to crawl out of a fourth-story window? Couldn't he at least tell distance from the size of the cars? No, you must be visually familiar with objects to use their size to judge distance. Try holding your left hand a few inches in front of your nose and your right hand at arm's length. Your right hand should appear to be about half the size of your left hand. Still, you know your right hand did not suddenly shrink, because you have seen it many times at various distances. We call this **size constancy:** The perceived

Visual perception involves finding meaningful patterns in complex stimuli. If you look closely at this painting by the artist Yvaral, you will see that it is entirely made up of small, featureless squares. An infant or newly sighted person would see only a jumble of meaningless colors. But because the squares form a familiar pattern, you should easily see Marilyn Monroe's face. (Or is that Madonna?) ("Marilyn Numerisée," 1990, courtesy Circle Gallery.)

Almost everyone's family album has at least one photo like this. Extreme viewing angles can make maintaining size constancy difficult, even for familiar objects.

Size constancy The perceived size of an object remains constant, despite changes in its retinal image.

size of an object remains the same, even though the size of its image on the retina changes.

To perceive your hand accurately, you had to draw on past experience. Some perceptions are so basic they seem to be *native* (inborn). An example is the ability to see a line on a piece of paper. Likewise, even newborn babies show some evidence of size constancy (Slater, Mattock, & Brown, 1990). However, many of our perceptions are *empirical,* or based on prior experience. For instance, cars, houses, and people look like toys when seen from a great distance or from an unfamiliar perspective, such as from the top of a skyscraper. This suggests that although some size constancy is innate, it is also affected by learning (Granrud, 2004).

In **shape constancy** the shape of an object remains stable, even though the shape of its retinal image changes. You can demonstrate shape constancy by looking at this page from directly overhead and then from an angle. Obviously, the page is rectangular, but most of the images that reach your eyes are distorted. Yet, though the book's image changes, your perception of its shape remains constant. (For additional examples, see ● Fig. 4.28.) On the highway, alcohol intoxication impairs size and shape constancy, adding to the accident rate among drunk drivers (Farrimond, 1990).

Let's say that you are outside in bright sunlight. Beside you, a friend is wearing a gray skirt and a white blouse. Suddenly a cloud shades the sun. It might seem that the blouse would grow dimmer, but it still appears to be bright white. This happens because the blouse continues to reflect a larger *proportion* of light than nearby objects. **Brightness constancy** refers to the fact that the brightness of objects appears to stay the same as lighting conditions change. However, this holds true only if the blouse and other objects are all illuminated by the same amount of light. You could make an area on your friend's gray skirt look whiter than the shaded blouse by shining a bright spotlight on the skirt.

To summarize, the energy patterns reaching our senses are constantly changing, even when they come from the same object. Size, shape, and brightness constancy rescue us from a confusing world in which objects would seem to shrink and grow, change shape as if made of rubber, and light up or fade like neon lamps. Gaining these constancies was only one of the hurdles Mr. S. B. faced in learning to see. In the next section, we will consider some others.

Perceptual Organization— Getting It All Together

SURVEY QUESTION: *What basic principles do we use to group sensations into meaningful patterns?*

Mr. S. B. soon learned to tell time from a large clock and to read block letters he had known only from touch. At a zoo, he recognized an elephant from descriptions he had heard. However, handwriting meant nothing to him for more than a year after he regained sight, and many objects were meaningless until he touched them. Thus, Mr. S. B. slowly learned to organize his sensations into meaningful perceptions.

How are sensations organized? The Gestalt psychologists (see Module 1.3) proposed that the simplest organization involves grouping some sensations into an object, or figure, that stands out on a plainer background. **Figure-ground organization** is probably inborn, because it is the first perceptual ability to appear after cataract patients regain sight. In normal figure-ground perception, only one figure is seen. In *reversible figures,* however, figure and ground can be switched. In ● Figure 4.29 it is equally possible to see either a wineglass figure on a dark background or two face profiles on a light background. As you shift from one pattern to the other, you should get a clear sense of what figure-ground organization means.

Are there other Gestalt organizing principles? The Gestalt psychologists identified several other principles that bring some order to your perceptions (● Fig. 4.30).

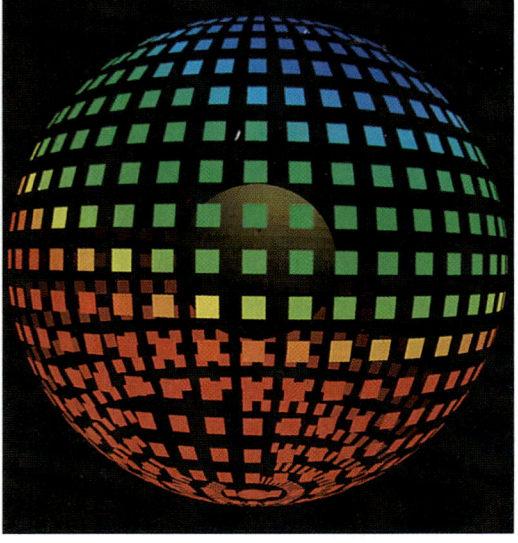

● **FIGURE 4.28** Shape constancy. *(a)* When a door is open, its image actually forms a trapezoid. Shape constancy is indicated by the fact that it is still perceived as a rectangle. *(b)* With great effort you may be able to see this design as a collection of flat shapes. However, if you maintain shape constancy, the distorted squares strongly suggest the surface of a sphere. (From *Spherescapes-1* by Scott Walter and Kevin McMahon, 1983.)

● **FIGURE 4.29** A reversible figure-ground design. Do you see two faces in profile, or a wineglass?

1. **Nearness.** All other things being equal, stimuli that are near each other tend to be grouped together (Kubovy & Gepshtein, 2003). Thus, if three people stand near each other and a fourth person stands 10 feet away, the adjacent three will be seen as a group and the distant person as an outsider. (See Fig. 4.30*a*.)
2. **Similarity.** "Birds of a feather flock together," and stimuli that are similar in size, shape, color, or form tend to be grouped together. (See Fig. 4.30*b*.) Picture two bands marching side by side. If their uniforms are the same colors, the bands will be seen as one large group, not as two separate groups.
3. **Continuation, or continuity.** Perceptions tend toward simplicity and continuity. In Figure 4.30*c* it is easier to visualize a wavy line on a squared-off line than it is to see a complex row of shapes.
4. **Closure.** Closure refers to the tendency to *complete* a figure, so that it has a consistent overall form. Each of the drawings in Figure 4.30*d* has one or more gaps, yet each is perceived as a recognizable figure. Our tendency to form shapes—even with minimal cues—is powerful.
5. **Contiguity.** A principle that can't be shown in Figure 4.30 is contiguity, or nearness in time *and* space. Contiguity is often responsible for the perception that one thing has *caused* another (Buehner & May, 2003). A psychologist friend of ours demonstrates this principle in class by knocking on his head with one hand while knocking on a wooden table (out of sight) with the other. The knocking sound is perfectly timed with the movements of his visible hand. This leads to the irresistible perception that his head is made of wood.
6. **Common region.** As you can see in Figure 4.30*e*, stimuli that are found within a common area tend to be seen as a group (Palmer, 1992). On the basis of similarity and nearness, the stars in Figure 4.30*e* should be one group and the dots another. However, the colored backgrounds define regions that create three groups of objects (four stars, two stars plus two dots, and four dots). Perhaps the principle of common region explains why we tend to mentally group together people from a particular country, state, province, or geographic region.

Clearly, the Gestalt principles shape our day-to-day perceptions, but so does learning and past experience. Take a moment and look for the camouflaged animal pictured in ● Figure 4.31. (Camouflage patterns break up figure-ground organization). If you had never seen similar animals before, could you have located this one? Mr. S. B. would have been at a total loss to find meaning in such a picture.

In a way, we are all detectives, seeking patterns in what we see. In this sense, a meaningful pattern represents a **perceptual hypothesis,** or initial guess about how to organize sensations. Have you ever seen a "friend" in the distance, only to have the person turn into a stranger as you drew closer? Pre-existing ideas and expectations *actively* guide our interpretation of sensations (Most et al., 2005).

The active nature of perception is perhaps most apparent for *ambiguous stimuli* (patterns allowing more than one interpretation). If you look at a cloud, you may discover dozens of ways to organize its contours into fanciful shapes and scenes. Even clearly defined stimuli may permit more than one interpretation. Look at Necker's cube in ● Fig. 4.32 if you doubt that perception is an active process. Visualize the top cube as a wire box. If you stare at the cube, its organization will change. Sometimes it will seem to project upward, like the lower left cube; other times it will project downward. The difference lies in how your brain interprets the same information. In short, we actively *construct* meaningful perceptions;

Shape constancy The perceived shape of an object is unaffected by changes in its retinal image.
Brightness constancy The apparent (or relative) brightness of objects remains the same as long as they are illuminated by the same amount of light.
Figure-ground organization Part of a stimulus appears to stand out as an object (figure) against a less prominent background (ground).
Perceptual hypothesis An initial guess regarding how to organize (perceive) a stimulus pattern.

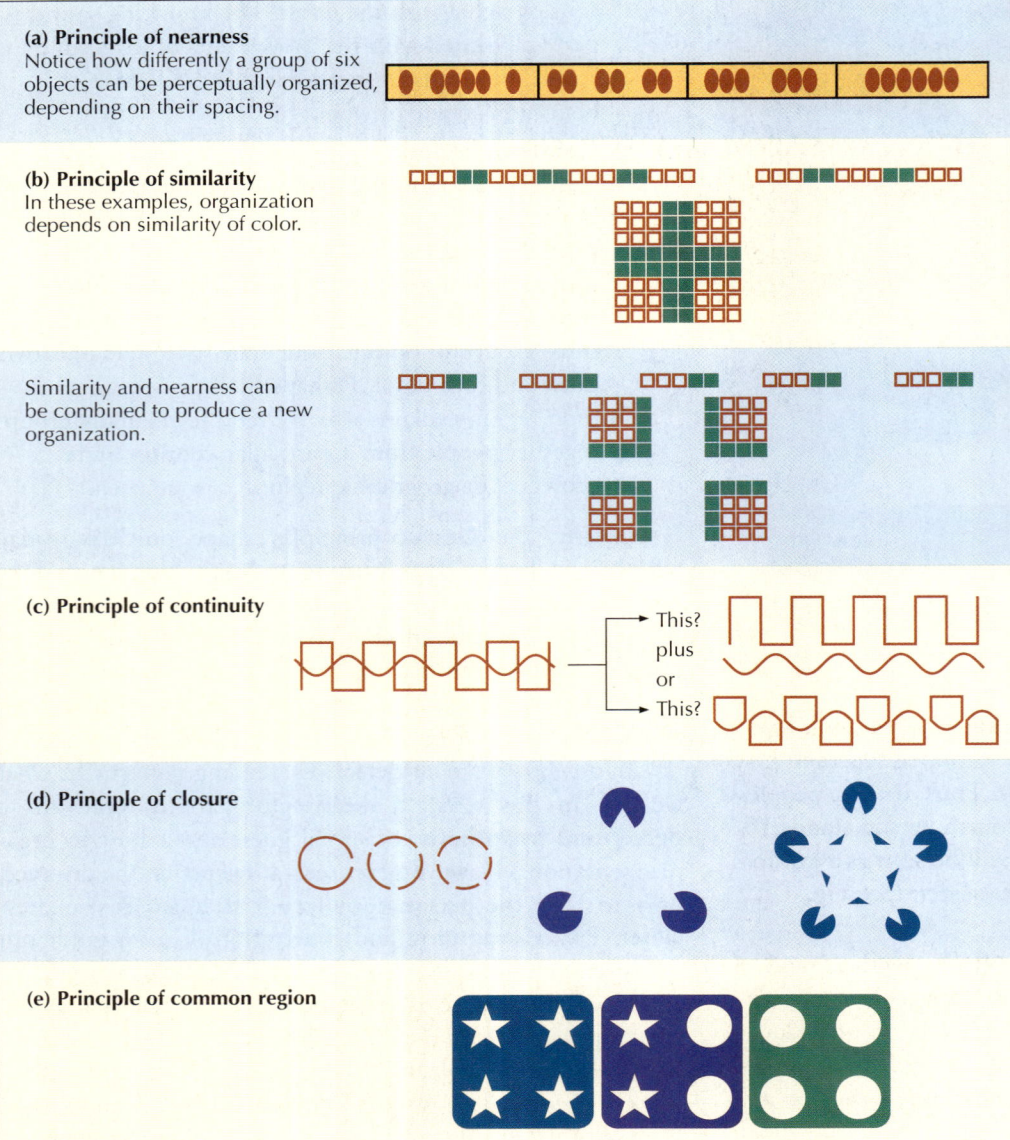

● **FIGURE 4.30** How we organize perceptions.

● **FIGURE 4.31** A challenging example of perceptual organization. Once the camouflaged insect (known as a giant walkingstick) becomes visible, it is almost impossible to view the picture again without seeing the insect.

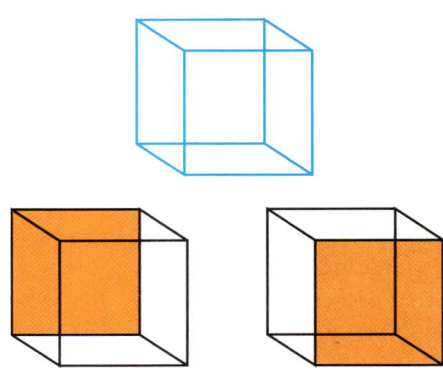

● **FIGURE 4.32** Necker's cube.

● **FIGURE 4.33** *(Left)* An impossible figure—the "three-pronged widget." *(Right)* It might seem that including more information in a drawing would make perceptual conflicts impossible. However, Japanese artist Shigeo Fukuda has shown otherwise. ("Disappearing Column" © Shigeo Fukuda, 1985.)

we do not passively record the events and stimuli around us (Coren, Ward, & Enns, 2004).

In some instances, a stimulus may offer such conflicting information that perceptual organization becomes impossible. For example, the tendency to make a three-dimensional object out of a drawing is frustrated by the "three-pronged widget" (● Fig. 4.33), an *impossible figure.* Such patterns cannot be organized into stable, consistent, or meaningful perceptions. If you cover either end of the drawing in Fig. 4.33, it makes sense perceptually. However, a problem arises when you try to organize the entire drawing. Then, conflicting information prevents you from forming a stable perception.

One of the most amazing perceptual feats is our capacity to create three-dimensional space from flat retinal images. We'll explore that topic in the next module, but first here's a summary and a chance to rehearse what you've learned.

MODULE 4.4 Summary

How do perceptual constancies affect our perceptions?
- Perception is the process of assembling sensations into a usable mental representation of the world.
- In vision, the image projected on the retina is constantly changing, but the external world appears stable and undistorted because of size, shape, and brightness constancy.

What basic principles do we use to group sensations into meaningful patterns?
- Separating figure and ground is the most basic perceptual organization.
- The following Gestalt principles also help organize sensations: nearness, similarity, continuity, closure, contiguity, and common region.
- A perception represents a hypothesis, or initial guess, about how to organize sensations.

KNOWLEDGE BUILDER

Perceptual Constancies and Perceptual Organization

Recite

1. Which among the following are subject to basic perceptual constancy?
   a. figure-ground organization
   b. size
   c. ambiguity
   d. brightness
   e. continuity
   f. closure
   g. shape
   h. nearness

2. The first and most basic perceptual organization to emerge when sight is restored to a blind person is
   a. continuity
   b. nearness constancy
   c. recognition of numbers and letters
   d. figure-ground

3. Which of the following is least likely to contribute to the formation of a perceptual figure?
   a. continuity
   b. closure
   c. similarity
   d. separation

4. At times, meaningful perceptual organization represents a _____, or "guess," held until the evidence contradicts it.

5. The design known as Necker's cube is a good example of an impossible figure. T or F?

Reflect

Critical Thinking

6. People who have taken psychedelic drugs, such as LSD or mescaline, often report that the objects and people they see appear to be changing in size, shape, and brightness. This suggests that such drugs disrupt what perceptual process?

Relate

If you needed to explain the perceptual constancies to a friend, what would you say? Why are the constancies important for maintaining a stable perceptual world?

As you look around the area in which you are now, how are the Gestalt principles helping to organize your perceptions? Try to find a specific example for each principle.

Link

Internet addresses frequently change. To find the sites listed here, visit **http://www.thomsonedu.com/psychology/coon** for an updated list of Internet addresses and direct links to relevant sites.

- **Size Constancy in a Photograph** Explore a series of photographs that illustrate size constancy.
- **Form and Contour** Explore interactive demonstrations of the Gestalt principles and other curious phenomena.
- **Figure/Ground in Graphic Design** Explore the use of the figure-ground principle in graphic design.

ANSWERS

1. b, d, g 2. d 3. d 4. hypothesis 5. F 6. Perceptual constancies (size, shape, and brightness).

MODULE 4.5 Depth Perception

CLOSE ONE OF YOUR EYES, hold your head very still, and stare at a single point across the room. If you don't move your head or eyes, your surroundings will appear to be almost flat, like a painting or photograph. But even under these conditions you will still have some sense of depth. Now, open both eyes and move your head and eyes as usual. Suddenly, the "3-D" perceptual world returns. This module discusses the mechanisms that underlie our ability to perceive depth and space.

Depth Perception—What If the World Were Flat?

SURVEY QUESTION: *How is it possible to see depth and judge distance?*

Depth perception is the ability to see three-dimensional space and to accurately judge distances. Without depth perception, you would be unable to drive a car or ride a bicycle, play catch, shoot baskets, thread a needle, or simply navigate around a room (Howard & Rogers, 2001a). The world would look like a flat surface.

Mr. S. B. had trouble with depth perception after his sight was restored. Is depth perception learned? Studies done with a *visual cliff* suggest that depth perception is partly learned and partly innate (Witherington et al., 2005). Basically, a visual cliff is a glass-topped table (● Fig. 4.34). On one side a checkered surface lies directly beneath the glass. On the other side, the checkered surface is 4 feet below. This makes the glass look like a tabletop on one side and a cliff, or drop-off, on the other.

To test for depth perception, 6- to 14-month-old infants were placed in the middle of the visual cliff. This gave them a choice of crawling to the shallow side or the deep side. (The glass prevented them from doing any "skydiving" if they chose the deep side.) Most infants chose the shallow side. In fact, most refused the deep side even when their mothers tried to call them toward it (Gibson & Walk, 1960).

If the infants were at least 6 months old when they were tested, isn't it possible that they learned to perceive depth? Yes. More recent research has shown that depth perception begins to develop as early as 2 weeks of age (Yonas, Elieff, & Arterberry, 2002). It is very likely that at least a basic level of depth perception is innate (Aslin & Smith, 1988). Yet, the development of depth perception is not complete until about 6 months, suggesting that it depends on both brain maturation and individual experience.

We also learn to use a variety of *depth cues* as aids to perceiving three-dimensional space. **Depth cues** are features of

● **FIGURE 4.34** Human infants and newborn animals refuse to go over the edge of the visual cliff.

the environment and messages from the body that supply information about distance and space. Some cues require two eyes (**binocular depth cues**), whereas others will work with just one eye (**monocular depth cues**).

Depth perception The ability to see three-dimensional space and to accurately judge distances.

Depth cues Features of the environment and messages from the body that supply information about distance and space.

Binocular depth cues Perceptual features that impart information about distance and three-dimensional space which require two eyes.

Monocular depth cues Perceptual features that impart information about distance and three-dimensional space which require just one eye.

Binocular Depth Cues

The most basic source of depth perception is *retinal disparity* (a discrepancy in the images that reach the right and left eyes). Retinal disparity, which is a binocular cue, is based on the fact that the eyes are about 2.5 inches apart. Because of this, each eye receives a slightly different view of the world. Try this: put a finger in front of your eyes and as close to your nose as you can. First close one eye and then the other, over and over again. You should notice that your finger seems to jump back and forth as you view the different images reaching each eye. However, when the two different images are fused into one overall image, **stereoscopic vision** (three-dimensional sight) occurs (Howard & Rogers, 2001b). The result is a powerful sensation of depth (● Fig. 4.35 and ● Fig. 4.36).

Convergence is a second binocular depth cue. When you look at a distant object, the lines of vision from your eyes are parallel. However, when you look at something 50 feet or less in distance, your eyes must converge (turn in) to focus the object (● Fig. 4.37).

You can feel convergence by exaggerating it: Focus on your fingertip and bring it toward your eyes until they almost cross. You can actually feel the muscles that control eye movement working harder and harder as your fingertip gets closer. If you repeat this little exercise with one eye shut, you

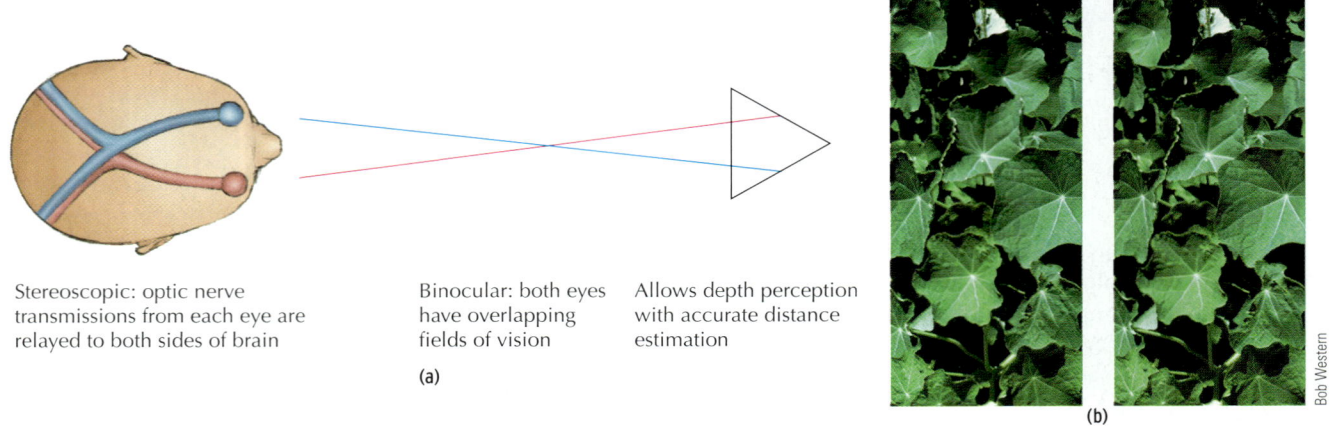

● **FIGURE 4.35** (a) Stereoscopic vision. (b) The photographs show what the right and left eyes would see when viewing a plant. Hold the page about 6 to 8 inches from your eyes. Allow your eyes to cross and focus on the overlapping image between the two photos. Then try to fuse the leaves into one image. If you are successful, the third dimension will appear like magic.

● **FIGURE 4.36** This computer-generated art creates a 3-D illusion by superimposing two patterns. There are mismatches between some areas of the two patterns. This simulates retinal disparity and creates a sensation of depth. To get the 3-D effect, hold the stereogram about 8 inches from the end of your nose. Relax your eyes and look *through* the art, as if you were focusing on something in the distance. If you're patient, you may see a dragon. (© 2008 Magic Eye Inc., www.magiceye.com.)

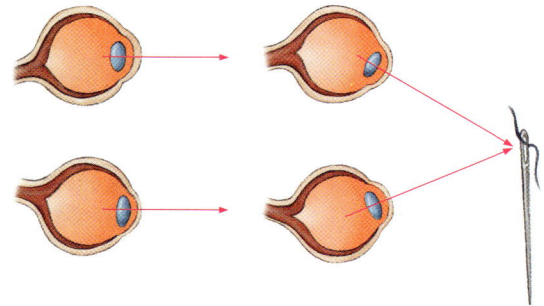

● **FIGURE 4.37** The eyes must converge, or turn in toward the nose, to focus on close objects.

will feel no increase in muscle tension as your finger gets closer. It takes *both* eyes to converge. This is why we say convergence is a binocular depth cue.

You are normally not aware of it, but whenever you estimate a distance under 50 feet (as when you play catch or zap flies with your personal laser), you are using convergence. How? Muscles attached to the eyeball feed information on eye position to the brain to help it judge distance.

Can a person with one eye perceive depth? Yes, but not as well as a person with two eyes. Overall, stereoscopic vision is 10 times better for judging depth than perception based on just one eye (Rosenberg, 1994). Try driving a car or riding a bicycle with one eye closed. You will find yourself braking too soon or too late, and you will have difficulty estimating your speed. ("But officer, my psychology text said to . . .") Despite this, you will be able to drive, although it will be more difficult than usual. This is possible because your single eye is making use of monocular depth cues.

Monocular Depth Cues

As their name implies, monocular depth cues can be perceived with just one eye. One such cue is *accommodation,* the bending of the lens to focus on nearby objects. Sensations from muscles attached to each lens flow back to the brain. Changes in these sensations help us judge distances within about 4 feet of the eyes. This information is available even if you are just using one eye, so accommodation is a monocular cue. Beyond 4 feet, accommodation has limited value. Obviously, it is more important to a watchmaker or a person trying to thread a needle than it is to a basketball player or someone driving an automobile. Other monocular depth cues are also referred to as pictorial depth cues, because a good movie, painting, or photograph can create a convincing sense of depth where none exists.

How is the illusion of depth created on a two-dimensional surface? **Pictorial depth** cues are monocular depth cues found in paintings, drawings, and photographs that impart information about space, depth, and distance. To understand how these cues work, imagine that you are looking outdoors through a window. If you trace everything you see onto the glass, you will have an excellent drawing, with convincing depth. Then, if we analyze what is on the glass, we will find the following features (● Fig. 4.38).

1. **Linear perspective.** This cue is based on the apparent convergence of parallel lines in the environment. If you stand between two railroad tracks, they appear to meet near the horizon. Because you know they are parallel, their convergence implies great distance. (See Fig. 4.38*a.*)

2. **Relative size.** If an artist wishes to depict two objects of the same size at different distances, the artist makes the more distant object smaller. (See Fig. 4.38*b.*) Special effects in films create sensational illusions of depth by rapidly changing the image size of planets, airplanes, monsters, or what have you. (Also see ● Fig. 4.39.)

3. **Height in the picture plane.** Objects that are placed higher (closer to the horizon line) in a drawing tend to be perceived as more distant. In the upper frame of Figure 4.38*b* the black columns look like they are receding into the distance partly because they become smaller, but also because they move higher in the drawing.

4. **Light and shadow.** Most objects are lighted in ways that create clear patterns of light and shadow. Copying such patterns of light and shadow can give a two-dimensional design a three-dimensional appearance. (See Fig. 4.38*c.*) (Also, look ahead to ● Fig. 4.40 for more information on light and shadow.)

5. **Overlap.** Overlap (or *interposition*) occurs when one object partially blocks another object. Hold your hands up and ask a friend across the room which is nearer. Relative size will give the answer if one hand is much nearer to your friend than the other. But if one hand is only slightly closer than the other, your friend may not be able to tell—until you slide one hand in front of the other. Overlap then removes any doubt. (See Fig. 4.38*d.*)

6. **Texture gradients.** Changes in texture also contribute to depth perception. If you stand in the middle of a cobblestone street, the street will look coarse near your feet. However, its texture will get smaller and finer if you look into the distance. (See Fig. 4.38*e.*)

Stereoscopic vision Perception of space and depth caused chiefly by the fact that the eyes receive different images.

Pictorial depth cues Monocular depth cues found in paintings, drawings, and photographs that impart information about space, depth, and distance.

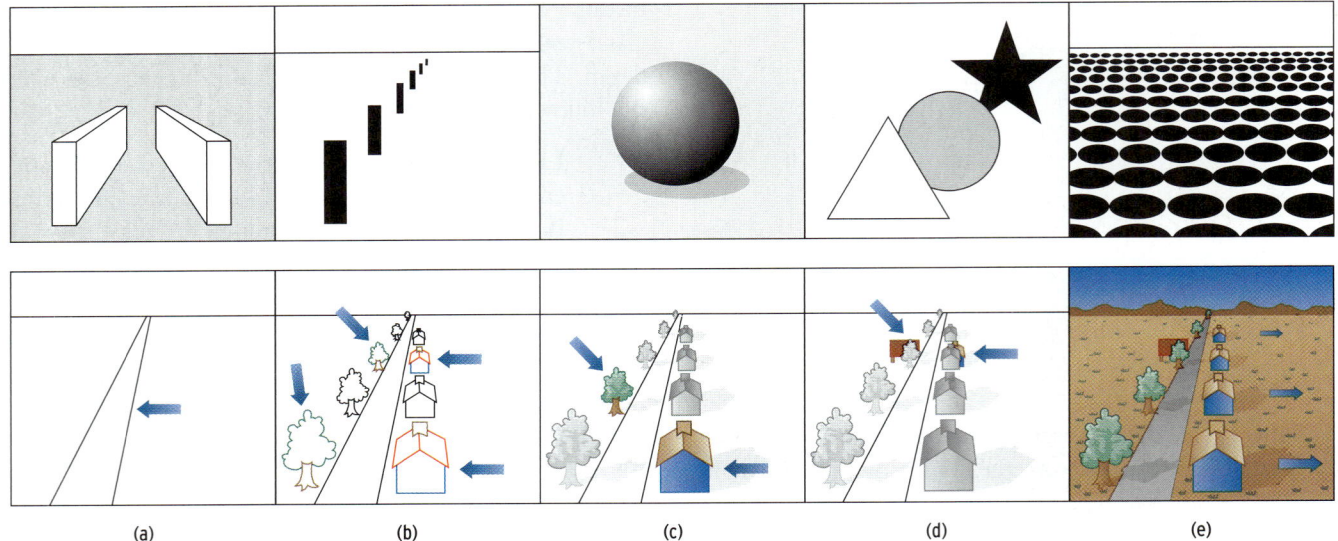

● **FIGURE 4.38** (a) Linear perspective. (b) Relative size. (c) Light and shadow. (d) Overlap. (e) Texture gradients. Drawings in the top row show fairly "pure" examples of each of the pictorial depth cues. In the bottom row, the pictorial depth cues are used to assemble a more realistic scene.

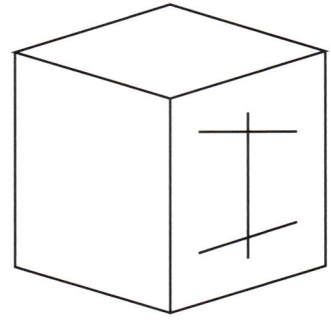

Linear perspective is a very powerful cue for depth. Because of the depth cues implied in this drawing, the upper cross on the vertical line appears to be diagonal. It is actually a right angle. The lower cross, which appears to be a right angle, is actually diagonal to the vertical line. (Adapted from Enns & Coren, 1995.)

● **FIGURE 4.39** On a dry lake bed, relative size is just about the only depth cue available for judging the camera's distance from this vintage aircraft. What do you estimate the distance to be? For the answer, look ahead to Figure 4.43.

7. **Aerial perspective.** Smog, fog, dust, and haze add to the apparent distance of an object. Because of aerial perspective, distant objects tend to be hazy, washed out in color, and lacking in detail. Aerial haze is often most noticeable when it is missing. If you have ever seen a distant mountain range on a crystal-clear day, it might have looked like it was only a few miles away. In reality, you could have been viewing them through 50 miles of crystal-clear air.

8. **Relative motion.** Relative motion, also known as *motion parallax* (PAIR-ah-lax), can be seen by looking out a window and moving your head from side to side. Notice that nearby objects appear to move a sizable distance as your head moves. Trees, houses, and telephone poles that are farther away appear to move slightly in relation to the background. Distant objects like hills, mountains, or clouds don't seem to move at all.

When combined, pictorial cues can create a powerful illusion of depth. (See ■ Table 4.1 for a summary of all the depth cues we have discussed.)

Is motion parallax really a pictorial cue? Strictly speaking it is not, except in the two-dimensional world of movies, television, or animated cartoons. However, when parallax is present, we almost always perceive depth. Much of the apparent depth of a good movie comes from relative motion captured by the camera. ● Figure 4.41 illustrates an interesting feature of motion parallax. Imagine that you are in a bus and watching the passing scenery (with your gaze at a right angle

● **FIGURE 4.40** *(Above)* When judging depth, we usually assume that light comes mainly from one direction, usually from above. Squint a little to blur the image you see here. You should perceive a collection of globes projecting outward. If you turn this page upside down, the globes should become cavities. (Adapted from Ramachandran, 1995.) *(Below)* The famed Dutch artist M. C. Escher violated our assumptions about light to create the dramatic illusions of depth found in his 1955 lithograph *Convex and Concave*. In this print, light appears to come from all sides of the scene. (M. C. Escher's "Convex and Concave" © 2002 Cordon Art B. V.–Baarn–Holland. All rights reserved.)

■ **TABLE 4.1** Summary of Visual Depth Cues

Binocular Cues
- Retinal disparity
- Convergence

Monocular Cues
- Accommodation
- Pictorial depth cues (listed below)
  Linear perspective
  Relative size
  Height in the picture plane
  Light and shadow
  Overlap
  Texture gradients
  Aerial perspective
  Relative motion (motion parallax)

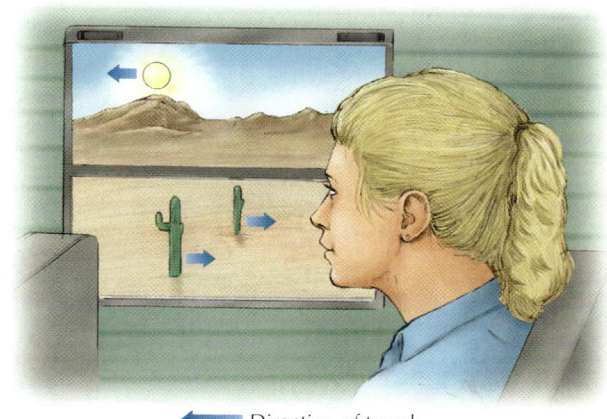

← Direction of travel

● **FIGURE 4.41** The apparent motion of objects viewed during travel depends on their distance from the observer. Apparent motion can also be influenced by an observer's point of fixation. At middle distances, objects closer than the point of fixation appear to move backward; those beyond the point of fixation appear to move forward. Objects at great distances, such as the sun or moon, always appear to move forward.

to the road). Under these conditions, nearby objects will appear to rush *backward*. Those farther away, such as distant mountains, will seem to move very little or not at all. Objects that are more remote, such as the sun or moon, will appear to move in the *same* direction you are traveling. (That's why the moon appears to "follow" you when you take a stroll at night.)

The Moon Illusion How do the depth perception cues relate to daily experience? We constantly use both pictorial cues and bodily cues to sense depth and judge distances. Consider an intriguing effect called the *moon illusion* (perceiving the moon as larger when it is low in the sky). When the moon is on the horizon, it tends to look like a silver dollar. When it is directly overhead, it looks more like a dime. Contrary to what some people believe, the moon is not magnified by the atmosphere. But the moon *looks* nearly twice as large when it's low in the sky (Ross & Plug, 2002). This occurs, in part, because the moon's *apparent distance* is greater when it is near the horizon than when it is overhead (Kaufman & Kaufman, 2000).

But if it seems farther away, shouldn't it look smaller? No. When the moon is overhead, few depth cues surround it. In contrast, when you see the moon on the horizon, it is behind houses, trees, telephone poles, and mountains. These objects add numerous depth cues, which cause the horizon to seem more distant than the sky overhead. Picture two balloons, one 10 feet away and the second 20 feet away. Suppose the more distant balloon is inflated until its image matches the image of the nearer balloon. How do we know the more distant balloon is larger? Because its image is the same size as a balloon that is closer. Similarly, the moon makes the same-size image on the horizon as it does overhead. However, the horizon seems more distant because more depth cues are present. As a result, the horizon moon must be perceived as larger (Kaufman & Kaufman, 2000). (See ● Fig. 4.42.)

This explanation is known as the **apparent-distance hypothesis** (the horizon seems more distant than the night sky). You can test it by removing depth cues while looking at a horizon moon. Try looking at the moon through a rolled-up paper tube, or make your hands into a "telescope" and look at the next large moon you see. It will immediately appear to shrink when viewed without depth cues (Ross & Plug, 2002). (See ● Fig. 4.43.)

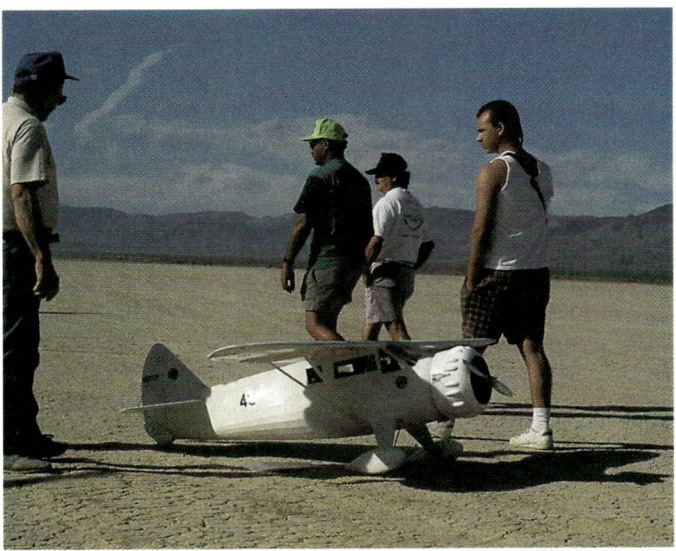

● **FIGURE 4.43** Before you can use familiar size to judge distance, objects must actually be the size you assume they are. Either these men are giants, or the model airplane was closer than you may have thought when you looked at Figure 4.39.

MODULE 4.5 Summary

How is it possible to see depth and judge distance?
- A basic, innate capacity for depth perception is present soon after birth.
- Depth perception depends on binocular depth cues of retinal disparity and convergence.
- Depth perception also depends on the monocular depth cue of accommodation. Other things depth perception depends on include the following: the monocular "pictorial" depth cues of linear perspective, relative size, height in the picture plane, light and shadow, overlap, texture gradients, aerial haze, and motion parallax.
- The moon illusion can be explained by the apparent-distance hypothesis, which emphasizes that many depth cues are present when the moon is near the horizon, and few are present when it is overhead.

● **FIGURE 4.42** The Ponzo illusion may help you understand the moon illusion. Picture the two white bars as resting on the railroad tracks. In the drawing, the upper bar is the same length as the lower bar. However, because the upper bar appears to be farther away than the lower bar, we perceive it as longer. The same logic applies to the moon illusion.

KNOWLEDGE BUILDER

Depth Perception

Recite

1. The visual cliff is used to test for infant sensitivity to linear perspective. T or F?
2. Write an *M* or a *B* after each of the following to indicate if it is a monocular or binocular depth cue.

    accommodation ____ convergence ____ retinal disparity ____ linear perspective ____ motion parallax ____ overlap ____ relative size ____

3. Which of the depth cues listed in Question 2 are based on muscular feedback? _____.
4. Interpretation of pictorial depth cues requires no prior experience. T or F?
5. The apparent-distance hypothesis provides a good explanation of the
    a. moon illusion
    b. horizontal-vertical illusion
    c. Zulu illusion
    d. effects of inattentional blindness

Reflect
Critical Thinking

6. Scientists believe that the famous Dutch artist Rembrandt had a visual defect that prevented him from perceiving depth. (He had a wandering eye.) How might this have aided him as an artist?

Relate

Part of the rush of excitement produced by action movies and video games is based on the sense of depth they create. Return to the list of pictorial depth cues. What cues have you seen used to portray depth? Try to think of specific examples in a movie or game you have seen recently.

Link

Internet addresses frequently change. To find the sites listed here, visit http://www.thomsonedu.com/psychology/coon for an updated list of Internet addresses and direct links to relevant sites.

- **The Third Dimension** Explore a variety of depth cues.
- **Gallery of Illusions** An interesting and fun website that presents illusory stimuli that are fun to view and that provides a basis to learn about sensation and perception.
- **3-D Stereograms** Find the 3-D images hidden in these pictures.

ANSWERS

1. F 2. accommodation (M), convergence (B), retinal disparity (B), linear perspective (M), motion parallax (M), overlap (M), relative size (M) 3. accommodation or convergence 4. F 5. a 6. An artist must transfer a three-dimensional scene onto a flat canvas. Because Rembrandt could not see depth, it might have been easier for him to put what he saw onto a two-dimensional surface.

Apparent-distance hypothesis An explanation of the moon illusion stating that the horizon seems more distant than the night sky.

MODULE 4.6 Perception and Objectivity

AS MENTIONED IN MODULE 2.1, it takes a split second (about 50 milliseconds) for a visual signal to move from the retina to the brain. Therefore, perceptions always lag slightly behind events in the "real world." An event that happens quickly, like the pop of a flashbulb, may be over by the time you perceive it. In fact, various processes distort our perceptions, which are far from being a perfect model of the world. Let's investigate some factors that affect the accuracy of our perceptual experiences.

Perception and Objectivity—Believing Is Seeing

SURVEY QUESTION: *How is perception altered by expectations, motives, emotions, and learning?*

At the beginning of this chapter one of your authors described an apparent murder that turned out to be something quite different. If he had never returned to "the scene of the crime," he would have sworn that he had seen a homicide. The girl's description completely shaped his own perceptions. This perhaps is understandable. But he'll never forget the added shock he felt when he met the "murderer"—the man he had seen a few moments before as huge, vicious, and horrible-looking. The man was not a stranger. He was a neighbor who your author had seen dozens of times before and knows by name. Stories such as this show that our experiences are **perceptual constructions** or mental models of external events. Perceptions are filtered through our needs, expectations, attitudes, values, and beliefs (● Fig. 4.44). Clearly, we don't just believe what we see. We also see what we believe. Let's explore the process of perceptual construction and some factors that shape or even distort it. (Also see "The Boiled Frog Syndrome.")

On a piece of paper, draw a circle about 3 inches in diameter. Inside the circle, above and to the left of center, make a large black dot, about one-half inch in diameter. Make another dot inside the circle above and to the right of center. Now, still inside the circle, draw an arc, curved upward and about 2 inches long just below the center of the circle. If you followed these instructions, your reaction might now be, "Oh! Why didn't you just say to draw a happy face?"

Like the happy face drawing, perceptual construction seems to proceed in two major ways. In **bottom-up processing**, we analyze information starting at the "bottom" with small sensory units (features) and build upward to a complete perception. The reverse also seems to occur. In **top-down processing**, pre-existing knowledge is used to rapidly

● **FIGURE 4.44** It is difficult to look at this simple drawing without perceiving depth. Yet, the drawing is nothing more than a collection of flat shapes. Turn this page counterclockwise 90 degrees and you will see three C's, one within another. When the drawing is turned sideways, it seems nearly flat. However, if you turn the page upright again, a sense of depth will reappear. Clearly, you have used your knowledge and expectations to *construct* an illusion of depth. The drawing itself would only be a flat design if you didn't invest it with three-dimensional meaning.

organize features into a meaningful whole. Bottom-up processing is like putting together a picture puzzle you've never seen before: You must assemble small pieces until a recognizable pattern appears. Top-down processing is like putting together a puzzle you have solved many times: After only a few pieces are in place you begin to see outlines of the final picture.

Both types of processing are illustrated by ● Figure 4.45. Also, return to Figure 4.31, the giant walkingstick. The first time you saw the photo you probably processed it bottom-up, picking out features until the insect was recognizable. This time, because of top-down processing, you should see the insect instantly. Another good example of top-down processing is found in perceptual expectancies.

Perceptual Expectancies

What is a perceptual expectancy? A runner in the starting blocks at a track meet is *set* to respond in a certain way. Likewise, past experience, motives, context, or suggestions may create a **perceptual expectancy** (or **set**) that prepares you to perceive in a certain way. If a car backfires, runners at a track meet may jump the gun. As a matter of fact, we all frequently jump the gun when perceiving. In essence, an expectancy is a perceptual hypothesis we are *very likely* to apply to a stimulus—even if applying it is inappropriate.

CRITICAL THINKING

The Boiled Frog Syndrome

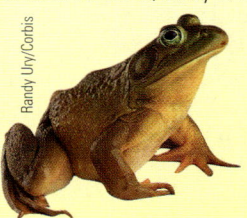

Perception can blind us to very slow events and gradual changes. Humans evolved to detect sharp changes, such as the sudden appearance of a lion, a potential mate, or sources of food. However, many of the threats facing us today develop very slowly. Examples include global warming, degradation of the environment, the stockpiling of nuclear warheads, global deforestation, erosion of the ozone layer, and runaway human population growth.

Robert Ornstein, a psychologist, and Paul Ehrlich, a biologist, believe that many of the large-scale threats we face are similar to the "boiled frog syndrome." Frogs placed in a pan of water that is slowly heated cannot detect the gradual rise in temperature. They will sit still until they die. Like the doomed frogs, many people seem unable to detect gradual but deadly trends in modern civilization (Ornstein & Ehrlich, 1989).

To avoid disasters, it may take a conscious effort by large numbers of people to construct the "big picture" and reverse lethal but easily overlooked patterns (O'Neill, 2005). The relatively new field of *community psychology* is dedicated to helping overcome our own narrow perspectives to perceive important larger patterns (Nelson & Prilleltensky, 2005). Understanding how perception shapes "reality" may ultimately prove to be a matter of life or death. Are you paying attention?

● **FIGURE 4.45** This painting by abstract artist Al Held is 9 feet by 9 feet. If you process the painting "bottom-up," all you will see is two small dark geometric shapes. Would you like to try some top-down processing? Knowing the painting's title will allow you to apply your knowledge and see the painting in an entirely different way. The title? It's *The Big N*. Can you see it now? (Courtesy The Museum of Modern Art, New York.)

as you draw nearer, the words on the sign become FOOD AHEAD. Most people have had similar experiences in which expectations altered their perceptions. To observe perceptual expectancies firsthand, perform the demonstration described in ● Figure 4.46.

Perceptual expectancies are frequently created by *suggestion*. This is especially true of perceiving other people. In one classic experiment, a psychology professor arranged for a guest lecturer to teach his class. Half the students in the class were given a page of notes that described the lecturer as a "rather *cold* person, industrious, critical, practical, and determined." The other students got notes describing him as a "rather *warm* person, industrious, critical, practical, and determined" (Kelley, 1950; italics added). Students who received the "cold" description perceived the lecturer as unhappy and irritable and didn't volunteer in class discussion. Those who got the "warm" description saw the lecturer as happy and good natured, and they actively took part in discussion with him. In the same way, labels such as "punk," "mental patient," "queer," "illegal immigrant," "bitch," and so on, are very likely to distort perceptions.

Perceptual sets often lead us to see what we *expect* to see. One of your authors thought he saw a murder in the supermarket because he had just heard the girl's description of what was happening. Here's another example: Let's say you are driving across the desert and you're very low on gas. Finally, you see a sign approaching. On it are the words FUEL AHEAD. You relax, knowing you will not be stranded. But

Perceptual construction A mental model of external events.
Bottom-up processing Organizing perceptions by beginning with low-level features.
Top-down processing Applying higher-level knowledge to rapidly organize sensory information into a meaningful perception.
Perceptual expectancy (or set) A readiness to perceive in a particular manner, induced by strong expectations.

View I   View II   View III

● **FIGURE 4.46** "Young woman/old woman" illustrations. As an interesting demonstration of perceptual expectancy, show some of your friends view I and some view II (cover all other views). Next show your friends view III and ask them what they see. Those who saw view I should see the old woman in view III; those who saw view II should see the young woman in view III. Can you see both? (Adapted from Leeper, 1935.)

Motives, Emotions, and Perception

Our motives and emotions also play a role in shaping our perceptions. For example, if you are hungry, food-related words are more likely to gain your attention than nonfood words (Mogg et al., 1998). Advertisers take advantage of two motives that are widespread in our society: *anxiety* and *sex*. Everything from mouthwash to automobile tires is merchandised by using sex to gain attention. Other ads combine sex with anxiety. Deodorant, soaps, toothpaste, and countless other articles are pushed in ads that play on desires to be attractive, to have "sex appeal," or to avoid embarrassment.

By directing attention, motives may alter what is perceived. As part of a supposed study of "the dating practices of college students," male volunteers were shown a picture of a female student and asked to give a first impression of how attractive she was. Before making these ratings, each person read one of two short written passages: One was sexually arousing and the other was not. The important finding was that men who read the more arousing passage rated the female as more attractive (Stephan, Berscheid, & Walster, 1971). This result may come as no surprise if you have ever been infatuated with someone and then fallen out of love. A person who once seemed highly attractive may look quite different when your feelings change.

Our emotions can also shape our perceptions. According to psychologist Barbara Frederickson, negative emotions generally narrow our perceptual focus, increasing the likelihood of inattentional blindness, whereas positive emotions can actually broaden the scope of attention (Fredrickson & Branigan, 2005). For example, positive emotions can affect how well people recognize people from other races. In recognizing faces, a consistent *other-race effect* occurs. This is a sort of "They all look alike to me" bias in perceiving persons from other racial and ethnic groups. In tests of facial recognition, people are much better at recognizing faces of their own race than others. But when people are in positive moods, their ability to recognize people from other races improves (Johnson & Fredrickson, 2005).

Another reason for the other-race effect is that we typically have more experience with people from our own race. As a result, we become very familiar with the features that help us recognize different persons. For other groups, we lack the perceptual expertise needed to accurately separate one face from another (Sporer, 2001). This indicates the importance of perceptual learning, a topic we turn to next.

Perceptual Learning

England is one of the few countries in the world where people drive on the left side of the road. In view of this reversal, it is not unusual for visitors to step off curbs in front of cars—after carefully looking for traffic in the *wrong* direction. As this example suggests, learning has a powerful impact on perception.

How does learning affect perception? The term **perceptual learning** refers to changes in the brain that alter how we process sensory information (Fahle & Poggio, 2002). For example, to use a computer, you must learn to pay attention to specific stimuli, such as icons and cursors. We also learn to tell the difference between stimuli that seemed identical at first. An example is the novice chef who discovers how to tell the difference between dried basil, oregano, and tarragon. In other situations, we learn to focus on just one part of a group of stimuli. This saves us from having to process all the stimuli in the group. For instance, a linebacker in football may be able to tell if the next play will be a run or a pass by watching one or two key players, rather than the entire opposing team (Seitz & Watanabe, 2005).

Module 4.6 • PERCEPTION AND OBJECTIVITY   189

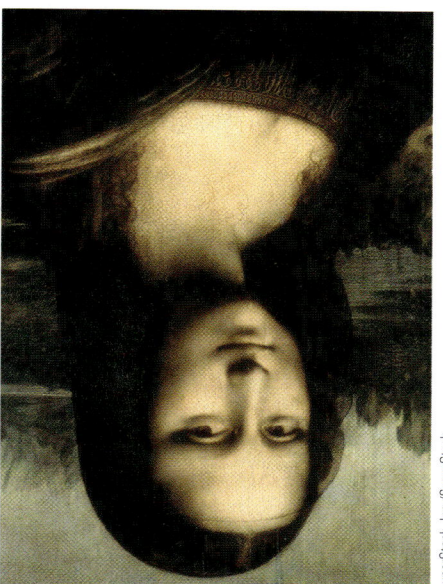

• **FIGURE 4.47** The effects of prior experience on perception. The doctored face looks far worse when viewed right side up because it can be related to past experience.

Illusions Perceptual learning is responsible for a number of *illusions*. In an **illusion**, length, position, motion, curvature, or direction is consistently misjudged. For example, you are probably in the perceptual habit of assuming that a room is shaped roughly like a box. This need not be true, however. An *Ames room* (named for the man who designed it) is a lopsided space that appears square when viewed from a certain point (• Fig. 4.48). This illusion is achieved by carefully distorting the proportions of the walls, floor, ceiling, and windows. Because the left corner of the Ames room is farther from a viewer than the right, a person standing in that corner looks very small; one standing in the nearer, shorter right corner looks very large. A person who walks from the left to the right corner will seem to "magically" grow larger.

Note that illusions are distorted perceptions of stimuli that actually exist. In a **hallucination**, people perceive objects or events that have no external reality (Lepore, 2002). For example, they hear voices that are not there (see "Staying in Touch with Reality"). If you think you are experiencing an illusion or a hallucination, try engaging in some reality testing.

What do you mean by reality testing? In any situation having an element of doubt or uncertainty, **reality testing** involves obtaining additional information to check your perceptions. If you think you see a 3-foot-tall butterfly, you can confirm you are hallucinating by trying to touch its wings. To detect an illusion, you may have to measure a drawing or apply a straightedge to it. • Figure 4.49 shows a powerful illusion called Fraser's spiral. What appears to be a spiral is actually made up of a series of closed circles. Most people cannot spontaneously see this reality. Instead, they must carefully trace one of the circles to confirm what is "real" in the design.

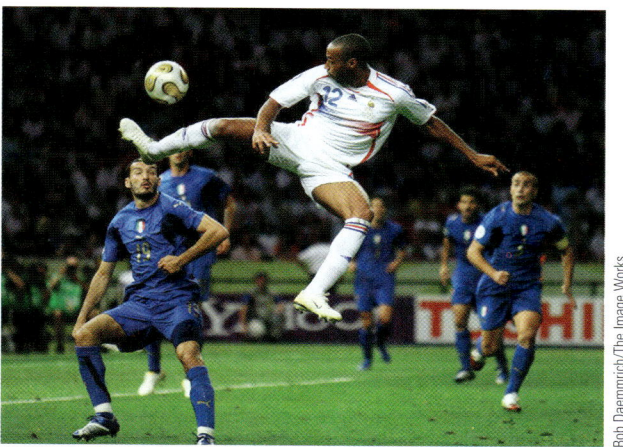

In many sports, expert players are much better than beginners at paying attention to key information. Compared with novices, experts scan actions and events more quickly, and they focus on only the most meaningful information. This allows experts to make decisions and react more quickly (Bard, Fleury, & Goulet, 1994).

In general, learning creates *perceptual habits* (ingrained patterns of organization and attention) that affect our daily experience. Stop for a moment and look at • Figure 4.47. The left face looks somewhat unusual, to be sure. But the distortion seems mild—until you turn the page upside down. Viewed this way, the face looks quite grotesque. Why is there a difference? Apparently, most people have little experience with upside-down faces. Perceptual learning, therefore, has less impact on our perceptions of an upside-down face. With a face in the normal position, you know what to expect and where to look. Also, you tend to see the entire face as a recognizable pattern. When a face is inverted, we are forced to perceive its individual features separately (Bartlett & Searcy, 1993).

Perceptual learning Changes in perception that can be attributed to prior experience; a result of changes in how the brain processes sensory information.
Illusion A misleading or distorted perception.
Hallucination An imaginary sensation—such as seeing, hearing, or smelling something that does not exist in the external world.
Reality testing Obtaining additional information to check on the accuracy of perceptions.

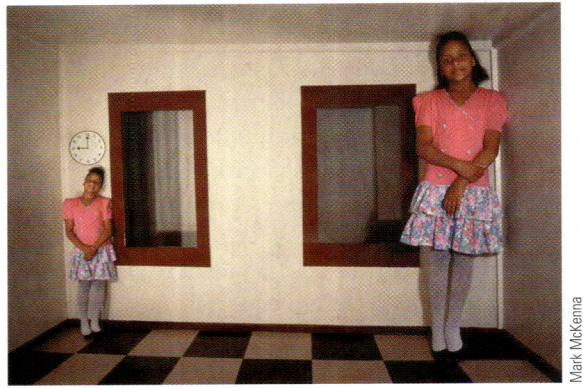

● **FIGURE 4.48** The Ames room. From the front, the room looks normal; actually, the right-hand corner is very short, and the left-hand corner is very tall. In addition, the left side of the room slants away from viewers. The diagram shows the shape of the room and reveals why people appear to get bigger as they cross the room toward the nearer, shorter right corner.

● **FIGURE 4.49** The limits of pure perception. Even simple designs are easily misperceived. Fraser's spiral is actually a series of concentric circles. The illusion is so powerful that people who try to trace one of the circles sometimes follow the illusory spiral and jump from one circle to the next. (Adapted from Seckel, 2000.)

(a) Which of the horizontal lines is longer?

(b) Is the diagonal a single straight line? Check it with a ruler.

(c) Is this a drawing of a staircase descending from upper left to lower right . . . or is it the view of the underneath of a staircase from lower right to upper left?

(d) Are these lines parallel? Cover some of the slash marks to see.

(e) Which line is longer, horizontal or vertical?

(f) Notice how the background distorts the square.

(g) Which quadrilateral is larger?

(h) Which column is shortest? Which is longest?

● **FIGURE 4.50** Some interesting perceptual illusions. Such illusions are a normal part of visual perception.

THE CLINICAL FILE
Staying in Touch with Reality

Just imagine that often, and without warning, you hear a voice shouting "Buckets of blood!" or see blood spattering across the walls of your bedroom. Chances are people would think you are mentally disturbed. Hallucinations are a major symptom of psychosis, dementia, epilepsy, migraine headaches, alcohol withdrawal, and drug intoxication (Spence & David, 2004). They are also one of the clearest signs that a person has "lost touch with reality."

Yet consider the case of mathematician John Nash (the subject of *A Beautiful Mind*, the winner of the 2002 Oscar for best film). Even though Nash suffered from schizophrenia, he eventually learned to use his ability to engage in reality testing to sort out which of his experiences were perceptions and which were hallucinations. Unlike John Nash, most people who experience full-blown hallucinations also have a limited ability to reality test (Hohwy & Rosenberg, 2005).

Curiously, "sane hallucinations" also occur. *Charles Bonnet syndrome* is a rare condition that afflicts mainly older people who are partially blind but not mentally disturbed. They may "see" people, animals, buildings, plants, and other objects appear and disappear in front of their eyes. One older man suffering from partial blindness and leukemia complained of seeing animals in his house, including cattle and bears (Jacob et al., 2004). However, people experiencing "sane hallucinations" can more easily tell that their hallucinations aren't real because their capacity to reality test is not impaired.

Such unusual experiences show how powerfully the brain seeks meaningful patterns in sensory input and the role reality testing plays in our normal perceptual experience.

● **FIGURE 4.51** Why does line *(b)* in the Müller-Lyer illusion look longer than line *(a)*? Probably because it looks more like a distant corner than a nearer one. Because the vertical lines form images of the same length, the more "distant" line must be perceived as larger. As you can see in the drawing on the right, additional depth cues accentuate the Müller-Lyer illusion. (Adapted from Enns & Coren, 1995.)

Can illusions be explained? Not in all cases, or to everyone's satisfaction. In general, size and shape constancy, habitual eye movements, continuity, and perceptual habits combine in various ways to produce the illusions in Figure 4.50. Rather than attempt to explain all of them, let's focus on one deceptively simple example.

Consider the drawing in ● Figure 4.50*a*. This is the familiar **Müller-Lyer** (MEOO-ler-LIE-er) **illusion** in which the horizontal line with arrowheads appears shorter than the line with V's. A quick measurement will show that they are the same length. How can we explain this illusion? Evidence suggests it is based on a lifetime of experience with the edges and corners of rooms and buildings. Richard Gregory (1990) believes you see the horizontal line with the V's as if it were the corner of a room viewed from inside (● Fig. 4.51). The line with arrowheads, on the other hand, suggests the corner

Müller-Lyer illusion Two equal-length lines tipped with inward or outward pointing V's appear to be of different lengths.

of a room or building seen from outside. In other words, cues that suggest a three-dimensional space alter our perception of a two-dimensional design (Enns & Coren, 1995).

Earlier, to explain the moon illusion, we said that if two objects make images of the same size, the more distant object must be larger. This is known formally as *size-distance invariance* (the size of an object's image is precisely related to its distance from the eyes). Gregory believes the same concept explains the Müller-Lyer illusion. If the V-tipped line looks farther away than the arrowhead-tipped line, you must compensate by seeing the V-tipped line as longer. This explanation presumes that you have had years of experience with straight lines, sharp edges, and corners—a pretty safe assumption in our culture.

Is there any way to show that past experience causes the illusion? If we could test someone who saw only curves and wavy lines as a child, we would know if experience with a "square" culture is important. Fortunately, the Zulus, a group of people in South Africa, live in a "round" culture. In their daily lives, Zulus rarely encounter a straight line: Their houses are shaped like rounded mounds and arranged in a circle, tools and toys are curved, and there are few straight roads or square buildings.

What happens if a Zulu looks at the Müller-Lyer design? The typical Zulu villager does not experience the illusion. At most, she or he sees the V-shaped line as *slightly* longer than the other (Gregory, 1990). This seems to confirm the importance of perceptual habits in determining our view of the world.

In the next section, we will go beyond normal perception to ask, Is extrasensory perception possible? Before we do that, here's a chance to answer the question, Is remembering the preceding discussion possible?

MODULE 4.6 Summary

How is perception altered by expectations, motives, emotions, and learning?

- Perception is an active construction of events.
- Perceptions may be based on top-down or bottom-up processing of information.
- Suggestion, motives, emotions, attention, and prior experience combine in various ways to create perceptual sets, or expectancies.
- Personal motives and values often alter perceptions by changing the evaluation of what is seen or by altering attention to specific details.
- Perceptual learning influences the ways in which we organize and interpret sensations.
- One of the most familiar of all illusions, the Müller-Lyer illusion, seems to be related to perceptual learning, linear perspective, and size-distance invariance relationships.

KNOWLEDGE BUILDER

Perception and Objectivity

Recite

1. Perceptual habits may become so ingrained that they lead us to misperceive a stimulus. T or F?
2. Perceptual learning seems to program the brain for sensitivity to important _____ of the environment.
3. The Ames room is used to test infants for depth perception. T or F?
4. Size-distance relationships appear to underlie which two illusions? _____ and _____
5. Research shows that heightened sexual arousal can cause a person to perceive members of the opposite sex as more physically attractive. T or F?
6. In top-down processing of information, individual features are analyzed and assembled into a meaningful whole. T or F?
7. When a person is prepared to perceive events in a particular way, it is said that a perceptual expectancy or _____ exists.

Reflect

Critical Thinking

8. What size object do you think you would have to hold at arm's length to cover up a full moon?
9. Cigarette advertisements in the United States are required to carry a warning label about the health risks of smoking. How have tobacco companies made these labels less visible?

Relate

How has perceptual learning affected your ability to safely drive a car? For example, what do you pay attention to at intersections? Where do you habitually look as you are driving?

If you spent a year hiking the Amazon River Basin, what effect might it have on your perception of the Müller-Lyer illusion?

You have almost certainly misperceived a situation at some time because of a perceptual expectancy or the influence of motives. How were your perceptions influenced?

Link

Internet addresses frequently change. To find the sites listed here, visit **http://www.thomsonedu.com/psychology/coon** for an updated list of Internet addresses and direct links to relevant sites.

- **Context and Expectations** Read about the effect of context on perception.
- **Perceptual Learning** Explore an example of perceptual learning through wine tasting.
- **Ames Room** Explore the Ames room illusion.

ANSWERS

1. T 2. features 3. F 4. moon illusion, Müller-Lyer illusion 5. T 6. F 7. set 8. The most popular answers range from a quarter to a softball. Actually, a pea held in the outstretched hand will cover a full moon (Kunkel, 1993). If you listed an object larger than a pea, be aware that perceptions, no matter how accurate they seem, may distort reality. 9. Advertisers place health warnings in the corners of ads, where they attract the least possible attention. Also, the labels are often placed on "busy" backgrounds so that they are partially camouflaged. Finally, the main images in ads are designed to strongly attract attention. This further distracts readers from seeing the warnings.

MODULE 4.7 Extrasensory Perception

ABOUT HALF OF THE GENERAL PUBLIC believes in the existence of extrasensory perception (Wiseman & Watt, 2006). Very few psychologists share this belief. Actually, it's surprising that even more people aren't believers. ESP and other paranormal events are treated as accepted facts in many movies and television programs. What is the evidence for and against extrasensory perception?

Extrasensory Perception—Do You Believe in Magic?

SURVEY QUESTION: *Is extrasensory perception possible?*

Uri Geller, a self-proclaimed "psychic," once agreed to demonstrate his claimed paranormal abilities. During testing, it seemed that Geller could sense which of 10 film canisters contained a hidden object, he correctly guessed the number that would come up on a die shaken in a closed box, and he reproduced drawings sealed in envelopes.

Was Geller cheating, or was he using some ability beyond normal perception? There is little doubt that Geller was cheating (Randi, 1997). But how? The answer lies in a discussion of **extrasensory perception (ESP)**—the purported ability to perceive events in ways that cannot be explained by known sensory capacities.

Parapsychology is the study of ESP and other **psi phenomena** (events that seem to defy accepted scientific laws). (Psi is pronounced like "sigh.") Parapsychologists seek answers to the questions raised by three basic forms that ESP could take. These are:

1. **Telepathy.** The purported ability to communicate directly with another person's mind. When the other person is dead, the communications are called *mediumship*.
2. **Clairvoyance.** The purported ability to perceive events or gain information in ways that appear unaffected by distance or normal physical barriers.
3. **Precognition.** The purported ability to perceive or accurately predict future events. Precognition may take the form of prophetic dreams that foretell the future.

While we are at it, we might as well toss in another purported psi ability:

4. **Psychokinesis.** The purported ability to exert influence over inanimate objects by willpower ("mind over matter"). (Psychokinesis cannot be classed as a type of ESP, but it is frequently studied by parapsychologists.)

An Appraisal of ESP

Psychologists as a group are highly skeptical about psi abilities. If you've ever had an apparent clairvoyant or telepathic experience, you might be convinced that ESP exists. However, the difficulty of excluding *coincidence* makes such experiences less conclusive than they might seem. Consider a typical "psychic" experience: During the middle of the night, a woman away for a weekend visit suddenly had a strong impulse to return home. When she arrived she found the house on fire with her husband asleep inside (Rhine, 1953). An experience like this is striking, but it does not confirm the reality of ESP. If, by coincidence, a hunch turns out to be correct, it may be *reinterpreted* as precognition or clairvoyance (Marks, 2000; Wiseman & Watt, 2006). If it is not confirmed, it will simply be forgotten. Most people don't realize it, but such coincidences occur quite often.

Formal investigation of psi events owes much to the late J. B. Rhine, who tried to study ESP objectively. Many of

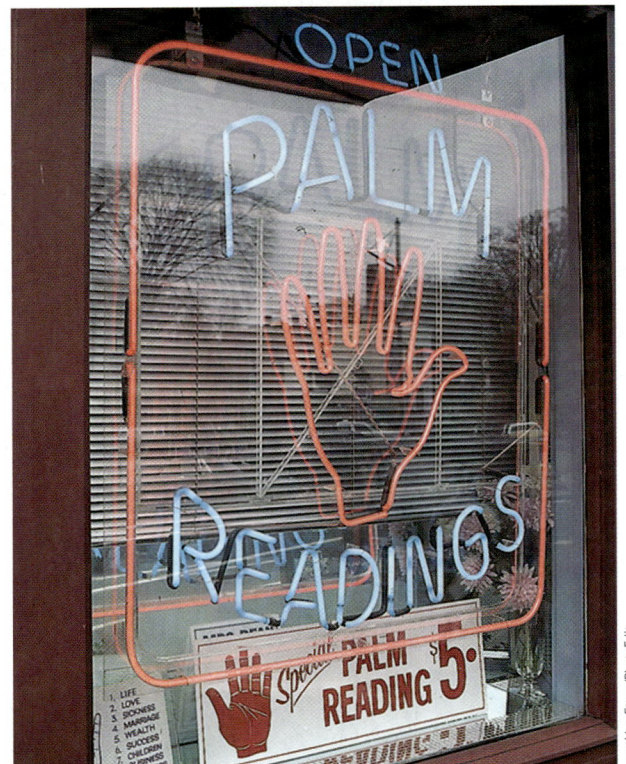

Most so-called psychics are simply keen observers. The "psychic" begins a "reading" by making general statements about a person. The "psychic" then plays "hot and cold" by attending to the person's facial expressions, body language, or tone of voice. When the "psychic" is "hot" (on the right track), the "psychic" continues to make similar statements about the person. If the person's reactions signal that the "psychic" is "cold," the psychic drops that topic or line of thought and tries another (Schouten, 1994).

Rhine's experiments made use of the *Zener cards* (a deck of 25 cards, each bearing one of five symbols) (● Fig. 4.52). In a typical clairvoyance test, people tried to guess the symbols on the cards as they were turned up from a shuffled deck. Pure guessing in this test will produce an average score of 5 "hits" out of 25 cards.

Fraud and Skepticism Unfortunately, some of Rhine's most dramatic early experiments used badly printed Zener cards that allowed the symbols to show faintly on the back. It is also very easy to cheat, by marking cards with a fingernail or by noting marks on the cards caused by normal use. Even if this were not the case, there is evidence that early experimenters sometimes unconsciously gave people cues about cards with their eyes, facial gestures, or lip movements. In short, none of the early studies in parapsychology were done in a way that eliminated the possibility of fraud or "leakage" of helpful information (Alcock, Burns, & Freeman, 2003).

Modern parapsychologists are now well aware of the need for double-blind experiments, security and accuracy in record keeping, meticulous control, and repeatability of experiments (Milton & Wiseman, 1997; O'Keeffe & Wiseman, 2005). In the last 10 years, hundreds of experiments have been reported in parapsychological journals. Many of them seem to support the existence of psi abilities.

Then why do most psychologists remain skeptical about psi abilities? Fraud continues to plague the field. As one critic put it, positive ESP results usually mean "Error Some Place" (Marks, 2000). The more closely psi experiments are examined, the more likely it is that claimed successes will evaporate (Alcock, 2003; Stokes, 2001).

The need for skepticism is especially great anytime there's money to be made from purported psychic abilities. For example, the owners of the "Miss Cleo" TV-psychic operation were convicted of felony fraud in 2002. "Miss Cleo," supposedly a Jamaican-accented psychic, was really just an actress from Los Angeles. People who paid $4.99 a minute for a "reading" from "Miss Cleo" actually reached one of several hundred operators. These people were hired through ads that read "No experience necessary." Despite being entirely faked, the "Miss Cleo" scam brought in more than $1 billion before it was shut down.

Anyone can learn to do "cold readings" (Wood et al., 2003) well enough to produce satisfied customers. *Cold reading* is a set of techniques that are used to lead people to believe in the truth of what a psychic or medium is saying about them. These include a reliance on many of the same techniques used by practitioners of the horoscope, such as uncritical acceptance, positive instances, and the Barnum effect. (See Module 1.2.) To do a cold reading, you would begin by making general statements about a person. Then you would expand on anything the person responds to in a positive way. For instance you might say, "I sense that you experienced a serious loss in childhood." If the person silently nods "yes," you would continue to talk about childhood loss. If the person looks dubious, you would change to another topic.

Statistics and Chance Inconsistency is another major problem in psi research. For every study with positive results, there are many others that fail and are never published (Alcock, 2003). It is rare—in fact, almost unheard of—for a person to maintain psi ability over any sustained period (Alcock, Burns, & Freeman, 2003). ESP researchers believe this "decline effect" shows that parapsychological skills are very fragile. But critics argue that a person who only temporarily scores above chance has just received credit for a **run of luck** (a statistically unusual outcome that could occur by chance alone). When the run is over, it is not fair to assume that ESP is temporarily gone. We must count *all* attempts.

To understand the run-of-luck criticism, imagine that you flip a coin 100 times and record the results. You then flip another coin 100 times, again recording the results. The two lists are compared. For any 10 pairs of flips, we would expect heads or tails to match 5 times. Let's say that you go through the list and find a set of 10 pairs where 9 out of 10 matched. This is far above chance expectation. But does it mean that the first coin "knew" what was going to come up on the second coin? The idea is obviously silly.

Now, what if a person guesses 100 times what will come up on a coin. Again, we might find a set of 10 guesses that matches the results of flipping the coin. Does this mean that the person, for a time, had precognition—then lost it? Parapsychologists tend to believe the answer is yes. Skeptics assume that nothing more than random matching occurred, as in the two-coin example.

Inconclusive Research Unfortunately, many of the most spectacular findings in parapsychology simply cannot be replicated (reproduced or repeated) (Hyman, 1996a). Even the

● **FIGURE 4.52** ESP cards used by J. B. Rhine, an early experimenter in parapsychology.

Extrasensory perception (ESP) The purported ability to perceive events in ways that cannot be explained by known capacities of the sensory organs.
Psi phenomena Events that seem to lie outside the realm of accepted scientific laws.
Run of luck A statistically unusual outcome (as in getting five heads in a row when flipping a coin) that could still occur by chance alone.

same researchers using the same experimental subjects typically can't get similar results every time (Schick & Vaughn, 2001). More importantly, improved research methods usually result in fewer positive results (Hyman, 1996b; O'Keeffe & Wiseman, 2005).

Reinterpretation is also a problem in psi experiments. For example, ex-astronaut Edgar Mitchell claimed he did a successful telepathy experiment from space. Yet news accounts never mentioned that on some trials Mitchell's "receivers" scored above chance, and on others they scored *below* chance. Although you might assume that below chance trials were failures to find telepathy, Mitchell reinterpreted them as "successes," claiming that they represented intentional "psi missing." But, as skeptics have noted, if both high scores and low scores count as successes, how can you lose?

Of course, in many ESP tests the outcome is beyond debate. A good example is provided by recent ESP experiments done through newspapers, radio, and television. In these mass media studies, people attempted to identify ESP targets from a distance. The results of one study of over 1.5 million ESP trials done through the mass media are easy to summarize: There was no significant ESP effect (Milton & Wiseman, 1999). Zero. Zip. Nada. Clearly, state lottery organizers have nothing to fear!

Stage ESP

Stage ESP simulates ESP for the purpose of entertainment. If psychic phenomena do occur, they certainly can't be controlled well enough to be used by entertainers. Like stage magic, it is based on sleight of hand, deception, and patented gadgets (● Fig. 4.53). A case in point is Uri Geller, a former nightclub magician who "astounded" audiences—and some scientists—with apparent telepathy, psychokinesis, and precognition.

It's now clear that tests of Geller's performance were incredibly sloppy. For instance, Geller reproduced sealed drawings in a room next to the one where the drawings were made. Original reports failed to mention that there was a hole in the wall between the rooms, through which Geller could have heard descriptions of the pictures as they were being drawn. Likewise, in the "die in the box" tests Geller was allowed to hold the box, shake it, and have the honor of opening it (Randi, 1997).

Why weren't such details reported? Sensational and uncritical reporting of apparent paranormal events is widespread. Hundreds of books, articles, and television programs are produced each year by people who are getting rich by promoting unsupported claims. If a person did have psychic powers, he or she would not have to make a living by entertaining others. A quick trip to a casino would allow the person to retire for life.

Implications After close to 130 years of investigation, it is still impossible to say conclusively whether psi events occur. As we have seen, a close look at psi experiments often reveals serious problems of evidence, procedure, and scientific rigor (Alcock, Burns, & Freeman, 2003; Hyman, 1996b; Stokes, 2001). Yet, being a skeptic does not mean a person is against something. It means that you are unconvinced. The purpose of this discussion, then, has been to counter the *uncritical* acceptance of psi events that is rampant in the media. (But then, you already knew we were going to say that, didn't you!)

  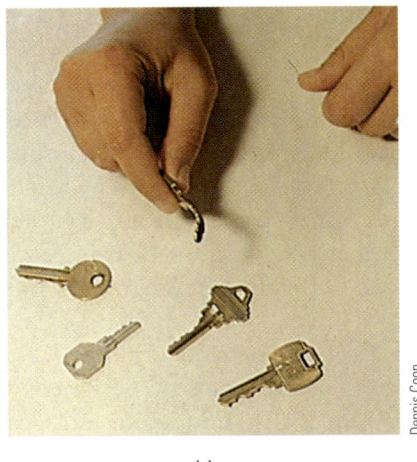

(a)　　　　　　　　　　　(b)　　　　　　　　　　　(c)

● **FIGURE 4.53** Fake psychokinesis. *(a)* The performer shows an observer several straight keys. While doing so, he bends one of the keys by placing its tip in the slot of another key. Normally, this is done out of sight, behind the "psychic's" hand. It is clearly shown here so you can see how the deception occurs. *(b)* Next, the "psychic" places the two keys in the observer's hand and closes it. By skillful manipulation, the observer has been kept from seeing the bent key. The performer then "concentrates" on the keys to "bend them with psychic energy." *(c)* The bent key is revealed to the observer. "Miracle" accomplished! (Adapted from Randi, 1983.)

What would it take to scientifically demonstrate the existence of ESP? Quite simply, a set of instructions that would allow any competent, unbiased observer to produce a psi event under standardized conditions that rule out any possibility of fraud (Schick & Vaughn, 2001). In fact, professional magician and skeptic James Randi even offers a $1,000,000 prize to anyone who can demonstrate evidence of psi events under standardized conditions. No one has claimed the prize yet. (You can read all about it if you google the James Randi Educational Foundation.)

A Look Ahead In this chapter we have moved from basic sensations to the complexities of perceiving people and events. We have also probed some of the controversies concerning ESP. In the Psychology in Action module, we will return to "everyday" perception, for a look at perceptual awareness.

MODULE 4.7 Summary

Is extrasensory perception possible?

- Parapsychology is the study of purported psi phenomena, including telepathy (as well as mediumship) clairvoyance, precognition, and psychokinesis.
- Research in parapsychology remains controversial because of a variety of problems and shortcomings. The bulk of the evidence to date is against the existence of ESP.
- The more carefully controlled an ESP experiment is, the less likely it is to produce evidence that ESP occurs.
- Stage ESP is based on deception and tricks.

KNOWLEDGE BUILDER

Extrasensory Perception

Recite

1. Four purported psi events investigated by parapsychologists are clairvoyance, telepathy, precognition, and _____.
2. The Zener cards were used in early studies of
   a. psi phenomena
   b. inattentional blindness
   c. the Müller-Lyer illusion
   d. top-down processing
3. Natural, or "real life," occurrences are regarded as the best evidence for the existence of ESP. T or F?
4. Skeptics attribute positive results in psi experiments to statistical runs of luck. T or F?
5. Replication rates are very high for ESP experiments. T or F?

Reflect
Critical Thinking

6. What would you estimate is the chance that two people will have the same birthday (day and month, but not year) in a group of 30 people?
7. A "psychic" on television offers to fix broken watches for viewers. Moments later, dozens of viewers call the station to say that their watches miraculously started running again. What have they overlooked?

Relate

Let's say that a friend of yours is an avid fan of TV shows that feature paranormal themes. See if you can summarize for her or him what is known about ESP. Be sure to include evidence for and against the existence of ESP and some of the thinking errors associated with nonskeptical belief in the paranormal.

Link

Internet addresses frequently change. To find the sites listed here, visit http://www.thomsonedu.com/psychology/coon for an updated list of Internet addresses and direct links to relevant sites.

- **James Randi Education Foundation** Win $1,000,000 dollars for proving, under scientifically controlled conditions, that you have ESP.
- **The Skeptic's Dictionary: ESP** Read more about the responses of skeptics to claims of paranormal abilities.
- **The Skeptic's Dictionary: Cold Reading** Learn to recognize when purported psychics are using cold reading techniques.

ANSWERS

1. psychokinesis 2. a 3. F 4. T 5. F 6. Most people assume that this would be a relatively rare event. Actually there is a 71 percent chance that two people will share a birthday in a group of 30. Most people probably underestimate the natural rate of occurrence of many seemingly mysterious coincidences (Alcock, 2003). 7. When psychologists handled watches awaiting repair at a store, 57 percent began running again, with no help from a "psychic." Believing the "psychic's" claim also overlooks the impact of big numbers: If the show reached a large audience, at least a few "broken" watches would start working merely by chance.

Stage ESP The simulation of ESP for the purpose of entertainment.

MODULE *Psychology in Action*
4.8 Becoming a Better Eyewitness to Life

SURVEY QUESTION: *How can I learn to perceive events more accurately?*

In the courtroom, the claim "I saw it with my own eyes" still carries a lot of weight with a jury. Too many jurors (unless they have taken a psychology course) tend to assume that eyewitness testimony is nearly infallible (Durham & Dane, 1999). Even U.S. judges are vulnerable to overoptimism about eyewitness testimony (Wise & Safer, 2004). But to put it bluntly, eyewitness testimony is frequently wrong (Wells & Olson, 2003). Recall, for instance, that one of your authors would have sworn in court that he had seen a murder taking place at the supermarket—*if* he hadn't received more information to correct his misperceptions.

What about witnesses who are certain that their perceptions were accurate? Should juries believe them? Actually, having confidence in your testimony has almost no bearing on its accuracy (Brewer & Wells, 2006)! Psychologists are gradually convincing lawyers, judges, and police that eyewitness errors are common (Yarmey, 2003). Even so, thousands of people have been wrongfully convicted (Scheck, Neufeld, & Dwyer, 2000).

Unfortunately, perception rarely provides an "instant replay" of events. Impressions formed when a person is surprised, threatened, or under stress are especially prone to distortion. One study of eyewitness cases found that the *wrong person* was chosen from police lineups 25 percent of the time (Levi, 1998).

Even in broad daylight, eyewitness testimony is untrustworthy. In 2001 an airliner crashed near Kennedy International Airport in New York. Hundreds of people saw the plane go down. Half of them said the plane was on fire. Flight recorders showed there was no fire. One witness in five saw the plane make a right turn. An equal number saw it make a left turn! As one investigator noted, the best witness may be a "kid under 12 years old who doesn't have his parents around." Adults, it seems, are easily swayed by their expectations.

Wouldn't the victim of a crime remember more than a mere witness? Not necessarily. A revealing study found that eyewitness accuracy is virtually the same for witnessing a crime (seeing a pocket calculator stolen) as it is for being a victim (seeing one's own watch stolen) (Hosch & Cooper, 1982). Placing more weight on the testimony of victims may be a serious mistake. In many crimes, victims fall prey to *weapon focus*. Understandably, they fix their entire attention on the knife, gun, or other weapon used by an attacker. In doing so, they fail to notice details of appearance, dress, or other clues to identity (Pickel, French, & Betts, 2003). Additional factors that consistently lower eyewitness accuracy are summarized in ■ Table 4.2 (Kassin et al., 2001; Wells & Olson, 2003).

Implications Now that DNA testing is available, more than 200 people who were convicted of murder, rape, and other crimes in the United States have been exonerated. Most of these innocent people were convicted mainly on the basis of eyewitness testimony. Each also spent *years* in prison before being cleared (Foxhall, 2000). How often are everyday perceptions as inaccurate or distorted as those of an emotional eyewitness? The answer is, very frequently. Bearing this in mind may help you be more tolerant of the views of others and more cautious about your own objectivity. It may also encourage more frequent reality testing on your part.

If you have ever concluded that someone was angry, upset, or unfriendly without checking the accuracy of your perceptions, you have fallen into a subtle trap. Personal objectivity is an elusive quality, requiring frequent reality testing to maintain. At the very least, it pays to ask a person what she or he is feeling when you are in doubt. Clearly, most of us could learn to be better "eyewitnesses" to daily events.

Positive Psychology: Perceptual Awareness

Do some people perceive things more accurately than others? Humanistic psychologist Abraham Maslow (1969) believed that some people perceive themselves and others with unusual accuracy. Maslow characterized these people as especially alive, open, aware, and mentally healthy. He found that their perceptual styles were marked by immersion in the present; a lack of self-consciousness; freedom from selecting, criticizing, or evaluating; and a general "surrender" to experience. The kind of perception Maslow described is like that of a mother with her newborn infant, a child at Christmas, or two people in love.

TABLE 4.2 Factors Affecting the Accuracy of Eyewitness Perceptions

SOURCES OF ERROR	SUMMARY OF FINDINGS
1. Wording of questions	An eyewitness's testimony about an event can be affected by how the questions put to that witness are worded.
2. Postevent information	Eyewitness testimony about an event often reflects not only what was actually seen but also information obtained later on.
3. Attitudes, expectations	An eyewitness's perception and memory for an event may be affected by his or her attitudes and expectations.
4. Alcohol intoxication	Alcohol intoxication impairs later ability to recall events.
5. Cross-racial perceptions	Eyewitnesses are better at identifying members of their own race than they are at identifying people of other races.
6. Weapon focus	The presence of a weapon impairs an eyewitness's ability to accurately identify the culprit's face.
7. Accuracy-confidence	An eyewitness's confidence is not a good predictor of his or her accuracy.
8. Exposure time	The less time an eyewitness has to observe an event, the less well she or he will perceive and remember it.
9. Unconscious transference	Eyewitnesses sometimes identify as a culprit someone they have seen in another situation or context.
10. Color perception	Judgments of color made under monochromatic light (such as an orange street light) are highly unreliable.
11. Stress	Very high levels of stress impair the accuracy of eyewitness perceptions.

Adapted from Kassin et al., 2001.

In daily life, we quickly **habituate** (respond less) to predictable and unchanging stimuli. Habituation is a type of learning—basically, we learn to cease paying attention to familiar stimuli. For instance, when you download a new MP3, the music initially holds your attention all the way through. But when the MP3 becomes "old," the song may play without your really attending to it. When a stimulus is repeated *without change,* our response to it habituates, or decreases. Interestingly, creative people habituate *more slowly* than average. We might expect that they would rapidly become bored with a repeated stimulus. Instead, it seems that creative people actively attend to stimuli, even those that are repeated (Colin, Moore, & West, 1996).

The Value of Paying Attention Whereas the average person has not reached perceptual restriction of the "if you've seen one tree, you've seen them all" variety, the fact remains that most of us tend to look at a tree and classify it into the perceptual category of "trees in general" without really appreciating the miracle standing before us. How, then, can we bring about **dishabituation** (a reversal of habituation) on a day-to-day basis? Does perceptual clarity require years of effort? Fortunately, a more immediate avenue is available. The deceptively simple key to dishabituation is: Pay attention. The following story summarizes the importance of attention:

One day a man of the people said to Zen Master Ikkyu: "Master, will you please write for me some maxims of the highest wisdom?"

Ikkyu immediately took his brush and wrote the word "Attention."

"Is that all?" asked the man. "Will you not add something more?"

Ikkyu then wrote twice running: "Attention. Attention."

"Well," remarked the man rather irritably, "I really don't see much depth or subtlety in what you have just written."

Then Ikkyu wrote the same word three times running: "Attention. Attention. Attention." Half angered, the man demanded, "What does that word 'Attention' mean anyway?"

And Ikkyu answered gently: "Attention means attention." (Kapleau, 1966)

To this we can add only one thought, provided by the words of poet William Blake: "If the doors of perception were cleansed, man would see everything as it is, infinite."

Habituation A decrease in perceptual response to a repeated stimulus.
Dishabituation A reversal of habituation.

How to Become a Better "Eyewitness" to Life

Here's a summary of ideas from this chapter to help you maintain and enhance perceptual awareness and accuracy.

1. *Remember that perceptions are constructions of reality.* Learn to regularly question your own perceptions. Are they accurate? Could another interpretation fit the facts? What assumptions are you making? Could they be false? How might your assumptions be distorting your perceptions?

2. *Break perceptual habits and interrupt habituation.* Each day, try to do some activities in new ways. For example, take different routes when you travel to work or school. Do routines, such as brushing your teeth or combing your hair, with your nonpreferred hand. Try to look at friends and family members as if they are persons you just met for the first time.

3. *Shift adaptation levels and broaden frames of reference by seeking out-of-the-ordinary experiences.* The possibilities here range from trying foods you don't normally eat to reading opinions very different from your own. Experiences ranging from a quiet walk in the woods to a trip to an amusement park may be perceptually refreshing.

4. *Beware of perceptual sets.* Anytime you pigeonhole people, objects, or events, there is a danger that your perceptions will be distorted by expectations or pre-existing categories. Be especially wary of labels and stereotypes. Try to see people as individuals and events as unique, one-time occurrences.

5. *Be aware of the ways in which motives and emotions influence perceptions.* It is difficult to avoid being swayed by your own interests, needs, desires, and emotions. But be aware of this trap and actively try to see the world through the eyes of others. Taking the other person's perspective is especially valuable in disputes or arguments. Ask yourself, "How does this look to her or him?"

6. *Make a habit of engaging in reality testing.* Actively look for additional evidence to check the accuracy of your perceptions. Ask questions, seek clarifications, and find alternate channels of information. Remember that perception is not automatically accurate. You could be wrong—we all are frequently.

7. *Pay attention.* Make a conscious effort to pay attention to other people and your surroundings. Don't drift through life in a haze. Listen to others with full concentration. Watch their facial expressions. Make eye contact. Try to get in the habit of approaching perception as if you are going to have to testify later about what you saw and heard.

MODULE 4.8 Psychology in Action Summary

How can I learn to perceive events more accurately?

- The perceptions of eyewitnesses are surprisingly unreliable. Eyewitness accuracy is further damaged by weapon focus and a number of similar factors.
- When a stimulus is repeated without change, our response to it undergoes habituation.
- Perceptual accuracy is enhanced by reality testing, dishabituation, and conscious efforts to pay attention.
- It is also valuable to break perceptual habits, to broaden frames of reference, to beware of perceptual sets, and to be aware of the ways in which motives and emotions influence perceptions.

KNOWLEDGE BUILDER

Perceptual Awareness and Accuracy

Recite

1. Most perceptions can be described as active constructions of external reality. T or F?
2. Inaccuracies in eyewitness perceptions obviously occur in "real life," but they cannot be reproduced in psychology experiments. T or F?
3. Accuracy scores for facts provided by witnesses to staged crimes may be as low as 25 percent correct. T or F?
4. Victims of crimes are more accurate eyewitnesses than are impartial observers. T or F?
5. *Reality testing* is another term for dishabituation. T or F?
6. A good antidote to perceptual habituation can be found in conscious efforts to
   a. reverse sensory gating
   b. pay attention
   c. achieve visual accommodation
   d. counteract shape constancy

Reflect
Critical Thinking

7. Return for a moment to the incident described at the beginning of this chapter. What perceptual factors were involved in the first version of the "murder"? How did the girl affect what one of your authors saw?

Relate

Because perceptions are reconstructions or models of external events, we should all engage in more frequent reality testing. Can you think of a recent event when a little reality testing would have saved you from misjudging a situation?

In order to improve your own perceptual awareness and accuracy, which strategies would you emphasize first?

Link

Internet addresses frequently change. To find the sites listed here, visit **http://www.thomsonedu.com/psychology/coon** for an updated list of Internet addresses and direct links to relevant sites.

- **What Jennifer Saw** Explore the evidence in a case of mistaken identity.
- **The Innocence Project** Read about real cases of people convicted through eyewitness testimony but later exonerated by DNA evidence.
- **Avoiding Habituation** Read about how advertisers apply the idea of habituation to the design of advertisements.

ANSWERS

1. T 2. F 3. T 4. F 5. F 6. b 7. The girl's misperception, communicated so forcefully to your author, created a powerful expectancy that influenced what he perceived. Also, the event happened quickly (the exposure time was brief) and the stressful or emotional nature of the incident encouraged your author's misperception.

Interactive Learning

Psychology: Active Learning Modules Book Companion Website

http://www.thomsonedu.com/psychology/coon

Visit your Book Companion Website, where you will find flash cards, practice quizzes, Internet links, and more to help you study.

ThomsonNOW

Just What You Need to Know NOW!

Spend time on what you need to master rather than on information you already have learned. Take a pre-test for this chapter, and ThomsonNOW will generate a personalized study plan based on your results. The study plan will identify the topics you need to review and direct you to online resources to help you master those topics. You can then take a post-test to help you determine the concepts you have mastered and what you will need to work on. Try it out! Go to **www.thomsonedu.com/login** to sign in with an access code or to purchase access to this product.

5 States of Consciousness

MODULE 5.1 Altered States and Sleep
SURVEY QUESTION: What is an altered state of consciousness?
SURVEY QUESTION: What are the effects of sleep loss or changes in sleep patterns?
SURVEY QUESTION: Are there different stages of sleep?

MODULE 5.2 Sleep Disturbances and Dreaming
SURVEY QUESTION: What are the causes of sleep disorders and unusual sleep events?
SURVEY QUESTION: Do dreams have meaning?

MODULE 5.3 Hypnosis, Meditation, and Sensory Deprivation
SURVEY QUESTION: How is hypnosis done, and what are its limitations?

SURVEY QUESTION: What are meditation and sensory deprivation? Do they have any benefits?

MODULE 5.4 Psychoactive Drugs
SURVEY QUESTION: What are the effects of the more commonly used psychoactive drugs?

MODULE 5.5 Psychology in Action: Exploring and Using Dreams
SURVEY QUESTION: How are dreams used to promote personal understanding?

A Visit to Several States (of Consciousness)

In New Zealand, a Maori tohunga (priest) performs a nightlong ritual to talk to the spirits who created the world in the mythical period the Aborigines call Dreamtime.

In Toronto, Canada, three businesswomen head for a popular tavern after a particularly stressful day.

In the American Southwest, a Navajo elder gives his congregation peyote tea, a sacrament in the Native American Church, as a drumbeat resounds in the darkness.

In Big Bend National Park in southern Texas, a college student spends a day walking through the wilderness, in a quiet state of mindfulness meditation.

In Northern Ireland, a nun living in a convent spends an entire week in silent prayer and contemplation.

In Los Angeles, California, an aspiring actor consults a hypnotist for help in reducing her stage fright.

In Berkeley, California, an artist spends 2 hours in a flotation chamber to clear her head before resuming work on a large painting.

At a park in Amsterdam, a group of street musicians smoke a joint and sing for spare change.

In Tucson, Arizona, one of your authors pours himself another cup of coffee.

Each of these people seeks to alter consciousness—in different ways, to different degrees, and for different reasons. As these examples suggest, consciousness can take many forms. In the discussion that follows, we will begin with the familiar realms of sleep and dreaming and then move to more exotic states of consciousness.

© Hank Morgan/Rainbow

MODULE 5.1 Altered States and Sleep

AN UNCONSCIOUS PERSON will die without constant care. Yet, as crucial as consciousness is, we can't really explain how it occurs. On the other hand, we can identify various states of consciousness and explore the role they play in our lives. This is especially true of sleep and dreaming, two states that psychologists have studied in detail. This first module introduces a number of altered states of consciousness and provides a guided tour of sleep and dreaming.

States of Consciousness—The Many Faces of Awareness

SURVEY QUESTION: *What is an altered state of consciousness?*

To be conscious means to be aware. **Consciousness** consists of all the sensations, perceptions, memories, and feelings you are aware of at any instant (Koch, 2004). (See "What Is It Like to Be a Bat?") We spend most of our lives in **waking consciousness,** a state of clear, organized alertness. In waking consciousness we perceive times, places, and events as real, meaningful, and familiar. But states of consciousness related to fatigue, delirium, hypnosis, drugs, and euphoria may differ markedly from "normal" awareness. Everyone experiences at least some altered states, such as sleep, dreaming, and daydreaming (Blackmore, 2004). In everyday life, changes in consciousness may also accompany long-distance running, listening to music, making love, or other circumstances.

Altered States of Consciousness

How are altered states distinguished from normal awareness? During an **altered state of consciousness** (**ASC**) changes occur in the *quality* and *pattern* of mental activity. Typically there are distinct shifts in our perceptions, emotions, memories, time sense, thoughts, feelings of self-control, and suggestibility (Siegel, 2005). Definitions aside, most people know when they have experienced an ASC.

Are there other causes of ASCs? In addition to the ones mentioned, we could add sensory overload (for example, a rave, Mardi Gras crowd, or mosh pit), monotonous stimulation (such as "highway hypnotism" on long drives), unusual physical conditions (high fever, hyperventilation, dehydration, sleep loss, near-death experiences), restricted sensory input, and many other possibilities. In some instances, altered states have important cultural meanings. (See "Consciousness and Culture" for more information.) Let's begin with a look at the most common altered state, sleep and dreaming.

Sleep—A Nice Place to Visit

SURVEY QUESTION: *What are the effects of sleep loss or changes in sleep patterns?*

Each of us will spend some 25 years of life asleep. Contrary to common belief, you are not totally unresponsive during sleep. For instance, you are more likely to awaken if you hear your own name spoken, instead of another. Likewise, a sleeping mother may ignore a jet thundering overhead but wake at the slightest whimper of her child. It's even possible to do simple tasks while asleep. In one experiment, people learned to avoid an electric shock by touching a switch each time a tone sounded. Eventually, they could do it without waking. (This is much like the basic survival skill of turning off your alarm clock without waking.) Of course, sleep does impose limitations. Don't expect to learn math, a foreign language, or other complex skills while asleep—especially if the snooze takes place in class (Druckman & Bjork, 1994; Froufe & Schwartz, 2001). But do expect that a good sleep will help you to consolidate what you learned the day before (Fenn, Nusbaum, & Margoliash, 2003).

Because sleep is familiar, many people think they know all about it. Before reading more, test your knowledge with the following Sleep Quiz. Were you surprised by any of the answers? Let's see what we know about our "daily retreat from the world."

Sleep Quiz

1. People can learn to sleep for just a few hours a night and still function well. T or F?
2. Everyone dreams every night. T or F?
3. The brain rests during sleep. T or F?
4. Resting during the day can replace lost sleep. T or F?
5. As people get older they sleep more. T or F?
6. Alcohol may help a person get to sleep, but it disturbs sleep later during the night. T or F?
7. If a person goes without sleep long enough, death will occur. T or F?
8. Dreams mostly occur during deep sleep. T or F?
9. A person prevented from dreaming would soon go crazy. T or F?
10. Sleepwalking occurs when a person acts out a dream. T or F?

Answers: 1. F 2. T 3. F 4. F 5. F 6. T 7. T 8. F 9. F 10. F

CRITICAL THINKING

What Is It Like to Be a Bat?

Imagine hurtling through the air on leather wings while shrieking noisily. Suddenly, the faint echo of your own voice draws your attention to a moth that is frantically trying to evade you. You careen after it, twisting through the pitch-black jungle. Dodging trees and other bats, you catch the moth and savor your first meal of the still-young night.

In his famous essay, "What Is It Like to Be a Bat?" Thomas Nagel (1974) points out that we can learn a lot about bats from an objective, *third-person* point of view. Scientifically, we know that bats use echolocation (they emit sounds and interpret the echoes to locate objects) to hunt insects at night. But what does that *feel* like from a subjective, *first-person* point of view? Have you ever been curious about what it is like to be a bat, or a dog, or a cat? What runs through Rover's mind when he sniffs other dogs? Does Fluffy have dreams? Are they as strange as ours? Do cats ever worry about the future? Do they like music? Do animals feel joy?

According to Nagel, we cannot directly know the first-person experience of animals (or even other people, for that matter). The difficulty of knowing other minds is why the early behaviorists distrusted introspection. (Remember Module 1.3?) A key challenge for psychology is to use objective studies of the brain and behavior to help us understand the mind and consciousness, which are basically private phenomena (Blackmore, 2004; Koch, 2004). This chapter summarizes some of what we have learned about states of consciousness.

The Need for Sleep

How strong is the need for sleep? Sleep is an innate **biological rhythm** that can never be entirely ignored (Lavie, 2001; Mistlberger, 2005). Of course, sleep will give way temporarily, especially at times of great danger. As comedian and filmmaker Woody Allen once put it, "The lion and the lamb shall lie down together, but the lamb will not be very sleepy." However, there are limits to how long humans can go without sleep. A rare disease that prevents sleep always ends with stupor, coma, and death (Dauvilliers et al., 2004). (See ● Fig. 5.1.)

Imagine placing an animal on a moving treadmill, over a pool of water. Even under these conditions, animals soon drift into repeated microsleeps. A **microsleep** is a brief shift in brain activity to the pattern normally recorded during sleep. When you drive, remember that microsleeps can lead to macro-accidents. Even if your eyes are open, you can fall asleep for a few seconds. A hundred thousand traffic accidents every year are caused by sleepiness (Rau, 2005). Although coffee helps (Kamimori et al., 2005), if you are struggling to stay awake while driving, you should stop, quit fighting it, and take a short nap.

Sleep Deprivation *How long could a person go without sleep?* With few exceptions, 4 days or more without sleep becomes hell for everyone. For example, a disc jockey named Peter Tripp once stayed awake for 200 hours to raise money for charity. After 100 hours, Tripp began to hallucinate: He saw cobwebs in his shoes and watched in terror as a tweed coat became a suit of "furry worms." By the end of 200 hours, Tripp was unable to distinguish between his hallucinations and reality (Luce, 1965). Despite Tripp's breakdown, longer sleepless periods are possible. The world record is held by Randy Gardner—who at age 17 went 264 hours (11 days)

● **FIGURE 5.1** Not all animals sleep, but like humans, those that do have powerful sleep needs. For example, dolphins must voluntarily breathe air, which means they face the choice of staying awake or drowning. The dolphin solves this problem by sleeping on just one side of its brain at a time! The other half of the brain, which remains awake, controls breathing (Jouvet, 1999).

without sleep. Surprisingly, Randy needed only 14 hours of sleep to recover. As Randy found, most symptoms of **sleep deprivation** (sleep loss) are reversed by a single night's rest. (In 2007, a man named Tony Wright claimed that he set a new record by going 266 hours without sleep. However, *The*

> **Consciousness** Mental awareness of sensations, perceptions, memories, and feelings.
> **Waking consciousness** A state of clear, organized alertness.
> **Altered state of consciousness (ASC)** A condition of awareness distinctly different in quality or pattern from waking consciousness.
> **Biological rhythm** Any repeating cycle of biological activity, such as sleep and waking cycles or changes in body temperature.
> **Microsleep** A brief shift in brainwave patterns to those of sleep.
> **Sleep deprivation** Being prevented from getting desired or needed amounts of sleep.

HUMAN DIVERSITY

Consciousness and Culture

Throughout history, people have found ways to alter consciousness (Siegel, 2005). A dramatic example is the sweat lodge ceremony of the Sioux Indians. During the ritual, several men sit in total darkness inside a small chamber heated by coals. Cedar smoke, bursts of steam, and sage fill the air. The men chant rhythmically. The heat builds. At last they can stand it no more. The door is thrown open. Cooling night breezes rush in. And then? The cycle begins again—often to be repeated four or five times more.

Like the yoga practices of Hindu mystics or the dances of the Whirling Dervishes of Turkey, the ritual "sweats" of the Sioux are meant to cleanse the mind and body. When they are especially intense, they bring altered awareness and personal revelation.

People seek some altered states for pleasure, as is often true of drug intoxication. Yet as the Sioux illustrate, many cultures regard altered consciousness as a pathway to personal enlightenment. Indeed, all cultures and most religions recognize and accept some alterations of consciousness. However, the meaning given to these states varies greatly—from signs of "madness" and "possession" by spirits to life-enhancing breakthroughs. Thus, cultural conditioning greatly affects what altered states we recognize, seek, consider normal, and attain (de Rios & Grob, 2005).

In many cultures, rituals of healing, prayer, purification, or personal transformation are accompanied by altered states of consciousness.

Guinness Book of Records no longer recognizes sleep deprivation competitions because of possible health risks, so Randy still holds the "official" record.)

What are the costs of sleep loss? Age and personality make a big difference. Although Peter Tripp's behavior became quite bizarre, Randy Gardner and Tony Wright were less impaired. However, make no mistake: Sleep is a necessity. At various times, Randy's speech was slurred, and he couldn't concentrate, remember clearly, or name common objects (Coren, 1996). Sleep loss also typically causes trembling hands, drooping eyelids, inattention, irritability, staring, increased pain sensitivity, and general discomfort (Doran, Van Dongen, & Dinges, 2001).

Most people who have not slept for 2 or 3 days can still do interesting or complex mental tasks. But they have trouble paying attention, staying alert, and doing simple or boring routines (Belenky et al., 2003). For a driver, pilot, or machine operator, this can spell disaster (Hardaway & Gregory, 2005). If a task is monotonous (such as factory work or air traffic control), no amount of sleep loss is safe. In fact, if you lose just 1 hour of sleep a night, it can affect your mood, memory, ability to pay attention, and even your health (Maas, 1999). (See "Teenage Sleep Zombies.")

How can I tell how much sleep I really need? Pick a day when you feel well rested. Then sleep that night until you wake without an alarm clock. If you feel rested when you wake up, that's your natural sleep need. If you're sleeping fewer hours than you need, you're building up a sleep debt (Maas, 1999).

Severe sleep loss can cause a temporary **sleep-deprivation psychosis** (loss of contact with reality) like Peter Tripp suffered. Confusion, disorientation, delusions, and hallucinations are typical of this reaction. Fortunately, such "crazy" behavior is uncommon. Hallucinations and delusions rarely appear before 60 hours of wakefulness (Naitoh, Kelly, & Englund, 1989).

Sleep Patterns

Sleep was described as an innate biological rhythm. What does that mean? Daily sleep and waking periods create a variety of sleep patterns. Rhythms of sleep and waking are so steady that they continue

THE CLINICAL FILE

Teenage Sleep Zombies

Did you ever have to fight to stay awake in a high school class? *Hypersomnia* (hi-per-SOM-nee-ah: excessive daytime sleepiness) is a common problem during adolescence (Carskadon, Acebo, & Jenni, 2004). The reason? Rapid physical changes during puberty increase the need for sleep. However, the quality and quantity of sleep time tends to *decrease* during the teen years (Fukuda & Ishihara, 2001). At a time when they need more sleep, many adolescents get less.

If teenagers are sleep deprived, why don't they just sleep more? As children enter puberty, they begin to stay up later at night. However, they must get up early to attend school, regardless of when they went to bed. As a result, many teens are seriously sleep deprived during the week. Then, on the weekend, they sleep longer and get up late in the morning (LaBerge et al., 2001). After sleeping extra amounts for 2 days, many teens have difficulty falling asleep Sunday night. On Monday, they have to get up early for school, and the sleep loss cycle begins again.

What can be done about teenage sleep deprivation? Psychologists have persuaded some school districts to start classes later so that high school students can sleep longer. Studies suggest that this schedule improves learning and reduces behavior problems. In fact, it looks like some of the "storm and stress" of adolescence may be ordinary grouchiness caused by sleep loss (Mitru, Millrood, & Mateika, 2002).

---

for many days, even when clocks and light-dark cycles are removed. However, under such conditions, humans eventually shift to a sleep-waking cycle that averages slightly more than 24 hours (Czeisler et al., 1999). (See ● Fig. 5.2.) This suggests that external time markers, especially light and dark, help tie our sleep rhythms to days that are exactly 24 hours long. Otherwise, many of us would drift into our own unusual sleep cycles (Duffy & Wright, Jr., 2005).

● **FIGURE 5.2** Sleep rhythms. Bars show periods of sleep during the fourth, fifth, and sixth weeks of an experiment with a human subject. During unscheduled periods, the subject was allowed to select times of sleep and lighting. The result was a sleep rhythm of about 25 hours. Notice how this free-running rhythm began to advance around the clock as they fell asleep later each day. When periods of darkness (shaded area) were imposed during the fifth week, the rhythm quickly resynchronized with 24-hour days. (Adapted from Czeisler et al., 1981.)

What is the normal range of sleep? A few rare individuals can get by on an hour or two of sleep a night—and feel perfectly fine. Only a small percentage of the population are **short sleepers,** averaging 5 hours of sleep or less per night. On the other end of the scale we find **long sleepers,** who doze 9 hours or more (Grandner & Kripke, 2004). The majority of us sleep on a familiar 7- to 8-hour-per-night schedule. For a few people, however, it is quite normal to sleep as little as 5 hours per night or as much as 11. Urging everyone to sleep 8 hours would be like advising everyone to wear medium-size shoes.

We need less sleep as we get older, right? Yes, total sleep time declines throughout life. Those older than 50 average only 6 hours of sleep a night. In contrast, infants spend up to 20 hours a day sleeping, usually in 2- to 4-hour cycles.

As they mature, most children go through a "nap" stage and eventually settle into a steady cycle of sleeping once a day (● Fig. 5.3). Perhaps we should all continue to take an afternoon "siesta." Midafternoon sleepiness is a natural part of the sleep cycle. Brief, well-timed naps can help maintain alertness in people like truck drivers and hospital interns, who often must fight to stay alert (Garbarino et al., 2004).

Busy people may be tempted to sleep less. However, people on *shortened* cycles—for example, 3 hours of sleep to 6 hours awake—often can't get to sleep when the cycle calls for it. That's why astronauts continue to sleep on their normal earth schedule while in space. Adapting to *longer-*than-normal days is more promising. Such days can be tailored to

Sleep-deprivation psychosis A major disruption of mental and emotional functioning brought about by sleep loss.
Short sleeper A person averaging 5 hours of sleep or less per night.
Long sleeper A person averaging 9 hours of sleep or more per night.

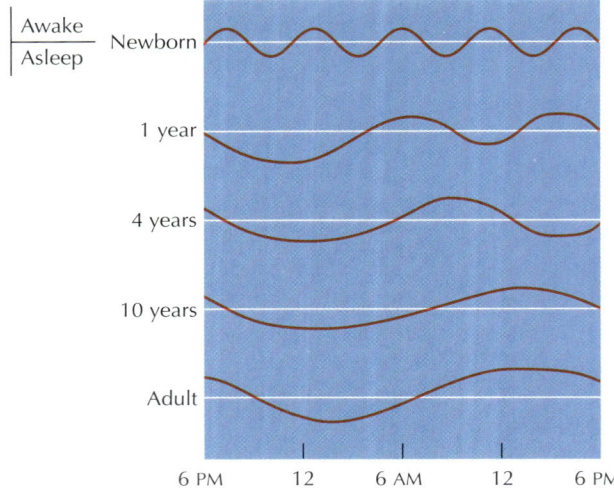

● **FIGURE 5.3** Development of sleep patterns. Short cycles of sleep and waking gradually become the night-day cycle of an adult. Although most adults don't take naps, midafternoon sleepiness is a natural part of the sleep cycle. (Adapted from Williams, Agnew, & Webb, 1964.)

● **FIGURE 5.4** These conjoined twins share the same blood supply, yet one sleeps while the other is awake. (Photo by Yale Joel, *Life Magazine*. © 1954 Time, Inc.)

● **FIGURE 5.5** (a) Photograph of an EEG recording session. The man in the background is asleep. (b) Changes in brainwave patterns associated with various stages of sleep. Actually, most wave types are present at all times, but they occur more or less frequently in various sleep stages.

match natural sleep patterns, which have a ratio of 2 to 1 between time awake and time asleep (16 hours awake and 8 hours asleep). For instance, one study showed that 28-hour "days" work for some people. Overall, however, sleep is a "gentle tyrant." Sleep patterns may be bent and stretched, but they rarely yield entirely to human whims (Akerstedt et al., 1993).

Stages of Sleep—The Nightly Roller-Coaster Ride

SURVEY QUESTION: *Are there different stages of sleep?*

What causes sleep? Early sleep experts thought that something in the bloodstream must cause sleep. But conjoined twins, whose bodies are joined at birth, show that this is false. It's not unusual for one twin to be asleep while the second is awake (● Fig. 5.4). During waking hours, a **sleep hormone** (sleep-promoting chemical) collects in the brain and spinal cord, *not* in the blood. If this substance is extracted from one animal and injected into another, the second animal will sleep deeply for many hours (Cravatt et al., 1995). Notice, however, that this explanation is incomplete. For example, why would a well-rested person have to fight to stay awake during a boring midday meeting?

Whether you are awake or asleep right now depends on the *balance* between separate sleep and waking systems. Brain circuits and chemicals in one of the systems promote sleep. A network of brain cells in the other system responds to chemicals that inhibit sleep. The two systems seesaw back and forth, switching the brain between sleep and wakefulness

● **FIGURE 5.6** (a) Average proportion of time adults spend daily in REM sleep and NREM sleep. REM periods add up to about 20 percent of total sleep time. (b) Typical changes in stages of sleep during the night. Notice that dreams mostly coincide with REM periods.

(Lavie, 2001). Note that the brain does not "shut down" during sleep. Rather, the *pattern* of activity changes.

Stages of Sleep

How does brain activity change when you fall asleep? Sleep activity can be measured with an **electroencephalograph** (eh-LEK-tro-en-SEF-uh-lo-graf) or **EEG**. The brain generates tiny electrical signals (brainwaves) that can be amplified and recorded. When you are awake and alert, the EEG reveals a pattern of small fast waves called **beta waves** (● Fig. 5.5). Immediately before sleep, the pattern shifts to larger and slower waves called **alpha waves**. (Alpha waves also occur when you are relaxed and allow your thoughts to drift.) As the eyes close, breathing becomes slow and regular, the pulse rate slows, and body temperature drops. Soon after, four separate **sleep stages** occur.

Stage 1 As you enter **light sleep** (stage 1 sleep), your heart rate slows even more. Breathing becomes more irregular. The muscles of your body relax. This may trigger a reflex muscle twitch called a *hypnic* (HIP-nik: sleep) *jerk*. (This is quite normal, so have no fear about admitting to your friends that you fell asleep with a hypnic jerk.) In stage 1 sleep the EEG is made up mainly of small, irregular waves with some alpha. Persons awakened at this time may or may not say they were asleep.

Stage 2 As sleep deepens, body temperature drops further. Also, the EEG begins to include **sleep spindles,** which are short bursts of distinctive brainwave activity (Fogel et al., 2007). Spindles seem to mark the true boundary of sleep. Within 4 minutes after spindles appear, most people will say they were asleep.

Stage 3 In stage 3, a new brainwave called delta begins to appear. **Delta waves** are very large and slow. They signal a move to deeper sleep and a further loss of consciousness.

Stage 4 Most people reach **deep sleep** (the deepest level of normal sleep) in about an hour. Stage 4 brainwaves are almost pure delta, and the sleeper is in a state of oblivion. If you make a loud noise during stage 4, the sleeper will wake up in a state of confusion and may not remember the noise. After spending some time in stage 4, the sleeper returns (through stages 3 and 2) to stage 1. Further shifts between deeper and lighter sleep occur throughout the night (● Fig. 5.6).

Two Basic Kinds of Sleep

If you watch a person sleep, you will soon notice that the sleeper's eyes occasionally move under the eyelids. These **rapid eye movements (REMs)** are associated with dreaming. (See Fig. 5.6b.) Roughly 85 percent of the time, people awakened during REMs report vivid dreams. In addition to rapid eye movements, **REM sleep** is marked by a return to fast,

---

Sleep hormone A sleep-promoting substance found in the brain and spinal cord.

Electroencephalograph (EEG) A device designed to detect, amplify, and record electrical activity in the brain.

Beta waves Small, fast brainwaves associated with being awake and alert.

Alpha waves Large, slow brainwaves associated with relaxation and falling asleep.

Sleep stages Levels of sleep identified by brainwave patterns and behavioral changes.

Light sleep Stage 1 sleep, marked by small, irregular brainwaves and some alpha waves.

Sleep spindles Distinctive bursts of brainwave activity that indicate a person is asleep.

Delta waves Large, slow brainwaves that occur in deeper sleep (stages 3 and 4).

Deep sleep Stage 4 sleep; the deepest form of normal sleep.

Rapid eye movements (REMs) Swift eye movements during sleep.

REM sleep Sleep marked by rapid eye movements and a return to stage 1 EEG patterns.

irregular EEG patterns similar to stage 1 sleep. In fact, the brain is so active during REM sleep that it looks as if the person is awake (Rock, 2004). Some eye movements correspond to dream activities: Dream that you are watching a tennis match, and you will probably move your eyes from side to side. However, people who were born blind still have REMs, so eye movements are not just a result of "watching" dream images (Shafton, 1995). REM sleep is easy to observe in pets, such as dogs and cats. Watch for eye and face movements and irregular breathing. (You can forget about your pet iguana, though. Reptiles show no signs of REM sleep.)

REM and NREM Sleep The two most basic states of sleep are REM sleep, with its associated dreaming, and **non-REM (NREM) sleep,** which occurs during stages 1, 2, 3, and 4 (Rock, 2004). NREM sleep is dream free about 90 percent of the time. Your first period of stage 1 sleep usually lacks REMs and dreams. Each later return to stage 1 is usually accompanied by rapid eye movements. Dreams during REM sleep tend to be longer, clearer, more detailed, more bizarre, and more "dream-like" than thoughts and images that occur in NREM sleep (Hobson, Pace-Schott, & Stickgold, 2000). Also, brain areas associated with imagery and emotion become more active during REM sleep. This may explain why REM dreams tend to be more vivid than NREM dreams (Braun, Balkin, & Herscovitch, 1998; Rock, 2004).

What is the function of NREM sleep? NREM sleep increases after physical exertion and may help us recover from bodily fatigue. In comparison, daytime stress tends to increase REM sleep. REM sleep totals only about 90 minutes per night. Yet, its link with dreaming makes it as important as NREM sleep. REM sleep may rise dramatically when there is a death in the family, trouble at work, a marital conflict, or other emotionally charged events.

CRITICAL THINKING

Abducted by Space Aliens?

Imagine opening your eyes shortly before dawn, attempting to roll over in your bed, and suddenly realizing that you are entirely paralyzed. While lying helplessly on your back and unable to cry out for help, you become aware of sinister figures lurking in your bedroom. As they move closer to your bed, your heart begins to pound violently and you feel as if you are suffocating. You hear buzzing sounds, and feel electrical sensations shooting throughout your body. Within moments, the visions vanish and you can move once again. Terrified, you wonder what has just happened. (McNally & Clancy, 2005, p.114)

Sleep paralysis, which normally prevents us from moving during REM sleep, can also occur just as you begin to wake up. During such episodes, people sometimes have *hypnopompic* (hip-neh-POM-pik: "upon awakening") hallucinations. According to psychologist Al Cheyne, these hallucinations may include bizarre experiences, such as sensing that an alien being is in your bedroom; feeling something pressing on your chest, suffocating you; or feeling like you are floating out of your body (Cheyne, 2005; Cheyne, Rueffer, & Newby-Clark, 1999).

Although most of us shrug off these weird experiences, some people try to make sense of them. Earlier in history, people interpreted these hallucinated intruders as angels, demons, or witches\ and believed that their out-of-body experiences were real. However, as our culture changes, so do our interpretations of sleep experiences. Today, for example, some people who have sleep-related hallucinations believe they have been abducted by aliens or sexually abused (McNally & Clancy, 2005).

Folklore and legends often develop as attempts to explain human experiences, including some of the stranger aspects of sleep. By studying hypnopompic hallucinations, psychologists hope to offer natural explanations for many experiences that might otherwise seem supernatural or paranormal (Cheyne, Rueffer, & Newby-Clark, 1999).

Swiss artist Henry Fuseli drew on hypnopompic imagery as an inspiration for his famous painting *The Nightmare*.

REM Sleep and Dreaming *What happens to the body when a person dreams?* REM sleep is a time of high emotion. The heart beats irregularly. Blood pressure and breathing waver. Both males and females appear to be sexually aroused: Men usually have an erection, and genital blood flow increases in women. This occurs for all REM sleep, so it is not strictly related to erotic dreams (Jouvet, 1999).

During REM sleep your body becomes quite still, as if you were paralyzed. Imagine for a moment the results of acting out some of your recent dreams. Very likely, REM-sleep paralysis prevents some hilarious—and dangerous—nighttime escapades. When it fails, some people thrash violently, leap out of bed, and may attack their bed partners. A lack of muscle paralysis during REM sleep is called *REM behavior disorder* (Ochoa & Pulido, 2005). One patient suffering from the disorder tied himself to his bed every night. That way, he couldn't jump up and crash into furniture or walls (Shafton, 1995). And yet, sometimes sleep paralysis can go a little too far. (See "Abducted by Space Aliens?")

In a moment we will survey some additional sleep problems—if you are still awake. First, here are a few questions to check your memory of our discussion so far.

MODULE 5.1 Summary

What is an altered state of consciousness?
- Consciousness is a core feature of mental life.
- Altered states of consciousness are defined by changes in the quality and pattern of mental activity.
- Cultural conditioning greatly affects what altered states a person recognizes, seeks, considers normal, and attains.

What are the effects of sleep loss or changes in sleep patterns?
- Sleep is an innate biological rhythm necessary for survival. Sleep-deprived people experience microsleeps.
- Moderate sleep loss mainly lowers performance on routine or boring tasks. Extended sleep loss can (somewhat rarely) produce a temporary sleep-deprivation psychosis.
- Sleep patterns show some flexibility, but 7 to 8 hours is the average. The amount of daily sleep decreases steadily from birth to old age.

Are there different stages of sleep?
- Sleep occurs in four stages. Stage 1 is light sleep, and stage 4 is deep sleep. The sleeper alternates between stages 1 and 4 (passing through stages 2 and 3) several times each night.
- The two most basic sleep states are rapid eye movement (REM) sleep and non-REM (NREM) sleep. REM sleep is strongly associated with dreaming.
- Dreaming and REMs occur mainly during light sleep, similar to stage 1. Dreaming is accompanied by emotional arousal but relaxation of the muscles.

Non-REM (NREM) sleep Non-rapid eye movement sleep characteristic of stages 1, 2, 3, and 4.

KNOWLEDGE BUILDER

Altered States and Sleep

Recite

1. Changes in the quality and pattern of mental activity define
   a. an EEG
   b. an REM
   c. SIDS
   d. an ASC

2. Alyssa experiences a microsleep while driving. Most likely, this indicates that she
   a. was producing mostly beta waves
   b. had high levels of sleep hormones in her bloodstream
   c. switched from delta waves to alpha waves
   d. was sleep deprived

3. Delusions and hallucinations typically continue for several days after a sleep-deprived individual returns to normal sleep. T or F?

4. Older adults, and particularly the elderly, sleep more than children do because the elderly are more easily fatigued. T or F?

5. Which of the following would normally be most incompatible with moving your arms and legs while asleep?
   a. REM sleep
   b. sleep spindles
   c. delta waves
   d. NREM sleep

6. Rapid eye movements indicate that a person is in deep sleep. T or F?

7. Alpha waves are to presleep drowsiness as _____ _____ are to stage 4 sleep.

Reflect
Critical Thinking

8. Why might it be better for the unscheduled human sleep-waking cycle to average more than 24 hours, instead of less?

9. Biologically, what advantages might sleeping provide?

Relate

Make a quick list of some altered states of consciousness you have experienced. What do they have in common? How are they different? What conditions caused them?

Imagine that you are a counselor at a sleep clinic. You must explain the basics of sleep and dreaming to a new client who knows little about these topics. Can you do it?

Link

Internet addresses frequently change. To find the sites listed here, visit http://www.thomsonedu.com/psychology/coon for an updated list of Internet addresses and direct links to relevant sites.

- **Sleepless at Stanford** What all undergraduates should know about how their sleeping lives affect their waking lives.
- **Sleep Patterns** Are you an owl or a lark?
- **Sleep Paralysis** Read about hypnopompic and hypnagogic experiences.

ANSWERS

1. d 2. d 3. F 4. F 5. a 6. F 7. delta waves 8. Sleep experts theorize that the 25-hour average leaves a little "slack" in the cycle. External time markers can then retard the body cycle slightly to synchronize it with light-dark cycles. If the body cycle were shorter than 24 hours, we all might have to "stretch" every day to adjust. 9. Lowering body activity and metabolism during sleep may help conserve energy and lengthen life. Also, natural selection may have favored sleep because animals that remained active at night probably had a higher chance of being killed. (We'll bet they had more fun, though.)

MODULE 5.2 Sleep Disturbances and Dreaming

SLEEP QUALITY has taken a beating in North America. Artificial lighting, frenetic schedules, exciting pastimes, smoking, drinking, overstimulation, and many other factors have contributed to a near epidemic of sleep problems. Sleep disturbances are a serious risk to health and happiness (Shneerson, 2005). This module begins with a look at some common sleep problems. After that, we will address the intriguing question: How meaningful are dreams?

Sleep Disturbances—Showing Nightly: Sleep Wars!

SURVEY QUESTION: *What are the causes of sleep disorders and unusual sleep events?*

Sleep clinics treat thousands of people each year who suffer from sleep disorders or complaints. These disturbances range from daytime sleep attacks to sleepwalking and terrifying nightmares. (See ■ Table 5.1.) Let's explore some of the more interesting problems these people face.

Insomnia

Staring at the ceiling at 2 A.M. is pretty low on most people's list of favorite pastimes. Yet, about 30 percent of all adults have had insomnia. Roughly 9 percent have a serious or chronic problem. **Insomnia** includes difficulty in going to sleep, frequent nighttime awakenings, waking too early, or a combination of these problems. Insomnia can harm people's work, health, and relationships (Sateia & Nowell, 2004).

Types and Causes of Insomnia Worry, stress, and excitement can cause *temporary insomnia* and a self-defeating cycle. First, excess mental activity ("I can't stop turning things over in my mind") and heightened arousal block sleep. Then, frustration and anger over not being able to sleep cause more worry and arousal. This further delays sleep, which causes more frustration, and so on (Espie, 2002). A good way to beat this cycle is to avoid fighting it. It is usually best to get up and do something useful or satisfying when you can't sleep. (Reading a textbook might be a good choice of useful activities.) Return to bed only when you begin to feel that you are struggling to stay awake. If sleeping problems last for more than 3 weeks, then a diagnosis of *chronic insomnia* can be made.

Drug-dependency insomnia (sleep loss caused by withdrawal from sleeping pills) can also occur. North Americans spend a billion dollars a year on sleeping pills. There is real irony in this expense. Nonprescription sleeping pills such as

■ **TABLE 5.1 Sleep Disturbances—Things That Go Wrong in the Night**

Hypersomnia Excessive daytime sleepiness. This can result from depression, insomnia, narcolepsy, sleep apnea, sleep drunkenness (a very slow transition to waking), periodic limb movements, drug abuse, and other problems.

Insomnia Difficulty in getting to sleep or staying asleep; also, not feeling rested after sleeping.

Narcolepsy Sudden, irresistible, daytime sleep attacks that may last anywhere from a few minutes to a half hour. Victims may fall asleep while standing, talking, or even driving.

Nightmare disorder Vivid, recurrent nightmares that significantly disturb sleep.

Periodic limb movement syndrome Muscle twitches (primarily affecting the legs) that occur every 20 to 40 seconds and severely disturb sleep.

REM behavior disorder A failure of normal muscle paralysis, leading to violent actions during REM sleep.

Restless legs syndrome An irresistible urge to move the legs in order to relieve sensations of creeping, tingling, prickling, aching, or tension.

Sleep apnea During sleep, breathing stops for 20 seconds or more until the person wakes a little, gulps in air, and settles back to sleep; this cycle may be repeated hundreds of times per night.

Sleep drunkenness A slow transition to clear consciousness after awakening; sometimes associated with irritable or aggressive behavior.

Sleep terror disorder The repeated occurrence of night terrors that significantly disturb sleep.

Sleep-wake schedule disorder A mismatch between the sleep-wake schedule demanded by a person's body rhythm and that demanded by the environment.

Sleepwalking disorder Repeated incidents of leaving bed and walking about while asleep.

Sominex, Nytol, and Sleep-Eze have little sleep-inducing effect. Barbiturates are even worse. These prescription sedatives decrease both stage 4 sleep and REM sleep, drastically lowering sleep quality. In addition, many users become "sleeping-pill junkies" who need an ever-greater number of pills to get to sleep. Victims must be painstakingly weaned from their sleep medicines. Otherwise, terrible nightmares and "rebound insomnia" may drive them back to drug use. It's worth remembering that although alcohol and other depressant drugs may help a person get to sleep, they greatly reduce sleep quality (Nau & Lichstein, 2005).

Insomnia Difficulty in getting to sleep or staying asleep.

Behavioral Remedies for Insomnia *If sleeping pills are a poor way to treat insomnia, what can be done?* Sleep specialists prefer to treat insomnia with lifestyle changes and behavioral techniques (Montgomery & Dennis, 2004). Treatment for chronic insomnia usually begins with a careful analysis of a patient's sleep habits, lifestyle, stress levels, and medical problems. All the approaches discussed in the following list are helpful for treating insomnia (Nau & Lichstein, 2005). Of the methods listed, stimulus control and sleep restriction are the most effective (Chesson et al., 1999):

1. **Stimulus control.** One of the best ways to combat insomnia is also the simplest. Insisting on a regular schedule helps establish a firm body rhythm, greatly improving sleep. This is best achieved by exercising **stimulus control,** which refers to linking a response with specific stimuli. It is important to get up and go to sleep at the same time each day, including weekends (Bootzin & Epstein, 2000). (As noted earlier regarding adolescent sleep loss, many people upset their sleep rhythms by staying up late on weekends.) In addition, insomniacs are told to avoid doing anything but sleeping when they are in bed. They are not to study, eat, watch TV, read, pay the bills, worry, or even think in bed. (Lovemaking is okay, however.) In this way, only sleeping and relaxation become associated with going to bed at specific times (Bootzin & Epstein, 2000).

2. **Sleep restriction.** Even if an entire night's sleep is missed, it is important not sleep late in the morning, nap more than an hour, sleep during the evening, or go to bed early the following night. Instead, restricting sleep to normal bedtime hours avoids fragmenting sleep rhythms (Shneerson, 2005).

3. **Paradoxical intention.** Another helpful approach is to remove the pressures of trying to go to sleep. Instead, the goal becomes trying to keep the eyes open (in the dark) and stay awake as long as possible (Nau & Lichstein, 2005). This allows sleep to come unexpectedly and lowers performance anxiety (Espie, 2002).

4. **Relaxation.** Some insomniacs lower their arousal before sleep by using a physical or mental strategy for relaxing, such as progressive muscle relaxation (see Module 13.3), meditation, or blotting out worries with calming images. It is also helpful to schedule time in the early evening to write down worries or concerns and plan what to do about them the next day, in order to set them aside before going to bed.

4. **Exercise.** Strenuous exercise during the day promotes sleep. It is best if done about 6 hours before bedtime (Maas, 1999). However, exercise in the evening is helpful only if it is very light.

5. **Food intake.** What you eat can affect how easily you get to sleep. Eating starchy foods increases the amount of tryptophan (TRIP-tuh-fan: an amino acid) reaching the brain. More tryptophan, in turn, increases the amount of serotonin in the brain, which is associated with relaxation, a positive mood, and sleepiness. Thus, to promote sleep, try eating a starchy snack, such as cookies, bread, pasta, oatmeal, pretzels, or dry cereal. If you really want to drop the bomb on insomnia, try eating a baked potato (which may be the world's largest sleeping pill!) (Sahelian, 1998).

6. **Stimulants.** Stimulants, such as coffee and cigarettes, should be avoided.

Sleepwalking, Sleeptalking, and Sleepsex

Sleepsex? As strange as it may seem, many waking behaviors can be engaged in while asleep, such as driving a car, cooking, playing a musical instrument, and eating (Plazzi, et al., 2005). The most famous, sleepwalking, is eerie and fascinating in its own right. **Somnambulists** (som-NAM-bue-lists: those who sleepwalk) avoid obstacles, descend stairways, and on rare occasions may step out of windows or in front of automobiles. Sleepwalkers have been observed jumping into lakes, urinating in garbage pails or closets (phew!), shuffling furniture around, and even wielding weapons (Schenck & Mahowald, 2005).

The sleepwalker's eyes are usually open, but a blank face and shuffling feet reveal that the person is still asleep. If you find someone sleepwalking, you should gently guide the person back to bed. Awakening a sleepwalker does no harm, but it is not necessary.

Does sleepwalking occur during dreaming? No. Remember that people are normally immobilized during REM sleep. EEG studies have shown that somnambulism occurs during NREM stages 3 and 4 (Stein & Ferber, 2001). Sleeptalking also occurs mostly in NREM stages of sleep. The link with deep sleep explains why sleeptalking makes little sense and why sleepwalkers are confused and remember little when awakened (DSM-IV-TR, 2000).

Oh, yes, you're curious about sleepsex. There is, of course, an official name for it: *sexsomnia* (Shapiro, Trajanovic, & Fedoroff, 2003). Sexsomnia is not as exciting as it might sound: Just imagine being the startled I-was-sleeping-but-I'm-now-wide-awake partner of someone attempting to have sex with you while he or she is actually sleeping (Mangan, 2004). It is not uncommon for sexual assault charges to be laid against such sleeping perpetrators (Shapiro, Trajanovic, & Fedoroff, 2003).

Nightmares and Night Terrors

Stage 4 sleep is also the realm of night terrors. These frightening episodes are quite different from ordinary nightmares. A **nightmare** is simply a bad dream that takes place during REM sleep. Frequently occurring nightmares (one a week or more) are associated with higher levels of psychological distress (Levin & Fireman, 2002). During stage 4 **night terrors,** a person suffers total panic and may hallucinate frightening dream images into the bedroom. An attack may last 15 or 20 minutes. When it is over, the person awakens drenched in sweat but only vaguely remembers the terror. Because night terrors occur during NREM sleep (when the body is not immobilized), victims may sit up, scream, get out of bed, or run around the room. Victims remember little afterward. (Other family members, however, may have a story to tell.) Night terrors are most common in childhood, but they continue to plague about 2 out of every 100 adults (Kataria, 2004; Ohayon, Guilleminault, & Priest, 1999).

How to Eliminate a Nightmare *Is there any way to stop a recurring nightmare?* A bad nightmare can be worse than any horror movie. It's easy to leave a theater, but we often remain trapped in terrifying dreams. Nevertheless, most nightmares can be banished by following three simple steps. First, write down your nightmare, describing it in detail. Next, change the dream any way you wish, being sure to spell out the details of the new dream. The third step is *imagery rehearsal,* in which you mentally rehearse the changed dream before you fall asleep again (Krakow & Zadra, 2006). Imagery rehearsal may work because it makes upsetting dreams familiar, while a person is awake and feeling safe. Or perhaps it mentally "reprograms" future dream content. In any case, the technique has helped many people (Krakow & Krakow, 2002).

Narcolepsy

One of the most dramatic sleep problems is **narcolepsy** (NAR-koe-lep-see), or sudden, irresistible sleep attacks. These last anywhere from a few minutes to a half hour. Victims may fall asleep while standing, talking, or even driving. Emotional excitement, especially laughter, commonly triggers narcolepsy. (Tell an especially good joke and a narcoleptic may fall asleep.) More than half of all victims also suffer from **cataplexy** (CAT-uh-plex-see), a sudden temporary paralysis of the muscles, leading to complete body collapse. It's easy to understand why narcolepsy can devastate careers and relationships (Thorpy, 2006).

Because sudden paralysis happens during dreaming, is there a connection between narcolepsy and REM sleep? Yes, narcoleptics tend to fall directly into REM sleep. Thus, the narcoleptic's sleep attacks and paralysis appear to occur when REM sleep intrudes into the waking state (Mignot, 2001).

Fortunately, narcolepsy is rare. It runs in families, which suggests that it is hereditary (Chabas et al., 2003). In fact, this has been confirmed by breeding several generations of narcoleptic dogs. (These dogs, by the way, are simply outstanding at learning the trick "Roll over and play dead.") There is no known cure for narcolepsy, but a drug named sodium oxybate reduces the frequency and intensity of attacks (Thorpy, 2006).

Sleep Apnea

Some sage once said, "Laugh and the whole world laughs with you; snore and you sleep alone." Nightly "wood sawing" is often harmless, but it can signal a serious problem. A person who snores loudly, with short silences and loud gasps or snorts, may suffer from apnea (AP-nee-ah: interrupted breathing). In **sleep apnea,** breathing stops for periods of 20 seconds to 2 minutes. As the need for oxygen becomes intense, the person wakes a little and gulps in air. She or he then settles back to sleep. But soon, breathing stops again. This cycle is repeated hundreds of times a night. As you might guess, apnea victims are extremely sleepy during the day (Collop, 2005).

What causes sleep apnea? Some cases occur because the brain stops sending signals to the diaphragm to maintain breathing. Another cause is blockage of the upper air passages. The most effective treatments are the use of a continuous positive airway pressure (CPAP) mask to aid breathing during sleep, weight loss, and surgery for breathing obstructions (Collop, 2005).

SIDS Sleep apnea is suspected as one cause of **sudden infant death syndrome (SIDS),** or "crib death." Each year 1 out of every 500 babies is a victim of SIDS. In the "typical" crib death, a slightly premature or small baby with some signs of a cold or cough is bundled up and put to bed. A short time later, parents find the child has died. A baby deprived of air will normally struggle to begin breathing again. However, SIDS babies seem to have a weak arousal reflex. This prevents them from changing positions and resuming breathing after an episode of apnea (Horne et al., 2001).

Stimulus control Linking a particular response with specific stimuli.
Somnambulism Sleepwalking; occurs during NREM sleep.
Nightmare A bad dream that occurs during REM sleep.
Night terror A state of panic during NREM sleep.
Narcolepsy A sudden, irresistible sleep attack.
Cataplexy A sudden temporary paralysis of the muscles.
Sleep apnea Repeated interruption of breathing during sleep.
Sudden infant death syndrome (SIDS) The sudden, unexplained death of an apparently healthy infant.

Babies at risk for SIDS must be carefully watched for the first 6 months of life. To aid parents in this task, a special monitor may be used that sounds an alarm when breathing or pulse becomes weak (• Fig. 5.7). The list that follows gives some danger signals for SIDS.

- The mother is a teenager.
- The baby is premature.
- The baby has a shrill, high-pitched cry.
- The baby engages in "snoring," breath-holding, or frequent awakening at night.
- The baby breathes mainly through an open mouth.
- The baby remains passive when its face rolls into a pillow or blanket.
- The baby's bed contains soft objects such as pillows, quilts, comforters, or sheepskins.
- Parents or other adults in the home are smokers.

"Back to Sleep" Pop quiz: Should babies be placed facedown or face up in bed? Sleeping position is another major risk factor for SIDS. Healthy infants are better off sleeping on their backs or sides. (Premature babies, those with respiratory problems, and those who often vomit may need to sleep facedown. Ask a pediatrician for guidance.) At least one third of all SIDS cases involve babies who were placed facedown. Remember, "*back* to sleep" is the safest position for most infants (Hauck et al., 2002).

Dreams—A Separate Reality?

SURVEY QUESTION: *Do dreams have meaning?*

When REM sleep was discovered in 1952, it ushered in a "Golden Era" of dream inquiry. To conclude our discussion of sleep, let's consider some age-old questions about dreaming.

• **FIGURE 5.7** Infants at risk for SIDS are often attached to devices that monitor breathing and heart rate during sleep. An alarm sounds to alert parents if either pulse or respiration falters. SIDS rarely occurs after an infant is 1 year old. Babies at risk for SIDS should be placed on their sides or on their backs.

Does everyone dream? Do dreams occur in an instant? Most people dream four or five times a night, but not all people remember their dreams. "Nondreamers" are often surprised by their dreams when first awakened during REM sleep. Dreams are usually spaced about 90 minutes apart. The first dream lasts only about 10 minutes; the last averages 30 minutes and may run as long as 50. Dreams, therefore, occur in real time, not as a "flash" (Shafton, 1995).

REM Sleep Revisited

How important is REM sleep? Is it essential for normal functioning? To answer these questions, sleep expert William Dement awakened volunteers each time they entered REM sleep. Soon, their need for "dream time" grew more urgent. By the fifth night, many had to be awakened 20 or 30 times to prevent REM sleep. When the volunteers were finally allowed to sleep undisturbed, they dreamed extra amounts. This effect, called a **REM rebound,** explains why alcoholics have horrible nightmares after they quit drinking. Alcohol reduces sleep quality by suppressing REM sleep, thus setting up a powerful rebound when it is withdrawn (Stein & Friedmann, 2005).

Dement's volunteers complained of memory lapses, poor concentration, and anxiety. For a while, it was thought that people deprived of REM sleep might go crazy. But later experiments showed that missing *any* sleep stage can cause a rebound for that stage. In general, daytime disturbances are related to the *total amount* of sleep lost, not to the *type* of sleep lost (Devoto et al., 1999).

The Value of REM Sleep What, then, is the purpose of REM sleep? Early in life, REM sleep may stimulate the developing brain. Newborn babies spend a hearty 8 or 9 hours a day in REM sleep. That's about 50 percent of their total sleep time. In adulthood, REM sleep may prevent sensory deprivation during sleep, and it may help us process emotional events. REM sleep also seems to help us sort and integrate memories; especially memories about strategies that help us solve problems (Walker & Stickgold, 2006). Speaking very loosely, it's as if the dreaming brain were reviewing messages left on a telephone answering machine, to decide which are worth keeping. During the day, when information is streaming in, the brain may be too busy to efficiently select useful memories. When the conscious brain is "offline," we are better able to build new memories. Although we have much to learn, it's clear that REM sleep and dreaming are valuable for keeping the brain in good working order.

Dream Worlds

Most dreams reflect everyday events (Hall, 1966; Pesant & Zadra, 2006). For example, athletes dream about athletic activities of the previous day (Erlacher & Schredl, 2004). The favorite dream setting is a familiar room in a house. Action usually takes place between the dreamer and two or three other emotionally important people—friends, enemies, loved ones, or employers. Dream actions are also mostly familiar: running, jumping, riding, sitting, talking, and watching. About half of all dreams have sexual elements. Dreams of flying, floating, and falling occur less frequently.

Are most dreams happy or sad? If you ask people in the morning what they dreamed about, they mention more unpleasant emotions than pleasant emotions (Merritt et al., 1994). However, it may be that dreams of fear, anger, or sadness are easier to remember. When people are awakened during REM sleep, they report equal numbers of positive and negative emotions (Fosse, Stickgold, & Hobson, 2001).

Dream Theories

How meaningful are dreams? Most theorists agree that dreams reflect our waking thoughts, fantasies, and emotions (Beck, 2004). Thus, the real question might be, How deep should we dig in interpreting dreams? Some theorists believe that dreams have deeply hidden meanings. Others regard dreams as nearly meaningless. Let's examine both views.

Psychodynamic Dream Theory Theory Sigmund Freud's landmark book, *The Interpretation of Dreams* (1900), first advanced the idea that many dreams are based on *wish fulfillment* (an expression of unconscious desires). Thus, a student who is angry with a teacher might dream of embarrassing the teacher in class; a lonely person may dream of romance; or a hungry child may dream of food.

Freud's **psychodynamic theory** of dreaming emphasizes internal conflicts and unconscious forces. Although many of his ideas are attractive, there is evidence against them. For example, volunteers in a study of starvation showed no particular increase in dreams about food and eating. In general, dreams show few signs of directly expressing hidden wishes (Domhoff, 2003; Fisher & Greenberg, 1996).

Freud's response to critics, no doubt, would have been that dreams rarely express needs so directly. One of Freud's key insights is that ideas in dreams are expressed as images or pictures, rather than in words. Freud believed that dreams express unconscious desires and conflicts as disguised **dream symbols** (images that have deeper symbolic meaning). For instance, death might be symbolized by a journey, children by small animals, or sexual intercourse by horseback riding or dancing. Similarly, a woman sexually attracted to her best friend's husband might dream of stealing her friend's wedding ring and placing it on her own hand, an indirect symbol of her true desires.

Do all dreams have hidden meanings? Probably not. Even Freud realized that some dreams are trivial "day residues" or

According to Freudian theory, dream imagery often has symbolic meaning. How would you interpret Chilean artist Matias Morales's dreamlike image, titled *Dream in Blue*? The fact that dreams don't have a single unambiguous meaning is one of the shortcomings of Freudian dream theory.

carryovers from ordinary waking events. On the other hand, dreams do tend to reflect a person's current concerns, so Freud wasn't entirely wrong.

The Activation-Synthesis Hypothesis Psychiatrists Allan Hobson and Robert McCarley have a radically different view of dreaming. They believe that during REM sleep, brain cells are activated that normally control eye movements, balance, and actions. However, messages from the cells are blocked from reaching the body, so no movement occurs. Nevertheless, the cells continue to tell higher brain areas of their activities. Struggling to interpret this information, the brain searches through stored memories and manufactures a dream (Hobson, 2000; 2005).

How does that help explain dream content? Let's use the classic chase dream as an example. In such dreams we feel we are running but not going anywhere. This occurs because the brain is told the body is running, but it gets no feedback from the motionless legs. To make sense of this information, the brain creates a chase drama. A similar process probably explains dreams of floating or flying.

Hobson and McCarley call their view the **activation-synthesis hypothesis.** Hobson explains that several parts of

---

REM rebound The occurrence of extra rapid eye movement sleep following REM sleep deprivation.

Psychodynamic theory Any theory of behavior that emphasizes internal conflicts, motives, and unconscious forces.

Dream symbols Images in dreams that serve as visible signs of hidden ideas, desires, impulses, emotions, relationships, and so forth.

Activation-synthesis hypothesis An attempt to explain how dream content is affected by motor commands in the brain that occur during sleep but are not carried out.

the brain are "turned on" (activated) during REM sleep. This triggers sensations, motor commands, and memories. The cortex of the brain, which also becomes more active during REM sleep, synthesizes this activity into stories and visual images. However, frontal areas of the cortex, which control higher mental abilities, are mostly shut down during REM sleep. This explains why dreams are more primitive and more bizarre than daytime thoughts (Hobson, 2000). Viewed this way, dreams are merely a different type of thinking that occurs during sleep (McCarley, 1998).

Note that the activation-synthesis hypothesis doesn't rule out the idea that dreams have meaning. Because dreams are created from memories and past experiences, they can tell us quite a lot about each person's mental life, emotions, and concerns (Hobson, 2000). Regardless, many psychologists continue to believe that dreams have deeper meaning (White & Taytroe, 2003; Wilkinson, 2006).

There seems to be little doubt that dreams can make a difference in our lives: Veteran sleep researcher William Dement once dreamed that he had lung cancer. In the dream a doctor told Dement he would die soon. At the time, Dement was smoking two packs of cigarettes a day. He says, "I will never forget the surprise, joy, and exquisite relief of waking up. I felt reborn." Dement quit smoking the following day. (For more information about dreaming, see the Psychology in Action module later in this chapter.)

MODULE 5.2 Summary

What are the causes of sleep disorders and unusual sleep events?

- Sleep loss and sleep disorders are serious health problems that should be corrected when they persist.
- Sleepwalking and sleeptalking occur during NREM sleep. Night terrors occur in NREM sleep, whereas nightmares occur in REM sleep.
- Narcolepsy (sleep attacks) and cataplexy (a sudden temporary paralysis of the muscles) are caused by a sudden shift to stage 1 REM patterns during normal waking hours.
- Sleep apnea (interrupted breathing) is one source of insomnia and daytime hypersomnia (sleepiness).
- Apnea is suspected as one cause of sudden infant death syndrome (SIDS). With only a few exceptions, healthy infants should sleep face up or on their sides.
- Insomnia may be temporary or chronic. Behavioral approaches to managing insomnia, such as sleep restriction and stimulus control, are quite effective.

Do dreams have meaning?

- In addition to other functions, REM sleep appears to help us process useful memories.
- Most dream content is about familiar settings, people, and actions. Positive and negative emotions occur about equally in dreams.
- According to the Freudian (psychodynamic) view, dreams express unconscious wishes through dream symbols.
- Many theorists have questioned Freud's view of dreams. For example, the activation-synthesis model portrays dreaming as a physiological process.
- Because the frontal lobes of the brain are less active during sleep, dreams may be more revealing than waking thoughts. However, the idea that dreams have deep symbolic meaning is debatable.

KNOWLEDGE BUILDER

Sleep Disturbances and Dreaming

Recite

1. People who suffer from sudden daytime sleep attacks have which sleep disorder?
   a. narcolepsy
   b. REM behavior disorder
   c. somnambulism
   d. sleep spindling

2. Eating a snack that is nearly all starch can promote sleep because it increases _____ in the brain.
   a. beta waves
   b. tryptophan
   c. EEG activity
   d. hypnic cycling

3. Night terrors, sleepwalking, and sleeptalking all occur during stage 1, NREM sleep. T or F?

4. Sleep _____ is suspected as one cause of SIDS.

5. Which of the following is *not* a behavioral remedy for insomnia?
   a. daily hypersomnia
   b. stimulus control
   c. progressive relaxation
   d. paradoxical intention

6. The favored setting for dreams is
   a. work
   b. school
   c. outdoors or unfamiliar places
   d. familiar rooms

7. Sorting and integrating memories is one function of
   a. activation-synthesis cycles
   b. REM sleep
   c. deep sleep
   d. NREM sleep

8. According to the activation-synthesis model of dreaming, dreams are constructed from _____ to explain messages received from nerve cells controlling eye movement, balance, and bodily activity.

Reflect
Critical Thinking

9. Even without being told that somnambulism is an NREM event, you could have predicted that sleepwalking doesn't occur during dreaming. Why?

Relate

Almost everyone suffers from insomnia at least occasionally. Are any of the techniques for combating insomnia similar to strategies you have discovered on your own?

How many sleep disturbances can you name (including those listed in Table 5.1)? Are there any that you have experienced? Which do you think would be most disruptive?

Do you think the activation-synthesis theory provides an adequate explanation of your own dreams? Have you had dreams that seem to reflect Freudian wish fulfillment? Do you think your dreams have symbolic meaning?

Link

Internet addresses frequently change. To find the sites listed here, visit http://www.thomsonedu.com/psychology/coon for an updated list of Internet addresses and direct links to relevant sites.

- **The National Sleep Foundation** The NSF is dedicated to improving public health and safety by achieving understanding of sleep and sleep disorders and by supporting education, sleep-related research, and advocacy.

- **Sleep Apnea** Find out more about sleep apnea.

- **Sudden Infant Death and Other Infant Death** Information about SIDS, with links to related topics.

ANSWERS

1. a 2. b 3. F 4. apnea 5. a 6. d 7. b 8. memories 9. Because people are immobilized during REM sleep and REM sleep is strongly associated with dreaming. This makes it unlikely that sleepwalkers are acting out dreams.

MODULE 5.3 Hypnosis, Meditation, and Sensory Deprivation

WHAT DO YOU KNOW ABOUT HYPNOSIS? Which of your beliefs are true? Which are myths? Is hypnosis real? Does it have any value? You'll find out in this module.

Meditation is a centuries-old method for altering consciousness. Some forms of meditation take years to master. Yet, one of the simplest techniques may be among the most useful. We'll also look at the effects of sensory deprivation (restricted sensory input). Depending on circumstances, sensory deprivation can be stressful and unpleasant or relaxing and beneficial.

Hypnosis—Look into My Eyes

SURVEY QUESTION: *How is hypnosis done, and what are its limitations?*

"Your body is becoming heavy. You can barely keep your eyes open. You are so tired you can't move. Relax. Let go. Relax. Close your eyes and relax." These are the last words a textbook should ever say to you, and the first a hypnotist might say.

Interest in hypnosis began in the 1700s with Austrian doctor Franz Mesmer, whose name gave us the term *mesmerize* (to hypnotize). Mesmer believed he could cure disease with magnets. Mesmer's strange "treatments" are related to hypnosis because they actually relied on the power of suggestion, not magnetism (Waterfield, 2002). For a time, Mesmer enjoyed quite a following. In the end, however, his theories of "animal magnetism" were rejected and he was branded a fraud.

The term *hypnosis* was later coined by English surgeon James Braid. The Greek word *hypnos* means "sleep," and Braid used it to describe the hypnotic state. Today we know that hypnosis is *not* sleep. Confusion about this point remains because some hypnotists give the suggestion, "Sleep, sleep." However, EEG patterns recorded during hypnosis are different from those observed when a person is asleep or pretending to be hypnotized (Barabasz, 2000).

Theories of Hypnosis

If hypnosis isn't sleep, then what is it? That's a good question. **Hypnosis** is often defined as an altered state of consciousness, characterized by narrowed attention and an increased openness to suggestion (Kallio & Revonsuo, 2003; Kosslyn et al., 2000). Notice that this definition assumes hypnosis is a distinct state of consciousness.

The best-known *state theory* of hypnosis was proposed by Ernest Hilgard (1904–2001), who argued that hypnosis causes a *dissociative state*, or "split" in awareness. To illustrate, he asked hypnotized subjects to plunge one hand into a painful bath of ice water. Subjects told to feel no pain said they felt none. The same subjects were then asked if there was any part of their mind that did feel pain. With their free hand, many wrote, "It hurts," or "Stop it, you're hurting me," while they continued to act pain-free (Hilgard, 1977, 1994). Thus, one part of the hypnotized person says there is no pain and acts as if there is none. Another part, which Hilgard calls the *hidden observer*, is aware of the pain but remains in the background. The **hidden observer** is a detached part of the hypnotized person's awareness that silently observes events.

In contrast, *nonstate theorists* argue that hypnosis is not a distinct state at all. Instead it is merely a blend of conformity, relaxation, imagination, obedience, and role-playing (Kirsch, 2005). For example, many theorists believe that all hypnosis is really self-hypnosis (*autosuggestion*). From this perspective, a hypnotist merely helps another person to follow a series of suggestions. These suggestions, in turn, alter sensations, perceptions, thoughts, feelings, and behaviors (Lynn & Kirsch, 2006). (See "Swinging Suggestions.")

Regardless of which theoretical approach finally prevails, hypnosis can be explained by normal principles. It is not mysterious or "magical," despite what stage hypnotists might have you think.

Stage Hypnosis

On stage the hypnotist intones, "When I count to three, you will imagine that you are on a train to Disneyland and growing younger and younger as the train approaches." Responding to these suggestions, grown men and women begin to giggle and squirm like children on their way to a circus.

How do stage entertainers use hypnosis to get people to do strange things? They don't. Little or no hypnosis is needed to do a good hypnosis act. **Stage hypnosis** is often merely a simulation of hypnotic effects. Stage hypnotists make use of several features of the stage setting to perform their act (Barber, 2000).

1. **Waking suggestibility.** We are all more or less open to suggestion, but on stage people are unusually cooperative because they don't want to "spoil the act." As a result, they will readily follow almost any instruction given by the entertainer.

DISCOVERING PSYCHOLOGY

Swinging Suggestions

Here's a demonstration you can use to gain insight into hypnosis. Tie a short length of string (about 6 inches) to a small, heavy object, such as a ring or a small metal nut. Hold the ring at eye level, about a foot from your face. Concentrate on the ring and notice that it will begin to move, ever so slightly. As it does, focus all your attention on the ring. Narrow your attention to a beam of energy and mentally push the ring away from you. Each time the ring swings away, push on it, using only mental force. Then release it and let it swing back toward you. Continue to mentally push and release the ring until it is swinging freely. For the best results, try this now, before reading more.

Did the ring move? If it did, you used *autosuggestion* to influence your own behavior in a subtle way. Suggestions that the ring would swing caused your hand to make tiny micromuscular movements. These, in turn, caused the ring to move—no special mental powers or supernatural forces are involved.

As is true of hypnotic suggestion, the ring's movement probably seemed to be automatic. Obviously, you could just intentionally swing the ring. However, if you responded to sugges-

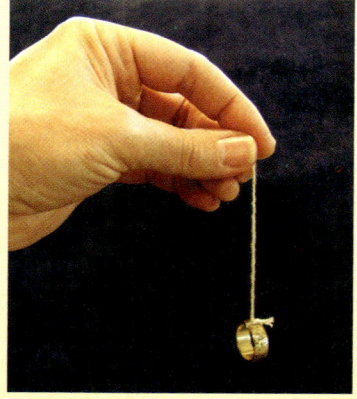

tion, the movement seemed to happen without any effort on your part. In the same way, when people are hypnotized, their actions seem to occur without any voluntary intent. Incidentally, autosuggestion likely underlies other phenomena such as how Ouija boards spell out answers to questions despite no apparent conscious interference. Autosuggestion also plays a role in many forms of self-therapy.

2. **Selection of responsive subjects.** Participants in stage hypnotism (all *volunteers*) are first "hypnotized" as a group. Then, anyone who doesn't yield to instructions is eliminated.

3. **The hypnosis label disinhibits.** Once a person has been labeled "hypnotized," she or he can sing, dance, act silly, or whatever, without fear or embarrassment. On stage, being "hypnotized" takes away personal responsibility for one's actions.

4. **The hypnotist as a "director."** After volunteers loosen up and respond to a few suggestions, they find that they are suddenly the stars of the show. Audience response to the antics on stage brings out the "ham" in many people. All the "hypnotist" needs to do is direct the action.

5. **The stage hypnotist uses tricks.** Stage hypnosis is about 50 percent taking advantage of the situation and 50 percent deception. One of the more impressive stage tricks is to rigidly suspend a person between two chairs. This is astounding only because the audience does not question it. Anyone can do it, as is shown in the photographs and instructions in ● Figure 5.8. Try it!

To summarize, hypnosis is real, and it can significantly alter private experience. Hypnosis is a useful tool in a variety of settings. Nightclubs, however, are not one of these settings. Stage "hypnotists" entertain; they rarely hypnotize. Let's conclude our exploration of hypnosis by looking into how it is done and what effects it has.

● **FIGURE 5.8** Arrange three chairs as shown. Have someone recline as shown. Ask him to lift slightly while you remove the middle chair. Accept the applause gracefully! (Concerning hypnosis and similar phenomena, the moral, of course, is "Suspend judgment until you have something solid to stand on.")

Hypnosis An altered state of consciousness characterized by narrowed attention and increased suggestibility.

Hidden observer A detached part of the hypnotized person's awareness that silently observes events.

Stage hypnosis Use of hypnosis to entertain; often, merely a simulation of hypnosis for that purpose.

The Reality of Hypnosis

How is hypnosis done? Could I be hypnotized against my will? Hypnotists use many different methods. Still, all techniques encourage a person (1) to focus attention on what is being said, (2) to relax and feel tired, (3) to "let go" and accept suggestions easily, and (4) to use vivid imagination (Druckman & Bjork, 1994). Basically, you must cooperate to become hypnotized.

What does it feel like to be hypnotized? You might be surprised at some of your actions during hypnosis. You also might have mild feelings of floating, sinking, anesthesia, or separation from your body. Personal experiences vary widely. A key element in hypnosis is the **basic suggestion effect** (a tendency of hypnotized persons to carry out suggested actions as if they were involuntary). Hypnotized persons feel like their actions and experiences are *automatic*—they seem to happen without effort. Here is how one person described his hypnotic session:

> I felt lethargic, my eyes going out of focus and wanting to close. My hands felt real light. . . . I felt I was sinking deeper into the chair. . . . I felt like I wanted to relax more and more. . . . My responses were more automatic. I didn't have to *wish* to do things so much or *want* to do them . . . I just did them . . . . I felt floating . . . very close to sleep. (Hilgard, 1968)

Contrary to the way hypnosis is portrayed in movies, hypnotized people generally remain in control of their behavior and aware of what is going on. For instance, most people will not act out hypnotic suggestions that they consider immoral or repulsive (such as disrobing in public or harming someone) (Kirsch & Lynn, 1995).

Hypnotic Susceptibility *Can everyone be hypnotized?* About 8 people out of 10 can be hypnotized, but only 4 out of 10 will be good hypnotic subjects. People who are imaginative and prone to fantasy are often highly responsive to hypnosis (Kallio & Revonsuo, 2003). But people who lack these traits may also be hypnotized. If you are willing to be hypnotized, chances are good that you could be. Hypnosis depends more on the efforts and abilities of the hypnotized person than the skills of the hypnotist. But make no mistake; people who are hypnotized are not merely faking their responses.

Hypnotic susceptibility refers to how easily a person can become hypnotized. It is measured by giving a series of suggestions and counting the number of times a person responds. A typical hypnotic test is the *Stanford Hypnotic Susceptibility Scale,* shown in ■ Table 5.2. In the test, various suggestions are made, and the person's response is noted. For instance, you might be told that your left arm is becoming more and more rigid and that it will not bend. If you can't bend your arm during the next 10 seconds, you have shown susceptibility to hypnotic suggestions. (Also see ● Fig. 5.9.)

Effects of Hypnosis *What can (and cannot) be achieved with hypnosis?* Many abilities have been tested during hypnosis, leading to the following conclusions (Burgess & Kirsch, 1999; Chaves, 2000):

1. **Superhuman acts of strength.** Hypnosis has no more effect on physical strength than instructions that encourage a person to make his or her best effort.
2. **Memory.** There is some evidence that hypnosis can enhance memory (Wagstaff et al., 2004). However, it frequently increases the number of false memories as well. For this reason, many states now bar persons from testifying in court if they were hypnotized to improve their memory of a crime they witnessed.
3. **Amnesia.** A person told not to remember something heard during hypnosis may claim not to remember. In some instances this may be nothing more than a deliberate attempt to avoid thinking about specific ideas. However, brief memory loss of this type actu-

■ TABLE 5.2 Standard Hypnotic Susceptibility Scale

SUGGESTED BEHAVIOR	CRITERION OF PASSING
1. Postural sway	Falls without forcing
2. Eye closure	Closes eyes without forcing
3. Hand lowering (left)	Lowers at least 6 inches by end of 10 seconds
4. Immobilization (right arm)	Arm rises less than 1 inch in 10 seconds
5. Finger lock	Incomplete separation of fingers at end of 10 seconds
6. Arm rigidity (left arm)	Less than 2 inches of arm bending in 10 seconds
7. Hands moving together	Hands at least as close as 6 inches after 10 seconds
8. Verbal inhibition (name)	Name unspoken in 10 seconds
9. Hallucination (fly)	Any movement, grimacing, acknowledgment of effect
10. Eye catalepsy	Eyes remain closed at end of 10 seconds
11. Posthypnotic (changes chairs)	Any partial movement response
12. Amnesia test	Three or fewer items recalled

Source: Adapted from Weitzenhoffer & Hilgard, 1959.

Module 5.3 • HYPNOSIS, MEDITATION, AND SENSORY DEPRIVATION

● **FIGURE 5.9** In one test of hypnotizability, subjects attempt to pull their hands apart after hearing suggestions that their fingers are "locked" together.

ally does seem to occur (Barnier, McConkey, & Wright, 2004).

4. **Pain relief.** Hypnosis can relieve pain (Keefe, Abernethy, & Campbell, 2005). It can be especially useful when chemical painkillers are ineffective. For instance, hypnosis can reduce phantom limb pain (Oakley, Whitman, & Halligan, 2002). (As discussed in Module 4.3, amputees sometimes feel phantom pain that seems to come from a missing limb.)

5. **Age regression.** Given the proper suggestions, some hypnotized people appear to "regress" to childhood. However, most theorists now believe that "age-regressed" subjects are only acting out a suggested role.

6. **Sensory changes.** Hypnotic suggestions concerning sensations are among the most effective. Given the proper instructions, a person can be made to smell a small bottle of ammonia and respond as if it were a wonderful perfume. It is also possible to alter color vision, hearing sensitivity, time sense, perception of illusions, and many other sensory responses.

Hypnosis is a valuable tool. It can help people relax, feel less pain, and make better progress in therapy (Chapman, 2006). Generally, hypnosis is more successful at changing subjective experience than it is at modifying behaviors such as smoking or overeating.

Meditation—Chilling, the Healthy Way

SURVEY QUESTION: *What are meditation and sensory deprivation? Do they have any benefits?*

Throughout history, meditation and sensory deprivation have been widely used means of altering consciousness by relaxing. Let's see what they have in common and how they differ.

Meditation

Meditation is a mental exercise used to alter consciousness. In general, meditation focuses attention and interrupts the typical flow of thoughts, worries, and analysis. People who use meditation to reduce stress often report less daily physical tension and anxiety (Andresen, 2000). PET and fMRI scans reveal changes in the activity of the frontal lobes of the brain during meditation, which suggests that it may represent a distinct state of consciousness (Cahn & Polich, 2006).

Meditation takes two major forms. In **concentrative meditation,** you attend to a single focal point, such as an object, a thought, or your own breathing. In contrast, **mindfulness meditation** is "open," or expansive. In this case, you widen your attention to embrace a total, nonjudgmental awareness of the world (Lazar, 2005). An example is losing all self-consciousness while walking in the wilderness with a quiet and receptive mind. Although it may not seem so, mindfulness meditation is more difficult to attain than concentrative meditation. For this reason, we will discuss concentrative meditation as a practical self-control method.

Performing Concentrative Meditation *How is concentrative meditation done?* The basic idea is to sit still and quietly focus on some external object or on a repetitive internal stimulus, such as your own breathing or humming (Blackmore, 2004). As an alternative, you can silently repeat a *mantra* (a word used as the focus of attention in concentrative meditation). Typical mantras are smooth, flowing sounds that are easily repeated. A widely used mantra is the word "om." A mantra could also be any pleasant word or a phrase from a familiar

---

Basic suggestion effect The tendency of hypnotized persons to carry out suggested actions as if they were involuntary.

Hypnotic susceptibility One's capacity for becoming hypnotized.

Meditation A mental exercise for producing relaxation or heightened awareness.

Concentrative meditation Mental exercise based on attending to a single object or thought.

Mindfulness meditation Mental exercise based on widening attention to become aware of everything experienced at any given moment.

song, poem, or prayer. If other thoughts arise as you repeat a mantra, just return attention to it as often as necessary to maintain meditation.

The Relaxation Response The benefits of meditation include lowered heart rate, blood pressure, muscle tension, and other signs of stress (Lazar et al., 2000). Medical researcher Herbert Benson believes that the core of meditation is the **relaxation response**—an innate physiological pattern that opposes your body's fight-or-flight mechanisms. Benson feels, quite simply, that most of us have forgotten how to relax deeply. People in his experiments learned to produce the relaxation response by following these instructions:

> Sit quietly and comfortably. Close your eyes. Relax your muscles, beginning at your feet and progressing up to your head. Relax them deeply. Become aware of breathing through your nose. As you breathe out, say a word like "peace" silently to yourself. Don't worry about how successful you are in relaxing deeply. Just let relaxation happen at its own pace. Don't be surprised by distracting thoughts. When they occur, ignore them and continue repeating "peace." (Adapted from Benson, 1977; Lazar et al., 2000)

As a stress-control technique, meditation may be a good choice for people who find it difficult to "turn off" upsetting thoughts when they need to relax. In one study, a group of college students who received just 90 minutes of training in the relaxation response experienced greatly reduced stress levels (Deckro et al., 2002). The physical benefits of meditation include lowered heart rate, blood pressure, muscle tension, and other signs of stress (Lazar et al., 2000), as well as improved immune system activity (Davidson et al., 2003).

According to Shauna Shapiro and Roger Walsh (2006), meditation has benefits beyond relaxation. Practiced regularly, meditation may foster mental well-being and positive mental skills such as clarity, concentration, and calm. In this sense, meditation may share much in common with psychotherapy. Indeed, research has shown that mindfulness meditation relieves a variety of psychological disorders, from insomnia to anxiety disorders. It can also reduce aggression and the illegal use of psychoactive drugs (Shapiro & Walsh, 2006). Regular meditation may even help people develop self-awareness and maturity (Travis, Arenander, & DuBois, 2004).

Sensory Deprivation

The relaxation response can also be produced by brief sensory deprivation. **Sensory deprivation (SD)** refers to any major reduction in the amount or variety of sensory stimulation.

What happens when stimulation is greatly reduced? A hint comes from reports by prisoners in solitary confinement, arctic explorers, high-altitude pilots, long-distance truck drivers, and radar operators. When faced with limited or monotonous stimulation, people sometimes have bizarre sensations, dangerous lapses in attention, and wildly distorted perceptions. Oddly enough, brief periods of sensory restriction can be very relaxing.

Psychologists have explored the possible benefits of sensory restriction using small isolation tanks like the one pictured in ● Figure 5.10. An hour or two spent in a flotation tank, for instance, causes a large drop in blood pressure, muscle tension, and other signs of stress (van Dierendonck & Te Nijenhuis, 2005). Of course, it could be argued that a warm bath has the same effect. Nevertheless, brief sensory deprivation appears to be one of the surest ways to induce deep relaxation (Suedfeld & Borrie, 1999).

Like meditation, sensory restriction may also help with more than relaxation. Mild sensory deprivation can help people quit smoking, lose weight, and reduce their use of alcohol and drugs (van Dierendonck & Te Nijenhuis, 2005). Psychologist Peter Suedfeld calls such benefits **Restricted Environmental Stimulation Therapy (REST).** Deep relaxation makes people more open to suggestion, and sensory restriction interrupts habitual behavior patterns. As a result, REST can "loosen" belief systems and make it easier to change bad habits (Suedfeld & Borrie, 1999).

REST also shows promise as a way to stimulate creative thinking (Norlander, Bergman, & Archer, 1998). Other researchers have reported that REST sessions can enhance performance in skilled sports, such as gymnastics, tennis, basketball, darts, and marksmanship (Druckman & Bjork, 1994; Norlander, Bergman, & Archer, 1999). There is also evidence that REST can relieve chronic pain and reduce stress (Bood et al., 2006). Clearly, there is much yet to be learned from studying "nothingness."

Summary To summarize, research suggests that meditation and sensory deprivation are ways to elicit the relaxation response. For many people, sitting quietly and "resting" can be

● **FIGURE 5.10** A sensory isolation chamber. Small flotation tanks like the one pictured have been used by psychologists to study the effects of mild sensory deprivation. Subjects float in darkness and silence. The shallow body-temperature water contains hundreds of pounds of Epsom salts, so that subjects float near the surface. Mild sensory deprivation produces deep relaxation.

as effective. Similar stress reduction occurs when people set aside time daily to engage in other restful activities, such as muscle relaxation, positive daydreaming, and even leisure reading. However, if you are the type of person who finds it difficult to ignore upsetting thoughts, then concentrative meditation might be a good way to promote relaxation. Practiced regularly, meditation and REST may even help improve overall mental health—something almost everyone could use in our fast-paced society.

Positive Psychology: Mindfulness and Well-Being

Did you "space out" anytime today? Most of us have occasional moments of reduced awareness. **Mindfulness** is the opposite of such mindless moments: It involves an open, nonjudgmental awareness of current experience. In other words, mindfulness is the same state that people who practice receptive meditation are trying to achieve. A person who is mindful is fully present, moment by moment. She or he is acutely aware of every thought, emotion, or sensation, but does not judge it or react to it. The person is fully "awake" and attuned to immediate reality.

Psychologists interested in positive mental states have begun to study the effects of mindfulness. For example, cancer patients who are taught mindfulness meditation have lower levels of distress and a greater sense of well-being. Such benefits apply to healthy people, too. In general, mindfulness is associated with self-knowledge and well-being (Brown & Ryan, 2003). Anyone who has a tendency to sleepwalk through life—and that's most of us at times—would be wise to be mindful of the value of mindfulness.

MODULE 5.3 Summary

How is hypnosis done, and what are its limitations?

- Hypnosis is an altered state characterized by narrowed attention and increased suggestibility. (Not all psychologists agree that hypnotic effects require an alteration of consciousness.)
- Stage hypnotism takes advantage of typical stage behavior and uses deception to simulate hypnosis.
- Hypnosis appears capable of producing relaxation, controlling pain, and altering perceptions.
- Hypnosis alters perceptions and behavior, but it is more capable of changing subjective experiences than habits, such as smoking.

What are meditation and sensory deprivation? Do they have any benefits?

- Concentrative meditation can be used to focus attention, alter consciousness, and reduce stress.
- Major benefits of meditation are its ability to interrupt anxious thoughts and to elicit the relaxation response.
- Brief exposure to sensory deprivation can also elicit the relaxation response. Under proper conditions, sensory deprivation may help break long-standing habits.

Relaxation response The pattern of internal bodily changes that occurs at times of relaxation.
Sensory deprivation (SD) Any major reduction in the amount or variety of sensory stimulation.
Restricted Environmental Stimulation Therapy (REST) A form of sensory deprivation that results in a variety of psychological benefits.
Mindfulness A state of open, nonjudgmental awareness of current experience.

KNOWLEDGE BUILDER

Hypnosis, Meditation, and Sensory Deprivation

Recite

1. The term *hypnotism* was coined by a British surgeon named
   a. Franz Mesmer
   b. James Stanford
   c. T. A. Kreskin
   d. James Braid

2. Tests of hypnotic susceptibility measure a person's tendency to respond to
   a. suggestion
   b. imagery rehearsal
   c. stimulus control techniques
   d. the activation-synthesis effect

3. Which of the following can most definitely be achieved with hypnosis?
   a. unusual strength
   b. pain relief
   c. improved memory
   d. sleep-like brainwaves

4. The focus of attention in concentrative meditation is "open," or expansive. T or F?

5. Mantras are words said silently to oneself to end a session of meditation. T or F?

6. Which terms do not belong together?
   a. concentrative meditation–relaxation response
   b. receptive meditation–mantra
   c. sensory deprivation–REST
   d. receptive meditation–mindfulness

7. The most immediate benefit of meditation appears to be its capacity for producing the relaxation response. T or F?

8. Prolonged periods of extreme sensory deprivation lower anxiety and induce deep relaxation. T or F?

Reflect

Critical Thinking

9. What kind of control group would you need in order to identify the true effects of hypnosis?

10. Regular meditators report lower levels of stress and a greater sense of well-being. What other explanations must we eliminate before this effect can be regarded as genuine?

Relate

How have your beliefs about hypnosis changed after reading the preceding section? Can you think of specific examples in which hypnosis was misrepresented? For example, in high school assemblies, stage acts, movies, or TV dramas?

Various activities can produce the relaxation response. When do you experience states of deep relaxation, coupled with a sense of serene awareness? What similarities do these occurrences have to meditation?

Have you experienced any form of sensory restriction or sensory deprivation? How did you react? Would you be willing to try REST in order to break a bad habit?

Link

Internet addresses frequently change. To find the sites listed here, visit **http://www.thomsonedu.com/psychology/coon** for an updated list of Internet addresses and direct links to relevant sites.

- **Hypnosis and Self-Hypnosis** Frequently asked questions; includes a self-hypnosis induction script.
- **Meditation for Stress Reduction** Find out more about how to meditate.
- **Introduction to Floating** Read more about REST (Restricted Environmental Stimulation Therapy).

ANSWERS

1. d 2. a 3. b 4. F 5. F 6. b 7. T 8. F 9. Most experiments on hypnosis include a control group in which people are asked to simulate being hypnotized. Without such controls, the tendency of subjects to cooperate with experimenters makes it difficult to identify true hypnotic effects. 10. Studies on the effects of meditation must control for the placebo effect and the fact that those who choose to learn meditation may not be a representative sample of the general population.

MODULE 5.4 Psychoactive Drugs

DRUG ABUSE has been one of the most persistent of all social problems in Western nations. The problem is that prescription drugs that can ease pain, induce sleep, or end depression have a high potential for abuse (Goldberg, 2006). Add alcohol and illicit drugs to the menu and it's little wonder that so many lives are damaged by drug use. This module provides an overview of commonly abused substances.

Drug-Altered Consciousness—The High and Low of It

SURVEY QUESTION: *What are the effects of the more commonly used psychoactive drugs?*

The surest way to alter human consciousness is to administer a **psychoactive drug** (a substance capable of altering attention, judgment, memory, time sense, self-control, emotion, or perception). Psychoactive drugs alter consciousness by directly influencing brain function (Julien, 2005). (See "How Addictive Drugs Affect the Brain.")

The fact that most Americans regularly use psychoactive drugs attests to the popularity of altering consciousness (don't forget that caffeine, alcohol, and nicotine are mildly psychoactive). Because of their profound effects, the more powerful psychoactive drugs are controlled substances. Nevertheless, more than 20 million Americans are currently illicit drug users (SAMHAS, 2005). Most psychoactive drugs can be placed on a scale ranging from stimulation to depression. A **stimulant** is a substance that increases activity in the body and nervous system. A **depressant** does the reverse. ● Figure 5.11 shows various drugs and their approximate effects. A more complete summary of frequently abused psychoactive drugs is given in ■ Table 5.3.

Dependence

Drug dependence falls into two broad categories. When a person compulsively uses a drug to maintain bodily comfort, a **physical dependence** (addiction) exists. Addiction occurs most often with drugs that cause **withdrawal symptoms** (physical illness that follows removal of a drug) (Julien, 2005). Withdrawal from drugs such as alcohol, barbiturates, and opiates can cause violent flu-like symptoms of nausea, vomiting, diarrhea, chills, sweating, and cramps. Addiction is often accompanied by a **drug tolerance** (reduced response to a drug). This leads users to take larger and larger doses to get the desired effect.

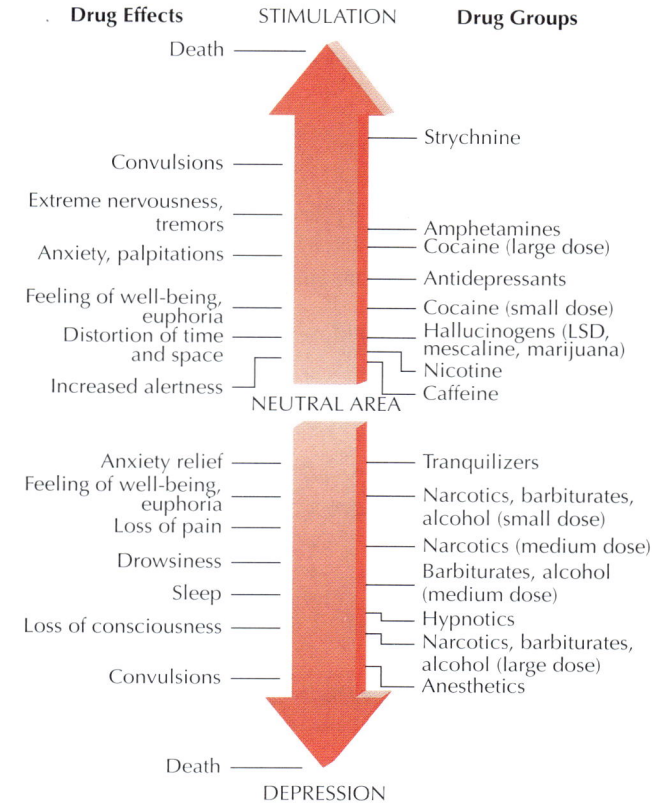

● **FIGURE 5.11** Spectrum and continuum of drug action. Many drugs can be rated on a stimulation-depression scale according to their effects on the central nervous system. Although LSD, mescaline, and marijuana are listed here, the stimulation-depression scale is less relevant to these drugs. The principal characteristic of such hallucinogens is their mind-altering quality.

Persons who develop a **psychological dependence** feel that a drug is necessary to maintain feelings of comfort or well-being. Usually, they intensely crave the drug and its rewarding qualities (Winger et al., 2005). Psychological dependence can be just as powerful as physical addiction. That's

---

Psychoactive drug A substance capable of altering attention, memory, judgment, time sense, self-control, mood, or perception.

Stimulant A substance that increases activity in the body and nervous system.

Depressant A substance that decreases activity in the body and nervous system.

Physical dependence Physical addiction, as indicated by the presence of drug tolerance and withdrawal symptoms.

Withdrawal symptoms Physical illness and discomfort following the withdrawal of a drug.

Drug tolerance A reduction in the body's response to a drug.

Psychological dependence Drug dependence that is based primarily on emotional or psychological needs.

TABLE 5.3 Comparison of Psychoactive Drugs

NAME	CLASSIFICATION	MEDICAL USE	USUAL DOSE	DURATION OF EFFECT
Alcohol	Sedative-hypnotic	Solvent, antiseptic	Varies	1-4 hours
Amphetamines	Stimulant	Relief of mild depression, control of narcolepsy and hyperactivity	2.5-5 milligrams	4 hours
Barbiturates	Sedative-hypnotic	Sedation, relief of high blood pressure, anticonvulsant	50-100 milligrams	4 hours
Benzodiazepines	Anxiolytic (antianxiety drug)	Tranquilizer	2-100 milligrams	10 minutes-8 hours
Caffeine	Stimulant	Counteract depressant drugs, treatment of migraine headaches	Varies	Varies
Cocaine	Stimulant, local anesthetic	Local anesthesia	Varies	Varied, brief periods
Codeine	Narcotic	Ease pain and coughing	30 milligrams	4 hours
GHB	Sedative-hypnotic	Experimental treatment of narcolepsy, alcoholism	1-3 grams (powder)	1-3 hours
Heroin	Narcotic	Pain relief	Varies	4 hours
LSD	Hallucinogen	Experimental study of mental function, alcoholism	100-500 milligrams	10 hours
Marijuana (THC)	Relaxant, euphoriant; in high doses, hallucinogen	Treatment of glaucoma and side effects of chemotherapy	1-2 cigarettes	4 hours
MDMA	Stimulant/hallucinogen	None	125 milligrams	4-6 hours
Mescaline	Hallucinogen	None	350 micrograms	12 hours
Methadone	Narcotic	Pain relief	10 milligrams	4-6 hours
Morphine	Narcotic	Pain relief	15 milligrams	6 hours
PCP	Anesthetic	None	2-10 milligrams	4-6 hours, plus 12-hour recovery
Psilocybin	Hallucinogen	None	25 milligrams	6-8 hours
Tobacco (nicotine)	Stimulant	Emetic (nicotine)	Varies	Varies

Question marks indicate conflict of opinion. It should be noted that illicit drugs are frequently adulterated and thus pose unknown hazards to the user.

why some psychologists define addiction as any compulsive habit pattern. By this definition, a person who has lost control over drug use, for whatever reason, is addicted. In fact, most people who answer yes to both of the following questions have an alcohol or drug problem and should seek professional help (Brown et al., 1997):

- In the last year, did you ever drink or use drugs more than you meant to?
- Have you felt you wanted or needed to cut down on your drinking or drug use in the last year?

Drugs of Abuse Some drugs, of course, have a higher potential for abuse than others. Heroin is certainly more dangerous than caffeine. However, this is only one side of the picture. It can be as useful to classify drug-taking *behavior* as it is to rate drugs. For example, some people remain social drinkers for life, whereas others become alcoholics within weeks of taking

TABLE 5.3 Comparison of Psychoactive Drugs

EFFECTS SOUGHT	LONG-TERM SYMPTOMS	PHYSICAL DEPENDENCE POTENTIAL	PSYCHOLOGICAL DEPENDENCE POTENTIAL	ORGANIC DAMAGE POTENTIAL
Sense alteration, anxiety reduction, sociability	Cirrhosis, toxic psychosis, neurologic damage, addiction	Yes	Yes	Yes
Alertness, activeness	Loss of appetite, delusions, hallucinations, toxic psychosis	Yes	Yes	Yes
Anxiety reduction, euphoria	Addiction with severe withdrawal symptoms, possible convulsions, toxic psychosis	Yes	Yes	Yes
Anxiety relief	Irritability, confusion, depression, sleep disorders	Yes	Yes	No, but can affect fetus
Wakefulness, alertness	Insomnia, heart arrhythmias, high blood pressure	No?	Yes	Yes
Excitation, talkativeness	Depression, convulsions	Yes	Yes	Yes
Euphoria, prevent withdrawal discomfort	Addiction, constipation, loss of appetite	Yes	Yes	No
Intoxication, euphoria, relaxation	Anxiety, confusion, insomnia, hallucinations, seizures	Yes	Yes	No?
Euphoria, prevent withdrawal discomfort	Addiction, constipation, loss of appetite	Yes	Yes	No*
Insightful experiences, exhilaration, distortion of senses	May intensify existing psychosis, panic reactions	No	No?	No?
Relaxation; increased euphoria, perceptions, sociability	Possible lung cancer, other health risks	No	Yes	Yes?
Excitation, euphoria	Personality change, hyperthermia, liver damage	No	Yes	Yes
Insightful experiences, exhilaration, distortion of senses	May intensify existing psychosis, panic reactions	No	No?	No?
Prevent withdrawal discomfort	Addiction, constipation, loss of appetite	Yes	Yes	No
Euphoria, prevent withdrawal discomfort	Addiction, constipation, loss of appetite	Yes	Yes	No*
Euphoria	Unpredictable behavior, suspicion, hostility, psychosis	Debated	Yes	Yes
Insightful experiences, exhilaration, distortion of senses	May intensify existing psychosis, panic reactions	No	No?	No?
Alertness, calmness, sociability	Emphysema, lung cancer, mouth and throat cancer, cardiovascular damage, loss of appetite	Yes	Yes	Yes

*Persons who inject drugs under nonsterile conditions run a high risk of contracting AIDS, hepatitis, abscesses, or circulatory disorders.

their first drink (Robinson & Berridge, 2003). In this sense, drug use can be classified as *experimental* (short-term use based on curiosity), *social-recreational* (occasional social use for pleasure or relaxation), *situational* (use to cope with a specific problem, such as needing to stay awake), *intensive* (daily use with elements of dependence), or *compulsive* (intense use and extreme dependence). The last three categories of drug taking tend to be damaging no matter what drug is used.

Note in Table 5.3 that the drugs most likely to lead to physical dependence are alcohol, amphetamines, barbiturates, cocaine, codeine, heroin, methadone, morphine, and tobacco (nicotine). Using *any* of the drugs listed in Table 5.3 can result in psychological dependence. Note too that people who take drugs intravenously are at high risk for developing hepatitis and AIDS. (See Module 14.3.) The discussion that follows focuses on the drugs most often abused by students.

BRAINWAVES

How Addictive Drugs Affect the Brain

Psychoactive drugs influence the activity of brain cells (Kalat, 2007). Typically, drugs imitate or alter the effects of neurotransmitters, the chemicals that carry messages between brain cells. Some drugs, such as Ecstasy, amphetamines, and some antidepressants, cause more neurotransmitters to be released, increasing the activity of brain cells. Other drugs, such as cocaine, slow the removal of neurotransmitters after they are released. This prolongs the action of transmitter chemicals and typically has a stimulating effect. Other drugs, such as nicotine and opiates, directly stimulate brain cells by mimicking neurotransmitters. Another possibility is illustrated by alcohol and tranquilizers. These drugs affect certain types of brain cells that cause relaxation and relieve anxiety. Some drugs fill receptor sites on brain cells and block incoming messages. Other possibilities also exist, which is why drugs can have such a wide variety of effects on the brain (Julien, 2005).

Nearly all addictive drugs stimulate the brain's reward circuitry, producing feelings of pleasure (Kalat, 2007). In particular, addictive drugs stimulate a brain region called the *nucleus accumbens* to release the neurotransmitter dopamine, which results in intensified feelings of pleasure (● Fig. 5.12). As one expert put it, addictive drugs fool brain-reward pathways: "As a result, the reward pathway signals, 'That felt good. Let's do it again. Let's remember exactly how we did it.'" This creates a compulsion to repeat the drug experience. It's the hook that eventually snares the addict (Restak, 2001). In the end, the addictive drug physically changes the brain's reward circuitry, making it even harder for the addict to overcome his or her addiction (Robinson & Berridge, 2003). Adolescents are especially susceptible to addiction because brain systems that restrain risk-taking are not as mature as those that reward pleasure seeking (Chambers, Taylor, & Potenza, 2003).

● **FIGURE 5.12** Addictive drugs increase dopamine activity in the medial forebrain bundle and the nucleus accumbens, stimulating the frontal cortex and giving rise to intensified feelings of pleasure.

Uppers—Amphetamines, Cocaine, MDMA, Caffeine, Nicotine

Amphetamines

Amphetamines are synthetic stimulants. Common street names for amphetamine are "speed," "bennies," "dexies," "go," and "uppers." These drugs were once widely prescribed for weight loss or depression. Today, the main legitimate medical use of amphetamines is to treat childhood hyperactivity and overdoses of depressant drugs. Illicit use of amphetamines is widespread, however, especially by people seeking to stay awake and by those who think drugs can improve mental or physical performance (Iversen, 2006).

Methamphetamine is a more potent variation of amphetamine. It can be snorted, injected, or eaten. Of the various types of amphetamine, methamphetamine has created the largest drug problem. "Bergs," "glass," "meth," or "crystal," as it is known on the street, can be made cheaply in backyard labs and sold for massive profits. In addition to ruining lives through addiction, it has fueled a violent criminal subculture.

Amphetamines rapidly produce a drug tolerance. Most abusers end up taking ever-larger doses to get the desired effect. Eventually, some users switch to injecting methamphetamine directly into the bloodstream. True speed freaks typically go on binges lasting several days, after which they "crash" from lack of sleep and food.

Abuse *How dangerous are amphetamines?* Amphetamines pose many dangers. Large doses can cause nausea, vomiting, extremely high blood pressure, fatal heart attacks, and disabling strokes. It is important to realize that amphetamines speed up the use of the body's resources; they do not magically supply energy. After an amphetamine binge, people suffer from crippling fatigue, depression, confusion, uncontrolled irritability, and aggression. Repeated amphetamine use damages the brain. Amphetamines can also cause *amphetamine psychosis*, a loss of contact with reality. Affected users have paranoid delusions that someone is out to get them. Acting on these delusions, they may become violent, resulting in suicide, self-injury, or injury to others (Iversen, 2006).

A potent smokable form of crystal methamphetamine has added to the risks of stimulant abuse. This drug, known as "ice" on the street, is highly addictive. Like "crack," the smokable form of cocaine, it produces an intense high. But also like crack (discussed in a moment), crystal methamphetamine leads very rapidly to compulsive abuse and severe drug dependence.

Cocaine

Cocaine ("coke," "snow," "blow," "snuff") is a powerful central nervous system stimulant extracted from the leaves of the coca plant. Cocaine produces feelings of alertness, euphoria, well-being, power, boundless energy, and pleasure (Julien, 2005). At the turn of the twentieth century, dozens of nonprescription potions and cure-alls contained cocaine. It was during this time that Coca-Cola was indeed the "real thing." From 1886 until 1906, when the U.S. Pure Food and Drug Act was passed, Coca-Cola contained cocaine (which has since been replaced with caffeine).

How does cocaine differ from amphetamines? The two are very much alike in their effects on the central nervous system. The main difference is that amphetamine lasts several hours; cocaine is snorted and quickly metabolized, so its effects last only about 15 to 30 minutes.

Abuse *How dangerous is cocaine?* Cocaine is one of the most dangerous drugs of abuse. When rats and monkeys are given free access to cocaine, they find it irresistible. Many, in fact, end up dying of convulsions from self-administered over-

Cocaine was the main ingredient in many nonprescription elixirs before the turn of the twentieth century. Today cocaine is recognized as a powerful and dangerous drug. Its high potential for abuse has damaged the lives of countless users.

doses of the drug. Cocaine increases the chemical messengers dopamine (DOPE-ah-meen) and noradrenaline (nor-ah-DREN-ah-lin). Noradrenaline arouses the brain, and dopamine produces a "rush" of pleasure. This combination is so powerfully rewarding that cocaine users run a high risk of becoming compulsive abusers (Ridenour et al., 2005). Even casual or first-time users risk having convulsions, a heart attack, or a stroke (Lacayo, 1995).

A person who stops using cocaine does not experience heroin-like withdrawal symptoms. But cocaine can be highly addictive. The brain adapts to cocaine abuse in ways that upset its chemical balance, causing depression when cocaine is withdrawn. First, there is a jarring "crash" of mood and energy. Within a few days, the person enters a long period of fatigue, anxiety, paranoia, boredom, and **anhedonia** (an-he-DAWN-ee-ah: an inability to feel pleasure). Before long, the urge to use cocaine becomes intense. So, although cocaine does not fit the classic pattern of addiction, it is ripe for compulsive abuse. Even a person who gets through withdrawal may crave cocaine months or years later (Withers et al., 1995). If cocaine were cheaper, 9 out of 10 users would progress to compulsive abuse. In fact, rock cocaine ("crack," "rock," or *"roca"*), which is cheaper, produces very high abuse rates. Here are some signs of cocaine abuse:

- *Compulsive use.* If cocaine is available—say, at a party—you can't say no to it.
- *Loss of control.* Once you have had some cocaine, you will keep using it until you are exhausted or the cocaine is gone.

Anhedonia An inability to feel pleasure.

- *Disregarding consequences.* You don't care if the rent gets paid, your job is endangered, your lover disapproves, or your health is affected; you'll use cocaine anyway.

Cocaine's capacity for abuse and social damage rivals that of heroin. Anyone who thinks she or he has a cocaine problem should seek advice at a drug clinic or a Cocaine Anonymous meeting. Quitting cocaine is extremely difficult (Sinha et al., 2006). Nevertheless, three out of four cocaine abusers who remain in treatment do succeed in breaking their coke dependence (Simpson et al., 1999).

MDMA ("Ecstasy")

The drug MDMA (methylenedioxymethamphetamine, or "Ecstasy") is also chemically similar to amphetamine. In addition to producing a rush of energy, users say it makes them feel closer to others and heightens sensory experiences. Ecstasy causes brain cells to release extra amounts of serotonin. The physical effects of MDMA include dilated pupils, elevated blood pressure, jaw clenching, loss of appetite, and elevated body temperature (Braun, 2001). Although some users believe that Ecstasy increases sexual pleasure, it diminishes sexual performance, impairing erection in 40 percent of men and retarding orgasm in both men and women (Zemishlany, Aizenberg, & Weizman, 2001).

Abuse Ecstasy use in North America has declined slightly from a peak around 2002, perhaps because of widespread negative publicity. Regardless, every year more than half a million Americans try Ecstasy for the first time (SAMHSA, 2005). Every year, emergency room doctors see many MDMA cases, including MDMA-related deaths. Some of these incidents are caused by elevated body temperature (hyperthermia) or heart arrhythmias, which can lead to collapse. Ecstasy users at "rave" parties try to prevent overheating by drinking water to cool themselves. This may help to a small degree, but the risk of fatal heat exhaustion is real. MDMA can also cause severe liver damage, which can be fatal (Braun, 2001). In addition, Ecstasy users are more likely to abuse alcohol and other drugs, to neglect studying, to party excessively, and to engage in risky sex (Strote, Lee, & Wechsler, 2002). Ironically, Ecstasy use at "rave" parties actually does intensify the impact of the music. We say ironically because the end result is often overstimulation of the brain, which can result in a "rebound" depression (Michelangelo et al., 2006).

It may take another decade before Ecstasy's full impact on health emerges. For now, we know that repeated use of MDMA damages serotonergic brain cells. This damage lasts for years. It leads to feelings of anxiety or depression that can persist for months after a person stops taking Ecstasy. In addition, heavy users typically do not perform well in tests of learning and memory and show signs of underlying brain damage (Quednow et al., 2006). Despite its street name, Ecstasy may be a ticket to agony for many users (Iversen, 2006; Kuhn & Wilson, 2001).

Caffeine

Caffeine is the most frequently used psychoactive drug in North America. (And that's not counting Seattle!) Caffeine stimulates the brain by blocking chemicals that normally inhibit or slow nerve activity (Julien, 2005). Its effects become apparent with doses as small as 50 milligrams, the amount found in about one-half cup of brewed coffee. Physically, caffeine causes sweating, talkativeness, tinnitus (ringing in the ears), and hand tremors (Nehlig, 2004). Psychologically, caffeine suppresses fatigue or drowsiness and increases feelings of alertness (Wesensten, 2002). Some people have a hard time starting a day (or writing another paragraph) without it.

How much caffeine did you consume today? It is common to think of coffee as the major source of caffeine, but there are many others. Caffeine is found in tea, many soft drinks (especially colas), chocolate, and cocoa (■ Table 5.4). More than 2,000 nonprescription drugs also contain caffeine, including stay-awake pills, cold remedies, and many name-brand aspirin products.

Abuse *Are there any serious drawbacks to using caffeine?* Overuse of caffeine may result in an unhealthy dependence known as **caffeinism.** Insomnia, irritability, loss of appetite, chills, racing heart, and elevated body temperature are all signs of caffeinism. Many people with these symptoms drink 15 or 20 cups of coffee a day. However, even at lower dosages, caffeine can intensify anxiety and other psychological problems (Hogan, Hornick, & Bouchoux, 2002).

■ **TABLE 5.4 Average Caffeine Content of Various Foods**

Instant coffee (5 ounces or 1 cup), 64 milligrams
Percolated coffee (5 ounces or 1 cup), 108 milligrams
Drip coffee (5 ounces or 1 cup), 145 milligrams
Decaffeinated coffee (5 ounces or 1 cup), 3 milligrams
Black tea (5 ounces or 1 cup), 42 milligrams
Canned ice tea (17 ounces), 30 milligrams
Cocoa drink (6 ounces or 1 cup), 8 milligrams
Chocolate drink (8 ounces or 1 carton), 14 milligrams
Sweet chocolate (1-ounce square), 20 milligrams
Colas (12 ounces or 1 can), 50 milligrams
Soft drinks (12 ounces or 1 can), 0–52 milligrams

Caffeine poses a variety of health risks. Caffeine encourages the growth of breast cysts in women, and it may contribute to bladder cancer, heart problems, and high blood pressure. Pregnant women should consider giving up caffeine entirely because of a suspected link between caffeine and birth defects. Pregnant women who consume as little as 2 cups coffee a day increase the risk of having a miscarriage (Cnattingius et al., 2000).

It is customary to think that caffeine is not a drug. But as few as 2.5 cups of coffee a day (or the equivalent) can be a problem. People who consume even such modest amounts may experience anxiety, depression, fatigue, headaches, and flu-like symptoms during withdrawal (Juliano & Griffiths, 2004). About half of all caffeine users show some signs of dependence (Hughes et al., 1998). It is wise to remember that caffeine *is* a drug and use it in moderation.

Nicotine

Nicotine is a natural stimulant found mainly in tobacco. Next to caffeine and alcohol, it is the most widely used psychoactive drug (Julien, 2005).

How does nicotine compare with other stimulants? Nicotine is a potent drug. It is so toxic that it is sometimes used to kill insects! In large doses it causes stomach pain, vomiting and diarrhea, cold sweats, dizziness, confusion, and muscle tremors. In very large doses, nicotine may cause convulsions, respiratory failure, and death. For a nonsmoker, 50 to 75 milligrams of nicotine taken in a single dose could be lethal. (Chain-smoking about 17 to 25 cigarettes will produce this dosage.) Most first-time smokers get sick on one or two cigarettes. In contrast, a heavy smoker may inhale 40 cigarettes a day without feeling ill. This indicates that regular smokers build a tolerance for nicotine.

Abuse *How addictive is nicotine?* A vast array of evidence confirms that nicotine is very addictive (Spinella, 2005). The average age of first use is 15, and it takes about a year before dependence sets in (Baker, Brandon, & Chassin, 2004). Among regular smokers who are 15 to 24 years old, 60 percent are addicted (Breslau et al., 2001). For many smokers, withdrawal from nicotine causes headaches, sweating, cramps, insomnia, digestive upset, irritability, and a sharp craving for cigarettes (Killen & Fortmann, 1997; NIDA, 2006). These symptoms may last from 2 to 6 weeks and may be worse than heroin withdrawal. Indeed, relapse patterns are nearly identical for alcoholics, heroin addicts, cocaine abusers, and smokers who try to quit (Stolerman & Jarvis, 1995). Up to 90 percent of people who quit smoking relapse within a year, and 20 percent relapse even after 2 years of abstinence (Krall, Garvey, & Garcia, 2002).

Impact on Health *How serious are the health risks of smoking?* If you think smoking is harmless, or that there's no connection between smoking and cancer, you're kidding yourself. A burning cigarette releases a large variety of potent *carcinogens* (car-SIN-oh-jins: cancer-causing substances). According to the U.S. Surgeon General (USDHHS, 2004), "smoking harms nearly every organ of the body," leading to an increased risk of many cancers (such as lung cancer), cardiovascular diseases (such as stroke), respiratory diseases (such as chronic bronchitis), and reproductive disorders (such as decreased fertility). Together, these health risks combine to reduce the life expectancy of the average smoker by 10 to 15 years. (Skeptics please note: Wayne McLaren, who portrayed the rugged "Marlboro Man" in cigarette ads, died of lung cancer at age 51.) More people die every year from tobacco use than from motor vehicle injuries, murders, suicides, alcohol use, illegal drug use, and AIDS *combined* (NCCDPHP, 2004).

By the way, urban cowboys and Skol bandits, the same applies to chewing tobacco and snuff. A 30-minute exposure to one pinch of smokeless tobacco is equivalent to smoking three or four cigarettes. Along with all the health risks of

Actress and comedienne Lily Tomlin, here shown portraying one of her comedic characters, Ernestine, once took up smoking for a role in a movie (*Shadows and Fog*) and developed a 4-pack-a-day habit. As Tomlin's experience shows, the best way to avoid developing a nicotine addiction is to not begin smoking in the first place.

Caffeinism Excessive consumption of caffeine, leading to dependence and a variety of physical and psychological complaints.

smoking, users of smokeless tobacco also run a higher risk of developing oral cancer (American Lung Association, 2006).

Smokers don't just risk their own health; they also endanger those who live and work nearby. Secondary smoke causes about 3,000 lung cancer deaths and as many as 62,000 heart disease deaths each year in the United States alone. It is particularly irresponsible of smokers to expose young children, who are especially vulnerable, to secondhand smoke (American Lung Association, 2006).

Quitting Smoking *What is the best way to quit smoking?* Most people try to quit by themselves. Some try to quit cold turkey, whereas others try to taper down gradually. Although going cold turkey has its advocates, gradually quitting works better for more people.

Going cold turkey makes quitting an all-or-nothing proposition. Smokers who smoke even one cigarette after "quitting forever" tend to feel they've failed. Many figure they might just as well resume smoking. Those who quit gradually accept that success may take many attempts, spread over several months. If you are going to quit by going cold turkey, you will have a better chance of success if you decide to quit *now* rather than at some time in the future (West & Sohal, 2006).

The best way to taper off is *scheduled gradual reduction* (Riley et al., 2002). There are many ways in which smoking can be gradually reduced. For example, the smoker can (1) delay having a first cigarette in the morning and then try to delay a little longer each day, (2) gradually reduce the total number of cigarettes smoked each day, or (3) quit completely, but for just 1 week, then quit again, a week at a time, for as many times as necessary to make it stick. Deliberately scheduling the gradually stretching of time periods between cigarettes is a key part of this program. Scheduled smoking apparently helps people learn to cope with the urge to smoke. As a result, people using this method are more likely to succeed. Also, they more often remain permanent nonsmokers than people using other approaches (Cinciripini, Wetter, & McClure, 1997).

Whatever approach is taken, quitting smoking is not easy (Abrams et al., 2003). Many people find that using nicotine patches or gum helps them get through the withdrawal period (Shiffman et al., 2006). Also, as we have noted, anyone trying to quit should be prepared to make several attempts before succeeding. But the good news is tens of millions of people have quit.

Downers—Sedatives, Tranquilizers, and Alcohol

How do downers differ from the stimulant drugs? The most widely used downers, or depressant drugs, are alcohol, barbiturates, GHB, and benzodiazepine (ben-zoe-die-AZ-eh-peen) tranquilizers. These drugs are much alike in their effects. In fact, barbiturates and tranquilizers are sometimes referred to as "solid alcohol." Let's examine the properties of each.

Barbiturates

Barbiturates are sedative drugs that depress brain activity. Common barbiturates include amobarbital, pentobarbital, secobarbital, and tuinal. On the street they are known as "downers," "blue heavens," "yellow jackets," "lows," "goof balls," "reds," "pink ladies," "rainbows," or "tooies." Medically, barbiturates are used to calm patients or to induce sleep. At mild dosages, barbiturates have an effect similar to alcohol intoxication. Higher dosages can cause severe mental confusion or even hallucinations. Barbiturates are often taken in excess amounts because a first dose may be followed by others, as the user becomes uninhibited or forgetful. Overdoses first cause a loss of consciousness. Then they severely depress brain centers that control heartbeat and breathing. The result is death (McKim, 2003).

GHB

Would you swallow a mixture of degreasing solvent and drain cleaner to get high? Apparently, a lot of people would. A mini-epidemic of GHB (gamma-hydroxybutyrate) use has taken place in recent years, especially at nightclubs and raves. GHB ("goop," "scoop," "max," "Georgia Home Boy") is a central nervous system depressant that relaxes and sedates the body. Users describe its effects as being similar to alcohol. Mild GHB intoxication tends to produce euphoria, a desire to socialize, and a mild loss of inhibitions. GHB's intoxi-

"And then when we turn 30 and get lung cancer, we can sue the tobacco companies."

cating effects typically last 3 to 4 hours, depending on the dosage.

Abuse At lower dosages, GHB can relieve anxiety and produce relaxation. However, as the dose increases, its sedative effects may result in nausea, a loss of muscle control, and either sleep or a loss of consciousness. Potentially fatal doses of GHB are only three times the amount typically taken by users. This narrow margin of safety has led to numerous overdoses, especially when GHB was combined with alcohol. An overdose causes coma, breathing failure, and death. Also, GHB inhibits the gag reflex, so some users choke to death on their own vomit.

In 2000, the U.S. government classified GHB as a controlled substance, making its possession a felony. Clinical evidence increasingly suggests that GHB is addictive and a serious danger to users. Two out of three frequent users have lost consciousness after taking GHB. Heavy users who stop taking GHB have withdrawal symptoms that include anxiety, agitation, tremor, delirium, and hallucinations (Miotto et al., 2001).

As if the preceding weren't enough reason to be leery of GHB, here's one more to consider: GHB is often manufactured in homes with recipes and ingredients purchased on the Internet. As mentioned earlier, it can be produced by combining degreasing solvent with drain cleaner (Falkowski, 2000). If you want to degrease your brain, GHB will do the trick.

Tranquilizers

A **tranquilizer** is a drug that lowers anxiety and reduces tension. Doctors prescribe benzodiazepine tranquilizers to alleviate nervousness and stress. Valium is the best-known drug in this family; others are Xanax, Halcion, and Librium. Even at normal dosages these drugs can cause drowsiness, shakiness, and confusion. When used at too high a dosage or for too long, benzodiazepines have strong addictive potential (McKim, 2003).

A drug sold under the trade name Rohypnol (ro-HIP-nol) has added to the problem of tranquilizer abuse. This drug, which is related to Valium, is cheap and 10 times more potent. It lowers inhibitions and produces relaxation or intoxication. Large doses induce short-term amnesia and sleep. "Roofies," as they are known on the street, are odorless and tasteless. They have been used to spike drinks, which are given to the unwary. Victims of this "date rape" drug are then sexually assaulted or raped while they are unconscious. (Be aware, however, that drinking too much alcohol is by far the most common prelude to rape.)

Abuse Repeated use of barbiturates can cause physical dependence. Some abusers suffer severe emotional depression that may end in suicide. Similarly, when tranquilizers are used at too high a dosage or for too long, addiction can occur. Many people have learned the hard way that their legally prescribed tranquilizers are as dangerous as many illicit drugs (McKim, 2003).

Combining barbiturates or tranquilizers with alcohol is especially risky. When mixed, the effects of both drugs are multiplied by a **drug interaction** (one drug enhances the effect of another). Drug interactions are responsible for many hundreds of fatal drug overdoses every year (Goldberg, 2006). All too often, depressants are gulped down with alcohol or added to a spiked punch bowl. This is the lethal brew that left a young woman named Karen Ann Quinlan in a coma that lasted 10 years, ending with her death. It is no exaggeration to restate that mixing depressants with alcohol can be deadly.

Alcohol

Alcohol is the common name for ethyl alcohol, the intoxicating element in fermented and distilled liquors. Contrary to popular belief, alcohol is not a stimulant. The noisy animation at drinking parties is due to alcohol's effect as a *depressant*. As ● Figure 5.13 shows, small amounts of alcohol reduce inhibitions and produce feelings of relaxation and euphoria. Larger amounts cause ever-greater impairment of the brain until the drinker loses consciousness. Alcohol is also not an aphrodisiac. Rather than enhancing sexual arousal, it usually impairs performance, especially in males. As William Shakespeare observed long ago, drink "provokes the desire, but it takes away the performance."

Abuse Alcohol, the world's favorite depressant, breeds our biggest drug problem. More than 20 million people in the United States and Canada have serious drinking problems. One American dies every 20 minutes in an alcohol-related car crash. The level of alcohol abuse among adolescents and young adults is alarming. Of 18-year-olds, 15 percent are heavy drinkers and 40 percent have engaged in binge drinking (SAMHAS, 2005). For fraternity and sorority members, the figure is much higher. **Binge drinking** is defined as downing five or more drinks in a short time (four drinks for women). Apparently, many students think it's entertaining to get completely wasted and throw up on their friends. However, binge drinking is a serious sign of alcohol abuse. It is responsible for 1,400 college student deaths each year and thousands of trips to the ER (Wechsler et al., 2002).

Tranquilizer A drug that lowers anxiety and reduces tension.

Drug interaction A combined effect of two drugs that exceeds the addition of one drug's effects to the other.

Binge drinking Consuming five or more drinks in a short time.

● **FIGURE 5.13** The behavioral effects of alcohol are related to blood alcohol content and the resulting suppression of higher mental function. Arrows indicate the typical threshold for legal intoxication in the United States. (From Jozef Cohen (1969). *Eyewitness Series in Psychology*, p. 44. © Rand McNally and Company. Reprinted by permission.)

Binge drinking is of special concern because the brain continues to develop into the early 20s. Research has shown that teenagers and young adults who drink too much may lose as much as 10 percent of their brain power—especially their memory capacity (Brown et al., 2000). Such losses can have a long-term impact on a person's chances for success in life. In short, getting drunk is a slow but sure way to get stupid (Wechsler & Wuethrich, 2002).

Positive reinforcement—drinking for pleasure—motivates most people who consume alcohol. What sets alcohol abusers apart from other drinkers is that they also drink to cope with negative emotions, such as anxiety and depression. That's why alcohol abuse increases with the level of stress in people's lives. People who drink to cope with bad feelings are at risk of becoming alcoholics (Kenneth, Carpenter, & Hasin, 1998).

Recognizing Problem Drinking *What are the signs of alcohol abuse?* Because alcohol abuse is such a common problem, it is important to recognize the danger signals. If you can answer yes to even one of the following questions, you may have a problem with drinking (adapted from the College Alcohol Problems Scale, revised; Maddock et al., 2001):

AS A RESULT OF DRINKING ALCOHOLIC BEVERAGES I . . .
1. engaged in unplanned sexual activity.
2. drove under the influence.
3. did not use protection when engaging in sex.
4. engaged in illegal activities associated with drug use.
5. felt sad, blue, or depressed.
6. was nervous or irritable.
7. felt bad about myself.
8. had problems with appetite or sleeping.

And remember, research has shown that you are likely to overestimate how much your fellow students are drinking (Maddock & Glanz, 2005). So don't let yourself be lured into overdrinking just because you have the (probably false) impression that other students are drinking more than you. Limiting your own drinking may help others as well. When people are tempted to drink too much, their main reason for stopping is that "other people were quitting and deciding they'd had enough" (Johnson, 2002).

Treatment Treatment for alcohol dependence begins with sobering up the person and cutting off the supply. This phase is referred to as **detoxification** (literally, "to remove poison"). It frequently produces all the symptoms of drug withdrawal and can be extremely unpleasant. The next step is to try to restore the person's health. Heavy abuse of alcohol usually causes severe damage to body organs and the nervous system. After alcoholics have "dried out" and some degree of health has been restored, they may be treated with tranquilizers, antidepressants, or psychotherapy. Unfortunately, the success of these procedures has been limited.

One mutual-help approach that has been fairly successful is Alcoholics Anonymous (AA). AA takes a spiritual approach while acting on the premise that it takes a former alcoholic to understand and help a current alcoholic. Participants at AA meetings admit that they have a problem, share feelings, and resolve to stay "dry" one day at a time. Other group members provide support for those struggling to end dependency. (Other "12-step" programs, such as Cocaine Anonymous and Narcotics Anonymous, use the same approach.)

Eighty percent of those who remain in AA for more than 1 year get through the following year without a drink. However, AA's success rate may simply reflect the fact that members join voluntarily, meaning they have admitted they have a serious problem (Morgenstern et al., 1997). Sadly, it seems that alcohol abusers will often not face their problems until they have "hit rock bottom." If they are willing, though, AA presents a practical approach to the problem (Vaillant, 2005).

Other groups offer a rational, nonspiritual approach to alcohol abuse that better fits the needs of some people. Examples include Rational Recovery and Secular Organizations for Sobriety (SOS). Other alternatives to AA include medical treatment, group therapy, and individual psychotherapy (Buddie, 2004). There is a strong tendency for abusive drinkers to deny they have a problem. The sooner they seek help, the better.

Binge drinking and alcohol abuse have become serious problems among college students. Many alcohol abusers regard themselves as "moderate" drinkers, which suggests that they are in denial about how much they actually drink (Grant & Dawson, 1997).

Moderated Drinking Many social-recreational drinkers could do a far better job of managing their use of alcohol. Almost everyone has been to a party spoiled by someone who drank too much too fast. Those who avoid overdrinking have a better time, and so do their friends. But how do you avoid drinking too much? After all, as one wit once observed, "The conscience dissolves in alcohol." It takes skill to regulate drinking in social situations, where the temptation to drink can be strong. If you choose to drink, here are some guidelines that may be helpful (adapted from Miller & Munoz, 2005; Vogler & Bartz, 1992):

PACED DRINKING
1. Think about your drinking beforehand and plan how you will manage it.
2. Drink slowly, eat while drinking or drink on a full stomach, and make every other drink (or more) a nonalcoholic beverage.
3. Limit drinking primarily to the first hour of a social event or party.
4. Practice how you will politely but firmly refuse drinks.
5. Learn how to relax, meet people, and socialize without relying on alcohol.

Detoxification In the treatment of alcoholism, the withdrawal of the patient from alcohol.

Hallucinogens—Tripping the Light Fantastic

Marijuana is the most popular illicit drug in America (SAMHAS, 2005). The main active chemical in marijuana is tetrahydrocannabinol (tet-rah-hydro-cah-NAB-ih-nol), or THC for short. THC is a mild **hallucinogen** (hal-LU-sin-oh-jin: a substance that alters sensory impressions). Other hallucinogenic drugs include LSD and PCP.

LSD and PCP

The drug LSD (lysergic acid diethylamide, or "acid") is perhaps the best-known hallucinogen. Even when taken in tiny amounts, LSD can produce hallucinations and psychotic-like disturbances in thinking and perception. Two other common hallucinogens are mescaline (peyote) and psilocybin ("magic mushrooms," or "shrooms"). Incidentally, the drug PCP (phencyclidine, or "angel dust") can have hallucinogenic effects. However, PCP, which is an anesthetic, also has stimulant and depressant effects. This potent combination can cause extreme agitation, disorientation, violence—and too often, tragedy. All the hallucinogens, including marijuana, typically affect neurotransmitter systems that carry messages between brain cells (Julien, 2005).

Marijuana

Marijuana and hashish are derived from the hemp plant *Cannabis sativa*. Marijuana ("pot," "grass," "Ganja," "MJ") consists of the dried leaves and flowers of the hemp plant. Hashish is a resinous material scraped from *Cannabis* leaves. Marijuana's psychological effects include a sense of euphoria or well-being, relaxation, altered time sense, and perceptual distortions. At high dosages, however, paranoia, hallucinations, and delusions can occur (Ksir, Hart, & Ray, 2006). All considered, marijuana intoxication is relatively subtle by comparison to drugs such as LSD or alcohol. Despite this, driving a car while high on marijuana can be extremely hazardous. As a matter of fact, driving under the influence of any intoxicating drug is dangerous.

No overdose deaths from marijuana have been reported. However, marijuana cannot be considered harmless. Particularly worrisome is the fact that THC accumulates in the body's fatty tissues, especially in the brain and reproductive organs. Even if a person smokes marijuana just once a week, the body is never entirely free of THC. Scientists have located a specific receptor site on the surface of brain cells where THC binds to produce its effects (● Fig. 5.14). These receptor sites are found in large numbers in the cerebral cortex, which is the seat of human consciousness (Julien, 2005). In addition, THC receptors are found in areas involved in the control of skilled movement. Naturally occurring chemicals similar to THC may help the brain cope with pain and stress. However, when THC is used as a drug, high dosages can cause paranoia, hallucinations, and dizziness.

Does marijuana produce physical dependence? Yes, according to recent studies (Lichtman & Martin, 2006). Frequent users of marijuana find it very difficult to quit, so dependence is a risk (Budney & Hughes, 2006). But marijuana's potential

Artists have tried at times to capture the effects of hallucinogens. Here, the artist depicts visual experiences he had while under the influence of LSD.

● **FIGURE 5.14** This thin slice of a rat's brain has been washed with a radioactive THC-like drug. Yellowish areas show where the brain is rich in THC receptors. In addition to the cortex, or outer layer of the brain, THC receptors are found in abundance in areas involved in the control of coordinated movement. Naturally occurring chemicals similar to THC may help the brain cope with pain and stress. However, when THC is used as a drug, high doses can cause paranoia, hallucinations, and dizziness (Julien, 2005).

for abuse lies primarily in the realm of psychological dependence, not physical addiction.

Dangers of Marijuana Use *There have been very alarming reports in the press about the dangers of marijuana. Are they accurate?* In the past it was widely reported that marijuana causes brain damage, genetic damage, and a loss of motivation. Each of these charges can be criticized for being based on poorly done or inconclusive research. But that doesn't mean that marijuana gets a clean bill of health. For about a day after a person smokes marijuana, his or her attention, coordination, and short-term memory are impaired (Pope, Gruber, & Yurgelun-Todd, 1995). Frequent marijuana users show small declines in learning, memory, attention, and thinking abilities (Solowij et al., 2002). When surveyed at age 29, nonusers are healthier, earn more, and are more satisfied with their lives than people who smoke marijuana regularly (Ellickson, Martino, & Collins, 2004).

People who smoke five or more joints a week score 4 points lower on IQ tests. This is enough to dull their learning capacity. In fact, many people who have stopped using marijuana say they quit because they were bothered by short-term memory loss and concentration problems. Fortunately, IQ scores and other cognitive measures rebound in about a month after a person quits using marijuana (Grant et al., 2001). In other words, people who smoke dope may act like dopes, but if they quit, there's a good chance they will regain their mental abilities.

Health Risks After many years of conflicting information, some of marijuana's health hazards are also being clarified. Marijuana's long-term effects include the following health risks.

1. Marijuana smoke contains 50 percent more cancer-causing hydrocarbons and 16 times more tar than tobacco smoke does. Thus, smoking several joints a week may be the equivalent of smoking a dozen cigarettes a day. In regular users, marijuana increases the risk of a variety of cancers, including prostate and cervical cancer (Hashibe, 2005).

2. Marijuana temporarily lowers sperm production in males, and users produce more abnormal sperm. This could be a problem for a man who is marginally fertile and wants to have a family (Schuel et al., 1999).

3. In experiments with female monkeys, THC causes abnormal menstrual cycles and disrupts ovulation. Other animal studies show that THC causes a higher rate of miscarriages and that it can reach the developing fetus. As is true for so many other drugs, it appears that marijuana should be avoided during pregnancy.

4. THC can suppress the body's immune system, increasing the risk of disease.

5. In animals, marijuana causes genetic damage within cells of the body. It is not known to what extent this happens in humans, but it does suggest that marijuana can be detrimental to health.

6. Activity levels in the cerebellum are lower than normal in marijuana abusers. This may explain why chronic marijuana users tend to show some loss of coordination (Volkow et al., 1996).

7. There is some evidence that THC damages parts of the brain important for memory (Chan et al., 1998).

8. Children whose mothers smoked marijuana during pregnancy show lowered ability to succeed in challenging, goal-oriented activities (Fried & Smith, 2001; Noland et al., 2005).

Although much is still unknown, marijuana appears to pose a wide range of health risks, as do two other potent drugs in widespread use—tobacco and alcohol. Only future research will tell for sure "what's in the pot."

Summary

Why is drug abuse such a common problem? People seek drug experiences for many reasons, ranging from curiosity and a desire to belong to a group, to a search for meaning or an escape from feelings of inadequacy. The best predictors of adolescent drug use and abuse are drug use by peers, parental

An outdated antimarijuana poster demonstrates the kind of misinformation that has long been attached to this drug. Research has finally begun to sort out what risks are associated with use of marijuana.

Hallucinogen A substance that alters or distorts sensory impressions.

drug use, delinquency, parental maladjustment, poor self-esteem, social nonconformity, and stressful life changes. One study found that adolescents who abuse drugs tend to be maladjusted, alienated, impulsive, and emotionally distressed (Masse & Tremblay, 1997). Antisocial behavior, school failure, and risky sexual behavior are also commonly associated with drug abuse (Ary et al., 1999). Such patterns make it clear that taking drugs is a symptom, rather than a cause, of personal and social maladjustment (Ksir, Hart, & Ray, 2006).

Many abusers turn to drugs in a self-defeating attempt to cope with life. All the frequently abused drugs produce immediate feelings of pleasure. The negative consequences follow much later. This combination of immediate pleasure and delayed punishment allows abusers to feel good on demand. In time, of course, most of the pleasure goes out of drug abuse and the abuser's problems get worse. But if an abuser merely feels better (however briefly) after taking a drug, drug taking can become compulsive (Higgins et al., 2004). In contrast, people who stop using drugs often say that they quit because the drawbacks had come to exceed the benefits (Toneatto et al., 1999).

Although billions of dollars have been spent on drug enforcement in recent years, there has been an increase in the overall level of drug use in the United States. Most drug use begins in early adolescence (Chen & Kandel, 1995). Given this fact, some experts believe that prevention through education and early intervention is the answer to drug problems (Julien, 2005). What do you think?

A Look Ahead

Of the many states of consciousness we have discussed, dreaming remains one of the most familiar—and the most surprising. Are there lessons to be learned from dreams? What personal insights lie hidden in the ebb and flow of your dream images? Let's find out in the upcoming Psychology in Action module.

MODULE 5.4 Summary

What are the effects of the more commonly used psychoactive drugs?

- A psychoactive drug is a substance that affects the brain in ways that alter consciousness. Most psychoactive drugs can be placed on a scale ranging from stimulation to depression.
- Drugs may cause a physical dependence (addiction) or a psychological dependence, or both. The physically addicting drugs are alcohol, amphetamines, barbiturates, cocaine, codeine, GHB, heroin, methadone, morphine, nicotine, and tranquilizers. All psychoactive drugs can lead to psychological dependence.
- Drug use can be classified as experimental, recreational, situational, intensive, and compulsive. Drug abuse is most often associated with the last three.
- Stimulant drugs are readily abused because of the period of depression that often follows stimulation. The greatest risks are associated with amphetamines (especially methamphetamine), cocaine, MDMA, and nicotine, but even caffeine can be a problem. Nicotine includes the added risk of lung cancer, heart disease, and other health problems.
- Barbiturates and tranquilizers are depressant drugs whose action is similar to that of alcohol.
- The overdose level for barbiturates and GHB is close to the intoxication dosage, making them dangerous drugs. Mixing barbiturates, tranquilizers, or GHB and alcohol may result in a fatal drug interaction.
- Alcohol is the most heavily abused drug in common use today. Binge drinking is a problem among college students. It is possible to pace the consumption of alcohol.
- Marijuana is subject to an abuse pattern similar to alcohol. Studies have linked chronic marijuana use with lung cancer, various mental impairments, and other health problems.

Well-crafted information and education can discourage drug use. This poster emphasizes the dangers of secondhand smoke. Research has shown that this is one of several issues that motivates children and adolescents to resist pressures to begin smoking.

KNOWLEDGE BUILDER

Psychoactive Drugs

Recite

1. Which of the drugs listed below are known to cause a physical dependence?
   a. heroin
   b. morphine
   c. codeine
   d. methadone
   e. barbiturates
   f. alcohol
   g. marijuana
   h. amphetamines
   i. nicotine
   j. cocaine
   k. GHB

2. Amphetamine psychosis is similar to extreme _____, in which the individual feels threatened and suffers from delusions.

3. Cocaine is very similar to which of the following in its effects on the central nervous system?
   a. Seconal
   b. codeine
   c. Cannabis
   d. amphetamine

4. Drug interaction is a special danger when a person combines
   a. marijuana and amphetamine
   b. barbiturates and alcohol
   c. alcohol and cocaine
   d. marijuana and THC

5. College students may overdrink as they try to keep up with how much they falsely imagine that their peers drink. T or F?

6. Treatment for alcohol dependence begins with sobering up the person and cutting off the supply. This is referred to as
   a. "hitting bottom"
   b. the crucial phase
   c. detoxification
   d. clinical anhedonia

7. Addictive drugs stimulate the brain's reward circuitry by affecting
   a. neurotransmitters
   b. alpha waves
   c. tryptophan levels
   d. delta spindles

Reflect
Critical Thinking

8. The U.S. government, which helps fund anti-smoking campaigns and smoking-related health research, also continues to subsidize tobacco growers. Can you explain this contradiction?

9. Why do you think there is such a contrast between the laws regulating marijuana and those regulating alcohol and tobacco?

Relate

What legal drugs did you use in the last year? Did any have psychoactive properties? How do psychoactive drugs differ from other substances in their potential for abuse?

Link

Internet addresses frequently change. To find the sites listed here, visit http://www.thomsonedu.com/psychology/coon for an updated list of Internet addresses and direct links to relevant sites.

- **Higher Education Center** The Higher Education Center's purpose is to help college and community leaders develop, implement, and evaluate programs and policies to reduce student problems related to alcohol and other drug use and interpersonal violence.
- **National Council on Alcoholism and Drug Dependence, Inc.** This site provides education, information, help, and hope to the public.
- **Drugs and Behavior Links** Comprehensive links to topics in drugs and behavior.

ANSWERS

1. All of them do. 2. paranoia 3. d 4. b 5. T 6. c 7. a 8. Neither can we. 9. Drug laws in Western societies reflect cultural values and historical patterns of use. Inconsistencies in the law often cannot be justified on the basis of pharmacology, health risks, or abuse potential.

MODULE **Psychology in Action**

5.5 Exploring and Using Dreams

SURVEY QUESTION: *How are dreams used to promote personal understanding?*

In many ways, dreams can be thought of as a message *from* yourself *to* yourself. Thus, the way to understand dreams is to remember them, write them down, look for the messages they contain, and become deeply acquainted with *your own* symbol system. Here's how:

HOW TO CATCH A DREAM

1. Before going to sleep, plan to remember your dreams. Keep a pen and paper or a tape recorder beside your bed.
2. If possible, arrange to awaken gradually without an alarm. Natural awakening almost always follows soon after a REM period.
3. If you rarely remember your dreams, you may want to set an alarm clock to go off an hour before you usually awaken. Although less desirable than awakening naturally, this may let you catch a dream.
4. Upon awakening, lie still and review the dream images with your eyes closed. Try to recall as many details as possible.
5. If you can, make your first dream record (whether by writing or by tape) with your eyes closed. Opening your eyes will disrupt dream recall.
6. Review the dream again and record as many additional details as you can remember. Dream memories disappear quickly. Be sure to describe feelings as well as the plot, characters, and actions of the dream.
7. Put your dreams into a permanent dream diary. Keep dreams in chronological order and review them periodically. This procedure will reveal recurrent themes, conflicts, and emotions. It almost always produces valuable insights.
8. Remember, a number of drugs suppress dreaming by interfering with REM sleep. (See Table 5.5.)

Dream Work

At one time or another almost everyone has had a dream that seemed to have deep meaning (Rock, 2004). Exploring everyday dream life can be a source of personal enrichment and personal growth (Cartwright & Lamberg, 1992). What strategies do psychologists use to interpret dreams? Let's start with Sigmund Freud's pioneering approach.

To unlock dreams, Freud identified four **dream processes,** or mental filters, that disguise the meanings of dreams. The

TABLE 5.5 Effects of Selected Drugs on Dreaming

DRUG	EFFECT ON REM SLEEP
Alcohol	Decrease
Amphetamines	Decrease
Barbiturates	Decrease
Caffeine	None
Cocaine	Decrease
LSD	Slight increase
Marijuana	Slight decrease or no effect
Opiates	Decrease
Valium	Decrease

first is **condensation,** in which several people, objects, or events are combined into a single dream image. A dream character that looks like a teacher, acts like your father, talks like your mother, and is dressed like your employer might be a condensation of authority figures in your life.

Displacement is a second way of disguising dream content. Displacement may cause important emotions or actions of a dream to be redirected toward safe or seemingly unimportant images. Thus, a student angry at his parents might dream of accidentally wrecking their car instead of directly attacking them.

A third dream process is **symbolization.** As mentioned earlier, Freud believed that dreams are often expressed in images that are symbolic rather than literal. That's why it helps to ask what feelings or ideas a dream image might symbolize. Let's say, for example, that a student dreams of coming to class naked. A literal interpretation would be that the student is an exhibitionist! A more likely symbolic meaning is that the student feels vulnerable or unprepared in the class.

Secondary elaboration is the fourth method by which dream meanings are disguised. **Secondary elaboration** is the tendency to make a dream more logical and to add details when remembering it. The fresher a dream memory is, the more useful it is likely to be.

Looking for condensation, displacement, symbolization, and secondary elaboration may help you unlock your dreams. But there are other techniques that may be more effective. Dream theorist Calvin Hall (1974) preferred to think of dreams as plays and the dreamer as a playwright. Although Hall points out that dream images and ideas tend to be more primitive than waking thoughts, much can be learned by

How would you try to find the meaning of this dream? A traditional approach is to look for symbolic messages, as well as literal meanings. If you find yourself wearing a mask in a dream, for instance, it could relate to important roles that you play at school, work, or home. It could also mean that you want to hide or that you are looking forward to a costume party. However, to accurately interpret a dream, it is important to learn your own "vocabulary" of dream images and meanings. Keeping a dream diary is the first step toward gaining valuable insights.

simply considering the *setting, cast of characters, plot,* and *emotions* portrayed in a dream.

Another dream theorist, Rosalind Cartwright, suggests that dreams are primarily "feeling statements." According to her, the overall *emotional tone* (underlying mood) of a dream is a major clue to its meaning (Cartwright & Lamberg, 1992). Is the dream comical, threatening, joyous, or depressing? Were you lonely, jealous, frightened, in love, or angry?

Because each dream has several possible meanings or levels of meaning, there is no fixed way to work with it. Telling the dream to others and discussing its meaning can be a good start. Describing it may help you relive some of the feelings in the dream. Also, family members or friends may be able to offer interpretations to which you would be blind. Watch for verbal or visual puns and other playful elements in dreams. For example, if you dream that you are in a wrestling match and your arm is pinned behind your back, it may mean that you feel someone is "twisting your arm" in real life.

The meaning of most dreams will yield to a little detective work. Try asking a series of questions about dreams you would like to understand:

PROBING DREAMS

1. Who was in the dream? Were there humans, animals, or mythical characters? Do you recognize any of the characters?
2. What social interactions were taking place? Were those interactions friendly? Aggressive? Sexual?
3. What activities were taking place? Were they physical activities or not?
4. Was there striving? Was the striving successful or not?
5. Was the dream about good fortune or misfortune?
6. What emotions were present in the dream? Was there anger, apprehension, confusion, happiness, or sadness?
7. What were the physical surroundings like? What was the setting? Were there any physical objects present? (Adapted from the Hall-Van de Castle system of dream content analysis; Domhoff, 2003.)

If you still have trouble seeing the meaning of a dream, you may find it helpful to use a technique developed by Fritz Perls. Perls, the originator of Gestalt therapy, considered most dreams a special message about what's missing in our lives, what we avoid doing, or feelings that need to be "re-owned." Perls believed that dreams are a way of filling in gaps in personal experience (Perls, 1969).

An approach that Perls found helpful is to "take the part of" or "speak for" each of the characters and objects in the dream. In other words, if you dream about a strange man standing behind a doorway, you would speak aloud to the man, then answer for him. To use Perls's method, you would even speak for the door, perhaps saying something like, "I am a barrier. I keep you safe, but I also keep you locked inside. The stranger has something to tell you. You must risk opening me to learn it."

A particularly interesting dream exercise is to continue a dream as waking fantasy so that it may be concluded or carried on to a more meaningful ending. As the world of dreams and your personal dream language become more familiar, you will doubtless find many answers, paradoxes, intuitions, and insights into your own behavior.

Using Your Dreams

It is possible to learn to use our dreams for our own purposes. For example, as mentioned previously (see Module 5.2), nightmare sufferers can use imagery rehearsal to modify their

Dream processes Mental filters that hide the true meanings of dreams.
Condensation Combining several people, objects, or events into a single dream image.
Displacement Directing emotions or actions toward safe or unimportant dream images.
Symbolization The nonliteral expression of dream content.
Secondary elaboration Making a dream more logical and complete while remembering it.

own nightmares (Germain et al., 2004; Krakow & Zadra, 2006). Similarly, it is possible to use your dreams to enhance creativity (Stickgold & Walker, 2004).

Dreams and Creativity

History is full of cases where dreams have been a pathway to creativity and discovery. A striking example is provided by Dr. Otto Loewi, a pharmacologist and winner of a Nobel Prize. Loewi had spent years studying the chemical transmission of nerve impulses. A tremendous breakthrough in his research came when he dreamed of an experiment three nights in a row. The first two nights he woke up and scribbled the experiment on a pad. But the next morning, he couldn't tell what the notes meant. On the third night, he got up after having the dream. This time, instead of making notes he went straight to his laboratory and performed the crucial experiment. Loewi later said that if the experiment had occurred to him while awake he would have rejected it.

Loewi's experience gives some insight into using dreams to produce creative solutions. Inhibitions are reduced during dreaming, which may be especially useful in solving problems that require a fresh point of view. Even unimaginative people may create amazing worlds each night in their dreams. For many of us, this rich ability to create is lost in the daily rush of sensory input.

Being able to take advantage of dreams for problem solving is improved if you "set" yourself before retiring. Before you go to bed, try to visualize or think intently about a problem you wish to solve. Steep yourself in the problem by stating it clearly and reviewing all relevant information. Then use the suggestions listed previously to catch your dreams. Although this method is not guaranteed to produce a novel solution or a new insight, it is certain to be an adventure. About half of a group of college students using the method for 1 week recalled a dream that helped them solve a personal problem (Barrett, 1993).

Lucid Dreaming If you would like to press further into the territory of dreams, you may want to learn lucid dreaming, a relatively rare but fascinating experience. During a **lucid dream** a person feels as if she or he is fully awake within the dream world and capable of normal thought and action. If you ask yourself, "Could this be a dream?" and answer "Yes," you are having a lucid dream (LaBerge, 2000; Holzinger, LaBerge, & Levitan, 2006).

Stephen LaBerge and his colleagues at the Stanford University Sleep Research Center have used a unique approach to show that lucid dreams are real and that they occur during REM sleep. In the sleep lab, lucid dreamers agree to make prearranged signals when they become aware they are dreaming. One such signal is to look up abruptly in a dream, causing a distinct upward eye movement. Another signal is to clench the right and left fists (in the dream) in a prearranged pattern. In other words, lucid dreamers can partially overcome REM sleep paralysis. Such signals show very clearly that lucid dreaming and voluntary action in dreams is possible (LaBerge, 2000).

How can a person learn to have lucid dreams? Try following this simple routine: When you awaken spontaneously from a dream, take a few minutes to try to memorize it. Next, engage in 10 to 15 minutes of reading or any other activity requiring full wakefulness. Then while lying in bed and returning to sleep, say to yourself, "Next time I'm dreaming, I want to remember I'm dreaming." Finally, visualize yourself lying in bed asleep while in the dream you just rehearsed. At the same time, picture yourself realizing that you are dreaming. Follow this routine each time you awaken (substitute a dream memory from another occasion if you don't awaken from a dream). Researchers have also found that stimulation from the vestibular system tends to increase lucidity. Thus, sleeping in a hammock, a boat, or on a waterbed might increase the number of lucid dreams you have (Leslie & Ogilvie, 1996).

Why would anyone want to have more lucid dreams? Researchers are interested in lucid dreams because they provide a tool for understanding dreaming (Paulsson & Parker, 2006). Using subjects who can signal while they are dreaming makes it possible to explore dreams with firsthand data from the dreamer's world itself.

On a more personal level, lucid dreaming can convert dreams into a nightly "workshop" for emotional growth. Consider, for example, a recently divorced woman who kept dreaming that she was being swallowed by a giant wave. Rosalind Cartwright asked the woman to try swimming the next time the wave engulfed her. She did, with great determination, and the nightmare lost its terror. More important, her revised dream made her feel that she could cope with life again. For reasons such as this, people who have lucid dreams tend to feel a sense of emotional well-being (Wolpin et al., 1992). Dream expert Allan Hobson believes that learning to voluntarily enter altered states of consciousness (through lucid dreaming or self-hypnosis, for example) has allowed him to have enlightening experiences without the risks of taking mind-altering drugs (Hobson, 2001). So, day or night, don't be afraid to dream a little.

KNOWLEDGE BUILDER

Exploring and Using Dreams

Recite

1. Which is NOT one of the four dream processes identified by Freud?
   a. condensation
   b. lucidity
   c. displacement
   d. symbolization
2. In secondary elaboration, one dream character stands for several others. T or F?
3. Calvin Hall's approach to dream interpretation emphasizes the setting, cast, plot, and emotions portrayed in a dream. T or F?
4. Rosalind Cartwright stresses that dreaming is a relatively mechanical process having little personal meaning. T or F?
5. Both alcohol and LSD cause a slight increase in dreaming. T or F?
6. "Taking the part of" or "speaking for" dream elements is a dream interpretation technique originated by Fritz Perls. T or F?
7. Recent research shows that lucid dreaming occurs primarily during NREM sleep or microawakenings. T or F?

Reflect
Critical Thinking

8. The possibility of having a lucid dream raises an interesting question: If you were dreaming right now, how could you prove it?

Relate

Some people are very interested in remembering and interpreting their dreams. Others pay little attention to dreaming. What importance do you place on dreams? Do you think dreams and dream interpretation can increase self-awareness?

Link

Internet addresses frequently change. To find the sites listed here, visit **http://www.thomsonedu.com/psychology/coon** for an updated list of Internet addresses and direct links to relevant sites.

- **Dreams and Lucid Dreams** Provides links to frequently asked questions and articles regarding dreaming and lucid dreams.
- **Dream Dictionary** One attempt to provide standardized interpretations of common dream symbols.
- **How to Keep a Diary of Dreams** Find out how to keep your own dream diary.

ANSWERS

1. b 2. F 3. T 4. F 5. F 6. T 7. F 8. In waking consciousness, our actions have consequences that produce immediate sensory feedback. Dreams lack such external feedback. Thus, trying to walk through a wall or doing similar tests would reveal if you were dreaming.

MODULE 5.5 Summary

How are dreams used to promote personal understanding?

- Freud held that the meaning of dreams is hidden by condensation, displacement, symbolization, and secondary elaboration. Hall emphasizes the setting, cast, plot, and emotions of a dream. Cartwright's view of dreams as feeling statements and Perls's technique of speaking for dream elements are also helpful.
- Dreams may be used for creative problem solving, especially when dream awareness is achieved through lucid dreaming.

Interactive Learning

Psychology: Active Learning Modules Book Companion Website

http://www.thomsonedu.com/psychology/coon

Visit your book companion website, where you will find flash cards, practice quizzes, Internet links, and more to help you study.

ThomsonNOW

Just What You Need to Know NOW!

Spend time on what you need to master rather than on information you already have learned. Take a pre-test for this chapter, and ThomsonNOW will generate a personalized study plan based on your results. The study plan will identify the topics you need to review and direct you to online resources to help you master those topics. You can then take a post-test to help you determine the concepts you have mastered and what you will need to work on. Try it out! Go to **www.thomsonedu.com/login** to sign in with an access code or to purchase access to this product.

Lucid dream A dream in which the dreamer feels awake and capable of normal thought and action.

6 Conditioning and Learning

MODULE 6.1 Learning and Classical Conditioning
SURVEY QUESTION: What is learning?
SURVEY QUESTION: How does classical conditioning occur?
SURVEY QUESTION: Does conditioning affect emotions?

MODULE 6.2 Operant Conditioning
SURVEY QUESTION: How does operant conditioning occur?
SURVEY QUESTION: Are there different kinds of operant reinforcement?

MODULE 6.3 Partial Reinforcement and Stimulus Control
SURVEY QUESTION: How are we influenced by patterns of reward?

MODULE 6.4 Punishment
SURVEY QUESTION: What does punishment do to behavior?

MODULE 6.5 Cognitive Learning and Imitation
SURVEY QUESTION: What is cognitive learning?
SURVEY QUESTION: Does learning occur by imitation?

MODULE 6.6 Psychology in Action: Behavioral Self-Management—A Rewarding Project
SURVEY QUESTION: How does conditioning apply to practical problems?

What Did You Learn in School Today?

When one of your authors was in college, he and other students discovered an intriguing flaw in the dorm plumbing: Flush a toilet while someone was taking a shower and the cold water pressure would suddenly drop. This caused the shower to become scalding hot. Naturally, the shower victim screamed in terror as his reflexes caused him to leap backward in pain. Soon it was discovered that if *all* the toilets were flushed at once, the effects were multiplied many times over!

A toilet has to be one of the world's most uninspiring stimuli. But for a time, a whole flock of college students twitched involuntarily whenever they heard a toilet flush. Their reactions were the result of classical conditioning, a basic type of learning. Classical conditioning is one of the topics of this chapter.

Now, let's say that you are at school and you feel like you are "starving to death." You locate a vending machine and deposit your last bit of change to buy a candy bar. Then you press the button, and . . . nothing happens. Being civilized and in complete control, you press the other buttons, try the coin return, and look for an attendant. Still nothing. Your stomach growls. Impulsively, you give the machine a little kick (just to let it know how you feel). Then, as you turn away, out pops a candy bar plus 75 cents change. Once this happens, chances are good that you will repeat the "kicking response" in the future. If it pays off several times more, kicking vending machines may become a regular feature of your behavior. In this case, learning is based on operant conditioning (also called instrumental learning).

Classical and operant conditioning reach into every corner of our lives. Are you ready to learn more about learning? If so, read on!

David R. Frazier/PhotoEdit

MODULE 6.1 Learning and Classical Conditioning

MOST BEHAVIOR is learned. Imagine if you suddenly lost all you had ever learned. What could you do? You would be unable to read, write, or speak. You couldn't feed yourself, find your way home, drive a car, play the bassoon, or "party." Needless to say, you would be totally incapacitated. (Dull, too!) How do the most fundamental types of learning occur?

What Is Learning—Does Practice Make Perfect?

SURVEY QUESTION: *What is learning?*

Learning is a relatively permanent change in behavior due to experience (Domjan, 2006). Notice that this definition excludes temporary changes caused by motivation, fatigue, maturation, disease, injury, or drugs. Each of these can alter behavior, but none qualifies as learning.

Isn't learning the result of practice? It depends on what you mean by practice. Merely repeating a response will not necessarily produce learning. You could close your eyes and swing a tennis racket hundreds of times without learning anything about tennis. Reinforcement is the key to learning. **Reinforcement** refers to any event that increases the probability that a response will occur again. A response is any identifiable behavior. Responses may be observable actions, such as blinking, eating a piece of candy, or turning a doorknob. They can also be internal, such as having a faster heartbeat.

To teach a dog a trick, we could reinforce correct responses by giving the dog some food each time it sits up. Similarly, you could teach a child to be neat by praising him for picking up his toys. Learning can also occur in other ways. For instance, if a girl gets stung by a bee, she may learn to associate pain with bees and to fear them. In this case, the girl's fear is reinforced by the discomfort she feels immediately after seeing the bee. Later, you'll discover how such varied experiences lead to learning.

Antecedents and Consequences Unlocking the secrets of learning begins with noting what happens before and after a response. Events that precede a response are called **antecedents.** For example, Ashleigh, who is 3, has learned that when she hears a truck pull into the driveway, it means that daddy is home. Ashleigh runs to the front door, where she gets a hug from her father. Effects that follow a response are **consequences.** The hug is what reinforces Ashleigh's tendency to run to the door. As this suggests, paying careful attention to the "before and after" of learning is a key to understanding it.

Classical Conditioning

Classical conditioning is based on what happens before we respond. It begins with a stimulus that reliably triggers a response. Imagine, for example, that a puff of air (the stimulus) is aimed at your eye. The air puff will make you blink (a response) every time. The eye blink is a **reflex** (automatic, nonlearned response).

Now, assume that we sound a horn (another stimulus) just before each puff of air hits your eye. If the horn and the air puff occur together many times, what happens? Soon, the horn alone will make you blink. Clearly, you've learned something. Before, the horn didn't make you blink. Now it does. Similarly, if your mouth waters each time you eat a cookie, you may learn to salivate when you merely *see* a cookie, a picture of cookies, a cookie jar, or other stimuli that preceded salivation.

In **classical conditioning,** an antecedent stimulus that doesn't produce a response is linked with one that does (a horn is associated with a puff of air to the eye, for example). We can say that learning has occurred when the new stimulus will also *elicit* (bring forth) responses (● Fig. 6.1).

Operant Conditioning

In **operant conditioning,** learning is based on the consequences of responding. A response may be followed by a reinforcer (such as food). Or by punishment. Or by nothing.

● **FIGURE 6.1** In classical conditioning, a stimulus that does not produce a response is paired with a stimulus that does elicit a response. After many such pairings, the stimulus that previously had no effect begins to produce a response. In the example shown, a horn precedes a puff of air to the eye. Eventually the horn alone will produce an eye blink. In operant conditioning, a response that is followed by a reinforcing consequence becomes more likely to occur on future occasions. In the example shown, a dog learns to sit up when it hears a whistle.

These results determine whether a response is likely to be made again. (See Fig. 6.1.) For example, if you wear a particular hat and get lots of compliments (reinforcement), you are likely to wear it more often. If people snicker, insult you, call the police, or scream (punishment), you will probably wear it less often.

Now that you have an idea of what happens in the two basic kinds of learning, let's look at classical conditioning in more detail.

Classical Conditioning—Does the Name Pavlov Ring a Bell?

SURVEY QUESTION: *How does classical conditioning occur?*

At the beginning of the twentieth century, something happened in the lab of Russian physiologist Ivan Pavlov that brought him the Nobel Prize: Pavlov's subjects drooled at him.

Actually, Pavlov was studying digestion. To observe salivation, he placed meat powder or some tidbit on a dog's tongue. After doing this many times, Pavlov noticed that his dogs were salivating *before* the food reached their mouths (Schultz & Schultz, 2005). Later, the dogs even began to salivate when they saw Pavlov enter the room. Was this misplaced affection? Pavlov knew better. Salivation is normally a reflex. For the animals to salivate at the mere sight of food, some type of learning must have occurred. Pavlov called it conditioning (● Fig. 6.2). Because of its importance in psychology's history, it is now called classical conditioning (also known as *Pavlovian conditioning* or *respondent conditioning*) (Mackintosh, 2003).

Pavlov's Experiment

How did Pavlov study conditioning? After Pavlov observed that food made his dogs salivate, he began his classic experiments. (See Fig. 6.2.) To begin, he rang a bell. At first, the bell was a neutral stimulus (the dogs did not respond to it by salivating). Immediately after Pavlov rang the bell, he placed meat powder on the dog's tongue, which caused reflex salivation. This sequence was repeated a number of times: bell, meat powder, salivation; bell, meat powder, salivation. Eventually (as conditioning took place), the dogs began to salivate when they heard the bell (● Fig. 6.3). By association, the bell, which before had no effect, began to evoke the same response that food did. This was shown by sometimes ringing the bell alone. Then the dog salivated even though no food had been placed in its mouth.

Psychologists use several terms to describe these events. The meat powder is an **unconditioned stimulus (US)** (a stimulus innately capable of producing a response; salivation in this case). Notice that the dog did not have to learn to respond to the US. Such stimuli naturally trigger reflexes or emotional reactions. Because a reflex is innate, or "built in," it is called an **unconditioned** (nonlearned) **response (UR).** Reflex salivation was the UR in Pavlov's experiment.

The bell starts out as a **neutral stimulus (NS).** In time, the bell becomes a **conditioned stimulus (CS)** (a stimulus that, because of learning, will elicit a response). When Pavlov's bell also produced salivation, the dog was making a new response. Thus, salivation had also become a **conditioned** (learned) **response (CR).** (See Fig. 6.3.) ■ Table 6.1 summarizes the important elements of classical conditioning.

Are all these terms really necessary? Yes, because they help us recognize similarities in various instances of learning. Let's summarize the terms, using an earlier example:

BEFORE CONDITIONING	EXAMPLE
US → UR	Puff of air → eye blink
NS → no effect	Horn → no effect
AFTER CONDITIONING	**EXAMPLE**
CS → CR	Horn → eye blink

Learning Any relatively permanent change in behavior that can be attributed to experience.

Reinforcement Any event that increases the probability that a particular response will occur.

Antecedents Events that precede a response.

Consequences Effects that follow a response.

Reflex An innate, automatic response to a stimulus; for example, an eye blink.

Classical conditioning A form of learning in which reflex responses are associated with new stimuli.

Operant conditioning Learning based on the consequences of responding.

Unconditioned stimulus A stimulus innately capable of eliciting a response.

Unconditioned response An innate reflex response elicited by an unconditioned stimulus.

Neutral stimulus A stimulus that does not evoke a response.

Conditioned stimulus A stimulus that evokes a response because it has been repeatedly paired with an unconditioned stimulus.

Conditioned response A learned response elicited by a conditioned stimulus.

● **FIGURE 6.2** An apparatus for Pavlovian conditioning. A tube carries saliva from the dog's mouth to a lever that activates a recording device (far left). During conditioning, various stimuli can be paired with a dish of food placed in front of the dog. The device pictured here is more elaborate than the one Pavlov used in his early experiments.

● **FIGURE 6.3** The classical conditioning procedure.

■ TABLE 6.1	Elements of Classical Conditioning		
ELEMENT	**SYMBOL**	**DESCRIPTION**	**EXAMPLE**
Unconditioned stimulus	US	A stimulus innately capable of eliciting a response	Meat powder
Unconditioned response	UR	An innate reflex response elicited by an unconditioned stimulus	Reflex salivation
Neutral stimulus NS		A stimulus that does not evoke a response	Bell
Conditioned stimulus	CS	A stimulus that evokes a response because it has been repeatedly paired with an unconditioned stimulus	Bell
Conditioned response	CR	A learned response elicited by a conditioned stimulus	Salivation

Now let's see if we can explain the shower and flushing toilet example described earlier. The unconditioned, or non-learned, response (UR) was a reflex jump from the hot water. The unconditioned stimulus (US) was the hot water. The conditioned stimulus (CS) was the sound of a flushing toilet. That is, the flushing sound was at first neutral. But as a result of conditioning, it became capable of triggering a learned reflex. See "Coping with Chemo" for an example of how classical conditioning is being used to solve a clinical problem.

● **FIGURE 6.4** Acquisition and extinction of a conditioned response. (Adapted from Pavlov, 1927.)

Principles of Classical Conditioning— The Boy and the Bell

Imagine a boy named Johnny. To observe conditioning, you could ring a bell and squirt lemon juice into Johnny's mouth. By repeating this procedure several times, you could condition Johnny to salivate to the bell. Johnny might then be used to explore other aspects of classical conditioning. Let's see how conditioning occurs.

Acquisition

During **acquisition,** or training, a conditioned response must be reinforced (strengthened) (● Fig. 6.4). Classical conditioning is *reinforced* when the CS is followed by, or paired with, an unconditioned stimulus. This type of reinforcement is known as **respondent reinforcement**. For Johnny, the bell is the CS, salivating is the UR, and the sour lemon juice is a US. To reinforce salivating to the bell, we must link the bell with the lemon juice. Conditioning will be most rapid if the US (lemon juice) follows *immediately* after the CS (the bell). With most reflexes, the optimal delay between CS and US is from one-half second to about 5 seconds (Chance, 2006).

Higher Order Conditioning Once a response is learned, it can bring about **higher order conditioning.** In this case, a well-learned CS is used to reinforce further learning. That is, the CS has become strong enough to be used like an unconditioned stimulus. Let's illustrate again with our salivating child.

As a result of earlier learning, the bell now makes Johnny salivate. (No lemon juice is needed.) To go a step further, you

THE CLINICAL FILE
Coping with Chemo

Our hearts go out to children with cancer. Even the treatment, chemotherapy, makes them miserable because it causes nausea and vomiting. In a cruel twist, after a few treatments, nausea can occur even when no chemotherapy is scheduled. Typically, it is triggered by certain sights or tastes, like the sight of the treatment center or the taste of a food the child ate before an earlier chemotherapy session.

In classical conditioning terms, chemotherapy is a US that leads to nausea, which is a UR. The sight of the treatment center or the taste of food eaten before treatment is initially a neutral stimulus that becomes associated with nausea and vomiting, making it a CS. These sights or tastes can now elicit anticipatory nausea (a CR) even at times when the child doesn't receive chemotherapy (Chance, 2006).

In nature, many species are *biologically prepared* to associate specific locations and tastes with nausea. If animals eat contaminated food and then get sick and vomit, later the same locations or tastes may trigger anticipatory nausea and vomiting. These reactions discourage animals from eating potentially dangerous food. Unfortunately, conditioned nausea only complicates treatment for young cancer patients. If Gita eats pepperoni pizza, her favorite meal, before she has a chemotherapy session, the taste of pizza may come to make her feel sick.

Is there any way to prevent conditioned nausea? No, but classical conditioning can provide some relief (Taylor, 2002). Meals eaten before chemotherapy can be strongly flavored with an unusual taste, such as peppermint. The unique flavor overshadows other tastes, which don't become linked with nausea (Bovbjerg et al., 1992). In this way, Gita can continue to enjoy her pepperoni pizza, because the nausea becomes conditioned to the unusual taste.

● **FIGURE 6.5** Higher order conditioning takes place when a well-learned conditioned stimulus is used as if it were an unconditioned stimulus. In this example, a child is first conditioned to salivate to the sound of a bell. In time, the bell will elicit salivation. At that point, you could clap your hands and then ring the bell. Soon, after repeating the procedure, the child would learn to salivate when you clapped your hands.

tisers use this effect by pairing images that evoke good feelings (such as people smiling and having fun) with pictures of their products. They hope that you will learn, by association, to feel good when you see their products (Priluck & Till, 2004).

Expectancies

Many psychologists believe that classical conditioning is related to information that might aid survival. According to this **informational view,** we look for associations among events. Doing so creates new mental **expectancies,** or expectations about how events are interconnected.

How does classical conditioning alter expectancies? Notice that the conditioned stimulus reliably precedes the unconditioned stimulus. Because it does, the CS *predicts* the US (Rescorla, 1987). During conditioning, the brain learns to *expect* that the US will follow the CS. As a result, the brain prepares the body to respond to the US. Here's an example: When you are about to get a shot with a hypodermic needle,

could clap your hands and then ring the bell. (Again, no lemon juice would be used.) Through higher order conditioning, Johnny would soon learn to salivate when you clapped your hands (● Fig. 6.5). (This little trick could be a real hit with friends and neighbors.)

Higher order conditioning extends learning one or more steps beyond the original conditioned stimulus. Many adver-

Acquisition The period in conditioning during which a response is reinforced.
Respondent reinforcement Reinforcement that occurs when an unconditioned stimulus closely follows a conditioned stimulus.
Higher order conditioning Classical conditioning in which a conditioned stimulus is used to reinforce further learning; that is, a CS is used as if it were a US.
Informational view Perspective that explains learning in terms of information imparted by events in the environment.
Expectancy An anticipation concerning future events or relationships.

your muscles tighten and there is a catch in your breathing. Why? Because your body is preparing for pain. You have learned to expect that getting poked with a needle will hurt. This expectancy, which was acquired during classical conditioning, changes your behavior.

Extinction and Spontaneous Recovery

After conditioning has occurred, what would happen if the US no longer followed the CS? If the US never again follows the CS, conditioning will extinguish, or fade away. Let's return to the boy and the bell. If you ring the bell many times and do not follow it with lemon juice, Johnny's expectancy that "bell precedes lemon juice" will weaken. As it does, he will lose his tendency to salivate when he hears the bell. Thus, we see that classical conditioning can be weakened by removing the connection between the conditioned and unconditioned stimulus. (See Fig. 6.4.) This process is called **extinction.**

If conditioning takes a while to build up, shouldn't it take time to reverse? Yes. In fact, it may take several extinction sessions to completely reverse conditioning. Let's say that we ring the bell until Johnny quits responding. It might seem that extinction is complete. However, Johnny will probably respond to the bell again on the following day, at least at first (Rescorla, 2004). The return of a learned response after apparent extinction is called **spontaneous recovery.** It explains why people who have had car accidents may need many slow, calm rides before their fear of driving extinguishes.

Generalization

After conditioning, other stimuli similar to the CS may also trigger a response. This is called **stimulus generalization.** For example, we might find that Johnny salivates to the sound of a ringing telephone or doorbell, even though they were never used as conditioning stimuli.

It is easy to see the value of stimulus generalization. Consider the child who burns her finger while playing with matches. Most likely, lighted matches will become conditioned fear stimuli for her. But will she fear only matches? Because of stimulus generalization, she may also have a healthy fear of flames from lighters, fireplaces, stoves, and so forth. It's fortunate that generalization extends learning to related situations. Otherwise, we would all be far less adaptable.

As you may have guessed, stimulus generalization has limits. As stimuli become less like the original CS, responding decreases. If you condition a person to blink each time you play a particular note on a piano, blinking will decline as you play higher or lower notes. If the notes are *much* higher or lower, the person will not respond at all (● Fig. 6.6). Stimulus generalization explains why many stores carry imitations of nationally known products. For many customers, positive attitudes conditioned to the real products tend to generalize to the cheaper knockoffs (Till & Priluck, 2000).

Discrimination

Let's consider one more idea with Johnny (who by now must be ready to hide in the closet). Suppose we again condition Johnny, with a bell as the CS. As an experiment, we occasionally sound a buzzer instead of ringing the bell. However, the buzzer is never followed by the US (lemon juice). At first, Johnny salivates when he hears the buzzer (because of generalization). But after we sound the buzzer several times more, Johnny will stop responding to it. Why? In essence, Johnny's generalized response to the buzzer has extinguished. As a result, he has learned to *discriminate,* or respond differently, to the bell and the buzzer.

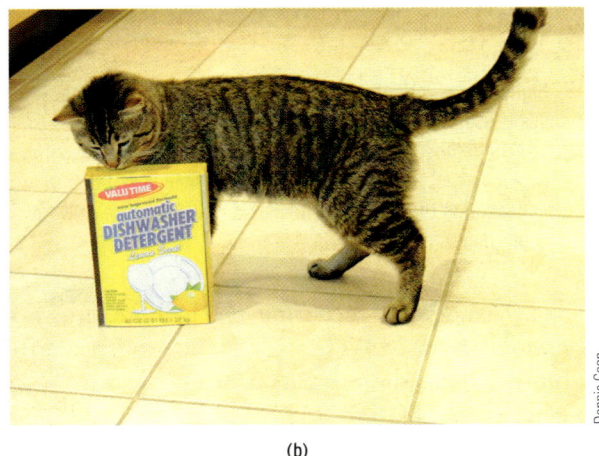

● **FIGURE 6.6** *(a)* Stimulus generalization. Stimuli similar to the CS also elicit a response. *(b)* This cat has learned to salivate when it sees a cat food box. Because of stimulus generalization, it also salivates when shown a similar-looking detergent box.

Stimulus discrimination is the ability to respond differently to various stimuli. As an example, you might remember the feelings of anxiety or fear you had as a child when your mother's or father's voice changed to its you're-in-a-heap-of-trouble tone. (Or the dreaded give-me-that-Wii-controller tone.) Most children quickly learn to discriminate voice tones associated with punishment from those associated with praise or affection.

Classical Conditioning in Humans— An Emotional Topic

SURVEY QUESTION: *Does conditioning affect emotions?*

How much human learning is based on classical conditioning? At its simplest, classical conditioning depends on unconditioned reflex responses. As mentioned earlier, a reflex is a dependable, inborn stimulus-and-response connection. For example, your hand reflexively draws back from pain. Bright light causes the pupil of the eye to narrow. A puff of air directed at your eye will make you blink. Various foods elicit salivation. Any of these reflexes, and others as well, can be associated with a new stimulus. At the very least, you have probably noticed how your mouth waters when you see or smell a bakery. Even pictures of food may make you salivate (a photo of a sliced lemon is great for this).

Conditioned Emotional Responses

In addition to simple reflexes, more complex *emotional*, or "gut," responses may be linked to new stimuli. For instance, if your face reddened when you were punished as a child, you may blush now when you are embarrassed or ashamed. Or think about the effects of associating pain with a dentist's office during your first visit. On later visits, did your heart pound and your palms sweat *before* the dentist began?

Many *involuntary*, autonomic nervous system responses ("fight-or-flight" reflexes) are linked with new stimuli and situations by classical conditioning. For example, learned reactions worsen many cases of hypertension (high blood pressure). Traffic jams, arguments with a spouse, and similar situations can become conditioned stimuli that trigger a dangerous rise in blood pressure (Reiff, Katkin, & Friedman, 1999).

Of course, emotional conditioning also applies to animals. One of the most common mistakes people make with pets (especially dogs) is hitting them if they do not come when called. Calling the animal then becomes a conditioned stimulus for fear and withdrawal. No wonder the pet disobeys when called on future occasions. Parents who belittle, scream at, or physically abuse their children make the same mistake.

Learned Fears Some phobias (FOE-bee-ahs) are also based on emotional conditioning. A *phobia* is a fear that persists even when no realistic danger exists. Fears of animals, water, heights, thunder, fire, bugs, elevators, and the like are common. Psychologists believe that many phobias begin as **conditioned emotional responses** (**CERs**), learned emotional reactions to a previously neutral stimulus. People who have phobias can often trace their fears to a time when they were frightened, injured, or upset by a particular stimulus, especially in childhood (King, Muris, & Ollendick, 2005). Just one bad experience in which you were frightened or disgusted by a spider may condition fears that last for years (de Jong & Muris, 2002).

Stimulus generalization and higher order conditioning can spread CERs to other stimuli (Gewirtz & Davis, 1998). As a result, what began as a limited fear may become a disabling phobia (● Fig. 6.7). However, a therapy called *desensitization* is now widely used to extinguish fears, anxieties, and phobias. This is done by gradually exposing the phobic person to feared stimuli while she or he remains calm and relaxed. For example, people have been desensitized for acrophobia (fear of heights) through *virtual reality exposure*, the use of computers to safely simulate, in this case, the experience of heights (Wiederhold & Wiederhold, 2005). (See Modules 13.3 & 13.4 for more information about therapies based on learning principles.)

Undoubtedly, we acquire many of our likes, dislikes, and fears as conditioned emotional responses. As noted before, advertisers try to achieve the same effect by pairing products with pleasant images and music. So do many students on a first date.

Vicarious, or Secondhand, Conditioning

Conditioning also occurs indirectly, which adds to its impact on us. Let's say, for example, that you watch another person get an electric shock. Each time, a signal light comes on before the shock is delivered. Even if you don't receive a shock yourself, you will soon develop a CER to the light. Children who learn to fear thunder by watching their parents react to it have un-

---

Extinction The weakening of a conditioned response through removal of reinforcement.

Spontaneous recovery The reappearance of a learned response after its apparent extinction.

Stimulus generalization The tendency to respond to stimuli similar to, but not identical to, a conditioned stimulus.

Stimulus discrimination The learned ability to respond differently to similar stimuli.

Conditioned emotional response (CER) An emotional response that has been linked to a previously nonemotional stimulus by classical conditioning.

● **FIGURE 6.7** Hypothetical example of a CER becoming a phobia. Child approaches dog (a) and is frightened by it (b). Fear generalizes to other household pets (c) and later to virtually all furry animals (d).

dergone similar conditioning. Many Americans were traumatized as a consequence of watching media coverage of the September 11 terrorist attacks in New York and Washington (Blanchard et al., 2004). Similarly, people who counsel traumatized victims of sexual abuse can themselves develop vicarious trauma (Rothschild & Rand, 2006; Way et al., 2004).

Vicarious classical conditioning occurs when we learn to respond emotionally to a stimulus by observing another person's emotional reactions. Such "secondhand" learning affects feelings in many situations. For example, "horror" movies filled with screaming actors probably add to fears of snakes, caves, spiders, heights, and other terrors. If movies can affect us, we might expect the emotions of parents, friends, and relatives to have even more impact. How, for instance, does a city child learn to fear snakes and respond emotionally to mere pictures of them? Being told that "snakes are dangerous" may not explain the child's *emotional* response. More likely, the child has observed others reacting fearfully to the word *snake* or to snake images on television (King, Muris, & Ollendick, 2005).

The emotional attitudes we develop toward foods, political parties, ethnic groups, escalators—whatever—are probably conditioned not only by direct experiences, but vicariously as well. No one is born prejudiced—all attitudes are learned. Parents may do well to look in a mirror if they wonder how or where a child "picked up" a particular fear or emotional attitude.

MODULE **6.1 Summary**

What is learning?
- Learning is a relatively permanent change in behavior due to experience. Learning depends on reinforcement, which increases the probability that a particular response will occur.
- Classical conditioning and operant conditioning are responsible for basic learning capacity in humans and animals.
- In classical conditioning, a neutral stimulus is followed by an unconditioned stimulus. With repeated pairings, the neutral stimulus begins to elicit a response.
- In operant conditioning, responses that are followed by reinforcement occur more frequently.

How does classical conditioning occur?
- Classical conditioning, studied by Pavlov, occurs when a neutral stimulus (NS) is associated with an unconditioned stimulus (US).
- The US triggers a reflex called the unconditioned response (UR). If the NS is consistently paired with the US, it becomes a conditioned stimulus (CS). After conditioning, a CS is capable of producing a conditioned (learned) response (CR).
- When the conditioned stimulus is followed by the unconditioned stimulus, conditioning is reinforced (strengthened).
- When the CS is repeatedly presented alone, conditioning is extinguished (weakened or inhibited).
- In classical conditioning, the CS creates an expectancy that the US will follow, which alters behavior.
- In higher order conditioning, a well-learned conditioned stimulus is used as if it were an unconditioned stimulus, which leads to further learning.
- Through stimulus generalization, stimuli similar to the conditioned stimulus will also produce a response. Stimulus discrimination occurs when we learn to respond to a particular stimulus, but not to others that are similar.

Does conditioning affect emotions?
- Conditioning applies to visceral or emotional responses as well as simple reflexes. As a result, conditioned emotional responses (CERs) also occur.
- Irrational fears called phobias may begin as CERs. Conditioning of emotional responses can occur vicariously (secondhand) as well as directly.

KNOWLEDGE BUILDER

Learning and Classical Conditioning

Recite

1. The concept of reinforcement applies to both
   a. antecedents and consequences
   b. neutral stimuli and rewards
   c. classical and operant conditioning
   d. acquisition and spontaneous recovery
2. Classical conditioning, studied by the Russian physiologist _____, is also referred to as _____ conditioning.
3. You smell the odor of cookies being baked and your mouth waters. Apparently, the odor of cookies is a _____ and your salivation is a _____.
   a. CR, CS
   b. CS, CR
   c. consequence, neutral stimulus
   d. reflex, CS
4. The informational view says that classical conditioning is based on changes in mental _____ about the CS and US.
5. After you have acquired a conditioned response, it may be weakened by
   a. spontaneous recovery
   b. stimulus generalization
   c. removing reinforcement
   d. following the CS with a US
6. When a conditioned stimulus is used to reinforce the learning of a second conditioned stimulus, higher order conditioning has occurred. T or F?
7. Psychologists theorize that many phobias begin when a CER generalizes to other, similar situations. T or F?
8. Three-year-old Josh sees his 5-year-old sister get chased by a neighbor's dog. Now Josh is as afraid of the dog as his sister is. Josh's fear is a result of
   a. stimulus discrimination
   b. vicarious conditioning
   c. spontaneous recovery
   d. higher order conditioning

Reflect
Critical Thinking

9. Lately you have been getting a shock of static electricity every time you touch a door handle. Now there is a hesitation in your door-opening movements. Can you analyze this situation in terms of classical conditioning?

Relate

US, CS, UR, CR—How will you remember these terms? First, you should note that we are interested in either a stimulus (S) or a response (R). What else do we need to know? Each S or R can be either conditioned (C) or unconditioned (U).

Can a stimulus provoke a response before any learning has occurred? If it can, then it's a US. Do you have to learn to respond to the stimulus? Then it's a CS.

Does a response occur without being learned? Then it's a UR. If it has to be learned, then it's a CR.

Link

Internet addresses frequently change. To find the sites listed here, visit http://www.thomsonedu.com/psychology/coon for an updated list of Internet addresses and direct links to relevant sites.

- **Ivan Pavlov** Read a short biography of the man who discovered classical conditioning.
- **Classical Conditioning Experiment** Try this demonstration of classical conditioning.
- **Conditioned Emotional Responses** Read the classic 1920 paper on Little Albert.

ANSWERS

1. c 2. Pavlov, respondent 3. b 4. expectancies 5. c 6. T 7. T 8. b 9. Door handles have become conditioned stimuli that elicit the reflex withdrawal and muscle tensing that normally follows getting a shock. This conditioned response has also generalized to other handles.

Vicarious classical conditioning Classical conditioning brought about by observing another person react to a particular stimulus.

MODULE 6.2 Operant Conditioning

THE PRINCIPLES of operant learning are among the most powerful tools in psychology. You won't regret learning how to use them. Operant conditioning applies to all living creatures and explains much day-to-day behavior. Operant conditioning can be used to alter the behavior of pets, children, and other adults, and your own behavior, too.

Operant Conditioning— Can Pigeons Play Ping-Pong?

SURVEY QUESTION: *How does operant conditioning occur?*

As stated earlier, in **operant conditioning** (or instrumental learning) we associate responses with their consequences. The basic principle is simple: Acts that are reinforced tend to be repeated (Mazur, 2006). Pioneer learning theorist Edward L. Thorndike called this the **law of effect**; the probability of a response is altered by the effect it has (Schultz & Schultz, 2005). Learning is strengthened each time a response is followed by a satisfying state of affairs. Think of the earlier example of the vending machine. Because kicking the machine had the effect of producing food and money, the odds of repeating the "kicking response" increased. Likewise, if you like jokes, you are much more likely to tell a joke to several different friends if each of them laughs at it. If the first three people frown when they hear the joke, you may not tell it again.

Classical conditioning is passive. It simply "happens to" the learner when a US follows a CS. In operant conditioning, the learner actively "operates on" the environment. Thus, operant conditioning refers mainly to learning *voluntary* responses. For example, pushing buttons on a TV remote control is a learned operant response. Pushing a particular button is reinforced by gaining the consequence you desire, such as changing channels or muting an obnoxious commercial. (See ■ Table 6.2 for a further comparison of classical and operant conditioning.)

Positive Reinforcement

The idea that reward affects learning is certainly nothing new to parents (and other trainers of small animals). However, parents, as well as teachers, politicians, supervisors, and even you, may use reward in ways that are inexact or misguided. A case in point is the term *reward*. To be correct, it is better to say *reinforcer*. Why? Because rewards do not always increase responding. If you try to give licorice candy to a child as a "reward" for good behavior, it will work only if the child likes licorice. What is reinforcing for one person may not be for another. As a practical rule of thumb, psychologists define an **operant reinforcer** as any event that follows a response and increases its probability of occurring again (● Fig. 6.8).

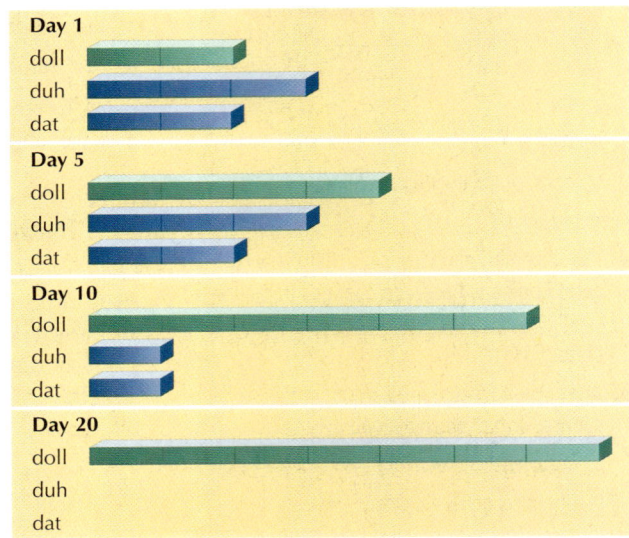

● **FIGURE 6.8** Assume that a child who is learning to talk points to her favorite doll and says either "doll," "duh," or "dat" when she wants it. Day 1 shows the number of times the child uses each word to ask for the doll (each block represents one request). At first, she uses all three words interchangeably. To hasten learning, her parents decide to give her the doll only when she names it correctly. Notice how the child's behavior shifts as operant reinforcement is applied. By day 20, saying "doll" has become the most probable response.

■ **TABLE 6.2** Comparison of Classical and Operant Conditioning

	CLASSICAL CONDITIONING	OPERANT CONDITIONING
Nature of response	Involuntary, reflex	Spontaneous, voluntary
Reinforcement	Occurs *before* response (CS paired with US)	Occurs *after* response (response is followed by reinforcing stimulus or event)
Role of learner	Passive (response is *elicited* by US)	Active (response is emitted)
Nature of learning	Neutral stimulus becomes a CS through association with a US	Probability of making a response is altered by consequences that follow it
Learned expectancy	US will follow CS	Response will have a specific effect

Acquiring an Operant Response

Many studies of instrumental learning have been done in a conditioning chamber, an apparatus designed to study operant conditioning in animals (Skinner, 1938). This device is also called a Skinner box, after B. F. Skinner, who invented it (● Fig. 6.9). A look into a typical Skinner box will clarify the process of operant conditioning.

> **THE ADVENTURES OF EINSTEIN THE RAT**
> A hungry (but smart) rat is placed in a small cage-like chamber. The walls are bare except for a metal lever and a tray into which food pellets can be dispensed. (See Fig. 6.9.)

Frankly, there's not much to do in a Skinner box. This increases the chances that our subject will make the response we want to reinforce, which is pressing the bar. Also, hunger keeps the animal motivated to seek food and actively *emit,* or freely give off, a variety of responses. Now let's take another look at our subject.

> **FURTHER ADVENTURES OF EINSTEIN THE RAT**
> For a while our subject walks around, grooms, sniffs at the corners, or stands on his hind legs—all typical rat behaviors. Then it happens. He places his paw on the lever to get a better view of the top of the cage. *Click!* The lever depresses, and a food pellet drops into the tray. The rat walks to the tray, eats the pellet, and then grooms himself. Up and exploring the cage again, he leans on the lever. *Click!* After a trip to the food tray, he returns to the bar and sniffs it, then puts his foot on it. *Click!* Soon the rat settles into a smooth pattern of frequent bar pressing.

Notice that the rat did not acquire a new skill in this situation. He was already able to depress the bar. Reinforcement only alters how *frequently* he presses the bar. In operant conditioning, new behavior patterns are molded by changing the probability that various responses will be made.

Information and Contingency Like classical conditioning, operant learning is based on information and expectancies. In operant conditioning, *we learn to expect that a certain response will have a certain effect at certain times* (Pierce & Cheney, 2004). That is, we learn that a particular response is associated with reinforcement (Hergenhahn & Olson, 2005). Further, operant reinforcement works best when it is *response contingent* (kon-TIN-jent). That is, it must be given only after a desired response has occurred. From this point of view, a reinforcer tells a person or an animal that a response was "right" and worth repeating.

● Figure 6.10 shows how operant reinforcement can change behavior. The results are from an effort to teach a severely disturbed 9-year-old child to say "Please," "Thank you," and "You're welcome." As you can see, during the initial, baseline period, the child rarely used the word *please*. Typically, he just grabbed objects and became angry if he couldn't have them. However, when he was reinforced for saying "Please," he soon learned to use the word nearly every time he wanted something. When the child said "Please" he was reinforced in three ways: He received the object he asked for (a crayon, for example); he was given a small food treat, such as a piece of candy, popcorn, or a grape; and he was praised for his good behavior (Matson et al., 1990).

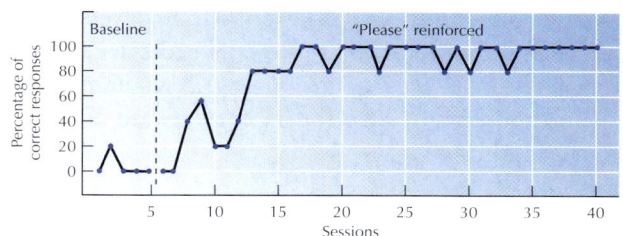

● **FIGURE 6.10** Reinforcement and human behavior. The percentage of times that a severely disturbed child said "Please" when he wanted an object was increased dramatically by reinforcing him for making a polite request. Reinforcement produced similar improvements in saying "Thank you" and "You're welcome," and the boy applied these terms in new situations as well. (Adapted from Matson et al., 1990.)

● **FIGURE 6.9** The Skinner box. This simple device, invented by B. F. Skinner, allows careful study of operant conditioning. When the rat presses the bar, a pellet of food or a drop of water is automatically released. (A photograph of a Skinner box appears in Module 1.3.)

Operant conditioning Learning based on the consequences of responding.
Law of effect Responses that lead to desirable effects are repeated; those that produce undesirable results are not.
Operant reinforcer Any event that reliably increases the probability or frequency of responses it follows.

The Timing of Reinforcement

Operant reinforcement is most effective when it rapidly follows a correct response (Mazur, 2006). For rats in a Skinner box, little learning occurs, if any, when the delay between bar pressing and receiving food exceeds 50 seconds (● Fig. 6.11). In general, you will be most successful if you present a reinforcer *immediately* after a response you wish to change. Thus, a child who is helpful or courteous should be immediately praised for her good behavior.

Let's say I work hard all semester in a class to get an A grade. Wouldn't the delay in reinforcement keep me from learning anything? No, for several reasons. First, as a mature human you can anticipate future reward. Second, you get reinforced by quiz and test grades all through the semester. Third, a single reinforcer can often maintain a long *response chain* (a linked series of actions that lead to reinforcement). A classic example of **response chaining** is provided by Barnabus, a rat trained by psychologists at Brown University.

THE GREAT BARNABUS

By carefully working from the last response to the first, Barnabus was trained to make an ever-longer chain of responses to obtain a single food pellet. When in top form, Barnabus was able to climb a spiral staircase, cross a narrow bridge, climb a ladder, pull a toy car with a chain, get into the car, pedal it to a second staircase, climb the staircase, wriggle through a tube, climb onto an elevator and descend to a platform, press a lever to receive a food pellet, and . . . start over! (Pierrel & Sherman, 1963)

Many of the things we do every day involve similar response chains. The long series of events necessary to prepare a meal is rewarded by the final eating. A violinmaker may carry out thousands of steps for the final reward of hearing a first musical note. And as a student, you have built up a long response chain for the final reward of a good grade (right?).

Are You Superstitious? Reinforcers affect not only the specific response they follow but also other responses that occur shortly before. This helps explain many human superstitions. If a golfer taps her club on the ground three times and then hits a great shot, what happens? The successful shot reinforces not only the correct swing but also the three taps. During operant training, animals often develop similar unnecessary responses. If this happens a few times more, the golfer may superstitiously tap her club three times before every shot. Some examples of actual superstitious behaviors of professional baseball players include drawing four lines in the dirt before getting in the batter's box, eating chicken before each game, and always playing in the same athletic supporter—for 4 years (phew!) (Burger & Lynn, 2005).

Superstitious behaviors are repeated because they appear to produce reinforcement, even though they are actually unnecessary (Burger & Lynn, 2005). If you walk under a ladder and then break a leg, you may avoid ladders in the future. Each time you avoid a ladder and nothing bad happens, your superstitious action is reinforced. Belief in magic can also be explained along such lines. Rituals to bring rain, ward off illness, or produce abundant crops very likely earn the faith of participants because they occasionally appear to succeed. Besides, better safe than sorry.

Shaping

How is it possible to reinforce responses that rarely occur? Even in a barren Skinner box, it could take a long time for a rat (even one as smart as Einstein) to accidentally press the bar and get a food pellet. We might wait forever for more complicated responses to occur. For example, you would have to wait a long time for a duck to accidentally walk out of its cage, turn on a light, play a toy piano, turn off the light, and walk back to its cage. If this is what you wanted to reward, you would never get the chance.

Then how are the animals on TV and at amusement parks taught to perform complicated tricks? The answer lies in **shaping,** which is the gradual molding of responses to a desired pattern. Let's look again at our subject, Einstein.

EINSTEIN THE RAT SHAPES UP

Assume that Einstein has not yet learned to press the bar. He also shows no signs of interest in the bar. Instead of waiting for the first accidental bar press, we can shape his behavior. At first, we settle for just getting him to face the bar. Any time he turns toward the bar, he is reinforced with a bit of food. Soon Einstein spends much of his time facing the bar. Next, we reinforce him every time he takes

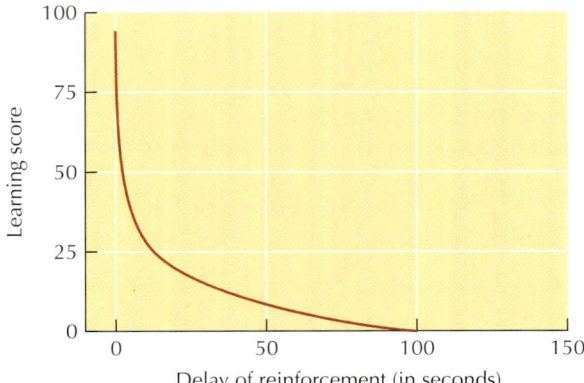

● **FIGURE 6.11** The effect of delay of reinforcement. Notice how rapidly the learning score drops when reward is delayed. Animals learning to press a bar in a Skinner box showed no signs of learning if food reward followed a bar press by more than 100 seconds (Perin, 1943).

a step toward the bar. If he turns toward the bar and walks away, nothing happens. But when he faces the bar and takes a step forward, *click!* His responses are being shaped.

By changing the rules about what makes a successful response, we can gradually train the rat to approach the bar and press it. In other words, *successive approximations* (ever-closer matches) to a desired response are reinforced during shaping. B. F. Skinner once taught two pigeons to play Ping-Pong in this way (● Fig. 6.12). Shaping applies to humans, too. Let's say you want to study more, clean the house more often, or exercise more. In each case, it would be best to set a series of gradual, daily goals. Then you can reward yourself for small steps in the right direction (Watson & Tharp, 2007).

Operant Extinction

Would a rat stop bar pressing if no more food arrived? Yes, but not immediately. Through **operant extinction,** learned responses that are not reinforced gradually fade away. Just as acquiring an operant response takes time, so does extinction. For example, if a TV program repeatedly bores you, watching the program will probably extinguish over time.

Even after extinction seems complete, the previously reinforced response may return. If a rat is removed from a Skinner box after extinction and given a short rest, the rat will press the bar again when returned to the box. Similarly, a few weeks after they give up on buying state lottery tickets, many people are tempted to try again.

Does extinction take as long the second time? If reinforcement is still withheld, a rat's bar pressing will extinguish again, usually more quickly. The brief return of an operant response after extinction is another example of spontaneous recovery (mentioned earlier regarding classical conditioning). Spontaneous recovery is very adaptive. After a rest period, the rat responds again in a situation that produced food in the past: "Just checking to see if the rules have changed!"

Marked changes in behavior occur when reinforcement and extinction are combined. For example, parents often unknowingly reinforce children for *negative attention seeking* (using misbehavior to gain attention). Children are generally ignored when they are playing quietly. They get attention when they become louder and louder, yell "Hey, Mom!" at the top of their lungs, throw tantrums, show off, or break something. Granted, the attention they get is often a scolding, but attention is a powerful reinforcer, nevertheless. Parents report dramatic improvements when they *ignore* their children's disruptive behavior and praise or attend to a child who is quiet or playing constructively.

Negative Reinforcement

Until now, we have stressed **positive reinforcement,** which occurs when a pleasant or desirable event follows a response. How else could operant learning be reinforced? The time has come to consider **negative reinforcement,** which occurs when making a response removes an unpleasant event. Don't be fooled by the word *negative.* Negative reinforcement also increases responding. However, it does so by ending (negating) discomfort.

Let's say that you have a headache and take an aspirin. Your aspirin taking will be negatively reinforced if the headache stops. Likewise, a rat could be taught to press a bar to get food (positive reinforcement), or the rat could be given a continuous mild shock (through the floor of its cage) that is turned off by a bar press (negative reinforcement). Either way, the rat will learn to press the bar more often. Why? Because it leads to a desired state of affairs (food or an end to pain). Here are two additional examples of negative reinforcement:

While walking outside, your hands get so cold they hurt. You take a pair of gloves out of your backpack and put them on, ending the pain. (Putting on the gloves is negatively reinforced.)

A politician who irritates you is being interviewed on the evening news. You change channels so you won't have to listen to him. (Channel changing is negatively reinforced.)

● **FIGURE 6.12** Operant conditioning principles were used to train these pigeons to play Ping-Pong.

> **Response chaining** The assembly of separate responses into a series of actions that lead to reinforcement.
> **Superstitious behavior** A behavior repeated because it seems to produce reinforcement, even though it is actually unnecessary.
> **Shaping** Gradually molding responses to a final desired pattern.
> **Operant extinction** The weakening or disappearance of a nonreinforced operant response.
> **Positive reinforcement** Occurs when a response is followed by a reward or other positive event.
> **Negative reinforcement** Occurs when a response is followed by an end to discomfort or by the removal of an unpleasant event.

Punishment

Many people mistake negative reinforcement for punishment. However, **punishment** refers to following a response with an *aversive* (unpleasant) consequence. Punishment *decreases* the likelihood that the response will occur again. As noted, negative reinforcement *increases* responding. The difference can be seen in a hypothetical example. Let's say you live in an apartment and your neighbor's stereo is blasting so loudly that your ears hurt. If you pound on the wall and the volume suddenly drops (negative reinforcement), future wall pounding will be more likely. But if you pound on the wall and the volume increases (punishment) or if the neighbor comes over and pounds on you (more punishment), wall pounding becomes less likely. Here are two more examples of punishment, in which an unpleasant result follows a response:

> You are driving your car too fast. You are caught in a radar trap and given a speeding ticket. Henceforth, you will be less likely to speed. (Speeding was punished by a fine.)
>
> Every time you give advice to a friend she suddenly turns cold and distant. Lately, you've stopped offering her advice. (Giving advice was punished by rejection.)

Isn't it also punishing to have privileges, money, or other positive things taken away for making a particular response? Yes. Punishment also occurs when a reinforcer or positive state of affairs is removed, such as losing privileges. This second type of punishment is called **response cost**. Parents who "ground" their teenage children for misbehavior are applying response cost. Parking tickets and other fines are also based on response cost. For your convenience, ■ Table 6.3 summarizes four basic consequences of making a response.

Operant Reinforcers— What's Your Pleasure?

SURVEY QUESTION: *Are there different kinds of operant reinforcement?*

For humans, learning may be reinforced by anything from an M&M candy to a pat on the back. In categorizing reinforcers, useful distinctions can be made between *primary reinforcers, secondary reinforcers,* and *feedback*. Operant reinforcers of all types have a large impact on our lives. Let's examine them in more detail.

Primary Reinforcers

Primary reinforcers are natural, nonlearned, and rooted in biology: They produce comfort, end discomfort, or fill an immediate physical need. Food, water, and sex are obvious examples. Every time you open the refrigerator, walk to a drinking fountain, turn up the heat, or order a double latte, your actions reflect primary reinforcement.

In addition to obvious examples, there are other, less obvious, primary reinforcers, such as psychoactive drugs. One of the most powerful is *intracranial self-stimulation* (ICS). ICS involves the direct activation of "pleasure centers" in the brain. (See "Tickling Your Own Fancy.")

Secondary Reinforcers

Much human learning is still strongly tied to food, water, and other primary reinforcers. Regardless, humans also respond to a much broader range of rewards and reinforcers. Money, praise, attention, approval, success, affection, grades, and the like all serve as learned or **secondary reinforcers.**

How does a secondary reinforcer gain its ability to promote learning? Some secondary reinforcers are simply associated with a primary reinforcer. For example, if you would like to train a dog to follow you ("heel") when you take a walk, you could reward the dog with small food treats for staying near you. If you praise the dog each time you give it a treat, praise will become a secondary reinforcer. In time, you will be able to skip giving treats and simply praise your pup for doing the right thing. The same principle applies to children. One reason that parents' praise becomes a secondary reinforcer is because it is frequently associated with food, candy, hugs, and other primary reinforcers.

Tokens Secondary reinforcers that can be *exchanged* for primary reinforcers gain their value more directly (Mazur, 2006). Printed money obviously has little or no value of its own. You can't eat it, drink it, or sleep with it. However, it can be exchanged for food, water, lodging, and other necessities.

A **token reinforcer** is a tangible secondary reinforcer, such as money, gold stars, poker chips, and the like. In a series of classic experiments, chimpanzees were taught to work for tokens. The chimps were first trained to put poker chips into a "Chimp-O-Mat" vending machine. Each chip dispensed a few grapes or raisins. Once the animals had learned to exchange tokens for food, they would learn new tasks to earn the chips. To maintain the value of the tokens, the chimps were occasionally allowed to use the "Chimp-O-Mat" (● Fig. 6.14) (Cowles, 1937; Wolfe, 1936).

A major advantage of tokens is that they don't lose reinforcing value as quickly as primary reinforcers do. For instance, if you use candy to reinforce a developmentally disabled child for correctly naming things, the child might lose interest once he is satiated (fully satisfied) or no longer hungry. It would be better to use tokens as immediate rewards for learning. Later, the child can exchange his tokens for candy, toys, or other treats.

BRAINWAVES

Tickling Your Own Fancy

Suppose you could have an electrode permanently implanted in your brain and connected to an iPod-style controller. Twirl the controller and electrical impulses stimulate one of your brain's "pleasure centers." The very few humans who have ever had a chance to try direct brain stimulation report feeling intense pleasure that is better than food, water, sex, drugs, or any other primary reinforcer (Heath, 1963). (See ● Fig. 6.13.)

Most of what we know about intracranial self-stimulation comes from studying rats with similar implants (Olds & Fobes, 1981). A rat "wired for pleasure" can be trained to press the bar in a Skinner box to deliver electrical stimulation to its own limbic system. (Refer back to Fig. 2.27.) Some rats will press the bar thousands of times per hour to obtain brain stimulation. After 15 or 20 hours of constant pressing, animals sometimes collapse from exhaustion. When they revive, they begin pressing again. If the reward circuit is not turned off, an animal will ignore food, water, and sex in favor of bar pressing.

Many natural primary reinforcers activate the same pleasure pathways in the brain that make ICS so powerful (McBride, Murphy, & Ikemoto, 1999). So do psychoactive drugs, such as alcohol and cocaine (Eisler, Justice, Jr., & Neill, 2004; Rodd et al., 2005). In fact, rats will also self-administer nicotine. When they do, they are even more likely to engage in ICS (Kenny & Markou, 2006). Apparently, nicotine further increases the sensitivity of pleasure pathways in the brain.

One shudders to think what might happen if brain implants were easy and practical to do. (They are not.) Every company from Playboy to Microsoft would have a device on the market, and we would have to keep a closer watch on politicians than usual!

● **FIGURE 6.13** Humans have been "wired" for brain stimulation, as shown in *(a)*. However, in humans, this has been done only as an experimental way to restrain uncontrollable outbursts of violence. Implants have not been done merely to produce pleasure. Most research has been carried out with rats. Using the apparatus shown in *(b)*, the rat can press a bar to deliver mild electric stimulation to a "pleasure center" in the brain.

■ TABLE 6.3 Behavioral Effects of Various Consequences

	CONSEQUENCE OF MAKING A RESPONSE	EXAMPLE	EFFECT ON RESPONSE PROBABILITY
Positive reinforcement	Positive event begins	Food given	Increase
Negative reinforcement	Negative event ends	Pain stops	Increase
Punishment	Negative event begins	Pain begins	Decrease
Punishment (response cost)	Positive event ends	Food removed	Decrease
Nonreinforcement	Nothing	—	Decrease

Tokens have been used with troubled children and adults in special programs, and even in ordinary elementary school classrooms (Spiegler & Guevremont, 2003) (● Fig. 6.15). In each case the goal is to provide an immediate reward for learning. Typically, tokens may be exchanged for food, special privileges, or trips to movies, amusement parks, and so forth. Many parents find that tokens greatly reduce discipline problems with younger children. For example, children can earn points or gold stars during the week for good behavior. If they earn enough tokens, they are allowed on Sunday to choose one item out of a "grab bag" of small prizes.

Punishment Any event that follows a response and *decreases* its likelihood of occurring again.

Response cost Removal of a positive reinforcer after a response is made.

Primary reinforcers Nonlearned reinforcers; usually those that satisfy physiological needs.

Secondary reinforcer A learned reinforcer; often one that gains reinforcing properties by association with a primary reinforcer.

Token reinforcer A tangible secondary reinforcer such as money, gold stars, poker chips, and the like.

● **FIGURE 6.14** Poker chips normally have little or no value for chimpanzees, but this chimp will work hard to earn them once he learns that the "Chimp-O-Mat" will dispense food in exchange for them.

● **FIGURE 6.15** Reinforcement in a token economy. This graph shows the effects of using tokens to reward socially desirable behavior in a mental hospital ward. Desirable behavior was defined as cleaning, making the bed, attending therapy sessions, and so forth. Tokens earned could be exchanged for basic amenities such as meals, snacks, coffee, game-room privileges, or weekend passes. The graph shows more than 24 hours per day because it represents the total number of hours of desirable behavior performed by all patients in the ward. (Adapted from Ayllon & Azrin, 1965.)

Social Reinforcers As we have noted, learned desires for attention and approval, which are called **social reinforcers,** often influence human behavior. This fact can be used in a classic, if somewhat mischievous, demonstration.

SHAPING A TEACHER

For this activity, about one half (or more) of the students in a classroom must participate. First, select a target behavior. This should be something like "lecturing from the right side of the room." (Keep it simple, in case your teacher is a slow learner.) Begin training in this way: Each time the instructor turns toward the right or takes a step in that direction, participating students should look *really* interested. Also, smile, ask questions, lean forward, and make eye contact. If the teacher turns to the left or takes a step in that direction, participating students should lean back, yawn, check out their split ends, close their eyes, or generally look bored. Soon, without being aware of why, the instructor should be spending most of his or her time each class period lecturing from the right side of the classroom.

This trick has been a favorite of psychology graduate students for decades. For a time, one of your author's professors delivered all her lectures from the right side of the room while toying with the cords on the window shades. (We added the cords the second week!) The point to remember from this example is that attention and approval can change the behavior of children, family members, friends, roommates, and co-workers. Be aware of what you are reinforcing.

Feedback

His eyes, driven and blazing, dart from side to side. His left hand twitches, dances, rises, and strikes, hitting its target again and again. At the same time, his right hand furiously spins in circular motions. Does this describe some strange neurological disorder? Actually, it depicts 10-year-old Vikram as he plays his favorite video game, an animated skateboarding adventure!

How did Vikram learn the complex movements needed to excel at virtual skateboarding? After all, he was not rewarded with food or money. The answer lies in the fact that Vikram's favorite video game provides *feedback,* a key element that underlies learning. **Feedback** (information about the effect a response had) is particularly important in human learning (Lefrançois, 2006).

Every time a player moves, a video game responds instantly with sounds, animated actions, and a higher or lower score. The machine's responsiveness and the information flow it provides can be very motivating if you want to win. The

DISCOVERING PSYCHOLOGY

Conditioning and Conservation

Psychologists enjoy seeing behavioral principles used to solve practical problems. One area of behavior very much in need of attention is our "throw-away" society. We burn fossil fuels; destroy forests; use chemical products; and strip, clear, and farm the land. In doing so, we alter the very face of the Earth. What can be done? One approach involves changing the *consequences* of wasteful energy use, polluting, and the like. For example, energy taxes can be used to increase the cost of using fossil fuels (response cost). On the reinforcement side of the equation, rebates can be offered for installing insulation, or buying energy-efficient appliances or cars, and tax breaks can be given to companies that take steps to preserve the environment.

On a daily level, people can help recycle materials such as paper, steel, glass, aluminum, and plastic. Again, behavioral principles come into play. For instance, people who set their own goals for recycling tend to meet them. Likewise, when families, work groups, factories, and dorms receive feedback, on a weekly basis, about how much they recycled, they typically recycle more. Recycling is also more effective when entire families participate, with some family members (usually mom, of course) reinforcing the recycling behavior of other family members (Meneses & Beerlipalacio, 2005). We also know that people are more likely to continue recycling if they feel a sense of satisfaction from helping protect the environment (Ewing, 2001). Is such satisfaction sufficiently reinforcing to encourage more people to reduce, reuse, and recycle? We certainly hope so.

---

same principle applies to many other learning situations: If you are trying to learn to use a computer, to play a musical instrument, to cook, or to solve math problems, reinforcement comes from feedback that you achieved a desired result.

The adaptive value of feedback helps explain why much human learning occurs in the absence of obvious reinforcers, such as food or water. Humans readily learn responses that merely have a desired effect or that bring a goal closer. Let's explore this idea further.

Knowledge of Results Imagine that you are asked to throw darts at a target. Each dart must pass over a screen that prevents you from telling if you hit the target. If you threw 1,000 darts, we would expect little improvement in your performance because no feedback is provided. Vikram's video game did not explicitly reward him for correct responses. Yet, because it provided feedback, rapid learning took place.

How can feedback be applied? Increased feedback (also called **knowledge of results, or KR**) almost always improves learning and performance (Horn et al., 2005). If you want to learn to play a musical instrument, to sing, to speak a second language, or to deliver a speech, recorded feedback can be very helpful. In sports, videos replays are used to provide feedback on everything from tennis serves to pick-off moves in baseball. Whenever you are trying to learn a complex skill, it pays to get more feedback (Wulf et al., 2002). (Also, see "Conditioning and Conservation.")

Learning Aids

How do these techniques make use of feedback? Feedback is most effective when it is *frequent, immediate,* and *detailed. Programmed instruction* teaches students in a format that presents information in small amounts, gives immediate practice, and provides continuous feedback to learners. Frequent feedback keeps learners from practicing errors. It also lets students work at their own pace. (A small sample of programmed instruction is shown in ● Figure 6.16 so that you can see what the format looks like.) Programmed learning can be done in book form, presented on a CD-ROM or through the web (Emurian, 2005; McDonald, Yanchar, & Osguthorpe, 2005).

In *computer-assisted instruction (CAI),* learning is aided by computer-presented information and exercises. In addition to giving learners immediate feedback, the computer can give hints about why an answer was wrong and what is needed to correct it (Timmerman & Kruepke, 2006). Although the final level of skill or knowledge gained is not necessarily higher, CAI can save much time and effort. In addition, people often do better with feedback from a computer because they can freely make mistakes and learn from them (Luyben, Hipworth, & Pappas, 2003; Norton, 2003). For example, CAI can give medical students unlimited practice at diagnosing diseases from symptoms, such as "acute chest pain" (Papa, Aldrich, & Schumacker, 1999).

Some CAI programs, called *serious games,* make use of instructional games in which stories, competition with a partner, sound effects, and game-like graphics increase interest and motivation (Michael & Chen, 2006) (● Fig. 6.17). Educational simulations allow students to explore an imagi-

---

Social reinforcer Reinforcement based on receiving attention, approval, or affection from another person.

Feedback Information returned to a person about the effects a response has had; also known as knowledge of results.

Knowledge of results (KR) Informational feedback.

Types of Conditioning	
classical reflex voluntary	Much _____ conditioning involves involuntary _____ responses. In contrast, operant conditioning affects spontaneous, or _____, responses.
response CS	Reinforcement occurs before the _____ in classical conditioning as the _____ is paired with the US.
reinforcement after reinforcer	In operant conditioning, _____ occurs _____ the response. In this case, the response is followed by a _____.
passive elicited	In classical conditioning, the learner is _____ because responses are _____ by the US.
learner emits	In operant conditioning, the _____ actively _____ responses that are affected by reinforcement.

• **FIGURE 6.16** To sample a programmed instruction format, try covering the terms on the left with a piece of paper. As you fill in the blanks, uncover one new term for each response. In this way, your correct (or incorrect) responses will be followed by immediate feedback.

nary situation or "microworld" that simulates real-world problems. By seeing the effects of their choices, students discover basic principles of physics, biology, psychology, or other subjects (Grabe, 2006).

As psychologists fully explore the value and limits of computer-assisted instruction, it seems likely that their efforts will improve not only education but our understanding of human learning as well. Let's pause now for some learning exercises so that you can get some feedback about your mastery of the preceding ideas.

MODULE 6.2 Summary

How does operant conditioning occur?
- To understand why people behave as they do, it is important to identify how their responses are being reinforced.
- Operant conditioning occurs when a voluntary action is followed by a reinforcer, which increases the frequency of the response. Operant learning is based on the law of effect.
- Delaying reinforcement greatly reduces its effectiveness, but long chains of responses may be maintained by a single reinforcer.
- Superstitious behaviors often become part of response chains because they *appear* to be associated with reinforcement.
- By rewarding successive approximations to a particular response, behavior can be shaped into desired patterns.
- If an operant response is not reinforced, it may extinguish (disappear). But after extinction seems complete, it may temporarily reappear (spontaneous recovery).
- Both positive reinforcement and negative reinforcement increase the likelihood that a response will be repeated. Punishment decreases the likelihood that the response will occur again.

Are there different kinds of operant reinforcement?
- Operant learning may be based on primary reinforcers or secondary reinforcers.
- Feedback, or knowledge of results, also aids learning and improves performance.
- Programmed instruction breaks learning into a series of small steps and provides immediate feedback. Computer-assisted instruction (CAI) does the same but has the added advantage of providing alternative exercises and information when needed.

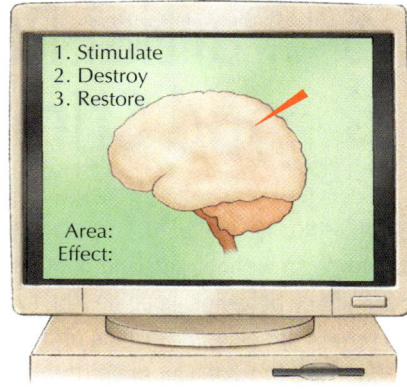

● **FIGURE 6.17** Computer-assisted instruction. The screen on the left shows a typical drill-and-practice math problem, in which students must find the hypotenuse of a triangle. The center screen presents the same problem as an instructional game to increase interest and motivation. In the game, a child is asked to set the proper distance on a ray gun in the hovering space ship to "vaporize" an attacker. The screen on the right depicts an educational simulation. Here, students place a "probe" at various spots in a human brain. They then "stimulate," "destroy," or "restore" areas. As each area is altered, it is named on the screen and the effects on behavior are described. This allows students to explore basic brain functions on their own.

KNOWLEDGE BUILDER

Operant Conditioning

Recite

1. Responses in operant conditioning are _____ or _____, whereas those in classical conditioning are passive, _____, or _____ responses.

2. Changing the rules in small steps so that an animal (or person) is gradually trained to respond as desired is called _____.

3. Extinction in operant conditioning is also subject to _____ of a response.
   a. successive approximations
   b. shaping
   c. automation
   d. spontaneous recovery

4. Positive reinforcers increase the rate of responding, and negative reinforcers decrease it. T or F?

5. Primary reinforcers are those learned through classical conditioning. T or F?

6. Which is a correct match?
   a. social reinforcer-primary reinforcement
   b. token reinforcer-secondary reinforcement
   c. ICS-secondary reinforcement
   d. negative reinforcer-punishment

7. Superstitious responses are those that are
   a. shaped by secondary reinforcement
   b. extinguished
   c. prepotent
   d. unnecessary to obtain reinforcement

8. Knowledge of results, or KR, is also known as _____.

9. CAI is based on the same principles as
   a. negative reinforcement
   b. programmed instruction
   c. higher order conditioning
   d. stimulus generalization

Reflect
Critical Thinking

10. How might operant conditioning principles be used to encourage people to pick up litter? (What rewards could be offered, and how might the cost of rewards be kept low?)

Relate

How have your thoughts about the effects of "rewards" changed now that you've read about operant conditioning? Can you explain the difference between positive reinforcement, negative reinforcement, and punishment? Can you give an example of each concept from your own experience?

A friend of yours punishes his dog all the time. What advice would you give him about how to use reinforcement, extinction, and shaping, instead of punishment?

Link

Internet addresses frequently change. To find the sites listed here, visit **http://www.thomsonedu.com/psychology/coon** for an updated list of Internet addresses and direct links to relevant sites.

- **B.F. Skinner** Read about the life and work of B. F. Skinner in his own words.
- **Clicker Training for Animals** One approach to using operant conditioning to train animals.
- **Hardwired for Happiness** Are our brains hardwired for happiness?

ANSWERS

1. voluntary, involuntary or emitted, elicited 2. shaping 3. d 4. F 5. F 6. b 7. d 8. feedback 9. b 10. A strategy that has been used with some success is to hold drawings for various prizes, such as movie or concert passes. Each time a person turns in a specific amount of litter, he or she receives one chance (a token) to enter in the drawing. Giving refunds for cans and bottles is another way to reinforce recycling of litter.

MODULE 6.3 Partial Reinforcement and Stimulus Control

ANYONE WISHING TO INFLUENCE operant learning would be ill equipped to do so without knowing how various patterns of reinforcement affect behavior. Imagine, for example, that a mother wants to reward her child for turning off the lights when he leaves a room. Contrary to what you might think, she would be well advised to reinforce only some of her son's correct responses. Why would this be so? You'll find the answer in this module. You'll also learn how antecedent stimuli control our behavior in a stop-and-go fashion.

Partial Reinforcement—Las Vegas, a Human Skinner Box?

SURVEY QUESTION: *How are we influenced by patterns of reward?*

Until now, we have treated operant reinforcement as if it were continuous. *Continuous reinforcement* means that a reinforcer follows every correct response. This is fine for the lab, but it has little to do with the real world. Most of our responses are more inconsistently rewarded. In daily life, learning is usually based on **partial reinforcement,** in which reinforcers do not follow every response. Partial reinforcement can be given in several patterns, called **schedules of reinforcement** (plans for determining which responses will be reinforced). Each has a distinct effect on behavior. In addition to these (which will be explored in a moment), there is a general effect: Responses acquired by partial reinforcement are highly resistant to extinction (Svartdal, 2003). For some obscure reason, lost in the lore of psychology, this is called the **partial reinforcement effect.**

How does getting reinforced part of the time make a habit stronger? If you have ever visited Las Vegas or a similar gambling mecca, you have probably seen row after row of people playing slot machines. To gain insight into partial reinforcement, imagine that you are making your first visit to Las Vegas. You put a dollar in a slot machine and pull the handle. Ten dollars spills into the tray. Using one of your newly won dollars, you pull the handle again. Another payoff! Let's say this continues for 15 minutes. Every pull is followed by a payoff. Suddenly each pull is followed by nothing. Obviously, you would respond several times more before giving up. However, when continuous reinforcement is followed by extinction, the message soon becomes clear: No more payoffs.

The one-armed bandit (slot machine) is a dispenser of partial reinforcement.

Contrast this with partial reinforcement. Again, imagine that this is your first encounter with a slot machine. You put a dollar in the machine five times without a payoff. You are just about to quit, but decide to play once more. Bingo! The machine returns $20. After this, payoffs continue on a partial schedule; some are large, and some are small. All are unpredictable. Sometimes you hit 2 in a row, and sometimes 20 or 30 pulls go unrewarded.

Now let's say the payoff mechanism is turned off again. How many times do you think you would respond this time before your handle-pulling behavior extinguished? Because you have developed the expectation that any play may be "the one," it will be hard to resist just one more play . . . and one more . . . and one more. Also, because partial reinforcement includes long periods of nonreward, it will be harder to discriminate between periods of reinforcement and extinction. It is no exaggeration to say that the partial reinforcement effect has left many people penniless. Even psychologists visiting Las Vegas may get "cleaned out" (not your authors, of course!).

Schedules of Partial Reinforcement

Partial reinforcement can be given in many different patterns (Domjan, 2006). Let's consider the four most basic, which have some interesting effects on us. Typical responses to each pattern are shown in ● Figure 6.18. Results such as these are obtained when a cumulative recorder is connected to a Skinner box. The device consists of a moving strip of paper and a mechanical pen that jumps upward each time a response is made. Rapid responding causes the pen to draw a steep line; a horizontal line indicates no response. Small tick marks on the lines show when a reinforcer was given.

Fixed Ratio (FR) What would happen if a reinforcer followed only every other response? Or what if we followed every third, fourth, fifth, or other number of responses with reinforcement? Each of these patterns is a **fixed ratio (FR) schedule** (a set number of correct responses must be made to obtain a reinforcer). Notice that in an FR schedule the ratio of reinforcers to responses is fixed: FR-2 means that every other response is rewarded; FR-3 means that every third response is reinforced; in an FR-10 schedule, exactly 10 responses must be made to obtain a reinforcer.

Fixed ratio schedules produce *very high response rates.* (See Fig. 6.18.) A hungry rat on an FR-10 schedule will quickly run off 10 responses, pause to eat, and then run off 10 more. A similar situation occurs when factory or farm workers are paid on a piecework basis. When a fixed number of items must be produced for a set amount of pay, work output is high.

Variable Ratio (VR) In a **variable ratio (VR) schedule** a varied number of correct responses must be made to get a reinforcer. Instead of reinforcing every fourth response (FR-4), for example, a person or animal on a VR-4 schedule gets rewarded *on the average* every fourth response. Sometimes 2 responses must be made to obtain a reinforcer; sometimes it's 5, sometimes 4, and so on. The actual number varies, but it averages out to 4 (in this example). Variable ratio schedules also produce high response rates.

VR schedules seem less predictable than FR. Does that have any effect on extinction? Yes. Because reinforcement is less predictable, VR schedules tend to produce greater resistance to extinction than fixed ratio schedules. Playing a slot machine is an example of behavior maintained by a variable ratio schedule. Another would be a child asking for a "treat" at the supermarket. The number of times the child must ask before getting reinforced varies, so the child becomes quite persistent. Golf, tennis, baseball, and many other sports are also reinforced on a variable ratio basis: Even the best batters in baseball rarely hit more than an average of 3 out of every 10 balls pitched to them.

Fixed Interval (FI) In another pattern, reinforcement is given only when a correct response is made after a fixed amount of time has passed. This time interval is measured from the last reinforced response. Responses made during the time interval are not reinforced. In a **fixed interval (FI) schedule** the first correct response made after the time period has passed is reinforced. Thus, a rat on an FI-30-second schedule has to wait 30 seconds after the last reinforced response before a bar press will pay off again. The rat can press the bar as often as it wants during the interval, but it will not be rewarded.

Fixed interval schedules produce *moderate response rates.* These are marked by spurts of activity mixed with periods of inactivity. Animals working on an FI schedule seem to develop a keen sense of the passage of time (Eckerman, 1999). (See "Are Animals Stuck in Time?") For example:

> **EINSTEIN THE RAT TAKES A BREAK**
> Einstein, trained on an FI-60-second schedule, has just been reinforced for a bar press. What does he do? He saunters around the cage, grooms himself, hums, whistles, reads magazines, and polishes his

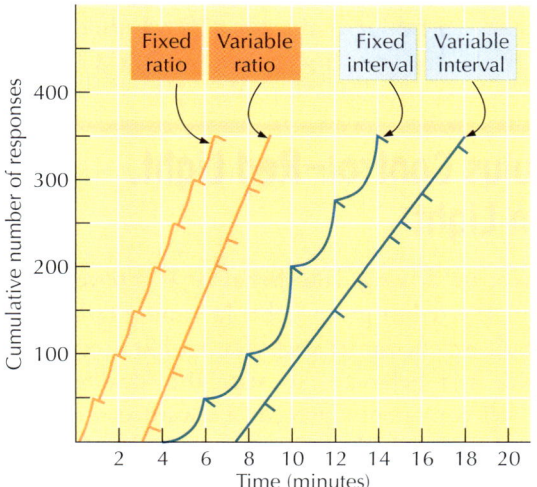

● **FIGURE 6.18** Typical response patterns for reinforcement schedules.

> **Partial reinforcement** A pattern in which only a portion of all responses are reinforced.
> **Schedule of reinforcement** A rule or plan for determining which responses will be reinforced.
> **Partial reinforcement effect** Responses acquired with partial reinforcement are more resistant to extinction.
> **Fixed ratio (FR) schedule** A set number of correct responses must be made to get a reinforcer. For example, a reinforcer is given for every four correct responses.
> **Variable ratio (VR) schedule** A varied number of correct responses must be made to get a reinforcer. For example, a reinforcer is given after three to seven correct responses; the actual number changes randomly.
> **Fixed interval (FI) schedule** A reinforcer is given only when a correct response is made after a set amount of time has passed since the last reinforced response. Responses made during the time interval are not reinforced.

CRITICAL THINKING

Are Animals Stuck in Time?

We humans are *cognitive time travelers*, regularly zooming back and forth through time in our minds. You can, for example, think about past events, such as what you had for breakfast this morning. We can also imagine events in the future. Brides-to-be are famous for planning their weddings down to the last detail. But what about animals? Are they cognitive time travelers or are they "stuck in time" (Roberts, 2002; Zentall, 2005)? Do dogs ever think about how hot it was yesterday or what they plan to do tomorrow? To answer such questions, psychologists have used operant conditioning as a research tool.

Conditioning studies have repeatedly shown that animals are sensitive to the passage of time (Zentall, 2005). For example, pigeons and rats reinforced on fixed interval schedules stop responding immediately after they receive a reinforcer and do not start again until just before the next scheduled reinforcement (Roberts, 2002). In one study, pigeons were put in a Skinner box with a pecking key on each wall. They quickly learned to peck only at Key 1 if it was 9:30 in the morning and at Key 3 if it was 4:00 in the afternoon (Saksida & Wilkie, 1994).

Another study focused on scrub jays. These birds are hoarders; they store excess food at different locations and then go back later to eat it. Scrub jays were allowed to hoard some nuts in one location and some worms in another. If they were released 4 hours later, they went directly to the worms. However, if they are released 5 days later, they went straight for the nuts. Worms are a scrub jay's favorite food, which explains their choice after 4 hours. But worms decay after a day or so, while nuts stay edible. It seems that the jays knew exactly where they stored each type of food and how much time had passed (Clayton, Yu, & Dickinson, 2001).

While these studies are suggestive, they are part of an ongoing debate about whether or not animals are stuck in time (Roberts & Roberts, 2002). Nevertheless, be careful if you

Florida scrub jays are food hoarders. Does their food hoarding behavior prove they are not "trapped in time"?

forget to feed your beloved dog, Rover, at his usual mealtime. If he has been conditioned to think it's time to eat, he may settle for your favorite flip-flops instead of dog food!

---

nails. After 50 seconds, he walks to the bar and gives it a press—just testing. After 55 seconds, he gives it two or three presses, but there's still no payoff. Fifty-eight seconds, and he settles down to rapid pressing, 59 seconds, 60 seconds, and he hits the reinforced press. After one or two more presses (unrewarded), he wanders off again for the next interval.

Is getting paid weekly an FI schedule? Pure examples of fixed interval schedules are rare, but getting paid each week at work does come close. Notice, however, that most people do not work faster just before payday, as an FI schedule predicts. A closer parallel would be having a report due every 2 weeks for a class. Right after turning in a paper, your work would probably drop to zero for a week or more (Chance, 2006).

Variable Interval (VI) **Variable interval (VI)** schedules are a variation on fixed intervals. Here, reinforcement is given for the first correct response made after a varied amount of time. On a VI-30-second schedule, reinforcement is available after an interval that *averages* 30 seconds.

VI schedules produce *slow, steady response rates* and tremendous resistance to extinction (Lattal, Reilly, & Kohn, 1998). When you dial a phone number and get a busy signal, reward (getting through) is on a VI schedule. You may have to wait 30 seconds or 30 minutes. If you are like most people, you will doggedly dial over and over again until you get a connection. Success in fishing is also on a VI schedule—which may explain the bulldog tenacity of many anglers (Chance, 2006).

Stimulus Control—Red Light, Green Light

When you are driving, your behavior at intersections is controlled by the red or green light. In similar fashion, many of the stimuli we encounter each day act like stop or go signals that guide our behavior. To state the idea more formally, stimuli that consistently precede a rewarded response tend to influence when and where the response will occur. This effect is called **stimulus control.** Notice how it works with our friend Einstein.

LIGHTS OUT FOR EINSTEIN THE RAT
While learning the bar-pressing response, Einstein has been in a Skinner box illuminated by a bright light. During several training sessions, the light is alternately turned on and off. When the light is on, a bar press will produce food. When the light is off, bar pressing goes unrewarded. We soon observe that the rat presses vigorously when the light is on and ignores the bar when the light is off.

In this example, the light signals what consequences will follow if a response is made. Evidence for stimulus control could be shown by turning the food delivery *on* when the light is *off*. A well-trained animal might never discover that the rules had changed. A similar example of stimulus control would be a child learning to ask for candy when her mother is in a good mood, but not asking at other times. Likewise, we pick up phones that are ringing, but rarely answer phones that are silent. Thus, a simplified summary of stimulus control is: Notice something, do something, get something (Powell, Symbaluk, & Macdonald, 2005).

Generalization Two important aspects of stimulus control are generalization and discrimination. Let's return to the example of the vending machine (from the chapter preview) to illustrate these concepts. First, generalization.

Is generalization the same in operant conditioning as it is in classical conditioning? Basically, yes. **Operant stimulus generalization** is the tendency to respond to stimuli similar to those that preceded operant reinforcement. That is, a reinforced response tends to be made again when similar antecedents are present. Assume, for instance, that you have been reliably rewarded for kicking one particular vending machine. Your kicking response tends to occur in the presence of that machine. It has come under stimulus control. Now let's say that there are three other machines on campus identical to the one that pays off. Because they are similar, your kicking response may well transfer to them. If each of these machines also pays off when kicked, your kicking response may *generalize* to other machines only mildly similar to the original. Similar generalization explains why children may temporarily call all men *daddy*—much to the embarrassment of their parents.

Discrimination Meanwhile, back at the vending machine. . . . As stated earlier, to discriminate means to respond differently to varied stimuli. Because one vending machine reinforced your kicking response, you began kicking other identical machines (generalization). Because these also paid off, you began kicking similar machines (more generalization). If kicking these new machines has no effect, the kicking response that generalized to them will extinguish because of nonreinforcement. Thus, your response to machines of a particular size and color is consistently rewarded, whereas the same response to different machines is extinguished. Through **operant stimulus discrimination** you have learned to differentiate between antecedent stimuli that signal reward and nonreward. As a result, your response pattern will shift to match these **discriminative stimuli** (stimuli that precede reinforced and nonreinforced responses).

A discriminative stimulus that most drivers are familiar with is a police car on the freeway. This stimulus is a clear signal that a specific set of reinforcement contingencies applies. As you have probably observed, the presence of a police car brings about rapid reductions in driving speed, lane changes, and tailgating.

The role of discriminative stimuli may be clarified by an interesting feat achieved by Jack, a psychologist friend of one of your authors. Here is his account of what Jack did:

> Jack decided to teach his cat to say its name. To begin, he gave the cat a pat on the back. If the cat meowed in a way that sounded anything like its name, Jack immediately gave the cat a small amount of food. If the cat made this unusual meow at other times, it received nothing. This process was repeated many times each day.
>
> By gradual shaping, the cat's meow was made to sound very much like its name. Also, this peculiar meow came under stimulus control: When it received a pat on the back, the cat said its name; without the pat, it remained silent or meowed normally.
>
> I should add at this point that I was unaware that Jack had a new cat or that he had trained it. I went to visit him one night and met the cat on the front steps. I gave the cat a pat on the back and said, "Hi kitty, what's your name?" Imagine my surprise when the cat immediately replied, "Ralph"!

Variable interval (VI) schedule A reinforcer is given for the first correct response made after a varied amount of time has passed since the last reinforced response. Responses made during the time interval are not reinforced.

Stimulus control Stimuli present when an operant response is acquired tend to control when and where the response is made.

Operant stimulus generalization The tendency to respond to stimuli similar to those that preceded operant reinforcement.

Operant stimulus discrimination The tendency to make an operant response when stimuli previously associated with reward are present and to withhold the response when stimuli associated with nonreward are present.

Discriminative stimuli Stimuli that precede rewarded and nonrewarded responses in operant conditioning.

Stimulus control. Operant shaping was used to teach this whale to "bow" to an audience. Fish were used as reinforcers. Notice the trainer's hand signal, which serves as a discriminative stimulus to control the performance.

Psychologists symbolize a stimulus that precedes reinforced responses as an S+. Discriminative stimuli that precede unrewarded responses are symbolized as S− (Chance, 2006). Thus, ● Figure 6.19 summarizes Ralph's training.

Stimulus discrimination is also aptly illustrated by the "sniffer" dogs that locate drugs and explosives at airports and border crossings. Operant discrimination is used to teach these dogs to recognize contraband. During training, they are reinforced only for approaching containers baited with drugs or explosives.

Stimulus discrimination clearly has a tremendous impact on human behavior. Learning to recognize different automobile brands, birds, animals, wines, types of music, and even the answers on psychology tests all depends, in part, on operant discrimination learning.

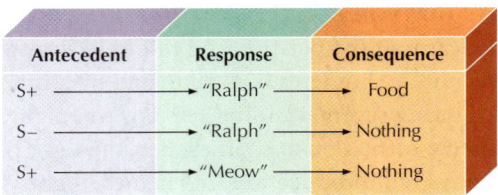

● **FIGURE 6.19** A diagram of Ralph the cat's discrimination training.

MODULE 6.3 Summary

How are we influenced by patterns of reward?
- Reward or reinforcement may be given continuously (after every response) or on a schedule of partial reinforcement. Partial reinforcement produces greater resistance to extinction.
- Five basic schedules of reinforcement are continuous, fixed ratio, variable ratio, fixed interval, and variable interval. Each schedule produces a different pattern of responding.
- Stimuli that precede a reinforced response tend to control when and where operant responses occur (stimulus control). Two aspects of stimulus control are generalization and discrimination.
- In generalization, an operant response tends to occur when stimuli similar to those preceding reinforcement are present.
- In discrimination, responses are given in the presence of discriminative stimuli associated with reinforcement (S+) and withheld in the presence of stimuli associated with nonreinforcement (S−).

KNOWLEDGE BUILDER

Partial Reinforcement and Stimulus Control

Recite

1. Two aspects of stimulus control are _____ and _____.
2. Responding tends to occur in the presence of discriminative stimuli associated with reinforcement and tends not to occur in the presence of discriminative stimuli associated with nonreinforcement. T or F?
3. *Stimulus generalization* refers to making an operant response in the presence of stimuli similar to those that preceded reinforcement. T or F?
4. Moderate response rates that are marked by spurts of activity and periods of inactivity are characteristic of
   a. FR schedules
   b. VR schedules
   c. FI schedules
   d. VI schedules
5. Partial reinforcement tends to produce slower responding and reduced resistance to extinction. T or F?
6. The schedule of reinforcement associated with playing slot machines and other types of gambling is
   a. fixed ratio
   b. variable ratio
   c. fixed interval
   d. variable interval

Reflect
Critical Thinking

7. A business owner who pays employees an hourly wage wants to increase productivity. How could the owner make more effective use of reinforcement?
8. How could you use conditioning principles to teach a dog or a cat to come when called?

Relate

Think of something you do that is reinforced only part of the time. Do you pursue this activity persistently? How have you been affected by partial reinforcement?

See if you can think of at least one everyday example of the five basic schedules of reinforcement.

Doors that are meant to be pushed outward have metal plates on them. Those that are meant to be pulled inward have handles. Do these discriminative stimuli affect your behavior? (If they don't, how's your nose doing?)

Link

Internet addresses frequently change. To find the sites listed here, visit **http://www.thomsonedu.com/psychology/coon** for an updated list of Internet addresses and direct links to relevant sites.

- **Schedules of Reinforcement** Read more about partial reinforcement schedules.
- **Stimuli** Explore the different functions stimuli can serve.
- **Positive and Negative Discriminative Stimuli in Animal Training** Read about the application of discriminative stimuli in animal training.

ANSWERS

1. generalization, discrimination 2. T 3. T 4. c 5. F 6. b 7. Continuing to use fixed interval rewards (hourly wage or salary) would guarantee a basic level of income for employees. To reward extra effort, the owner could add some fixed ratio reinforcement (such as incentives, bonuses, commissions, or profit sharing) to employees' pay. 8. An excellent way to train a pet to come when you call is to give a distinctive call or whistle each time you feed the animal. This makes the signal a secondary reinforcer and a discriminative stimulus for reward (food). Of course, it also helps to directly reinforce an animal with praise, petting, or food for coming when called.

MODULE 6.4 Punishment

SPANKINGS, reprimands, fines, jail sentences, firings, failing grades, and the like are commonly used to control behavior. Clearly, the story of learning is unfinished without a return to the topic of punishment.

Punishment—Putting the Brakes on Behavior

SURVEY QUESTION: *What does punishment do to behavior?*

Recall that **punishment** lowers the probability that a response will occur again. To be most effective, punishment must be given contingently (only after an undesired response occurs). Punishers, like reinforcers, are defined by observing their effects on behavior. A **punisher** is any consequence that reduces the frequency of a target behavior. It is not always possible to know ahead of time what will act as a punisher for a particular person. For example, when Jason's mother reprimanded him for throwing toys, he stopped doing it. In this instance, the reprimand was a punisher. However, Chris is starved for attention of any kind from his parents, who both work full-time. For Chris, a reprimand, or even a spanking, might actually reinforce toy throwing. Remember, too, that a punisher can be either the onset of an unpleasant event or the removal of a positive state of affairs (response cost).

Variables Affecting Punishment

How effective is punishment? Although many people assume that punishment stops unacceptable behavior, the effectiveness of punishers depends greatly on their *timing, consistency,* and *intensity.* Punishment works best when it occurs as the response is being made or *immediately* afterward (timing), and when it is given *each time* a response occurs (consistency). Thus, you could effectively (and humanely) punish a dog that barks incessantly by spraying water on its nose each time it barks. About 10 to 15 such treatments are usually enough to greatly reduce barking. This would not be the case if you applied punishment haphazardly or long after the barking stopped. If you discover that your dog dug up a tree and ate it while you were gone, punishing the dog hours later will do little good. Likewise, the commonly heard childhood threat, "Wait 'til your father comes home, then you'll be sorry," just makes the father a feared brute; it doesn't effectively punish an undesirable response.

Severe punishment (following a response with an intensely aversive or unpleasant stimulus) can be extremely effective in stopping behavior. If 3-year-old Beavis sticks his finger in a light socket and gets a shock, that may be the last time he *ever* tries it. However, mild punishment only temporarily *suppresses* a response. If the response is still reinforced, punishment may be particularly ineffective.

This fact was demonstrated by slapping rats on the paw as they were bar pressing in a Skinner box. Two groups of well-trained rats were placed on extinction. One group was punished with a slap for each bar press, and the other group was not. It might seem that the slap would cause bar pressing to extinguish more quickly. Yet, this was not the case, as you can see in ● Figure 6.20. Punishment temporarily slowed responding, but it did not cause more rapid extinction. Slapping the paws of rats or children has little permanent effect on a reinforced response.

Similarly, if 7-year-old Alissa sneaks a snack from the refrigerator before dinner and is punished for it, she may pass up snacks for a short time. But because snack sneaking was also rewarded by the sneaked snack, she will probably try

Punishers are consequences that lower the probability that a response will be made again. Receiving a traffic citation is directly punishing because the driver is delayed and reprimanded. Paying a fine and higher insurance rates add to the punishment in the form of response cost.

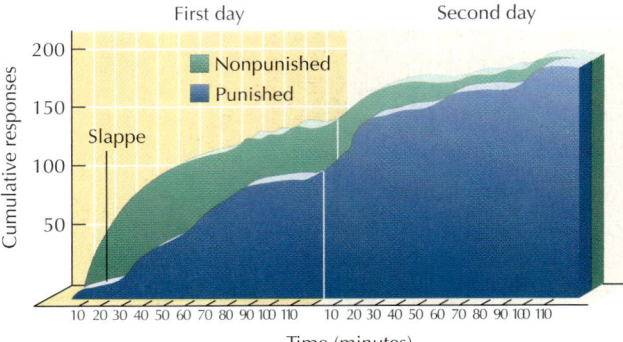

● **FIGURE 6.20** The effect of punishment on extinction. Immediately after punishment, the rate of bar pressing is suppressed, but by the end of the second day, the effects of punishment have disappeared. (From B. F. Skinner, *The Behavior of Organisms.* © 1938. D. Appleton-Century Co., Inc. Reprinted by permission of Prentice-Hall, Inc.)

sneaky snacking again, sometime later (the sneaky little devil). But seriously, to reiterate, intense punishment may permanently suppress responding, even for actions as basic as eating. Animals severely punished while eating may never eat again (Bertsch, 1976).

Side Effects of Punishment

Are there drawbacks to using punishment? There are several, all of which become more of a problem as punishment increases in severity. Basically, punishment is *aversive* (painful or uncomfortable). As a result, people and situations associated with punishment tend, through classical conditioning, to become feared, resented, or disliked. The aversive nature of punishment makes it especially poor to use when teaching children to eat politely or in toilet training.

Escape and Avoidance A second major problem is that aversive stimuli encourage escape and avoidance learning (Brennan, Beck, & Servatius, 2003). In **escape learning** we learn to make a response in order to end an aversive stimulus. For example, if you work with a loud and obnoxious person, you may at first escape from conversations with him to obtain relief. (Notice that escape learning is based on negative reinforcement.) Later you may dodge him altogether. This is an example of **avoidance learning** (making a response in order to postpone or prevent discomfort). Each time you sidestep him, your avoidance is again reinforced by a sense of relief. In many situations involving frequent punishment, similar desires to escape and avoid are activated. For example, children who run away from punishing parents (escape) may soon learn to lie about their behavior (avoidance) or to spend as much time away from home as possible (also an avoidance response).

Aggression A third problem with punishment is that it can greatly increase *aggression*. Animals react to pain by attacking whomever or whatever else is around. A common example is the faithful dog that nips its owner during a painful procedure at the veterinarian's office. Likewise, humans who are in pain have a tendency to lash out at others.

We also know that one of the most common responses to frustration is aggression. Generally speaking, punishment is painful, frustrating, or both. Punishment, therefore, sets up a powerful environment for learning aggression. When spanked, a child may feel angry, frustrated, and hostile. What if that child then goes outside and hits a brother, a sister, or a neighbor? The danger is that aggressive acts may feel good because they release anger and frustration. If so, aggression has been rewarded and will tend to occur again in other frustrating situations.

One study found that children who are physically punished are more likely to engage in aggressive, impulsive, antisocial behavior (Thomas, 2004). Similarly, a classic study of angry adolescent boys found that they were severely punished at home. This suppressed their misbehavior at home but made them more aggressive elsewhere. Parents were often surprised to learn that their "good boys" were in trouble for fighting at school (Bandura & Walters, 1959). Fortunately, at least for younger children, if parents change to less punitive parenting, their children's levels of aggression will decline (Thomas, 2004).

In the classroom, physical punishment, yelling, and humiliation are also generally ineffective. Positive reinforcement, in the form of praise, approval, and reward, is much more likely to quell classroom disruptions, defiance, and inattention (Alberto & Troutman, 2006).

Using Punishment Wisely

In light of its limitations and drawbacks, should punishment be used to control behavior? Parents, teachers, animal trainers, and the like have three basic tools to control simple learning: (1) Reinforcement strengthens responses; (2) nonreinforcement causes responses to extinguish; (3) punishment suppresses responses. (Consult ● Figure 6.21 to refresh your

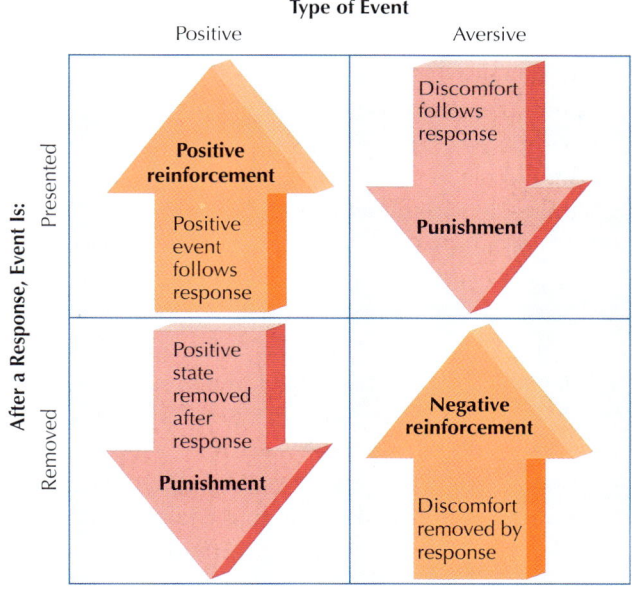

● **FIGURE 6.21** Types of reinforcement and punishment. The impact of an event depends on whether it is presented or removed after a response is made. Each square defines one possibility: Arrows pointing upward indicate that responding is increased; downward-pointing arrows indicate that responding is decreased.

Punishment The process of suppressing a response.
Punisher Any event that decreases the probability or frequency of responses it follows.
Escape learning Learning to make a response in order to end an aversive stimulus.
Avoidance learning Learning to make a response in order to postpone or prevent discomfort.

memory about the different types of reinforcement and punishment.) These tools work best in combination. It is usually best to begin by making liberal use of positive reinforcement, especially praise, to encourage good behavior. Also, try extinction first: See what happens if you ignore a problem behavior, or shift attention to a desirable activity and then reinforce it with praise. Remember, it is much more effective to strengthen and encourage desirable behaviors than it is to punish unwanted behaviors (Gershoff, 2002). When all else fails, it may be necessary to use punishment to help manage the behavior of an animal, child, or even another adult. For those times, here are some tips to keep in mind:

1. *Apply punishment during, or immediately after, misbehavior.* Of course, immediate punishment is not always possible. With older children and adults, you can bridge the delay by clearly stating what act you are punishing. If you cannot punish an animal or young child immediately, wait for the next instance of misbehavior.
2. *Be consistent.* Be very clear about what you regard as misbehavior. Punish every time the misbehavior occurs. Don't punish for something one day and ignore it the next. If you are usually willing to give a child three chances, don't change the rule and explode without warning after a first offense. Both parents should try to punish their children for the same things and in the same way.
3. *Use the minimum punishment necessary to suppress misbehavior.* If punishment is used at all, it should always be mild. In a situation that poses immediate danger, such as when a child reaches for something hot or a dog runs into the street, mild punishment may prevent disaster. Punishment in such cases works best when it produces actions *incompatible* with the response you want to suppress. Let's say a child reaches toward a stove burner. Would a swat on the bottom serve as an effective punisher? Probably so. It would be better, however, to slap the child's outstretched hand so that it will be *withdrawn* from the source of danger. Taking away privileges or other positive reinforcers (response cost) is usually best for older children and adults. Often, a verbal rebuke or a scolding is enough.
4. *Avoid harsh punishment.* Harsh or excessive punishment has serious negative drawbacks (never slap a child's face, for instance). "Sparing the rod" will not spoil a child. In fact, the reverse is true. As we just discussed, harsh punishment can lead to negative emotional reactions, avoidance and escape behaviors, and increased aggression (Aucoin, Frick, & Bodin, 2006). It can even lead to long-term mental health problems (Afifi et al., 2006).

What about spanking? Parents should minimize spanking or avoid it entirely (Gershoff, 2002). Although most children show no signs of long-term damage from spanking if it is backed up by supportive parenting, emotional damage does occur if spankings are severe, frequent, or coupled with harsh parenting (Baumrind, Larzelere, & Cowan, 2002). Like all harsh punishment, frequent spanking tends to increase aggression and leads to more problem behaviors, not fewer (McLoyd & Smith, 2002; Saadeh, Rizzo, & Roberts, 2002). In fact, antispanking laws have been passed in a number of countries around the world.

5. *Don't rely exclusively on punishment.* Mild punishment tends to be ineffective if reinforcers are still available in the situation. That's why it is best to also reward an alternate, desired response. For example, a child who has a habit of taking toys from her sister should not just be reprimanded for it. She should also be praised for cooperative play and sharing her toys with others. Besides, punishment only tells a person or an animal that a response was "wrong." Punishment does not say what the "right" response is, so it *does not teach new behaviors.* If reinforcement is missing, punishment becomes less effective (Gershoff, 2002).
6. *Expect anger from a punished person.* Briefly acknowledge this anger but be careful not to reinforce it. Be willing to admit your mistake if you wrongfully punish someone or if you punished too severely.
7. *Punish with kindness and respect.* Allow the punished person to retain self-respect. For instance, do not punish a person in front of others, if possible. A strong, trusting relationship tends to minimize behavior problems. Ideally, others should want to behave well to get your praise, not because they fear punishment.

To summarize, the most common error in using punishment is to over-rely on it for training or discipline. The overall emotional adjustment of a child or pet disciplined mainly by reward is usually superior to one disciplined mainly by punishment. Frequent punishment makes a person or an animal unhappy, confused, anxious, aggressive, and fearful.

Parents and teachers should also be aware that using punishment can be "habit forming." When children are being noisy, messy, disrespectful, or otherwise misbehaving, the temptation to punish them can be strong. The danger is that punishment often works. When it does, a sudden end to the adult's irritation acts as a negative reinforcer. This encourages the adult to use punishment more often in the future (Alberto & Troutman, 2006). Immediate silence may be "golden," but its cost can be very high in terms of a child's emotional health.

MODULE 6.4 Summary

What does punishment do to behavior?
- Punishment decreases responding. Punishment occurs when a response is followed by the onset of an aversive event or by the removal of a positive event (response cost).
- Punishment is most effective when it is immediate, consistent, and intense.
- Although severe punishment can virtually eliminate a particular behavior, mild punishment usually only temporarily suppresses responding. Reinforcement must be used to make lasting changes in the behavior of a person or an animal.
- Punishment tends to produce escape and avoidance learning, and it encourages the learning of aggressive responses.

KNOWLEDGE BUILDER

Punishment

Recite
1. Negative reinforcement increases responding; punishment suppresses responding. T or F?
2. Three factors that greatly influence the effects of punishment are timing, consistency, and _____.
3. Mild punishment tends to only temporarily _____ a response that is also reinforced.
   a. enhance
   b. aggravate
   c. replace
   d. suppress
4. Three undesired side effects of punishment are (1) conditioning of fear and resentment, (2) encouragement of aggression, and (3) the learning of escape or _____ responses.
5. Using punishment can be "habit forming" because putting a stop to someone else's irritating behavior can _____ _____ the person who applies the punishment.

Reflect
Critical Thinking
6. Using the concept of partial reinforcement, can you explain why inconsistent punishment is especially ineffective?
7. Escape and avoidance learning have been applied to encourage automobile seat belt use. Can you explain how?

Relate
Think of how you were punished as a child. Was the punishment immediate? Was it consistent? What effect did these factors have on your behavior? Was the punishment effective? Which of the side effects of punishment have you witnessed or experienced?

Link
Internet addresses frequently change. To find the sites listed here, visit **http://www.thomsonedu.com/psychology/coon** for an updated list of Internet addresses and direct links to relevant sites.
- **Ten Reasons Not to Hit Your Kids** Read more about the limitations of spanking.
- **Guidelines for Using Time Out with Children and Preteens** Read about the use of response cost as an effective form of punishment.
- **Reinforcement vs Punishment in the Training of Animals** Learn why punishment should be avoided in the training of animals.

ANSWERS
1. T 2. intensity 3. d 4. avoidance 5. negatively reinforce 6. An inconsistently punished response will continue to be reinforced on a partial schedule, which makes it even more resistant to extinction. 7. Many automobiles have an unpleasant buzzer that sounds if the ignition key is turned before the driver's seat belt is fastened. Most drivers quickly learn to fasten the belt to stop the annoying sound. This is an example of escape conditioning. Avoidance conditioning is evident when a driver learns to buckle up before the buzzer sounds.

MODULE 6.5 Cognitive Learning and Imitation

MUCH LEARNING can be explained by classical and operant conditioning. But, as we have seen, even basic conditioning has "mental" elements. As a human, you can anticipate future reward or punishment and react accordingly. (You may wonder why this doesn't seem to work when a doctor or dentist says, "This won't hurt a bit." Here's why: They lie!). In this module we will move beyond conditioning into the realm of cognitive learning.

Cognitive Learning—Beyond Conditioning

SURVEY QUESTION: *What is cognitive learning?*

There is no doubt that human learning includes a large *cognitive,* or mental, dimension (Lefrançois, 2006). As humans, we are greatly affected by information, expectations, perceptions, mental images, and the like. Loosely speaking, **cognitive learning** refers to understanding, knowing, anticipating, or otherwise making use of information-rich higher mental processes. Cognitive learning extends beyond basic conditioning into the realms of memory, thinking, problem solving, and language. Because these topics are covered in later chapters, our discussion here is limited to a first look at learning beyond conditioning.

Cognitive Maps

How do you navigate around the town you live in? Have you constructed an overall mental picture of how the town is laid out. This *cognitive map* acts as a guide even when you must detour or take a new

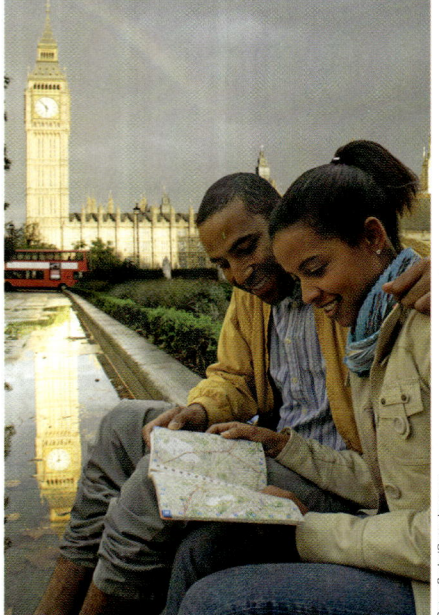

It's easy to get lost when visiting a new city if you don't have a cognitive map of the area. Printed maps help, but they may still leave you puzzled until you begin to form a mental representation of major landmarks and directions.

route (Foo et al., 2005). A **cognitive map** is an internal representation of an area, such as a maze, city, or campus. Even the lowly rat—not exactly a mental giant (well, except for Einstein the rat)—learns *where* food is found in a maze, not just which turns to make to reach the food (Tolman, Ritchie, & Kalish, 1946). If you have ever learned your way through some of the levels found in many video games, you will have a good idea of what a cognitive map is. In a sense, cognitive maps also apply to other kinds of knowledge. For instance, it could be said that you have been developing a "map" of psychology while reading this book. That's why students sometimes find it helpful to draw pictures or diagrams of how they envision concepts fitting together.

Latent Learning

Cognitive learning is also revealed by latent (hidden) learning. **Latent learning** occurs without obvious reinforcement and remains hidden until reinforcement is provided (Davidson, 2000). Here's an example from a classic animal study: Two groups of rats were allowed to explore a maze. The animals in one group found food at the far end of the maze. Soon, they learned to rapidly make their way through the maze when released. Rats in the second group were unrewarded and showed no signs of learning. But later, when the "uneducated" rats were given food, they ran the maze as quickly as the rewarded group (Tolman & Honzik, 1930). Although there was no outward sign of it, the unrewarded animals had learned their way around the maze. Their learning, therefore, remained latent at first (● Fig. 6.22).

How did they learn if there was no reinforcement? Just satisfying curiosity can be enough to reward learning (Harlow

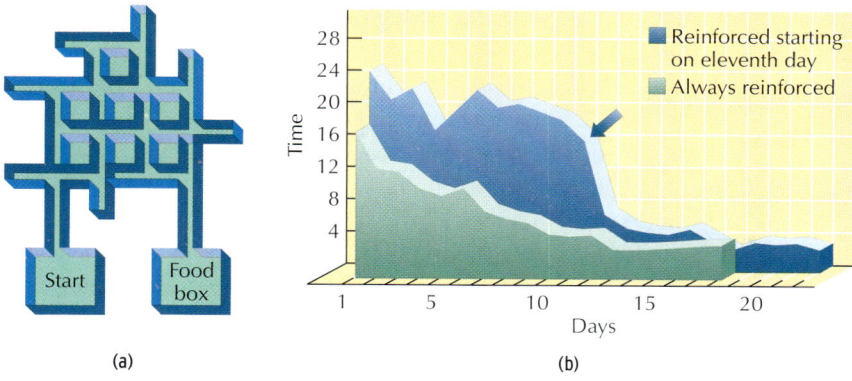

● **FIGURE 6.22** Latent learning. *(a)* The maze used by Tolman and Honzik to demonstrate latent learning by rats. *(b)* Results of the experiment. Notice the rapid improvement in performance that occurred when food was made available to the previously unreinforced animals. This indicates that learning had occurred but that it remained hidden or unexpressed. (Adapted from Tolman & Honzik, 1930.)

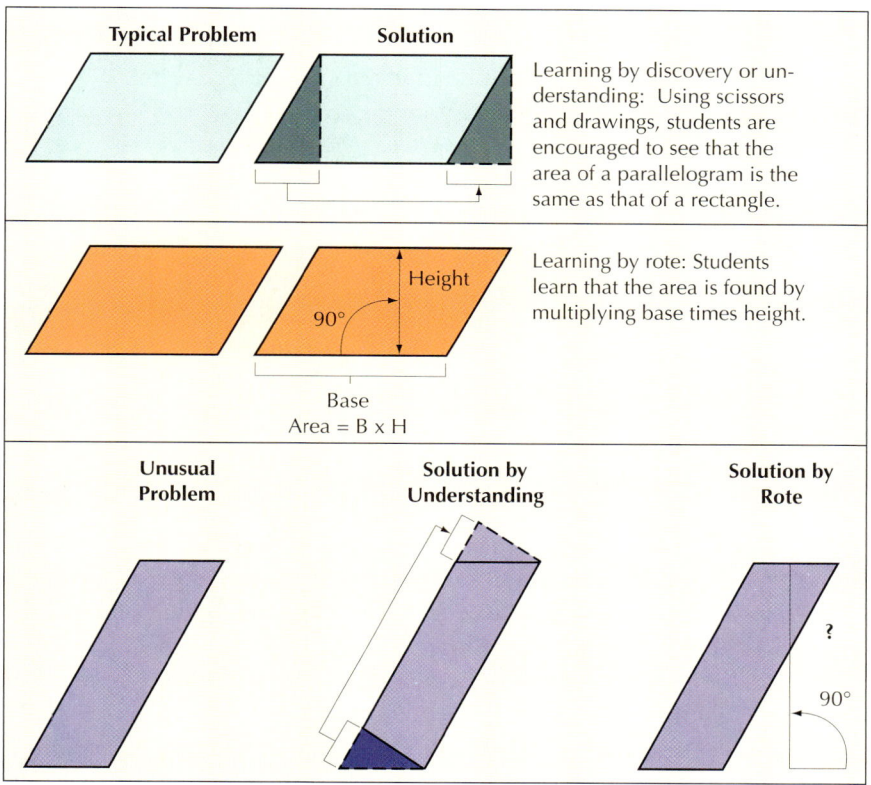

● **FIGURE 6.23** Learning by understanding and by rote. For some types of learning, understanding may be superior, although both types of learning are useful. (Adapted from Wertheimer, 1959.)

people *discover* facts and principles on their own. In **discovery learning**, skills are gained by insight and understanding instead of by rote (Swaak, de Jong, & van Joolingen, 2004).

As long as learning occurs, what difference does it make if it is by discovery or by rote?
● Figure 6.23 illustrates the difference. Two groups of students were taught to calculate the area of a parallelogram by multiplying the height by the length of the base. Some were encouraged to see that a "piece" of a parallelogram could be "moved" to create a rectangle. Later, they were better able to solve unusual problems in which the height times base formula didn't seem to work. Students who simply memorized a rule were confused by the same problems (Wertheimer, 1959). As this implies, discovery can lead to a better understanding of new or unusual problems. When possible, people should try new strategies and discover new solutions during learning. However, this doesn't mean that students are supposed to stumble around and rediscover the principles of math, physics, or chemistry. The best teaching strategies are based on *guided discovery,* in which students are

& Harlow, 1962). In humans, latent learning is related to higher-level abilities, such as anticipating future reward. For example, if you give an attractive classmate a ride home, you may make mental notes about how to get to his or her house, even if a date is only a remote future possibility.

Discovery Learning Much of what is meant by cognitive learning is summarized by the word *understanding*. Each of us has, at times, learned ideas by **rote** (repetition and memorization). Although rote learning is efficient, many psychologists believe that learning is more lasting and flexible when

Cognitive learning Higher level learning involving thinking, knowing, understanding, and anticipation.
Cognitive map Internal images or other mental representations of an area (maze, city, campus, and so forth) that underlie an ability to choose alternative paths to the same goal.
Latent learning Learning that occurs without obvious reinforcement and that remains unexpressed until reinforcement is provided.
Rote learning Learning that takes place mechanically, through repetition and memorization, or by learning rules.
Discovery learning Learning based on insight and understanding.

given enough freedom to actively think about problems and enough guidance so that they gain useful knowledge (Mayer, 2004).

Modeling—Do as I Do, Not as I Say

SURVEY QUESTION: *Does learning occur by imitation?*

Many skills are learned by what Albert Bandura (1971) calls *observational learning,* or *modeling*. **Observational learning** is achieved by watching and imitating the actions of another person or by noting the consequences of the person's actions. In other words, modeling is any process in which information is imparted by example, before direct practice is allowed (Lefrançois, 2006).

The value of learning by observation is obvious: Imagine trying to *tell* someone how to tie a shoe, do a dance step, or play a guitar. Bandura believes that anything that can be learned from direct experience can be learned by observation. Often, this allows a person to skip the tedious trial-and-error stage of learning.

Observational Learning

It seems obvious that we learn by observation, but how does it occur? By observing a **model** (someone who serves as an example), a person may (1) learn new responses, (2) learn to carry out or avoid previously learned responses (depending on what happens to the model for doing the same thing), or (3) learn a general rule that can be applied to various situations (Lefrançois, 2006).

For observational learning to occur, several things must take place. First, the learner must pay *attention* to the model and *remember* what was done. (A beginning auto mechanic might be interested enough to watch an entire tuneup but unable to remember all the steps.) Next, the learner must be able to *reproduce* the modeled behavior. (Sometimes this is a matter of practice, but it may be that the learner will never be able to perform the behavior. We may admire the feats of world-class gymnasts, but most of us could never reproduce them, no matter how much we practiced.) If a model is *successful* at a task or *rewarded* for a response, the learner is more likely to imitate the behavior. In general, models who are attractive, trustworthy, capable, admired, powerful, or high in status also tend to be imitated (Brewer & Wann, 1998). Finally, once a new response is tried, *normal reinforcement determines whether it will be repeated thereafter.* (Notice the similarity to latent learning, described earlier.)

Imitating Models Modeling has a powerful effect on behavior. In a classic experiment, children watched an adult attack a large blowup "Bo-Bo the Clown" doll. Some children saw an adult sit on the doll, punch it, hit it with a hammer, and kick it around the room. Others saw a movie of these actions. A third group saw a cartoon version of the aggression. Later, the children were frustrated by having some attractive toys taken away from them. Then they were allowed to play with the Bo-Bo doll. Most imitated the adult's attack (● Fig. 6.24). Some even added new aggressive acts of their own! Interestingly, the cartoon was only slightly less effective in encouraging aggression than the live adult model and the filmed model (Bandura, Ross, & Ross, 1963).

Then do children blindly imitate adults? No. Remember that observational learning only prepares a person to duplicate a response. Whether it is actually imitated depends on whether the model was rewarded or punished for what was done. Nevertheless, when parents tell a child to do one thing but model a completely different response, children tend to imitate what the parents *do,* and *not* what they *say*. Thus, through modeling, children learn not only attitudes, gestures, emotions, and personality traits, but fears, anxieties, and bad habits as well. A good example is the adolescent smoker, who is much more likely to begin smoking if her parents, siblings, and friends smoke (Wilkinson & Abraham, 2004).

Now, consider a typical situation: Little Raymond has just been interrupted at play by his older brother, Robert.

Observational learning often imparts large amounts of information that would be difficult to obtain by reading instructions or memorizing rules.

● **FIGURE 6.24** A nursery school child imitates the aggressive behavior of an adult model he has just seen in a movie. (Photos courtesy of Albert Bandura.)

Angry and frustrated, he screams at Robert. This behavior interrupts his father Frank's TV watching. Father promptly spanks little Raymond, saying, "This will teach you to hit your big brother." And it will. Because of modeling effects, it is unrealistic to expect a child to "Do as I say, not as I do." The message Frank has given the child is clear: "You have frustrated me; therefore, I will hit you." The next time little Raymond is frustrated, it won't be surprising if he imitates his father and hits his brother (so why does everybody love Raymond, anyway?).

Modeling and the Media

Does television promote observational learning? Today's 8- to 18-year-olds spend an average of 44.5 hours a week engaged with various media, including television, video games, movies, the Internet, music, and print media (Roberts, Foehr, & Rideout, 2005). Although overall use is falling, television still consumes the lion's share of media attention, averaging 21 hours every week.

By the time the average person has graduated from high school, she or he will have viewed some 15,000 hours of TV, compared with only 11,000 hours spent in the classroom. In that time, viewers will have seen some 18,000 murders and countless acts of robbery, arson, bombing, torture, and beatings. Even G-rated cartoons average 10 minutes of violence per hour (Yokota & Thompson, 2000). In short, typical TV viewers are exposed to a massive dose of media violence, which tends to promote observational learning of aggression (Bushman & Anderson, 2001).

Televised Aggression The last finding comes as no surprise. Studies show conclusively that if large groups of children watch a great deal of televised violence, they will be more prone to behave aggressively (Anderson et al., 2003; Bushman & Anderson, 2001). In other words, not all children will become more aggressive, but many will. More ominously, the effect can last into early adulthood. A group of primary school students with known television viewing habits were later contacted in early adulthood (Huesmann et al., 2003). Those who watched more violence on television as elementary schoolers were more aggressive as adults 15 years later (● Fig. 6.25).

Does the same conclusion apply to video games? Oh, yes. Children tend to imitate what they observe in all media. From professional wrestling (Bernthal, 2003) to rap music (Wing-

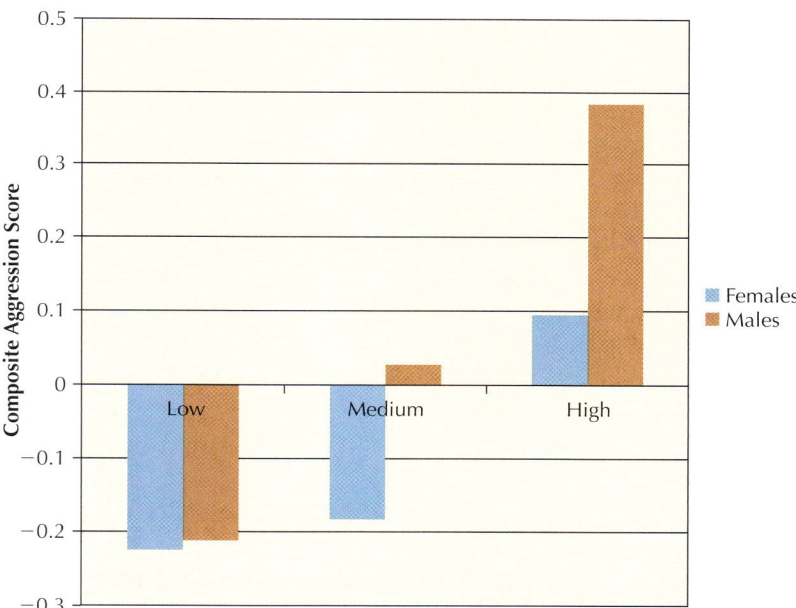

● **FIGURE 6.25** This graph shows that preschoolers who watched low levels of television violence were less aggressive than average as young adults when contacted 15 years later. In contrast, preschoolers who watched high levels of television violence were more aggressive than average as young adults. The composite aggression score includes measures of indirect aggression (e.g., verbal abusiveness) and direct aggression (physical aggression). (Data adapted from Huesmann et al., 2003.)

Observational learning Learning achieved by watching and imitating the actions of another or noting the consequences of those actions.

Model A person who serves as an example in observational learning.

CRITICAL THINKING

You Mean Video Games Might Be Bad for Me?

Today's kids can experience more gore in a day than most people used to experience in a lifetime, even during military combat. For example, in one video game you can kill an entire marching band with a flamethrower. Some of your victims won't die right away. They will just writhe in pain, begging you to finish them off.

What effects do such experiences have on people who play violent video games? Reviews have concluded that violent video games increase aggressive behavior in children and young adults (Anderson & Bushman, 2001; Anderson, 2004). As with TV, young children are especially susceptible to fantasy violence in video games (Anderson et al., 2003; Bensley & Van Eenwyk, 2001).

One study illustrates the impact of video game violence. First, college students played a violent (Mortal Kombat) or nonviolent (PGA Tournament Golf) video game. Next, they competed with another student (actually an actor) in a task that allowed aggression and retaliation to take place. Students who played Mortal Kombat were much more likely to aggress, by punishing their competitor (Bartholow & Anderson, 2002). (Don't mess with someone who just played Mortal Kombat!)

How does video game violence increase aggressive behavior? One possibility is that repeated exposure to violence desensitizes players, making them less likely to react negatively to violence and, hence, more prone to engage in it (Bartholow, Sestir, & Davis, 2005; Funk, 2005). Another possibility is that by practicing violence against other people, players may learn to be aggressive in real life (Unsworth & Ward, 2001). (Before you write off video games altogether, read "You Mean Video Games Might Be Good For Me?" in Module 9.1.)

ood et al., 2003) to video games (Carnagey & Anderson, 2004), children have plenty of opportunity to observe and imitate both the good and the bad. (See "You Mean Video Games Might Be Bad for Me?" for some recent evidence.)

Is it fair to say, then, that media violence causes aggression in consumers, especially children? Fortunately, that would be an exaggeration (Kirsh, 2005). Media violence can make aggression more *likely,* but it does not invariably "cause" it to occur for any given child. Many other factors affect the chances that hostile thoughts will be turned into actions. Youngsters who believe that aggression is an acceptable way to solve problems, who believe that TV violence is realistic, and who identify with TV characters are most likely to copy televised aggression (Huesmann et al., 2003). It is particularly troubling to find media *heroes* behaving aggressively, as well as villains. Younger children, in particular, are more likely to be influenced because they don't fully recognize that media characters and stories are fantasies (McKenna & Ossoff, 1998).

In view of such findings, it is understandable that countries like Canada, Norway, and Switzerland have restricted the amount of permissible violence on television. Should all countries do the same?

A Look Ahead Conditioning principles are often derived from animal experiments. However, it should be apparent that the same principles apply to human behavior. Perhaps the best way to appreciate this fact is to observe how reinforcement affects your own behavior. With this in mind, the upcoming Psychology in Action section proposes a personal experiment in operant conditioning. Don't miss this coming attraction!

TV heroes can act as powerful models for observational learning of aggression.

MODULE 6.5 Summary

What is cognitive learning?

- Cognitive learning involves higher mental processes, such as memory, thinking, problem solving, understanding, knowing, and anticipating.
- Even in relatively simple learning situations, animals and people seem to form cognitive maps (internal representations of relationships).
- In latent learning, learning remains hidden or unseen until a reward or incentive for performance is offered.
- Discovery learning emphasizes insight and understanding, in contrast to rote learning.

Does learning occur by imitation?

- Learning can occur by merely observing and imitating the actions of another person or by noting the consequences of the person's actions.
- Observational learning is influenced by the personal characteristics of the model and the success or failure of the model's behavior. Aggression is readily learned and released by modeling.
- Television characters can act as powerful models for observational learning. Televised violence increases the likelihood of aggression by viewers.

KNOWLEDGE BUILDER

Cognitive Learning and Imitation

Recite

1. An internal representation of relationships is referred to as a _____ _____.
2. Learning that suddenly appears when a reward or incentive for performance is given is called
   a. discovery learning
   b. latent learning
   c. rote learning
   d. reminiscence
3. Psychologists use the term _____ to describe observational learning.
4. If a model is successful, rewarded, attractive, or high in status, his or her behavior is
   a. difficult to reproduce
   b. less likely to be attended to
   c. more likely to be imitated
   d. subject to positive transfer
5. Children who observed a live adult behave aggressively became more aggressive; those who observed movie and cartoon aggression did not. T or F?
6. Children are most likely to imitate TV characters with whom they identify. T or F?
7. Children who watch a great deal of televised violence are more prone to be aggressive, an effect that is best explained by
   a. negative reinforcement
   b. shaping and successive approximations
   c. observational learning
   d. vicarious classical conditioning

Reflect
Critical Thinking

8. Draw a map of your school's campus as you picture it now. Draw a map of the campus as you pictured it after your first visit. Why do the maps differ?
9. Children who watch many aggressive programs on television tend to be more aggressive than average. Why doesn't this observation prove that televised aggression causes aggressive behavior?

Relate

Try to think of at least one personal example of each of these concepts: cognitive map, latent learning, discovery learning.

Describe a skill you have learned primarily through observational learning. How did modeling help you learn?

What entertainment or sports personalities did you identify with when you were a child? How did it affect your behavior?

Link

Internet addresses frequently change. To find the sites listed here, visit http://www.thomsonedu.com/psychology/coon for an updated list of Internet addresses and direct links to relevant sites.

- **Social Learning Theory and Criminality** Explore the hypothesis that cognitive learning underlies much criminal behavior.
- **Mirror Neurons and Imitation Learning** Read about a possible neural basis for imitation learning.
- **Media Violence** How much do children learn by imitating what they see in the media?

ANSWERS

1. cognitive map 2. b 3. modeling 4. c 5. F 6. T 7. c 8. Your cognitive map of the campus has undoubtedly become more accurate and intricate over time as you have added details to it. Your drawings should reflect this change. 9. Because the observation is based on a correlation. Children who are already aggressive may choose to watch more aggressive programs, rather than being made aggressive by them. It took experimental studies to verify that televised aggression promotes aggression by viewers.

MODULE **Psychology in Action**

6.6 Behavioral Self-Management– A Rewarding Project

SURVEY QUESTION: *How does conditioning apply to practical problems?*

This discussion could be the start of one of the most personal applications of psychology in this book. This is an invitation to carry out a self-management project of your own (Watson & Tharp, 2007). Would you like to increase the number of hours you spend studying each week? Would you like to exercise more, attend more classes, concentrate longer, or read more books? All these activities and many others can be improved by applying the principles described here.

Self-Managed Behavior

The principles of operant conditioning can be adapted to manage your own behavior (Martin & Pear, 2003). Here's how:

1. **Choose a target behavior.** Identify the activity you want to change.
2. **Record a baseline.** Record how much time you currently spend performing the target activity or count the number of desired or undesired responses you make each day.
3. **Establish goals.** Remember the principle of shaping, and set realistic goals for gradual improvement on each successive week. Also, set daily goals that add up to the weekly goal.
4. **Choose reinforcers.** If you meet your daily goal, what reward will you allow yourself? Daily rewards might be watching television, eating a candy bar, socializing with friends, listening to your iPod, or whatever you enjoy. Also establish a weekly reward. If you reach your weekly goal, what reward will you allow yourself? A movie? A dinner out? Some time playing a game like Guitar Hero? A weekend hike?
5. **Record your progress.** Keep accurate records of the amount of time spent each day on the desired activity or the number of times you make the desired response.
6. **Reward successes.** If you meet your daily goal, collect your reward. If you fall short, be honest with yourself and skip the reward. Do the same for your weekly goal.

7. **Adjust your plan as you learn more about your behavior.** Overall progress will reinforce your attempts at self-management.

If you have trouble finding rewards, remember that anything done often can serve as reinforcement. This is known as the *Premack principle*. It is named after David Premack, a psychologist who popularized its use. For example, if you like to watch television every night and want to study more, make it a rule not to turn on the set until you have studied for an hour (or whatever length of time you choose). Then lengthen the requirement each week. Here is a sample of one student's plan:

1. *Target behavior:* number of hours spent studying for school.
2. *Recorded baseline:* an average of 25 minutes per day for a weekly total of 3 hours.
3. *Goal for the first week:* an increase in study time to 40 minutes per day; weekly goal of 5 hours total

study time. *Goal for second week:* 50 minutes per day and 6 hours per week. *Goal for third week:* 1 hour per day and 7 hours per week. *Ultimate goal:* to reach and maintain 14 hours per week study time.

4. *Daily reward for reaching goal:* 1 hour of guitar playing in the evening; no playing if the goal is not met. *Weekly reward for reaching goal:* going to a movie or buying a DVD.

Self-Recording

Even if you find it difficult to give and withhold rewards, you are likely to succeed. Simply knowing that you are reaching a desired goal can be reward enough. The key to any self-management program, therefore, is **self-recording** (keeping records of response frequencies, a form of feedback). The concept was once demonstrated by students in a psychology course. Some of the students recorded their study time and graphed their daily and weekly study behavior. Even though no extra rewards were offered, these students earned better grades than others who were not required to keep records (Johnson & White, 1971).

Feedback can help you decrease bad habits as well as increase desirable responses. Keep track of the number of times daily that you arrive late to class, smoke a cigarette, watch an hour of TV, drink a cappuccino, bite your fingernails, swear, or whatever you are interested in changing. A simple tally on a piece of paper will do, or you can get a small mechanical counter like those used to keep golf scores or count calories. Record keeping helps break patterns, and the feedback can be motivating as you begin to make progress.

Good Ways to Break Bad Habits

How can I use learning principles to break a bad habit? By using the methods we have discussed, you can reinforce yourself for *decreasing* unwanted behaviors. However, breaking bad habits may require some additional techniques. Here are four strategies to help you change bad habits.

Alternate Responses

A good strategy for change is to try to get the same reinforcement with a new response.

Example: Marta often tells jokes at the expense of others. Her friends sometimes feel hurt by her sharp-edged humor. Marta senses this and wants to change. What can she do? Usually, Marta's joke telling is reinforced by attention and approval. She could just as easily get the same reinforcement by giving other people praise or compliments. Making a change in her behavior should be easy because she will continue to receive the reinforcement she seeks.

Extinction

Try to discover what is reinforcing an unwanted response and remove, avoid, or delay the reinforcement.

Example: Fatima has developed a habit of taking longer and longer "breaks" to watch TV when she should be studying. Obviously, TV watching is reinforcing her break taking. To improve her study habits, Fatima could delay reinforcement by studying at the library or some other location a good distance from her TV.

Response Chains

Break up response chains that precede an undesired behavior; this will help break the bad habit. The key idea is to scramble the chain of events that leads to an undesired response (Watson & Tharp, 2007).

Example: Most nights Ignacio comes home from work, turns on the TV, and eats a whole bag of cookies or chips. He then takes a shower and changes clothes. By dinner time he has lost his appetite. Ignacio realizes he is substituting junk food for dinner. Ignacio could solve the problem by breaking the response chain that precedes dinner. For instance, he could shower immediately when he gets home or avoid turning on the television until after dinner.

Cues and Antecedents

Try to avoid, narrow down, or remove stimuli that elicit the bad habit.

Example: Brandon wants to cut down on smoking. He can take many smoking cues out of his surroundings by removing ashtrays, matches, and extra cigarettes from his house, car, and office. Drug cravings are strongly related to cues conditioned to the drug, such as the odor of cigarettes (Lazev, Herzog, & Brandon, 1999). Brandon can narrow antecedent stimuli even more. He could begin by smoking only in the lounge at work, never in his office or in his car. He could then limit his smoking to home. Then to only one room at home. Then to one chair at home. If he succeeds in getting this far, he may want to limit his smoking to only one unpleasant place, such as a bathroom, basement, or garage (Riley et al., 2002).

Contracting

If you try the techniques described here and have difficulty sticking with them, you may want to try behavioral contracting. In a **behavioral contract,** you state a specific problem

---

Self-recording Self-management based on keeping records of response frequencies.

Behavioral contract A formal agreement stating behaviors to be changed and consequences that apply.

behavior you want to control, or a goal you want to achieve. Also state the rewards you will receive, privileges you will forfeit, or punishments you must accept. The contract should be signed by you and a person you trust.

A behavioral contract can be quite motivating, especially when mild punishment is part of the agreement. Here's a classic example, reported by Nurnberger and Zimmerman (1970): A student working on his Ph.D. had completed all requirements but his dissertation, yet for 2 years had not written a single page. A contract was drawn up for him in which he agreed to meet weekly deadlines on the number of pages he would complete. To make sure he would meet the deadlines, he wrote postdated checks. These were to be forfeited if he failed to reach his goal for the week. The checks were made out to organizations he despised (the Ku Klux Klan and American Nazi Party). From the time he signed the contract until he finished his degree, the student's work output was greatly improved.

Getting Help

Attempting to manage or alter your own behavior may be more difficult than it sounds. If you feel you need more information, consult the books listed below. You will also find helpful advice in the Psychology in Action module of Chapter 13. If you do try a self-modification project but find it impossible to reach your goals, be aware that professional advice is available.

Where to Obtain More Information:

Watson, D. L., & Tharp, R. G. (2007). *Self-directed behavior* (9th ed.). Belmont, CA: Wadsworth.

Williams, R. L., & Long, J. D. (1991). *Toward a self-managed life style.* Boston: Houghton Mifflin.

MODULE 6.6 Psychology in Action Summary

How does conditioning apply to practical problems?
- By applying operant conditioning principles, it is possible to change or manage your own behavior.
- When managing behavior, self-reinforcement, self-recording, feedback, and behavioral contracting are all helpful.
- Four strategies that can help change bad habits are reinforcing alternative responses, promoting extinction, breaking response chains, and avoiding antecedent cues.

KNOWLEDGE BUILDER

Behavioral Self-Management

Recite

1. After a target behavior has been selected for reinforcement, it's a good idea to record a baseline so that you can set realistic goals for change. T or F?
2. Self-recording, even without the use of extra rewards, can bring about desired changes in target behaviors. T or F?
3. The Premack principle states that behavioral contracting can be used to reinforce changes in behavior. T or F?
4. A self-management plan should make use of the principle of shaping by setting a graduated series of goals. T or F?
5. Eleni ends up playing dozens of solitaire games on her computer each time she tries to work on a term paper for her history class. Eventually she does get to work on the paper, but only after a long delay. To break this bad habit Eleni removes the solitaire icon from her computer screen so that she won't see it when she begins work. Eleni has used which strategy for breaking bad habits?
   a. alternative responses
   b. extinction
   c. avoid cues
   d. contracting

Reflect
Critical Thinking

6. How does setting daily goals in a behavioral self-management program help maximize the effects of reinforcement?

Relate

Even if you don't expect to carry out a self-management project right now, outline a plan for changing your own behavior. Be sure to describe the behavior you want to change, set goals, and identify reinforcers.

Link

Internet addresses frequently change. To find the sites listed here, visit **http://www.thomsonedu.com/psychology/coon** for an updated list of Internet addresses and direct links to relevant sites.

- **Psychological Self-Tools** An online self-help book.
- **Self-Management** Explore some self-management techniques.
- **Behavior Contract** An example of a behavioral contract from a school setting.

ANSWERS

1. T 2. T 3. F 4. T 5. c 6. Daily performance goals and rewards reduce the delay of reinforcement, which maximizes its impact.

Interactive Learning

Psychology: Active Learning Modules Book Companion Website

http://www.thomsonedu.com/psychology/coon

Visit your Book Companion Website, where you will find flash cards, practice quizzes, Internet links, and more to help you study.

ThomsonNOW™

Just What You Need to Know NOW!

Spend time on what you need to master rather than on information you already have learned. Take a pre-test for this chapter, and ThomsonNOW will generate a personalized study plan based on your results. The study plan will identify the topics you need to review and direct you to online resources to help you master those topics. You can then take a post-test to help you determine the concepts you have mastered and what you will need to work on. Try it out! Go to www.thomsonedu.com/login to sign in with an access code or to purchase access to this product.

7 Memory

MODULE 7.1 Memory Systems
SURVEY QUESTION: Is there more than one type of memory?

MODULE 7.2 STM and LTM
SURVEY QUESTION: What are the features of short-term memory?
SURVEY QUESTION: What are the features of long-term memory?
SURVEY QUESTION: Is there more than one type of long-term memory?

MODULE 7.3 Measuring Memory
SURVEY QUESTION: How is memory measured?

MODULE 7.4 Forgetting
SURVEY QUESTION: What causes forgetting?
SURVEY QUESTION: What happens in the brain when memories are formed?

MODULE 7.5 Exceptional Memory and Improving Memory
SURVEY QUESTION: What are "photographic" memories?
SURVEY QUESTION: How can I improve my memory?

MODULE 7.6 Psychology in Action: Mnemonics—Memory Magic
SURVEY QUESTION: Are there any tricks to help me with my memory?

"What the Hell's Going on Here?"

It's February and Steven is cross-country skiing on the ice of Lake Michigan. He realizes he is very cold and decides to turn back. In a few minutes comes a new realization: He is lost. Wandering on the ice, he grows numb and very, very tired.

Put yourself in Steven's shoes, and you will appreciate the shock of what happened next. Steven clearly recalls wandering lost and alone on the ice. Immediately after that, he remembers waking up in a field. But as he looked around, Steven knew something was wrong. It was a warm spring day! In his backpack he found running shoes, swimming goggles, and a pair of glasses—all unfamiliar. As he looked at his clothing—also unfamiliar—Steven thought to himself, "What the hell's going on here?" Fourteen months had passed since he left to go skiing (Loftus & Loftus, 1980). How did he get to the field? Steven couldn't say. He had lost more than a year of his life to total amnesia.

As Steven's amnesia vividly shows, life without memory would be meaningless. Imagine the terror of having all your memories wiped out. You would have no identity, no knowledge, and no life history (Behrend, Beike, & Lampinen, 2004). You wouldn't recognize friends or family members. When you looked in a mirror, a stranger would stare back at you. In a very real sense, we are our memories.

This chapter discusses memory and forgetting. By reading it you'll almost certainly discover ways to improve your memory.

MODULE 7.1 Memory Systems

DO YOU REMEMBER what you had for breakfast this morning? The last friend you instant messaged? Or what happened on September 11, 2001? Of course you do. But how is it possible for us to so easily travel back in time? Let's begin with a look at basic memory systems. An interesting series of events must occur before we can say "I remember."

Stages of Memory—Do You Have a Mind Like a Steel Trap? or a Sieve?

SURVEY QUESTION: *Is there more than one type of memory?*

Many people think of memory as "a dusty storehouse of facts." In reality, **memory** is an active system that receives, stores, organizes, alters, and recovers information (Lieberman, 2004). In some general ways memory acts like a computer (● Fig. 7.1). Incoming information is first **encoded,** or changed into a usable form. This step is like typing data into a computer. Next, information is **stored,** or held, in the system. (As we will see in a moment, human memory can be pictured as three separate storage systems.) Finally, memories must be **retrieved,** or taken out of storage to be useful. If you're going to remember all the 9,856 new terms on your next psychology exam, you must successfully encode, store, and retrieve them.

What are the three separate memory systems just mentioned? Psychologists have identified three stages of memory in a model known as the *Atkinson-Schiffrin model* (Atkinson & Schiffrin, 1968; Goldstein, 2008). To be stored for a long time, information must pass through all three stages (● Fig. 7.2).

Sensory Memory

Let's say a friend asks you to pick up several things at a market. How will you remember them? Information first enters **sensory memory,** which can hold an exact copy of what you see or hear, for a few seconds or less. We are normally unaware of the functioning of our sensory memories. For instance, look at a flower and then quickly close your eyes. If you are lucky, you might just notice that an **iconic** (eye-KON-ick) **memory,** or fleeting mental image, of the flower will persist for about one-half second (Keysers et al., 2005). Similarly, when you hear information, sensory memory stores it as an *echoic memory* for up to 2 seconds (Haenschel et al., 2005). (An **echoic memory** is a brief flurry of activity in the auditory system.) In general, sensory memory holds information just long enough to move it to the second memory system, short-term memory (Neath & Surprenant, 2003).

Short-Term Memory

Not everything we see or hear stays in memory. Imagine that a radio is playing in the background as your friend reads her shopping list. Will you remember what the announcer says, too? Probably not, because *selective attention* (focusing on a selected portion of sensory input) controls what information moves on to short-term memory. **Short-term memory (STM)** holds small amounts of information in conscious awareness for a dozen seconds or so. By paying attention to your friend, you will place her shopping list in short-term memory (while you ignore the voice on the radio saying, "Buy Burpo Butter").

How are short-term memories encoded? Short-term memories can be stored as images. But more often they are stored *phonetically* (by sound), especially in recalling words and letters (Page et al., 2007). If you are introduced to Tim at a party and you forget his name, you are more likely to call him by a name that sounds like Tim (Jim, Kim, or Slim, for instance), rather than a name that sounds different, such as Bob or Mike. Your friend with the shopping list may be lucky if you don't bring home jam instead of ham and soap instead of soup!

Short-term memory briefly stores small amounts of information. When you dial a phone number or briefly remember a shopping list, you are using STM. Notice that information is quickly "dumped" from STM and forever lost. Short-term memory prevents our minds from storing useless names, dates, telephone numbers, and other trivia.

● **FIGURE 7.1** In some ways, a computer acts like a mechanical memory system. Both systems process information, and both allow encoding, storage, and retrieval of data.

● **FIGURE 7.2** The Atkinson-Shiffrin model. Remembering is thought to involve at least three steps. Incoming information is first held for a second or two by sensory memory. Information selected by attention is then transferred to temporary storage in short-term memory (STM). If new information is not rapidly encoded, or rehearsed, it is forgotten. If it is transferred to long-term memory (LTM), it becomes relatively permanent, although retrieving it may be a problem. The preceding is a useful, but highly simplified, *model* of memory; it may not be literally true of what happens in the brain (Atkinson & Shiffrin, 1968; Goldstein, 2008).

As you may have noticed when dialing a telephone, STM is very sensitive to *interruption*, or *interference*. You've probably had something like this happen: Someone leaves a phone number on your answering machine. You repeat the number to yourself as you start to dial. Then the doorbell rings and you rush to see who is there. When you return to the phone, you have completely forgotten the number. You listen to the message again and memorize the number. This time as you begin to dial, someone asks you a question. You answer, turn to the phone, and find that you have forgotten the number. Notice again that STM can handle only small amounts of information. It is very difficult to do more than one task at a time in STM (Miyake, 2001; Oberauer & Göthe, 2006).

Working Memory Short-term memory is often used for more than just storing information. When STM is combined with other mental processes, it provides an area of **working memory** where we do much of our thinking. Working memory acts as a sort of "mental scratchpad." It briefly holds the information we need when we are thinking and solving problems (Holmes & Adams, 2006). Whenever you do mental arithmetic, put together a puzzle, plan a meal, follow directions, or read a book, you are using working memory (Baddeley, 2003).

Long-Term Memory

If STM is so limited, how do we remember for longer periods? Information that is important or meaningful is transferred to **long-term memory** (**LTM**), which acts as a lasting storehouse for knowledge. LTM contains everything you know about the world—from aardvark to zucchini, math to *Desperate Housewives*, facts to fantasy. Yet, there appears to be no danger of running out of room. LTM can hold nearly limitless amounts of information. In fact, the more you know, the easier it becomes to add new information to memory. This is the reverse of what we would expect if LTM could be "filled up" (Goldstein, 2008). It is also one of many reasons for getting an education.

Are long-term memories also encoded as sounds? They can be. But typically, long-term memories are stored on the basis of *meaning*, not sound. If you make an error in LTM, it will probably be related to meaning. For example, if you are trying to recall the word *barn* from a memorized list, you are more likely to mistakenly say *shed* or *farm* than *yarn* or *darn*. If you can link information in STM to knowledge already stored in LTM, it gains meaning. This makes it easier to remember. As an example, try to memorize this story:

> With hocked gems financing him, our hero bravely defied all scornful laughter. "Your eyes deceive," he had said. "An egg, not a table, correctly typifies this unexplored planet." Now three sturdy sisters sought proof. Forging along, days became weeks as many doubters spread fearful rumors about the edge. At last from nowhere welcome winged creatures appeared, signifying momentous success. (Adapted from Dooling & Lachman, 1971.)

Memory The mental system for receiving, encoding, storing, organizing, altering, and retrieving information.
Encoding Converting information into a form in which it will be retained in memory.
Storage Holding information in memory for later use.
Retrieval Recovering information from storage in memory.
Sensory memory The first, normally unconscious, stage of memory, which holds an exact record of incoming information for a few seconds or less.
Iconic memory A mental image or visual representation.
Echoic memory A brief continuation of sensory activity in the auditory system after a sound is heard.
Short-term memory (**STM**) The memory system used to hold small amounts of information in our conscious awareness for about a dozen seconds.
Working memory Another name for short-term memory, especially as it is used for thinking and problem solving.
Long-term memory (**LTM**) The memory system used for relatively permanent storage of meaningful information.

HUMAN DIVERSITY

Cows, Memories, and Culture

If you were on a farm and saw 20 cows walk by, do you think you could remember the age, color, gender, and condition of all of them? Unless you are a dairy farmer, doing so would be quite a feat of memory. As noted, we are most likely to remember information that is personally important or meaningful. However, for a Maasai person from East Africa, it would be easier. Livestock are very important in Maasai culture; a Maasai's wealth is measured by the number of cattle owned. Thus, the Maasai are prepared to encode and store information about cattle that would be difficult for most people in the United States to remember.

Culture affects our memories in other interesting ways. For example, American culture emphasizes individuals, whereas Chinese culture emphasizes membership in groups. In one study, European-American and Chinese adults were asked to recall 20 memories from any time in their lives. As expected, American memories tended to be self-centered: Most people remembered surprising events and what they did during the events. Chinese adults, in contrast, remembered important social or historical events and their own interactions with family members, friends, and others (Wang & Conway, 2004). Thus, in the United States, personal memories tend to be about "me"; in China they tend to be about "us."

This odd story emphasizes the impact that meaning has on memory. People given the title of the story were able to remember it far better than those not given a title. See if the title helps you as much as it did them: "Columbus Discovers America."

Dual Memory Although sensory memory is involved every time we use our memory, we are most likely to notice STM and LTM. To summarize their connection, picture short-term memory as a small desk at the front of a huge warehouse full of filing cabinets (LTM). As information enters the warehouse, it is first placed on the desk. Because the desk is small, it must be quickly cleared off to make room for new information. Unimportant items are simply tossed away. Meaningful or personally important information is placed in the files (LTM). (See "Cows, Memories, and Culture.")

When we want to use knowledge from LTM to answer a question, the information is returned to STM. Or, in our analogy, a folder is taken out of the files (LTM) and moved to the desk (STM), where it can be used. Now that you have a general picture of memory it is time to explore STM and LTM in more detail. But first, here's a chance to rehearse what you've learned.

MODULE 7.1 Summary

Is there more than one type of memory?
- Memory systems allow us to encode, store, and retrieve information.
- The three stages of memory (sensory memory, short-term memory, and long-term memory) hold information for increasingly longer periods.
- The best way to remember depends, to an extent, on which memory system you are using.
- Sensory memories are encoded as iconic memories or echoic memories. Short-term memories tend to be encoded by sound, and long-term memories by meaning.

KNOWLEDGE BUILDER

Memory Systems

Recite
Learning Check

Match: **A.** Sensory memory **B.** STM **C.** LTM

1. ____ Information tends to be stored phonetically
2. ____ Holds information for a few seconds or less
3. ____ Stores an iconic memory or echoic memory
4. ____ Permanent, unlimited capacity
5. ____ Temporarily holds small amounts of information
6. ____ Selective attention determines its contents
7. STM is improved by interruption, or interference, because attention is more focused at such times. T or F?

Reflect
Critical Thinking

8. Why is sensory memory important to filmmakers?

Relate

Wave a pencil back and forth in front of your eyes while focusing on something in the distance. The pencil's image looks transparent. Why? (Because sensory memory briefly holds an image of the pencil. This image persists after the pencil passes by.)

Think of a time today when you used short-term memory (such as briefly remembering a phone number, an Internet address, or someone's name). How long did you retain the information? How did you encode it? How much do you remember now?

How is long-term memory helping you read this sentence? If the words weren't already stored in LTM, could you read at all? How else have you used LTM today?

Link

Internet addresses frequently change. To find the sites listed here, visit **http://www.thomsonedu.com/psychology/coon** for an updated list of Internet addresses and direct links to relevant sites.

- **Playing Games With Memory** Try some activities to test your memory.
- **The Atkinson-Schiffrin model** Further explore the three-store model of memory.
- **Working Memory, Language and Reading** Use the concept of working memory to better understand the process or reading.

ANSWERS

1. B 2. A 3. A 4. C 5. B 6. B 7. F 8. Without sensory memory, a movie would look like a series of still pictures. The split-second persistence of visual images helps blend one motion-picture frame into the next.

MODULE 7.2 STM and LTM

TO MAKE GOOD USE OF YOUR MEMORY, it is valuable to know more about the quirks and characteristics of both STM and LTM. It's time to dig deeper into the inner workings of our dual memory system.

Short-Term Memory—Do You Know the Magic Number?

SURVEY QUESTION: *What are the features of short-term memory?*

How much information can be held in short-term memory? For an answer, read the following numbers once. Then close the book and write as many as you can in the correct order.

8 5 1 7 4 9 3

This is called a digit-span test. It is a measure of attention and short-term memory. If you were able to correctly repeat 7 digits, you have an average short-term memory. Now try to memorize the following list, again reading it only once.

7 1 8 3 5 4 2 9 1 6 3 4

This series was probably beyond your short-term memory capacity. Psychologist George Miller found that short-term memory is limited to the "magic number" 7 (plus or minus 2) **information bits** (Miller, 1956). A bit is a single meaningful "piece" of information, such as a digit. It is as if short-term memory has 7 "slots" or "bins" into which separate items can be placed. Actually, a few people can remember up to 9 bits, and for some types of information 5 bits is the limit. Thus, an *average* of 7 information bits can be held in short-term memory (Neath & Surprenant, 2003).

When all of the "slots" in STM are filled, there is no room for new information. Picture how this works at a party: Let's say your hostess begins introducing everyone who is there, "Chun, Dasia, Marco, Roseanna, Cholik, Shawn, Kyrene. . . ." "Stop," you think to yourself. But she continues, "Nelia, Jay, Efren, Frank, Marietta, Jorge, Patty, Amit, Ricky." The hostess leaves, satisfied that you have met everyone. And you spend the evening talking with Chun, Dasia, and Ricky, the only people whose names you remember!

Chunking

Before we continue, try your short-term memory again, this time on letters. Read the following letters once, then look away and try to write them in the proper order.

T V I B M U S N Y M C A

Notice that there are 12 letters, or "bits" of information. This should be beyond the 7-item limit of STM. However, because the letters are in four groups, or *chunks* of information, many students are able to memorize them. **Information chunks** are made up of bits of information grouped into larger units.

How does chunking help? Chunking *recodes* (reorganizes) information into units that are already in LTM. For example, you may have noticed that NY is the abbreviation for New York. If so, the two bits N and Y became one chunk. In a classic experiment that used lists like this one, people remembered best when the letters were read as familiar meaningful chunks: TV, IBM, USN, YMCA (Bower & Springston, 1970). If you recoded the letters this way, you probably remembered the entire list.

Chunking suggests that STM holds about 5 to 7 of whatever units we are using. A single chunk could be made up of numbers, letters, words, phrases, or familiar sentences. Picture STM as a small desk again. Through chunking, we combine several items into one "stack" of information. This allows us to place 7 stacks on the desk, where before there was only room for 7 separate items. While you are studying, try to find ways to link 2, 3, or more separate facts or ideas into larger chunks, and your short-term memory will improve. Psychologist Nelson Cowan (2001, 2005) believes that STM may actually hold only 4 items, unless some chunking has occurred. The clear message is that creating information chunks is the key to making good use of your short-term memory (Gobet, 2005).

Rehearsing Information

How long do short-term memories last? They disappear very rapidly. However, you can prolong a memory by silently repeating it, a process called **maintenance rehearsal.** You have probably briefly remembered an address or telephone number this way. In a sense, rehearsing information allows you to "hear" it many times, not just once (Nairne, 2002). The more times a short-term memory is rehearsed, the greater its chances of being stored in LTM (Goldstein, 2008).

What if rehearsal is prevented, so a memory cannot be recycled or moved to LTM? Without maintenance rehearsal, STM is quite brief. In one experiment, subjects heard meaningless syllables like XAR followed by a number like 67. As soon as subjects heard the number, they began counting backward by threes (to prevent them from repeating the syllable). After a delay of between 12 and 18 seconds, their memory for the syllables fell to zero (Peterson & Peterson, 1959).

After *12 to 18 seconds* without rehearsal, the short-term memories were gone forever! Part of this rapid loss can be explained by the testing procedures used (Goldstein, 2008). In daily life, short-term memories usually last longer. Just the same, if you are introduced to someone, and the name slips out of STM, it is gone forever. To escape this awkward situation you might try saying something like, "I'm curious, how do you spell your name?" Unfortunately, the response is often an icy reply like, "B-O-B S-M-I-T-H, it's really not too difficult." To avoid embarrassment, pay careful attention to the name, repeat it to yourself several times, and try to use it in the next sentence or two—before you lose it (Neath & Surprenant, 2003).

Elaborative rehearsal, which makes information more meaningful, is a far better way to form lasting memories. Elaborative rehearsal links new information to memories that are already in LTM. When you are studying, you will remember more if you elaborate, extend, and reflect about the meaning of the information. As you read, try to reflect frequently. Ask yourself "why" questions, such as "Why would that be true?" (Toyota & Kikuchi, 2005; Willoughby et al., 1997). Also, try to relate new ideas to your own experiences and knowledge (Hartlep & Forsyth, 2000).

● **FIGURE 7.3** Exposed cerebral cortex of a patient undergoing brain surgery. Numbers represent points that reportedly produced "memories" when electrically stimulated. A critical evaluation of such reports suggests that they are more like dreams than memories. This fact raises questions about claims that long-term memories are permanent. (From Penfield, 1958. Courtesy of the author and Charles C Thomas, Publisher, Springfield, Illinois.)

Long-Term Memory— Where the Past Lives

SURVEY QUESTIONS: *What are the features of long-term memory? Is there more than one type of long-term memory?*

An electrode touched the patient's brain. Immediately she said, "Yes, sir, I think I heard a mother calling her little boy somewhere. It seemed to be something happening years ago. It was somebody in the neighborhood where I live." A short time later the electrode was applied to the same spot. Again the patient said, "Yes, I hear the same familiar sounds, it seems to be a woman calling, the same lady" (Penfield, 1958). A woman undergoing brain surgery made these statements. There are no pain receptors in the brain, so the patient was awake as her brain was electrically stimulated (● Fig. 7.3). When activated, some brain areas seemed to produce vivid memories of long-forgotten events.

Permanence *Are all our experiences permanently recorded in memory?* Results like those described led neurosurgeon Wilder Penfield to claim that the brain records the past like a "strip of movie film, complete with sound track" (Penfield, 1957). But as you know, this is an exaggeration. Many events never get past short-term memory. Also, brain stimulation produces memory-like experiences in only about 3 percent of cases. Most reports resemble dreams more than memories, and many are clearly imaginary. Memory experts now believe that long-term memories are only *relatively* permanent (Goldstein, 2008). Perfect, eternal memories are a myth.

TRY IT YOURSELF: HOW'S YOUR MEMORY?
To better appreciate the next topic, pause for a moment and read the words you see here. Read through the list once. Then continue reading the next section of this module.

bed   dream   blanket   doze   pillow   nap   snore   mattress   alarm   clock   rest   slumber   nod   sheet   bunk   cot   cradle   groggy

Constructing Memories

There's another reason for doubting that all our experiences are permanently recorded. As new long-term memories are stored, older memories are often updated, changed, lost, or

Information bits Meaningful units of information, such as numbers, letters, words, or phrases.
Information chunks Information bits grouped into larger units.
Maintenance rehearsal Silently repeating or mentally reviewing information to hold it in short-term memory.
Elaborative rehearsal Rehearsal that links new information with existing memories and knowledge.

CRITICAL THINKING

Do You Like Jam With Your Memory?

Have you ever wondered why famous companies, which already sell huge amounts of familiar products (such as soft drinks or beer), continue to advertise as heavily as they do? If you believe the point of the advertising is to familiarize people with a product or to inform them about it, this *is* a mystery. But if you think about the constructive nature of memory, the mystery is solved. According to economist Jesse Shapiro (2006), the intent of much advertising is to "jam" your memory with positive impressions of a product.

How does "memory jamming" work? How many times have you had a bottle or can of your favorite beer or soft drink? And how many commercials for those beverages have you watched? Every extra commercial adds one more positive memory of the beverage to your long-term memory. Here's a typical commercial: Boy goes to cool party, sees hot girl, flashes favorite beer, gets girl. (Yes, beer commercials mainly target young men.) Because we cannot easily tell which recollection is fact and which is fiction, storing enough of these commercials can eventually create "memories" that never happened. For example, you might remember enjoying a particular beverage more than you actually did, in fact.

According to Shapiro (2006), the more positive fictional commercials we see, the less likely we are to remember an actual negative experience with a product. In effect, the positive, fictional memories "jam," or block, our ability to remember actual negative memories when deciding whether to buy a product. Braun-LaTour & LaTour (2004) add that long-term advertising campaigns create a "brand" memory that can be remarkably strong. This appears to be especially true when the ads are first viewed in early childhood. So perhaps you have been having jam with your memories ever since you were a baby.

---

revised (Lieberman, 2004). To illustrate this point, Elizabeth Loftus and John Palmer (1974) showed people a filmed automobile accident. Afterward, some participants were asked to estimate how fast the cars were going when they "smashed" into each other. For others the words "bumped," "contacted," or "hit" replaced "smashed." One week later, each person was asked, "Did you see any broken glass?" Those asked earlier about the cars that "smashed" into each other were more likely to say yes. (No broken glass was shown in the film.) The new information ("smashed") was included in memories and altered them.

Eyewitness memories are notoriously inaccurate. By the time witnesses are asked to testify in court, information they learned after an incident may blend into their original memories.

TRY IT YOURSELF: OLD OR NEW?
Now, without looking back to the list of words you read a few minutes ago, see if you can tell which of the following are "old" words (items from the list you read) and which are "new" words (items that weren't on the list). Mark each of the following words as old or new:

sofa   sleep   lamp   kitchen

Updating memories is called **constructive processing.** Gaps in memory, which are common, may be filled in by logic, guessing, or new information (Schacter, Norman, & Koutstaal, 1998). Indeed, it is possible to have "memories" for things that never happened (such as remembering broken glass at an accident when there was none) (Loftus, 2003a, 2003b). In one study, people who had visited a Disney resort were shown several fake ads for Disney that featured Bugs Bunny. Later, about 16 percent of the people who saw these fake ads claimed that they had met Bugs at Disneyland. This is impossible, of course, because Bugs Bunny is a Warner Brothers character that would never be found at Disneyland (Braun, Ellis, & Loftus, 2002).

Could constructive processing be used to deliberately manipulate memory? Bingo. According to one theory, advertisers do it all the time. See "Do You Like Jam With Your Memory?" for more information.

TRY IT YOURSELF: AND NOW, THE RESULTS
Return now and look at the labels you wrote on the "old or new" word list. Contrary to what you may think you "remembered," all of the listed words are "new." None was on the original list!

CRITICAL THINKING

Telling Wrong from Right in Forensic Memory

Imagine that you are a forensic psychologist, investigating a crime. Unfortunately, your witness can't remember much of what happened. As a "memory detective," what can you do to help?

Could hypnosis improve the witness's memory? It might seem so. In one case in California, 26 children were abducted from a school bus and held captive for ransom. Under hypnosis, the bus driver recalled the license plate number of the kidnappers' van. This memory helped break the case. Such successes seem to imply that hypnosis can improve memory. But does it?

Research has shown that hypnosis increases false memories more than it does true ones. Eighty percent of the new memories produced by hypnotized subjects in one classic experiment were *incorrect* (Dywan & Bowers, 1983). This is in part because a hypnotized person is more likely than normal to use imagination to fill in gaps in memory. Also, if a questioner asks misleading or suggestive questions, hypnotized persons tend to weave the information into their memories (Scoboria et al., 2002). To make matters worse, even when a memory is completely false, the hypnotized person's confidence in it can be unshakable (Burgess & Kirsch, 1999).

Thus, hypnosis sometimes uncovers more information, as it did with the bus driver (Schreiber & Schreiber, 1999). However, in the absence of corroborating evidence, there is no sure way to tell which of these memories are false and which are true (Newman & Thompson, 2001).

Is there a better way to improve eyewitness memory? To help police detectives, R. Edward Geiselman and Ron Fisher created the **cognitive interview,** a technique for jogging the memory of eyewitnesses (Fisher & Geiselman, 1987). The key to this approach is recreating the crime scene. Witnesses revisit the scene in their imaginations or in person. That way, aspects of the crime scene, such as sounds, smells, and objects, provide helpful retrieval cues (stimuli associated with a memory). Back in the context of the crime, the witness is encouraged to recall events in different orders and from different viewpoints. Every new memory, no matter how trivial it may seem, can serve as a cue to trigger the retrieval of yet more memories. (Later, in Module 7.4, we will see why such cues are so effective for jogging memories.)

When used properly, the cognitive interview produces 35 percent more correct information than standard questioning (Davis, McMahon, & Greenwood, 2005; Geiselman et al., 1986). This improvement comes without adding to the number of false memories elicited, as occurs with hypnosis. The result is a procedure that is more effective in actual police work (Ginet & Py, 2001; Kebbell & Wagstaff, 1998) and in different cultures (Stein & Memon, 2006).

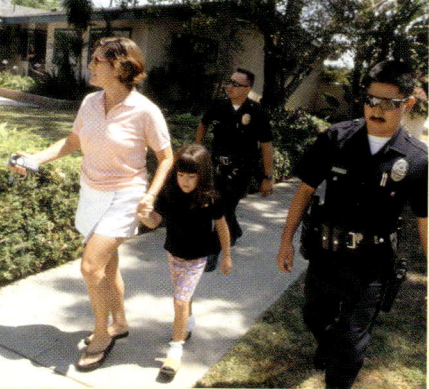

Some police detectives, following the advice of psychologists, recreate crime scenes to help witnesses remember what they saw. Typically, people return to the scene at the time of day the crime occurred. They are also asked to wear the same clothing they wore and go through the same motions as they did before the crime. With so many memory cues available, witnesses sometimes remember key items of information they hadn't recalled before.

If you thought you "remembered" that "sleep" was on the original list, you had a false memory. The word *sleep* is associated with most of the words on the original list, which creates a strong impression that you saw it before (Roediger & McDermott, 1995).

As the preceding examples show, thoughts, inferences, and mental associations may be mistaken for true memories (Loftus, 2003a, 2003b). People in Elizabeth Loftus's experiments who had these *pseudomemories* (false memories) were often quite upset to learn they had given false "testimony" (Loftus & Ketcham, 1994).

False long-term memories are a common problem in police work. For example, a witness may select a photo of a suspect from police files or see a photo in the news. Later, the witness identifies the suspect in a lineup or in court. Did the witness really remember the suspect from the scene of the crime? Or was it from the more recently seen photograph?

Does new information "overwrite" existing memories? No, the real problem is that we often can't remember the *source* of a memory (Simons et al, 2004). This can lead witnesses to "remember" a face that they actually saw somewhere other than the crime scene (Ruva, McEvoy, & Bryant, 2007). Many tragic cases of mistaken identity occur this way. One famous example involved memory expert Donald Thomson.

Constructive processing Reorganizing or updating memories on the basis of logic, reasoning, or the addition of new information.

Cognitive interview Use of various cues and strategies to improve the memory of eyewitnesses.

After appearing live on Australian television, he was accused of rape. It turns out that the victim was watching him on TV when the actual rapist broke into her apartment (Schacter, 1996, 2001).

Is there any way to avoid such problems? Forensic psychologists have tried a variety of techniques to help improve the memory of witnesses. "Telling Wrong from Right in Forensic Memory" examines research on this important question.

To summarize, forming and using long-term memories is an active, creative, highly personal process. Our memories are colored by emotions, judgments, and quirks of personality. If you and a friend were joined at the hip and you went through life side-by-side, you would still have different memories. What we remember depends on what we pay attention to, what we regard as meaningful or important, and what we feel strongly about (Schacter, 2000).

Organizing Memories

Long-term memory stores huge amounts of information during a lifetime. How are we able to quickly find specific memories? The answer is that each person's "memory index" is highly organized.

Do you mean that information is arranged alphabetically, as in a dictionary? Not a chance! If we ask you to name a black-and-white animal that lives on ice, is related to a chicken, and cannot fly, you don't have to go from aardvark to zebra to find the answer. You will probably only think of black-and-white birds living in the Antarctic. *Voila,* the answer is penguin.

Information in LTM may be arranged according to rules, images, categories, symbols, similarity, formal meaning, or personal meaning (Lieberman, 2004). In recent years, psychologists have begun to develop a picture of the *structure,* or organization, of memories. *Memory structure* refers to the pattern of associations among items of information. For example, assume that you are given two statements, to which you must answer yes or no: (1) *A canary is an animal.* (2) *A canary is a bird.* Which do you answer more quickly? Most people can say that *A canary is a bird* faster than they can recognize that *A canary is an animal* (Collins & Quillian, 1969). Why should this be so? Psychologists believe that a **network model** of memory explains why. According to this view, LTM is organized as a network of linked ideas (● Fig. 7.4). When ideas are "farther" apart, it takes a longer chain of associations to connect them. The more two items are separated, the longer it takes to answer. In terms of information links, *canary* is probably "close" to *bird* in your "memory files." *Animal* and *canary* are farther apart. Remember though, this has nothing to do with alphabetical order. We are talking about a system of linked meanings.

Redintegrative Memories Networks of associated memories may also help explain a common experience: Imagine finding a picture taken on your sixth birthday or tenth Christmas. As you look at the photo, one memory leads to another, which leads to another, and another. Soon you have unleashed a flood of seemingly forgotten details. This process is called redintegration (ruh-DIN-tuh-GRAY-shun).

Redintegrative memories seem to spread through the "branches" of memory networks. Many people find that such memories are also touched off by distinctive odors out of the past—from a farm visited in childhood, Grandma's kitchen, the seashore, a doctor's office, the perfume or aftershave of a former lover, and so on. The key idea in redintegration is that

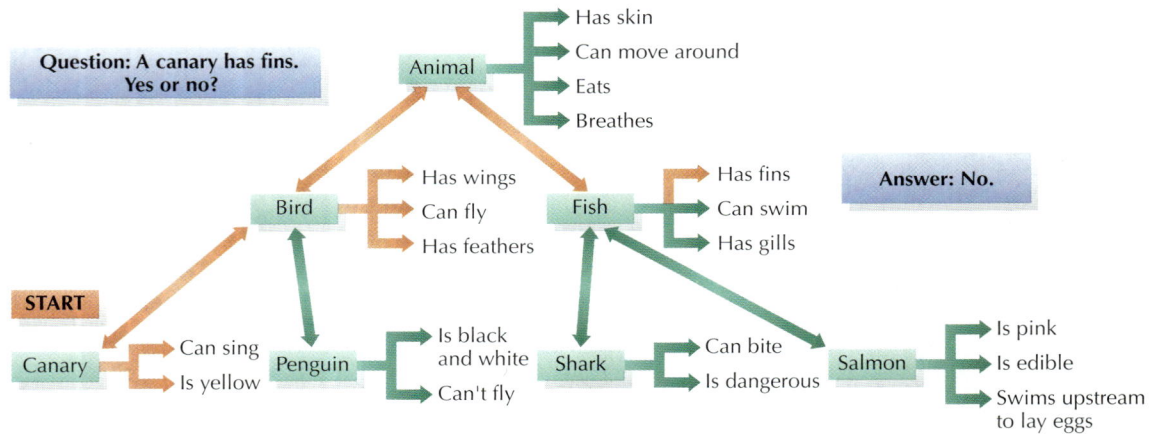

● **FIGURE 7.4** A hypothetical network of facts about animals shows what is meant by the structure of memory. Small networks of ideas such as this are probably organized into larger and larger units and higher levels of meaning. (Adapted from Collins & Quillian, 1969.)

one memory serves as a cue to trigger another. As a result, an entire past experience may be reconstructed from one small recollection.

Skill Memory and Fact Memory

How many types of long-term memory are there? It is becoming clear that more than one type of long-term memory exists. For example, a curious thing happens to many people who develop amnesia. Amnesic patients may be unable to learn a telephone number, an address, or a person's name. Yet, the same patients can learn to solve complex puzzles in a normal amount of time (Cavaco et al., 2004) (● Fig. 7.5). These and other observations have led many psychologists to conclude that long-term memories fall into at least two categories. One is called *procedural memory* (or skill memory). The other is *declarative memory* (also sometimes called fact memory).

Skills **Procedural memory** includes basic conditioned responses and learned actions, such as those involved in typing, driving, or swinging a golf club. Memories such as these can be fully expressed only as actions (or "know-how"). It is likely that skill memories register in "lower" brain areas, especially the cerebellum. They represent the more basic "automatic" elements of conditioning, learning, and memory (Hermann et al., 2004).

Facts **Declarative memory** stores specific factual information, such as names, faces, words, dates, and ideas. Declarative memories are expressed as words or symbols. For example, knowing that Peter Jackson directed both the *Lord of the Rings* trilogy and the latest remake of *King Kong* is a declarative memory. This is the type of memory that a person with amnesia lacks and that most of us take for granted. Declarative memory can be further divided into *semantic memory* and *episodic memory* (Tulving, 2002).

Semantic Memory Most of our basic factual knowledge about the world is almost totally immune to forgetting. The names of objects, the days of the week or months of the year, simple math skills, the seasons, words and language, and other general facts are all quite lasting. Such impersonal facts make up a part of LTM called **semantic memory.** Semantic memory serves as a mental dictionary or encyclopedia of basic knowledge.

Episodic Memory Semantic memory has no connection to times or places. It would be rare, for instance, to remember when and where you first learned the names of the seasons. In contrast, **episodic** (ep-ih-SOD-ik) **memory** is an "autobiographical" record of personal experiences. It stores life events (or "episodes") day after day, year after year. Can you remember your seventh birthday? Your first date? An accident you witnessed? What you did yesterday? All are episodic memories. Note that episodic memories are about the "what," "where," and "when" of our lives. More than a simple ability to store information, they make it possible for us to mentally travel back in time and *re-experience* events (Tulving, 2002).

Are episodic memories as lasting as semantic memories? In general, episodic memories are more easily forgotten than semantic memories. In fact, it is the forgetting of episodic information that results in the formation of semantic memories. At first, you remembered when and where you were when you learned the names of the seasons. Over time you forgot the episodic details but will likely remember the names for the rest of your life.

New information constantly pours into episodic memory. Stop for a moment and remember where and when you

● **FIGURE 7.5** The tower puzzle. In this puzzle, all the colored disks must be moved to another post without ever placing a larger disk on a smaller one. Only one disk may be moved at a time, and a disk must always be moved from one post to another (it cannot be held aside). An amnesic patient learned to solve the puzzle in 31 moves, the minimum possible. Even so, each time he began, he protested that he did not remember ever solving the puzzle before and that he did not know how to begin. Evidence like this suggests that memories for skills are distinct from memories for facts. (Adapted from Squire & Zola-Morgan, 1988.)

Network model A model of memory that views it as an organized system of linked information.

Redintegrative memories Memories that are reconstructed or expanded by starting with one memory and then following chains of association to other, related memories.

Procedural memory Long-term memories of conditioned responses and learned skills.

Declarative memory That part of long-term memory containing specific factual information.

Semantic memory A subpart of declarative memory that records impersonal knowledge about the world.

Episodic memory A subpart of declarative memory that records personal experiences that are linked with specific times and places.

● **FIGURE 7.6** In the model shown here, long-term memory is divided into procedural memory (learned actions and skills) and declarative memory (stored facts). Declarative memories can be either semantic (impersonal knowledge) or episodic (personal experiences associated with specific times and places).

first met your best friend. That was an episodic memory. Notice that you now remember that you just remembered something. You have a new episodic memory in which you remember that you remembered while reading this text! It's easy to see how much we ask of our memory.

How Many Types of Memory? In answer to the question posed at the beginning of this section, it is very likely that three kinds of long-term memories exist: procedural memory and two types of declarative memory, semantic and episodic (Lieberman, 2004) (● Fig. 7.6). Although other types of memory may be discovered, it appears that some pieces of the puzzle are falling into place.

MODULE 7.2 Summary

What are the features of short-term memory?
- Selective attention determines what information moves from sensory memory, which is exact but very brief, on to STM.
- STM has a capacity of about 5 to 7 bits of information, but this limit can be extended by chunking. Short-term memories are brief and very sensitive to interruption or interference. However, they can be kept alive by maintenance rehearsal.

What are the features of long-term memory?
- LTM serves as a general storehouse for meaningful information. Elaborative rehearsal helps us form lasting, long-term memories.
- Long-term memories are relatively permanent. LTM seems to have an almost unlimited storage capacity.
- Constructive processing tends to alter memories. Remembering is an active process. Our memories are frequently lost, altered, revised, or distorted.
- LTM is highly organized. The structure of memory networks is the subject of current research.
- Redintegrative memories are reconstructed, as one bit of information leads to others, which then serve as cues for further recall.

Is there more than one type of long-term memory?
- LTM contains procedural (skill) and declarative (fact) memories. Declarative memories can be semantic or episodic.

KNOWLEDGE BUILDER

STM and LTM

Recite

1. Information is best transferred from STM to LTM when a person engages in
   a. maintenance chunking
   b. maintenance recoding
   c. elaborative networking
   d. elaborative rehearsal
2. Constructive processing is often responsible for creating pseudomemories. T or F?
3. Electrical stimulation of the brain has shown conclusively that all memories are stored permanently but not all memories can be retrieved. T or F?
4. Memories elicited under hypnosis are more vivid, complete, and reliable than normal. T or F?
5. The existence of redintegrative memories is best explained by _____ models of memory.
   a. network
   b. integrative
   c. implicit
   d. chunking
6. Which of the following is a synonym for skill memory?
   a. semantic memory
   b. declarative memory
   c. episodic memory
   d. procedural memory

Reflect

Critical Thinking

7. Parents sometimes warn children not to read comic books, fearing that they will learn less in school if they "fill their heads up with junk." Why is this warning unnecessary?

Relate

Telephone numbers are divided into an area code (3 digits) and a 7-digit number that is divided into 3 digits, plus 4 more. Can you relate this practice to STM? How about to chunking and recoding?

Think about how you've used your memory in the last hour. See if you can identify an example of each of the following: a procedural memory, a declarative memory, a semantic memory, and an episodic memory.

Link

Internet addresses frequently change. To find the sites listed here, visit **http://www.thomsonedu.com/psychology/coon** for an updated list of Internet addresses and direct links to relevant sites.

- **The Magical Number Seven, Plus or Minus Two** Read George Miller's original paper on capacity limits in short-term memory.
- **Questions and Answers about Memories of Childhood Abuse** Read a summary of the repressed memory issue from the American Psychological Association.
- **False Memory Syndrome Foundation** This site provides information about false memory and its devastating effects, explanations of how it works, and aid to those who are affected.

ANSWERS

1. d 2. T 3. F 4. F 5. a 6. d 7. Because the more information you have in long-term memory, the greater the possibilities for linking new information to it. Generally, the more you know, the more you can learn—even if some of what you know is "junk."

MODULE 7.3 Measuring Memory

WHETHER YOU HAVE "REMEMBERED" depends on how you are tested. Also, various types of testing have revealed much of what is known about memory. For example, unconscious memories are revealed by a special technique called priming. In this module we will consider various ways of measuring memory.

Measuring Memory—The Answer Is on the Tip of My Tongue

SURVEY QUESTION: *How is memory measured?*

You either remember something or you don't, right? Wrong. Partial memories are common. For instance, have you ever tried to remember something only to find yourself stuck in a **tip-of-the-tongue (TOT) state?** This is the feeling that a memory is available but not quite retrievable (Schwartz, 2002). It is as if an answer or a memory is just out of reach—on the "tip of your tongue." In a classic TOT study, university students read the definitions of words such as *sextant, sampan,* and *ambergris*. Students who "drew a blank" and couldn't name a defined word were asked to give any other information they could. Often, they could guess the first and last letter and the number of syllables of the word they were seeking. They also gave words that sounded like or meant the same thing as the defined word (Brown & McNeill, 1966). In another study, people listened to theme music from popular TV shows. Then they tried to name the program the tune came from. This produced TOT experiences for about 1 out of 5 tunes (Riefer, Keveri, & Kramer, 1995).

The items listed next may induce the TOT state. See if you can name the defined words. (*Answers are at the bottom of this page.)

WHAT'S ON THE TIP OF YOUR TONGUE?

1. A person who collects and studies postage stamps
2. To officially renounce a throne
3. A nylon strip surfaced with tiny hooks that fasten to another strip surfaced with uncut pile
4. Produced by humans rather than natural
5. The pictorial system of writing used in ancient Egypt
6. A small fish that attaches itself to a shark

Closely related to the TOT state is the fact that people can often tell beforehand if they are likely to remember something. This is called the **feeling of knowing** (Widner, Jr., Otani, & Winkelman, 2005). Feeling-of-knowing reactions are easy to observe on TV game shows, where they occur just before contestants are allowed to answer. *Déjà vu,* the experience that you have previously experienced a new situation, is yet another example of partial retrieval. A déjà vu experience likely occurs when a new experience triggers the retrieval of a past experience without yielding *any* of the details (Brown, 2004).

Because memory is not an all-or-nothing event, there are several ways of measuring it. Three commonly used *memory tasks* (tests of memory) are recall, recognition, and relearning. Let's see how they differ.

Recalling Information

What is the name of the first song on your favorite CD? Who won the World Series last year? Who wrote *Hamlet?* If you can answer these questions you are using **recall,** a direct retrieval of facts or information. Tests of recall often require *verbatim* (word-for-word) memory. If you study a poem until you can recite it without looking at it, you are recalling it. If you complete a fill-in-the-blank question, you are using recall. When you answer an essay question by providing facts and ideas, you are also using recall, even though you didn't learn your essay verbatim.

The order in which information is memorized has an interesting effect on recall. To experience it, try to memorize the following list, reading it only once:

bread, apples, soda, ham, cookies, rice, lettuce, beets, mustard, cheese, oranges, ice cream, crackers, flour, eggs

If you are like most people, it will be hardest for you to recall items from the middle of the list. ● Figure 7.7 shows the results of a similar test. Notice that most errors occur with middle items of an ordered list. This is the **serial position effect.** You can remember the last items on a list because they are still in STM. The first items are also remembered well because they entered an "empty" short-term memory. This allows you to rehearse the items so they move into long-term memory (Addis & Kahana, 2004). The middle items are neither held in short-term memory nor moved to long-term memory, so they are often lost.

Recognizing Information

Try to write down everything you can remember learning from a class you took last year. If you actually did this, you might conclude that you had learned very little. However, a

---

* 1. philatelist 2. abdicate 3. Velcro 4. artificial 5. hieroglyphics 6. remora

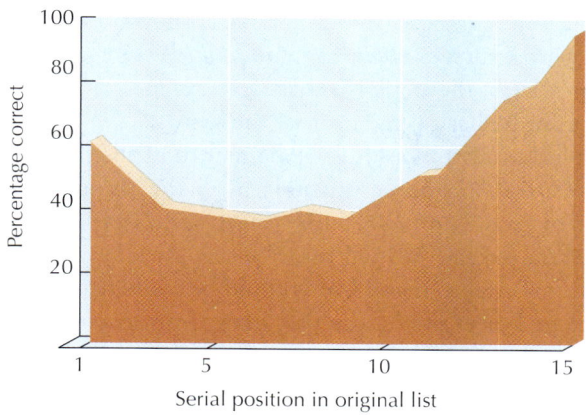

● **FIGURE 7.7** The serial position effect. The graph shows the percentage of subjects correctly recalling each item in a 15-item list. Recall is best for the first and last items. (Data from Craik, 1970.)

more sensitive test based on recognition could be used. In **recognition memory,** previously learned material is correctly identified. For instance, you could take a multiple-choice test on facts and ideas from the course. Because you would only have to recognize correct answers, you would probably find that you had learned a lot.

Recognition memory can be amazingly accurate for pictures and photographs (Whitehouse, Maybery, & Durkin, 2006). In one classic study, the investigator showed people 2,560 photographs at a rate of one every 10 seconds. Each person was then shown 280 pairs of photographs. Each pair included an "old" picture (from the first set of photos) and a similar "new" image. Subjects could tell 85 to 95 percent of the time which photograph they had seen before (Haber, 1970). This finding may explain why we rarely need to see our friends' vacation photos more than once.

Recognition is usually superior to recall. That's why people so often say, "I may forget a name, but I never forget a face." (You recall the name but recognize the face.) That's also why police departments use photographs or a lineup to identify criminal suspects. Witnesses who disagree when they try to recall a suspect's height, weight, age, or eye color often agree completely when they merely need to recognize the person.

Is recognition always superior? It depends greatly on the kind of *distractors* used (Flowe & Ebbese, 2007). These are false items included with an item to be recognized. If distractors are very similar to the correct item, memory may be poor. A reverse problem occurs when only one choice looks like it could be correct. This can produce a *false positive,* or false sense of recognition, like the false memory you had earlier when you thought you remembered seeing the word *sleep.*

There have been instances in which witnesses described a criminal as black, tall, or young. Then a lineup was held in which a suspect was the only African American among

whites, the only tall suspect, or the only young person. In such cases a false identification is very likely. A better method is to have *all* the distractors look like the person witnesses described. Also, to reduce false positives, witnesses should be warned that the culprit *may not be present.* Many hundreds of people have been put in jail on the basis of mistaken eyewitness memories (Wells, Memon, & Penrod, 2006). To avoid tragic mistakes, it's far better to show witnesses one photo at a time (a sequential lineup). For each photo, the witness must decide whether the person is the culprit before another photo is shown (Wells, 2001; Wells & Olsen, 2003).

Relearning Information

In another classic experiment, a psychologist read a short passage in Greek to his son every day when the boy was between 15 months and 3 years of age. At age 8, the boy was asked if he remembered the Greek passage. He showed no evidence of recall. He was then shown selections from the passage he heard and selections from other Greek passages. Could he recognize the one he heard as an infant? "It's all Greek to me!" he said, indicating a lack of recognition (and drawing a frown from everyone in the room).

Had the psychologist stopped, he might have concluded that no memory of the Greek remained. However, the child was then asked to memorize the original quotation and oth-

Police lineups make use of the sensitivity of recognition memory. However, unless great care is taken, false identifications are still possible (Wells, 2001).

Tip-of-the-tongue (TOT) state The feeling that a memory is available but not quite retrievable.
Feeling of knowing The ability to predict beforehand whether one will be able to remember something.
Recall To supply or reproduce memorized information with a minimum of external cues.
Serial position effect The tendency to make the most errors in remembering the middle items of an ordered list.
Recognition memory An ability to correctly identify previously learned information.

ers of equal difficulty. This time his earlier learning became evident. The boy memorized the passage he had heard in childhood 25 percent faster than the others (Burtt, 1941). As this experiment suggests, **relearning** is typically the most sensitive measure of memory.

When a person is tested by relearning, how do we know a memory still exists? As with the boy described, relearning is measured by a *savings score* (the amount of time saved when relearning information). Let's say it takes you 1 hour to memorize all the names in a telephone book. (It's a small town.) Two years later you relearn them in 45 minutes. Because you "saved" 15 minutes, your savings score would be 25 percent (15 divided by 60 times 100). Savings of this type are a good reason for studying a wide range of subjects. It may seem that learning algebra, history, or a foreign language is wasted if you don't use the knowledge immediately. But when you do need such information, you will be able to relearn it quickly.

Implicit and Explicit Memories

Many memories remain outside of conscious awareness. For example, if you know how to type, it is apparent that you know where the letters are on the keyboard. But how many typists could correctly label blank keys in a drawing of a keyboard? Many people find that they cannot directly remember such information, even though they "know" it.

Who were the last three presidents of the United States? What did you have for breakfast today? What is the title of The Black Eyed Peas' latest album? Explicit memory is used in answering each of these questions. **Explicit memories** are past experiences that are consciously brought to mind. Recall, recognition, and the tests you take in school rely on explicit memories. In contrast, **implicit memories** lie outside of awareness (Roediger & Amir, 2005). That is, we are not aware that a memory exists. Nevertheless, implicit memories—such as unconsciously knowing where the letters are on a keyboard—greatly influence our behavior (Neath & Surprenant, 2003).

Priming *How is it possible to show that a memory exists if it lies outside of awareness?* Psychologists first noticed implicit memory while studying memory loss caused by brain injuries. Let's say, for example, that a patient is shown a list of common words, such as *chair, tree, lamp, table,* and so on. A few minutes later, the patient is asked to recall words from the list. Sadly, he has no memory of the words.

Now, instead of asking the patient to explicitly recall the list, we could "prime" his memory by giving him the first two letters of each word. "We'd like you to say a word that begins with these letters," we tell him. "Just say whatever comes to mind." Of course, many words could be made from each pair of letters. For example, the first item (from *chair*) would be the letters *CH*. The patient could say "child," "chalk," "chain," "check," or many other words. Instead, he says "chair," a word from the original list. The patient is not aware that he is remembering the list, but as he gives a word for each letter pair, almost all are from the list. Apparently, the letters **primed** (activated) hidden memories, which then influenced his answers.

Similar effects have been found for people with normal memories. As the preceding example implies, implicit memories are often revealed by giving a person limited cues, such as the first letter of words or partial drawings of objects. Typically, the person believes that he or she is just saying whatever comes to mind. Nevertheless, information previously seen or heard affects his or her answers (Rueckl & Galantucci, 2005). Some nutritionists like to say, "You are what you eat." In the realm of memory it appears that we are what we experience—to a far greater degree than once realized.

MODULE 7.3 Summary

How is memory measured?
- The tip-of-the-tongue state shows that memory is not an all-or-nothing event. Memories may therefore be revealed by recall, recognition, relearning, or priming.
- In recall, memories are retrieved without explicit cues, as in an essay exam. Recall of listed information often reveals a serial position effect.
- A common test of recognition is the multiple-choice question.
- In relearning, material that seems to be forgotten is learned again, and memory is revealed by a savings score.
- Recall, recognition, and relearning mainly measure explicit memories. Other techniques, such as priming, are necessary to reveal implicit memories.

Can you label the letter keys on this blank keyboard? If you can, you probably used implicit memory to do it.

KNOWLEDGE BUILDER

Measuring Memory

Recite

Unless you have a memory like Mr. S's, it might be a good idea to see if you can answer these questions before reading on.

1. Four techniques for measuring or demonstrating memory are _____, _____, _____, _____.
2. Essay tests require _____ of facts or ideas.
3. As a measure of memory, a savings score is associated with
   a. recognition
   b. eidetic images
   c. relearning
   d. reconstruction
4. The two most sensitive tests of memory are
   a. recall and redintegration
   b. recall and relearning
   c. recognition and relearning
   d. recognition and digit-span
5. Priming is used to reveal which type of memories?
   a. explicit
   b. sensory
   c. skill
   d. implicit

Reflect
Critical Thinking

6. When asked to explain why they may have failed to recall some information, people often claim it must be because the information is no longer in their memory. Why does the existence of implicit memories challenge this explanation?

Relate

Have you experienced the TOT state recently? Were you able to retrieve the word you were searching for? If not, what could you remember about it?

Do you prefer tests based primarily on recall or recognition? Have you observed a savings effect while relearning information you studied in the past (such as in high school)?

Can you think of things you do that are based on implicit memories? For instance, how do you know which way to turn various handles in your house, apartment, or dorm? Do you have to explicitly think, "Turn it to the right," before you act?

Link

Internet addresses frequently change. To find the sites listed here, visit http://www.thomsonedu.com/psychology/coon for an updated list of Internet addresses and direct links to relevant sites.

- **What is Déjà Vu?** Links to more information on this fascinating form of partial retrieval.
- **A New Theoretical Framework for Explicit and Implicit Memory** An excellent article exploring a new framework for understanding and measuring explicit and implicit memory functions.
- **Free Recall Test** Test your free recall ability.

ANSWERS

1. recall, recognition, relearning, priming 2. recall 3. c 4. c 5. d 6. It is possible to have an implicit memory that cannot be consciously recalled. Memories like these (*available* in memory even though they are not consciously *accessible*) show that failing to recall something does not mean it is no longer in memory (Aliik, 2000). The *feeling of knowing* is related. Have you ever left an examination unable to recall the correct answer to a question *knowing* that you know the answer? That's because the answer was available but not accessible at the time of the exam.

Relearning Learning again something that was previously learned. Used to measure memory of prior learning.

Explicit memory A memory that a person is aware of having; a memory that is consciously retrieved.

Implicit memory A memory that a person does not know exists; a memory that is retrieved unconsciously.

Priming Facilitating the retrieval of an implicit memory by using cues to activate hidden memories.

MODULE 7.4 Forgetting

WHY ARE SOME MEMORIES lost so quickly? For example, why is it hard to remember information a week or two after taking a test in class? Forgetting is one of the more vexing aspects of memory. Why do we forget? Again, the more you know about how we "lose" memories, the better you will be able to hang on to them.

Forgetting—Why We, Uh, Let's See; Why We, Uh . . . Forget!

SURVEY QUESTION: *What causes forgetting?*

Most forgetting tends to occur immediately after memorization. Herman Ebbinghaus (1885) famously tested his own memory at various intervals after learning. Ebbinghaus wanted to be sure he would not be swayed by prior learning, so he memorized *nonsense syllables*. These are meaningless three-letter words such as CEF, WOL, and GEX. The importance of using meaningless words is shown by the fact that OMO, FAB, and DUZ are no longer used on memory tests. People who recognize these words as detergent names find them very easy to remember. This is another reminder that relating new information to what you already know can improve memory.

By waiting various lengths of time before testing himself, Ebbinghaus plotted a **curve of forgetting.** This graph shows the amount of information remembered after varying lengths of time (●Fig. 7.8). Notice that forgetting is rapid at first and is then followed by a slow decline (Hintzman, 2005). The same applies to meaningful information, but the forgetting curve is stretched over a longer time. As you might expect,
recent events are recalled more accurately than those from the remote past (O'Connor et al., 2000). Thus, you are more likely to remember that *The Departed* won the "Best Picture" Academy Award for 2006 than you are to remember that *A Beautiful Mind* was the 2001 winner.

As a student, you should note that a short delay between studying and taking a test minimizes forgetting. However, this is no reason for cramming. Most students make the error of only cramming. If you cram, you don't have to remember for very long, but you may not learn enough in the first place. If you use short, daily study sessions and review intensely before a test, you will get the benefit of good preparation and a minimum time lapse.

The Ebbinghaus curve shows less than 30 percent remembered after only 2 days have passed. Is forgetting really that rapid? No, not always. Meaningful information is not lost nearly as quickly as nonsense syllables. After 3 years, students who took a university psychology had forgotten about 30 percent of the facts they learned. After that, little more forgetting occurred (Conway, Cohen, & Stanhope, 1992). Actually, as learning grows stronger, some knowledge may become nearly permanent (Berntsen & Thomsen, 2005).

"I'll never forget old, old . . . oh, what's his name?" Forgetting is both frustrating and embarrassing. Why *do* we forget? The Ebbinghaus curve gives a general picture of forgetting, but it doesn't explain it. For explanations, we must search further. Before we do, look at "Card Magic!" where you will find an interesting demonstration.

When Encoding Fails

Whose head is on a U.S. penny? Which way is it facing? What is written at the top of a penny? Can you accurately draw and label a penny? In an interesting experiment, Ray Nickerson and Marilyn Adams (1979) asked a large group of students to draw a penny. Few could. Well then, could the students at least recognize a drawing of a real penny among fakes? (See ●Fig. 7.11.) Again, few could.

The most obvious reason for forgetting is also the most commonly overlooked. Obviously, few of us ever encode the details of a penny. In many cases, we "forget" because of **encoding failure.** That is, a memory was never formed in the first place (the card trick you just saw is another example). If you are bothered by frequent forgetting or absentmindedness, it is wise to ask yourself, "Have I been storing the information in the first place?" (Schacter, 2001). When 140 college professors were asked what they do to improve their memory, the favorite technique was to *write things down* (Park, Smith, & Cavanaugh, 1990). Making notes prevents

● **FIGURE 7.8** The curve of forgetting. This graph shows the amount remembered (measured by relearning) after varying lengths of time. Notice how rapidly forgetting occurs. The material learned was nonsense syllables. Forgetting curves for meaningful information also show early losses followed by a long gradual decline, but overall, forgetting occurs much more slowly. (Adapted from Ebbinghaus, 1885.)

DISCOVERING PSYCHOLOGY

Card Magic!

● **FIGURE 7.9**

Pick a card from the six shown in ● Figure 7.9 above. Look at it closely and be sure you can remember which card is yours. Now, snap your fingers and look at the cards in Figure 7.10, below. Poof! Only five cards remain, and the card you chose has disappeared. Obviously, you could have selected any one of the six cards in Figure 7.9. How did we know which one to remove?

This trick is based entirely on an illusion of memory. Recall that you were asked to concentrate on one card among the six cards in Figure 7.9. That prevented you from paying attention to the other cards, so they weren't stored in your memory (Mangels, Picton, & Craik, 2001; Naveh-Benjamin, Guez, & Sorek, 2007). The five cards you see below are all new (none is shown above in Figure 7.9). Because you couldn't find your card in the "remaining five," it looked like your card disappeared. What looked like "card magic" is actually memory magic. Now return to "When Encoding Fails" and continue reading to learn more about forgetting.

● **FIGURE 7.10**

(a) (b) (c) (d) (e)
(f) (g) (h) (i) (j)

● **FIGURE 7.11** Some of the distractor items used in a study of recognition memory and encoding failure. Penny A is correct but was seldom recognized. Pennies G and J were popular wrong answers. (Adapted from Nickerson & Adams, 1979.)

information from slipping out of short-term memory before you can review it and store it more permanently. By the way, if you like to study while watching television or instant messaging, beware. Dividing your attention like that also leads to encoding failure (Naveh-Benjamin, Guez, & Sorek, 2007).

College Students: They're All Alike! Encoding failures also affect our memories of people. Imagine yourself in this situation: As you are walking on campus, a young man who looks like a college student approaches you and asks for directions. While you are talking, two workers carrying a door pass between you and the young man. While your view is blocked by the door, another man takes the place of the first. Now you are facing a different person than the one who was there just seconds earlier. If this happened to you, do you think you would notice the change? Remarkably, only half the people tested in this way noticed the switch (Simons & Levin, 1998)!

How could anyone fail to notice that one stranger had been replaced by another? The people who didn't remember the first man were all older adults. College students weren't fooled by the switch. Apparently, older adults encoded the first man in very general terms as a "college student." As a result, that's all they remembered about him. Because his replacement also looked like a college student, they thought he was the same person (Simons & Levin, 1998).

Curve of forgetting A graph that shows the amount of memorized information remembered after varying lengths of time.

Encoding failure Failure to store sufficient information to form a useful memory.

Actually, we all tend to categorize strangers in general terms: Is the person young or old, male or female, a member of my ethnic group or another? This tendency is one reason why eyewitnesses are better at identifying members of their own ethnic group than persons from other groups (Burgess & Weaver, 2003; Michel, Caldara, & Rossion, 2006). It may seem harsh to say so, but during brief social contacts, people really do act as if members of other ethnic groups "all look alike." Of course, this bias disappears when people get acquainted and learn more about one another as individuals (McKone et al., 2007).

Memory Decay

One view of forgetting holds that **memory traces** (changes in nerve cells or brain activity) decay (fade or weaken) over time. **Memory decay** appears to be a factor in the loss of sensory memories. Such fading also applies to short-term memory. Information stored in STM seems to initiate a brief flurry of activity in the brain that quickly dies out. Short-term memory therefore operates like a "leaky bucket": New information constantly pours in, but it rapidly fades away and is replaced by still newer information. Let's say that you are trying to remember a short list of letters, numbers, or words after seeing or hearing them once. If it takes you more than 4 to 6 seconds to repeat the list, you will forget some of the items (Dosher & Ma, 1998).

Disuse Is it possible that the decay of memory traces also explains long-term forgetting? That is, could long-term memory traces fade from **disuse** (infrequent retrieval) and eventually become too weak to retrieve? There is evidence that memories not retrieved and "used" or rehearsed become weaker over time (Schacter, 2001). However, disuse alone cannot fully explain forgetting.

Disuse doesn't seem to account for our ability to recover seemingly forgotten memories through redintegration, relearning, and priming. It also fails to explain why some unused memories fade, whereas others are carried for life. A third contradiction will be recognized by anyone who has spent time with the elderly. People growing senile may become so forgetful that they can't remember what happened a week ago. Yet at the same time your Uncle Oscar's recent memories are fading, he may have vivid memories of trivial and long-forgotten events from the past. "Why, I remember it as clearly as if it were yesterday," he will say, forgetting that the story he is about to tell is one he told earlier the same day. In short, disuse offers no more than a partial explanation of long-term forgetting.

If decay and disuse don't fully explain forgetting from long-term memory, what does? Let's briefly consider some additional possibilities.

Cue-Dependent Forgetting

Often, memories appear to be *available* but not *accessible*. An example is having an answer on the "tip of your tongue." You know the answer is there (it is available), but it remains just "out of reach" (it is inaccessible). This suggests that many memories are "forgotten" because **memory cues** (stimuli associated with a memory) are missing when the time comes to retrieve information. For example, if you were asked, "What were you doing on Monday afternoon of the third week in May 2 years ago?" your reply might be, "Come on, how should I know?" However, if you were reminded, "That was the day the courthouse burned," or "That was the day Stacy had her automobile accident," you might remember immediately.

The presence of appropriate cues almost always enhances memory (Nairne, 2002). In theory, for instance, memory will be best if you study in the same room where you will be tested. Because this is often impossible, when you study, try to visualize the room where you will be tested. Doing so can enhance memory later (Jerabek & Standing, 1992). Similarly, people remember better if the same odor (such as lemon or lavender) is present when they study and are tested (Parker, Ngu, & Cassaday, 2001). If you wear a particular perfume or cologne while you prepare for a test, it might be wise to wear it when you take the test.

State-Dependent Learning Have you heard the story about the drunk who misplaced his wallet and had to get drunk again to find it? Although this tale is often told as a joke, it is not too far-fetched. The bodily state that exists during learn-

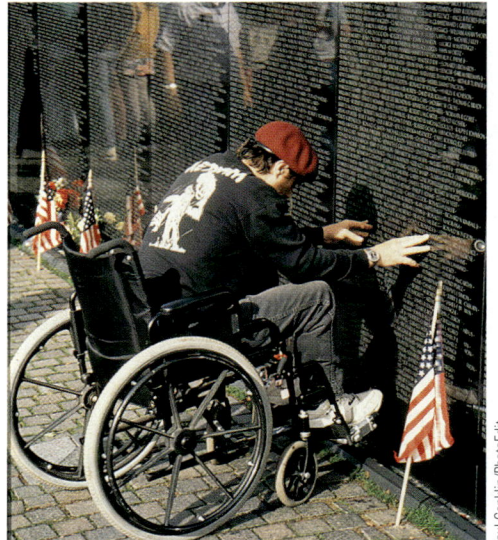

External cues like those found in a photograph, in a scrapbook, or during a walk through an old neighborhood often aid recall of seemingly lost memories. For many veterans, finding a familiar name engraved in the Vietnam Veterans Memorial unleashes a flood of memories.

ing can be a strong cue for later memory, an effect known as **state-dependent learning** (Neath & Surprenant, 2003). Being very thirsty, for instance, might prompt you to remember events that took place on another occasion when you were thirsty. Because of such effects, information learned under the influence of a drug is best remembered when the drugged state occurs again (Slot & Colpaert, 1999).

A similar effect applies to emotional states (Wessel & Wright, 2004). For instance, Gordon Bower (1981) found that people who learned a list of words while in a happy mood recalled them better when they were again happy. People who learned while they felt sad remembered best when they were sad (● Fig. 7.12). Similarly, if you are in a happy mood, you are more likely to remember recent happy events. If you are in a bad mood, you will tend to have unpleasant memories. Such links between emotional cues and memory could explain why couples who quarrel often end up remembering—and rehashing—old arguments.

Interference

Further insight into forgetting comes from a classic experiment in which college students learned lists of nonsense syllables. After studying, students in one group slept for 8 hours and were then tested for memory of the lists. A second group stayed awake for 8 hours and went about business as usual. When members of the second group were tested, they remembered *less* than the group that slept (● Fig. 7.13). This difference is based on the fact that new learning can interfere with previous learning. **Interference** refers to the tendency for new memories to impair retrieval of older memories (and the reverse). It seems to apply to both short-term and long-term memory (Lustig, May, & Hasher, 2001; Nairne, 2002).

It is not completely clear if new memories alter existing memory traces or if they make it harder to "locate" (retrieve)

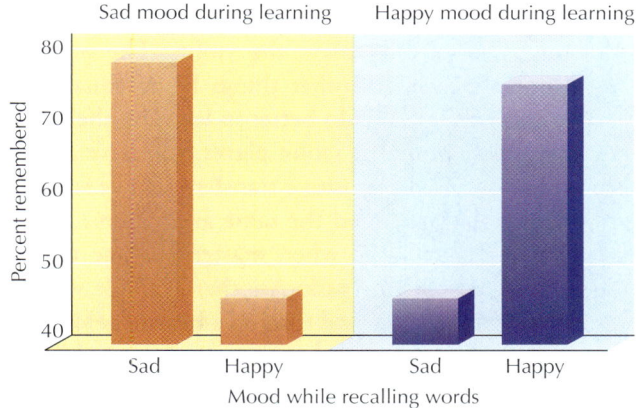

● **FIGURE 7.12** The effect of mood on memory. Subjects best remembered a list of words when their mood during testing was the same as their mood was when they learned the list. (Adapted from Bower, 1981.)

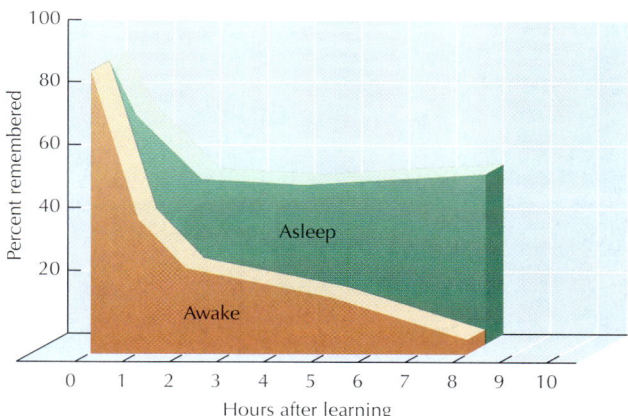

● **FIGURE 7.13** The amount of forgetting after a period of sleep or of being awake. Notice that sleep causes less memory loss than activity that occurs while one is awake. (Adapted from Jenkins & Dallenbach, 1924.)

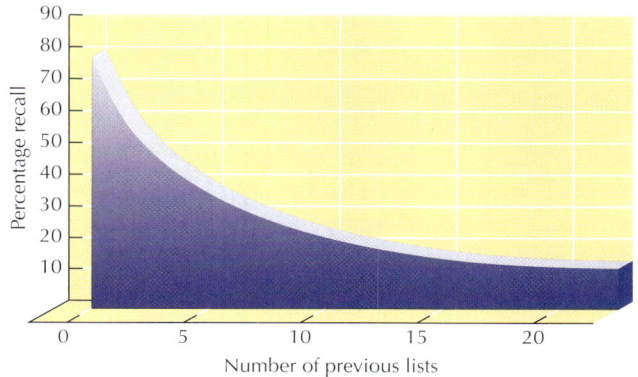

● **FIGURE 7.14** Effects of interference on memory. A graph of the approximate relationship between percentage recalled and number of different word lists memorized. (Adapted from Underwood, 1957.)

earlier memories. In any case, there is no doubt that interference is a major cause of forgetting (Neath & Surprenant, 2003). College students who memorized 20 lists of words (one list each day) were able to recall only 15 percent of the last list. Students who learned only one list remembered 80 percent (Underwood, 1957) (● Fig. 7.14).

Memory traces Physical changes in nerve cells or brain activity that take place when memories are stored.
Memory decay The fading or weakening of memories assumed to occur when memory traces become weaker.
Disuse Theory that memory traces weaken when memories are not periodically used or retrieved.
Memory cue Any stimulus associated with a particular memory. Memory cues usually enhance retrieval.
State-dependent learning Memory influenced by one's bodily state at the time of learning and at the time of retrieval. Improved memory occurs when the bodily states match.
Interference The tendency for new memories to impair retrieval of older memories, and the reverse.

How could anyone lose something as large as a car? If you park your car in a different place every day, you may have experienced forgetting caused by interference. Today's memory about your car's location is easily confused with memories from yesterday, and the day before, and the day before that.

Order Effects The sleeping college students remembered more because retroactive (RET-ro-AK-tiv) interference was held to a minimum. **Retroactive interference** refers to the tendency for new learning to inhibit retrieval of old learning. Avoiding new learning prevents retroactive interference. This doesn't exactly mean you should hide in a closet after you study for an exam. However, you should avoid studying other subjects until the exam. Sleeping after study can help you retain memories, and reading, writing, or even watching TV may cause interference.

Retroactive interference is easily demonstrated in the laboratory by this arrangement:

Experimental group: Learn A   Learn B   Test A
Control group: Learn A   Rest   Test A

● **FIGURE 7.15** Retroactive and proactive interference. The order of learning and testing shows whether interference is retroactive (backward) or proactive (forward).

Imagine yourself as a member of the experimental group. In task A, you learn a list of telephone numbers. In task B, you learn a list of Social Security numbers. How do you score on a test of task A (the telephone numbers)? If you do not remember as much as the control group that learns *only* task A, then retroactive interference has occurred. The second thing learned interfered with memory of the first thing learned; the interference went "backward," or was "retroactive" (● Fig. 7.15).

Proactive (pro-AK-tiv) interference is a second basic source of forgetting. **Proactive interference** occurs when prior learning inhibits recall of later learning. A test for proactive interference would take this form:

Experimental group: Learn A   Learn B   Test B
Control group: Rest   Learn B   Test B

Let's assume that the experimental group remembers less than the control group on a test of task B. In that case, learning task A interfered with memory for task B.

Then proactive interference goes "forward"? Yes. For instance, if you cram for a psychology exam and then later the same night cram for a history exam, your memory for the second subject studied (history) will be less accurate than if you had studied only history. (Because of retroactive interference, your memory for psychology would probably also suffer.) The greater the similarity in the two subjects studied, the more interference takes place. The moral, of course, is don't procrastinate in preparing for exams. The more you can avoid competing information, the more likely you are to recall what you want to remember (Anderson & Bell, 2001; Wixted, 2004).

The interference effects we have described apply primarily to memories of verbal information, such as the contents of this chapter. When you are learning a skill, similarity can sometimes be beneficial, rather than disruptive. The next section explains how this occurs.

Transfer of Training Two people begin mandolin lessons. One already plays the violin. The other is a trumpet player. All other things being equal, which person will initially do better in learning the mandolin? If you chose the violin player, you have an intuitive grasp of what positive transfer is. (The strings on a mandolin are tuned the same as a violin.) **Positive transfer** takes place when mastery of one task aids mastery of a second task. Another example would be learning to balance and turn on a bicycle before learning to ride a motorcycle or motor scooter. Likewise, surfing and skateboarding skills transfer to snowboarding.

Is there such a thing as negative transfer? There is indeed. In **negative transfer,** skills developed in one situation conflict with those required to master a new task. Learning to back a car with a trailer attached to it is a good example. Normally, when you are backing a car, the steering wheel is turned in the direction you want to go, the same as when moving forward. However, when backing a trailer, you must turn the steering wheel *away* from the direction you want the trailer to go. This situation results in negative transfer and often creates comical scenes at campgrounds and boat launching ramps.

On a more serious note, many tragic crashes caused by negative transfer finally led to greater standardization of airplane cockpits. Fortunately, negative transfer is usually brief, and it occurs less often than positive transfer. Negative transfer is most likely to occur when a new response must be made to an old stimulus (Besnard & Cacitti, 2005). If you have ever encountered a pull-type handle on a door that must be pushed open, you will appreciate this point.

Repression and Suppression of Memories

Take a moment and scan over the events of the last few years of your life. What kinds of things most easily come to mind? Many people remember happy, positive events better than disappointments and irritations (Moore & Zoellner, 2007). A clinical psychologist would call this tendency **repression,** or motivated forgetting. Through repression, painful, threatening, or embarrassing memories are held out of consciousness (Anderson et al., 2004). An example is provided by soldiers who have repressed some of the horrors they saw during combat (Karon & Widener, 1997).

The forgetting of past failures, upsetting childhood events, the names of people you dislike, or appointments you don't want to keep may reveal repression. People prone to repression tend to be extremely sensitive to emotional events. As a result, they use repression to protect themselves from threatening thoughts (McNally, Clancy, & Barrett, 2004). See "The Recovered Memory/False Memory Debate" for further cautions.

If I try to forget a test I failed, am I repressing it? No. Repression can be distinguished from **suppression,** an active, conscious attempt to put something out of mind. By not thinking about the test, you have merely suppressed a memory. If you choose to, you can remember the test. Clinicians consider true repression an *unconscious* event. When a memory is repressed we may be unaware that forgetting has even occurred.

Although some psychologists have questioned whether repression exists (Court & Court, 2001), evidence suggests that we can choose to actively suppress remembering upsetting information (Anderson, 2001). If you have experienced a painful emotional event, you will probably avoid all thoughts associated with it. This tends to keep cues out of

It is highly likely that you have a flashbulb memory about where you were when you first learned about the terrorist attack on the World Trade Center in New York. If someone alerted you about the news, you will remember that person's call and you will have clear memories about how you reacted to seeing the collapse of the towers.

mind that could trigger a painful memory. In time, your active suppression of the memory may become true repression (Anderson & Green, 2001).

Flashbulb Memories

Why are some traumatic events vividly remembered, whereas others are repressed? Psychologists use the term **flashbulb memories** to describe images that seem to be frozen in

---

Retroactive interference The tendency for new memories to interfere with the retrieval of old memories.
Proactive interference The tendency for old memories to interfere with the retrieval of newer memories.
Positive transfer Mastery of one task aids learning or performing another.
Negative transfer Mastery of one task conflicts with learning or performing another.
Repression Unconsciously pushing unwanted memories out of awareness.
Suppression A conscious effort to put something out of mind or to keep it from awareness.
Flashbulb memories Memories created at times of high emotion that seem especially vivid.

THE CLINICAL FILE

The Recovered Memory/False Memory Debate

Many sexually abused children develop problems that persist into adulthood. In some instances, they repress all memory of the abuse. According to some psychologists, uncovering these hidden memories can be an important step toward regaining emotional health (Palm & Gibson, 1998).

Although the preceding may be true, the search for repressed memories of sexual abuse has itself been a problem. Cases have surfaced in which families were torn apart by accusations of sexual abuse that later turned out to be completely false (Porter et al., 2003). For example, Gary Ramona lost his marriage and his $400,000-a-year job when his daughter Holly alleged that he molested her throughout her childhood. To prove to Holly that her memories were true, the therapists gave her the drug Amytal, and told her that it was a "truth drug." (Amytal is a hypnotic drug that induces a twilight state of consciousness. People do not automatically tell the truth while under its influence.) Ramona sued Holly's therapists, claiming that they had been irresponsible. After reviewing the evidence, a jury awarded Gary Ramona $500,000 in damages. In a way, Gary Ramona was lucky. Most people who are falsely accused have no way to prove their innocence (Loftus & Ketcham, 1994).

Why would anyone have false memories about such disturbing events? Several popular

Gary Ramona's life was shattered by "recovered" memories that turned out to be false.

books and a few misguided therapists have actively encouraged people to find repressed memories of abuse. Hypnosis, guided visualization, suggestion, age regression, and similar techniques can elicit fantasies that are mistaken for real memories. As we saw in Module 7.2, it is easy to create false memories, especially by using hypnosis (Loftus, 2003b; Loftus & Bernstein, 2005).

In an effort to illustrate how easy it is to create false memories, and to publicize *false memory syndrome*, memory expert Elizabeth Loftus once deliberately implanted a false memory in actor Alan Alda. As the host of the television series *Scientific American Frontiers*, he was scheduled to interview Loftus. Before the interview, Alda was asked to fill out a questionnaire about his tastes in food. When he arrived, Loftus told Alda that his answers revealed that he must once have gotten sick after eating hard-boiled eggs (which was false). Later that day, at a picnic, Alda would not eat hard-boiled eggs (Loftus, 2003a).

Certainly, some memories of abuse that return to awareness are genuine and must be dealt with. However, there is little doubt that some "recovered" memories are pure fantasy. No matter how real a recovered memory may seem, it could be false, unless it can be verified by others or by court or medical records (Olio, 2004).

A few years ago, an "epidemic" of recovered memories took place. Today, psychologists have developed new guidelines for therapists to minimize the risk of influencing clients' memories. Nevertheless, false claims about childhood abuse still occasionally make the news. The saddest thing about such claims is that they deaden public sensitivity to actual abuse. Childhood sexual abuse is widespread. Awareness of its existence must not be repressed.

---

memory at times of personal tragedy, accident, or other emotionally significant events (Niedzwienska, 2004).

Depending on your age, you may have a "flashbulb" memory for the assassinations of John F. Kennedy and Martin Luther King, the *Challenger* or *Columbia* space shuttle disasters, or the terrorist attack on the World Trade Center in New York (Curci & Luminet, 2006). Flashbulb memories are most often formed when an event is surprising, important, or emotional (Paradis et al., 2004). They are frequently associated with public tragedies, but memories of positive events may also have "flashbulb" clarity.

Flashbulb memories seem to be very detailed. Often, they focus primarily on how you reacted to the event. ■ Table 7.1 lists some memories that had "flashbulb" clarity for at least 50 percent of a group of college students. How vivid are the memories they trigger for you? (Note again that both positive and negative events are listed.)

The term *flashbulb memories* was first used to describe recollections that seemed to be unusually vivid and permanent. It has become clear, however, that flashbulb memories are not always accurate (Greenberg, 2004). More than anything else, what sets flashbulb memories apart is that we tend to place great *confidence* in them—even when they are wrong (Niedzwienska, 2004). Perhaps that's because we review emotionally charged events over and over and tell others about them. Also, public events such as wars, earthquakes, and assassinations reappear many times in the news, which highlights them in memory. Over time, flashbulb memories tend to crystallize into consistent, if not entirely accurate, landmarks in our lives (Schmolck, Buffalo, & Squire, 2000).

TABLE 7.1 Bright Flashes of Memory

MEMORY CUE	PERCENTAGE OF STUDENTS WITH FLASHBULB MEMORIES
A car accident you were in or witnessed	85
When you first met your college roommate	82
The night of your high school graduation	81
The night of your senior prom (if you went or not)	78
An early romantic experience	77
A time you had to speak in front of an audience	72
When you first got your college admissions letter	65
Your first date–the moment you met him/her	57

Source: From Rubin, 1985.

Memory and the Brain—Some "Shocking" Findings

SURVEY QUESTION: *What happens in the brain when memories are formed?*

One possibility overlooked in our discussion of forgetting is that memories may be lost as they are being formed (Papanicolaou, 2006). For example, a head injury may cause a "gap" in memories preceding the accident. **Retrograde amnesia,** as this is called, involves forgetting events that occurred before an injury or trauma. In contrast, **anterograde amnesia** involves forgetting events that follow an injury or trauma (Behrend, Beike, & Lampinen, 2004). (An example of this type of amnesia is discussed in a moment.)

Consolidation

Retrograde amnesia can be understood if we assume that it takes a certain amount of time to form a lasting memory through a process called **consolidation** (Vogel, Woodman, & Luck, 2006). You can think of consolidation as being somewhat like writing your name in wet concrete. Once the concrete is set, the information (your name) is fairly lasting. But while it is setting, it can be wiped out (amnesia) or scribbled over (interference).

Consider a classic experiment on consolidation, in which a rat is placed on a small platform. The rat steps down to the floor and receives a painful electric shock. After one shock, the rat can be returned to the platform repeatedly, but it will not step down. Obviously, the rat remembers the shock. Would it remember if consolidation were disturbed?

Interestingly, one way to prevent consolidation is to give a different kind of shock called electroconvulsive shock (ECS). ECS is a mild electric shock to the brain. It does not harm the animal, but it does destroy any memory that is being formed. If each painful shock (the one the animal remembers) is followed by ECS (which wipes out memories during consolidation), the rat will step down over and over. Each time, ECS will erase the memory of the painful shock. (ECS is employed as a psychiatric treatment for severe depression in humans.)

What would happen if ECS were given several hours after the learning? Recent memories are more easily disrupted than older memories. If enough time is allowed to pass between learning and ECS, the memory will be unaffected because consolidation is already complete. That's why people with mild head injuries lose only memories from just before the accident and older memories remain intact (Lieberman, 2004). Likewise, you would forget more if you studied, stayed awake 8 hours, and then slept 8 hours than you would if you studied, slept 8 hours, and were awake for 8 hours. Either way, 16 hours would pass. However, less forgetting would occur in the second instance because more consolidation would occur before interference begins (Wixted, 2005).

Where does consolidation take place in the brain? Actually, many parts of the brain are responsible for memory, but the **hippocampus** is particularly important (Sutherland et al., 2006). The hippocampus acts as a sort of "switching station" between short-term and long-term memory (Squire, 2004). The hippocampus does this, in part, by growing new neurons and by making new connections within the brain (Eichenbaum & Fortin, 2005). If the memory in question is particularly emotional, as are many flashbulb memories, activity in the *amygdala*, another part of the limbic system, appears to intensify the process of consolidation (McGaugh, 2004).

Humans who have hippocampal damage usually develop anterograde amnesia, showing a striking inability to consolidate new memories (Zola & Squire, 2001). A patient described by Brenda Milner provides a vivid example. Two years after an operation damaged his hippocampus, the 29-year-old patient continued to give his age as 27. He also reported that it seemed as if the operation had just taken place

---

Retrograde amnesia Loss of memory for events that preceded a head injury or other amnesia-causing event.

Anterograde amnesia Loss of the ability to form or retrieve memories for events that occur after an injury or trauma.

Consolidation Process by which relatively permanent memories are formed in the brain.

Hippocampus A brain structure associated with emotion and the transfer of information from short-term memory to long-term memory.

(Milner, 1965). His memory of events before the operation remained clear, but he found forming new long-term memories almost impossible. When his parents moved to a new house a few blocks away on the same street, he could not remember the new address. Month after month, he read the same magazines over and over without finding them familiar. If you were to meet this man, he would seem fairly normal because he still has short-term memory. But if you were to leave the room and return 15 minutes later, he would act as if he had never seen you before. Years ago his favorite uncle died, but he suffers the same grief anew each time he is told of the death. Lacking the ability to form new lasting memories, he lives eternally in the present (Corkin, 2002).

The Brain and Long-Term Memory

Somewhere within the 3-pound mass of the human brain lies all we know: ZIP codes, faces of loved ones, history, favorite melodies, the taste of an apple, and much, much more. Where is this information? According to neuroscientist Richard Thompson (2005), many parts of the brain can become active when we learn and form long-term memories, but usually one area is more critical for each particular form of memory.

Some areas of the cerebral cortex *are* more important to long-term memory than others. Patterns of blood flow in the cerebral cortex (the wrinkled outer layer of the brain) can be used to map brain activity. ● Figure 7.16 shows the results of measuring blood flow while people were thinking about a semantic memory *(a)* or an episodic memory *(b)*. In the map, green indicates areas that are more active during semantic thinking. Reds show areas of greater activity during episodic thinking. The brain in view *c* shows the difference in activity between views *a* and *b*. The resulting pattern indicates that the front of the cortex is related to episodic memory. Back areas are more associated with semantic memory (Tulving, 2002).

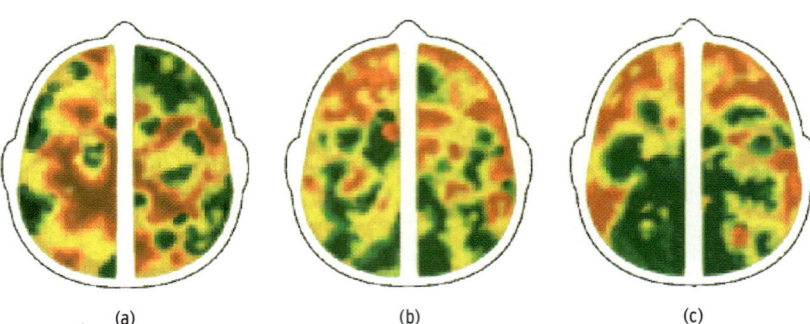

● **FIGURE 7.16** Patterns of blood flow in the cerebral cortex associated with semantic memories and episodic memories. (© Tulving, E. (1989). Remembering and knowing the past. *American Scientist*, 77(4), 361-367.)

To summarize (and simplify greatly), the hippocampus handles memory consolidation (Zola & Squire, 2001). Once declarative long-term memories are formed, they appear to be stored in the cortex of the brain (Squire, 2004). In contrast, long-term procedural (skill) memories are likely stored in the cerebellum (Hermann et al., 2004).

How are memories recorded in the brain? Scientists are beginning to identify the exact ways in which nerve cells record information. For example, Eric Kandel and his colleagues have studied learning in the marine snail *aplysia* (ah-PLEEZ-yah). Kandel found that learning in *aplysia* occurs when certain nerve cells in a circuit alter the amount of transmitter chemicals they release (Bailey & Kandel, 2004). Learning also alters the activity, structure, and chemistry of brain cells. Such changes determine which connections get stronger and which become weaker. This "reprograms" the brain and records information (Abel & Lattal, 2001; Squire, 2004).

Scientists continue to study various chemicals, especially neurotransmitters, that affect memory. If their research succeeds, it may be possible to help the millions of persons who suffer from memory impairment (Elli & Nathan, 2001). (See "The Long-Term Potential of a Memory Pill.")

An *aplysia*. The relatively simple nervous system of this sea animal allows scientists to study memory as it occurs in single nerve cells.

MODULE 7.4 Summary

What causes forgetting?

- Herman Ebbinghaus found that forgetting is most rapid immediately after learning, as shown by the curve of forgetting.
- Failure to encode information is a common cause of "forgetting."

CRITICAL THINKING

The Long-Term Potential of a Memory Pill

At long last, scientists may have found the chemical "signature" that records memories in everything from snails to rats to humans. If two or more interconnected brain cells become more active at the same time, the connections between them grow stronger (Squire & Kandel, 2000). This process is called *long-term potentiation*. After it occurs, an affected brain cell will respond more strongly to messages from the other cells. The brain appears to use this mechanism to form lasting memories (García-Junco-Clemente, Linares-Clemente, & Fernández-Chacón, 2005).

How has that been demonstrated? Electrically stimulating parts of the brain involved in memory, such as the hippocampus, can decrease long-term potentiation (Ivanco & Racine, 2000). For example, using electroconvulsive shock to overstimulate memory areas in the brains of rats interferes with long-term potentiation (Trepel & Racine, 1999). It also causes memory loss—just as it does when humans are given ECS for depression.

Will researchers ever produce a "memory pill" for people with normal memory? It's a growing possibility. Drugs that *increase* long-term potentiation also tend to improve memory (Shakesby, Anwyl, & Rowan, 2002). For example, rats administered such drugs could remember the correct path through a maze better than rats not given the drug (Service, 1994). Such findings suggest that memory can be and will be artificially enhanced (Schacter, 2000). However, the possibility of something like a "physics pill" or a "math pill" still seems remote.

- Forgetting in sensory memory and STM probably reflects a weakening (decay) of memory traces. Decay of memory traces may also explain some LTM losses.
- Forgetting is often based on a lack of memory cues. State-dependent learning is related to the effects of memory cues.
- Much forgetting in STM and LTM is caused by interference.
- In retroactive interference, new learning interferes with the ability to remember earlier learning.
- Proactive interference occurs when old learning interferes with new learning.

- Memories can be consciously suppressed and they may be unconsciously repressed.

  What happens in the brain when memories are formed?

- It takes time to consolidate memories. Lasting memories are recorded by changes in the activity, structure, and chemistry of brain cells.
- In the brain, memory consolidation takes place in the hippocampus. After memories have been consolidated, they appear to be stored in the cortex of the brain.

KNOWLEDGE BUILDER

Forgetting

Recite

1. According to the Ebbinghaus curve of forgetting, we forget slowly at first and then a rapid decline occurs. T or F?
2. Which explanation seems to account for the loss of short-term memories?
   a. decay
   b. disuse
   c. repression
   d. interference
3. When memories are available but not accessible, forgetting may be cue dependent. T or F?
4. When learning one thing makes it more difficult to recall another, forgetting may be caused by _____.
5. You are asked to memorize long lists of telephone numbers. You learn a new list each day for 10 days. When tested on list 3, you remember less than a person who only learned the first three lists. Your larger memory loss is probably caused by
   a. disuse
   b. retroactive interference
   c. regression
   d. proactive interference
6. If you consciously succeed at putting a painful memory out of mind, you have used
   a. redintegration
   b. suppression
   c. negative rehearsal
   d. repression
7. Flashbulb memories could be thought of as the reverse of
   a. repressed memories
   b. proactive memories
   c. retroactive memories
   d. episodic memories
8. Retrograde amnesia results when consolidation is speeded up. T or F?

Reflect
Critical Thinking

9. Based on state-dependent learning, why do you think that music often strongly evokes memories?
10. You must study French, Spanish, psychology, and biology in one evening. What do you think would be the best order in which to study these subjects so as to minimize interference?
11. There may be another way to explain why flashbulb memories are so long lasting. Can you think of one?

Relate

Which of the following concepts best explain why you have missed some answers on psychology tests: encoding failure, decay, disuse, memory cues, interference?

Do you know someone whose name you have a hard time remembering? Do you like or dislike that person? Do you think your difficulty is an instance of repression? Suppression? Interference? Encoding failure?

Have you had a flashbulb memory? How vivid is the memory today? How accurate do you think it is?

Here's a mnemonic tip: Elephants are supposed to have good memories, but a *hippo campus* is the place to go if you want to learn to consolidate memories.

Link

Internet addresses frequently change. To find the sites listed here, visit **http://www.thomsonedu.com/psychology/coon** for an updated list of Internet addresses and direct links to relevant sites.

- **Memory: A Contribution to Experimental Psychology** Read Hermann Ebbinghaus' original article.
- **About Education: Fundamental Concepts of Forgetting and Learning** Relate ideas about forgetting to education.
- **Memory Loss & the Brain** Read issues of a free newsletter.

ANSWERS

1. F 2. a and d 3. T 4. interference 5. b 6. b 7. a 8. F 9. Music tends to affect the mood that a person is in, and moods tend to affect memory (Miranda & Kihlstrom, 2005). 10. Any order that separates French from Spanish and psychology from biology would work (for instance: French, psychology, Spanish, biology). 11. Memories of emotionally significant events may be unusually strong because such memories are rehearsed more frequently. People usually mentally review emotionally charged events many times.

MODULE 7.5 Exceptional Memory and Improving Memory

IN THIS MODULE we explore exceptional memories. Is superior memory a biological gift, such as having a "photographic" memory? Or do excellent memorizers merely make better-than-average use of normal memory capacities? Regardless of how good your memory may be, there are probably times when you wish it were better. While we're waiting around for the arrival of a memory pill, this module also describes some ways to immediately improve your memory skills.

Exceptional Memory—Wizards of Recall

SURVEY QUESTION: *What are "photographic" memories?*

Can you remember how many doors there are in your house or apartment? To answer a question like this, many people form **mental images** (mental pictures) of each room and count the doorways they visualize. As this example implies, many memories are stored as mental images (Roeckelein, 2004).

Stephen Kosslyn, Thomas Ball, and Brian Reiser (1978) found an interesting way to show that memories do exist as images. Participants first memorized a sort of treasure map similar to the one shown in • Figure 7.17a. They were then asked to picture a black dot moving from one object, such as one of the trees, to another, such as the hut at the top of the island. Did people really form an image to do this task? It seems they did. As shown in Figure 7.17b, the time it took to "move" the dot was directly related to actual distances on the map.

Is the "treasure map" task an example of photographic memory? In some ways, internal memory images do have "photographic" qualities. However, the term *photographic memory* is more often used to describe a memory ability called eidetic imagery.

Eidetic Imagery

Eidetic (eye-DET-ik) **imagery** occurs when a person has visual images clear enough to be "scanned" or retained for at least 30 seconds. Internal memory images can be "viewed" mentally with the eyes closed. In contrast, eidetic images are "projected" out in front of a person. That is, they are best "seen" on a plain surface, such as a blank piece of paper. In this respect, eidetic images are somewhat like the afterimages you might have after looking at a flashbulb or a brightly lit neon sign (Haber & Haber, 2000).

Eidetic memory is more common in childhood, with about 8 children in 100 having eidetic images. In one series of tests, children were shown a picture from *Alice's Adventures in Wonderland* (• Fig. 7.18). To test your eidetic imagery, look at the picture and read the instructions there.

Now, let's see how much you remember. Can you say (without looking again) which of Alice's apron strings is longer? Are the cat's front paws crossed? How many stripes are on the cat's tail? After the picture was removed from view, one 10-year-old boy was asked what he saw. He replied, "I see the tree, gray tree with three limbs. I see the cat with stripes around its tail." Asked to count the stripes, the boy replied, "There are about 16" (a correct count!). The boy then went

> **Mental images** Mental pictures or visual depictions used in memory and thinking.
> **Eidetic imagery** The ability to retain a "projected" mental image long enough to use it as a source of information.

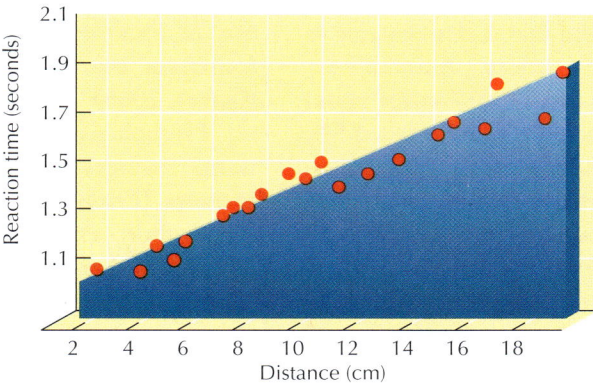

• **FIGURE 7.17** (a) "Treasure map" similar to the one used by Kosslyn, Ball, and Reiser (1978) to study images in memory. (b) This graph shows how long it took subjects to move a visualized spot various distances on their mental images of the map. (See text for explanation.)

(a)   (b)

● **FIGURE 7.18** A test picture like that used to identify children with eidetic imagery. To test your eidetic imagery, look at the picture for 30 seconds. Then look at a blank surface and try to "project" the picture onto it. If you have good eidetic imagery, you will be able to see the picture in detail. Return now to the text and try to answer the questions there. (Redrawn from an illustration in Lewis Carroll's *Alice's Adventures in Wonderland*.)

on to describe the remainder of the picture in striking detail (Haber, 1969).

Don't be disappointed if you didn't do too well when you tried your eidetic skills. Most eidetic imagery disappears during adolescence and becomes rare by adulthood (Haber & Haber, 2000).

A Case of Photographic Memory

Let's return now to the concept of mental images. In rare instances, such images may be so vivid that it is reasonable to say that a person has "photographic memory." A notable example was reported by Aleksandr Luria (1968) in his book, *The Mind of a Mnemonist*. Luria studied a man he called Mr. S, who had practically unlimited memory for visual images. Mr. S could remember almost everything that ever happened to him with incredible accuracy. Luria tried to test Mr. S's memory by using longer and longer lists of words or numbers. However, he soon discovered that no matter how long the list, Mr. S was able to recall it without error. Mr. S could memorize, with equal ease, strings of digits, meaningless consonants, mathematical formulas, and poems in foreign languages. His memory was so powerful that he had to devise ways to *forget*—such as writing information on a piece of paper and then burning it.

Mr. S's abilities might seem fantastic to any college student. However, Mr. S remembered so much that he couldn't separate important facts from trivia or facts from fantasy (Neath & Surprenant, 2003). For instance, if you asked him to read this chapter, he might remember every word. Yet, he might also recall all the images each word made him think of and all the sights, sounds, and feelings that occurred as he was reading. Therefore, finding the answer for a specific question, writing a logical essay, or even understanding a single sentence was very difficult for him. If you didn't have selective memory, you would recall all the ingredients on your cereal box, every street number you've seen, and countless other scraps of information.

Few people in history have possessed memory abilities like Mr. S's. Instead most people with good memories have learned effective strategies for remembering. Let's investigate further.

Strategies for Remembering

At first, a student volunteer named Steve could remember 7 digits—a typical score for a college student. Could he improve with practice? For 20 months Steve practiced memorizing ever-longer lists of digits. Ultimately, he was able to memorize approximately 80 digits, like this sample:

92842048050842268953990190252912807999970
66065747173106010805852697260263577332135

How did Steve do it? Basically, he worked by chunking digits into meaningful groups containing 3 or 4 digits each. Steve's avid interest in long-distance running helped greatly. For instance, to him the first 3 digits above represented 9 minutes and 28 seconds, a good time for a 2-mile run. When running times wouldn't work, Steve used other associations, such as ages or dates, to chunk digits (Ericsson & Chase, 1982). It seems apparent that Steve's success was based on learned strategies. By using similar memory systems, other people have trained themselves to equal Steve's feat (Bellezza, Six, & Phillips, 1992). In fact, the ability to organize information into chunks underlies expertise in many fields (Gobet, 2005).

Psychologist Anders Ericsson believes that most exceptional memory is merely a learned extension of normal memory (Ericsson et al., 2004). As evidence, he notes that Steve's short-term memory did not improve during months of practice. For example, Steve could still memorize only 7 consonants. Steve's phenomenal memory for numbers grew as he figured out new ways to chunk digits at encoding and store them in LTM.

Researchers studying Rajan Mahadevan have drawn similar conclusions about his spectacular memory for long strings of digits. In 1981 Rajan earned a place in the *Guinness Book of World Records* by reciting the first 31,811 digits of *pi!* Yet, like Steve, Rajan's memory for most other types of information is average. His exceptional memory seems to be based on highly practiced strategies for encoding and storing digits (Thompson, Cowan, & Frieman, 1993). By using similar memory systems, college students have even managed to duplicate some of Mr. S's feats, such as memorizing a 50-digit matrix in 3 minutes (Higbee, 1997).

Steve and Rajan began with normal memory for digits. Both extended their memory abilities by diligent practice. Clearly, exceptional memory can be learned (Ericsson et al., 2004). However, we still have to wonder, do some people have naturally superior memories?

Memory Champions

Each year the World Memory Championship is held in England. Contestants must rapidly memorize daunting amounts of information, such as long lists of unrelated words and numbers. Psychologists John Wilding and Elizabeth Valentine saw this event as an opportunity to study exceptional memory and persuaded the contestants to take some additional memory tests. These ranged from ordinary (recall a story), to challenging (recall the telephone numbers of 6 different people), to diabolical (recall 48 numerals arranged in rows and columns; recognize 14 previously seen pictures of snowflakes among 70 new photos) (Maguire et al., 2003; Wilding & Valentine, 1994).

Exceptional memorizers were found to:

- Use memory strategies and techniques
- Have specialized interests and knowledge that make certain types of information easier to encode and recall
- Have naturally superior memory abilities, often including vivid mental images
- Not have superior intellectual abilities or different brains

```
8 7 3 7 9 2 6 8
2 0 1 1 7 4 9 5
0 1 7 5 8 7 8 3
1 9 4 7 6 0 6 9
3 6 1 6 8 1 5 4
4 5 2 4 0 2 9 7
```

This number matrix is similar to the ones contestants in the World Memory Championship had to memorize. To be scored as correct, digits had to be recalled in their proper positions (Wilding & Valentine, 1994).

The first two points confirm what we learned from Steve's acquired memory ability. Many of the contestants, for example, actively used memory strategies, including special memory "tricks" called *mnemonics* (nee-MON-iks). Specialized interests and knowledge also helped for some tasks. For example, one contestant, who is a mathematician, was exceedingly good at memorizing numbers (Wilding & Valentine, 1994).

Several of the memory contestants were able to excel on tasks that prevented the use of learned strategies and techniques. This observation implies that superior memory ability can be a "gift" as well as a learned skill. Wilding and Valentine conclude that exceptional memory may be based on either natural ability or learned strategies. Usually it requires both.

Improving Memory— Keys to the Memory Bank

SURVEY QUESTION: *How can I improve my memory?*

Most super memorizers use strategies to augment whatever natural talents they have. Some of their strategies are described in the remainder of this module. Further, mnemonics are explored in this chapter's Psychology in Action section. Please do remember to read it.

Memory Strategies

As we have seen in this chapter, memory is not like a tape recorder or a video camera. Information is frequently lost, and memories change as they are stored and retrieved. This can be frustrating at times, but it's also a good thing. The flexibility of human memory allows us to focus on what's important and meaningful, even though it also contributes to some inaccuracies. Making full use of memory requires effort and practice. Let's see how you can improve your memory.

Knowledge of Results Learning proceeds best when feedback, or knowledge of results, allows you to check your progress. Feedback can help you identify ideas that need extra practice. In addition, knowing that you have remembered or answered correctly is rewarding. A prime way to provide feedback for yourself while studying is *recitation*.

Recitation If you are going to remember something, eventually you will have to retrieve it. *Recitation* refers to summarizing aloud while you are learning. Recitation forces you to practice retrieving information. When you are reading a text, you should stop frequently and try to remember what you have just read by restating it in your own words. In one classic experiment, the best memory score was earned by a group of students who spent 80 percent of their time reciting and only 20 percent reading (Gates, 1958). Maybe students who talk to themselves aren't crazy after all.

Rehearsal The more you *rehearse* (mentally review) information as you read, the better you will remember it. But remember that maintenance rehearsal alone is not very effective. Elaborative rehearsal, in which you look for connections to existing knowledge, is far better. Thinking about facts helps link them together in memory. To learn college-level information, you must make active use of more reflective rehearsal strategies (Santrock & Halonen, 2007).

Selection The Dutch scholar Erasmus said that a good memory should be like a fish net: It should keep all the big fish and let the little ones escape. If you boil down the paragraphs in most textbooks to one or two important terms or ideas, your memory chores will be more manageable. Practice very selective marking in your texts and use marginal notes to further summarize ideas. Most students mark their texts too much instead of too little. If everything is underlined, you haven't been selective. And, very likely, you didn't pay much attention in the first place (Peterson, 1992).

Organization Assume that you must memorize the following list of words: north, man, red, spring, woman, east, autumn, yellow, summer, boy, blue, west, winter, girl, green, south. This rather difficult list could be reorganized into *chunks* as follows: north-east-south-west, spring-summer-autumn-winter, red-yellow-green-blue, man-woman-boy-girl. Organizing class notes and summarizing chapters can be quite helpful (Hettich, 2005). You may even want to summarize your summaries, so that the overall network of ideas becomes clearer and simpler. Summaries improve memory by encouraging better encoding of information (Hadwin, Kirby, & Woodhouse, 1999).

Whole Versus Part Learning If you have to memorize a speech, is it better to try to learn it from beginning to end? Or in smaller parts like paragraphs? Generally it is better to practice whole packages of information rather than smaller parts (*whole learning*). This is especially true for fairly short, organized information. An exception is that learning parts may be better for extremely long, complicated information. In *part learning,* subparts of a larger body of information are studied (such as sections of a textbook chapter). To decide which approach to use, remember to study the *largest meaningful amount of information* you can at one time.

For very long or complex material, try the *progressive part method,* by breaking a learning task into a series of short sections. At first, you study part A until it is mastered. Next, you study parts A and B; then A, B, and C; and so forth. This is a good way to learn the lines of a play, a long piece of music, or a poem (Ash & Holding, 1990). After the material is learned, you should also practice by starting at points other than A (at C, D, or B, for example). This helps prevent getting "lost" or going blank in the middle of a performance.

Serial Position Whenever you must learn something in *order,* be aware of the serial position effect. As you will recall, this is the tendency to make the most errors in remembering the middle of a list. If you are introduced to a long line of people, the names you are likely to forget will be those in the middle, so you should make an extra effort to attend to them. You should also give extra practice to the middle of a list, poem, or speech. Try to break long lists of information into short sublists, and make the middle sublists the shortest of all.

Cues The best memory cues (stimuli that aid retrieval) are those that were present during encoding (Anderson, 2005). For example, students in one study had the daunting task of trying to recall a list of 600 words. As they read the list (which they did not know they would be tested on), the students gave three other words closely related in meaning to each listed word. In a test given later, the words each student supplied were used as cues to jog memory. The students recalled an astounding 90 percent of the original word list (Mantyla, 1986). Now read the following sentence:

The fish bit the swimmer.

If you were tested a week from now, you would be more likely to recall the sentence if you were given a memory cue. And, surprisingly, the word *shark* would work better as a reminder than *fish* would. The reason for this is that most people think of a shark when they read the sentence. As a result, *shark* becomes a potent memory cue (Schacter, 2000).

The preceding example shows, once again, that it often helps to *elaborate* information as you learn. When you study, try to use new names, ideas, or terms in several sentences. Also, form images that include the new information, and relate it to knowledge you already have. Your goal should be to knit meaningful cues into your memory code to help you retrieve information when you need it (● Fig. 7.19).

Overlearning Numerous studies have shown that memory is greatly improved when you *overlearn.* That is, when study is continued beyond bare mastery. After you have learned material well enough to remember it once without error, you should continue studying. Overlearning is your best insurance against going blank on a test because of being nervous.

Spaced Practice To keep boredom and fatigue to a minimum, try alternating short study sessions with brief rest periods. This pattern, called **spaced practice,** is generally supe-

● **FIGURE 7.19** Actors can remember large amounts of complex information for many months, even when learning new roles in between. During testing, they remember their lines best when they are allowed to move and gesture as they would when performing. Apparently their movements supply cues that aid recall (Noice & Noice, 1999).

rior to **massed practice,** in which little or no rest is given between learning sessions. By improving attention and consolidation, three 20-minute study sessions can produce more learning than 1 hour of continuous study. There's an old joke that goes, "How do you get to Carnegie Hall?" The answer is, "Practice, practice, practice." A better answer would be "Practice, wait awhile, practice, wait awhile, practice" (Neath & Surprenant, 2003).

Perhaps the best way to make use of spaced practice is to *schedule* your time. To make an effective schedule, designate times during the week before, after, and between classes when you will study particular subjects. Then treat these times just as if they are classes you have to attend.

Sleep and Memory Remember that sleeping after study reduces interference. However, unless you are a "night person," late evening may not be a very efficient time for you to study. Also, you obviously can't sleep after every study session or study everything just before you sleep. That's why your study schedule should include ample breaks between subjects as described earlier. (See "Spaced Practice.") The breaks and free time in your schedule are as important as your study periods.

Hunger and Memory People who are hungry almost always score lower on memory tests. So, mother was right—it's a good idea to make sure you've had a good breakfast or lunch before you take tests at school (Smith, Clark, & Gallagher, 1999). And a coffee won't hurt your test performance, either (Smith, 2005).

Extend How Long You Remember When you are learning new information, test yourself repeatedly. As you do, gradually lengthen the amount of time that passes before you test yourself again. For example, if you are studying German words on flash cards, look at the first card and then move it a few cards back in the stack. Do the same with the next few cards. When you get to the first "old" card, test yourself on it and check the answer. Then, move it farther back in the stack. Do the same with other "old" cards as they come up. When "old" cards come up for the third time, put them clear to the back of the stack (Cull, Shaughnessy, & Zechmeister, 1996).

Review If you have spaced your practice and overlearned, review will be like icing on your study cake. Reviewing shortly before an exam cuts down the time during which you must remember details that may be important for the test. When reviewing, hold the amount of new information you try to memorize to a minimum. It may be realistic to take what you have actually learned and add a little more to it at the last minute by cramming. But remember that more than a little new learning may interfere with what you already know.

Using a Strategy to Aid Recall Successful recall is usually the result of a planned *search* of memory (Herrmann et al., 2006). For example, one study found that students were most likely to recall names that eluded them if they made use of partial information (Reed & Bruce, 1982). The students were trying to answer questions such as, "He is best remembered as the scarecrow in the Judy Garland movie *The Wizard of Oz*." (The answer is Ray Bolger.) Partial information that helped students remember included impressions about the length of the name, letter sounds within the name, similar names, and related information (such as the names of other characters in the movie). A similar helpful strategy is to go through the alphabet, trying each letter as the first sound of a name or word you are seeking.

The *cognitive interview* described in Module 7.2 (see "Telling Wrong from Right in Forensic Memory") offers some further hints for recapturing context and jogging memories:

1. Say or write down *everything* you can remember that relates to the information you are seeking. Don't worry about how trivial any of it seems; each bit of information you remember can serve as a cue to bring back others.

Spaced practice A practice schedule that alternates study periods with brief rests.

Massed practice A practice schedule in which studying continues for long periods, without interruption.

2. Try to recall events or information in different orders. Let your memories flow out backward or out of order, or start with whatever impressed you the most.

3. Recall from different viewpoints. Review events by mentally standing in a different place. Or try to view information as another person would remember it. When taking a test, for instance, ask yourself what other students or your professor would remember about the topic.

4. Mentally put yourself back in the situation where you learned the information. Try to mentally recreate the learning environment or relive the event. As you do, include sounds, smells, details of weather, nearby objects, other people present, what you said or thought, and how you felt as you learned the information (Fisher & Geiselman, 1987; Milne & Bull, 2002).

A Look Ahead Psychologists still have much to learn about the nature of memory and how to improve it. For now, one thing stands out clearly: People who have good memories excel at organizing information and making it meaningful. Sometimes, however, you are faced with the need to memorize information without much inherent meaning. For example, a shopping list is just a list of more or less unrelated items. There isn't much of a meaningful relationship between carrots, toilet paper, TV dinners, and Twinkies except that you need more of them. With this in mind, the Psychology in Action discussion for this chapter tells how you can use mnemonics to better memorize when meaning-based memory strategies, like those described in this module, are not helpful.

MODULE 7.5 Summary

What are "photographic" memories?
- Eidetic imagery (photographic memory) occurs when a person is able to project an image onto a blank surface.
- Eidetic imagery is rarely found in adults. However, many adults have internal memory images, which can be very vivid.
- Exceptional memory may be based on natural ability or learned strategies. Usually it involves both.

How can I improve my memory?
- Excellent memory abilities are based on using strategies and techniques that make learning efficient and that compensate for natural weaknesses in human memory.
- Some people have naturally superior memories, but even they find it beneficial to use memory strategies.
- Memory can be improved by using feedback, recitation, and rehearsal, by selecting and organizing information, and by using the progressive part method, spaced practice, overlearning, and active search strategies.
- When you are studying or memorizing, you should also keep in mind the effects of serial position, sleep, review, cues, and elaboration.

KNOWLEDGE BUILDER

Exceptional Memory and Improving Memory

Recite

1. Children with eidetic imagery typically have no better than average long-term memory. T or F?
2. For most people, having an especially good memory is based on
   a. maintenance rehearsal
   b. constructive processing
   c. phonetic imagery
   d. learned strategies
3. To improve memory, it is reasonable to spend as much or more time reciting as reading. T or F?
4. Organizing information while studying has little effect on memory because long-term memory is already highly organized. T or F?
5. The progressive part method of study is best suited to long and complex learning tasks. T or F?
6. As new information is encoded and rehearsed it is helpful to elaborate on its meaning and connect it to other information. T or F?
7. The cognitive interview helps people remember more by providing
   a. memory cues
   b. a serial position effect
   c. phonetic priming
   d. massed practice

Reflect

Critical Thinking

8. Mr. S had great difficulty remembering faces. Can you guess why?
9. What advantages would there be to taking notes as you read a textbook, as opposed to underlining words in the text?

Relate

What kinds of information are you good at remembering? Why do you think your memory is better for those topics?

Return to the topic headings in the preceding pages that list techniques for improving memory. Place a check mark next to those that you have used recently. Review any you didn't mark and think of a specific example of how you could use each technique at school, at home, or at work.

Link

Internet addresses frequently change. To find the sites listed here, visit **http://www.thomsonedu.com/psychology/coon** for an updated list of Internet addresses and direct links to relevant sites.

- **Does No One Have a Photographic Memory?** A discussion of the impossibility of photographic memory.
- **Famous Mnemonists** Read about some of history's most famous memorizers.
- **Memory Strategies** Read about a useful list of memory strategies for studying.

ANSWERS

1. T 2. d 3. T 4. F 5. T 6. T 7. a 8. Mr. S's memory was so specific that faces seemed different and unfamiliar if he saw them from a new angle or if a face had a different expression on it than when Mr. S last saw it. 9. Note-taking is a form of recitation; it encourages elaborative rehearsal and facilitates the organization and selection of important ideas, and your notes can be used for review.

MODULE 7.6 Psychology in Action
Mnemonics–Memory Magic

SURVEY QUESTION: *Are there any tricks to help me with my memory?*

Just imagine the poor biology or psychology student who is required to learn the names of the 12 cranial nerves (in order, of course). Although the spinal nerves connect the brain to the body through the spinal cord, the cranial nerves do so directly. Just in case you wanted to know, the names of the 12 cranial nerves are: olfactory, optic, oculomotor, trochlear, trigeminal, abducens, facial, vestibulocochlear, glossopharyngeal, vagus, spinal accessory, and hypoglossal.

As you might imagine, most of us find it difficult to memorize this list. In the absence of any obvious meaningful relationship among these terms, many students find it difficult to apply the memory strategies we discussed in the last module and instead turn to *rote* learning (learning by simple repetition). Fortunately, there *is* an alternative: mnemonics (nee-MON-iks) (Lieberman, 2004; Neath & Surprenant, 2003). A **mnemonic** is any kind of memory system or aid. The superiority of mnemonic learning as opposed to rote learning has been demonstrated many times (Carney & Levin, 2003; Manalo, 2002). Some mnemonic systems are so common that almost everyone knows them. If you are trying to remember how many days there are in a month, you may find the answer by reciting, "Thirty days hath September. . . ." Physics teachers often help students remember the colors of the spectrum by giving them the mnemonic "Roy G. Biv": **R**ed, **O**range, **Y**ellow, **G**reen, **B**lue, **I**ndigo, **V**iolet. The budding sailor who has trouble telling port from starboard may remember that port and left both have four letters or may remind herself, "I *left* port." And what beginning musician hasn't remembered the notes represented by the lines and spaces of the musical staff by learning "F-A-C-E" and "**E**very **G**ood **B**oy **D**oes **F**ine"?

Generations of students have learned the names of the spinal nerves by memorizing the sentence "**O**n **O**ld **O**lympus **T**owering **T**op **A** **F**amous **V**ocal **G**erman **V**iewed **S**ome **H**ops. This mnemonic, which uses the first letter of each of the cranial nerves to generate a nonsense sentence, indeed produces better recall of the cranial nerves. Such *acrostics* are even more effective if you make up your own (Bloom & Lamkin, 2006). By practicing mnemonics you should be able to greatly improve your memory with little effort.

Here, then, are the basic principles of mnemonics.

1. **Use mental pictures.** Visual pictures, or images, are generally easier to remember than words. Turning information into mental pictures is therefore very helpful. Make these images as vivid as possible (Neath & Surprenant, 2003).

2. **Make things meaningful.** Transferring information from short-term memory to long-term memory is aided by making it meaningful. If you encounter technical terms that have little or no immediate meaning for you, *give* them meaning, even if you have to stretch the term to do so. (This point is clarified by the examples following this list.)

3. **Make information familiar.** Connect it to what you already know. Another way to get information into long-term memory is to connect it to information already stored there. If some facts or ideas in a chapter seem to stay in your memory easily, associate other more difficult facts with them.

4. **Form bizarre, unusual, or exaggerated mental associations.** Forming images that make sense is better in most situations. However, when associating two ideas, terms, or especially mental images, you may find that the more outrageous and exaggerated the association, the more likely you are to remember. Bizarre images make stored information more *distinctive* and therefore easier to retrieve (Worthen & Marshall, 1996). Imagine, for example, that you have just been introduced to Mr. Rehkop. To remember his name, you could picture him wearing a police uniform. Then replace his nose with a ray gun. This bizarre image will provide two hints when you want to remember Mr. Rehkop's name: *ray* and *cop*. This technique works for other kinds of information, too. College students who used exaggerated mental associations to remember the names of unfamiliar animals outperformed students who just used rote memory (Carney & Levin, 2001). Bizarre images mainly help improve immediate memory, and they work best for fairly simple information (Fritz et al., 2007; Robinson-Riegler & McDaniel, 1994). Nevertheless, they can be a first step toward learning.

A sampling of typical applications of mnemonics should make these four points clearer to you.

Example 1 Let's say you have 30 new vocabulary words to memorize in Spanish. You can proceed by rote memorization (repeat them over and over until you begin to get them), or you can learn them with little effort by using the keyword method (Fritz et al., 2007; Pressley, 1987). In the **keyword method** a familiar word or image is used to link two other words or items. To remember that the word *pájaro* (pronounced PAH-hah-ro) means bird, you can link it to a "key"

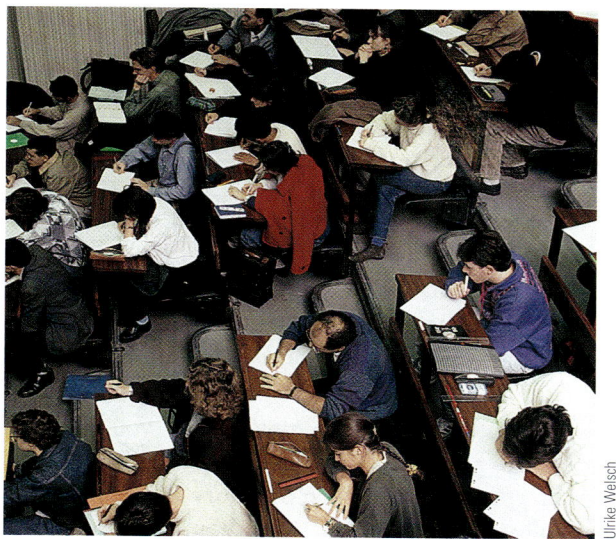

Mnemonics can be an aid in preparing for tests. However, because mnemonics help most in the initial stages of storing information, it is important to follow through with other elaborative learning strategies.

word in English: *Pajaro* (to me) sounds like "parked car-o." Therefore, to remember that *pajaro* means bird, you might visualize a parked car jam-packed full of birds. You should try to make this image as vivid and exaggerated as possible, with birds flapping and chirping and feathers flying everywhere. Similarly, for the word *carta* (which means "letter"), you might imagine a shopping *cart* filled with postal letters.

If you link similar keywords and images for the rest of the list, you may not remember them all, but you will get most without any more practice. As a matter of fact, if you have formed the *pajaro* and *carta* images just now, it is going to be almost impossible for you to ever see these words again without remembering what they mean. The keyword method is also superior when you want to work "backward" from an English word to a foreign vocabulary word (Hogben & Lawson, 1992).

What about a year from now? How long do keyword memories last? Mnemonic memories work best in the short run. Later, they may be more fragile than conventional memories. That's why it's usually best to use mnemonics during the initial stages of learning (Carney & Levin, 2003). To create more lasting memories, you'll need to use the techniques discussed earlier in this chapter.

Exaggerated mental images can link two words or ideas in ways that aid memory. Here, the keyword method is used to link the English word *letter* with the Spanish word *carta*.

Example 2 Let's say you have to learn the names of all the bones and muscles in the human body for biology. You are trying to remember that the jawbone is the *mandible*. This one is easy because you can associate it to a *man nibbling*, or maybe you can picture a *man dribbling* a basketball with his jaw (make this image as ridiculous as possible). If the muscle name *latissimus dorsi* gives you trouble, familiarize it by turning it into *"the ladder misses the door, sigh."* Then picture a ladder glued to your back where the muscle is found. Picture the ladder leading up to a small door at your shoulder. Picture the ladder missing the door. Picture the ladder sighing like an animated character in a cartoon.

This seems like more to remember, not less; and it seems like it would cause you to misspell things. Mnemonics are not a complete substitute for normal memory; they are an aid to normal memory. Mnemonics are not likely to be helpful unless you make extensive use of *images* (Willoughby et al., 1997). Your mental pictures will come back to you easily. As for misspellings, mnemonics can be thought of as a built-in hint in your memory. Often, when taking a test, you will find that the slightest hint is all you need to remember correctly. A mnemonic image is like having someone leaning over your shoulder who says, "Psst, the name of that muscle sounds like 'ladder misses the door, sigh.'" If misspelling continues to be a problem, try to create memory aids for spelling, too.

Here are two more examples to help you appreciate the flexibility of a mnemonic approach to studying.

Example 3 Your art history teacher expects you to be able to name the artist when you are shown slides as part of exams. You have seen many of the slides only once before in class. How will you remember them? As the slides are shown in class, make each artist's name into an object or image. Then picture the object *in* the paintings done by the artist. For example, you can picture Van Gogh as a *van* (automobile) *going* through the middle of each Van Gogh painting. Picture the van running over things and knocking things over. Or, if you remember that Van Gogh cut off his ear, picture a giant bloody ear in each of his paintings.

Example 4 If you have trouble remembering history, try to avoid thinking of it as something from the dim past. Picture each historical personality as a person you know right now (a friend, teacher, parent, and so on). Then picture these people doing whatever the historical figures did. Also, try visualizing battles or other events as if they were happening

Mnemonic Any kind of memory system or aid.
Keyword method As an aid to memory, using a familiar word or image to link two items.

in your town or make parks and schools into countries. Use your imagination.

How can mnemonics be used to remember things in order? Here are three techniques that are helpful.

1. **Form a story or a chain.** To remember lists of ideas, objects, or words in order, try forming an exaggerated association (mental image) connecting the first item to the second, then the second to the third, and so on. To remember the following short list in order—elephant, doorknob, string, watch, rifle, oranges—picture a full-size *elephant* balanced on a *doorknob* playing with a *string* tied to him. Picture a *watch* tied to the string, and a *rifle* shooting *oranges* at the watch. This technique can be used quite successfully for lists of 20 or more items. In one test, people who used a linking mnemonic did much better at remembering lists of 15 and 22 errands (Higbee et al., 1990). Try it next time you go shopping and leave your list at home. Another helpful strategy is to make up a short story that links all the items on a list you want to remember (McNamara & Scott, 2001).

2. **Take a mental walk.** Ancient Greek orators had an interesting way to remember ideas in order when giving a speech. Their method was to take a mental walk along a familiar path. As they did, they associated topics with the images of statues found along the walk. You can do the same thing by "placing" objects or ideas along the way as you mentally take a familiar walk (Neath & Surprenant, 2003).

3. **Use a system.** As we have already seen, many times the first letters or syllables of words or ideas can be formed into another word that will serve as a reminder of order. "Roy G. Biv" is an example. As an alternative, learn the following: 1 is a bun, 2 is a shoe, 3 is a tree, 4 is a door, 5 is a hive, 6 is sticks, 7 is heaven, 8 is a gate, 9 is a line, 10 is a hen. To remember a list in order, form an image associating bun with the first item on your list. For example, if the first item is *frog*, picture a "frog-burger" on a bun to remember it. Then, associate shoe with the second item, and so on.

If you have never used mnemonics, you may still be skeptical, but give this approach a fair trial. Most people find they can greatly extend their memory through the use of mnemonics. But remember, like most things worthwhile, remembering takes effort.

MODULE 7.6 Psychology in Action Summary

Are there any tricks to help me with my memory?

- Memory systems (mnemonics) greatly improve immediate memory. However, conventional learning tends to create the most lasting memories.
- Mnemonic systems use mental images and unusual associations to link new information with familiar memories already stored in LTM.
- Effective mnemonics tend to rely on mental images and bizarre or exaggerated mental associations.

KNOWLEDGE BUILDER

Mnemonics

Recite

1. Memory systems and aids are referred to as _____.
2. Which of the following is least likely to improve memory?
   a. using exaggerated mental images
   b. forming a chain of associations
   c. turning visual information into verbal information
   d. associating new information to information that is already known or familiar
3. Bizarre images make stored information more distinctive and therefore easier to retrieve. T or F?
4. Bower's 1973 study showed that, in general, mnemonics only improve memory for related words or ideas. T or F?
5. The keyword method is a commonly used
   a. cognitive interviewing technique
   b. massed practice strategy
   c. mnemonic technique
   d. first step in the progressive-part method

Reflect
Critical Thinking

6. How are elaborative rehearsal and mnemonics alike?

Relate

The best mnemonics are your own. As an exercise, see if you can create a better acrostic for the 12 cranial nerves. One student generated **O**ld **O**tto **O**ctavius **T**ried **T**rigonometry **A**fter **F**acing **V**ery **G**rim **V**irgin's **S**ad **H**usbands (Bloom & Lamkin, 2006).

Come up with mnemonics for the words *iconic memory, implicit memory,* and *mnemonic.* Here are some examples to help you get started. An iconic memory is a visual image: Picture an *eye* in a *can* to remember that iconic memories store visual information. Implicit memories are "hidden": Picture an *imp* hiding in memory. A mnemonic is a memory aid: Imagine writing a phone number on your knee to remember it. Imagine your *knee moaning,* "Ick, you shouldn't write on me."

Now, go through the glossary items in this chapter and make up mnemonics for any terms you have difficulty remembering.

Link

Internet addresses frequently change. To find the sites listed here, visit **http://www.thomsonedu.com/psychology/coon** for an updated list of Internet addresses and direct links to relevant sites.

- **Memory Techniques and Mnemonics** Follow links to information on mnemonics.
- **Memory Training Technique** Test your memory using the mnemonic technique of taking a mental walk.
- **Online Memory Improvement Course** Learn more details about several useful mnemonic techniques.

ANSWERS

1. mnemonics 2. c 3. T 4. F 5. c 6. Both attempt to relate new information to information stored in LTM that is familiar or already easy to retrieve.

Interactive Learning

Psychology: Active Learning Modules Book Companion Website

http://www.thomsonedu.com/psychology/coon

Visit your Book Companion Website, where you will find flash cards, practice quizzes, Internet links, and more to help you study.

ThomsonNOW

Just What You Need to Know NOW!

Spend time on what you need to master rather than on information you already have learned. Take a pre-test for this chapter, and ThomsonNOW will generate a personalized study plan based on your results. The study plan will identify the topics you need to review and direct you to online resources to help you master those topics. You can then take a post-test to help you determine the concepts you have mastered and what you will need to work on. Try it out! Go to www.thomsonedu.com/login to sign in with an access code or to purchase access to this product.

8 Intelligence, Cognition, Language, and Creativity

MODULE 8.1 Intelligence
SURVEY QUESTION: How is human intelligence defined and measured?
SURVEY QUESTION: How much does intelligence vary from person to person?
SURVEY QUESTION: What are some controversies in the study of intelligence?

MODULE 8.2 Imagery, Concepts, and Language
SURVEY QUESTION: What is the nature of thought?
SURVEY QUESTION: In what ways are images related to thinking?
SURVEY QUESTION: How do we learn concepts?
SURVEY QUESTION: What is the role of language in thinking?

MODULE 8.3 Problem Solving
SURVEY QUESTION: What do we know about problem solving?

MODULE 8.4 Creative Thinking and Intuition
SURVEY QUESTION: What is creative thinking?
SURVEY QUESTION: How accurate is intuition?

MODULE 8.5 Psychology in Action: Culture, Race, IQ, and You
SURVEY QUESTION: Are IQ tests fair to all cultural and racial groups?

Meet the Rain Man

Meet Kim Peek, the model for Dustin Hoffman's character in the Academy Award-winning movie *Rain Man*. Kim began memorizing books at 18 months of age. Today, he can recite from memory more than 9,000 books. He knows all the zip codes and area codes in America and can give accurate travel directions between any two major U.S. cities. He can also discuss hundreds of pieces of classical music in detail and is even learning to play all that music. Amazingly, though, for someone with such skills, Kim has difficulty with abstract thinking and tests of general intelligence. He is poorly coordinated and cannot button his own clothes (Treffert & Christensen, 2005).

Kim Peek is an autistic savant. His *autism* involves impairments in intelligence, communication, and social interaction, as well as repetitive behavior patterns (Dawson & Toth, 2006). Paradoxically, Kim is also a *savant* (highly knowledgeable person). Despite their impaired intelligence, autistic savants may have exceptional abilities in music, mechanics, math, memory, or other mental tasks.

The striking contrast between Kim's limited intelligence and his unusual talents raises many questions. What is intelligence? Is it all in our genes? How do we think? How are we able to solve problems? How do people create works of art, science, and literature? For some preliminary answers, we will investigate intelligence, thinking, problem solving, language, and creativity in the following pages.

Richard Green

MODULE 8.1 Intelligence

WHAT DO WE MEAN when we say that a person is "bright" or "smart"? Can intelligence be measured? Can intelligence tests predict success in life? What are the consequences of having extremely high or low intelligence? These questions and others concerning intelligence have fascinated psychologists for more than 100 years. Let's see what has been learned and what issues are still debated.

Human Intelligence—The IQ and You

SURVEY QUESTION: *How is human intelligence defined and measured?*

Like many important concepts in psychology, intelligence cannot be observed directly. Nevertheless, we feel certain it exists. Let's compare two children:

> When she was 14 months old, Anne H. wrote her own name. She taught herself to read at age 2. At age 5, she astounded her kindergarten teacher by bringing a notebook computer to class—on which she was reading an encyclopedia. At 10 she breezed through an entire high school algebra course in 12 hours.
>
> Billy A., who is 10 years old, can write his name and can count, but he has trouble with simple addition and subtraction problems and finds multiplication impossible. He has been held back in school twice and is still incapable of doing the work his 8-year-old classmates find easy.

Anne is considered a genius; Billy, a slow learner. There seems little doubt that they differ in intelligence.

Wait! Anne's ability is obvious, but how do we know that Billy isn't just lazy? This is the same question that Alfred Binet faced in 1904 (Jarvin & Sternberg, 2003). The minister of education in Paris had asked Binet to find a way to distinguish slower students from the more capable (or the capable but lazy). In a flash of brilliance, Binet and an associate created a test made up of "intellectual" questions and problems. Next, they learned which questions an average child could answer at each age. By giving children the test, they could tell if a child was performing up to his or her potential (Kaufman, 2000).

Binet's approach gave rise to modern intelligence tests. At the same time, it launched nearly 100 years of heated debate. Part of the debate is related to the basic difficulty of defining intelligence (Sternberg, Grigorenko, & Kidd, 2005).

The power of intelligence is beautifully expressed by Stephen W. Hawking, a theoretical physicist and one of the best-known scientific minds of modern times. Hawking has suffered since age 13 from Lou Gehrig's disease. Today, he can only control his left hand, and he cannot speak. Nevertheless, his brain remains fiercely active. With courage and determination, he has used his intellect to advance our understanding of the universe.

Defining Intelligence

Isn't there an accepted definition of intelligence? Yes, **intelligence** is the global capacity to act purposefully, to think rationally, and to deal effectively with the environment. The core of intelligence consists of *general mental abilities* (called the **g-factor**) in the areas of reasoning, problem solving, knowledge, memory, and successful adaptation to one's surroundings (Sternberg, 2004). Beyond this there is much disagreement. In fact, many psychologists simply accept an *operational definition* of

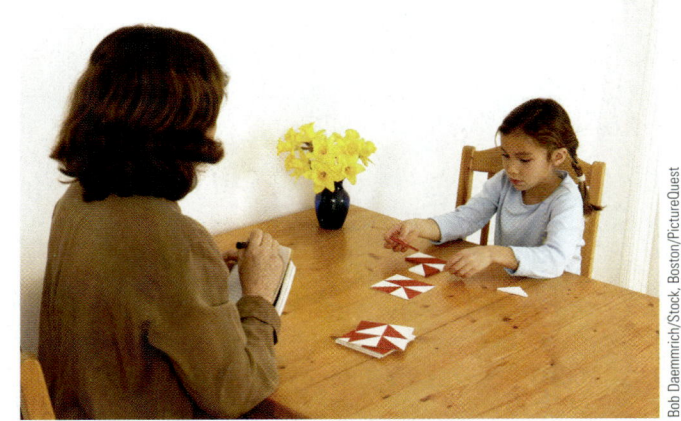

Modern intelligence tests are widely used to measure intellectual abilities. When properly administered, such tests provide an operational definition of intelligence.

HUMAN DIVERSITY

Intelligence—How Would a Fool Do It?

You have been asked to sort some objects into categories. Wouldn't it be smart to put the clothes, containers, implements, and foods in separate piles? Not necessarily. When members of the Kpelle culture in Liberia were asked to sort objects, they grouped them together by function. For example, a potato (food) would be placed together with a knife (implement). When the Kpelle were asked why they grouped the objects this way, they often said that's how a wise man would do it. The researchers finally asked the Kpelle, "How would a fool do it?" Only then did the Kpelle sort the objects into the nice, neat categories we Westerners prefer.

This anecdote, related by cultural psychologist Patricia Greenfield (1997), raises serious questions about general definitions of intelligence. For example, among the Cree of Northern Canada, "smart" people are the ones who have visual skills needed to find food on the frozen tundra (Darou, 1992). For the Puluwat people in the South Pacific, being smart means having ocean-going navigation skills necessary to get from island to island (Sternberg, 2004). And so it goes, as each culture teaches its children the kinds of "intelligence" valued in that culture—how the wise man would do it, not a fool (Correa-Chávez, Rogoff, & Arauz, 2005).

In view of such differences, psychologists have tried to create "culture-fair" intelligence tests. Some have even questioned the value of intelligence testing itself. We'll discuss both these ideas in this chapter's "Psychology in Action" module.

---

intelligence by spelling out the procedures they use to measure it. Thus, by selecting items for an intelligence test, a psychologist is saying in a very direct way, "This is what I mean by intelligence." A test that measures memory, reasoning, and verbal fluency offers a very different definition of intelligence than one that measures strength of grip, shoe size, length of the nose, or the person's best *Too Human* video game score. (For a glimpse at how other cultures define "intelligent" behavior, see "Intelligence—How Would a Fool Do It?")

Intelligence Tests

American psychologists quickly saw the value of Alfred Binet's test. In 1916, Lewis Terman and others at Stanford University revised it for use in North America. After more revisions, the *Stanford-Binet Intelligence Scales, Fifth Edition* continues to be widely used. The original Stanford-Binet assumed that a child's intellectual abilities improve with each passing year. Today, the Stanford-Binet (or SB5) is still primarily made up of age-ranked questions. Naturally, these questions get a little harder at each age level. The SB5 is appropriate for people from age 2 to 85+ years (Roid, 2003).

The SB5 measures five cognitive factors (types of mental abilities) that make up general intelligence. These are *fluid reasoning, knowledge, quantitative reasoning, visual-spatial processing,* and *working memory*. Each factor is measured with verbal questions (those involving words and numbers) and nonverbal questions (items that use pictures and objects). Let's see what each factor looks like.

Fluid Reasoning
Fluid Reasoning tests reasoning ability with questions like the following:

> How are an apple, a plum, and a banana different from a beet?
>
> An apprentice is to a master as a novice is to an _____.
>
> "I knew my bag was going to be in the last place I looked, so I looked there first." What is silly or impossible about that?

Other items ask people to fill in the missing shape in a group of shapes and to tell a story that explains what's going on in a series of pictures.

Knowledge
The Knowledge factor assesses the person's knowledge about a wide range of topics.

> Why is yeast added to bread dough?
> What does cryptic mean?
> What is silly or impossible about this picture? (For example, a bicycle has square wheels.)

Quantitative Reasoning
Test items for Quantitative Reasoning measure a person's ability to solve problems involving numbers. Here are some samples:

> If I have six marbles and you give me another one, how many marbles will I have?
> Given the numbers 3, 6, 9, 12, what number would come next?
> If a shirt is being sold for 50 percent of the normal price, and the price tag is $60, what is the cost of the shirt?

Intelligence An overall capacity to think rationally, act purposefully, and deal effectively with the environment.

g-factor A general ability factor or core of general intellectual ability that involves reasoning, problem-solving ability, knowledge, memory, and successful adaptation to one's surroundings.

Visual-Spatial Processing People who have visual-spatial skills are good at putting picture puzzles together and copying geometric shapes (such as triangles, rectangles, and circles). Visual-Spatial Processing questions ask test takers to reproduce patterns of blocks and choose pictures that show how a piece of paper would look if it were folded or cut. Verbal questions can also require visual-spatial abilities:

> Suppose that you are going east, then turn right, then turn right again, then turn left. In what direction are you facing now?

Working Memory The Working Memory part of the SB5 measures the ability to use short-term memory. Some typical memory tasks include the following:

> Correctly remember the order of colored beads on a stick.
> After hearing several sentences, name the last word from each sentence.
> Repeat a series of digits (forward or backward) after hearing them once.

If you were to take the SB5, it would yield a score for your general intelligence, verbal intelligence, nonverbal intelligence, and each of the five cognitive factors (Bain & Allin, 2005).

Intelligence Quotients

Imagine that a child named Yuan can answer questions that an average 7-year-old can answer. How smart is she? Actually, we can't say yet, because we don't know how old Yuan is. If she is 10, she's not very smart. If she's 5, she is very bright. Thus, to estimate a child's intelligence we need to know both her **mental age** (average intellectual performance) and her **chronological age** (age in years).

Mental age is based on the level of age-ranked questions a person can answer. For example, at ages 8 or 9, very few children can define the word *connection*. At age 10, 10 percent can. At age 13, 60 percent can. Thus, a 13-year-old of average ability can define *connection*. If we had only this one item to test children with, those who answered correctly would be given a mental age of 13. When scores from many such items are combined, a child's overall mental age can be found. ■ Table 8.1 is a sample of items that persons of average intelligence can answer at various ages.

Mental age is a good measure of actual ability. But mental age says nothing about whether overall intelligence is high or low compared with other people of the same age. To find out what a particular mental age means, we must relate mental age to actual age. This yields an **intelligence quotient**, or **IQ**. A quotient results from dividing one number into another. When the Stanford-Binet was first used, IQ was defined as mental age (MA) divided by chronological age (CA) and multiplied by 100. (Multiplying by 100 changes the IQ into a whole number, rather than a decimal.)

$$\frac{MA}{CA} \times 100 = IQ$$

An advantage of the original IQ calculation was that intelligence could be compared among children with different chronological and mental ages. For instance, 10-year-old Justin has a mental age of 12. Thus, his IQ is 120:

$$\frac{(MA)\ 12}{(CA)\ 10} \times 100 = 120\ (IQ)$$

Justin's friend Suke also has a mental age of 12. However, Suke's chronological age is 12, so his IQ is 100:

$$\frac{(MA)\ 12}{(CA)\ 12} \times 100 = 100\ (IQ)$$

The IQ shows that 10-year-old Justin is brighter than his 12-year-old friend Suke, even though their intellectual skills are about the same. Notice that a person's IQ will be 100 when mental age equals chronological age. An IQ score of 100 is therefore defined as average intelligence.

TABLE 8.1 Sample Items from the Stanford-Binet Intelligence Scale

Age	Items
2 years old	On a large paper doll, points out the hair, mouth, feet, ears, nose, hands, and eyes. When shown a tower built of four blocks, builds one like it.
3 years old	When shown a bridge built of three blocks, builds one like it. When shown a drawing of a circle, copies it with a pencil.
4 years old	Fills in the missing word when asked, "Brother is a boy; sister is a _____." "In daytime it is light; at night it is _____." Answers correctly when asked, "Why do we have houses?" "Why do we have books?"
5 years old	Defines *ball*, *hat*, and *stove*. When shown a drawing of a square, copies it with a pencil.
9 years old	Answers correctly when examiner says, "In an old graveyard in Spain they have discovered a small skull which they believe to be that of Christopher Columbus when he was about 10 years old. What is foolish about that?" Answers correctly when asked, "Tell me the name of a color that rhymes with head." "Tell me a number that rhymes with tree."
Adult	Can describe the difference between laziness and idleness, poverty and misery, character and reputation. Answers correctly when asked, "Which direction would you have to face so your right hand would be toward the north?"

(From L. Terman & M. Merrill, *Stanford-Binet Intelligence Scale*, 1937. Revised edition, 1960. Houghton Mifflin Co. Used with permission.)

Then does a person with an IQ score below 100 have below average intelligence? Not unless the IQ is well below 100. An IQ of 100 is the *mathematical* average (or mean) for such scores. However, average intelligence is usually defined as any score from 90 to 109. The important point is that IQ scores will be over 100 when mental age is higher than age in years (● Fig. 8.1). IQ scores below 100 occur when a person's age in years exceeds his or her mental age. An example of the second situation would be a 15-year-old with an MA of 12:

$$\frac{12}{15} \times 100 = 80 \text{ (IQ)}$$

Deviation IQs The preceding examples may give you insight into IQ scores. However, it's no longer necessary to directly calculate IQs. Instead, modern tests use **deviation IQs.** These scores are based on a person's relative standing in his or her age group. That is, they tell how far above or below average the person's score falls. (For more information, see the Statistics appendix near the end of this book.) Tables supplied with the test are then used to convert a person's relative standing in the group to an IQ score. For example, if you score at the fiftieth percentile, half the people your age who take the test score higher than you and half score lower. In this case, your IQ score is 100. If you score at the eighty-fourth percentile, your IQ score is 115. If you score at the ninety-seventh percentile, your IQ score is 130.

The Wechsler Tests

Is the Stanford-Binet the only intelligence test? A widely used alternative is the *Wechsler Adult Intelligence Scale–Third Edition* (WAIS-III). A version for children is called the *Wechsler Intelligence Scale for Children–Fourth Edition* (WISC-IV) (Baron, 2005).

The Wechsler tests are similar to the Stanford-Binet but differ in important ways. For one thing, the WAIS-III was specifically designed to test adult intelligence. The original Stanford-Binet was better suited for children and adolescents. The latest Stanford-Binet (the SB5) can now be used for all ages, but the WAIS was the first "adult" IQ test. Like the Stanford-Binet, the Wechsler tests yield a single overall IQ. In addition, the WAIS and WISC give separate scores for **performance** (nonverbal) **intelligence** and **verbal** (language- or symbol-oriented) **intelligence**. (Note that this feature was also recently added to the SB5.) The abilities measured by the Wechsler tests and some sample test items are listed in ■ Table 8.2.

Group Tests

The SB5 and the Wechsler tests are **individual intelligence tests,** which must be given to a single person by a trained specialist. In contrast, **group intelligence tests** can be given to large groups of people with minimal supervision. Group tests usually require people to read, to follow instructions, and to solve problems of logic, reasoning, mathematics, or spatial skills. If you're wondering if you have ever taken an intelligence test, the answer is probably yes. The well-known *Scholastic Assessment Test* (SAT) measures aptitudes for language, math, and reasoning. The SAT is designed to predict your chances for success in college. Because it measures a number of different mental aptitudes, it can also be used to estimate general intelligence (Frey & Detterman, 2004).

● **FIGURE 8.1** With a score of 230, Marilyn vos Savant has the highest IQ ever officially recorded. When she was only 7 years and 9 months old, vos Savant could answer questions that the average 13-year-old can answer. At ages 8, 9, and 10, she got perfect scores on the Stanford-Binet scale. Now in her 60s, she is a well-published author and recently became the host of an *Ask Marilyn* segment for CBS TV News.

Mental age The average mental ability people display at a given age.
Chronological age A person's age in years.
Intelligence quotient (IQ) An index of intelligence defined as a person's mental age divided by his or her chronological age and multiplied by 100.
Deviation IQ An IQ obtained statistically from a person's relative standing in his or her age group; that is, how far above or below average the person's score was relative to other scores.
Performance intelligence Intelligence measured by solving puzzles, assembling objects, completing pictures, and other nonverbal tasks.
Verbal intelligence Intelligence measured by answering questions involving vocabulary, general information, arithmetic, and other language- or symbol-oriented tasks.
Individual intelligence test A test of intelligence designed to be given to a single individual by a trained specialist.
Group intelligence test Any intelligence test that can be administered to a group of people with minimal supervision.

TABLE 8.2 Sample Items Similar to Those Used on the WAIS-III

VERBAL SUBTESTS	SAMPLE ITEMS
Information	How many wings does a bird have? Who wrote *Paradise Lost*?
Digit span	Repeat from memory a series of digits, such as 3 1 0 6 7 4 2 5, after hearing it once.
General comprehension	What is the advantage of keeping money in the bank? Why is copper often used in electrical wires?
Arithmetic	Three men divided 18 golf balls equally among themselves. How many golf balls did each man receive? If 2 apples cost 15¢, what will be the cost of a dozen apples?
Similarities	In what way are a lion and a tiger alike and/or unalike? In what way are a saw and a hammer alike and/or unalike?
Vocabulary	What is a guitar? What does "robin" mean?
Letter-number sequencing	Repeat a list of mixed numbers and letters, numbers first, in numerical order, and letters second, in alphabetical order.
PERFORMANCE SUBTESTS	**DESCRIPTION OF ITEM**
Picture arrangement	Arrange a series of cartoon panels to make a meaningful story.
Picture completion	What is missing from these pictures?
Block design	Copy designs with blocks.
Object assembly	Put together a jigsaw puzzle.
Digit symbol	Fill in the symbols.
Matrix reasoning	Select the item that completes the matrix.
Symbol search	Match symbols appearing in separate groups.

Wechsler Adult Intelligence Scale®–Third Edition. Copyright © 2007 by Harcourt Assessment, Inc. Reproduced with permission. All rights reserved.

Variations in Intelligence— Curved like a Bell

SURVEY QUESTION: *How much does intelligence vary from person to person?*

IQ scores are classified as shown in ■ Table 8.3. A look at the percentages reveals a definite pattern. The distribution (or scattering) of IQ scores approximates a **normal** (bell-shaped) **curve.** That is, most scores fall close to the average and very few are found at the extremes. ● Figure 8.2 shows this characteristic of measured intelligence.

TABLE 8.3 Distribution of Adult IQ Scores on WAIS-III

IQ	DESCRIPTION	PERCENT
Above 130	Very superior	2.2
120-129	Superior	6.7
110-119	Bright normal	16.1
90-109	Average	50.0
80-89	Dull normal	16.1
70-79	Borderline	6.7
Below 70	Intellectual disabled	2.2

The Mentally Gifted

How high is the IQ of a genius? Only 2 people out of 100 score above 130 on IQ tests. These bright individuals are usually described as "gifted." Less than one-half of 1 percent of the population scores above 140. These people are certainly gifted or perhaps even "geniuses." However, some psychologists reserve the term *genius* for people with even higher IQs or those who are exceptionally creative (Hallahan & Kauffman, 2006).

Gifted Children *Do high IQ scores in childhood predict later ability?* To directly answer this question, Lewis Terman selected 1,500 children with IQs of 140 or more. Terman followed this gifted group (the "Termites" as he called them) into adulthood and found that most were quite successful. A majority finished college, earned advanced degrees, or held professional positions, and many had written books or scientific articles (Terman & Oden, 1959).

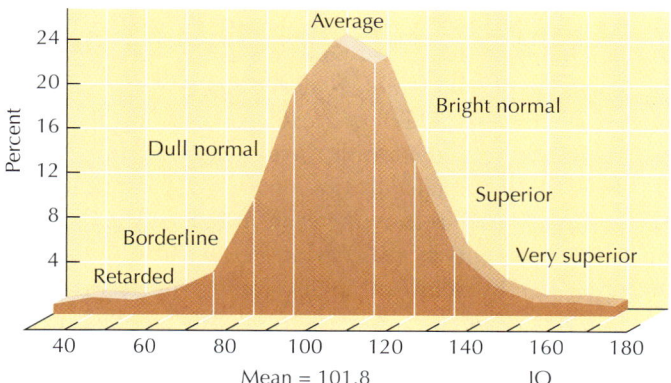

● **FIGURE 8.2** Distribution of Stanford-Binet Intelligence Test scores for 3,184 children. (Adapted from Terman & Merrill, 1960.)

In general, the correlation between IQ scores and school grades is 0.50, a sizable association. The link would be even stronger, but motivation, special talents, off-campus learning, and many other factors also affect grades. The same is true of "real world" success beyond school. IQ is not at all good at predicting success in art, music, writing, dramatics, science, and leadership. Creativity is much more strongly related to doing well in these areas (Preckel, Holling, & Wiese, 2006; Runco, 2004). Regardless, when people score in the gifted range, their chances for high achievement do seem to rise (Shurkin, 1992).

Were all the gifted children superior as adults? No. Some had committed crimes, were unemployable, or were emotionally troubled. Remember that a high IQ reveals *potential*. It does not guarantee success. Marilyn vos Savant, with an IQ of 230, has contributed little to science, literature, or art. Nobel prize–winning physicist Richard Feynman, whom many regarded as a genius, had an IQ of 122 (Michalko, 1998).

How did Terman's more successful Termites differ from the less successful? Most of them had educated parents who taught them to value learning. They also had *intellectual determination*, which is a desire to know, to excel, and to persevere (Winner, 2003). Thus, successful gifted persons tend to be *persistent* and *motivated* to learn. No one is paid to sit around being *capable* of achievement. What you do is always more important than what you should be able to do. That's why a child's talents are most likely to blossom when they are nurtured with support, encouragement, education, and effort (Callahan, 2006).

Identifying Gifted Children How might a parent spot an unusually bright child? Early signs of giftedness are not always purely "intellectual." **Giftedness** can be either the possession of a high IQ or special talents or aptitudes, such as creativity. Remember, Kim Peek is remarkably gifted *in some ways*.

The following signs may reveal that a child is gifted: A tendency to seek out older children and adults; an early fascination with explanations and problem solving; talking in complete sentences as early as 2 or 3 years of age; an unusually good memory; precocious talent in art, music, or number skills; an early interest in books, along with early reading (often by age 3); showing of kindness, understanding, and cooperation toward others (Alvino & Editors, 1996; Distin, 2006).

Notice that this list goes beyond straight g-factor, or "academic" intelligence. In fact, if artistic talent, mechanical aptitude, musical aptitude, athletic potential, and so on are considered, many children have a special "gift" of one kind or another. Limiting giftedness to high IQ can shortchange children with special talents. This is especially true of ethnic minority children, who may be the victims of subtle biases in standardized intelligence tests. These children, as well as children with physical disabilities, are less likely to be recognized as gifted (Ford & Moore, 2006; Robinson & Clinkenbeard, 1998).

Intellectual Disability

A person with mental abilities far below average is termed **intellectually disabled** (a related term, **mentally retarded**, is seen by many as offensive). Intellectual disability begins at an IQ of approximately 70 or below. However, a person's ability

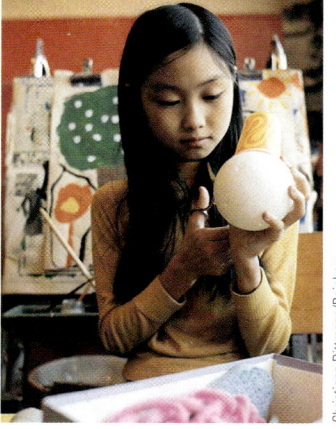

It is wise to remember that there are many ways in which a child may be gifted. Many schools now offer Gifted and Talented Education programs for students with a variety of special abilities—not just for those who score well on IQ tests.

Normal curve A bell-shaped curve characterized by a large number of scores in a middle area, tapering to very few extremely high and low scores.

Giftedness The possession of a high IQ or special talents or aptitudes.

Intellectual disability (formerly mental retardation) The presence of a developmental disability, a formal IQ score below 70, or a significant impairment of adaptive behavior.

TABLE 8.4 Levels of Intellectual Disability

IQ RANGE	DEGREE OF INTELLECTUAL DISABILITY	EDUCATIONAL CLASSIFICATION	REQUIRED LEVEL OF SUPPORT
50-55 to 70	Mild	Educable	Intermittent
35-40 to 50-55	Moderate	Trainable	Limited
20-25 to 35-40	Severe	Dependent	Extensive
Below 20-25	Profound	Life support	Pervasive

(DSM-IV-TR, 2000; Hodapp, 1994.)

to perform *adaptive behaviors* (basic skills such as dressing, eating, communicating, shopping, and working) also figures into evaluating this disability (DSM-IV-TR, 2000; Hallahan & Kauffman, 2006). (See ■ Table 8.4.)

It's important to realize that intellectually disabled persons have no handicap where feelings are concerned. They are easily hurt by rejection, teasing, or ridicule. Likewise, they respond warmly to love and acceptance. They have a right to self-respect and a place in the community (AAIDD, 2004). This is especially important during childhood, when support from others adds greatly to the person's chances of becoming a well-adjusted member of society.

Causes of Intellectual Disability *What causes intellectual disability?* About half of all cases of intellectual disability are *organic,* or related to physical disorders (Das, 2000). These include *fetal damage* (prenatal damage from teratogens such as disease, infection, or drugs) and *birth injuries* (such as lack of oxygen during delivery). *Metabolic disorders,* which affect energy production and use in the body, also cause intellectual disability. Some forms of intellectual disability are linked to *genetic abnormalities,* such as missing genes, extra genes, or defective genes. Malnutrition and exposure to lead, PCBs, and other toxins early in childhood can also cause organic intellectual disability (Beirne-Smith, Patton, & Shannon, 2006).

In 30 to 40 percent of cases, no known biological problem can be identified. In many such instances, the degree of intellectual disability is mild, in the 50 to 70 IQ range. Often, other family members are also mildly intellectually disabled. *Familial intellectual disability,* as this is called, occurs mostly in very poor households where nutrition, intellectual stimulation, medical care, and emotional support may be inadequate. This suggests that familial intellectual disability is based largely on an impoverished environment. Thus, better nutrition, education, and early childhood enrichment programs could prevent many cases of intellectual disability (Beirne-Smith, Patton, & Shannon, 2006).

Questioning Intelligence—How Intelligent Are Intelligence Tests?

SURVEY QUESTION: *What are some controversies in the study of intelligence?*

Defining intelligence as a g-factor (general ability) has been controversial. As we noted earlier in our discussion of "intelligent" behavior in other cultures, there are many ways to be smart. For example, consider William, a grade-school student 2 years behind in reading, who shows his teacher how to solve a difficult computer-programming problem. Or what about his classmate, Malika, who performs poorly in math but plays intricate pieces of piano music? Both these children show clear signs of intelligence. And yet, each might score below average on a traditional IQ test. And, as we have seen, autistic savants like Kim Peek have even more extreme intellectual strengths and weaknesses. Such observations have convinced many psychologists that it is time to forge new, broader definitions of intelligence. Their basic goal is to better predict "real-world" success—not just the likelihood of success in school (Sternberg & Grigorenko, 2006).

Multiple Intelligences

One such psychologist is Howard Gardner of Harvard University. Gardner (2003, 2004) theorizes that there are actually eight distinctly different kinds of intelligence. These are different mental "languages" that people use for thinking. Each is listed below, with examples of pursuits that make use of them.

1. *Language* (linguistic abilities)—writer, lawyer, comedian

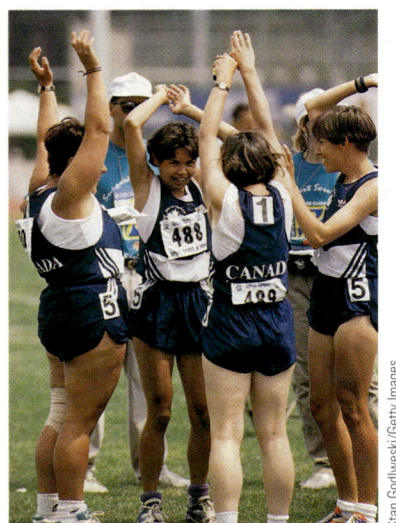

These youngsters are participants in the Special Olympics—an athletic event for the intellectually disabled. It is often said of the Special Olympics that "everyone is a winner—participants, coaches, and spectators."

2. *Logic and math* (numeric abilities)—scientist, accountant, programmer
3. *Visual and spatial* (pictorial abilities)—engineer, inventor, artist
4. *Music* (musical abilities)—composer, musician, music critic
5. *Bodily-kinesthetic* (physical abilities)—dancer, athlete, surgeon
6. *Intrapersonal* (self-knowledge)—poet, actor, minister
7. *Interpersonal* (social abilities)—psychologist, teacher, politician
8. *Naturalist* (an ability to understand the natural environment)—biologist, medicine man, organic farmer

To simplify a great deal, people can be "word smart," "number smart," "picture smart," "musically smart," "body smart," "self smart," "people smart," and/or "nature smart."

Most of us are probably strong in only a few types of intelligence. In contrast, geniuses like Albert Einstein seem to be able to use nearly all of the intelligences, as needed, to solve problems.

If Gardner's theory of **multiple intelligences** is correct, traditional IQ tests measure only a part of real-world intelligence—namely, linguistic, logical-mathematical, and spatial abilities. A further implication is that our schools may be wasting a lot of human potential (Campbell, Campbell, & Dickinson, 2003). For example, some children might find it easier to learn math or reading if these topics were tied into art, music, dance, drama, and so on. Already, many schools are using Gardner's theory to cultivate a wider range of skills and talents (Campbell, Campbell, & Dickinson, 2003; Kornhaber & Gardner, 2006). Before we return to human intelligence, let's see what we can learn from some smart machines.

Artificial Intelligence: I Compute, Therefore I Am

How smart are computers and robots? Just as people like Kim Peek challenge our understanding of general intelligence, so too does the prospect of creating intelligent machines. Let's say you are exchanging instant messages over the Internet with someone you don't know. You are allowed to make any comments and ask any questions you like, for as long as you like. In reality, the "person" you are communicating with is a computer. Do you think a computer could fool you into believing it was human? If it did, wouldn't that qualify it as "intelligent"? You may be surprised to learn that, to date, no machine has come close to passing this test (Moor, 2003).

The problem computers face is that we humans can mentally "shift gears" from one topic to another with incredible flexibility. In contrast, machine "intelligence" is currently "blind" outside its underlying set of rules. As a tiny example, u cann understnd wrds thet ar mizpeld. Computers are very literal and easily stymied by such errors.

Regardless, artificial intelligence has been successful at very specific tasks. **Artificial intelligence (AI)** usually refers

According to Howard Gardner's theory, bodily-kinesthetic skills reflect one of eight distinct types of intelligence.

 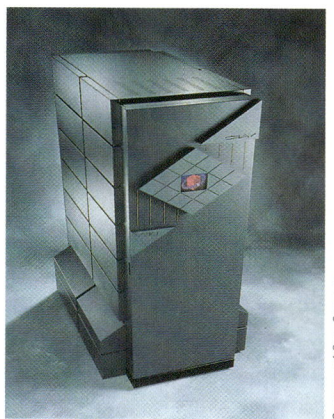

Two composers. The one on the left was a genius who wrote sublime, multi-voiced harmonies. The one on the right has created reasonably good, if uninspired, music. Computer models of thought can approximate intelligent human behavior. However, rule-based computer "thinking" still lacks the flexibility, creativity, and common sense of human intelligence.

Multiple intelligences Howard Gardner's theory that there are several specialized types of intellectual ability.

Artificial intelligence Any artificial system (often a computer program) that is capable of human-like problem solving or intelligent responding.

to computer programs capable of doing things that require intelligence when done by people (Russell & Norvig, 2003). For example, listeners sometimes mistake music created by Kemal Ebcioglu for that written by Johann Sebastian Bach, the eighteenth-century German composer. Ebcioglu wrote a computer program that creates harmonies remarkably similar to Bach's. By analyzing Bach's music, Ebcioglu came up with 350 rules that govern harmonization. The result is a program that displays artificial intelligence in a specific area.

Much of current artificial intelligence is based on the fact that many tasks—from harmonizing music to diagnosing disease—can be reduced to a set of rules applied to a collection of information. AI is valuable in situations where speed, vast memory, and persistence are required. In fact, AI programs are better at some tasks than humans are. An example is world chess champion Garry Kasparov's loss, in 1997, to a computer called Deep Blue.

AI and Cognition Although AI is a long way from duplicating general human intelligence, artificial intelligence offers a way to probe some of our specific cognitive skills, or intelligences. For instance, computer simulations and expert systems provide good examples of how AI is being used as a research tool.

Computer simulations are programs that attempt to duplicate specific human behaviors, especially thinking, decision making, or problem solving. Here, the computer acts as a "laboratory" for testing models of cognition. If a computer program behaves as humans do (including making the same errors), then the program may be a good model of how we think.

Expert systems are computer programs that respond as a human expert would (Giarratano & Riley, 2005). They have demystified some human abilities by converting complex skills into clearly stated rules a computer can follow. Expert systems can predict the weather, analyze geological formations, diagnose disease, play chess, read, tell when to buy or sell stocks, and perform many other tasks.

Eventually, AI will almost certainly lead to robots that recognize voices and that speak and act "intelligently" in specific areas of ability. To achieve this, should intelligence be directly programmed into computers? Or should computers be designed to learn from experience, like the human brain does (McClelland & Rogers, 2003)? Only time will tell. For now, it's interesting to note that these questions mirror another area of controversy—whether human intelligence is inherited or learned from experience.

Heredity, Environment, and Intelligence

Is intelligence inherited? Most people are aware that there is a moderate similarity in the intelligence of parents and their children, or between brothers and sisters. As ● Figure 8.3 shows, the similarity in IQ scores among relatives grows in proportion to how close they are on the family tree.

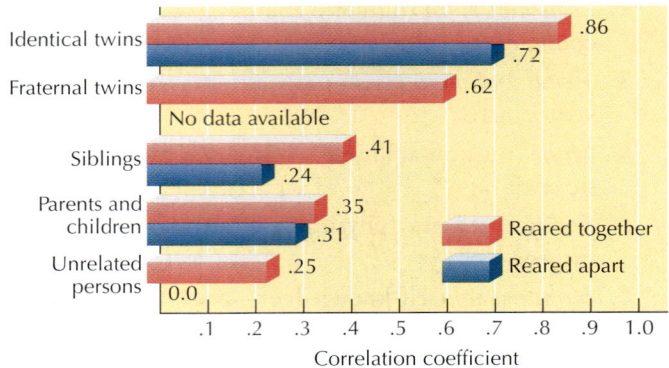

● **FIGURE 8.3** Approximate correlations between IQ scores for persons with varying degrees of genetic and environmental similarity. Notice that the correlations grow smaller as the degree of genetic similarity declines. Also note that a shared environment increases the correlation in all cases. (Estimates from Bouchard, 1983; Henderson, 1982.)

Does this indicate that intelligence is hereditary? Not necessarily. Brothers, sisters, and parents share similar environments as well as similar heredity. To separate nature and nurture, **twin studies** may be done. Such studies compare the IQs of twins who were raised together or separated at birth. This allows us to estimate how much heredity and environment affect intelligence.

Twin Studies Notice in Figure 8.3 that the IQs of fraternal twins are more alike than the IQs of ordinary siblings. *Fraternal twins* come from two separate eggs fertilized at the same time. Genetically, they are no more alike than ordinary siblings. Why, then, should the twins' IQs be more similar? The reason is environmental: Parents treat twins more alike than ordinary siblings, resulting in a closer match in IQs.

More striking similarities are observed with *identical twins,* who develop from a single egg and have identical genes. At the top of Figure 8.3 you can see that identical twins who grow up in the same family have highly correlated IQs. This is what we would expect with identical heredity and very similar environments. Now, let's consider what happens when identical twins are reared apart. As you can see, the correlation drops, but only from 0.86 to 0.72. Psychologists who emphasize genetics believe these figures show that adult intelligence is roughly 50 percent hereditary (Grigorenko & Sternberg, 2003).

How do environmentalists interpret the figures? They point out that the IQs of some separated twins differ by as much as 20 points. Such IQ gaps occur when the twins grow up with big educational and environmental differences. It is more common for separated twins to be placed in homes socially and educationally similar to their biological parents. This fact

CRITICAL THINKING

You Mean Video Games Might Be Good for Me?

Although rapidly rising Western IQ scores suggest that environmental factors influence intelligence (Schooler, 1998), we are left with the question, Which factors? Writer Steven Johnson (2005) believes that popular culture is responsible. Although he agrees that much popular media content is too violent or sexual in nature, he points out that video games, the Internet, and even television are becoming more complex. As a result, they demand ever-greater cognitive effort from us. In other words, it is as important to understand *how* we experience the environment as it is to understand *what* we experience.

For example, early video games, such as Pong or Pac Man, offered simple, repetitive visual experiences. In contrast, today's popular games, such as The World of Warcraft or Second Life, offer rich, complicated experiences that can take many hours of intense problem solving to complete. Furthermore, players must usually figure out the rules by themselves. Instructions that fans have written for popular games are typically much longer than chapters in this book. Only a complex and engaging game would prompt players to use such instructions, much less write them for others to use (Johnson, 2005).

According to Johnson, other forms of popular culture have also become more complex, including the Internet, computer software, and even popular television. For example, compared with television dramas of the past, modern dramas weave plot lines and characters through an entire season of programs. In the end, popular culture may well be inviting us to read, reflect, and problem-solve more than ever before. (Before you uncritically embrace video games, read "You Mean Video Games Might Be Bad For Me?" in Module 6.5.)

would tend to inflate apparent genetic effects by making the separated twins' IQs more alike. Another frequently overlooked fact is that twins grow up in the same environment *before birth* (in the womb). If we take such environmental similarities into account, intelligence would seem to be less than 50 percent hereditary (Devlin, Daniels, & Roeder, 1997; Turkheimer et al., 2003).

IQ and Environment *How much can environment alter intelligence?* Strong evidence for an environmental view of intelligence comes from adoption studies. Consider families having one adopted child and one biological child. As ● Figure 8.4 shows, parents contribute genes *and* environment to their biological child. With an adopted child they contribute only environment. If intelligence is highly genetic, the IQs of biological children should be more like their parents' IQs than are the IQs of adopted children. However, one study found that children reared by the same mother tend to resemble her IQ to the same degree. It does not matter whether or not they share her genes (Kamin, 1981; Weinberg, 1989).

In another study, striking increases in IQ occurred in 25 children who were moved from an orphanage and were eventually adopted by parents who gave them love, a family, and a stimulating home environment. Once considered intellectually disabled and unadoptable, the children gained an average of 29 IQ points. A second group of initially less "intellectually disabled" children, who stayed in the orphanage, *lost* an average of 26 IQ points (Skeels, 1966)!

A particularly dramatic environmental effect is the fact that Westernized nations have shown average IQ gains of 15 points during the last 30 years (Dickens & Flynn, 2001). These IQ boosts occurred in far too short a time for genetics to explain them. It is more likely that the gains reflect environmental forces, such as improved education and nutrition and living in a technologically complex society (Johnson, 2005). If you've ever tried to play a computer game or set up a wireless network in your home, you'll understand why people may be getting better at answering IQ test questions. (See "You Mean Video Games Might Be Good for Me?")

Summary In the final analysis, intelligence reflects development as well as potential, nurture as well as nature (Grigorenko, 2005). Moreover, the fact that intelligence is partly determined by heredity tells us little of any real value. Genes are fixed at birth. Improving the environments in which children learn and grow is the main way in which we can assure that they reach their full potential (Grigorenko & Sternberg, 2003; White, 2006).

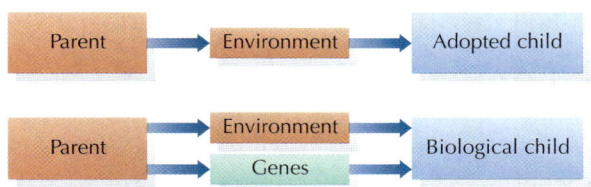

● **FIGURE 8.4** Comparison of an adopted child and a biological child reared in the same family. (Adapted from Kamin, 1981.)

Twin study A comparison of the characteristics of twins who were raised together or separated at birth; used to identify the relative impact of heredity and environment.

MODULE 8.1 Summary

How is human intelligence defined and measured?

- Intelligence refers to the general capacity (or g-factor) to act purposefully, think rationally, and deal effectively with the environment. In practice, intelligence is operationally defined by intelligence tests.
- The first intelligence test was assembled by Alfred Binet. A modern version of Binet's test is the *Stanford-Binet Intelligence Scale*.
- Intelligence is expressed as an intelligence quotient (IQ), defined as mental age divided by chronological age and then multiplied by 100. The distribution of IQ scores approximates a normal curve.
- Another major intelligence test is the *Wechsler Adult Intelligence Scale* (WAIS). The WAIS measures both verbal and performance intelligence. Group intelligence tests are also available.

How much does intelligence vary from person to person?

- People with IQs in the gifted or "genius" range of above 140 tend to be superior in many respects. However, by criteria other than IQ, many children can be considered gifted or talented in one way or another.
- The term *intellectually disabled* is applied to those whose IQ falls below 70 or who lack various adaptive behaviors. About 50 percent of the cases of intellectual disability are organic. The remaining cases are of undetermined cause. Many of these cases are thought to reflect familial intellectual disability.

What are some controversies in the study of intelligence?

- Many psychologists have begun to forge new, broader definitions of intelligence. Howard Gardner's theory of multiple intelligences is a good example.
- *Artificial intelligence* refers to any artificial system that can perform tasks that require intelligence when done by people. Two principal areas of artificial intelligence research on particular human skills are computer simulations and expert systems.
- Intelligence is partially determined by heredity. However, environment is also important, as revealed by IQ increases induced by education and stimulating environments.

KNOWLEDGE BUILDER

Intelligence

Recite

1. Which modern intelligence test originated with attempts to measure the mental abilities of children in Paris?
   a. SB5
   b. WAIS
   c. SAT
   d. WISC

2. If we define intelligence by writing a test, we are using a(n) _____ definition.

3. By definition, a person has average intelligence when
   a. MA = CA
   b. CA = 100
   c. MA = 100
   d. MA × CA = 100

4. The WAIS-III is a group intelligence test. T or F?

5. The distribution of IQs approximates a _____ (bell-shaped) curve.

6. One thing that the mentally gifted and the intellectually disabled have in common is that both have
   a. a tendency to suffer from metabolic disorders
   b. to be tested with the WAIS, rather than the SB5
   c. MAs that are higher than their CAs
   d. extreme IQ scores

7. Many cases of intellectual disability without known organic causes appear to be _____.

8. From a practical point of view, intelligence can most readily be increased by
   a. genetics
   b. teaching adaptive behaviors
   c. stimulating environments
   d. applying deviation IQs

Reflect

Critical Thinking

9. Is it ever accurate to describe a machine as "intelligent"?

10. Some people treat IQ as if it were a fixed number, permanently stamped on the forehead of each child. Why is this view in error?

Relate

If you were going to write an intelligence test, what kinds of questions would you include? How much would they resemble the questions found on the SB5, the WAIS-III, or culture-fair tests?

How has your understanding of the following concepts changed: IQ, giftedness, intellectual disability?

A friend says to you, "I think intelligence is entirely inherited from parents." What could you tell your friend to make sure she or he is better informed?

Link

Internet addresses frequently change. To find the sites listed here, visit **http://www.thomsonedu.com/psychology/coon** for an updated list of Internet addresses and direct links to relevant sites.

- **American Mensa** Mensa is an international society that has one qualification only for membership: an IQ score in the top 2 percent of the population on a standardized intelligence test.
- **Intellectual Disabilities** Learn more about intellectual disability from the American Association on Intellectual and Developmental Disabilities (AAIDD).
- **Multiple Intelligences in Education** Learn more about Gardner's theory of multiple intelligences and how it is being applied in education.

ANSWERS

1. a 2. operational 3. a 4. F 5. normal 6. d 7. familial 8. c 9. Rule-driven expert systems may appear "intelligent" within a narrow range of problem solving. However, they are "stone stupid" at everything else. This is usually not what we have in mind when discussing human intelligence. 10. Because one's IQ depends on the intelligence test used to measure it: Change the test and you will change the score. Also, heredity establishes a range of possibilities; it does not automatically preordain a person's intellectual capacities.

MODULE 8.2 Imagery, Concepts, and Language

HUMAN INTELLIGENCE allows us to be highly adaptable creatures. We live in deserts, jungles, mountains, frenzied cities, placid retreats, and space stations. Unlike other species, our success owes more to intelligence and thinking abilities than it does to physical strength or speed (Solso, MacLin, & MacLin, 2005). Let's see how concepts, language, and mental images make abstract thinking possible.

What Is Thinking?—It's All in Your Head!

SURVEY QUESTION: *What is the nature of thought?*

Cognition refers to mentally processing information. Our thoughts take many forms, including daydreaming, problem solving, and reasoning (to name but a few). Although thinking is not limited to humans, imagine trying to teach an animal to match the feats of Shakuntala Devi, who once set a "world's record" for mental calculation by multiplying two randomly chosen 13-digit numbers (7,686,369,774,870 times 2,465,099,745,779) in her head, giving the answer in 28 seconds. (That's 18,947,668,104,042,434,089,403,730 if you haven't already figured it out.)

Some Basic Units of Thought

At its most basic, thinking is an *internal representation* (mental expression) of a problem or situation. (Picture a chess player who mentally tries out several moves before actually touching a chess piece.) The power of being able to mentally represent problems is dramatically illustrated by chess grand master Miguel Najdorf, who once simultaneously played 45 chess games while blindfolded. How did Najdorf do it? Like most people, he used the basic units of thought: images, concepts, and language (or symbols). **Images** are picture-like mental representations. **Concepts** are ideas that represent categories of objects or events. **Language** consists of words or symbols, and rules for combining them. Thinking often involves all three units. For example, blindfolded chess players rely on visual images, concepts ("Game 2 begins with a strategy called an English opening"), and the notational system, or "language," of chess.

In a moment we will delve further into imagery, concepts, and language. Be aware, however, that thinking involves attention, pattern recognition, memory, decision making, intuition, knowledge, and more. The rest of this module is just a sample of what cognitive psychology is about.

Mental Imagery— Does a Frog Have Lips?

SURVEY QUESTION: *In what ways are images related to thinking?*

Almost everyone has visual and auditory images. More than half have imagery for movement, touch, taste, smell, and pain. Thus, mental images are sometimes more than just "pictures." For example, your image of a bakery may also include its delicious odor. Some people have a rare form of imagery called *synaesthesia* (sin-es-THEE-zyah). For these individuals, images cross normal sensory barriers (Martino & Marks, 2001). For instance, listening to music may produce a burst of colors or tastes, as well as sound sensations (Robertson & Sagiv, 2005). Despite such variations, most of us use images to think, remember, and solve problems. For instance, we may use mental images to:

- Make a decision or solve a problem (choosing what clothes to wear; figuring out how to arrange furniture in a room).
- Change feelings (thinking of pleasant images to get out of a bad mood; imagining yourself as thin to stay on a diet).
- Improve a skill or prepare for some action (using images to improve a swimming stroke; mentally rehearsing how you will ask for a raise).
- Aid memory (picturing Mr. Cook wearing a chef's hat, so you can remember his name).

The Nature of Mental Images

Mental images are not flat, like photographs. Researcher Stephen Kosslyn showed this by asking people, "Does a frog have lips and a stubby tail?" Unless you often kiss frogs, you will probably tackle this question by using mental images. Most people picture a frog, "look" at its mouth, and then mentally "rotate" the frog in mental space to check its tail (Kosslyn, 1983). Mental rotation is partly based on imagined movements (● Fig. 8.5). That is, we mentally "pick up" an object and turn it around (Wraga et al., 2005).

"Reverse Vision" What happens in the brain when a person has visual images? Seeing something in your "mind's eye" is similar to seeing real objects. Information from the eyes normally activates the brain's primary visual area, creating an image (● Fig. 8.6). Other brain areas then help us recognize the image by relating it to stored knowledge. When you form

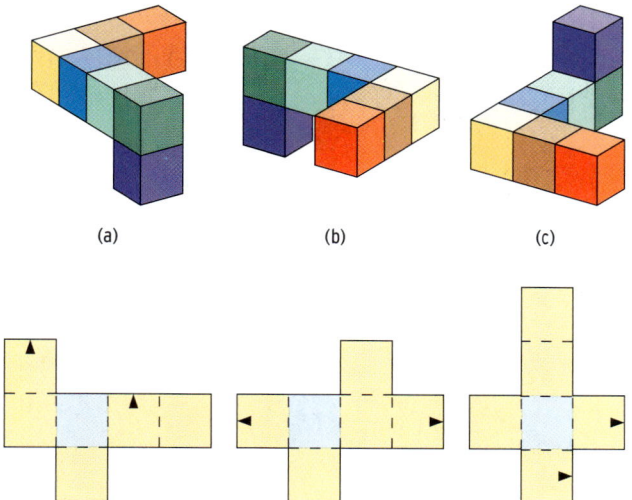

● **FIGURE 8.5** Imagery in thinking. *(Top)* Subjects were shown a drawing similar to *(a)* and drawings of how *(a)* would look in other positions, such as *(b)* and *(c)*. Subjects could recognize *(a)* after it had been "rotated" from its original position. However, the more *(a)* was rotated in space, the longer it took to recognize it. This result suggests that people actually formed a three-dimensional image of *(a)* and rotated the image to see if it matched (Shepard, 1975). *(Bottom)* Try your ability to manipulate mental images: Picture each of these shapes as a piece of paper that can be folded to make a cube. After they have been folded, on which cubes do the arrow tips meet (Kosslyn, 1985)?

a mental image, the system works in reverse. Brain areas where memories are stored send signals back to the visual cortex, where once again, an image is created (Ganis, Thompson, & Kosslyn, 2004; Kosslyn, 2005). For example, if you visualize a friend's face right now, the area of your brain that specializes in perceiving faces will become more active (O'Craven & Kanwisher, 2000).

Using Mental Images *How are images used to solve problems?* We use *stored images* (information from memory) to apply past experiences to problem solving. Let's say you are asked, "How many ways can you use an empty egg carton?" You might begin by picturing uses you have already seen, such as sorting buttons into a carton. To give more original answers, you will probably need to use *created* images, which are assembled or invented, rather than simply remembered. Thus, an artist may completely picture a proposed sculpture before beginning work. People with good imaging abilities tend to score higher on tests of creativity (Morrison & Wallace, 2001). In fact, Albert Einstein, Thomas Edison, Lewis Carroll, and many other of history's most original intellects relied heavily on imagery (West, 1991).

Does the "size" of a mental image affect thinking? To find out, first picture a cat sitting beside a housefly. Now try to "zoom in" on the cat's ears so you see them clearly. Next, picture a rabbit sitting beside an elephant. How quickly can you "see" the rabbit's front feet? Did it take longer than picturing the cat's ears?

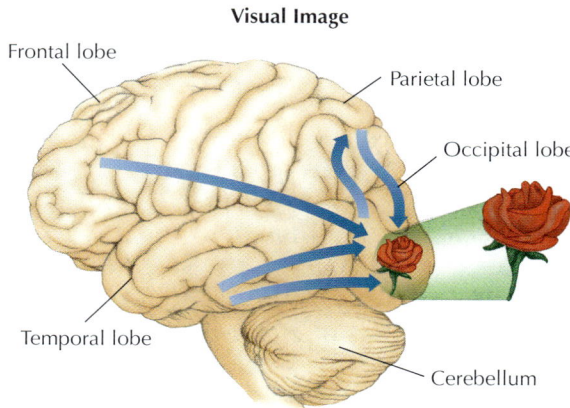

● **FIGURE 8.6** When you see a flower, its image is represented by activity in the primary visual area of the cortex, at the back of the brain. Information about the flower is also relayed to other brain areas. If you form a mental image of a flower, information follows a reverse path. The result, once again, is activation of the primary visual area.

When a rabbit is pictured with an elephant, the rabbit's image must be small because the elephant is large. Using such tasks, Stephen Kosslyn found that the smaller an image is, the harder it is to "see" its details. To put this finding to use, try forming oversize images of things you want to think about. For example, to understand electricity, picture the wires as large pipes with electrons the size of golf balls moving through them; to understand the human ear, explore it (in your mind's eye) like a large cave; and so forth.

Cognition The process of thinking or mentally processing information (images, concepts, words, rules, and symbols).

Image Most often, a mental representation that has picture-like qualities; an icon.

Concept A generalized idea representing a category of related objects or events.

Language Words or symbols, and rules for combining them, that are used for thinking and communication.

The Church of the Sacred Family in Barcelona, Spain, was designed by Antonio Gaudi. Could a person lacking mental imagery design such a masterpiece? Three people out of 100 find it impossible to produce mental images, and 3 out of 100 have very strong imagery. Most artists, architects, designers, sculptors, and filmmakers have excellent visual imagery.

A study found that rock climbers use kinesthetic imagery to learn climbing routes and to plan their next few moves (Smyth & Waller, 1998).

Kinesthetic Imagery *Do muscular responses relate to thinking?* In a sense, we think with our bodies as well as our heads. *Kinesthetic images* are created from muscular sensations (Holmes & Collins, 2001). Such images help us think about movements and actions. As you think and talk, kinesthetic sensations can guide the flow of ideas. For example, if you try to tell a friend how to make bread, you may move your hands as if kneading the dough. Or, try answering this question: Which direction do you turn the hot-water handle in your kitchen to shut off the water? Most people haven't simply memorized the words "Turn it clockwise" or "Turn it counterclockwise." Instead you will probably "turn" the faucet in your imagination before answering. You may even make a turning motion with your hand before answering.

Kinesthetic images are especially important in music, sports, dance, skateboarding, martial arts, and other movement-oriented skills. People with good kinesthetic imagery (or high *bodily-kinesthetic intelligence*) learn such skills faster than those with poor imagery (Glisky, Williams, & Kihlstrom, 1996).

Concepts—I'm Positive, It's a Whatchamacallit

SURVEY QUESTION: *How do we learn concepts?*

A *concept* is an idea that represents a category of objects or events. Concepts help us identify important features of the world. That's why experts in various areas of knowledge are good at classifying objects. Bird watchers, tropical fish fanciers, 5-year-old dinosaur enthusiasts, and other experts all learn to look for identifying details that beginners tend to miss. If you are knowledgeable about a topic, such as horses, flowers, or football, you literally see things differently than less well-informed people do (Johnson & Mervis, 1997; Ross, 2006).

Forming Concepts

How are concepts learned? **Concept formation** is the process of classifying information into meaningful categories (Ashby & Maddox, 2005). At its most basic, concept formation is based on experience with *positive* and *negative instances* (examples that belong, or do not belong, to the concept class).

Concept formation is not as simple as it might seem. Imagine a child learning the concept of *dog*.

DOG DAZE

A child and her father go for a walk. At a neighbor's house, they see a medium-size dog. The father says, "See the dog." As they pass the next yard, the child sees a cat and says, "Dog!" Her father corrects her, "No, that's a *cat*." The child now thinks, "Aha, dogs are large and cats are small." In the next yard, she sees a Pekingese and says, "Cat!" "No, that's a dog," replies her father.

The child's confusion is understandable. At first she might even mistake a Pekingese for a dust mop. However, with more positive and negative instances, the child will eventually recognize everything from Great Danes to Chihuahuas as members of the same category—dogs.

As adults, we often acquire concepts by learning or forming rules. A **conceptual rule** is a guideline for deciding whether objects or events belong to a concept class. For example, a triangle must be a closed shape with three sides made of straight lines. Rules are an efficient way to learn concepts, but examples remain important. It's unlikely that memorizing rules would allow a new listener to accurately categorize *punk, hip-hop, fusion, salsa, metal, country,* and *rap* music.

Types of Concepts

Are there different kinds of concepts? Yes, **conjunctive concepts,** or "and" concepts, are defined by the presence of two or more features (Reed, 2007). In other words, an item must have "this feature *and* this feature *and* this feature." For example, a *motorcycle* must have two wheels *and* an engine *and* handlebars.

Relational concepts are based on how an object relates to something else, or how its features relate to one another. All of the following are relational concepts: *larger, above, left, north,* and *upside down.* Another example is *sister,* which is defined as "a female considered in her relation to another person having the same parents."

Disjunctive concepts have *at least one* of several possible features. These are "either/or" concepts. To belong to the category, an item must have "this feature *or* that feature *or* another feature." For example, in baseball, a *strike* is *either* a swing and a miss *or* a pitch over the plate *or* a foul ball. The either/or quality of disjunctive concepts makes them hard to learn.

Prototypes When you think of the concept *bird,* do you mentally list the features that birds have? Probably not. In addition to rules and features, we use **prototypes,** or ideal models, to identify concepts (Burnett et al., 2005; Rosch, 1977). A robin, for example, is a prototypical bird; an ostrich is not. In other words, some items are better examples of a concept than others are. Which of the drawings in ● Figure 8.7 best represents a cup? At some point, as a cup grows taller or wider it becomes a vase or a bowl. How do we know when the line is crossed? Probably, we mentally compare objects to an "ideal" cup, like number 5. That's why it's hard to identify concepts when we can't come up with relevant prototypes. What, for example, are the objects shown in ● Figure 8.8? As you can see, prototypes are especially helpful when we try to categorize complex stimuli (Minda & Smith, 2001).

Faulty Concepts Using inaccurate concepts often leads to thinking errors. For example, *social stereotypes* are oversimplified concepts of groups of people. Stereotypes about men, African Americans, women, conservatives, liberals, police officers, or other groups often muddle thinking about members of the group. A related problem is *all-or-nothing thinking* (one-dimensional thought). In this case, we classify things as absolutely right or wrong, good or bad, fair or unfair, black or white, honest or dishonest. Thinking this way prevents us from appreciating the subtleties of most life problems (Bastian & Haslam, 2006).

● **FIGURE 8.7** When does a cup become a bowl or a vase? Deciding if an object belongs to a conceptual class is aided by relating it to a prototype, or ideal example. Subjects in one experiment chose number 5 as the "best" cup. (Adapted from Labov, 1973.)

Concept formation The process of classifying information into meaningful categories.

Conceptual rule A formal rule for deciding if an object or event is an example of a particular concept.

Conjunctive concept A class of objects that have two or more features in common. (For example, to qualify as an example of the concept an object must be both red *and* triangular.)

Relational concept A concept defined by the relationship between features of an object or between an object and its surroundings (for example, "greater than," "lopsided").

Disjunctive concept A concept defined by the presence of at least one of several possible features. (For example, to qualify an object must be either blue *or* circular.)

Prototype An ideal model used as a prime example of a particular concept.

• **FIGURE 8.8** Use of prototypes in concept identification. Even though its shape is unusual, item (a) can be related to a model (an ordinary set of pliers) and thus recognized. But what are items (b) and (c)? If you don't recognize them, look ahead to Figure 8.10. (Adapted from Bransford & McCarrell, 1977.)

Connotative Meaning Generally speaking, concepts have two types of meaning. The **denotative meaning** of a word or concept is its exact definition. The **connotative meaning** is its emotional or personal meaning. The denotative meaning of the word *naked* (having no clothes) is the same for a nudist as it is for a movie censor, but we could expect their connotations to differ. Connotative differences can influence how we think about important issues. For example, the term *enhanced radiation device* has a more positive connotation than *neutron bomb* does (Gruner & Tighe, 1995).

Can you clarify what a connotative meaning is? Yes, connotative meaning can be measured with a technique called the *semantic differential*, as shown in • Figure 8.9. When we rate words or concepts, most of their connotative meaning

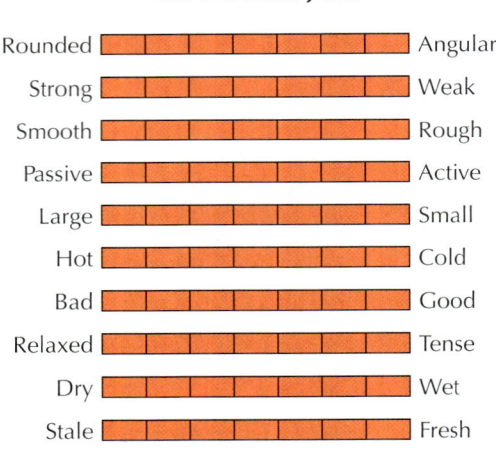

• **FIGURE 8.9** This is an example of Osgood's semantic differential. The connotative meaning of the word *jazz* can be established by rating it on the scales. Mark your own rating by placing dots or X's in the spaces. Connect the marks with a line; then have a friend rate the word and compare your responses. It might be interesting to do the same for *rock and roll, classical,* and *rap.* You also might want to try the word *psychology.* (From *Psychological Bulletin,* Vol. 49, No. 3, May 1952.)

• **FIGURE 8.10** Context can substitute for a lack of appropriate prototypes in concept identification.

boils down to the dimensions *good/bad, strong/weak,* and *active/passive.* (Sounds like a good movie title, doesn't it: *The Good, the Bad, the Strong, the Weak, the Active, the Passive.*) These dimensions give words very different connotations, even when their denotative meanings are similar. For example, I am *conscientious;* you are *careful;* he is *nitpicky!* Because we are conscientious (not nitpicky, right?), let's further explore language.

Language—Don't Leave Home without It

SURVEY QUESTION: *What is the role of language in thinking?*

As we have seen, thinking may occur without language. Everyone has searched for a word to express an idea that exists as a vague image or feeling. Nevertheless, most thinking relies heavily on language, because words *encode* (translate) the world into mental symbols that are easy to manipulate (• Fig. 8.11).

The study of meaning in words and language is known as **semantics.** It is here that the link between words and thinking becomes most evident. Suppose, on an intelligence test, you were asked to circle the word that does not belong in this series:

SKYSCRAPER   CATHEDRAL
TEMPLE   PRAYER

If you circled *prayer,* you answered as most people do. Now try another problem, again circling the odd item:

CATHEDRAL   PRAYER   TEMPLE
SKYSCRAPER

Did you circle *skyscraper* this time? The new order subtly alters the meaning of the last word (Mayer, 1995). This occurs because words get much of their meaning from *context.* For example, the word *shot* means different things when we are thinking of marksmanship, bartending, medicine, photography, or golf (Carroll, 2008; Miller, 1999).

Likewise, the words we use can greatly affect our thinking: Has one country's army "invaded" another or "effected a

● **FIGURE 8.11** Wine tasting illustrates the encoding function of language. To communicate their experiences to others, wine connoisseurs must put taste sensations into words. The wine you see here is "Marked by deeply concentrated nuances of plum, blackberry, and currant, with a nice balance of tannins and acid, building to a spicy oak finish." (Don't try this with a Pop-tart!)

protective incursion"? Is the city reservoir "half full" or "half empty"? Would you rather eat "rare prime beef" or "bloody slab of dead cow"?! More subtle effects also occur. For example, most people have difficulty quickly naming the color of the ink used to print the words in the bottom two rows of ● Figure 8.12. The word meanings are just too strong to ignore.

Language also plays a major role in defining ethnic communities and other social groups. Thus, language can be a bridge or a barrier between cultures. Translating languages can cause a rash of semantic problems. Perhaps the San Jose, California, public library can be excused for once displaying a large banner that was supposed to say "You are welcome" in a native Philippine language. The banner actually said "You are circumcised." However, in more important situations, such as in international business and diplomacy, avoiding

● **FIGURE 8.12** The Stroop interference task. Test yourself by naming the colors in the top two rows as quickly as you can. Then name the colors of the *ink* used to print the words in the bottom two rows (do not read the words themselves). Was it harder to name the ink colors in the bottom rows? (Adapted from MacLeod, 2005.)

semantic confusion may be vital. (See "Bilingualism—*Si o No, Oui ou Non,* Yes or No?")

The Structure of Language

What does it take to make a language? First, a language must provide *symbols* that stand for objects and ideas (Jay, 2003). The symbols we call words are built out of **phonemes** (FOE-neems: basic speech sounds) and **morphemes** (MOR-feems: speech sounds collected into meaningful units, such as syllables or words). For instance, in English the sounds *m, b, w,* and *a* cannot form a syllable *mbwa*. In Swahili, they can. (Also, see ● Fig. 8.13.)

Next, a language must have a **grammar,** or set of rules for making sounds into words and words into sentences (Reed, 2007). One part of grammar, known as **syntax,** concerns

Albanian	mak, mak
Chinese	gua, gua
Dutch	rap, rap
English	quack, quack
French	coin, coin
Italian	qua, qua
Spanish	cuá, cuá
Swedish	kvack, kvack
Turkish	vak, vak

● **FIGURE 8.13** Animals around the world make pretty much the same sounds. Notice, however, how various languages use slightly different phonemes to express the sound a duck makes.

Denotative meaning The exact, dictionary definition of a word or concept; its objective meaning.
Connotative meaning The subjective, personal, or emotional meaning of a word or concept.
Semantics The study of meanings in words and language.
Phonemes The basic speech sounds of a language.
Morphemes The smallest meaningful units in a language, such as syllables or words.
Grammar A set of rules for combining language units into meaningful speech or writing.
Syntax Rules for ordering words when forming sentences.

HUMAN DIVERSITY

Bilingualism—*Si o No, Oui ou Non,* Yes or No?

Are there advantages to being able to speak more than one language? Definitely. **Bilingualism** is the ability to speak two languages. Studies have found that students who learn to speak two languages well have better mental flexibility, general language skills, control of attention, and problem-solving abilities (Bialystok, 2001; Craik & Bialystok, 2005; Cromdal, 1999).

Unfortunately, millions of minority American children who do not speak English at home experience *subtractive bilingualism*. Immersed in English-only classrooms, where they are expected to "sink or swim," they usually end up losing some of their native language skills. Such children risk becoming less than fully competent in *both* their first and second languages. In addition, they tend to fall behind educationally. As they struggle with English, their grasp of arithmetic, social studies, science, and other subjects may also suffer. In short, English-only instruction can leave them poorly prepared to succeed in the majority culture (Genesee, Paradis, & Crago, 2004; Matthews & Matthews, 2004).

For majority group children, the picture can be quite different, because learning a second language is almost always beneficial. It poses no threat to the child's home language and improves a variety of cognitive skills. This has been called *additive bilingualism* because learning a second language adds to a child's overall competence (Hinkel, 2005).

An approach called **two-way bilingual education** offers a way to retain the benefits of bilingualism and avoid its drawbacks (Lessow-Hurley, 2005). In such programs, native speakers and children with limited English skills are taught part of the day in English and part in a second language. Both native and minority language speakers become fluent in two languages, and they perform as well or better than single-language students in English and general academic abilities.

Then why isn't two-way bilingual education more widely used? Bilingual education tends to be politically unpopular among majority language speakers. Language is an important sign of group membership. Even where the majority culture is highly dominant, some of its members may feel that recent immigrants and "foreign languages" are eroding their culture. Regardless, an ability to think and communicate in a second language is a wonderful gift.

Although minority children are certainly at a disadvantage if they do not become proficient in English, native English speakers may be short-changed by English-only schools as well. Given the cognitive benefits, fostering bilingualism may turn out to be one of the best ways to improve competitiveness in our rapidly globalizing information economy.

---

rules for word order. Syntax is important because rearranging words almost always changes the meaning of a sentence: "Dog bites man" versus "Man bites dog."

Traditional grammar is concerned with "surface" language—the sentences we actually speak. Linguist Noam Chomsky has focused instead on the unspoken rules we use to change core ideas into various sentences. Chomsky (1986) believes that we do not learn all the sentences we might ever say. Rather, we actively *create* them by applying **transformation rules** to universal, core patterns. We use these rules to change a simple declarative sentence to other voices or forms (past tense, passive voice, and so forth). For example, the core sentence "Dog bites man" can be transformed to these patterns (and others as well):

Past: The dog bit the man.
Passive: The man was bitten by the dog.
Negative: The dog did not bite the man.
Question: Did the dog bite the man?

Children seem to be using transformation rules when they say things such as "I runned home." That is, the child applied the normal past tense rule to the irregular verb *to run*.

A true language is also *productive*—it can generate new thoughts or ideas. In fact, words can be rearranged to produce a nearly infinite number of sentences. Some are silly: "Please don't feed me to the goldfish." Some are profound: "We hold these truths to be self-evident, that all men are created equal." In either case, the productive quality of language makes it a powerful tool for thinking.

Gestural Languages Contrary to common belief, language is not limited to speech. Consider the case of Ildefonso, a young man who was born deaf. At age 24, Ildefonso had never communicated with another human, except by mime. Then at last, Ildefonso had a breakthrough: After much hard work with a sign language teacher, he understood the link between a cat and the gesture for it. At that magic moment, he grasped the idea that "cat" could be communicated to another person, just by signing the word.

American Sign Language (ASL), a gestural language, made Ildefonso's long-awaited breakthrough possible. ASL is not pantomime or a code. It is a true language, like German, Spanish, or Japanese (Liddell, 2003). In fact, those who use other gestural languages, such as French Sign, Chinese Sign, or Old Kentish Sign, do not understand ASL.

Although ASL has a *spatial* grammar, syntax, and semantics all its own (● Fig. 8.14), both speech and signing follow similar universal language patterns. Signing children pass through the stages of language development at about the

● **FIGURE 8.14** ASL has only 3,000 root signs, compared with roughly 600,000 words in English. However, variations in signs make ASL a highly expressive language. For example, the sign LOOK-AT can be varied in ways to make it mean look at me, look at her, look at each, stare at, gaze, watch, look for a long time, look at again and again, reminisce, sightsee, look forward to, predict, anticipate, browse, and many more variations.

same age as speaking children do. Some psychologists now believe that speech evolved from gestures, far back in human history (Corballis, 2002). Gestures help us string words together as we speak (Morsella & Krauss, 2004). Some people would have difficulty speaking with their hands tied to their sides. Do you ever make hand gestures when you are speaking on the phone? If so, you may be displaying a remnant of the gestural origins of language. Perhaps that's also why the same brain areas become more active when a person speaks or signs (Emmorey et al., 2003).

Sign languages naturally arise out of a need to communicate visually. But they also embody a personal identity and define a distinct community. Those who "speak" sign share not just a language, but a rich culture as well (Singleton & Newport, 2004).

Infants can express the idea "pick me up" in gestures before they can make the same request in words. Their progression from gestures to speech may mirror the evolution of human language abilities (Stokoe, 2001).

The Animal Language Debate

Do animals use language? Animals do communicate. The cries, gestures, and mating calls of animals have broad meanings immediately understood by other animals of the same species (Searcy & Nowicki, 2005). For the most part, however, natural animal communication is quite limited. Even apes and monkeys make only a few dozen distinct cries, which carry messages such as "attack," "flee," or "food here." More important, animal communication lacks the productive quality of human language. For example, when a monkey gives an "eagle distress call," it means something like, "I see an eagle." The monkey has no way of saying, "I don't see an eagle," or "Thank heavens that wasn't an eagle," or "That sucker I saw yesterday was some huge eagle" (Pinker & Jackendoff, 2005). Let's consider some of psychology's successes and failures in trying to teach animals to use language.

Talking Chimps Early attempts to teach chimps to talk were a dismal failure. The world record was held by Viki, a chimp who could say only four words (*mama, papa, cup,* and *up*) after 6 years of intensive training (Fleming, 1974; Hayes, 1951). (Actually, all four words sounded something like a belch.) Then there was a breakthrough. Beatrix and Allen Gardner used operant conditioning and imitation to teach a female chimp named Washoe to use American Sign Language. Washoe was soon able to put together primitive sentence strings like "Come-gimme sweet," "Out please," "Gimme tickle," and "Open food drink." At her peak, Washoe could construct six-word sentences and use about 240 signs (Gardner & Gardner, 1989).

A chimp named Sarah was another well-known pupil of human language. David Premack taught Sarah to use 130 "words" consisting of plastic chips arranged on a magnetized board (● Fig. 8.15). From the beginning of her training, Sarah was required to use proper word order. She learned to answer questions; to label things "same" or "different"; to classify objects by color, shape, and size; and to form compound sentences (Premack & Premack, 1983). One of Sarah's top achievements was her use of conditional sentences. A *conditional statement* contains a qualification, often in the if/then form: "If Sarah take apple, then Mary give Sarah chocolate." "If Sarah take banana, then Mary no give Sarah chocolate" (● Fig. 8.16).

Bilingualism An ability to speak two languages.

Two-way bilingual education A program in which English-speaking children and children with limited English proficiency are taught half the day in English and half in a second language.

Transformation rules Rules by which a simple declarative sentence may be changed to other voices or forms (past tense, passive voice, and so forth).

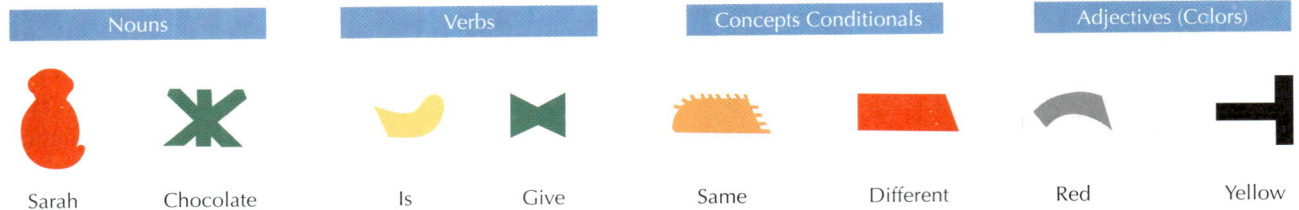

● **FIGURE 8.15** Here is a sample of some of the word-symbols that Sarah the chimpanzee used to communicate with humans. (Adapted from Premack & Premack, 1972.)

● **FIGURE 8.16** After reading the message "Sarah insert apple pail banana dish" on the magnetic board, Sarah performed the actions as directed. (From "Teaching Language to an Ape," by Ann J. Premack and David Premack. © 1972 Scientific American, Inc. Reprinted by permission of Eric Mose Jr.)

Can it be said with certainty that the chimps understand such interchanges? Most researchers working with chimps believe that they have indeed communicated with them. Especially striking are the chimps' spontaneous responses. Washoe once "wet" on psychologist Roger Fouts's back while riding on his shoulders. When Fouts asked, with some annoyance, why she had done it, Washoe signed, "It's funny!"

Criticisms Such interchanges are impressive. But communication and real language usage are different things. Even untrained chimps use simple gestures to communicate with humans. For example, a chimp will point at a banana that is out of reach, while glancing back and forth between the banana and a person standing nearby (Leavens & Hopkins, 1998). (The meaning of the gesture is clear. The meaning of the exasperated look on the chimp's face is less certain, but it probably means, "Yes, give me the banana, you idiot.")

Also, problems with syntax (word order) have plagued almost all animal language studies. For example, when a chimp named Nim Chimpsky (no relation to Noam Chomsky) wanted an orange, he would typically signal a grammarless string of words: "Give orange me give eat orange me eat orange give me eat orange give me you." This might be communication, but it is not language.

Lexigrams More recently, Kanzi, a pygmy chimpanzee studied by Duane Rumbaugh and Sue Savage-Rumbaugh, has learned to communicate by pushing buttons on a computer keyboard. Each of the 250 buttons is marked with a *lexigram,* or geometric word-symbol (● Fig. 8.17). Using the lexigrams, Kanzi can create primitive sentences several words long. He can also understand about 650 spoken sentences. During testing, Kanzi hears spoken words over headphones, so his caretakers cannot visually prompt him (Savage-Rumbaugh & Lewin, 1996; Savage-Rumbaugh, Shanker, & Taylor, 1998).

Kanzi's sentences consistently follow correct word order. Like a child learning language, Kanzi picked up some rules from his caregivers (Segerdahl, Fields, & Savage-Rumbaugh, 2005). However, he has developed other patterns on his own. For example, Kanzi usually places action symbols in the order he wants to carry them out, such as "chase tickle" or "chase hide." In this respect, Kanzi's grammar is on a par with that of a 2-year-old child (Savage-Rumbaugh et al., 1993).

Kanzi's ability to invent a simple grammar may help us better understand the roots of human language. It is certainly the strongest answer yet to critics (Benson et al., 2002). On

● **FIGURE 8.17** Kanzi's language learning has been impressive. He can comprehend spoken English words. He can identify lexigram symbols when he hears corresponding words. He can use lexigrams when the objects they refer to are absent, and he can, if asked, lead someone to the object. All these skills were acquired through observation, not conditioning (Savage-Rumbaugh et al., 1990).

the other hand, Chomsky insists that if chimps were biologically capable of language they would use it on their own. Although the issue is far from resolved, such research may unravel the mysteries of language learning.

MODULE 8.2 Summary

What is the nature of thought?
- Thinking is an internal representation of external stimuli or situations.
- Three basic units of thought are images, concepts, and language (or symbols).

In what ways are images related to thinking?
- Images may be retrieved from memory or created to solve problems.
- Images can be three-dimensional, they can be rotated in space, and their size may change.
- Kinesthetic images are used to represent movements and actions. Kinesthetic sensations help structure the flow of thoughts for many people.

How do we learn concepts?
- A concept is a generalized idea of a class of objects or events.
- Concept formation may be based on positive and negative instances or rule learning.
- Concept identification frequently makes use of prototypes, or ideal models.
- Concepts may be conjunctive ("and" concepts), disjunctive ("either/or" concepts), or relational.
- The denotative meaning of a word or concept is its dictionary definition. Connotative meaning is personal or emotional.

What is the role of language in thinking?
- Language encodes events as symbols, for easy mental manipulation. The study of meaning in language is called *semantics*.
- Bilingualism is a valuable ability. Two-way bilingual education allows children to develop additive bilingualism while in school.
- Language carries meaning by combining a set of symbols according to a set of rules (grammar), which includes rules about word order (syntax).
- True languages are productive and can be used to generate new ideas or possibilities.
- Complex gestural systems, such as American Sign Language, are true languages.
- Chimpanzees and other primates have been taught American Sign Language and similar systems. This suggests to some that primates are capable of very basic language use. Others question this conclusion.

KNOWLEDGE BUILDER

Imagery, Concepts, and Language

Recite

1. List three primary units of thought: _____ _____ _____

2. Our reliance on imagery in thinking means that problem solving is impaired by the use of language or symbols. T or F?

3. A person doing mental rotation would need to use which basic unit of thought?
   a. concepts
   b. language
   c. images
   d. symbols

4. Our ability to think about movements and actions is aided by
   a. kinesthetic imagery
   b. rotational concepts
   c. mental calculation
   d. relational concepts

5. A *mup* is defined as anything that is small, blue, and hairy. *Mup* is a _____ concept.

6. The connotative meaning of the word *naked* is "having no clothes." T or F?

7. True languages are _____ because they can be used to generate new possibilities.

8. The basic speech sounds are called _____; the smallest meaningful units of speech are called _____.

9. Noam Chomsky believes that we use _____ to change core declarative sentences into other voices and forms.
   a. phonemes
   b. transformation rules
   c. conditional statements
   d. conjunctive encoding

Reflect

Critical Thinking

10. A Democrat and a Republican are asked to rate the word *democratic* on the semantic differential. Under what conditions would their ratings be most alike?

11. Chimpanzees and other apes are intelligent and entertaining animals. If you were doing language research with a chimp, what major problem would you have to guard against?

Relate

Name some ways in which you have used imagery in the thinking you have done today.

Write a conceptual rule for the following idea: *unicycle*. Were you able to define the concept with a rule? Would positive and negative instances help make the concept clearer for others?

A true sports car has two seats, a powerful engine, good brakes, and excellent handling. What kind of a concept is the term *sports car*? What do you think of as a prototypical sports car?

Here's some mnemonic help: You use a *phone* to send *phonemes*. To *morph* them into words you have to hit them with a *grammar*. What wrong is with sentence this? (The answer is not a *sin tax*, but it still may tax you.)

You must learn to communicate with an alien life form whose language cannot be reproduced by the human voice. Do you think it would be better to use a gestural language or lexigrams? Why?

Link

Internet addresses frequently change. To find the sites listed here, visit **http://www.thomsonedu.com/psychology/coon** for an updated list of Internet addresses and direct links to relevant sites.

- **Amoeba Web Psychology Resources: Cognitive Psychology** Go to the "Cognitive Psychology" link on this web page and you will find numerous other links to articles/information on many areas of cognitive psychology.
- **International Dyslexia Association** The goals of this organization are to provide the most comprehensive forum for parents, educators, and researchers to share their experience, methods, and knowledge about dyslexia. Also includes events, news, and articles.
- **Koko.org** View the sign language (and art!) of Koko, the gorilla.

ANSWERS

1. images, concepts, language or symbols (others could be listed) 2. F 3. c 4. a 5. conjunctive 6. F 7. productive 8. phonemes, morphemes 9. b 10. If they both assume the word refers to a form of government, not a political party or a candidate. 11. The problem of anthropomorphizing (ascribing human characteristics to animals) is especially difficult to avoid when researchers spend many hours "conversing" with chimps.

MODULE 8.3 Problem Solving

WE ALL SOLVE MANY PROBLEMS every day. Problem solving can be as commonplace as figuring out how to make a nonpoisonous meal out of leftovers or as significant as developing a cure for cancer. How do we solve such problems?

Problem Solving—Getting an Answer in Sight

SURVEY QUESTION: *What do we know about problem solving?*

A good way to start a discussion of problem solving is to solve a problem. Give this one a try.

> A famous ocean liner (the *Queen Latifah*) is steaming toward port at 20 miles per hour. The ocean liner is 50 miles from shore when a seagull takes off from its deck and flies toward port. At the same instant, a speedboat leaves port at 30 miles per hour. The bird flies back and forth between the speedboat and the *Queen Latifah* at a speed of 40 miles per hour. How far will the bird have flown when the two boats pass?

If you don't immediately see the answer to this problem, read it again. (The answer is revealed in the "Insightful Solutions" section.)

Mechanical Solutions

For routine problems, a **mechanical solution** may be adequate. Mechanical solutions are achieved by trial and error or by rote. If you forget the combination to your bike lock, you may be able to discover it by trial and error. In an era of high-speed computers, many trial-and-error solutions are best left to machines. A computer could generate all possible combinations of the five numbers on the lock in a split second. (Of course, it would take a long time to try them all.) When a problem is solved by *rote,* thinking is guided by an **algorithm,** or learned set of rules that always leads to a correct solution. A simple example of an algorithm is the steps needed to divide one number into another (by doing arithmetic, not by using a calculator).

If you have a good background in math, you may have solved the problem of the bird and the boats by rote. (Your authors hope you didn't. There is an easier solution.)

Solutions by Understanding

Many problems cannot be solved mechanically. In that case, **understanding** (deeper comprehension of a problem) is necessary. Try this problem:

> A person has an inoperable stomach tumor. A device is available that produces rays that at high intensity will destroy tissue (both healthy and diseased). How can the tumor be destroyed without damaging surrounding tissue? (Also see the sketch in ● Figure 8.18.)

What does this problem show about problem solving? German psychologist Karl Duncker gave college students this problem in a classic series of studies. Duncker asked them to think aloud as they worked. He found that successful students first had to discover the *general properties* of a correct solution. A **general solution** defines the requirements for success but not in enough detail to guide further action. This phase was complete when students realized that the intensity of the rays had to be lowered on their way to the tumor. Then, in the second phase, they proposed a number of **functional** (workable) **solutions** and selected the best one (Duncker, 1945). (One solution is to focus weak rays on the tumor from several angles. Another is to rotate the person's body, to minimize exposure of healthy tissue.)

It might help to summarize with a more familiar example. Almost everyone who has tried the Rubik's Cube puzzle begins at the mechanical, *trial-and-error level.* If you want to take the easy route, printed instructions are available that give the steps for a *rote* solution. In time, those who persist begin to *understand* the *general properties* of the puzzle. After that, they can solve it consistently.

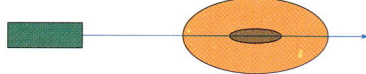

● **FIGURE 8.18** A schematic representation of Duncker's tumor problem. The dark spot represents a tumor surrounded by healthy tissue. How can the tumor be destroyed without injuring surrounding tissue? (Adapted from Duncker, 1945.)

Mechanical solution A problem solution achieved by trial and error or by a fixed procedure based on learned rules.

Algorithm A learned set of rules that always leads to the correct solution of a problem.

Understanding In problem solving, a deeper comprehension of the nature of the problem.

General solution A solution that correctly states the requirements for success but not in enough detail for further action.

Functional solution A detailed, practical, and workable solution.

Heuristics

"You can't get there from here," or so it often seems when facing a problem. Solving problems often requires a strategy. If the number of alternatives is small, a **random search strategy** may work. This is another example of trial-and-error thinking in which all possibilities are tried, more or less randomly. Imagine that you are traveling and decide to look up an old friend, J. Smith, in a city you are visiting. You open the phone book and find 47 J. Smiths listed. Of course, you could dial each number until you find the right one. "Forget it," you say to yourself. "Is there any way I can narrow the search?" "Oh, yeah! I remember hearing that Janet lives by the beach." Then you take out a map and call only the numbers with addresses near the waterfront (Hunt & Ellis, 2004).

The approach used in this example is a **heuristic** (hew-RIS-tik: a strategy for identifying and evaluating problem solutions). Typically, a heuristic is a "rule of thumb" that *reduces the number of alternatives* thinkers must consider (Solso, MacLin, & MacLin, 2005). Although this raises the odds of success, it does not guarantee a solution. Here are some heuristic strategies that often work:

- Try to identify how the current state of affairs differs from the desired goal. Then find steps that will reduce the difference.
- Try working backward from the desired goal to the starting point or current state.
- If you can't reach the goal directly, try to identify an intermediate goal or sub-problem that at least gets you closer.
- Represent the problem in other ways, with graphs, diagrams, or analogies, for instance.
- Generate a possible solution and test it. Doing so may eliminate many alternatives, or it may clarify what is needed for a solution.

Experts and Novices Research has shown that expert skills are based on *acquired strategies* (learned heuristics) and specific *organized knowledge* (systematic information). Although experts are much more likely than novices to have heuristics available for solving problems, what really sets master players apart is their ability to intuitively recognize *patterns* that suggest what lines of play should be explored next (Anderson, 2005). This helps eliminate a large number of possible moves. The chess master, therefore, does not waste time exploring unproductive pathways (Ross, 2006). Experts are better able to see the true nature of problems and to define them in terms of general principles (Anderson, 2005).

In other words, becoming a star performer does not come from some general strengthening of the mind. Master chess players don't necessarily have better memories than beginners (except for realistic chess positions) (Gobet & Simon, 1996; Solso, MacLin, & MacLin, 2005). (See ● Fig. 8.19.) And, typically, they don't explore more moves ahead than lesser players.

Expertise also allows more *automatic processing,* or fast, fairly effortless thinking based on experience with similar problems. Automatic processing frees "space" in short-term memory, making it easier to work on the problem. At the highest skill levels, expert performers tend to rise above rules and plans. Their decisions, thinking, and actions become rapid and fluid. Thus, when a chess master recognizes a pattern on the chessboard, the most desirable tactic comes to mind almost immediately.

Mind you, this capacity comes at a price. Expert chess players can automatically recognize 50,000 to 100,000 patterns, a level of skill that takes about 10 years to build up (Ross, 2006). Many other kinds of expertise take this long to develop, suggesting that American inventor Thomas Edison was right when he said, "Genius is one percent inspiration and ninety-nine percent perspiration."

Insightful Solutions

A thinker who suddenly solves a problem has experienced **insight.** Insight is so rapid and clear that we may wonder why we didn't see the solution sooner (Schilling, 2005). Insights are usually based on reorganizing a problem. This allows us to see problems in new ways and makes their solutions seem obvious (Robertson, 2001).

Let's return now to the problem of the boats and the bird. The best way to solve it is by insight. Because the boats will cover the 50-mile distance in exactly 1 hour, and the bird flies 40 miles per hour, the bird will have flown 40 miles when the boats meet. Very little math is necessary if you have

● **FIGURE 8.19** The left chessboard shows a realistic game. The right chessboard is a random arrangement of pieces. Expert chess players can memorize the left board at a glance, yet they are no better than beginners at memorizing the random board (Ross, 2006). Expert performance at most thinking tasks is based on acquired strategies and knowledge. If you would like to excel at a profession or a mental skill, plan on adding to your knowledge every day (Solso, MacLin, & MacLin, 2005).

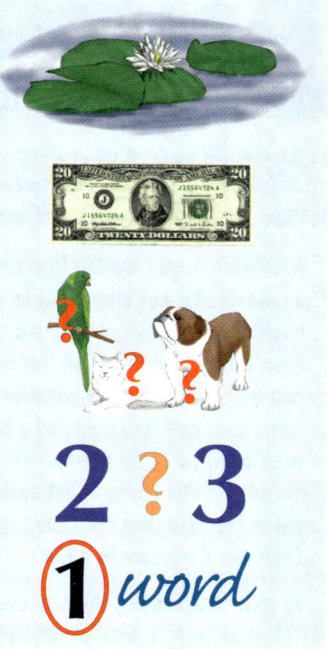

Water lilies

Problem: Water lilies growing in a pond double in area every 24 hours. On the first day of spring, only one lily pad is on the surface of the pond. Sixty days later, the pond is entirely covered. On what day is the pond half-covered?

Twenty dollars

Problem: Jessica and Blair both have the same amount of money. How much must Jessica give Blair so that Blair has $20 more than Jessica?

How many pets?

Problem: How many pets do you have if all of them are birds except two, all of them are cats except two, and all of them are dogs except two?

Between 2 and 3

Problem: What one mathematical symbol can you place between 2 and 3 that results in a number greater than 2 and less than 3?

One word

Problem: Rearrange the letters NEWDOOR to make one word.

● **FIGURE 8.20**

insight into this problem. ● Figure 8.20 lists some additional insight problems you may want to try (The answers can be found in ■ Table 8.5).

The Nature of Insight Psychologists Robert Sternberg and Janet Davidson (1982) believe that insight involves three abilities. The first is *selective encoding,* which refers to selecting information that is relevant to a problem, while ignoring distractions. For example, consider the following problem:

> If you have white socks and black socks in your drawer, mixed in the ratio of 4 to 5, how many socks will you have to take out to ensure you have a pair of the same color?

A person who recognizes that "mixed in a ratio of 4 to 5" is irrelevant will be more likely to come up with the correct answer of 3 socks.

■ **TABLE 8.5 Solutions to Insight Problems**

Water lilies: Day 59

Twenty dollars: $10

How many pets?: Three (one bird, one cat, and one dog)

Between 2 and 3: A decimal point

One word: ONE WORD (You may object that the answer is two words, but the problem called for the answer to be "one word," and it is.)

Insight also relies on *selective combination,* or bringing together seemingly unrelated bits of useful information. Try this sample problem:

> With a 7-minute hourglass and an 11-minute hourglass, what is the simplest way to time the boiling of an egg for 15 minutes?

The answer requires using both hourglasses in combination. First, the 7-minute and the 11-minute hourglasses are started. When the 7-minute hourglass runs out, it's time to begin boiling the egg. At this point, 4 minutes remain on the 11-minute hourglass. Thus, when it runs out it is simply turned over. When it runs out again, 15 minutes will have passed.

A third source of insights is *selective comparison.* This is the ability to compare new problems with old information or with problems already solved. A good example is the hat rack problem, in which subjects must build a structure that can support an overcoat in the middle of a room. Each person is given only two long sticks and a C-clamp to work with. The solution,

Random search strategy Trying possible solutions to a problem in a more or less random order.

Heuristic Any strategy or technique that aids problem solving, especially by limiting the number of possible solutions to be tried.

Insight A sudden mental reorganization of a problem that makes the solution obvious.

HUMAN DIVERSITY

How to Weigh an Elephant

Does the culture we grow up in affect our ability to use selective comparison to solve problems? See if you can solve this problem:

> A treasure hunter wanted to explore a cave, but he was afraid that he might get lost. Obviously, he did not have a map of the cave; all that he had with him were some common items such as a flashlight and a bag. What could he do to make sure he did not get lost trying to get back out of the cave later? (Adapted from Chen, Mo, & Honomichl, 2004.)

To solve his problem, the man could leave a trail of small objects, such as pebbles or sand, while traveling through the cave, and then follow this trail out to exit.

Seventy-five percent of American college students, but only 25 percent of Chinese students, were able to solve the cave problem. Why was there such a difference in the two groups? It seems that American students benefited from having heard the story of Hansel and Gretel when they were growing up. As you may recall, Hansel and Gretel were able to find their way out of the woods because Hansel made a trail of bread crumbs that led back home (Chen, Mo, & Honomichl, 2004).

Now try this problem:

> In a village by a river, the chief of a tribe guards a sacred stone statue. Every year, the chief goes downriver to the next village to collect taxes. There, he places the statue in a tub at one end of a hanging balance. To pay their taxes, the villagers have to fill a tub at the other end of the scale with gold coins until the scale balances. This year, the chief forgot to bring his balance scale. How can he figure out how much gold to collect to match the statue's weight? (Adapted from Chen, Mo, & Honomichl, 2004.)

To solve this problem, the chief could put a tub in the river, and place the statue in the tub. Then he could mark the water level on the outside of the tub. To pay their taxes, the villagers would have to put gold coins in the tub until it sank to the same level as it did when the statue was in it.

Sixty-nine percent of Chinese students, but only 8 percent of American students, were able to solve this problem. Again, it seems that being exposed to a similar problem in the past was helpful. Most Chinese are familiar with a traditional tale about weighing an elephant that is too big to put on a scale. In the story, the elephant is placed in a boat and the water level is marked. After the elephant is removed, the boat is filled with small stones until the water again reaches the mark. Then each of the stones is weighed on a small scale and the total weight of the elephant is calculated (Chen, Mo, & Honomichl, 2004).

Every culture prepares its members to solve some types of problems more easily than others. As a result, learning about other cultures can make us more flexible and resourceful thinkers—and that's no fairy tale.

---

shown in ● Figure 8.21, is to clamp the two sticks together so that they are wedged between the floor and ceiling. If you were given this problem, you would be more likely to solve it if you first thought of how pole lamps are wedged between floor and ceiling. (See "How to Weigh an Elephant.")

Fixations One of the most important barriers to problem solving is **fixation,** the tendency to get "hung up" on wrong solutions or to become blind to alternatives. Usually this occurs when we place unnecessary restrictions on our thinking (German & Barrett, 2005). How, for example, could you plant four small trees so that each is an equal distance from all the others? (The answer is shown in ● Figure 8.22.)

A prime example of restricted thinking is **functional fixedness.** This is an inability to see new uses (functions) for familiar objects or for things that were used in a particular way (German & Barrett, 2005). If you have ever used a dime as a screwdriver, you've overcome functional fixedness.

How does functional fixedness affect problem solving? Karl Duncker illustrated the effects of functional fixedness by asking students to mount a candle on a vertical board so the candle could burn normally. Duncker gave each student three candles, some matches, some cardboard boxes, some thumbtacks, and other items. Half of Duncker's subjects received these items *inside* the cardboard boxes. The others were given all the items, including the boxes, spread out on a tabletop.

Duncker found that when the items were in the boxes, solving the problem was very difficult. Why? If students saw the boxes as *containers,* they didn't realize the boxes might be part of the solution. (If you haven't guessed the solution,

● **FIGURE 8.21** A solution to the hat rack problem.

● **FIGURE 8.22** Four trees can be placed equidistant from one another by piling dirt into a mound. Three of the trees are planted equal distances apart around the base of the mound. The fourth tree is planted on the top of the mound. If you were fixated on arrangements that involve level ground, you may have been blind to this three-dimensional solution.

check ● Figure 8.23.) Undoubtedly, we could avoid many fixations by being more flexible in categorizing the world (Langer, 2000). For instance, creative thinking could be facilitated in the container problem by saying "This *could be* a box," instead of "This *is* a box." When tested with the candle problem, 5-year-old children show no signs of functional fixedness. Apparently, this is because they have had less experience with the use of various objects. It is sometimes said that to be more creative, you should try to see the world without preconceptions, as if through the eyes of a child. In the case of functional fixedness that may actually be true (German & Defeyter, 2000).

Common Barriers to Problem Solving

Functional fixedness is just one of the mental blocks that prevent insight. Here's an example of another: A $5 bill is placed on a table, and a stack of objects is balanced precariously on top of the bill. How can the bill be removed without touching or moving the objects? A good answer is to split the bill on one of its edges. Gently pulling from opposite ends will tear the bill in half and remove it without toppling the objects. Many people fail to see this solution because they have learned not to destroy money (Adams, 1988). Notice again the impact of placing something in a category, in this case, "things of value" (which should not be destroyed). Other common mental blocks can hinder problem solving, too, as listed here.

1. **Emotional barriers:** inhibition and fear of making a fool of oneself, fear of making a mistake, inability to tolerate ambiguity, excessive self-criticism
   Example: An architect is afraid to try an unconventional design because she fears that other architects will think it is frivolous.
2. **Cultural barriers:** values that hold that fantasy is a waste of time; that playfulness is for children only; that reason, logic, and numbers are good; that feelings, intuitions, pleasure, and humor are bad or have no value in the serious business of problem solving
   Example: A corporate manager wants to solve a business problem but becomes stern and angry when members of his marketing team joke playfully about possible solutions.
3. **Learned barriers:** conventions about uses (functional fixedness), meanings, possibilities, taboos
   Example: A cook doesn't have any clean mixing bowls and fails to see that he could use a frying pan as a bowl.
4. **Perceptual barriers:** habits leading to a failure to identify important elements of a problem
   Example: A beginning artist concentrates on drawing a vase of flowers without seeing that the "empty" spaces around the vase are part of the composition, too.

(a) (b) (c)

● **FIGURE 8.23** Materials for solving the candle problem were given to subjects in boxes *(a)* or separately *(b)*. Functional fixedness caused by condition *(a)* interfered with solving the problem. The solution to the problem is shown in *(c)*.

Fixation The tendency to repeat wrong solutions or faulty responses, especially as a result of becoming blind to alternatives.

Functional fixedness A rigidity in problem solving caused by an inability to see new uses for familiar objects.

MODULE 8.3 Summary

What do we know about problem solving?
- The solution to a problem may be arrived at mechanically (by trial and error or by rote application of rules), but mechanical solutions are often inefficient.
- Solutions by understanding usually begin with discovery of the general properties of an answer, followed by a functional solution.
- Problem solving is aided by heuristics, which narrow the search for solutions.
- Expert problem solving is based on learned mental heuristics and highly organized knowledge.
- When understanding leads to a rapid solution, insight has occurred. Three elements of insight are selective encoding, selective combination, and selective comparison.
- Insight can be blocked by fixations. Functional fixedness is a common fixation, but emotional blocks, cultural values, learned conventions, and perceptual habits are also problems.

KNOWLEDGE BUILDER

Problem Solving

Recite

1. Insight refers to rote, or trial-and-error, problem solving. T or F?
2. After you find a general solution to a problem you must usually also find a
   a. heuristic
   b. search strategy
   c. fixation
   d. functional solution
3. Problem-solving strategies that guide the search for solutions are called _____.
4. A common element underlying insight is that information is encoded, combined, and compared
   a. mechanically
   b. by rote
   c. functionally
   d. selectively
5. Functional fixedness is a major barrier to
   a. insightful problem solving
   b. using random search strategies
   c. mechanical problem solving
   d. achieving fixations through problem solving
6. Organized knowledge, acquired heuristics, and the ability to recognize patterns are all characteristics of human expertise. T or F?

Reflect
Critical Thinking

7. Do you think that it is true that "a problem clearly defined is a problem half solved"?
8. Sea otters select suitably sized rocks and use them to hammer shellfish loose for eating. They then use the rock to open the shell. Does this qualify as thinking?

Relate

Identify at least one problem you have solved mechanically or by rote. Now identify a problem you solved by understanding. Did the second problem involve finding a general solution or a functional solution? Or both? What heuristics did you use to solve the problem?

What is the best insightful solution you've ever come up with? Did it involve selective encoding, combination, or comparison?

Can you think of a time when you overcame functional fixedness to solve a problem?

Link

Internet addresses frequently change. To find the sites listed here, visit **http://www.thomsonedu.com/psychology/coon** for an updated list of Internet addresses and direct links to relevant sites.

- **Classic Problems** Try to solve some classic problems.
- **How Experts Differ from Novices** Read more about the differences between experts and novices.
- **Functional Fixedness** Read about tool use and functional fixedness.

ANSWERS

1. F 2. d 3. heuristics 4. d 5. a 6. T 7. Although this might be an overstatement, it is true that clearly defining a starting point and the desired goal can serve as a heuristic in problem solving. 8. Psychologist Donald Griffin (1992) believes it does because thinking is implied by actions that appear to be planned with an awareness of likely results.

MODULE 8.4 Creative Thinking and Intuition

ORIGINAL IDEAS have changed the course of human history. Much of what we now take for granted in art, medicine, music, technology, and science was once regarded as radical or impossible. How do creative thinkers achieve the breakthroughs that advance us into new realms? Creativity is elusive. Nevertheless, psychologists have learned a great deal about how creativity occurs and how to promote it, as you will soon learn.

Creative Thinking—Down Roads Less Traveled

SURVEY QUESTION: *What is creative thinking?*

We have seen that problem solving may be mechanical, insightful, or based on understanding. To this we can add that thinking may be **inductive** (going from specific facts or observations to general principles) or **deductive** (going from general principles to specific situations). Thinking may also be **logical** (proceeding from given information to new conclusions on the basis of explicit rules) or **illogical** (intuitive, associative, or personal).

What distinguishes creative thinking from more routine problem solving? Creative thinking involves all these thinking styles, plus *fluency, flexibility,* and *originality*. Let's say that you would like to find creative uses for the millions of automobile tires discarded each year. The creativity of your suggestions could be rated in this way: **Fluency** is defined as the total number of suggestions you are able to make. **Flexibility** is the number of times you shift from one class of possible uses to another. **Originality** refers to how novel or unusual your ideas are. By counting the number of times you showed fluency, flexibility, and originality, we could rate your creativity, or capacity for *divergent thinking* (Baer, 1993; Runco, 2004).

In routine problem solving or thinking, there is one correct answer, and the problem is to find it (Cropley, 2006). This leads to **convergent thinking** (lines of thought converge on the answer). **Divergent thinking** is the reverse, in which many possibilities are developed from one starting point (Baer, 1993). (See ■ Table 8.6 for some examples.) Rather than repeating learned solutions, creative thinking produces new answers, ideas, or patterns (Davidovitch & Milgram, 2006).

Tests of Creativity

Divergent thinking can be measured in several ways. In the *Unusual Uses Test,* you would be asked to think of as many uses as possible for some object, such as the tires mentioned earlier. In the *Consequences Test,* you would list the consequences that would follow a basic change in the world. For example, you might be asked, "What would hap-

The first paper clip was patented in 1899. Competition for sales, combined with divergent thinking, has resulted in a remarkable array of alternative designs. These are drawings of just a few of the variations that have appeared over the years. (Adapted from Kim, 2000.)

Fluency is an important part of creative thinking. Mozart produced more than 600 pieces of music. Picasso (shown here) created more than 20,000 artworks. Shakespeare wrote 154 sonnets. Not all of these works were masterpieces. However, a fluent outpouring of ideas fed the creative efforts of each of these geniuses.

Inductive thought Thinking in which a general rule or principle is gathered from a series of specific examples; for instance, inferring the laws of gravity by observing many falling objects.

Deductive thought Thought that applies a general set of rules to specific situations; for example, using the laws of gravity to predict the behavior of a single falling object.

Logical thought Drawing conclusions on the basis of formal principles of reasoning.

Illogical thought Thought that is intuitive, haphazard, or irrational.

Fluency In tests of creativity, *fluency* refers to the total number of solutions produced.

Flexibility In tests of creativity, flexibility is indicated by the number of different types of solutions produced.

Originality In tests of creativity, *originality* refers to how novel or unusual solutions are.

Convergent thinking Thinking directed toward discovery of a single established correct answer; conventional thinking.

Divergent thinking Thinking that produces many ideas or alternatives; a major element in original or creative thought.

TABLE 8.6 Convergent and Divergent Problems

Convergent Problems
- What is the area of a triangle that is 3 feet wide at the base and 2 feet tall?
- Erica is shorter than Zoey but taller than Carlo, and Carlo is taller than Jared. Who is the second tallest?
- If you simultaneously drop a baseball and a bowling ball from a tall building, which will hit the ground first?

Divergent Problems
- What objects can you think of that begin with the letters BR?
- How could discarded aluminum cans be put to use?
- Write a poem about fire and ice.

little correlation between creativity tests and IQ test scores (Preckel, Holling, & Wiese, 2006).

Creativity tests have been useful, but they are not the whole story. If you want to predict whether a person will be creative in the future, it helps to look at two more kinds of information (Feldhusen & Goh, 1995):

- The *products* of creative thinking (such as essays, poems, drawings, or constructed objects) are often more informative than test results. When creative people are asked to actually produce something, others tend to judge their work as creative.
- A simple listing of a person's *past creative activities and achievements* is an excellent guide to the likelihood that she or he will be creative in the future.

pen if everyone suddenly lost their sense of balance and could no longer stay upright?" People try to list as many reactions as possible. If you were to take the *Anagrams Test,* you would be given a word such as *creativity* and asked to make as many new words as possible by rearranging the letters. Each of these tests can be scored for fluency, flexibility, and originality. (For an example of other tests of divergent thinking, see ● Figure 8.24.) Tests of divergent thinking seem to tap something quite different from intelligence. Generally, there is

Isn't creativity more than divergent thought? What if a person comes up with a large number of useless answers to a problem? A good question. Divergent thinking is an important part of creativity, but there is more to it. To be creative, the solution to a problem must be more than novel, unusual, or original. It must also be *practical* if it is an invention and *sensible* if it is an idea. This is the dividing line between a "harebrained scheme" and a "stroke of genius." In other words, the creative person brings reasoning and critical thinking to bear on new ideas once they are produced (Runco, 2003).

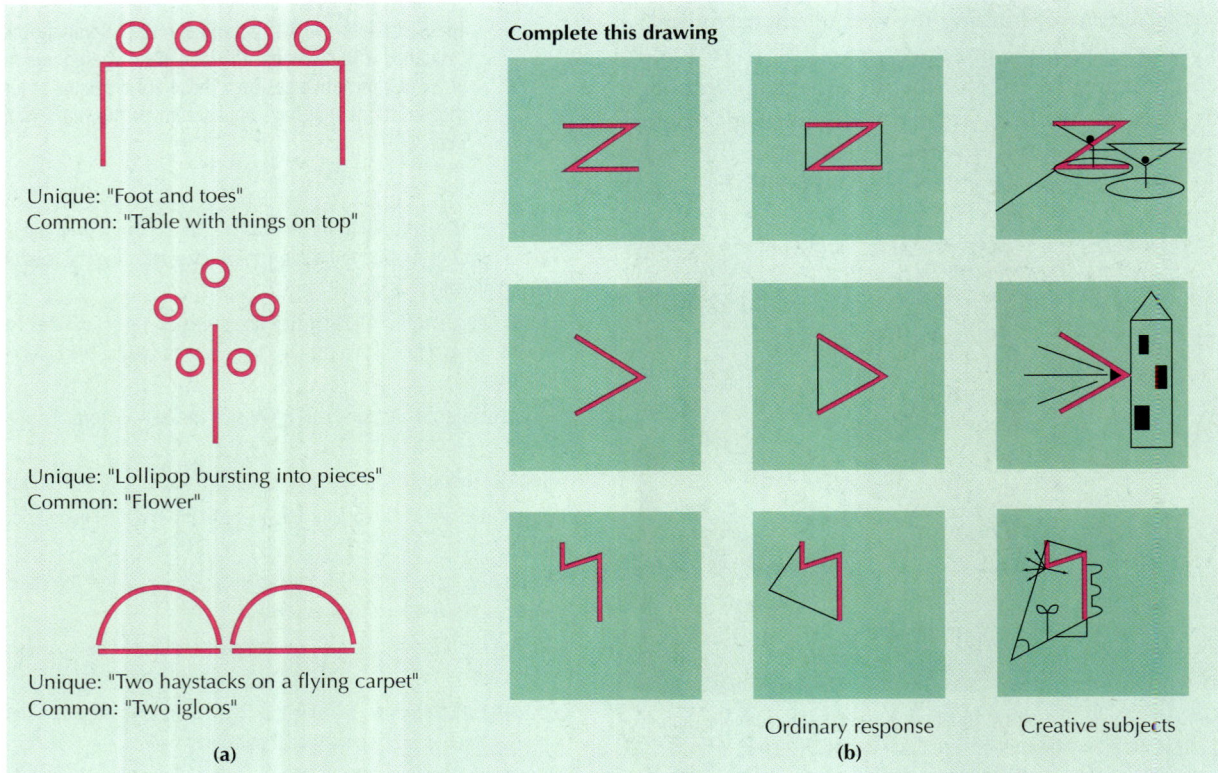

● **FIGURE 8.24** Some tests of divergent thinking. Creative responses are more original and more complex. ((a) Adapted from Wallach & Kogan, 1965; (b) adapted from Barron, 1958.)

Hat-tipping device. According to the patent, it is for "automatically effecting polite salutations by the elevation and rotation of the hat on the head of the saluting party when said person bows to the person or persons saluted." In addition to being original or novel, a creative solution must fit the demands of the problem. Is this a creative solution to the "problem" of hat tipping? (U.S. Patent No. 556,248. From *Absolutely Mad Inventions*, by A. E. Brown and H. A. Jefcott, Jr., Dover, 1970.)

Stages of Creative Thought

Is there any pattern to creative thinking? Typically, five stages occur during creative problem solving:

1. **Orientation.** As a first step, the person defines the problem and identifies its most important dimensions.
2. **Preparation.** In the second stage, creative thinkers saturate themselves with as much information about the problem as possible.
3. **Incubation.** Most major problems produce a period during which all attempted solutions will be futile. At this point, problem solving may proceed on a subconscious level: Although the problem seems to have been set aside, it is still "cooking" in the background.
4. **Illumination.** The stage of incubation is often ended by a rapid insight or series of insights. These produce the "Aha!" experience, often depicted in cartoons as a lightbulb appearing over the thinker's head.
5. **Verification.** The final step is to test and critically evaluate the solution obtained during the stage of illumination. If the solution proves faulty, the thinker reverts to the stage of incubation.

Of course, creative thought is not always so neat. Nevertheless, the stages listed are a good summary of the most typical sequence of events.

You may find it helpful to relate the stages to the following more or less true story. Legend has it that the king of Syracuse (a city in ancient Greece) once suspected that his goldsmith had substituted cheaper metals for some of the gold in a crown and kept the extra gold. Archimedes, a famous mathematician and thinker, was given the problem of discovering whether the king had been cheated.

Archimedes began by defining the problem *(orientation)*: "How can I tell what metals have been used in the crown without damaging it?" He then checked all known methods of analyzing metals *(preparation)*. All involved cutting or melting the crown, so he was forced to temporarily set the problem aside *(incubation)*. Then one day as he stepped into

The development of modern aircraft has been highly creative and quite rapid. Even so, it has been marked more by continuous incremental progress than by dramatic breakthroughs.

his bath, Archimedes suddenly knew he had the solution *(illumination)*. He was so excited he is said to have run naked through the streets shouting, "Eureka, eureka!" (I have found it, I have found it!).

On observing his own body floating in the bath, Archimedes realized that different metals of equal weight would displace different amounts of water. A pound of brass, for example, occupies more space than a pound of gold, which is denser. All that remained was to test the solution *(verification)*. Archimedes placed an amount of gold (equal in weight to that given the goldsmith) in a tub of water. He marked the water level and removed the gold. He then placed the crown in the water. Was the crown pure gold? If it was, it would raise the water to exactly the same level. Unfortunately, the purity of the crown and the fate of the goldsmith are to this day unknown! (Too bad Archimedes didn't grow up in China. If he had heard the "weighing-the-elephant" tale, he might have quickly solved the crown problem.)

The preceding account is a good general description of creative thinking. However, rather than springing from sudden insights, much creative problem solving is incremental. That is, it is the end result of many small steps. This is certainly true of many inventions, which build on earlier ideas. Some authors believe that truly exceptional creativity requires a rare combination of thinking skills, personality, and a supportive social environment. This mix, they believe, accounts for creative giants such as Edison, Freud, Mozart, Picasso, and others (Runco, 2004; Tardif & Sternberg, 1988).

Positive Psychology: The Creative Personality

What makes a person creative? According to the popular stereotype, highly creative people are eccentric, introverted, neurotic, socially inept, unbalanced in their interests, and on the edge of madness. Although some artists and musicians cultivate this public image, there is little truth in it. Direct studies of creative individuals paint a very different picture (Winner, 2003):

1. There is a small positive correlation between creativity and IQ. In other words, smarter people have a slight tendency to be more creative. But, for the most part, at any given level of IQ, some people are creative and some are not (Preckel, Holling, & Wiese, 2006).
2. Creative people usually have a greater-than-average range of knowledge and interests, and they are more fluent in combining ideas from various sources. They are also good at using mental images and metaphors in thinking (Riquelme, 2002).
3. Creative people are open to a wide variety of experiences. They accept irrational thoughts and are uninhibited about their feelings and fantasies. They tend to use broad categories, to question assumptions, to break mental sets, and they find order in chaos. They also experience more unusual states of consciousness, such as vivid dreams and mystical experiences (Ayers, Beaton, & Hunt, 1999).
4. Creative people enjoy symbolic thought, ideas, concepts, and possibilities. They tend to be interested in truth, form, and beauty, rather than in fame or success. Their creative work is an end in itself (Sternberg & Lubart, 1995).
5. Creative people value their independence and prefer complexity. However, they are unconventional and nonconforming primarily in their work; otherwise they do not have unusual, outlandish, or bizarre personalities.

Living More Creatively

Can creativity be learned? It is beginning to look as if some creative thinking skills can be learned. In particular, you can become more creative by practicing divergent thinking and by taking risks, analyzing ideas, and seeking unusual connections between ideas (Baer, 1993; Sternberg, 2001). Psychologist Mihalyi Csikszentmihalyi (sik-sent-me-HALE-yee) (1997) makes these recommendations about how to become more creative:

- Find something that surprises you every day.
- Try to surprise at least one person every day.
- If something sparks your interest, follow it.
- Make a commitment to doing things well.
- Seek challenges.
- Take time for thinking and relaxing.
- Start doing more of what you really enjoy, less of what you dislike.
- Try to look at problems from as many viewpoints as you can.

Even if you don't become more creative by following these suggestions, they are still good advice. Life is not a standardized test with a single set of correct answers. It is more like a blank canvas on which you can create designs that uniquely express your talents and interests. To live more creatively, you must be ready to seek new ways of doing things. Try to surprise at least one person today—yourself, if no one else.

Intuitive Thought—Mental Shortcut? Or Dangerous Detour?

SURVEY QUESTION: *How accurate is intuition?*

At the same time that irrational, intuitive thought may contribute to creative problem solving, it can also lead to think-

CRITICAL THINKING

Have You Ever Thin Sliced Your Teacher?

Think back to your least favorite teacher (not your current one, of course!). How long did it take you to figure out that he or she wasn't going to make your list of star teachers?

In an intriguing study, psychologist Nalini Ambady asked people to watch video clips of teachers they did not know. After watching three 10-second segments, participants were asked to rate the teachers. Amazingly, their ratings correlated highly with year-end course evaluations made by actual students (Ambady & Rosenthal, 1993). Ambady obtained the same result when she presented an even thinner "slice" of teaching behavior, just three 2-second clips. A mere 6 seconds is all that participants needed to form intuitive judgments of the instructors' teaching!

In his book *Blink*, Malcolm Gladwell (2005) argues that this was not a case of hurried irrationality. Instead, it was "thin-slicing," or quickly making sense of thin slivers of experience. According to Gladwell, these immediate, intuitive reactions can sometimes form the basis of more carefully reasoned judgments. They are a testament to the power of the *cognitive unconscious*, which is a part of the brain that does automatic, unconscious processing (Wilson, 2002). Far from being irrational, intuition may be an important part of how we think.

The trick, of course, is figuring out when thin slicing can be trusted and when it can't. After all, first impressions aren't always right. For example, have you ever had a teacher you came to appreciate only after classes were well under way or only after the course was over? In many circumstances, quick impressions are most valuable when you take the time to verify them through further observation.

---

ing errors. To see how this can happen, try the following problems.

> *Problem 1* An epidemic breaks out, and 600 people are about to die. Doctors have two choices. If they give drug A, 200 lives will be saved. If they give drug B, there is a one-third chance that 600 people will be saved and a two-thirds chance that none will be saved. Which drug should they choose?

> *Problem 2* Again, 600 people are about to die, and doctors must make a choice. If they give drug A, 400 people will die. If they give drug B, there is a one-third chance that no one will die and a two-thirds chance that 600 will die. Which drug should they choose?

Most people choose drug A for the first problem and drug B for the second. This is fascinating because the two problems are identical. The only difference is that the first is stated in terms of lives saved, the second in terms of lives lost. Yet, even people who realize that their answers are contradictory find it difficult to change them (Kahneman & Tversky, 1972, 1973).

Intuition

As the example shows, we often make decisions intuitively, rather than logically or rationally. **Intuition** is quick, impulsive thought. It may provide fast answers, but it can also be misleading and sometimes disastrous. (See "Have You Ever Thin Sliced Your Teacher?")

Two noted psychologists, Daniel Kahneman (KON-eh-man) and Amos Tversky (tuh-VER-ski) (1937–1996), studied how we make decisions in the face of uncertainty. They found that human judgment is often seriously flawed (Kahneman, 2003; Kahneman, Slovic, & Tversky, 1982). Let's explore some common intuitive thinking errors, so you will be better prepared to avoid them.

Representativeness One very common pitfall in judgment is illustrated by this question: Which is more probable?

> **A.** Tiger Woods will not be in the lead after the first round of golf of a tournament but will win the tournament.
>
> **B.** Tiger Woods will not be in the lead after the first round of golf of a tournament.

Tversky and Kahneman (1982) found that most people regard statements like A as more probable than B. However, this intuitive answer overlooks an important fact: The likelihood of two events occurring together is lower than the probability of either one alone. (For example, the probability of getting one head when flipping a coin is one half, or 0.5. The probability of getting two heads when flipping two coins is one fourth, or 0.25.) Therefore, A is less likely to be true than B.

According to Tversky and Kahneman, such faulty conclusions are based on the **representativeness heuristic**. That

---

Intuition Quick, impulsive thought that does not make use of formal logic or clear reasoning.

Representativeness heuristic A tendency to select wrong answers because they seem to match pre-existing mental categories.

is, we tend to give a choice greater weight if it seems to be representative of what we already know. Thus, you probably compared the information about Tiger Woods with your mental model of what a golf pro's behavior should be like. Answer A seems to better represent the model. Therefore, it seems more likely than answer B, even though it isn't. In courtrooms, jurors are more likely to think a defendant is guilty if the person appears to fit the profile of a person likely to commit a crime (Davis & Follette, 2002). For example, a young single male from a poor neighborhood would be more likely to be judged guilty of theft than a middle-aged married father from an affluent suburb.

Emotion Feelings also tend to affect good judgment. When we must make a choice, our emotional reactions to various alternatives can determine what intuitively seems to be the right answer. Emotions such as fear, hope, anxiety, liking, or disgust can eliminate possibilities from consideration or promote them to the top of the list (Kahneman, 2003). For many people, choosing which political candidate to vote for is a good example of how emotions can cloud clear thinking. Rather than comparing candidates' records and policies, it is tempting to vote for the person we like, rather than the person who is most qualified for the job.

Underlying Odds A second common error in judgment involves ignoring the **base rate,** or underlying probability of an event. People in one experiment were told that they would be given descriptions of 100 people—70 lawyers and 30 engineers. Subjects were then asked to guess, without knowing anything about a person, whether she or he was an engineer or a lawyer. All correctly stated the probabilities as 70 percent for lawyer and 30 percent for engineer. Participants were then given this description:

> Dick is a 30-year-old man. He is married with no children. A man of high ability and high motivation, he promises to be quite successful in his field. He is well liked by his colleagues.

Notice that the description gives no new information about Dick's occupation. He could still be either an engineer or a lawyer. Therefore, the odds should again be estimated as 70-30. However, most people changed the odds to 50-50. Intuitively it seems that Dick has an equal chance of being either an engineer or a lawyer. But this guess completely ignores the underlying odds.

Perhaps it is fortunate that we do at times ignore underlying odds. Were this not the case, how many people would get married in the face of a 50-percent divorce rate? Or how many would start high-risk businesses? On the other hand, people who smoke, drink and then drive, or skip wearing auto seat belts ignore rather high odds of injury or illness. In many high-risk situations, ignoring base rates is the same as thinking you are an exception to the rule.

Framing

The most general conclusion about intuition is that the way a problem is stated, or **framed,** affects decisions (Tversky & Kahneman, 1981). As the first example in this discussion revealed, people often give different answers to the same problem if it is stated in slightly different ways. To gain some added insight into framing, try another thinking problem:

> A couple are divorcing. Both parents seek custody of their only child, but custody can be granted to just one parent. If you had to make a decision based on the following information, to which parent would you award custody of the child?
>
> **Parent A:** average income, average health, average working hours, reasonable rapport with the child, relatively stable social life.
>
> **Parent B:** above-average income, minor health problems, lots of work-related travel, very close relationship with the child, extremely active social life.

Most people choose to award custody to Parent B, the parent who has some drawbacks but also several advantages (such as above-average income). That's because people tend to look for *positive qualities* that can be *awarded* to the child. However, how would you choose if you were asked this question: Which parent should be denied custody? In this case, most people choose to deny custody to Parent B. Why is Parent B a good choice one moment and a poor choice the next? It's because the second question asked who should be *denied* custody. To answer this question, people tend to look for *negative qualities* that would *disqualify* a parent. As you can see, the way a question is framed can channel us down a narrow path so we attend to only part of the information provided, rather than weighing all the pros and cons (Shafir, 1993).

Usually, the *broadest* way of framing or stating a problem produces the best decisions. However, people often state problems in increasingly narrow terms until a single, seemingly "obvious" answer emerges. For example, to select a career, it would be wise to consider pay, working conditions, job satisfaction, needed skills, future employment outlook, and many other factors. Instead, such decisions are often narrowed to thoughts such as, "I like to write, so I'll be a journalist," "I want to make good money and law pays well," or "I can be creative in photography." Framing decisions so narrowly greatly increases the risk of making a poor choice. If you would like to think more critically and analytically, it is important to pay attention to how you are defining problems before you try to solve them. Remember, shortcuts to answers often short-circuit clear thinking.

Wisdom

People can be intelligent without being wise. For example, a person who does well in school and on IQ tests may make a total mess of her life. Likewise, people can be intelligent without being creative, and clear, rational thinking can lead to correct, but uninspired, answers (Solomon, Marshall, & Gardner, 2005). In many areas of human life, wisdom represents a mixture of convergent thinking, intelligence, and reason, spiced with creativity and originality. People who are wise approach life with openness and tolerance (Helson & Srivastava, 2002).

MODULE 8.4 Summary

What is creative thinking?

- To be creative, a solution must be practical and sensible as well as original. Creative thinking requires divergent thought, characterized by fluency, flexibility, and originality. Tests of creativity measure these qualities.
- Five stages often seen in creative problem solving are orientation, preparation, incubation, illumination, and verification. Not all creative thinking fits this pattern.
- Studies suggest that the creative personality has a number of characteristics, most of which contradict popular stereotypes. There is only a very small correlation between IQ and creativity.
- Some creative thinking skills can be learned.

How accurate is intuition?

- Intuitive thinking often leads to errors. Wrong conclusions may be drawn when an answer seems highly representative of what we already believe is true.
- Emotions also lead to intuitive thinking and poor choices.
- Another problem is ignoring the base rate (or underlying probability) of an event.
- Clear thinking is usually aided by stating or framing a problem in broad terms.

Base rate The basic rate at which an event occurs over time; the basic probability of an event.

Framing In thought, the terms in which a problem is stated or the way that it is structured.

KNOWLEDGE BUILDER

Creative Thinking and Intuition

Recite

1. Fluency, flexibility, and originality are characteristics of
   a. convergent thought
   b. deductive thinking
   c. creative thought
   d. trial-and-error solutions

2. List the typical stages of creative thinking in the correct order.

   _____ _____
   _____ _____
   _____

3. Reasoning and critical thinking tend to block creativity; these are noncreative qualities. T or F?

4. To be creative, an original idea must also be practical or feasible. T or F?

5. Intelligence and creativity are highly correlated; the higher a person's IQ, the more likely he or she is to be creative. T or F?

6. Kate is single, outspoken, and very bright. As a college student, she was deeply concerned with discrimination and other social issues and participated in several protests. Which statement is more likely to be true?
   a. Kate is a bank teller.
   b. Kate is a bank teller and a feminist.

7. Our decisions are greatly affected by the way a problem is stated, a process called
   a. framing
   b. base rating
   c. induction
   d. selective encoding

Reflect

Critical Thinking

8. A coin is flipped four times with one of the following results: (a) H T T H, (b) T T T T, (c) H H H H, (d) H H T H. Which sequence would most likely precede getting a head on the fifth coin flip?

Relate

Make up a question that would require convergent thinking to answer. Now do the same for divergent thinking.

Which of the tests of creativity described in the text do you think you would do best on? (Look back if you can't remember them all.)

To better remember the stages of creative thinking, make up a short story that includes these words: *orient, prepare, in Cuba, illuminate, verify*.

Explain in your own words how representativeness and base rates contribute to thinking errors.

Link

Internet addresses frequently change. To find the sites listed here, visit **http://www.thomsonedu.com/psychology/coon** for an updated list of Internet addresses and direct links to relevant sites.

- **Creativity Web** Multiple links to resources on creativity.
- **Creative Thinking Techniques** Try to apply a variety of creative thinking and lateral thinking techniques.
- **Thin Slicing** Read what Malcolm Gladwell, the author of *Blink*, has to say about rapid cognition.

ANSWERS

1. c 2. orientation, preparation, incubation, illumination, verification 3. F 4. T 5. F 6. a 7. a 8. The chance of getting a head on the fifth flip is the same in each case. Each time you flip a coin, the chance of getting a head is 50 percent, no matter what happened before. However, many people intuitively think that b is the answer because a head is "overdue," or that c is correct because the coin is "on a roll" for heads.

MODULE 8.5 Psychology in Action
Culture, Race, IQ, and You

SURVEY QUESTION: *Are IQ tests fair to all cultural and racial groups?*

Do you consider yourself intelligent? Okay, then give the Dove Test a try.

If you scored 14 on this exam, your IQ is approximately 100, indicating average intelligence. If you scored 10 or less, you are intellectually disabled. With luck and the help of a special educational program, you may be able to learn a few simple skills!

Isn't the Dove Test a little unfair? No, it is *very* unfair. It was written in 1971 by African-American sociologist Adrian Dove as "a half serious attempt to show that we're just not talking the same language." Dove tried to slant his test as much in favor of urban African-American culture as he believes typical IQ tests are biased toward a white middle-class background (Jones, 2003). (Because of its age, the test is probably now also unfair for African Americans under 40.)

Dove's test is a thought-provoking reply to the fact that African-American children score an average of about 15 points lower on standardized IQ tests than European-American children. By reversing the bias, Dove has shown that intelligence tests are not equally valid for all groups. As psychologist Jerome Kagan once said, "If the Wechsler and Binet scales were translated into Spanish, Swahili, and Chinese and given to every 10-year-old in Latin America, East Africa, and China, the majority would obtain IQ scores in the intellectually disabled range."

Culture-Fair Testing

Certainly we cannot believe that children of other cultures are all intellectually disabled. The fault must lie in the test (White, 2006). As noted earlier, cultural values, knowledge, language patterns, and traditions can greatly affect performance on tests designed for Western cultures (Neisser et al.,

DOVE COUNTERBALANCE INTELLIGENCE TEST

Time limit: 5 minutes.

Circle the correct answer.

1. T-bone Walker got famous for playing what?
   a. trombone b. piano c. T-flute d. guitar e. "hambone"

2. A "gas head" is a person who has a
   a. fast-moving car. b. stable of "lace." c. "process." d. habit of stealing cars. e. long jail record for arson

3. If you throw the dice and 7 is showing on the top, what is facing down?
   a. 7 b. snake eyes c. boxcars d. little joes e. 11

4. Cheap chitlings (not the kind you purchase at a frozen-food counter) will taste rubbery unless they are cooked long enough. How soon can you quit cooking them to eat and enjoy them?
   a. 45 minutes b. 2 hours c. 24 hours d. 1 week (on a low flame) e. 1 hour

5. Bird or Yardbird was the jacket jazz lovers from coast to coast hung on
   a. Lester Young b. Peggy Lee c. Benny Goodman d. Charlie Parker e. Birdman of Alcatraz

6. A "handkerchief head" is
   a. a cool cat b. a porter c. an Uncle Tom d. a hoddi e. a preacher

7. Jet is
   a. an East Oakland motorcycle club b. one of the gangs in West Side Story c. a news and gossip magazine d. a way of life for the very rich

8. "Bo Diddly" is a
   a. game for children b. down-home cheap wine c. down-home singer d. new dance e. Moejoe call

9. Which word is most out of place here?
   a. splib b. blood c. gray d. spook e. black

10. If a pimp is uptight with a woman who gets state aid, what does he mean when he talks about "Mother's Day"?
    a. second Sunday in May b. third Sunday in June c. first of every month d. none of these e. first and fifteenth of every month

11. Many people say that "Juneteenth" (June 10) should be made a legal holiday because this was the day when
    a. the slaves were freed in the United States b. the slaves were freed in Texas c. the slaves were freed in Jamaica d. the slaves were freed in California e. Martin Luther King was born f. Booker T. Washington died

12. If a man is called a "blood," then he is a
    a. fighter b. Mexican-American c. Black d. hungry hemophile e. red man or Indian

13. What are the Dixie Hummingbirds?
    a. a part of the KKK b. a swamp disease c. a modern gospel group d. a Mississippi Negro paramilitary strike force e. deacons

14. The opposite of square is
    a. round. b. up c. down d. hip e. lame

ANSWERS

1. d 2. c 3. a 4. c 5. d 6. c 7. c 8. c 9. c 10. c 11. b 12. c 13. c 14. d

1996; Sternberg & Grigorenko, 2005). To avoid this problem, some psychologists have tried to develop culture-fair tests that do not disadvantage certain groups. A **culture-fair test** is designed to minimize the importance of skills and knowledge that may be more common in some cultures than in others. (For a sample of culture-fair test items, see ● Figure 8.25.)

Culture-fair tests attempt to measure intelligence without, as much as possible, being influenced by a person's verbal skills, cultural background, and educational level. Their value lies not just in testing people from other cultures. They are also useful for testing children in the United States who come from poor communities, rural areas, or ethnic minority families (Stephens et al., 1999). However, no intelligence test can be entirely free of cultural influences. For instance, our culture is very "visual," because children are constantly exposed to television, movies, video games, and the like. Thus, compared with children in developing countries, a child who grows up in the United States may be better prepared to take *both* nonverbal tests and traditional IQ tests.

Because the concept of intelligence exhibits such diversity across cultures, many psychologists have begun to stress the need to rethink the concept of intelligence itself (Greenfield, 1997; Sternberg & Grigorenko, 2005). If we are to find a truly culture-fair way to measure intelligence, we first need to identify those core cognitive skills, or multiple intelligences, that lie at the heart of human intelligence the world around (Sternberg & Grigorenko, 2006).

The Politics of Race, Culture, and IQ

Biased tests are not the only IQ issue African Americans have confronted. One persistent claim is that African Americans score below average in IQ because of their "genetic heritage" and that they are genetically incapable of climbing out of poverty (Hernstein & Murray, 1994; Rushton & Jensen, 2005). Psychologists have responded to such claims with a number of counterarguments.

First, it is no secret that as a group African Americans are more likely than European Americans to live in environments that are physically, educationally, and intellectually impoverished. As we saw earlier in this chapter, when unequal education is part of the equation, IQs tell us little about how heredity affects intelligence (Sternberg, Grigorenko, & Kidd, 2005; Suzuki & Aronson, 2005). Indeed, one study found that placing poor African-American children into better-off European-American adoptive families increased the children's IQs by an average of 13 points, bringing them into line with those of European-American children (Nisbett, 2005). That is, providing African-American children with the same environmental experiences available to European-American children erased IQ differences.

Second, the point made by the Dove Test is often overlooked. The assumptions, biases, and content of standard IQ tests do not always allow meaningful comparisons between ethnic, cultural, or racial groups (Fagan & Holland, 2007; Suzuki & Aronson, 2005). As Leon Kamin (1981) says, "The important fact is that we cannot say which sex (or race) might be more intelligent, because we have no way of measuring 'intelligence.' We have only IQ tests." Kamin's point is that the makers of IQ tests decided in advance to use test items that would give men and women equal IQ scores. It would be just as easy to put together an IQ test that would give African Americans and European Americans equal scores. Differences in IQ scores are not a fact of nature, but a decision by the test makers. That's why European Americans do better on IQ tests written by European Americans, and African Americans do better on IQ tests devised by African Americans.

Third, although IQ predicts school performance, it does not predict later career success (McClelland, 1994). In this regard, "street smarts," or what psychologist Robert Sternberg calls *practical intelligence* (Stemler & Sternberg, 2006), may be seen by minority cultures as more important than "book learning," or what Sternberg calls *analytic intelligence* (Sankofa et al., 2005).

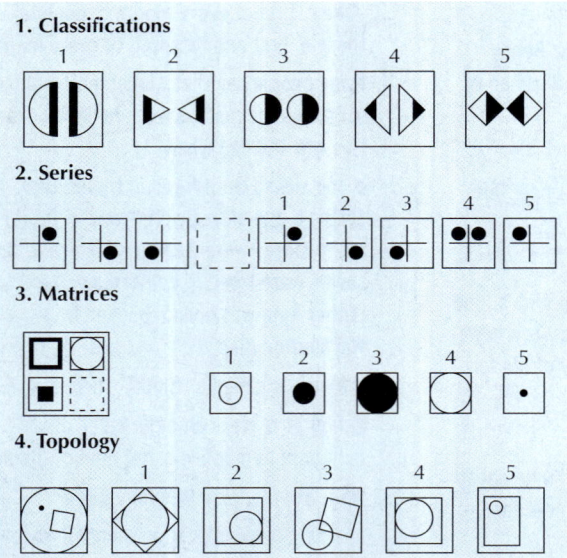

● **FIGURE 8.25** Sample items from a culture-fair test. **1.** Which pattern is different from the remaining four? (Number 3.) **2.** Which of the five figures on the right would properly continue the three on the left–that is, fill the blank? (Number 5.) **3.** Which of the figures on the right should go in the square on the left to make it look right? (Number 2.) **4.** At left, the dot is outside the square and inside the circle. In which of the figures on the right could you put a dot outside the square and inside the circle? (Number 3.) ("Cultural Fair Test Sample Items," from R. B. Cattell, *Culture Free Intelligence Test, Scale 1, Handbook*. Reprinted by permission of R. B. Cattell.)

Most psychologists have concluded there is no scientific evidence that group differences in average IQ are based on genetics. In fact, studies that used actual blood group testing found no significant correlations between ethnic ancestry and IQ scores. According to Bonham, Warshauer-Baker, and Collins (2005), this is because it does not even make genetic sense to talk about "races" at all because obvious external markers, like skin color, have little to do with underlying genetic differences. Group differences in IQ scores are based on cultural and environmental differences, as much as on heredity (Neisser et al., 1996; Nisbett, 2005). To conclude otherwise reflects political beliefs and biases, not scientific facts.

Thinking Beyond the Numbers Game

African Americans are not the only segment of the population with reason to question the validity of intelligence testing and the role of heredity in determining intelligence. The clarifications they have won extend to others as well.

Consider the 9-year-old child confronted with this question on an intelligence test: "Which of the following does not belong with the others? Roller skates, airplane, train, bicycle." If the child fails to answer "airplane," does it reveal a lack of intelligence? It can be argued that an intelligent choice could be based on any of these alternatives: Roller skates are not typically used for transportation; an airplane is the only non-land item; a train can't be steered; a bicycle is the only item with just two wheels. The parents of a child who misses this question may have reason to be angry because educational systems tend to classify children and then make the label stick.

In response to such concerns, court decisions have led some states to outlaw the use of intelligence tests in public schools.

High-Stakes Testing

Widespread reliance on standardized intelligence tests and aptitude tests has raised questions about the relative good and harm they do. On the positive side, tests can open opportunities as well as close them. A high test score may allow a disadvantaged youth to enter college, or it may identify a child who is bright but emotionally disturbed. Test scores may also be fairer and more objective than arbitrary judgments made by admissions officers or employment interviewers. Also, tests *do* accurately predict academic performance. The fact that academic performance *does not* predict later success may call for an overhaul of college course work, not an end to testing.

On the negative side, mass testing can sometimes exclude people of obvious ability. Other complaints relate to the frequent appearance of bad or ambiguous questions on standardized tests, overuse of class time to prepare students for the tests (instead of teaching general skills), and in the case of intelligence tests, the charge that tests are often biased. Also, most standardized tests demand passive recognition of facts, assessed with a multiple-choice format. They do not, for the most part, test a person's ability to think critically or creatively or to apply knowledge to solve problems.

Conclusion

An application of the preceding discussion to your personal understanding of intelligence can be summarized in this way: Intelligence tests are a double-edged sword; we have learned much from their use, yet they have the potential to do great harm. In the final analysis, it is important to remember—as Howard Gardner has pointed out—that creativity, motivation, physical health, mechanical aptitude, artistic ability, and numerous other qualities not measured by intelligence tests contribute to the achievement of life goals. Also remember that IQ is not intelligence. IQ is an *index* of intelligence (as narrowly defined by a particular test). Change the test and you change the score. An IQ is not some permanent number stamped on your forehead (or the foreheads of your friends and classmates) that forever determines your potential. The real issue is what skills people have and how they apply them, not what their test scores are (White, 2006).

MODULE 8.5 Psychology in Action Summary

Are IQ tests fair to all cultural and racial groups?
- Traditional IQ tests often suffer from a degree of cultural bias. For this and other reasons, it is wise to remember that IQ is merely an index of intelligence and that intelligence is narrowly defined by most tests.
- IQ is related to achievement in school, but many other factors are also important. Outside school, the connection between IQ and achievement is even weaker.
- The use of standard IQ tests for educational placement of students (especially into special education classes) has been prohibited by law in some states.

Culture-fair test A test (such as an intelligence test) designed to minimize the importance of skills and knowledge that may be more common in some cultures than in others.

KNOWLEDGE BUILDER

Culture, Race, IQ, and You

Recite

1. The WAIS-III, SB5, and Dove Test are all culture-fair intelligence scales. T or F?
2. The claim that heredity accounts for racial differences in average IQ ignores environmental differences and the cultural bias inherent in standard IQ tests. T or F?
3. IQ scores predict school performance. T or F?
4. IQ is not intelligence; it is one index of intelligence. T or F?

Reflect
Critical Thinking

5. Assume that a test of memory for words is translated from English to Spanish. Would the Spanish version of the test be equal in difficulty to the English version?

Relate

Do you think it would be possible to create an intelligence test that is universally culture-fair? What would its questions look like? Can you think of any type of question that wouldn't favor the mental skills emphasized by some culture, somewhere in the world?

Funding for schools in some states varies greatly in rich and poor neighborhoods. Imagine that a politician opposes spending more money on disadvantaged students because she believes it would "just be a waste." What arguments can you offer against her assertion?

In your own opinion, what are the advantages of using standardized tests to select applicants for college, graduate school, and professional schools? What are the disadvantages?

Link

Internet addresses frequently change. To find the sites listed here, visit **http://www.thomsonedu.com/psychology/coon** for an updated list of Internet addresses and direct links to relevant sites.

- **Be Careful of How You Define Intelligence** An article about cross-cultural differences in intelligence.
- **The Knowns and Unknowns of Intelligence** From the APA, what is known about intelligence and intelligence tests.
- **The Bell Curve** Read critical responses to *The Bell Curve*, a book widely criticized for its controversial conclusions about race and intelligence.

ANSWERS

1. F 2. T 3. T 4. T 5. Probably not, because the Spanish words might be longer or shorter than the same words in English. The Spanish words might also sound more or less alike than words on the original test. Translating an intelligence test into another language can subtly change the meaning and difficulty of test items.

Interactive Learning

Psychology: Active Learning Modules Book Companion Website

http://www.thomsonedu.com/psychology/coon

Visit your Book Companion Website, where you will find flash cards, practice quizzes, Internet links, and more to help you study.

ThomsonNOW™

Just What You Need to Know NOW!

Spend time on what you need to master rather than on information you already have learned. Take a pre-test for this chapter, and ThomsonNOW will generate a personalized study plan based on your results. The study plan will identify the topics you need to review and direct you to online resources to help you master those topics. You can then take a post-test to help you determine the concepts you have mastered and what you will need to work on. Try it out! Go to www.thomsonedu.com/login to sign in with an access code or to purchase access to this product.

9 Motivation and Emotion

MODULE 9.1 Overview of Motivation
SURVEY QUESTIONS: What is motivation? Are there different types of motives?

MODULE 9.2 Hunger, Thirst, Pain, and Sex
SURVEY QUESTION: What causes hunger? Overeating? Eating disorders?
SURVEY QUESTIONS: Is there more than one type of thirst? In what ways are pain avoidance and the sex drive unusual?

MODULE 9.3 Arousal, Achievement, and Growth Needs
SURVEY QUESTION: How does arousal relate to motivation?
SURVEY QUESTIONS: What are social motives? Why are they important?
SURVEY QUESTION: Are some motives more basic than others?

MODULE 9.4 Emotion and Physiological Arousal
SURVEY QUESTION: What happens during emotion?
SURVEY QUESTION: Can "lie detectors" really detect lies?

MODULE 9.5 Emotional Expression and Theories of Emotion
SURVEY QUESTION: How accurately are emotions expressed by the face and "body language"?
SURVEY QUESTION: How do psychologists explain emotions?

MODULE 9.6 Psychology in Action: Emotional Intelligence—The Fine Art of Self-Control
SURVEY QUESTION: What does it mean to have "emotional intelligence"?

Moved by the Music of Life

Robert was in his doctor's waiting room when he suffered a "strange attack." Robert recalls that the "atmosphere changed, the walls seemed to close in, and the voices of other patients became a buzz." However, months of therapy were no help because Robert simply couldn't talk about his feelings. When asked how he felt, Robert might reply "Fine" or "I don't know." Or he might describe a bodily sensation, replying "My stomach hurts" (Lumley, 2004). The scientific name for Robert's problem is *alexithymia* (a-LEX-ih-THIGH-me-ah), from the Latin for "can't name emotions."

It could be said that emotion is the "music" that defines the rhythms of our lives. Sadly, Robert is not moved by the music of life as intensely as most of us are. Not only is Robert unable to name his emotions, he is only vaguely aware of them in the first place. It's even hard for him to imagine emotions. As you might suspect, Robert cannot easily empathize with the emotions of others. People like Robert find it hard to form close relationships with others. Their lack of inner awareness can also lead to health problems, such as depression or addictive behaviors (Lumley, 2004).

This chapter is about the motives that provide the drumbeat of human behavior and the emotions that are its rhythm. Derived from the Latin word *movere* (to move), motivation and emotion play complex roles in our everyday lives. Even "simple" motivated activities, such as eating, are not solely under the control of the body. In many instances, external cues, expectations, learning, cultural values, and other factors influence our motives and our emotions (R. C. Beck, 2004).

Let's begin with basic motives, such as hunger and thirst, and then explore how emotions affect us. Although emotions can be the music of life, they are sometimes the music of death as well. Read on to find out why.

MODULE 9.1 Overview of Motivation

WHAT DO YOU PLAN TO DO TODAY? What are your goals? Why do you pursue them? How vigorously do you try to reach them? When are you satisfied? When do you give up? These are all questions about motivation, or why we act as we do. Let's begin with a basic model of motivation and an overview of types of motives.

Motivation—Forces that Push and Pull

SURVEY QUESTIONS: *What is motivation? Are there different types of motives?*

Motivation refers to the dynamics of behavior—the ways in which our actions are *initiated, sustained, directed,* and *terminated* (Franken, 2007).

Can you clarify that? Yes. Imagine that Kendra is studying psychology in the library. Her stomach begins to growl and she can't concentrate. She grows restless and decides to buy an apple from a vending machine. The machine is empty, so she goes to the cafeteria. Closed. Kendra drives home, where she cooks a meal and eats it. At last her hunger is satisfied, and she resumes studying. Notice how Kendra's food seeking was *initiated* by a bodily need. Her search was *sustained* because her need was not immediately met, and her actions were *directed* by possible sources of food. Finally, her food seeking was *terminated* by achieving her goal.

A Model of Motivation

Many motivated activities begin with a **need,** or internal deficiency. The need that initiated Kendra's search was a shortage of key substances in her body. Needs cause a **drive** (an energized motivational state) to develop. The drive was hunger, in Kendra's case. Drives activate a **response** (an action or series of actions) designed to attain a **goal** (the "target" of motivated behavior). Reaching a goal that satisfies the need will end the chain of events. Thus, a simple model of motivation can be shown in this way:

Aren't needs and drives the same thing? No, because the strength of needs and drives can differ (Franken, 2007). If you begin fasting today, your bodily need for food will increase every day. However, you would probably feel less "hungry" on the seventh day of fasting than you did on the first. Whereas your need for food steadily increases, the hunger drive comes and goes.

Now let's observe Kendra again. It's Saturday night: For dinner, Kendra has soup, salad, a large steak, a baked potato, four pieces of bread, two pieces of cheesecake, and three cups of coffee. After dinner, she complains that she is "too full to move." Soon after, Kendra's roommate arrives with a strawberry pie. Kendra exclaims that strawberry pie is her favorite dessert and eats three large pieces! Is this hunger? Certainly, Kendra's dinner satisfied her biological needs for food.

How does that change the model of motivation? Kendra's "pie lust" illustrates that motivated behavior can be energized by the "pull" of external stimuli, as well as by the "push" of internal needs.

Incentives The "pull" of a goal is called its **incentive value** (the goal's appeal beyond its ability to fill a need). Some goals are so desirable (strawberry pie, for example) that they can motivate behavior in the absence of an internal need. Other goals are so low in incentive value that they may be rejected even if they meet the internal need. Fresh, live grubworms, for instance, are highly nutritious. However, it is doubtful that you would eat one no matter how hungry you might be.

Usually, our actions are energized by a mixture of internal needs *and* external incentives. That's why a strong need may change an unpleasant incentive into a desired goal. Perhaps you've never eaten a grubworm, but we'll bet you've eaten some pretty horrible leftovers when the refrigerator was bare. The incentive value of goals also helps explain motives that don't seem to come from internal needs, such as drives for success, status, or approval (● Fig. 9.1).

Types of Motives For our purposes, motives can be divided into three major categories:

1. **Primary motives** are based on biological needs that must be met for survival. The most important primary motives are hunger, thirst, pain avoidance, and needs for air, sleep, elimination of wastes, and regulation of body temperature. Primary motives are innate.

2. **Stimulus motives** express our needs for stimulation and information. Examples include activity, curiosity, exploration, manipulation, and physical contact. Although such motives also appear to be innate, they are not strictly necessary for survival.

3. **Secondary motives** are based on learned needs, drives, and goals. Learned motives help explain many human activities, such as making music, blogging, or trying to win the skateboarding finals in the

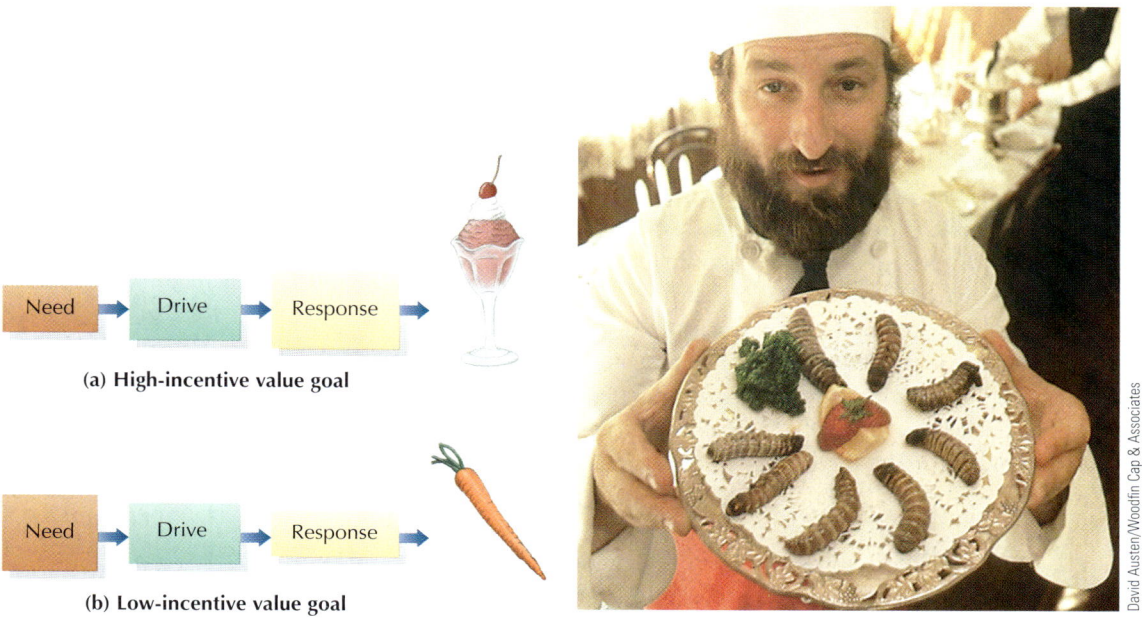

FIGURE 9.1 Needs and incentives interact to determine drive strength *(left)*. *(a)* Moderate need combined with a high-incentive goal produces a strong drive. *(b)* Even when a strong need exists, drive strength may be moderate if a goal's incentive value is low. It is important to remember, however, that incentive value lies "in the eye of the beholder" *(photo)*. No matter how hungry, few people would be able to eat the pictured grubworms.

X Games. Many secondary motives are related to learned needs for power, affiliation (the need to be with others), approval, status, security, and achievement. Fear and aggression also appear to be greatly affected by learning.

Primary Motives and Homeostasis

How important is air in your life? Water? Sleep? Food? Temperature regulation? Finding a public rest room? For most of us, satisfying biological needs is so routine that we tend to overlook how much of our behavior they direct. But exaggerate any of these needs through famine, shipwreck, poverty, near drowning, bitter cold, or drinking 10 cups of coffee, and their powerful grip on behavior becomes evident. We are, after all, still animals in many ways.

Biological drives are essential because they maintain *homeostasis* (HOE-me-oh-STAY-sis), or bodily equilibrium (Cannon, 1932).

What is homeostasis? The term **homeostasis** means "standing steady," or "steady state." Optimal levels exist for body temperature, for chemicals in the blood, for blood pressure, and so forth (Levin, 2006). When the body deviates from these "ideal" levels, automatic reactions begin to restore equilibrium (Deckers, 2005). Thus, it might help to think of homeostasis as being similar to a thermostat set at a particular temperature.

A (VERY) SHORT COURSE ON THERMOSTATS
The thermostat in your house constantly compares the actual room temperature to a *set point*, or ideal temperature, which you can control. When room temperature falls below the set point, the heat is automatically turned on to warm the room. When the heat equals or slightly exceeds the set point, it is automatically turned off or the air conditioning is turned on. In this way room temperature is kept in a state of equilibrium hovering around the set point.

The first reactions to disequilibrium in the human body are also automatic. For example, if you become too hot, more blood will flow through your skin and you will begin to perspire, thus lowering body temperature. Usually, we are not aware of such changes, unless continued disequilibrium drives us to seek shade, warmth, food, or water.

Motivation Internal processes that initiate, sustain, and direct activities.
Need An internal deficiency that may energize behavior.
Drive The psychological expression of internal needs or valued goals—for example, hunger, thirst, or a drive for success.
Response Any action, glandular activity, or other identifiable behavior.
Goal The target or objective of motivated behavior.
Incentive value The value of a goal above and beyond its ability to fill a need.
Primary motives Innate motives based on biological needs.
Stimulus motives Innate needs for stimulation and information.
Secondary motives Motives based on learned needs, drives, and goals.
Homeostasis A steady state of body equilibrium.

Circadian Rhythms

Our needs and drives can change from moment to moment. After eating, our motivation to eat more food tends to diminish, and a few minutes in the hot sun can leave us feeling thirsty. But our motivation can also vary over longer cycles. Scientists have long known that body activity is guided by internal "biological clocks." Every 24 hours, your body undergoes a cycle of changes called **circadian** (SUR-kay-dee-AN) **rhythms** (*circa*: about; *diem*: a day) (Beersma & Gordijn, 2007). Throughout the day, activities in the liver, kidneys, and endocrine glands undergo large changes. Body temperature, blood pressure, and amino acid levels also shift from hour to hour. These activities, and many others, peak once a day (● Fig. 9.2). People are usually more motivated and alert at the high point of their circadian rhythms (Antle & Mistlberger, 2005).

Shift Work and Jet Lag Circadian rhythms are most noticeable after a major change in time schedules. Businesspersons, athletes, and other time zone travelers tend to perform poorly when their body rhythms are disturbed. If you travel great distances east or west, the peaks and valleys of your circadian rhythms will be out of phase with the sun and clocks. For example, you might be wide awake at midnight and feel like you're sleepwalking during the day. (Return to Fig. 9.2.) Shift work has the same effect, causing fatigue, irritability, upset stomach, and depression (Garbarino, 2002; Shen et al., 2006).

How fast do people adapt to rhythm changes? For major time zone shifts (5 hours or more) it can take up to 2 weeks to resynchronize. The *direction* of travel also affects adaptation (Herxheimer & Waterhouse, 2003). If you fly west, adapting is relatively easy; if you fly east, adapting takes much longer (● Fig. 9.3). When you fly east, the sun comes up *earlier* relative to your "home" time. Let's say that you live in Seattle and fly to Washington. If you get up at 7 A.M. in Washington, it's 4 A.M. back in Seattle—and your body knows it. If you fly west, the sun comes up later. In this case, it is easier for people to "advance" (stay up later and sleep in) than it is to shift backward.

Adjusting to jet lag is slowest when you stay indoors, where you can sleep and eat on "home time." Getting outdoors speeds adaptation. A few intermittent 5-minute periods of exposure to bright light early in the morning are also helpful for resetting your circadian rhythm (Duffy & Wright, Jr., 2005).

How does this affect those of us who are not world travelers? There are few college students who have not at one time or another "burned the midnight oil," especially for final exams. At such times it is wise to remember that departing from your regular schedule usually costs more than it's worth. You may be motivated to do as much during 1 hour in the morning as you could have done in 3 hours of work after midnight. You might just as well go to sleep 2 hours earlier.

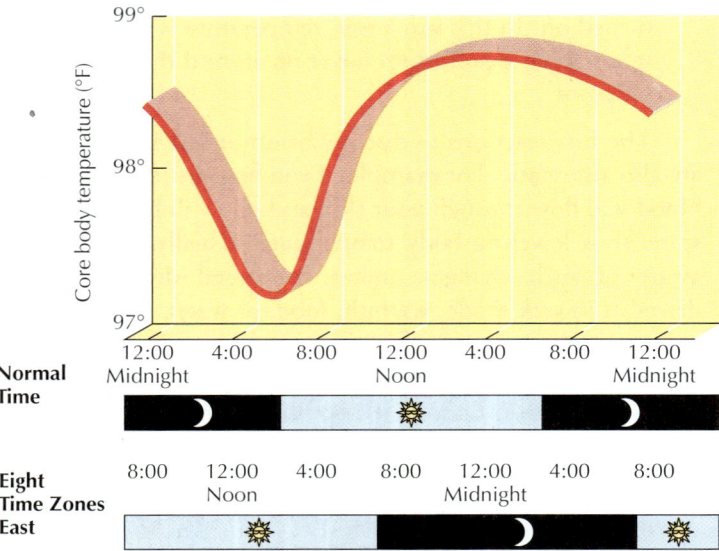

● **FIGURE 9.2** Core body temperature is a good indicator of a person's circadian rhythm. Most people reach a low point 2 to 3 hours before their normal waking time. It's no wonder that both the Chernobyl and Three Mile Island nuclear power plant accidents occurred around 4 A.M. Rapid travel to a different time zone, shift work, depression, and illness can throw sleep and waking patterns out of synchronization with the body's core rhythm. Mismatches of this kind are very disruptive (Hauri & Linde, 1990).

● **FIGURE 9.3** Time required to adjust to air travel across six time zones. The average time to resynchronize was shorter for westbound travel than for eastbound flights. (Data from Beljan et al., 1972; cited by Moore-Ede et al., 1982.)

In general, if you can anticipate an upcoming body rhythm change, it is best to preadapt to your new schedule. *Preadaptation* refers to gradually matching your sleep–waking cycle to a new time schedule. Before traveling, for instance, you should go to sleep 1 hour later (or earlier) each day until your sleep cycle matches the time at your destination.

MODULE 9.1 Summary

What is motivation?
- Motives initiate, sustain, and direct activities. Many motives involve the following sequence: need, drive, goal, and goal attainment (need reduction).
- Behavior can be activated either by needs (push) or by goals (pull).
- The attractiveness of a goal and its ability to initiate action are related to its incentive value.

Are there different types of motives?
- Three basic categories of motives are primary motives, stimulus motives, and secondary motives.
- Most primary motives operate to maintain homeostasis.
- Circadian rhythms are closely tied to sleep, activity, and energy cycles. Time zone travel and shift work can seriously disrupt motivation, sleep, and bodily rhythms.

KNOWLEDGE BUILDER

Overview of Motivation

Recite

Classify the following needs or motives by placing the correct letter in the blank.
A. Primary motive **B.** Stimulus motive **C.** Secondary motive

1. ____ curiosity
2. ____ status
3. ____ sleep
4. ____ thirst
5. ____ achievement
6. ____ physical contact
7. Motives _____, sustain, and _____ activities.
8. The maintenance of bodily equilibrium is called thermostasis. T or F?
9. Desirable goals are motivating because they are high in
   a. secondary value
   b. stimulus value
   c. homeostatic value
   d. incentive value
10. The term *jet lag* is commonly used to refer to disruptions of
    a. the inverted U function
    b. circadian rhythms
    c. any of the episodic drives
    d. the body's set point

Reflect

Critical Thinking

11. Many people mistakenly believe that they suffer from "hypoglycemia" (low blood sugar), which is often blamed for fatigue, difficulty concentrating, irritability, and other symptoms. Why is it unlikely that many people actually have hypoglycemia?

Relate

Motives help explain why we do what we do. See if you can think of something you do that illustrates the concepts of need, drive, response, and goal. Does the goal in your example vary in incentive value? What effects do high and low incentive value goals have on your behavior?

Mentally list some primary motives you have satisfied today. Then list some stimulus motives and secondary motives. How did each influence your behavior?

Link

Internet addresses frequently change. To find the sites listed here, visit http://www.thomsonedu.com/psychology/coon for an updated list of Internet addresses and direct links to relevant sites.

- **Theories of Motivation** Because no single theory can account for all aspects of biological aspects of motivation, this site examines the major approaches to understanding motivation and includes discussions of both the strengths and weaknesses of each theory.
- **Sleeplessness and Circadian Rhythm Disorder** Read what happens when your biological clock malfunctions and what you can do about it.
- **Drive Reduction Theory and Incentives in the Regulation of Food Intake** Using eating behavior as an example, explore the roles of drive reduction and incentives.

ANSWERS

1. b 2. c 3. a 4. a 5. c 6. b 7. initiate, direct 8. F 9. d 10. b 11. Because of homeostasis: Blood sugar is normally maintained within narrow bounds. Although blood sugar levels fluctuate enough to affect hunger, true hypoglycemia is an infrequent medical problem.

Circadian rhythms Cyclical changes in body functions and arousal levels that vary on a schedule approximating a 24-hour day.

MODULE 9.2 Hunger, Thirst, Pain, and Sex

YOU GET HUNGRY, you find food, you eat: Hunger might seem like a "simple" motive, but only recently have we begun to understand it. Hunger provides a good model of how internal and external factors direct our behavior. Many of the principles that explain hunger also apply to thirst. However, pain avoidance and the sex drive have unusual characteristics that make them interesting and instructive.

Hunger—Pardon Me, My Hypothalamus Is Growling

SURVEY QUESTION: *What causes hunger? Overeating? Eating disorders?*

Like almost every other human motive, our hunger levels are affected by both internal bodily factors and external environmental and social ones. To understand how this works, let's begin with a survey of some of the internal factors controlling our hunger.

Internal Factors in Hunger

Don't our feelings of hunger originate in our stomach? To find out, Walter Cannon and A. L. Washburn (1912) decided to see if stomach contractions cause hunger. In an early study, Washburn trained himself to swallow a balloon, which could be inflated through an attached tube. This allowed Cannon to record the movements of Washburn's stomach (● Fig. 9.4). When Washburn's stomach contracted, he reported that he felt "hunger pangs." In view of this, the two scientists concluded that hunger is nothing more than the contractions of an empty stomach. (However, this proved to be an inflated conclusion.)

For many people, hunger produces an overall feeling of weakness or shakiness, rather than a "growling" stomach. Of course, eating *does* slow when the stomach is stretched or distended (full). (Remember last Thanksgiving?) However, we now know that the stomach is not essential for feeling hunger. Even people who have had their stomachs removed for medical reasons continue to feel hungry and eat regularly (Woods et al., 2000).

Then what does cause hunger? Many different factors combine to promote and suppress hunger. The brain receives many signals from parts of the digestive system, ranging from the tongue and stomach to the intestines and the liver.

The liver? Yes, as the levels of blood sugar (glucose) drop, the liver responds by sending nerve impulses to the brain. These "messages" contribute to a desire to eat (Woods et al., 2000).

Brain Mechanisms

What part of the brain controls hunger? When you are hungry, many parts of the brain are affected, so no single "hunger thermostat" exists. However, a small area called the **hypothalamus** (HI-po-THAL-ah-mus) regulates many motives, including hunger, thirst, and the sex drive (● Fig. 9.5).

The hypothalamus is sensitive to levels of sugar in the blood (and other substances described in a moment). It also receives neural messages from the liver and the stomach. When combined, these signals determine if you are hungry or not (Woods et al., 2000).

● **FIGURE 9.4** In Walter Cannon's early study of hunger, a simple apparatus was used to simultaneously record hunger pangs and stomach contractions. (Adapted from Cannon, 1934.)

● **FIGURE 9.5** Location of the hypothalamus in the human brain.

One part of the hypothalamus acts as a *feeding system* that initiates eating. If the *lateral hypothalamus* is "turned on" with an electrified probe, even a well-fed animal will immediately begin eating. (The term *lateral* simply refers to the *sides* of the hypothalamus. See ● Figure 9.6.) If the same area is destroyed, the animal will never eat again.

The lateral hypothalamus is normally activated in a variety of ways. For example, when you are hungry your stomach lining produces ghrelin (GREL-in), a hormone that activates your lateral hypothalamus (Olszewski et al., 2003). (If your stomach is growlin', it's probably releasing ghrelin.) Ghrelin also activates parts of your brain involved in learning. This means you should consider studying before you eat, not immediately afterward (Diano et al., 2006).

A second area in the hypothalamus is part of a *satiety system,* or "stop mechanism" for eating. If the *ventromedial hypothalamus* (VENT-ro-MEE-dee-al) is destroyed, dramatic overeating results. (*Ventromedial* refers to the bottom middle of the hypothalamus.) Rats with such damage will eat until they balloon up to weights of 1,000 grams or more (● Fig. 9.7). A normal rat weighs about 180 grams. To put this weight gain in human terms, picture someone you know who weighs 180 pounds growing to a weight of 1,000 pounds.

The *paraventricular* (PAIR-uh-ven-TRICK-you-ler) *nucleus* of the hypothalamus also affects hunger. (See Fig. 9.4.) This area helps keep blood sugar levels steady by both starting and stopping eating. The paraventricular nucleus is sensitive to a substance called neuropeptide Y (NPY). If NPY is present in large amounts, an animal will eat until it cannot hold another bite (Williams et al., 2004). Incidentally, the hypothalamus also responds to a chemical in marijuana, which can produce intense hunger (the "munchies") (Di Marzo et al., 2001).

How do we know when to stop eating? A chemical called glucagon-like peptide 1 (GLP-1) causes eating to cease. After

● **FIGURE 9.6** This is a cross section through the middle of the brain (viewed from the front of the brain). Indicated areas of the hypothalamus are associated with hunger and the regulation of body weight.

● **FIGURE 9.7** Damage to the hunger satiety system in the hypothalamus can produce a very fat rat, a condition called hypothalamic *hyperphagia* (HI-per-FAGE-yah: overeating). This rat weighs 1,080 grams. (The pointer has gone completely around the dial and beyond.) (Photo courtesy of Neal Miller.)

Hypothalamus A small area at the base of the brain that regulates many aspects of motivation and emotion, especially hunger, thirst, and sexual behavior.

BRAINWAVES

Your Brain's "Fat Point"

A thermostat set to, say, 72 degrees will constantly turn the heat and/or air conditioning on and off to maintain the temperature at that set point. Like a thermostat, your brain maintains a **set point** in order to control your weight over the long term. It does this by monitoring the amount of fat stored in your body (Ahima & Osei, 2004).

Your set point is the weight you maintain when you are making no effort to gain or lose weight. When your body weight goes below its set point, you will feel hungry most of the time. On the other hand, fat cells release a substance called *leptin* when your "spare tire" is well inflated. Leptin is carried in the bloodstream to the hypothalamus, where it tells us to eat less (Williams et al., 2004).

Can you change your fat set point? Good question. Your leptin levels are partly under genetic control. In rare cases mice (and we humans) inherit a genetic defect that reduces leptin levels in the body, leading to obesity. In such cases, the administration of leptin can help (Williamson et al., 2005).

For the rest of us, the news is not so encouraging because there is currently no known way to lower your set point for fat. To make matters worse, radical diets do not help (but you knew that already, didn't you?). They may even raise the set point for fat, resulting in *diet-induced obesity* (Ahima & Osei, 2004). You may not be able to lose weight by resetting your hypothalamus, but psychologists have studied other approaches to weight loss; we will examine some later in this module.

The mouse on the left has a genetic defect that prevents its fat cells from producing normal amounts of leptin. Without this chemical signal, the mouse's body acts as if its set point for fat storage is, shall we say, rather high.

---

you eat a meal, GLP-1 is released by the intestines. From there, it travels in the bloodstream to the brain. When enough GLP-1 arrives, your desire to eat ends (Nori, 1998). It takes at least 10 minutes for the hypothalamus to respond after you begin eating. That's why you are less likely to overeat if you eat slowly, which gives your brain time to get the message that you've had enough (Liu et al., 2000).

In addition to knowing when to start eating and when meals are over, your brain also controls your weight over longer periods. (See "Your Brain's 'Fat Point.'")

The substances we have reviewed are only some of the chemical signals that start and stop eating (Geary, 2004). Others continue to be discovered. In time, they may make it possible to artificially control hunger. If so, better treatments for extreme obesity and self-starvation could follow (Batterham et al., 2003).

External Factors in Hunger and Obesity

Our "hunger" is affected by more than just our bodily needs for food. In fact, if internal needs alone controlled eating, fewer people would overeat. Let's consider some external influences on hunger and their role in obesity, a major health risk and, for many, a source of social stigma and low self-esteem. Roughly 65 percent of adults in the United States are overweight (● Fig. 9.8). As a result, obesity is overtaking smoking as a cause of needless deaths (Murray, 2001).

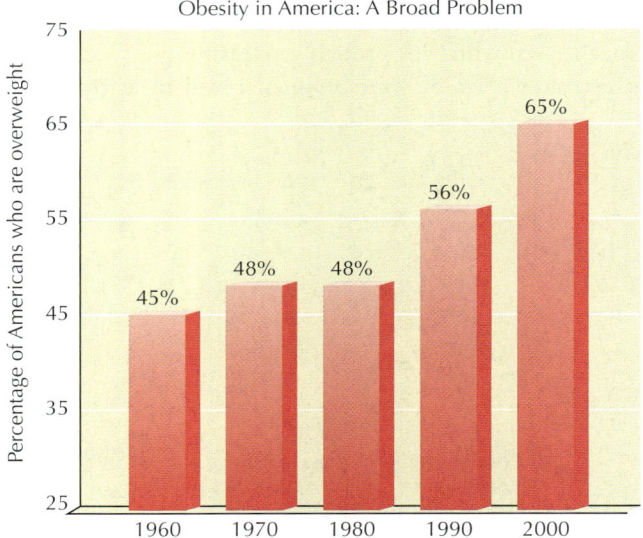

● **FIGURE 9.8** A near epidemic of obesity has occurred in the United States during the last 20 years, with 65 percent of all Americans now classified as overweight (CDC, 2002).

External Eating Cues

Most of us are sensitive to *external eating cues*. These are signs and signals linked with food. For example, do you tend to eat more when food is highly visible and easy to get? If so, then external cues affect your food intake. In cultures like ours, where food is plentiful, eating cues add greatly to the risk of overeating (Woods et al., 2000). Many college freshmen gain weight rapidly during their first 3 months on campus (the famous "Frosh 15"). All-you-can-eat dining halls in the dorms and nighttime snacking appear to be the culprits (Levitsky et al., 2003). The presence of others can also affect whether people overeat (or undereat) depending on how much everyone else is eating and how important it is to impress them (Pliner & Mann, 2004).

Taste The availability of a variety of tasty foods can also lead to overeating and obesity in societies where such foods are plentiful. Normally, tastes for foods vary considerably. For example, if you are well fed, leptin dulls the tongue's sensitivity to sweet tastes (Kawai et al., 2000). If you have noticed that you lose your "sweet tooth" when you are full, you may have observed this effect. Actually, if you eat too much of any particular food, it will become less appealing. This probably helps us maintain variety in our diets. However, it also encourages obesity. If you overdose on fried chicken or French fries, moving on to some cookies or chocolate cheesecake certainly won't do your body much good (Pinel, Assanand, & Lehman, 2000).

It is easy to acquire a **taste aversion,** or active dislike, for a particular food. This can happen if a food causes sickness or if it is merely associated with nausea (Jacobsen et al., 1993). Not only do we learn to avoid such foods, but they too can become nauseating. A friend of one of your authors once became ill after eating a cheese Danish (well, actually, *several*) and has never again been able to come face to face with this delightful pastry.

If getting sick occurs long after eating, how does it become associated with a particular food? A good question. Taste aversions are a type of classical conditioning. As stated in Module 6.1, a long delay between the conditioned stimulus (CS) and the unconditioned stimulus (US) usually prevents conditioning. However, psychologists theorize that we have a biological tendency to associate an upset stomach with foods eaten earlier. Such learning is usually protective. Yet, as we saw previously (in Module 6.1), many cancer patients suffer taste aversions long after the nausea of their drug treatments has passed (Chance, 2006; Stockhorst, Klosterhalfen, & Steingrueber, 1998).

Taste aversions may also help people avoid severe nutritional imbalances. For example, if you go on a fad diet and eat only grapefruit, you will eventually begin to feel ill. In time, associating your discomfort with grapefruit may create an aversion to it and restore some balance to your diet.

Emotional Eating *Is it true that people also overeat when they are emotionally upset?* Yes. People with weight problems are prone to overeat when they are anxious, angry, or sad (Geliebter & Aversa, 2003). Furthermore, obese individuals are often unhappy in our fat-conscious culture. The result is overeating that leads to emotional distress and still more overeating. This makes weight control extremely difficult (Rutledge & Linden, 1998).

Cultural Factors Learning to think of some foods as desirable and others as revolting has a large impact on what we eat. In North America we would never consider eating the eyes out of the steamed head of a monkey, but in some parts of the world they are considered a delicacy. By the same token, vegans and vegetarians think it is barbaric to eat any kind of meat. In short, cultural values greatly affect the *incentive value* of foods.

Dieting

A diet is not just a way to lose weight. Your current diet is defined by the types and amounts of food you regularly eat. Some diets actually encourage overeating. For instance, placing animals on a "supermarket" diet leads to gross obesity. In one experiment, rats were given meals of chocolate chip cookies, salami, cheese, bananas, marshmallows, milk chocolate, peanut butter, and fat. These pampered rodents overate, gaining almost three times as much weight as rats that ate only laboratory chow (Sclafani & Springer, 1976). (Rat chow is a dry mixture of several bland grains. If you were a rat, you'd probably eat more cookies than rat chow, too.)

People are also sensitive to dietary content. In general, *sweetness,* high *fat content,* and *variety* tend to encourage overeating (Lucas & Sclafani, 1990). Sadly, our culture provides the worst kinds of foods for people who suffer from obesity. Restaurant and fat food tends to be higher in fat and calories than meals made at home (Brownell, 2003).

"Supersized" meals are another problem. For example, food portions at restaurants in the United States are 25 percent larger, or more, than they are in France. Far fewer people are obese in France, most likely because they simply eat less. The French also take longer to eat a meal, which discourages overeating (Rozin et al., 2003).

An added problem faced by people who want to control their weight concerns "yo-yo" dieting.

The Paradox of Yo-Yo Dieting If dieting works, why are hundreds of "new" diets published each year? The answer is that although dieters do lose weight, most regain it soon after they stop dieting. In fact, many people end up weighing even more than before. Why should this be so? Dieting (starving) slows the body's rate of metabolism (the rate at which energy is used up). In effect, a dieter's body becomes highly efficient

Set point The proportion of body fat that tends to be maintained by changes in hunger and eating.

Taste aversion An active dislike for a particular food.

"Supersized" portions contribute to overeating. A fast food meal consisting of a hamburger, medium fries, and a medium soda averages 1,200 calories, which is more than half the daily caloric need for an adult. Make that a double burger, add cheese, and super-size the fries and the drink and you will consume two thirds of the food you need in a day in just one meal. Notice, too, that people tend to eat all the food they have paid for, even if it is more than they need.

at *conserving* calories and storing them as fat (Pinel, Assanand, & Lehman, 2000).

Apparently, evolution prepared us to save energy when food is scarce and to stock up on fat when food is plentiful. Briefly starving yourself, therefore, may have little lasting effect on weight. "Yo-yo dieting," or repeatedly losing and gaining weight, is especially dangerous. Frequent changes in weight can dramatically slow the body's metabolic rate. As noted earlier, this may raise the body's set point for fat and makes it harder to lose weight each time a person diets and easier to regain weight when the diet ends. Frequent weight changes also increase the risk of heart disease and premature death (Wang & Brownell, 2005). To avoid bouncing between feast and famine requires a permanent change in eating habits and exercise.

To summarize, eating and overeating are related to internal and external influences, diet, emotions, genetics, exercise, and many other factors. People become obese in different ways and for different reasons. We live in a culture that provides inexpensive, good-tasting food everywhere and have a brain that evolved to say "Eat whenever food is available." Clearly, scientists are still a long way from winning the "battle of the bulge." Nevertheless, many people have learned to take control of eating by applying psychological principles. (See "Behavioral Dieting.")

Eating Disorders

Under the sheets of her hospital bed Krystal looks like a skeleton. If her **anorexia nervosa** (AN-uh-REK-see-yah ner-VOH-sah: self-starvation) cannot be stopped, Krystal may die of malnutrition. Victims of anorexia, who are mostly adolescent females, suffer devastating weight losses from severe, self-inflicted dieting (Cooper, 2005).

Do anorexics lose their appetite? Although the compulsive attempt to lose weight causes them to not seek or desire food, they often still feel physical hunger. Often, anorexia starts with "normal" dieting that slowly begins to dominate the person's life. In time, anorexics suffer debilitating health problems. From 5 to 8 percent (more than 1 in 20) die of malnutrition (Polivy & Herman, 2002). ■ Table 9.1 lists the symptoms of anorexia nervosa.

■ **TABLE 9.1 Recognizing Eating Disorders**

Anorexia Nervosa
- Body weight below 85 percent of normal for one's height and age
- Refusal to maintain body weight in normal range
- Intense fear of becoming fat or gaining weight, even though underweight
- Disturbance in one's body image or perceived weight
- Self-evaluation is unduly influenced by body weight
- Denial of seriousness of abnormally low body weight
- Absence of menstrual periods
- Purging behavior (vomiting or misuse of laxatives or diuretics)

Bulimia Nervosa
- Normal or above-normal weight
- Recurring binge eating
- Eating within an hour or two an amount of food that is much larger than most people would consume
- Feeling a lack of control over eating
- Purging behavior (vomiting or misuse of laxatives or diuretics).
- Excessive exercise to prevent weight gain
- Fasting to prevent weight gain
- Self-evaluation unduly influenced by body weight

Source: Adapted from DSM-IV-TR, 2000.

Kirstie Alley, the star of the television series "Fat Actress," has been a lifelong yo-yo dieter who tried many different diets. Ironically, her show poked fun at the anxieties women like her suffer as they struggle with their weight. As a spokeswoman for a national weight-loss program, Kirstie again lost weight. Will she maintain her weight loss now that she has reached her target weight?

DISCOVERING PSYCHOLOGY

Behavioral Dieting

As we have noted, dieting is usually followed by rapid weight gain. If you really want to lose weight, you must overhaul your eating habits, an approach called **behavioral dieting**. Here are some helpful behavioral techniques.

1. **Get yourself committed to weight loss.** Involve other people in your efforts. Programs such as Overeaters Anonymous or Take Off Pounds Sensibly can be a good source of social support.

2. **Exercise.** No diet can succeed for long without an increase in exercise, because exercise burns calories. To lose weight, you must use more calories than you take in. Add activity to your routine in every way you can think of. Stop saving steps and riding elevators. Burning just 200 extra calories a day can help prevent rebound weight gains. The more frequently and vigorously you exercise, the more weight you will lose (Jeffery & Wing, 2001).

3. **Learn your eating habits by observing yourself and keeping a "diet diary."** Begin by making a complete, 2-week record of when and where you eat, what you eat, and the feelings and events that occur just before and after eating. Is a roommate, relative, or spouse encouraging you to overeat? What are your most "dangerous" times and places for overeating?

4. **Learn to weaken your personal eating cues.** When you have learned when and where you do most of your eating, avoid these situations. Try to restrict your eating to one room, and do not read, watch TV, study, or talk on the phone while eating. Require yourself to interrupt what you are doing in order to eat.

5. **Count calories, but don't starve yourself.** To lose weight, you must eat less, and calories allow you to keep a record of your food intake. If you have trouble eating less every day, try dieting 4 days a week. People who diet intensely every other day lose as much as those who diet moderately every day (Viegener et al., 1990).

6. **Develop techniques to control the act of eating.** Begin by taking smaller portions. Carry to the table only what you plan to eat. Put all other food away before leaving the kitchen. Eat slowly, sip water between bites of food, leave food on your plate, and stop eating before you are completely full. Be especially wary of the extra large servings at fast-food restaurants. Saying "super-size me" too often can, indeed, leave you super sized (Murray, 2001).

7. **Avoid snacks.** It is generally better to eat several small meals a day than three large ones because more calories are burned (Assanand, Pinel, & Lehman, 1998). However, high-calorie snacks tend to be eaten *in addition to* meals. If you have an impulse to snack, set a timer for 20 minutes and see if you are still hungry then. Delay the impulse to snack several times if possible. Dull your appetite by filling up on raw carrots, bouillon, water, coffee, or tea.

8. **Chart your progress daily.** Record your weight, the number of calories eaten, and whether you met your daily goal. Set realistic goals by cutting down calories gradually. Losing about a pound per week is realistic, but remember, you are changing habits, not just dieting. Diets don't work!

9. **Set a "threshold" for weight control.** Maintaining weight loss can be even more challenging than losing weight. It is easier to maintain weight losses if you set a regain limit of 3 pounds or less. In other words, if you gain more than 2 or 3 pounds, you immediately begin to make corrections in your eating habits and amount of exercise (Brownell, 2003).

Be patient with this program. It takes years to develop eating habits. You can expect it to take at least several months to change them. If you are unsuccessful at losing weight with these techniques, you might find it helpful to seek the aid of a psychologist familiar with behavioral weight-loss techniques.

Bulimia nervosa (bue-LIHM-ee-yah) is a second major eating disorder. Bulimic persons gorge on food, then vomit or take laxatives to avoid gaining weight. (See Table 9.1.) Like anorexia, most victims of bulimia are girls or women. Approximately 5 percent of college women are bulimic, and as many as 60 percent have milder eating problems. Bingeing and purging can seriously damage health. Typical risks include sore throat, hair loss, muscle spasms, kidney damage,

Anorexia nervosa Active self-starvation or a sustained loss of appetite that has psychological origins.

Behavioral dieting Weight reduction based on changing exercise and eating habits, rather than temporary self-starvation.

Bulimia nervosa Excessive eating (gorging) usually followed by self-induced vomiting and/or taking laxatives.

Anorexia nervosa is far more dangerous than many people realize. This haunting photo shows popular singer Karen Carpenter shortly before she died of starvation-induced heart failure. Many other celebrities have struggled with eating disorders, including Paula Abdul, Kirstie Alley, Fiona Apple, Victoria Beckham (Posh Spice), Princess Diana, Tracey Gold, Janet Jackson, and Mary-Kate Olsen.

dehydration, tooth erosion, swollen salivary glands, menstrual irregularities, loss of sex drive, and even heart attack.

Eating Disorders in Men The prevalence of eating disorders is on the rise among men. Currently, one third of men want less fat on their bodies while another third want more muscles (McCabe & Ricciardelli, 2004). As a result, more and more men are deliberately adjusting their eating patterns. Many are going too far: about 10 percent of anorexics and 25 percent of bulimics are now men (Weltzin et al., 2005). It is worth noting that men are also tend to react to their body image concerns by engaging in excessive exercise.

Causes What causes anorexia and bulimia? Women and men who suffer from eating disorders are extremely dissatisfied with their bodies (Crisp et al., 2006). Usually, they have distorted views of themselves, exaggerated fears of becoming fat, and low self-esteem. Many overestimate their body size by 25 percent or more. As a result, they think they are disgustingly "fat" when they are actually wasting away (● Fig. 9.9) (Polivy & Herman, 2002).

Many of these problems are related to the idealized body images presented in the media (Levine & Harrison, 2004). Girls who spend a lot of time reading fashion magazines are more likely to have distorted body images and unrealistic ideas about how they compare with others (Martinez-Gonzalez et al., 2003).

The current popularity of fitness, exercise, and sports has also contributed as more men and women now change their diets in their search for a lean, muscled look. People engaged in sports that require low body fat or extremes of weight loss (such as wrestling, pole vaulting, high jumping, and even cycling) are particularly vulnerable to developing eating disorders (Weltzin et al., 2005).

People with eating disorders appear to be trying to gain some measure of control. Anorexic teens girls are usually described as "perfect" daughters—helpful, considerate, conforming, and obedient. They seem to be seeking perfect control in their lives by being perfectly slim (Castro et al., 2004). People suffering from bulimia are also concerned with control. Typically they are obsessed with thoughts of weight, food, eating, and ridding themselves of food. As a result, they feel guilt, shame, self-contempt, and anxiety. Vomiting reduces their anxiety, which makes purging highly reinforcing (Powell & Thelen, 1996).

Treatment Most people suffering from eating disorders will not seek help on their own. This is especially true for men because eating disorders are still widely perceived to be female disorders (Weltzin et al., 2005). Typically, it takes strong urging by family or friends to get victims into treatment.

Treatment for anorexia usually begins with giving drugs to relieve obsessive fears of gaining weight. Then a medical diet is used to restore weight and health. Next, a counselor may help patients work on the emotional conflicts that led to weight loss. For bulimia, behavioral counseling may include self-monitoring of food intake. A related cognitive-behavioral approach focuses on changing the thinking patterns and beliefs about weight and body shape

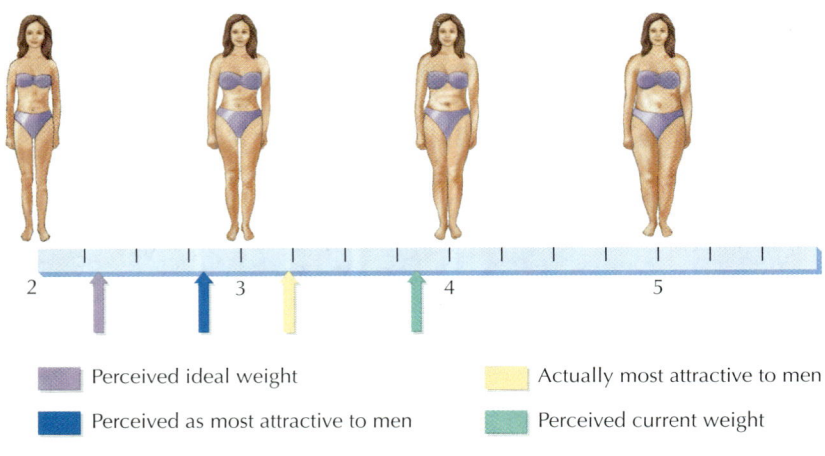

Perceived ideal weight · Actually most attractive to men
Perceived as most attractive to men · Perceived current weight

● **FIGURE 9.9** Women with abnormal eating habits were asked to rate their body shape on a scale similar to the one you see here. As a group, they chose ideal figures much thinner than what they thought their current weights were. (Most women say they want to be thinner than they currently are, but to a lesser degree than women with eating problems.) Notice that the women with eating problems chose an ideal weight that was even thinner than what they thought men prefer. This is not typical of most women. In this study, only women with eating problems wanted to be thinner than what they thought men find attractive (Zellner, Harner, & Adler, 1989).

that perpetuate eating disorders (Byrne & McLean, 2002; Cooper, 2005).

Primary Motives Revisited—Thirst, Pain, and Sex

SURVEY QUESTIONS: *Is there more than one type of thirst? In what ways are pain avoidance and the sex drive unusual?*

Most biological motives work in ways that are similar to hunger. For example, thirst is only partially controlled by dryness of the mouth. If you were to take a drug that made your mouth constantly wet, or dry, your water intake would remain normal. Like hunger, thirst is regulated by separate *thirst* and *thirst satiety* systems in the hypothalamus. Also like hunger, thirst is strongly affected by learning and cultural values.

Thirst

You may not have noticed, but there are actually two kinds of thirst. **Extracellular thirst** occurs when water is lost from the fluids surrounding the cells of your body. Bleeding, vomiting, diarrhea, sweating, and drinking alcohol cause this type of thirst (Franken, 2007). When a person loses both water and minerals in any of these ways—especially by perspiration—a slightly salty liquid may be more satisfying than plain water.

Why would a thirsty person want to drink salty water? The reason is that before the body can retain water, minerals lost through perspiration (mainly salt) must be replaced. In lab tests, animals greatly prefer saltwater after salt levels in their bodies are lowered (Strickler & Verbalis, 1988). Similarly, some nomadic peoples of the Sahara Desert prize blood as a beverage, probably because of its saltiness. (Maybe they should try Gatorade?)

A second type of thirst occurs when you eat a salty meal. In this instance your body does not lose fluid. Instead, excess salt causes fluid to be drawn out of cells. As the cells "shrink," **intracellular thirst** is triggered. Thirst of this type is best quenched by plain water.

The drives for food, water, air, sleep, and elimination are all similar in that they are generated by a combination of activities in the body and the brain, and they are influenced by various external factors. However, the drive to avoid pain and the sex drive and are more unusual.

Pain

How is the drive to avoid pain different? Hunger, thirst, and sleepiness come and go in a fairly regular cycle each day. Pain avoidance, by contrast, is an **episodic drive** (ep-ih-SOD-ik). That is, it occurs in distinct episodes when bodily damage takes place or is about to occur. Most drives prompt us to actively seek a desired goal (food, drink, warmth, and

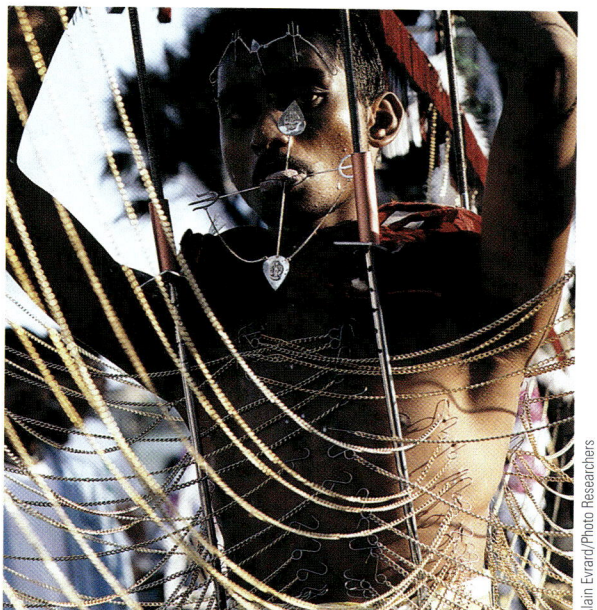

Tolerance for pain and the strength of a person's motivation to avoid discomfort are greatly affected by cultural practices and beliefs.

so forth). Pain prompts us to *avoid* or *eliminate* sources of discomfort.

Some people feel they must be "tough" and not show any distress. Others complain loudly at the smallest ache or pain. The first attitude raises pain tolerance, and the second lowers it. As this suggests, the drive to avoid pain is partly learned. That's why members of some societies endure cutting, burning, whipping, tattooing, and piercing of the skin that would agonize most people (but apparently not devotees of piercing and "body art"). In general, we learn how to react to pain by observing family members, friends, and other role models (McMahon & Koltzenburg, 2005).

The Sex Drive

Many psychologists do not think of sex as a primary motive, because sex (contrary to anything your personal experience might suggest) is not necessary for *individual* survival. It is necessary, of course, for *group* survival.

The term **sex drive** refers to the strength of one's motivation to engage in sexual behavior. In lower animals the sex drive is directly related to hormones. Female mammals (other than humans) are interested in mating only when their fertil-

> **Extracellular thirst** Thirst caused by a reduction in the volume of fluids found between body cells.
> **Intracellular thirst** Thirst triggered when fluid is drawn out of cells due to an increased concentration of salts and minerals outside the cell.
> **Episodic drive** A drive that occurs in distinct episodes.
> **Sex drive** The strength of one's motivation to engage in sexual behavior.

ity cycles are in the stage of **estrus,** or "heat." Estrus is caused by a release of **estrogen** (a female sex hormone) into the bloodstream. Hormones are important in males as well. In most animals, castration will abolish the sex drive. But in contrast to females, the normal male animal is almost always ready to mate. His sex drive is primarily aroused by the behavior and scent of a receptive female. Therefore, in many species mating is closely tied to female fertility cycles.

How much do hormones affect human sex drives? Hormones affect the human sex drive, but not as directly as in animals (Crooks & Baur, 2008). The sex drive in men is related to the amount of **androgens** (male hormones such as testosterone) provided by the testes. When the supply of androgens dramatically increases at puberty, so does the male sex drive. Likewise, the sex drive in women is related to their estrogen levels (Hyde & DeLamater, 2006). However, "male" hormones also affect the female sex drive. In addition to estrogen, a woman's body produces small amounts of androgens. When their androgen levels increase, many women experience a corresponding increase in sex drive (Van Goozen et al., 1995). Testosterone levels decline with age, and various medical problems can lower sexual desire. In some instances, taking testosterone supplements can restore the sex drive in both men and women (Crooks & Baur, 2008).

Does alcohol increase the sex drive? In general, no. Alcohol is a *depressant.* As such, it may, in small doses, stimulate erotic desire by lowering inhibitions. This effect no doubt accounts for alcohol's reputation as an aid to seduction. (Humorist Ogden Nash once summarized this bit of folklore by saying "Candy is dandy, but liquor is quicker.") However, in larger doses alcohol suppresses orgasm in women and erection in men. Getting drunk *decreases* sexual desire, arousal, pleasure, and performance (McKay, 2005).

Numerous other drugs are reputed to be *aphrodisiacs* (af-ruh-DEEZ-ee-aks: substances that increase sexual desire or pleasure). However, like alcohol, many other drugs actually impair sexual response, rather than enhance it (McKay, 2005). Some examples are amphetamines, amyl nitrite, barbiturates, cocaine, Ecstasy, LSD, and marijuana. In the end, love is the best aphrodisiac (Crooks & Baur, 2008).

Perhaps the most interesting fact about the sex drive is that it is largely *nonhomeostatic* (relatively independent of bodily need states). In humans, the sex drive can be aroused at virtually any time by almost anything. It therefore shows no clear relationship to deprivation (the amount of time since the drive was last satisfied). Certainly, an increase in desire may occur as time passes. But recent sexual activity does not prevent sexual desire from occurring again. Notice, too, that people may seek to arouse the sex drive as well as to reduce it. This unusual quality makes the sex drive capable of motivating a wide range of behaviors. It also explains why sex is used to sell almost everything imaginable.

MODULE 9.2 Summary

What causes hunger? Overeating? Eating disorders?
- Hunger is influenced by a complex interplay between fullness of the stomach, blood sugar levels, metabolism in the liver, and fat stores in the body.
- The most direct control of eating comes from the hypothalamus, which is sensitive to both neural and chemical messages that affect eating.
- Other factors influencing hunger are the body's set point, external eating cues, the attractiveness and variety of diet, emotions, learned taste preferences and aversions, and cultural values.
- Obesity is the result of internal and external influences, diet, emotions, genetics, and exercise.
- Behavioral dieting is based on techniques that change eating patterns and exercise habits.
- Anorexia nervosa and bulimia nervosa are two prominent eating disorders. Both tend to involve conflicts about self-image, self-control, and anxiety.

Is there more than one type of thirst? In what ways are pain avoidance and the sex drive unusual?
- Like hunger, thirst and other basic motives are primarily under the central control of the hypothalamus. Thirst may be either intracellular or extracellular.
- Pain avoidance is episodic as opposed to cyclic. Pain avoidance and pain tolerance are partially learned.
- The sex drive is unusual because it is nonhomeostatic.

KNOWLEDGE BUILDER

Hunger, Thirst, Pain, and Sex

Recite

1. The hunger satiety system in the hypothalamus signals the body to start eating when it receives signals from the liver or detects changes in blood sugar. T or F?
2. Maintaining your body's set point for fat is closely linked with the amount of _____ in the bloodstream.
    a. hypothalamic factor-1
    b. ventromedial peptide-1
    c. NPY
    d. leptin
3. People who frequently diet tend to benefit from practice: They lose weight more quickly each time they diet. T or F?
4. Bingeing and purging are most characteristic of people who have
    a. taste aversions
    b. anorexia
    c. bulimia
    d. strong sensitivity to external eating cues
5. In addition to changing eating habits, a key element of behavioral dieting is
    a. exercise
    b. well-timed snacking
    c. better eating cues
    d. commitment to "starving" every day
6. A cancer patient has little appetite for food several weeks after the nausea caused by chemotherapy has ended. Her loss of appetite is probably best explained by
    a. increased NPY in the brain
    b. a conditioned taste aversion
    c. the aftereffects of yo-yo dieting
    d. a loss of extracellular hunger
7. Thirst may be either intracellular or _____.
8. Pain avoidance is an _____ drive.
9. Sexual behavior in animals is largely controlled by estrogen levels in the female and the occurrence of estrus in the male. T or F?

Reflect
Critical Thinking

10. Kim, who is overweight, is highly sensitive to external eating cues. How might her wristwatch contribute to her overeating?

Relate

Think of the last meal you ate. What caused you to feel hungry? What internal signals told your body to stop eating? How sensitive are you to external eating cues? How were you influenced by portion size? Have you developed any taste aversions?

A friend of yours seems to be engaging in yo-yo dieting. Can you explain to her or him why such dieting is ineffective? Can you summarize how behavioral dieting is done?

If you wanted to provoke extracellular thirst in yourself, what would you do? How could you make intracellular thirst occur?

Link

Internet addresses frequently change. To find the sites listed here, visit http://www.thomsonedu.com/psychology/coon for an updated list of Internet addresses and direct links to relevant sites.

- **Eating Disorders Web Site** Home page of a self-help group for those afflicted with eating disorders.
- **Healthy Dieting** Find you body mass index as you learn more about healthy dieting.
- **The Facts About Aphrodisiacs** Find out if aphrodisiacs increase the sex drive.

ANSWERS

1. F 2. d 3. F 4. c 5. a 6. b 7. extracellular 8. episodic 9. F 10. The time of day can influence eating, especially for externally cued eaters, who tend to get hungry at mealtimes, irrespective of their internal needs for food.

Estrus Changes in the sexual drives of animals that create a desire for mating; particularly used to refer to females in heat.
Estrogen Any of a number of female sex hormones.
Androgen Any of a number of male sex hormones, especially testosterone.

MODULE 9.3 Arousal, Achievement, and Growth Needs

ARE YOU FULL OF ENERGY RIGHT NOW? Are you feeling tired? Clearly, the level of arousal you are experiencing is closely linked with your motivation. Are there ideal levels of arousal for different people and different activities? Let's find out.

Stimulus Drives—Skydiving, Horror Movies, and the Fun Zone

SURVEY QUESTION: *How does arousal relate to motivation?*

Most people enjoy a steady "diet" of new movies, novels, tunes, fashions, games, news, web sites, and adventures. Yet stimulus drives, which reflect needs for information, exploration, manipulation, and sensory input, go beyond mere entertainment. Stimulus drives also help us survive. As we scan our surroundings, we constantly identify sources of food, danger, shelter, and other key details. The drive for stimulation is already present during infancy. By the time a child can walk, there are few things in the home that have not been tasted, touched, viewed, handled, or, in the case of toys, destroyed!

Stimulus drives are readily apparent in animals as well as humans. For example, monkeys will quickly learn to solve a mechanical puzzle made up of interlocking metal pins, hooks, and latches (Butler, 1954) (● Fig. 9.10). No food treats or other external rewards are needed to get them to explore and manipulate their surroundings. The monkeys seem to work for the sheer fun of it.

Arousal Theory

Are stimulus drives homeostatic? Yes. According to **arousal theory** we try to keep arousal at an optimal level (Franken, 2007; Hancock & Ganey, 2003). In other words, when your level of arousal is too low or too high, you will seek ways to raise or lower it.

What do you mean by arousal? Arousal refers to activation of the body and the nervous system. Arousal is zero at death; it is low during sleep; it is moderate during normal daily activities; and it is high at times of excitement, emotion, or panic. Arousal theory assumes that we become uncomfortable when arousal is too low ("I'm bored") or when it is too high, as in fear, anxiety, or panic ("The dentist will see you now"). Most adults vary their activities to maintain a comfortable level of activation. Music, parties, sports, conversation, sleep, surfing the web, and the like, are combined to keep arousal at moderate levels. The right mix of activities prevents boredom *and* overstimulation (Csikszentmihalyi, Abuhamdeh, & Nakamura, 2005).

Sensation Seekers *Do people vary in their needs for stimulation?* Picture a city dweller who is visiting the country. Before long, she begins to complain that it is "too quiet" and seeks some "action." Now imagine a country dweller who is visiting the city. Very soon, she finds the city "overwhelming" and seeks peace and quiet. These examples are extremes, but arousal theory also suggests that people learn to seek particular levels of arousal.

Sensation seeking is a trait of people who prefer high levels of stimulation (Gray & Wilson, 2007). Whether you are high or low in sensation seeking is probably based on how your body responds to new, unusual, or intense stimulation (Zuckerman, 2002). People high in sensation seeking tend to be bold and independent, and they value change. They also report more sexual partners than low scorers, they are more likely to smoke, and they prefer spicy, sour, and crunchy foods over bland foods. Low sensation seekers are orderly, nurturant, and giving, and they enjoy the company of others. Which are you? (Most people fall somewhere between the extremes. See "Xtreme!")

● **FIGURE 9.10** Monkeys happily open locks that are placed in their cage. Because no reward is given for this activity, it provides evidence for the existence of stimulus needs. (Photo courtesy of Harry F. Harlow.)

HUMAN DIVERSITY

Xtreme!

Where would you prefer to go on your next summer vacation? How about a week with your best friends at a cottage on a nearby lake? Or a shopping and museum trip to New York City? Better yet, how about cage diving with great white sharks in South Africa? If the shark adventure attracts you, you are probably high in sensation seeking and would be interested in a vacation that includes activities like bungee jumping, scuba diving, skiing, surfing, sky diving, or white-water rafting (Pizam et al., 2004).

Thrill seeking is an element of the sensation-seeking personality.

Marvin Zuckerman (1990, 2000) has devised a test to measure differences in sensation seeking. His *Sensation-Seeking Scale* (SSS) includes statements like the samples shown here (from Zuckerman, 1996):

Thrill and adventure seeking
- I would like to try parachute jumping.
- I think I would enjoy the sensations of skiing very fast down a high mountain slope.

Experience seeking
- I like to explore a strange city or section of town myself, even if it means getting lost.
- I like to try new foods that I have never tasted before.

Disinhibition
- I like wild, "uninhibited" parties.
- I often like to get high (drinking liquor or smoking marijuana).

Boredom susceptibility
- I can't stand watching a movie that I've seen before.
- I like people who are sharp and witty, even if they do sometimes insult others.

So who are the potential cage divers? Perhaps it's not surprising that SSS scores tend to be higher among men and younger people (Butkovic & Bratko, 2003; Roberti, 2004). SSS scores also vary across cultures. In one study of 11 different cultures, people from America, Israel, and Ireland scored higher on the SSS than people from South Africa, Slovakia, Sicily, or Gabon (Pizam et al., 2004).

Exciting lives aside, there is a dark side to sensation seeking as well. High sensation seekers are also more likely to engage in high-risk behaviors such as substance abuse (Horvath et al., 2004) and casual unprotected sex (Gullette & Lyons, 2005).

Levels of Arousal

Is there an ideal level of arousal for peak performance? If we set aside individual differences, most people perform best when their arousal level is *moderate*. Let's say that you have to take an essay exam. If you are feeling sleepy or lazy (arousal level too low), your performance will suffer. If you are in a state of anxiety or panic about the test (arousal level too high), you will also perform below par. Thus, the relationship between arousal and performance forms an *inverted* U function (a curve in the shape of an upside-down U) (● Fig. 9.11) (Hancock & Ganey, 2003).

The inverted U tells us that at very low levels of arousal you're not sufficiently energized to perform well. Performance will improve as your arousal level increases, up to the middle of the curve. Then it begins to drop off, as you become emotional, frenzied, or disorganized. For example, imagine trying to start a car stalled on a railroad track, with a speeding train bearing down on you. That's what the high-arousal end of the curve feels like.

Is performance always best at moderate levels of arousal? No, the ideal level of arousal depends on the complexity of a task. If a task is relatively simple, it is best for arousal to be high. When a task is more complex, your best performance will occur at lower levels of arousal. (See Fig. 9.11.) This relationship is called the **Yerkes-Dodson law.** It applies to a wide variety of tasks and to measures of motivation other than arousal.

For example, at a track meet, it is almost impossible for sprinters to get too aroused for a race. The task is direct and simple: Run as fast as you can for a short distance. On the other hand, a golfer making a tournament-deciding putt faces a more sensitive and complex task. Excessive arousal is almost certain to hurt his or her performance. In school, most students have had experience with "test anxiety," a familiar example of how too much arousal can lower performance.

Arousal theory Assumes that people prefer to maintain ideal, or comfortable, levels of arousal.

Yerkes-Dodson law A summary of the relationships among arousal, task complexity, and performance.

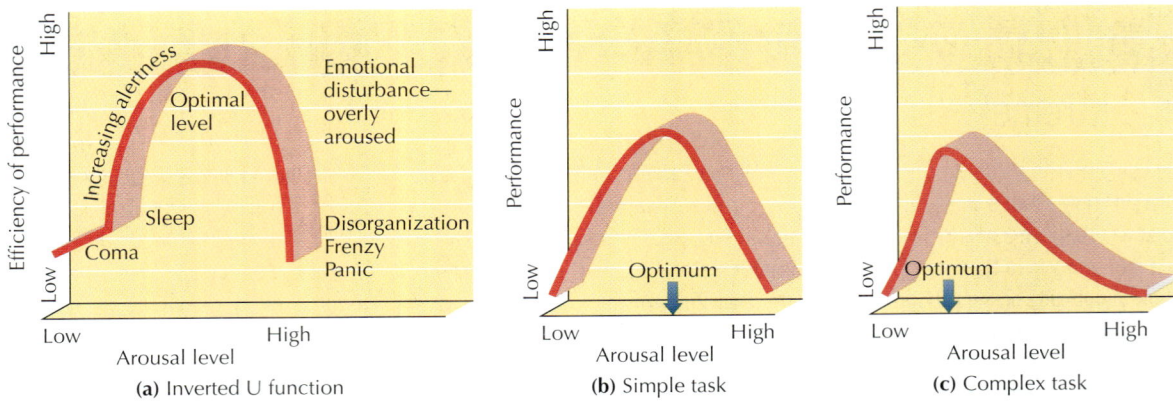

● **FIGURE 9.11** (a) The general relationship between arousal and efficiency can be described by an inverted U curve. The optimal level of arousal or motivation is higher for a simple task (b) than for a complex task (c).

Coping with Test Anxiety

Then is it true that by learning to calm down, a person would do better on tests? Usually, but not always. To begin with, some arousal is healthy; it focuses us on the task at hand. It is only when arousal interferes with performance that we refer to anxiety. **Test anxiety** is a mixture of *heightened physiological arousal* (nervousness, sweating, pounding heart) and *excessive worry*. This combination—arousal plus worry—tends to distract students with a rush of upsetting thoughts and feelings (Stipek, 2001).

Also, studies show that students are typically most anxious when they don't know the material (Cassady, 2004). If this is the case, calming down simply means you will remain calm while failing. Here are some suggestions for coping with test anxiety:

Preparation *Hard work* is the most direct antidote for test anxiety. Many anxious students simply study too little, too late. That's why improving your study skills is a good way to reduce test anxiety (Cassady, 2004). The best solution is to *overprepare* by studying long before the "big day." Well-prepared students score higher, worry less, and are less likely to panic (Zohar, 1998).

Relaxation Learning to relax is another way to lower test anxiety (Ricketts & Galloway, 1984). You can learn self-relaxation skills by looking at Module 13.6, where a relaxation technique is described. Emotional support also helps (Stöber, 2004). If you are test anxious, discuss the problem with your professors or study for tests with a supportive classmate.

Rehearsal To reduce nervousness, rehearse how you will cope with upsetting events. Before taking a test, imagine yourself going blank, running out of time, or feeling panicked. Then calmly plan how you will handle each situation—by keeping your attention on the task, by focusing on one question at a time, and so forth (Watson & Tharp, 2007).

Restructuring Thoughts Another helpful strategy involves listing the upsetting thoughts you have during exams. Then you can learn to combat these worries with calming, rational replies (Jones & Petruzzi, 1995). (These are called *coping statements*; see Module 11.5 for more information.) Let's say you think, "I'm going to fail this test and everybody will think I'm stupid." A good reply to this upsetting thought would be to say, "If I prepare well and control my worries, I will probably pass the test. Even if I don't, it won't be the end of the world. My friends will still like me, and I can try to improve on the next test."

Students who cope well with exams usually try to do the best they can, even under trying circumstances. Becoming a more confident test taker can actually increase your scores, because it helps you remain calm. With practice, most people can learn to be less testy at test-taking time (Smith, 2002).

Social Motives—In Pursuit of Excellence

SURVEY QUESTIONS: *What are social motives? Why are they important?*

Some of your friends are more interested than others in success, achievement, competition, money, possessions, status, love, approval, grades, dominance, power, or belonging to groups—all of which are *social motives* or goals. We acquire **social motives** in complex ways, through socialization and cultural conditioning (Franken, 2007). The behavior of outstanding artists, scientists, athletes, educators, and leaders is best understood in terms of such learned needs, particularly the need for achievement.

The Need for Achievement

To many people, being "motivated" means being interested in achievement (Wigfield & Eccles, 2002). In a later chapter we will investigate aggression, helping, affiliation, seeking approval, and other social motives. For now, let us focus on the

need for achievement (nAch), which is a desire to meet an internal standard of excellence (McClelland, 1961). People with a high need for achievement strive to do well any time they are evaluated.

Is that like the aggressive businessperson who strives for success? Not necessarily. Needs for achievement may lead to wealth and prestige, but people who are high achievers in art, music, science, or amateur sports may excel without seeking riches. Such people typically enjoy challenges, and they relish a chance to test their abilities (Puca & Schmalt, 1999).

Power The need for achievement differs from the **need for power,** which is a desire to have impact or control over others (McClelland, 1975). People with strong needs for power want their importance to be visible: They buy expensive possessions, wear prestigious clothes, and exploit relationships. In some ways, the pursuit of power and financial success is the dark side of the American dream. People whose main goal in life is to make lots of money tend to be poorly adjusted and unhappy (Kasser & Ryan, 1993).

Characteristics of Achievers Using a simple measure, David McClelland (1917–1998) found that he could predict the behavior of high and low achievers. For instance, McClelland compared people's occupations with scores on an achievement test they took as college sophomores. Fourteen years later, those who scored high in nAch tended to have jobs that involved risk and responsibility (McClelland, 1965).

Here's a test: In front of you are five targets. Each is placed at an increasing distance from where you are standing. You are given a beanbag to toss at the target of your choice. Target A, anyone can hit; target B, most people can hit; target C, some people can hit; target D, very few people can hit; target E is rarely if ever hit. If you hit A, you will receive $2; B, $4; C, $8; D, $16; and E, $32. You get only one toss. Which one would you choose? McClelland's research suggests that if you have a high need for achievement, you will select C or perhaps D. Those high in nAch are *moderate* risk takers. When faced with a problem or a challenge, persons high in nAch avoid goals that are too easy.

Why do they pass up sure success? They do it because easy goals offer no sense of satisfaction. They also avoid long shots either because there is no hope of success or because "winning" will be due to luck rather than skill. Persons low in nAch select sure things or impossible goals. Either way, they don't have to take any responsibility for failure.

Desires for achievement and calculated risk taking lead to success in many situations. People high in nAch complete difficult tasks, they earn better grades, and they tend to excel in their occupations. College students high in nAch attribute success to their own ability, and failure to insufficient effort. Thus, high nAch students are more likely to renew their ef-

The person with high needs for achievement strives to do well in any situation in which evaluation takes place.

forts when they perform poorly. When the going gets tough, high achievers get going.

The Key to Success

What does it take to achieve extraordinary success? Psychologist Benjamin Bloom studied America's top concert pianists, Olympic swimmers, sculptors, tennis players, mathematicians, and research neurologists. Bloom (1985) found that drive and determination, not great natural talent, led to exceptional success.

The first steps toward high achievement began when parents exposed their children to music, swimming, scientific ideas, and so forth, "just for fun." At first, many of the children had very ordinary skills. One Olympic swimmer, for instance, remembers repeatedly losing races as a 10-year-old. At some point, however, the children began to actively cultivate their abilities. Before long, parents noticed the child's rapid progress and found an expert instructor or coach. After more successes, the youngsters began "living" for their talent and practiced many hours daily. This continued

> **Test anxiety** High levels of arousal and worry that seriously impair test performance.
> **Social motives** Learned motives acquired as part of growing up in a particular society or culture.
> **Need for achievement (nAch)** The desire to excel or meet some internalized standard of excellence.
> **Need for power** The desire to have social impact and control over others.

for many years before they reached truly outstanding heights of achievement.

The upshot of Bloom's work is that talent is nurtured by dedication and hard work (Beck, 2004). It is most likely to blossom when parents actively support a child's special interests and emphasize doing one's best at all times. Studies of child prodigies and eminent adults also show that intensive practice and expert coaching are common ingredients of high achievement. Elite performance in music, sports, chess, the arts, and many other pursuits typically requires at least 10 years of dedicated practice (Ericsson & Charness, 1994; Ross, 2006). The belief that talent will magically surface on its own is largely a myth.

Self-Confidence Achieving elite performance may be reserved for the dedicated few. Nevertheless, like elite athletes, you may be able to improve your motivation by increasing your self-confidence (Hanton, Mellalieu, & Hall, 2004). People with self-confidence believe they can successfully carry out an activity or reach a goal. To enhance self-confidence, it is wise to do the following (Druckman & Bjork, 1994):

- Set goals that are specific and challenging but attainable.
- Visualize the steps you need to take to reach your goal.
- Advance in small steps.
- When you first acquire a skill, your goal should be to make progress in learning. Later, you can concentrate on improving your performance, compared with other people.
- Get expert instruction that helps you master the skill.
- Find a skilled model (someone good at the skill) to emulate.
- Get support and encouragement from an observer.
- If you fail, regard it as a sign that you need to try harder, not that you lack ability.

Self-confidence affects motivation by influencing the challenges you will undertake, the effort you will make, and how long you will persist when things don't go well. You can be confident that self-confidence is worth cultivating.

Motives in Perspective— A View from the Pyramid

SURVEY QUESTION: *Are some motives more basic than others?*

As you may recall from Module 1.3, Abraham Maslow called the full use of personal potential *self-actualization*. Maslow also described a **hierarchy of human needs,** in which some needs are more basic or powerful than others. Think about the needs that influence your own behavior. Which seem strongest? Which do you spend the most time and energy satisfying? Now look at Maslow's hierarchy (●Fig. 9.12). Note that physiological needs are at the base of the pyramid. Because these needs must be met if we are to survive, they tend to be *prepotent,* or dominant over the higher needs. It could be said, for example, that "to a starving person, food is god."

Maslow believed that higher, more fragile needs are expressed only after we satisfy our physiological needs. This is also true of needs for safety and security. Until they are met, we may have little interest in higher pursuits. For instance, a person who is extremely thirsty might have little interest in writing poetry or even talking with friends. For this reason, Maslow described the first four levels of the hierarchy as **basic needs.** Other basic needs include love and belonging (family, friendship, caring), and needs for esteem and self-esteem (recognition and self-respect).

All the basic needs are *deficiency* motives. That is, they are activated by a *lack* of food, water, security, love, esteem, or other basic needs. At the top of the hierarchy we find **growth needs,** which are expressed as a need for self-actualization. The need for self-actualization is not based on deficiencies. Rather, it is a positive, life-enhancing force for personal growth (Reiss & Havercamp, 2005). Like other humanistic psychologists, Maslow believed that people are basically good. If our basic needs are met, he said, we will tend to move on to actualizing our potentials.

How are needs for self-actualization expressed? Maslow called the less powerful but humanly important actualization motives **meta-needs** (Maslow, 1970). Meta-needs are an expression of tendencies to fully develop your personal potentials. The meta-needs are:

1. Wholeness (unity)
2. Perfection (balance and harmony)
3. Completion (ending)
4. Justice (fairness)
5. Richness (complexity)
6. Simplicity (essence)
7. Aliveness (spontaneity)
8. Beauty (rightness of form)
9. Goodness (benevolence)
10. Uniqueness (individuality)
11. Playfulness (ease)
12. Truth (reality)
13. Autonomy (self-sufficiency)
14. Meaningfulness (values)

According to Maslow, we tend to move up through the hierarchy of needs, toward the meta-needs. When the meta-needs are unfulfilled, people fall into a "syndrome of decay" marked by despair, apathy, and alienation.

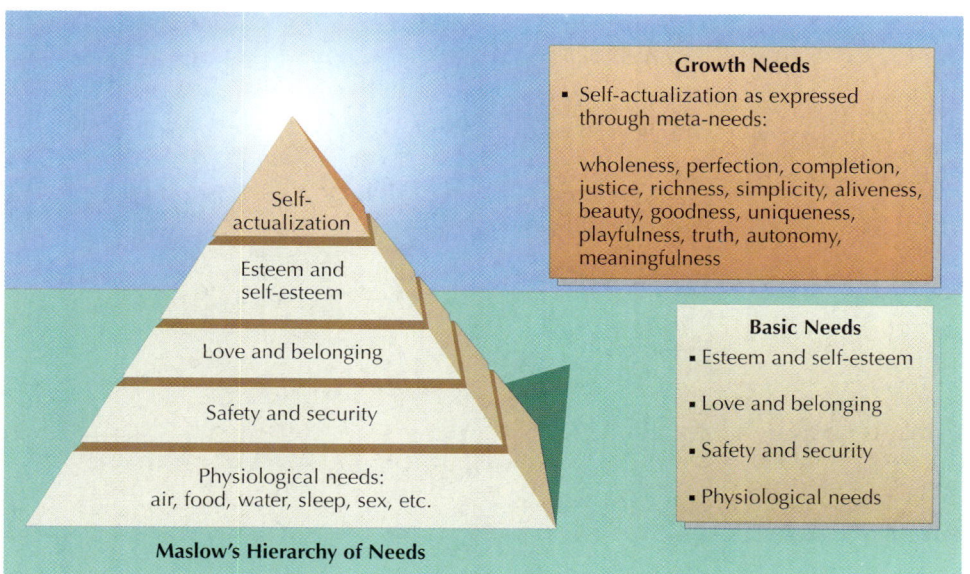

● **FIGURE 9.12** Maslow believed that lower needs in the hierarchy are dominant. Basic needs must be satisfied before growth motives are fully expressed. Desires for self-actualization are reflected in various meta-needs (see text).

Maslow's point is that mere survival or comfort is usually not enough to make a full and satisfying life. It's interesting to note, in this regard, that college students who are primarily concerned with money, personal appearance, and social recognition score lower than average in vitality, self-actualization, and general well-being (Kasser & Ryan, 1996).

Maslow's hierarchy is not well documented by research and parts of it are questionable. How, for instance, do we explain the actions of a person who fasts as part of a social protest? How can the meta-need for justice overcome the more basic need for food? (Perhaps the answer is that fasting is temporary and self-imposed.) Despite such objections, Maslow's views are a good way to understand and appreciate the rich interplay of human motives.

Are many people motivated by meta-needs? Maslow estimated that few people are primarily motivated by needs for self-actualization. Most of us are more concerned with esteem, love, or security. Perhaps this is because rewards in our society tend to encourage conformity, uniformity, and security in schools, jobs, and relationships. When was the last time you met a meta-need?

Intrinsic and Extrinsic Motivation

Some people cook for a living and consider it hard work. Others cook for pleasure and dream of opening a restaurant. For some people, mountain biking, gardening, writing, photography, or jewelry making is fun. For others the same activities are drudgery they must be paid to do. How can the same activity be "work" for one person and "play" for another?

When you do something for enjoyment or to improve your abilities, your motivation is usually *intrinsic*. **Intrinsic motivation** occurs when we act without any obvious external rewards. We simply enjoy an activity or see it as an opportunity to explore, learn, and actualize our potentials. In contrast, **extrinsic motivation** stems from external factors, such as pay, grades, rewards, obligations, and approval. Most of the activities we think of as "work" are extrinsically rewarded (Baard, Deci, & Ryan, 2004; Ryan & Deci, 2000).

Turning Play into Work

Don't extrinsic incentives strengthen motivation? Yes, they can, but not always. In fact, *excessive* rewards can decrease intrinsic motivation and spontaneous interest. For instance, in one classic study, children who were lavishly rewarded for drawing with felt-tip pens later showed little interest in playing with the

Wheelchair athletes engage in vigorous competition. Maslow considered such behavior an expression of the need for self-actualization.

Hierarchy of human needs Abraham Maslow's ordering of needs, based on their presumed strength or potency.

Basic needs The first four levels of needs in Maslow's hierarchy; lower needs tend to be more potent than higher needs.

Growth needs In Maslow's hierarchy, the higher level needs associated with self-actualization.

Meta-needs In Maslow's hierarchy, needs associated with impulses for self-actualization.

Intrinsic motivation Motivation that comes from within, rather than from external rewards; motivation based on personal enjoyment of a task or activity.

Extrinsic motivation Motivation based on obvious external rewards, obligations, or similar factors.

People who are intrinsically motivated feel free to explore creative solutions to problems. (*Left,* Dean Kaman, inventor of the Segway personal transportation device. *Right,* "Caffiends at the Beach," an entrant in the Great Arcata to Ferndale World Championship Cross Country Kinetic Sculpture Race.)

pens again (Greene & Lepper, 1974). Apparently, "play" can be turned into "work" by *requiring* people to do something they would otherwise enjoy. When we are coerced or "bribed" to act, we tend to feel as if we are "faking it." Employees who lack initiative and teenagers who reject school and learning are good examples of such reactions (Ryan & Deci, 2000).

Creativity People are more likely to be creative when they are intrinsically motivated. On the job, for instance, salaries and bonuses may increase the amount of work done. However, work *quality* is affected more by intrinsic factors, such as personal interest and freedom of choice (Nakamura & Csikszentmihalyi, 2003). When a person is intrinsically motivated, a certain amount of challenge, surprise, and complexity makes a task rewarding. When extrinsic motivation is stressed, people are less likely to solve tricky problems and come up with innovative ideas (Amabile, Hadley, & Kramer, 2002).

How can the concept of intrinsic motivation be applied? Both types of motivation are necessary. But extrinsic motivation shouldn't be overused, especially with children. To summarize: (1) If there's no intrinsic interest in an activity to begin with, you have nothing to lose by using extrinsic rewards; (2) if basic skills are lacking, extrinsic rewards may be necessary at first; (3) extrinsic rewards can focus attention on an activity so real interest will develop; (4) if extrinsic rewards are used, they should be small and phased out as soon as possible (Cameron & Pierce, 2002; Greene & Lepper, 1974). It also helps to tell children they seem to be *really interested* in drawing, playing the piano, learning a language, or whatever activity you are rewarding (Cialdini et al., 1998).

At work, it is valuable for managers to find out what each employee's interests and career goals are. People are not solely motivated by money. A chance to do challenging, interesting, and intrinsically rewarding work is often just as important. In many situations it is important to encourage intrinsic motivation, especially when children are learning new skills.

MODULE 9.3 Summary

How does arousal relate to motivation?
- Many activities are related to needs for stimulation and our efforts to maintain desired levels of arousal.
- Drives for stimulation are partially explained by arousal theory, which states that people seek to maintain ideal levels of bodily arousal. People vary in their desired level of arousal or stimulation, as measured by the Sensation-Seeking Scale.
- Optimal performance usually occurs at moderate levels of arousal, as described by an inverted U function. The Yerkes-Dodson law further states that the ideal arousal level is higher for simple tasks and lower for complex tasks.

What are social motives? Why are they important?
- Social motives, which are learned, account for much of the diversity of human motivation.
- One prominent social motive is the need for achievement (nAch). High nAch is correlated with moderate risk taking and success in many situations.
- Self-confidence greatly affects motivation in everyday life.

Are some motives more basic than others?
- Maslow's hierarchy of motives categorizes needs as either basic or growth oriented. Lower needs are assumed to be prepotent (dominant) over higher needs. Self-actualization, the highest and most fragile need, is reflected in meta-needs.
- Meta-needs are closely related to intrinsic motivation. In some situations, external rewards can undermine intrinsic motivation, enjoyment, and creativity.

KNOWLEDGE BUILDER

Arousal, Achievement, and Growth Needs

Recite

1. Exploration, manipulation, and curiosity provide evidence for the existence of _____ drives.
2. People who score high on the SSS tend to be extroverted, independent, and individuals who value change. T or F?
3. Complex tasks, such as taking a classroom test, tend to be disrupted by high levels of arousal, an effect predicted by
   a. the Sensation-Seeking Scale
   b. the Yerkes-Dodson law
   c. studies of circadian arousal patterns
   d. studies of the need for achievement
4. Two key elements of test anxiety that must be controlled are _____ and excessive _____.
5. People high in nAch
   a. prefer long shots
   b. prefer sure things
   c. are moderate risk takers
   d. prefer change and high levels of stimulation
6. The highest level of Maslow's hierarchy of motives involves
   a. meta-needs
   b. needs for safety and security
   c. needs for love and belonging
   d. extrinsic needs
7. Intrinsic motivation is often undermined in situations in which obvious external rewards are applied to a naturally enjoyable activity. T or F?
8. Which of the following is *not* a characteristic of people who score high on the Sensation-Seeking Scale?
   a. boredom susceptibility
   b. experience seeking
   c. inhibition
   d. thrill seeking

Reflect
Critical Thinking

9. Many U.S. college freshmen say that "being well-off financially" is an essential life goal and that "making more money" was a very important factor in their decision to attend college. Which meta-needs are fulfilled by "making more money"?

Relate

Does arousal theory seem to explain any of your own behavior? Think of at least one time when your performance was impaired by arousal that was too low or too high. Now think of some personal examples that illustrate the Yerkes-Dodson law.

In situations involving risk and skill, do you like to "go for broke"? Or do you prefer sure things? Do you think you are high, medium, or low in nAch?

Which levels of Maslow's hierarchy of needs occupy most of your time and energy?

Name an activity you do that is intrinsically motivated and one that is extrinsically motivated. How do they differ?

Link

Internet addresses frequently change. To find the sites listed here, visit http://www.thomsonedu.com/psychology/coon for an updated list of Internet addresses and direct links to relevant sites.

- **Sensation-Seeking Scale** Find out if you are high or low in sensation seeking.
- **The Yerkes-Dodson Law** Read more about the Yerkes-Dodson law.
- **Achievement Motivation in Business.** Find out if people high in the need for achievement make good managers.

ANSWERS

1. stimulus 2. T 3. b 4. arousal, worry 5. c 6. a 7. T 8. c 9. None of them.

MODULE 9.4 Emotion and Physiological Arousal

PICTURE THE FACES OF TERRIFIED PEOPLE fleeing the collapse of the World Trade Center towers in New York and it's easy to see that motivation and emotion are closely related. Emotions shape our relationships and color our daily activities. What are the basic parts of an emotion? How does the body respond during emotion? Let's find out.

Inside an Emotion—How Do You Feel?

SURVEY QUESTION: *What happens during emotion?*

If a mad scientist replaced your best friend's brain with a computer, how would you know that something was wrong? An absence of emotion might be one of the first telltale signs. **Emotion** is characterized by physiological arousal and changes in facial expressions, gestures, posture, and subjective feelings. As mentioned earlier, the word *emotion* derives from the Latin word meaning "to move." First, your body is physically aroused during emotion. Such bodily stirrings are what cause us to say we were "moved" by a play, a funeral, or an act of kindness. Second, we are often motivated, or moved to take action, by emotions such as fear, anger, or joy. Many of the goals we seek make us feel good. Many of the activities we avoid make us feel bad. We feel happy when we succeed and sad when we fail (Kalat & Shiota, 2007).

Emotions are linked to many basic **adaptive behaviors,** such as attacking, fleeing, seeking comfort, helping others, and reproducing. Such behaviors help us survive and adjust to changing conditions (Plutchik, 2003). However, it is also apparent that emotions can have negative effects. Stage fright or "choking" in sports can spoil performances. Hate, anger, contempt, disgust, and fear disrupt behavior and relationships. But more often, emotions aid survival. As social animals, it would be impossible for humans to live in groups, cooperate in raising children, and defend one another without positive emotional bonds of love, caring, and friendship (Buss, 2000).

A pounding heart, sweating palms, "butterflies" in the stomach, and other bodily reactions are a major element of fear, anger, joy, and other emotions. Typical **physiological changes** include changes in heart rate, blood pressure, perspiration, and other bodily stirrings. Most are caused by activity in the sympathetic nervous system and by the hormone *adrenaline*, which the adrenal glands release into the bloodstream.

Emotional expressions, or outward signs of what a person is feeling, are another ingredient of emotion. For example, when you are intensely afraid, your hands tremble, your face contorts, your posture becomes tense and defensive, and your voice changes. In general, these expressions serve to tell others what emotions we are experiencing (Hortman, 2003). **Emotional feelings** (a person's private emotional experience) are a final major element of emotion. This is the part of emotion with which we are usually most familiar.

Primary Emotions

Are some emotions more basic than others? Yes. Robert Plutchik (2003) has identified eight **primary emotions.** These are fear, surprise, sadness, disgust, anger, anticipation, joy, and trust (acceptance). If the list seems too short, it's because each emotion

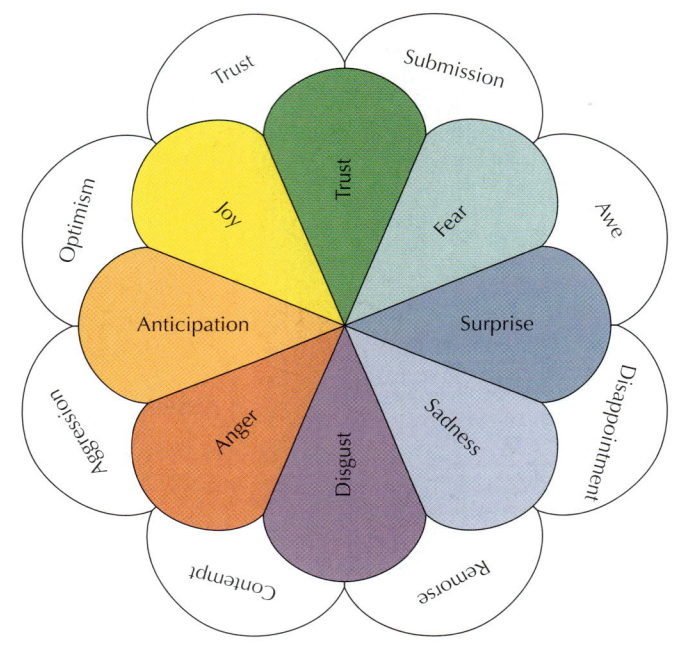

Less intense	Primary emotion	More intense
Interest	Anticipation	Vigilance
Serenity	Joy	Ecstasy
Acceptance	Trust	Admiration
Apprehension	Fear	Terror
Distraction	Surprise	Amazement
Pensiveness	Sadness	Grief
Boredom	Disgust	Loathing
Annoyance	Anger	Rage

● **FIGURE 9.13** Primary and mixed emotions. In Robert Plutchik's model there are eight primary emotions, as listed in the inner areas. Adjacent emotions may combine to give the emotions listed around the perimeter. Mixtures involving more widely separated emotions are also possible. For example, fear plus anticipation produces anxiety. (Adapted from Plutchik, 2003.)

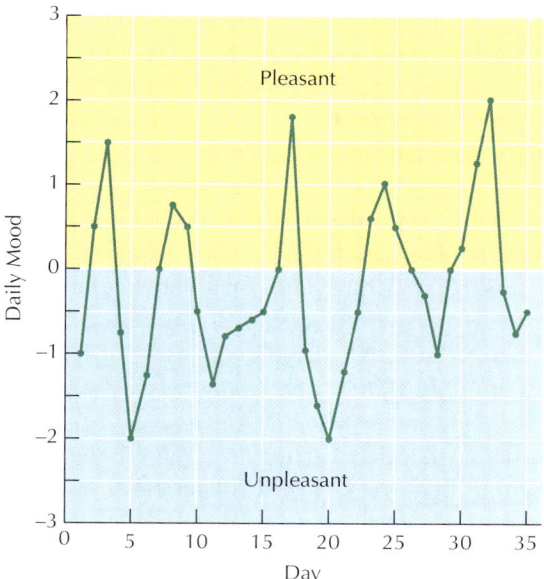

● **FIGURE 9.14** Folklore holds that people who work or attend school on a weekly schedule experience their lowest moods on "Blue Monday." Actually, moods tend to be generally lower for *most* weekdays than they are on weekends. The graph shown here plots the average daily mood ratings made by a group of college students over a 5-week period. As you can see, many people find that their moods rise and fall on a 7-day cycle. For most students, a low point tends to occur around Monday or Tuesday and a peak on Friday or Saturday. (Adapted from Larsen & Kasimatis, 1990.) In other words, moods are often entrained (pulled along) by weekly schedules.

can vary in *intensity*. When you're angry, for instance, you may feel anything from rage to simple annoyance. (See ● Fig. 9.13.)

As shown in Figure 9.13, each pair of adjacent primary emotions can be mixed to yield a third, more complex emotion. Other mixtures are also possible. For example, 5-year-old Tupac feels both joy and fear as he eats a cookie he stole from mom's cookie jar. The result? Guilt—as you may recall from your own childhood. Likewise, jealousy could be a mixture of love, anger, and fear.

A *mood* is the mildest form of emotion (● Fig. 9.14). **Moods** are low-intensity emotional states that can last for many hours or even days. Moods often affect day-to-day behavior by preparing us to act in certain ways. For example, when your neighbor Roseanne is in an irritable mood, she may react angrily to almost anything you say. When she is in a happy mood, she can easily laugh off an insult. Happy, positive moods tend to make us more adaptable in several ways. For example, when you are in a good mood, you are likely to make better decisions and you will be more helpful, efficient, creative, and peaceful (Compton, 2005).

Like our motives, our moods are closely tied to circadian rhythms. When your body temperature is at its daily low point, you are more likely to feel "down" emotionally. When body temperature is at its peak, your mood is likely to be positive—even if you missed a night of sleep (Boivin, Czeisler, & Waterhouse, 1997).

The Brain and Emotion

Emotions can be either positive or negative. Ordinarily, we might think that positive and negative emotions are mutually exclusive. But this is not the case. As Tupac's "cookie guilt" implies, it is possible to have positive and negative emotions at the same time. How is that possible? In the brain, positive emotions are processed mainly in the left hemisphere. In contrast, negative emotions are processed in the right hemisphere. The fact that positive and negative emotions are based on different brain areas helps explain why we can feel happy and sad at the same time (Canli et al., 1998). It also explains why your right foot is more ticklish than your left foot! The left hemisphere controls the right side of the body and processes positive emotions (Smith & Cahusac, 2001). Thus, most people are more ticklish on their right side. If you really want to tickle someone, be sure to "do it right."

Later we will attempt to put all the elements of emotion together into a single picture. But first, we need to look more closely at bodily arousal and emotional expressions.

Physiology and Emotion—Arousal, Sudden Death, and Lying

SURVEY QUESTION: *Can "lie detectors" really detect lies?*

An African Bushman frightened by a lion and a city dweller frightened by a prowler will react in much the same way. Such encounters usually produce muscle tension, a pounding heart, irritability, dryness of the throat and mouth, sweating, butterflies in the stomach, frequent urination, trembling, restlessness, sensitivity to loud noises, and numerous other body changes. These reactions are nearly universal because they are innate. Specifically, they are caused by the **autonomic nervous system** (**ANS**) (the neural system that connects the brain with internal organs and glands). As you

Emotion A state characterized by physiological arousal, changes in facial expression, gestures, posture, and subjective feelings.
Adaptive behaviors Actions that aid attempts to survive and adapt to changing conditions.
Physiological changes (in emotion) Alterations in heart rate, blood pressure, perspiration, and other involuntary responses.
Emotional expression Outward signs that an emotion is occurring.
Emotional feelings The private, subjective experience of having an emotion.
Primary emotions According to Robert Plutchik's theory, the most basic emotions are fear, surprise, sadness, disgust, anger, anticipation, joy, and acceptance.
Mood A low-intensity, long-lasting emotional state.
Autonomic nervous system (ANS) The system of nerves that connects the brain with the internal organs and glands.

may recall from Chapter 2, activity of the ANS is *automatic*, rather than voluntary (Kalat & Shiota, 2007).

Fight or Flight

The ANS has two divisions, the sympathetic branch and the parasympathetic branch. The two branches are active at all times. Whether you are relaxed or aroused at any moment depends on the combined activity of both branches.

What does the ANS do during emotion? In general, the **sympathetic branch** activates the body for emergency action—for "fighting or fleeing." It does this by arousing some body systems and inhibiting others (● Fig. 9.15). These changes have a purpose. Sugar is released into the bloodstream for quick energy, the heart beats faster to supply blood to the muscles, digestion is temporarily slowed, blood flow in the skin is restricted to reduce bleeding, and so forth. Such reactions improve the chances of surviving an emergency.

The **parasympathetic branch** reverses emotional arousal. This calms and relaxes the body. After a period of high emotion, the heart is slowed, the pupils return to normal size, blood pressure drops, and so forth. In addition to restoring balance, the parasympathetic system helps build up and conserve the body's energy.

The parasympathetic system responds much more slowly than the sympathetic system. That's why a pounding heart, muscle tension, and other signs of arousal don't fade for 20 or 30 minutes after you feel an intense emotion, such as fear. Moreover, after a strong emotional shock, the parasympathetic system may overreact and lower blood pressure too much. This can cause you to become dizzy or faint after seeing something shocking, such as a horrifying accident.

Sudden Death An overreaction to intense emotion is called a **parasympathetic rebound.** If the rebound is severe, it can sometimes cause death. In times of war, for instance, combat can be so savage that some soldiers literally die of fear (Moritz & Zamchech, 1946). Apparently, such deaths occur because the parasympathetic nervous system slows the heart to a stop. Even in civilian life this is possible. In one case, a terrified young woman was admitted to a hospital because she felt she was going to die. A backwoods midwife had predicted that the woman's two sisters would die before their sixteenth and twenty-first birthdays. Both died as predicted. The midwife also predicted that this woman would die before her twenty-third birthday. She was found dead in her hospital bed the day after she was admitted. It was 2 days before her twenty-third birthday (Seligman, 1989). The woman was an apparent victim of her own terror.

Is the parasympathetic nervous system always responsible for such deaths? Probably not. For older persons or those with heart problems, sympathetic effects may be enough to bring about heart attack and collapse. For example, five times more people than usual died of heart attacks on the day of a major 1994 earthquake in Los Angeles (Leor, Poole, & Kloner, 1996). In Asia, the number 4 is

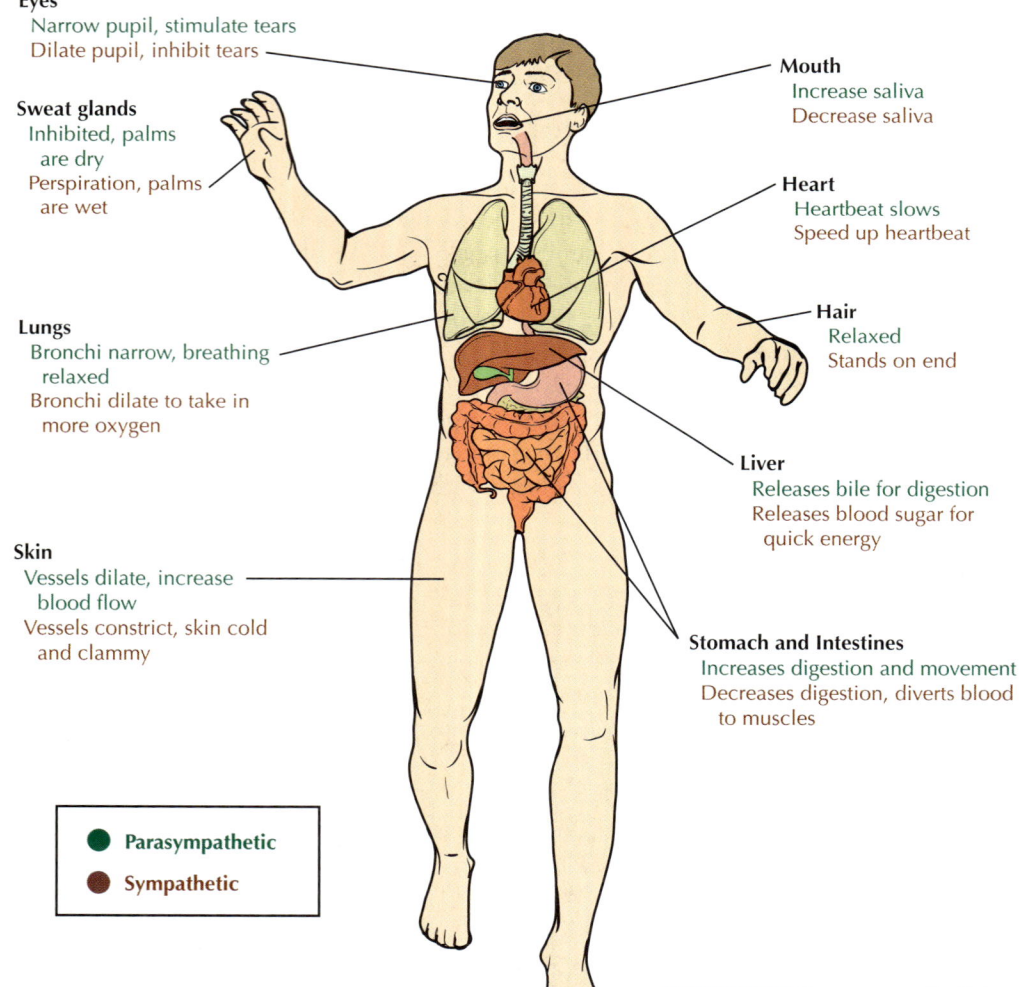

● **FIGURE 9.15** The parasympathetic branch of the ANS calms and quiets the body. The sympathetic branch arouses the body and prepares it for emergency action.

● **FIGURE 9.16** *(left)* A typical polygraph includes devices for measuring heart rate, blood pressure, respiration, and galvanic skin response. Pens mounted on the top of the machine make a record of bodily responses on a moving strip of paper. *(right)* Changes in the area marked by the arrow indicate emotional arousal. If such responses appear when a person answers a question he or she may be lying, but other causes of arousal are also possible.

considered unlucky, and more heart patients die on the fourth day of the month than any other day. Because they fear they will die on an "unlucky day," their chance of dying actually increases (Phillips et al., 2001).

Lie Detectors

We know that people are not always truthful. As many as 25 percent of all wrongful convictions include false confessions as evidence (Kassin, 2005). If you can't count on someone's word, what can you trust? The most popular method for detecting falsehoods measures the bodily changes that accompany emotion. However, the accuracy of "lie detector" tests is doubtful, and they can be a serious invasion of privacy (Lykken, 2001; National Academy of Sciences, 2002).

What is a lie detector? Do lie detectors really detect lies? The lie detector is more accurately called a **polygraph,** a word that means "many writings" (● Fig. 9.16). The polygraph was invented in 1915 by psychologist William Marston, who also created the comic book character *Wonder Woman,* a superhero whose "magic lasso" could force people to tell the truth (Grubin & Madsen, 2005). Although the polygraph is popularly known as a lie detector because the police use it for that purpose, in reality the polygraph is not a lie detector at all (Bunn, 2007). The device only records *general emotional arousal*—it can't tell the difference between lying and fear, anxiety, or excitement (Lykken, 2001).

A typical polygraph records changes in heart rate, blood pressure, breathing, and the galvanic skin response. The galvanic skin response (GSR) is recorded from the hand by electrodes that measure skin conductance or, more simply, sweating.

When trying to detect a lie, the polygraph operator begins by asking irrelevant (neutral, nonemotional) questions, such as, "Is your name (person's name)?" "Did you eat lunch today?" and so forth. This establishes a "baseline" for normal emotional responses. Then the examiner asks relevant questions: "Did you murder Hensley?" Presumably, only a guilty person will become anxious or emotional if they lie when answering relevant questions.

Wouldn't a person be nervous just from being questioned? Yes, but to minimize this problem, skilled polygraph examiners ask a series of questions with critical items mixed among them. An innocent person may respond emotionally to the whole procedure, but only a guilty person is supposed to respond more to key questions. For example, a suspected bank robber might be shown several pictures and asked, "Was it the teller who was robbed this person? Was it this person?"

As an alternative, subjects may be asked **control questions,** which are designed to make almost anyone anxious: "Have you ever stolen anything from your place of work?" Typically, such questions are very difficult to answer truthfully with an unqualified no. In theory they show how a person reacts to doubt or misgivings. The person's reaction to critical questions can then be compared with responses to control questions.

Even when questioning is done properly, lie detection may be inaccurate (Grubin & Madsen, 2005). For example, a man named Floyd Fay was convicted of murdering his friend Fred Ery. To prove his innocence, Fay volunteered to take a lie detector test, which he failed. Fay spent 2 years in prison before the real killer confessed to the crime. Psychologist David Lykken (1998, 2001) has documented many cases in which innocent people were jailed after being convicted on the basis of polygraph evidence.

If Floyd Fay was innocent, why did he fail the test? Put yourself in his place, and it's easy to see why. Imagine the

---

Sympathetic branch A part of the ANS that activates the body at times of stress.

Parasympathetic branch A part of the autonomic system that quiets the body and conserves energy.

Parasympathetic rebound Excess activity in the parasympathetic nervous system following a period of intense emotion.

Polygraph A device for recording heart rate, blood pressure, respiration, and galvanic skin response; commonly called a "lie detector."

Control questions In a polygraph exam, questions that almost always provoke anxiety.

CRITICAL THINKING

To Catch a Terrorist

An airport check-in agent asks a passenger if he packed his own luggage. He says he did, but he is sitting in a booth that records infrared images of the heat patterns on his face. The images reveal stress, suggesting that he is lying. His luggage is searched and an otherwise undetectable explosive device is confiscated, averting a potential disaster.

Although the above scenario is not yet a reality, it is not as far-fetched as you might think. The growing realization that polygraph tests are not very accurate could not have come at a worse time for national security (Knight, 2005). The infrared scanner is just one alternative currently under development. Preliminary research indicates that infrared face scans are at least as accurate as polygraphs at detecting lying (Pavlidis, Eberhardt, & Levine, 2002).

Other new techniques look directly at brain activity, thus bypassing the traditional approach of measuring indirect signs of emotional arousal. For example, psychologist Daniel Langleben theorizes that a liar must inhibit telling the truth in order to lie (Langleben et al., 2002). Thus, extra brain areas must be activated to tell a lie, which can be seen in fMRI brain images (see Module 2.2) when people are lying.

Even if new methods are used, the key problem remains: How can we avoid falsely classifying liars as truth tellers and truth tellers as liars? Until that can be done with acceptable accuracy, the new techniques may have no more value than the polygraph does.

---

examiner asking, "Did you kill Fred?" Because you knew Fred, and you are a suspect, it's no secret that this is a critical question. What would happen to *your* heart rate, blood pressure, breathing, and perspiration under such circumstances?

Proponents of lie detection claim it is 95 percent accurate. But in one study, accuracy was dramatically lowered when people thought about past emotional experiences as they answered irrelevant questions (Ben-Shakhar & Dolev, 1996). Similarly, the polygraph may be thrown off by self-inflicted pain, by tranquilizing drugs, or by people who can lie without anxiety (Waid & Orne, 1982). Worst of all, the test is much more likely to label an innocent person guilty, rather than a guilty person innocent. In studies involving real crimes, an average of 1 innocent person in 5 was rated as guilty by the lie detector (Lykken, 2001). For such reasons, the National Academy of Sciences recently concluded that polygraph tests should not be used to screen employees (National Academy of Sciences, 2002).

Despite the lie detector's flaws, you may be tested for employment or for other reasons. Should this occur, the best advice is to remain calm; then actively challenge the results if the machine wrongly questions your honesty. And beware; newer, possibly more accurate, methods of detecting lies are under development. (See "To Catch a Terrorist.")

MODULE 9.4 Summary

What happens during emotion?

- Emotions can be disruptive, but overall they help us to adapt and survive. An emotion consists of physiological changes, adaptive behavior, emotional expressions, and emotional feelings.
- The primary emotions of fear, surprise, sadness, disgust, anger, anticipation, joy, and acceptance can be mixed to produce more complex emotional experiences.
- Body changes that occur during emotion are caused by the hormone adrenaline and by activity in the autonomic nervous system (ANS).
- The sympathetic branch of the ANS is primarily responsible for arousing the body, the parasympathetic branch for quieting it.
- *Can "lie detectors" really detect lies?*
- The polygraph, or "lie detector," measures emotional arousal (rather than lying) by monitoring heart rate, blood pressure, breathing rate, and the galvanic skin response (GSR).
- Under some circumstances, the accuracy of the lie detector can be quite low.

KNOWLEDGE BUILDER

Emotion and Physiological Arousal

Recite

1. Many of the physiological changes associated with emotion are caused by secretion of the hormone
   a. atropine
   b. adrenaline
   c. attributine
   d. amoduline
2. Emotional _____ often serve to communicate a person's emotional state to others.
3. Awe, remorse, and disappointment are among the primary emotions listed by Robert Plutchik. T or F?
4. Emotional arousal is closely related to activity of the _____ nervous system.
5. Preparing the body for "fighting or fleeing" is largely the job of the
   a. paraventricular nucleus
   b. sympathetic branch
   c. GSR
   d. left hemisphere
6. The parasympathetic system inhibits digestion and raises blood pressure and heart rate. T or F?
7. What body changes are measured by a polygraph?

Reflect
Critical Thinking
8. Can you explain why people "cursed" by shamans or "witch doctors" sometimes actually die?

Relate

How did your most emotional moment of the past week affect your behavior, expressions, feelings, and bodily state? Could you detect both sympathetic and parasympathetic effects?

Make a list of the emotions you consider to be most basic. To what extent do they agree with Plutchik's list?

What did you think about lie detector tests before reading this chapter? What do you think now?

Link

Internet addresses frequently change. To find the sites listed here, visit http://www.thomsonedu.com/psychology/coon for an updated list of Internet addresses and direct links to relevant sites.

- **The Affective System** An overview of the affective system that provides information about how particular parts of the brain are associated with different aspects of emotion, a classification of basic emotions, and an explanation of how emotions impact our behavior.
- **When a Patient Has No Story To Tell** Read the case histories of several people with alexithymia.
- **Learn the Truth about Lie Detectors** Read arguments against the use of polygraph testing.

ANSWERS

1. b 2. expressions 3. F 4. autonomic 5. b 6. F 7. heart rate, blood pressure, breathing rate, galvanic skin response 8. In cultures where there is deep belief in magic or voodoo, a person who thinks that she or he has been cursed may become uncontrollably emotional. After several days of intense terror, a parasympathetic rebound is likely. If the rebound is severe enough, it can lead to physical collapse and "voodoo death."

MODULE 9.5 Emotional Expression and Theories of Emotion

NEXT TO OUR OWN FEELINGS, the expressions of others are the most familiar aspect of emotion. In this module we will address such questions as: Are emotional expressions universal? Do they really reveal what others are feeling? How are they affected by culture and learning? In addition, we will explore several theories of emotion. Explanations of emotion are important because the better you understand your emotions, the better you will be able to manage them.

● **FIGURE 9.18** Is anger expressed the same way in different cultures? Masks that are meant to be frightening or threatening are strikingly similar around the world. Most have an open, downward-curved mouth and diagonal or triangular eyes, eyebrows, nose, cheeks, and chin. (Keep this list in mind next Halloween.) Obviously, the pictured mask is not meant to be warm and cuddly. Your ability to "read" its emotional message suggests that basic emotional expressions have universal biological roots (Aronoff, Barclay, & Stevenson, 1988).

Expressing Emotions—Making Faces and Talking Bodies

SURVEY QUESTION: *How accurately are emotions expressed by the face and "body language"?*

Next to our own feelings, the expressions of others are the most familiar part of emotion. Are emotional expressions a carryover from human evolution? Charles Darwin thought so. Darwin (1872) observed that angry tigers, monkeys, dogs, and humans all bare their teeth in the same way. Psychologists believe that emotional expressions evolved to communicate our feelings to others, which aids survival. Such messages give valuable hints about what other people are likely to do next (Kalat & Shiota, 2007). For instance, in one study, people were able to detect angry and scheming faces faster than happy, sad, or neutral faces (● Fig. 9.17). Presumably, we are especially sensitive to threatening faces because they warn us of possible harm (Tipples, Atkinson, & Young, 2002).

Facial Expressions

Are emotional expressions the same for all people? Basic expressions appear to be fairly universal (● Fig. 9.18). Facial expressions of *fear, anger, disgust, sadness, surprise,* and *happiness*

Angry Sad Happy Scheming Neutral

● **FIGURE 9.17** When shown groups of simplified faces (without labels), the angry and scheming faces "jumped out" at people faster than sad, happy, or neutral faces. An ability to rapidly detect threatening expressions probably helped our ancestors survive. (Adapted from Tipples, Atkinson, & Young, 2002.)

(enjoyment) are recognized around the world (Smith et al., 2005). *Contempt* and *interest* may also be universal, but researchers are less certain of these expressions (Ekman, 1993). Notice that this list covers most of the primary emotions described earlier. Children who are born blind have little opportunity to learn emotional expressions from others. Even so, they also display basic expressions in the same way sighted people do (Galati, Scherer, & Ricci-Bitti, 1997). It's also nice to note that a smile is the most universal and easily recognized facial expression of emotion.

Some facial expressions are shaped by learning and may be found only in specific cultures. Among the Chinese, for example, sticking out the tongue is a gesture of surprise, not of disrespect or teasing. If a person comes from another culture, it is wise to remember that you may easily misunderstand his or her expressions. At such times, knowing the social *context* in which an expression occurs helps clarify its meaning (Carroll & Russell, 1996; Kalat & Shiota, 2007).

Your face can produce some 20,000 different expressions, which makes it the most expressive part of your body. Most of these are *facial blends* (a mixture of two or more basic expressions). Imagine, for example, that you just received an F on an unfair test. Quite likely, your eyes, eyebrows, and forehead would reveal anger, and your mouth would be turned downward in a frown.

Most of us believe we can fairly accurately tell what others are feeling by observing their facial expressions. If thousands

400

of facial blends occur, how do we make such judgments? The answer is that facial expressions can be boiled down to three basic dimensions: *pleasantness-unpleasantness, attention-rejection,* and *activation* (or arousal) (Schlosberg, 1954). By smiling when you give a friend a hard time, you add an emotional message of acceptance to the verbal insult, which changes it's meaning. As they say in movie Westerns, it makes a big difference to "Smile when you say that, partner."

Cultural Differences in Emotion

How many times have you been angry this week? If it was more than once, you're not unusual. Anger is a very common emotion in Western cultures. Very likely this is because our culture emphasizes personal independence and a free expression of individual rights and needs. In North America, anger is widely viewed as a "natural" reaction to feeling that you have been treated unfairly.

In contrast, many Asian cultures place a high value on group harmony. In Asia, expressing anger in public is less common and anger is regarded as less "natural." The reason for this is that anger tends to separate people. Thus, being angry is at odds with a culture that values cooperation. Culture also influences positive emotions. In America, we tend to have positive feelings such as pride, happiness, and superiority, which emphasize our role as *individuals*. In Japan, positive feelings are more often linked with membership in groups (friendly feelings, closeness to others, and respect) (Kitayama, Markus, & Kurokawa, 2000; Markus et al., 2006).

It is common to think of emotion as an individual event. However, as you can see, emotion is shaped by cultural ideas, values, and practices (Mesquita & Markus, 2004).

Gender and Emotion *Women have a reputation for being "more emotional" than men. Are they?* Compared with women, men in Western cultures are more likely to have difficulty expressing their emotions. According to psychologist Ronald Levant, although male babies start out life more emotionally expressive than female babies, little boys soon learn to "toughen up," beginning in early childhood (Levant et al., 2006). As a result, men have learned to curtail the expression of most of their emotions, although not to the extent of Robert, the alexithymic man we met at the beginning of the chapter. Whereas girls are encouraged to express sadness, fear, shame, and guilt, boys are more likely to be allowed to express only anger and hostility (Fischer et al., 2004).

But does this mean that men experience emotions less than women? Ronald Levant believes that men who fail to express emotions become less aware of their own emotions. For many men, an inability to express feelings or to even be aware of them is a major barrier to having close, satisfying relationships with others (Levant, 2003). Blunted emotions may even contribute to tragedies like the mass murders at Columbine High School in Littleton, Colorado. For many young males, anger is the only emotion they can freely feel and express.

The expression of emotion is strongly influenced by learning. As you have no doubt observed, women cry more often, longer, and more intensely than men do. Men begin learning early in childhood to suppress crying—possibly to the detriment of their emotional health (Levant, 2003). Many men are especially unwilling to engage in public displays of emotion, in contrast to these women, who are grieving for the victims of a 2005 school siege in Beslan, Russia, which left nearly 200 children dead.

Body Language

If a friend walked up to you and said, "Hey, ugly, what are you doing?" would you be offended? Probably not, because such remarks are usually delivered with a big grin. The facial and bodily gestures of emotion speak a language all their own and add to what a person says.

Kinesics (kih-NEEZ-iks) is the study of communication through body movement, posture, gestures, and facial expres-

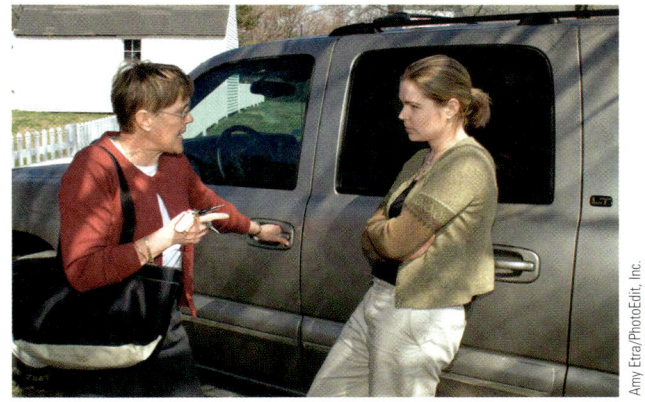

Emotions are often unconsciously revealed by gestures and body positioning.

Kinesics Study of the meaning of body movements, posture, hand gestures, and facial expressions; commonly called "body language."

sions (Harrigan, 2006). Informally, we call it body language. To see a masterful use of body language, turn off the sound on a television and watch a popular entertainer or politician at work.

What kinds of messages are sent with body language? Again, it is important to realize that cultural learning affects the meaning of gestures. What, for instance, does it mean if you touch your thumb and first finger together to form a circle? In North America it means "Everything is fine" or "A-okay." In France and Belgium it means "You're worth zero." In southern Italy it means "You're an ass!" When the layer of culturally defined meanings is removed, it is more realistic to say that body language reveals an overall emotional tone (underlying emotional state).

The body telegraphs other feelings. The most general "messages" involve *relaxation* or *tension* and *liking* or *disliking*. Relaxation is expressed by casually positioning the arms and legs, leaning back (if sitting), and spreading the arms and legs. Liking is expressed mainly by leaning toward a person or object. Thus, body positioning can reveal feelings that would normally be concealed. Who do you "lean toward"?

Theories of Emotion—Several Ways to Fear a Bear

SURVEY QUESTION: *How do psychologists explain emotions?*

Is it possible to explain what takes place during emotion? How are arousal, behavior, cognition, expressions, and feelings interrelated? Theories of emotion offer different answers to these questions. Let's explore five views. Each appears to have a part of the truth, so we will try to put them all together in the end.

The James-Lange Theory

You're hiking in the woods when a bear suddenly steps out onto the trail. What will happen next? Common sense tells us that we will then feel fear, become aroused, and run (and sweat and yell). But is this the true order of events? In the 1880s, William James and Carl Lange (LON-geh) proposed that common sense had it backward. According to the **James-Lange theory,** bodily arousal (such as increased heart rate) does not *follow* a feeling such as fear. Instead, they argued, *emotional feelings follow bodily arousal.* Thus, we see a bear, run, are aroused, and *then* feel fear as we become aware of our bodily reactions (● Fig. 9.19).

To support his ideas, James pointed out that we often do not experience an emotion until after reacting. For example, imagine that you are driving. Suddenly a car pulls out in front of you. You swerve and skid to an abrupt halt at the side of the road. Only after you have come to a stop do you notice

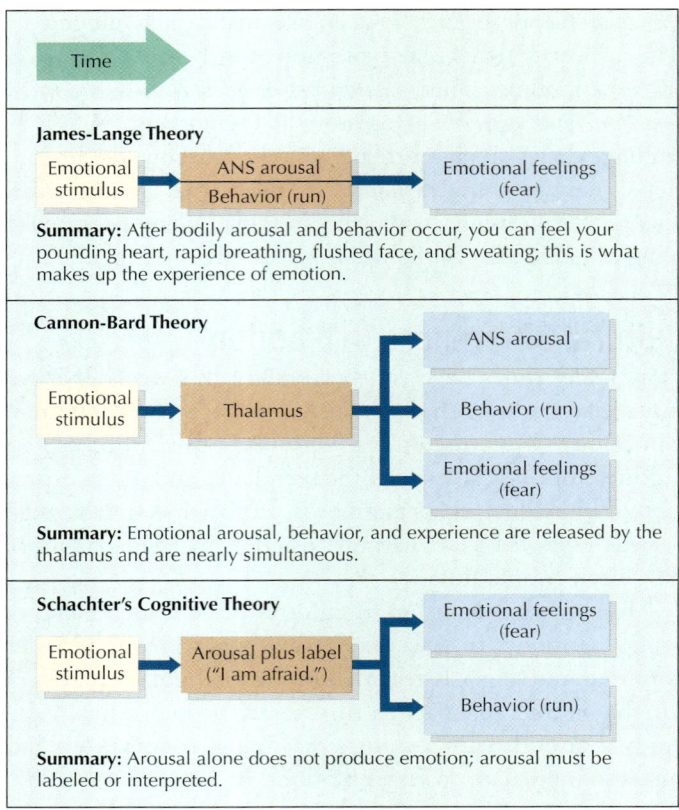

● **FIGURE 9.19** Earlier theories of emotion.

your pounding heart, rapid breathing, and tense muscles—and recognize your fear.

The Cannon-Bard Theory

Walter Cannon (1932) and Phillip Bard disagreed with the James-Lange theory. According to the **Cannon-Bard theory,** emotional feelings and bodily arousal *occur at the same time.* Cannon and Bard believed that seeing a bear activates the thalamus in the brain. The thalamus, in turn, alerts the cortex and the hypothalamus for action. The cortex produces our emotional feelings and emotional behavior. The hypothalamus triggers a chain of events that arouses the body. Thus, if you see a dangerous-looking bear, brain activity will simultaneously produce bodily arousal, running, and a feeling of fear. (See Fig. 9.19.)

Schachter's Cognitive Theory of Emotion

The previous theories are mostly concerned with our physical responses. Stanley Schachter realized that cognitive (mental) factors also enter into emotion. According to **Schachter's cognitive theory,** emotion occurs when we apply a particular *label* to general physical *arousal*. Schachter believed that when we are aroused, we have a need to interpret our feelings. Assume, for instance, that someone sneaks up behind you on a dark street and says "Boo!" No matter who the person is, your body will be aroused (pounding heart, sweating palms, and so on). If the person is a total stranger, you might interpret this arousal as fear; if the person is a close friend, the arousal may be labeled as surprise or delight. The label (such as anger, fear, or happiness) you apply to bodily arousal is influenced by your past experiences, the situation, and the reactions of others. (See Fig. 9.19.)

Support for the cognitive theory of emotion comes from an experiment in which people watched a slapstick movie (Schachter & Wheeler, 1962). Before viewing the movie, one third of the people received an arousing injection of adrenaline, one third got a placebo (salt water) injection, and one third were given a tranquilizer. People who received the adrenaline rated the movie funniest and laughed the most while watching it. In contrast, those given the tranquilizer were least amused. The placebo group fell in between.

According to the cognitive theory of emotion, individuals who received adrenaline had a stirred-up body but no explanation for what they were feeling. Consequently, they became happy when the movie implied that their arousal was due to amusement. This and similar experiments make it clear that emotion is much more than just an agitated body. Perception, experience, attitudes, judgment, and many other mental factors also affect the emotions we feel. Schachter's theory would predict, then, that if you met a bear, you would be aroused. If the bear seemed unfriendly, you would interpret your arousal as fear, and if the bear offered to shake your "paw," you would be happy, amazed, and relieved!

Attribution We now move from slapstick movies and fear of bear bodies to an appreciation of bare bodies. Researcher Stuart Valins (1967) added an interesting wrinkle to Schachter's theory of emotion. According to Valins, arousal can be attributed to various sources—a process that alters our perceptions of emotion. To demonstrate **attribution,** Valins (1966) showed male college students a series of photographs of nude females. While watching the photographs, each student heard an amplified heartbeat that he believed was his own. In reality, students were listening to a recorded heartbeat carefully designed to beat *louder* and *stronger* when some (but not all) of the slides were shown.

After watching the slides, each student was asked to say which was most attractive. Students who heard the false heartbeat consistently rated slides paired with a "pounding heart" as the most attractive. In other words, when a student saw a slide and heard his heart beat louder, he attributed his "emotion" to the slide. His interpretation seems to have been, "Now that one I like!" His next reaction, perhaps, was "But why?" Later research suggests that subjects persuaded themselves that the slide really was more attractive in order to explain their apparent arousal (Truax, 1983).

That seems somewhat artificial. Does it really make any difference what arousal is attributed to? Yes. To illustrate attribution in the "real world," consider what happens when parents interfere with the budding romance of a son or daughter. Often, trying to separate a young couple *intensifies* their feelings. Meddling parents add frustration, anger, and fear or excitement (as in seeing each other "on the sly") to the couple's feelings. Because they already care for each other, they are likely to attribute all this added emotion to "true love" (Walster, 1971).

Attribution theory predicts that you are most likely to "love" someone who gets you stirred up emotionally (Foster et al., 1998). This is true even when fear, anger, frustration, or rejection is part of the formula. Thus, if you want to successfully propose marriage, take your intended to the middle of a narrow, windswept suspension bridge over a deep chasm and look deeply into his or her eyes. As your beloved's heart pounds wildly (from being on the bridge, not from your irresistible charms), say, "I love you." Attribution theory predicts that your companion will conclude, "Oh wow, I must love you, too."

The preceding is not as farfetched as it may seem. In an ingenious study, a female psychologist interviewed men in a park. Some were on a swaying suspension bridge 230 feet above a river. The rest were on a solid wooden bridge just 10 feet above the ground. After the interview, the psychologist

Which theory of emotion best describes the reactions of these people? Given the complexity of emotion, each theory appears to possess an element of truth.

James-Lange theory States that emotional feelings follow bodily arousal and come from awareness of such arousal.
Cannon-Bard theory States that activity in the thalamus causes emotional feelings and bodily arousal to occur simultaneously.
Schachter's cognitive theory States that emotions occur when physical arousal is labeled or interpreted on the basis of experience and situational cues.
Attribution The mental process of assigning causes to events. In emotion, the process of attributing arousal to a particular source.

gave each man her telephone number, so he could "find out about the results" of the study. Men interviewed on the suspension bridge were much more likely to give the "lady from the park" a call (Dutton & Aron, 1974). Apparently, these men experienced heightened arousal, which they interpreted as attraction to the experimenter—a clear case of love at first fright!

The Facial Feedback Hypothesis

Schachter added thinking and interpretation (cognition) to our view of emotion, but the picture still seems incomplete. What about expressions? How do they influence emotion? As Charles Darwin observed, the face is very central to emotion—perhaps it is more than just an "emotional billboard."

Psychologist Carrol Izard (1977, 1990) was among the first to suggest that the face does, indeed, affect emotion. According to Izard, emotions cause innately programmed changes in facial expression. Sensations from the face then provide cues to the brain that help us determine what emotion we are feeling. This idea is known as the **facial feedback hypothesis** (Soussignan, 2002). Stated another way, it says that having facial expressions and becoming aware of them is what influences our private emotional experience. Exercise, for instance, arouses the body, but we don't experience this arousal as emotion because it does not trigger emotional expressions.

Psychologist Paul Ekman takes this idea one step further. He believes that "making faces" can actually cause emotion (Ekman, 1993). In one study, participants were guided as they arranged their faces, muscle by muscle, into expressions of surprise, disgust, sadness, anger, fear, and happiness (● Fig. 9.20). At the same time, each person's bodily reactions were monitored.

Contrary to what you might expect, "making faces" can affect the autonomic nervous system, as shown by changes in heart rate and skin temperature. In addition, each facial expression produces a different pattern of activity. An angry face, for instance, raises heart rate and skin temperature, whereas disgust lowers both (Ekman, Levenson, & Friesen et al., 1983). Other studies have confirmed that posed expressions alter emotions and bodily activity (Duclos & Laird, 2001; Soussignan, 2002).

In a fascinating experiment on facial feedback, people rated how funny they thought cartoons were while holding a pen crosswise in their mouths. Those who held the pen in their teeth thought the cartoons were funnier than did people who held the pen in their lips. Can you guess why? The answer is that if you hold a pen with your teeth, you are forced to form a smile. Holding it with the lips makes a frown. As predicted by the facial feedback hypothesis, emotional experiences were influenced by the facial expressions that people made (Strack, Martin, & Stepper, 1988). Next time you're feeling sad, bite a pen!

It appears, then, that not only do emotions influence expressions, but expressions influence emotions, as shown here (Duclos & Laird, 2001).

Contracted Facial Muscles	Felt Emotion
Forehead	Surprise
Brow	Anger
Mouth (down)	Sadness
Mouth (smile)	Joy

This could explain an interesting effect you have probably observed. When you are feeling "down," forcing yourself to smile will sometimes be followed by an actual improvement in your mood (Kleinke, Peterson, & Rutledge, 1998).

If smiling can improve a person's mood, is it a good idea to inhibit negative emotions? For an answer, see "Suppressing Emotion—Don't Turn Off the Music."

Emotional Appraisal

According to Richard Lazarus (1991a, 1991b), the emotions you experience are greatly influenced by how you think about an event in the first place. **Emotional appraisal** refers to evaluating the personal meaning of a stimulus: Is it good/bad,

● **FIGURE 9.20** Facial feedback and emotion. Participants in Ekman's study formed facial expressions like those normally observed during emotion. When they did this, emotion-like changes took place in their body activity. (Adapted from Ekman et al., 1983.)

THE CLINICAL FILE

Suppressing Emotion—Don't Turn Off the Music

According to popular media, we are supposed to be happy all the time (Hecht, 2007). Thus, while sharing a beautiful day with friends, you can freely express your happiness. Yet real emotional life has its ups and downs. Often we try to appear less emotional than we really are, especially when we are feeling negative emotions. Have you ever been angry with a friend in public? Embarrassed by someone's behavior at a party? Disgusted by someone's table manners? In such circumstances, people are quite good at suppressing outward signs of emotion.

However, restraining emotion can actually increase activity in the sympathetic nervous system. In other words, hiding emotion requires a lot of effort. Suppressing emotions can also impair thinking and memory, as you devote energy to self-control. Thus, although suppressing emotion allows us to appear calm and collected on the outside, this cool appearance comes at a high cost (Richards & Gross, 2000). People who suppress emotions cope poorly with life and are prone to depression and other problems (Lynch et al., 2001).

Conversely, people who express their emotions generally experience better emotional and physical health (Lumley, 2004; Pennebaker, 2004). Paying attention to our negative emotions can also lead us to think more clearly about the positive *and* the negative. The end result is better decision making, which can increase our overall happiness in the long run (Norem, 2002). Usually, it's better to manage emotions than it is to suppress them. You will find some suggestions for managing emotions in the upcoming "Psychology in Action" section.

threatening/supportive, relevant/irrelevant, and so on. Some examples of emotional appraisals and the emotions they give rise to can be found in ■ Table 9.2.

A Contemporary Model of Emotion

To summarize, James and Lange were right that feedback from arousal and behavior adds to our emotional experiences. Cannon and Bard were right about the timing of events. Schachter showed us that cognition is important. In fact, psychologists are increasingly aware that how you *appraise* a situation greatly affects your emotions (Strongman, 2003). Richard Lazarus stressed the importance of emotional appraisal. Let's put these ideas together in a single model of emotion (● Fig. 9.21).

Imagine that a large snarling dog lunges at you with its teeth bared. A modern view of your emotional reactions goes

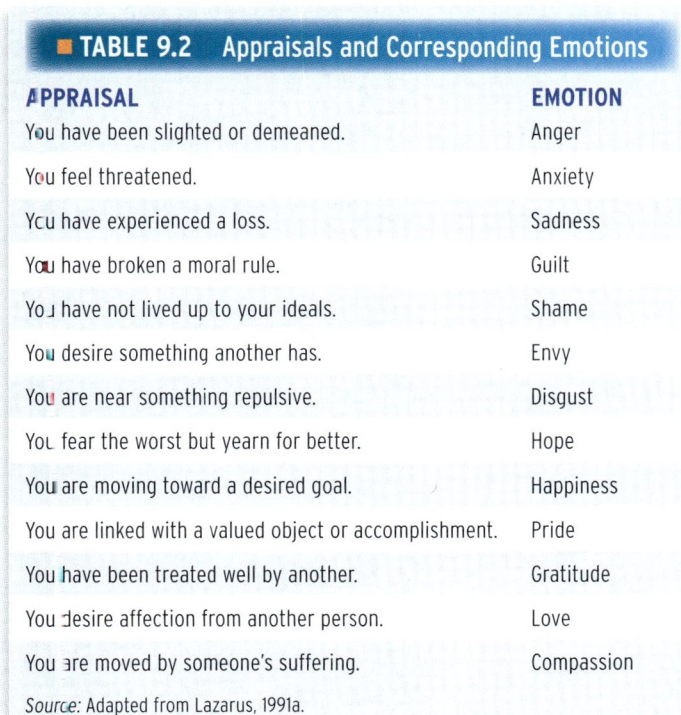

■ **TABLE 9.2** Appraisals and Corresponding Emotions

APPRAISAL	EMOTION
You have been slighted or demeaned.	Anger
You feel threatened.	Anxiety
You have experienced a loss.	Sadness
You have broken a moral rule.	Guilt
You have not lived up to your ideals.	Shame
You desire something another has.	Envy
You are near something repulsive.	Disgust
You fear the worst but yearn for better.	Hope
You are moving toward a desired goal.	Happiness
You are linked with a valued object or accomplishment.	Pride
You have been treated well by another.	Gratitude
You desire affection from another person.	Love
You are moved by someone's suffering.	Compassion

Source: Adapted from Lazarus, 1991a.

● **FIGURE 9.21** A contemporary model of emotion.

Facial feedback hypothesis States that sensations from facial expressions help define what emotion a person feels.

Emotional appraisal Evaluating the personal meaning of a stimulus or situation.

something like this: An *emotional stimulus* (the dog) is *appraised* (judged) as a threat or other cause for emotion. (You think to yourself, "Uh oh, big trouble!") Your appraisal gives rise to *ANS arousal* (your heart pounds, and your body becomes stirred up) and *cognitive labeling*. The appraisal also releases *innate emotional expressions*. (Your face twists into a mask of fear, and your posture becomes tense.) At the same time, your appraisal leads to *adaptive behavior*. (You run from the dog.) It also causes a change in consciousness that you recognize as the subjective experience of fear. (The intensity of this *emotional feeling* is directly related to the amount of ANS arousal taking place in your body.)

Each element of emotion—ANS arousal, labeling, adaptive behavior, subjective experience, and your emotional expressions—may further alter your emotional appraisal of the situation, as well as your thoughts, judgments, and perceptions. Thus, according to the facial feedback hypothesis, your facial expression will further influence your emotion. Such changes affect each of the other reactions, which again alters your appraisal and interpretation of events. Thus, emotion may blossom, change course, or diminish as it proceeds. Note too that the original emotional stimulus can be external, like the attacking dog, or internal, such as a memory of being chased by a dog, rejected by a lover, or praised by a friend. That's why mere thoughts and memories can make us fearful, sad, or happy (Strongman, 2003).

Our discussion suggests that emotion is greatly influenced by how you think about an event. For example, if another driver "cuts you off" on the highway, you could become very angry. But if you do, you will add 15 minutes of emotional upset to your day. By changing your appraisal, you could just as easily choose to laugh at the other driver's childish behavior—and minimize the emotional wear-and-tear (Gross, 2001).

A Look Ahead In the "Psychology in Action" section of this chapter we will look further at the impact of emotional appraisals. Before we continue, you might want to appraise your learning with the exercises that follow.

MODULE 9.5 Summary

How accurately are emotions expressed by the face and "body language"?

- Basic facial expressions of fear, anger, disgust, sadness, and happiness are universal. Contempt, surprise, and interest may be, too.
- Body gestures and movements (body language) express general emotional tone rather than specific universal messages.
- Facial expressions reveal pleasantness versus unpleasantness, attention versus rejection, and a person's degree of emotional activation. Body positioning expresses relaxation or tension and liking or disliking.

How do psychologists explain emotions?

- The James-Lange theory says that emotional experience follows bodily reactions. In contrast, the Cannon-Bard theory says that bodily reactions and emotional experiences occur at the same time.
- Schachter's cognitive theory emphasizes that labeling bodily arousal can determine what emotion you feel. Emotions are also influenced by attribution (ascribing arousal to a particular source).
- The facial feedback hypothesis holds that facial expressions help define the emotions we feel.
- Contemporary views of emotion emphasize the effects of cognitive appraisals. Also, our feelings and actions change as each element of emotion interacts with others. One of the best ways to manage emotion is to change your emotional appraisal of a situation.

KNOWLEDGE BUILDER

Emotional Expression and Theories of Emotion

Recite

1. Charles Darwin held that emotional expressions aid survival for animals. T or F?
2. A formal term for "body language" is _____.
3. Which three dimensions of emotion are communicated by facial expressions?
   a. pleasantness-unpleasantness
   b. complexity
   c. attention-rejection
   d. anger
   e. curiosity-disinterest
   f. activation
4. According to the James-Lange theory, emotional experience precedes physical arousal and emotional behavior. (We see a bear, are frightened, and run.) T or F?
5. The Cannon-Bard theory of emotion says that bodily arousal and emotional experience occur _____.
6. The idea that labeling arousal helps define what emotions we experience is associated with
   a. the James-Lange theory
   b. Schachter's cognitive theory
   c. the Cannon-Bard theory
   d. Darwin's theory of innate emotional expressions
7. Subjects in Valins's false heart rate study attributed increases in their heart rate to the action of a placebo. T or F?
8. As you try to wiggle your ears, you keep pulling the corners of your mouth back into a smile. Each time you do, you find yourself giggling. Which of the following provides the best explanation for this reaction?
   a. attribution
   b. the Cannon-Bard theory
   c. appraisal
   d. facial feedback

Reflect

Critical Thinking

9. People with high spinal injuries may feel almost no signs of physiological arousal from their bodies. Nevertheless they still feel emotion, which can be intense at times. What theory of emotion does this observation contradict?

Relate

Write a list of emotions that you think you can accurately detect from facial expressions. Does your list match Paul Ekman's? Would you be more confident in rating pleasantness-unpleasantness, attention-rejection, and activation? Why?

Which theory seems to best explain your own emotional experiences? Try frowning or smiling for 5 minutes. Did facial feedback have any effect on your mood? Cover the left column of Table 9.2. Read each emotional label in the right column. What appraisal do you think would lead to the listed emotion? Do the appraisals in the table match your predictions?

Link

Internet addresses frequently change. To find the sites listed here, visit http://www.thomsonedu.com/psychology/coon for an updated list of Internet addresses and direct links to relevant sites.

- **The Expression of the Emotions in Man and Animals** Read Charles Darwin's original book.
- **What's in a Face?** Read an APA article about facial expressions.
- **Controlling Anger** Discusses anger and some strategies for its control.

ANSWERS

1. T 2. kinesics 3. a, c, f 4. F 5. simultaneously 6. b 7. F 8. d 9. The James-Lange theory and Schachter's cognitive theory. The facial feedback hypothesis also helps explain the observation.

MODULE *Psychology in Action*

9.6 Emotional Intelligence—The Fine Art of Self-Control

SURVEY QUESTION: *What does it mean to have "emotional intelligence"?*

The Greek philosopher Aristotle had a recipe for handling relationships smoothly: "Be angry with the right person, to the right degree, at the right time, for the right purpose, and in the right way." Psychologists Peter Salovey and John Mayer call such self-control **emotional intelligence,** a combination of skills, such as empathy, self-control, and self-awareness (Salovey & Mayer, 1997). Such skills can make us more flexible, adaptable, and emotionally mature (Bonanno et al., 2004).

People who excel in life tend to be emotionally intelligent (Mehrabian, 2000). If our emotions are the music of life, then emotionally intelligent people are good musicians. They do not stifle their emotions or overindulge in them. Instead, they compose them into sustaining life rhythms that mesh well with other people. They are more *agreeable* than people with low emotional skills (Haas et al., 2007).

Indeed, the costs of poor emotional skills can be high. They range from problems in marriage and parenting to poor physical health. A lack of emotional intelligence can ruin careers and sabotage achievement. Perhaps the greatest toll falls on children and teenagers. For them, having poor emotional skills can contribute to depression, eating disorders, unwanted pregnancy, aggression, violent crime, and poor academic performance (Parker, 2005). Thus, in many life circumstances emotional intelligence is as important as IQ (Dulewicz & Higgs, 2000).

What specific skills make up emotional intelligence? Many elements contribute to emotional intelligence (Larsen & Prizmic, 2004; Mayer et al., 2001). A description of some of the most important skills follows.

Self-Awareness Emotionally intelligent people are tuned in to their own feelings (Taylor & Taylor-Allan, 2007). For example, they are able to recognize quickly if they are angry, or envious, or feeling guilty, or depressed. This is valuable because many people have disruptive emotions without being able to pinpoint why they are uncomfortable.

Empathy Empathetic people accurately perceive emotions in others and sense what others are feeling. They are good at "reading" facial expressions, tone of voice, and other signs of emotion.

Managing Emotions Emotional intelligence involves an ability to manage your own emotions and those of others. For example, you know how to calm down when you are angry and you also know how to calm others. As Aristotle noted so long ago, people who are emotionally intelligent have an ability to amplify or restrain emotions, depending on the situation (Bonanno et al., 2004).

Understanding Emotions Emotions contain useful information. For instance, anger is a cue that something is wrong; anxiety indicates uncertainty; embarrassment communicates shame; depression means we feel helpless; enthusiasm tells us we're excited. People who are emotionally intelligent know what causes various emotions, what they mean, and how they affect behavior.

Using Emotion People who are emotionally intelligent use their feelings to enhance thinking and decision making. For example, if you can remember how you reacted emotionally in the past, it can help you react better to new situations. You can also use emotions to promote personal growth and improve relationships with others. For instance, you may have noticed that helping someone else makes you feel better, too. Likewise, when good fortune comes their way, people who are emotionally smart share the news with others. Almost always, doing so strengthens relationships and increases emotional well being (Gable et al., 2004).

Emotional Flexibility

In general, being emotionally intelligent means accepting that emotions are an essential part of who we are and how we survive. There is a natural tendency to enjoy positive emotions like joy or love, while treating negative emotions as unwelcome misery. However, negative emotions can also be valuable and constructive. For example, persistent distress may impel a person to seek help, mend a relationship, or find a new direction in life (Plutchik, 2003).

Often, the "right" choices in life can only be defined by taking personal values, needs, and emotions into account. Extremely rational approaches to making choices can produce sensible but emotionally empty decisions. Good decisions often combine emotion with reason. In short, emotional intelligence is the ability to consciously make your emotions work for you.

Positive Psychology and Positive Emotions

It's obvious that joy, interest, contentment, love, and similar emotions are pleasant and rewarding. However, as psychologist Barbara Fredrickson has pointed out, positive emotions have other benefits. Negative emotions are associated with actions that probably helped our ancestors save their skins: escaping, attacking, expelling poison, and the like. As useful as these reactions may be, they tend to narrow our focus of attention and limit our ideas about possible actions. In contrast, positive emotions tend to broaden our focus (Fredrickson & Branigan, 2005). This opens up new possibilities and builds up our personal resources. For instance, emotions such as joy, interest, and contentment create an urge to play, to be creative, to explore, to savor life, to seek new experiences, to integrate, and to grow.

In short, positive emotions are not just a pleasant side effect of happy circumstances. They also encourage personal growth and social connection. Happiness can be cultivated by using the strengths we already possess—including kindness, originality, humor, optimism, and generosity. Such strengths are natural buffers against misfortune, and they can help people live more positive, genuinely happy lives (Seligman, 2002). A capacity for having positive emotions is a basic human strength, and cultivating good feelings is a part of emotional intelligence (Fredrickson, 2003).

Becoming Emotionally Smart

How would a person learn the skills that make up emotional intelligence? Psychologists are still unsure how to teach emotional intelligence. Nevertheless, it's clear that emotional skills can be learned. Accepting that emotions are valuable is an important first step. There are many valuable lessons to learn from paying close attention to your emotions and the emotions of others. It's a good bet that many of the people you admire the most are not just smart, but also emotionally smart. They are people who know how to offer a toast at a wedding, tell a joke at a roast, comfort the bereaved at a funeral, add to the fun at a party, or calm a frightened child. These are skills worth cultivating.

MODULE 9.6 Psychology in Action Summary

What does it mean to have "emotional intelligence"?
- Emotional intelligence is the ability to consciously make your emotions work for you in a wide variety of life circumstances.
- Important elements of emotional intelligence include self-awareness, empathy, an ability to manage emotions, understanding emotion, and knowing how to use emotions to enhance thinking, decision making, and relationships.
- Positive emotions are valuable because they tend to broaden our focus and they encourage personal growth and social connection.

Emotional intelligence Emotional competence, including empathy, self-control, self-awareness, and other skills.

KNOWLEDGE BUILDER

Emotional Intelligence

Recite

1. People who rate high in emotional intelligence tend to be highly aware of their own feelings and unaware of emotions experienced by others. T or F?
2. Using the information imparted by emotional reactions can enhance thinking and decision making. T or F?
3. Positive emotions may be pleasant, but they tend to narrow our focus of attention and limit the range of possible actions we are likely to consider. T or F?
4. Which of the following is *not* an element of emotional intelligence?
   a. empathy
   b. self-control
   c. misattribution
   d. self-awareness

Reflect
Critical Thinking

5. You are angry because a friend borrowed money from you and hasn't repaid it. What would be an emotionally intelligent response to this situation?

Relate

Think of a person you know who is smart but low in emotional intelligence. Think of another person who is smart cognitively and emotionally. How does the second person differ from the first? Which person do you think would make a better parent, friend, supervisor, roommate, or teacher?

Link

Internet addresses frequently change. To find the sites listed here, visit **http://www.thomsonedu.com/psychology/coon** for an updated list of Internet addresses and direct links to relevant sites.

- **Emotional IQ Test** Measure your emotional intelligence.
- **Emotional Intelligence** This site provides information about emotional intelligence and why some people may be better at handling emotions than others and offers a useful set of guidelines for doing just this.
- **Emotional Intelligence Links** Explore a comprehensive set of links on the topic of emotional intelligence.

ANSWERS

1. F 2. T 3. F 4. c 5. There's no single right answer to this question. However, rather than being angry it might be better to reflect on whether friendship or money is more important in life. If you appreciate your friend's virtues, accept that no one is perfect and reappraise the loan as a gift; you could save a valued relationship and reduce your anger at the same time.

Interactive Learning

Psychology: Active Learning Modules Book Companion Website

http://www.thomsonedu.com/psychology/coon

Visit your Book Companion Website, where you will find flash cards, practice quizzes, Internet links, and more to help you study.

ThomsonNOW

Just What You Need to Know NOW!

Spend time on what you need to master rather than on information you already have learned. Take a pre-test for this chapter, and ThomsonNOW will generate a personalized study plan based on your results. The study plan will identify the topics you need to review and direct you to online resources to help you master those topics. You can then take a post-test to help you determine the concepts you have mastered and what you will need to work on. Try it out! Go to www.thomsonedu.com/login to sign in with an access code or to purchase access to this product.

10 Personality

MODULE 10.1 Overview of Personality
SURVEY QUESTIONS: How do psychologists use the term *personality*? What core concepts make up the psychology of personality?

MODULE 10.2 Trait Theories
SURVEY QUESTION: Are some personality traits more basic or important than others?

MODULE 10.3 Psychoanalytic Theory
SURVEY QUESTION: How do psychodynamic theories explain personality?

MODULE 10.4 Behavioral and Social Learning Theories
SURVEY QUESTION: What do behaviorists and social learning theorists emphasize in personality?

MODULE 10.5 Humanistic Theories
SURVEY QUESTION: How do humanistic theories differ from other perspectives?

MODULE 10.6 Personality Assessment
SURVEY QUESTION: How do psychologists measure personality?

MODULE 10.7 Psychology in Action: Barriers and Bridges—Understanding Shyness
SURVEY QUESTIONS: What causes shyness? What can be done about it?

The Hidden Essence

Rural Colorado. The car banged over one last, brain-jarring rut and lurched toward the dilapidated farmhouse. Annette, a friend of one of your authors, was on the porch, hooting and whooping and obviously happy to see old friends arrive.

If anyone was suited for a move to the "wilds" of Colorado, it was Annette, a strong and resourceful woman. Still, it was hard to imagine a more radical change. After separating from her husband, she had traded a comfortable life in the city for rough times in the high country. Annette was working as a ranch hand and a lumberjack (lumberjill?), trying to make it through some hard winters.

So radical were the changes in Annette's life, we worried that she might be entirely different. She was, on the contrary, more her "old self" than ever.

Perhaps you have had a similar experience. After several years of separation, it is always intriguing to see an old friend. At first you may be struck by how the person has changed. ("Where did you get that haircut!?") Soon, however, you will probably be delighted to discover that the semi-stranger before you is still the person you once knew. It is exactly this core of consistency that psychologists have in mind when they use the term *personality*.

Without doubt, personality touches our daily lives. Falling in love, choosing friends, getting along with co-workers, voting for a president, or coping with your zaniest relatives all raise questions about personality.

What is personality? How does it differ from temperament, character or attitudes? Is it possible to measure personality? Can we change our personality? We'll address these questions and more in this chapter.

Andre Forget/AP/Wide World Photo

MODULE 10.1 Overview of Personality

EACH PERSON HAS A UNIQUE PATTERN OF THINKING, behaving, and expressing feelings. In short, everyone has a unique personality. As psychologists, we would like to better understand Annette's personality. What concepts and theories can we use?

The Psychology of Personality— Do You Have Personality?

SURVEY QUESTIONS: *How do psychologists use the term* personality? *What core concepts make up the psychology of personality?*

"Annette has a very optimistic personality." "Ramiro's not handsome, but he has a great personality." "My father's business friends think he's a nice guy. They should see him at home where his real personality comes out." "It's hard to believe Tanya and Nikki are sisters. They have such opposite personalities."

It's obvious that we all frequently use the term *personality*. But if you think that personality means "charm," "charisma," or "style," you have misused the term. Psychologists regard **personality** as a person's unique pattern of thinking, emotions, and behavior (Burger, 2008; Mischel, 2004). In other words, *personality* refers to the consistency in who you are, have been, and will become. It also refers to the special blend of talents, values, hopes, loves, hates, and habits that makes each of us a unique person.

How is that different from the way most people use the term? Many people confuse personality with *character*. The term **character** implies that a person has been evaluated, not just described (Skipton, 1997). If, by saying someone has "personality," you mean the person is friendly, outgoing, and attractive, you are describing what we regard as good character in our culture. But in some cultures it is deemed good for people to be fierce, warlike, and cruel. So, whereas everyone in a particular culture has personality, not everyone has character—or at least not good character. (Do you know any good characters?)

Personality is also distinct from *temperament*, the "raw material" from which personalities are formed. **Temperament** refers to the hereditary aspects of your personality, such as your sensitivity, irritability, distractibility, and typical mood (Kagan, 2004). Judging from Annette's adult personality, you might guess that she was an active, happy baby.

Psychologists use a large number of terms to explain personality. It might be wise, therefore, to start with a few key concepts. These ideas should help you keep your bearings as you read this chapter.

Traits

We use the idea of traits every day to talk about personality. For instance, Dan is *sociable, orderly,* and *intelligent.* His sister Kayla is *shy, sensitive,* and *creative.* As we observed in our reunion with Annette, personality traits like these are usually quite stable (Gustavsson et al., 1997; Hergenhahn & Olson, 2007). Think about how little the traits of your best friends have changed in the last 5 years. It would be strange indeed to feel like you were talking with a different person every time you met a friend or an acquaintance. In general, then,

Does this man have personality? Do you?

Psychologists and employers are especially interested in the personality traits of individuals who hold high-risk, high-stress positions involving public safety, such as police, air-traffic controllers, and nuclear power plant employees.

CRITICAL THINKING

The Amazing Twins

Many reunited twins in the Minnesota study have displayed similarities far beyond what would be expected on the basis of heredity. The "Jim twins," James Lewis and James Springer, are one famous example. Both Jims had married and divorced women named Linda. Both had undergone police training. One named his firstborn son James Allan, the other named *his* firstborn son James Alan. Both drove Chevrolets and vacationed at the same beach each summer. Both listed carpentry and mechanical drawing among their hobbies. Both had built benches around trees in their yards. And so forth (Holden, 1980).

Are all identical twins so, well, identical? No, they aren't. Consider identical twins Carolyn Spiro and Pamela Spiro Wagner who, unlike the "Jim Twins," lived together throughout their childhood. While in sixth grade, they found out that President Kennedy had been assassinated. Carolyn wasn't sure why everyone was so upset. Pamela heard voices announcing that she was responsible for his death. After years of hiding her voices from everyone, Pamela tried to commit suicide while the twins were attending Brown University. She was diagnosed with schizophrenia. Never to be cured, she has gone on to write award-winning poetry. Carolyn eventually became a Harvard psychiatrist (Spiro Wagner & Spiro, 2005). Some twins reared apart appear very similar; some reared together appear rather different.

So why are some identical twins, like the Jim Twins, so much alike even if they were reared apart? Although genetics is important, it is preposterous to suggest that there are child-naming genes and bench-building genes. How, then, do we explain the eerie similarities in some separated twins' lives? Imagine that you were separated at birth from a twin brother or sister. If you were reunited with your twin today, what would you do? Quite likely, you would spend the next several days comparing every imaginable detail of your lives. Under such circumstances it is virtually certain that you and your twin would notice and compile a long list of similarities. ("Wow! I use the same brand of toothpaste you do!") Yet, two unrelated persons of the same age, sex, and race could probably rival your list—*if* they were as motivated to find similarities.

In fact, one study compared twins to unrelated pairs of students. The unrelated pairs, who were the same age and sex, were almost as alike as the twins. They had highly similar political beliefs, musical interests, religious preferences, job histories, hobbies, favorite foods, and so on (Wyatt et al., 1984). Why were the unrelated students so similar? Basically, it's because people of the same age and sex live in the same historical times and select from similar societal options. As just one example, in nearly every elementary school classroom you will find several children with the same first name.

It appears then that many of the seemingly "astounding" coincidences shared by reunited twins may be a special case of the fallacy of positive instances, described in Module 1.2. Reunited twins tend to notice the similarities and ignore the differences.

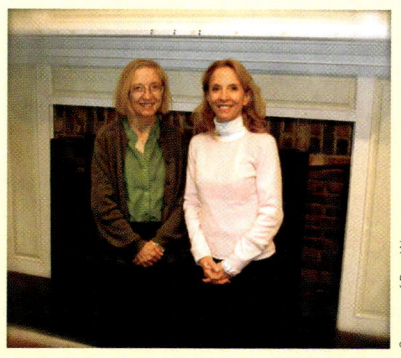

Identical twins Pam (left) and Carolyn (right) were raised together. Regardless, Carolyn became a psychiatrist while Pamela developed schizophrenia and went on to become an award-winning poet (Spiro Wagner & Spiro, 2005). Their story illustrates the complex interplay of forces which shape our adult personalities.

---

personality traits like these are stable qualities that a person shows in most situations (Matthews, Deary, & Whiteman, 2003).

Typically, traits are inferred from behavior. If you see Dan talking to strangers—first at a supermarket and later at a party—you might deduce that he is "sociable." Once personality traits are identified, they can be used to predict future behavior. For example, noting that Dan is outgoing might lead you to predict that he will be sociable at school or at work. In fact, such consistencies can span many years (McAdams & Pals, 2006). A study of women who appeared to be happy in their college yearbook photos (they had genuine smiles) found that most were still happy people 30 years later (Harker & Keltner, 2001).

At what age are personality traits firmly established? Personality starts to stabilize at around age 3 and continues to "harden" though age 50 (Caspi, Roberts, & Shiner, 2005). Personality slowly matures during old age as most people continue to become more conscientious and agreeable. It appears that stereotypes of the "grumpy old man" and "cranky old woman" are largely unfounded (Roberts, Walton, & Viechtbauer, 2006; Srivastava et al., 2003).

> **Personality** A person's unique and relatively stable behavior patterns.
> **Character** Personal characteristics that have been judged or evaluated; a person's desirable or undesirable qualities.
> **Temperament** The hereditary aspects of personality, including sensitivity, activity levels, prevailing mood, irritability, and adaptability.
> **Personality trait** A stable, enduring quality that a person shows in most situations.

Do We Inherit Personality?

Does the stability of personality traits mean that they are affected by heredity? Some breeds of dogs have reputations for being friendly, aggressive, intelligent, calm, or emotional. Such differences fall in the realm of **behavioral genetics,** the study of inherited behavioral traits. We know that facial features, eye color, body type, and many other physical characteristics are inherited. So are many of our behavioral tendencies (Bouchard, 2004; Kalat, 2007). Genetic studies have shown that intelligence, some mental disorders, temperament, and other complex qualities are influenced by heredity. In view of such findings, we also might wonder, Do genes affect personality?

Wouldn't comparing the personalities of identical twins help answer the question? It would indeed—especially if the twins were separated at birth or soon after.

Twins and Traits For several decades, psychologists at the University of Minnesota have been studying identical twins who grew up in different homes. Medical and psychological tests reveal that reunited twins are very much alike, even when they are reared apart (Bouchard, 2004; Bouchard et al., 1990). They may even be similar in appearance, voice quality, facial gestures, hand movements, and nervous tics, such as nail biting. Separated twins also tend to have similar talents. If one twin excels at art, music, dance, drama, or athletics, the other is likely to as well—despite wide differences in childhood environment. However, as "The Amazing Twins" explains, it's wise to be cautious about some reports of extraordinary similarities in reunited twins.

Summary Studies of twins make it clear that heredity has a sizable effect on each of us. All told, it seems reasonable to conclude that heredity is responsible for about 25 to 50 percent of the variation in many personality traits (Caspi, Roberts, & Shiner, 2005; Loehlin et al., 1998). Notice, however, that the same figures imply that personality is shaped as much, or more, by environment as it is by heredity.

Each personality is a unique blend of heredity and environment, biology and culture. We are not—thank goodness—genetically programmed robots whose behavior and personality traits are "wired in" for life. Where you go in life is the result of the choices you make. Although these choices are influenced by inherited tendencies, they are not merely a product of your genes (Funder, 2006).

Types

Have you ever asked the question, "What type of person is she (or he)?" A **personality type** refers to people who have *several traits in common* (Larsen & Buss, 2005). Informally, your own thinking might include categories such as the executive type, the athletic type, the motherly type, the hip-hop type, the techno geek, and so forth. If you tried to define these informal types, you would probably list a different collection of traits for each one.

How valid is it to speak of personality "types"? Over the years, psychologists have proposed many ways to categorize personalities into types. For example, Swiss psychiatrist Carl Jung (yoong) proposed that people are either *introverts* or *extroverts.* An **introvert** is a shy, reserved person whose attention is focused inward. An **extrovert** is a bold, outgoing person whose attention is directed outward. These terms are so widely used that you may think of yourself and your friends as being one type or the other. However, the wildest, wittiest, most party-loving "extrovert" you know is introverted at times. Likewise, extremely introverted persons are assertive and sociable in some situations. In short, two categories (or even several) are often inadequate to fully capture differences in personality. That's why rating people on a list of traits tends to be more informative than classifying them into two or three types.

Even though types tend to oversimplify personality, they do have value. Most often, types are a shorthand way of labeling people who have several key traits in common. For example, in Module 11.4 we discuss Type A and Type B personalities. Type A's are people who have personality traits that increase their chance of suffering a heart attack; Type B's take a more laid-back approach to life (● Fig. 10.1). Similarly, you will read in

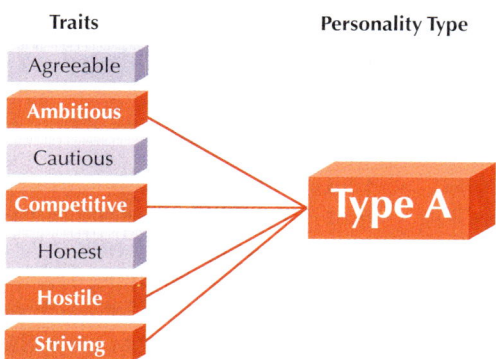

● **FIGURE 10.1** Personality types are defined by the presence of several specific traits. For example, several possible personality traits are shown in the left column. A person who has a Type A personality typically possesses all or most of the highlighted traits. Type A persons are especially prone to heart disease. (See Module 11.4.)

Module 12.2 about unhealthy personality types such as the paranoid personality, the dependent personality, and the antisocial personality. Each problem type is defined by a specific collection of maladaptive traits.

Self-Concept

Self-concepts provide another way of understanding personality. The rough outlines of your self-concept could be revealed by this request: "Please tell us about yourself." In other words, your **self-concept** consists of all your ideas, perceptions, stories, and feelings about who you are. It is the mental "picture" you have of your own personality (Swann, Chang-Schneider, & Larsen McClarty, 2007).

We creatively build our self-concepts out of daily experiences. Then we slowly revise them as we have new experiences. Once a stable self-concept exists, it tends to guide what we pay attention to, remember, and think about. Because of this, self-concepts can greatly affect our behavior and personal adjustment—especially when they are inaccurate (Ryckman, 2008). For instance, Alesha is a student who thinks she is stupid, worthless, and a failure, despite getting good grades. With such an inaccurate self-concept, she tends to be depressed regardless of how well she does.

Self-Esteem
Note that in addition to having a faulty self-concept, Alesha has low **self-esteem** (a negative self-evaluation). A person with high self-esteem is confident, proud, and self-respecting. One who has low self-esteem is insecure, lacking in confidence, and self-critical. Like Alesha, people with low self-esteem are usually anxious and unhappy.

Self-esteem tends to rise when we experience success or praise. A person who is competent and effective and who is loved, admired, and respected by others will almost always

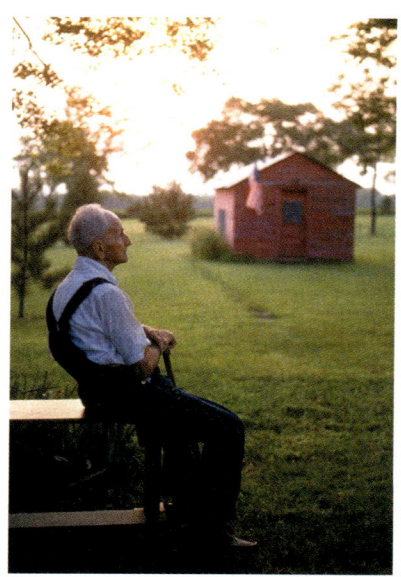

Self-concepts can be remarkably consistent. In an interesting study, very old people were asked how they had changed over the years. Almost all thought they were essentially the same person they were when they were young (Troll & Skaff, 1997).

have high self-esteem (Baumeister et al., 2003). (The reasons for having high self-esteem can vary in different cultures. See "Self-Esteem and Culture" for more information.)

What if you "think you're hot," but you're not? Genuine self-esteem is based on an accurate appraisal of your strengths and weaknesses. A positive self-evaluation that is bestowed too easily may not be healthy (Twenge & Campbell, 2001). People who think very highly of themselves (and let others know it) may at first seem confident, but their arrogance quickly turns off other people (Paulhus, 1998).

Personality Theories

As you can already see, it would be easy to get lost without a framework for understanding personality. How do our thoughts, actions, and feelings relate to one another? How does personality develop? Why do some people suffer from psychological problems? How can they be helped? To answer such questions, psychologists have created a dazzling array of

Behavioral genetics The study of inherited behavioral traits and tendencies.
Personality type A style of personality defined by a group of related traits.
Introvert A person whose attention is focused inward; a shy, reserved, self-centered person.
Extrovert A person whose attention is directed outward; a bold, outgoing person.
Self-concept A person's perception of his or her own personality traits.
Self-esteem Regarding oneself as a worthwhile person; a positive evaluation of oneself.

HUMAN DIVERSITY

Self-Esteem and Culture—Hotshot or Team Player?

You and some friends are playing soccer. Your team wins, in part because you make some good plays. After the game, you bask in the glow of having performed well. You don't want to brag about being a hotshot, but your self-esteem gets a boost from your personal success.

In Japan, Shinobu and some of his friends are playing soccer. His team wins, in part because he makes some good plays. After the game Shinobu is happy because his team did well. However, Shinobu also dwells on the ways in which he let his team down. He thinks about how he could improve, and he resolves to be a better team player.

These sketches illustrate a basic difference in Eastern and Western psychology. In individualistic cultures such as the United States, self-esteem is based on personal success and outstanding performance (Lay & Verkuyten, 1999). For us, the path to higher self-esteem lies in self-enhancement. We are pumped up by our successes and tend to downplay our faults and failures (Ross et al., 2005).

Japanese and other Asian cultures place a greater emphasis on collectivism, or interdependence among people. For them, self-esteem is based on a secure sense of belonging to social groups. As a result, people in Asian cultures are more apt to engage in self-criticism (Ross et al., 2005). By correcting personal faults, they add to the well-being of the group (Kitayama, Markus, & Kurokawa, 2000). And when the *group* succeeds, individual members feel better about themselves, which raises their self-esteem.

Perhaps self-esteem is still based on success in both Eastern and Western cultures. However, it is fascinating that cultures define success in such different ways (Schmitt & Allik, 2005). The North American emphasis on winning is not the only way to feel good about yourself.

---

theories. A **personality theory** is a system of concepts, assumptions, ideas, and principles proposed to explain personality (● Fig. 10.2). In this chapter, we can only explore a few of the many personality theories. These are the four major perspectives we will consider:

1. **Trait theories** attempt to learn what traits make up personality and how they relate to actual behavior.
2. **Psychodynamic theories** focus on the inner workings of personality, especially internal conflicts and struggles.
3. **Behavioristic and social learning theories** place importance on the external environment and on the effects of conditioning and learning. Social learning theories attribute differences in personality to socialization, expectations, and mental processes.
4. **Humanistic theories** stress private, subjective experience, and personal growth.

Which personality theory is right? To date, each theory has added to our understanding by providing a sort of lens through which human behavior can be viewed. Nevertheless, theories can't be fully proved or disproved. We can only ask, Does the evidence tend to support this theory or disconfirm it? Yet, although theories are neither true nor false, their implications or predictions may be. The best way to judge a theory, then, is in terms of its *usefulness*. Does the theory adequately explain behavior? Does it stimulate new research? Does it suggest how to treat psychological disorders? Each theory has fared differently in these areas (Pervin, Cervone, & John, 2005). ■ Table 10.1 provides an overview of the four principal approaches to personality. In the final analysis, the challenge now facing

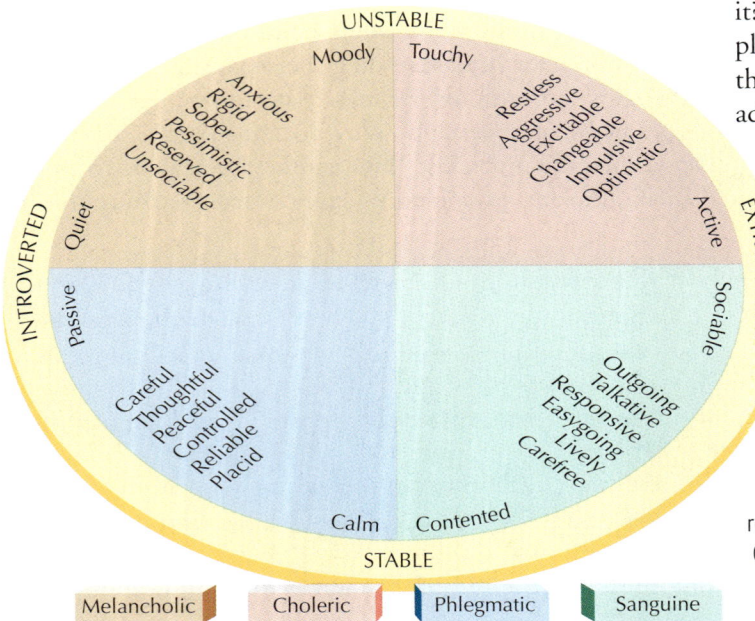

● **FIGURE 10.2** English psychologist Hans Eysenck (1916–1997) believed that many personality traits are related to whether you are mainly introverted or extroverted and whether you tend to be emotionally stable or unstable (highly emotional). These characteristics, in turn, are related to four basic types of temperament first recognized by the early Greeks. The types are: *melancholic* (sad, gloomy), *choleric* (hot-tempered, irritable), *phlegmatic* (sluggish, calm), and *sanguine* (cheerful, hopeful). (Adapted from Eysenck, 1981.)

TABLE 10.1 Comparison of Personality Theories

	TRAIT THEORIES	PSYCHOANALYTIC THEORY	BEHAVIORISTIC AND SOCIAL LEARNING THEORIES	HUMANISTIC THEORY
View of human nature	Neutral	Negative	Neutral	Positive
Is behavior free or determined?	Determined	Determined	Determined	Free choice
Principal motives	Depends on one's traits	Sex and aggression	Drives of all kinds	Self-actualization
Personality structure	Traits	Id, ego, superego	Habits, expectancies	Self
Role of unconscious	Minimized	Maximized	Practically nonexistent	Minimized
Conception of conscience	Traits of honesty, etc.	Superego	Self-reinforcement, punishment history	Ideal self, valuing process
Developmental emphasis	Combined effects of heredity and environment	Psychosexual stages	Critical learning situations, identification, and imitation	Development of self-image
Barriers to personal growth	Unhealthy traits	Unconscious conflicts, fixations	Maladaptive habits, unhealthy environment	Conditions of worth, incongruence

personality theorists is how to integrate the four major perspectives into a unified, systematic explanation of personality (Mayer, 2005; McAdams & Pals, 2006). With these broad perspectives in mind, let's take a deeper look at personality.

MODULE 10.1 Summary

How do psychologists use the term personality? *What core concepts make up the psychology of personality?*

- *Personality* refers to a person's unique pattern of thinking, emotion, and behavior.
- *Character* is personality evaluated, or the possession of desirable qualities.
- *Temperament* refers to the hereditary aspects of one's emotional nature.
- Traits are lasting personal qualities that are inferred from behavior.
- Behavioral genetics and studies of identical twins show that heredity contributes significantly to personality traits.
- Personality types group people into categories on the basis of shared traits.
- Behavior is influenced by self-concept and self-esteem.
- Personality theories combine interrelated assumptions, ideas, and principles to explain personality.
- Four main types of personality theories are trait, psychodynamic, behavioristic and social learning, and humanistic.

Personality theory A system of concepts, assumptions, ideas, and principles used to understand and explain personality.

KNOWLEDGE BUILDER

Overview of Personality

Recite

1. When someone's personality has been evaluated, we are making a judgment about his or her
   a. temperament
   b. character
   c. extroversion
   d. self-esteem
2. A personality type is usually defined by the presence of
   a. all five personality dimensions
   b. a stable self-concept
   c. several specific traits
   d. a source trait
3. The research methods of _____ have been used to study the extent to which we inherit personality characteristics.
   a. behavioral genetics
   b. social learning theory
   c. factor analysis
   d. trait profiling
4. Heredity is more important than environment in shaping personality. T or F?
5. Our self-concept affects our behavior and _____.
   a. temperament
   b. extraversion
   c. personality type
   d. personal adjustment

Reflect
Critical Thinking

6. In what way would memory contribute to the formation of an accurate or inaccurate self-image?

Relate

See if you can define or describe the following terms in your own words: personality, character, temperament, trait, type, self-concept, self-esteem.

Meet with another student in your psychology class to explore your similarities. Did you find any similarities as surprising as those shared by the "Jim Twins"?

Link

Internet addresses frequently change. To find the sites listed here, visit **http://www.thomsonedu.com/psychology/coon** for an updated list of Internet addresses and direct links to relevant sites.

- **Personality Theories** Explore an electronic textbook about personality theories.
- **The Personality Project** Access a wide variety of information on personality.
- **Personality: Theory & Perspectives** An undergraduate psychology course about individual differences.

ANSWERS

1. b 2. c 3. a 4. F 5. D 6. As discussed in Chapter 7, memory is highly selective, and long-term memories are often distorted by recent information. Such properties add to the moldability of self-concept.

MODULE 10.2 Trait Theories

THE DOMINANT APPROACH to the study of personality is currently the trait approach. Trait theories seek to describe personality in terms of a small number of underlying personality traits or factors. Of the various trait theories, The Big Five is currently the most influential. According to this theory, all personalities can be described as varying along five key factors: *extroversion, agreeableness, conscientiousness, neuroticism,* and *openness to experience* (Costa & McCrae, 2006).

The Trait Approach—Describe Yourself in 18,000 Words or Less

SURVEY QUESTION: *Are some personality traits more basic or important than others?*

How many words can you think of to describe the personality of a close friend? Your list might be long: More than 18,000 English words refer to personal characteristics. As we have noted, traits are stable qualities that a person shows in most situations (Matthews, Deary, & Whiteman, 2003). For example, if you are usually friendly, optimistic, and cautious, these qualities are traits of your personality.

What if I am also sometimes shy, pessimistic, or uninhibited? The original three qualities are still traits as long as they are most *typical* of your behavior. Let's say our friend Annette approaches most situations with optimism but tends to expect the worst each time she applies for a job. If her pessimism is limited to this situation or just a few others, it is still accurate and useful to describe her as an optimistic person.

Predicting Behavior

As we have noted, separating people into broad types, such as "introvert" or "extrovert," may oversimplify personality. However, introversion/extroversion can also be thought of as a trait. Knowing how you rate on this single dimension would allow us to predict how you will behave in a variety of settings. Where, for example, do you prefer to meet people, face-to-face or through the Internet? Researchers have found that students high in the trait of introversion are more likely to prefer the Internet because they find it easier to talk with people online (Koch & Pratarelli, 2004). (Other interesting links exist between traits and behavior. See "What's Your Musical Personality?")

Describing People

In general, psychologists try to identify traits that best describe a person. Take a moment to check the traits in ■ Table 10.2 that describe your personality. Are the traits you checked of equal importance? Are some stronger or more basic than others? Do any overlap? For example, if you checked "dominant," did you also check "confident" and "bold"? Answers to these questions would interest a trait theorist. To better understand personality, **trait theorists** attempt to analyze, classify, and interrelate traits.

Classifying Traits

Are there different types of traits? Yes, psychologist Gordon Allport (1961) identified several kinds. **Common traits** are characteristics shared by most members of a culture. Common traits tell us how people from a particular nation or culture are similar or which traits a culture emphasizes. In America, for example, competitiveness is a fairly common trait. Among the Hopi of Northern Arizona, however, it is relatively rare.

Of course, common traits don't tell us much about individuals. Although many people are competitive in American culture, various people you know may rate high, medium, or low in this trait. Usually we are also interested in **individual traits**, which describe a person's unique qualities.

■ TABLE 10.2 Adjective Checklist

Check the traits you feel are characteristic of your personality. Are some more basic than others?

aggressive	organized	ambitious	clever
confident	loyal	generous	calm
warm	bold	cautious	reliable
sensitive	mature	talented	jealous
sociable	honest	funny	religious
dominant	dull	accurate	nervous
humble	uninhibited	visionary	cheerful
thoughtful	serious	helpful	emotional
orderly	anxious	conforming	good-natured
liberal	curious	optimistic	kind
meek	neighborly	passionate	compulsive

Trait theorist A psychologist interested in classifying, analyzing, and interrelating traits to understand personality.

Common traits Personality traits that are shared by most members of a particular culture.

Individual traits Personality traits that define a person's unique individual qualities.

DISCOVERING PSYCHOLOGY

What's Your Musical Personality?

Even if you like all kinds of music, you probably prefer some styles to others. Of the styles listed here, which three do you enjoy the most? (Circle your choices.)

blues jazz classical folk rock alternative heavy metal country sound track religious pop rap/hip-hop soul/funk electronic/dance

In one study, Peter Rentfrow and Samuel Gosling found that the types of music people prefer tend to be associated with their personality characteristics. See if your musical tastes match their findings (Rentfrow & Gosling, 2003).

People who value aesthetic experiences, have good verbal abilities, and are liberal and tolerant of others tend to like music that is reflective and complex (blues, jazz, classical, and folk music).

People who are curious about new experiences, enjoy taking risks, and are physically active prefer intense, rebellious music (rock, alternative, and heavy metal music).

People who are cheerful, conventional, extroverted, reliable, helpful, and conservative tend to enjoy upbeat conventional music (country, sound track, religious, and pop music).

People who are talkative, full of energy, forgiving, and physically attractive and who reject conservative ideals tend to prefer energetic, rhythmic music (rap/hip-hop, soul/funk, and electronic/dance music).

Unmistakably, personality traits affect our everyday behavior.

Here's an analogy to help you separate common traits from individual traits: If you decide to buy a pet dog, you will want to know the general characteristics of the dog's breed (its common traits). In addition, you will want to know about the "personality" of a specific dog (its individual traits) before you decide to take it home.

Allport also made distinctions between *cardinal traits, central traits,* and *secondary traits.* **Cardinal traits** are so basic that all of a person's activities can be traced to the trait. For instance, compassion was an overriding trait of Mother Teresa's personality. Likewise, Abraham Lincoln's personality was dominated by the cardinal trait of honesty. According to Allport, few people have cardinal traits.

Central Traits *How do central and secondary traits differ from cardinal traits?* **Central traits** are the basic building blocks of personality. A surprisingly small number of central traits can capture the essence of a person. For instance, just six traits would provide a good description of Annette's personality: dominant, sociable, honest, cheerful, intelligent, and optimistic. When college students were asked to describe someone they knew well, they mentioned an average of seven central traits (Allport, 1961).

Secondary traits are more superficial personal qualities, such as food preferences, attitudes, political opinions, musical tastes, and so forth. In Allport's terms, a personality description might therefore include the following items:

Name: Jane Doe
Age: 22
Cardinal traits: None
Central traits: Possessive, autonomous, artistic, dramatic, self-centered, trusting
Secondary traits: Prefers colorful clothes, likes to work alone, politically liberal, always late

Source Traits *How can you tell if a personality trait is central or secondary?* Raymond B. Cattell (1906–1998) tried to answer this question by directly studying the traits of a large number of people. Cattell began by measuring visible features of personality, which he called **surface traits.** Soon, Cattell noticed that these surface traits often appeared together in groups. In fact, some traits appeared together so often that they seemed to represent a single, more basic trait. Cattell called these deeper characteristics, or dimensions, **source traits** (Cattell, 1965). They are the core of each individual's personality.

How do source traits differ from Allport's central traits? Allport classified traits subjectively, and it's possible that he was wrong at times. Cattell used *factor analysis* to look for connections among traits. **Factor analysis** is a statistical technique used to correlate multiple measurements and identify general underlying factors. For example, he found that imaginative people are almost always *inventive, original, curious, creative, innovative,* and *ingenious.* Thus, *imaginative* is a source trait. If you are an imaginative person, we automatically know that you have several other traits, too.

Cattell identified 16 source traits. According to him, all 16 are needed to fully describe a personality. Source traits are measured by a test called the *Sixteen Personality Factor Questionnaire* (often referred to as the 16 PF). Like many personality tests, the 16 PF can be used to produce a **trait profile,** or graph of a person's score on each trait. Trait profiles draw a "picture" of individual personalities, which makes it easier to compare them (● Fig. 10.3).

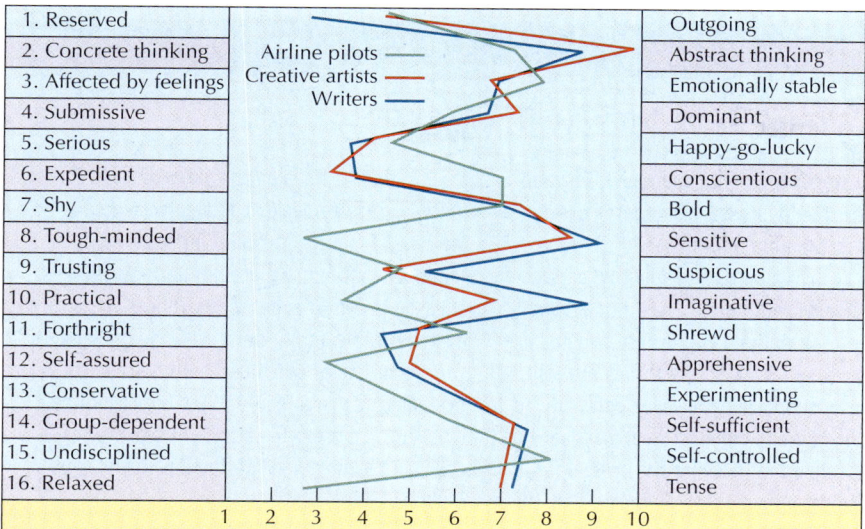

● **FIGURE 10.3** The 16 source traits measured by Cattell's 16 PF are listed beside the graph. Scores can be plotted as a profile for an individual or a group. The profiles shown here are group averages for airline pilots, creative artists, and writers. Notice the similarity between artists and writers and the difference between these two groups and pilots. (Cattell, R. B., "Personality Pinned Down," 1973. Reprinted by permission of Dr. R. B. Cattell.)

The Big Five

Noel is outgoing and friendly, conscientious, even-tempered, and curious. His brother Joel is reserved, hostile, irresponsible, temperamental, and disinterested in ideas. You will be spending a week in a space capsule with either Noel or Joel. Who would you choose? If the answer seems obvious, it's because Noel and Joel were described with the **five-factor model,** a system that identifies the five most basic dimensions of personality.

The "Big Five" factors listed in ● Figure 10.4 attempt to further reduce Cattell's 16 factors to just five universal dimensions, or source traits (Costa & McCrae, 2006). The Big Five may be the best answer of all to the question, What is the essence of human personality (McCrae & Terracciano, 2005)?

Five Key Dimensions If you would like to compare the personalities of two people, try rating them informally on the five dimensions shown in Figure 10.4. For factor 1, *extroversion,* rate how introverted or extroverted each person is. Factor 2, *agreeableness,* refers to how friendly, nurturant, and caring a person is, as opposed to cold, indifferent, self-centered, or spiteful. A person who is *conscientious* (factor 3) is self-disciplined, responsible, and achieving. People low on this factor are irresponsible, careless, and undependable. Factor 4, *neuroticism,* refers to negative, upsetting emotions. People who are high in neuroticism tend to be anxious, emotionally "sour," irritable, and unhappy. Finally, people who rate high on factor 5, *openness to experience,* are intelligent and open to new ideas (McCrae & Costa, 2001).

The beauty of the Big-Five model is that almost any trait you can name will be related to one of the five factors. If you were selecting a college roommate, hiring an employee, or answering a singles ad, you would probably like to know all

● **FIGURE 10.4** The Big Five. According to the five-factor model, basic differences in personality can be "boiled down" to the dimensions shown here. The five-factor model answers these essential questions about a person: Is she or he extroverted or introverted? Agreeable or difficult? Conscientious or irresponsible? Emotionally stable or unstable? Smart or unintelligent? These questions cover a large measure of what we might want to know about someone's personality. (Trait descriptions adapted from McCrae & Costa, 2001.)

Cardinal trait A personality trait so basic that all of a person's activities relate to it.
Central traits The core traits that characterize an individual personality.
Secondary traits Traits that are inconsistent or relatively superficial.
Surface traits The visible or observable traits of one's personality.
Source traits Basic underlying traits, or dimensions, of personality; each source trait is reflected in a number of surface traits.
Factor analysis A statistical technique used to correlate multiple measurements and identify general underlying factors.
Trait profile A graph of the scores obtained on several personality traits.
Five-factor model Proposes that there are five universal dimensions of personality.

THE CLINICAL FILE

Perfectly Miserable

Up to a point, conscientiousness is associated with high achievement. However, having impossibly high standards, a trait called perfectionism, can be a problem. As you might expect, college students who are perfectionists tend to get good grades. Yet some students cross the line into maladaptive perfectionism, which typically *lowers* performance at school and elsewhere (Accordino, Accordino, & Slaney, 2000).

People who suffer from unhealthy perfectionism set unattainably high standards for themselves. This causes them to feel as if they are always failing. Perfectionistic students are self-critical, terrified of making mistakes, and often seriously depressed (Grzegorek et al., 2004; Sumi & Kanda, 2002).

For many students, maladaptive perfectionism begins with harsh, perfectionistic parenting. There's nothing wrong with having parents who expect a lot of you—if they are also emotionally supportive. However, parents who are demanding and highly critical may leave a student feeling that nothing she or he does is ever quite good enough. As already noted, this is a recipe for self-doubt and depression.

Authentic Navajo rugs always have a flaw in their intricate designs. Navajo weavers intentionally make a "mistake" in each rug as a reminder that humans are not perfect. There is a lesson in this: It is not always necessary, or even desirable, to be "perfect." To learn from your experiences you must feel free to make mistakes (Castro & Rice, 2003). Success, in the long run, is more often based on seeking "excellence," rather than "perfection" (Enns, Cox, & Clara, 2005).

---

the personal dimensions covered by the Big Five. Such traits predict how people will act in various circumstances. For example, people who score high in conscientiousness tend to perform well at work, do well in school, and rarely have automobile accidents (Arthur & Doverspike, 2001; Barrick, Moun, & Judge, 2001; Chamorro-Premuzic & Furnham, 2003). They even live longer (Martin, Friedman, & Schwartz, 2007). (Is it possible to be too conscientious? See "Perfectly Miserable" for an answer.)

Before you read the next section, take a moment to answer the questions that follow. Doing so will add to your understanding of a long-running controversy in the psychology of personality.

Knowing where a person stands on the "Big Five" personality factors helps predict his or her behavior. For example, people who score high on conscientiousness tend to be safe drivers who are unlikely to have automobile accidents (Arthur & Doverspike, 2001).

Rate Yourself: How Do You View Personality?

1. My friends' actions are fairly consistent from day to day and in different situations. T or F?
2. Whether a person is honest or dishonest, kind or cruel, a hero or a coward depends mainly on circumstances. T or F?
3. Most people I have known for several years have pretty much the same personalities now as they did when I first met them. T or F?
4. The reason that people in some professions (such as teachers, lawyers, or doctors) seem so much alike is because their work requires that they act in particular ways. T or F?
5. One of the first things I would want to know about a potential roommate is what the person's personality is like. T or F?
6. I believe that immediate circumstances usually determine how people act at any given time. T or F?
7. To be comfortable in a particular job, a person's personality must match the nature of the work. T or F?
8. Almost anyone would be polite at a wedding reception; it doesn't matter what kind of personality the person has. T or F?

Now count the number of times you marked true for the odd-numbered items. Do the same for the even-numbered items.

If you agreed with most of the odd-numbered items, you tend to view behavior as strongly influenced by personality traits or lasting personal dispositions.

If you agreed with most of the even-numbered items, you view behavior as strongly influenced by external situations and circumstances.

What if I answered true about equally for odd and even items? Then you place equal weight on traits and situations as ways to explain behavior. This is the view now held by many personality psychologists (Funder, 2006; Mischel & Shoda, 1998).

Traits, Consistency, and Situations

Does that mean that to predict how a person will act, it is better to focus on both personality traits and external circumstances? Yes, it's best to take both into account. Personality traits are quite consistent. Also, they can predict such things as job performance, dangerous driving, or a successful marriage (Funder, 2006). Yet, *situations* also greatly influence our behavior. For instance, it would be unusual for you to dance at a movie or read a book at a football game. Likewise, few people sleep in roller coasters or tell off-color jokes at funerals. However, your personality traits may predict whether you choose to read a book, go to a movie, or attend a football game in the first place. Typically, traits *interact* with situations to determine how we will act (Mischel, 2004).

In a **trait-situation interaction,** external circumstances influence the expression of a personality trait. For instance, imagine what would happen if you moved from a church to a classroom to a party to a football game. As the setting changed, you would probably become louder and more boisterous. This change would show situational effects on behavior. At the same time, your personality traits would also be apparent: If you were quieter than average in church and class, you would probably be quieter than average in the other settings, too.

MODULE 10.2 Summary

Are some personality traits more basic or important than others?

- Trait theories identify lasting and consistent personal characteristics.
- Allport made distinctions between common traits and individual traits and among cardinal, central, and secondary traits.
- Cattell's theory attributes visible surface traits to the existence of 16 underlying source traits.
- The five-factor model identifies the following five universal dimensions of personality: extroversion, agreeableness, conscientiousness, neuroticism, and openness to experience.
- Traits and situations interact to determine how we behave.

Trait-situation interaction The influence that external settings or circumstances have on the expression of personality traits.

KNOWLEDGE BUILDER

Trait Theories

Recite

1. A trait can be used to describe someone's personality if that trait is _____ descriptive of his or her behavior.
   a. always
   b. typically
   c. occasionally
   d. rarely
2. Central traits are those shared by most members of a culture. T or F?
3. Cattell believes that clusters of _____ traits reveal the presence of underlying _____ traits.
4. Which of the following is *not* one of the Big Five personality factors?
   a. submissiveness
   b. agreeableness
   c. extroversion
   d. neuroticism
5. Conscientious people tend to be perfectionists. T or F?
6. To understand personality, it is wise to remember that traits and situations _____ to determine our behavior.

Reflect

Critical Thinking

7. Are situations equally powerful in their impact on behavior?

Relate

List six or seven traits that best describe your personality. Which system of traits seems to best match your list, Allport's, Cattell's, or the Big Five?

Choose a prominent trait from your list. Does its expression seem to be influenced by specific situations? Do you think that heredity contributed to the trait?

Link

Internet addresses frequently change. To find the sites listed here, visit **http://www.thomsonedu.com/psychology/coon** for an updated list of Internet addresses and direct links to relevant sites.

- **Raymond Cattell** Read about Raymond Cattell and his Sixteen Personality Factor Questionnaire.
- **Internet Personality Inventory** Test yourself on the Big Five.
- **The Big Five Dimensions** Provides additional information about the Big Five, with links to related sites.

ANSWERS

1. a or b 2. F 3. surface, source 4. a 5. F 6. interact 7. No. Circumstances can have a strong or weak influence. In some situations, almost everyone will act the same, no matter what their personality traits may be. In other situations, traits may be of greater importance.

MODULE 10.3 Psychoanalytic Theory

PSYCHODYNAMIC THEORISTS are not content with studying traits. Instead, they try to probe under the surface of personality—to learn what drives, conflicts, and energies animate us. Psychodynamic theorists believe that many of our actions are based on hidden, or unconscious, thoughts, needs, and emotions.

Psychoanalytic Theory— Id Came to Me in a Dream

SURVEY QUESTION: *How do psychodynamic theories explain personality?*

Psychoanalytic theory, the best-known psychodynamic approach, grew out of the work of Sigmund Freud, a Viennese physician. As a doctor, Freud was fascinated by patients whose problems seemed to be more emotional than physical. From about 1890 until he died in 1939, Freud evolved a theory of personality that deeply influenced modern thought (Jacobs, 2003). Let's consider some of its main features (Schultz & Schultz, 2005).

The Structure of Personality

How did Freud view personality? Freud's model portrays personality as a dynamic system directed by three mental structures, the **id,** the **ego,** and the **superego.** According to Freud, most behavior involves activity of all three systems. (Freud's theory includes a large number of concepts. For your convenience, they are defined in ■ Table 10.3 rather than in glossary boxes.)

The Id The id is made up of innate biological instincts and urges. It is self-serving, irrational, impulsive, and totally unconscious. The id operates on the **pleasure principle.** That is, it seeks to freely express pleasure-seeking urges of all kinds.

Psychoanalytic theory Freudian theory of personality that emphasizes unconscious forces and conflicts.

■ TABLE 10.3 Key Freudian Concepts

Anal stage The psychosexual stage corresponding roughly to the period of toilet training (ages 1 to 3).
Anal-expulsive personality A disorderly, destructive, cruel, or messy person.
Anal-retentive personality A person who is obstinate, stingy, or compulsive and who generally has difficulty "letting go."
Conscience The part of the superego that causes guilt when its standards are not met.
Conscious The region of the mind that includes all mental contents a person is aware of at any given moment.
Ego The executive part of personality that directs rational behavior.
Ego ideal The part of the superego representing ideal behavior; a source of pride when its standards are met.
Electra conflict A girl's sexual attraction to her father and feelings of rivalry with her mother.
Erogenous zone Any body area that produces pleasurable sensations.
Eros Freud's name for the "**life instincts.**"
Fixation A lasting conflict developed as a result of frustration or overindulgence.
Genital stage Period of full psychosexual development, marked by the attainment of mature adult sexuality.
Id The primitive part of personality that remains unconscious, supplies energy, and demands pleasure.
Latency According to Freud, a period in childhood when psychosexual development is more or less interrupted.
Libido In Freudian theory, the force, primarily pleasure oriented, that energizes the personality.
Moral anxiety Apprehension felt when thoughts, impulses, or actions conflict with the superego's standards.
Neurotic anxiety Apprehension felt when the ego struggles to control id impulses.
Oedipus conflict A boy's sexual attraction to his mother and feelings of rivalry with his father.
Oral stage The period when infants are preoccupied with the mouth as a source of pleasure and means of expression.
Oral-aggressive personality A person who uses the mouth to express hostility by shouting, cursing, biting, and so forth. Also, one who actively exploits others.
Oral-dependent personality A person who wants to passively receive attention, gifts, love, and so forth.
Phallic personality A person who is vain, exhibitionistic, sensitive, and narcissistic.
Phallic stage The psychosexual stage (roughly ages 3 to 6) when a child is preoccupied with the genitals.
Pleasure principle A desire for immediate satisfaction of wishes, desires, or needs.
Preconscious An area of the mind containing information that can be voluntarily brought to awareness.
Psyche The mind, mental life, and personality as a whole.
Psychosexual stages The oral, anal, phallic, and genital stages, during which various personality traits are formed.
Reality principle Delaying action (or pleasure) until it is appropriate.
Superego A judge or censor for thoughts and actions.
Thanatos The **death instinct** postulated by Freud.
Unconscious The region of the mind that is beyond awareness, especially impulses and desires not directly known to a person.

If we were solely under control of the id, the world would be chaotic beyond belief.

The id acts as a well of energy for the entire **psyche** (sigh-KEY), or personality. This energy, called **libido** (lih-BEE-doe), flows from the **life instincts** (or **Eros**). According to Freud, libido underlies our efforts to survive, as well as our sexual desires and pleasure seeking. Freud also described a **death instinct. Thanatos,** as he called it, produces aggressive and destructive urges. Freud offered humanity's long history of wars and violence as evidence of such urges. Most id energies, then, are aimed at discharging tensions related to sex and aggression.

The Ego The ego is sometimes described as the "executive," because it directs energies supplied by the id. The id is like a blind king or queen whose power is awesome but who must rely on others to carry out orders. The id can only form mental images of things it desires. The ego wins power to direct behavior by relating the desires of the id to external reality.

Are there other differences between the ego and the id? Yes. Recall that the id operates on the pleasure principle. The ego, in contrast, is guided by the **reality principle.** The ego is the system of thinking, planning, problem solving, and deciding. It is in conscious control of the personality and often delays action until it is practical or appropriate.

The Superego *What is the role of the superego?* The superego acts as a judge or censor for the thoughts and actions of the ego. One part of the superego, called the **conscience,** reflects actions for which a person has been punished. When standards of the conscience are not met, you are punished internally by *guilt* feelings.

A second part of the superego is the **ego ideal.** The ego ideal reflects all behavior one's parents approved of or rewarded. The ego ideal is a source of goals and aspirations. When its standards are met, we feel *pride*.

The superego acts as an "internalized parent" to bring behavior under control. In Freudian terms, a person with a weak superego will be a delinquent, criminal, or antisocial personality. In contrast, an overly strict or harsh superego may cause inhibition, rigidity, or unbearable guilt.

The Dynamics of Personality

How do the id, ego, and superego interact? Freud didn't picture the id, ego, and superego as parts of the brain or as "little people" running the human psyche. Instead, they are conflicting mental processes. Freud theorized a delicate balance of power among the three. For example, the id's demands for immediate pleasure often clash with the superego's moral restrictions. Perhaps an example will help clarify the role of each part of the personality.

> **FREUD IN A NUTSHELL**
> Let's say you are sexually attracted to an acquaintance. The id clamors for immediate satisfaction of its sexual desires but is opposed by the superego (which finds the very thought of sex shocking). The id says, "Go for it!" The superego icily replies, "Never even think that again!" And what does the ego say? The ego says, "I have a plan!"

Of course, this is a drastic simplification, but it does capture the core of Freudian thinking. To reduce tension, the ego could begin actions leading to friendship, romance,

Freud considered personality an expression of two conflicting forces: life instincts and the death instinct. Both are symbolized in this drawing by Allan Gilbert. (If you don't immediately see the death symbolism, stand farther from the drawing.)

courtship, and marriage. If the id is unusually powerful, the ego may give in and attempt a seduction. If the superego prevails, the ego may be forced to *displace* or *sublimate* sexual energies to other activities (sports, music, dancing, push-ups, cold showers). According to Freud, internal struggles and rechanneled energies typify most personality functioning.

Is the ego always caught in the middle? Basically yes, and the pressures on it can be intense. In addition to meeting the conflicting demands of the id and superego, the overworked ego must deal with external reality.

According to Freud, you feel anxiety when your ego is threatened or overwhelmed. Impulses from the id cause **neurotic anxiety** when the ego can barely keep them under control. Threats of punishment from the superego cause **moral anxiety.** Each person develops habitual ways of calming these anxieties, and many resort to using *ego-defense mechanisms* to lessen internal conflicts. Defense mechanisms are mental processes that deny, distort, or otherwise block out sources of threat and anxiety. (The ego defense mechanisms that Freud identified are used as a form of protection against stress, anxiety, and threatening events. See Module 11.3.)

Levels of Awareness Like other psychodynamic theorists, Freud believed that our behavior often expresses unconscious (or hidden) forces. The **unconscious** holds repressed memories and emotions, plus the instinctual drives of the id. Interestingly, modern scientists have found that the brain's limbic system does, in fact, seem to trigger unconscious emotions and memories (LeDoux, 1996).

Even though they are beyond awareness, unconscious thoughts, feelings, or urges may slip into behavior in disguised or symbolic form. For example, if you meet someone you would like to know better, you may unconsciously leave a book or a jacket at that person's house to ensure another meeting.

Are the actions of the ego and superego also unconscious, like the id? At times, yes, but they also operate on two other levels of awareness (● Fig. 10.5). The **conscious** level includes everything you are aware of at a given moment, including thoughts, perceptions, feelings, and memories. The **preconscious** contains material that can be easily brought to awareness. If you stop to think about a time when you felt angry or rejected, you will be moving this memory from the preconscious to the conscious level of awareness.

The superego's activities also reveal differing levels of awareness. At times we consciously try to live up to moral codes or standards. Yet, at other times a person may feel guilty without knowing why. Psychoanalytic theory credits such guilt to unconscious workings of the superego. Indeed, Freud believed that the unconscious origins of many feelings cannot be easily brought to awareness.

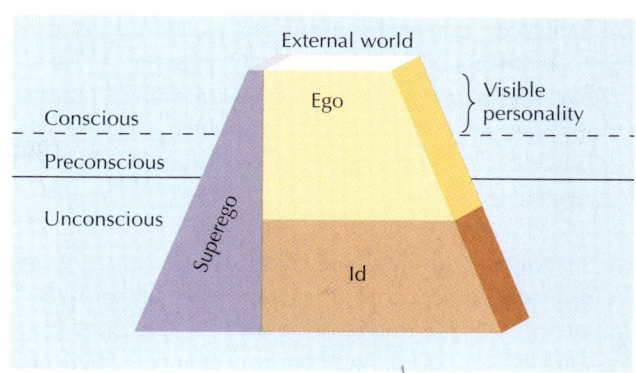

● **FIGURE 10.5** The approximate relationship between the id, ego, and superego, and the levels of awareness.

Personality Development

How does psychoanalytic theory explain personality development? Freud theorized that the core of personality is formed before age 6 in a series of **psychosexual stages.** Freud believed that erotic urges in childhood have lasting effects on development. As you might expect, this is a controversial idea. However, Freud used the terms *sex* and *erotic* very broadly to refer to many physical sources of pleasure.

A Freudian Fable? Freud identified four psychosexual stages, the **oral, anal, phallic,** and **genital.** (He also described a period of "latency" between the phallic and genital stages. Latency is explained in a moment.) At each stage, a different part of the body becomes a child's primary **erogenous zone** (an area capable of producing pleasure). Each area then serves as the main source of pleasure, frustration, and self-expression.

Was Freud's ever-present cigar a sign of an oral fixation? Was it a phallic symbol? Was it both? Or was it neither? An inability to say for sure is one of the shortcomings of psychoanalytic theory.

Freud believed that many adult personality traits can be traced to **fixations** in one or more of the stages.

What is a fixation? A fixation is an unresolved conflict or emotional hang-up caused by overindulgence or by frustration. As we describe the psychosexual stages you'll see why Freud considered fixations important.

The Oral Stage During the first year of life, most of an infant's pleasure comes from stimulation of the mouth. If a child is overfed or frustrated, oral traits may be created. Adult expressions of oral needs include gum chewing, nail biting, smoking, kissing, overeating, and alcoholism.

What if there is an oral fixation? Fixation early in the oral stage produces an **oral-dependent** personality. Oral-dependent persons are gullible (they swallow things easily!) and passive and need lots of attention (they want to be mothered and showered with gifts). Frustrations later in the oral stage may cause aggression, often in the form of biting. Fixations here create cynical, **oral-aggressive** adults who exploit others. They also like to argue. ("Biting sarcasm" is their forte!)

The Anal Stage Between the ages of 1 and 3, the child's attention shifts to the process of elimination. When parents attempt toilet training, the child can gain approval or express rebellion or aggression by "holding on" or by "letting go." Therefore, harsh or lenient toilet training can cause an anal fixation that may lock such responses into personality. Freud described the **anal-retentive** (holding-on) personality as obstinate, stingy, orderly, and compulsively clean. The **anal-expulsive** (letting-go) personality is disorderly, destructive, cruel, or messy.

The Phallic Stage Adult traits of the **phallic personality** are vanity, exhibitionism, sensitive pride, and narcissism (self-love). Freud theorized that phallic fixations develop between the ages of 3 and 6. At this time, increased sexual interest causes the child to be physically attracted to the parent of the opposite sex. In males this attraction leads to an **Oedipus conflict.** In it, the boy feels a rivalry with his father for the affection of his mother. Freud believed that the male child feels threatened by the father (specifically, the boy fears castration). To ease his anxieties, the boy must *identify* with the father. Their rivalry ends when the boy seeks to become more like his father. As he does, he begins to accept the father's values and forms a conscience.

What about the female child? Girls experience an **Electra conflict.** In this case, the girl loves her father and competes with her mother. However, according to Freud, the girl identifies with the mother more gradually.

Freud believed that females already feel castrated. Because of this, they are less driven to identify with their mothers than boys are with their fathers. This, he said, is less effective in creating a conscience. This particular part of Freudian thought has been thoroughly (and rightfully) rejected by modern experts in the psychology of women. It is probably best understood as a reflection of the male-dominated times in which Freud lived.

Latency According to Freud there is a period of **latency** from age 6 to puberty. Latency is not actually a stage. Rather, it is a quiet time during which psychosexual development is dormant. Freud's belief that psychosexual development is "on hold" at this time is hard to accept. Nevertheless, Freud saw latency as a relatively quiet time compared with the stormy first 6 years of life.

The Genital Stage At puberty an upswing in sexual energies activates all the unresolved conflicts of earlier years. This upsurge, according to Freud, is the reason why adolescence can be filled with emotion and turmoil. The genital stage begins at puberty. It is marked, during adolescence, by a growing capacity for responsible social-sexual relationships. The genital stage ends with a mature capacity for love and the realization of full adult sexuality.

Critical Comments As bizarre as Freud's theory might seem, it has been influential for several reasons. First, it pioneered the idea that the first years of life help shape adult personality. Second, it identified feeding, toilet training, and early sexual experiences as critical events in personality formation. Third, Freud was among the first to propose that development proceeds through a series of stages. (Erik Erikson's psycho*social* stages, which cover development from birth to old age, are a modern offshoot of Freudian thinking. See Module 3.7.)

Is the Freudian view of development widely accepted? Few psychologists wholeheartedly embrace Freud's theory today. In some cases Freud was clearly wrong. His portrayal of the elementary school years (latency) as free from sexuality and unimportant for personality development is hard to believe. His idea of the role of a stern or threatening father in the development of a strong conscience in males has also been challenged. Studies show that a son is more likely to develop a strong conscience if his father is affectionate and accepting, rather than stern and punishing. Freud also overemphasized sexuality in personality development. Other motives and cognitive factors are of equal importance.

Freud has been criticized for his views of patients who believed they were sexually molested as children. Freud assumed that such events were merely childhood fantasies. This view led to a long-standing tendency to disbelieve children who have been molested and women who have been raped (Brannon, 1996).

Another important criticism is that Freud's concepts are almost impossible to verify scientifically. The theory provides numerous ways to explain almost any thought, action, or feeling *after* it has occurred. However, it leads to few predictions, which makes its claims difficult to test. Although more criticisms of Freud could be listed, the fact remains that there is an element of truth to much of what he said (Jacob, 2003). Because of this, some clinical psychologists continue to regard Freudian theory as a useful way to think about human problems.

MODULE 10.3 Summary

How do psychodynamic theories explain personality?
- Psychodynamic theories emphasize internal (and often unconscious) forces and mental activities.
- According to Sigmund Freud's psychoanalytic theory, personality consists of three mental systems: the id, the ego, and the superego.
- Libido, derived from the life instincts, is the primary source of energy within the personality.
- Internal conflicts may cause neurotic anxiety or moral anxiety and lead to the use of ego-defense mechanisms.
- Personal awareness operates on three levels: conscious, preconscious, and unconscious.
- According to Freud, personality development occurs in four psychosexual stages: oral, anal, phallic, and genital.
- Fixation at any stage of psychosexual development can leave a lasting imprint on adult personality.

KNOWLEDGE BUILDER

Psychoanalytic Theory

Recite

1. Freud stated that the mind functions on three levels: the conscious, the unconscious, and the
   a. psyche
   b. preconscious
   c. superego
   d. subconscious
2. List the three divisions of personality postulated by Freud. _____ _____ _____
3. Which division is totally unconscious? _____
4. Which division is responsible for moral anxiety? _____
5. Freud proposed the existence of a life instinct known as Thanatos. T or F?
6. Freud's view of personality development is based on the concept of _____ stages.
7. Arrange these stages in the proper order: phallic, anal, genital, oral. _____
8. Freudian theory states that a person who is passive, dependent, and needs lots of attention has a fixation in the
   a. oral stage
   b. superego
   c. Oedipal stage
   d. genital stage

Reflect
Critical Thinking

9. Many adults would find it embarrassing or humiliating to drink from a baby bottle. Can you explain why?

Relate

Try to think of at least one time when your thoughts, feelings, or actions seemed to reflect the workings of each of the following: the id, the ego, and the superego.
 Do you know anyone who seems to have oral, anal, or phallic personality traits? Do you think Freud's concept of fixation explains their characteristics?
 Do any of your personal experiences support the existence of an Oedipus conflict or an Electra conflict? If not, is it possible that you have repressed feelings related to these conflicts?

Link

Internet addresses frequently change. To find the sites listed here, visit http://www.thomsonedu.com/psychology/coon for an updated list of Internet addresses and direct links to relevant sites.
- **Sigmund Freud and the Freud Archives** This site provides an extensive collection of links to Internet resources related to Sigmund Freud and his works. Included in this collection are libraries, museums, and biographical materials as well as materials in the Brill Library archives.
- **Freud & Women** Read about the controversy surrounding Freud's views on women.
- **Psychodynamic and Neo-Freudian Theories** Freud's followers did not always agree with his views. Read about their views on personality.

ANSWERS

1. b 2. id, ego, superego 3. id 4. superego 5. F 6. psychosexual 7. oral, anal, phallic, genital 8. a 9. A psychoanalytic theorist would say that it is because the bottle rekindles oral conflicts and feelings of vulnerability and dependence.

MODULE 10.4 Behavioral and Social Learning Theories

UNLIKE PSYCHOANALYTIC THEORISTS, behavioral theorists explain personality through concepts such as learning, reinforcement, and imitation. Behavioral and social learning theories are based on scientific research, which makes them powerful ways of looking at personality.

Learning Theories of Personality— Habit I Seen You Before?

SURVEY QUESTION: *What do behaviorists and social learning theorists emphasize in personality?*

How do behaviorists approach personality? According to some critics, behaviorists approach personality as if people are robots like Data of *Star Trek* fame. Actually, the behaviorist position is not nearly that mechanistic, and its value is well established. Behaviorists have shown repeatedly that children can *learn* things like kindness, hostility, generosity, or destructiveness. What does this have to do with personality? Everything, according to the behavioral viewpoint.

Behavioral personality theories emphasize that personality is no more (or less) than a collection of learned behavior patterns. Personality, like other learned behavior, is acquired through classical and operant conditioning, observational learning, reinforcement, extinction, generalization, and discrimination. When Mother says, "It's not nice to make mud pies with Mommy's blender. If we want to grow up to be a big girl, we won't do it again, will we?" she serves as a model and in other ways shapes her daughter's personality.

Strict **learning theorists** reject the idea that personality is made up of traits. They would assert, for instance, that there is no such thing as a trait of "honesty" (Mischel, 2004).

Certainly some people are honest and others are not. How can honesty not be a trait? Learning theorists recognize that some people are honest *more often* than others. But knowing this does not allow us to predict whether a person will be honest in a specific situation. It would not be unusual, for example, to find that a person honored for returning a lost wallet had cheated on a test, bought a term paper, or broken the speed limit. If you were to ask a learning theorist, "Are you an honest person?" the reply might be, "In what situation?"

As you can see, learning theorists are interested in the **situational determinants** (external causes) of our actions. A good example of how situations can influence behavior is a study in which people were intentionally overpaid for doing an assigned task. Under normal circumstances, 80 percent kept the extra money without mentioning it. But as few as 17 percent were dishonest if the situation was altered. For instance, if people thought the money was coming out of the pocket of the person doing the study, far fewer were dishonest (Bersoff, 1999). Thus, situations always interact with our prior learning to activate behavior.

Situations vary greatly in their impact. Some are powerful. Others are trivial and have little effect on behavior. The more powerful the situation, the easier it is to see what is meant by *situational determinants*. For example, each of the following situations would undoubtedly have a strong influence on your behavior: an armed terrorist walks onto your bus; you accidentally sit on a lighted cigarette; you find your lover in bed with your best friend. Yet even these situations could provoke very different reactions from different personalities. That's why behavior is always a product of both prior learning and the situations in which we find ourselves (Mischel, Shoda, & Smith, 2004).

Ultimately, what is predictable about personality is that we respond in consistent ways to certain *types of situations*. Consider, for example, two people who are easily angered: One person might get angry when she is delayed (for example, in traffic or a checkout line) but not when she misplaces something at home; the other person might get angry whenever she misplaces things but not when she is delayed. Overall, the two women are equally prone to anger, but their anger tends to occur in different patterns and different types of situations.

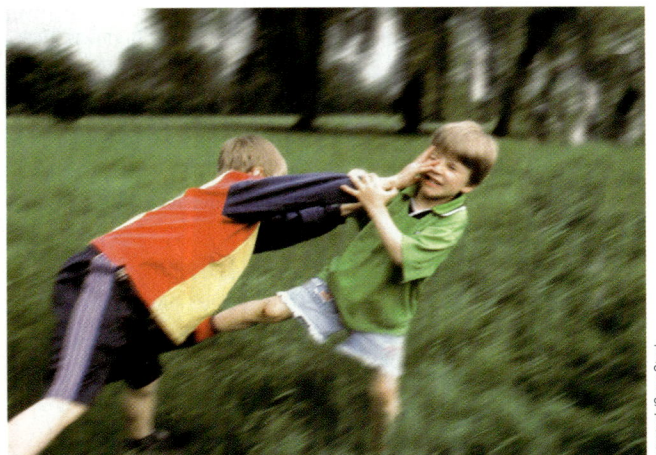

Freud believed that aggressive urges are "instinctual." In contrast, behavioral theories assume that personal characteristics such as aggressiveness are learned. Is this boy's aggression the result of observational learning, harsh punishment, or prior reinforcement?

Seventy-five percent of American college students admit that they have been academically dishonest in one way or another. What can be done about these high rates of dishonesty? The behavioral perspective holds that honesty is determined as much by circumstances as it is by personality. In line with this, simple measures like announcing in classes that integrity codes will be enforced can significantly reduce cheating. Using multiple forms of exams and web-based plagiarism software and educating students about plagiarism also tend to deter dishonesty (Altschuler, 2001; McKeever, 2006).

Personality = Behavior

How do learning theorists view the structure of personality? The behavioral view of personality can be illustrated with an early theory proposed by John Dollard and Neal Miller (1950). In their view, **habits** (learned behavior patterns) make up the structure of personality. As for the dynamics of personality, habits are governed by four elements of learning: *drive, cue, response,* and *reward.* A **drive** is any stimulus strong enough to goad a person to action (such as hunger, pain, lust, frustration, or fear). **Cues** are signals from the environment. These signals guide **responses** (actions) so that they are most likely to bring about **reward** (positive reinforcement).

How does that relate to personality? Let's say a child named Katrina is frustrated by her older brother Kelvin, who takes a toy from her. Katrina could respond in several ways: She could throw a temper tantrum, hit Kelvin, tell Mother, and so forth. The response she chooses is guided by available cues and the previous effects of each response. If telling Mother has paid off in the past and the mother is present, telling again may be her immediate response. If a different set of cues exists (if Mother is absent or if Kelvin looks particularly menacing), Katrina may select some other response. To an outside observer, Katrina's actions seem to reflect her personality. To a learning theorist, they simply express the combined effects of drive, cue, response, and reward.

Doesn't this analysis leave out a lot? Yes. Learning theorists first set out to provide a simple, clear model of personality. But in recent years they have had to face a fact that they originally tended to overlook: People think. The new breed of behavioral psychologists—who include perception, thinking, expectations, and other mental events in their views—are called social learning theorists. Learning principles, modeling, thought patterns, perceptions, expectations, beliefs, goals, emotions, and social relationships are combined in **social learning theory** to explain personality (Mischel, Shoda, & Smith, 2004).

Social Learning Theory

The "cognitive behaviorism" of social learning theory can be illustrated by three concepts proposed by Julian Rotter: the psychological situation, expectancy, and reinforcement value (Rotter & Hochreich, 1975). Let's examine each.

Someone trips you. How do you respond? Your reaction probably depends on whether you think it was planned or an accident. It is not enough to know the setting in which a person responds. We also need to know the person's **psychological situation** (how the person interprets or defines the situation). As another example, let's say you score low on an exam. Do you consider it a challenge to work harder, a sign that you should drop the class, or an excuse to get drunk? Again, your interpretation is important.

Our actions are affected by an **expectancy,** or anticipation, that making a response will lead to reinforcement. To continue the example, if working harder has paid off in the past, it is a likely reaction to a low test score. But to predict your response, we would also have to know if you *expect* your efforts to pay off in the present situation. In fact, expected

---

Behavioral personality theory Any model of personality that emphasizes learning and observable behavior.

Learning theorist A psychologist interested in the ways that learning shapes behavior and explains personality.

Situational determinants External conditions that strongly influence behavior.

Habit A deeply ingrained, learned pattern of behavior.

Drive Any stimulus (especially an internal stimulus such as hunger) strong enough to goad a person to action.

Cue External stimuli that guide responses, especially by signaling the presence or absence of reinforcement.

Response Any behavior, either observable or internal.

Reward Anything that produces pleasure or satisfaction; a positive reinforcer.

Social learning theory An explanation of personality that combines learning principles, cognition, and the effects of social relationships.

Psychological situation A situation as it is perceived and interpreted by an individual, not as it exists objectively.

Expectancy Anticipation about the effect a response will have, especially regarding reinforcement.

Through self-reinforcement we reward ourselves for personal achievements and other "good" behavior.

reinforcement may be more important than actual past reinforcement. And what about the *value* you attach to grades, school success, or personal ability? The third concept of **reinforcement value** states that we attach different subjective values to various activities or rewards. This, too, must be taken into account to understand personality.

Self-Efficacy An ability to control your own life is the essence of what it means to be human. Because of this, Albert Bandura believes that one of the most important expectancies we develop concerns **self-efficacy** (EF-uh-keh-see: a capacity for producing a desired result). You're attracted to someone in your anthropology class. Will you ask him or her out? You're thinking about learning to snowboard. Will you try it this winter? You're beginning to consider a career in psychology. Will you take the courses you need to get into graduate school? You'd like to exercise more on the weekends. Will you join a hiking club? In these and countless other situations, efficacy beliefs play a key role in shaping our lives by influencing the activities and environments we choose (Bandura, 2001; Schultz & Schultz, 2005).

Self-Reinforcement One more idea deserves mention. At times, we all evaluate our actions and may reward ourselves with special privileges or treats for "good behavior." With this in mind, social learning theory adds the concept of self-reinforcement to the behavioristic view. **Self-reinforcement** refers to praising or rewarding yourself for having made a particular response (such as completing a school assignment). Thus, habits of self-praise and self-blame become an important part of personality (Schultz & Schultz, 2005). In fact, self-reinforcement can be thought of as the social learning theorist's counterpart to the superego.

Rate Yourself: Self-Reinforcement

Check the statements in the list that apply to you.

__ I often think positive thoughts about myself.

__ I frequently meet standards that I set for myself.

__ I try not to blame myself when things go wrong.

__ I usually don't get upset when I make mistakes because I learn from them.

__ I can get satisfaction out of what I do even if it's not perfect.

__ When I make mistakes I take time to reassure myself.

__ I don't think talking about what you've done right is too boastful.

__ Praising yourself is healthy and normal.

__ I don't think I have to be upset every time I make a mistake.

__ My feelings of self-confidence and self-esteem stay pretty steady.

People who agree with most of these statements tend to have high rates of self-reinforcement (Heiby, 1983).

Self-reinforcement is closely related to high self-esteem. The reverse is also true: Mildly depressed college students tend to have low rates of self-reinforcement. It is not known if low self-reinforcement leads to depression, or the reverse. In either case, self-reinforcement is associated with less depression and greater life satisfaction (Seybolt & Wagner, 1997). From a behavioral viewpoint, there is value in learning to be "good to yourself."

Behavioristic View of Development

How do learning theorists account for personality development? Many of Freud's ideas can be restated in terms of learning theory. Dollard and Miller (1950) agree with Freud that the first 6 years are crucial for personality development, but for different reasons. Rather than thinking in terms of psychosexual urges and fixations, they ask, "What makes early learning experiences so lasting in their effects?" Their answer is that childhood is a time of urgent drives, powerful rewards and punishments, and crushing frustrations. Also important is **social reinforcement,** which is based on praise, attention, or approval from others. These forces combine to shape the core of personality.

Critical Situations Dollard and Miller believe that during childhood four **critical situations** are capable of leaving a lasting imprint on personality. These are (1) feeding, (2) toilet or cleanliness training, (3) sex training, and (4) learning to express anger or aggression.

Why are these of special importance? Feeding serves as an illustration. If children are fed when they cry, it encourages them to actively manipulate their parents. The child allowed to cry without being fed learns to be passive. Thus, a basic active or passive orientation toward the world may be created by early feeding experiences. Feeding can also affect later social relationships because the child learns to associate people with pleasure or with frustration and discomfort.

Toilet and cleanliness training can be a particularly strong source of emotion for both parents and children. Rashad's parents were aghast the day they found him smearing feces about with joyful abandon. They reacted with sharp punishment, which frustrated and confused Rashad. Many attitudes toward cleanliness, conformity, and bodily functions are formed at such times. Studies have also long shown that severe, punishing, or frustrating toilet training can have undesirable effects on personality development (Christophersen & Mortweet, 2003). Because of this, toilet and cleanliness training demand patience and a sense of humor.

What about sex and anger? When, where, and how a child learns to express anger and sexual feelings can leave an imprint on personality. Specifically, permissiveness for sexual and aggressive behavior in childhood is linked to adult needs for power (McClelland & Pilon, 1983). This link probably occurs because permitting such behaviors allows children to get pleasure from asserting themselves. Sex training also involves learning socially defined "male" and "female" gender roles—which also affect personality (Pervin, Cervone, & John, 2005).

Personality and Gender From birth onward, children are labeled as boys or girls and encouraged to learn sex-appropriate behavior (Denmark, Rabinowitz, & Sechzer, 2005).

What does it mean to have a "masculine" or "feminine" personality? According to social learning theory, identification and imitation contribute greatly to personality development and to sex training. **Identification** refers to the child's emo-

Adult personality is influenced by identification with parents and imitation of their behavior.

tional attachment to admired adults, especially those who provide love and care. Identification typically encourages **imitation,** a desire to act like the admired person. Many "male" or "female" traits come from children's attempts to imitate a same-sex parent with whom they identify.

If children are around parents of both sexes, why don't they imitate behavior typical of the opposite sex as well as of the same sex? You may recall from Chapter 6 that learning takes place vicariously as well as directly. This means that we can learn

> **Reinforcement value** The subjective value a person attaches to a particular activity or reinforcer.
> **Self-efficacy** Belief in your capacity to produce a desired result.
> **Self-reinforcement** Praising or rewarding oneself for having made a particular response (such as completing a school assignment).
> **Social reinforcement** Praise, attention, approval, and/or affection from others.
> **Critical situations** Situations during childhood that are capable of leaving a lasting imprint on personality.
> **Identification** Feeling emotionally connected to a person and seeing oneself as like him or her.
> **Imitation** An attempt to match one's own behavior to another person's behavior.

without direct reward by observing and remembering the actions of others. But the actions we choose to imitate depend on their outcomes. For example, boys and girls have equal chances to observe adults and other children acting aggressively. However, girls are less likely than boys to imitate directly aggressive behavior (shouting at or hitting). Instead, girls are more likely to rely on indirectly aggressive behavior (excluding others from friendship, spreading rumors). This may well be because the expression of direct aggression is thought to be inappropriate for girls. As a consequence, girls rarely see direct female aggression rewarded or approved (Richardson & Green, 1999). In others words, "girlfighting" is likely a culturally reinforced pattern (Brown, 2005). Intriguingly, over the last few years, girls have become more willing to engage in direct aggression as popular culture presents more and more images of directly aggressive women (Artz, 2005).

Historically, parents and other adults in Western countries like the United States tended to encourage boys to engage in **instrumental** (goal-directed) **behaviors,** to be directly aggressive, to hide their emotions, and to prepare for the world of work. Girls, on the other hand, were encouraged in **expressive** (emotion-oriented) **behaviors** and, to a lesser degree, were socialized for motherhood and to be indirectly aggressive. Thus, from an early age males and females tended to grow up in different, gender-defined cultures (Martin & Fabes, 2001). However, it is important to note that these differences are fading as more people redefine traditional male and female gender roles.

We have considered only a few examples of the links between social learning and personality. Nevertheless, the connection is unmistakable. When parents accept their children and give them affection, the children become sociable, positive, and emotionally stable, and they have high self-esteem. When parents are rejecting, punishing, sarcastic, humiliating, or neglectful, their children become hostile, unresponsive, unstable, and dependent and have impaired self-esteem (Triandis & Suh, 2002).

MODULE 10.4 Summary

What do behaviorists and social learning theorists emphasize in personality?

- Behavioral theories of personality emphasize learning, conditioning, and the situational determinants of behavior.
- Learning theorists John Dollard and Neal Miller consider habits the basic core of personality.
- Habits express the combined effects of drive, cue, response, and reward.
- To explain personality, social learning theory combines learning with thinking, expectations, and other mental processes.
- Social learning theory is exemplified by Julian Rotter's concepts of the psychological situation, expectancies, and reinforcement value.
- The behavioristic view of personality development holds that social reinforcement in four situations is critical: feeding, toilet or cleanliness training, sex training, and anger or aggression training.
- Identification and imitation are of particular importance in learning to be "male" or "female."

KNOWLEDGE BUILDER

Behavioral and Social Learning Theories

Recite

1. Learning theorists believe that personality "traits" really are _____ acquired through prior learning. They also emphasize _____ determinants of behavior.
2. Dollard and Miller consider cues the basic structure of personality. T or F?
3. To explain behavior, social learning theorists include mental elements, such as _____ (the anticipation that a response will lead to reinforcement).
4. Self-reinforcement is to behavioristic theory as superego is to psychoanalytic theory. T or F?
5. Which of the following is *not* a "critical situation" in the behaviorist theory of personality development?
   a. feeding
   b. sex training
   c. language training
   d. anger training
6. In addition to basic rewards and punishments, a child's personality is also shaped by _____ reinforcement.
7. Social learning theories of development emphasize the impact of identification and _____.

Reflect

Critical Thinking

8. Rotter's concept of *reinforcement value* is closely related to a motivational principle discussed in Module 9.1. Can you name it?

Relate

What is your favorite style of food? Can you relate Miller and Dollard's concepts of habit, drive, cue, response, and reward to explain your preference?

Some people love to shop. Others hate it. How have the psychological situation, expectancy, and reinforcement value affected your willingness to "shop 'til you drop"?

Who did you identify with as a child? What aspects of that person's behavior did you imitate?

Link

Internet addresses frequently change. To find the sites listed here, visit **http://www.thomsonedu.com/psychology/coon** for an updated list of Internet addresses and direct links to relevant sites.

- **Julian Rotter** Read about Julian Rotter and his social learning theory.
- **Information on Self-Efficacy** Read about Albert Bandura and the idea of self-efficacy.
- **Controlling Your Own Study Behavior** Apply the concept of self-reinforcement to your own studying.

ANSWERS

1. habits, situational 2. F 3. expectancies 4. T 5. c 6. social 7. imitation 8. Incentive value.

Instrumental behaviors Behaviors directed toward the achievement of some goal; behaviors that are instrumental in producing some effect.

Expressive behaviors Behaviors that express or communicate emotion or personal feelings.

MODULE 10.5 Humanistic Theories

AT THE BEGINNING OF THIS CHAPTER you met Annette, an interesting personality. A few years ago, Annette and her husband spent a year riding mules across the country as a unique way to see America and get to know themselves better. Where do such desires for personal growth come from? Humanistic theories pay special attention to the fuller use of human potentials, and they help bring balance to our overall views of personality.

Humanistic Theory—Peak Experiences and Personal Growth

SURVEY QUESTION: *How do humanistic theories differ from other perspectives?*

Humanism focuses on human experience, problems, potentials, and ideals. It is a reaction to the rigidity of traits, the pessimism of psychoanalytic theory, and the mechanical nature of learning theory. At its core is a positive image of what it means to be human. Humanists reject the Freudian view of personality as a battleground for instincts and unconscious forces. Instead, they view human nature as inherently good. (**Human nature** consists of the traits, qualities, potentials, and behavior patterns most characteristic of the human species.) Humanists also oppose the machine-like overtones of behaviorism. We are not, they say, merely a bundle of moldable responses. Rather, we are creative beings capable of **free choice** (an ability to choose that is not determined by genetics, learning, or unconscious forces). In short, humanists seek ways to encourage our potentials to blossom.

To a humanist the person you are today is largely the product of all the choices you have made. Humanists also emphasize immediate **subjective experience** (private perceptions of reality), rather than prior learning. They believe that there are as many "real worlds" as there are people. To understand behavior, we must learn how a person subjectively views the world—what is "real" for her or him.

Who are the major humanistic theorists? Many psychologists have added to the humanistic tradition. Of these, the best known are Carl Rogers (1902–1987) and Abraham Maslow (1908–1970). Because Maslow's idea of self-actualization was introduced in Chapter 1, let's begin with a more detailed look at this facet of his thinking.

Maslow and Self-Actualization

Abraham Maslow became interested in people who were living unusually effective lives. How were they different? To find an answer, Maslow began by studying the lives of great men and women from history, such as Albert Einstein, William James, Jane Addams, Eleanor Roosevelt, Abraham Lincoln, John Muir, and Walt Whitman. From there he moved on to directly study living artists, writers, poets, and other creative individuals.

Along the way, Maslow's thinking changed radically. At first he studied only people of obvious creativity or high achievement. However, it eventually became clear that a housewife, clerk, student, or someone like our friend Annette could live a rich, creative, and satisfying life. Maslow referred to the process of fully developing personal potentials as **self-actualization** (Maslow, 1954). The heart of self-actualization is a continuous search for personal fulfillment (Ewen, 2003; Reiss & Havercamp, 2005).

Characteristics of Self-Actualizers A **self-actualizer** is a person who is living creatively and fully using his or her potentials. In his studies, Maslow found that self-actualizers share many similarities. Whether famous or unknown, well-schooled or uneducated, rich or poor, self-actualizers tend to fit the following profile.

1. **Efficient perceptions of reality.** Self-actualizers are able to judge situations correctly and honestly. They are very sensitive to the fake and dishonest.
2. **Comfortable acceptance of self, others, nature.** Self-actualizers accept their own human nature with all its flaws. The shortcomings of others and the contradictions of the human condition are accepted with humor and tolerance.
3. **Spontaneity.** Maslow's subjects extended their creativity into everyday activities. Actualizers tend to be unusually alive, engaged, and spontaneous.
4. **Task centering.** Most of Maslow's subjects had a mission to fulfill in life or some task or problem outside of themselves to pursue. Humanitarians such as Albert Schweitzer and Mother Teresa represent this quality.
5. **Autonomy.** Self-actualizers are free from reliance on external authorities or other people. They tend to be resourceful and independent.
6. **Continued freshness of appreciation.** The self-actualizer seems to constantly renew appreciation of life's basic goods. A sunset or a flower will be experienced as intensely time after time as it was at first. There is an "innocence of vision," like that of an artist or child.

7. **Fellowship with humanity.** Maslow's subjects felt a deep identification with others and the human situation in general.
8. **Profound interpersonal relationships.** The interpersonal relationships of self-actualizers are marked by deep, loving bonds (Hanley & Abell, 2002).
9. **Comfort with solitude.** Despite their satisfying relationships with others, self-actualizing persons value solitude and are comfortable being alone (Sumerlin & Bundrick, 1996).
10. **Nonhostile sense of humor.** This refers to the wonderful capacity to laugh at oneself. It also describes the kind of humor a man like Abraham Lincoln had. Lincoln probably never made a joke that hurt anybody. His wry comments were a gentle prodding of human shortcomings.
11. **Peak experiences.** All of Maslow's subjects reported the frequent occurrence of **peak experiences** (temporary moments of self-actualization). These occasions were marked by feelings of ecstasy, harmony, and deep meaning. Self-actualizers reported feeling at one with the universe, stronger and calmer than ever before, filled with light, beautiful and good, and so forth.

In summary, self-actualizers feel safe, nonanxious, accepted, loved, loving, and alive.

Maslow's choice of self-actualizing people for study seems pretty subjective. Is it really a fair representation of self-actualization? Although Maslow tried to investigate self-actualization empirically, his choice of people for study was subjective. Undoubtedly there are many ways to make full use of personal potential. Maslow's primary contribution was to draw our attention to the possibility of lifelong personal growth.

What steps can be taken to promote self-actualization? Maslow made few specific recommendations about how to proceed. There is no magic formula for leading a more creative life. Self-actualization is primarily a *process,* not a goal or an end point. As such, it requires hard work, patience, and commitment. Nevertheless, some helpful suggestions can be gleaned from his writings (Maslow, 1954, 1967, 1971). Here are some ways to begin:

1. **Be willing to change.** Begin by asking yourself, "Am I living in a way that is deeply satisfying to me and that truly expresses me?" If not, be prepared to make changes in your life. Indeed, ask yourself this question often and accept the need for continual change.
2. **Take responsibility.** You can become an architect of self by acting as if you are personally responsible for every aspect of your life. Shouldering responsibility in this way helps end the habit of blaming others for your own shortcomings.
3. **Examine your motives.** Self-discovery involves an element of risk. If your behavior is restricted by a desire for safety or security, it may be time to test some limits. Try to make each life decision a choice for growth, not a response to fear or anxiety.
4. **Experience honestly and directly.** Wishful thinking is another barrier to personal growth. Self-actualizers trust themselves enough to accept all kinds of information without distorting it to fit their fears and desires. Try to see yourself as others do. Be willing to admit, "I was wrong," or, "I failed because I was irresponsible."
5. **Make use of positive experiences.** Maslow considered peak experiences temporary moments of self-actualization. Therefore, you might actively repeat activities that have caused feelings of awe, amazement, exaltation, renewal, reverence, humility, fulfillment, or joy.
6. **Be prepared to be different.** Maslow felt that everyone has a potential for "greatness," but most fear becoming what they might. As part of personal growth, be prepared to trust your own impulses and feelings; don't automatically judge yourself by the standards of others. Accept your uniqueness.
7. **Get involved.** With few exceptions, self-actualizers tend to have a mission or "calling" in life. For these people, "work" is not done just to fill deficiency needs, but to satisfy higher yearnings for truth, beauty, community, and meaning. Get personally involved and committed. Turn your attention to problems outside yourself.
8. **Assess your progress.** There is no final point at which one becomes self-actualized. It's important to gauge your progress frequently and to renew your efforts. If you feel bored at school, at a job, or in a relationship, consider it a challenge. Have you been taking responsibility for your own personal growth? Almost any activity can be used as a chance for self-enhancement if it is approached creatively.

Humanism An approach that focuses on human experience, problems, potentials, and ideals.
Human nature Those traits, qualities, potentials, and behavior patterns most characteristic of the human species.
Free choice The ability to freely make choices that are not controlled by genetics, learning, or unconscious forces.
Subjective experience Reality as it is perceived and interpreted, not as it exists objectively.
Self-actualization The process of fully developing personal potentials.
Self-actualizer One who is living creatively and making full use of his or her potentials.
Peak experiences Temporary moments of self-actualization.

Positive Psychology: Positive Personality Traits

It could be said that self-actualizing people are thriving, not just surviving. In recent years, proponents of positive psychology have tried to scientifically study positive personality traits that contribute to happiness and well-being (Keyes & Haidt, 2003; Seligman, 2003). Although their work does not fall within the humanistic tradition, their findings are relevant here.

Martin Seligman, Christopher Peterson, and others have identified six human strengths that contribute to well-being and life satisfaction. Each strength is expressed by the positive personality traits listed here (Peterson & Seligman, 2004).

- **Wisdom and knowledge:** Creativity, curiosity, open-mindedness, love of learning, perspective
- **Courage:** Bravery, persistence, integrity, vitality
- **Humanity:** Love, kindness, social intelligence
- **Justice:** Citizenship, fairness, leadership
- **Temperance:** Forgiveness, humility, prudence, self-control
- **Transcendence:** Appreciation of beauty and excellence, gratitude, hope, humor, spirituality

Which of the positive personality traits are most closely related to happiness? A recent study found that traits of hope, vitality, gratitude, love, and curiosity are strongly associated with life satisfaction (Park, Peterson, & Seligman, 2004). These characteristics, in combination with Maslow's descriptions of self-actualizers, provide a good guide to the characteristics that help people live happy, meaningful lives.

Carl Rogers' Self Theory

Carl Rogers, another well-known humanist, also emphasized the human capacity for inner peace and happiness. The **fully functioning person**, he said, lives in harmony with his or her deepest feelings and impulses. Such people are open to their experiences, and they trust their inner urges and intuitions (Rogers, 1961). Rogers believed that this attitude is most likely to occur when a person receives ample amounts of love and acceptance from others.

Personality Structure and Dynamics Rogers' theory emphasizes the **self**, a flexible and changing perception of personal identity. Much behavior can be understood as an attempt to maintain consistency between our *self-image* and our actions. (Your **self-image** is a total subjective perception of your body and personality.) For example, people who think of themselves as kind tend to be considerate in most situations.

Let's say I know a person who thinks she is kind, but she really isn't. How does that fit Rogers' theory? According to

Humanists consider self-image a central determinant of behavior and personal adjustment.

Rogers, we allow experiences that match our self-image into awareness, where they gradually change the self. Information or feelings inconsistent with the self-image are said to be incongruent. Thus, a person who thinks she is kind but really isn't is in a state of **incongruence.** In other words, there is a discrepancy between her experiences and her self-image. As another example, it would be incongruent to believe that you are a person who "never gets angry" if you spend much of each day seething inside.

Experiences seriously incongruent with the self-image can be threatening and are often distorted or denied conscious recognition. Blocking, denying, or distorting experiences prevents the self from changing. This creates a gulf between the self-image and reality. As the self-image grows more unrealistic, the **incongruent person** becomes confused, vulnerable, dissatisfied, or seriously maladjusted (● Fig. 10.6). In line with Rogers' observations, a study of college students confirmed that being *authentic* is vital for healthy functioning. That is, we need to feel that our behavior accurately expresses who we are (Sheldon et al., 1997). Please note, however, that being authentic doesn't mean you can do whatever you want. Being true to yourself is no excuse for acting irresponsibly or ignoring the feelings of others.

When your self-image is consistent with what you really think, feel, do, and experience, you are best able to actualize your potentials. Rogers also considered it essential to have congruence between the self-image and the **ideal self.** The ideal self is similar to Freud's ego ideal. It is an image of the person you would most like to be.

Is it really incongruent not to live up to your ideal self? Rogers was aware that we never fully attain our ideals. Nevertheless, the greater the gap between the way you see yourself and the way you would like to be, the more tension and anxiety you will experience.

● **FIGURE 10.6** Incongruence occurs when there is a mismatch between any of these three entities: the ideal self (the person you would like to be), your self-image (the person you think you are), and the true self (the person you actually are). Self-esteem suffers when there is a large difference between one's ideal self and self-image. Anxiety and defensiveness are common when the self-image does not match the true self.

THE CLINICAL FILE
Telling Stories about Ourselves

You know these two student types: the carefree party animal and the conscientious bookworm. Perhaps you even think of yourself as one or the other. Is there any truth to these (stereo)types? Can you change your type?

There is little doubt that college life creates a conflict between new opportunities for fun with friends and the need to study hard (McGregor, McAdams, & Little, 2006). In general, our personality traits are relatively stable lifelong characteristics (McAdams & Pals, 2006). As a result, a person high in the Big Five traits of extraversion and agreeableness will tend to embrace a carefree college lifestyle. In comparison, someone high in conscientiousness will find it easier to hit the books (McGregor, McAdams, & Little, 2006).

Does that mean a partyer can't become a bookworm (or vice versa)? It depends: Do you mean over a week? Or a lifetime? As we saw in Module 10.1, personality traits do slowly change as we age. In particular, we tend to become more agreeable and conscientious as we grow older (Roberts, Walton, & Viechtbauer, 2006).

Oh, you need to change by the end of the semester? That's a taller order. One promising approach is to tell yourself stories about possible selves you could become. The *narrative approach* to personality asserts that our personalities are shaped by the stories we tell about ourselves (Pals, 2006). In other words, alternate life stories are not just fantasies or daydreams. They actually influence who we are and who we become. Narratives may even underlie successful psychotherapy. Rather than trying to change personality traits, effective therapists help clients tell better stories about their lives (McAdams & Pals, 2006).

So, if you feel that you are being too careless and carefree at school, start imagining yourself studying more, getting to classes on time, and getting good grades. Listen to the stories of successful students and use them to revise your own story. Visit your campus counseling center to learn more about how to succeed at school. In other words, imagine yourself as a bit more of a bookworm. (Don't worry, your carefree nature won't desert you!)

If you feel you are too conscientious and working too hard, imagine yourself going out to socialize more often. Listen to the stories of your extraverted friends. Imagine the benefits of balancing work and play in your life. If you are shy or perfectionistic, visit your campus counseling center to learn how to become more social or relaxed. And, again, don't worry: Having more fun doesn't mean you will suddenly become irresponsible.

Whatever possible self you choose to pursue, you are more likely to become what you imagine if you elaborate your story, making it more detailed and "real" as you gradually adopt new patterns. You *can* create a new story for yourself, and you *can* make it yours.

Rogers emphasized that to maximize our potentials, we must accept information about ourselves as honestly as possible. In accord with his thinking, researchers have found that people with a close match between their self-image and ideal self tend to be socially poised, confident, and resourceful. Those with a poor match tend to be depressed, anxious, and insecure (Boldero et al., 2005).

According to psychologists Hazel Markus and Paula Nurius (1986), our ideal self is only one of a number of **possible selves** (persons we could become or are afraid of becoming). Annette, who was described earlier, is an interesting personality, to say the least. Annette is one of those people who seems to have lived many lives in the time that most of

Fully functioning person A person living in harmony with her or his deepest feelings, impulses, and intuitions.
Self A continuously evolving conception of one's personal identity.
Self-image Total subjective perception of one's body and personality (another term for self-concept).
Incongruence State that exists when there is a discrepancy between one's experiences and self-image or between one's self-image and ideal self.
Incongruent person A person who has an inaccurate self-image or whose self-image differs greatly from the ideal self.
Ideal self An idealized image of oneself (the person one would like to be).
Possible self A collection of thoughts, beliefs, feelings, and images concerning the person one could become.

us manage only one. Like Annette, you may have pondered many possible personal identities. (See "Telling Stories about Ourselves.")

Possible selves translate our hopes, fears, fantasies, and goals into specific images of who we *could* be. Thus, a beginning law student might picture herself as a successful attorney, an enterprising college student might imagine himself as an Internet entrepreneur, and a person on a diet might imagine both slim and grossly obese possible selves. Such images tend to direct our future behavior (Oyserman et al., 2004).

Of course, almost everyone over age 30 has probably felt the anguish of becoming aware that some cherished possible selves will never be realized. Nevertheless, there is value in asking yourself not just "Who am I?" but also "Who would I like to become?" As you do, remember Maslow's advice that everyone has a potential for "greatness," but most fear becoming what they might.

Humanistic View of Development

Why do mirrors, photographs, video cameras, and the reactions of others hold such fascination and threat for many people? Carl Rogers's theory suggests it is because they provide information about one's self. The development of a self-image depends greatly on information from the environment. It begins with a sorting of perceptions and feelings: my body, my toes, my nose, I want, I like, I am, and so on. Soon, it expands to include self-evaluation: I am a good person, I did something bad just now, and so forth.

How does development of the self contribute to later personality functioning? Rogers believed that positive and negative evaluations by others cause children to develop internal standards of evaluation called **conditions of worth.** In other words, we learn that some actions win our parents' love and approval whereas others are rejected. More important, parents may label some *feelings* as bad or wrong. For example, a child might be told that it is wrong to feel angry toward a brother or sister—even when anger is justified. Likewise, a little boy might be told that he must not cry or show fear, two very normal emotions.

Learning to evaluate some experiences or feelings as "good" and others as "bad" is directly related to a later capacity for self-esteem, positive self-evaluation, or **positive self-regard,** to use Rogers' term. To think of yourself as a good, lovable, worthwhile person, your behavior and experiences must match your internal conditions of worth. The problem is that this can cause incongruence by leading to the denial of many true feelings and experiences.

To put it simply, Rogers blamed many adult emotional problems on attempts to live by the standards of others. He believed that congruence and self-actualization are encouraged by replacing conditions of worth with **organismic valuing** (a natural, undistorted, full-body reaction to an experience). Organismic valuing is a direct, gut-level response to life that avoids the filtering and distortion of incongruence. It involves trusting one's own feelings and perceptions. Organismic valuing is most likely to develop, Rogers felt, when children (or adults) receive **unconditional positive regard** (unshakable love and approval) from others. That is, when they are "prized" as worthwhile human beings, just for being themselves, without any conditions or strings attached. Although this may be a luxury few people enjoy, we are more likely to move toward our ideal selves if we receive affirmation and support from a close partner (Drigotas et al., 1999).

MODULE 10.5 Summary

How do humanistic theories differ from other perspectives?

- Humanistic theories stress subjective experience, free choice, self-actualization, and positive models of human nature.
- Abraham Maslow's study of self-actualizers showed that they share traits that range from efficient perceptions of reality to frequent peak experiences.
- Self-actualization is best viewed as an ongoing process of personal growth, rather than a final destination.
- Positive psychologists have identified six human strengths that contribute to well-being and life satisfaction: wisdom and knowledge, courage, humanity, justice, temperance, and transcendence.
- Carl Rogers viewed the self as an entity that emerges from personal experience. Optimal functioning occurs when there is a good match between your true self, your self-image, and your ideal self.
- The incongruent person has an unrealistic self-image and/or a mismatch between the self-image and the ideal self. The congruent or fully functioning person is flexible and open to experiences and feelings.
- In the development of personality, humanists are interested in the emergence of a self-image and in self-evaluations.
- As parents apply conditions of worth to children's behavior, thoughts, and feelings, children begin to do the same. Internalized conditions of worth then contribute to incongruence.
- Positive self-regard is nurtured by organismic valuing and by receiving unconditional positive regard.

KNOWLEDGE BUILDER

Humanistic Theories

Recite

1. Humanists view human nature as basically good, and they emphasize the effects of subjective learning and unconscious choice. T or F?
2. Maslow used the term _____ to describe the tendency of certain individuals to fully use their talents and potentials.
3. According to Rogers, a close match between the self-image and the ideal self creates a condition called incongruence. T or F?
4. Markus and Nurius describe alternative self-concepts that a person may have as "possible selves." T or F?
5. Carl Rogers believed that personal growth is encouraged when conditions of worth are replaced by
   a. self-efficacy
   b. instrumental worth
   c. latency
   d. organismic valuing
6. According to Maslow, a preoccupation with one's own thoughts, feelings, and needs is characteristic of self-actualizing individuals. T or F?
7. Maslow thought of peak experiences as temporary moments of
   a. congruence
   b. positive self-regard
   c. self-actualization
   d. self-reinforcement
8. Which of the following is *not* one of the six human strengths identified by positive psychologists?
   a. congruence
   b. courage
   c. justice
   d. transcendence

Reflect
Critical Thinking

9. What role would "possible selves" have in the choice of a college major?

Relate

How do your views of human nature and free choice compare with those of the humanists?

Do you know anyone who seems to be making especially good use of his or her personal potentials? Does that person fit Maslow's profile of a self-actualizer?

How much difference do you think there is between your self-image, your ideal self, and your true self? Do you think Rogers is right about the effects of applying conditions of worth to your perceptions and feelings?

Link

Internet addresses frequently change. To find the sites listed here, visit **http://www.thomsonedu.com/psychology/coon** for an updated list of Internet addresses and direct links to relevant sites.

- **About Humanistic Psychology** Discusses the history and future of humanistic psychology.
- **Maslow's Hierarchy of Needs** Read more about Maslow's hierarchy of needs and self-actualization.
- **Some Observations on the Organization of Personality** Read an original article by Carl Rogers.

ANSWERS

1. F 2. self-actualization 3. F 4. T 5. d 6. F 7. c 8. a 9. Career decisions almost always involve, in part, picturing oneself occupying various occupational roles.

Conditions of worth Internal standards used to judge the value of one's thoughts, actions, feelings, or experiences.
Positive self-regard Thinking of oneself as a good, lovable, worthwhile person.
Organismic valuing A natural, undistorted, full-body reaction to an experience.
Unconditional positive regard Unshakable love and approval given without qualification.

MODULE 10.6 Personality Assessment

MEASURING PERSONALITY can help predict how people will behave at work, at school, and in therapy. However, painting a detailed picture can be a challenge. In many instances, it requires several of the techniques described in this module. To capture a personality as unique as Annette's, it might take all of them!

Personality Assessment—Psychological Yardsticks

SURVEY QUESTION: *How do psychologists measure personality?*

Psychologists use interviews, observation, questionnaires, and projective tests to assess personality (Burger, 2008). Each method has strengths and limitations. For this reason, they are often used in combination.

Formal personality measures are refinements of more casual ways of judging a person. At one time or another, you have probably "sized up" a potential date, friend, or roommate by engaging in conversation (interview). Perhaps you have asked a friend, "When I am delayed I get angry. Do you?" (questionnaire). Maybe you watch your professors when they are angry or embarrassed to learn what they are "really" like when they're caught off-guard (observation). Or possibly you have noticed that when you say, "I think people feel . . . ," you may be expressing your own feelings (projection). Let's see how psychologists apply each of these methods to probe personality.

The Interview

In an **interview,** direct questioning is used to learn about a person's life history, personality traits, or current mental state (Sommers-Flanagan & Sommers-Flanagan, 2002). In an **unstructured interview,** conversation is informal and topics are taken up freely as they arise. In a **structured interview,** information is gathered by asking a planned series of questions.

How are interviews used? Interviews are used to identify personality disturbances; to select people for jobs, college, or special programs; and to study the dynamics of personality. Interviews also provide information for counseling or therapy. For instance, a counselor might ask a depressed person, "Have you ever contemplated suicide? What were the circumstances?" The counselor might then follow by asking, "How did you feel about it?" or, "How is what you are now feeling different from what you felt then?"

In addition to providing information, interviews make it possible to observe a person's tone of voice, hand gestures, posture, and facial expressions. Such "body language" cues are important because they may radically alter the message sent, as when a person claims to be "completely calm" but trembles uncontrollably.

Limitations Interviews give rapid insight into personality, but they have limitations. For one thing, interviewers can be swayed by preconceptions. A person identified as a "housewife," "college student," "high school athlete," "punk," "geek," or "ski bum" may be misjudged because of an interviewer's personal biases. Second, an interviewer's own personality, or even gender, may influence a client's behavior. When this occurs, it can accentuate or distort the person's apparent traits (Pollner, 1998). A third problem is that people sometimes try to deceive interviewers. For example, a person accused of a crime might try to avoid punishment by pretending to be mentally disabled.

A fourth problem is the **halo effect,** which is the tendency to generalize a favorable (or unfavorable) impression to an entire personality (Lance, LaPointe, & Stewart, 1994). Because of the halo effect, a person who is likable or physically attractive may be rated more mature, intelligent, or mentally healthy than she or he actually is.

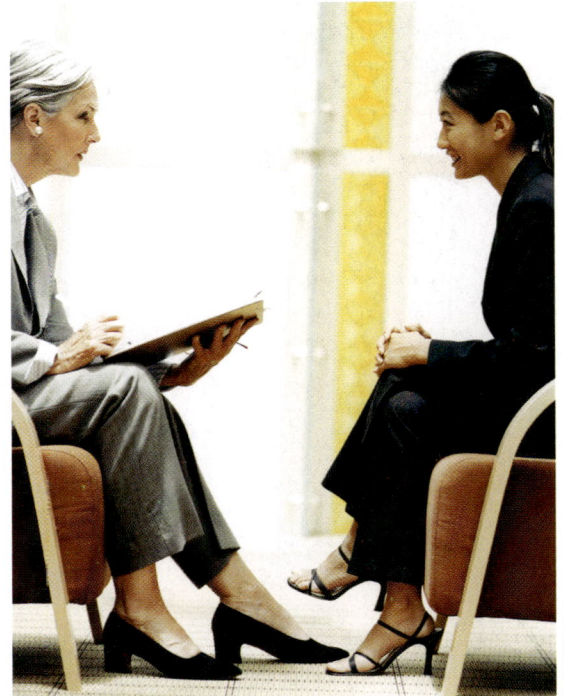

What is your initial impression of the person wearing the black suit? If you think that she looks friendly, attractive, or neat, your subsequent perceptions might be altered by a positive first impression. Interviewers are often influenced by the halo effect (see text).

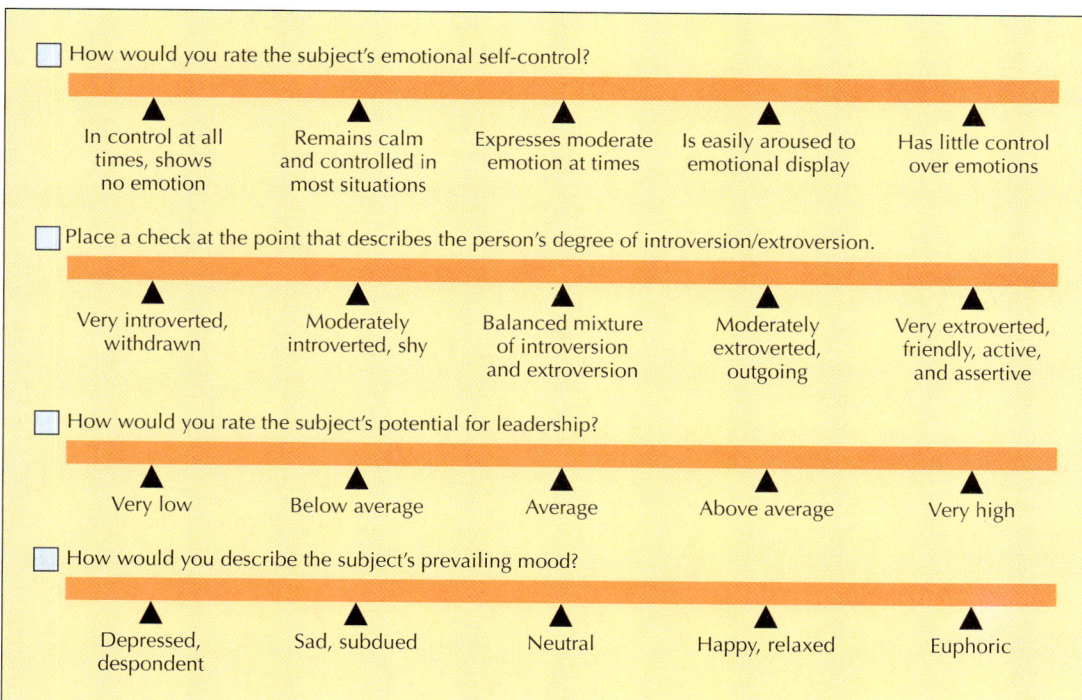

● **FIGURE 10.7** Sample rating scale items. To understand how the scale works, imagine someone you know well. Where would you place check marks on each of the scales to rate that person's characteristics?

Even with their limitations, interviews are a respected method of assessment. In many cases, interviews are the first step in evaluating personality and an essential prelude to therapy. Nevertheless, interviews are usually not enough and must be supplemented by other measures and tests (Meyer et al., 2001).

Direct Observation and Rating Scales

Are you fascinated by airports, bus depots, parks, taverns, subway stations, or other public places? Many people relish a chance to observe the actions of others. When used for assessment, **direct observation** (looking at behavior) is a simple extension of this natural interest in "people watching." For instance, a psychologist might arrange to observe a disturbed child as she plays with other children. Is the child withdrawn? Does she become hostile or aggressive without warning? By careful observation, the psychologist can identify the girl's personality traits and clarify the nature of her problems.

Wouldn't observation be subject to the same problems of misperception as an interview? Yes. Misperceptions can be a difficulty, which is why rating scales are sometimes used (● Fig. 10.7). A **rating scale** is a list of personality traits or aspects of behavior that can be used to evaluate a person. Rating scales limit the chance that some traits will be overlooked while others are exaggerated (Synhorst et al., 2005). Perhaps they should be a standard procedure for choosing a roommate, spouse, or lover!

An alternative approach is to do a **behavioral assessment** by counting the frequency of specific behaviors. In this case, observers record *actions,* not what traits they think a person has (Ramsay, Reynolds, & Kamphaus, 2002). For example, a psychologist working with hospitalized mental patients might note the frequency of a patient's aggression, self-care, speech, and unusual behaviors. Behavioral assessments can also be used to probe thought processes. In one study, for example, couples were assessed while communicating with each other about their sexuality. Couples with sexual difficulties were less likely to be receptive to talking about their sexuality and more likely to blame each other than were couples with no sexual difficulties (Kelly, Strassberg, & Turner, 2006).

Interview (personality) A face-to-face meeting held for the purpose of gaining information about an individual's personal history, personality traits, current psychological state, and so forth.
Unstructured interview An interview in which conversation is informal and topics are taken up freely as they arise.
Structured interview An interview that follows a prearranged plan, usually a series of planned questions.
Halo effect The tendency to generalize a favorable or unfavorable first impression to unrelated details of personality.
Direct observation Assessing behavior through direct surveillance.
Rating scale A list of personality traits or aspects of behavior on which a person is rated.
Behavioral assessment Recording the frequency of various behaviors.

Situational Testing In **situational testing,** real-life conditions are simulated so that a person's spontaneous reactions can be observed. Such tests assume that the best way to learn how people react is to put them in realistic situations and watch what happens. Situational tests expose people to frustration, temptation, pressure, boredom, or other conditions capable of revealing personality characteristics (Olson-Buchanan & Drasgow, 2006; Weekley & Jones, 1997). Some popular "reality TV" programs, such as *American Idol, Survivor,* and *The Amazing Race* bear some similarity to situational tests—which may account for their ability to attract millions of viewers.

How are situational tests done? An interesting example of situational testing is the judgmental firearms training provided by many police departments. At times, police officers must make split-second decisions about using their weapons. A mistake could be fatal. In a typical shoot/don't-shoot test, actors play the part of armed criminals. As various high-risk scenes are acted out live, on videotape, or by computer, officers must decide to shoot or hold fire. A newspaper reporter who once took the test (and failed it) gives this account (Gersh, 1982):

> I judged wrong. I was killed by a man in a closet, a man with a hostage, a woman interrupted when kissing her lover, and a man I thought was cleaning a shotgun. . . . I shot a drunk who reached for a comb, and a teenager who pulled out a black water pistol. Looked real to me.

In addition to the training it provides, situational testing uncovers police cadets who lack the good judgment needed to carry a gun out on the street.

Personality Questionnaires

Personality questionnaires are paper-and-pencil tests that reveal personality characteristics. Questionnaires are more objective than interviews or observation. (An **objective test** gives the same score when different people correct it.) Questions, administration, and scoring are all standardized so that scores are unaffected by any biases an examiner may have. However, this is not enough to ensure accuracy. A good test must also be reliable and valid. A test is **reliable** if it yields close to the same score each time it is given to the same person. A test has **validity** if it measures what it claims to measure. Unfortunately, many personality tests you will encounter, such as those in magazines or on the Internet, have little or no validity.

Dozens of personality tests are available, including the *Guilford-Zimmerman Temperament Survey,* the *California Psychological Inventory,* the *Allport-Vernon Study of Values,* the 16 PF, and many more. One of the best-known and most widely used objective tests is the **Minnesota Multiphasic Personality Inventory-2** (**MMPI-2**) (Butcher, 2005). The MMPI-2 is composed of 567 items to which a test taker must respond "true" or "false." Items include statements such as the following.

> Everything tastes the same.
> I am very normal, sexually.
> I like birds.
> I usually daydream in the afternoon.
> Mostly I stay away from other people.
> Someone has been trying to hurt me.
> Sometimes I think strange thoughts.*

How can these items show anything about personality? For instance, what if a person has a cold so that "everything tastes the same"? For an answer (and a little bit of fun), read the following items. Answer "Yes," "No," or "Don't bother me, I can't cope!"

> I would enjoy the work of a chicken flicker.
> My eyes are always cold.
> Frantic screaming makes me nervous.
> I believe I smell as good as most people.
> I use shoe polish to excess.
> The sight of blood no longer excites me.
> As an infant I had very few hobbies.
> Dirty stories make me think about sex.
> I stay in the bathtub until I look like a raisin.
> I salivate at the sight of mittens.
> I never finish what I†

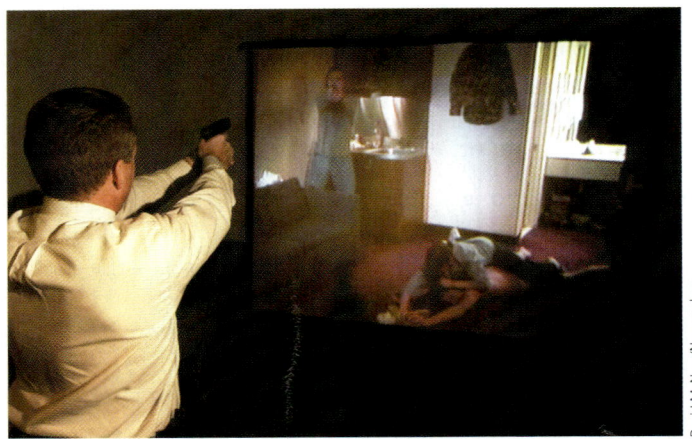

A police officer undergoes judgmental firearms training. Variations on this situational test are used by a growing number of police departments. All officers must score a passing grade.

*MMPI-2 statements themselves cannot be reproduced to protect the validity of the test.
†Art Buchwald quotation courtesy of Art Buchwald, *Washington Post.*

These items were written by humorist Art Buchwald (1965) to satirize personality questionnaires. Such questions may seem ridiculous, but they are not very different from the real thing. How, then, do the items on tests such as the MMPI-2 reveal anything about personality? The answer is that a single item tells little about personality. For example, a person who agrees that "Everything tastes the same" might simply have a cold. It is only through *patterns* of response that personality dimensions are revealed.

Items on the MMPI-2 were selected for their ability to correctly identify persons with particular psychological problems (Butcher, 2005). For instance, if depressed persons consistently answer a series of items in a particular way, it is assumed that others who answer the same way are also prone to depression. As silly as the gag items in the preceding lists may seem, it is possible that some could actually work in a legitimate test. But before an item could be part of a test, it would have to be shown to correlate highly with some trait or dimension of personality.

The MMPI-2 measures 10 major aspects of personality (listed in ■ Table 10.4). After the MMPI-2 is scored, results are charted graphically as an **MMPI-2 profile** (● Fig. 10.8). By comparing a person's profile to scores produced by typical, normal adults, a psychologist can identify various personality disorders. Additional scales can identify substance abuse, eat-

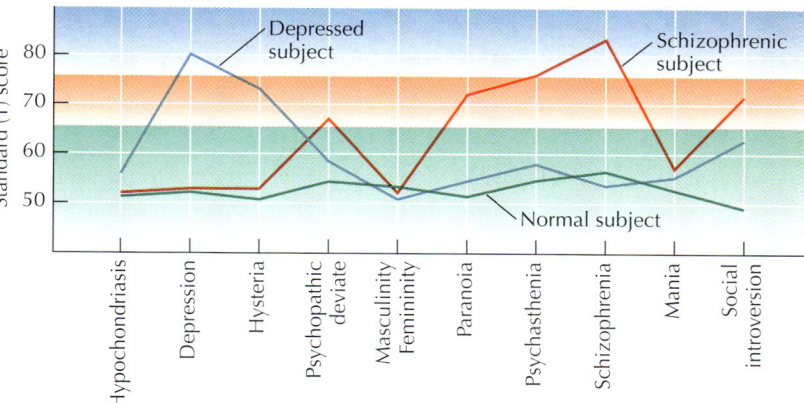

● **FIGURE 10.8** An MMPI-2 profile showing hypothetical scores indicating normality, depression, and psychosis. High scores begin at 66 and very high scores at 76. An unusually low score (40 and below) may also reveal personality characteristics or problems.

ing disorders, Type A (heart-attack prone) behavior, repression, anger, cynicism, low self-esteem, family problems, inability to function in a job, and other problems (Butcher, 2005).

How accurate is the MMPI-2? Personality questionnaires are only accurate if people tell the truth about themselves. Because of this, the MMPI-2 has additional **validity scales** that reveal whether a person's scores should be discarded. The validity scales detect attempts by test takers to "fake good" (make themselves look good) or "fake bad" (make it look like they have problems). Other scales uncover defensiveness or tendencies to exaggerate shortcomings and troubles. When taking the MMPI-2, it is best to answer honestly, without trying to second-guess the test.

A clinical psychologist trying to decide if a person has emotional problems would be wise to take more than the MMPI-2 into account. Test scores are informative, but they

■ **TABLE 10.4** MMPI-2 Basic Clinical Subscales

1. **Hypochondriasis** (HI-po-kon-DRY-uh-sis). Exaggerated concern about one's physical health.
2. **Depression.** Feelings of worthlessness, hopelessness, and pessimism.
3. **Hysteria.** The presence of physical complaints for which no physical basis can be established.
4. **Psychopathic deviate.** Emotional shallowness in relationships and a disregard for social and moral standards.
5. **Masculinity/femininity.** One's degree of traditional "masculine" aggressiveness or "feminine" sensitivity.
6. **Paranoia.** Extreme suspiciousness and feelings of persecution.
7. **Psychasthenia** (sike-as-THEE-nee-ah). The presence of obsessive worries, irrational fears (phobias), and compulsive (ritualistic) actions.
8. **Schizophrenia.** Emotional withdrawal and unusual or bizarre thinking and actions.
9. **Mania.** Emotional excitability, manic moods or behavior, and excessive activity.
10. **Social introversion.** One's tendency to be socially withdrawn.

(Reproduced by permission. © 1943, renewed 1970 by the University of Minnesota. Published by the Psychological Corporation, New York. All rights reserved.)

Situational test Simulating real-life conditions so that a person's reactions may be directly observed.
Personality questionnaire A paper-and-pencil test consisting of questions that reveal aspects of personality.
Objective test A test that gives the same score when different people correct it.
Reliability The ability of a test to yield nearly the same score each time it is given to the same person.
Validity The ability of a test to measure what it purports to measure.
Minnesota Multiphasic Personality Inventory-2 (MMPI-2) One of the best-known and most widely used objective personality questionnaires.
MMPI-2 profile A graphic representation of an individual's scores on each of the primary scales of the MMPI-2.
Validity scales Scales that tell whether test scores should be invalidated for lying, inconsistency, or "faking good."

CRITICAL THINKING

Honesty Tests—Do They Tell the Truth?

Each year, millions of anxious job seekers take paper-and-pencil honesty tests given by companies that hope to avoid hiring dishonest workers (Spector, 2005). **Honesty tests** (also known as integrity tests) assume that poor attitudes toward dishonest acts predispose a person to dishonest behavior. Examples include attitudes toward taking office supplies home or leaving work early. Most of the tests also ask people how honest they think the average person is and how honest they are in comparison. Surprisingly, many job applicants willingly rate their own honesty as below average (Neuman & Baydoun, 1998). (You have to admire them for being honest about it!) Honesty tests also ask about prior brushes with the law, past acts of theft or deceit, and attitudes toward alcohol and drug use.

Is honesty testing valid? This question is still very much in dispute. Some psychologists believe that the best honesty tests are sufficiently valid to be used for making hiring decisions (Ones & Viswesvaran, 2001). Others, however, remain unconvinced. Most studies have failed to demonstrate that honesty tests can accurately *predict* if a person will be a poor risk on the job (Horn, Nelson, & Brannick, 2004; Ones, Viswesvaran, & Schmidt, 2003). Psychologists are also concerned because honesty tests are often administered by untrained people.

Yet another cause for concern is the fact that 96 percent of test takers who fail are *falsely labeled* as dishonest (Camara & Schneider, 1994). In North America alone, that means well over a million workers a year are wrongly accused of being dishonest (Rieke & Guastello, 1995).

Some states have banned the use of honesty tests as the sole basis for deciding whether to hire a person. Yet, it's easy to understand why employers want to do whatever they can to reduce theft and dishonesty in the workplace. The pressures to use honesty tests are intense. No doubt, the debate about honesty testing will continue. Honest.

can incorrectly label some people (Urbina, 2004). ("Honesty Tests" discusses a related problem.) Fortunately, clinical judgments usually rely on information from interviews, tests, and other sources. Also, despite their limitations, it is reassuring to note that psychological assessments are at least as accurate as commonly used medical tests (Meyer et al., 2001).

Projective Tests of Personality—Inkblots and Hidden Plots

Projective tests take a different approach to personality. Interviews, observation, rating scales, and inventories try to directly identify overt, observable traits (Leichtman, 2004). By contrast, projective tests seek to uncover deeply hidden or *unconscious* wishes, thoughts, and needs.

As a child you may have delighted in finding faces and objects in cloud formations. Or perhaps you have learned something about your friends' personalities from their reactions to movies or paintings. If so, you will have some insight into the rationale for projective tests. In a **projective test,** a person is asked to describe ambiguous stimuli or make up stories about them. Describing an unambiguous stimulus (a picture of an automobile, for example) tells little about your personality. But when you are faced with an unstructured stimulus, you must organize what you see in terms of your own life experiences. Everyone sees something different in a projective test, and what is perceived can reveal the inner workings of personality.

Projective tests have no right or wrong answers, which makes them difficult to fake (Leichtman, 2004). Moreover, projective tests can be a rich source of information, because responses are not restricted to simple true/false or yes/no answers.

The Rorschach Inkblot Test

Is the inkblot test a projective technique? The inkblot test, or **Rorschach Technique** (ROAR-shock), is one of the oldest and most widely used projective tests. Developed by Swiss psychologist Hermann Rorschach in the 1920s, it consists of 10 standardized inkblots. These vary in color, shading, form, and complexity.

How does the test work? First, a person is shown each blot and asked to describe what she or he sees in it (● Fig. 10.9). Later the psychologist may return to a blot, asking the person to identify specific sections of it, to expand previous descriptions, or to give new impressions about what it contains. Obvious differences in content—such as "blood dripping from a dagger" versus "flowers blooming in a basket"—are important for identifying personal conflicts and fantasies. But surprisingly, content is less important than what parts of the inkblot are used to organize images. These factors allow psychologists to detect emotional disturbances by observing how a person perceives the world (Hilsenroth, 2000).

The Thematic Apperception Test

Another popular projective test is the **Thematic Apperception Test** (**TAT**) developed by personality theorist Henry Murray (1893–1988).

How does the TAT differ from the Rorschach? The TAT consists of 20 sketches depicting various scenes and life situ-

● **FIGURE 10.9** Inkblots similar to those used on the Rorschach. What do you see?

ations (● Fig. 10.10). During testing, a person is shown each sketch and asked to make up a story about the people in it. Later, the person looks at each sketch a second or a third time and elaborates on previous stories or creates new stories.

To score the TAT, a psychologist analyzes the content of the stories. Interpretations focus on how people feel, how they interact, what events led up to the incidents depicted in the sketch, and how the story will end. For example, TAT stories told by bereaved college students typically include themes of death, grief, and coping with loss (Balk et al., 1998).

A psychologist might also count the number of times the central figure in a TAT story is angry, overlooked, apathetic, jealous, or threatened. Here is a story written by a student to describe Figure 10.10:

● **FIGURE 10.10** This is a picture like those used for the Thematic Apperception Test. If you wish to simulate the test, tell a story that explains what led up to the pictured situation, what is happening now, and how the action will end.

The girl has been seeing this guy her mother doesn't like. The mother is telling her that she better not see him again. The mother says, "He's just like your father." The mother and father are divorced. The mother is smiling because she thinks she is right. But she doesn't really know what the girl wants. The girl is going to see the guy again, anyway.

As this example implies, the TAT is especially good at revealing feelings about a person's social relationships (Alvarado, 1994; Aronow, Altman Weiss, & Reznikoff, 2001).

Limitations of Projective Testing Although projective tests have been popular, their validity is considered lowest among tests of personality (Lilienfeld, 1999; Wood et al., 2003). Objectivity and reliability (consistency) are also low for different users of the TAT and Rorschach. Note that after a person interprets an ambiguous stimulus, the scorer must interpret the person's (sometimes) ambiguous responses. In a sense, the interpretation of a projective test may be a projective test for the scorer!

Despite their drawbacks, projective tests still have value (Hilsenroth, 2000). This is especially true when they are used as part of a **test battery** (collection of assessment devices and interviews). In the hands of a skilled clinician, projective tests

---

Honesty test A paper-and-pencil test designed to detect attitudes, beliefs, and behavior patterns that predispose a person to dishonest behavior.
Projective tests Psychological tests making use of ambiguous or unstructured stimuli.
Rorschach Technique A projective test comprised of 10 standardized inkblots.
Thematic Apperception Test (TAT) A projective test consisting of 20 different scenes and life situations about which respondents make up stories.
Test battery A group of tests and interviews given to the same individual.

can be a good way to detect major conflicts, to get clients to talk about upsetting topics, and to set goals for therapy (O'Roark, 2001).

Sudden Murderers—A Research Example

Personality assessments provide us with clues to some of the most perplexing human events. Consider Fred Cowan, a model student in school and described by those who knew him as quiet, gentle, and a man who loved children. Despite his size (6 feet tall, 250 pounds), Fred was described by a coworker as "someone you could easily push around."

Fred Cowan represents a puzzling phenomenon: We occasionally read in the news about sudden murderers—gentle, quiet, shy, good-natured people who explode without warning into violence (Cartwright, 2002a; Lee, Zimbardo, & Bertholf, 1977). Two weeks after he was suspended from his job, Fred returned to work determined to get even with his supervisor. Unable to find the man, he killed four co-workers and a policeman before taking his own life.

Isn't such behavior contrary to the idea of personality traits? It might seem that sudden murderers are newsworthy simply because they are unlikely candidates for violence. On the contrary, research conducted by Melvin Lee, Philip Zimbardo, and Minerva Bertholf suggests that sudden murderers explode into violence *because* they are shy, restrained, and inexpressive, not in spite of it. These researchers studied prisoners at a California prison. Ten were inmates whose homicide was an unexpected first offense. Nine were criminals with a record of habitual violence prior to murder. Sixteen were inmates convicted of nonviolent crimes.

Did the inmates differ in personality makeup? Each of the inmates took a battery of tests, including the MMPI, a measure of shyness, and an adjective checklist (in which inmates described themselves by selecting relevant adjectives from a list of adjectives used to describe people). Personal interviews were also done with each inmate. As expected, the sudden murderers were passive, shy, and over-controlled (restrained) individuals. The habitually violent inmates were "masculine" (aggressive), under-controlled (impulsive), and less likely to view themselves as shy than the inmates convicted of nonviolent crimes (Lee, Zimbardo, & Bertholf, 1977).

Psychologists have learned that quiet, over-controlled individuals are likely to be especially violent if they ever lose control. Their attacks are usually triggered by a minor irritation or frustration, but the attack reflects years of unexpressed feelings of anger and belittlement. When sudden murderers finally release the strict controls they have maintained on their overcontrolled behavior, a furious and frenzied attack ensues (Cartwright, 2002b). Usually it is totally out of proportion to the offense against them and many have amnesia for their violent actions.

In comparison, the previously violent murderers showed very different reactions. Although they killed, their violence was moderate—usually only enough to do the necessary damage. Typically, they felt they had been cheated or betrayed and that they were doing what was necessary to remedy the situation or maintain their manhood (Lee, Zimbardo, & Bertholf, 1977).

A Look Ahead The preceding example illustrates how some of the concepts and techniques discussed in this chapter can be applied to further our understanding. The "Psychology in Action" module that follows should add balance to your view of personality. Don't be shy. Read on!

MODULE 10.6 Summary

How do psychologists measure personality?

- Personality is typically assessed with interviews, direct observation, questionnaires, and projective tests.
- Structured and unstructured interviews provide much information, but they are subject to interviewer bias, misperceptions, and the halo effect.
- Direct observation, sometimes involving situational tests, behavioral assessment, or rating scales, allows psychologists to evaluate a person's actual behavior.
- To have any value, personality measures must be reliable and valid.
- Personality questionnaires, such as the Minnesota Multiphasic Personality Inventory-2 (MMPI-2), are objective and reliable, but their validity is open to question.
- Projective tests ask a person to project thoughts or feelings to an ambiguous stimulus or unstructured situation.
- The Rorschach Technique, or inkblot test, is a well-known projective technique. A second is the Thematic Apperception Test (TAT).
- Projective tests are low in validity and objectivity. Nevertheless, they are considered useful by many clinicians.
- Accurate measures of personality often require the use of a test battery (collection of assessment devices and interviews).

KNOWLEDGE BUILDER

Personality Assessment

Recite

1. The halo effect can be a serious problem in accurate personality assessment that is based on
   a. projective testing
   b. behavioral recording
   c. interviewing
   d. the TAT
2. Which of the following is considered the most objective measure of personality?
   a. rating scales
   b. personality questionnaires
   c. projective tests
   d. TAT
3. Situational testing allows direct _____ of personality characteristics.
4. A psychotic person would probably score highest on which MMPI-2 scale?
   a. depression
   b. hysteria
   c. schizophrenia
   d. mania
5. The use of ambiguous stimuli is most characteristic of
   a. interviews
   b. projective tests
   c. personality inventories
   d. direct observation
6. The content of one's responses to the MMPI-2 is considered an indication of unconscious wishes, thoughts, and needs. T or F?
7. Doing a behavioral assessment requires direct observation of the person's actions or a direct report of the person's thoughts. T or F?
8. Which of the following items *does not* belong with the others?
   a. Rorschach Technique
   b. TAT
   c. MMPI-2
   d. projective testing
9. A surprising finding is that sudden murderers are usually under-controlled, very masculine, and more impulsive than average. T or F?
10. A test is considered valid if it consistently yields the same score when the same person takes it on different occasions. T or F?

Reflect
Critical Thinking

11. Can you think of one more reason why personality traits may not be accurately revealed by interviews?
12. Projective testing would be of greatest interest to which type of personality theorist?

Relate

How do *you* assess personality? Do you informally make use of any of the methods described in this chapter?

You are a candidate for a desirable job. Your personality is going to be assessed by a psychologist. What method (or methods) would you prefer that she or he use? Why?

Link

Internet addresses frequently change. To find the sites listed here, visit **http://www.thomsonedu.com/psychology/coon** for an updated list of Internet addresses and direct links to relevant sites.

- **Personality and IQ Tests** Multiple links to personality tests and IQ tests that are scored online.
- **MMPI** Explore a research project about the MMPI.
- **The Classical Rorschach** Explore Hermann Rorschach and his famous inkblot test.

ANSWERS

1. c 2. b 3. observation 4. c 5. b 6. F 7. T 8. c 9. F 10. F 11. Because of trait-situation interactions, a person may not behave in a normal fashion while being evaluated in an interview. 12. Psychodynamic, because projective testing is designed to uncover unconscious thoughts, feelings, and conflicts.

MODULE 10.7 Psychology in Action
Barriers and Bridges— Understanding Shyness

SURVEY QUESTIONS: *What causes shyness? What can be done about it?*

As a personality trait, **shyness** refers to a tendency to avoid others, as well as feelings of anxiety, preoccupation, and social inhibition (uneasiness and strain when socializing) (Bruch, 2001). Shy persons fail to make eye contact, retreat when spoken to, speak too quietly, and display little interest or animation in conversations. Do you:

- Find it hard to talk to strangers?
- Lack confidence with people?
- Feel uncomfortable in social situations?
- Feel nervous with people who are not close friends?

Mild shyness may be no more than a nuisance. However, extreme shyness is often associated with depression, loneliness, fearfulness, social anxiety, inhibition, and low self-esteem (Derlega, Winstead, & Jones, 2005; Jackson et al., 2002).

Elements of Shyness

What causes shyness? To begin with, shy persons often lack **social skills** (proficiency at interacting with others). Many simply have not learned how to meet people or how to start a conversation and keep it going. **Social anxiety** (a feeling of apprehension in the presence of others) is also a factor in shyness. Almost everyone feels nervous in some social situations

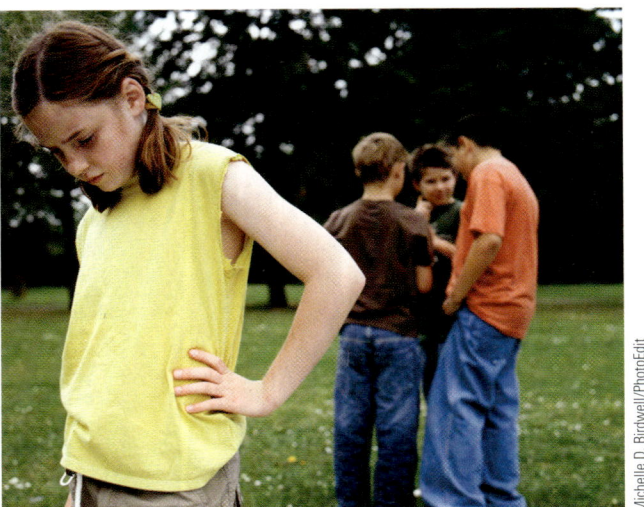

(such as meeting an attractive stranger). Typically, this is a reaction to **evaluation fears** (fears of being inadequate, embarrassed, ridiculed, or rejected). Although fears of rejection are common, they are much more frequent or intense for shy persons (Bradshaw, 2006; Jackson, Towson, & Narduzzi, 1997). A third problem for shy persons is a **self-defeating bias** (distortion) in their thinking. Specifically, shy persons almost always blame themselves when a social encounter doesn't go well. They are unnecessarily self-critical in social situations (Lundh et al., 2002).

Situational Causes of Shyness Shyness is most often triggered by *novel* or *unfamiliar* social situations. A person who does fine with family or close friends may become shy and awkward when meeting a stranger. Shyness is also magnified by formality, meeting someone of higher status, being noticeably different from others, or being the focus of attention (as in giving a speech) (Larsen & Buss, 2005).

Don't most people become cautious and inhibited in such circumstances? Yes. That's why we need to see how the personalities of shy and not-shy persons differ.

Dynamics of the Shy Personality

There is a tendency to think that shy persons are wrapped up in their own feelings and thoughts. But surprisingly, researchers Jonathan Cheek and Arnold Buss (1979) found no connection between shyness and **private self-consciousness** (attention to inner feelings, thoughts, and fantasies). Instead, they discovered that shyness is linked to **public self-consciousness** (acute awareness of oneself as a social object).

Persons who rate high in public self-consciousness are intensely concerned about what others think of them (Cowden, 2005). They worry about saying the wrong thing or appearing foolish. In public, they may feel "naked" or as if others can "see through them." Such feelings trigger anxiety or outright fear during social encounters, leading to awkwardness and inhibition (Cowden, 2005). The shy person's anxiety, in turn, often causes her or him to misperceive others in social situations (Schroeder, 1995).

As mentioned, almost everyone feels anxious in at least some social situations. But there is a key difference in the way shy and not-shy persons *label* this anxiety. Shy persons tend to consider their social anxiety a *lasting personality trait.* Shyness, in other words, becomes part of their self-concept. In contrast, not-shy persons believe that *external situations* cause their occasional feelings of shyness. When not-shy persons feel anxiety or "stage fright," they assume that almost anyone would feel as they do under the same circumstances (Zimbardo, Pilkonis, & Norwood, 1978).

Labeling is important because it affects *self-esteem*. In general, not-shy persons tend to have higher self-esteem than shy persons. This is because not-shy persons give themselves credit for their social successes and they recognize that failures are often due to circumstances. In contrast, shy people blame themselves for social failures, never give themselves credit for successes, and expect to be rejected (Jackson et al., 2002).

Shy Beliefs

What can be done to reduce shyness? Shyness is often maintained by unrealistic or self-defeating beliefs (Antony, 2004; Butler, 2001). Here's a sample of such beliefs.

1. *If you wait around long enough at a social gathering, something will happen.*
   Comment: This is really a cover-up for fear of starting a conversation. For two people to meet, at least one has to make an effort, and it might as well be you.
2. *Other people who are popular are just lucky when it comes to being invited to social events or asked out.*
   Comment: Except for times when a person is formally introduced to someone new, this is false. People who are more active socially typically make an effort to meet and spend time with others. They join clubs, invite others to do things, strike up conversations, and generally leave little to luck.
3. *The odds of meeting someone interested in socializing are always the same, no matter where I am.*
   Comment: This is another excuse for inaction. It pays to seek out situations that have a higher probability of leading to social contact, such as clubs, teams, and school events.
4. *If someone doesn't seem to like you right away, they really don't like you and never will.*
   Comment: This belief leads to much needless shyness. Even when a person doesn't show immediate interest, it doesn't mean the person dislikes you. Liking takes time and opportunity to develop.

Unproductive beliefs like the preceding can be replaced with statements such as the following.

1. I've got to be active in social situations.
2. I can't wait until I'm completely relaxed or comfortable before taking a social risk.
3. I don't need to pretend to be someone I'm not; it just makes me more anxious.
4. I may think other people are harshly evaluating me, but actually I'm being too hard on myself.
5. I can set reasonable goals for expanding my social experience and skills.
6. Even people who are very socially skillful are never successful 100 percent of the time. I shouldn't get so upset when an encounter goes badly. (Adapted from Antony, 2004; Butler, 2001.)

Social Skills

Learning social skills takes practice (Carducci & Fields, 2007). There is nothing "innate" about knowing how to meet people or start a conversation. Social skills can be directly practiced in a variety of ways. It can be helpful, for instance, to get a tape recorder and listen to several of your conversations. You may be surprised by the way you pause, interrupt, miss cues, or seem disinterested. Similarly, it can be useful to look at yourself in a mirror and exaggerate facial expressions of surprise, interest, dislike, pleasure, and so forth. By such methods, most people can learn to put more animation and skill into their self-presentation. (For a discussion of related skills, see the section on self-assertion in Module 15.3.)

Conversation

One of the simplest ways to make better conversation is by learning to ask questions. A good series of questions shifts attention to the other person and shows you are interested. Nothing fancy is needed. You can do fine with questions such as, "Where do you (work, study, live)? Do you like (dancing, travel, music)? How long have you (been at this school, worked here, lived here)?" After you've broken the ice, the

---

Shyness A tendency to avoid others plus uneasiness and strain when socializing.
Social skills Proficiency at interacting with others.
Social anxiety A feeling of apprehension in the presence of others.
Evaluation fears Fears of being inadequate, embarrassed, ridiculed, or rejected.
Self-defeating bias A distortion of thinking that impairs behavior.
Private self-consciousness Preoccupation with inner feelings, thoughts, and fantasies.
Public self-consciousness Intense awareness of oneself as a social object.

best questions are often those that are *open ended* (they can't be answered "yes" or "no"):

"What parts of the country have you seen?" (as opposed to: "Have you ever been to Florida?")

"What's it like living on the West Side?" (as opposed to: "Do you like living on the West Side?")

"What kinds of food do you like?" (as opposed to: "Do you like Chinese cooking?")

It's easy to see why open-ended questions are helpful. In replying to open-ended questions, people often give "free information" about themselves. This extra information can be used to ask other questions or to lead into other topics of conversation.

This brief sampling of ideas is no substitute for actual practice. Overcoming shyness requires a real effort to learn new skills and test old beliefs and attitudes. It may even require the help of a counselor or therapist. At the very least, a shy person must be willing to take social risks. Breaking down the barriers of shyness will always include some awkward or unsuccessful encounters. Nevertheless, the rewards are powerful: human companionship and personal freedom.

MODULE 10.7 Psychology in Action Summary

What causes shyness? What can be done about it?
- Shyness typically involves social anxiety, evaluation fears, self-defeating thoughts, public self-consciousness, and a lack of social skills.
- Shyness is marked by heightened public self-consciousness and a tendency to regard one's shyness as a lasting trait.
- Shyness can be reduced by replacing self-defeating beliefs with more supportive thoughts and by learning social skills.

KNOWLEDGE BUILDER

Understanding Shyness

Recite
1. Shy individuals normally do not lack social skills.
2. Social anxiety and evaluation fears are seen almost exclusively in shy individuals; the not-shy rarely have such experiences. T or F?
3. Unfamiliar people and situations most often trigger shyness. T or F?
4. Contrary to what many people think, shyness is *not* related to
   a. private self-consciousness
   b. social anxiety
   c. self-esteem
   d. blaming oneself for social failures
5. Shy persons tend to consider their social anxiety to be a
   a. situational reaction
   b. personality trait
   c. public efficacy
   d. habit
6. Changing personal beliefs and practicing social skills can be helpful in overcoming shyness. T or F?

Reflect
Critical Thinking
7. Shyness is a trait of Vonda's personality. Like most shy people, Vonda is most likely to feel shy in unfamiliar social settings. Vonda's shy behavior demonstrates that the expression of traits is governed by what concept?

Relate
If you are shy, see if you can summarize how social skills, social anxiety, evaluation fears, self-defeating thoughts, and public self-consciousness contribute to your social inhibition. If you're not shy, imagine how you would explain these concepts to a shy friend.

Link
Internet addresses frequently change. To find the sites listed here, visit http://www.thomsonedu.com/psychology/coon for an updated list of Internet addresses and direct links to relevant sites.
- **The Shyness Home Page** Try several shyness surveys.
- **Shake Your Shyness** Get some tips for dealing with shyness.
- **Understanding Shyness** The "frequently asked questions" list for alt.support.shyness on Usenet.

ANSWERS

1. F 2. F 3. T 4. a 5. b 6. T 7. trait-situation interactions (again)

Interactive Learning

Psychology: Active Learning Modules Book Companion Website

http://www.thomsonedu.com/psychology/coon
Visit your Book Companion Website, where you will find flash cards, practice quizzes, Internet links, and more to help you study.

ThomsonNOW™
Just what you need to know NOW!

Spend time on what you need to master rather than on information you already have learned. Take a pre-test for this chapter, and ThomsonNOW will generate a personalized study plan based on your results. The study plan will identify the topics you need to review and direct you to online resources to help you master those topics. You can then take a post-test to help you determine the concepts you have mastered and what you will need to work on. Try it out! Go to **www.thomsonedu.com/login** to sign in with an access code or to purchase access to this product.

11 Health, Stress, and Coping

MODULE **11.1 Health Psychology**
SURVEY QUESTIONS: What is health psychology? How does behavior affect health?

MODULE **11.2 Stress, Frustration, and Conflict**
SURVEY QUESTIONS: What is stress? What factors determine its severity?
SURVEY QUESTION: What causes frustration, and what are typical reactions to it?
SURVEY QUESTIONS: Are there different types of conflict? How do people react to conflict?

MODULE **11.3 Defenses, Helplessness, and Depression**
SURVEY QUESTION: What are defense mechanisms?
SURVEY QUESTION: What do we know about coping with feelings of helplessness and depression?

MODULE **11.4 Stress and Health**
SURVEY QUESTION: How is stress related to health and disease?

MODULE **11.5 Psychology in Action: Stress Management**
SURVEY QUESTION: What are the best strategies for managing stress?

Violet's Series of Unfortunate Events

Somehow, Violet had managed to survive the rush of make-or-break term papers, projects, and classroom speeches. Then it was on to finals, where her tests seemed perfectly timed to inflict as much suffering as possible. Her two hardest exams fell on the same day! Great.

On the last day of finals, Violet got caught in a traffic jam on her way to school. Two drivers cut her off, and another gave her a one-finger salute. When Violet finally got to campus the parking lot was swarming with frantic students. Most of them, like her, were within minutes of missing a final exam. At last, Violet spied an empty space. As she started toward it, a Mini Cooper darted around the corner and into "her" place. The driver of the car behind her began to honk impatiently. For a moment, Violet was seized by a colossal desire to run over anything in sight.

Finally, after a week and a half of stress, pressure, and frustration, Violet's finals were over. Sleep deprivation, gallons of coffee, junk food, and equal portions of cramming and complaining had carried her through. She was off for the summer. At last, she could kick back, relax, and have some fun. Or could she? Just 4 days after the end of school, Violet got a bad cold, followed by bronchitis that lasted for nearly a month.

Violet's experience illustrates what happens when stress, emotion, personal habits, and health collide. Though the timing of her cold might have been a coincidence, odds are it wasn't. Periods of stress are frequently followed by illness (Lyons & Chamberlain, 2006).

In the first part of this chapter we will explore a variety of behavioral health risks. Then we will look more closely at what stress is and how it affects us. After that, we will emphasize ways of coping with stress, so you can do a better job of staying healthy than Violet did.

MODULE 11.1 Health Psychology

HEALTH IS PRICELESS. It's also free. Despite the high cost of healthcare, one of the most important sources of health is free for the taking. Health psychologists have shown that many of the diseases that bedevil us are caused by unhealthy behavior. Let's see which personal habits contribute the most to leading a long, healthy, and happy life.

Health Psychology—Here's to Your Good Health

SURVEY QUESTIONS: *What is health psychology? How does behavior affect health?*

Most people agree that health is important—especially their own. Yet, half of all deaths in North America are primarily due to unhealthy behavior (Mokdad et al., 2004). **Health psychology** aims to do something about such deaths by using behavioral principles to prevent illness and promote health. Psychologists working in the allied field of **behavioral medicine** apply psychology to manage medical problems, such as diabetes or asthma. Their interests include pain control, helping people cope with chronic illness, stress-related diseases, self-screening for diseases (such as breast cancer), and similar topics (Brannon & Feist, 2007).

Behavioral Risk Factors

A century ago, people primarily died from infectious diseases and accidents. Today, people generally die from **lifestyle diseases,** which are related to health-damaging personal habits (Mokdad et al., 2004). Examples include heart disease, stroke, and lung cancer (● Fig. 11.1). Clearly, some lifestyles promote health, whereas others lead to illness and death. As one observer put it, "We have met the enemy and he is us."

What are some unhealthy behaviors? Some causes of illness are beyond our control, but many behavioral risks can be reduced. **Behavioral risk factors** are actions that increase the chances of disease, injury, or early death. For example, approximately 438,000 people die every year from smoking-related diseases (CDC, 2005). Similarly, being overweight *doubles* the chance of dying from cancer or heart disease. Roughly 65 percent of all American adults are overweight (CDC, 2003). As a result, obesity may soon overtake smoking as the main cause of preventable deaths. Being fat is not just a matter of fashion—in the long run it could kill you. A person who is overweight at age 20 can expect to lose 5 to 20 years of life expectancy (Fontaine et al., 2003).

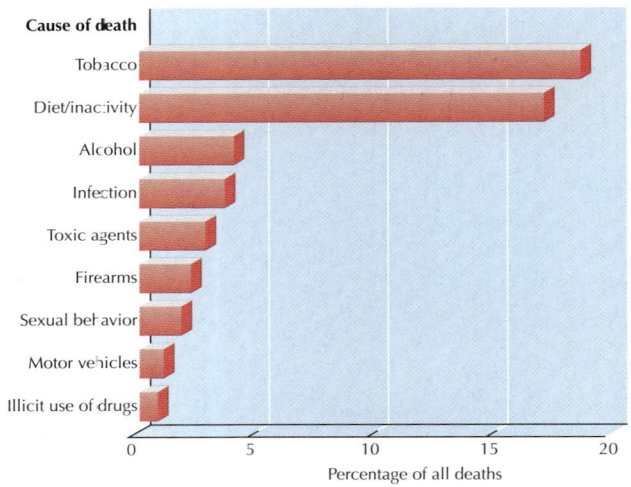

● **FIGURE 11.1** The nine leading causes of death in the United States are shown in this graph. As you can see, eight of the top nine causes are directly related to behavioral risk factors (infection is the exception). At least 45 percent of all deaths can be traced to unhealthful behavior. The percentage of day-to-day health problems related to unhealthful behavior is even higher. (Data from Mokdad et al., 2004.)

Each of the following factors is a major behavioral risk (Baum & Posluszny, 1999): high levels of stress, untreated high blood pressure, cigarette smoking, abuse of alcohol or other drugs, overeating, inadequate exercise, unsafe sexual behavior, exposure to toxic substances, violence, excess sun exposure, reckless driving, and disregarding personal safety (accidents). Seventy percent of all medical costs are related to just six of the listed factors—smoking, alcohol and drug abuse, poor diet, insufficient exercise, and risky sexual practices (Orleans, Gruman, & Hollendonner, 1999).

The personal habits you have by the time you are 18 or 19 greatly affect your health, happiness, and life expectancy years later (Gurung, 2006; Vaillant & Mukamal, 2001). ■ Table 11.1 shows how many high school students in the United States engage in various kinds of risky behaviors.

Specific risk factors are not the only concern. Some people have a general **disease-prone personality** that leaves them depressed, anxious, hostile, and . . . frequently ill. In contrast, people who are intellectually resourceful, compassionate, optimistic, and nonhostile tend to enjoy good health (Taylor, 2006; Taylor et al., 2000). Depression, in particular, is likely to damage health (Luppa et al., 2007). People who are depressed eat poorly, sleep poorly, rarely exercise, fail to use seat belts in cars, smoke more, and so on (Allgower, Wardle, & Steptoe, 2001).

Lifestyle In your mind's eye, fast-forward an imaginary film of your life all the way to old age. Do it twice—once with a

TABLE 11.1 Percentage of U.S. High School Students Who Engaged in Health-Endangering Behaviors

RISKY BEHAVIOR IN THE PREVIOUS 30 DAYS	PERCENTAGE
Rode with drinking driver	30
Were in a physical fight	33
Carried a weapon	17
Drank alcohol	45
Used marijuana	22
Engaged in sexual intercourse	47
Did not use condom during last sexual intercourse	37
Smoked cigarettes	22
Did not eat enough fruits and vegetables	78
Did not get enough physical exercise	3

Source: Grunbaum et al., 2004.

In some cases, lifestyle diseases can be treated or prevented by making specific, minor changes in behavior. For example, hypertension (high blood pressure) can be deadly. Yet, consuming less sodium (salt) can help fend off this "silent killer." (Losing weight, using alcohol sparingly, and getting more exercise will also help [Georgiades et al., 2000].)

In addition to removing specific risk factors, psychologists are interested in getting people to increase behaviors that promote health. Health-promoting behaviors include such obvious practices as getting regular exercise, controlling smoking and alcohol use, maintaining a balanced diet, getting good medical care, and managing stress (Zarcadoolas, Pleasant, & Greer, 2006). In one study, the risk of dying was cut by 65 percent during a 10-year period for adults who were careful about diet, alcohol, exercise, and smoking (Knoops et al., 2004).

Health-promoting behaviors don't have to be restrictive or burdensome. For instance, maintaining a healthy diet doesn't mean surviving on tofu and wheat grass. The healthiest people in the study just described ate a tasty "Mediterra-

lifestyle including a large number of behavioral risk factors, and again without them. It should be obvious that many small risks can add up, dramatically raising the chance of illness. If stress is a frequent part of your life, visualize your body seething with emotion, day after day. If you smoke, picture a lifetime's worth of cigarette smoke blown through your lungs in a week. If you drink, take a lifetime of alcohol's assaults on the brain, stomach, and liver and squeeze them into a month: Your body would be poisoned, ravaged, and soon dead. If you eat a high-fat, high-cholesterol diet, fast-forward a lifetime of heart-killing plaque clogging your arteries.

We don't mean to sermonize. We just want to remind you that risk factors make a difference. To make matters worse, unhealthy lifestyles almost always create multiple risks. That is, people who smoke are also likely to drink excessively. Those who overeat usually do not get enough exercise, and so on (Straub, 2006). Even infectious diseases are often linked to behavioral risks. For example, pneumonia and other infections occur at high rates in people who have cancer, heart disease, lung disease, or liver disease. Thus, many deaths attributed to infections can actually be traced to smoking, poor diet, or alcohol abuse (Mokdad et al., 2004).

Health-Promoting Behaviors

To prevent disease, health psychologists first try to remove behavioral risk factors. All the medicine in the world may not be enough to restore health without changes in behavior. We all know someone who has had a heart attack or lung disease who couldn't change the habits that led to his or her illness.

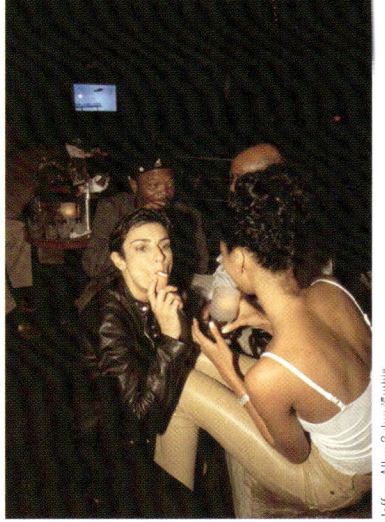

In the long run, behavioral risk factors and lifestyles do make a difference in health and life expectancy.

Health psychology Study of the ways in which behavioral principles can be used to prevent illness and promote health.
Behavioral medicine The study of behavioral factors in medicine, physical illness, and medical treatment.
Lifestyle disease A disease related to health-damaging personal habits.
Behavioral risk factors Behaviors that increase the chances of disease, injury, or premature death.
Disease-prone personality A personality type associated with poor health; marked by persistent negative emotions, including anxiety, depression, and hostility.

nean diet" high in fruit, vegetables, and fish and low in red meat and dairy products. Likewise, you don't need to exercise like an Olympic athlete to benefit from physical activity. All you need is 30 minutes of exercise (the equivalent of a brisk walk) three or four times a week. Almost everyone can fit such "lifestyle physical activity" into his or her schedule (Pescatello, 2001).

What about alcohol? Moderation in drinking doesn't mean that you must be a teetotaler. Consuming one or two alcoholic drinks per day is generally safe for most people, especially if you remain alcohol free 2 or 3 days a week. However, having three or more drinks a day greatly increases the risk of stroke, cirrhosis of the liver, cancer, high blood pressure, heart disorders, and other diseases (Knoops et al., 2004).

To summarize, a small number of behavioral patterns accounts for many common health problems (Grunbaum et al., 2004). ■ Table 11.2 lists several major ways to promote good health.

Early Prevention

Of the behavioral risks we have discussed, smoking is the largest preventable cause of death and the single most lethal factor (Mokdad et al., 2004). As such, it illustrates the prospect for preventing illness.

What have health psychologists done to lessen the risks? Attempts to "immunize" youths against pressures to start smoking are a good example. The smoker who says "Quitting is easy, I've done it dozens of times" states a basic truth—only 1 smoker in 10 has long-term success at quitting. Thus, the best way to deal with smoking is to prevent it before it becomes a lifelong habit. For example, school-based prevention programs have used quizzes about smoking, antismoking art contests, poster and T-shirt giveaways, antismoking pamphlets for parents, and questions for students to ask their parents (Zarcadoolas, Pleasant, & Greer, 2006). Such efforts are designed to persuade kids that smoking is dangerous and "uncool." Apparently, many teens are getting the message, as attitudes toward smoking are now more negative than they were 20 years ago (Chassin et al., 2003).

Some antismoking programs include **refusal skills training**. In this case, youths learn to resist pressures to begin smoking (or using other drugs). For example, junior high students can role play ways to resist smoking pressures from peers, adults, and cigarette ads. Similar methods can be applied to other health risks, such as sexually transmitted diseases and teen pregnancy (Wandersman & Florin, 2003).

Many health programs also teach students general life skills. The idea is to give kids skills that will help them cope with day-to-day stresses. That way, they will be less tempted to escape problems through drug use or other destructive

■ **TABLE 11.2** Major Health-Promoting Behaviors

SOURCE	DESIRABLE BEHAVIORS
Nutrition	Eating a balanced, low-fat diet; appropriate caloric intake; maintenance of healthy body weight
Exercise	At least 30 minutes of aerobic exercise, 5 days per week
Blood pressure	Lower blood pressure with diet and exercise, or medicine if necessary
Alcohol and drugs	No more than two drinks per day; abstain from using drugs
Tobacco	Do not smoke; do not use smokeless tobacco
Sleep and relaxation	Avoid sleep deprivation; provide for periods of relaxation every day
Sex	Practice safer sex; avoid unplanned pregnancy
Injury	Curb dangerous driving habits, use seat belts; minimize sun exposure; forgo dangerous activities
Stress	Learn stress management; lower hostility

behaviors. **Life skills training** includes practice in stress reduction, self-protection, decision making, goal setting, self-control, and social skills (Tobler et al., 2000).

Community Health

In addition to early prevention, health psychologists have had some success with **community health campaigns**. These are community-wide education projects designed to lessen major risk factors. Health campaigns inform people of risks such as stress, alcohol abuse, high blood pressure, high cholesterol, smoking, sexually transmitted diseases, or excessive sun exposure. This is followed by efforts to motivate people to change their behavior. Campaigns sometimes provide *role models* (positive examples) who show people how to improve their own health. They also direct people to services for health screening, advice, and treatment. Health campaigns may

Celebrities can also help persuade young people to not start smoking in the first place.

reach people through the mass media, public schools, health fairs, their work, or self-help programs. Such programs are increasingly successful in helping people make healthful changes in their behavior (Orleans, 2000).

Positive Psychology: Wellness

Health is not just an absence of disease (Allen, Carlson, & Ham, 2007). People who are truly healthy enjoy a positive state of **wellness** or well-being. Maintaining wellness is a lifelong pursuit and, hopefully, a labor of love. People who attain optimal wellness are both physically and psychologically healthy. They are happy, optimistic, self-confident individuals who can bounce back emotionally from adversity (Tugade, Fredrickson, & Barrett, 2004).

People who enjoy a sense of well-being also have supportive relationships with others, they do meaningful work, and they live in a clean environment. Many of these aspects of wellness are addressed elsewhere in this book. In this chapter we will give special attention to the effect that stress has on health and sickness. Understanding stress and learning to control it can improve not only your health, but the quality of your life as well (Suinn, 2001). For these reasons, a discussion of stress and stress management follows.

MODULE 11.1 Summary

What is health psychology? How does behavior affect health?

- Health psychologists study lifestyle diseases, which are related to health-damaging personal habits and behavioral risk factors.
- A surprisingly small number of health-promoting behaviors have a major effect on general health and life expectancy.
- At the minimum, it is important to maintain healthy habits with respect to diet, alcohol, exercise, and smoking.
- Health psychologists try to prevent unhealthy habits from becoming established early in life. They also seek to improve well-being through community health campaigns.
- Maintaining wellness is a lifelong personal responsibility.

Refusal skills training Program that teaches youths how to resist pressures to begin smoking. (Can also be applied to other drugs and health risks.)

Life skills training A program that teaches stress reduction, self-protection, decision making, self-control, and social skills.

Community health campaign A community-wide education program that provides information about how to lessen risk factors and promote health.

Wellness A positive state of good health; more than the absence of disease.

KNOWLEDGE BUILDER

Health Psychology

Recite

1. Adjustment to chronic illness and the control of pain are topics that would more likely be of interest to a specialist in _____ _____ _____ rather than to a health psychologist.
2. With respect to health, which of the following is *not* a major behavioral risk factor?
   a. over-exercise
   b. cigarette smoking
   c. stress
   d. high blood pressure
3. Lifestyle diseases related to just six behaviors account for 70 percent of all medical costs. The behaviors are smoking, alcohol and drug abuse, poor diet, insufficient exercise, and
   a. driving too fast
   b. excessive sun exposure
   c. unsafe sex
   d. exposure to toxins
4. Health-promoting behaviors that combat hypertension include the following: lose weight, consume less sodium, use alcohol sparingly, and get more
   a. sleep
   b. exercise
   c. carbohydrates
   d. cholesterol
5. Health psychologists tend to prefer _____ _____ rather than modifying habits (like smoking) that become difficult to break once they are established.
6. The disease-prone personality is marked by _____, anxiety, and hostility.

Reflect

Critical Thinking

7. The general public is increasingly well informed about health risks and healthful behavior. Can you apply the concept of reinforcement to explain why so many people fail to act on this information?

Relate

If you were to work as a health psychologist, would you be more interested in preventing disease or managing it?

Make a list of the major behavioral risk factors that apply to you. Are you laying the foundation for a lifestyle disease?

Which of the health-promoting behaviors listed in Table 11.2 would you like to increase?

If you were designing a community health campaign, who would you use as role models of healthful behavior?

Link

Internet addresses frequently change. To find the sites listed here, visit **http://www.thomsonedu.com/psychology/coon** for an updated list of Internet addresses and direct links to relevant sites.

- **Division 38** Visit the website of the health psychology division of the American Psychological Association.
- **Careers in Health Psychology** Learn more about careers in health psychology.
- **The Longevity Game** Find out how long you might live; explore your options.

ANSWERS

1. behavioral medicine 2. a 3. c 4. b 5. prevention 6. depression 7. Many of the health payoffs are delayed by months or years, greatly lessening the immediate rewards for healthful behavior.

MODULE 11.2 Stress, Frustration, and Conflict

ALTHOUGH STRESS IS A NATURAL PART OF LIFE, it can be a major behavioral risk factor if it is prolonged or severe. It might seem that stressful events "happen to" people. Although this is sometimes the case, more often stress is a matter of how we perceive events and react to them. Because of this, stress can often be managed or controlled. This unit explains how stress occurs and describes typical reactions to it.

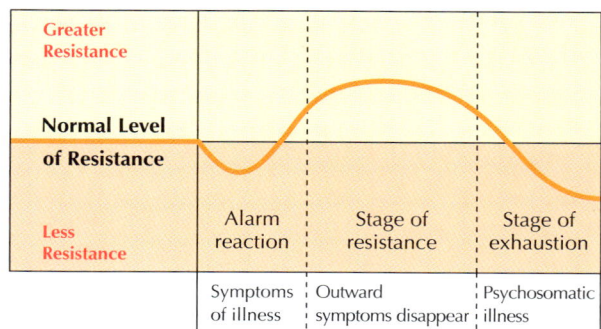

● **FIGURE 11.2** The general adaptation syndrome. During the initial alarm reaction to stress, resistance falls below normal. It rises again as bodily resources are mobilized, and it remains high during the stage of resistance. Eventually, resistance falls again as the stage of exhaustion is reached. (From *The Stress of Life* by Hans Selye. Copyright © 1976 by Hans Selye. Used by permission of McGraw-Hill Book Company.)

Stress—Thrill or Threat?

SURVEY QUESTIONS: *What is stress? What factors determine its severity?*

Stress can be dangerous if it is prolonged or severe, but it isn't always bad. As Canadian stress research pioneer Hans Selye (SEL-yay) (1976) observed, "To be totally without stress is to be dead." That's because **stress** is the mental and physical condition that occurs when we adjust or adapt to the environment. Unpleasant events such as work pressures, marital problems, or financial woes naturally produce stress. But so do travel, sports, a new job, mountain climbing, dating, and other positive activities. Even if you aren't a thrill seeker, a healthy lifestyle may include a fair amount of *eustress* (good stress). Activities that provoke "good stress" are usually challenging, rewarding, and energizing.

A **stress reaction** begins with the same autonomic nervous system arousal that occurs during emotion. Imagine you are standing at the top of a wind-whipped ski jump for the first time. Internally, you would experience a rapid surge in your heart rate, blood pressure, respiration, muscle tension, and other ANS responses. *Short-term* stresses of this kind can be uncomfortable, but they rarely do any damage. (Your landing might, however.) *Long-term* stresses are another matter entirely (Sternberg, E. M., 2000).

General Adaptation Syndrome

The impact of long-term stresses can be understood by examining the body's defenses against stress, a pattern known as the general adaptation syndrome.

The **general adaptation syndrome (GAS)** is a series of bodily reactions to prolonged stress. Selye (1976) noticed that the first symptoms of almost any disease or trauma (poisoning, infection, injury, or stress) are almost identical. The body responds in the same way to any stress, be it infection, failure, embarrassment, a new job, trouble at school, or a stormy romance.

How does the body respond to stress? The GAS consists of three stages: an alarm reaction, a stage of resistance, and a stage of exhaustion (● Fig. 11.2) (Selye, 1976).

In the **alarm reaction,** your body mobilizes its resources to cope with added stress. The pituitary gland signals the adrenal glands to produce more adrenaline, noradrenaline, and cortisol. As these stress hormones are dumped into the bloodstream, some bodily processes are speeded up and others are slowed. This allows bodily resources to be applied where they are needed (Lyons & Chamberlain, 2006).

We should all be thankful that our bodies automatically respond to emergencies. But brilliant as this emergency system is, it can also cause problems. In the first phase of the alarm reaction, people have such symptoms as headache, fever, fatigue, sore muscles, shortness of breath, diarrhea, upset stomach, loss of appetite, and a lack of energy. Notice that these are also the symptoms of being sick, of stressful travel, of high-altitude sickness, of final exams week, and (possibly) of falling in love!

> **Stress** The mental and physical condition that occurs when a person must adjust or adapt to the environment.
> **Stress reaction** The physical response to stress, consisting mainly of bodily changes related to autonomic nervous system arousal.
> **General adaptation syndrome (GAS)** A series of bodily reactions to prolonged stress; occurs in three stages: alarm, resistance, and exhaustion.
> **Alarm reaction** First stage of the GAS, during which bodily resources are mobilized to cope with a stressor.

463

During the **stage of resistance,** bodily adjustments to stress stabilize. As the body's defenses come into balance, symptoms of the alarm reaction disappear. Outwardly, everything seems normal. However, this appearance of normality comes at a high cost. The body is better able to cope with the original stressor, but its resistance to other stresses is lowered. For example, animals placed in extreme cold become more resistant to the cold but more susceptible to infection. It is during the stage of resistance that the first signs of psychosomatic disorders (physical disorders triggered by psychological factors) begin to appear.

Continued stress leads to the **stage of exhaustion,** in which the body's resources are drained and stress hormones are depleted. Some of the typical signs or symptoms of impending exhaustion include the following (Friedman, 2002):

Emotional signs: Anxiety, apathy, irritability, mental fatigue

Behavioral signs: Avoidance of responsibilities and relationships, extreme or self-destructive behavior, self-neglect, poor judgment

Physical signs: Excessive worry about illness, frequent illness, exhaustion, overuse of medicines, physical ailments and complaints

The GAS may sound melodramatic if you are young and healthy or if you've never endured prolonged stress. However, stress should not be taken lightly. Unless a way of relieving stress is found, the result will be a psychosomatic disease, a serious loss of health, or complete collapse. When Selye examined animals in the later stages of the GAS, he found that their adrenal glands were enlarged and discolored. There was intense shrinkage of internal organs, such as the thymus, spleen, and lymph nodes, and many animals had stomach ulcers. In addition to such direct effects, stress can disrupt the body's immune system, as described next.

Stress, Illness, and Your Immune System

How can prolonged stress result in a physical illness? An answer can be found in your body's immune system, which mobilizes defenses (such as white blood cells) against invading microbes and other disease agents. The immune system is regulated, in part, by the brain. Because of this link, stress and upsetting emotions can affect the immune system in ways that increase susceptibility to disease (Miller, Cohen, & Ritchey, 2002). By the way, the study of links among behavior, stress, disease, and the immune system is called **psychoneuroimmunology** (Daruna, 2004). (Try dropping that into a conversation sometime if you want to see a stress reaction!)

Studies show that the immune system is weakened in students during major exam times. Immunity is also lowered

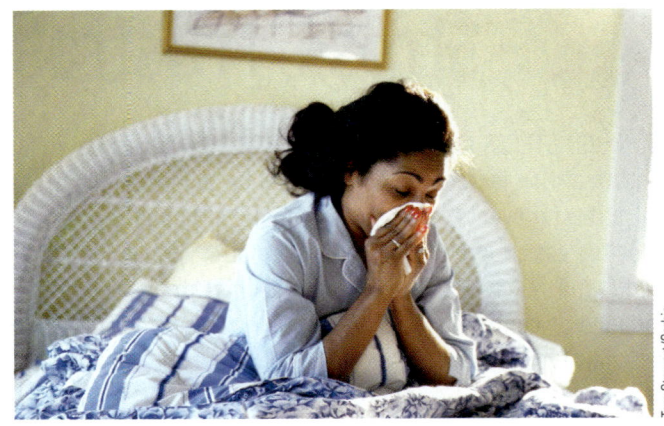

Stress and negative emotions lower immune system activity and increase inflammation. This, in turn, raises our vulnerability to infection, worsens illness, and delays recovery.

by divorce, bereavement, a troubled marriage, job loss, poor sleep, depression, and similar stresses (Deinzer et al., 2000; Motivala & Irwin, 2007; Segerstrom & Miller, 2004). Lowered immunity explains why the "double whammy" of getting sick when you are trying to cope with prolonged or severe stress is so common (Lyons & Chamberlain, 2006). Stress causes the body to release substances that increase inflammation. This is part of the body's self-protective response to threats, but it can prolong infections and delay healing (Kiecolt-Glaser et al., 2002). It's also worth noting again the value of positive emotions. Happiness, laughter, and delight tend to strengthen immune system response. Doing things that make you happy can also protect your health (Rosenkranz et al., 2003).

Could reducing stress help prevent illness? Yes. Various psychological approaches, such as support groups, relaxation exercises, guided imagery, and stress management training, can actually boost immune system functioning (Dougall & Baum, 2003). By doing so, they help promote and restore health. For example, stress management reduced the severity of cold and flu symptoms in a group of university students (Reid, Mackinnon, & Drummond, 2001).

There is even evidence that stress management can improve the chances of survival in people with life-threatening diseases, such as cancer, heart disease, and human immunodeficiency virus/acquired immunodeficiency syndrome (HIV/AIDS) (Schneiderman et al., 2001). With some successes to encourage them, psychologists are now searching for the best combination of treatments to help people resist disease (Miller & Cohen, 2001).

When Is Stress a Strain?

It goes almost without saying that some events are more likely to cause stress than others. A **stressor** is a condition or event that challenges or threatens a person. Police officers, for instance, suffer from a high rate of stress-related diseases. The threat of injury or death, plus occasional confrontations with angry, drunk, or hostile citizens, takes a toll. A major factor is the *unpredictable* nature of police work. An officer who stops a car to issue a traffic ticket never knows if a cooperative citizen or an armed gang member is waiting inside.

A revealing study shows how unpredictability adds to stress. In a series of 1-minute trials, college students breathed air through a mask. In some trials, the air contained 20 percent more carbon dioxide (CO_2) than normal. If you were to inhale this air, you would feel anxious, stressed, and a little like you were suffocating. Students tested this way hated the "surprise" doses of CO_2. They found it much less stressful to be told in advance which trials would include a choking whiff of CO_2 (Lejuez et al., 2000).

Pressure is another element of stress, especially job stress. **Pressure** occurs when a person must meet *urgent* external demands or expectations (Weiten, 1998). For example, we feel pressured when activities must be speeded up, when deadlines must be met, when extra work is added, or when we must work near maximum capacity for long periods. Most students who have survived final exams are familiar with the effects of pressure.

What if I set deadlines for myself? Does it make a difference where the pressure comes from? Yes. People generally feel more stress in situations over which they have little or no control (Taris et al., 2005). In one study, nurses with a high sense of control were less likely to get sick, both physically and mentally, than were nurses with a low sense of control (Ganster, Fox, & Dwyer, 2001).

To summarize, when emotional "shocks" are *intense* or *repeated, unpredictable, uncontrollable,* and linked to *pressure,* stress will be magnified and damage is likely to result. At work, people face many of these sources of stress every day. (See ■ Table 11.3 for a list of the most common sources of stress at work.) In fact, chronic job stress sometimes results in *burnout,* a pattern of emotional exhaustion. (See "Burnout—The High Cost of Caring.")

Appraising Stressors

Our reactions to stressful events are greatly affected by how we appraise situations. (See Module 9.5 for a discussion of how appraisal influences emotions.) That's why some people are distressed by events that others view as a thrill or a challenge (eustress). Ultimately, stress depends on how you perceive a situation. Our friend Akihito would find it stressful to listen to five of his son's hip-hop CDs in a row. His son Takashi would find it stressful to listen to *one* of his father's opera CDs. To know if you are stressed, we must know what meaning you place on events. As we will see in a moment, whenever a stressor is appraised as a *threat* (potentially harmful), a powerful stress reaction follows (Folkman & Moskowitz, 2004; Lazarus, 1991).

■ **TABLE 11.3 The Top 10 Work Stresses**

WORK STRESS	RANK
Workload	1
Feeling undervalued	2
Deadlines	3
Type of work people have to do	4
Having to take on other people's work	5
Lack of job satisfaction	6
Lack of control over the working day	7
Having to work long hours	8
Frustration with the working environment	9
Performance targets	10

Source: Data from Skillsoft, 2006.

Air-traffic control is stressful work. Employees must pay intense attention for long periods, they have little control over the pace of work, and the consequences of making a mistake can be dire.

Stage of resistance Second stage of the GAS, during which bodily adjustments to stress stabilize, but at a high physical cost.

Stage of exhaustion Third stage of the GAS, at which time the body's resources are exhausted and serious health consequences occur.

Psychoneuroimmunology Study of the links among behavior, stress, disease, and the immune system.

Stressor A specific condition or event in the environment that challenges or threatens a person.

Pressure A stressful condition that occurs when a person must meet urgent external demands or expectations.

THE CLINICAL FILE

Burnout—The High Cost of Caring

Margo, a young nurse, realizes with dismay that she has "lost all patience with her patients" and wishes they would "go somewhere else to be sick." Margo's feelings are a clear sign of job **burnout,** a condition in which workers are physically, mentally, and emotionally drained (Greenglass, Burke, & Moore, 2003). Burnout has three aspects (Maslach, Schaufeli, & Leiter, 2001):

- Emotional exhaustion: Affected persons are fatigued, tense, apathetic, and suffer from physical ailments. They feel "used up" and "empty."
- Cynicism or detachment: Burned-out workers have an "I don't give a damn anymore" attitude, and they treat clients coldly, as if they were objects.
- Feelings of reduced personal accomplishment: Burned-out workers do poor work and feel helpless, hopeless, or angry.

Burnout may occur in any job, but it is a special problem in emotionally demanding helping professions, such as nursing, teaching, social work, childcare, counseling, or police work. Often, the most idealistic and caring workers are the ones who burn out. As some say, "You have to be on fire to burn out" (Maslach, Schaufeli, & Leiter, 2001).

If we wish to keep caring people in the helping professions, it may be necessary to adjust workloads, rewards, and the amount of control people have in their jobs (Leiter & Maslach, 2005). In general, social support helps people from many cultures resist burnout (Pines et al., 2002). For example, support groups at work help caregivers deal with stress by allowing them to talk about their feelings and problems at work (Greenglass, Burke, & Konarski, 1998).

Can college students experience burnout? Yes, they can. If you have a negative attitude toward your studies and feel that your college workload is too heavy, you may be vulnerable to burnout (Jacobs & Dodd, 2003). On the other hand, if you have a positive attitude toward your studies, participate in extracurricular activities, and enjoy good social support from your friends, rock on!

The helping professions require empathy, caring, and emotional involvement. As a result, caregivers risk depleting their emotional resources and ability to cope. Over time, this can lead to burnout.

"Am I Okay or in Trouble?" You have been selected to give a speech to 300 people. Or, a doctor tells you that you must undergo a dangerous and painful operation. Or, the one true love of your life walks out the door. What would your emotional response to these events be? How do you cope with a threat?

According to Richard Lazarus (1991), there are two important steps in managing a threat. The first is a **primary appraisal,** in which you decide if a situation is relevant or irrelevant, positive or threatening. In essence, this step answers the question, "Am I okay or in trouble?" Then you make a **secondary appraisal,** in which you assess your resources and choose a way to meet the threat or challenge. ("What can I do about this situation?") Thus, the way a situation is "sized up" greatly affects our ability to cope with it (• Fig. 11.3). Public speaking, for instance, can be appraised as an intense threat or as a chance to perform. Emphasizing the threat—by imagining failure, rejection, or embarrassment—obviously invites disaster (Strongman, 2003).

The Nature of Threat What does it mean to feel threatened by a stressor? Certainly in most day-to-day situations it doesn't mean you think your life is in danger. (Unless, of course, you owe money to "Eddie The Enforcer.") Threat has more to do with the idea of control. We are particularly prone to feel stressed when we can't—or think we can't—control our immediate environment. In short, a *perceived* lack of control is just as threatening as an actual lack of control. For example, college students who feel overloaded experience stress even though their workload may not actually be heavier than that of their classmates (Jacobs & Dodd, 2003).

THE CLINICAL FILE

Coping with Traumatic Stress

Traumatic experiences produce psychological injury or intense emotional pain. Victims of **traumatic stresses,** such as war, torture, rape, assassination, plane crashes, natural disasters, or street violence, may suffer from nightmares, flashbacks, insomnia, irritability, nervousness, grief, emotional numbing, and depression. There is little doubt that the 2005 hurricane season caused these effects in the Gulf Coast states. Like most traumatic stresses, the impact, especially of hurricanes Katrina and Rita, was and continues to be overwhelming.

People who personally witness or survive a disaster are most affected by traumatic stress. Twenty percent of the people who lived close to Ground Zero in New York suffered serious stress disorders (Galea et al., 2002). Yet even those who experience horror at a distance may be traumatized (Galea & Resnick, 2005). Forty-four percent of U.S. adults who only saw the September 11 terrorist attacks on television had at least some stress symptoms (Schuster et al., 2001). Indirect exposure to such terrorist attacks, coupled with the ongoing risk of more attacks, such as those in Spain and England, has ensured that many people will suffer ongoing stress into the foreseeable future (Marshall et al., 2007).

Traumatic stress produces feelings of helplessness and vulnerability (Fields & Margolin, 2001). Victims realize that disaster could strike again without warning. In addition to feeling threatened, many victims sense that they are losing control of their lives (Scurfield, 2002).

What can people do about such reactions? Psychologists recommend the following:

- Identify what you are feeling and talk to others about your fears and concerns.
- Think about the skills that have helped you overcome adversity in the past and apply them to the present situation.
- Continue to do the things that you enjoy and that make life meaningful (LeDoux & Gorman, 2001).
- Get support from others. This is a major element in recovery from all traumatic events.
- Give yourself time to heal. Fortunately, most people are more resilient than they think.

When traumatic stresses are severe or repeated, some people have even more serious symptoms. They suffer from crippling anxiety or become emotionally numb. Typically, they can't stop thinking about the disturbing event, they anxiously avoid anything associated with the event, and they are constantly fearful or nervous. (These are the symptoms of *stress disorders*, which are discussed in Module 12.2.) Such reactions can leave victims emotionally handicapped for months or years after a disaster. The consequences can last a lifetime for children who are the victims of trauma (Gillespie & Nemeroff, 2007). If you feel that you are having trouble coping with a severe emotional shock, consider seeking help from a psychologist or other professional (Bisson et al., 2007).

There can be little doubt that Hurricane Katrina's assault on New Orleans was a traumatically stressful event. Even people who merely witnessed the disaster on television suffered from stress symptoms.

● **FIGURE 11.3** Stress is the product of an interchange between a person and the environment.

A sense of control also comes from believing you can reach desired goals. It is threatening to feel that we lack *competence* to cope with life's demands (Bandura, 2001). Because of this, the intensity of your body's stress reaction often depends on what you think and tell yourself about a stressor. That's why it's valuable to learn to think in ways that ward off the body's stress response. (Some strategies for controlling upsetting thoughts are described in the "Psychology in Action" module.)

> **Burnout** A job-related condition of mental, physical, and emotional exhaustion.
> **Primary appraisal** Deciding if a situation is relevant to oneself and if it is a threat.
> **Secondary appraisal** Deciding how to cope with a threat or challenge.
> **Traumatic stresses** Extreme events that cause psychological injury or intense emotional pain.

Coping with Threat

You have appraised a situation as threatening. What will you do next? You have two major choices. Both involve thinking and acting in ways that help us handle stressors. In **emotion-focused coping,** we try to control our emotional reactions to the situation. For example, a distressed person may distract herself by listening to music, taking a walk to relax, or seeking emotional support from others. In contrast, **problem-focused coping** is aimed at managing or correcting the distressing situation itself. Some examples are making a plan of action or concentrating on your next step (Folkman & Moskowitz, 2004).

Couldn't both types of coping occur together? Yes. Sometimes the two types of coping aid one another. For instance, quieting your emotions may make it easier for you find a way to solve a problem. Say, for example, that a woman feels anxious as she steps to the podium to give a speech. If she does some deep breathing to reduce her anxiety (emotion-focused coping), she will be better able to glance over her notes to improve her delivery (problem-focused coping).

It is also possible for coping efforts to clash. For instance, if you have to make a difficult decision, you may suffer intense emotional distress. In such circumstances there is a temptation to make a quick, ill-advised choice, just to end the suffering. Doing so may allow you to cope with your emotions, but it shortchanges problem-focused coping.

In general, problem-focused coping tends to be especially useful when you are facing a controllable stressor—that is, a situation you can actually do something about. Emotion-focused efforts are best suited to managing your reaction to stressors you cannot control (Folkman & Moskowitz, 2004). To improve your chances of coping effectively, the stress-fighting strategies described in this chapter include a mixture of both techniques.

So far, our discussion has focused on everyday stresses. How do people react to the extreme stresses imposed by war, violence, or disaster? "Coping with Traumatic Stress" discusses this important topic.

Frustration—Blind Alleys and Lead Balloons

SURVEY QUESTION: *What causes frustration, and what are typical reactions to it?*

Do you remember how frustrated Violet was when she couldn't find a parking place? **Frustration** is a negative emotional state that occurs when people are prevented from reaching desired goals. In Violet's case, the goal of finding a parking space was blocked by another car.

Obstacles of many kinds cause frustration. A useful distinction can be made between external and personal sources of frustration. *External frustration* is based on conditions outside a person that impede progress toward a goal. All of the following are external frustrations: getting stuck with a flat tire; having a marriage proposal rejected; finding the cupboard bare when you go to get your poor dog a bone; finding the refrigerator bare when you go to get your poor tummy a T-bone; finding the refrigerator gone when you return home; being chased out of the house by your starving dog. In other words, external frustrations are based on *delays, failure, rejection, loss,* and other direct blocking of motivated behavior.

Notice that external obstacles can be either *social* (slow drivers, tall people in theaters, people who cut into lines) or *nonsocial* (stuck doors, a dead battery, rain on the day of the game). If you ask your friends what has frustrated them recently, most will probably mention someone's behavior ("My sister wore one of my dresses when I wanted to wear it," "My supervisor is unfair," "My history teacher grades too hard"). As social animals, we humans are highly sensitive to social sources of frustration (Taylor, 2006). That's probably why unfair treatment associated with racial or ethnic prejudice is a major source of frustration and stress in the lives of many African Americans and other minority group members (Clark, et al., 1999; Gurung, 2006).

Frustration usually increases as the *strength, urgency,* or *importance* of a blocked motive increases. Violet was especially frustrated in the parking lot because she was late for an exam. Likewise, an escape artist submerged in a tank of water and bound with 200 pounds of chain would become *quite* frustrated if a trick lock jammed. Remember, too, that motivation becomes stronger as we near a goal. As a result, frustration is more intense when a person runs into an obstacle very close to a goal. If you've ever missed an A grade by 5 points, you were probably very frustrated. If you've missed an A by 1 point—well, frustration builds character, right?

A final factor affecting frustration is summarized by the old phrase "the straw that broke the camel's back." The effects of *repeated* frustrations can accumulate until a small irritation sets off an unexpectedly violent response. A case in point is the fact that people with long daily commutes are more likely to display "road rage" (angry, aggressive driving) (Harding et al., 1998).

Personal frustrations are based on personal characteristics. If you are 4 feet tall and aspire to be a professional basketball player, you very likely will be frustrated. If you want to go to medical school but can earn only D grades, you will likewise be frustrated. In both examples, frustration is actually based on personal limitations. Yet, failure may be *perceived* as externally caused. We will return to this point in a discussion of stress management. In the meantime, let's look at some typical reactions to frustration.

Reactions to Frustration

Aggression is any response made with the intent of harming a person or an object. It is one of the most persistent and frequent responses to frustration (Anderson & Bushman, 2002).

Does frustration always cause aggression? Aren't there other reactions? Although the connection is strong, frustration does not always incite aggression. More often, frustration is met first with *persistence,* often in the form of more vigorous efforts and varied responses (● Fig. 11.4). For example, if you put your last quarter in a vending machine and pressing the button has no effect, you will probably press harder and faster (vigorous effort). Then you will press all the other buttons (varied response). Persistence may help you reach your goal by getting *around* a barrier. However, if the machine *still* refuses to deliver, or return your quarter, you may become aggressive and kick the machine (or at least tell it what you think of it).

Persistence can be very adaptive. Overcoming a barrier ends the frustration and allows the need or motive to be satisfied. The same is true of aggression that removes or destroys a barrier. Picture a small band of nomadic humans, parched by thirst but separated from a water hole by a menacing animal. It is easy to see that attacking the animal may ensure their survival. In modern society such direct aggression is seldom acceptable. If you find a long line at the drinking fountain, aggression is hardly appropriate. Because direct aggression is discouraged, it is frequently *displaced.*

How is aggression displaced? Directing aggression toward a source of frustration may be impossible, or it may be too dangerous. If you are frustrated by your boss at work or by a teacher at school, the cost of direct aggression may be too high (losing your job or failing a class). Instead, the aggression may be displaced, or redirected, toward whomever or whatever is available. Targets of **displaced aggression** tend to be safer, or less likely to retaliate, than the original source of frustration. At one time or another, you have probably lashed out at a friend or relative who was not the real cause of your annoyance. As this suggests, excessive anger over a minor irritation is a common form of displaced aggression (Miller et al., 2003).

Psychologists attribute much hostility to displaced aggression. A disturbing example is the finding that unemployment and divorce are associated with increased child abuse (Weissman, Jogerst, & Dawson, 2003). In a pattern known as **scapegoating**, a person or a group is blamed for conditions not of their making. A *scapegoat* is a person who has become a habitual target of displaced aggression. Despite recent progress, many minority groups continue to face hostility based on scapegoating. Think, for example, about the hostility expressed toward illegal immigrants during times of economic hardship. In many communities, layoffs and job losses are closely linked to increased violence (Catalano, Novaco, & McConnell, 1997). Or think about the hostility expressed toward anyone in the United States who looked even vaguely "foreign" right after the September 11 terrorist attacks.

I have a friend who dropped out of school to hitchhike around the country. He seemed very frustrated before he quit. What type of response to frustration is that? Another major reaction to frustration is escape, or withdrawal. It is stressful and unpleasant to be frustrated. If other reactions do not reduce frustration, a person may try to escape. **Escape** may mean

● **FIGURE 11.4** Frustration and common reactions to it.

Emotion-focused coping Managing or controlling one's emotional reaction to a stressful or threatening situation.
Problem-focused coping Directly managing or remedying a stressful or threatening situation.
Frustration A negative emotional state that occurs when one is prevented from reaching a goal.
Aggression Any response made with the intent of causing harm.
Displaced aggression Redirecting aggression to a target other than the actual source of one's frustration.
Scapegoating Blaming a person or a group of people for conditions not of their making.
Escape Reducing discomfort by leaving frustrating situations or by psychologically withdrawing from them.

Bumper cars seem to bring out aggressive impulses in many drivers. Wild smash-ups are part of the fun, but are some drivers displacing aggressive urges related to frustration in other areas of their lives?

actually leaving a source of frustration (dropping out of school, quitting a job, leaving an unhappy marriage), or it may mean psychologically escaping. Two common forms of psychological escape are feigned apathy (pretending not to care) and the use of drugs such as cocaine, alcohol, marijuana, or narcotics. (Notice that these are examples of *ineffective* emotion-focused coping.) (See Fig. 11.4 for a summary of common reactions to frustration.)

Coping with Frustration

In a classic experiment, a psychologist studying frustration placed rats on a small platform at the top of a tall pole. Then he forced them to jump off the platform toward two elevated doors, one locked and the other unlocked. If the rat chose the correct door, it swung open and the rat landed safely on another platform. Rats who chose the locked door bounced off it and fell into a net far below.

The problem of choosing the open door was made unsolvable and very frustrating by randomly alternating which door was locked. After a time, most rats adopted a stereotyped response. That is, they chose the same door every time. This door was then permanently locked. All the rat had to do was to jump to the other door to avoid a fall, but time after time the rat bounced off the locked door (Maier, 1949).

Isn't that an example of persistence? No. Persistence that is *inflexible* can turn into "stupid," stereotyped behavior like that of a rat on a jumping stand. When dealing with frustration, you must know when to quit and establish a new direction. Here are some suggestions to help you avoid needless frustration.

1. Try to identify the source of your frustration. Is it external or personal?
2. Is the source of frustration something that can be changed? How hard would you have to work to change it? Is it under your control at all?
3. If the source of your frustration can be changed or removed, are the necessary efforts worth it?

The answers to these questions help determine if persistence will be futile. There is value in learning to accept gracefully those things that cannot be changed.

It is also important to distinguish between *real* barriers and *imagined* barriers. All too often we create our own imaginary barriers. For example, Corazon wants a part-time job to earn extra money. At the first place she applied, she was told that she didn't have enough "experience." Now she complains of being frustrated because she wants to work but cannot. She needs "experience" to work but can't get experience without working. She has quit looking for a job.

Is Corazon's need for experience a real barrier? Unless she applies for *many* jobs it is impossible to tell if she has overestimated its importance. For her the barrier is real enough to prevent further efforts, but with persistence she might locate an "unlocked door." If a reasonable amount of effort does show that experience is essential, it might be obtained in other ways—through temporary volunteer work, for instance.

Conflict—Yes, No, Yes, No, Yes, No, Well, Maybe

SURVEY QUESTIONS: *Are there different types of conflict? How do people react to conflict?*

Conflict occurs whenever a person must choose between contradictory needs, desires, motives, or demands. Choosing between college and work, marriage and single life, or study and failure are common conflicts. There are four basic forms of conflict. As we will see, each has its own properties (● Fig. 11.5 and ● Fig. 11.6).

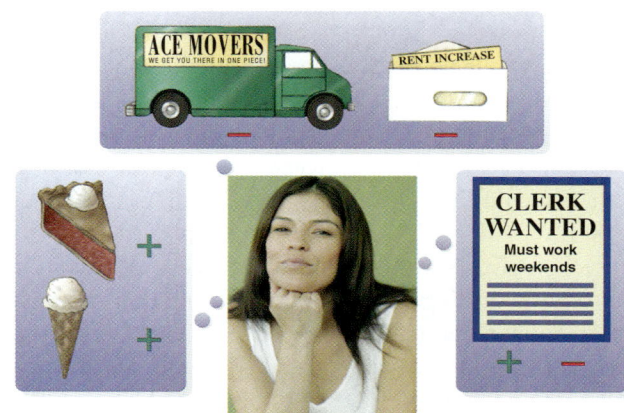

● **FIGURE 11.5** Three basic forms of conflict. For this woman, choosing between pie and ice cream is a minor approach-approach conflict; deciding whether to take a job that will require weekend work is an approach-avoidance conflict; and choosing between paying higher rent and moving is an avoidance-avoidance conflict. (Photo: Royalty-Free/Corbis)

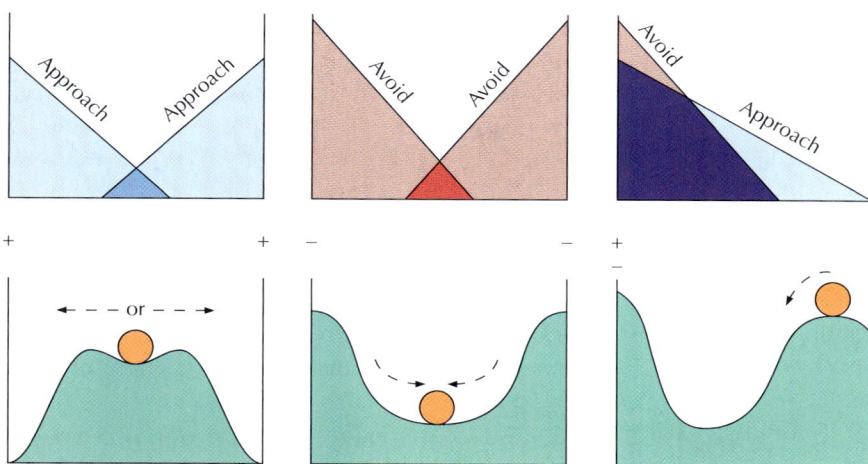

● **FIGURE 11.6** Conflict diagrams. As shown by the colored areas in the graphs, desires to approach and to avoid increase near a goal. The effects of these tendencies are depicted below each graph. The "behavior" of the ball in each example illustrates the nature of the conflict above it. An approach conflict *(left)* is easily decided. Moving toward one goal will increase its attraction *(graph)* and will lead to a rapid resolution. (If the ball moves in either direction, it will go all the way to one of the goals.) In an avoidance conflict *(center)*, tendencies to avoid are deadlocked, resulting in inaction. In an approach-avoidance conflict *(right)*, approach proceeds to the point where desires to approach and avoid cancel each other. Again, these tendencies are depicted *(below)* by the action of the ball. (Graphs adapted from Miller, 1944.)

Approach-Approach Conflicts A simple **approach-approach conflict** comes from having to choose between two positive, or desirable, alternatives. Choosing between tutti-frutti-coconut-mocha-champagne ice and orange-marmalade-peanut-butter-coffee swirl at your favorite ice cream parlor may throw you into a temporary conflict. However, if you really like both choices, your decision will be quickly made. Even when more important decisions are at stake, approach-approach conflicts tend to be the easiest to resolve. The old fable about the mule that died of thirst and starvation while standing between a bucket of water and a bucket of oats is obviously unrealistic. When both options are positive, the scales of decision are easily tipped one direction or the other.

Avoidance-Avoidance Conflicts Being forced to choose between two negative, or undesirable, alternatives creates an **avoidance-avoidance conflict**. A person in an avoidance conflict is caught between "the devil and the deep blue sea," "the frying pan and the fire," or "a rock and a hard place." In real life, double-avoidance conflicts involve dilemmas such as choosing between unwanted pregnancy and abortion, the dentist and tooth decay, a monotonous job and poverty, or dorm food and starvation.

Suppose I don't object to abortion. Or suppose that I consider any pregnancy sacred and not to be tampered with? Like many other stressful situations, these examples can be defined as conflicts only on the basis of personal needs and values. If a woman wants to end a pregnancy and does not object to abortion, she experiences no conflict. If she would not consider abortion under any circumstances, there is also no conflict.

Avoidance conflicts often have a "damned if you do, damned if you don't" quality. In other words, both choices are negative, but *not choosing* may be impossible or equally undesirable. To illustrate, imagine the plight of a person trapped in a hotel fire 20 stories from the ground. Should she jump from the window and almost surely die on the pavement? Or should she try to dash through the flames and almost surely die of smoke inhalation and burns? When faced with a choice such as this, it is easy to see why people often *freeze,* finding it impossible to decide or take action. In actual disasters of this sort, people are often found dead in their rooms, victims of an inability to take action.

Indecision, inaction, and freezing are not the only reactions to double-avoidance conflicts. Because avoidance conflicts are stressful and difficult to solve, people sometimes pull out of them entirely. This reaction, called *leaving the field,* is another form of escape. It may explain the behavior of a student who could not attend school unless he worked. However, if he worked he could not earn passing grades. His solution after much conflict and indecision? He joined the navy.

Approach-Avoidance Conflicts Approach-avoidance conflicts are also difficult to resolve. A person in an **approach-avoidance conflict** is "caught" by being attracted to, and repelled by, the same goal or activity. Attraction keeps the person in the situation, but its negative aspects cause turmoil and distress. For example, a high school student arrives to pick up his date for the first time. He is met at the door by her father, who is a professional wrestler—7 feet tall, 300 pounds, and entirely covered with hair. The father gives the boy a crushing handshake and growls that he will break him in half if the girl is not home on time. The student considers the girl attractive and has a good time. But does he ask her out again? It depends on the relative strength of his attraction and his fear. Almost certainly he will feel *ambivalent* about

---

Conflict A stressful condition that occurs when a person must choose between incompatible or contradictory alternatives.

Approach-approach conflict Choosing between two positive, or desirable, alternatives.

Avoidance-avoidance conflict Choosing between two negative, undesirable alternatives.

Approach-avoidance conflict Being attracted to and repelled by the same goal or activity.

asking her out again, knowing that another encounter with her father awaits him.

Ambivalence (mixed positive and negative feelings) is a central characteristic of approach-avoidance conflicts. Ambivalence is usually translated into *partial approach* (Miller, 1944). Because our student is still attracted to the girl, he may spend time with her at school and elsewhere. But he may not actually date her again. Some more realistic examples of approach-avoidance conflicts are planning to marry someone your parents strongly disapprove of, wanting to be in a play but suffering stage fright, wanting to buy a car but not wanting to make monthly payments, and wanting to eat when you're already overweight. Many of life's important decisions have approach-avoidance dimensions.

Multiple Conflicts *Aren't real-life conflicts more complex than the ones described here?* Yes. Conflicts are rarely as clear-cut as those described. People in conflict are usually faced with several dilemmas at once, so several types of conflict may be intermingled. The fourth type of conflict moves us closer to reality.

In a **double approach-avoidance conflict**, each alternative has both positive and negative qualities. For example, you are offered two jobs: One has good pay but poor hours and dull work; the second has interesting work and excellent hours but low pay. Which do you select? This situation is more typical of the choices we must usually make. It offers neither completely positive nor completely negative options.

As with single approach-avoidance conflicts, people faced with double approach-avoidance conflicts feel ambivalent about each choice. This causes them to *vacillate,* or waver between the alternatives. Just as you are about to choose one such alternative, its undesirable aspects tend to loom large. So, what do you do? You swing back toward the other choice. If you have ever been romantically attracted to two people at once—each having qualities you like and dislike—then you have probably experienced vacillation. Another example that may be familiar is trying to decide between two college majors, each with advantages and disadvantages.

In real life it is common to face **multiple approach-avoidance conflicts** in which several alternatives each have positive and negative features. An example would be trying to choose which automobile to buy among several brands. When multiple approach-avoidance conflicts involve major life decisions, such as choosing a career, a school, a mate, or a job, they can add greatly to the amount of stress we experience.

Managing Conflicts

How can I handle conflicts more effectively? Most of the suggestions made earlier concerning frustration also apply to conflicts. However, here are some additional things to remember when you are in conflict or must make a difficult decision.

1. Don't be hasty when making important decisions. Hasty decisions are often regretted. Even if you do make a faulty decision, it will trouble you less if you know that you did everything possible to avoid a mistake.

2. Try out important decisions *partially* when possible. If you are thinking about moving to a new town, try to spend a few days there first. If you are choosing between colleges, do the same. If classes are in progress, sit in on some. If you want to learn to scuba dive, rent equipment for a reasonable length of time before buying.

3. Look for workable compromises. Again, it is important to get all available information. If you think that you have only one or two alternatives and they are undesirable or unbearable, seek the aid of a teacher, counselor, minister, or social service agency. You may be overlooking possible alternatives these people will know about.

4. When all else fails, make a decision and live with it. Indecision and conflict exact a high cost. Sometimes it is best to select a course of action and stick with it unless it is very obviously wrong after you have taken it.

Conflicts are a normal part of life. With practice you can learn to manage many of the conflicts you will face.

MODULE 11.2 Summary

What is stress? What factors determine its severity?

- Stress occurs when demands are placed on an organism to adjust or adapt. Stress always represents an interaction between a person and the environment.
- The body reacts to stress in a series of stages called the general adaptation syndrome (GAS).
- The stages of the GAS are alarm, resistance, and exhaustion. Bodily reactions in the GAS follow the pattern observed in the development of psychosomatic disorders.
- Studies of psychoneuroimmunology show that stress lowers the body's resistance to disease by weakening the immune system.
- Events tend to be more stressful when they involve pressure, a lack of control, unpredictability, and intense or repeated emotional shocks.
- Stress is intensified when a situation is perceived as a threat and the person does not feel competent to cope with it.
- In work settings, prolonged stress can lead to burnout.

- Making a primary appraisal greatly affects our emotional responses to a situation.
- During a secondary appraisal we select problem-focused coping or emotion-focused coping (or both) as a way of managing stress.

What causes frustration, and what are typical reactions to it?

- Frustration is a negative emotional state that occurs when we are prevented from reaching desired goals.
- Frustration becomes more intense as the strength, urgency, or importance of a blocked motive increases.
- Major behavioral reactions to frustration include persistence, more vigorous responding, circumvention, direct aggression, displaced aggression (including scapegoating), and escape or withdrawal.

Are there different types of conflict? How do people react to conflict?

- Contradictory needs, desires, motives, or demands, create psychological conflicts.
- Four major types of conflict are approach-approach, avoidance-avoidance, approach-avoidance, and multiple conflicts (double approach-avoidance and multiple approach-avoidance).

Double approach-avoidance conflict Being simultaneously attracted to and repelled by each of two alternatives.

Multiple approach-avoidance conflict Being simultaneously attracted to and repelled by each of several alternatives.

KNOWLEDGE BUILDER

Stress, Frustration, and Conflict

Recite

1. The first signs of psychosomatic disorders begin to appear during the stage of
   a. alarm
   b. exhaustion
   c. resistance
   d. appraisal

2. Students taking stressful final exams are more susceptible to the cold virus, a pattern best explained by
   a. the disease-prone personality
   b. psychoneuroimmunology
   c. emotion-focused coping
   d. reaction formation

3. Whereas stressful incidents suppress the immune system, stress management techniques have almost no effect on immune system functioning. T or F?

4. Emotional exhaustion, cynicism, and reduced accomplishment are characteristics of job _____.

5. Stress tends to be greatest when a situation is appraised as a _____ and a person does not feel _____ to cope with the situation.

6. According to Richard Lazarus, choosing a way to meet a threat or challenge takes place during the
   a. primary stress reaction
   b. secondary stress reaction
   c. primary appraisal
   d. secondary appraisal

7. Which of the following is *not* a common reaction to frustration?
   a. ambivalence
   b. aggression
   c. displaced aggression
   d. persistence

8. Displaced aggression is closely related to the pattern of behavior known as
   a. scapegoating
   b. leaving the field
   c. stereotyped responding
   d. burnout

9. You would be most likely to experience vacillation if you found yourself in
   a. an approach-approach conflict
   b. an avoidance-avoidance conflict
   c. a double approach-avoidance conflict
   d. the condition called emotion-focused coping

Reflect
Critical Thinking

10. Which do you think would produce more stress: (a) Appraising a situation as mildly threatening but feeling like you are totally incompetent to cope with it? Or (b) appraising a situation as very threatening but feeling that you have the resources and skills to cope with it?

11. Being frustrated is unpleasant. If some action, including aggression, ends frustration, why might we expect the action to be repeated on other occasions?

Relate

Can you say "psychoneuroimmunology"? Have you impressed anyone with the word yet?

What impact did pressure, control, predictability, repetition, and intensity have on your last stress reaction?

What type of coping do you tend to use when you face a stressor such as public speaking or taking an important exam?

Think of a time when you were frustrated. What was your goal? What prevented you from reaching it? Was your frustration external or personal?

Have you ever displaced aggression? Why did you choose another target for your hostility?

Review the major types of conflict and think of a conflict you have faced that illustrates each type. Did your reactions match those described in the text?

Link

Internet addresses frequently change. To find the sites listed here, visit **http://www.thomsonedu.com/psychology/coon** for an updated list of Internet addresses and direct links to relevant sites.

- **The Discovery of Stress** Read more about Hans Selye's discovery of stress.
- **Psychoneuroimmunology** Read an article on psychoneuroimmunology from the American Psychological Association.
- **Burnout** Read about job burnout symptoms and fixes.

ANSWERS

1. a 2. b 3. F 4. burnout 5. threat, competent 6. d 7. d 8. a 9. c 10. There is no correct answer here because individual stress reactions vary greatly. However, the secondary appraisal of a situation often determines just how stressful it is. Feeling incapable of coping is very threatening. 11. If a response ends discomfort, the response has been negatively reinforced. This makes the response more likely to occur in the future. (See Module 6.2.)

MODULE 11.3 Defenses, Helplessness, and Depression

STRESSFUL AND THREATENING EXPERIENCES often produce anxiety. How do we handle this unpleasant state? Psychodynamic psychologists have identified various defense mechanisms that shield us from anxiety. You might not always be aware of it, but you have probably used several of the defenses described here. You'll also find an interesting perspective on helplessness and depression in this module, with a special section on the "college blues."

Psychological Defense—Mental Karate?

SURVEY QUESTION: *What are defense mechanisms?*

Threatening situations tend to produce **anxiety.** When you are anxious you feel tense, uneasy, apprehensive, worried, and vulnerable. This unpleasant state can lead to emotion-focused coping that is *defensive* in nature (Lazarus, 1991). Psychodynamic psychologists have identified various defenses that shield us from anxiety. Defense mechanisms allow us to reduce anxiety caused by stressful situations or our own shortcomings.

What are psychological defense mechanisms, and how do they reduce anxiety? A **defense mechanism** is any mental process used to avoid, deny, or distort sources of threat or anxiety, especially threats to one's self-image. Many of the defenses were first identified by Sigmund Freud, who assumed they operate *unconsciously.* Often, defense mechanisms create large blind spots in awareness. For instance, you might know an extremely stingy person who is completely unaware that he is a tightwad.

Everyone has at one time or another used defense mechanisms. Let's consider some of the most common. (A more complete listing is given in ■ Table 11.4.)

Denial One of the most basic defenses is **denial** (protecting oneself from an unpleasant reality by refusing to accept it or believe it). We are prone to deny death, illness, and similar painful and threatening events. For instance, if you were told that you had only 3 months to live, how would you react? Your first thoughts might be "Aw, come on, someone must have mixed up the X-rays" or "The doctor must be mistaken" or simply "It can't be true!" Similar denial and disbelief are common reactions to the unexpected death of a friend or relative: "It's just not real. I just don't believe it!"

Repression Freud noticed that his patients had tremendous difficulty recalling shocking or traumatic events from child-

■ TABLE 11.4 Psychological Defense Mechanisms

Compensation Counteracting a real or imagined weakness by emphasizing desirable traits or seeking to excel in the area of weakness or in other areas.

Denial Protecting oneself from an unpleasant reality by refusing to perceive it.

Fantasy Fulfilling unmet desires in imagined achievements or activities.

Identification Taking on some of the characteristics of an admired person, usually as a way of compensating for perceived personal weaknesses or faults.

Intellectualization Separating emotion from a threatening or anxiety-provoking situation by talking or thinking about it in impersonal "intellectual" terms.

Isolation Separating contradictory thoughts or feelings into "logic-tight" mental compartments so that they do not come into conflict.

Projection Attributing one's own feelings, shortcomings, or unacceptable impulses to others.

Rationalization Justifying your behavior by giving reasonable and "rational," but false, reasons for it.

Reaction formation Preventing dangerous impulses from being expressed in behavior by exaggerating opposite behavior.

Regression Retreating to an earlier level of development or to earlier, less demanding habits or situations.

Repression Unconsciously preventing painful or dangerous thoughts from entering awareness.

Sublimation Working off unmet desires, or unacceptable impulses, in activities that are constructive.

Anxiety Apprehension, dread, or uneasiness similar to fear but based on an unclear threat.

Defense mechanism A habitual and often unconscious psychological process used to reduce anxiety.

hood. It seemed that powerful forces were holding these painful memories from awareness. Freud called this **repression**, our tendency to protect ourselves by repressing threatening thoughts and impulses. Feelings of hostility toward a family member, the names of people we dislike, and past failures are common targets of repression. Research suggests that you are most likely to repress information that threatens your self-image (Mendolia, 2002).

Reaction Formation In a **reaction formation**, impulses are not just repressed; they are also held in check by exaggerating opposite behavior. For example, a mother who unconsciously resents her children may, through reaction formation, become absurdly overprotective and overindulgent. Her real thoughts of "I hate them" and "I wish they were gone" are replaced by "I love them" and "I don't know what I would do without them." The mother's hostile impulses are traded for "smother" love, so that she won't have to admit she hates her children. Thus, the basic idea in a reaction formation is that the individual acts out an opposite behavior to block threatening impulses or feelings.

Regression In its broadest meaning, **regression** refers to any return to earlier, less demanding situations or habits. Most parents who have a second child have to put up with at least some regression by the older child. Threatened by a new rival for affection, an older child may regress to childish speech, bedwetting, or infantile play after the new baby arrives. If you've ever seen a child get homesick at summer camp or on a vacation, you've observed regression. The child wants to go home, where it's "safe." An adult who throws a temper tantrum or a married adult who "goes home to mother" is also regressing.

Projection Projection is an unconscious process that protects us from the anxiety we would feel if we were to discern our faults. A person who is projecting tends to see his or her own feelings, shortcomings, or unacceptable impulses in others. **Projection** lowers anxiety by exaggerating negative traits in others. This justifies one's own actions and directs attention away from personal failings.

One of your authors once worked for a greedy shop owner who cheated many of his customers. This same man considered himself a pillar of the community and very religious. How did he justify to himself his greed and dishonesty? He believed that everyone who entered his store was bent on cheating *him* any way they could. In reality, few, if any, of his customers shared his motives, but he projected his own greed and dishonesty onto them.

Rationalization Every teacher is familiar with this strange phenomenon: On the day of an exam, an incredible wave of disasters sweeps through the city. Mothers, fathers, sisters, brothers, aunts, uncles, grandparents, friends, relatives, and pets become ill or die. Motors suddenly fall out of cars. Books are lost or stolen. Alarm clocks go belly-up and ring no more. All manner of computer equipment malfunctions.

The making of excuses comes from a natural tendency to explain our behavior. **Rationalization** refers to justifying personal actions by giving "rational" but false reasons for them. When the explanation you give for your behavior is reasonable and convincing—but not the real reason—you are *rationalizing*. For example, Violet failed to turn in an assignment made at the beginning of the semester in one of her classes. Here's the explanation she gave her professor:

> My car broke down 2 days ago, and I couldn't get to the library until yesterday. Then I couldn't get all the books I needed because some were checked out, but I wrote what I could. Then last night, as the last straw, the ink cartridge in my printer ran out, and since all the stores were closed, I couldn't finish the paper on time.

When asked why she left the assignment until the last minute (the real reason it was late), Violet offered another set of rationalizations. Like many people, Violet had difficulty seeing herself without the protection of her rationalizations.

All the defense mechanisms described seem pretty undesirable. Do they have a positive side? People who overuse defense mechanisms become less adaptable, because they consume great amounts of emotional energy to control anxiety and maintain an unrealistic self-image. Defense mechanisms do have value, though. Often, they help keep us from being overwhelmed by immediate threats. This can provide time for a person to learn to cope in a more effective, problem-focused manner. If you recognize some of your own behavior in the descriptions here, it is hardly a sign that you are hopelessly defensive. As noted earlier, most people occasionally use defense mechanisms.

Two defense mechanisms that have a decidedly more positive quality are compensation and sublimation.

Compensation Compensatory reactions are defenses against feelings of inferiority. A person who has a defect or weakness (real or imagined) may go to unusual lengths to overcome the weakness or to *compensate* for it by excelling in other areas. One of the pioneers of "pumping iron" in America is Jack LaLanne, who opened the first modern health spa in America. LaLanne made a successful career out of bodybuilding in spite of the fact that he was thin and sickly as a young man. Or perhaps it would be more accurate to say *because* he was thin and sickly. You can find dozens of examples of **compensation** at work. A childhood stutterer may excel in debate at college. As a child, Helen Keller was unable to see or hear, but she became an outstanding thinker and writer. Perhaps Ray Charles, Stevie Wonder, Andrea Bocelli, and other blind entertainers were drawn to music because of their handicap.

Module 11.3 • DEFENSES, HELPLESSNESS, AND DEPRESSION 477

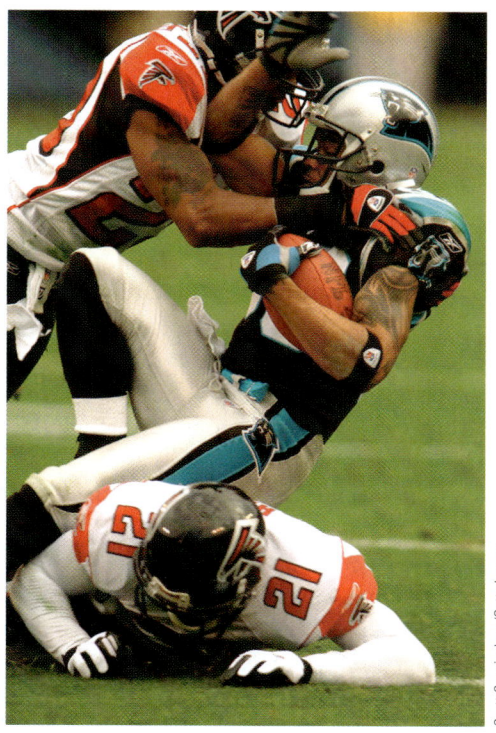

For some players—and fans—football probably allows sublimation of aggressive urges. *Grand Theft Auto* and similar computer games may serve the same purpose.

Sublimation The defense called **sublimation** (sub-lih-MAY-shun) is defined as working off frustrated desires (especially sexual desires) through socially acceptable activities. Freud believed that art, music, dance, poetry, scientific investigation, and other creative activities could serve to rechannel sexual energies into productive behavior. Freud also felt that almost any strong desire could be sublimated. For example, a very aggressive person may find social acceptance as a professional soldier, boxer, or football player. Greed may be refined into a successful business career. Lying may be sublimated into storytelling, creative writing, or politics.

Sexual motives appear to be the most easily and widely sublimated (Jacobs, 2003). Freud would have had a field day with such modern pastimes as surfing, motorcycle riding, drag racing, and dancing to or playing rock music, to name but a few. People enjoy each of these activities for a multitude of reasons, but it is hard to overlook the rich sexual symbolism apparent in each.

Learned Helplessness—Is There Hope?

SURVEY QUESTION: *What do we know about coping with feelings of helplessness and depression?*

What would happen if a person's defenses failed or if the person appraised a threatening situation as hopeless? Martin Seligman studied the case of a young marine who seemed to have adapted to the stresses of being held prisoner during the Vietnam War. The marine's health was related to a promise made by his captors: If he cooperated, they said, he would be released on a certain date. As the date approached, his spirits soared. Then came a devastating blow. He had been deceived. His captors had no intention of ever releasing him. He immediately lapsed into a deep depression, refused to eat or drink, and died shortly thereafter.

That seems like an extreme example. Does anything similar occur outside of concentration camps? Apparently so. For example, researchers in San Antonio, Texas, asked older people if they were hopeful about the future. Those who answered "No" died at elevated rates (Stern, Dhanda, & Hazuda, 2001).

To explain such patterns psychologists have focused on the concept of **learned helplessness,** an acquired inability to overcome obstacles and avoid aversive stimuli (Seligman, 1989). To observe learned helplessness, let's see what happens when animals are tested in a shuttle box (● Fig. 11.7). If placed in one side of a divided box, dogs will quickly learn to leap to the other side to escape an electric shock. If they are given a warning before the shock occurs (for example, a light that dims), most dogs learn to avoid the shock by leaping the barrier before the shock arrives. This is true of most dogs, but not those who have learned to feel helpless (Overmier & LoLordo, 1998).

How is a dog made to feel helpless? Before being tested in the shuttle box, a dog can be placed in a harness (from which the dog cannot escape) and then given several painful shocks. The animal is helpless to prevent these shocks. When placed in the shuttle box, dogs prepared this way react to the first shock by crouching, howling, and whining. None of them try to escape. They helplessly resign themselves to their fate. After all, they have already learned that there is nothing they can do about shock.

As the shuttle box experiments suggest, helplessness is a psychological state that occurs when events *appear to be uncontrollable* (Seligman, 1989). Helplessness also afflicts humans. It is a common reaction to repeated failure and to unpredictable or unavoidable punishment. A prime example is college students who feel helpless about their schoolwork. Such students tend to procrastinate, give up easily, and drop out of school (Perry, 2003).

Where humans are concerned, attributions (discussed in Module 9.5) have a large effect on helplessness. Persons who are made to feel helpless in one situation are more likely to act helpless in other situations if they attribute their failure to *lasting, general* factors. An example would be concluding "I

Learned helplessness A learned inability to overcome obstacles or to avoid punishment; learned passivity and inaction to aversive stimuli.

● **FIGURE 11.7** In the normal course of escape and avoidance learning, (a) a light dims shortly before the floor is electrified. (b) Because the light does not yet have meaning for the dog, the dog receives a shock (noninjurious, by the way) and leaps the barrier. Dogs soon learn (c) to watch for the dimming of the light and (d) to jump before receiving a shock. Dogs made to feel "helpless" rarely even learn to escape shock, much less to avoid it.

must be stupid" after doing poorly on a test in a biology class. In contrast, attributing a low score to specific factors in the situation ("I'm not too good at the type of test my biology professor uses" or "I'm not very interested in biology") tends to prevent learned helplessness from spreading (Peterson & Vaidya, 2001).

Depression

Seligman and others have pointed out the similarities between learned helplessness and **depression**. Both are marked by feelings of despondency, powerlessness, and hopelessness. "Helpless" animals display decreased activity, lowered aggression, blunted appetite, and a loss of sex drive. Humans suffer from similar effects and also tend to see themselves as failing, even when they're not (LoLordo, 2001; Seligman, 1989).

Depression is one of the most widespread emotional problems, and it undoubtedly has many causes. However, learned helplessness seems to explain many cases of depression and hopelessness. For example, Seligman (1972) describes the fate of Archie, a 15-year-old boy. For Archie, school is an unending series of shocks and failures. Other students treat him as if he's stupid; in class he rarely answers questions because he doesn't know some of the words. He feels knocked down everywhere he turns. These may not be electric shocks, but they are certainly emotional "shocks," and Archie has learned to feel helpless to prevent them. When he leaves school his chances of success will be poor. He has learned to passively endure whatever shocks life has in store for him. Archie is not alone in this regard. Hopelessness is almost always a major element of depression (Ciarrochi, Dean, & Anderson, 2002).

Hope *Does Seligman's research give any clues about how to "unlearn" helplessness?* With dogs, an effective technique is to forcibly drag them away from shock into the "safe" compartment. After this is done several times, the animals regain "hope" and feelings of control over the environment. Just how this can be done with humans is a question psychologists are exploring. It seems obvious, for instance, that someone like Archie would benefit from an educational program that would allow him to "succeed" repeatedly.

In **mastery training,** responses are reinforced that lead to mastery of a threat or control over one's environment. Animals who undergo such training become more resistant to learned helplessness (Volpicelli et al., 1983). For example, animals that first learn to escape shock become more persistent in trying to flee inescapable shock. In effect, they won't give up, even when the situation really is "hopeless."

Such findings suggest that we might be able to "immunize" people against helplessness and depression by allowing them to master difficult challenges. The Outward Bound schools, in which people pit themselves against the rigors of mountaineering, white-water canoeing, and wilderness survival, might serve as a model for such a program.

The value of hope should not be overlooked. As fragile as this emotion seems to be, it is a powerful antidote to depres-

Mastery training can occur informally when people learn to cope with challenges. For example, 18- to 21-year-old trainees on a transatlantic sailing voyage showed marked improvements in their ability to cope with stress (Norris & Weinman, 1996).

sion and helplessness. As an individual, you may find hope in religion, nature, human companionship, or even technology. Wherever you find it, remember its value: Hope is among the most important of all human emotions. Having positive beliefs, such as optimism, hope, and a sense of meaning and control, is closely related to overall well-being (Taylor et al., 2000, 2003).

Depression: Why Students Get the Blues

During the school year, many college students suffer some symptoms of depression, which can exert a toll on academic performance. In one study, students diagnosed with depression scored half a grade point below nondepressed students (Hysenbegasi, Hass, & Rowland, 2005). Why do students get "blue"? Various problems contribute to depressive feelings. Here are some of the most common:

1. Stresses from college work and pressures to choose a career can leave students feeling that they are missing out on fun or that all their hard work is meaningless.
2. Isolation and loneliness are common when students leave their support groups behind. In the past, family, a circle of high school friends, and often a boyfriend or girlfriend could be counted on for support and encouragement.
3. Problems with studying and grades frequently trigger depression. Many students start college with high aspirations and little prior experience with failure. At the same time, many lack basic skills necessary for academic success and are afraid of failure (Martin & Marsh, 2003).
4. Depression can be triggered by the breakup of an intimate relationship, either with a former boyfriend or girlfriend or with a newly formed college romance.
5. Students who find it difficult to live up to their idealized images of themselves are especially prone to depression (Scott & O'Hara, 1993).
6. An added danger is that depressed students are more likely to abuse alcohol, which is a depressant (Weitzman, 2004).

Recognizing Depression Most people know, obviously enough, when they are "down." Aaron Beck, an authority on depression, suggests you should assume that more than a minor fluctuation in mood is involved when five conditions exist (Beck & Greenberg, 1974):

1. You have a consistently negative opinion of yourself.
2. You engage in frequent self-criticism and self-blame.
3. You place negative interpretations on events that usually wouldn't bother you.

In a survey, college students reported that they were depressed from one to two times a month. These episodes lasted from a few hours to several days.

4. The future looks bleak and negative.
5. You feel that your responsibilities are overwhelming.

What can be done to combat depression? Bouts of the college blues are closely related to stressful events. Learning to manage college work and to challenge self-critical thinking can help alleviate mild school-related depression.

Attacks of the college blues are common and should be distinguished from more serious cases of depression. Severe depression is a serious problem that can lead to suicide or a major impairment of emotional functioning. In such cases it would be wise to seek professional help.

Coping with Depression

If you don't do well on a test or a class assignment, how do you react? If you see it as a small, isolated setback, you probably won't feel too bad. However, if you feel like you have "blown it" in a big way, depression may follow. Students who strongly link everyday events to long-term goals (such as a successful career or high income) tend to overreact to day-to-day disappointments (McIntosh, Harlow, & Martin, 1995).

What does the preceding tell us about the college blues? The implication is that it's important to take daily tasks one step at a time and chip away at them. That way, you are less likely to feel overwhelmed, helpless, or hopeless. One classic suggestion comes from Aaron Beck and Ruth Greenberg (1974): When you feel "blue," you should make a *daily schedule* for yourself. Try to schedule activities to fill up every hour during

Depression A state of despondency marked by feelings of powerlessness and hopelessness.

Mastery training Reinforcement of responses that lead to mastery of a threat or control over one's environment.

the day. It is best to start with easy activities and progress to more difficult tasks. Check off each item as it is completed. That way, you will begin to break the self-defeating cycle of feeling helpless and falling further behind. (Depressed students spend much of their time sleeping.) A series of small accomplishments, successes, or pleasures may be all that you need to get going again. However, if you are lacking skills needed for success in college, ask for help in getting them. Don't remain "helpless."

Feelings of worthlessness and hopelessness are usually supported by self-critical or negative thoughts. Beck and Greenberg recommend writing down such thoughts as they occur, especially those that immediately precede feelings of sadness. After you have collected these thoughts, write a rational answer to each. For example, the thought "No one loves me" should be answered with a list of those who do care. One more point to keep in mind is this: When events begin to improve, try to accept it as a sign that better times lie ahead. Positive events are most likely to end depression if you view them as stable and continuing, rather than temporary and fragile (Needles & Abramson, 1990).

MODULE 11.3 Summary

What are defense mechanisms?
- Defense mechanisms are mental processes used to avoid, deny, or distort sources of threat or anxiety, including threats to one's self-image.
- Overuse of defense mechanisms makes people less adaptable.
- A large number of defense mechanisms have been identified, including compensation, denial, fantasy, intellectualization, isolation, projection, rationalization, reaction formation, regression, repression, and sublimation.

What do we know about coping with feelings of helplessness and depression?
- Learned helplessness can be used as a model for understanding depression. Mastery training, optimism, and hope all act as antidotes for learned helplessness.
- Depression is a major, and surprisingly common, emotional problem. Actions and thoughts that counter feelings of helplessness tend to reduce depression.
- The college blues are a relatively mild form of depression. Learning to manage college work and to challenge self-critical thinking can help alleviate the college blues.

KNOWLEDGE BUILDER

Defenses, Helplessness, and Depression

Recite

1. The psychological defense known as denial refers to the natural tendency to explain or justify one's actions. T or F?
2. Fulfilling frustrated desires in imaginary achievements or activities defines the defense mechanism of
   a. compensation
   b. isolation
   c. fantasy
   d. sublimation
3. In compensation, one's own undesirable characteristics or motives are attributed to others. T or F?
4. Of the defense mechanisms, two that are considered relatively constructive are
   a. compensation
   b. denial
   c. isolation
   d. projection
   e. regression
   f. rationalization
   g. sublimation
5. Depression in humans is similar to _____ _____ observed in animal experiments.
6. Learned helplessness tends to occur when events appear to be
   a. frustrating
   b. in conflict
   c. uncontrollable
   d. problem focused
7. At any given time, more than half the college student population suffers symptoms of depression. T or F?
8. Frequent self-criticism and self-blame are a natural consequence of doing college work. T or F?

Reflect
Critical Thinking

9. Learned helplessness is most closely related to which of the factors that determine the severity of stress?

Relate

We tend to be blind to our own reliance on defense mechanisms. Return to the definitions in Table 11.4 and see if you can think of one example of each defense that you have observed someone else using.

Have you ever felt helpless in a particular situation? What caused you to feel that way? Does any part of Seligman's description of learned helplessness match your own experience?

Imagine that a friend of yours is suffering from the college blues. What advice would you give your friend?

Link

Internet addresses frequently change. To find the sites listed here, visit **http://www.thomsonedu.com/psychology/coon** for an updated list of Internet addresses and direct links to relevant sites.

- **Defense Mechanisms** Try to role play various defense mechanisms.
- **Learned Helplessness** Read more about Seligman's discovery of learned helplessness.
- **Depression and Control** Explore the relationship between learned helplessness and depression.

ANSWERS

1. F 2. c 3. F 4. a, g 5. learned helplessness 6. c 7. F 8. F 9. Feelings of incompetence and lack of control.

MODULE 11.4 Stress and Health

AT THE BEGINNING OF THIS CHAPTER you read about Violet, a student who became ill after a stressful final exam period. Was Violet's illness a coincidence? Psychologists have now firmly established that stress affects our health. Let's see how this occurs. We will also explore some factors that limit the health risks we face. Because we live in a fast-paced and often stressful society, these are topics worth stressing.

Stress and Health—Unmasking a Hidden Killer

SURVEY QUESTION: *How is stress related to health and disease?*

Disaster, depression, and sorrow often precede illness (Brannon & Feist, 2007). As Violet (our intrepid student) learned after finals week, stressful events reduce the body's natural defenses against disease. More surprising is the finding that *life changes*—both good and bad—can increase susceptibility to accidents or illness. Major changes in our surroundings or routines require us to be vigilant, on guard, and ready to react. Over long periods, this can be quite stressful (Sternberg, 2000).

Marriage is usually a positive life event. Nevertheless, the many changes it brings can be stressful.

Life Events and Stress

How can I tell if I am subjecting myself to too much stress? Psychiatrist Thomas Holmes and graduate student Richard Rahe developed the first rating scale to estimate the health hazards we face when stresses add up (Holmes & Rahe, 1967). A version of the *Social Readjustment Rating Scale* (**SRRS**) is reprinted in ■ Table 11.5. Notice that the impact of life events is expressed in **life change units** (**LCUs**) (numerical values assigned to each life event).

As you read the scale, note again that positive life events may be as costly as disasters. Marriage rates 50 life change units, even though it is usually a happy event. You'll also see many items that read "Change in . . . ." This means that an improvement in life conditions can be as costly as a decline. A stressful adjustment may be required in either case.

To use the scale shown in Table 11.5, add up the LCUs for all life events you have experienced during the last year and compare the total to the following standards.

0–150:	No significant problems
150–199:	Mild life crisis (33 percent chance of illness)
200–299:	Moderate life crisis (50 percent chance of illness)
300 or more:	Major life crisis (80 percent chance of illness)

According to Holmes, there is a high chance of illness or accident when your LCU total exceeds 300 points. A more conservative rating of stress can be obtained by totaling LCU points for only the previous 6 months.

Many of the listed life changes don't seem relevant to young adults or college students. Does the SRRS apply to them? The SRRS tends to be more appropriate for older, more established adults. The health of college students is also affected by stressful events, such as entering college, changing majors, or the breakup of a steady relationship. (For a student-oriented rating of stress, see Table 11.8 in Module 11.5 on stress management.)

Evaluation People differ greatly in their reactions to the same event. For such reasons, the SRRS is at best a rough index of stress. Nevertheless, it's hard to ignore a classic study in which people were deliberately exposed to the virus that causes common colds. The results were nothing to sneeze at: If a person had a high stress score, she or he was much more likely to actually get a cold (Cohen et al., 1993). In view of

TABLE 11.5 Social Readjustment Rating Scale

RANK	LIFE EVENT	LIFE CHANGE UNITS	RANK	LIFE EVENT	LIFE CHANGE UNITS
1	Death of spouse or child	119	23	Mortgage or loan greater than $10,000	44
2	Divorce	98	24	Change in responsibilities at work	43
3	Death of close family member	92	25	Change in living conditions	42
4	Marital separation	79	26	Change in residence	41
5	Fired from work	79	27	Begin or end school	38
6	Major personal injury or illness	77	28	Trouble with in-laws	38
7	Jail term	75	29	Outstanding personal achievement	37
8	Death of close friend	70	30	Change in work hours or conditions	36
9	Pregnancy	66	31	Change in schools	35
10	Major business readjustment	62	32	Christmas	30
11	Foreclosure on a mortgage or loan	61	33	Trouble with boss	29
12	Gain of new family member	57	34	Change in recreation	29
13	Marital reconciliation	57	35	Mortgage or loan less than $10,000	28
14	Change in health or behavior of family member	56	36	Change in personal habits	27
15	Change in financial state	56	37	Change in eating habits	27
16	Retirement	54	38	Change in social activities	27
17	Change to different line of work	51	39	Change in number of family get-togethers	26
18	Change in number of arguments with spouse	51	40	Change in sleeping habits	26
19	Marriage	50	41	Vacation	25
20	Spouse begins or ends work	46	42	Change in church activities	22
21	Sexual difficulties	45	43	Minor violations of the law	22
22	Child leaving home	44			

Source: Reprinted from *Journal of Psychosomatic Research*, Vol. 43, No. 3, 1997, pp. 279-292, T. H. Homes & R. H. Rahe, © 1997 Elsevier Science. Reprinted by permission.

such findings, a high LCU score should be taken seriously. If your score goes much over 300, an adjustment in your activities or lifestyle may be needed. Remember, "To be forewarned is to be forearmed."

The Hazards of Hassles *There must be more to stress than major life changes. Isn't there a link between ongoing stresses and health?* In addition to having a direct impact, major life events spawn countless daily frustrations and irritations (Pillow, Zautra, & Sandler, 1996). Also, many of us face ongoing stresses at work or at home that do not involve major life changes (Pett & Johnson, 2005). Such minor but frequent stresses are called **hassles**, or **microstressors**. (See ■ Table 11.6 for some examples of hassles faced by college students.)

In a yearlong study, 100 men and women recorded the hassles they endured. Participants also reported on their physical and mental health. Frequent and severe hassles turned out to be better predictors of day-to-day health than major life events were. However, major life events did predict changes in health 1 or 2 years after the events took place. It appears that daily hassles are closely linked to immediate health and psychological well-being (Crowther et al., 2001). Major life changes have more of a long-term impact.

Social Readjustment Rating Scale (SRRS) A scale that rates the impact of various life events on the likelihood of illness.

Life change units (LCUs) Numerical values assigned to each life event on the SRRS.

Hassle (microstressor) Any distressing, day-to-day annoyance.

HUMAN DIVERSITY

Acculturative Stress–Stranger in a Strange Land

Around the world, an increasing number of emigrants and refugees must adapt to dramatic changes in language, dress, values, and social customs. For many, the result is a period of culture shock or **acculturative stress** (stress caused by adapting to a foreign culture). Typical reactions to acculturative stress are anxiety, hostility, depression, alienation, physical illness, or identity confusion (Rummens, Beiser, & Noh, 2003). For many young immigrants, acculturative stress is a major source of mental health problems (Yeh, 2003).

The severity of acculturative stress is related, in part, to how a person adapts to a new culture. There are four main patterns of adaptation (Berry, 1990; Berry et al., 2005):

Integration—maintain your old cultural identity but participate in the new culture
Separation—maintain your old cultural identity and avoid contact with the new culture
Assimilation—adopt the new culture as your own and have contact with its members
Marginalization—reject your old culture but suffer rejection by members of the new culture

To illustrate each pattern, let's consider a family that has immigrated to the United States from the imaginary country of Farlandia.

The father favors integration. He is learning English and wants to get involved in American life. At the same time, he is a leader in the Farlandian-American community and spends much of his leisure time with other Farlandian Americans. His level of acculturative stress is low.

The mother only speaks Farlandish and only interacts with other Farlandian Americans. She remains almost completely separate from American society. Her stress level is high.

The teenage daughter is annoyed by hearing Farlandish spoken at home, by her mother's serving only Farlandian food, and by having to spend her leisure time with her extended Farlandian family. She would prefer to speak English and to be with her American friends. Her desire to assimilate creates moderate stress.

The son doesn't particularly value his Farlandian heritage, yet his schoolmates reject him because he speaks with a Farlandian accent. He feels trapped between two cultures. His position is marginal, and his stress level is high.

To summarize, those who feel marginalized tend to be highly stressed; those who seek to remain separate are also highly stressed; those who pursue integration into their new culture are minimally stressed; and those who assimilate are moderately stressed.

As you can see, integration and assimilation are the best options. However, a big benefit of assimilating is that people who embrace their new culture experience fewer social difficulties. For many, this justifies the stress of adopting new customs and cultural values (Gurung, 2006; Ward & Rana-Deuba, 1999).

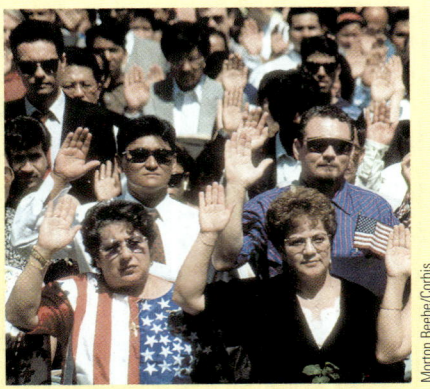

One of the best antidotes for acculturative stress is a society that tolerates or even celebrates ethnic diversity. Although some people find it hard to accept new immigrants, the fact is, nearly everyone's family tree includes people who were once strangers in a strange land.

One way to guarantee that you will experience a large number of life changes and hassles is to live in a foreign culture. "Acculturative Stress" offers a brief glimpse into some of the consequences of culture shock.

What can be done about a high LCU score or feeling excessively hassled? A good response is to use stress management skills. For serious problems, stress management should be learned directly from a therapist or a stress clinic. When ordinary stresses are involved, there is much you can do on your own. An upcoming discussion of stress management will give you a start. In the meantime, take it easy!

Psychosomatic Disorders

As we have seen, chronic or repeated stress can damage physical health as well as upset emotional well-being. Prolonged stress reactions are closely related to a large number of psychosomatic (SIKE-oh-so-MAT-ik) illnesses. In **psychosomatic disorders** (*psyche:* mind; *soma:* body), psychological factors contribute to actual bodily damage or to damaging changes in bodily functioning (Asmundson & Taylor, 2005). Psychosomatic problems, therefore, are *not* the same as hypochondria. **Hypochondriacs** (HI-po-KON-dree-aks) imagine that they have diseases. There is nothing imaginary about asthma, a migraine headache, or high blood pressure. Severe psychosomatic disorders can be fatal. The person who says, "Oh, it's *just* psychosomatic" doesn't understand how serious stress-related diseases really are. (See "Its All in Your Mind.")

The most common psychosomatic problems are gastrointestinal and respiratory (stomach pain and asthma, for example), but many others exist. Typical problems include eczema (skin rash), hives, migraine headaches, rheumatoid arthritis, hypertension (high blood pressure), colitis (ulcer-

TABLE 11.6 Examples of Common Hassles Faced by College Students

Too many things to do
Not enough money for housing
Feeling discriminated against
People making gender jokes
Communication problems with friends
Driving to school
People making fun of my religion
Fear of losing valuables
Work schedule
Getting into shape
Parents' expectations

Source: Pett & Johnson, 2005.

ation of the colon), and heart disease. Actually, these are only the major problems. Many lesser health complaints are also stress related. Typical examples include sore muscles, headaches, neckaches, backaches, indigestion, constipation, chronic diarrhea, fatigue, insomnia, premenstrual problems, and sexual dysfunctions (Taylor, 2006). For some of these problems biofeedback may be helpful. The next section explains how.

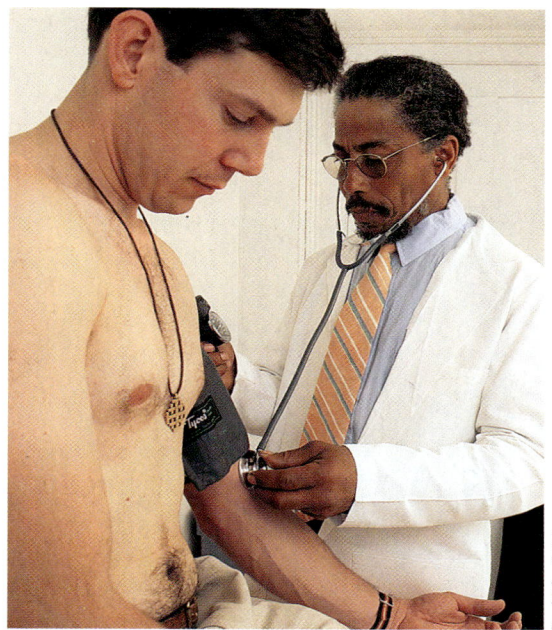

It is estimated that at least half of all patients who see a doctor have a psychosomatic disorder or an illness that is complicated by psychosomatic symptoms.

● **FIGURE 11.8** In biofeedback training, bodily processes are monitored and processed electronically. A signal is then routed back to the patient through headphones, signal lights, or other means. This information helps the patient alter bodily activities not normally under voluntary control.

Biofeedback

Psychologists have discovered that people can learn to control bodily activities once thought to be involuntary. This is done by applying informational feedback to bodily control, a process called **biofeedback.** If I were to say to you, "Raise the temperature of your right hand," you probably couldn't, because you wouldn't know if you were succeeding. To make your task easier, we could attach a sensitive thermometer to your hand. The thermometer could be wired so that an increase in temperature would activate a signal light. Then all you would have to do is try to keep the light on as much as possible. With practice and the help of biofeedback, you could learn to raise your hand temperature at will.

Biofeedback holds promise as a way to treat some psychosomatic problems (● Fig. 11.8). For instance, people have been trained to prevent migraine headaches with biofeedback. Sensors are taped to patients' hands and foreheads. Patients then learn to redirect blood flow away from the head to their extremities. Because migraine headaches involve excessive blood flow to the head, biofeedback helps patients reduce the frequency of their headaches (Andrasik, 2003; Larsson et al., 2005).

Early successes led many to predict that biofeedback would offer a cure for psychosomatic illnesses, anxiety, pho-

Acculturative stress Stress caused by the many changes and adaptations required when a person moves to a foreign culture.

Psychosomatic disorders Illnesses in which psychological factors contribute to bodily damage or to damaging changes in bodily functioning.

Hypochondriac A person who complains about illnesses that appear to be imaginary.

Biofeedback Information given to a person about his or her ongoing bodily activities; aids voluntary regulation of bodily states.

CRITICAL THINKING

Its All in Your Mind

Have you ever had someone dismiss a health concern by saying, "Its all in your mind," as if your problem might be imaginary? For centuries the *medical model* has dominated Western thinking. From this perspective, health is an absence of illness and your body is a complex biological machine that can break down and become ill. Sometimes, you inflict the damage yourself through poor lifestyle choices, such as smoking or overeating. Sometimes, an external cause, such as a virus, is the culprit. In either event, the problem is physical and your mind has little to do with it. Moreover, physical problems call for physical treatments ("Take your medicine"), so your mind has little to do with your recovery.

Over the last 50 years, the medical model has slowly given way to the *biopsychosocial model*. This view states that diseases are caused by a combination of biological, psychological, and social factors. Most importantly, the biopsychosocial model defines health as a state of well-being that we can *actively* attain and maintain (Oakley, 2004). Instead of passively getting treatments from a doctor, this model says that you play a role in fostering your own health. Thus, it may no longer be inaccurate to say, "It's all in your mind," *if* you mean that a person's beliefs—which affect behavior—can have a dramatic impact on health. So, as you take responsibility for your own well-being, remember that in some ways health is all in your mind!

---

bias, drug abuse, and a long list of other problems. In reality, biofeedback has proved helpful but not an instant cure (Schwartz & Andrasik, 2003). Biofeedback can help relieve muscle-tension headaches, migraine headaches, and chronic pain (Middaugh & Pawlick, 2002). It shows promise for lowering blood pressure and controlling heart rhythms (Rau, Bührer, & Weitkunat, 2003). The technique has been used with some success to control epileptic seizures and hyperactivity in children (Demos, 2005). Insomnia also responds to biofeedback therapy (Gathchel & Oordt, 2003).

How does biofeedback help? Some researchers believe that many of its benefits arise from *general relaxation*. Others stress that there is no magic in biofeedback itself. The method simply acts as a "mirror" to help a person perform tasks involving *self-regulation*. Just as a mirror does not comb your hair, biofeedback does not do anything by itself. It can, however, help people make desired changes in their behavior (Weems, 1998).

The Cardiac Personality

It would be a mistake to assume that stress is the sole cause of psychosomatic diseases. Genetic differences, organ weaknesses, and learned reactions to stress combine to do damage. Personality also enters the picture. As mentioned earlier, a general disease-prone personality type exists. To a degree, there are also "headache personalities," "asthma personalities," and so on. The best documented of such patterns is the "cardiac personality"—a person at high risk for heart disease.

Two cardiologists, Meyer Friedman and Ray Rosenman, offer a glimpse at how some people create stress for themselves. In a landmark study of heart problems, Friedman and Rosenman (1983) classified people as either **Type A personalities** (those who run a high risk of heart attack) or **Type B personalities** (those who are unlikely to have a heart attack). Then they did an 8-year follow-up, finding more than twice the rate of heart disease in Type A's than in Type B's (Rosenman et al., 1975).

Type A *What is the Type A personality like?* Type A people are hard driving, ambitious, highly competitive, achievement oriented, and striving. Type A people believe that with enough effort they can overcome any obstacle, and they "push" themselves accordingly.

Perhaps the most telltale signs of a Type A personality are *time urgency* and chronic *anger* or *hostility*. Type A's seem to chafe at the normal pace of events. They hurry from one activity to another, racing the clock in self-imposed urgency. As they do, they feel a constant sense of frustration and anger.

Individuals with Type A personalities feel a continuous sense of anger, irritation, and hostility.

Feelings of anger and hostility, in particular, are strongly related to increased risk of heart attack (Boyle et al., 2004; Bunde & Suls, 2006). One study found that 15 percent of a group of 25-year-old doctors and lawyers who scored high on a hostility test were dead by age 50. The most damaging pattern may occur in hostile persons who keep their anger "bottled up." Such people seethe with anger but don't express it outwardly. This increases their pulse rate and blood pressure and puts a tremendous strain on the heart (Bongard, al'Absi, & Lovallo, 1998).

To summarize, there is growing evidence that anger or hostility may be the core lethal factor of Type A behavior (Krantz & McCeney, 2002; Niaura et al., 2002). To date, hundreds of studies have supported the validity of the Type A concept. In view of this, Type A's would be wise to take their increased health risks seriously.

How are Type A people identified? Characteristics of Type A people are summarized in the short self-identification test presented in ■ Table 11.7. If most of the list applies to you, you might be a Type A. However, confirmation of your type would require more powerful testing methods. Also, remember that the original definition of Type A behavior was probably too broad. The key psychological factors that increase heart disease risk appear to be anger, hostility, and mistrust (Krantz & McCeney, 2002; Smith et al., 2004). Also although Type A behavior appears to promote heart disease, depression or distress may be what finally triggers a heart attack (Denollet & Van Heck, 2001; Dinan, 2001).

Because our society places a premium on achievement, competition, and mastery, it is not surprising that many people develop Type A personalities. The best way to avoid the self-made stress this causes is to adopt behavior that is the opposite of that listed in Table 11.7 (Williams, Barefoot, & Schneiderman, 2003). It is entirely possible to succeed in life without sacrificing your health or happiness in the process. People who frequently feel angry and hostile toward others may benefit from the advice of Redford Williams, a physician interested in Type A behavior.

Strategies for Reducing Hostility According to Redford Williams, reducing hostility involves three goals. First, you must stop mistrusting the motives of others. Second, you must find ways to reduce how often you feel anger, indignation, irritation, and rage. Third, you must learn to be kinder and more considerate. Based on his clinical experience, Williams (1989) recommends 12 strategies for reducing hostility and increasing trust:

1. Become aware of your angry, hostile, and cynical thoughts by logging them in a notebook. Record what happened, what you thought and felt, and what actions you took. Review your hostility log at the end of each week.
2. Admit to yourself and to someone you trust that you have a problem with excessive anger and hostility.
3. Interrupt hostile, cynical thoughts whenever they occur. (Module 13.6 explains a thought-stopping method you can use for this step.)
4. When you have an angry, hostile, or cynical thought about someone, silently look for the ways in which it is irrational or unreasonable.
5. When you are angry, try to mentally put yourself in the other person's shoes.
6. Learn to laugh at yourself and use humor to defuse your anger.

■ TABLE 11.7 Characteristics of the Type A Person

Check the items that apply to you. Do you:

- ____ Have a habit of explosively accentuating various key words in ordinary speech even when there is no need for such accentuation (I HATE it when you do THAT!)?
- ____ Finish other persons' sentences for them?
- ____ *Always* move, walk, and eat rapidly?
- ____ Quickly skim reading material and prefer summaries or condensations of books?
- ____ Become easily angered by slow-moving lines or traffic?
- ____ Feel an impatience with the rate at which most events take place?
- ____ Tend to be unaware of the details or beauty of your surroundings?
- ____ Frequently strive to think of or do two or more things simultaneously?
- ____ Almost always feel vaguely guilty when you relax, vacation, or do absolutely nothing for several days?
- ____ Tend to evaluate your worth in quantitative terms (number of A's earned, amount of income, number of games won, and so forth)?
- ____ Have nervous gestures or muscle twitches, such as grinding your teeth, clenching your fists, or drumming your fingers?
- ____ Attempt to schedule more and more activities into less time and in so doing make fewer allowances for unforeseen problems?
- ____ Frequently think about other things while talking to someone?
- ____ Repeatedly take on more responsibilities than you can comfortably handle?

Source: Shortened and adapted from Friedman and Ray H. Rosenman, *Type A Behavior and Your Heart*, Alfred A. Knopf, Inc., © 1983. Reprinted with permission.

Type A personality A personality type with an elevated risk of heart disease; characterized by time urgency, anger, and hostility.

Type B personality All personality types other than Type A; a low-cardiac-risk personality.

7. Learn reliable ways to relax. Two methods are described in this chapter's "Psychology in Action" module. Another can be found in the "Psychology in Action" discussion of Module 13.6.
8. Practice trusting others more. Begin with situations where no great harm will be done if the person lets you down.
9. Make an effort to listen more to others and to really understand what they are saying.
10. Learn to be assertive, rather than aggressive, in upsetting situations. (See Module 15.3 for information about self-assertion skills.)
11. Rise above small irritations by pretending that today is the last day of your life.
12. Rather than blaming people for mistreating you, and becoming angry over it, try to forgive them. We all have shortcomings.

Hardy Personality

How do Type A people who do not develop heart disease differ from those who do? Psychologist Salvatore Maddi has studied people who have a **hardy personality.** Such people seem to be unusually resistant to stress. The first study of hardiness began with two groups of managers at a large utility company. All the managers held high-stress positions. Yet, some tended to get sick after stressful events, whereas others were rarely ill. How did the people who were thriving differ from their "stressed-out" colleagues? Both groups seemed to have traits typical of the Type A personality, so that wasn't the explanation. They were also quite similar in most other respects. The main difference was that the hardy group seemed to hold a worldview that consisted of three traits (Maddi, 2006):

1. They had a sense of personal *commitment* to self, work, family, and other stabilizing values.
2. They felt that they had *control* over their lives and their work.
3. They had a tendency to see life as a series of *challenges,* rather than as a series of threats or problems.

How do such traits protect people from the effects of stress? Persons strong in *commitment* find ways of turning whatever they are doing into something that seems interesting and important. They tend to get involved rather than feeling alienated.

Persons strong in *control* believe that they can more often than not influence the course of events around them. This prevents them from passively seeing themselves as victims of circumstance.

Finally, people strong in *challenge* find fulfillment in continual growth. They seek to learn from their experiences, rather than accepting easy comfort, security, and routine (Maddi, 2006). Indeed, many "negative" experiences can actually enhance personal growth—if you have support from others and the skills needed to cope with challenge (Armeli, Gunthert, & Cohen, 2001).

Positive Psychology: Hardiness, Optimism, and Happiness

Good and bad events occur in all lives. What separates happy people from those who are unhappy is largely a matter of attitude. Happy people tend to see their lives in more positive terms, even when trouble comes their way. For example, happier people tend to find humor in disappointments. They look at setbacks as challenges. They are strengthened by losses (Lyubomirsky & Tucker, 1998). In short, happiness tends to be related to hardiness (Maddi, 2006). Why is there a connection? As psychologist Barbara Fredrickson has pointed out, positive emotions tend to broaden our mental focus. Emotions such as joy, interest, and contentment create an urge to play, to be creative, to explore, to savor life, to seek new experiences, to integrate, and to grow. When you are stressed, experiencing positive emotions can make it more likely that you will find creative solutions to your problems. Positive emotions also tend to reduce the bodily arousal that occurs when we are stressed, possibly limiting stress-related damage (Fredrickson, 2003).

Elsewhere in this chapter, we have noted the value of optimism, which goes hand in hand with hardiness and happiness. Optimists tend to expect that things will turn out well. This motivates them to actively cope with adversity. They are less likely to be stopped by temporary setbacks, and more likely to deal with problems head-on. Pessimists are more likely to ignore or deny problems. The result of such differences is that optimists are less stressed and anxious than pessimists. They are also in better health than pessimists. In general, optimists tend to take better care of themselves because they believe that their efforts to stay healthy will succeed (Peterson & Chang, 2003).

The Value of Social Support

Social support (close, positive relationships with others) provides one more important antidote to stress. People with close, supportive relationships tend to be happy, hardy, optimistic, and healthy (Kiecolt-Glaser et al., 2002). Apparently, support from family and friends serves as a buffer to cushion the impact of stressful events. (See "Feeling Stressed? You've Got a Friend.")

Women tend to make better use of social support than men do. Women who are stressed seek support, and they nurture others. Men are more likely to become aggressive or to withdraw emotionally (Taylor et al., 2000). This may be

DISCOVERING PSYCHOLOGY

Feeling Stressed? You've Got a Friend

Here's an interesting exercise to try: Briefly answer the following four questions about a specific person you are currently close to—someone you can turn to when you need help, advice, or encouragement.

1. What do you value or appreciate most about this person?
2. What does this person value or appreciate most about you?
3. What does this person do for you that is supportive or helpful?
4. How do you feel about this person after being away from her or him for a few hours or a few days? (Adapted from Smith, Ruiz, & Uchino, 2004.)

Do you feel more relaxed and at ease after answering these questions? In a recent study, the questions were used to get people to think about a close, supportive person for a few minutes. After that, subjects had to give a stressful speech. For some participants, thinking about a supportive person helped lower their stress levels (Smith, Ruiz, & Uchino, 2004).

The preceding study suggests that you may be able to reduce the stress you feel in difficult situations by thinking about a person who supports and encourages you. If that doesn't help, and you own a pet, there may be a good alternative strategy. Many people view their pets as loving, supportive companions who are better, in some ways, than humans. In another study, some people were asked to do stressful tasks alone, whereas others had a friend, a spouse, or a pet present. Under these conditions, the greatest amount of stress relief occurred when a pet (dog or cat) was present (Allen, Blascovich, & Mendes, 2002). Thus, if you have a pet, you might find it helpful to imagine the animal by your side when you face a stressful situation. Silently talking to your furry friend can be quite calming. In any case, whether your comfort comes from a human or an animal companion, it's valuable to remind yourself that "you've got a friend."

why "manly men" won't ask for help, whereas women in trouble call their friends! Where stress is concerned, many men could benefit from adopting women's tendency to tend to and befriend others.

How else might social support help? Most people share positive events, such as marriages, births, graduations, and birthdays, with others. When things go well, we like to tell others about them. Sharing such events tends to amplify positive emotions and to further increase social support. In many ways, the sharing of good news is an important means by which positive events contribute to individual well-being (Gable et al., 2004).

Support from family and friends acts as a major buffer against stress.

A Look Ahead The work we have reviewed here has drawn new attention to the fact that each of us has a personal responsibility for maintaining and promoting health. In the "Psychology in Action" module that follows, we will look at what you can do to better cope with stress and the health risks that it entails. But first, the following questions may help you maintain a healthy grade on your next psychology test.

MODULE 11.4 Summary

How is stress related to health and disease?

- The *Social Readjustment Rating Scale* rates the impact of life changes on long-range susceptibility to accident or illness.
- Immediate psychological and mental health is related to the intensity and severity of daily hassles or microstressors.
- Intense or prolonged stress may cause damage in the form of psychosomatic problems.
- During biofeedback training, bodily processes are monitored and converted to a signal that tells what the body is doing. Biofeedback allows people to alle-

Hardy personality A personality style associated with superior stress resistance.

Social support Close, positive relationships with other people.

viate some psychosomatic illnesses by altering bodily activities.

- People with Type A personalities are competitive, striving, hostile, impatient, and prone to having heart attacks.

- People who have traits of the hardy personality seem to be resistant to stress, even if they also have Type A traits.

- Optimism, positive emotions, and social support tend to buffer stress.

KNOWLEDGE BUILDER

Stress and Health

Recite

1. Ratings on the SRRS are based on the total number of _____ a person experienced in the preceding year.
   a. hassles
   b. LCUs
   c. STDs
   d. psychosomatic illnesses

2. Holmes's SRRS appears to predict long-range changes in health, whereas the frequency and severity of daily microstressors is closely related to immediate ratings of health. T or F?

3. Ulcers, migraine headaches, and hypochondria are all frequently psychosomatic disorders. T or F?

4. Which of the following is *not* classified as a psychosomatic disorder?
   a. hypertension
   b. colitis
   c. eczema
   d. thymus

5. Two major elements of biofeedback training appear to be relaxation and self-regulation. T or F?

6. Anger, hostility, and mistrust appear to be the core lethal factors in
   a. hypochondria
   b. learned helplessness
   c. the GAS
   d. Type A behavior

7. A sense of commitment, challenge, and control characterizes the hardy personality. T or F?

Reflect
Critical Thinking

8. People with a hardy personality type appear to be especially resistant to which of the problems discussed earlier in this chapter?

Relate

Pick a year from your life that was unusually stressful. Use the SRRS to find your LCU score for that year. Do you think there was a connection between your LCU score and your health? Or have you observed more of a connection between microstressors and your health?

Mindy complains about her health all the time, but she actually seems to be just fine. An acquaintance of Mindy's dismisses her problems by saying, "Oh, she's not really sick. It's just psychosomatic." What's wrong with this use of the term *psychosomatic*?

Do you think you are basically a Type A or a Type B personality? To what extent do you possess traits of the hardy personality?

Link

Internet addresses frequently change. To find the sites listed here, visit **http://www.thomsonedu.com/psychology/coon** for an updated list of Internet addresses and direct links to relevant sites.

- **SRRS** Fill out an online version of the Social Readjustment Rating Scale.
- **Stress, Anxiety, Fears, and Psychosomatic Disorders** A comprehensive source on stress, anxiety, and related disorders.
- **Type A Behavior** Describes Type A behavior, with links to an online test and related sites.

ANSWERS

1. b 2. T 3. F 4. d 5. T 6. d 7. T 8. Learned helplessness.

MODULE **Psychology in Action**

11.5 Stress Management

SURVEY QUESTION: *What are the best strategies for managing stress?*

Stress management is the use of behavioral strategies to reduce stress and improve coping skills. As promised, this section describes strategies for managing stress. Before you continue reading, you may want to assess your level of stress again, this time using a scale developed for undergraduate students (■ Table 11.8). Like the SRRS, high scores on the *College Life Stress Inventory* suggest that you have been exposed to health-threatening levels of stress (Renner & Mackin, 1998).

The *College Life Stress Inventory* is scored by adding the ratings for all the items that have happened to you in the last year. The following scale is an approximate guide to the meaning of your score. But remember, stress is an internal state. If you are good at coping with stressors, a high score may not be a problem for you.

0–150: Very low
151–590: Low
591–1030: Below average
1031–1470: Average
1471–1910: High
1911–2350: Very high
2351 or more: Extremely high

Now that you have a picture of your current level of stress, what can you do about it? The simplest way of coping with stress is to modify or remove its source—by leaving a stressful job, for example. Obviously this is often impossible, which is why learning to manage stress is so important.

As shown in ● Figure 11.9, stress triggers *bodily effects, upsetting thoughts,* and *ineffective behavior.* Also shown is the fact that each element worsens the others in a vicious cycle. Indeed, the basic idea of the "Stress Game" is that once it begins, *you lose*—unless you take action to break the cycle. The information that follows tells how.

Managing Bodily Reactions

Much of the immediate discomfort of stress is caused by fight-or-flight emotional responses. The body is ready to act, with tight muscles and a pounding heart. If action is prevented, we merely remain "uptight." A sensible remedy is to learn a reliable, drug-free way of relaxing.

● **FIGURE 11.9** The stress game. (Adapted from Rosenthal and Rosenthal, 1980.)

Stress management The application of behavioral strategies to reduce stress and improve coping skills.

TABLE 11.8 College Life Stress Inventory

Circle the "stress rating" number for any item that has happened to you in the last year, then add them.

EVENT	STRESS RATING	EVENT	STRESS RATING
Being raped	100	Lack of sleep	69
Finding out that you are HIV positive	100	Change in housing situation (hassles, moves)	69
Being accused of rape	98	Competing or performing in public	69
Death of a close friend	97	Getting in a physical fight	66
Death of a close family member	96	Difficulties with a roommate	66
Contracting a sexually transmitted disease (other than AIDS)	94	Job changes (applying, new job, work hassles)	65
Concerns about being pregnant	91	Declaring a major or concerns about future plans	65
Finals week	90	A class you hate	62
Concerns about your partner being pregnant	90	Drinking or use of drugs	61
Oversleeping for an exam	89	Confrontations with professors	60
Flunking a class	89	Starting a new semester	58
Having a boyfriend or girlfriend cheat on you	85	Going on a first date	57
Ending a steady dating relationship	85	Registration	55
Serious illness in a close friend or family member	85	Maintaining a steady dating relationship	55
Financial difficulties	84	Commuting to campus or work, or both	54
Writing a major term paper	83	Peer pressures	53
Being caught cheating on a test	83	Being away from home for the first time	53
Drunk driving	82	Getting sick	52
Sense of overload in school or work	82	Concerns about your appearance	52
Two exams in one day	80	Getting straight A's	51
Cheating on your boyfriend or girlfriend	77	A difficult class that you love	48
Getting married	76	Making new friends; getting along with friends	47
Negative consequences of drinking or drug use	75	Fraternity or sorority rush	47
Depression or crisis in your best friend	73	Falling asleep in class	40
Difficulties with parents	73	Attending an athletic event (e.g., football game)	20
Talking in front of a class	72		

Source: "Teaching of Psychology" by Michael J. Renner and R. S. Mackin, © 1998 Lawrence Erlbaum Associates and the authors. Reprinted by permission.

Exercise Stress-based arousal can be dissipated by using the body. Any full-body exercise can be effective. Swimming, dancing, jumping rope, yoga, most sports, and especially walking are valuable outlets. Regular exercise alters hormones, circulation, muscle tone, and a number of other aspects of physical functioning. Together, such changes can reduce anxiety and lower the risks for disease (Linden, 2005; Salmon, 2001).

Be sure to choose activities that are vigorous enough to relieve tension, yet enjoyable enough to be done repeatedly. Exercising for stress management is most effective when it is done daily. As little as 30 minutes of total exercise per day, even if it occurs in short 10- to 20-minute sessions, can improve mood and energy (Hansen, Stevens, & Coast, 2001).

Meditation Many stress counselors recommend *meditation* for quieting the body and promoting relaxation. Meditation and its effects were discussed in Module 5.3. For now, it is enough to restate that meditation is easy to learn—taking an expensive commercial course is unnecessary.

Meditation is one of the most effective ways to relax (Deckro et al., 2002). But be aware that listening to or playing music, taking nature walks, enjoying hobbies, and the like can be meditations of sorts. Anything that reliably interrupts upsetting thoughts and promotes relaxation can be helpful.

Progressive Relaxation It is possible to relax systematically, completely, and by choice. To learn the details of how this is done, consult Module 13.3 of this book. The basic idea of **progressive relaxation** is to tighten all the muscles in a given area of your body (the arms, for instance) and then voluntarily relax them. By first tensing and relaxing each area of the body (also called the *tension-release method*), you can learn what muscle tension feels like. Then when each area is relaxed, the change is more noticeable and more controllable. In this way it is possible, with practice, to greatly reduce tension.

Guided Imagery In a technique called **guided imagery**, people visualize images that are calming, relaxing, or beneficial in other ways. Relaxation, for instance, can be promoted by visualizing peaceful scenes. Pick several places where you feel safe, calm, and at ease. Typical locations might be a beach or lake, the woods, floating on an air mattress in a warm pool, or lying in the sun at a quiet park. To relax, vividly imagine yourself in one of these locations. In the visualized scene, you should be alone and in a comfortable position. It is important to visualize the scene as realistically as possible. Try to feel, taste, smell, hear, and see what you would actually experience in the calming scene. Practice forming such images several times a day for about 5 minutes each time. When your scenes become familiar and detailed they can be used to reduce anxiety and encourage relaxation (Rosenthal, 1993). Remember, too, that imagining that a supportive friend or a loving pet is nearby can reduce tension and anxiety (Allen, Blascovich, & Mendes, 2002; Smith, Ruiz, & Uchino, 2004).

Modifying Ineffective Behavior

Stress is often made worse by our misguided responses to it. The following suggestions may help you deal with stress more effectively.

Slow Down Remember that stress can be self-generated. Try to deliberately do things at a slower pace—especially if your pace has speeded up over the years. Tell yourself, "What counts most is not if I get there first, but if I get there at all" or "My goal is distance, not speed."

Organize Disorganization creates stress. Try to take a fresh look at your situation and get organized. Setting priorities can be a real stress fighter. Ask yourself what's really important, and concentrate on the things that count. Learn to let go of trivial but upsetting irritations. And above all, when you are feeling stressed, remember to KIS: **K**eep **I**t **S**imple. (Some people prefer KISS: Keep It Simple, Stupid.)

Strike a Balance Work, school, family, friends, interests, hobbies, recreation, community, church—there are many important elements in a satisfying life. Damaging stress often comes from letting one element—especially work or school—get blown out of proportion. Your goal should be quality in life, not quantity. Try to strike a balance between challenging "good stress" and relaxation. Remember, when you are "doing nothing" you are actually doing something very important: Set aside time for "me acts" such as loafing, browsing, puttering, playing, and napping.

Recognize and Accept Your Limits Many of us set unrealistic and perfectionist goals. Given that no one can ever be perfect, this attitude leaves many people feeling inadequate, no matter how well they have performed. Set gradual, achievable goals for yourself. Also, set realistic limits on what you try to do on any given day. Learn to say no to added demands or responsibilities.

Write About Your Feelings If you don't have someone you can talk to about stressful events, you might try expressing your thoughts and feelings in writing. Several studies have found that students who write about their upsetting experiences, thoughts, and feelings are better able to cope with stress. They also experience fewer illnesses, and they get better grades (Esterling et al., 1999; Pennebaker, 2004). Writing about your feelings tends to leave your mind clearer. This makes it easier to pay attention to life's challenges and come up with effective coping strategies (Klein & Boals, 2001a, 2001b). Thus, after you write about your feelings, it helps to make specific plans for coping with upsetting experiences (Pennebaker & Chung, 2007).

As an alternative, you might want to try writing about positive experiences. In one study, college students who wrote about intensely positive experiences had fewer illnesses over the next 3 months. Writing just 20 minutes a day for 3 days improved the students' moods and had a surprisingly long-lasting effect on their health (Burton & King, 2004).

Progressive relaxation A method for producing deep relaxation of all parts of the body.

Guided imagery Intentional visualization of images that are calming, relaxing, or beneficial in other ways.

Avoiding Upsetting Thoughts

Assume you are taking a test. Suddenly you realize that you are running short of time. If you say to yourself, "Oh no, this is terrible, I've blown it now," your body's response will probably be sweating, tenseness, and a knot in your stomach. On the other hand, if you say, "I should have watched the time, but getting upset won't help; I'll just take one question at a time," your stress level will be much lower.

As stated earlier, stress is greatly affected by the views we take of events. Physical symptoms and a tendency to make poor decisions are increased by negative thoughts or "self-talk." In many cases what you say to yourself can be the difference between coping and collapsing (Matheny et al., 1996).

Coping Statements Psychologist Donald Meichenbaum has popularized a technique called **stress inoculation.** In it, clients learn to fight fear and anxiety with an internal monologue of positive coping statements. First, clients learn to identify and monitor **negative self-statements** (self-critical thoughts that increase anxiety). Negative thoughts are a problem because they tend to directly elevate physical arousal. To counter this effect, clients learn to replace negative statements with coping statements from a supplied list. Eventually they are encouraged to make their own lists (Saunders et al., 1996).

How are coping statements applied? **Coping statements** are reassuring and self-enhancing. They are used to block out, or counteract, negative self-talk in stressful situations. Before giving a short speech, for instance, you would replace "I'm scared," "I can't do this," "My mind will go blank and I'll panic," or "I'll sound stupid and boring" with "I'll give my speech on something I like," or "I'll breathe deeply before I start my speech," or "My pounding heart just means I'm psyched up to do my best." Additional examples of coping statements follow.

Preparing for Stressful Situation

I'll just take things one step at a time.
If I get nervous, I'll just pause a moment.
Tomorrow I'll be through it.
I've managed to do this before.
What exactly do I have to do?

Confronting the Stressful Situation

Relax now, this can't really hurt me.
Stay organized; focus on the task.
There's no hurry. Take it step by step.
Nobody's perfect; I'll just do my best.
It will be over soon; just be calm.

Meichenbaum cautions that saying the "right" things to yourself may not be enough to improve stress tolerance. You must practice this approach in actual stress situations. Also, it is important to develop your own personal list of coping statements by finding what works for you. Ultimately, the value of learning this, and other stress management skills, ties back into the idea that much stress is self-generated. Knowing that you can manage a demanding situation is in itself a major antidote for stress. In a recent study, college students who learned stress inoculation not only had less anxiety and depression, but better self-esteem as well (Schiraldi & Brown, 2001).

Lighten Up Humor is worth cultivating as a way to reduce stress. A good sense of humor can lower your distress/stress reaction to difficult events (Lefcourt, 2003). In addition, an ability to laugh at life's ups and downs is associated with better immunity to disease (McClelland & Cheriff, 1997). Don't be afraid to laugh at yourself and at the many ways in which we humans make things difficult for ourselves. You've probably heard the following advice about everyday stresses: "Don't sweat the small stuff" and "It's all small stuff." Humor is one of the best antidotes for anxiety and emotional distress because it helps put things into perspective (Henman, 2001; Szabo, 2003). The vast majority of events are only as stressful as you allow them to be. Have some fun. It's perfectly healthy.

MODULE 11.5 Psychology in Action Summary

What are the best strategies for managing stress?

- The damaging effects of stress can be reduced with stress management techniques.
- All of the following are good ways to manage bodily reactions to stress: exercise, meditation, progressive relaxation, and guided imagery.
- To minimize ineffective behavior when you are stressed, you can slow down, get organized, balance work and relaxation, accept your limits, and write about your feelings.
- Learning to use coping statements is a good way to combat upsetting thoughts.

KNOWLEDGE BUILDER

Stress Management

Recite

1. Exercise, meditation, and progressive relaxation are considered effective ways of countering negative self-statements. T or F?
2. A person using progressive relaxation for stress management is most likely trying to control which component of stress?
   a. bodily reactions
   b. upsetting thoughts
   c. ineffective behavior
   d. the primary appraisal
3. Exercise, meditation, progressive relaxation, and guided imagery would be least likely to help a person who is in the GAS stage of
   a. alarm
   b. resistance
   c. exhaustion
   d. adaptation
4. While taking a stressful classroom test you say to yourself, "Stay organized; focus on the task." It's obvious that you are using
   a. guided imagery
   b. coping statements
   c. LCUs
   d. guided relaxation

Reflect
Critical Thinking

5. Steve always feels extremely pressured when the due date arrives for his major term papers. How could he reduce stress in such instances?

Relate

If you were going to put together a "tool kit" for stress management, what items would you include?

Link

Internet addresses frequently change. To find the sites listed here, visit **http://www.thomsonedu.com/psychology/coon** for an updated list of Internet addresses and direct links to relevant sites.

- **Self-Growth.Com** Explore a self-improvement and personal growth website that provides many links to stress management resources, including online articles and information on related topics such as biofeedback and stress.
- **Preventive Health Center** A general source of information on how to maintain health and prevent disease.
- **Stress Management Resources** A site that helps you deal with job-related stress.

ANSWERS

1. F 2. a 3. c 4. b 5. The stress associated with doing term papers can be almost completely eliminated by breaking up a long-term assignment into many small daily or weekly assignments. Students who habitually procrastinate are often amazed at how pleasant college work can be once they renounce "brinkmanship."

Interactive Learning

Psychology: Active Learning Modules Book Companion Website

http://www.thomsonedu.com/psychology/coon

Visit your Book Companion Website, where you will find flash cards, practice quizzes, Internet links, and more to help you study.

ThomsonNOW

Just What You Need to Know NOW!

Spend time on what you need to master rather than on information you already have learned. Take a pre-test for this chapter, and ThomsonNOW will generate a personalized study plan based on your results. The study plan will identify the topics you need to review and direct you to online resources to help you master those topics. You can then take a post-test to help you determine the concepts you have mastered and what you will need to work on. Try it out! Go to www.thomsonedu.com/login to sign in with an access code or to purchase access to this product.

Stress inoculation Use of positive coping statements to control fear and anxiety.

Negative self-statements Self-critical thoughts that increase anxiety and lower performance.

Coping statements Reassuring, self-enhancing statements that are used to stop self-critical thinking.

12 Psychological Disorders

MODULE 12.1 Normality and Psychopathology
SURVEY QUESTIONS: How is normality defined? What are the major psychological disorders?

MODULE 12.2 Personality Disorders and Anxiety-Based Disorders
SURVEY QUESTION: What is a personality disorder?
SURVEY QUESTION: What problems result when a person suffers high levels of anxiety?
SURVEY QUESTION: How do psychologists explain anxiety-based disorders?

MODULE 12.3 Psychosis, Delusional Disorders, and Schizophrenia
SURVEY QUESTION: What are the general characteristics of psychotic disorders?

SURVEY QUESTION: What is the nature of a delusional disorder?
SURVEY QUESTIONS: What forms does schizophrenia take? What causes it?

MODULE 12.4 Mood Disorders
SURVEY QUESTIONS: What are mood disorders? What causes depression?

MODULE 12.5 Psychology in Action: Suicide—Lives on the Brink
SURVEY QUESTIONS: Why do people commit suicide? Can suicide be prevented?

Beware the Helicopters

"The helicopters. Oh no, not the helicopters. Have come to tear the feathers out of my frontal lobes. Help me, nurse, help me, can't you hear them? Gotta get back into my body to save it.... The doctor is thinking I would make good glue."

These are the words of Carol North, a psychiatrist who survived schizophrenia. In addition to being plagued by hallucinated helicopters, Carol heard voices that said: "Be good," "Do bad," "Stand up," "Sit down," "Collide with the other world," "Do you want a cigar?" (North, 1987).

Carol North's painful journey into the shadows of madness left her incapacitated for nearly 20 years. Wonderfully, she has since forged her career as an eminent psychiatrist concerned with helping others escape the maze of mental illness (see, for example, North et al., 2006). Her case is but one hint of the magnitude of mental health problems. Here are some facts on psychological disorders (NIMH, 2006b):

- 1 in 4 American adults suffers from a diagnosable mental disorder in any given year.
- Mental disorders are the leading cause of disability for Americans and Canadians ages 15 to 44.
- Anxiety disorders are often accompanied by depression and/or substance abuse.
- In 2002, almost 32,000 Americans committed suicide.
- More than 20,000,000 Americans suffer from mood disorders in any given year.

What does it mean to be "crazy"? A hundred years ago, doctors and nonprofessionals alike used terms such as "crazy," "insane," "cracked," and "lunatic" quite freely. The "insane" were thought of as bizarre and definitely different from the rest of us. Today, our understanding of psychological disorders is more sophisticated. To draw the line between normal and abnormal, we must weigh some complex issues. We'll explore some of them in this chapter, as well as an array of psychological problems.

MODULE 12.1 Normality and Psychopathology

DECIDING IF A PERSON'S BEHAVIOR is abnormal is harder than it might seem. The conservative, churchgoing housewife down the street might be flagrantly psychotic and a lethal danger to her children. The reclusive eccentric who hangs out at the park could be the sanest person in town. Let's begin our discussion with some basic factors that affect judgments of normality. Then in upcoming modules we'll survey some of the major disorders that psychologists diagnose and treat.

Normality—What Is Normal?

SURVEY QUESTIONS: *How is normality defined? What are the major psychological disorders?*

"That guy is really wacko. His porch lights are dimming." "Yeah, the butter's sliding off his waffle. He's ready to go postal." Informally, it's tempting to make such snap judgments about mental health. But to seriously classify people as psychologically unhealthy raises complex and age-old issues.

The scientific study of mental, emotional, and behavioral disorders is known as **psychopathology**. The term also refers to mental disorders themselves, such as schizophrenia or depression, and to behavior patterns that make people unhappy and impair their personal growth (Butcher, Mineka, & Hooley, 2007). Defining abnormality can be tricky. We might begin by saying that psychopathology is characterized by *subjective discomfort* (private feelings of pain, unhappiness, or emotional distress) like Carol North endured.

But couldn't a person be seriously disturbed without feeling discomfort? Yes. Psychopathology doesn't always cause personal anguish. A person suffering from mania might feel elated and "on top of the world." Also, a *lack* of discomfort may reveal a problem. For example, if you showed no signs of grief after the death of a close friend, we might suspect psychopathology. In practice, subjective discomfort explains most instances in which people voluntarily seek professional help.

Some psychologists use statistics to define normality more objectively. **Statistical abnormality** refers to scoring very high or low on some dimension, such as intelligence, anxiety, or depression. Anxiety, for example, is a feature of several psychological disorders. To measure it, we could create a test to learn how many people show low, medium, or high levels of anxiety. Usually, the results of such tests will form a *normal* (bell-shaped) *curve*. (*Normal* in this case refers only to the *shape* of the curve.) Notice that most people score near the middle of a normal curve; very few have extremely high and low scores (● Fig. 12.1). A person who deviates from the average by being anxious all the time (high anxiety) might be abnormal. So, too, might a person who never feels anxiety.

Then statistical abnormality tells us nothing about the meaning of deviations from the norm? Right. It is as statistically "abnormal" (unusual) for a person to score above 145 on an IQ test as it is to score below 55. However, only the lower score is regarded as "abnormal" or undesirable. In the same sense, it is unusual for a person to speak four languages or to win an event at the Olympics, but these are desirable, if rare, accomplishments.

Statistical definitions also can't tell us *where to draw the line* between normality and abnormality. To take a new example, we could obtain the average frequency of sexual intercourse for persons of a particular age, sex, sexual orientation, and marital status. Clearly, a person who feels driven to have sex dozens of times a day has a problem. But as we move back toward the norm we face the problem of drawing lines. How often does normal behavior have to occur before it becomes abnormal? As you can see, statistical boundary lines tend to be somewhat arbitrary (Comer, 2005).

Atypical behavior or nonconformity may underlie some disorders. **Social nonconformity** refers to disobeying public standards for acceptable conduct. Extreme nonconformity can lead to destructive or self-destructive behavior. (Think, for instance, of a drug abuser or a prostitute.) However, we must be careful to separate unhealthy nonconformity from creative lifestyles. Many eccentric "characters" are charming and emotionally stable. Note, too, that strictly following social norms is no guarantee of mental health. In some cases, psychopathology involves rigid conformity. (See "Crazy for a Day.")

A young woman ties a thick rubber cord around her ankles, screams hysterically, and jumps head first off a bridge. Thirty years ago, the woman's behavior might have seemed

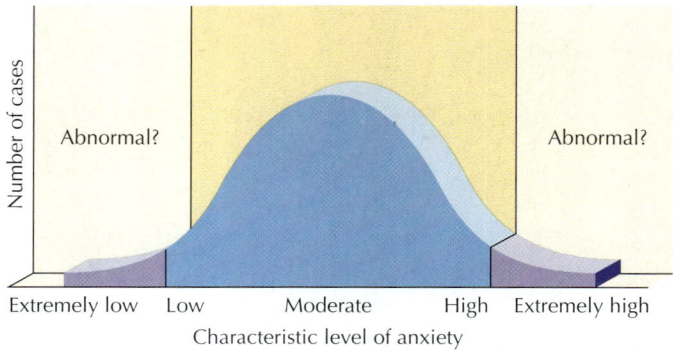

● **FIGURE 12.1** The number of people displaying a personal characteristic may help define what is statistically abnormal.

DISCOVERING PSYCHOLOGY

Crazy for a Day

Performing a mildly abnormal behavior is a good way to get a sense of how social norms define "normality" in daily life. Here's your assignment: Do something strange in public and observe how people react to you. (Please don't do anything dangerous, harmful, or offensive—and don't get arrested!) Here are some deviant behaviors that other students have staged:

- Sit in the dining area of a fast-food restaurant and loudly carry on a conversation with an imaginary companion.
- Stand in a busy hallway on campus and adopt a Kung Fu stance. Remain in that position for 10 minutes.
- Walk around campus on a sunny day while wearing a raincoat and carrying an open umbrella. Keep the umbrella over your head when you are inside buildings.
- Stick one finger in your nose and another in your ear. Walk through a busy shopping mall.
- Cover your head with aluminum foil for a day.

Does the idea of performing any of these actions make you uncomfortable? If so, you may not need to do anything more to appreciate how powerfully social norms constrain our actions. As we have noted, social nonconformity is just one facet of abnormal behavior. Nevertheless, actions that are regarded as "strange" within a particular culture are often the first sign to others that a person has a problem.

completely crazy. Today, it is a routine form of entertainment (called "bungee jumping"). Before any behavior can be defined as abnormal, we must consider the *situational context* (social situation, behavioral setting, or general circumstances) in which it occurs. Is it normal to stand outside and water a lawn with a hose? It depends on whether it is raining or not. Is it abnormal for a grown man to remove his pants and expose himself to another man or woman in a place of business? It depends on whether the other person is a bank clerk or a doctor!

Almost any imaginable behavior can be considered normal in some contexts. In 1972, an airplane carrying a rugby team crashed in the snow-capped Andes of South America. Incredibly, 16 of the 45 people onboard survived 73 days in deep snow and subfreezing temperatures. They were forced to use extremely grim measures to do so—they ate the bodies of those who died in the crash.

As implied by our earlier discussion of social norms, culture is one of the most influential contexts in which any behavior is judged (Fabrega, 2004). In some cultures it is considered normal to defecate or urinate in public or to appear naked in public. In our culture such behaviors would be considered unusual or abnormal. In Muslim cultures, women who remain completely housebound are considered normal or even virtuous. In Western cultures they might be diagnosed as suffering from a disorder called agoraphobia. (Agoraphobia is described later in this chapter.)

Thus, *cultural relativity* (the idea that judgments are made relative to the values of one's culture) can affect the diagnosis of psychological disorders. (See "A Disease Called Freedom.") Still, *all* cultures classify people as abnormal if they fail to communicate with others or are consistently unpredictable in their actions.

Core Features of Disordered Behavior

If abnormality is so hard to define, how are judgments of psychopathology made? Although the standards we have discussed are *relative*, abnormal behavior does have two core features. First, it is **maladaptive**. Rather than helping people cope successfully, abnormal behavior makes it more difficult for them to meet the demands of day-to-day life. Second, people suffering from psychological disorders *lose the ability to control* their thoughts, behaviors, or feelings adequately. For exam-

Social nonconformity does not automatically indicate psychopathology.

Psychopathology The scientific study of mental, emotional, and behavioral disorders; also, abnormal or maladaptive behavior.

Statistical abnormality Abnormality defined on the basis of an extreme score on some dimension, such as IQ or anxiety.

Social nonconformity Failure to conform to societal norms or the usual minimum standards for social conduct.

Maladaptive behavior Behavior that makes it difficult to adapt to the environment and meet the demands of day-to-day life.

HUMAN DIVERSITY

A Disease Called Freedom

The year is 1840. You are a slave who has tried repeatedly to escape from a cruel and abusive master. You want to be free. An expert is consulted about your "abnormal" behavior. His conclusion? You are suffering from "drapetomania," a mental "disorder" that causes slaves to run away (Wakefield, 1992). Your "cure"? The expert will cut off your toes.

As this example suggests, psychiatric terms are easily abused. Historically, some have been applied to culturally disapproved behaviors that are not really disorders. Another of our personal favorites is the long-outdated diagnosis of "anarchia," a form of insanity that leads one to seek a more democratic society (Brown, 1990).

All of the following were also once considered disorders: childhood masturbation, lack of vaginal orgasm, self-defeating personality (applied mainly to women), homosexuality, and nymphomania (a woman with a healthy sexual appetite) (Wakefield, 1992). Even today, race, gender, and social class continue to affect the diagnosis of various disorders (Durand & Barlow, 2006; Poland & Caplan, 2004).

Gender is probably the most common source of bias in judging normality because standards tend to be based on males (Nolen-Hoeksema, 2007; Widiger, 2005). According to psychologist Paula Caplan (1995) and others, women are penalized both for conforming to female stereotypes and for ignoring them. If a woman is independent, aggressive, and unemotional, she may be considered "unhealthy." Yet at the same time, a woman who is vain, emotional, irrational, and dependent on others (all "feminine" traits in our culture) may be classified as having a personality disorder (Bornstein, 1996). Indeed, a majority of persons classified as having dependent personality disorder are women. In view of this, Paula Caplan asks, why isn't there a category called "delusional dominating personality disorder" for obnoxious men (Caplan, 1995)?

Because culture can influence perceptions of disorder and normality, it is worth being cautious before you leap to conclusions about the mental health of others (DSM-IV-TR, 2000). (They might be doing an assignment for their psychology class!)

---

ple, gambling is not a problem if people bet for entertainment and can maintain self-control. However, compulsive gambling is a sign of psychopathology. The voices that Carol North kept hearing are a prime example of what it means to lose control of one's thoughts. In the most extreme cases, people become a danger to themselves or others, which is clearly maladaptive (Hansell, 2007).

In practice, deciding that a person needs help usually occurs when the person *does something* (hits a person, hallucinates, stares into space, collects rolls of toilet paper, and so forth) that *annoys* or *gains the attention* of a person in a *position of power* in the person's life (an employer, teacher, parent, spouse, or the person himself or herself). That person then *does something* about it. (A police officer may be called, the person may be urged to see a psychologist, a relative may start commitment proceedings, or the person may voluntarily seek help.)

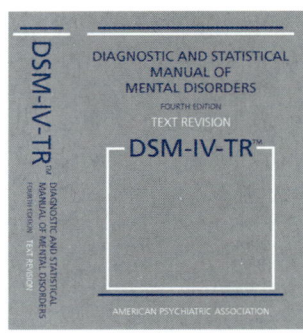

DSM-IV-TR is not the only system for classifying mental disorders. Nevertheless, most activities in mental health settings—from diagnosis to therapy to billing of insurance companies—are influenced by the *DSM*. *DSM-IV-TR* is both a scientific document and a social one. Major disorders are well-documented problems. Some problems, however, have little to do with "mental illness." Instead, they are primarily socially disapproved behaviors. (From the *Diagnostic and Statistical Manual of Mental Disorders*, Fourth Edition, Text Revision, © 2000 American Psychiatric Association.)

Classifying Mental Disorders— Problems by the Book

Psychological problems are classified by using the *Diagnostic and Statistical Manual of Mental Disorders* (DSM-IV-TR, 2000). The *DSM* helps psychologists correctly identify mental disorders and select the best therapies to treat them (First & Pincus, 2002).

A **mental disorder** is a significant impairment in psychological functioning. If you were to glance through the *DSM-IV-TR*, you would see many disorders described, including those in ■ Table 12.1. It's impossible here to discuss all of these problems. Major disorders are listed in the table so you can see the types of problems found in the *DSM*. (You don't need to memorize all of them.) The descriptions that follow will give you an overview of some selected problems.

TABLE 12.1 Major *DSM-IV-TR* Categories

- DISORDERS USUALLY FIRST DIAGNOSED IN INFANCY, CHILDHOOD, OR ADOLESCENCE
  Mental retardation
    Example: Mild mental retardation
  Learning disorders
    Example: Reading disorder
  Motor skills disorder
    Example: Developmental coordination disorder
  Communication disorders
    Example: Stuttering
  Pervasive developmental disorders
    Example: Autistic disorder
  Attention-deficit and disruptive behavior disorders
    Example: Attention-deficit/hyperactivity disorder
  Feeding and eating disorders of infancy or early childhood
    Example: Pica (eating inedible substances)
  Tic disorders
    Example: Tourette's disorder
  Elimination disorders
    Example: Enuresis (bedwetting)
  Other disorders of infancy, childhood, or adolescence
    Example: Separation anxiety disorder

- DELIRIUM, DEMENTIA, AMNESTIC, AND OTHER COGNITIVE DISORDERS
  Delirium
    Example: Delirium due to a general medical condition
  Dementia
    Example: Dementia of the Alzheimer's type
  Amnestic disorders (memory loss)
    Example: Amnestic disorder due to a general medical condition
  Cognitive disorder not otherwise specified

- MENTAL DISORDERS DUE TO A GENERAL MEDICAL CONDITION NOT ELSEWHERE CLASSIFIED
  Catatonic disorder due to a general medical condition
  Personality change due to a general medical condition
  Mental disorder not otherwise specified due to a general medical condition

- SUBSTANCE-RELATED DISORDERS
    Example: Cocaine use disorders

- SCHIZOPHRENIA AND OTHER PSYCHOTIC DISORDERS
  Schizophrenia
    Example: Schizophrenia, paranoid type
  Schizophreniform disorder
  Schizoaffective disorder
  Delusional disorder
    Example: Delusional disorder, grandiose type
  Brief psychotic disorder
  Shared psychotic disorder (folie á deux)
  Psychotic disorder due to a general medical condition
  Substance-induced psychotic disorder
  Psychotic disorder not otherwise specified

- MOOD DISORDERS
  Depressive disorders
    Example: Major depressive disorder
  Bipolar disorders
    Example: Bipolar I disorder
  Mood disorder due to a general medical condition
  Substance-induced mood disorder
  Mood disorder not otherwise specified

- ANXIETY DISORDERS
    Example: Panic disorder

- SOMATOFORM DISORDERS
    Example: Conversion disorder

- FACTITIOUS DISORDERS (FAKED DISABILITY OR ILLNESS)
    Example: Factitious disorder

- DISSOCIATIVE DISORDERS
    Example: Dissociative identity disorder

- SEXUAL AND GENDER IDENTITY DISORDERS
  Sexual dysfunctions
    Example: Sexual arousal disorders
  Paraphilias
    Example: Voyeurism
  Sexual disorder not otherwise specified
  Gender identity disorders
    Example: Gender identity disorder

- EATING DISORDERS
    Example: Anorexia nervosa

- SLEEP DISORDERS
  Primary sleep disorders
  Dyssomnias
    Example: Primary insomnia
  Parasomnias
    Example: Sleep terror disorder
  Sleep disorders related to another mental disorder
    Example: Insomnia related to posttraumatic stress disorder
  Other sleep disorders
    Example: Substance-induced sleep disorder

- IMPULSE CONTROL DISORDERS NOT ELSEWHERE CLASSIFIED
    Example: Kleptomania

- ADJUSTMENT DISORDERS
    Example: Adjustment disorder

- PERSONALITY DISORDERS
    Example: Antisocial personality disorder

Mental disorder A significant impairment in psychological functioning.

An Overview of Psychological Disorders

People suffering from **psychotic disorders** have "retreated from reality." That is, they suffer from hallucinations and delusions and are socially withdrawn. Psychotic disorders are severely disabling and often lead to hospitalization. Typically, psychotic patients cannot control their thoughts and actions. For example, David often heard the voice of his Uncle Bill: "He told me to turn off the TV. He said, 'It's too damn loud, turn it down, turn it down.' Other times he talks about fishing. 'Good day for fishing. Got to go fishing'" (Durand & Barlow, 2006). Psychotic symptoms occur in schizophrenia, delusional disorders, and some mood disorders. Also, psychosis may be related to medical problems, drug abuse, and other conditions. (■ Table 12.2 provides a simplified list of major disorders.)

Organic mental disorders are problems caused by brain pathology; that is, by drug damage, diseases of the brain, injuries, poisons, and so on (● Fig. 12.2). A person with organic disorders may have severe emotional disturbances, impaired thinking, memory loss, personality changes, delirium, or psychotic symptoms (Nolen-Hoeksema, 2007).

In reality, almost all mental disorders are partly biological (Hansell, 2007). That's why *DSM-IV-TR* does not list "organic mental disorders" as a separate category. Nevertheless, all of the following problems are closely associated with organic damage: delirium, dementia, amnesia, and other cognitive disorders; mental disorders due to a general medical condition; and substance-related disorders (drug abuse).

● **FIGURE 12.2** This MRI scan of a human brain (viewed from the top) reveals a tumor (dark spot). Mental disorders sometimes have organic causes of this sort. However, in many instances no organic damage can be found.

Mood disorders are primarily defined by the presence of extreme, intense, and long-lasting emotions. Afflicted persons may be *manic,* meaning agitated, elated, and hyperactive, or they may be *depressed.* Some people with mood disorders alternate between mania and depression, and they may have psychotic symptoms as well.

■ TABLE 12.2 Some Selected Categories of Psychopathology

PROBLEM	PRIMARY SYMPTOM	TYPICAL SIGNS OF TROUBLE
Psychotic disorders	Loss of contact with reality	You hear or see things that others don't; your mind has been playing tricks on you.
Mood disorders	Mania or depression	You feel sad and hopeless; or you talk too loud and too fast and have a rush of ideas and feelings that others think are unreasonable.
Anxiety disorders	High anxiety or anxiety-based	You have anxiety attacks and distortions of behavior; you feel like you are going to die; or you are afraid to do things that most people can do; or you spend unusual amounts of time doing things like washing your hands or counting your heartbeats.
Somatoform disorders	Bodily complaints without an organic (physical) basis	You feel physically sick, but your doctor says nothing is wrong with you; or you suffer from pain that has no physical basis; or you are preoccupied with thoughts about being sick.
Dissociative disorders	Amnesia, feelings of unreality, multiple identities	There are major gaps in your memory of events; you feel like you are a robot or a stranger to yourself; others tell you that you have done things that you don't remember doing.
Personality disorders	Unhealthy personality patterns	Your behavior patterns repeatedly cause problems at work, school, and in your relationships with others.
Sexual and gender identity disorders	Disturbed gender identity, deviant sexual behavior, problems in sexual adjustment	You feel that you are a man trapped in a woman's body (or the reverse); or you can only gain sexual satisfaction by engaging in highly atypical sexual behavior; or you have problems with sexual desire, arousal, or performance.
Substance-related disorders	Disturbances related to drug abuse or dependence	You have been drinking too much, using illegal drugs, or taking prescription drugs more often than you should.

The self-portraits shown here were painted by Andy Wilf between 1978 and 1981. During that time, Wilf is said to have increasingly abused drugs and alcohol. This dramatic series of images is a record of his self-destructive descent into a private hell. The third painting shows a shrouded skull—and foretells the artist's fate. Wilf died of a drug overdose. Drug abuse is but one of the many psychopathologies, or "problems in living," psychologists seek to alleviate. (Courtesy of Ulrike Kantor, Ulrike Kantor Gallery.)

Anxiety disorders are marked by fear or anxiety and by distorted behavior. Some anxiety disorders involve feelings of panic. Others take the form of phobias (irrational fears) or just overwhelming anxiety and nervousness. Two additional anxiety disorders are posttraumatic stress disorder and acute stress disorder. Obsessive-compulsive behavior patterns are also associated with high anxiety. (These problems are described later in this chapter.)

Somatoform (so-MAT-oh-form) **disorders** occur when a person has physical symptoms that mimic disease or injury (paralysis, blindness, illness, or chronic pain, for example), for which there is no identifiable physical cause. In such cases, psychological factors appear to explain the symptoms.

A person with a **dissociative disorder** may have temporary amnesia or multiple personalities. Also included in this category are frightening episodes of depersonalization, in which people feel like they are outside their bodies, are behaving like robots, or are lost in a dream world.

Personality disorders are deeply ingrained, unhealthy personality patterns. Such patterns usually appear in adolescence and continue through much of adult life. They include paranoid (overly suspicious), narcissistic (self-loving), dependent, borderline, and antisocial personality types, as well as others.

Sexual and gender identity disorders include any of a wide range of difficulties with sexual identity, deviant sexual behavior, or sexual adjustment. In gender identity disorders, sexual identity does not match a person's physical sex and the person may seek a sex-change operation. Deviations in sexual behavior known as *paraphilias* include exhibitionism, fetishism, voyeurism, and so on. Also found in this category are a variety of *sexual dysfunctions* (problems in sexual desire, arousal, or response). (Sexual dysfunctions are discussed in Module 14.4.)

Substance-related disorders involve abuse of, or dependence on, psychoactive drugs. Typical culprits include alcohol, barbiturates, opiates, cocaine, amphetamines, hallucinogens, marijuana, and nicotine. A person with a substance-related disorder cannot stop using the drug and may also suffer from withdrawal symptoms, delirium, dementia, amnesia, psychosis, emotional outbursts, sexual problems, and sleep disturbances. (Problems with drug abuse and dependence are discussed in Module 5.4.)

Shouldn't neurosis be listed here? Neurosis was once a recognized mental disorder. However, it is no longer included in the DSM because the term *neurosis* is too imprecise. Behavior that psychologists used to refer to as "neurotic" is now a part of anxiety, somatoform, or dissociative disorders. Even though **neurosis** is an outdated term, you may still hear it used to loosely refer to problems involving excessive anxiety.

In addition to the formal mental disorders we have reviewed, many cultures have names for "unofficial" psychological "disorders." See "Running Amok with Cultural Maladies" for some examples.

Psychotic disorder A severe mental disorder characterized by a retreat from reality, by hallucinations and delusions, and by social withdrawal.
Organic mental disorder A mental or emotional problem caused by brain diseases or injuries.
Mood disorder A major disturbance in mood or emotion, such as depression or mania.
Anxiety disorder Disruptive feelings of fear, apprehension, or anxiety, or distortions in behavior that are anxiety related.
Somatoform disorder Physical symptoms that mimic disease or injury for which there is no identifiable physical cause.
Dissociative disorder Temporary amnesia, multiple personality, or depersonalization.
Personality disorder A maladaptive personality pattern.
Sexual and gender identity disorders Any of a wide range of difficulties with sexual identity, deviant sexual behavior, or sexual adjustment.
Substance-related disorder Abuse of or dependence on a mood- or behavior-altering drug.
Neurosis An outdated term once used to refer, as a group, to anxiety disorders, somatoform disorders, dissociative disorders, and some forms of depression.

HUMAN DIVERSITY

Running Amok with Cultural Maladies

Every culture recognizes the existence of psychopathology, and most have at least a few folk names for afflictions you won't find in the *DSM-IV-TR*. Called *culture-bound syndromes*, here are some examples from around the world (Durand & Barlow, 2006; López & Guarnaccia, 2000; Sumathipala, Siribaddana, & Bhugra, 2004):

- **Amok** Men in Malaysia, Laos, the Philippines, and Polynesia who believe they have been insulted are sometimes known to go *amok*. After a period of brooding they erupt into an outburst of violent, aggressive, or homicidal behavior randomly directed at people and objects.
- **Susto** Among Latin Americans, the symptoms of susto include insomnia, irritability, phobias, and an increase in sweating and heart rate. Susto can result if someone is badly frightened by a black magic curse. In extreme cases, *voodoo death* can result, as the person is literally scared to death.
- **Ghost sickness** Among many American Indian tribes, people who become preoccupied with death and the deceased are said to suffer from *ghost sickness*. The symptoms of ghost sickness include bad dreams, weakness, loss of appetite, fainting, dizziness, fear, anxiety, hallucinations, loss of consciousness, confusion, feelings of futility, and a sense of suffocation.
- **Koro** In southern and eastern Asia, a man may experience sudden and intense anxiety that his penis (or, in females, the vulva and nipples) will recede into the body. In addition to the terror this incites, victims also believe that advanced cases of *koro* can cause death. A similar fear of shrinking genitals has also been reported from West Africa (Dzokoto & Adams, 2005).
- **Zar** In North African and Middle Eastern societies, zar is said to occur when spirits possess an individual. Zar is marked by shouting, laughing, hitting the head against a wall, singing, or weeping. Victims may become apathetic or withdrawn and they may refuse to eat or carry out daily tasks.
- **Dhat** In Indian society, *dhat* is the fear of the loss of semen during nocturnal emissions. A man suffering from dhat will feel anxious and perhaps also guilty. He may also experience fatigue, loss of appetite, weakness, anxiety, and sexual dysfunction.

It's clear that people have a need to label and categorize disturbed behavior. As you can see, however, folk terminology tends to be vague. The terms listed here provide little guidance about the true nature of a person's problems or the best ways to treat them. That's why the *DSM* is based on empirical data and clinical observations. Otherwise, psychologists and psychiatrists would be no better than folk healers when making diagnoses (Ancis, Chen, & Schultz, 2004). By the way, culture-bound disorders occur in all societies. For example, American psychologists Pamela Keel and Kelly Klump believe that bulimia is primarily a syndrome of Western cultures, including the United States (Keel & Klump, 2003).

General Risk Factors

What causes psychological disorders like those listed in Table 12.2? We will soon explore the causes of some specific problems. For now, here are some general risk factors that contribute to psychopathology, including the following factors:

- **Social conditions:** poverty, stressful living conditions, homelessness, social disorganization, overcrowding
- **Family factors:** parents who are immature, mentally disturbed, criminal, or abusive; severe marital strife; extremely poor child discipline; disordered family communication patterns
- **Psychological factors:** stress, low intelligence, learning disorders, lack of control or mastery
- **Biological/physical factors:** genetic defects or inherited vulnerabilities, poor prenatal care, very low birth weight, chronic physical illness or disability, exposure to toxic chemicals or drugs, head injuries

Insanity

Which of the mental disorders causes insanity? None. **Insanity** is a legal term. It refers to an inability to manage one's affairs or foresee the consequences of one's actions. People who are declared insane are not legally responsible for their actions. If necessary, they can be involuntarily committed to a mental hospital.

Legally, insanity is established by testimony from *expert witnesses* (psychologists and psychiatrists) recognized by a court of law as being qualified to give opinions on a specific topic. Involuntary commitments happen most often when people are brought to emergency rooms. People who are involuntarily committed are usually judged to be a danger to themselves or to others, or they are severely mentally disabled (Luchins et al., 2004).

An Important Note—You're Okay, Really! In upcoming modules we will explore some selected problems in more detail, beginning with personality disorders. As your authors, we hope that you will not fall prey to "medical student's disease." Medical students, it seems, have a predictable tendency to notice in themselves the symptoms of each dreaded disease they study. As a psychology student you may notice what seem to be abnormal tendencies in your own behavior. If so, don't panic. In most instances, this only shows that pathological behavior is an *exaggeration* of normal defenses and reactions, not that your behavior is abnormal.

MODULE 12.1 Summary

How is normality defined, and what are the major psychological disorders?

- *Psychopathology* refers to maladaptive behavior and to the scientific study of mental disorders.
- Factors that typically affect judgments of abnormality include subjective discomfort, statistical abnormality, nonconformity, context, and culture.
- Two key elements of mental disorder are that abnormal behavior is maladaptive and it involves a loss of self-control.
- Judgments of normality are relative, but psychological disorders clearly exist and they need to be classified, explained, and treated.
- A widely used system for classifying mental disorders is found in the *Diagnostic and Statistical Manual of Mental Disorders (DSM)*.
- Major mental problems include psychotic disorders, organic disorders, mood disorders, anxiety disorders, somatoform disorders, dissociative disorders, personality disorders, sexual or gender identity disorders, and substance-related disorders.
- *Insanity* is a legal term defining whether a person may be held responsible for his or her actions. Sanity is determined in court on the basis of testimony by expert witnesses.

Insanity A legal term that refers to a mental inability to manage one's affairs or to be aware of the consequences of one's actions.

KNOWLEDGE BUILDER

Normality and Psychopathology

Recite

1. The core feature of abnormal behavior is that it is
   a. statistically unusual
   b. maladaptive
   c. socially nonconforming
   d. a source of subjective discomfort

2. One of the most powerful contexts in which judgments of normality and abnormality are made is
   a. the family
   b. occupational settings
   c. religious systems
   d. culture

3. Amnesia, multiple identities, and depersonalization are possible problems in
   a. mood disorders
   b. somatoform disorders
   c. psychosis
   d. dissociative disorders

4. Which among the following is not a major psychological problem listed in the DSM-IV-TR?
   a. mood disorders
   b. personality disorders
   c. insanity
   d. anxiety disorders

5. People are said to have "retreated from reality" when they suffer from
   a. psychotic disorders
   b. mood disorders
   c. somatoform disorders
   d. personality disorders

6. Koro and dhat are
   a. somatoform disorders
   b. forms of psychosis
   c. folk terminology
   d. organic mental disorders

7. Someone who engages in one of the paraphilias has what type of disorder?
   a. dissociative
   b. somatoform
   c. substance
   d. sexual

8. Which of the following is a legal concept?
   a. neurosis
   b. psychosis
   c. drapetomania
   d. insanity

Reflect
Critical Thinking

9. Brian, a fan of grunge rock, occasionally wears a skirt in public. Does Brian's cross-dressing indicate that he has a mental disorder?

10. Many states began to restrict use of the insanity defense after John Hinkley, Jr., who tried to murder former U.S. President Ronald Reagan, was acquitted by reason of insanity. What does this trend reveal about insanity?

Relate

Think of an instance of abnormal behavior you have witnessed. By what formal standards would the behavior be regarded as abnormal? In what way was the behavior maladaptive?

What disorders would the following sentences help you remember? An anxious psychotic in a bad mood asked for an organic substance. "First you have to fill out a somato form and tell us what sex or gender you are," he was told. "Don't diss my personality," he replied.

Link

Internet addresses frequently change. To find the sites listed here, visit **http://www.thomsonedu.com/psychology/coon** for an updated list of Internet addresses and direct links to relevant sites.

- **Against All Odds** Read an article about Carol North, the psychiatrist who overcame schizophrenia.
- **The Insanity Defense** Follow some of the history of the insanity defense.
- **Psychiatric Disorders** Explore a complete listing of the DSM-IV-TR diagnostic categories.

ANSWERS

1. b 2. d 3. d 4. c 5. a 6. c 7. d 8. d 9. Probably not. Undoubtedly, Brian's cross-dressing is socially disapproved of by many people. Nevertheless, to be classified as a mental disorder it must cause him to feel disabling shame, guilt, depression, or anxiety. The cultural relativity of behavior like Brian's is revealed by the fact that it is fashionable and acceptable for women to wear men's clothing. 10. It emphasizes that insanity is a legal concept, not a psychiatric diagnosis. Laws reflect community standards. When those standards change, lawmakers may seek to alter definitions of legal responsibility.

MODULE 12.2 Personality Disorders and Anxiety-Based Disorders

YOU PROBABLY KNOW SOMEONE whose personality characteristics make life difficult for her or him. Imagine that person's traits becoming even more extreme. If they did, the person would have a personality disorder, our first topic in this unit.

Now imagine that you are waiting to take an extremely important test, waiting to give a speech to a large audience, or waiting to find out if you or a loved one has a serious illness. You've almost certainly felt anxiety in similar situations. If so, then you will understand why anxiety-based disorders are so debilitating. People who suffer from extreme anxiety are miserable most of the time, and their behavior becomes distorted and self-defeating. In this module, we'll also discuss anxiety disorders and why they occur.

Personality Disorders—Blueprints for Maladjustment

SURVEY QUESTION: *What is a personality disorder?*

"Get out of here and leave me alone so I can die in peace," Judy screamed at her nurses in the seclusion room of the psychiatric hospital. On one of her arms, long dark red marks mingled with the scars of previous suicide attempts. Judy once bragged that her record was 67 stitches. Today, the nurses had to strap her into restraints to keep her from gouging her own eyes. She was given a sedative and slept for 12 hours. She woke calmly and asked for her therapist—even though her latest outburst began when he canceled a morning appointment and changed it to afternoon.

Judy has a condition called *borderline personality disorder*. Although she is capable of working, Judy has repeatedly lost jobs because of her turbulent relationships with other people. At times she can be friendly and a real charmer. At other times she is extremely unpredictable, moody, and even suicidal. Being a friend to Judy can be a fearsome challenge. Canceling an appointment, forgetting a special date, a wrong turn of phrase—these and similar small incidents may trigger Judy's rage or a suicide attempt. Like other people with borderline personality disorder, Judy is extremely sensitive to ordinary criticism, which leaves her feeling rejected and abandoned. Typically, she reacts with anger, self-hatred, and impulsive behavior. These "emotional storms" damage her personal relationships and leave her confused about who she is (Siever & Koenigsberg, 2000).

Maladaptive Personality Patterns

As stated earlier, a person with a personality disorder has maladaptive personality traits. For example, people with a paranoid personality disorder are suspicious, hypersensitive, and wary of others. Narcissistic persons need constant admiration, and they are lost in fantasies of power, wealth, brilliance, beauty, or love. Celebrities appear to more likely to be narcissistic than noncelebrities (Young & Pinsky, 2006). The dependent personality suffers from extremely low self-confidence. Dependent persons allow others to run their lives, and they place everyone else's needs ahead of their own. People with a histrionic personality disorder constantly seek attention by dramatizing their emotions and actions.

Typically, patterns such as the ones just described begin during adolescence or even childhood. Thus, personality disorders are deeply rooted and usually span many years. The list of personality disorders is long (■ Table 12.3), so let us focus on a single frequently misunderstood problem, the antisocial personality.

Antisocial Personality

What are the characteristics of an antisocial personality? A person with an **antisocial personality** lacks a conscience. Such people are impulsive, selfish, dishonest, emotionally shallow, and manipulative. Antisocial persons, who are sometimes called *sociopaths* or *psychopaths,* are poorly socialized and seem to be incapable of feeling guilt, shame, fear, loyalty, or love (DSM-IV-TR, 2000).

Are sociopaths dangerous? Sociopaths tend to have a long history of conflict with society. Many are delinquents or criminals who may be a threat to the general public (Ogloff, 2006). However, sociopaths are rarely the crazed murderers you may have seen portrayed on TV and in movies. In fact, many sociopaths are "charming" at first. Their "friends" only gradually become aware of the sociopath's lying and self-serving manipulation. One study found that psychopaths are "blind" to signs of disgust in others. This may add to their capacity for cruelty and their ability to use others (Kosson et al., 2002). Many successful businesspersons, entertainers, politicians, and other seemingly normal people have psycho-

> **Antisocial personality** A person who lacks a conscience; is emotionally shallow, impulsive, selfish; and tends to manipulate others.

TABLE 12.3 Personality Disorders: Maladaptive Patterns and Degree of Impairment

MODERATE IMPAIRMENT

Dependent You lack confidence, and you are extremely submissive and dependent on others (clinging).

Histrionic You are dramatic and flamboyant; you exaggerate your emotions to get attention from others.

Narcissistic You think you are wonderful, brilliant, important, and worthy of constant admiration.

Antisocial You are irresponsible, lack guilt or remorse, and engage in antisocial behavior, such as aggression, deceit, or recklessness.

HIGH IMPAIRMENT

Obsessive-compulsive You demand order, perfection, control, and rigid routine at all times.

Schizoid You feel very little emotion and can't form close personal relationships with others.

Avoidant You are timid, uncomfortable in social situations, and fear evaluation.

SEVERE IMPAIRMENT

Borderline Your self-image, moods, and impulses are erratic, and you are extremely sensitive to any hint of criticism, rejection, or abandonment by others.

Paranoid You deeply distrust others and are suspicious of their motives, which you perceive as insulting or threatening.

Schizotypal You are a loner, you engage in extremely odd behavior, and your thought patterns are bizarre, but you are not actively psychotic.

Sources: DSM-IV-TR, 2000; Millon, 1981.

Studies show that more than 65 percent of all persons with antisocial personalities have been arrested, usually for crimes such as robbery, vandalism, or rape.

pathic leanings. Basically, antisocial persons coldly use others and cheat their way through life (Ogloff, 2006).

Causes *What causes sociopathy?* Typically, people with antisocial personalities showed similar problems in childhood (Burt et al., 2007). Many were emotionally deprived and physically abused as children (Pollock et al., 1990). Adult sociopaths also display subtle neurological problems (● Fig. 12.3). For example, they have unusual brainwave patterns that suggest under-arousal of the brain. This may explain why sociopaths tend to be thrill seekers. Quite likely, they are searching for stimulation strong enough to overcome their chronic under-arousal and feelings of "boredom" (Hare, 2006).

In a revealing study, psychopaths were shown extremely grisly and unpleasant photographs of mutilations. The photos were so upsetting that they visibly startled normal people. The psychopaths, however, showed no startle response to the photos (Levenston et al., 2000). (They didn't "bat an eyelash.") Those with antisocial personalities might therefore be described as *emotionally cold*. They simply do not feel normal pangs of conscience, guilt, or anxiety (Blair et al., 2006).

Again, this coldness seems to account for an unusual ability to calmly lie, cheat, steal, or take advantage of others.

Can sociopathy be treated? Antisocial personality disorders are rarely treated with success (Hare, 2006). All too often, sociopaths manipulate therapy, just like any other situation. If it is to their advantage to act "cured," they will do so. However, they return to their former behavior patterns as soon as possible. On a more positive note, antisocial behavior does tend to decline somewhat after age 40, even without treatment, because people tend to become more "mellow" as they age (Laub & Sampson, 2003).

● **FIGURE 12.3** Using PET scans, Canadian psychologist Robert Hare found that the normally functioning brain *(left)* lights up with activity when a person sees emotion-laden words such as "maggot" or "cancer." But the brain of a psychopath *(right)* remains inactive, especially in areas associated with feelings and self-control. When Dr. Hare showed the bottom image to several neurologists, one asked, "Is this person from Mars?" (Images courtesy of Robert Hare.)

An individual with an antisocial personality feels very little anxiety. At the other end of the scale, people who have lots of anxiety also suffer from debilitating problems, as described next.

Anxiety-Based Disorders— When Anxiety Rules

SURVEY QUESTION: *What problems result when a person suffers high levels of anxiety?*

Anxiety refers to feelings of apprehension, dread, or uneasiness. We all feel anxiety, but anxiety that is out of proportion to a situation may reveal a problem. An example is a college student named Jian, who became unbearably anxious when he took exams. By the time Jian went to see a counselor, he had skipped several tests and was in danger of dropping out of school. In general, people with anxiety-related problems like Jian's display the following characteristics:

- High levels of anxiety and/or restrictive, self-defeating behavior patterns
- A tendency to use elaborate defense mechanisms or avoidance responses to get through the day
- Pervasive feelings of stress, insecurity, inferiority, and dissatisfaction with life

People with anxiety-related problems feel threatened and often can't do anything constructive about it. They struggle to control themselves, but they remain ineffective and unhappy (Rachman, 2004). In any given year, roughly 18 percent of the adult population suffers from an anxiety disorder (NIMH, 2006b).

If anxiety is a normal emotion, when does it signify a problem? A problem exists when intense anxiety prevents people from doing what they want or need to do. Also, their anxieties are out of control—they simply cannot stop worrying.

Adjustment Disorders

Do such problems cause a "nervous breakdown"? People suffering from anxiety-based problems may be miserable, but they rarely experience a "breakdown." Actually, the term *nervous breakdown* has no formal meaning. Nevertheless, a problem known as an *adjustment disorder* does come close to being something of a "breakdown."

Adjustment disorders occur when ordinary stresses push people beyond their ability to cope with life. Examples of such stresses are losing a job, intense marital strife, and chronic physical illness. People suffering from an adjustment disorder may be extremely irritable, anxious, apathetic, or depressed. They also have trouble sleeping, lose their appetite, and suffer from various physical complaints. Often, their problems can be relieved by rest, sedation, supportive counseling, and a chance to "talk through" their fears and anxieties (DSM-IV-TR, 2000).

How is an adjustment disorder different from an anxiety disorder? The outward symptoms are similar. However, adjustment disorders disappear when a person's life circumstances improve. People suffering from anxiety disorders seem to generate their own misery, regardless of what's happening around them. They feel that they must be on guard against *future* threats that *could happen* at any time (Barlow, 2000).

Anxiety Disorders

In most anxiety disorders, distress seems greatly out of proportion to a person's circumstances. For example, consider the following description of Adrian H:

> She becomes very anxious that her children "might have been hurt or killed if they were out of the neighborhood playing and she hadn't heard from them in a couple of hours." She also worries all the time about her job performance and her relationships with men. Adrian believes that men rarely call back after a date or two because "They can sense I'm not a fun person." She never really relaxes, has difficulty focusing at work, has frequent headaches, and suffers from insomnia. (Adapted from Brown & Barlow, 2007.)

Distress like Adrian H's is a key ingredient in anxiety disorders. It also may underlie dissociative and somatoform disorders, where maladaptive behavior serves to reduce anxiety and discomfort. To deepen your understanding, let's first examine the anxiety disorders themselves (■ Table 12.4). Then we will see how anxiety contributes to other problems.

Generalized Anxiety Disorder A person with a **generalized anxiety disorder** has been extremely anxious and worried for at least 6 months. Sufferers typically complain of sweating, a racing heart, clammy hands, dizziness, upset stomach, rapid breathing, irritability, and poor concentration. Overall, more women than men have these symptoms (Brown & Barlow, 2007).

Adjustment disorder An emotional disturbance caused by ongoing stressors within the range of common experience.

Generalized anxiety disorder A chronic state of tension and worry about work, relationships, ability, or impending disaster.

TABLE 12.4 Anxiety Disorders

TYPE OF DISORDER	TYPICAL SIGNS OF TROUBLE
Generalized anxiety disorder	You have been extremely anxious or worried for 6 months.
Panic disorder (without agoraphobia)	You are anxious much of the time and have sudden panic attacks.
Panic disorder (with agoraphobia)	You have panic attacks and are afraid that they might occur in public places, so you rarely leave home.
Agoraphobia (without a history of panic disorder)	You fear that something extremely embarrassing will happen if you leave home (but you don't have panic attacks).
Specific phobia	You have an intense fear of specific objects, activities, or locations.
Social phobia	You fear social situations where people can watch, criticize, embarrass, or humiliate you.
Obsessive-compulsive disorder	Your thoughts make you extremely nervous and compel you to rigidly repeat certain actions or routines.
Acute stress disorder	You are tormented for less than a month by the emotional aftereffects of horrible events you have experienced.
Posttraumatic stress disorder	You are tormented for more than a month by the emotional aftereffects of horrible events you have experienced.

Source: DSM-IV-TR, 2000.

Was Adrian H's problem a generalized anxiety disorder? Yes. However, if she also experienced *anxiety attacks,* then she would likely be diagnosed with panic disorder.

Panic Disorder (without Agoraphobia) In a **panic disorder (without agoraphobia)** people are highly anxious and also feel sudden, intense, unexpected panic. During a panic attack, victims experience chest pain, a racing heart, dizziness, choking, feelings of unreality, trembling, or fears of losing control. Many believe that they are having a heart attack, are going insane, or are about to die. Needless to say, this pattern leaves victims unhappy and uncomfortable much of the time. Again, the majority of people who suffer from panic disorder are women (Foot & Koszycki, 2004).

To get an idea of how a panic attack feels, imagine that you are trapped in your stateroom on a sinking ocean liner (the *Titanic?*). The room fills with water. When only a small air space remains near the ceiling and you are gasping for air, you'll know what a panic attack feels like.

Panic Disorder (with Agoraphobia) In a **panic disorder (with agoraphobia)** people suffer from chronic anxiety and sudden panic. In addition, they have agoraphobia (ah-go-rah-FOBE-ee-ah), which is an intense *fear that a panic attack will occur* in a public place or unfamiliar situation. That is, agoraphobics intensely fear leaving their home and familiar surroundings. Typically, they find ways of avoiding places that frighten them—such as crowds, open roads, supermarkets, automobiles, and so on. As a result, some agoraphobics are prisoners in their own homes (DSM-IV-TR, 2000).

Agoraphobia The problem known as **agoraphobia** can also occur without panic. In this case, people *fear that something extremely embarrassing will happen* if they leave home or enter an unfamiliar situation. For example, an agoraphobic person may refuse to go outside because he or she fears having a sudden attack of dizziness, or diarrhea, or shortness of breath. Going outside the home alone, being in a crowd, standing in line, crossing a bridge, or riding in a car can be impossible for an agoraphobic person (DSM-IV-TR, 2000). About 4.2 percent of all adults suffer from agoraphobia (with or without panic) during their lifetime (Grant et al., 2006).

Specific Phobia As we noted earlier, phobias are intense, irrational fears that a person cannot shake off, even when there is no real danger. In a **specific phobia,** the person's fear, anxiety, and avoidance are focused on particular objects, activities, or situations. People affected by phobias recognize that their fears are unreasonable, but they cannot control them. For example, a person with a spider phobia would find it impossible to ignore a *picture* of a spider, even though a photograph can't bite anyone (Miltner et al., 2004). Specific phobias can be linked to nearly any object or situation. Many have been given names, such as these:

- Acrophobia—fear of heights
- Astraphobia—fear of storms, thunder, lightning
- Arachnophobia—fear of spiders
- Aviophobia—fear of airplanes
- Claustrophobia—fear of closed spaces
- Hematophobia—fear of blood
- Microphobia—fear of germs
- Nyctophobia—fear of darkness
- Pathophobia—fear of disease
- Triskaidekaphobia—fear of the number 13
- Xenophobia—fear of strangers
- Zoophobia—fear of animals

By combining the appropriate root word with the word *phobia,* any number of unlikely fears can be named. Some are *zemmiphobia,* fear of the great mole rat; *phobosophobia,* fear of fear; *arachibutyrophobia,* fear of peanut butter sticking to the roof of the mouth; and *hippopotomonstrosesquipedaliophobia,* fear of long words!

For a person with a strong fear of snakes (ophidiophobia), merely looking at this picture may be unsettling.

The severe obsessions and compulsions of billionaire Howard Hughes led him to live as a recluse for more than 20 years. Hughes had an intense fear of contamination. To avoid infection, he constructed sterile, isolated environments in which his contact with people and objects was strictly limited by complicated rituals. Before handling a spoon, for instance, Hughes had his attendants wrap the handle in tissue paper and seal it with tape. A second piece of tissue was then wrapped around the first before he would touch it (Hodgson & Miller, 1982). A spoon prepared as Hughes required is shown at right.

Almost everyone has a few mild phobias, such as fearing heights, closed spaces, or bugs and crawly things. A phobic disorder differs from such garden-variety fears in that it produces overwhelming fear. True phobias may lead to vomiting, wild climbing and running, or fainting. For a phobic disorder to exist, the person's fear must disrupt his or her daily life. Phobic persons are so threatened that they will go to almost any length to avoid the feared object or situation, such as driving 50 miles out of the way to avoid crossing a bridge. About 8 percent of all adults have phobic disorders during their lifetime (NIMH, 2006a).

Social Phobia In a **social phobia,** people fear situations in which they can be observed, evaluated, embarrassed, or humiliated by others. This leads them to avoid certain social situations, such as eating, writing, using the rest room, or speaking in public. When such situations cannot be avoided, people endure them with intense anxiety or distress. It is common for them to have uncomfortable physical symptoms, such as a pounding heart, shaking hands, sweating, diarrhea, mental confusion, and blushing. Social phobias greatly impair a person's ability to work, attend school, and form personal relationships (DSM-IV-TR, 2000). About 7 percent of all adults are affected by social phobias in a given year (NIMH, 2006b).

Obsessive-Compulsive Disorder People who suffer from **obsessive-compulsive disorder** are preoccupied with certain distressing thoughts and feel compelled to perform certain behaviors. You have probably experienced a mild obsessional thought, such as a song or stupid commercial jingle that repeats over and over in your mind. This may be irritating, but it's usually not terribly disturbing. True obsessions are images or thoughts that force their way into awareness against a person's will. They are so disturbing that they cause intense anxiety. The most common obsessions are about violence or harm (such as poisoning one's spouse or being hit by a car), about being "dirty" or "unclean," about whether one has performed some action (such as turning off the stove), and about committing immoral acts (Barlow, 2002).

Obsessions usually give rise to compulsions. These are irrational acts that a person feels driven to repeat. Often, compulsive acts help control or block out anxiety caused by an obsession. For example, a minister who finds profanities popping into her mind might start compulsively counting her heartbeat. Doing this would prevent her from thinking "dirty" words.

Panic disorder (without agoraphobia) A chronic state of anxiety and also brief moments of sudden, intense, unexpected panic.
Panic disorder (with agoraphobia) A chronic state of anxiety and brief moments of sudden panic. The person fears that these panic attacks will occur in public places or unfamiliar situations.
Agoraphobia (without panic) The fear that something extremely embarrassing will happen if one leaves the house or enters unfamiliar situation.
Specific phobia An intense, irrational fear of specific objects, activities, or situations.
Social phobia An intense, irrational fear of being observed, evaluated, embarrassed, or humiliated by others in social situations.
Obsessive-compulsive disorder An extreme preoccupation with certain thoughts and compulsive performance of certain behaviors.

Many compulsive people are *checkers* or *cleaners.* For instance, a young mother who repeatedly pictures a knife plunging into her baby might check once an hour to make sure all the knives in her house are locked away. Doing so may reduce her anxieties, but it will probably also take over her life. Likewise, a person who feels "contaminated" from touching ordinary objects because "germs are everywhere" may be driven to wash his hands hundreds of times a day.

Of course, not all obsessive-compulsive disorders are so dramatic. Many simply involve extreme orderliness and rigid routine. Compulsive attention to detail and rigidly following rules helps keep activities totally under control and makes the highly anxious person feel more secure. (Notice that if such patterns are long-standing, but less intense, they are classified as a personality disorder.)

Stress Disorders

Stress disorders occur when people experience stresses outside the range of normal human experience, such as floods, tornadoes, earthquakes, or horrible accidents. They affect many political hostages; combat veterans; prisoners of war; victims of terrorism, torture, violent crime, child molestation, rape, or domestic violence; or people who have witnessed a death or serious injury (Brown & Barlow, 2007).

Symptoms of stress disorders include repeatedly reliving the traumatic event, avoiding reminders of the event, and blunted emotions. Also common are insomnia, nightmares, wariness, poor concentration, irritability, and explosive anger or aggression. If such reactions last *less* than a month after a traumatic event, the problem is called an **acute stress disorder.** If they last *more* than a month, the person is suffering from **posttraumatic stress disorder (PTSD)** (Nemeroff et al., 2006).

In December 2004 a tsunami killed more than 250,000 people in southern Asia. In the aftermath of such disasters, many survivors suffer from acute stress reactions. For some, the flare-up of anxiety and distress lasts for months or years after the stressful event, an example of a posttraumatic stress reaction.

If a situation causes distress, anxiety, or fear, we tend to avoid it in the future. This is a normal survival instinct. However, victims of PTSD fail to recover from these reactions. Military combat accounts for more than a quarter of the cases of PTSD among American men (Prigerson, Maciejewski, & Rosenheck, 2002). The constant threat of death and the gruesome sights and sounds of war take a terrible toll. Psychologists are already seeing high rates of PTSD among soldiers involved in combat in Iraq (Hoge et al., 2004). Sadly, 8 percent of military veterans still suffer from PTSD decades after they were in combat (Dirkzwager, Bramsen, & Van Der Ploeg, 2001). About 3.5 percent of adults suffer from posttraumatic stress in any given year (NIMH, 2006b).

Dissociative Disorders

In dissociative reactions we see striking episodes of *amnesia, fugue,* or *multiple identity.* **Dissociative amnesia** is an inability to recall one's name, address, or past. **Dissociative fugue** (FEWG) involves sudden, unplanned travel away from home and confusion about personal identity. Dissociations are often triggered by highly traumatic events (McLewin & Muller, 2006). In such cases, forgetting personal identity and fleeing unpleasant situations appear to be defenses against intolerable anxiety.

A person suffering from a **dissociative identity disorder** has two or more separate identities or personality states. (Note that identity disorders are not the same as schizophrenia. Schizophrenia, which is a psychotic disorder, is discussed later in this chapter.) One famous and dramatic example of multiple identities is described in the book *Sybil* (Schreiber, 1973). Sybil reportedly had 16 different personality states. Each identity had a distinct voice, vocabulary, and posture. One personality could play the piano (not Sybil), but the others could not.

When an identity other than Sybil was in control, Sybil experienced a "time lapse," or memory blackout. Sybil's amnesia and alternate identities first appeared during childhood. As a girl she was beaten, locked in closets, perversely tortured, sexually abused, and almost killed. Sybil's first dissociations allowed her to escape by creating another person who would suffer torture in her place. Identity disorders often begin with unbearable childhood experiences, like Sybil endured. A history of childhood trauma, especially sexual abuse, is found in a high percentage of persons whose personalities split into multiple identities (McLewin & Muller, 2006; Simeon et al., 2002).

Flamboyant cases like Sybil's have led some experts to question the existence of multiple personalities (Casey, 2001). However, a majority of psychologists continue to believe that multiple identity is a real, if rare, problem (Cormier & Thelen, 1998).

THE CLINICAL FILE

Sick of Being Sick

At 14, Ben was in the hospital again for his sinus problem. He had already undergone 40 surgeries since the age of 8. In addition, he had been diagnosed at various times with bipolar disorder, oppositional defiant disorder, and attention deficit disorder. Ben was taking 19 different medications, and his mother said she desperately wanted him to be "healed." She sought numerous tests and never missed an appointment. But at long last, it became clear that there was nothing wrong with Ben. Left alone with doctors, Ben revealed that he was "sick of being sick."

In reality, it was Ben's mother who was sick. She was eventually diagnosed as suffering from **Munchausen syndrome by proxy** (Awadallah, et al., 2005). This is a pattern in which a person fakes the medical problems of someone in his or her care. (In **Munchausen syndrome,** the person fakes his or her own medical problems.) As in Ben's case, most people with the syndrome are mothers who fabricate their children's illnesses. Sometimes they even deliberately harm their children. For example, one mother injected her son with 7-Up (Reisner, 2006).

But why? People who suffer from Munchausen syndrome and Munchausen by proxy appear to have a pathological need to seek attention and sympathy from medical professionals. They may also win praise for being health conscious or a good parent (DSM-IV-TR, 2000).

Munchausen by proxy illustrates another point about psychological disorders: Sam's mother was eventually diagnosed with several disorders, including Munchausen by proxy, schizoaffective disorder, and borderline personality disorder. As this suggests, many disturbed people are *comorbid*. That is, they suffer from more than one disorder at a time. Not only does comorbidity increase their misery, it makes it more difficult for health care providers to diagnose and treat them.

Therapy for dissociative identity disorders may make use of hypnosis, which allows contact with the various personality states. The goal of therapy is *integration* and *fusion* of the identities into a single, balanced personality. Fortunately, multiple identity disorders are far rarer in real life than they are in TV dramas!

Somatoform Disorders

Have you ever known someone who appeared to be healthy but seemed to constantly worry about disease? These people are preoccupied with bodily functions, such as their heartbeat or breathing or digestion. Minor physical problems—even a small sore or an occasional cough—may convince them that they have cancer or some other dreaded disease. Typically, they can't give up their fears of illness, even if doctors can find no medical basis for their complaints (Korol, Craig, & Firestone, 2003).

Are you describing hypochondria? Yes. In **hypochondriasis** (HI-po-kon-DRY-uh-sis), people interpret normal bodily sensations as proof that they have a terrible disease (see "Sick of Being Sick" for a related disorder with a curious twist). In a related problem called **somatization disorder** (som-ah-tuh-ZAY-shun), people express their anxieties through various bodily complaints. That is, they suffer from problems such as vomiting or nausea, shortness of breath, difficulty swallowing, or painful menstrual periods. Typically, the person feels ill much of the time and visits doctors repeatedly. Most sufferers take medicines or other treatments, but no physical cause can be found for their distress. Similarly, a person with **pain disorder** is disabled by pain that has no identifiable physical basis.

Stress disorder A significant emotional disturbance caused by stresses outside the range of normal human experience.

Acute stress disorder A psychological disturbance lasting up to 1 month following stresses that would produce anxiety in anyone who experienced them.

Posttraumatic stress disorder (PTSD) A psychological disturbance lasting more than 1 month following stresses that would produce anxiety in anyone who experienced them.

Dissociative amnesia Loss of memory (partial or complete) for important information related to personal identity.

Dissociative fugue Sudden travel away from home, plus confusion about one's personal identity.

Dissociative identity disorder The presence of two or more distinct personalities (multiple personality).

Hypochondriasis A preoccupation with fears of having a serious disease. Ordinary physical signs are interpreted as proof that the person has a disease, but no physical disorder can be found.

Somatization disorder Afflicted persons have numerous physical complaints. Typically, they have consulted many doctors, but no organic cause for their distress can be identified.

Pain disorder Pain that has no identifiable physical cause and appears to be of psychological origin.

Munchausen syndrome by proxy An affected person fakes the medical problems of someone in his or her care in order to gain attention.

Munchausen syndrome An affected person fakes his or her own medical problems in order to gain attention.

A rarer somatoform disorder ("body-form" disorder) is called a *conversion reaction.* In a **conversion disorder,** severe emotional conflicts are "converted" into symptoms that actually disturb physical functioning or closely resemble a physical disability. For instance, a soldier might become deaf or lame or develop "glove anesthesia" just before a battle.

What is "glove anesthesia"? "Glove anesthesia" is a loss of sensitivity in the areas of the skin that would normally be covered by a glove. Glove anesthesia shows that conversion symptoms often contradict known medical facts. The system of nerves in the hands does not form a glove-like pattern and could not cause such symptoms (● Fig. 12.4).

If symptoms disappear when a victim is asleep, hypnotized, or anesthetized, a conversion reaction must be suspected (Russo et al., 1998). Another sign to watch for is that victims of conversion reactions are strangely unconcerned about suddenly being disabled.

Uncontrollable sneezing, which may continue for days or weeks, is often a conversion disorder. In such cases, sneezing is atypical in rate and rhythm. In addition, the person's eyes do not close during a sneeze and sneezing does not occur during sleep. (A normal sneeze is shown here.) All these signs suggest that the cause of the sneezing is psychological, not physical (Fochtmann, 1995).

Anxiety and Disorder—Four Pathways to Trouble

SURVEY QUESTION: *How do psychologists explain anxiety-based disorders?*

What causes anxiety disorders? Susceptibility to anxiety-based disorders appears to be partly inherited (Rachman, 2004). Studies show that being high strung, nervous, or emotional runs in families. For example, 60 percent of children born to parents suffering from panic disorder have a fearful, inhibited temperament. Such children are irritable and wary as infants, shy and fearful as toddlers, and quiet and cautious introverts in elementary school. By the time they reach adulthood, they are at high risk for anxiety problems, such as panic attacks (Barlow, 2000; Durand & Barlow, 2006).

At least four major psychological perspectives on the causes of dissociative, anxiety-based, and somatoform disor-

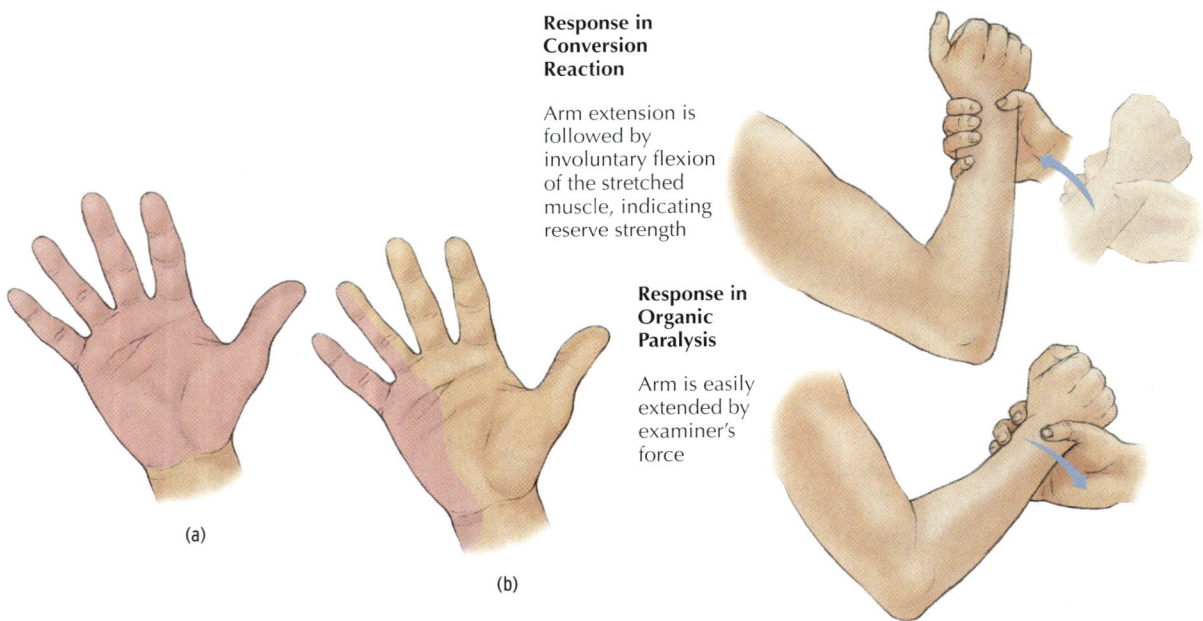

● **FIGURE 12.4** *(left)* "Glove" anesthesia is a conversion reaction involving loss of feeling in areas of the hand that would be covered by a glove *(a).* If the anesthesia were physically caused, it would follow the pattern shown in *(b). (right)* To test for organic paralysis of the arm, an examiner can suddenly extend the arm, stretching the muscles. A conversion reaction is indicated if the arm pulls back involuntarily. (Adapted from Weintraub, 1983.)

ders exist. These are (1) the *psychodynamic* approach, (2) the *humanistic-existential* approach, (3) the *behavioral* approach, and (4) the *cognitive* approach.

Psychodynamic Approach

The term *psychodynamic* refers to internal motives, conflicts, unconscious forces, and other dynamics of mental life. Freud was the first to propose a psychodynamic explanation for what he called "neurosis." According to Freud, disturbances like those we have described represent a raging conflict among subparts of the personality—the id, ego, and superego.

Freud emphasized that intense anxiety can be caused by forbidden id impulses for sex or aggression that threaten to break through into behavior. The person constantly fears doing something "crazy" or forbidden. She or he may also be tortured by guilt, which the superego uses to suppress forbidden impulses. Caught in the middle, the ego is eventually overwhelmed. This forces the person to use rigid defense mechanisms and misguided, inflexible behavior to prevent a disastrous loss of control. (See Module 11.3.)

Humanistic-Existential Approaches

Humanistic theories emphasize subjective experience, human problems, and personal potentials. Humanistic psychologist Carl Rogers regarded emotional disorders as the end product of a faulty self-image or self-concept (Rogers, 1959). Rogers believed that anxious individuals have built up unrealistic mental images of themselves. This leaves them vulnerable to contradictory information. Let's say, for example, that an essential part of Cheyenne's self-image is the idea that she is highly intelligent. If Cheyenne does poorly in school, she may deny or distort her perceptions of herself and the situation. Should Cheyenne's anxiety become severe, she may resort to using defense mechanisms. A conversion reaction, anxiety attacks, or similar symptoms could also result from threats to her self-image. These symptoms, in turn, would become new threats that provoke further distortions. Soon, she would fall into a vicious cycle of maladjustment and anxiety that feeds on itself once started.

Existentialism focuses on the elemental problems of existence, such as death, meaning, choice, and responsibility. Psychologists who take a more existential view stress that unhealthy anxiety reflects a loss of *meaning* in one's life. According to them, we must show *courage* and *responsibility* in our choices if life is to have meaning. Too often, they say, we give in to "existential anxiety" and back away from life-enhancing choices. Existential anxiety is the unavoidable anguish that comes from knowing we are personally responsible for our lives. Hence, we have a crushing need to choose wisely and courageously as we face life's empty and impersonal void.

From the existential view, people who are anxious are living in "bad faith." That is, they have collapsed in the face of the awesome responsibility to choose a meaningful existence. In short, they have lost their way in life. From this point of view, making choices that don't truly reflect what you value, feel, and believe can make you sick.

Behavioral Approach

Behaviorist approaches emphasize overt, observable behavior and the effects of learning and conditioning. Behaviorists assume that the "symptoms" we have discussed are learned, just as other behaviors are. You might recall from Chapter 6, for instance, that phobias can be acquired through classical conditioning. Similarly, anxiety attacks may reflect conditioned emotional responses that generalize to new situations and the hypochondriac's "sickness behavior" may be reinforced by the sympathy and attention he or she gets. One point that all theorists agree on is that disordered behavior is ultimately self-defeating because it makes the person more miserable in the long run, even though it temporarily lowers anxiety.

But if the person becomes more miserable in the long run, how does the pattern get started? The behavioral explanation is that self-defeating behavior begins with avoidance learning (described in Chapter 6). Avoidance learning occurs when making a response delays or prevents the onset of a painful or unpleasant stimulus. Here's a quick review to refresh your memory:

> An animal is placed in a special cage. After a few minutes a light comes on, followed a moment later by a painful shock. Quickly, the animal escapes into a second chamber. After a few minutes, a light comes on in this chamber, and the shock is repeated. Soon the animal learns to avoid pain by moving before the shock occurs. Once an animal learns to avoid the shock, it can be turned off altogether. A well-trained animal may avoid the nonexistent shock indefinitely.

The same analysis can be applied to human behavior. A behaviorist would say that the powerful reward of immediate relief from anxiety keeps self-defeating avoidance behaviors alive. This view, known as the **anxiety reduction hypothesis**, seems to explain why the behavior patterns we have discussed often look very "stupid" to outside observers.

Conversion disorder A bodily symptom that mimics a physical disability but is actually caused by anxiety or emotional distress.

Anxiety reduction hypothesis Explains the self-defeating nature of avoidance responses as a result of the reinforcing effects of relief from anxiety.

Cognitive Approach

The cognitive view is that distorted thinking causes people to magnify ordinary threats and failures, which leads to distress (Provencher, Dugas, & Ladouceur, 2004). For example, Bonnie, who is socially phobic, constantly has upsetting thoughts about being evaluated at school. One reason for this is that people with social phobias tend to be perfectionists. Like other social phobics, Bonnie is excessively concerned about mistakes. She also perceives criticism where none exists. Bonnie tends to avoid any social situation she perceives might focus too much attention on herself (Brown & Barlow, 2007). Even when socially phobic persons are successful, distorted thinking leads them to think they have failed (Barlow, 2002). In short, changing the thinking patterns of anxious individuals like Bonnie can greatly lessen their fears (Poulton & Andrews, 1996).

Implications All four psychological explanations probably contain a core of truth. For this reason, understanding anxiety-based disorders may be aided by combining parts of each perspective. Each viewpoint also suggests a different approach to treatment. Because many possibilities exist, therapy is discussed later, in Chapter 13.

MODULE 12.2 Summary

What is a personality disorder?

- Personality disorders are persistent, maladaptive personality patterns.
- Sociopathy is a common personality disorder. Antisocial persons lack a conscience, and they are emotionally cold, manipulative, shallow, and dishonest.

What problems result when a person suffers high levels of anxiety?

- Anxiety disorders, dissociative disorders, and somatoform disorders are characterized by high levels of anxiety, rigid defense mechanisms, and self-defeating behavior patterns.
- In an adjustment disorder, ordinary stresses push people beyond their ability to cope with life.
- Anxiety disorders include generalized anxiety disorder, panic disorder (with or without agoraphobia), agoraphobia, specific phobias, social phobia, obsessive-compulsive disorder, posttraumatic stress disorder, and acute stress disorder.
- High levels of anxiety also underlie the unhealthy distortions in behavior that occur in dissociative disorders and somatoform disorders.
- Dissociative disorders may take the form of amnesia, fugue, or multiple identities.
- Somatoform disorders center on physical complaints that mimic disease or disability. Four examples of somatoform disorders are hypochondriasis, somatization disorder, somatoform pain disorder, and conversion disorder.

How do psychologists explain anxiety-based disorders?

- Understanding anxiety-based disorders requires a combination of biological, psychodynamic, humanistic-existential, behavioral, and cognitive perspectives.

KNOWLEDGE BUILDER

Personality Disorders and Anxiety-Based Disorders

Recite

1. Which of the following personality disorders is associated with an inflated sense of self-importance and a constant need for attention and admiration?
   a. narcissistic
   b. antisocial
   c. paranoid
   d. manipulative

2. Antisocial personality disorders are difficult to treat, but there is typically a decline in antisocial behavior a year or two after adolescence. T or F?

3. When prolonged unemployment, a bad marriage, or physical illness pushes a person beyond his or her ability to cope, it is most likely that which of the following problems will occur?
   a. a dissociative disorder
   b. agoraphobia
   c. an adjustment disorder
   d. a conversion disorder

4. Panic disorder can occur with or without agoraphobia, but agoraphobia cannot occur alone, without the presence of a panic disorder. T or F?

5. Alice has a phobic fear of blood. What is the formal term for her fear?
   a. nyctophobia
   b. hematophobia
   c. pathophobia
   d. pyrophobia

6. A person who intensely fears eating, writing, or speaking in public suffers from _____ _____.

7. "Checkers" and "cleaners" suffer from which disorder?
   a. acarophobia
   b. panic disorder with agoraphobia
   c. generalized anxiety disorder
   d. obsessive-compulsive disorder

8. The symptoms of acute stress disorders last less than 1 month; posttraumatic stress disorders last more than 1 month. T or F?

9. Which of the following is not a dissociative disorder?
   a. fugue
   b. amnesia
   c. conversion reaction
   d. multiple identity

10. According to the _____ view, anxiety disorders are the end result of a faulty self-image.
    a. psychodynamic
    b. humanistic
    c. behaviorist
    d. cognitive

Reflect
Critical Thinking

11. Many of the physical complaints associated with anxiety disorders are closely related to activity of what part of the nervous system?

12. How could someone get away with Munchausen syndrome by proxy? Wouldn't doctors figure out that something was fishy with Ben long before he had 40 surgeries for a faked sinus disorder? (See "Sick of Being Sick.")

Relate

Many of the qualities that define personality disorders exist to a minor degree in normal personalities. Try to think of a person you know who has some of the characteristics described for each type of personality disorder.

Which of the anxiety disorders would you *least* want to suffer from? Why?

What minor obsessions or compulsions have you experienced?

What is the key difference between a stress disorder and an adjustment disorder? (Review both discussions if you don't immediately know the answer.)

Which of the four psychological explanations of anxiety-based disorders do you find most convincing?

Link

Internet addresses frequently change. To find the sites listed here, visit **http://www.thomsonedu.com/psychology/coon** for an updated list of Internet addresses and direct links to relevant sites.

- **Personality Disorders** Read more about the 10 personality disorders.
- **Anxiety Disorders** The website of the Anxiety Disorders Association of America.
- **Famous People with Phobias** Find out more about famous phobias and how to live with them.

ANSWERS

1. a 2. T 3. c 4. F 5. b 6. social phobia 7. d 8. T 9. c 10. b 11. The autonomic nervous system (ANS), especially the sympathetic branch of the ANS. 12. No one doctor tolerates false symptoms for long. Once a doctor refuses further treatment, the Munchausen sufferer will move on to another. Also, sometimes more than one doctor is being seen at one time.

MODULE 12.3 Psychosis, Delusional Disorders, and Schizophrenia

IMAGINE THAT A MEMBER OF YOUR FAMILY has been hearing voices, is talking strangely, has covered her head with aluminum foil, and believes that houseflies are speaking to her in code. If you observed such symptoms, would you be concerned? Of course you would, and rightly so. Psychotic disorders are among the most serious of all mental problems. They are also our next topic.

Psychotic Disorders—Life in the Shadow of Madness

SURVEY QUESTION: *What are the general characteristics of psychotic disorders?*

A person who is psychotic undergoes a number of striking changes in thinking, behavior, and emotion. Basic to all these changes is the fact that **psychosis** reflects a loss of contact with shared views of reality (psycho*sis*, singular; psycho*ses*, plural). The following comments, made by a psychotic patient, illustrate what is meant by a "split" from reality (Durand & Barlow, 2006):

> When you do the 25 of the clock, it means that you leave the house 25 after 1 to mail letters so they can check on you . . . and they know where you're at. That's the Eagle.

The Nature of Psychosis

What are the major features of psychotic disorders? Delusions and hallucinations are core features, but there are others as well.

People who suffer from **delusions** hold false beliefs that they insist are true, regardless of how much the facts contradict them. An example is a 43-year-old schizophrenic man who was convinced he was pregnant (Mansouri & Adityanjee, 1995).

Are there different types of delusions? Yes, some common types of delusions are: (1) *depressive* delusions, in which people feel that they have committed horrible crimes or sinful deeds; (2) *somatic* delusions, such as believing your body is "rotting away" or that it is emitting foul odors; (3) delusions of *grandeur,* in which people think they are extremely important; (4) delusions of *influence,* in which people feel they are being controlled or influenced by others or by unseen forces; (5) delusions of *persecution,* in which people believe that others are "out to get them"; and (6) delusions of *reference,* in which people give great personal meaning to unrelated events. For instance, delusional people sometimes think that television programs are giving them a special personal message (DSM-IV-TR, 2000).

Hallucinations are imaginary sensations, such as seeing, hearing, or smelling things that don't exist in the real world. The most common psychotic hallucination is hearing voices, like the voice that told Carol North to "Collide with the world." Sometimes these voices command patients to hurt themselves. Unfortunately, sometimes people obey (Barrowcliff & Haddock, 2006). More rarely, psychotic people may feel "insects crawling under their skin," taste "poisons" in their food, or smell "gas" their "enemies" are using to "get" them. Sensory changes, such as anesthesia (numbness, or a loss of sensation) or extreme sensitivity to heat, cold, pain, or touch, can also occur.

During a psychotic episode, emotions are often severely disturbed. For instance, the psychotic person may be wildly elated, depressed, hyperemotional, or apathetic. Sometimes psychotic patients display *flat affect,* a condition in which the face is frozen in a blank expression. Brain images from psychotic patients with "frozen faces" reveal that their brains process emotions abnormally (Fahim et al., 2005).

Some psychotic symptoms can be thought of as a primitive type of communication. That is, many patients can only

A psychotic individual in a state mental hospital.

use their actions to say "I need help" or "I can't handle it any more." Disturbed verbal communication is a nearly universal symptom of psychosis. In fact, psychotic speech tends to be so garbled and chaotic that it sometimes sounds like a "word salad."

Major disturbances such as those just described—as well as added problems with thinking, memory, and attention—bring about personality disintegration and a break with reality. *Personality disintegration* occurs when a person's thoughts, actions, and emotions are no longer coordinated. When psychotic disturbances and a fragmented personality are evident for weeks or months, the person has suffered a psychosis (DSM-IV-TR, 2000). (See ■ Table 12.5.)

Organic Psychosis In a sense, all psychoses are partly organic, involving physical changes in the brain. However, the general term *organic psychosis* is usually reserved for problems involving clear-cut brain injuries or diseases. For example, poisoning by lead or mercury can damage the brain and cause hallucinations, delusions, and a loss of emotional control (● Fig. 12.5). A particularly dangerous situation is found in old buildings that contain leaded paints. Lead tastes sweet. Thus, young children may be tempted to eat leaded paint flakes as if they were candy. Children who eat leaded paint can become psychotic or intellectually disabled (Mielke, 1999).

Leaded paints also release powdered lead into the air. Children may breathe the powder or eat it after handling contaminated toys. Other sources of lead are soldered water pipes, old lead-lined drinking fountains, lead-glazed pottery, and lead deposited years ago from automobile exhaust. On a much larger scale, "poisoning" of another type, in the form of drug abuse, can also produce psychotic symptoms (DSM-IV-TR, 2000).

● **FIGURE 12.5** The Mad Hatter, from Lewis Carroll's *Alice's Adventures in Wonderland*. History provides numerous examples of psychosis caused by toxic chemicals. Carroll's Mad Hatter character is modeled after an occupational disease of the eighteenth and nineteenth centuries. In that era, hatmakers were heavily exposed to mercury used in the preparation of felt. Consequently, many suffered brain damage and became psychotic, or "mad" (Kety, 1979).

The most common organic problem is **dementia** (duh-MEN-sha), a serious mental impairment in old age caused by deterioration of the brain. In dementia, we see major disturbances in memory, reasoning, judgment, impulse control, and personality. This combination usually leaves people con-

The soil and dust in cities and near busy streets is often heavily contaminated with lead. This lead came from automobile exhaust before leaded gasoline was banned. Young children frequently put objects and their hands in their mouths. This, then, is a major source of lead poisoning for many children. Paving play areas or covering them with clean soil can greatly reduce lead exposure (Mielke, 1999).

■ **TABLE 12.5 Warning Signs of Psychotic Disorders and Major Mood Disorders**

You express bizarre thoughts or beliefs that defy reality.

You have withdrawn from family members and other relationships.

You hear unreal voices or sees things others don't.

You are extremely sad, persistently despondent, or suicidal.

You are excessively energetic and have little need for sleep.

You lose your appetite, sleep excessively, and have no energy.

You exhibit extreme mood swings.

You believe someone is trying to get you.

You have engaged in antisocial, destructive, or self-destructive behavior.

Sources: Harvey et al., 1996; Sheehy & Cournos, 1992.

Psychosis A withdrawal from reality marked by hallucinations and delusions, disturbed thought and emotions, and personality disorganization.

Delusion A false belief held against all contrary evidence.

Hallucination An imaginary sensation, such as seeing, hearing, or smelling things that don't exist in the real world.

Dementia A serious mental impairment in old age caused by deterioration of the brain.

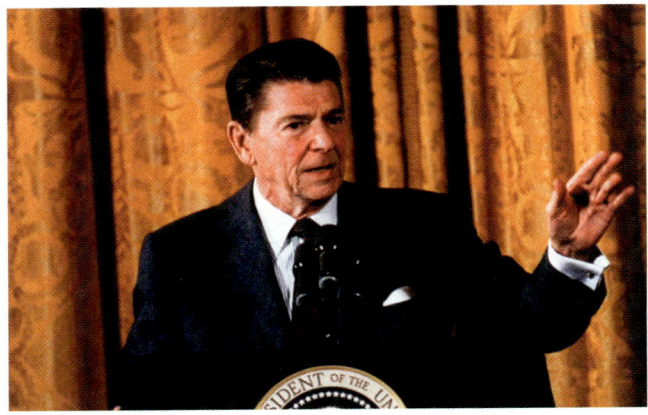

Former U.S. President Ronald Reagan was diagnosed with Alzheimer's disease in 1995. Like many Alzheimer's victims, Reagan slipped into a slow mental decline. He died in 2004.

fused, suspicious, apathetic, or withdrawn. Some common causes of dementia are circulatory problems, repeated strokes, or general shrinkage and atrophy of the brain. The majority of people who suffer from dementia slowly lose their mental abilities without becoming psychotic. However, some do develop delusions and lose contact with reality. The most common cause of dementia is *Alzheimer's disease.*

Alzheimer's disease (ALLS-hi-merz) is one of the most fearsome problems of aging. Alzheimer's victims slowly lose the ability to work, cook, drive, read, write, or do arithmetic. Eventually they are mute and bedridden. Alzheimer's disease appears to be caused by unusual webs and tangles in the brain that damage areas important for memory and learning (Ingram, 2003). Understandably, efforts to find a cure for Alzheimer's disease are expanding. For some of us, such efforts may be a race against time.

Are there specific kinds of psychotic disorders? Two major types of psychosis are *delusional disorders* and *schizophrenia.* As you will recall, mood disorders mainly involve emotional extremes. Nevertheless, psychotic symptoms can also occur in some mood disorders. You'll find information on each of these problems in upcoming discussions.

Delusional Disorders—An Enemy Behind Every Tree

SURVEY QUESTION: *What is the nature of a delusional disorder?*

People with delusional disorders usually do not suffer from hallucinations, emotional excesses, or personality disintegration. Even so, their break with reality is unmistakable. The main feature of **delusional disorders** is the presence of deeply held false beliefs, which may take the following forms (DSM-IV-TR, 2000):

- **Erotomanic type:** In this disorder, people have erotic delusions that they are loved by another person, especially by someone famous or of higher status.
- **Grandiose type:** In this case, people suffer from the delusion that they have some great, unrecognized talent, knowledge, or insight. They may also believe that they have a special relationship with an important person or with God or that they are a famous person. (If the famous person is alive, the deluded person regards her or him as an imposter.)
- **Jealous type:** An example of this type of delusion would be having an all-consuming, but unfounded, belief that your spouse or lover is unfaithful.
- **Persecutory type:** Delusions of persecution involve belief that you are being conspired against, cheated, spied on, followed, poisoned, maligned, or harassed.
- **Somatic type:** People suffering from somatic delusions typically believe that their bodies are diseased or rotting, or infested with insects or parasites, or that parts of their bodies are defective.

Although they are false, and sometimes far-fetched, all these delusions are about experiences that could occur in real life (Manschreck, 1996). In other types of psychosis, delusions tend to be more bizarre. For example, a person with schizophrenia might believe that space aliens have replaced all his internal organs with electronic monitoring devices. In contrast, people with ordinary delusions merely believe that someone is trying to steal their money, that they are being deceived by a lover, that the FBI is watching them, and the like (DSM-IV-TR, 2000).

Paranoid Psychosis

The most common delusional disorder, often called **paranoid psychosis,** centers on delusions of persecution. Many self-styled reformers, crank letter writers, conspiracy theorists, "UFO abductees," and the like suffer paranoid delusions. Paranoid individuals often believe that they are being cheated, spied on, followed, poisoned, harassed, or plotted against. Usually they are intensely suspicious, believing they must be on guard at all times.

The evidence such people find to support their beliefs usually fails to persuade others. Every detail of the paranoid person's existence is woven into a private version of "what's really going on." Buzzing during a telephone conversation may be interpreted as "someone listening"; a stranger who comes to the door asking for directions may be seen as "really trying to get information"; and so forth.

It is difficult to treat people suffering from paranoid delusions because it is almost impossible for them to accept that they need help. Anyone who suggests that they have a problem simply becomes part of the "conspiracy" to "persecute" them. Consequently, paranoid people frequently lead lonely, isolated, and humorless lives dominated by constant suspicion and hostility.

Although they are not necessarily dangerous to others, they can be. People who believe that the Mafia, "government agents," terrorists, or a street gang is slowly closing in on them may be moved to violence by their irrational fears. Imagine that a stranger comes to the door to ask a paranoid person for directions. If the stranger has his hand in his coat pocket, he could become the target of a paranoid attempt at "self-defense."

Delusional disorders are rare. By far, the most common form of psychosis is schizophrenia. Let's explore schizophrenia in more detail and see how it differs from a delusional disorder.

Schizophrenia—Shattered Reality

SURVEY QUESTIONS: *What forms does schizophrenia take? What causes it?*

Schizophrenia (SKIT-soh-FREN-ee-uh) is marked by delusions, hallucinations, apathy, thinking abnormalities, and a "split" between thought and emotion. In schizophrenia, emotions may become blunted or very inappropriate. For example, if a person with schizophrenia is told his mother just died, he might smile, or giggle, or show no emotion at all. Schizophrenic delusions may include the idea that the person's thoughts and actions are being controlled, that thoughts are being broadcast (so others can hear them), that thoughts have been "inserted" into the person's mind, or that thoughts have been removed. In addition, schizophrenia involves withdrawal from contact with others, a loss of interest in external activities, a breakdown of personal habits, and an inability to deal with daily events (Neufeld et al., 2003). One person in 100 has schizophrenia in any given year (NIMH, 2006b).

Many schizophrenic symptoms appear to be related to problems with *selective attention*. In other words, it is hard for people with schizophrenia to focus on one item of information at a time. Having an impaired "sensory filter" in their brains may be why they are overwhelmed by a jumble of thoughts, sensations, images, and feelings (Heinrichs, 2001).

Is there more than one type of schizophrenia? Schizophrenia appears to be a group of related disturbances. It has four major subtypes:

- **Disorganized type:** Schizophrenia marked by incoherence, grossly disorganized behavior, bizarre thinking, and flat or grossly inappropriate emotions.
- **Catatonic type:** Schizophrenia marked by stupor, rigidity, unresponsiveness, posturing, mutism, and, sometimes, agitated, purposeless behavior.
- **Paranoid type:** Schizophrenia marked by a preoccupation with delusions or by frequent auditory hallucinations related to a single theme, especially grandeur or persecution.
- **Undifferentiated type:** Schizophrenia in which there are prominent psychotic symptoms, but none of the specific features of catatonic, disorganized, or paranoid types.

Disorganized Schizophrenia

The disorder known as disorganized schizophrenia (sometimes called hebephrenic schizophrenia) comes close to matching the stereotyped images of "madness" seen in movies. In **disorganized schizophrenia**, personality disintegration is almost complete: Emotions, speech, and behavior are all highly disorganized. The result is silliness, laughter, and bizarre or obscene behavior, as shown by this intake interview of a patient named Edna:

Dr. I am Dr. _____. I would like to know something more about you.

Patient You have a nasty mind. Lord! Lord! Cats in a cradle.

Dr. Tell me, how do you feel?

Patient London's bell is a long, long dock. Hee! Hee! (Giggles uncontrollably.)

Dr. Do you know where you are now?

Patient D_____n! S_____t on you all who rip into my internals! The grudgerometer will take care of you all! (Shouting) I am the Queen, see my magic, I shall turn you all into smidgelings forever!

Dr. Your husband is concerned about you. Do you know his name?

Patient (Stands, walks to and faces the wall) Who am I, who are we, who are you, who are they, (turns) I . . . I . . . I . . . I! (Makes grotesque faces.)

Alzheimer's disease An age-related disease characterized by memory loss, mental confusion, and, in its later stages, a nearly total loss of mental abilities.

Delusional disorder A psychosis marked by severe delusions of grandeur, jealousy, persecution, or similar preoccupations.

Paranoid psychosis A delusional disorder centered especially on delusions of persecution.

Schizophrenia A psychosis characterized by delusions, hallucinations, apathy, and a "split" between thought and emotion.

Disorganized schizophrenia Schizophrenia marked by incoherence, grossly disorganized behavior, bizarre thinking, and flat or grossly inappropriate emotions.

Edna was placed in the women's ward where she proceeded to masturbate. Occasionally, she would scream or shout obscenities. At other times she giggled to herself. She was known to attack other patients. She began to complain that her uterus was attached to a "pipeline to the Kremlin" and that she was being "infernally invaded" by Communism. (Suinn, 1975*)

Disorganized schizophrenia typically develops in adolescence or young adulthood. Chances of improvement are limited, and social impairment is usually extreme (DSM-IV-TR, 2000).

Catatonic Schizophrenia

The catatonic person seems to be in a state of total panic (Fink & Taylor, 2003). **Catatonic schizophrenia** brings about a stuporous condition in which odd positions may be held for hours or even days. These periods of rigidity may be similar to the tendency to "freeze" at times of great emergency or panic. Catatonic individuals appear to be struggling desperately to control their inner turmoil. One sign of this is the fact that stupor may occasionally give way to agitated outbursts or violent behavior. The following excerpt describes a catatonic episode.

---

*All Suinn quotes in this chapter are from *Fundamentals of Behavior Pathology* by R. M. Suinn. Copyright © 1975. Reprinted by permission of John Wiley & Sons, Inc.

Manuel appeared to be physically healthy upon examination. Yet he did not regain his awareness of his surroundings. He remained motionless, speechless, and seemingly unconscious. One evening an aide turned him on his side to straighten out the sheet, was called away to tend to another patient, and forgot to return. Manuel was found the next morning, still on his side, his arm tucked under his body, as he had been left the night before. His arm was turning blue from lack of circulation, but he seemed to be experiencing no discomfort. (Suinn, 1975)

Notice that Manuel did not speak. *Mutism,* along with a marked decrease in responsiveness to the environment, makes patients with catatonic schizophrenia difficult to "reach." Fortunately, this bizarre disorder has become rare in Europe and North America (DSM-IV-TR, 2000).

Paranoid Schizophrenia

Paranoid schizophrenia is the most common schizophrenic disorder. As in paranoid delusional disorders, **paranoid schizophrenia** centers on delusions of grandeur and persecution. However, paranoid schizophrenics also hallucinate, and their delusions are more bizarre and unconvincing than those in a delusional disorder (Freeman & Garety, 2004).

Thinking that their minds are being controlled by God, the government, or "cosmic rays from space," or that someone is trying to poison them, people suffering from paranoid schizophrenia may feel forced into violence to "protect" themselves (● Fig. 12.6). An example is James Huberty, who brutally murdered 21 people at a McDonald's restaurant in

In disorganized schizophrenia, behavior is marked by silliness, laughter, and bizarre or obscene behavior.

Can the catatonic's rigid postures and stupor be understood in terms of abnormal body chemistry? Environment? Heredity? As is true of other forms of schizophrenia, the answer appears to be all three factors.

CRITICAL THINKING

Are the Mentally Ill Prone to Violence?

News reports and television programs tend to exaggerate the connection between mental illness and violence (Corrigan et al., 2005). Such media reports both create and reflect deeply held beliefs about mental disorders in our society. Such beliefs are important because they affect laws and personal attitudes toward the mentally ill. For example, people who strongly believe that the mentally ill are prone to violence are typically afraid to have former mental patients as neighbors, coworkers, or friends (Corrigan & Watson, 2005).

The reality is just the opposite. According to the largest study ever conducted on this question, mentally ill individuals who are not also substance abusers are no more prone to violence than are normal individuals (Monahan et al., 2001). There are only a few exceptions to this conclusion, and in those cases the risk is not very large (Lidz, et al., 2007; Noble, 1997; Rice, 1997):

- Only persons who are also involved with *substance abuse* are more prone to violence than nonpatients.
- Only persons who are *actively psychotic* are more violence prone than nonpatients. That is, if a person is experiencing delusions and hallucinations, the risk of violence is elevated. Other mental problems are unrelated to violence.
- Only persons *currently* experiencing psychotic symptoms are at increased risk for violence. Violent behavior is not related to having been a mental patient in the past or having had psychotic symptoms in the past.

Thus, most news stories give a false impression. Only a small minority of the actively mentally ill poses an increased risk. Even when we consider people who are actively psychotic,

we find that the vast majority are not violent. Former mental patients, in particular, are no more likely to be violent than people in general. No matter how disturbed a person may have been, she or he merits respect and compassion.

The risk of violence from mental patients is actually many times lower than that from persons who have the following attributes: young, male, poor, and intoxicated (Corrigan & Watson, 2005). Remember, people who are not mentally ill commit the overwhelming majority of violent crimes.

Many news stories give the impression that the mentally ill are dangerous. Consider, for example, the ghastly case of Jeffrey Dahmer, who killed, sexually molested, and then ate his victims. Like Dahmer, most of the mentally disordered persons who make the evening news have committed murder or some other horrible crime. This tends to give the impression that the mentally ill are violent and dangerous. Yet in reality, only a tiny percentage of all mentally disordered persons are more violent than average.

● **FIGURE 12.6** Over a period of years, Theodore Kaczynski mailed bombs to unsuspecting victims, many of whom were maimed or killed. As a young adult, Kaczynski was a brilliant mathematician. At the time of his arrest, he had become the Unabomber—a reclusive "loner" who deeply mistrusted other people and modern technology. After his arrest, Kaczynski was judged to be suffering from paranoid schizophrenia.

San Ysidro, California. Huberty, who had paranoid schizophrenia, felt persecuted and cheated by life. Shortly before he announced to his wife that he was "going hunting humans," Huberty had been hearing hallucinated voices.

How dangerous are the mentally ill? Horrific crimes, like the San Ysidro murders, lead many people to believe that the mentally ill are dangerous. Are they right? You might be surprised by the answer, found in "Are the Mentally Ill Prone to Violence?"

Catatonic schizophrenia Schizophrenia marked by stupor; rigidity; unresponsiveness; posturing; mutism; and, sometimes, agitated, purposeless behavior.

Paranoid schizophrenia Schizophrenia marked by a preoccupation with delusions or by frequent auditory hallucinations related to a single theme, especially grandeur or persecution.

Undifferentiated Schizophrenia

The three types of schizophrenia just described occur most often in textbooks. In reality, patients may shift from one pattern to another at different times. Many patients, therefore, are simply classified as suffering from **undifferentiated schizophrenia**, in which the specific features of catatonic, disorganized, or paranoid types are missing. Diagnosing schizophrenia is fairly subjective. All things considered, however, there is no doubt that schizophrenia is real or that its treatment is a major challenge.

The Causes of Schizophrenia

Former British Prime Minister Winston Churchill once described a question that perplexed him as "a riddle wrapped in a mystery inside an enigma." The same words might describe the causes of schizophrenia.

Environment *What causes schizophrenia?* An increased risk of developing schizophrenia may begin at birth or even before. Women who are exposed to the influenza (flu) virus or to rubella (German measles) during the middle of pregnancy have children who are more likely to become schizophrenic (Brown et al., 2001). Malnutrition during pregnancy and complications at the time of birth can have a similar impact. Possibly, such events disturb brain development, leaving people more vulnerable to a psychotic break with reality (Walker et al., 2004).

Early **psychological trauma** (a psychological injury or shock) may also add to the risk. Often, the victims of schizophrenia were exposed to violence, sexual abuse, death, divorce, separation, or other stresses in childhood (Walker et al., 2004). Living in a troubled family is a related risk factor. In a disturbed family environment, stressful relationships, communication patterns, and negative emotions prevail. Deviant communication patterns cause anxiety, confusion, anger, conflict, and turmoil. Typically, disturbed families interact in ways that are laden with guilt, prying, criticism, negativity, and emotional attacks (Bressi, Albonetti, & Razzoli, 1998; Davison & Neale, 2006).

Although they are attractive, environmental explanations alone are not enough to account for schizophrenia. For example, when the children of schizophrenic parents are raised away from their chaotic home environment, they are still more likely to become psychotic (Walker et al., 2004).

Heredity *Does that mean that heredity affects the risk of developing schizophrenia?* There is now little doubt that heredity is a factor in schizophrenia. It appears that some individuals inherit a potential for developing schizophrenia. They are, in other words, more vulnerable to the disorder than others are (Harrison & Weinberger, 2005; Walker et al., 2004).

How has that been shown? If one identical twin becomes schizophrenic (remember, identical twins have identical genes), then the other twin has a *48 percent* chance of also becoming schizophrenic (Lenzenweger & Gottesman, 1994). The figure for twins can be compared with the risk of schizophrenia for the population in general, which is about 1 percent. (See ● Fig. 12.7 for other relationships.) In general, schizophrenia is clearly more common among close relatives and it tends to run in families. There's even a case on record of *four* identical quadruplets *all* developing schizophrenia (Mirsky et al., 2000). In light of such evidence, researchers are now beginning to search for specific genes related to schizophrenia.

A problem exists with current genetic explanations of schizophrenia: Very few people with schizophrenia have children. How could a genetic defect be passed from one generation to the next if afflicted people don't reproduce? One possible answer is suggested by the fact that the older a man is (even if he doesn't suffer from schizophrenia) when he fathers a child, the more likely it is that the child will develop schizophrenia. Apparently, genetic mutations occur in aging

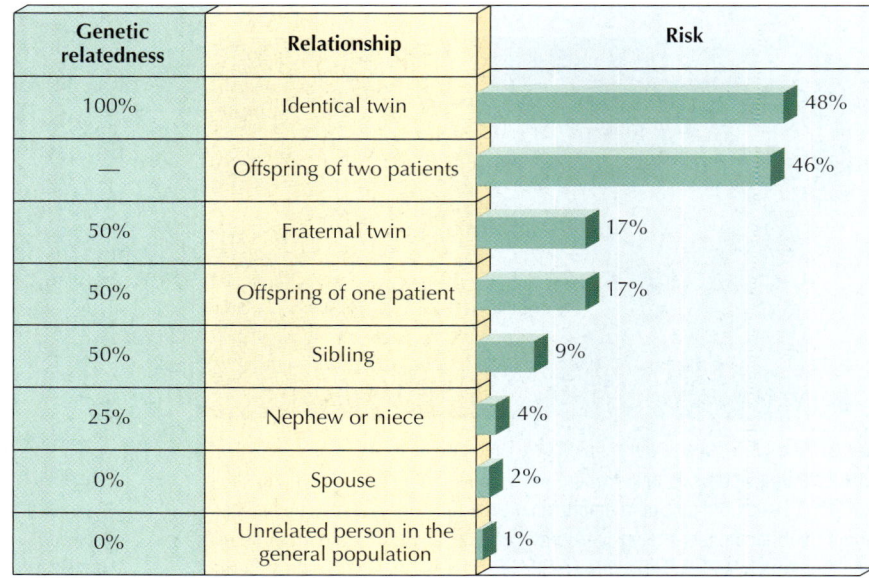

● **FIGURE 12.7** Lifetime risk of developing schizophrenia is associated with how closely a person is genetically related to a schizophrenic person. A shared environment also increases the risk. (Estimates from Lenzenweger & Gottesman, 1994.)

Genetic relatedness	Relationship	Risk
100%	Identical twin	48%
—	Offspring of two patients	46%
50%	Fraternal twin	17%
50%	Offspring of one patient	17%
50%	Sibling	9%
25%	Nephew or niece	4%
0%	Spouse	2%
0%	Unrelated person in the general population	1%

This series of paintings by Louis Wain reflects a troubled personality. Wain was a British illustrator who became schizophrenic in middle age. As Wain's psychosis progressed, his cat paintings became highly abstract and fragmented. In many ways, Wain's paintings resemble the perceptual changes caused by psychedelic drugs such as mescaline and LSD. Recent research suggests that psychosis may, in fact, be the result of mind-altering changes in brain chemistry.

male reproductive cells and increase the risk of schizophrenia (as well as other medical problems) (Malaspina et al., 2005; Sipos et al., 2004).

Brain Chemistry Amphetamine, LSD, PCP ("angel dust"), and similar drugs produce effects that partially mimic the symptoms of schizophrenia. Also, the same drugs (phenothiazines) used to treat LSD overdoses tend to alleviate psychotic symptoms. Facts such as these suggest that biochemical abnormalities (disturbances in brain chemicals or neurotransmitters) may occur in schizophrenic people. It is possible that the schizophrenic brain produces some substance similar to a *psychedelic* (mind-altering) drug. At present, one likely candidate is dopamine (DOPE-ah-meen), an important chemical messenger found in the brain.

Many researchers believe that schizophrenia is related to overactivity in brain dopamine systems (Durand & Barlow, 2006; Kapur & Lecrubier, 2003). Another possibility is that dopamine receptors become super-responsive to normal amounts of dopamine. Dopamine appears to trigger a flood of unrelated thoughts, feelings, and perceptions, which may account for the voices, hallucinations, and delusions of schizophrenia. The implication is that schizophrenic people may be on a sort of drug trip caused by their own bodies (● Fig. 12.8).

Dopamine is not the only brain chemical that has caught scientists' attention. The neurotransmitter glutamate also appears to be related to schizophrenia (van Elst et al., 2005). People who take the hallucinogenic drug PCP, which affects glutamate, have symptoms that closely mimic schizophrenia (Murray, 2002). This occurs because glutamate influences brain activity in areas that control emotions and sensory information (Tsai & Coyle, 2002). Another tantalizing connec-

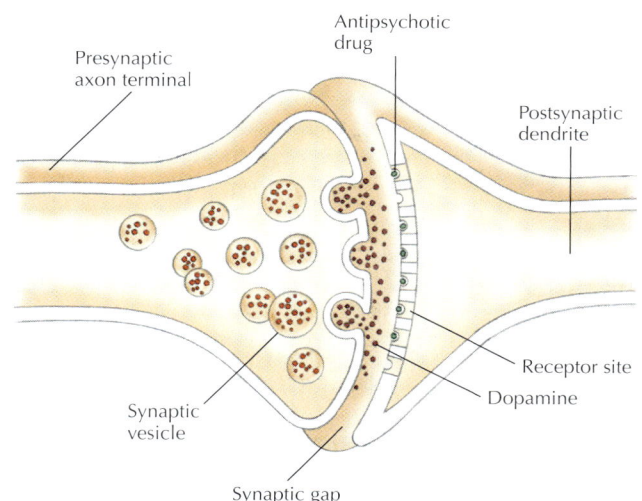

● **FIGURE 12.8** Dopamine normally crosses the synapse between two neurons, activating the second cell. Antipsychotic drugs bind to the same receptor sites as dopamine does, blocking its action. In people suffering from schizophrenia, a reduction in dopamine activity can quiet a person's agitation and psychotic symptoms.

tion is the fact that stress alters glutamate levels, which in turn alter dopamine systems (Moghaddam, 2002). The story is far from complete, but it appears that dopamine, glutamate, and other brain chemicals partly explain the devastating symptoms of schizophrenia (Walker et al., 2004). (See "The Schizophrenic Brain.")

Undifferentiated schizophrenia Schizophrenia lacking the specific features of catatonic, disorganized, or paranoid types.

Psychological trauma A psychological injury or shock, such as that caused by violence, abuse, neglect, separation, and so forth.

BRAINWAVES

The Schizophrenic Brain

Several brain imaging methods (remember Module 2.2?) have made it possible to directly observe the living schizophrenic brain. CT scans and MRI scans, which can reveal brain structure, suggest that the brains of schizophrenics have shrunk (atrophied). For example, ● Figure 12.9 shows a *CT scan* (*CT* stands for computed tomography, or computer-enhanced X-ray images) of the brain of John Hinkley, Jr., who shot former U.S. President Ronald Reagan and three other men in 1981. In the ensuing trial, Hinkley was declared insane. As you can see, his brain had wider-than-normal surface fissuring.

Similarly, *MRI* (magnetic resonance imaging) *scans* indicate that schizophrenic people tend to have enlarged ventricles (fluid-filled spaces within the brain), again suggesting that surrounding brain tissue has withered (Barkataki et al., 2006). One possible explanation is that the schizophrenic brain may be unable to continually create new neurons to replace old ones that have died (Toro & Deakin, 2007). Normal brains continue to produce new neurons (referred to as *neurogenesis*) throughout life (Toro & Deakin, 2007). It is telling that the affected areas are crucial for regulating motivation, emotion, perception, actions, and attention (Gur et al., 1998; Walker et al., 2004).

Other methods provide images of brain activity, including PET scans. To make a *PET* (positron emission tomography) *scan*, a radioactive sugar solution is injected into a vein. When the sugar reaches the brain, an electronic device measures how much is used in each area. These data are then translated into a color map, or scan, of brain activity (● Fig. 12.10). Researchers are finding patterns in such scans that are consistently linked with schizophrenia, affective disorders, and other problems. For instance, activity tends to be abnormally low in the frontal lobes of the schizophrenic brain (Durand & Barlow, 2006; Velakoulis & Pantelis, 1996). In the future, PET scans may be used to accurately diagnose schizophrenia. For now, such scans show that there is a clear difference in schizophrenic brain activity.

● **FIGURE 12.9** *(left)* CT scan of would-be presidential assassin John Hinkley, Jr., taken when he was 25. The X-ray image shows widened fissures in the wrinkled surface of Hinkley's brain. *(right)* CT scan of a normal 25-year-old's brain. In most young adults the surface folds of the brain are pressed together too tightly to be seen. As a person ages, surface folds of the brain normally become more visible. Pronounced brain fissuring in young adults may be a sign of schizophrenia, chronic alcoholism, or other problems.

  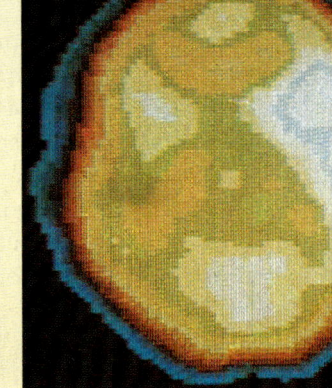

NORMAL SCHIZOPHRENIC MANIC-DEPRESSIVE

● **FIGURE 12.10** Positron emission tomography produces PET scans of the human brain. In the scans shown here, red, pink, and orange indicate lower levels of brain activity; white and blue indicate higher activity levels. Notice that activity in the schizophrenic brain is quite low in the frontal lobes (top area of each scan) (Velakoulis & Pantelis, 1996). Activity in the manic-depressive brain is low in the left brain hemisphere and high in the right brain hemisphere. The reverse is more often true of the schizophrenic brain. Researchers are trying to identify consistent patterns like these to aid diagnosis of mental disorders.

Implications

In summary, the emerging picture of psychotic disorders such as schizophrenia takes this form: Anyone subjected to enough stress may be pushed to a psychotic break. (Battlefield psychosis is an example.) However, some people inherit a difference in brain chemistry or brain structure that makes them more susceptible—even to normal life stresses.

Thus, the right mix of inherited potential and environmental stress brings about mind-altering changes in brain chemicals and brain structure. This explanation is called a **stress-vulnerability model.** It attributes psychotic disorders to a blend of environmental stress and inherited susceptibility (Walker et al., 2004). The model seems to apply to other forms of psychopathology as well, such as depression (● Fig. 12.11).

Despite advances in our understanding, psychosis remains "a riddle wrapped in a mystery inside an enigma." Let us hope that recent progress toward a cure for schizophrenia will continue.

MODULE 12.3 Summary

What are the general characteristics of psychotic disorders?

- Psychosis is a break in contact with reality that is marked by delusions, hallucinations, sensory changes, disturbed emotions, disturbed communication, and personality disintegration.
- An organic psychosis is based on known injuries or diseases of the brain.
- Some common causes of organic psychosis are poisoning, drug abuse, and dementia (especially Alzheimer's disease).

What is the nature of a delusional disorder?

- Delusional disorders are almost totally based on the presence of delusions of grandeur, persecution, infidelity, romantic attraction, or physical disease. The most common delusional disorder is paranoid psychosis.
- What forms does schizophrenia take? What causes it?
- Schizophrenia involves delusions, hallucinations, communication difficulties, and a split between thought and emotion.
- Disorganized schizophrenia is marked by extreme personality disintegration and silly, bizarre, or obscene behavior.
- Catatonic schizophrenia is associated with stupor, mutism, and odd postures. Sometimes violent and agitated behavior also occurs.
- In paranoid schizophrenia (the most common type), outlandish delusions of grandeur and persecution are coupled with psychotic symptoms and personality breakdown.
- Current explanations of schizophrenia emphasize a combination of prenatal injuries, early trauma, environmental stress, inherited susceptibility, and abnormalities in the brain.
- Heredity is a major factor in schizophrenia.
- Recent biochemical studies have focused on the brain transmitter dopamine and its receptor sites.
- The dominant explanation of schizophrenia, and other problems as well, is the stress-vulnerability model.

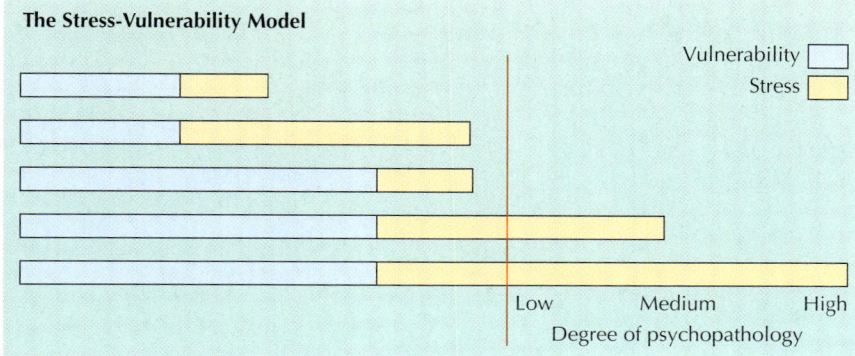

● **FIGURE 12.11** Various combinations of vulnerability and stress may produce psychological problems. The top bar shows low vulnerability and low stress. The result? No problem. The same is true of the next bar down, where low vulnerability is combined with moderate stress. Even high vulnerability (third bar) may not lead to problems if stress levels remain low. However, when high vulnerability combines with moderate or high stress (bottom two bars) the person "crosses the line" and suffers from psychopathology.

Stress-vulnerability model Attributes psychosis to a combination of environmental stress and inherited susceptibility.

KNOWLEDGE BUILDER

Psychosis, Delusional Disorders, and Schizophrenia

Recite

1. Carol wrongly believes that her body is "rotting away." She is suffering from
   a. depressive hallucinations
   b. a delusion
   c. flat affect
   d. Alzheimer's disease

2. Colin, who has suffered a psychotic break, is hearing voices. This symptom is referred to as
   a. flat affect
   b. hallucination
   c. a word salad
   d. organic delusions

3. A psychosis caused by lead poisoning would be regarded as an organic disorder. T or F?

4. Hallucinations and personality disintegration are the principal features of paranoid psychosis. T or F?

5. Which of the following is *not* one of the subtypes of schizophrenia?
   a. erotomanic type
   b. catatonic type
   c. paranoid type
   d. disorganized type

6. Environmental explanations of schizophrenia emphasize emotional trauma and
   a. manic parents
   b. schizoaffective interactions
   c. psychedelic interactions
   d. disturbed family relationships

7. The _____ _____ of a schizophrenic person runs a 48 percent chance of also becoming psychotic.

8. Biochemical explanations of schizophrenia have focused on excessive amounts of _____ in the brain.
   a. radioactive sugar
   b. webs and tangles
   c. PCP
   d. dopamine and glutamate

9. The stress-vulnerability model of psychosis explains mental disorders as a product of environmental stresses and
   a. psychological trauma
   b. deviant communication
   c. exposure to the flu virus during pregnancy
   d. heredity

Reflect
Critical Thinking

10. Researchers have found nearly double the normal number of dopamine receptor sites in the brains of schizophrenics. Why might that be important?

11. Enlarged surface fissures and ventricles are frequently found in the brains of chronic schizophrenics. Why is it a mistake to conclude that such features cause schizophrenia?

Relate

What did you think psychosis was like before you read about it? How has your understanding changed? If you were writing a "recipe" for psychosis, what would the main "ingredients" be?

If you were asked to play the role of a paranoid person for a theater production, what symptoms would you emphasize?

You have been asked to explain the causes of schizophrenia to the parents of a schizophrenic teenager. What would you tell them?

Link

Internet addresses frequently change. To find the sites listed here, visit **http://www.thomsonedu.com/psychology/coon** for an updated list of Internet addresses and direct links to relevant sites.

- **Psychotic Disorders** Read more about the psychotic disorders.
- **William Utermohlen's Self-Portraits** View these remarkable paintings by a man descending into Alzheimer's disease.
- **Schizophrenia** Explore this extensive website, which includes brain images and videos about schizophrenia.

ANSWERS

1. b 2. b 3. T 4. F 5. a 6. d 7. identical twin 8. d 9. d 10. Because of the extra receptors, schizophrenics may get psychedelic effects from normal levels of dopamine in the brain. 11. Because correlation does not confirm causation. Structural brain abnormalities are merely correlated with schizophrenia. They could be additional symptoms, rather than causes, of the disorder.

MODULE 12.4 Mood Disorders

FOR SOME PEOPLE, minor bouts of depression are as common as colds. But extreme swings of mood can be as disabling as a serious physical illness. In fact, depression can be deadly, because depressed persons may be suicidal. It is difficult to imagine how bleak and hopeless the world looks to a person who is deeply depressed, or how "crazy" it can be to ride a wave of mania. Let's explore mood disorders and their causes.

Mood Disorders—Peaks and Valleys

SURVEY QUESTIONS *What are mood disorders? What causes depression?*

Nobody loves you when you're down and out—or so it seems. Psychologists have come to realize that **mood disorders** (major disturbances in emotion) are among the most serious of all psychological conditions. In any given year, roughly 9.5 percent of the U.S. population suffers from a mood disorder (NIMH, 2006b).

Two general types of mood disorder are depressive disorders and bipolar disorders (Nevid & Greene, 2005). (See ■ Table 12.6.) In **depressive disorders,** sadness and despondency are exaggerated, prolonged, or unreasonable. Signs of a depressive disorder are dejection, hopelessness, and an inability to feel pleasure or to take interest in anything. Other common symptoms are fatigue, disturbed sleep and eating patterns, feelings of worthlessness, a very negative self-image, and thoughts of suicide. In **bipolar disorders,** people go both "up" and "down" emotionally (DSM-IV-TR, 2000).

Some mood disorders are long-lasting but relatively moderate problems. If a person is mildly depressed for at least 2 years, the problem is called a **dysthymic disorder** (dis-THY-mik). If depression alternates with periods when the person's mood is cheerful, expansive, or irritable, the problem is a **cyclothymic disorder** (SIKE-lo-THY-mik). Even at this level, mood disorders can be debilitating. However, major mood disorders are much more damaging.

Major Mood Disorders

Major mood disorders are characterized by emotional extremes. The person who only goes "down" emotionally suffers from a **major depressive disorder.** During major depressive episodes everything looks bleak and hopeless. The person has feelings of failure, worthlessness, and total despair. Suffering is intense, and the person may become extremely subdued, withdrawn, or intensely suicidal. Suicide attempted during a major depression is rarely a "plea for help." Usually, the person intends to succeed and may give no prior warning.

In major depressive disorders, suicidal impulses can be intense and despair total.

In a **bipolar I disorder,** people experience both extreme mania and deep depression. During manic episodes, the person is loud, elated, hyperactive, grandiose, and energetic.

Mood disorder Major disturbances in mood or emotion, such as depression or mania.

Depressive disorders Emotional disorders primarily involving sadness, despondency, and depression.

Bipolar disorders Emotional disorders involving both depression and mania or hypomania.

Dysthymic disorder Moderate depression that persists for 2 years or more.

Cyclothymic disorder Moderate manic and depressive behavior that persists for 2 years or more.

Major mood disorders Disorders marked by lasting extremes of mood or emotion and sometimes accompanied by psychotic symptoms.

Major depressive disorder A mood disorder in which the person has suffered one or more intense episodes of depression.

Bipolar I disorder A mood disorder in which a person has episodes of mania (excited, hyperactive, energetic, grandiose behavior) and also periods of deep depression.

TABLE 12.6 Major *DSM-IV-TR* Categories

PROBLEM	PRIMARY SYMPTOM	TYPICAL SIGNS OF TROUBLE
Depressive Disorders		
Major depressive disorder	Extreme emotional depression for at least 2 weeks	You feel extremely sad, worthless, fatigued, and empty; you are unable to feel pleasure; you are having thoughts of suicide.
Dysthymic disorder	Moderately depressed mood on most days during the last 2 years	You feel down and depressed more days than not; your self-esteem and energy levels have been low for many months.
Bipolar Disorders		
Bipolar I disorder	Extreme mania and depression	At times you have little need for sleep, can't stop talking, your mind races, and everything you do is of immense importance; at other times you feel extremely sad, worthless, and empty.
Bipolar II disorder	Emotional depression and at least one episode of mild mania	Most of the time you feel extremely sad, worthless, fatigued, and empty; however, at times you feel unusually good, cheerful, energetic, or "high."
Cyclothymic disorder	Periods of moderate depression and moderate mania for at least 2 years	You have been experiencing upsetting emotional ups and downs for many months.

Manic patients may go bankrupt in a matter of days, get arrested, or go on a binge of promiscuous sex. During periods of depression, the person is deeply despondent and possibly suicidal.

In a **bipolar II disorder** the person is mostly sad and guilt ridden but has had one or more mildly manic episodes (called *hypomania*). That is, in a bipolar II disorder both elation and depression occur, but the person's mania is not as extreme as in a bipolar I disorder. Bipolar II patients who are hypomanic usually just manage to irritate everyone around them. They are excessively cheerful, aggressive, or irritable, and they may brag, talk too fast, interrupt conversations, or spend too much money (Nolen-Hoeksema, 2007).

In serious cases of depression it is impossible for a person to function at work or at school. Sometimes, depressed individuals cannot even feed or dress themselves. In cases of depression and/or mania that are even more severe, the person may also lose touch with reality and display psychotic symptoms.

How do major mood disorders differ from dysthymic and cyclothymic disorders? As mentioned, the major mood disorders involve more severe emotional changes. Also, major mood disorders more often appear to be **endogenous** (en-DODGE-eh-nus: produced from within) rather than a reaction to external events.

What Causes Mood Disorders?

Depression and other mood disorders have resisted adequate explanation and treatment. Some scientists are focusing on the biology of mood changes. They are interested in brain chemicals and transmitter substances, especially serotonin, noradrenaline, and dopamine levels. Their findings are incomplete, but progress has been made. For example, the chemical *lithium carbonate* can be effective for treating some cases of bipolar depression.

Other researchers seek psychological explanations. Psychoanalytic theory, for instance, holds that depression is caused by repressed anger. This rage is displaced and turned inward as self-blame and self-hate. As discussed in Chapter 11, behavioral theories of depression emphasize learned helplessness (LoLordo, 2001; Seligman, 1989). Cognitive psychologists believe that self-criticism and negative, distorted, or self-defeating thoughts underlie many cases of depression. (This view is discussed in Module 13.4.) Clearly, life stresses trigger many mood disorders (Maier, 2001). This is especially true for people who have personality traits and thinking patterns that make them vulnerable to depression (Dozois & Dobson, 2002).

Gender and Depression Overall, women are twice as likely as men to experience depression (Kuehner, 2003). Researchers believe that social and environmental conditions are the main reason for this difference (Winstead & Sanchez, 2005). Factors that contribute to women's greater risk of depression include conflicts about birth control and pregnancy, work and parenting, and the strain of providing emotional support for others. Marital strife, sexual and physical abuse, and poverty are also factors. Nationwide, women and children are most likely to live in poverty. As a result, poor women frequently suffer the stresses associated with single parenthood, loss of control over their lives, poor housing, and dangerous neighborhoods (Stoppard & McMullen, 2003). One study found that women in the United States were most likely to be depressed if they lacked education, were unmarried, were Latina, had high stress levels, and experienced feelings of hopelessness (Myers et al., 2002).

Postpartum Depression One source of women's depression is fairly easy to identify. After pregnancy and childbirth, many women face a high risk of becoming depressed.

Two weeks after her child was born, Makemba realized something was wrong. She could no longer ignore that she was extremely irritable, fatigued, tearful, and depressed. "Shouldn't I be happy?" she wondered. "What's wrong with me?"

Many women are surprised to learn that they face a risk of depression after giving birth. The two most common forms of the problem are maternity blues and postpartum depression. (The term *postpartum* refers to the time following childbirth.)

An estimated 25 to 50 percent of all women experience *maternity blues,* a mild depression that usually lasts from 1 to 2 days after childbirth. These "third-day blues" are marked by crying, fitful sleep, tension, anger, and irritability. For most women, such reactions are a normal part of adjusting to childbirth. The depression is usually brief and not too severe.

For some women, maternity blues can be the beginning of a serious depression. Roughly 13 percent of all women who give birth develop **postpartum depression**, a moderately severe depression that begins within 3 months following childbirth. Typical signs of postpartum depression are mood swings, despondency, feelings of inadequacy, and an inability to cope with the new baby. Depression of this kind may last anywhere from 2 months to about a year. Women are not the only ones to suffer when postpartum depression strikes. A depressed mother can seriously retard her child's rate of development (Cooper & Murray, 2001).

Stress and anxiety before birth and negative attitudes toward child rearing increase the risk of postpartum depression. A troubled marriage and lack of support from the father are also danger signs. Part of the problem may be hormonal: After a woman gives birth, her estrogen levels can drop, altering her mood (Bloch, Daly, & Rubinow, 2003).

Women who become depressed tend to see their husbands as unsupportive. Therefore, educating new parents about the importance of supporting one another may reduce the risk of depression. Groups where new mothers can discuss their feelings are also helpful. If depression is severe or long lasting, new mothers should seek professional help.

Biology and Depression *Does the fact that major mood disorders appear to be endogenous imply that heredity is involved?* Yes, especially in bipolar disorders (McGuffin et al., 2003). As a case in point, if one identical twin is depressed, the other has a 67 percent chance of suffering depression, too. For fraternal twins the probability is 19 percent. This difference may be related to the recent finding that people who have a particular version of a gene are more likely to become depressed when they are stressed (Caspi et al., 2003). As we have noted, psychological causes are important in many cases of depression. But for major mood disorders, biological factors seem to play a larger role. Surprisingly, one additional source of depression is related to the seasons.

Seasonal Affective Disorder Unless you have experienced a winter of "cabin fever" in the far north, you may be surprised to learn that the rhythms of the seasons underlie some depressions. Researcher Norman Rosenthal has found that some people suffer from **seasonal affective disorder** (**SAD**), or depression that only occurs during the fall and winter months. Almost anyone can get a little depressed when days are short, dark, and cold. But when a person's symptoms are lasting and disabling, the problem may be SAD. Here are some of the major symptoms of SAD (Rosenthal, 1993):

- **Oversleeping and difficulty staying awake:** Your sleep patterns may be disturbed, and waking very early in the morning is common.
- **Fatigue:** You feel too tired to maintain a normal routine.
- **Craving:** You hunger for carbohydrates and sweets, leading to overeating and weight gain.
- **Inability to cope:** You feel irritable and stressed.
- **Social withdrawal:** You become unsocial in the winter but are socially active during other seasons.

Starting in the fall, people with SAD sleep longer but more poorly. During the day they feel tired and drowsy, and they tend to overeat. With each passing day they become more sad, anxious, irritable, and socially withdrawn.

Although their depressions are not severe, many victims of SAD face each winter with a sense of foreboding. SAD is especially prevalent in northern latitudes, where days are very short during the winter (Michalak & Lam, 2002) (● Fig. 12.12). For instance, one study found that 13 percent of college students living in northern New England showed signs of suffering from SAD (Low & Feissner, 1998). The students most likely to be affected were those who had moved from the South to attend college!

Bipolar II disorder A mood disorder in which a person is mostly depressed (sad, despondent, guilt ridden) but has also had one or more episodes of mild mania (hypomania).

Endogenous depression Depression that appears to be produced from within (perhaps by chemical imbalances in the brain), rather than as a reaction to life events.

Postpartum depression A mild to moderately severe depression that begins within 3 months following childbirth.

Seasonal affective disorder (SAD) Depression that occurs only during fall and winter; presumably related to decreased exposure to sunlight.

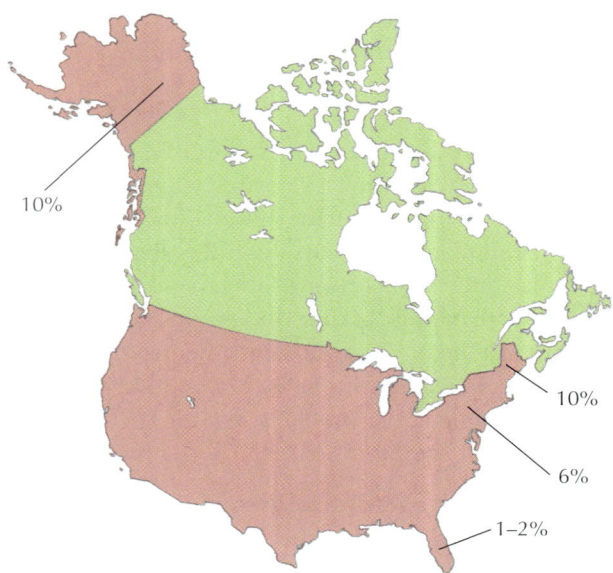

Rates of seasonal affective disorder, by latitude

● **FIGURE 12.12** Seasonal affective disorder appears to be related to reduced exposure to daylight during the winter. SAD affects 1 to 2 percent of Florida's population, about 6 percent of the people living in Maryland and New York City, and nearly 10 percent of the residents of New Hampshire and Alaska (Booker & Hellekson, 1992).

Seasonal depressions are related to the release of more melatonin during the winter. This hormone, which is secreted by the pineal gland in the brain, regulates the body's response to changing light conditions (Wehr et al., 2001). That's why 80 percent of SAD patients can be helped by extra doses of bright light, a remedy called phototherapy (● Fig. 12.13). **Phototherapy** involves exposing SAD patients to one or more hours of very bright fluorescent light each day (Neumeister, 2004). This is best done early in the morning, where it simulates dawn in the summer (Avery et al., 2001). For many SAD sufferers a hearty dose of morning "sunshine" appears to be the next best thing to vacationing in the tropics.

● **FIGURE 12.13** An hour or more of bright light a day can dramatically reduce the symptoms of seasonal affective disorder. Treatment is usually necessary from fall through spring. Light therapy typically works best when it is used early in the morning (Lewy et al., 1998).

Disorders in Perspective— Psychiatric Labeling

As we conclude our survey of psychological disorders, a caution is in order. The terms we have reviewed in this chapter aid communication about human problems. But if used carelessly, they can hurt people. Everyone has felt or acted "crazy" during brief periods of stress or high emotion. People with psychological disorders have problems that are more severe or long lasting than most of us experience. Otherwise, they may not be that different from you or me.

A fascinating classic study carried out by psychologist David Rosenhan illustrates the impact of psychiatric labeling. Rosenhan and several colleagues had themselves committed to mental hospitals with a diagnosis of "schizophrenia" (Rosenhan, 1973). After being admitted, each of these "pseudo-patients" dropped all pretense of mental illness. Yet, even though they acted completely normal, none of the researchers was ever recognized by hospital *staff* as a phony patient. Real patients were not so easily fooled. It was not unusual for a patient to say to one of the researchers, "You're not crazy, you're checking up on the hospital!" or "You're a journalist."

To record his observations, Rosenhan took notes by carefully jotting things on a small piece of paper hidden in his hand. However, he soon learned that stealth was totally unnecessary. Rosenhan simply walked around with a clipboard, recording observations. No one questioned this behavior. Rosenhan's note taking was just regarded as a symptom of his "illness." This observation clarifies why staff members failed to detect the fake patients. Because they were in a mental ward and because they had been *labeled* schizophrenic, anything the pseudo-patients did was seen as a symptom of psychopathology.

As Rosenhan's study shows, it is far better to label *problems* than to label people. Think of the difference in impact between saying, "You are experiencing a serious psychological disorder" and saying, "You're a schizophrenic." Which statement would you prefer to have said about yourself?

Social Stigma

An added problem with psychiatric labeling is that it frequently leads to prejudice and discrimination. That is, the mentally ill in our culture are often *stigmatized* (rejected and disgraced). People who have been labeled mentally ill (at any time in their lives) are less likely to be hired. They also tend to be denied housing, and they are more likely to be falsely accused of crimes. Thus, people who are grappling with mental illness may be harmed as much by social stigma as they are by their immediate psychological problems (Corrigan & Penn, 1999).

A Look Ahead Treatments for psychological problems range from counseling and psychotherapy to mental hospitalization and drug therapy. Because they vary greatly, a complete discussion of therapies is found in the next chapter. For now, it's worth noting that many milder mental disorders can be treated successfully. Even major disorders may respond well to drugs and other techniques. It is wrong to fear "former mental patients" or to exclude them from work, friendships, and other social situations. A struggle with major depression or a psychotic episode does not inevitably lead to lifelong dysfunction. Too often, however, it does lead to unnecessary rejection based on groundless fears (Sarason & Sarason, 2005).

Let's conclude with a look at a widely misunderstood problem: By the time you finish reading this page, someone in the United States will have attempted suicide. What can be done about suicide? The upcoming "Psychology in Action" module provides some answers.

MODULE 12.4 Summary

What are mood disorders? What causes depression?

- Mood disorders primarily involve disturbances of mood or emotion, producing manic or depressive states. Severe mood disorders may include psychotic features.
- In a dysthymic disorder, depression is long lasting, though moderate. In a cyclothymic disorder, people suffer from long-lasting, though moderate, swings between depression and elation.
- Bipolar disorders combine mania and depression. In a bipolar I disorder the person swings between severe mania and severe depression. In a bipolar II disorder the person is mostly depressed but has had periods of mild mania.
- A major depressive disorder involves extreme sadness and despondency but no signs of mania.
- Major mood disorders are partially explained by genetic vulnerability and changes in brain chemistry. Other important factors are loss, anger, learned helplessness, stress, and self-defeating thinking patterns.
- Many women experience a brief period of depression, called the maternity blues, shortly after giving birth. Some women suffer from a more serious and lasting condition called postpartum depression.
- Seasonal affective disorder (SAD), which occurs during the winter months, is another common form of depression. SAD is typically treated with phototherapy.

Phototherapy A treatment for seasonal affective disorder that involves exposure to bright, full-spectrum light.

KNOWLEDGE BUILDER

Mood Disorders

Recite

1. Dysthymic disorder is to depression as cyclothymic disorder is to manic-depression. T or F?
2. Major mood disorders, especially bipolar disorders, often appear to be endogenous. T or F?
3. Learned helplessness is emphasized by _____ theories of depression.
   a. humanistic
   b. biological
   c. behaviorist
   d. psychoanalytic
4. The fact that lithium carbonate is effective in treating some cases of bipolar depression suggests that the causes of bipolar disorders are at least partly _____.
   a. biological
   b. existential
   c. environmental
   d. exogenous
5. Roughly 13 percent of all new mothers experience the maternity blues, which are the first stage of postpartum depression. T or F?
6. Depression that occurs only in the winter is likely to be classified as
   a. SAD
   b. PTSD
   c. bipolar
   d. endogenous

Reflect
Critical Thinking

7. How might relationships contribute to the higher rates of depression experienced by women?

Relate

On a piece of paper write "Bipolar Disorders" and "Depressive Disorders." How much of Table 12.6 can you fill in under these headings? Keep reviewing until you can recreate the table (in your own words).

Link

Internet addresses frequently change. To find the sites listed here, visit **http://www.thomsonedu.com/psychology/coon** for an updated list of Internet addresses and direct links to relevant sites.

- **Depression** Take a depression test and find out more about depression.
- **Bipolar Disorder** Read more about bipolar disorder.
- **Seasonal Affective Disorder** Explore the website of the Seasonal Affective Disorder Association.

ANSWERS

1. T 2. T 3. c 4. a 5. F 6. a 7. Women tend to be more focused on relationships than men are. When listing the stresses in their lives, depressed women consistently report higher rates of relationship problems, such as loss of a friend, spouse, or lover, problems getting along with others, and illnesses suffered by people they care about. Depressed men tend to mention issues such as job loss, legal problems, or work problems (Kendler, Thornton, & Prescott, 2001).

MODULE **Psychology in Action**

12.5 Suicide–Lives on the Brink

SURVEY QUESTIONS: *Why do people commit suicide? Can suicide be prevented?*

"Suicide: A permanent solution to a temporary problem."

We tend to be very concerned about the high rates of murder in North America. Yet for every 3 people who die by homicide, 5 will kill themselves. And there may be as many as 25 attempts for every "successful" suicide (NIMH, 2003). Sooner or later you are likely to be affected by the suicide attempt of someone you know.

What factors affect suicide rates? Suicide rates vary greatly, but some general patterns do emerge.

Gender Men are "better" at suicide than women. Four times as many men as women *complete* suicide, but women make more attempts (NIMH, 2006b). Male suicide attempts are more lethal because men typically use a gun or an equally fatal method (Garland & Zigler, 1993). Women most often attempt a drug overdose, so there's a better chance of help arriving before death occurs. Sadly, women are beginning to use more deadly methods and may soon equal men in their likelihood of death by suicide.

Ethnicity Suicide rates vary dramatically from country to country. The rate in the United States is almost 10 times higher than the rate in Azerbaijan and, in turn, the rate in Hungary is more than 3 times the U.S. rate (Lester & Yang, 2005). Within the United States, Caucasians generally have higher suicide rates than do non-Caucasians (● Fig. 12.14), although rates have increased among African Americans in recent years (Griffin-Fennell & Williams, 2006). Sadly, the suicide rate among Native Americans is the highest in the country (suicide rates are equally high among the aboriginal peoples of Australia and New Zealand) (McKenzie, Serfaty, & Crawford, 2003).

Age Suicide rates increase with advancing age. More than half of all suicide victims are over 45 years old. (See Fig. 12.14.) White males 65 years and older are particularly at risk. Of particular concern is the rate of suicide among younger people. Between 1950 and 1990, suicide rates for adolescents and young adults doubled (Durand & Barlow, 2006). Among college students, suicide is the second leading cause of death (Jamison, 2001). School is a factor in some suicides, but only in the sense that suicidal students were not living up to their own extremely high standards. Many were good students. Other important factors in student suicide are cocaine or alcohol use (Garlow, Purselle, & Heninger, 2007), chronic health problems (real or imagined), and interpersonal difficulties (some who commit suicide are rejected lovers, but others are simply withdrawn and friendless people).

Marital Status Marriage (when successful) may be the best natural guard against suicidal

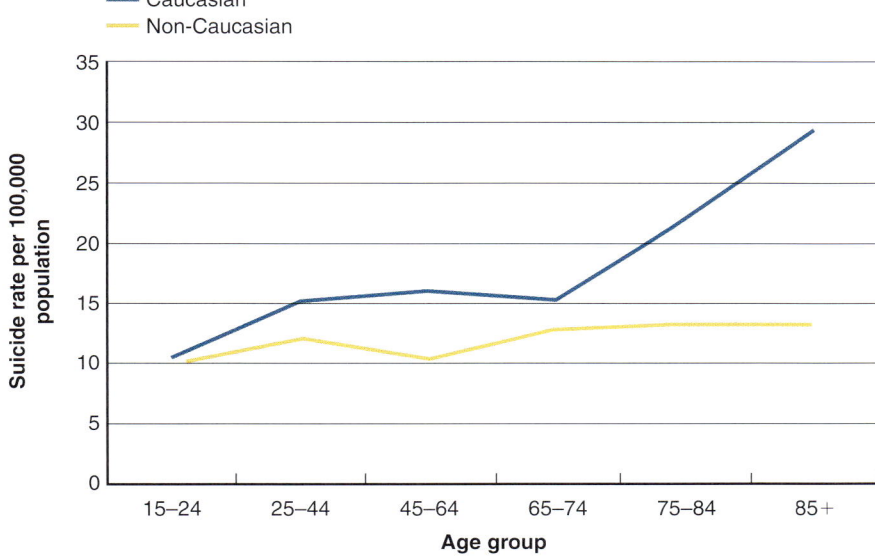

● **FIGURE 12.14** In the United States, suicide rates for Caucasians are higher than those for non-Caucasians. Also, older people have higher suicide rates than younger people (CDC, 2003).

impulses. Married individuals have lower rates than the divorced, the widowed, and single persons (Yip & Thorburn, 2004).

Immediate Causes of Suicide

Why do people try to kill themselves? The best explanation for suicide may simply come from a look at the conditions that precede it. A diagnosable mental disorder (usually depression or substance abuse disorder) is a factor in 90 percent of all suicides (NIMH, 2006b). Suicidal people usually have a history of trouble with family, a lover, or a spouse. Often they have drinking or drug abuse problems, sexual adjustment problems, or job difficulties.

The following are all major *risk factors* for suicide (NIMH, 2003; Rudd, Joiner, Jr., & Rajab, 2001): Drug or alcohol abuse; a prior suicide attempt; depression or other mood disorder; feelings of hopelessness or worthlessness; antisocial, impulsive, or aggressive behavior; severe anxiety; panic attacks; a family history of suicidal behavior; shame, humiliation, failure, or rejection; and the availability of a firearm.

Typically, suicidal people isolate themselves from others; feel worthless, helpless, and misunderstood; and want to die. An extremely negative self-image and severe feelings of *hopelessness* are warnings that the risk of suicide is very high (Beck et al., 1990; Heisel, Flett, & Hewitt, 2003). However, a long history of such conditions is not always necessary to produce a desire for suicide. Anyone may temporarily reach a state of depression severe enough to attempt suicide. Most dangerous for the average person are times of divorce, separation, rejection, failure, and bereavement. Each situation can seem intolerable and motivate an intense desire to die, to escape, or to obtain relief (Boergers, Spirito, & Donaldson, 1998). For young people, feelings of anger and hostility add to the danger. When the impulse to harm others is turned inward, the risk of suicide increases dramatically (Jamison, 2001).

Preventing Suicide

Is it true that people who talk about or threaten suicide are rarely the ones who try it? No, this is a major fallacy. Of every 10 potential suicides, 8 give warning beforehand. A person who threatens suicide should be taken seriously (● Fig. 12.15). A suicidal person may say nothing more than "I feel sometimes like I'd be better off dead." Warnings may also come indirectly. If a friend gives you a favorite ring and says, "Here, I won't be needing this anymore," or comments, "I guess I won't get my watch fixed—it doesn't matter anyway," it may be a plea for help.

● **FIGURE 12.15** Suicidal behavior usually progresses from suicidal thoughts, to threats, to attempts. A person is unlikely to make an attempt without first making threats. Thus, suicide threats should be taken seriously (Garland & Zigler, 1993).

The warning signs in the list that follows, especially if they are observed in combination, can signal an impending suicide attempt (Leenaars, Lester, & Wenckstern, 2005; Slaby, Garfinkel, & Garfinkel, 1994):

- Withdrawal from contact with others
- Sudden swings in mood
- Recent occurrence of life crisis or emotional shock
- Personality change
- Gift giving of prized possessions
- Depression/hopelessness
- Aggression and/or risk taking
- Single-car accident
- Preoccupation with death
- Drug use
- Death imagery in art
- Direct threats to commit suicide

Is it true that suicide can't be prevented, that the person will find a way to do it anyway? No. Suicide attempts usually come when a person is alone, depressed, and unable to view matters objectively. You *should* intervene if someone seems to be threatening suicide.

It is estimated that about two thirds of all suicide attempts are made by people who do not really want to die. Almost a third more are *ambivalent* or undecided about dying. Only 3 to 5 percent of suicide cases involve people who really want to die. Most people, therefore, are relieved when someone comes to their aid. Remember that suicide is almost always a cry for help and that you *can* help. As suicide expert Edwin Shneidman (1987a) puts it, "Suicidal behavior is often a form of communication, a cry for help born out of pain, with clues and messages of suffering and anguish and pleas for response."

How to Help

What is the best thing to do if someone hints they are thinking about suicide? It helps to know some of the common characteristics of suicidal thoughts and feelings (Leenaars, Lester, & Wenckstern, 2005; Shneidman, 1987b):

1. **Escape.** At times, everyone feels like running away from an upsetting situation. Running away from

home, quitting school, abandoning a marriage—these are all departures. Suicide, of course, is the ultimate escape. It helps when suicidal persons see that the natural wish for escape doesn't have to be expressed by ending it all.

2. **Unbearable psychological pain.** Emotional pain is what the suicidal person is seeking to escape. A goal of anyone hoping to prevent suicide should be to reduce the pain in any way possible. Ask the person, "Where does it hurt?" Suicide occurs when pain exceeds a person's resources for coping with pain.
3. **Frustrated psychological needs.** Often, suicide can be prevented if a distressed person's frustrated needs can be identified and eased. Is the person deeply frustrated in his or her search for love, achievement, trust, security, or friendship?
4. **Constriction of options.** The suicidal person feels helpless and decides that death is the *only* solution. The person has narrowed all his or her options solely to death. The rescuer's goal, then, is to help broaden the person's perspective. Even when all the choices are unpleasant, suicidal persons can usually be made to see that their *least unpleasant option* is better than death.

Knowing these patterns will give some guidance in talking to a suicidal person. In addition, your most important task may be to establish *rapport* (a harmonious connection) with the person. You should offer support, acceptance, and legitimate caring.

Remember that a suicidal person feels misunderstood. Try to accept and understand the feelings the person is expressing. Acceptance should also extend to the idea of suicide itself. It is completely acceptable to ask, "Are you thinking of suicide?"

Establishing communication with suicidal persons may be enough to carry them through a difficult time. You may also find it helpful to get day-by-day commitments from them to meet for lunch, share a ride, and the like. Let the person know you *expect* her or him to be there. Such commitments, even though small, can be enough to tip the scales when a person is alone and thinking about suicide.

Don't end your efforts too soon. A dangerous time for suicide is when a person suddenly seems to get better after a severe depression. This often means the person has finally decided to end it all. The improvement in mood is deceptive because it comes from an anticipation that suffering is about to end.

Crisis Intervention

Most cities have mental health crisis intervention teams or centers for suicide prevention. Both have staff members trained to talk with suicidal persons over the phone. Give a person who seems to be suicidal the number of one of these services. Urge the person to call you or the other number if she or he becomes frightened or impulsive. Or better yet, help the person make an appointment to get psychological treatment (Weishaar, 2006).

The preceding applies mainly to persons who are having mild suicidal thoughts. If a person actually threatens suicide, or if a suicide attempt seems to be imminent, don't worry about overreacting. Immediately seek professional assistance by calling the police, crisis intervention, or a rescue unit. If that is infeasible, ask how the person plans to carry out the suicide. A person who has a *specific, workable plan* and the means to carry it out should be asked to accompany you to the emergency ward of a hospital.

Needless to say, you should call immediately if a person is in the act of attempting suicide or if a drug has already been taken. The majority of suicide attempts come at temporary low points in a person's life and may never be repeated. Get involved—you may save a life!

MODULE 12.5 Psychology in Action Summary

Why do people commit suicide? Can suicide be prevented?

- Suicide is a relatively frequent cause of death that can, in many cases, be prevented.
- Suicide is statistically related to such factors as age, gender, and marital status.
- In individual cases, the potential for suicide is best identified by a desire to escape, unbearable psychological pain, and frustrated psychological needs.
- People contemplating suicide narrow their options until death seems like the only way out.
- The impulse to attempt suicide is usually temporary. Efforts to prevent suicide are worthwhile.

KNOWLEDGE BUILDER

Suicide and Suicide Prevention

Recite

1. More women than men use guns in their suicide attempts. T or F?
2. Although the overall suicide rate has remained about the same, there has been a decrease in adolescent suicides. T or F?
3. Suicide is equally a problem in all countries. T or F?
4. The highest suicide rates are found among the divorced. T or F?
5. The majority (two thirds) of suicide attempts are made by people who do not really want to die. T or F?
6. The risk that a person may attempt suicide is greatest if the person has
   a. a concrete, workable plan
   b. had a recent life crisis
   c. withdrawn from contact with others
   d. frustrated psychological needs

Reflect
Critical Thinking

7. If you follow the history of popular music, see if you can answer this question: What two major risk factors contributed to the 1994 suicide of Kurt Cobain, lead singer for the rock group Nirvana?

Relate

You're working a suicide hotline and you take a call from a very distressed young man. What risk factors will you look for as he tells you about his anguish?

What are the common characteristics of suicidal thoughts and feelings identified by Edwin Shneidman? If a friend of yours were to express any of these thoughts or feelings, how would you respond?

Link

Internet addresses frequently change. To find the sites listed here, visit **http://www.thomsonedu.com/psychology/coon** for an updated list of Internet addresses and direct links to relevant sites.

- **Suicide** Read all about suicide at suicide.org.
- **Suicide Prevention** Explore the website of the American Foundation for Suicide Prevention.
- **Are You Worried About a Friend or Loved One?** Visit this website if you are worried about someone near to you committing suicide.

ANSWERS

1. F 2. F 3. F 4. T 5. T 6. a 7. Drug or alcohol abuse and availability of a firearm.

Interactive Learning

 Psychology: Active Learning Modules Book Companion Website

http://www.thomsonedu.com/psychology/coon

Visit your Book Companion Website, where you will find flash cards, practice quizzes, Internet links, and more to help you study.

ThomsonNOW

Just What You Need to Know NOW!

Spend time on what you need to master rather than on information you already have learned. Take a pre-test for this chapter, and ThomsonNOW will generate a personalized study plan based on your results. The study plan will identify the topics you need to review and direct you to online resources to help you master those topics. You can then take a post-test to help you determine the concepts you have mastered and what you will need to work on. Try it out! Go to www.thomsonedu.com/login to sign in with an access code or to purchase access to this product.

13 Therapies

MODULE 13.1 Psychotherapy and Psychoanalysis
SURVEY QUESTION: How do psychotherapies differ?
SURVEY QUESTION: How did psychotherapy originate?
SURVEY QUESTION: Is Freudian psychoanalysis still used?

MODULE 13.2 Insight Therapies
SURVEY QUESTION: What are the major humanistic therapies?
SURVEY QUESTION: Can therapy be conducted at a distance?

MODULE 13.3 Behavior Therapy
SURVEY QUESTIONS: What is behavior therapy? How is behavior therapy used to treat phobias, fears, and anxieties?

MODULE 13.4 Operant Therapies and Cognitive Therapies
SURVEY QUESTION: What role does reinforcement play in behavior therapy?
SURVEY QUESTION: Can therapy change thoughts and emotions?

MODULE 13.5 Group Therapy, Therapy Skills, and Medical Therapies
SURVEY QUESTION: Can psychotherapy be done with groups of people?
SURVEY QUESTION: What do various therapies have in common?
SURVEY QUESTION: How do psychiatrists treat psychological disorders?

MODULE 13.6 Psychology in Action: Self-Management and Seeking Professional Help
SURVEY QUESTION: How are behavioral principles applied to everyday problems?
SURVEY QUESTION: How can a person find professional help?

Cold Terror on a Warm Afternoon

The warm Arizona sun was shining brightly. Outside, an assortment of small birds sang sweetly. Susan's psychology professor could hear them between her frightened sobs.

As psychologists, we meet many students with personal problems. Still, Susan's teacher was surprised to see her at his office door. Her excellent work in class and her healthy, casual appearance left him unprepared for her first words. "I feel like I'm losing my mind," she said. "Can I talk to you?"

In the next hour, Susan described her own personal hell. Her calm appearance hid a world of crippling fear, anxiety, and depression. At work, she was deathly afraid of talking to coworkers and customers. Her social phobia led to frequent absenteeism and embarrassing behavior. At each job she held, it was only a matter of time until she got fired.

At school Susan felt "different" and was sure that other students could tell she was "weird." Several disastrous romances had left her terrified of men. Lately she had been so depressed that she thought of suicide. Often, she became terrified for no apparent reason. Each time, her heart pounded wildly and she felt that she was about to completely lose control.

Susan's request for help was an important turning point. Emotional conflicts had made her existence a nightmare. At a time when she was becoming her own worst enemy, Susan realized she needed help from another person. In Susan's case, that person was a talented psychologist to whom her teacher referred her. With psychotherapy, the psychologist was able to help Susan come to grips with her emotions and regain her balance.

This chapter discusses methods used to alleviate problems like Susan's. First we will describe therapies that emphasize the value of gaining *insight* into personal problems. Then we will focus on *behavior therapies* and *cognitive therapies*, which directly change troublesome actions and thoughts. Later we will conclude with *medical therapies*, which are based on psychiatric drugs and other physical treatments.

© Hank Morgan/Rainbow

MODULE 13.1 Psychotherapy and Psychoanalysis

FORTUNATELY, the odds are that you will *not* experience an emotional problem like Susan's. But if you did, what help is available? In most cases, it would be some form of psychotherapy. This module introduces several basic types of therapy and provides a brief history of mental health care. It concludes with a discussion of psychoanalysis, the first fully developed psychotherapy.

Psychotherapy—Getting Better by the Hour

SURVEY QUESTION: *How do psychotherapies differ?*

Psychotherapy refers to any psychological technique that can bring about positive changes in personality, behavior, or personal adjustment. In most cases, psychotherapy is based on a dialogue between therapists and their clients. Some therapists also use learning principles to directly alter troublesome behaviors.

Therapists have many approaches to choose from: psychoanalysis, desensitization, Gestalt therapy, client-centered therapy, cognitive therapy, and behavior therapy—to name but a few. As we will see, each therapy emphasizes different concepts and methods. For this reason, the best approach for a particular person or problem may vary (Trull, 2005).

Dimensions of Therapy

The terms listed here describe basic aspects of various therapies (Sharf, 2008). Notice that more than one term may apply to a particular therapy. For example, it is possible to have a directive, action-oriented group therapy or a nondirective, individual, insight-oriented therapy.

- **Individual therapy:** A therapy involving only one client and one therapist.
- **Group therapy:** A therapy session in which several clients participate at the same time.
- **Insight therapy:** Any psychotherapy whose goal is to lead clients to a deeper understanding of their thoughts, emotions, and behavior.
- **Action therapy:** Any therapy designed to bring about direct changes in troublesome thoughts, habits, feelings, or behavior, without seeking insight into their origins or meanings.
- **Directive therapy:** Any approach in which the therapist provides strong guidance.
- **Nondirective therapy:** A style of therapy in which clients assume responsibility for solving their own problems; the therapist assists but does not guide or give advice.
- **Time-limited therapy:** Any therapy begun with the expectation that it will last only a limited number of sessions.
- **Supportive therapy:** An approach in which the therapist's goal is to offer support, rather than to promote personal change. A person trying to get through an emotional crisis or one who wants to solve day-to-day problems may benefit from supportive therapy.
- **Positive therapy:** Techniques designed to enhance personal strengths, rather than "fix" weaknesses.

Myths Psychotherapy has been depicted as a complete personal transformation—a sort of "major overhaul" of the psyche. But therapy is *not* equally effective for all problems. Chances of improvement are fairly good for phobias, low self-esteem, some sexual problems, and marital conflicts. More complex problems can be difficult to solve. For many people, the major benefit of therapy is that it provides comfort, support, and a way to make constructive changes (Bloch, 2006; Hellerstein et al., 1998).

In short, it is often unrealistic to expect psychotherapy to undo a person's entire past. Yet even when problems are severe, therapy may help a person gain a new perspective or learn behaviors to better cope with life. Psychotherapy can be hard work for both clients and therapists. But when it succeeds, few activities are more worthwhile.

It's also a mistake to think that psychotherapy is only used to solve problems or end a crisis. Even if a person is already doing well, therapy can be a way to promote personal growth (Bloch, 2006). Therapists in the positive psychology movement are developing ways to help people make use of their personal strengths. Rather than trying to fix what is "wrong" with a person, they seek to nurture positive traits and actively solve problems (Compton, 2005). ■ Table 13.1 lists some of the elements of positive mental health that therapists seek to restore or promote.

Origins of Therapy—Bored Skulls and Hysteria on the Couch

SURVEY QUESTION: *How did psychotherapy originate?*

Early treatments for mental problems give good reasons to appreciate modern therapies (Sharf, 2008). Archaeological findings dating to the Stone Age suggest that most primitive

TABLE 13.1 Elements of Positive Mental Health

- Personal autonomy and independence
- A sense of identity
- Feelings of personal worth
- Skilled interpersonal communication
- Sensitivity, nurturance, and trust
- Genuine and honest with self and others
- Self-control and personal responsibility
- Committed and loving personal relationships
- Capacity to forgive others and oneself
- Personal values and a purpose in life
- Self-awareness and motivation for personal growth
- Adaptive coping strategies for managing stresses and crises
- Fulfillment and satisfaction in work
- Good habits of physical health

Source: Adapted from Bergin, 1991.

(left) Supernatural explanations attributed abnormal behavior to the work of the devil or "possession" by demons. A modern analysis of "demonic possession" suggests that some victims were suffering from schizophrenia (Mirsky & Duncan, 2005). *(right)* Many other cases of "possession" in medieval Europe and "bewitchment" in colonial New England may be explained by the psychedelic effects of ergot fungus. An ear of rye infested with the fungus (dark areas) is shown here.

approaches were marked by fear and superstitious belief in demons, witchcraft, and magic. One of the more dramatic "cures" practiced by primitive "therapists" was a process called *trepanning* (treh-PAN-ing; also sometimes spelled *trephining*). In modern usage, trepanning is any surgical procedure in which a hole is bored in the skull. In the hands of primitive therapists it meant boring, chipping, or bashing holes into a patient's head. Presumably this was done to relieve pressure or release evil spirits (● Fig. 13.1). Actually, many "patients" didn't survive the "treatment," which suggests that trepanning may have simply been an excuse to kill people who were unusual.

During the Middle Ages, treatments for mental illness in Europe focused on **demonology,** the study of demons and persons plagued by spirits. Medieval "therapists" commonly blamed abnormal behavior on supernatural forces, such as possession by the devil, or on curses from witches and wizards. As a cure, they used exorcism to "cast out evil spirits." For the fortunate, exorcism was a religious ritual. More often, physical torture was used to make the body an inhospitable place for the devil to reside. Modern analyses of "demonic possession" suggest that many victims were suffering from epilepsy, schizophrenia (Mirsky & Duncan, 2005), dissociative disorders (van der Hart, Lierens, & Goodwin, 1996), and depression (Thase, 2006).

One reason for the rise of demonology may lie in *ergotism* (AIR-got-ism), a psychotic-like condition caused by ergot poisoning. In the Middle Ages, rye (grain) fields were often infested with ergot fungus. Ergot, we now know, is a natural source of LSD and other mind-altering chemicals. Eating tainted bread could have caused symptoms that were easily mistaken for bewitchment or madness. Pinching sensations, muscle twitches, facial spasms, delirium, and hallucinations are all signs of ergot poisoning (Matossian, 1982). Thus, many people "treated" by demonologists may have been doubly victimized.

It wasn't until 1793 that the emotionally disturbed were regarded as "mentally ill" and given compassionate treatment. That was the year a French doctor named Philippe Pinel changed the Bicêtre Asylum in Paris from a squalid "madhouse" into a mental hospital by unchaining the inmates

● **FIGURE 13.1** Primitive "treatment" for mental disorders sometimes took the form of boring a hole in the skull. This example shows signs of healing, which means the patient survived the treatment. Many didn't.

Psychotherapy Any psychological technique used to facilitate positive changes in a person's personality, behavior, or adjustment.

Demonology In medieval Europe, the study of demons and the treatment of persons "possessed" by demons.

(left) Many early asylums were no more than prisons with inmates held in chains. *(right)* One late-nineteenth-century "treatment" was based on swinging the patient in a harness—presumably to calm the patient's nerves.

(Harris, 2003). Although it has been more than 200 years since Pinel began humane treatment, the process of improving care continues today.

When was psychotherapy developed? The first true psychotherapy was created by Sigmund Freud more than 100 years ago (Jacobs, 2003). As a physician in Vienna, Freud was intrigued by cases of *hysteria*. People suffering from hysteria have physical symptoms (such as paralysis or numbness) for which no physical causes can be found. (Such problems are now called somatoform disorders, as discussed in Module 12.2.) Slowly, Freud became convinced that hysteria was related to deeply hidden unconscious conflicts. Based on this insight, Freud developed a therapy called *psychoanalysis*. Because it is the "granddaddy" of more modern therapies, let us examine psychoanalysis in some detail.

Psychoanalysis—Expedition into the Unconscious

SURVEY QUESTION: *Is Freudian psychoanalysis still used?*

Isn't psychoanalysis the therapy where the patient lies on a couch? Freud's patients usually reclined on a couch during therapy, while Freud sat out of sight taking notes and offering interpretations. This procedure was supposed to encourage a free flow of thoughts and images from the unconscious. However, it is the least important element of psychoanalysis and many modern analysts have abandoned it.

How did Freud treat emotional problems? Freud's theory stressed that "neurosis" and "hysteria" are caused by repressed memories, motives, and conflicts—particularly those stemming from instinctual drives for sex and aggression. Although they are hidden, these forces remain active in the personality, and they cause some people to develop rigid ego defenses and compulsive, self-defeating behavior. Thus, the main goal of **psychoanalysis** is to reduce internal conflicts that lead to emotional suffering (Marcus, 2002).

Freud developed on four basic techniques to uncover the unconscious roots of neurosis (Freud, 1949). These are *free association, dream analysis, analysis of resistance,* and *analysis of transference.*

Free Association Saying whatever comes to mind is the basis for **free association.** Patients must speak without worrying whether ideas are painful, embarrassing, or illogical. Thoughts are simply allowed to move freely from one idea to the next, without self-censorship. The purpose of free association is to lower defenses so that unconscious thoughts and feelings can emerge (Hoffer & Youngren, 2004).

Dream Analysis Freud believed that dreams provide a "royal road to the unconscious" because they freely express forbidden desires and unconscious feelings (Rock, 2004). Such feelings are found in the **latent content** (hidden, symbolic meaning) of dreams. Normally, we only remember a dream's **manifest content** (obvious, visible meaning), which tends to disguise information from the unconscious.

Freud was especially interested in unconscious messages revealed by **dream symbols** (images that have personal or

Pioneering psychotherapist Sigmund Freud's famous couch.

emotional meanings). Let's say a young man reports a dream in which he pulls a pistol from his waistband and aims at a target while his wife watches. The pistol repeatedly fails to discharge, and the man's wife laughs at him. Freud might have seen this as an indication of repressed feelings of sexual impotence, with the gun serving as a disguised image of the penis.

Analysis of Resistance When free associating or describing dreams, patients may *resist* talking about or thinking about certain topics. Such **resistances** (blockages in the flow of ideas) reveal particularly important unconscious conflicts. As analysts become aware of resistances, they bring them to the patient's awareness so the patient can deal with them realistically. Rather than being roadblocks in therapy, resistances can be challenges and guides (Engle & Arkowitz, 2006).

Analysis of Transference **Transference** is the tendency to "transfer" feelings to a therapist that match those the patient had for important persons in his or her past. At times, the patient may act as if the analyst is a rejecting father, an unloving or overprotective mother, or a former lover, for example. As the patient re-experiences repressed emotions, the therapist can help the patient recognize and understand them. Troubled persons often provoke anger, rejection, boredom, criticism, and other negative reactions from others. Effective therapists learn to avoid reacting as others do and playing the patient's habitual resistance and transference "games." This, too, contributes to therapeutic change (Marcus, 2002).

Psychoanalysis Today

What is the status of psychoanalysis today? Traditional psychoanalysis called for three to five therapy sessions a week, often for many years. Today, most patients are only seen once or twice per week, but treatment may still go on for years (Friedman et al., 1998). Because of the huge amounts of time and money this requires, psychoanalysts have become relatively rare. Nevertheless, psychoanalysis made a major contribution to modern therapies by highlighting the importance of unconscious conflicts (Friedman, 2006).

Many therapists have switched to doing **brief psychodynamic therapy,** which uses direct questioning to reveal unconscious conflicts (Binder, 2004). Modern therapists also actively provoke emotional reactions that will lower defenses and provide insights (Davanloo, 1995). Interestingly, brief therapy seems to accelerate recovery. Patients seem to realize that they need to get to the heart of their problems quickly (Messer & Kaplan, 2004).

Interpersonal Psychotherapy (IPT) One example of a brief dynamic psychotherapy is **interpersonal psychotherapy,** which was first developed to help people with depression by improving their relationships with others (Trull, 2005). Extensive empirical research has since confirmed the effectiveness of IPT in treating depressive disorders (de Mello, et al., 2005). It has also been used to help people with eating and substance abuse disorders, social phobias, and personality disorders (Hoffart, 2005; Markowitz, 2005; Trull, 2005).

Liona's therapy is a good example of IPT (Brown & Barlow, 2007). She was suffering from a depression that through her therapy she traced back to conflict between her mother and her father. When her father was absent, Liona adopted the role of her mother's protector and friend, but when her father was around she was expected to resume her role as "the daughter." She was angry with her father for abandoning her mother so frequently and upset at having to switch roles so often. Liona's IPT sessions (which sometimes included her mother) focused on clarifying Liona's family roles. She improved a lot after her mother urged her to stick to being "herself."

Is Traditional Psychoanalysis Effective? The development of newer, more streamlined dynamic therapies is in part due to questions about whether traditional psychoanalysis "works." In a classic criticism, Hans Eysenck (1994) suggested that psychoanalysis simply takes so long that patients experience a *spontaneous remission* of symptoms (improvement due to the mere passage of time). How could we tell if a particular therapy, or the passage of time, is responsible for a person's improvement? Typically, some patients are randomly assigned for treatment, and others are placed on a waiting list. If members of this *waiting-list control group,* who

---

Psychoanalysis A Freudian therapy that emphasizes the use of free association, dream interpretation, resistances, and transference to uncover unconscious conflicts.

Free association In psychoanalysis, the technique of having a client say anything that comes to mind, regardless of how embarrassing or unimportant it may seem.

Latent dream content The hidden or symbolic meaning of a dream, as revealed by dream interpretation and analysis.

Manifest dream content The surface, "visible" content of a dream; dream images as they are remembered by the dreamer.

Dream symbols Images in dreams whose personal or emotional meanings differ from their literal meanings.

Resistance A blockage in the flow of free association; topics the client resists thinking or talking about.

Transference The tendency of patients to transfer feelings to a therapist that correspond to those the patient had for important persons in his or her past.

Brief psychodynamic therapy A modern therapy based on psychoanalytic theory but designed to produce insights more quickly.

Interpersonal psychotherapy (IPT) A brief dynamic psychotherapy designed to help people by improving their relationships with other people.

receive no treatment, improve at the same rate as those in therapy, the therapy may be of little value.

How seriously should the possibility of spontaneous remission be taken? It's true that problems ranging from hyperactivity to anxiety improve with the passage of time. However, researchers have confirmed that psychoanalysis does, in fact, produce improvement in a majority of patients (Doidge, 1997).

The real value of Eysenck's critique is that it encouraged psychologists to try new ideas and techniques. Researchers began to ask: "When psychoanalysis works, why does it work? Which parts of it are essential and which are unnecessary?" Modern therapists have given surprisingly varied answers to these questions. Upcoming sections will acquaint you with some of the therapies currently in use.

MODULE 13.1 Summary

How do psychotherapies differ?
- Psychotherapy facilitates positive changes in personality, behavior, or adjustment.
- Psychotherapies may be classified as insight, action, directive, nondirective, supportive, or positive therapies or combinations of these.
- Therapies may be conducted either individually or in groups, and they may be time limited.

How did psychotherapy originate?
- Early approaches to mental illness were dominated by superstition and moral condemnation.
- Demonology attributed mental disturbance to supernatural forces, such as demonic possession, and prescribed exorcism as the cure.
- In some instances, the actual cause of bizarre behavior may have been ergot poisoning.
- More humane treatment began in 1793 with the work of Philippe Pinel in Paris.

Is Freudian psychoanalysis still used?
- As the first true psychotherapy, Freud's psychoanalysis gave rise to modern psychodynamic therapies.
- Psychoanalysis seeks to reveal unconscious thoughts, emotions, and conflicts.
- The psychoanalyst uses free association, dream analysis, and analysis of resistance and transference to reveal health-producing insights.
- Brief psychodynamic therapy (which relies on psychoanalytic theory but is brief and focused) is as effective as other major therapies. One example is interpersonal psychotherapy.
- Some critics argue that traditional psychoanalysis receives credit for spontaneous remissions of symptoms. However, psychoanalysis is successful for many patients.

KNOWLEDGE BUILDER

Psychotherapy and Psychoanalysis

Recite

Match:

____ 1. Directive therapies
____ 2. Action therapies
____ 3. Insight therapies
____ 4. Nondirective therapies

A. Change behavior
B. Place responsibility on the client
C. The client is guided strongly
D. Seek understanding

5. An approach that is incompatible with insight therapy is
   a. individual therapy
   b. action therapy
   c. nondirective therapy
   d. interpersonal psychotherapy

6. A scientific explanation of medieval "possessions" by "demons" is related to the effects of
   a. ergot poisoning
   b. trepanning
   c. exorcism
   d. unconscious transference

7. Pinel is famous for his use of exorcism. T or F?

8. In psychoanalysis, an emotional attachment to the therapist is called:
   a. free association
   b. manifest association
   c. resistance
   d. transference

Reflect

Critical Thinking

9. Waiting-list control groups help separate the effects of therapy from improvement related to the mere passage of time. What other type of control group might be needed to learn if therapy is truly beneficial?

Relate

How has your understanding of psychotherapy changed? How many types of therapy can you name?

Make a list describing what you think it means to be mentally healthy. How well does your list match the items in Table 13.1?

The use of trepanning, demonology, and exorcism all implied that the mentally ill are "cursed." To what extent are the mentally ill rejected and stigmatized today?

Try to free associate (aloud) for 10 minutes. How difficult was it? Did anything interesting surface?

Can you explain, in your own words, the role of dream analysis, resistances, and transference in psychoanalysis?

Link

Internet addresses frequently change. To find the sites listed here, visit http://www.thomsonedu.com/psychology/coon for an updated list of Internet addresses and direct links to relevant sites.

- **Pre-Columbian Trephination** Read about the first psychosurgery as a treatment for mental illness.
- **Phillipe Pinel** Read about Pinel's contribution to the history of the treatment of mental illness.
- **Freud and Psychoanalysis** Read about the history of psychoanalysis.

ANSWERS

1. C 2. A 3. D 4. B 5. b 6. a 7. F 8. d 9. Placebo therapy is sometimes used to assess the benefits of real therapy. Placebo therapy superficially resembles the real thing but lacks key elements that are thought to be therapeutic.

MODULE 13.2 Insight Therapies

WHEN MOST PEOPLE PICTURE CLINICAL PSYCHOLOGISTS at work, they probably imagine them doing insight therapy. As stated earlier, insight therapists help clients gain a deeper understanding of their thoughts, emotions, and behavior. Let's sample a variety of insight-oriented approaches, including therapies done at a distance (by telephone or over the Internet).

Humanistic Therapies—Restoring Human Potential

SURVEY QUESTION: *What are the major humanistic therapies?*

Better self-knowledge was the goal of traditional psychoanalysis. However, Freud claimed that his patients could expect only to change their "hysterical misery into common unhappiness"! Humanistic therapies are more optimistic. Most assume that it is possible for people to use their potentials fully and live rich, rewarding lives. Psychotherapy is seen as a way to give mental health a chance to emerge.

Client-Centered Therapy

What is client-centered therapy? How is it different from psychoanalysis? Psychoanalysts delve into the unconscious. Psychologist Carl Rogers (1902–1987) found it more beneficial to explore *conscious* thoughts and feelings. The psychoanalyst tends to take a position of authority, stating what dreams, thoughts, or memories "mean." In contrast, Rogers believed that what is right or valuable for the therapist may be wrong for the client. (Rogers preferred the term *client* to *patient* because *patient* implies that a person is "sick" and needs to be "cured.") Consequently, the client determines what will be discussed during each session. Thus, **client-centered therapy** (also called **person-centered therapy**) is nondirective and based on insights from conscious thoughts and feelings (Brodley, 2006; Schneider, 2002).

If the client runs things, what does the therapist do? The therapist's job is to create a safe "atmosphere of growth." The therapist provides opportunities for change, but the client must actively seek to solve his or her problems. The therapist cannot "fix" the client (Whitton, 2003).

Health-Promoting Conditions Rogers believed that effective therapists maintain four basic conditions. First, the therapist offers the client **unconditional positive regard** (unshakable personal acceptance). The therapist refuses to react with shock, dismay, or disapproval to anything the client says or feels. Total acceptance by the therapist is the first step to self-acceptance by the client.

Second, the therapist attempts to achieve genuine **empathy** by trying to see the world through the client's eyes and feeling some part of what the client is feeling.

As a third essential condition, the therapist strives to be **authentic** (genuine and honest). The therapist must not hide behind a professional role. Rogers believed that phony fronts destroy the growth atmosphere sought in client-centered therapy.

Fourth, the therapist does not make interpretations, propose solutions, or offer advice. Instead, the therapist **reflects** (rephrases, summarizes, or repeats) the client's thoughts and feelings. This allows the therapist to act as a psychological "mirror" so clients can see themselves more clearly. Rogers theorized that a person armed with a realistic self-image and greater self-acceptance will gradually discover solutions to life's problems.

Existential Therapy

According to the existentialists, "being in the world" (existence) creates deep anxiety. Each of us must deal with the realities of death. We must face the fact that we create our private world by making choices. We must overcome isolation on a vast and indifferent planet. Most of all, we must confront feelings of meaninglessness.

What do these concerns have to do with psychotherapy? **Existential therapy** focuses on the problems of existence, such as meaning, choice, and responsibility. Like client-centered therapy, it promotes self-knowledge. However, there are important differences. Client-centered therapy seeks to uncover a "true self" hidden behind a screen of defenses. In contrast, existential therapy emphasizes free will, the human ability to make choices. Accordingly, existential therapists believe you can *choose to become* the person you want to be.

Existential therapists try to give clients the *courage* to make rewarding and socially constructive choices. Typically, therapy focuses on *death, freedom, isolation,* and *meaninglessness,* the "ultimate concerns" of existence (van Deurzen & Kenward, 2005). These universal human challenges include

Psychotherapist Carl Rogers, who originated client-centered therapy.

an awareness of one's mortality, the responsibility that comes with freedom to choose, being alone in your own private world, and the need to create meaning in your life.

One example of existential therapy is Victor Frankl's logotherapy, which emphasizes the need to find and maintain meaning in life. Frankl (1904–1997) based his approach on experiences he had as a prisoner in a Nazi concentration camp. In the camp, Frankl saw countless prisoners break down as they were stripped of all hope and human dignity (Frankl, 1955). Those who survived with their sanity did so because they managed to hang on to a sense of meaning (logos). Even in less dire circumstances, a sense of purpose in life adds greatly to psychological well-being (Prochaska & Norcross, 2007).

What does the existential therapist do? The therapist helps clients discover self-imposed limitations in personal identity. To be successful, the client must fully accept the challenge of changing his or her life (Bretherton & Orner, 2004). Interestingly, Buddhists seek a similar state that they call "radical acceptance" (Brach, 2003). A key aspect of existential therapy is *confrontation,* in which clients are challenged to examine their values and choices and to take responsibility for the quality of their existence (Gerwood, 1998).

An important part of confrontation is the unique, intense, here-and-now *encounter* between two human beings. When existential therapy is successful, it brings about a renewed sense of purpose and a reappraisal of what's important in life. Some clients even experience an emotional rebirth, as if they had survived a close brush with death. As Marcel Proust wrote, "The real voyage of discovery consists not in seeing new landscapes but in having new eyes."

Gestalt Therapy

Gestalt therapy is based on the idea that perception, or *awareness,* is disjointed and incomplete in maladjusted persons. The German word *Gestalt* means "whole," or "complete." **Gestalt therapy** helps people rebuild thinking, feeling, and acting into connected wholes. This is achieved by expanding personal awareness; by accepting responsibility for one's thoughts, feelings, and actions; and by filling in gaps in experience (Joyce & Sills, 2001).

What do you mean by gaps in experience? Gestalt therapists believe that we often shy away from expressing or "owning" upsetting feelings. This creates a gap in self-awareness that may become a barrier to personal growth. For example, a person who feels anger after the death of a parent might go for years without fully expressing it. This and similar threatening gaps may impair emotional health.

The Gestalt approach is more directive than client-centered or existential therapy, and it emphasizes immediate experience. Working either one-to-one or in a group setting, the Gestalt therapist encourages clients to become more aware of their moment-to-moment thoughts, perceptions, and emotions (Staemmler, 2004). Rather than discussing *why* clients feel guilt, anger, fear, or boredom, they are encouraged to have these feelings in the "here and now" and become fully aware of them. The therapist promotes awareness by drawing attention to a client's posture, voice, eye movements, and hand gestures. Clients may also be asked to exaggerate vague feelings until they become clear. Gestalt therapists believe that expressing such feelings allows people to "take care of unfinished business" and break through emotional impasses (O'Leary, 2006).

Gestalt therapy is often associated with the work of Frederick (Fritz) Perls (1969). In all his writings, Perls' basic message comes through clearly: Emotional health comes from knowing what you *want* to do, not dwelling on what you *should* do, *ought* to do, or *should want* to do (Rosenberg & Lynch, 2002). Another way of stating this idea is that emotional health comes from taking full responsibility for one's feelings and actions. For example, it means changing "I can't" to "I won't," or "I must" to "I choose to."

How does Gestalt therapy help people discover their real wants? Above all else, Gestalt therapy emphasizes *present* experience. Clients are urged to stop intellectualizing and talking *about* feelings. Instead, they learn to live now; live here; stop imagining; experience the real; stop unnecessary thinking; taste and see; express rather than explain, justify, or judge; give in to unpleasantness and pain just as to pleasure; and surrender to being as you are. Gestalt therapists believe that, paradoxically, the best way to change is to become who you really are (Joyce & Sills, 2001).

Client-centered (or person-centered) therapy A nondirective therapy based on insights gained from conscious thoughts and feelings; emphasizes accepting one's true self.

Unconditional positive regard An unqualified, unshakable acceptance of another person.

Empathy A capacity for taking another's point of view; the ability to feel what another is feeling.

Authenticity In Carl Rogers's terms, the ability of a therapist to be genuine and honest about his or her own feelings.

Reflection In client-centered therapy, the process of rephrasing or repeating thoughts and feelings expressed by clients so they can become aware of what they are saying.

Existential therapy An insight therapy that focuses on the elemental problems of existence, such as death, meaning, choice, and responsibility; emphasizes making courageous life choices.

Gestalt therapy An approach that focuses on immediate experience and awareness to help clients rebuild thinking, feeling, and acting into connected wholes; emphasizes the integration of fragmented experiences.

Because of their emphasis on verbal interaction, humanistic therapies may be conducted at a distance, by telephone, e-mail, or videoconferencing. Let's investigate this possibility.

Therapy at a Distance—Psych Jockeys and Cybertherapy

SURVEY QUESTION: *Can therapy be conducted at a distance?*

How valid are psychological services offered at a distance? For better or worse, high-tech psychotherapy and counseling are rapidly becoming commonplace (Ormay, 2006). Today, psychological services are available through radio, telephone, e-mail, Internet chat rooms, and videoconferencing (Maheu et al., 2004). What are the advantages and disadvantages of getting help at a distance?

Media Psychologists

By now you have probably heard a phone-in radio psychologist or watched one on television. On a typical program, participants describe problems arising from child abuse, loneliness, love affairs, phobias, sexual adjustment, or depression. The media psychologist then offers reassurance, advice, or suggestions for getting help. Such talk-radio and television programs may seem harmless, but they raise some important questions. For instance, is it reasonable to give advice without knowing anything about a person's background? Could the advice do harm? What good can a psychologist do in 3 minutes or even an hour?

In their own defense, media psychologists point out that listeners and viewers may learn solutions to their problems by hearing others talk. Many also stress that their work is educational, not therapeutic. Nevertheless, the question arises: When does advice become therapy? The American Psychological Association urges media psychologists to discuss problems only of a general nature, instead of actually counseling anyone. For example, if a caller complains about insomnia, the radio psychologist should talk about insomnia in general, not probe the caller's personal life.

By giving information, advice, and social support, media psychologists do help some people. The well-known media psychologist Dr. Phil McGraw has even been awarded a President's Citation from the American Psychological Association for his work in publicizing mental health issues (Meyers, 2006). Even so, a good guide for anyone tempted to call a radio psychologist or accept advice from a TV psychologist might be "let the consumer beware."

Telephone Therapists

The same caution applies to commercial telephone therapists. These "counselors" can be reached through 900-number services for $3 to $4 per minute. To date, there is no evidence that commercial telephone counseling is effective.

It's important to note, however, that legitimate therapists may use the phone to calm, console, or advise their clients between therapy sessions. Others are experimenting with actually doing therapy by telephone. For example, after the attack on the World Trade Center towers, many rescue personnel needed counseling. To fill the need, a phone network was created to link emergency workers with psychologists all over the country (Murray, 2001; Shore, 2003).

A key feature of successful face-to-face therapy is the establishment of a continuing *relationship* between two people. In this regard, telephone therapy is seriously limited by a lack of visual cues, such as facial expressions and body language (Haas, Benedict, & Kobos, 1996). Regardless, under the right circumstances, telephone therapy can be as successful as face-to-face therapy (Day & Schneider, 2002). For example, in one study, telephone counseling helped improve success rates for smokers who wanted to quit (Rabius et al., 2004). Other studies have shown that depressed people benefit from telephone therapy (Mohr et al., 2005; Simon et al., 2004).

Internet Therapy

The ever-evolving Internet has provided new communication tools, including voice, text, graphics, and video. All these tools are being used to deliver therapy. Psychological advice, support groups, self-help magazines, and even online therapy

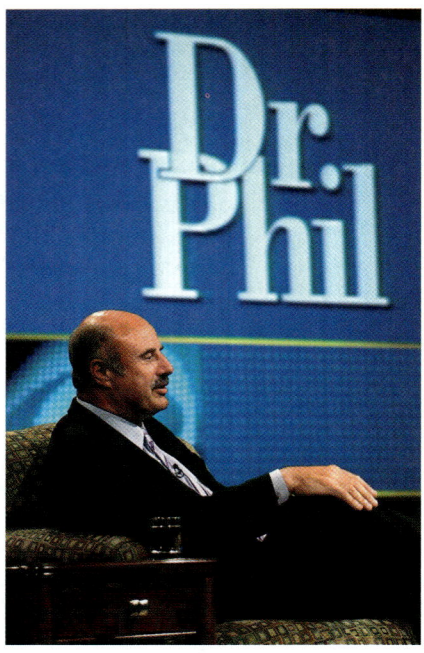

Media psychologists have been urged to educate without actually doing therapy. Some overstep this boundary, however. Do you think popular TV psychologist Dr. Phil sometimes goes too far?

are available via the Internet. Some services, such as support groups, are free. Online counseling or advice, in contrast, is typically offered for a fee. Some online therapists will "discuss" problems with you through e-mail messages (Chester & Glass, 2006). Others merely answer questions or give advice concerning specific problems.

Online counseling and advice services do have some advantages. For one thing, clients can remain anonymous. Thus, a person who might hesitate to see a psychologist can seek help privately, online. Likewise, the Internet can link people who live in rural areas with psychologists living in large cities. And, compared with traditional office visits, Internet therapy is less expensive.

As with radio talk shows and telephone counselors, many objections can be raised about online psychological services. Clearly, brief e-mail messages are no way to make a diagnosis. And forget about facial expressions or body language—not even tone of voice reaches the online therapist. Typing emotional icons (called *emoticons*) like little smiley faces (☺) or frowns (☹) is a poor substitute for real human interaction. Another problem is that e-mail counseling may not be completely confidential and could be intercepted and misused. Of special concern is the fact that "cybershrinks" may or may not be trained professionals (Bloom, 1998). And even if they are, questions exist about whether a psychologist licensed in one state can legally do therapy in another state via the Internet. Despite such objections, psychologists have demonstrated success providing therapy over the Internet, at least for certain types of problems (Carlbring et al., 2007; Klein, Richards, & Austin, 2006).

Many of the drawbacks we have discussed can be solved with videoconferencing. A two-way audio-video link allows the client and therapist to see one another on computer monitors and to talk via speakerphones. Doing therapy this way still lacks the close personal contact of face-to-face interaction. However, it does remove many of the objections to doing therapy at a distance. It's very likely that distance services will continue to evolve (Riva & Wiederhold, 2006) and become a major source of mental health care in coming years (Schopp, Demiris, & Glueckauf, 2006).

Implications As you can see, psychological services that rely on electronic communication may serve some useful purposes. However, the value of therapy offered by commercial telephone "counselors" and Internet "therapists" remains open to question. The very best advice given by media psychologists, telephone "counselors," or Internet "therapists" may be, "If at all possible, you should consider discussing this problem with a psychologist or counselor in your own community."

MODULE 13.2 Summary

What are the major humanistic therapies?
- Client-centered (or person-centered) therapy is non-directive, based on insights gained from conscious thoughts and feelings, and dedicated to creating an atmosphere of growth.
- Unconditional positive regard, empathy, authenticity, and reflection are combined to give the client a chance to solve his or her own problems.
- Existential therapies focus on the end result of the choices one makes in life. Clients are encouraged through confrontation and encounter to exercise free will and to take responsibility for their choices.
- Gestalt therapy emphasizes immediate awareness of thoughts and feelings. Its goal is to rebuild thinking, feeling, and acting into connected wholes and to help clients break through emotional blockages.

Can therapy be conducted at a distance?
- Media psychologists, telephone counselors, and cybertherapists may, on occasion, do some good. However, each has drawbacks, and the effectiveness of telephone counseling and cybertherapy has not been unambiguously established.
- Therapy by videoconferencing shows more promise as a way to provide mental health services at a distance.

KNOWLEDGE BUILDER

Insight Therapies

Recite

Match:

___ 1. Client-centered therapy   **A.** Electronic advice
___ 2. Gestalt therapy   **B.** Unconditional positive regard
___ 3. Existential therapy   **C.** Gaps in awareness
___ 4. Internet therapy   **D.** Choice and becoming

5. The Gestalt therapist tries to *reflect* a client's thoughts and feelings. T or F?
6. Filling in gaps in immediate self-awareness is one of the principal goals of
   a. supportive therapy
   b. existential therapy
   c. person-centered therapy
   d. Gestalt therapy
7. Confrontation and encounter are concepts of existential therapy. T or F?
8. To date, the most acceptable type of "distance therapy" is
   a. media psychology
   b. commercial telephone counseling
   c. Internet-based cybertherapy
   d. based on videoconferencing

Reflect

Critical Thinking

9. How might using the term *patient* affect the relationship between an individual and a therapist?

Relate

Here's a mnemonic for the elements of client-centered therapy: Picture a therapist saying "I ear u" to a client. The *E* stands for empathy, *A* for authenticity, *R* for reflection, and *U* for unconditional positive regard.

What would an existential therapist say about the choices you have made so far in your life? Should you be choosing more "courageously"?

You are going to play the role of a therapist for a classroom demonstration. How would you act if you were a client-centered therapist? An existential therapist? A Gestalt therapist?

A neighbor of yours is thinking about getting counseling on the Internet. What would you tell her about the pros and cons of distance therapy?

Link

Internet addresses frequently change. To find the sites listed here, visit **http://www.thomsonedu.com/psychology/coon** for an updated list of Internet addresses and direct links to relevant sites.

- **Carl Rogers** Read Rogers' original article some observations on the organization of personality.
- **Existential Therapy** Explore this extensive website about existential therapy.
- **Dr. Phil** See for yourself how Dr. Phil publicizes mental health issues.

ANSWERS

1. B 2. C 3. D 4. A 5. F 6. d 7. T 8. d 9. The terms *doctor* and *patient* imply a large gap in status and authority between the individual and his or her therapist. Client-centered therapy attempts to narrow this gap by making the person the final authority concerning solutions to his or her problems. Also, the word *patient* implies that a person is "sick" and needs to be "cured." Many regard this as an inappropriate way to think about human problems.

MODULE 13.3 Behavior Therapy

A BREAKTHROUGH OCCURRED when psychologists realized they could use learning principles to solve human problems. Behavior therapists directly change behavior patterns so that people can function more comfortably and effectively. This unit describes some innovative, and very successful, behavioral therapies.

Behavior Therapy—Healing by Learning

SURVEY QUESTIONS: *What is behavior therapy? How is behavior therapy used to treat phobias, fears, and anxieties?*

Jay repeatedly and vividly imagined himself going into a store to steal something. He then pictured himself being caught and turned over to the police, who handcuffed him and hauled him off to jail. Once there, he imagined calling his wife to tell her he had been arrested for shoplifting. He became very distressed as he faced her anger and his son's disappointment (Kohn & Antonuccio, 2002).

Why would anyone imagine such a thing? Jay's behavior is not as strange as it may seem. His goal was self-control: Jay is a *kleptomaniac* (a compulsive stealer). The method he chose (called *covert sensitization*) is a form of behavior therapy (Corsini, 2001). **Behavior therapy** is the use of learning principles to make constructive changes in behavior. Behavioral approaches include behavior modification, aversion therapy, desensitization, token economies, and other techniques (Forsyth & Savsevitz, 2002).

Behavior therapists believe that deep insight into one's problems is often unnecessary for improvement. Instead, they try to directly alter troublesome thoughts and actions. Jay didn't need to probe into his past or his emotions and conflicts; he simply wanted to break his shoplifting habit.

In general, how does behavior therapy work? Behavior therapists assume that people have *learned* to be the way they are. If they have learned responses that cause problems, then they can change them by *relearning* more appropriate behaviors. Broadly speaking, **behavior modification** refers to any use of classical or operant conditioning to directly alter human behavior (Miltenberger, 2008; Spiegler & Guevremont, 2003). (Some therapists prefer to call this approach *applied behavior analysis*.)

How does classical conditioning work? I'm not sure I remember. Classical conditioning is a form of learning in which simple responses (especially reflexes) are associated with new stimuli. Perhaps a brief review would be helpful. In classical conditioning, a neutral stimulus is followed by an *unconditioned stimulus (US)* that consistently produces an unlearned reaction, called the *unconditioned response (UR)*. Eventually, the previously neutral stimulus begins to produce this response directly. The response is then called a *conditioned response (CR)*, and the stimulus becomes a *conditioned stimulus (CS)*. Thus, for a child the sight of a hypodermic needle (CS) is followed by an injection (US), which causes anxiety or fear (UR). Eventually the sight of a hypodermic (the conditioned stimulus) may produce anxiety or fear (a conditioned response) *before* the child gets an injection. (For a more thorough review of classical conditioning, return to Module 6.1.)

What does classical conditioning have to do with behavior modification? Classical conditioning can be used to associate discomfort with a bad habit, as Jay did. More powerful versions of this approach are called aversion therapy.

Aversion Therapy

Imagine that you are eating an apple. Suddenly you discover that you just bit a large green worm in half. You vomit. Months later you cannot eat an apple again without feeling ill. It's apparent that you have developed a conditioned aversion to apples. (A *conditioned aversion* is a learned dislike or negative emotional response to some stimulus.)

How are conditioned aversions used in therapy? In **aversion therapy,** an individual learns to associate a strong aversion to an undesirable habit such as smoking, drinking, or gambling. Aversion therapy has been used to cure hiccups, sneezing, stuttering, vomiting, nail-biting, bed-wetting, compulsive hair-pulling, alcoholism, and the smoking of tobacco, marijuana, or crack cocaine. Actually, aversive conditioning happens every day. For example, not many physicians who treat lung cancer patients are smokers, nor do many emergency room doctors drive without using their seat belts (Eifert & Lejuez, 2000).

Puffing Up an Aversion The fact that nicotine is toxic makes it easy to create an aversion that helps people give up smoking. Behavior therapists have found that electric shock, nauseating drugs, and similar aversive stimuli are not required to make smokers uncomfortable. All that is needed is for the smoker to smoke—rapidly, for a long time, at a forced pace.

Behavior therapy Any therapy designed to actively change behavior.
Behavior modification The application of learning principles to change human behavior, especially maladaptive behavior.
Aversion therapy Suppressing an undesirable response by associating it with aversive (painful or uncomfortable) stimuli.

553

During *rapid smoking,* clients are told to smoke continuously, taking a puff every 6 to 8 seconds. Rapid smoking continues until the smoker is miserable and can stand it no more. By then, most people are thinking, "I never want to see another cigarette for the rest of my life."

Rapid smoking has long been known as an effective behavior therapy for smoking (McRobbie & Hajek, 2007). Nevertheless, anyone tempted to try rapid smoking should realize that it is very unpleasant. Without the help of a therapist, most people quit too soon for the procedure to succeed. In addition, rapid smoking can be dangerous. It should only be done with professional supervision. (An alternative method that is more practical is described in the "Psychology in Action" module of this chapter.)

Aversive Therapy for Drinking Another excellent example of aversion therapy was pioneered by Roger Vogler and his associates (1977). Vogler works with alcoholics who were unable to stop drinking. For many clients, aversion therapy is a last chance. While drinking an alcoholic beverage, clients receive a painful (although not injurious) electric shock to the hand. Most of the time, these shocks occur as the client is beginning to take a drink of alcohol.

These *response-contingent shocks* (shocks that are linked to a response) obviously take the pleasure out of drinking. Shocks also cause the alcohol abuser to develop a conditioned aversion to drinking. Normally, the misery caused by alcohol abuse comes long after the act of drinking—too late to have much effect. But if alcohol can be linked with *immediate* discomfort, then drinking will begin to make the individual very uncomfortable.

Is it really acceptable to treat clients this way? People are often disturbed (shocked?) by such methods. However, clients usually *volunteer* for aversion therapy because it helps them overcome a destructive habit. Indeed, commercial aversion programs for overeating, smoking, and alcohol abuse have attracted many willing customers. More important, aversion therapy can be justified by its long-term benefits. As behaviorist Donald Baer put it, "A small number of brief, painful experiences is a reasonable exchange for the interminable pain of a lifelong maladjustment."

Desensitization

How is behavior therapy used to treat phobias, fears, and anxieties? Assume that you are a swimming instructor who wants to help a child named Jamie overcome fear of the high diving board. How might you proceed? Directly forcing Jamie off the high board could be a psychological disaster. Obviously, a better approach would be to begin by teaching her to dive off the edge of the pool. Then she could be taught to dive off the low board, followed by a platform 6 feet above the water, and then an 8-foot platform. As a last step, Jamie could try the high board.

Who's Afraid of a Hierarchy? This rank-ordered series of steps is called a **hierarchy**. The hierarchy allows Jamie to undergo *adaptation*. Gradually, she adapts to the high dive and overcomes her fear. When Jamie has conquered her fear, we can say that *desensitization* (dee-SEN-sih-tih-ZAY-shun) has occurred (Spiegler & Guevremont, 2003).

Desensitization is also based on **reciprocal inhibition** (using one emotional state to block another) (Heriot & Pritchard, 2004). For instance, it is impossible to be anxious and relaxed at the same time. If we can get Jamie onto the high board in a relaxed state, her anxiety and fear will be inhibited. Repeated visits to the high board should cause fear to disappear in this situation. Again we would say that Jamie has been desensitized. Typically, **systematic desensitization** (a guided reduction in fear, anxiety, or aversion) is attained by gradually approaching a feared stimulus while maintaining relaxation.

What is desensitization used for? Desensitization is primarily used to help people unlearn phobias (intense, unrealistic fears) or strong anxieties. For example, each of these people might be a candidate for desensitization: a teacher with stage fright, a student with test anxiety, a salesperson who fears people, or a newlywed with an aversion to sexual intimacy.

Performing Desensitization *How is desensitization done?* First, the client and the therapist *construct a hierarchy*. This is a list of fear-provoking situations, arranged from least disturbing to most frightening. Second, the client is taught *exercises that produce deep relaxation.* (See "Feeling a Little Tense? Relax!") Once the client is relaxed, she or he proceeds

Programs for treating fears of flying combine relaxation, systematic desensitization, group support, and lots of direct and indirect exposure to airliners. Many such programs conclude with a brief flight, so that participants can "test their wings."

DISCOVERING PSYCHOLOGY

Feeling a Little Tense? Relax!

The key to desensitization is relaxation. To inhibit fear, you must *learn* to relax. One way to voluntarily relax is by using the **tension-release method.** To achieve deep-muscle relaxation, try the following exercise.

Tense the muscles in your right arm until they tremble. Hold them tight as you slowly count to 10 and then let go. Allow your hand and arm to go limp and to relax completely. Repeat the procedure. Releasing tension two or three times will allow you to feel whether or not your arm muscles have relaxed. Repeat the tension-release procedure with your left arm. Compare it with your right arm. Repeat until the left arm is equally relaxed. Apply the tension-release technique to your right leg; to your left leg; to your abdomen; to your chest and shoulders. Clench and release your chin, neck, and throat. Wrinkle and release your forehead and scalp. Tighten and release your mouth and face muscles. As a last step, curl your toes and tense your feet. Then release.

Practice the tension-release method until you can achieve complete relaxation quickly (5 to 10 minutes). After you have practiced relaxation once a day for a week or two, you will begin to be able to tell when your body (or a group of muscles) is tense. Also, you will begin to be able to relax on command. This is a valuable skill that you can apply in any situation that makes you feel tense or anxious.

---

to the third step by trying to *perform the least disturbing item* on the list. For a fear of heights (acrophobia), this might be: "(1) Stand on a chair." The first item is repeated until no anxiety is felt. Any change from complete relaxation is a signal that clients must relax again before continuing. Slowly, clients move up the hierarchy: "(2) Climb to the top of a small stepladder"; "(3) Look down a flight of stairs"; and so on, until the last item is performed without fear: "(20) Fly in an airplane."

For many phobias, desensitization works best when people are directly exposed to the stimuli and situations they fear (Bourne, 2005). For something like a simple spider phobia, this exposure can even be done in groups. Also, for some fears (such as fear of riding an elevator) desensitization may be completed in a single session (Sturges & Sturges, 1998).

Vicarious Desensitization *I understand how some fears could be desensitized by a gradual approach—as in the case of the child on the high dive. But what if it's not practical to directly act out the steps of a hierarchy?* For a fear of heights, the steps of the hierarchy might be acted out. However, if this is impractical, the problem can be handled by having clients observe *models* who are performing the feared behavior (Eifert & Lejuez, 2000) (• Fig. 13.2). A model is a person (either live or filmed) who serves as an example for observational learning. If such **vicarious desensitization** (secondhand learning) can't be used, there is yet another option. Fortunately, desensitization works almost as well when a person *vividly imagines* each step in the hierarchy (Yahnke, Sheikh, & Beckman, 2003). If the steps can be visualized without anxiety, fear in the actual situ-

• **FIGURE 13.2** Treatment of a snake phobia by vicarious desensitization. These classic photographs show models interacting with snakes. To overcome their own fears, phobic subjects observed the models (Bandura, Blanchard, & Ritter, 1969). (Photos courtesy of Albert Bandura.)

Hierarchy A rank-ordered series of higher and lower amounts, levels, degrees, or steps.

Reciprocal inhibition The presence of one emotional state can inhibit the occurrence of another, such as joy preventing fear or anxiety inhibiting pleasure.

Systematic desensitization A reduction in fear, anxiety, or aversion brought about by planned exposure to aversive stimuli.

Tension-release method A procedure for systematically achieving deep relaxation of the body.

Vicarious desensitization A reduction in fear or anxiety that takes place vicariously ("secondhand") when a client watches models perform the feared behavior.

ation is reduced. Because imagining feared stimuli can be done at a therapist's office, it is the most common way of doing desensitization.

Virtual Reality Exposure Desensitization is an *exposure therapy*. Like other such therapies, it involves exposing people to feared stimuli until their fears extinguish. In an important new development, psychologists are using virtual reality to treat phobias. Virtual reality is a computer-generated, three-dimensional "world" that viewers enter by wearing a head-mounted video display. **Virtual reality exposure** presents computerized fear stimuli to clients in a realistic, yet carefully controlled fashion (Wiederhold & Wiederhold, 2005). It has already been used to treat fears of flying, driving, and public speaking as well as acrophobia (fear of heights), claustrophobia, and spider phobias (Arbona et al., 2004; Giuseppe, 2005; Hoffman et al., 2003; Lee et al., 2002; Wald and Taylor, 2000). (See ● Fig. 13.3.)

Desensitization has been one of the most successful behavior therapies. A second new technique may provide yet another way to lower fears, anxieties, and psychological pain.

Eye Movement Desensitization Traumatic events produce painful memories. Disturbing flashbacks often haunts victims of accidents, disasters, molestations, muggings, rapes, or emotional abuse. Recently, Dr. Francine Shapiro developed **eye movement desensitization and reprocessing** (EMDR) to help ease traumatic memories and posttraumatic stress.

In a typical EMDR session, the client is asked to visualize the images that most upset her or him. At the same time, a pencil (or other object) is moved rapidly from side to side in front of the person's eyes. Watching the moving object causes the person's eyes to dart swiftly back and forth. After about 30 seconds, clients describe any memories, feelings, and thoughts that emerged and discuss them with the therapist. These steps are repeated until troubling thoughts and emotions no longer surface (Shapiro, 2001; Shapiro & Forrest, 2004).

A number of studies suggest that EMDR lowers anxieties and takes the pain out of traumatic memories (Seidler & Wagner, 2006; Silver et al., 2005). However, EMDR is highly controversial. Some studies, for example, have found that eye movements add nothing to the treatment. The apparent success of EMDR may simply be based on gradual exposure to upsetting stimuli, as in other forms of desensitization (Cahill, Carrigan, & Frueh, 1999; Davidson & Parker, 2001). On the other hand, some researchers continue to find that EMDR is superior to traditional therapies (Greenwald, 2006; Rogers & Silver, 2002).

Is EMDR a breakthrough? Given the frequency of traumas in modern society, it shouldn't be long before we find out.

MODULE 13.3 Summary

What is behavior therapy? How is behavior therapy used to treat phobias, fears, and anxieties?

- Behavior therapists use the learning principles of classical or operant conditioning to directly change human behavior.
- In aversion therapy, classical conditioning is used to associate maladaptive behavior (such as smoking or drinking) with pain or other aversive events in order to inhibit undesirable responses.
- In desensitization, exposure to fear stimuli, adaptation, and reciprocal inhibition are used to break the link between fear and particular situations.

● **FIGURE 13.3** *(left)* Dr. Barbara Rothbaum and Dr. Larry Hodges show how a virtual reality system is used to expose people to feared stimuli. Many clients would rather face feared stimuli in a virtual environment than in a real physical environment. *(right)* A computer image from a virtual elevator. Over an 8-week period, clients who suffered from acrophobia "rode" in the elevator. Each session took them to greater heights.

- Typical steps in desensitization are: Construct a fear hierarchy, learn to produce total relaxation, and perform items on the hierarchy (from least to most disturbing).
- Desensitization may be carried out in real settings, or it may be done by vividly imagining feared stimuli or by watching models perform the feared responses.
- In some cases, virtual reality exposure can be used to present fear stimuli in a controlled manner.
- A technique called eye movement desensitization and reprocessing (EMDR) shows promise as a treatment for traumatic memories and stress disorders. At present, however, EMDR is highly controversial.

KNOWLEDGE BUILDER

Behavior Therapy

Recite

1. What two types of conditioning are used in behavior modification? _____ and _____
2. Shock, pain, and discomfort play what role in conditioning an aversion?
   a. conditioned stimulus
   b. unconditioned response
   c. unconditioned stimulus
   d. conditioned response
3. If shock is used to control drinking, it must be _____ contingent.
4. What two principles underlie systematic desensitization? _____ and _____
5. When desensitization is carried out through the use of live or filmed models, it is called
   a. cognitive therapy
   b. flooding
   c. covert desensitization
   d. vicarious desensitization
6. The three basic steps in systematic desensitization are: construct a hierarchy, flood the person with anxiety, and imagine relaxation. T or F?
7. In EMDR therapy, computer-generated virtual reality images are used to expose clients to fear-provoking stimuli. T or F?

Reflect

Critical Thinking

8. Alcoholics who take a drug called Antabuse become ill after drinking alcohol. Why, then, don't they develop an aversion to drinking?
9. A natural form of desensitization often takes place in hospitals. Can you guess what it is?

Relate

Can you describe three problems for which you think behavior therapy would be an appropriate treatment?

A friend of yours has a dog that goes berserk during thunderstorms. You own an audiotape of a thunderstorm. How could you use the tape to desensitize the dog? (Hint: The tape player has a volume control.)

Have you ever become naturally desensitized to a stimulus or situation that at first made you anxious (for instance, heights, public speaking, or driving on freeways)? How would you explain your reduced fear?

Link

Internet addresses frequently change. To find the sites listed here, visit http://www.thomsonedu.com/psychology/coon for an updated list of Internet addresses and direct links to relevant sites.

- **Aversion therapy** Read more about aversion therapy.
- **Systematic Desensitization** Explore this self-administered procedure.
- **Virtual Reality Therapy** Learn more about VR therapy.

ANSWERS

1. classical (or respondent), operant 2. c 3. response 4. adaptation, reciprocal inhibition 5. d 6. F 7. F 8. Committed alcoholics may actually "drink through it" and learn to tolerate the nauseating effects. 9. Doctors and nurses learn to relax and remain calm at the sight of blood because of their frequent exposure to it.

Virtual reality exposure Use of computer-generated images to present fear stimuli. The virtual environment responds to a viewer's head movements and other inputs.

Eye movement desensitization and reprocessing (EMDR) A technique for reducing fear or anxiety; based on holding upsetting thoughts in mind while rapidly moving the eyes from side to side.

MODULE 13.4 Operant Therapies and Cognitive Therapies

IN THE NEXT MODULE, we will consider two contrasting approaches to human problems. Operant therapies are very behavioral: They directly reinforce some behaviors and seek to extinguish others. In contrast, cognitive therapists help people change harmful thinking patterns.

Operant Therapies—All the World Is a Skinner Box?

SURVEY QUESTION: *What role does reinforcement play in behavior therapy?*

Aversion therapy and desensitization are based on classical conditioning. Where does operant conditioning fit in? As you may recall, *operant conditioning* refers to learning based on the consequences of making a response. The operant principles most often used by behavior therapists to deal with human behavior are:

1. **Positive reinforcement.** Responses that are followed by reward tend to occur more frequently. If children whine and get attention, they will whine more frequently. If you get A's in your psychology class, you may become a psychology major.
2. **Nonreinforcement.** A response that is not followed by reward will occur less frequently.
3. **Extinction.** If a response is not followed by reward after it has been repeated many times, it will go away. After winning three times, you pull the handle on a slot machine 30 times more without a payoff. What do you do? You go away. So does the response of handle pulling (for that particular machine, at any rate).
4. **Punishment.** If a response is followed by discomfort or an undesirable effect, the response will be suppressed (but not necessarily extinguished).
5. **Shaping.** Shaping means rewarding actions that are closer and closer approximations to a desired response. For example, to reward an intellectually disabled child for saying "ball," you might begin by rewarding the child for saying anything that starts with a *b* sound.
6. **Stimulus control.** Responses tend to come under the control of the situation in which they occur. If you set your clock 10 minutes fast, it may be easier to leave the house on time in the morning. Your departure is under the stimulus control of the clock, even though you know it is fast.
7. **Time out.** A time-out procedure usually involves removing the individual from a situation in which reinforcement occurs. Time out is a variation of nonreinforcement: It prevents reward from following an undesirable response. For example, children who fight with each other can be sent to separate rooms and allowed out only when they are able to behave more calmly. (For a more thorough review of operant learning, return to Modules 6.2, 6.3, and 6.4.)

As simple as these principles may seem, they have been used very effectively to overcome difficulties in work, home, school, and industrial settings. Let's see how.

Nonreinforcement and Extinction

An extremely overweight mental patient had a persistent and disturbing habit: She stole food from other patients. No one could persuade her to stop stealing or to diet. For the sake of her health, a behavior therapist assigned her a special table in the ward dining room. If she approached any other table, she was immediately removed from the dining room. Because her attempts to steal food went unrewarded, they rapidly disappeared. Additionally, any attempt to steal from others caused the patient to miss her own meal (Ayllon, 1963).

What operant principles did the therapist in this example use? The therapist used *nonreward* to produce *extinction*. The most frequently occurring human behaviors lead to some form of reward. An undesirable response can be eliminated by *identifying* and *removing* the rewards that maintain it. But people don't always do things for food, money, or other obvious rewards. Most of the rewards maintaining human behavior are subtler. *Attention, approval,* and *concern* are common yet powerful reinforcers for humans (● Fig. 13.4).

Nonreward and extinction can eliminate many problem behaviors, especially in schools, hospitals, and institutions. Often, difficulties center around a limited number of particularly disturbing responses. Time out is a good way to remove such responses, usually by refusing to pay attention to a person who is misbehaving. For example, 14-year-old Terrel periodically appeared in the nude in the activity room of a training center for disturbed adolescents. This behavior

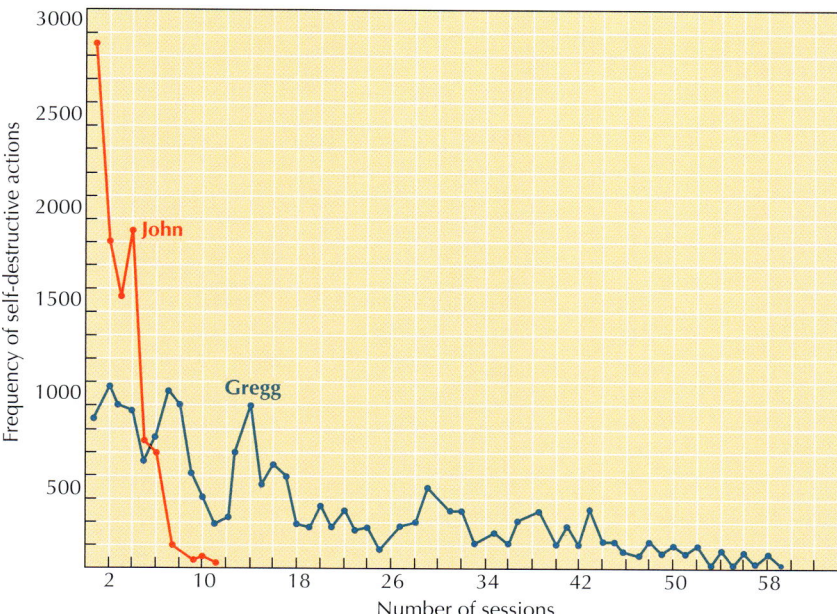

● **FIGURE 13.4** This graph shows extinction of self-destructive behavior in two autistic boys. Before extinction began, the boys received attention and concern from adults for injuring themselves. During extinction, the adults were taught to ignore the boys' self-damaging behavior. As you can see, the number of times that the boys tried to injure themselves declined rapidly. (Adapted from Lovaas & Simmons, 1969.)

always generated a great deal of attention from staff and other patients. Usually Terrel was returned to his room and confined there. During this "confinement," he often missed doing his usual chores. As an experiment he was placed on time out. The next time he appeared nude, counselors and other staff members greeted him normally and then ignored him. Attention from other patients rapidly subsided. Sheepishly he returned to his room and dressed.

Reinforcement and Token Economies

A distressing problem therapists sometimes face is how to break through to severely disturbed patients who won't talk. Conventional psychotherapy offers little hope of improvement for such patients.

What can be done for them? One widely used approach is based on *tokens* (symbolic rewards, such as plastic chips, that can be exchanged for real rewards). Tokens may be printed slips of paper, check marks, points, or gold stars. Whatever form they take, tokens serve as rewards because they may be exchanged for candy, food, cigarettes, recreation, or privileges, such as private time with a therapist, outings, or watching TV. Tokens are used in mental hospitals, half-way houses, schools for the intellectually disabled, programs for delinquents, and ordinary classrooms. They usually produce improvements in behavior (Dickerson, Tenhula, & Green-Paden, 2005; Reitman et al., 2004).

By using tokens, a therapist can *immediately reward* positive responses. For maximum impact, therapists select specific *target behaviors* (actions or other behaviors the therapist seeks to modify). Target behaviors are then reinforced with tokens. For example, a mute mental patient might first be given a token each time he or she says a word. Next, tokens may be given for speaking a complete sentence. Later, the patient could gradually be required to speak more often, then to answer questions, and eventually to carry on a short conversation in order to receive tokens. In this way, deeply withdrawn patients have been returned to the world of normal communication.

Full-scale use of tokens in an institutional setting produces a *token economy*. In a **token economy**, patients are rewarded with tokens for a wide range of socially desirable or productive activities (Spiegler & Guevremont, 2003). They must *pay* tokens for privileges and for engaging in problem behaviors (● Fig. 13.5). For example, tokens are given to patients who get out of bed, dress themselves, take required medication, arrive for meals on time, and so on. Constructive activities, such as gardening, cooking, or cleaning, may also earn tokens. Patients must *exchange* tokens for meals and private rooms, movies, passes, off-ward activities, and other privileges. They are *charged* tokens for staying in bed, disrobing in public, talking to themselves, fighting, crying, and similar target behaviors (Morisse et al., 1996).

Token economies can radically change a patient's overall adjustment and morale. Patients are given an incentive to change, and they are held responsible for their actions. The use of tokens may seem manipulative, but it actually empowers patients. Many "hopelessly" intellectually disabled, mentally ill, and delinquent people have been returned to productive lives by means of token economies (Field et al., 2004).

By the time they are ready to leave, patients may be earning tokens on a weekly basis for maintaining sane, responsible, and productive behavior (Miltenberger, 2008). Typically, the most effective token economies are those that gradually switch from tokens to *social rewards* such as praise, recognition, and approval. Such rewards are what patients will receive when they return to family, friends, and community.

Token economy A therapeutic program in which desirable behaviors are reinforced with tokens that can be exchanged for goods, services, activities, and privileges.

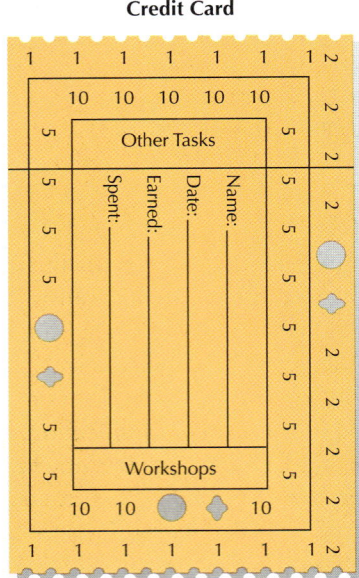

● **FIGURE 13.5** Shown here is a token used in one token economy system. In this instance the token is a card that records the number of credits eared by a patient. Also pictured is a list of credit values for various activities. Tokens may be exchanged for items or for privileges listed on the board. (Adapted from photographs by Robert P. Liberman.)

Cognitive Therapy—Think Positive!

SURVEY QUESTION: *Can therapy change thoughts and emotions?*

How would a behavior therapist treat a problem like depression? None of the techniques described seem to apply. As we have discussed, behavior therapists usually try to change troublesome actions. However, in recent years cognitive therapists have become interested in what people think, believe, and feel, as well as how they act. In general, **cognitive therapy** helps clients change thinking patterns that lead to troublesome emotions or behaviors (Hall, 2006). For example, compulsive hand-washing can be greatly reduced by changing a client's thoughts and beliefs about dirt and contamination (Jones & Menzies, 1998). Cognitive therapy has been used as a remedy for many problems, but it has been especially successful in treating depression (Chambless & Ollendick, 2001).

Cognitive Therapy for Depression

As you may recall from Module 12.4, cognitive psychologists believe that negative, self-defeating thoughts underlie depression. According to Aaron Beck (1991), depressed persons see themselves, the world, and the future in negative terms. Beck believes this occurs because of major distortions in thinking. The first is **selective perception**, which refers to perceiving only certain stimuli in a larger array. If five good things and three bad things happen during the day, depressed people focus only on the bad. A second thinking error in depression is **overgeneralization**, the tendency to think that an upsetting event applies to other, unrelated situations. An example would be considering yourself a total failure, or completely worthless, if you were to lose a part-time job or fail a test. To complete the picture, depressed persons tend to magnify the importance of undesirable events by engaging in **all-or-nothing thinking**. That is, they see events as completely good or bad, right or wrong, and themselves as either successful or failing miserably (Beck, 2002; Gilbert, 2001).

How do cognitive therapists alter such patterns? Cognitive therapists make a step-by-step effort to correct negative thoughts that lead to depression or similar problems. At first, clients are taught to recognize and keep track of their own thoughts. The client and therapist then look for ideas and beliefs that cause depression, anger, and avoidance. For example, here's how a therapist might challenge all-or-nothing thinking (Burns & Persons, 1982):

Client: I'm feeling even more depressed. No one wants to hire me, and I can't even clean up my apartment. I feel completely incompetent!

Therapist: I see. The fact that you are unemployed and have a messy apartment proves that you are completely incompetent?

Client: Well . . . I can see that doesn't add up.

Next, clients are asked to gather information to test their beliefs. For instance, a depressed person might list his or her activities for a week. The list is then used to challenge all-or-nothing thoughts, such as "I had a terrible week" or "I'm a complete failure." With more coaching, clients learn to alter their thoughts in ways that improve their moods, actions, and relationships.

Cognitive therapy is as effective as drugs for treating many cases of depression. More important, people who have adopted new thinking patterns are less likely to become depressed again—a benefit that drugs can't impart (Dozois & Dobson, 2004).

In an alternate approach, cognitive therapists look for an

DISCOVERING PSYCHOLOGY

Ten Irrational Beliefs—Which Do You Hold?

Rational-emotive behavior therapists have identified numerous beliefs that commonly lead to emotional upsets and conflicts. See if you recognize any of the following irrational beliefs:

1. I must be loved and approved by almost every significant person in my life or it's awful and I'm worthless.
   Example: "One of my roommates doesn't seem to like me. I must be a total zero."

2. I should be completely competent and achieving in all ways to be a worthwhile person.
   Example: "I don't understand my chemistry class. I guess I really am a stupid person."

3. Certain people I must deal with are thoroughly bad and should be severely blamed and punished for it.
   Example: "The old man next door is such a pain. I'm going to play my stereo even louder the next time he complains."

4. It is awful and upsetting when things are not the way I would very much like them to be.
   Example: "I should have gotten a B in that class. The teacher is unfair."

5. My unhappiness is always caused by external events; I cannot control my emotional reactions.
   Example: "You make me feel awful. I would be happy if it weren't for you."

6. If something unpleasant might happen, I should keep dwelling on it.
   Example: "I'll never forget the time my boss insulted me. I think about it every day at work."

7. It is easier to avoid difficulties and responsibilities than to face them.
   Example: "I don't know why my wife seems angry. Maybe it will just pass by if I ignore it."

8. I should depend on others who are stronger than I am.
   Example: "I couldn't survive if he left me."

9. Because something once strongly affected my life, it will do so indefinitely.
   Example: "My girlfriend dumped me during my junior year in college. I don't know if I can ever trust a woman again."

10. There is always a perfect solution to human problems, and it is awful if this solution is not found.
    Example: "I'm so depressed about politics in this country. It all seems hopeless."*

*Adapted from Beck, 2002; Ellis, 2004; Rohsenow & Smith, 1982.

If any of the listed beliefs sound familiar, you may be creating unnecessary emotional distress for yourself by holding on to unrealistic expectations.

---

absence of effective coping skills and thinking patterns, not for the *presence* of self-defeating thoughts (Dobson, Backs-Dermott, & Dozois, 2000). The aim is to teach clients how to cope with anger, depression, shyness, stress, and similar problems. Stress inoculation, which was described in Module 11.5, is a good example of this approach.

Cognitive therapy is a rapidly expanding specialty. Before we leave the topic, let's explore another widely used cognitive therapy.

Rational-Emotive Behavior Therapy

Rational-emotive behavior therapy (REBT) attempts to change irrational beliefs that cause emotional problems. According to Albert Ellis (1913–2007), the basic idea of rational-emotive behavior therapy is as easy as A-B-C (Ellis, 1995, 2004). Ellis assumes that people become unhappy and develop self-defeating habits because they have unrealistic or faulty *beliefs.*

How are beliefs important? Ellis analyzes problems in this way: The letter A stands for an *activating experience,* which the person assumes to be the cause of C, an *emotional consequence.* For instance, a person who is rejected (the activating experience) feels depressed, threatened, or hurt (the consequence). Rational-emotive behavior therapy shows the client that the real problem is what comes between A and C: In between is B, the client's irrational and unrealistic *beliefs.* In this example, an unrealistic belief leading to unnecessary suffering is: "I must be loved and approved by everyone at all times." REBT holds that events do not *cause* us to have feelings. We feel as we do because of our beliefs (Kottler, 2004). (For some examples, see "Ten Irrational Beliefs—Which Do You Hold?").

Ellis (1979, 2004) says that most irrational beliefs come

Cognitive therapy A therapy directed at changing the maladaptive thoughts, beliefs, and feelings that underlie emotional and behavioral problems.

Selective perception Perceiving only certain stimuli among a larger array of possibilities.

Overgeneralization Blowing a single event out of proportion by extending it to a large number of unrelated situations.

All-or-nothing thinking Classifying objects or events as absolutely right or wrong, good or bad, acceptable or unacceptable, and so forth.

Rational-emotive behavior therapy (REBT) An approach that states that irrational beliefs cause many emotional problems and that such beliefs must be changed or abandoned.

THE CLINICAL FILE

Overcoming the Gambler's Fallacy

Seventeen-year-old Jonathan just lost his shirt again. This time he did it playing online Blackjack. Jonathan started out making $5 bets and then doubled his bet over and over. Surely, he thought, his luck would eventually change. However, he ran out of money after just eight hands, having lost more than $1,000. Last week he lost a lot of money playing Texas Hold 'Em and slot machines. Now Jonathan is in tears—he has lost most of his summer earnings, and he is worried about having to drop out of school and tell his parents about his losses. Jonathan has had to admit that he had joined the growing ranks of underage gambling addicts (LaBrie & Shaffer, 2007; Wilber & Potenza, 2006).

Like many problem gamblers, Jonathan suffers from several cognitive distortions related to gambling. Here are some of his mistaken beliefs (adapted from Toneatto, 2002):

Magnified gambling skill: You have exaggerated self-confidence despite losing persistently.
Attribution errors: You credit your skill for wins but blame losses on bad luck.
Gambler's fallacy: You believe that losses soon must be followed by wins.
Selective memory: You remember times when you won but forget your losses.
Overinterpretation of cues: You put too much faith in irrelevant cues such as bodily sensations or an intuition that your next bet will be a winner.
Luck as a trait: You believe that you are a "lucky" person in general.
Probability biases: You have incorrect beliefs about randomness and chance events.

Do you have any of these mistaken beliefs? Taken together, Jonathan's cognitive distortions created an "illusion of control." That is, he believed that if he worked hard enough, he could figure out how to win. Fortunately, a cognitive therapist helped Jonathan *cognitively restructure* his beliefs. He now no longer believes he can control chance events. Jonathan still gambles a bit, but he only does so recreationally, keeping his losses within his budget and enjoying himself in the process.

---

from three core ideas, each of which is unrealistic:

1. I *must* perform well and be approved of by significant others. If I don't, then it is awful, I cannot stand it, and I am a rotten person.
2. You *must* treat me fairly. When you don't, it is horrible, and I cannot bear it.
3. Conditions *must* be the way I want them to be. It is terrible when they are not, and I cannot stand living in such an awful world.

It's easy to see that such beliefs can lead to much grief and needless suffering in a less than perfect world. Rational-emotive behavior therapists are very directive in their attempts to change a client's irrational beliefs and "self-talk." The therapist may directly attack clients' logic, challenge their thinking, confront them with evidence contrary to their beliefs, and even assign "homework." Here, for instance, are some examples of statements that dispute irrational beliefs (after Kottler, 2004):

- "Where is the evidence that you are a loser just because you didn't do well this one time?"
- "Who said the world should be fair? That's your rule."
- "What are you telling yourself to make yourself feel so upset?"
- "Is it really terrible that things aren't working out as you would like? Or is it just inconvenient?"

Many of us would probably do well to give up our irrational beliefs. Improved self-acceptance and a better tolerance of daily annoyances are the benefits of doing so. (See "Overcoming the Gambler's Fallacy.")

The value of cognitive approaches is further illustrated by three techniques (*covert sensitization, thought stopping,* and *covert reinforcement*) described in this chapter's "Psychology in Action" module. A little later you can see what you think of them.

MODULE 13.4 Summary

What role does reinforcement play in behavior therapy?

- Behavior modification makes use of operant principles, such as positive reinforcement, nonreinforcement, extinction, punishment, shaping, stimulus control, and time out. These principles are used to extinguish undesirable responses and to promote constructive behavior.
- Nonreward can extinguish troublesome behaviors. Often this is done by simply identifying and eliminating reinforcers, particularly attention and social approval.
- To apply positive reinforcement and operant shaping, tokens are often used to reinforce selected target behaviors.

- Full-scale use of tokens in an institutional setting produces a token economy. Toward the end of a token economy program, patients are shifted to social rewards such as recognition and approval.

Can therapy change thoughts and emotions?

- Cognitive therapy emphasizes changing thought patterns that underlie emotional or behavioral problems. Its goals are to correct distorted thinking and/or teach improved coping skills.
- Irrational beliefs are the core of many maladaptive thinking patterns. Changing such beliefs can have a positive impact on emotions and behavior.
- In a variation of cognitive therapy called rational-emotive behavior therapy (REBT), clients learn to recognize and challenge their irrational beliefs.

KNOWLEDGE BUILDER

Operant Therapies and Cognitive Therapies

Recite

1. Behavior modification programs aimed at extinction of an undesirable behavior typically make use of what operant principles?
   a. punishment and stimulus control
   b. punishment and shaping
   c. nonreinforcement and time out
   d. stimulus control and time out
2. Attention can be a powerful _____ for humans.
3. Token economies depend on the time-out procedure. T or F?
4. Tokens basically allow the operant shaping of desired responses or "target behaviors." T or F?
5. According to Beck, selective perception, overgeneralization, and _____ thinking are cognitive habits that underlie depression.
6. The B in the A-B-C of REBT stands for
   a. behavior
   b. belief
   c. being
   d. Beck
7. REBT teaches people to change the antecedents of irrational behavior. T or F?

Reflect

Critical Thinking

8. In Aaron Beck's terms, a belief such as "I must perform well or I am a rotten person" involves two thinking errors. What are they?

Relate

See if you can give a personal example of how the following principles have affected your behavior: positive reinforcement, extinction, punishment, shaping, stimulus control, and time out.

You are setting up a token economy for troubled elementary school children. What target behaviors will you attempt to reinforce? For what behaviors will you charge tokens?

We all occasionally engage in negative thinking. Can you remember a time recently when you engaged in selective perception? Overgeneralization? All-or-nothing thinking?

Which of REBT's irrational beliefs have affected your feelings? Which beliefs would you like to change?

Link

Internet addresses frequently change. To find the sites listed here, visit **http://www.thomsonedu.com/psychology/coon** for an updated list of Internet addresses and direct links to relevant sites.

- **Token Economies** Read about the use of token economies with autistic children.
- **The Beck Institute** Read about cognitive therapy and visit the rest of the Beck Institute website.
- **Albert Ellis Institute** Read about Albert Ellis and his rational-emotive behavior therapy.

ANSWERS

1. c 2. reinforcer 3. F 4. T 5. all-or-nothing 6. b 7. F 8. Overgeneralization and all-or-nothing thinking.

MODULE 13.5 Group Therapy, Therapy Skills, and Medical Therapies

TO COMPLETE OUR DISCUSSION OF PSYCHOTHERAPIES, we will begin with a brief look at group therapy. Group therapy has certain advantages, not the least of which is reduced cost. The middle portion of this module identifies the core features and helping skills that make psychotherapy "work." To conclude, we will explore medical approaches to treating mental disorders.

Group Therapy—People Who Need People

SURVEY QUESTION: *Can psychotherapy be done with groups of people?*

Group therapy is psychotherapy done with more than one person. Most of the therapies we have discussed can be adapted for use in groups (Corey, 2008). Psychologists first tried working with groups because there was a shortage of therapists. Surprisingly, group therapy has turned out to be just as effective as individual therapy, and it has some special advantages (Burlingame, Fuhriman, & Mosier, 2003).

What are the advantages? In group therapy, a person can *act out* or directly experience problems. Doing so often produces insights that might not occur from merely talking about an issue. In addition, other group members with similar problems can offer support and useful input. Group therapy is especially good for helping people understand their personal relationships (McCluskey, 2002). For reasons such as these, a number of specialized groups have emerged. Because they range from Alcoholics Anonymous to Marriage Encounter, we will sample only a few examples.

Psychodrama

One of the first group therapies was developed by Jacob L. Moreno (1953), who called his technique psychodrama. In **psychodrama,** clients act out personal conflicts with others who play supporting roles (Blatner, 2006). Through role playing, the client reenacts incidents that cause problems in real life. For example, Don, a disturbed teenager, might act out a typical family fight, with the therapist playing his father and with other clients playing his mother, brothers, and sisters. Moreno believed that insights gained in this way transfer to real-life situations.

Therapists using psychodrama often find that role reversals are helpful. A **role reversal** involves taking the part of another person to learn how he or she feels. For instance, Don might role play his father or mother to better understand their feelings. A related method is the **mirror technique,** in which clients observe another person reenact their behavior. Thus, Don might briefly join the audience and watch as another group member plays his role. This would allow him to see himself as others do. Later, the group may summarize what happened and reflect on its meaning (Turner, 1997).

Family Therapy

Family relationships are the source of great pleasure and, all too often, of great pain. In **family therapy,** husband, wife, and children work as a group to resolve the problems of each family member. Family therapy tends to be brief and focused on specific problems, such as frequent fights or a depressed teenager. For some types of problems, family therapy may be superior to other approaches (Capuzzi, 2003; Eisler et al., 2007).

Family therapists believe that a problem experienced by one family member is really the whole family's problem. If the entire pattern of behavior in a family doesn't change, improvements in any single family member may not last. Thus, family members work together to improve communication, to change destructive patterns, and to see themselves and each other in new ways. This helps them reshape distorted perceptions and interactions directly with the very persons with whom they have troubled relationships (Goldenberg & Goldenberg, 2004).

A group therapy session. Group members offer mutual support while sharing problems and insights.

Does the therapist work with the whole family at once? Family therapists treat the family as a unit, but they may not meet with the entire family at each session (Eisler et al., 2007). If a family crisis is at hand, the therapist may first try to identify the most resourceful family members, who can help solve the immediate problem. The therapist and family members may then work on resolving more basic conflicts and on improving family relationships (Griffin, 2002).

Group Awareness Training

During the 1960s and 1970s, the human potential movement led many people to seek personal growth experiences. Often, their interest was expressed by participation in sensitivity training or encounter groups.

What is the difference between sensitivity and encounter groups? Sensitivity groups tend to be less confrontational than encounter groups. Participants in **sensitivity groups** take part in exercises that gently enlarge self-awareness and sensitivity to others. For example, in a "trust walk," participants expand their confidence in others by allowing themselves to be led around while blindfolded.

Encounter groups are based on an honest expression of feelings, and intensely personal communication may take place. Typically, the emphasis is on tearing down defenses and false fronts. Because there is a danger of hostile confrontation, participation is safest when members are carefully screened and a trained leader guides the group. Encounter group "casualties" are rare, but they do occur (Shaffer & Galinsky, 1989).

In business settings, psychologists still use the basic principles of sensitivity and encounter groups—truth, self-awareness, and self-determination—to improve employee relationships. Specially designed encounter groups for married couples are also widely held (Harway, 2004).

There has also been much public interest in various forms of large-group awareness training. **Large-group awareness training** refers to programs that claim to increase self-awareness and facilitate constructive personal change. Lifespring, Actualizations, the Forum, and similar commercial programs are examples. Like the smaller groups that preceded them, large-group trainings combine psychological exercises, confrontation, new viewpoints, and group dynamics to promote personal change.

Are sensitivity, encounter, and awareness groups really psychotherapies? These experiences tend to be positive, but they produce only moderate benefits (Faith, Wong, & Carpenter, 1995). Moreover, many of the claimed benefits may simply result from a kind of **therapy placebo effect**, in which improvement is based on a client's belief that therapy will help. Positive expectations, a break in daily routine, and an excuse to act differently can have quite an impact. Also, less ambitious goals may be easier to attain. For example, one program succeeded in teaching stress-management techniques in a large group setting (Timmerman, Emmelkamp, & Sanderman, 1998). Because of their versatility, groups undoubtedly will continue to be a major tool for solving problems and improving lives (Corey, 2008).

Psychotherapy—An Overview

SURVEY QUESTION: *What do various therapies have in common?*

How effective is psychotherapy? Judging the outcome of therapy is tricky. In a national survey, nearly 9 out of 10 people who have sought mental health care say their lives improved as a result of the treatment (Kotkin, Daviet, & Gurin, 1996). Unfortunately you can't just take people's word for it. (See "How Do We Know Therapy Actually Works?") Fortunately, there is more direct evidence that therapy is beneficial. Hundreds of studies show a strong pattern of positive effects for psychotherapy, counseling, and other psychological treatments (Barlow, 2004; Lambert & Cattani-Thompson, 1996).

In general, then, psychotherapy works (Moras, 2002). Of course, results vary in individual cases. For some people therapy is immensely helpful; for others it is unsuccessful; overall it is effective for more people than not. Speaking more subjectively, a real success, in which a person's life is changed for the better, can be worth the frustration of several cases in which little progress is made.

Group therapy Psychotherapy conducted in a group setting to make therapeutic use of group dynamics.

Psychodrama A therapy in which clients act out personal conflicts and feelings in the presence of others who play supporting roles.

Role reversal Taking the role of another person to learn how one's own behavior appears from the other person's perspective.

Mirror technique Observing another person reenact one's own behavior, like a character in a play; designed to help persons see themselves more clearly.

Family therapy Technique in which all family members participate, both individually and as a group, to change destructive relationships and communication patterns.

Sensitivity group A group experience consisting of exercises designed to increase self-awareness and sensitivity to others.

Encounter group A group experience that emphasizes intensely honest interchanges among participants regarding feelings and reactions to one another.

Large-group awareness training Any of a number of programs (many of them commercialized) that claim to increase self-awareness and facilitate constructive personal change.

Therapy placebo effect Improvement caused not by the actual process of therapy but by a client's expectation that therapy will help.

CRITICAL THINKING

How Do We Know Therapy Actually Works?

Why is it risky to believe people who say their therapy was effective? An old joke among doctors is that a cold lasts a week without treatment and seven days with it. Perhaps the same is true of therapy. Someone who feels better after 6 months of therapy may have experienced a spontaneous remission—they just feel better because so much time has passed. Or perhaps the crisis that triggered the therapy is now nearly forgotten. Or maybe some sort of therapy placebo effect has occurred. Also, it's possible that the person has received help from other people, such as family, friends, or clergy.

In order to rule out similar explanations, we need to use some of the research methods described in Chapter 1. Ideally, we would randomly divide a group of clients into an experimental group that receives therapy and a control group that does not. When this is done, it is not unusual for the control group to show some improvement, even without receiving therapy (Lambert & Ogles, 2002). Thus, the therapy can be deemed effective only if the experimental group shows more improvement than the control group.

But isn't it unethical to withhold treatment from someone who really needs therapy? That's right. One way to deal with this is to use a *waiting-list control group* consisting of individuals who are waiting to see a therapist and who will eventually also receive therapy.

When the results of many experiments are combined, the effectiveness of therapy becomes clear (see, for example, Lipsey & Wilson, 1993). Recently, studies have shown that some therapies are most effective for specific disorders (Bradley et al., 2005; Eddy et al., 2004). For example, behavioral, cognitive-behavioral, and drug therapies are particularly helpful in treating obsessive-compulsive disorder.

Although it is common to think of therapy as a long, slow process, this is no longer normally the case (Shapiro et al., 2003). Research shows that about 50 percent of all clients feel better after between 13 and 18 weekly 1-hour therapy sessions (● Fig. 13.6). This means that the majority of clients improve after 6 months of therapy. Such rapid improvement is impressive in view of the fact that people often suffer for several years before seeking help. (Unfortunately, because of high costs and limited insurance coverage, the average client receives only 5 therapy sessions, after which only 20 percent of patients feel better [Hansen, Lambert, & Forman, 2002].)

Core Features of Psychotherapy

What do psychotherapies have in common? We have sampled only a few of the many therapies in use today. For a summary of major differences among psychotherapies, see ■ Table 13.2. To add to your understanding, let us briefly summarize what all techniques have in common.

Psychotherapies of various types share all or most of these goals: restoring hope, courage, and optimism; gaining insight; resolving conflicts; improving one's sense of self; changing unacceptable patterns of behavior; finding purpose; mending interpersonal relations; and learning to approach problems rationally (Frank & Frank, 2004; Seligman, 1998). To accomplish these goals, psychotherapies offer the following:

1. Therapy provides a *caring relationship* between the client and therapist, called a **therapeutic alliance.** Emotional rapport, warmth, friendship, understanding, acceptance, and empathy are the basis for this relationship. The therapeutic alliance unites the client and therapist as they work together to solve the client's problems. The strength of this alliance has a major impact on whether therapy succeeds (Kozart, 2002; Meier et al., 2006).

2. Therapy offers a *protected setting* in which emotional *catharsis* (release) can take place. Therapy is a sanctuary in which the client is free to express fears, anxieties, and personal secrets without fearing rejection or loss of confidentiality.

3. All therapies to some extent offer an *explanation* or *rationale* for the client's suffering. Additionally, they propose a line of action that will end this suffering.

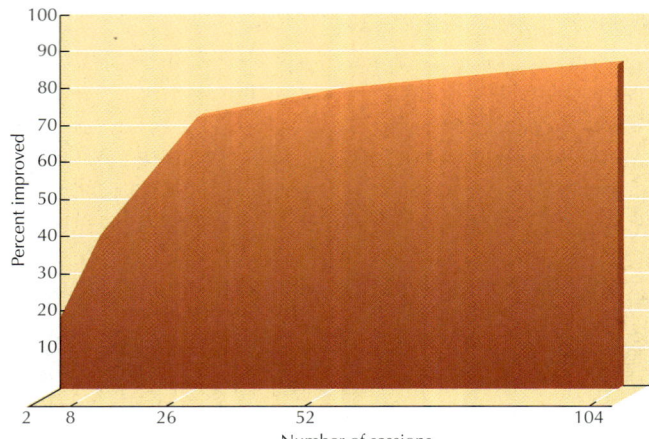

● **FIGURE 13.6** The dose-improvement relationship in psychotherapy. This graph shows the percentage of patients who improved after varying numbers of therapy sessions. Notice that the most rapid improvement took place during the first 6 months of once-a-week sessions. (From Howard et al., 1986.)

TABLE 13.2 Comparison of Psychotherapies

	INSIGHT OR ACTION?	DIRECTIVE OR NONDIRECTIVE?	INDIVIDUAL OR GROUP?	THERAPY'S STRENGTH*
Psychoanalysis	Insight	Directive	Individual	Searching honesty
Brief psychodynamic therapy	Insight	Directive	Individual	Productive use of conflict
Client-centered therapy	Insight	Nondirective	Both	Acceptance, empathy
Existential therapy	Insight	Both	Individual	Personal empowerment
Gestalt therapy	Insight	Directive	Both	Focus on immediate awareness
Behavior therapy	Action	Directive	Both	Observable changes in behavior
Cognitive therapy	Action	Directive	Individual	Constructive guidance
Rational-emotive behavior therapy	Action	Directive	Individual	Clarity of thinking and goals
Psychodrama	Insight	Directive	Group	Constructive re-enactments
Family therapy	Both	Directive	Group	Shared responsibility for problems

*This column based in part on Andrews (1989).

4. Therapy provides clients with a *new perspective* about themselves and their situations and a chance to practice *new behaviors* (Crencavage & Norcross, 1990; Prochaska & Norcross, 2007). Insights gained during therapy can bring about lasting changes in clients' lives (Grande et al., 2003).

If you recall that our discussion began with trepanning and demonology, it is clear that psychotherapy has come a long way. Still, the search for ways to improve psychotherapy remains an urgent challenge for those who devote their lives to helping others.

The Future of Psychotherapy

What will psychotherapy look like in the future? A group of experts predicted the following (Norcross, Hedges, & Prochaska, 2002):

- There will be an increase in the use of short-term therapy and solution-focused, problem-solving approaches.
- More therapy will be provided by master's-level practitioners (counselors, social workers, and psychiatric nurses).
- The use of lower-cost Internet services, telephone counseling, paraprofessionals, and self-help groups will grow.
- The use of psychiatrists and psychoanalysis will decrease.

As you might guess, many of these predicted changes are based on pressures to reduce the cost of mental health services. Another interesting cost-saving measure is the idea that computers may be able to treat some relatively minor problems. In one study, clients worked through 10 computer-guided sessions that helped them identify a problem, form a plan of action, and work through carrying out the plan. Most were satisfied with the help they received (Jacobs et al., 2001).

Basic Counseling Skills

A number of general helping skills can be distilled from the various approaches to therapy. These are points to keep in mind if you would like to comfort a person in distress, such as a troubled friend or relative (■ Table 13.3).

Active Listening People frequently talk "at" each other without really listening. A person with problems needs to be heard. Make a sincere effort to listen to and understand the person. Try to accept the person's message without judging it or leaping to conclusions. Let the person know you are listening, through eye contact, posture, your tone of voice, and your replies (Kottler, 2004).

Clarify the Problem People who have a clear idea of what is wrong in their lives are more likely to discover solutions. Try to understand the problem from the person's point of view. As you do, check your understanding often. For example,

Therapeutic alliance A caring relationship that unites a therapist and a client in working to solve the client's problems.

TABLE 13.3 Helping Behaviors

To help another person gain insight into a personal problem it is valuable to keep the following comparison in mind.

BEHAVIORS THAT HELP	BEHAVIORS THAT HINDER
Active listening	Probing painful topics
Acceptance	Judging/moralizing
Reflecting feelings	Criticism
Open-ended questioning	Threats
Supportive statements	Rejection
Respect	Ridicule/sarcasm
Patience	Impatience
Genuineness	Placing blame
Paraphrasing	Opinionated statements

Source: Adapted from Kottler, 2004.

you might ask, "Are you saying that you feel depressed just at school? Or in general?" Remember, a problem well defined is often half solved.

Focus on Feelings Feelings are neither right nor wrong. By focusing on feelings you can encourage the outpouring of emotion that is the basis for catharsis. Passing judgment on what is said just makes people defensive. For example, a friend confides that he has failed a test. Perhaps you know that he studies very little. If you say, "Just study more and you will do better," he will probably become defensive or hostile.

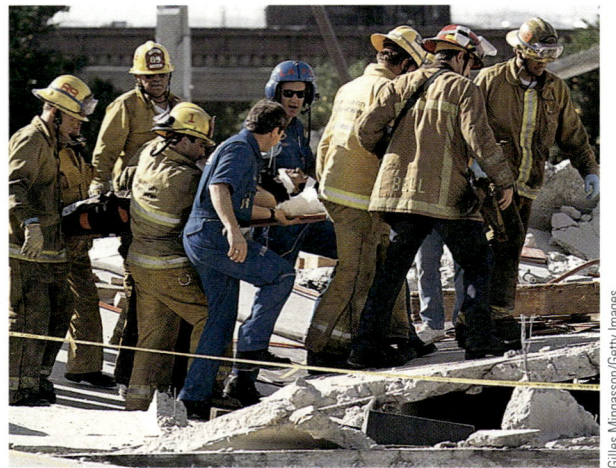

Teams of psychologists and counselors are often assembled to provide support to victims of major accidents and natural disasters. Because their work is stressful and often heart wrenching, relief workers also benefit from on-site counseling. Expressing emotions and talking about feelings are major elements of disaster counseling.

Much more can be accomplished by saying, "You must feel very frustrated" or simply, "How do you feel about it?"

Avoid Giving Advice Many people mistakenly think that they must solve problems for others. Remember that your goal is to provide understanding and support, not solutions. Of course, it is reasonable to give advice when you are asked for it, but beware of the trap of the "Why don't you . . . ? Yes, but . . ." game. According to psychotherapist Eric Berne (1964), this "game" follows a pattern: Someone says, "I have this problem." You say, "Why don't you do thus and so?" The person replies, "Yes, but . . ." and then tells you why your suggestion won't work. If you make a new suggestion the reply will once again be, "Yes, but . . ." Obviously, the person either knows more about his or her personal situation than you do or he or she has reasons for avoiding your advice. The student described earlier knows he needs to study. His problem is to understand why he doesn't *want* to study.

Accept the Person's Frame of Reference W. I. Thomas said, "Things perceived as real are real in their effects." Try to resist imposing your views on the problems of others. Because we all live in different psychological worlds, there is no "correct" view of a life situation. A person who feels that his or her viewpoint has been understood feels freer to examine it objectively and to question it. Accepting and understanding the perspective of another person can be especially difficult when cultural differences exist (Draguns, Gielen, & Fish, 2004). (See "Therapy and Culture—A Bad Case of 'Ifufunyane.'")

Reflect Thoughts and Feelings One of the best things you can do when offering support to another person is to give feedback by simply restating what is said. This is also a good way to encourage a person to talk. If your friend seems to be at a loss for words, *restate* or *paraphrase* his or her last sentence. Here's an example:

> *Friend:* I'm really down about school. I can't get interested in any of my classes. I flunked my Spanish test, and somebody stole my notebook for psychology.
>
> *You:* You're really upset about school, aren't you?
>
> *Friend:* Yeah, and my parents are hassling me about my grades again.
>
> *You:* You're feeling pressured by your parents?
>
> *Friend:* Yeah, damn.
>
> *You:* It must make you angry to be pressured by them.

HUMAN DIVERSITY

Therapy and Culture—A Bad Case of "Ifufunyane"

At the age of 23, the patient was clearly suffering from "ifufunyane," a form of bewitchment common in the Xhosa culture of South Africa. However, he was treated at a local hospital by psychiatrists, who said he had schizophrenia and gave him antipsychotic drugs. The drugs helped, but his family shunned his fancy medical treatment and took him to a traditional healer who gave him herbs for his ifufunyane. Unfortunately, he got worse and was readmitted to the hospital. This time, the psychiatrists included the patient's family in his treatment. Together, they agreed to treat him with a combination of antipsychotic drugs *and* traditional herbs. This time, the patient got much better and his ifufunyane was alleviated, too (Niehaus et al., 2005).

As this example illustrates, **culturally skilled therapists** are trained to work with clients from various cultural backgrounds. To be culturally skilled, a counselor must be able to do all of the following (APA, 2003; Draguns, Gielen, & Fish, 2004; Fowers & Davidov, 2006):

- Adapt traditional theories and techniques to meet the needs of clients from non-European ethnic or racial groups
- Be aware of his or her own cultural values and biases
- Establish rapport with a person from a different cultural background
- Be open to cultural differences without resorting to stereotypes
- Treat members of racial or ethnic communities as individuals
- Be aware of a client's ethnic identity and degree of acculturation to the majority society
- Use existing helping resources within a cultural group to support efforts to resolve problems

Cultural awareness has helped broaden our ideas about mental health and optimal development (Draguns, Gielen, & Fish, 2004). It is also worth remembering that cultural barriers apply to communication in all areas of life, not just therapy. Although such differences can be challenging, they are also frequently enriching (Uwe et al., 2006).

As simple as this sounds, it is very helpful to someone trying to sort out feelings. Try it. If nothing else, you'll develop a reputation as a fantastic conversationalist!

Silence Counselors tend to wait longer before responding than do people in everyday conversations. Pauses of 5 seconds or more are not unusual, and interrupting is rare. Listening patiently lets the person feel unhurried and encourages her or him to speak freely.

Questions Because your goal is to encourage free expression, *open questions* tend to be the most helpful. A *closed question* is one that can be answered yes or no. Open questions call for an open-ended reply. Say, for example, that a friend tells you, "I feel like my boss has it in for me at work." A closed question would be, "Oh yeah? So, are you going to quit?" Open questions, such as, "Do you want to talk about it?" or "How do you feel about it?" are more likely to be helpful.

Maintain Confidentiality Your efforts to help will be wasted if you fail to respect the privacy of someone who has confided in you. Put yourself in the person's place. Don't gossip.

These guidelines are not an invitation to play "junior therapist." Professional therapists are trained to approach serious problems with skills far exceeding those described here. However, the points made help define the qualities of a therapeutic relationship. They also emphasize that each of us can supply two of the greatest mental health resources available at any cost: friendship and honest communication.

Medical Therapies—Psychiatric Care

SURVEY QUESTION: *How do psychiatrists treat psychological disorders?*

Psychotherapy may be applied to anything from a brief crisis to a full-scale psychosis. However, most psychotherapists *do not* treat patients with major depressive disorders, schizophrenia, or other severe conditions. Major mental disorders are more often treated medically (Julien, 2004).

Three main types of **somatic** (bodily) **therapy** are *pharmacotherapy, electroconvulsive therapy,* and *psychosurgery*. Somatic therapy is often done in the context of psychiatric hospitalization. All the somatic approaches have a strong medical slant, and they are typically administered by psychiatrists.

Culturally skilled therapist A therapist who has the awareness, knowledge, and skills necessary to treat clients from diverse cultural backgrounds.
Somatic therapy Any bodily therapy, such as drug therapy, electroconvulsive therapy, or psychosurgery.

Drug Therapies

The atmosphere in psychiatric wards and mental hospitals changed radically in the mid-1950s with the widespread adoption of pharmacotherapy (FAR-meh-koe-THER-eh-pea). **Pharmacotherapy** refers to the use of drugs to treat emotional disturbances. Drugs may relieve the anxiety attacks and other discomforts of milder psychological disorders. More often, however, they are used to combat schizophrenia and major mood disorders.

What sort of drugs are used in pharmacotherapy? Three major types of drugs are used. **Anxiolytics** (such as Valium) produce relaxation or reduce anxiety. **Antidepressants** are mood-elevating drugs that combat depression. **Antipsychotics** (also called **major tranquilizers**) have tranquilizing effects and, in addition, reduce hallucinations and delusions. (See ■ Table 13.4 for examples of each class of drugs.)

Are drugs a valid approach to treatment? Drugs have shortened hospital stays, and they have greatly improved the chances that people will recover from major psychological disorders. Drug therapy has also made it possible for many people to return to the community, where they can be treated on an outpatient basis.

Limitations of Drug Therapy Few experts would argue for a return to the conditions that existed before pharmacotherapy became available. However, drugs do have drawbacks. For example, 15 percent of patients taking major tranquilizers for long periods develop a neurological disorder that causes rhythmic facial and mouth movements (Chakos et al., 1996). Newer drugs are often hailed as medical "miracles." However, all drugs involve a trade-off between benefits and risks. For example, the drug clozapine (Clozaril) can relieve the symptoms of schizophrenia in some previously "hopeless" cases. But Clozaril is also dangerous: 2 out of 100 patients taking the drug suffer from a potentially fatal blood disease (Ginsberg, 2006).

The work of artist Rodger Casier illustrates the value of psychiatric care. Despite having a form of schizophrenia, Casier produces artwork that has received public acclaim and has been featured in professional journals.

Is the risk worth it? Many experts think it is, because chronic schizophrenia robs people of almost everything that makes life worth living. It's possible, of course, that newer drugs will improve the risk/benefit ratio in the treatment of severe problems like schizophrenia. For example, the drug risperidone (Risperdal) appears to be as effective as Clozaril, without the lethal risk. But even the best new drugs are not cure-alls. They help some people and relieve some problems, but not all. It is noteworthy that for serious mental disorders a combination of medication and psychotherapy almost always works better than drugs alone. Nevertheless, where schizophrenia and major mood disorders are concerned, drugs will undoubtedly remain the primary mode of treatment (Vasa, Carlino, & Pine, 2006; Walker et al., 2004).

Electroshock

In **electroconvulsive therapy (ECT)** a 150-volt electrical current is passed through the brain for slightly less than a second. This rather drastic medical treatment for depression triggers a convulsion and causes the patient to lose consciousness for a short time. Muscle relaxants and sedative drugs are given before ECT to soften its impact. Treatments are given in a series of six to eight sessions spread over 3 to 4 weeks.

■ **TABLE 13.4 Commonly Prescribed Psychiatric Drugs**

CLASS	EXAMPLES (TRADE NAMES)	EFFECTS
Minor tranquilizers (antianxiety drugs)	Ativan, Halcion, Librium, Restoril, Valium, Xanax	Reduce anxiety, tension, fear
Antidepressants	Anafranil, Elavil, Nardil, Norpramin, Parnate, Paxil, Prozac, Tofranil, Zoloft	Counteract depression
Antipsychotics (major tranquilizers)	Clozaril, Haldol, Mellaril, Navane, Risperdal, Thorazine	Reduce agitation, delusions, hallucinations, thought disorders

In electroconvulsive therapy, electrodes are attached to the head and a brief electrical current is passed through the brain. ECT is used in the treatment of severe depression.

How does shock help? Actually, it is the seizure activity that is believed to be helpful. Proponents of ECT claim that shock-induced seizures alter the biochemical and hormonal balance in the brain and body, bringing an end to severe depression and suicidal behavior (Fink, 2000) as well as improving long-term quality of life (McCall et al., 2006). Others have charged that ECT works only by confusing patients so they can't remember why they were depressed.

The ECT Debate Not all professionals support the use of ECT. However, most experts seem to agree on the following: (1) At best, ECT produces only temporary improvement—it gets the patient out of a bad spot, but it must be combined with other treatments; (2) ECT can cause memory losses in some patients; (3) ECT should be used only after other treatments have failed; and (4) to lower the chance of a relapse, ECT should be followed by antidepressant drugs (Sackeim et al., 2001). All told, ECT is considered by many to be a valid treatment for selected cases of depression—especially when it rapidly ends wildly self-destructive or suicidal behavior (Pagnin et al., 2004). It's interesting to note that most ECT patients feel that the treatment helped them. Most, in fact, would have it done again (Bernstein et al., 1998).

Psychosurgery

The most extreme medical treatment is **psychosurgery** (any surgical alteration of the brain). The best-known psychosurgery is the lobotomy. In *prefrontal lobotomy* the frontal lobes are surgically disconnected from other brain areas. This procedure was supposed to calm persons who didn't respond to any other type of treatment.

When the lobotomy was first introduced in the 1940s, there were enthusiastic claims for its success. But later studies suggested that some patients were calmed, some showed no change, and some became mental "vegetables." Lobotomies also produced a high rate of undesirable side effects, such as seizures, blunted emotions, major personality changes, and stupor. At about the same time that such problems became apparent, the first antipsychotic drugs became available. Soon after, the lobotomy was abandoned (Mashour, Walker, & Martuza, 2005).

To what extent is psychosurgery used now? Psychosurgery is still considered valid by many neurosurgeons. However, most now use *deep lesioning,* in which small target areas are destroyed in the brain's interior. The appeal of deep lesioning is that it can have value as a remedy for some very specific disorders (Mashour, Walker, & Martuza, 2005). For instance, patients suffering from a severe type of obsessive-compulsive disorder may be helped by psychosurgery (Dougherty et al., 2002).

It is worth remembering that psychosurgery cannot be reversed. Whereas a drug can be given or taken away, you can't take back psychosurgery. Critics argue that psychosurgery should be banned altogether; others continue to report success with brain surgery. All things considered, it is perhaps most accurate, even after decades of use, to describe psychosurgery as an experimental technique. Nevertheless, it may have value as a remedy for some very specific disorders (Fenton, 1998; Mashour, Walker, & Martuza, 2005).

Hospitalization

Mental hospitalization for major mental disorders involves placing a person in a protected setting where medical therapy is provided. Hospitalization, by itself, can be a form of treatment. Staying in a hospital takes patients out of situations that may be sustaining their problems. For example, people with drug addictions may find it nearly impossible to resist

---

Pharmacotherapy The use of drugs to alleviate the symptoms of emotional disturbance.

Anxiolytics Drugs (such as Valium) that produce relaxation or reduce anxiety.

Antidepressants Mood-elevating drugs.

Antipsychotics Drugs that, in addition to having tranquilizing effects, also tend to reduce hallucinations and delusional thinking (also called major tranquilizers).

Electroconvulsive therapy (ECT) A treatment for severe depression, consisting of an electric shock passed directly through the brain, which induces a convulsion.

Psychosurgery Any surgical alteration of the brain designed to bring about desirable behavioral or emotional changes.

Mental hospitalization Placing a person in a protected, therapeutic environment staffed by mental health professionals.

the temptations for drug abuse in their daily lives. Hospitalization can help them make a clean break from their self-destructive behavior patterns (André et al., 2003).

At their best, hospitals are sanctuaries that provide diagnosis, support, refuge, and therapy. This is frequently true of psychiatric units in general hospitals and private psychiatric hospitals. At worst, confinement to an institution can be a brutal experience that leaves people less prepared to face the world than when they arrived. This is more often the case in large state mental hospitals (Gorman, 1996).

In most instances, hospitals are best used as a last resort, after other forms of treatment within the community have been exhausted. Actually, most psychiatric patients do as well with short-term hospitalization as they do with longer periods. For this reason, the average stay in psychiatric hospitals is now just 20 days, rather than 3 to 4 months, as it was 20 years ago.

Another trend in treatment is **partial hospitalization.** In this approach, some patients spend their days in the hospital but go home at night. Others attend therapy sessions during the evening. A major advantage of partial hospitalization is that patients can go home and practice what they've been learning. Eventually, most return to normal life. Overall, partial hospitalization can be just as effective as full hospitalization (Kiser, Heston, & Paavola, 2006).

Deinstitutionalization In the last 30 years the population in large mental hospitals has dropped by two thirds. This is largely a result of **deinstitutionalization,** or reduced use of full-time commitment to mental institutions. Long-term "institutionalization" can lead to dependency, isolation, and continued emotional disturbance (Chamberlin & Rogers, 1990). Deinstitutionalization was meant to remedy this problem.

How successful has deinstitutionalization been? In truth, its success has been limited (Talbott, 2004). Many states reduced mental hospital populations primarily as a way to save money. The upsetting result is that many chronic patients have been discharged to hostile communities without adequate care. Many former patients have joined the ranks of the homeless. Sadly, patients who trade hospitalization for unemployment, homelessness, and social isolation all too often end up rehospitalized or in jail (Goldman, 1998).

Large mental hospitals may no longer be warehouses for society's unwanted, but many former patients are no better off in bleak nursing homes, single-room hotels, board-and-care homes, shelters, or jails. One in five of the 2 million Americans who are in jail or prison are mentally ill—three times the number who are in mental hospitals (Human Rights Watch, 2003). These figures suggest that jails are replacing mental hospitals as our society's "solution" for mental illness. Yet, ironically, high-quality care is available in almost every community. As much as anything, a simple lack of money prevents large numbers of people from getting the help they need (Torrey, 1996).

Half-way houses may be a better way to ease a patient's return to the community (Soyez & Broekaert, 2003). **Half-way houses** are short-term group living facilities for people making the transition from an institution (mental hospital, prison, and so forth) to independent living. Typically, they offer supervision and support, without being as restricted and medically oriented as hospitals. They also keep people near their families. Most important, half-way houses can reduce a person's chances of being readmitted to a hospital (Coursey, Ward-Alexander, & Katz, 1990).

Depending on the quality of the institution, hospitalization may be a refuge or a brutalizing experience. Many state "asylums" or mental hospitals are antiquated and in need of drastic improvement.

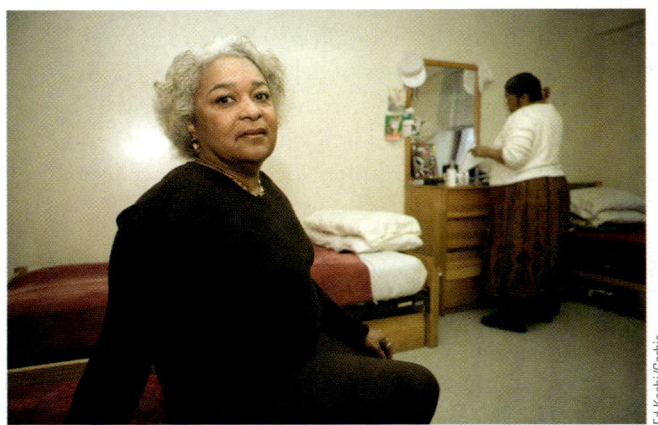

A well-run half-way house can be a humane and cost-effective way to ease former mental patients back into the community (Soyez & Broekaert, 2003).

Community Mental Health Programs

Community mental health centers are a bright spot in the area of mental health care. **Community mental health centers** offer a wide range of mental health services and psychiatric care. Such centers try to help people avoid hospitalization and find answers to mental health problems (Burns, 2004). Typically, they do this by providing short-term treatment, counseling, outpatient care, emergency services, and suicide prevention.

If it is like most, the primary aim of the mental health center in your community is to directly aid troubled citizens. Its second goal is likely to be *prevention*. Consultation, education, and **crisis intervention** (skilled management of a psychological emergency) are used to prevent problems before they become serious. Also, some centers attempt to raise the general level of mental health in a community by combating unemployment, delinquency, and drug abuse (Tausig, Michello, & Subedi, 2004).

Have community mental health centers succeeded in meeting their goals? In practice, they have concentrated much more on providing clinical services than they have on preventing problems. This appears to be primarily the result of wavering government support (translation: money). Overall, community mental health centers have succeeded in making psychological services more accessible than ever before. Many of their programs rely on **paraprofessionals** (individuals who work in a near-professional capacity under the supervision of more highly trained staff). Some paraprofessionals are ex-addicts, ex-alcoholics, or ex-patients who have "been there." Many more are persons (paid or volunteer) who have skills in tutoring, crafts, or counseling or who are simply warm, understanding, and skilled at communication. Often, paraprofessionals are more approachable than "doctors." This encourages people to seek mental health services that they might otherwise be reluctant to use (Everly, 2002).

A Look Ahead In the "Psychology in Action" module that follows we will return briefly to behavioral approaches. There you will find a number of useful techniques that you may be able to apply to your own behavior. You'll also find a discussion of when to seek professional help and how to find it. Here's your authors' professional advice: This is information you won't want to skip.

MODULE 13.5 Summary

Can psychotherapy be done with groups of people?
- Group therapy may be an extension of individual methods, or it may be based on special techniques developed for groups. Group therapy is especially good for relationship problems.
- In psychodrama, individuals enact roles and incidents resembling real-life problems. In family therapy, the family group is treated as a unit.
- Sensitivity and encounter groups encourage positive personality change. Large-group awareness training attempts to do the same, but the benefits of such programs are questionable.

What do various therapies have in common?
- Effective psychotherapies are based on the therapeutic alliance, a protected setting, catharsis, insights, new perspectives, and a chance to practice new behaviors.
- All of the following are helping skills that can be learned: active listening, acceptance, reflection, open-ended questioning, support, respect, patience, genuineness, and paraphrasing.
- The culturally skilled counselor must be able to establish rapport with a person from a different cultural background and adapt traditional theories and techniques to meet the needs of clients from non-European ethnic groups.

How do psychiatrists treat psychological disorders?
- Medical approaches to mental disorders, such as drugs, surgery, and hospitalization, are similar to medical treatments for physical ailments.
- Three somatic approaches to treatment are pharmacotherapy, electroconvulsive therapy (ECT), and psychosurgery.
- Community mental health centers seek to avoid or minimize mental hospitalization. They also seek to prevent mental health problems through education, consultation, and crisis intervention.

Partial hospitalization An approach in which patients receive treatment at a hospital during the day but return home at night.

Deinstitutionalization Reduced use of full-time commitment to mental institutions to treat mental disorders.

Half-way house A community-based facility for individuals making the transition from an institution (mental hospital, prison, and so forth) to independent living.

Community mental health center A facility offering a wide range of mental health services, such as prevention, counseling, consultation, and crisis intervention.

Crisis intervention Skilled management of a psychological emergency.

Paraprofessional An individual who works in a near-professional capacity under the supervision of a more highly trained person.

KNOWLEDGE BUILDER

Group Therapies, Helping Skills, and Medical Therapies

Recite

1. In psychodrama, people attempt to form meaningful wholes out of disjointed thoughts, feelings, and actions. T or F?
2. Most large-group awareness trainings make use of Gestalt therapy. T or F?
3. The mirror technique is frequently used in
   a. exposure therapy
   b. psychodrama
   c. family therapy
   d. ECT
4. Research shows that about half of all patients feel better after their first ___ therapy sessions.
   a. 8
   b. 16
   c. 24
   d. 26
5. Emotional rapport, warmth, understanding, acceptance, and empathy are the core of
   a. the therapeutic alliance
   b. large-group awareness training
   c. role reversals
   d. action therapy
6. Culturally skilled therapists do all but one of the following; which does not apply?
   a. Are aware of the client's degree of acculturation
   b. Use helping resources within the client's cultural group
   c. Adapt standard techniques to match cultural stereotypes
   d. Are aware of their own cultural values
7. ECT is a modern form of pharmacotherapy. T or F?
8. Currently, the frontal lobotomy is the most widely used form of psychosurgery. T or F?
9. Major tranquilizers are also known as
   a. anxiolytics
   b. antipsychotics
   c. antidepressants
   d. prefrontal sedatives
10. Deinstitutionalization is an advanced form of partial hospitalization. T or F?

Reflect
Critical Thinking

11. In your opinion, do psychologists have a duty to protect others who may be harmed by their clients? For example, if a patient has homicidal fantasies about his ex-wife, should she be informed?
12. Residents of Berkeley, California, once voted on a referendum to ban the use of ECT within city limits. Do you think that the use of certain psychiatric treatments should be controlled by law?

Relate

Would you rather participate in individual therapy or group therapy? What advantages and disadvantages do you think each has?

Based on your own experience, how valid do you think it is to say that within families "a problem for one is a problem for all"?

What lies at the "heart" of psychotherapy? How would you describe it to a friend?

Which of the basic counseling skills do you already use? Which would improve your ability to help a person in distress?

If a family member of yours became severely depressed, what therapies would be available to him or her? What are the pros and cons of each choice?

Link

Internet addresses frequently change. To find the sites listed here, visit http://www.thomsonedu.com/psychology/coon for an updated list of Internet addresses and direct links to relevant sites.

- **American Association for Marriage and Family Therapy** Visit the website of the AAMFT.
- **American Self-Help Group Clearinghouse** Explore this database of more than 1,000 self-help groups.
- **Lobotomy** Read a case study of lobotomy and the history of the transorbital lobotomy procedure.

ANSWERS

1. F 2. F 3. b 4. a 5. a 6. c 7. F 8. F 9. b 10. F 11. According to the law, there is a duty to protect others when a therapist could, with little effort, prevent serious harm. However, this duty can conflict with a client's rights to confidentiality and with client-therapist trust. Therapists often make difficult choices in such situations. 12. The question of who can prescribe drugs, perform surgery, and administer ECT is controlled by law. However, psychiatrists strongly object to residents, city councils, or government agencies making *medical* decisions.

MODULE *Psychology in Action*

13.6 Self-Management and Seeking Professional Help

SURVEY QUESTION: *How are behavioral principles applied to everyday problems?*

"Throw out the snake oil, ladies and gentlemen, and throw away your troubles. Doctor B. Havior Modification is here to put an end to all human suffering."

True? Well, not quite. Behavior therapy is not a cure-all. Its use is often quite complicated and requires a great deal of expertise. Still, behavior therapy offers a straightforward solution to many problems.

As mentioned elsewhere in this book, you should seek professional help when a significant problem exists. For lesser difficulties you may want to try applying behavioral principles yourself (Watson & Tharp, 2007). Let us see how this might be done.

COVERT REWARD AND PUNISHMENT—BOOSTING YOUR "WILLPOWER"

Therapist: "Have you ever decided to quit smoking cigarettes, watching television too much, eating too much, drinking too much, or driving too fast?"

Client: "Well, one of those applies. I have decided several times to quit smoking."

Therapist: "When have you decided?"

Client: "Usually after I am reminded of how dangerous smoking is—like when I heard that my uncle had died of lung cancer. He smoked constantly."

Therapist: "If you have decided to quit 'several times,' I assume you haven't succeeded."

Client: "No, the usual pattern is for me to become upset about smoking and then to cut down for a day or two."

Therapist: "You forget the disturbing image of your uncle's death, or whatever, and start smoking again."

Client: "Yes. I suppose if I had an uncle die every day or so, I might actually quit!"

The use of intensive behavioral principles, such as electric shock, to condition an aversion seems remote from everyday problems. Even naturally aversive actions are difficult to apply to personal behavior. As mentioned earlier, for instance, rapid smoking is difficult for most smokers to carry out on their own. And what about a problem like overeating? It would be difficult indeed to eat enough to create a lasting aversion to overeating. (Although it's sometimes tempting to try.)

In view of such limitations, psychologists have developed an alternative procedure that can be used to curb smoking, overeating, and other habits (Cautela & Kearney, 1986; Watson & Tharp, 2007).

Covert Sensitization In **covert sensitization,** aversive imagery is used to reduce the occurrence of an undesired response. Here's how it's done: Obtain six 3×5 cards and on each write a brief description of a scene related to the habit you wish to control. The scene should be so *disturbing* or *disgusting* that thinking about it would temporarily make you very uncomfortable about indulging in the habit. For smoking, the cards might read:

- "I am in a doctor's office. The doctor looks at some reports and tells me I have lung cancer. She says a lung will have to be removed and sets a date for the operation."
- "I am in bed under an oxygen tent. My chest feels caved in. There is a tube in my throat. I can barely breathe."
- "I wake up in the morning and smoke a cigarette. I begin coughing up blood."
- "My lover won't kiss me because my breath smells bad."
- Other cards would continue along the same line.

The trick, of course, is to get yourself to imagine or picture vividly each of these disturbing scenes *several times* a day. Imagining the scenes can be accomplished by placing them under *stimulus control*. Simply choose something you do *frequently* each day (such as getting a cup of coffee or getting up

Covert sensitization Use of aversive imagery to reduce the occurrence of an undesired response.

from your chair). Next make a rule: Before you can get a cup of coffee or get up from your chair, or whatever you have selected as a cue, you must take out your cards and *vividly picture* yourself engaging in the action you wish to curb (eating or smoking, for example). Then *vividly picture* the scene described on the top card. Imagine the scene for 30 seconds.

After visualizing the top card, move it to the bottom so the cards are rotated. Make up new cards each week. The scenes can be made much more upsetting than the samples given here. The samples are toned down to keep you from being "grossed out."

Covert sensitization can also be used directly in situations that test your self-control. If you are trying to lose weight, for instance, you might be able to turn down a tempting dessert in this way: As you look at the dessert, visualize maggots crawling all over it. If you make this image as vivid and nauseating as possible, losing your appetite is almost a certainty. If you want to apply this technique to other situations, be aware that vomiting scenes are especially effective. Covert sensitization may sound as if you are "playing games with yourself," but it can be a great help if you want to cut down on a bad habit (Cautela & Kearney, 1986). Try it!

Thought Stopping As discussed earlier, behavior therapists accept that thoughts, like visible responses, can also cause trouble. Think of times when you have repeatedly "put yourself down" mentally or when you have been preoccupied by needless worries, fears, or other negative and upsetting thoughts. If you would like to gain control over such thoughts, thought stopping may help you do it.

In **thought stopping,** aversive stimuli are used to interrupt or prevent upsetting thoughts. The simplest thought-stopping technique makes use of mild punishment to suppress upsetting mental images and internal "talk." Simply place a large, flat rubber band around your wrist. As you go through the day apply this rule: Each time you catch yourself thinking the upsetting image or thought, pull the rubber band away from your wrist and snap it. You need not make this terribly painful. Its value lies in drawing your attention to how often you form negative thoughts and in interrupting the flow of thoughts. Strong punishment is not required.

It seems like this procedure might be abandoned rapidly. Is there an alternative? A second thought-stopping procedure requires only that you interrupt upsetting thoughts each time they occur. Begin by setting aside time each day during which you will deliberately think the unwanted thought. As you begin to form the thought, shout "Stop!" aloud, with conviction. (Obviously, you should choose a private spot for this part of the procedure!)

Repeat the thought-stopping procedure 10 to 20 times for the first 2 or 3 days. Then switch to shouting "Stop!" covertly (to yourself) rather than aloud. Thereafter, thought stopping can be carried out throughout the day, whenever upsetting thoughts occur (Williams & Long, 1991). After several days of practice, you should be able to stop unwanted thoughts whenever they occur.

Covert Reinforcement Earlier we discussed how punishing images can be used to decrease undesirable responses, such as smoking or overeating. Many people also find it helpful to covertly *reinforce* desired actions. **Covert reinforcement** is the use of positive imagery to reinforce desired behavior. For example, suppose your target behavior is, once again, not eating dessert. If this were the case, you could do the following (Cautela & Kearney, 1986; Watson & Tharp, 2007):

> Imagine that you are standing at the dessert table with your friends. As dessert is passed, you politely refuse and feel good about staying on your diet.

These images would then be followed by imagining a pleasant, reinforcing scene:

> Imagine that you are your ideal weight. You look really slim in your favorite color and style. Someone you like says to you, "Gee, you've lost weight. I've never seen you look so good."

For many people, of course, actual direct reinforcement (as described in Module 6.6) is the best way to alter behavior. Nevertheless, covert or "visualized" reinforcement can have similar effects. To make use of covert reinforcement, choose one or more target behaviors and rehearse them mentally. Then follow each rehearsal with a vivid, rewarding image.

Self-Directed Desensitization— Overcoming Common Fears

You have prepared for 2 weeks to give a speech in a large class. As your turn approaches, your hands begin to tremble. Your heart pounds and you find it difficult to breathe. You say to your body, "Relax!" What happens? Nothing! That's why the first step in desensitization is learning to relax voluntarily, by using the tension-release method described in Module 13.3. As an alternative, you might want to try imagining a very safe, pleasant, and relaxing scene. Some people find such images as relaxing as the tension-release method (Rosenthal, 1993). Another helpful technique is to do some deep breathing. Typically, a person who is breathing deeply is relaxed. Shallow breathing involves little movement of the diaphragm. If you place your hand on your abdomen, it will move up and down if you are breathing deeply.

Once you have learned to relax, the next step is to identify the fear you would like to control and construct a hierarchy.

Procedure for Constructing a Hierarchy Make a list of situations (related to the fear) that make you anxious. Try to list at least 10 situations. Some should be very frightening and others only mildly frightening. Write a short description of each situation on a separate 3-by-5 card. Place the cards in order from the least disturbing situation to the most disturbing. Here is a sample hierarchy for a student afraid of public speaking:

1. Being given an assignment to speak in class
2. Thinking about the topic and the date the speech must be given
3. Writing the speech; thinking about delivering the speech
4. Watching other students speak in class the week before the speech date
5. Rehearsing the speech alone; pretending to give it to the class
6. Delivering the speech to my roommate; pretending my roommate is the teacher
7. Reviewing the speech on the day it is to be presented
8. Entering the classroom; waiting and thinking about the speech
9. Being called; standing up; facing the audience
10. Delivering the speech

Using the Hierarchy When you have mastered the relaxation exercises and have the hierarchy constructed, set aside time each day to work on reducing your fear. Begin by performing the relaxation exercises. When you are completely relaxed, visualize the scene on the first card (the least frightening scene). If you can *vividly* picture and imagine yourself in the first situation twice *without a noticeable increase in muscle tension*, proceed to the next card. Also, as you progress, relax yourself between cards.

Each day, stop when you reach a card that you cannot visualize without becoming tense in three attempts. Each day, begin one or two cards before the one on which you stopped the previous day. Continue to work with the cards until you can visualize the last situation without experiencing tension (techniques are based on Wolpe, 1974).

By using this approach you should be able to reduce the fear or anxiety associated with things such as public speaking, entering darkened rooms, asking questions in large classes, heights, talking to members of the opposite sex, and taking tests (Watson & Tharp, 2007). Even if you are not always able to reduce a fear, you will have learned to place relaxation under voluntary control. This alone is valuable because controlling unnecessary tension can increase energy and efficiency.

Seeking Professional Help—When, Where, and How?

SURVEY QUESTION: *How can a person find professional help?*

Chances are good that at some point you or someone in your family will benefit from mental health services of one kind or another. In one survey, half of all American households included someone who received mental health treatment during the preceding year (Chamberlin, 2004).

How would I know if I should seek professional help at some point in my life? Although there is no simple answer to this question, the following guidelines may be helpful.

1. If your level of psychological discomfort (unhappiness, anxiety, or depression, for example) is comparable to a level of physical discomfort that would cause you to see a doctor or dentist, you should consider seeing a psychologist or a psychiatrist.
2. Another signal to watch for is significant changes in behavior, such as the quality of your work (or schoolwork), your rate of absenteeism, your use of drugs (including alcohol), or your relationships with others.
3. Perhaps you have urged a friend or relative to seek professional help and were dismayed because he or she refused to do so. If you find friends or relatives making a similar suggestion, recognize that they may be seeing things more clearly than you are.
4. If you have persistent or disturbing suicidal thoughts or impulses, you should seek help immediately.

Locating a Therapist

If I wanted to talk to a therapist, how would I find one? Here are some suggestions that could help you get started.

1. *The Yellow Pages.* Psychologists are listed in the telephone book under "Psychologist" or in some cases under "Counseling Services." Psychiatrists are generally listed as a subheading under "Physicians." Counselors are usually found under the heading "Marriage and Family Counselors." These listings will usually put you in touch with individuals in private practice.
2. *Community or county mental health centers.* Most counties and many cities offer public mental health

Thought stopping Use of aversive stimuli to interrupt or prevent upsetting thoughts.
Covert reinforcement Using positive imagery to reinforce desired behavior.

services. (These are listed in the phone book.) Public mental health centers usually provide counseling and therapy services directly, and they can refer you to private therapists.

3. *Mental health associations.* Many cities have mental health associations organized by concerned citizens. Groups such as these usually keep listings of qualified therapists and other services and programs in the community.

4. *Colleges and universities.* If you are a student, don't overlook counseling services offered by a student health center or special student counseling facilities.

5. *Newspaper advertisements.* Some psychologists advertise their services in newspapers. Also, low-cost "outreach" clinics occasionally try to make their presence known to the public by advertising. In either case, you should carefully inquire into a therapist's training and qualifications. Without the benefit of a referral from a trusted person, it is wise to be cautious.

6. *Crisis hotlines.* The typical crisis hotline is a telephone service staffed by community volunteers. These people are trained to provide information concerning a wide range of mental health problems. They also have lists of organizations, services, and other resources in the community where you can go for help.

■ Table 13.5 summarizes all the sources for psychotherapy, counseling, and referrals we have discussed, as well as some additional possibilities.

■ TABLE 13.5 Mental Health Resources

- Family doctors
- Mental health specialists, such as psychiatrists, psychologists, social workers, or mental health counselors
- Religious leaders/counselors
- Health maintenance organizations
- Community mental health centers
- Hospital psychiatry departments and outpatient clinics
- University- or medical school-affiliated programs
- State hospital outpatient clinics
- Social service agencies
- Private clinics and facilities
- Employee assistance programs
- Local medical and/or psychiatric societies

Source: National Institute of Mental Health (2005).

Options *How would I know what kind of a therapist to see? How would I pick one?* The choice between a psychiatrist and a psychologist is somewhat arbitrary. Both are trained to do psychotherapy. Although a psychiatrist can administer somatic therapy and prescribe drugs, so can psychologists in New Mexico and Louisiana (Munsey, 2006). Besides, a psychologist can work in conjunction with a physician if such services are needed. Psychologists and psychiatrists can be equally effective as therapists (Seligman, 1995).

Fees for psychiatrists are usually higher, averaging about $160 to $200 an hour. Psychologists average about $100 an hour. Counselors and social workers typically charge about $80 per hour. Group therapy averages only about $40 an hour because the therapist's fee is divided among several people.

Be aware that most health insurance plans will pay for psychological services. If fees are a problem, keep in mind that many therapists charge on a sliding scale, or ability-to-pay basis, and that community mental health centers almost always charge on a sliding scale. In one way or another, help is almost always available for anyone who needs it.

Some communities and college campuses have counseling services staffed by sympathetic paraprofessionals or peer counselors. These services are free or very low cost. As mentioned earlier, paraprofessionals are people who work in a near-professional capacity under professional supervision. **Peer counselors** are nonprofessional persons who have learned basic counseling skills. There is a natural tendency, perhaps, to doubt the abilities of paraprofessionals. However, many studies have shown that paraprofessional counselors are often as effective as professionals (Christensen & Jacobson, 1994).

Also, don't overlook self-help groups, which can add valuable support to professional treatment. Members of a self-help group typically share a particular type of problem, such as eating disorders or coping with an alcoholic parent. **Self-help groups** offer members mutual support and a chance to discuss problems. In many instances helping others also serves as therapy for those who give help (Burlingame & Davies, 2002). For some problems, self-help groups may be the best choice of all (Fobair, 1997; Galanter et al., 2005).

Qualifications You can usually find out about a therapist's qualifications simply by asking. A reputable therapist will be glad to reveal his or her background. If you have any doubts, credentials may be checked and other helpful information can be obtained from local branches of any of the following organizations. You can also browse the websites listed here:

American Association for Marriage and Family Therapy (www.aamft.org)

American Family Therapy Association (www.afta.org)

American Psychiatric Association (www.psych.org)
American Psychological Association (www.apa.org)
Association of Humanistic Psychology (www.ahpweb.org)
Canadian Psychiatric Association (www.cpa-apc.org)
Canadian Psychological Association (www.cpa.ca)
National Mental Health Association (www.nmha.org)

The question of how to pick a particular therapist remains. The best way is to start with a short consultation with a respected psychiatrist, psychologist, or counselor. This will allow the person you consult to evaluate your difficulty and recommend a type of therapy or a therapist who is likely to be helpful. As an alternative you might ask the person teaching this course for a referral.

Evaluating a Therapist *How would I know whether or not to quit or ignore a therapist?* A balanced look at psychotherapies suggests that all *techniques* are about equally successful (Wampold et al., 1997). However, all *therapists* are not equally successful. Far more important than the approach used are the therapist's personal qualities (Okiishi et al., 2003; Prochaska & Norcross, 2007). The most consistently successful therapists are those who are willing to use whatever method seems most helpful for a client. They are also marked by personal characteristics of warmth, integrity, sincerity, and empathy. Former clients consistently rate the person doing the therapy as more important than the type of therapy used (Elliott & Williams, 2003).

It is perhaps most accurate to say that at this stage of development, psychotherapy is an art, not a science. The *relationship* between a client and therapist is the therapist's most basic tool (Hubble, Duncan, & Miller, 1999; Prochaska & Norcross, 2007). This is why you must trust and easily relate to a therapist for therapy to be effective. Here are some danger signals to watch for in psychotherapy:

- Sexual advances by therapist
- Therapist makes repeated verbal threats or is physically aggressive
- Therapist is excessively blaming, belittling, hostile, or controlling
- Therapist makes excessive small talk; talks repeatedly about his/her own problems
- Therapist encourages prolonged dependence on him/her
- Therapist demands absolute trust or tells client not to discuss therapy with anyone else

Clients who like their therapist are generally more successful in therapy (Talley et al., 1990). An especially important part of the therapeutic alliance is agreement about the goals of therapy (Meier et al., 2006). It is therefore a good idea to think about what you would like to accomplish by entering therapy. Write down your goals and discuss them with your therapist during the first session. Your first meeting with a therapist should also answer all of the following questions (Somberg, Stone, & Claiborn, 1993):

- Will the information I reveal in therapy remain completely confidential?
- What risks do I face if I begin therapy?
- How long do you expect treatment to last?
- What form of treatment do you expect to use?
- Are there alternatives to therapy that might help me as much or more?

It's always tempting to avoid facing up to personal problems. With this in mind, you should give a therapist a fair chance and not give up too easily. But don't hesitate to change therapists or to terminate therapy if you lose confidence in the therapist or if you don't relate well to the therapist as a person.

MODULE 13.6 Psychology in Action Summary

How are behavioral principles applied to everyday problems?

- Some personal problems can be successfully treated using self-management techniques, such as covert reinforcement, covert sensitization, thought stopping, and self-directed desensitization.
- In covert sensitization, aversive images are used to discourage unwanted behavior.
- Thought stopping uses mild punishment to prevent upsetting thoughts.
- Covert reinforcement is a way to encourage desired responses by mental rehearsal.
- Desensitization pairs relaxation with a hierarchy of upsetting images in order to lessen fears.

How could a person find professional help?

- Everyone should know how to obtain high-quality mental health care in his or her community.

Peer counselor A nonprofessional person who has learned basic counseling skills.
Self-help group A group of people who share a particular type of problem and provide mutual support to one another.

- Various psychotherapies are generally equally successful, but some therapists are more effective than others. If you need help, it is worth the effort required to find a well-qualified, highly recommended therapist.
- In most communities, a competent and reputable therapist can be located with public sources of information or through a referral.

KNOWLEDGE BUILDER

Self-Management and Seeking Professional Help

Recite

1. Covert sensitization and thought stopping combine aversion therapy and cognitive therapy. T or F?
2. Like covert aversion conditioning, covert reinforcement of desired responses is also possible. T or F?
3. The tension-release method is an important part of
   a. covert reinforcement
   b. thought stopping
   c. desensitization
   d. REBT
4. Items in a desensitization hierarchy should be placed in order from the least disturbing to the most disturbing. T or F?
5. The first step in desensitization is to place the visualization of disturbing images under stimulus control. T or F?
6. Persistent emotional discomfort is a clear sign that professional psychological counseling should be sought. T or F?
7. Community mental health centers rarely offer counseling or therapy themselves; they only do referrals. T or F?
8. In many instances a therapist's personal qualities have more of an effect on the outcome of therapy than does the type of therapy used. T or F?

Reflect

Critical Thinking

9. Would it be acceptable for a therapist to urge a client to break all ties with a troublesome family member?

Relate

How could you use covert sensitization, thought stopping, and covert reinforcement to change your behavior? Try to apply each technique to a specific example.

Just for practice, make a fear hierarchy for a situation you find frightening. Does vividly picturing items in the hierarchy make you tense or anxious? If so, can you intentionally relax using the tension-release method?

Assume that you want to seek help from a psychologist or other mental health professional. How would you proceed? Take some time to actually find out what mental health services are available to you.

Link

Internet addresses frequently change. To find the sites listed here, visit **http://www.thomsonedu.com/psychology/coon** for an updated list of Internet addresses and direct links to relevant sites.

- **Therapy Effectiveness** Read an article about the effectiveness of therapy.
- **Finding a Therapist in Your Hometown** Use the Internet to locate a local therapist.
- **Find a Therapist** Another Internet tool to help you locate a therapist.

ANSWERS

1. T 2. T 3. c 4. T 5. F 6. T 7. F 8. T 9. Such decisions must be made by clients themselves. Therapists can help clients evaluate important decisions and feelings about significant persons in their lives. However, actively urging a client to sever a relationship borders on unethical behavior.

Interactive Learning

Psychology: Active Learning Modules Book Companion Website

http://www.thomsonedu.com/psychology/coon

Visit your Book Companion Website, where you will find flash cards, practice quizzes, Internet links, and more to help you study.

ThomsonNOW

Just What You Need to Know NOW!

Spend time on what you need to master rather than on information you already have learned. Take a pre-test for this chapter, and ThomsonNOW will generate a personalized study plan based on your results. The study plan will identify the topics you need to review and direct you to online resources to help you master those topics. You can then take a post-test to help you determine the concepts you have mastered and what you will need to work on. Try it out! Go to www.thomsonedu.com/login to sign in with an access code or to purchase access to this product.

14 Gender and Sexuality

MODULE 14.1 Sex, Gender, and Androgyny
SURVEY QUESTIONS: What are the basic dimensions of sex? How does one's sense of maleness or femaleness develop?
SURVEY QUESTION: What is psychological androgyny (and is it contagious)?

MODULE 14.2 Sexual Behavior and Sexual Orientation
SURVEY QUESTION: What are the most typical patterns of human sexual behavior?

MODULE 14.3 Sexual Response, Attitudes, and Behavior
SURVEY QUESTION: To what extent do females and males differ in sexual response?

SURVEY QUESTION: What are the most common sexual disorders?
SURVEY QUESTION: Have recent changes in attitudes affected sexual behavior?
SURVEY QUESTION: What impacts have sexually transmitted diseases had on sexual behavior?

MODULE 14.4 Psychology in Action: Sexual Problems—When Pleasure Fades
SURVEY QUESTIONS: What are the most common sexual adjustment problems? How are they treated?

That Magic Word

Sex \seks\ n 1. One of the two divisions of organisms formed on the distinction of male and female.

"Sex" has many meanings: reproduction, lovemaking, sexual identity, and much more. Of the various meanings, the simplest would seem to be biological sex. What, really, could be simpler? Females are females and males are males, right? Wrong. Even something as basic as biological sex is many sided.

The complexity of sexual identity is illustrated by Michelle's journey from her early life as a man to her current life as a woman. Michelle is a transsexual who acted on her deeply held desire to change her sex, biologically, psychologically, and socially. About her transition, Michelle remarked, "Whatever it takes to create a foundation, I am happy for. It was hard for them (her parents) to have a gay boy, and then a gay boy into a girl, and then a gay girl who is dating a girl who is actually a boy. I think it has been about a year now that she (her mother) has been using, 'I love you' " (Kaufmann, 2007, p. 6).

Genetically Michelle is still male, but psychologically she is female, she has female genitals, and she functions socially as a female (Hyde & DeLamater, 2006). Is Michelle, then, female or male? You might view Michelle as an unfair example because transsexuals seek to alter their "natural" sex. For most people, the indicators of maleness or femaleness are in agreement. Nevertheless, it is not unusual to find ambiguities among various aspects of a person's sex.

Sex is probably a topic you already know a lot about. It should be interesting, then, for you to compare your knowledge with the information that follows. Sex and gender have a tremendous impact on relationships, personal identity, and health.

MODULE 14.1 Sex, Gender, and Androgyny

CONTRARY TO COMMON BELIEF, classifying a person as male or female is not a simple either/or proposition. To begin this module, we will consider the basic dimensions that define each person as male or female. In all societies, numerous facets of daily life are affected by whether you are female or male, masculine or feminine.

Sexual Development— Circle One: *XX* or *XY*?

SURVEY QUESTIONS: *What are the basic dimensions of sex? How does one's sense of maleness or femaleness develop?*

One thing we never forget about a person is his or her sex. Considering the number of activities, relationships, conflicts, and choices influenced by sex, it is no wonder that we pay such close attention to it (Hyde & DeLamater, 2006).

Being male or female is partly a matter of biology and partly psychological. The term **sex** refers to whether you are biologically female or male. In contrast, **gender** refers to all the psychological and social traits associated with being male or female (Crooks & Baur, 2008). In other words, after we establish that you are male or female, gender tells us if you are masculine or feminine (as defined by the culture in which you live). Two important aspects of gender are *gender roles* and *gender identity*, which we will discuss soon. As Michelle's story so clearly illustrates, biological sex does not always align with psychological and social gender. In **transsexuals**, a person's biological sex conflicts with his or her preferred psychological and social gender roles. For the moment, let's begin with two basic questions: Biologically, what does it mean to be female or male? How do male and female differences develop?

Female or Male?

Males and females differ in both *primary* and *secondary* sexual characteristics. **Primary sexual characteristics** refer to the sexual and reproductive organs themselves: the vagina, ovaries, and uterus in females and the penis, testes, and scrotum in males. (See ● Fig. 14.1 and ● Fig. 14.2. Also see ■ Table 14.1.) **Secondary sexual characteristics** are more superficial physical features that appear at puberty. These features develop in response to hormonal signals from the pituitary gland. In females, secondary sexual characteristics include breast development, broadening of the hips, and other changes in body shape. Males grow facial and body hair, and the voice deepens. These changes signal that a person is bio-

● **FIGURE 14.1** Cutaway view of internal and external male reproductive structures.

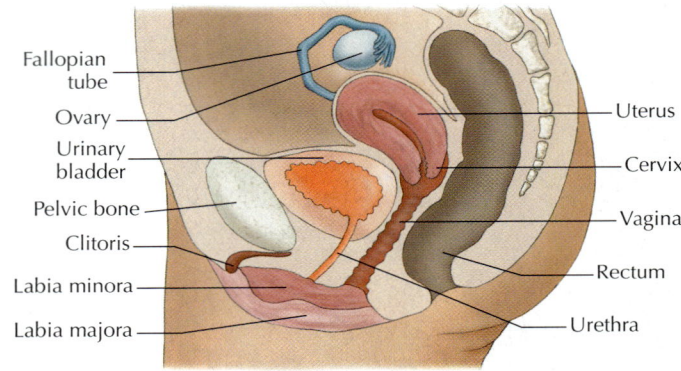

● **FIGURE 14.2** Cutaway view of internal and external female reproductive structures.

logically ready to reproduce. Reproductive maturity is especially evident in the female *menarche* (MEN-are-kee: the onset of menstruation). Soon after menarche, monthly ovulation begins. *Ovulation* refers to the release of ova (eggs) from the ovaries. From the first ovulation until *menopause* (the end of regular monthly fertility cycles in the late 40s or early 50s), women can bear children.

Sex Hormones *What causes the development of sex differences?* In general, sexual characteristics are related to the effects of sex hormones. (Hormones are chemical substances secreted by endocrine glands.) The **gonads** (or sex glands) affect sexual development and behavior by secreting **estrogens** (female hormones) and **androgens** (male hormones). The gonads in the male are the testes; female gonads are the ovaries. The adrenal glands (located above the kidneys) also supply sex hormones. At puberty, adrenal hormones add to the development of secondary sexual characteristics.

584

TABLE 14.1 Female and Male Sexual Anatomy

FEMALE REPRODUCTIVE STRUCTURES

Cervix (SER-vix) The lower end of the uterus that projects into the vagina.

Clitoris (KLIT-er-iss) Small, sensitive organ made up of erectile tissue; located above the vaginal opening.

Fallopian tube (feh-LOPE-ee-en) One of two tubes that carry eggs from the ovaries to the uterus.

Labia majora (LAY-bee-ah mah-JOR-ah) The larger outer lips of the vulva.

Labia minora (LAY-bee-ah mih-NOR-ah) Inner lips of the vulva, surrounding the vaginal opening.

Ovary (OH-vah-ree) One of the two female reproductive glands; ovaries are the source of hormones and eggs.

Uterus (YOO-ter-us) The pear-shaped muscular organ in which the fetus develops during pregnancy; also known as the womb.

Vagina (vah-JINE-ah) Tube-like structure connecting the external female genitalia with the uterus.

MALE REPRODUCTIVE STRUCTURES

Cowper's glands Two small glands that secrete a clear fluid into the urethra during sexual excitement.

Epididymis (ep-ih-DID-ih-mus) A coiled structure at the top of the testes in which sperm are stored.

External urethral orifice (yoo-REE-thral OR-ih-fis) The opening at the tip of the penis through which urine and semen pass.

Glans penis (glanz PEA-nis) The tip of the penis.

Prostate (PROSS-tate) A gland located at the base of the urinary bladder that supplies most of the fluid that makes up semen.

Scrotum (SKROE-tehm) The sac-like pouch that holds the testes.

Seminal vesicles (SEM-in-uhl VES-ih-kuhlz) These two small organs (one on each side of the prostate) supply fluid that becomes part of semen.

Testis (TES-tis, singular; testes, plural) One of the two male reproductive glands; the testes are a source of hormones and sperm.

Vas deferens (vaz DEH-fur-enz) The duct that carries sperm from the testes to the urethra.

RELATED STRUCTURES

Pelvic bone One of the bones at the front of the pelvis (the pelvis connects the spine with the legs).

Rectum The lowest section of the large intestine.

Urethra (yoo-REE-thra) The tube through which urine drains as it leaves the body. In males, semen also passes through the urethra.

Urinary bladder The sac that collects urine before it is eliminated from the body.

Interestingly, everyone normally produces both estrogens and androgens. Sex differences are related to the *proportion* of these hormones found in the body. In fact, prenatal development of male or female anatomy is largely due to the presence or absence of **testosterone** (tes-TOSS-teh-rone: one of the androgens, secreted mainly by the testes) (LeVay & Valente, 2006).

Then is biological sex determined by the sex hormones? Not entirely. As suggested by the chapter preview, sex cannot be reduced to a single dimension (Carroll, 2007).

Dimensions of Sex At the very least, classifying a person as female or male must take into account the following biological factors: (1) **genetic sex** (*XX* or *XY* chromosomes), (2) **gonadal sex** (ovaries or testes), (3) **hormonal sex** (predominance of androgens or estrogens), (4) **genital sex** (clitoris and vagina in females, penis and scrotum in males). An important nonbiological part of a person's sexual makeup is (5) **gender identity** (one's subjective sense of being male or female). To see why sex must be defined along these five dimensions, let's trace the events involved in becoming female or male.

Prenatal Sexual Development

Becoming male or female starts simply enough. Genetic sex is determined at the instant of conception: Two *X* **chromosomes** initiate female development; an *X* chromosome plus a *Y* **chromosome** produces a male. A woman's

---

Sex One's biological classification as female or male.

Gender Psychological and social characteristics associated with being male or female; defined especially by one's gender identity and learned gender roles.

Transsexual A person with a deep conflict between his or her biological sex and preferred psychological and social gender roles.

Primary sexual characteristics Sex as defined by the genitals and internal reproductive organs.

Secondary sexual characteristics Sexual features other than the genitals and reproductive organs—breasts, body shape, facial hair, and so forth.

Gonads The primary sex glands—the testes in males and ovaries in females.

Estrogen Any of a number of female sex hormones.

Androgen Any of a number of male sex hormones, especially testosterone.

Testosterone A male sex hormone, secreted mainly by the testes and responsible for the development of many male sexual characteristics.

Genetic sex Sex as indicated by the presence of *XX* (female) or *XY* (male) chromosomes.

Gonadal sex Sex as indicated by the presence of ovaries (female) or testes (male).

Hormonal sex Sex as indicated by a preponderance of estrogens (female) or androgens (male) in the body.

Genital sex Sex as indicated by the presence of male or female genitals.

Gender identity One's personal, private sense of maleness or femaleness.

***X* chromosome** The female chromosome contributed by the mother; produces a female when paired with another *X* chromosome and a male when paired with a *Y* chromosome.

***Y* chromosome** The male chromosome contributed by the father; produces a male when paired with an *X* chromosome. Fathers may give either an *X* or a *Y* chromosome to their offspring.

ovum always provides an *X* chromosome, because she has two *X*'s in her own genetic makeup. In contrast, one half of the male's sperm carry *X* chromosomes and the other half *Y*'s.

Genetic sex stays the same throughout life. But it alone does not determine biological sex. We must also consider hormonal effects before birth. For the first 6 weeks of prenatal growth, genetically female and male embryos look identical. However, if a *Y* chromosome is present, testes develop in the embryo and supply testosterone. This stimulates growth of the penis and other male structures (● Fig. 14.3). In the absence of testosterone, the embryo will develop female reproductive organs and genitals, regardless of genetic sex (LeVay & Valente, 2006). It might be said, then, that nature's primary impulse is to make a female. Without testosterone, we would all be women.

Prenatal growth usually matches genetic sex, but not always. A genetic male won't develop male genitals if too little testosterone is available. Even if testosterone is present, an inherited *androgen insensitivity* (unresponsiveness to testosterone) may exist. Again, the result is female development (LeVay & Valente, 2006).

Similarly, androgens must be at low levels or absent for an *XX* embryo to develop as a female. Thus, for both genetic females and males, hormonal problems before birth may produce an **intersexual person** (one who has ambiguous sexual anatomy). For instance, a developing female may be masculinized by the antimiscarriage drug progestin or by a problem known as *androgenital syndrome* (an-dro-JEN-ih-tal). In androgenital syndrome the child's body produces estrogen, but a genetic abnormality causes the adrenal glands to release too much androgen. In such cases, a female child may be born with genitals that are more male than female.

Can sex be assigned? For a variety of reasons, including transsexuality and intersexuality, it may make sense to reassign the sex of an individual. Surgery can reconfigure the external appearance of the genitals, hormone treatments can shift the chemical balance in the body, and a deliberate effort can be made to transform the person's sense of gender identity. But how successful are such measures? Experts are divided about the best way to treat such individuals. See "Bruce or Brenda—Can Sex Be Assigned?"

Gender Identity

As stated earlier, gender identity is your personal, private sense of being female or male. Gender identity is at least partly learned.

How is gender identity acquired? Obviously, it begins with *labeling* ("It's a girl," "It's a boy") (Eagly, 2001). Thereafter it is shaped by **gender role socialization** (the process of learning gender behaviors regarded as appropriate for one's sex in a given culture). Gender role socialization reflects all the subtle

(a) Undifferentiated

(b) Female *XX* Chromosomes

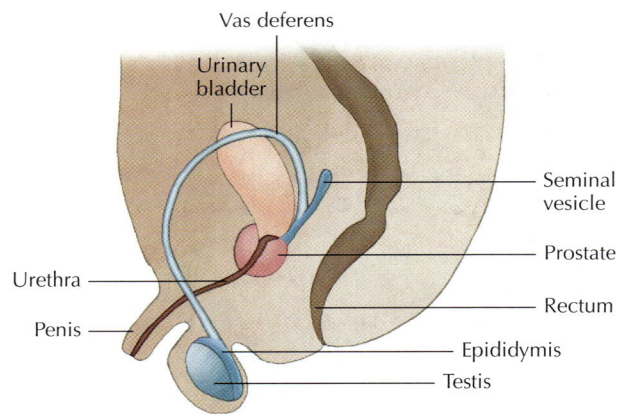

(c) Male *XY* Chromosomes

● **FIGURE 14.3** Prenatal development of the reproductive organs. Early development of ovaries or testes affects hormonal balance and alters sexual anatomy. (a) At first the sex organs are the same in the human female and male. (b) When androgens are absent, female structures develop. (c) Male sex organs are produced when androgens are present.

pressures from parents, peers, and cultural forces that urge boys to "act like boys" and girls to "act like girls." By the time they are just 2 years of age, children are aware of gender role differences (Witt, 1997). At 3 or 4 years of age, gender identity is usually well formed.

Don't intersexual children imply that biology also plays a role in gender identity? Yes, they do. The fact that trying to

THE CLINICAL FILE

Bruce or Brenda—Can Sex Be Assigned?

After Bruce was born, disaster struck. A normally routine circumcision destroyed his penis. Doctors suggested to his parents that Bruce should be sexually reassigned to become Brenda, a girl. With multiple surgeries and hormone treatments, the doctors said, Brenda would turn out just fine. Following their advice, Brenda wasn't told about the "accident" and she was raised as a girl. For many years, her case was considered a prime example of successful gender reassignment.

However, by puberty Brenda was miserable and suicidal, never quite fitting in with the other girls. In desperation, her parents told her the truth. Initially, Brenda was relieved. She opted for surgical reconstruction as a boy and took the name David. In 2000 David helped author John Colapinto tell his story in *As Nature Made Him* (Colapinto, 2000). After some initial successes as a man, David's marriage and finances failed. Tragically, he committed suicide in 2004.

Although many cases of sexual reassignment are successful, David's case is not unique. Of course, David was neither a transsexual nor an intersexual person. But even some intersexual children whose sex is changed have similar experiences. Like David, an intersexual child who is biologically male but raised as a girl may continue to feel that she is a boy, especially at puberty when "she" may begin growing a beard. If their "secret" is revealed, intersexual people may feel damaged—that their bodies were surgically altered without their permission (Cull, 2002).

As this discussion implies, a heated controversy exists about the treatment of sex and gender issues in young children (Williams, 2002). Supporters of early sex assignment argue that the benefits usually outweigh the long-term psychological costs (Slijper et al., 2000). Critics of early sex assignment believe that it is better for individuals to accept who they are and to realize that some bodies do not neatly fit into the categories of male and female (Holmes, 2002). Recently, critics have argued, with some success, that rather than impose the choice on them as children, it is better to wait until adulthood, when transsexual and intersexual individuals can then choose for themselves whether or not to have surgery and whether to live as a man or a woman (Thyen, et al., 2005).

Only time will tell which approach is more successful, and for which particular transsexual and intersex conditions. Because sex and gender are complex, the best course of treatment may prove to be different for different people (Rathus, Nevid, & Fichner-Rathus, 2005).

---

assign gender is not always successful suggests that hormones may "sex-type" the brain before birth (LeVay & Valente, 2006). Changes in the brain are then thought to alter the chances of developing feminine or masculine traits (Witelson, 1991). Direct evidence for this idea is provided by females exposed to androgens before birth. After birth, their hormones shift to female, and they are raised as girls. Nevertheless, the prenatal exposure to male hormones has a masculinizing effect. During childhood, such girls are typically "tomboys" who prefer the company of boys to girls. However, their masculinization usually does not persist. After adolescence, the girls' tomboyism usually gives way to female interests and gender characteristics. Cases like these make it clear that both prenatal hormones and later social factors contribute to adult sexual identity (Breedlove, Cooke, & Jordan, 1999).

Origins of Male-Female Differences

In animals, clear links exist between prenatal hormones and male or female behaviors. In humans, biology plays a similar role. That is, prenatal androgens and estrogens subtly influence development of the body, nervous system, and later behavior patterns. Although it would be a mistake to ignore this **biological biasing effect,** most human sex-linked behaviors are influenced much more by learning than is the case for animals (Helgeson, 2005).

At the risk of getting mired in the "battle of the sexes," let's consider one more idea. Some researchers believe that the biological biasing effect imparts different thinking abilities in women and men. Women, they say, are more often "left brained" and men "right brained." The left brain, you may recall, is largely responsible for language and rote learning. The right brain is superior at spatial reasoning. Thus, some psychologists think that biological differences explain why men (as a group) do slightly better on spatial tasks and math and why women are slightly better at language skills (Clements et al., 2006; Hiscock, Perachio, & Inch, 2001). Others, however, strongly reject this theory. To them, such claims are based on shaky evidence and sexist thinking. The most telling evidence on this point may be that female and male scores on the Scholastic Assessment Test (SAT) are rapidly becoming more alike. The same applies to tests of math ability (Halpern, 2001). The narrowing gap is probably ex-

Intersexual person A person who has genitals suggestive of both sexes.
Gender role socialization The process of learning gender behaviors considered appropriate for one's sex in a given culture.
Biological biasing effect Hypothesized effect that prenatal exposure to sex hormones has on development of the body, nervous system, and later behavior patterns.

plained by a growing similarity in male and female interests, experiences, and educational goals.

Note also that the differences that do exist between women and men are based on *averages* (● Fig. 14.4). Many women are better at math than most men are. Likewise, many men are better at verbal skills than most women are. Scores for women and men overlap so much that it is impossible to predict if any one person will be good or bad at math or language skills simply from knowing his or her sex. There is no biological basis for the unequal treatment women have faced at work, school, and elsewhere. Most male-female performance gaps can be traced to *social* differences in the power and opportunities given to men and women. Unequal power tends to exaggerate differences between men and women and then makes these artificial differences appear to be real (Goodwin & Fiske, 2001).

Gender Roles

Gender roles probably have as big an influence on sexual behavior as chromosomal, genital, or hormonal factors do. A **gender role** is the favored pattern of behavior expected of each sex. In our culture, boys are encouraged to be strong, fast, aggressive, dominant, and achieving. Traditional females are expected to be sensitive, intuitive, passive, emotional, and "naturally" interested in child rearing. All cultures define gender roles. This often leads to stereotyped thinking, as illustrated by the following riddle:

Question: How many men does it take to change a light bulb?

Answer: None. Real men aren't afraid of the dark.

This joke pokes fun at the North American stereotype of manhood. Despite much progress in the last 20 years, gender role stereotypes continue to have a major impact on women and men.

Gender role stereotypes are oversimplified beliefs about what men and women are actually like. Gender roles influence how we act. Gender role stereotypes, in contrast, treat gender roles as if they were real biological differences. That is, culturally defined ways of acting are turned into false beliefs about what men and women can and can't do.

Are women suited to be fighter pilots, corporate presidents, military commanders, or racecar drivers? A person with strong gender role stereotypes might say, "No, because women are not sufficiently aggressive, dominant, or mechanically inclined for such roles." Yet, today's women have performed successfully in virtually all realms. Nevertheless, gender role stereotypes persist. The United States has never had a woman president, although as we write this chapter Hillary Clinton is a frontrunner for the Democratic Party nomination for the 2008 elections.

Gender role stereotypes can be a major career obstacle. For many jobs, your chances of being hired could be reduced by your sex, be it male or female. Unequal pay for comparable work and experience is also a major problem for women. In the professions, women earn only about 76 cents for every dollar earned by men (NAFE, 2004). The rate for women of color is worse—65 cents for African American women and a measly 55 cents for Latinas. The male-female pay difference is even found in colleges, where greater awareness of gender fairness should prevail (Kite et al., 2001).

Like all stereotypes, those based on gender roles ignore the wonderful diversity of humanity. Fortunately, extreme gender stereotyping has declined somewhat in the last 20 years (Helwig, 1998; Kite et al., 2001). Just the same, in business, academia, medicine, law, sports, and politics, women continue to earn less money and achieve lower status than men. In other words, many women are still "running in place," hobbled by gender stereotyping (DeArmond et al., 2006). (See "Man's Work.")

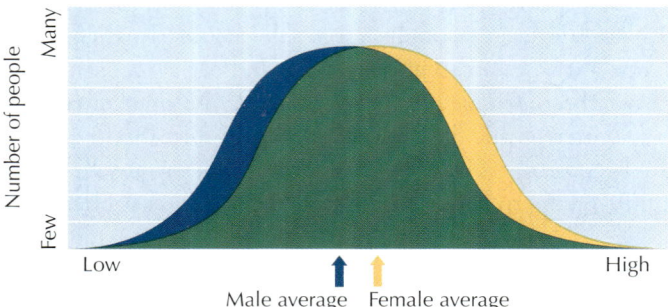

● **FIGURE 14.4** Recorded differences in various abilities that exist between women and men are based on *averages*. For example, if we were to record the number of men and women who have low, medium, or high scores on tests of language ability, we might obtain graphs like those shown. For other abilities, men would have a higher average. However, such average differences are typically small. As a result, the overlap in female abilities and male abilities is very large (Stewart & McDermott, 2004).

"The committee on women's rights will now come to order."

DISCOVERING PSYCHOLOGY

Man's Work

Andrea is the assistant vice president for sales at a large aircraft company. She is responsible for training and supervising junior executives, keeping up with industry trends, and finding new clients. Her work focuses on engine assemblies, hydraulic controls, fuel tanks, servos, and other mechanical parts. In a recent performance review, Andrea received high evaluations. She is regarded as a rising star, based on sales, the number of new client accounts she has produced, and actual dollars earned. Her performance is in the top 5 percent of all employees at her level.

Now that you know a little about Andrea, use the following scale to answer this question: How much do you think you would like this person? (Circle your rating.)

Not at All | Slightly | Somewhat | Moderately | More than Average | Quite a Lot | Very Much

Do you think your rating would be higher if the name *James* replaced *Andrea* in the job summary?

In a recent study, college students rated a woman and a man who were equally successful in a traditionally "male" job. The students consistently liked high-performing women *less* than they did men with identical jobs and achievements.

Why are women who are successful at "man's work" considered less likeable? The answer is that women tend to be punished for violating gender norms. Being successful in a "male" job implies that a woman has the "wrong" traits, which are better suited to males. That is, the self-assertive, achievement-oriented behaviors that are valued in men are frowned on in women. Despite the fact that women have shown that they can excel, many pay a social price for their success (DeArmond et al., 2006; Heilman et al., 2004).

Culture A look at other cultures shows that our gender roles are by no means "natural" or universal. For example, in many cultures women do the heavy work because men are considered too weak for it (Best, 2002). In Russia, roughly 75 percent of all medical doctors are women and women make up a large portion of the workforce. Many more examples could be cited, but one of the most interesting is anthropologist Margaret Mead's (1935) classic observations of the Tchambuli people of New Guinea.

Gender roles for the Tchambuli are a nearly perfect reversal of North American stereotypes. Tchambuli women do the fishing and manufacturing, and they control the power and economic life of the community. Women also take the initiative in courting and sexual relations. Tchambuli men, on the other hand, are expected to be dependent, flirtatious, and concerned with their appearance. Art, games, and theatrics occupy most of the Tchambuli males' time, and men are particularly fond of adorning themselves with flowers and jewelry.

As the Tchambuli show, men and women are expected to act in quite different ways in various cultures. The arbitrary nature of gender roles is also apparent. A man is no less a man if he cooks, sews, or cares for children. A woman is no less a woman if she excels in sports, succeeds in business, or works as an auto mechanic. Still, adult personality and gender identity are closely tied to cultural definitions of "masculinity" and "femininity."

An interesting side effect of gender role socialization is the imprint it leaves on activities that have nothing to do with sex. For example, it has long been thought that boys are more aggressive than girls and that girls have more emotional empathy than boys (Maccoby & Jacklin, 1974).

Gender Role Socialization

How are gender differences created? Learning gender roles begins immediately. Infant girls are held more gently and treated more tenderly than boys. Both parents play more

Behaviors that are considered typical and appropriate for each sex (gender roles) vary a great deal from culture to culture. Undoubtedly some cultures magnify sex differences more than others (Carroll, 2007).

Gender role The pattern of behaviors that are regarded as "male" or "female" by one's culture; sometimes also referred to as a sex role.

Gender role stereotypes Oversimplified and widely held beliefs about the basic characteristics of men and women.

roughly with sons than with daughters (who are presumed to be more "delicate"). Later, boys are allowed to roam over a wider area without special permission. They are also expected to run errands earlier than girls. Daughters are told that they are pretty and that "nice girls don't fight." Boys are told to be strong and that "tough guys don't cry." Sons are more often urged to control their emotions, except for anger and aggression, which parents tolerate more in boys than in girls.

Toys are strongly sex typed: Parents buy dolls for girls; trucks, tools, and sports equipment for boys. Fathers, especially, tend to encourage their children to play with "appropriate" sex-typed toys (Raag & Rackliff, 1998) (● Fig. 14.5). By the time children reach kindergarten they have learned to think that doctors, firefighters, and pilots are men and that nurses, secretaries, and hairdressers are women (Eagly, 2000; Stroeher, 1994). And why not? The workforce is still highly segregated by sex, and children learn from what they observe. Stereotyped gender roles are even the norm in TV commercials, children's picture books, and video games (Browne, 1998; Oppliger, 2007)!

"Female" and "Male" Behavior Overall, parents tend to encourage their sons to engage in **instrumental** (goal-directed) **behaviors**, to control their emotions, and to prepare for the world of work. Daughters, on the other hand, are encouraged in **expressive** (emotion-oriented) **behaviors** and, to a lesser degree, are socialized for motherhood.

When parents are told they treat girls and boys differently, many explain that the sexes are just "naturally" different. But what comes first, "natural differences" or the gender-based expectations that create them? In our culture, "male" seems—for many—to be defined as "not female." That is, parents often have a vague fear of expressive and emotional behavior in male children. To them, such behavior implies that a boy is effeminate or a sissy. Many parents who would not be troubled if their daughters engaged in "masculine" play might be upset if their sons played with dolls or imitated "female" mannerisms.

Differences between boys and girls are magnified by sex-segregated play. Beginning around age 3, boys start to play mostly with boys and girls play with girls. And how do they play? Girls tend to play indoors and near adults. They like to cooperate by playing house and other games that require lots of verbal give-and-take. Boys prefer superhero games and rough-and-tumble play outdoors. They tend to be concerned with dominance or who's the boss. Thus, from an early age males and females tend to grow up in different, gender-defined cultures (Martin & Fabes, 2001; Oppliger, 2007).

To summarize, gender role socialization in our society prepares children for a world in which men are expected to be instrumental, conquering, controlling, and unemotional. Women, in contrast, are expected to be expressive, emotional, passive, and dependent. Thus, gender role socialization teaches us to be highly competent in some respects and handicapped in others (Levant, 1996, 2003).

Of course, many people find traditional gender roles acceptable and comfortable. It seems evident, however, that just about everyone will benefit when the more stereotyped and burdensome aspects of gender roles are set aside. The next section explains why.

Androgyny—Are You Masculine, Feminine, or Androgynous?

SURVEY QUESTION: *What is psychological androgyny (and is it contagious)?*

Are you aggressive, ambitious, analytical, assertive, athletic, competitive, decisive, dominant, forceful, independent, individualistic, self-reliant, and willing to take risks? If so, you are quite "masculine." Are you affectionate, cheerful, child-like, compassionate, flatterable, gentle, gullible, loyal, sensitive, shy, soft spoken, sympathetic, tender, understanding, warm, and yielding? If so, then you are quite "feminine." What if you have traits from both lists? In that case, you may be *androgynous* (an-DROJ-ih-nus).

The two lists you just read are from the seminal work of psychologist Sandra Bem (1974). By combining 20 "masculine" traits (self-reliant, assertive, and so forth), 20 "feminine" traits (affectionate, gentle), and 20 neutral traits (truthful, friendly) Bem created the *Bem Sex Role Inventory* (BSRI). (Some psychologists prefer to use the term *sex role* instead of gender role.) Next, she and her associates gave the BSRI to

● **FIGURE 14.5** One study found that the mothers interacted differently with their infants sons and daughters as they played with gender-neutral toys. Mothers of girls engaged on more interpretation and conversation, whereas mothers of boys commented more and offered more instructions (Clearfield & Nelson, 2006).

thousands of people, asking them to say whether each trait applied to them. Of those surveyed, 50 percent fell into traditional feminine or masculine categories; 15 percent scored higher on traits of the opposite sex; and 35 percent were androgynous, getting high scores on both feminine and masculine items.

Psychological Androgyny

The word **androgyny** (an-DROJ-ih-nee) literally means "man-woman." Androgyny sounds as if it might have something to do with androids, asexuality, or sex-change operations, but it actually refers to having both feminine and masculine traits (Helgeson, 2005).

Bem is convinced that our complex society requires flexibility with respect to gender roles. She believes that it is necessary for men to be gentle, compassionate, sensitive, and yielding and for women to be forceful, self-reliant, independent, and ambitious—*as the situation requires.* In short, Bem feels that more people should be androgynous.

Adaptability Bem has shown that androgynous individuals are more adaptable. They seem especially to be less hindered by images of "feminine" or "masculine" behavior. For example, in one study people were given the choice of doing either a "masculine" activity (oil a hinge, nail boards together, and so forth) or a "feminine" activity (prepare a baby bottle, wind yarn into a ball, and so on). Masculine men and feminine women consistently chose to do gender-appropriate activities, even when the opposite choice paid more!

Bem has concluded that rigid gender stereotypes and gender roles can seriously restrict behavior, especially for men (Bem, 1975, 1981). She believes that masculine males have great difficulty expressing warmth, playfulness, and concern—even when they are appropriate. Masculine men, it seems, tend to view such feelings as unacceptably "feminine." Masculine men (let's call them "manly men") also find it hard to accept emotional support from others, particularly from women (Levant, 2001; 2003). They tend to be interested in sports, have mostly male friends, dislike feminists, and sit with their knees wide apart (really!). Problems faced by highly feminine women are the reverse of those faced by masculine men. Such women have trouble being independent and assertive, even when these qualities are desirable. In contrast, more androgynous individuals are higher in emotional intelligence (remember Module 9.6?) (Guastello & Guastello, 2003).

Over the years androgyny has been variously supported, attacked, and debated. Now, as the dust begins to settle, the picture looks like this:

Androgynous individuals adapt easily to both traditionally "feminine" and "masculine" situations.

- Having "masculine" traits primarily means that a person is independent and assertive. Scoring high in "masculinity," therefore, is related to high self-esteem and to success in many situations (Long, 1989).
- Having "feminine" traits primarily means that a person is nurturing and interpersonally oriented. People who score high in "femininity," therefore, are more likely to seek and receive social support. They tend to experience greater social closeness with others and more happiness in marriage (Reevy & Maslach, 2001).

In sum, there are advantages to possessing both "feminine" and "masculine" traits (Guastello & Guastello, 2003; Lefkowitz & Zeldow, 2006). In general, androgynous persons are more flexible when it comes to coping with difficult situations (Crooks & Baur, 2008; Spangenberg & Lategan, 1993). (See • Figure 14.6.) Androgynous persons also tend to be more satisfied with their lives. Apparently, they can use both instrumental and emotionally expressive capacities to enhance their lives and relationships (Lefkowitz & Zeldow, 2006; Ramanaiah, Detwiler, & Byravan, 1995).

Interestingly, some men appear to be moving toward more balanced definitions of manhood. For instance, more Mexican-American men than European-American men are androgynous (Sugihara & Warner, 1999). Along the same lines, some Asian-American men, especially those who were born in the United States, appear to be creating a more flexible masculinity free from male dominance. These men link their masculinity with a capacity for caring, and they are not

Instrumental behaviors Behaviors directed toward the achievement of some goal; behaviors that are instrumental in producing some effect.

Expressive behaviors Behaviors that express or communicate emotion or personal feelings.

Androgyny The presence of both "masculine" and "feminine" traits in a single person (as masculinity and femininity are defined within one's culture).

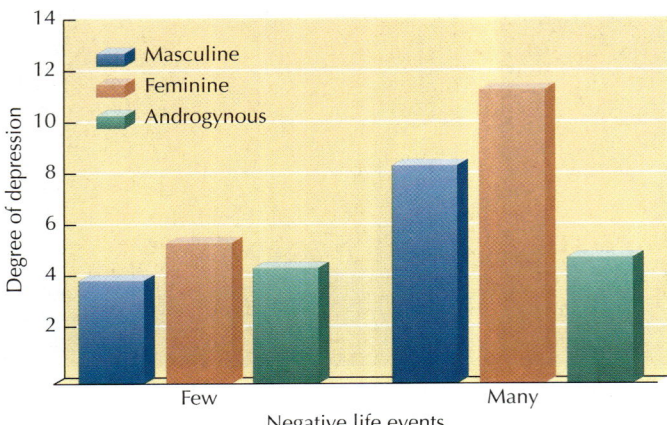

● **FIGURE 14.6** Another indication of the possible benefits of androgyny is found in a study of reactions to stress. When confronted with an onslaught of negative events, strongly masculine or feminine persons become more depressed than androgynous individuals do. (Adapted from Roos & Cohen, 1987.)

afraid of doing "feminine tasks," such as cooking or housework (Chua & Fujino, 1999).

It is worth saying again that many people remain comfortable with traditional views of gender. Nevertheless, "feminine" traits and "masculine" traits can exist in the same person, and androgyny can be a highly adaptive balance.

MODULE 14.1 Summary

What are the basic dimensions of sex? How does one's sense of maleness or femaleness develop?

- *Male* and *female* are not simple either/or categories. Sexual identity is complex, multifaceted, and influenced by biology, socialization, and learning.
- Physically, males and females differ in primary and secondary sexual characteristics.
- Estrogens (female sex hormones) and androgens (male sex hormones) influence the development of primary and secondary sexual characteristics.
- Biological sex consists of genetic sex, gonadal sex, hormonal sex, and genital sex. Sexual character is also affected by gender identity.
- Sexual development begins with genetic sex (*XX* or *XY* chromosomes) and is then influenced by prenatal hormone levels.
- Many researchers believe that prenatal hormones exert a biological biasing effect that combines with social factors to influence psychosexual development.
- In most psychological dimensions, women and men are more alike than they are different.
- Male and female behavior patterns are related to learned gender identity and gender role socialization.
- Gender role stereotypes often distort perceptions about the kinds of activities for which men and women are suited.
- Gender identity usually becomes stable by age 3 or 4 years.
- Gender role socialization accounts for most observed female/male gender differences. Parents tend to encourage boys in instrumental behaviors and girls in expressive behaviors.

What is psychological androgyny (and is it contagious)?
- Roughly one third of all persons are androgynous. Approximately 50 percent are traditionally feminine or masculine.
- There are some advantages to being feminine and other advantages to being masculine. Androgyny combines the best of both and contributes to greater behavioral adaptability.

KNOWLEDGE BUILDER

Sex, Gender, and Androgyny

Recite

1. _____ sexual characteristics refer to the sexual and reproductive organs; _____ sexual characteristics refer to other body changes that take place at puberty.
2. All individuals normally produce both androgens and estrogens, although the proportions differ in females and males. T or F?
3. The four basic dimensions of biological sex are:
   _____, _____,
   _____, _____
4. In females, intersexual anatomy may result from
   a. an androgen insensitivity
   b. androgenital syndrome
   c. excessive estrogen
   d. all of these
5. For humans, the biological biasing effect of prenatal hormones tends to override all other influences. T or F?
6. One's private sense of maleness or femaleness is referred to as _____ _____.
7. Traditional gender role socialization encourages _____ behavior in males.
   a. instrumental
   b. emotional
   c. expressive
   d. dependent
8. A person who is androgynous is one who scores high on ratings of traits usually possessed by the opposite sex. T or F?
9. For both women and men, having masculine traits is associated with greater happiness in marriage. T or F?

Reflect
Critical Thinking

10. Transsexualism exists when a person feels that she or he is trapped in a body of the wrong sex. This problem is therefore defined almost entirely on the basis of which dimension of gender?
11. As children are growing up, the male emphasis on instrumental behavior comes into conflict with the female emphasis on expressive behavior. At what age do you think such conflicts become prominent?
12. Could a person be androgynous in a culture where "masculine" and "feminine" traits differ greatly from those on Bem's list?

Relate

In 2007 the American Medical Association changed its antidiscrimination policies to include transgender people. This means, for example, that doctors can no longer refuse medical treatment to transgender patients. Do you agree or disagree with this change?

Can you remember an example of gender role socialization you experienced as a child? Do you think you were encouraged to engage more in instrumental behaviors or expressive behaviors?

Mentally change your male friends to females and your female friends to males. Can you separate the "human being" or "core person" from your friends' normal gender identities and gender roles?

Think of three people you know, one who is androgynous, one who is traditionally feminine, and one who is traditionally masculine. What advantages and disadvantages do you see in each collection of traits. How do you think you would be classified if you took the BSRI?

Link

Internet addresses frequently change. To find the sites listed here, visit **http://www.thomsonedu.com/psychology/coon** for an updated list of Internet addresses and direct links to relevant sites.

- **Human Sexual Reproduction** Read more about the biology of sex and sexual reproduction.
- **Sex and Gender** Read an article about the difference between sex and gender.
- **My Life as an Intersexual** Read the story of one person's life as an intersexual.

ANSWERS

1. Primary, secondary 2. T 3. genetic sex, gonadal sex, hormonal sex, genital sex 4. b 5. F 6. gender identity 7. a 8. F 9. F 10. Gender identity 11. Children segregate themselves into same-sex groups during much of childhood, which limits conflicts between male and female patterns of behavior. However, as children move into adolescence they begin to spend more time with members of the opposite sex. This brings the dominant, competitive style of boys into conflict with the nurturing, expressive style of girls, often placing girls at a disadvantage (Maccoby, 1990). 12. Yes. Being androgynous means having both masculine and feminine traits as they are defined within one's culture.

MODULE 14.2 Sexual Behavior and Sexual Orientation

SEXUALITY IS A NATURAL PART OF BEING HUMAN. With this in mind, we will discuss the human sex drive and typical patterns of sexual behavior. This unit also explores sexual orientation, which is a deep part of personal identity. Sexual orientation is a very basic dimension of human sexuality because it addresses the question, Who are you attracted to?

Sexual Behavior—Mapping the Erogenous Zone

SURVEY QUESTION: *What are the most typical patterns of human sexual behavior?*

A capacity for sexual arousal is apparent at birth or soon after. Researcher Alfred Kinsey verified instances of orgasm in boys as young as 5 months old and girls as young as 4 months (Kinsey, Pomeroy, & Martin, 1948, 1953). Kinsey also found that 2- to 5-year-old children spontaneously touch and exhibit their genitals.

Various sexual behaviors continue throughout childhood. But as a child matures, cultural norms place greater restrictions on sexual activities. Still, many females and males engage in preadolescent sex play. In adulthood, norms continue to shape sexual activity along socially approved lines. In our culture, sex between children, incest (sex between close relatives), prostitution, and extramarital sex are all discouraged.

As was true of gender roles, it's apparent that such restrictions are somewhat arbitrary. Sexual activities of all kinds are more common in cultures that place fewer restrictions on sexual behavior. Apart from cultural norms, it can be said that any sexual act engaged in by consenting adults is "normal" if it does not hurt anyone. (Atypical sexual behavior is discussed later in this chapter.)

Sexual Arousal

Human sexual arousal is complex. It may, of course, be produced by direct stimulation of the body's **erogenous zones** (eh-ROJ-eh-nus: productive of pleasure or erotic desire). Human erogenous zones include the genitals, mouth, breasts, ears, anus, and, to a lesser degree, the entire surface of the body. It is clear, however, that more than physical contact is involved: A urological or gynecological exam rarely results in any sexual arousal. Likewise, an unwanted sexual advance may produce only revulsion. Human sexual arousal obviously includes a large mental element.

Sexual Scripts In a restaurant we commonly expect certain things to occur. It could even be said that each of us has a restaurant "script" that defines a plot, the dialogue, and actions that should take place. We also learn a variety of **sexual scripts**, or unspoken mental plans that guide our sexual behavior. Such scripts determine when and where we are likely to express sexual feelings, and with whom (Lenton & Bryan, 2005). They provide a "plot" for the order of events in lovemaking, and they outline "approved" actions, motives, and outcomes.

When two people follow markedly different scripts, misunderstandings are almost sure to occur. Consider, for instance, what happens when a woman acting out a "friendly-first-date" script is paired with a man following a "seduction" script: The result is often anger, hurt feelings, or worse (Schleicher & Gilbert, 2005). Even newlyweds may find that their sexual "agendas" differ. In such cases, considerable "rewriting" of scripts is often needed for sexual compatibility. For humans the mind (or brain) is the ultimate erogenous zone.

Are men more easily sexually aroused than women? Overall, women and men have equal potential for sexual arousal and women are no less *physically* responsive than men. However, women tend to place more emphasis on emotional closeness with a lover than men do (Basson et al., 2005; Peplau, 2003).

In one study women watched excerpts from two erotic films. One was made by a man for male viewers. The other was directed by a woman and presented from a female point of view. Although women's physical arousal was nearly identical for both films, as measured by a medical recording device, their subjective experiences differed greatly. Many women reported being repulsed, disgusted, and decidedly not aroused by the male-oriented film. When they watched the film made for women, subjects reported more subjective feelings of sexual arousal, more positive emotions, and more interest in the film (Laan et al., 1994).

Why did the women respond so differently? Basically, the male-centered film was a macho fantasy in which the woman was little more than a sexual prop—her pleasure and fulfillment were portrayed as largely unimportant. In the woman-made film, the female character took the initiative in lovemaking and obviously enjoyed it. Clearly, women and men have equal potential for sexual arousal. However, a woman's subjective feelings of arousal tend to be more closely tied to her emotional response to erotic cues. It would appear that many women want to be active partners in lovemaking, and they want their needs and preferences to be acknowledged.

Based on the frequency of orgasm (from masturbation or intercourse), the peak of male sexual activity is at age 18. The peak rate of female sexual activity appears to occur a little later (Janus & Janus, 1993). However, male and female sexual patterns are rapidly becoming more alike. • Figure 14.7 presents some of the data on sexual behavior from a major national health survey of American men and women ages 25 to 44. As you can see, in any given year men and women do not differ in their average number of opposite-sex partners or in their overall pattern of sexual activity (Mosher, Chandra, & Jones, 2005). Exaggerating the differences between male and female sexuality is not only inaccurate, it can also create artificial barriers to sexual satisfaction (Wiederman, 2001). For example, assuming that men should always initiate sex denies the fact that women have comparable sexual interests and needs.

Sex Drive *What causes differences in sex drive?* The term **sex drive** refers to the strength of one's motivation to engage in sexual behavior. Attitudes toward sex, sexual experience, and recency of sexual activity are all important, but physical factors also play a role. As discussed in Module 9.2, a man's sex drive is related to the amount of androgens (especially testosterone) supplied by the testes (Crooks & Baur, 2008). The connection can be very direct: When a man chats with a woman he finds attractive, his testosterone levels actually increase (Roney, 2003). Likewise, the sex drive in women is related to estrogen levels (Graziottin, 1998). As you may also recall, testosterone also plays a role in female sexuality. A woman's sex drive is closely related to the testosterone level in her bloodstream. Of course, women produce much smaller amounts of testosterone than men do. But that doesn't mean their sex drive is weaker. Women's bodies are more sensitive to testosterone, and their sex drive is comparable to males. Testosterone levels decline with age, which can lower sexual desire. However, in some instances, testosterone supplements

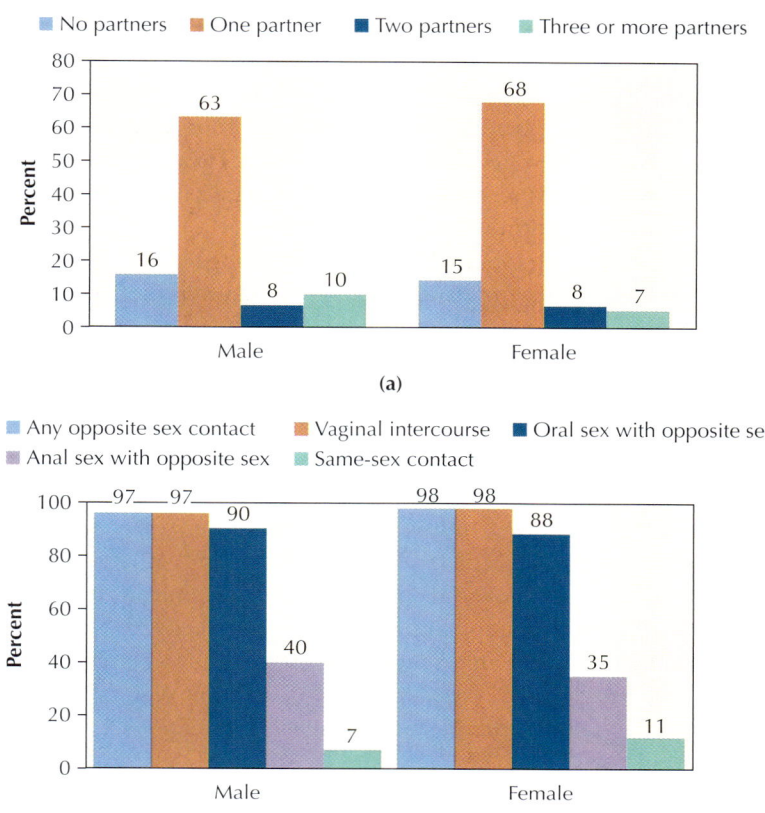

● **FIGURE 14.7** These graphs show the pattern of sexual behavior for American adults. *(a)* Men and women do not differ in their average number of sexual partners or *(b)* in their overall pattern of sexual activity. (Adapted from Mosher, Chandra, & Jones, 2005.)

can restore the sex drive in both men and women (Crooks & Baur, 2008).

Numerous drugs are reputed to be aphrodisiacs (af-ruh-DEEZ-ee-aks: substances that increase sexual desire or pleasure). However, like alcohol (see Module 9.2), many drugs actually impair sexual response, rather than enhance it. Some examples are amphetamines, amyl nitrite, barbiturates, cocaine, Ecstasy, LSD, and marijuana. As one expert observed, "Love, however you define it, seems to be the best aphrodisiac of all" (Crooks & Baur, 2008).

Does removal of the testes or ovaries abolish the sex drive? In lower animals, **castration** (surgical removal of the testicles or

---

Erogenous zones Areas of the body that produce pleasure and/or provoke erotic desire.

Sexual script An unspoken mental plan that defines a plot, dialogue, and actions expected to take place in a sexual encounter.

Sex drive The strength of one's motivation to engage in sexual behavior.

Castration Surgical removal of the testicles or ovaries.

ovaries) tends to abolish sexual activity in *inexperienced* animals. In humans, the effects of male and female castration vary. At first, some people experience a loss of sex drive; in others there is no change. (That's why castration of sex offenders is not likely to curb their behavior.) However, after several years almost all subjects report a decrease in sex drive unless they take hormone supplements.

The preceding observations have nothing to do with **sterilization** (surgery to make a man or woman infertile). The vast majority of women and men who choose surgically based birth control (such as a tubal ligation or a vasectomy) do not lose interest in sex. If anything, they may become more sexually active when pregnancy is no longer a concern.

What happens to the sex drive in old age? A natural decline in sex drive typically accompanies aging. As noted earlier, this is related to a reduced output of sex hormones, especially testosterone (Crooks & Baur, 2008) (● Fig. 14.8). However, sexual activity need not come to an end. Some people in their 80s and 90s continue to have active sex lives (Skoog, 1996). The crucial factor for an extended sex life appears to be regularity and opportunity. ("Use it or lose it.") People who fairly regularly engage in intercourse have little difficulty in later years (Janus & Janus, 1993).

Masturbation One of the most basic sexual behaviors is **masturbation** (self-stimulation that causes sexual pleasure or orgasm). Female masturbation most often involves rubbing the clitoris or areas near it. Male masturbation usually takes the form of rubbing or stroking the penis.

Do more men masturbate than women? Yes. Of the women who took part in a national survey, 89 percent reported that they had masturbated at some time. Of the males, 95 percent reported that they had masturbated. (Some cynics add, "And the other 5 percent lied!") As ● Figure 14.9 shows, masturbation is a regular feature of the sex lives of many people (Janus & Janus, 1993).

What purpose does masturbation serve? Through masturbation, people discover what pleases them sexually. Masturbation is an important part of the psychosexual development of most adolescents. Among other things, it provides a healthy substitute for sexual involvement at a time when young people are maturing emotionally.

Is it immature for masturbation to continue after marriage? If it is, there are many "immature" people around! Approximately 70 percent of married women and men masturbate at least occasionally. Generally speaking, masturbation is valid at any age and usually has no effect on marital relationships. Contrary to popular myths, people are not compelled to masturbate because they lack a sexual partner. Masturbation is just "one more item on the menu" for people with active sex lives (Laumann et al., 1994).

Is there any way in which masturbation can cause harm? Fifty years ago, a child might have been told that masturbation would cause insanity, acne, sterility, or other such nonsense. "Self-abuse," as it was often called, has enjoyed a long and unfortunate history of religious and medical disapproval. The modern view is that masturbation is a normal sexual behavior (Bockting & Coleman, 2003). Enlightened parents are well aware of this fact. Still, many children are punished or made to feel guilty for touching their genitals. This is unfortunate because masturbation itself is harmless. Typically, its only negative effects are feelings of fear, guilt, or anxiety that arise from learning to think of masturbation as "bad" or "wrong." In an age when people are urged to practice "safer sex," masturbation remains the safest sex of all.

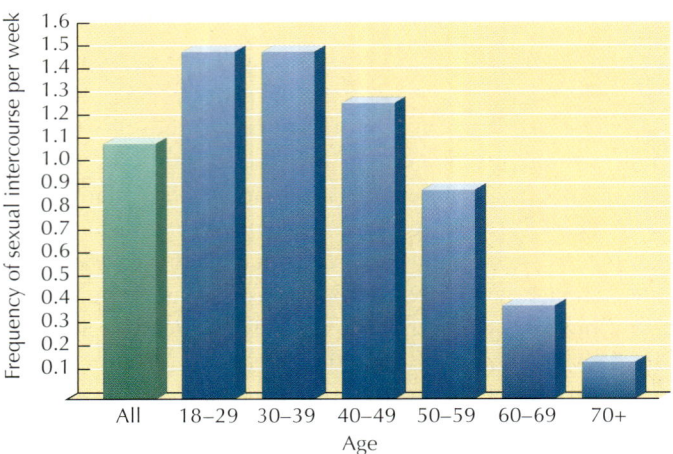

● **FIGURE 14.8** Average frequency of sexual intercourse per week for adults in the United States. Average intervals for intercourse decline from once every 4 to 5 days in young adulthood to once every 16 days for people in their 60s. Remember that averages such as these are lowered by the inclusion of people who are abstinent or who do not have sexual partners (such as many widowed persons). However, the age declines noted here also show up for people who are married, ranging from an average rate of intercourse of twice a week for couples under 30 to once every 3 weeks for those over 70. This suggests that the average frequency of intercourse does decline with advancing age (Smith, 1990).

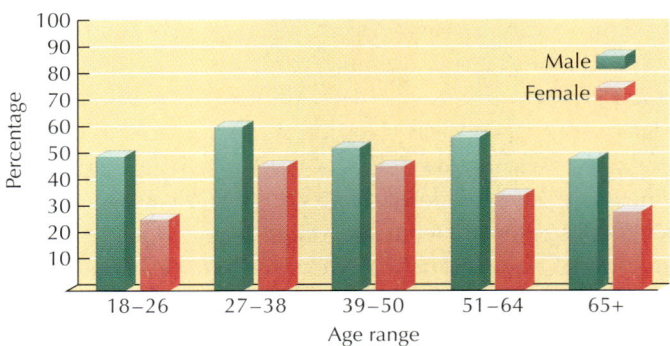

● **FIGURE 14.9** Percentage of women and men who masturbate. (Data from Janus & Janus, 1993.)

BRAINWAVES

Genes, the Brain, and Sexual Orientation

Why are some people attracted to the opposite sex whereas others prefer members of the same sex? Available evidence suggests that sexual orientation is at least partly hereditary (LeVay & Valente, 2006). One study found that if one identical twin is homosexual or bisexual, there is a 50-percent chance that the other twin is, too. Similar findings lead some researchers to estimate that sexual orientation is 30 to 70 percent genetic (Mustanski, Chivers, & Bailey, 2002).

Further research suggests that sexual orientation is influenced by a gene or genes found on the *X* chromosome. Thus, genetic tendencies for homosexuality may be passed from mothers to their children (Hu et al., 1995; Rahman & Wilson, 2003). During human evolution, homosexuality may have developed to reduce competition between males for a limited number of potential female mates (Schuiling, 2004).

How could genes affect sexual orientation? The most popular theory holds that genes affect hormone levels in the developing fetus (LeVay, 2006). According to the *prenatal hormonal theory of homosexuality,* some male fetuses are exposed to too little testosterone. Similarly, some female fetuses are exposed to too much testosterone. These differences, in turn, can impact sexual orientation (Mustanski, Chivers, & Bailey, 2002). Incidentally, many people mistakenly believe that homosexuality is caused by a hormone imbalance in adulthood. However, it is highly unlikely that adult hormone levels affect sexual orientation because the hormone levels of most gay men and lesbians are within the normal range (Banks & Gartrell, 1995).

Hormonal differences during pregnancy may alter areas of the brain that orchestrate sexual behavior. Support for this idea comes from the finding that parts of the hypothalamus, which is connected with sexual activity, differ in size in heterosexuals and homosexuals (Kinnunen et al., 2004; LeVay, 1993). Furthermore, differences in neurotransmitter levels have been detected in the hypothalamus in homosexual and heterosexual persons (Kinnunen et al., 2004).

Consistent with the biological view of sexual orientation, it is unlikely that parenting makes children homosexual. There is little difference between the development of children with gay or lesbian parents and those who have heterosexual parents (Patterson, 2002; Wainwright, Russell, & Patterson, 2004). Most lesbians and gay men were raised by heterosexual parents, and most children raised by gay or lesbian parents become heterosexual (Garnets, 2002).

All these findings tend to discredit myths about parents making children homosexual or claims that homosexuality is merely a choice. Although learning contributes to one's sexual orientation, it appears that nature strongly prepares people to be either homosexual or heterosexual (LeVay, 1993). In view of this, discriminating against homosexuals is much like rejecting a person for being blue eyed or left handed (Rathus, Nevid, & Fichner-Rathus, 2005).

Sexual Orientation—Who Do You Love?

Sexual behavior and romantic relationships are strongly influenced by a person's sexual orientation. **Sexual orientation** refers to your degree of emotional and erotic attraction to members of the same sex, opposite sex, or both sexes. **Heterosexual** people are romantically and erotically attracted to members of the opposite sex. Those who are **homosexual** are attracted to people whose sex matches their own. A person who is **bisexual** is attracted to both men and women. In short, sexual orientation answers these questions: Who are you attracted to? Who do you have erotic fantasies about? Do you love men, or women, or both (Garnets, 2002)?

Sexual orientation is a deep part of personal identity. Starting with their earliest erotic feelings, most people remember being attracted to either the opposite sex or the same sex. The chances are practically nil of an exclusively heterosexual or homosexual person being "converted" from one orientation to the other. If you are heterosexual, you are probably certain that nothing could ever make you have homoerotic feelings. If so, then you know how homosexual persons feel about the prospects for changing *their* sexual orientation (Seligman, 1994).

But what about people who have had both heterosexual and homosexual relationships? The fact that sexual orientation is usually quite stable doesn't rule out the possibility that for some people erotic feelings may change during the course of a lifetime. However, many such instances involve homosexual

---

Sterilization Medical procedures such as vasectomy or tubal ligation that make a man or a woman infertile.

Masturbation Producing sexual pleasure or orgasm by directly stimulating the genitals.

Sexual orientation One's degree of emotional and erotic attraction to members of the same sex, opposite sex, or both sexes.

Heterosexual A person romantically and erotically attracted to members of the opposite sex.

Homosexual A person romantically and erotically attracted to same-sex persons.

Bisexual A person romantically and erotically attracted to both men and women.

people who date or marry members of the opposite sex because of pressures to fit into heterosexual society. When these people realize they are being untrue to themselves, their identity and relationships may shift. Other apparent shifts in orientation probably involve people who are basically bisexual.

What determines a person's sexual orientation? Research suggests that hereditary and biological, social, cultural, and psychological influences combine to produce one's sexual orientation (Carroll, 2007; Garnets, 2002). As one author summarized, "Like much of human behavior, a combination of biological and social factors are most likely involved in the development of sexuality" (Rathus, Nevid, & Fichner-Rathus, 2005). "Genes, the Brain, and Sexual Orientation" summarizes some interesting findings about the origins of sexual orientation.

Homosexuality

As the preceding discussion implies, homosexuality is part of the normal range of variations in sexual orientation (Garnets, 2002). Gay men, lesbians, and bisexuals encounter hostility because they are members of minority groups, not because there is anything inherently wrong with them (Balsam & Mohr, 2007).

Based on a national survey, it is estimated that about 4 percent of all adults regard themselves as homosexual or bisexual (Mosher, Chandra, & Jones, 2005). Here are the figures:

	MEN	WOMEN
Heterosexual	90.2%	90.3%
Homosexual	2.3%	1.3%
Bisexual	1.8%	2.8%

A different survey of young men found that 6 percent identified themselves as homosexual, so the preceding figures may be low estimates (Bagley & Tremblay, 1998). Nevertheless, among men, *at least* 1 in 50 is homosexual. Among women, *at least* 1 in 100 is a lesbian. About 1 person in 50 is bisexual. Together, these percentages indicate that at least 4 persons out of every 100 are bisexual or homosexual (Mosher, Chandra, & Jones, 2005). That means about 12 million people in the United States alone are gay, lesbian, or bisexual. Millions of others have a family member who is homosexual. Historically, homosexuality has been a part of human sexuality since the dawn of time.

In contrast to heterosexuals, homosexual persons tend to discover their sexual orientation at a fairly late date—often not until early adolescence. Very likely, this is because they are surrounded by powerful cultural images that contradict their natural feelings. However, most homosexual persons begin to sense that they are different in childhood. By early adolescence, gay men and lesbians begin to feel an attraction to members of the same sex. Gradually, this leads them to question their sexual identity and accept their same-sex orientation (Diamond, 1998).

The problems faced by lesbians and gay men tend to be related to rejection by family and discrimination in hiring and housing. Such unfair treatment is based on homophobia and heterosexism in our society (Balsam & Mohr, 2007; Cowan et al., 2005). *Homophobia* refers to prejudice, fear, and dislike directed at homosexuals. *Heterosexism* is the belief that heterosexuality is better or more natural than homosexuality. Understandably, social rejection tends to produce higher rates of anxiety, depression, and suicidal thinking among gay and lesbian people (Cochran, 2001; Gilman et al., 2001; Lester, 2006). However, anyone facing discrimination and stigma would react in much the same way (Jorm et al., 2002). When such stresses are factored out, homosexual persons are no more likely to have emotional problems than heterosexual people (Goldfried, 2001). Homosexuality itself is not a problem (APA, 2004; Mays & Cochran, 2001).

Most homosexual people have at one time or another suffered verbal abuse—or worse—because of their sexual orientation (Balsam & Mohr, 2007; Cochran, 2001). Much of this rejection is based on false stereotypes about gay and lesbian people. The following points are a partial reply to such stereotypes. Gay and lesbian people:

- Do not try to convert others to homosexuality.
- Do not molest children.
- Are not mentally ill.
- Do not hate persons of the opposite sex.
- Do not, as parents, make their own children gay.
- Do have long-term, caring, monogamous relationships.
- Are no less able to contribute to society than heterosexuals.

Homosexual people are found in all walks of life, at all social and economic levels, and in all cultural groups. They are as diverse in terms of race, ethnicity, age, parenthood, relationships, careers, health, education, politics, and sexual behavior as the heterosexual community (Garnets, 2002). Perhaps as more people come to see gay and lesbian people in terms of their humanity, rather than their sexuality, the prejudices they have faced will wane.

MODULE 14.2 Summary

What are the most typical patterns of human sexual behavior?

- A wide range of sexual activities can be regarded as normal and characteristic of the human species.

However, social norms tend to define what is "acceptable" within various cultures.

- "Normal" sexual behavior is defined differently by various cultures. There appears to be little difference in sexual responsiveness between females and males.
- Sexual arousal is related to the body's erogenous zones. Sexual arousal is as much mental as it is physical.
- Evidence indicates that the sex drive peaks at a later age for females than it does for males, although this difference is diminishing.
- Castration may or may not influence sex drive in humans. Sterilization does not alter the sex drive.
- Frequency of sexual intercourse gradually declines with increasing age. However, many elderly persons remain sexually active, and large variations exist at all ages.
- Masturbation is a normal and completely acceptable behavior.
- *Sexual orientation* refers to one's degree of emotional and erotic attraction to members of the same sex, opposite sex, or both sexes. A person may be heterosexual, homosexual, or bisexual.
- Similar factors (heredity, biology, and socialization) underlie all sexual orientations.
- As a group, homosexual men and women do not differ psychologically from heterosexuals.
- All three sexual orientations (heterosexual, homosexual, bisexual) are part of the normal range of sexual behavior.

KNOWLEDGE BUILDER

Sexual Behavior and Sexual Orientation

Recite

1. A capacity for sexual arousal is apparent at birth or soon after. T or F?
2. Areas of the body that produce erotic pleasure are called _____ zones.
3. When exposed to erotic stimuli, men and women vary in their most common emotional reactions, but there appears to be no difference in their levels of physical arousal. T or F?
4. There is some evidence to suggest that sexual activity and sex drives peak later for males than they do for females. T or F?
5. It is possible (and normal) for sexual activity to continue to the age of 80 or 90. T or F?
6. More males than females report that they masturbate. T or F?
7. Masturbation can cause physical harm, according to the latest research reports. T or F?
8. Research suggests that homosexuality is closely related to hormonal imbalances found in roughly 4 percent of all adults. T or F?
9. Whether a person has erotic fantasies about women or men is a strong indicator of his or her sexual orientation. T or F?

Reflect

Critical Thinking

10. Why do you think that fidelity in marriage is strongly encouraged by law and custom?

Relate

How would you explain the following statement to students in a high school biology class: "Human sexual arousal obviously includes a large cognitive element"?

To what extent does the discussion of sexual arousal and sex drive agree with your own experiences and beliefs? What do you want to remember that you didn't know before?

Which of your prior beliefs about sexual orientation are true? Which are false?

Link

Internet addresses frequently change. To find the sites listed here, visit **http://www.thomsonedu.com/psychology/coon** for an updated list of Internet addresses and direct links to relevant sites.

- **Sexual Scripts** Read an article on the sexual scripts found in *Seventeen Magazine*.
- **Simon LeVay's Home Page** Read about the biology of sexual orientation.
- **Facts about Sexual Orientation** Read about sexual prejudice in our society.

ANSWERS

1. T 2. erogenous 3. T 4. F 5. T 6. T 7. F 8. F 9. T 10. Through marriage laws and customs, human societies tend to foster enduring bonds between sexual partners to help ensure that children are cared for and not just produced.

MODULE 14.3 Sexual Response, Attitudes, and Behavior

AN UNDERSTANDING OF HUMAN SEXUAL RESPONSE contributes greatly to healthy sexuality. The first part of this unit describes female and male sexual response from initial excitement through resolution. The next section discusses atypical, or psychologically unhealthy, sexual behaviors. Then we will investigate how changes in attitudes are affecting sexual behavior. An important final discussion focuses on responsible sexual behavior and sexually transmitted diseases.

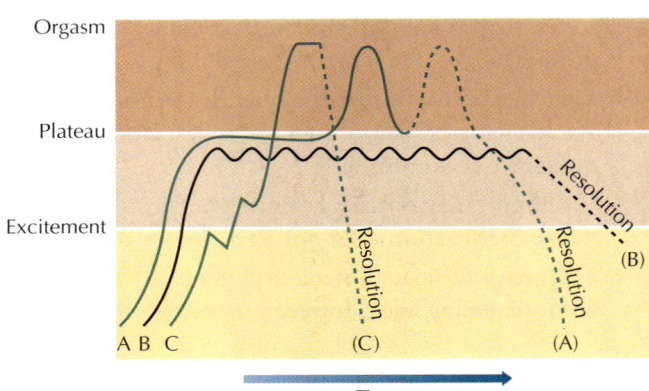

● **FIGURE 14.10** Female sexual response cycle. The green line shows that sexual arousal rises through the excitement phase and levels off for a time during the plateau phase. Arousal peaks during orgasm and then returns to pre-excitement levels. In pattern A, arousal rises from excitement through the plateau phase and peaks in orgasm. Resolution may be immediate, or it may first include a return to the plateau phase and a second orgasm (dotted line). In pattern B, arousal is sustained at the plateau phase and slowly resolved without sexual climax. Pattern C shows a fairly rapid rise in arousal to orgasm. Little time is spent in the plateau phase, and resolution is fairly rapid. (Reproduced by permission from Frank A. Beach [ed.], *Sex and behavior*, New York: John Wiley & Sons, Inc., 1965.)

Human Sexual Response– Sexual Interactions

SURVEY QUESTION: *To what extent do females and males differ in sexual response?*

The pioneering work of gynecologist William Masters and psychologist Virginia Johnson greatly expanded our understanding of sexual response (Masters & Johnson, 1966, 1970). In a series of experiments, interviews, and controlled observations, Masters and Johnson directly studied sexual intercourse and masturbation in nearly 700 males and females. This objective information has given us a much clearer picture of human sexuality.

According to Masters and Johnson, sexual response can be divided into four phases: (1) *excitement,* (2) *plateau,* (3) *orgasm,* and (4) *resolution* (● Fig. 14.10 and ● Fig. 14.11). These four phases can be described as follows:

Excitement phase The first level of sexual response, indicated by initial signs of sexual arousal.
Plateau phase The second level of sexual response, during which physical arousal intensifies.
Orgasm A climax and release of sexual excitement.
Resolution The final phase of sexual response, involving a return to lower levels of sexual tension and arousal.

The four phases are the same for people of all sexual orientations (Garnets & Kimmel, 1991).

Female Response In women, the excitement phase is marked by a complex pattern of changes in the body. The vagina is prepared for intercourse, the nipples become erect, pulse rate rises, and the skin may become flushed or reddened. If sexual stimulation ends, the excitement phase will gradually subside. If a woman moves into the plateau phase, physical changes and subjective feelings of arousal become more intense. Sexual arousal that ends during this phase tends to ebb more slowly, which may produce considerable frustration. Occasionally, women skip the plateau phase. (See Fig. 14.10.) For some women, this is almost always the case.

During orgasm, 3 to 10 muscular contractions of the vagina, uterus, and related structures discharge sexual tension. Somewhat rarely, a small amount of fluid is released from the urethra during orgasm (Whipple, 2000). Orgasm is usually followed by resolution, a return to lower levels of sexual tension and arousal. After orgasm, about 15 percent of all women return to the plateau phase and may have one or more additional orgasms (Mah & Binik, 2001).

Before the work of Masters and Johnson, theorists debated whether "vaginal orgasms" are different from those derived from stimulation of the clitoris. The clitoris is a small, sensitive organ located above the vaginal opening. Sigmund Freud claimed that a "clitoral orgasm" is an "immature" form of female response. Because the clitoris is the female structure comparable to the penis, Freud believed that women whose orgasms focused on the clitoris had not fully accepted their femininity.

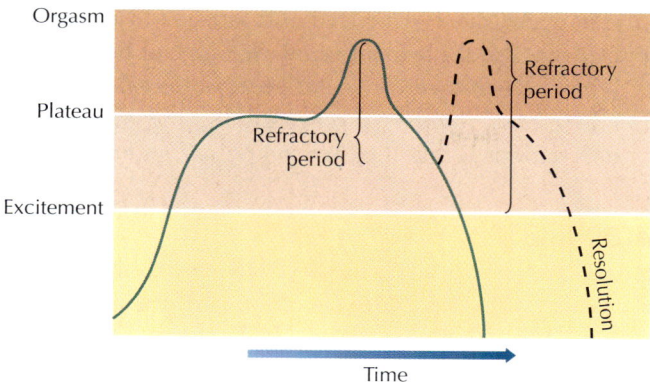

● **FIGURE 14.11** Male sexual response cycle. The green line shows that sexual arousal rises through the excitement phase and levels off for a time during the plateau phase. Arousal peaks during orgasm and then returns to pre-excitement levels. During the refractory period, immediately after orgasm, a second sexual climax is typically impossible. However, after the refractory period has passed, there may be a return to the plateau phase, followed by a second orgasm (dotted line). (Reproduced by permission from Frank A. Beach [ed.], *Sex and behavior*, New York: John Wiley & Sons, Inc., 1965.)

Masters and Johnson exploded the Freudian myth by showing that physical responses are the same no matter how an orgasm is produced (Mah & Binik, 2001). As a matter of fact, the inner two thirds of the vagina is relatively insensitive to touch. Most sensations during intercourse come from stimulation of the clitoris and other external areas.

Apparently, sensations from many sources are fused together into the total experience of orgasm. For most women, the clitoris is an important source of pleasurable sensations. Women in one study said that they enjoyed vaginal and clitoral stimulation equally. But if they were forced to choose, two thirds said they would prefer clitoral sensations (Fisher, 1973). Similarly, researcher Shere Hite reported that only 26 percent of women regularly reach orgasm during intercourse without separate massaging of the clitoris (Hite, 1976). Thus, to downgrade the "clitoral orgasm" ignores basic female biology.

Male Response Sexual arousal in the male is signaled by erection of the penis during the excitement phase. A rise in heart rate, increased blood flow to the genitals, enlargement of the testicles, erection of the nipples, and numerous other body changes also occur. As is true of female sexual response, continued stimulation moves the male into the plateau phase. Again, physical changes and subjective feelings of arousal become more intense. Further stimulation during the plateau phase brings about a reflex release of sexual tension, resulting in orgasm.

In the mature male, orgasm is usually accompanied by **ejaculation** (release of sperm and seminal fluid). Afterward, it is followed by a short **refractory period** during which a second orgasm is impossible. (Many men cannot even have an erection until the refractory phase has passed.) Only rarely is the male refractory period immediately followed by a second orgasm. Both orgasm and resolution in the male usually do not last as long as they do for females.

Comparing Male and Female Responses

Male and female sexual responses are generally quite similar. However, the differences that do exist can affect sexual adjustment. For example, women typically go through the sexual phases more slowly than men. During lovemaking, 10 to 20 minutes is often required for a woman to go from excitement to orgasm. Males may experience all four stages in as little as 4 minutes. However, there is much variation, especially in women. A study of married women found that 50 percent of them reached orgasm if intercourse lasted 1 to 11 minutes; when intercourse lasted 15 minutes or more, the rate increased to 66 percent. Twenty-five percent of the wives said that orgasm occurred within 1 minute of the start of intercourse (Brewer, 1981). (Note that these times refer only to intercourse, not to an entire arousal sequence.) Such differences should be kept in mind by couples seeking sexual compatibility.

Does that mean that a couple should try to time lovemaking to promote simultaneous orgasm? At one time simultaneous orgasm (both partners reaching sexual climax at the same time) was considered the "goal" of lovemaking. Now, it is regarded as an artificial concern that may reduce sexual enjoyment. It is more advisable for couples to seek mutual satisfaction through a combination of intercourse and erotic touching (*foreplay*) than it is to inhibit spontaneity, communication, and pleasure. A national survey found that the vast majority of American adults no longer feel that simultaneous orgasm is necessary for satisfying lovemaking (Janus & Janus, 1993).

Does the slower female response just described mean that women are less sexual than men? Definitely not. During masturbation, 70 percent of females reach orgasm in 4 minutes or less. This casts serious doubt on the idea that women respond more slowly. Slower female response during inter-

---

Excitement phase The first phase of sexual response, indicated by initial signs of sexual arousal.

Plateau phase The second phase of sexual response, during which physical arousal is further heightened.

Orgasm A climax and release of sexual excitement.

Resolution The fourth phase of sexual response, involving a return to lower levels of sexual tension and arousal.

Ejaculation The release of sperm and seminal fluid by the male at the time of orgasm.

Refractory period A short period after orgasm during which males are unable to again reach orgasm.

course probably occurs because stimulation to the clitoris is less direct. It might be said that men simply provide too little stimulation for more rapid female response, not that women are in any way inferior.

Does penis size affect female response? Think about it. If a woman's sexual satisfaction is related to her partner's attention to clitoral stimulation and foreplay, then why would his penis length matter? Besides, Masters and Johnson found that the vagina adjusts to the size of the penis and that subjective feelings of pleasure and intensity of orgasm are not related to penis size. They also found that although individual differences exist in flaccid penis size, there tends to be much less variation in size during erection. That's why erection has been called the "great equalizer." Contrary to popular belief, there is no relationship between penis size and male sexual potency. Lovemaking involves the entire body. Preoccupation with the size of a woman's breasts, a man's penis, and the like are based on myths that undermine genuine caring, sharing, and sexual satisfaction.

Men almost always reach orgasm during intercourse, but many women do not. Does this indicate that women are less sexually responsive? Again, the evidence argues against any lack of female sexual responsiveness. It is true that about 1 woman in 3 does not experience orgasm during the first year of marriage, and only about 30 percent regularly reach orgasm through intercourse alone. However, this does not imply lack of physical responsiveness, because 90 percent of all women reach orgasm when masturbating.

In another regard, women are clearly more responsive. Only about 5 percent of males are capable of multiple orgasm (and then only after an unavoidable refractory period). Most men are limited to a second orgasm at best. In contrast, Masters and Johnson's findings suggest that most women who regularly experience orgasm are capable of multiple orgasm. According to one survey, 48 percent of all women have had multiple orgasms (Darling, Davidson, & Passarello, 1992). Remember, though, that only about 15 percent regularly have multiple orgasms. A woman should not automatically assume that something is wrong if she isn't orgasmic or multiorgasmic. Many women have satisfying sexual experiences even when orgasm is not involved.

Atypical Sexual Behavior—Trench Coats, Whips, Leathers, and Lace

SURVEY QUESTION: *What are the most common sexual disorders?*

By strict standards (including the law in some states), any sexual activity other than face-to-face heterosexual intercourse between married adults is atypical or "deviant." But public standards are often at odds with private behavior. Just as the hunger drive is expressed and satisfied in many ways, the sex drive also leads to an immense range of behaviors.

When do variations in sexual behavior become sufficiently atypical to be a problem? Psychologically, the mark of true sexual deviations is that they are compulsive and destructive.

Paraphilias

Sexual deviations, or **paraphilias** (PAIR-eh-FIL-ih-ahs), typically cause guilt, anxiety, or discomfort for one or both participants. The paraphilias cover a wide variety of behaviors, including the following:

Pedophilia—sex with children, or child molesting

Fetishism—sexual arousal associated with inanimate objects

Exhibitionism—"flashing," or displaying the genitals to unwilling viewers

Voyeurism—"peeping," or viewing the genitals of others without their permission

Transvestic fetishism—achieving sexual arousal by wearing clothing of the opposite sex

Sexual sadism—deriving sexual pleasure from inflicting pain

Sexual masochism—desiring pain as part of the sex act

Frotteurism—sexually touching or rubbing against a nonconsenting person, usually in a public place such as a subway

Sexual deviance is a highly emotional subject, and many people have misconceptions about it. Two of the most misunderstood problems are exhibitionism and pedophilia. Check your understanding against the information that follows.

Exhibitionism Exhibitionism is a common problem. Roughly 35 percent of all sexual arrests are for "flashing." Exhibitionists are typically male and married, and most come from strict and repressive backgrounds. Exhibitionists have the highest repeat rate among sexual offenders. Most of them feel a deep sense of inadequacy, which produces a compulsive need to prove their "manhood" by frightening women. Although exhibitionists are usually harmless, those who approach closer than arm's reach may be dangerous. In general, a woman confronted by an exhibitionist can assume that his goal is to shock and alarm her. By becoming visibly upset she actually encourages him (Hyde & DeLamater, 2006).

Child Molestation Child molesters, who also are usually males, are often pictured as despicable perverts lurking in dark alleys. In fact, most are married and two thirds are fathers. Many are rigid, passive, puritanical, or religious. In most cases of pedophilia, the offender is a friend, acquaintance, or relative of the child (Abel & Harlow, 2001; Abel, Wiegel, & Osborn, 2007). Molesters are also often thought of as child rapists, but most molestations rarely exceed fondling (Sue, Sue, & Sue, 1996).

How serious are the effects of a molestation? The impact varies widely. It is affected by how long the abuse lasts and whether genital sexual acts are involved (Freize, 1987). Many authorities believe that a single incident of fondling is unlikely to cause severe emotional harm to a child. For most children the event is frightening but not a lasting trauma. That's why parents are urged not to overreact to such incidents or to become hysterical. Doing so only further frightens the child. This by no means implies, however, that parents should ignore hints from a child that a molestation may have occurred. Here are some hints of trouble that parents should watch for.

Recognizing Signs of Child Molestation
1. The child fears being seen nude (for instance, during bathing), when such fears were absent before.
2. The child develops physical complaints, such as headaches, stomachaches, and other stress symptoms.
3. The child displays anxiety, fidgeting, shame, or discomfort when any reference to sexual behavior occurs.
4. The child becomes markedly emotional and irritable.
5. The child engages in hazardous risk taking, such as jumping from high places or riding a bicycle dangerously in traffic.
6. The child reveals self-destructive or suicidal thoughts, or self-blame.
7. The child shows a loss of self-esteem or self-worth.

(Adapted from Frederick, 1987.)

How can children protect themselves? Children should be taught to shout "No" if an adult tries to engage them in sexual activity. If children are asked to keep a secret, they should reply that they don't keep secrets. Parents and children also need to be aware that some pedophiles now try to make contact with children on the Internet. If an adult suggests to a child online that they could meet in person, the child should immediately tell his or her parents.

It also helps if children know the tactics typically used by molesters. Interviews with convicted sex offenders revealed the following (Elliott, Browne, & Kilcoyne, 1995):

Tactics of Child Molesters
1. Most molesters act alone.
2. Most assaults take place in the abuser's home.
3. Many abusers gain access to the child through caretaking.
4. Children are targeted at first through bribes, gifts, and games.
5. The abuser tries to lull the child into participation through touch, talking about sex, and persuasion. (This can take place through e-mail or chat rooms on the Internet.)
6. The abuser then uses force, anger, threats, and bribes to gain continued compliance.

Repeated molestations, those that involve force or threats, and incidents that exceed fondling can leave lasting emotional scars. As adults, many victims of incest or molestation develop sexual phobias. For them, lovemaking may evoke vivid and terrifying memories of the childhood victimization. Serious harm is especially likely to occur if the molester is someone the child deeply trusts. Molestations by parents, close relatives, teachers, priests, youth leaders, and similar persons can be quite damaging. In such cases professional counseling is often needed (Saywitz et al., 2000).

As the preceding discussion suggests, the picture of sexual deviance that most often emerges is one of sexual inhibition and immaturity. Typically, some relatively infantile sexual expression (like exhibitionism or pedophilia) is selected because it is less threatening than more mature sexuality.

Many sadists, masochists, fetishists, and transvestites voluntarily associate with people who share their sexual interests. Thus, their behavior may not harm anyone, except when it is extreme. In contrast, pedophilia, exhibitionism, voyeurism, and frotteurism do victimize unwilling participants (Crooks & Baur, 2008).

All the paraphilias, unless they are very mild, involve compulsive behavior. As a result, they tend to emotionally handicap people. There is room in contemporary society for a large array of sexual behaviors. Nevertheless, any behavior that becomes compulsive (be it eating, gambling, drug abuse, or sex) is psychologically unhealthy.

Attitudes and Sexual Behavior— The Changing Sexual Landscape

SURVEY QUESTION: *Have recent changes in attitudes affected sexual behavior?*

Has there been a "sexual revolution"? If a woman and a man living 100 years ago could be transported to the present, what would they think about today's sexual values and practices? Undoubtedly, they would be stunned by the changes that

Paraphilias Compulsive or destructive deviations in sexual preferences or behavior.

Twenty years ago, television soap operas were tame, gossipy melodramas. Today they are sexy, gossipy melodramas that frequently feature steamy on-screen lovemaking.

have taken place. Unmarried couples falling into bed on television; advertisements for bras, skimpy men's underwear, tampons, and cures for "jock itch"; near nudity at the beaches; sexually explicit movies—these and many other elements of contemporary culture would shock a person from the Victorian era.

The word *revolution,* however, suggests rapid change. Has there been a sexual revolution? A look at social changes in the 1960s and 1970s makes it clear that some fundamental alterations have occurred. Liberalized sexual attitudes and access to effective birth control significantly changed sexual behavior. Compared with earlier times, the gap between sexual values and actual behavior has narrowed. For example, traditional morality called for female virginity before marriage. Yet, by the 1940s and 1950s as many as 75 percent of married women had engaged in premarital sex (Strong & DeVault, 1994).

Attitudes Changing attitudes can be seen in national polls about premarital intercourse. In a 1959 Roper poll, 88 percent of those interviewed agreed that premarital sex is wrong. By the 1990s, more than 70 percent of young men and women approved of premarital sex (Wells & Twenge, 2005). Similar changes have occurred in attitudes toward extramarital sex, homosexuality, sex education, and related issues.

Behavior *Have changing attitudes been translated into behavior?* Changes in attitudes are still larger than changes in actual sexual behavior. Mostly, there is greater *tolerance* for sexual activity, especially that *engaged in by others.* For example, a 1970s magazine poll found that 80 percent of all readers considered extramarital sex acceptable under some circumstances (Athenasiou, Shaver, & Tavris, 1970). But two other polls found that, in practice, only about 30 percent of married persons actually had extramarital sexual experience (Rubenstein, 1983; Rubenstein & Tavris, 1987). These are older studies, but the percentage has not changed greatly in the last 50 years. More important, faithfulness in marriage is a widely shared norm. Over a year, only about 4 percent of married people have sex partners other than their spouse. Americans actually seem to live up to the norm of marital fidelity fairly well (Mosher, Chandra, & Jones, 2005).

Teen premarital intercourse rates are a good indication of overall sexual activity. The social upheaval that began in the 1960s led to an especially sharp rise in sexual activity among teenagers. This increase continued into the 1980s but has reversed in recent years. In 1988, 60 percent of teenage males and 51 percent of teenage females had premarital intercourse by age 19. By 2002, the rates had dropped to 45 percent for both teenage males and females (CDC, 2002). The drop is especially pronounced among younger teens.

Encouragingly, the recent decline in sexual behavior during early adolescence has been accompanied by higher rates of contraceptive use and declining rates of teen pregnancy. Nevertheless, the United States still has one of the highest teenage pregnancy rates among all industrialized nations (CDC, 2002).

A partial solution to this problem may be to continue to give youths a better understanding of their sexuality. Research confirms that sex education *delays* the age at which young people first engage in sexual intercourse (Sawyer & Smith, 1996). Parents can encourage sexual responsibility in their children by providing close supervision and by stressing the value of delayed sexual involvement (Rosenthal et al., 2001).

Is the Revolution Over?

Talk of a sexual revolution has quieted in recent years, and a conservative counter-movement has been visible, especially among teenagers. Some of the reaction may reflect concern about sexually transmitted diseases. However, it is unlikely that the United States will undergo a wholesale return to less liberal times (Janus & Janus, 1993). An interesting trend is the fact that people today spend as much of their adult lives (on average) alone as they do in marriage. As a result, many people are involved in nonmarried sexual relationships (Mahay & Laumann, 2004).

CRITICAL THINKING

Are We Oversexualizing Young Girls?

As the sexual double standard continues to fade, women feel freer to express their sexuality. But there is a negative side: Many experts now fear that girls are being oversexualized by influences such as beauty pageants for very young girls and the public antics of female role models, such as Paris Hilton and Britney Spears (APA, 2007). Greater sexual freedom is positive only for those ready for it.

According to a recent American Psychological Association Task Force, unhealthy sexualization can be distinguished from healthy sexuality when one or more of the following conditions occurs (APA, 2007):

- A person is valued solely due to sexual appearance or behavior and not other characteristics.
- A person is led to narrowly equate sexual attractiveness with being "sexy."
- A person is objectified sexually (treated as an object for the gratification of other people).
- A person is inappropriately used sexually by another person.

Sexualization is especially unhealthy when it is imposed on younger children. From media images to popular fashions, young girls are more likely to be oversexualized than are young boys (APA, 2007). Oversexualization leads young girls to see themselves as having value only as sexual objects. This results in mental health problems, such as low self-esteem, eating disorders, depression, and feelings of shame (Ward, 2004). Some studies have even shown that sexualized girls perform more poorly on intellectual activities (Hebl, King, & Lin, 2004). Most worrisome is an increasing tendency for young girls to engage in risky sexual behaviors, such as unprotected oral sex (Atwood, 2006; Prinstein, Meade, & Cohen, 2003).

According to the APA Task Force, parents, educators, and others should encourage young girls to develop relationships based on their personalities and interests, rather than on how they look (APA, 2007).

What messages do beauty pageants send to these young girls?

In all, there is ample evidence that sexual behavior has generally increased in the last 40 years. Although this trend has brought problems, it does not seem to represent a wholesale move toward sexual promiscuity. Even premarital intercourse does not appear to represent a major rejection of traditional values and responsible behavior. The connection between sexuality and love or affection remains strong for most people. Both premarital sex and cohabitation are still widely viewed as preludes to marriage or as temporary substitutes for it. Likewise, other changes in attitudes and behavior appear to reflect a greater acceptance of sexuality rather than a total rejection of earlier values (Crooks & Baur, 2008).

Slow Death of the Double Standard A good summary of one major change that has occurred in sexual behavior is found in the phrase "the slow death of the double standard."

The *double standard* refers to using different rules to judge the appropriateness of male and female sexual behavior. In past decades, for example, males were largely forgiven for engaging in premarital sex. Young males who "sowed some wild oats" were widely tolerated. In fact, many were tacitly encouraged to seek casual sex as a step toward manhood. On the other hand, women who were sexually active before marriage ran the risk of being labeled "easy," "bad," or "promiscuous." Clearly, women are more aware of the double standard than men: 79 percent of men believe it exists, whereas 91 percent of women do (Janus & Janus, 1993).

Similar differences pervade sexual mores and frequently place women in a "separate but not equal" position with regard to sexual behavior (Sprecher & Hatfield, 1996). However, as the gap between female and male sexual patterns continues to close, it is increasingly likely that an end to the double standard is in sight (Schleicher & Gilbert, 2005).

Choices A more comfortable acceptance of human sexuality is the positive side of changing sexual attitudes and values. The negative side is revealed by the plight of people who are not ready for, or interested in, greater sexual freedom. (See "Are We

CRITICAL THINKING

Gender Role Stereotyping and Rape

Rape is related to traditional gender role socialization. Traditional feminine stereotypes include the idea that women should not show direct interest in sex. Traditional masculine stereotypes, on the other hand, include the ideas that a man should take the initiative and persist in attempts at sexual intimacy—even when the woman says no (Locke & Mahalik, 2005).

Psychologists James Check and Neil Malamuth (1983) believe that such attitudes create a "rape-supportive culture." In their view, rape is only an extreme expression of a system that condones coercive (forced) sexual intimacy. They point out, for instance, that the most used cries of rapists to their victims are "You know you want it," and afterward, "There now, you really enjoyed it, didn't you?"

In general, research has confirmed a link between acceptance of rape myths and sexual violence toward women (Forbes, Adams-Curtis, & White, 2004). In a classic experimental confirmation of the hypothesis that stereotyped images contribute to rape, male college students were classified as either high or low in gender role stereotyping. Each student then read one of three stories: The first described voluntary intercourse, the second depicted stranger rape, and the third described date rape.

As predicted, college males high in gender role stereotyping were more aroused by the rape stories. Their arousal patterns, in fact, were similar to those found among actual rapists. Moreover, a chilling 44 percent of those tested indicated they would consider rape—especially if they could be sure of not being caught (Check & Malamuth, 1983).

In view of such findings—and the continuing widespread belief that when a woman says no she means yes—it is little wonder that rape occurs every 6 minutes in the United States. Perhaps the time has come for our culture to make it clear that no means no. Educating men about rape myths has been one of the most successful ways of preventing sexual assault (King, 2005; Reppucci, Woolard, & Fried, 1999).

Oversexualizing Young Girls?") Apparently, some individuals feel pressured into sexual behavior because it is "expected." Six percent of first sexual intercourse experiences are against the person's will (Bajracharya, Sarvela, & Isberner, 1995).

Pressures to engage in sex probably come as much from the individual as from others. For a greater acceptance of sexuality to be constructive, people must feel that they have the right to say no, as well as the right to choose when, where, how, and with whom they will express their sexuality. As is true elsewhere, freedom must be combined with responsibility, commitment, and caring if it is to have meaning.

The Crime of Rape

Although it is commonly believed that rapists are usually strangers to the women they rape, nothing could be further from the truth. The importance of respecting the right to say no is underscored by the fact that 76 percent of American women who have been sexually or physically assaulted reported that the perpetrator was a husband, intimate partner, or acquaintance (FVPF, 2007). From 10 to 14 percent of all married women have experienced *marital rape*, which is usually accompanied by nonsexual violence (Martin, Taft, & Resick, 2007). Similarly, 5 to 15 percent of all female college students report having been raped. Roughly half of these rapes were **acquaintance (date) rapes** (forced intercourse that occurs in the context of a date or other voluntary encounter). In other words, they were carried out by first dates, casual dates, or romantic acquaintances (Fisher, Cullen, & Daigle, 2005; Koss, 2000).

Men who commit marital or date rape often believe they have done nothing wrong. A typical explanation is, "Her words were saying no, but her body was saying yes." (See "Gender Role Stereotyping and Rape.") But forced sex is rape, even if the rapist doesn't use a knife or become violent. The effects of rape by someone familiar are no less devastating than those of rape committed by a stranger.

Rape Myths A study of college men found that many tend to blame *women* for date rape. According to them, women who are raped by an acquaintance actually wanted to have sex. This is just one of several widely held beliefs that qualify as rape myths (Forbes, Adams-Curtis, & White, 2004; Jones, Russell, & Bryant, 1998). All these statements are myths:

- A woman who appears alone in public and dresses attractively is "asking for it."
- When a woman says no she really means yes.
- Many women who are raped actually enjoy it.
- If a woman goes home with a man on a first date, she is interested in sex.
- If a woman is sexually active, she is probably lying if she says she was raped.

Men who believe rape myths are more likely to misread a woman's resistance to unwanted sexual advances, assuming that she really means yes when she says no (Forbes, Adams-Curtis, & White, 2004). Add some alcohol to the situation and the risk of sexual assault is even greater: Men who believe rape myths and who have been drinking are especially likely to ignore signals that a woman wants sexual advances to stop (Bernat, Calhoun, & Stolp, 1998; Marx, Gross, & Adams, 1999).

Forcible Rape Date rape is coercive but not necessarily violent. Forcible rape, which is distressingly common, is carried out under the threat of bodily injury. Rapists often inflict more violence on their victims than is necessary to achieve their goal. Many women feel confident that their chances of being raped are low. But the facts tell a different story (CDC, 2007; FVPF, 2007; Koss, 1993):

- At least 1 woman in 7 will be raped in her lifetime. Because only 1 rape in 5 is reported, the true figure is much higher.
- In 75 percent of all cases the rapist is a friend or acquaintance of the victim.
- Pregnancy is one result of rape in 32,000 cases every year.
- Four to 30 percent of rape victims contract sexually transmitted diseases.

Most psychologists no longer think of forcible rape as a primarily sexual act. Rather, it is an act of brutality or aggression based on the need to debase others. Many rapists impulsively take what they want without concern for the feelings of the victim or guilt about their deed. Others harbor deep-seated resentment or outright hatred of women.

Quite often, the rapist's goal is not strictly sexual intercourse; it is to attack, subordinate, humiliate, and degrade the victim. Typical aftereffects for the victim include rage, guilt, depression, loss of self-esteem, shame, sexual adjustment problems, and, in many cases, a lasting mistrust of male-female relationships. The impact is so great that most women continue to report fear, anxiety, and sexual dysfunction a year or two after being raped. Even years later, rape survivors are more likely to suffer from depression, alcohol or drug abuse, and other emotional problems.

It is also important to be aware that men can also be the victims of rape, especially homosexual rape (Davies & McCartney, 2003). Any man who doubts the seriousness of rape should imagine himself mistakenly placed in jail, where he is violently raped (sodomized) by other inmates. There is no pleasure in rape for victims of either sex. It is truly a despicable crime.

STDs and Safer Sex—Choice, Risk, and Responsibility

SURVEY QUESTION: *What impacts have sexually transmitted diseases had on sexual behavior?*

In general, most adults favor greater freedom of choice for themselves, including choice about sexual behavior. Yet, there is some ambivalence toward greater sexual freedom. As the upcoming discussion of AIDS suggests, there are new and compelling reasons for caution in sexual behavior.

A **sexually transmitted disease (STD)** is an infection passed from one person to another by intimate physical contact. Sexually active people run a high risk of getting chlamydia (klah-MID-ee-ah), gonorrhea, hepatitis B, herpes, genital warts, syphilis, and other STDs (■ Table 14.2). Many people who carry STDs remain *asymptomatic* (a-SIMP-teh-mat-ik: lacking obvious symptoms). It is easy to have an infection without knowing it. Likewise, it is often impossible to tell if a sexual partner is infectious. Thus, risky sex is a serious hazard. A study of sexually active teenage girls engaging in risky sex is a case in point. Nearly 90 percent of the girls thought that they had virtually no chance of getting an STD. In reality, over the next 18 months 1 in 4 got chlamydia or gonorrhea (Ethier et al., 2003).

A major problem is the fact that people who are sexually active may have indirect contact with many other people. A recent study of sexual relationships at a high school in a Midwestern city found long chains of sexual contact between students. Thus, a student at the end of the chain might have had sex with only one person, but in reality she or he had indirect contact with dozens or even hundreds of others (Bearman, Moody, & Stovel, 2004).

For many sexually active people, the human immunodeficiency virus (HIV) has added a new threat. HIV is a sexually transmitted disease that disables the immune system. Whereas most STDs are treatable, HIV infections can be lethal. Check your knowledge about HIV against the following summary.

HIV/AIDS

Acquired immunodeficiency syndrome (AIDS) is caused by an HIV infection. As the immune system weakens, other "opportunistic" diseases invade the body. Most people with AIDS eventually die of multiple infections (although newer multidrug therapies have greatly improved the odds of survival). The first symptoms of AIDS may show up as little as 2 months after infection, but they typically don't appear for 10 years. Because of this long incubation period, infected persons often pass HIV on to others without knowing it. Medical tests can detect an HIV infection. However, for at least the first 6 months after becoming infected, a person can test negative while carrying the virus. A negative test result, therefore, is no guarantee that someone is a "safe" sex partner.

> **Acquaintance (date) rape** Forced intercourse that occurs in the context of a date or other voluntary encounter.
> **Sexually transmitted disease (STD)** A disease that is typically passed from one person to the next by intimate physical contact; a venereal disease.

TABLE 14.2 Common Sexually Transmitted Diseases

STD	MALE SYMPTOMS	FEMALE SYMPTOMS	PREVENTION	TREATMENT
Gonorrhea	Milky discharge from urethra; painful, frequent urination	Vaginal discharge and inflammation, painful urination	Condom/safer sex practices	Antibiotics
Chlamydia	Painful urination, discharge from urethra	Painful urination, discharge from vagina, abdominal pain	Condom/safer sex practices	Antibiotics
Syphilis	Painless sores on genitals, rectum, tongue, or lips; skin rash, fever, headache, aching bones and joints	Same	Condom/safer sex practices	Antibiotics
Genital herpes	Pain or itching on the penis; water blisters or open sores	Pain or itching in the genital area; water blisters or open sores	Condom/safer sex practices	Symptoms can be treated but not cured
Genital warts	Warty growth on genitals	Same	Condom/safer sex practices	Removal by surgery or laser
HIV/AIDS	Prolonged fatigue, swollen lymph nodes, fever lasting more than 10 days, night sweats, unexplained weight loss, purplish lesions on skin, persistent cough or sore throat, persistent colds, persistent diarrhea, easy bruising or unexplained bleeding	Same	Condom/safer sex practices	Can be treated with various drugs but cannot be cured
Hepatitis B	Mild cases may have no symptoms, but infection can cause chronic liver disease, cirrhosis of the liver, or liver cancer	Same	Vaccination	Non available
Pelvic inflammatory disease	Does not apply	Intense pain in lower back and/or abdomen, fever	Condom/safer sex practices	Antibiotics

HIV infections are spread by direct contact with body fluids—especially blood, semen, and vaginal secretions. HIV cannot be transmitted by casual contact. People do not get AIDS from shaking hands, touching or using objects touched by a person who has AIDS, eating food prepared by an infected person, social kissing, sweat or tears, sharing drinking glasses, sharing towels, and so forth.

HIV can be spread by all forms of sexual intercourse, and it has affected persons of all sexual orientations. Recently, the AIDS epidemic has spread more quickly among heterosexuals, women, African Americans, Hispanics, and children (Taylor-Seehafer & Rew, 2000). Around the world, almost half of all HIV cases are female (UNAIDS, 2006). HIV infection is the leading cause of death among women and men between the ages of 25 and 44 (Gayle, 2000). Worldwide, 2.9 million people die each year from HIV/AIDS and 4.3 million new infections occur (UNAIDS, 2006).

Populations at Risk In North America, those who are at greatest risk for HIV infection remain men who have had sex with other men (homosexual and bisexual men), people who have shared needles (for tattoos or for intravenous drug use), blood transfusion recipients (between 1977 and spring 1985), hemophiliacs (who require frequent blood transfusions), sexual partners of people in the preceding groups, and heterosexuals with a history of multiple partners. Thus, the vast majority of people are not at high risk of HIV infection. Still, 1.4 million people in North America are now infected with HIV, of whom 26 percent are women. Each year, 43,000 more people in the United States become infected (UNAIDS, 2006). In short, people who engage in unsafe sex are gambling with their lives—at very poor odds.

Behavioral Risk Factors

Sexually active people can do much to protect their own health. The behaviors listed here are risky when performed with an infected person.

Risky Behaviors
- Sharing drug needles and syringes
- Anal sex, with or without a condom
- Vaginal or oral sex with someone who injects drugs or engages in anal sex
- Sex with someone you don't know well or with someone you know has several partners
- Unprotected sex (without a condom) with an infected partner
- Having two or more sex partners (additional partners further increase the risk)

- Not engaging in sex while intoxicated
- Using a condom

Sexually active persons should practice safer sex until their partner's sexual history or health has been clearly established. And remember, a condom offers little or no protection if it is misused. Sadly, 1 of 3 sexually active teens don't know how to use a condom correctly (and virgins of both sexes are even more clueless) (Crosby & Yarber, 2001).

HIV and AIDS initially had a strong impact on sexual behavior in some groups. Among gay men there was a sharp decrease in risky sex and an increase in monogamous relationships. Unfortunately, this trend has recently reversed. Once again, STD rates are rising dramatically among gay men. In part, this may be due to the fact that new medical treatments are helping people with HIV live longer. Many victims simply do not look or act sick. This gives a false impression about the dangers of HIV infection and encourages foolish risk taking (Handsfield, 2001).

Other groups are also not getting the message. The AIDS epidemic has thus far had little impact on the willingness of high school and college age students to engage in risky behavior (casual sex) or to use condoms (Bauman, Karasz, & Hamilton, 2007). A study of heterosexual adults found that 62 percent did not practice safer sex with their last partner. Most of these "gamblers" knew too little about their partners to be sure they were not taking a big risk. ■ Table 14.3 lists the excuses they gave for engaging in risky sex (Kusseling et al., 1996). For many people, drinking alcohol greatly increases the likelihood of taking sexual risks (Corbin & Fromme, 2002).

Apparently, heterosexual people still don't feel that they are truly at risk. However, *75 percent* of people with HIV were infected through heterosexual sex. Over the next 20 to 30 years, heterosexual transmission is expected to become the primary means of spreading HIV. Over the next 15 years, 65 million more people will die of AIDS unless prevention efforts are greatly expanded (Altman, 2002).

The AIDS Memorial Quilt was begun in 1985 to commemorate those who have died from AIDS. Today the quilt has grown to immense size, symbolizing the extent of the AIDS epidemic. Originally the quilt memorialized only homosexual victims. It now includes heterosexual men, women, and children, signifying that AIDS respects no boundaries.

In the United States, between 2 and 4 of every 100 adults put themselves at high risk by engaging in the behaviors just listed (Gayle, 2000). It's important to remember that you can't tell from appearance if a person is infected. Many people would be surprised to learn that their partners have engaged in behavior that places them both at risk.

The preceding high-risk behaviors can be contrasted with the following list of safer sexual practices. Note, however, that unless a person completely abstains, sex can be made safer but not risk free.

Safer Sex Practices
- Not having sex
- Sex with one mutually faithful, uninfected partner
- Not injecting drugs
- Discussing contraception with partner
- Being selective regarding sexual partners
- Reducing the number of sexual partners
- Discussing partner's sexual health prior to engaging in sex

■ **TABLE 14.3 Common Excuses for Not Practicing Safer Sex**

REASONS FOR NOT HAVING SAFER SEX	PERCENTAGE GIVING EXCUSE
Condom not available	20
Didn't want to use a condom	19
"Couldn't stop ourselves"	15
Partner didn't want to use a condom	14
Alcohol or drug use	11

Source: Kusseling et al., 1996.

Risk and Responsibility

The threat of HIV/AIDS has forced many people to face new issues of risk and responsibility. Those who do not ensure their own safety are playing Russian roulette with their health. One chilling study of HIV patients—who knew they were infectious—found that 41 percent of those who were sexually active did not always use condoms (Sobel et al., 1996)! Thus, responsibility for "safer sex" rests with each sexually active individual. It is unwise to count on a sexual partner for protection against HIV infection.

A special risk that befalls people in committed relationships is that they often interpret practicing safer sex as a sign of mistrust. Taking precautions could, instead, be defined as a way of showing that you really care about the welfare of your partner (Hammer et al., 1996). Likewise, dating couples who have high levels of emotional, social, and intellectual intimacy are more likely to use contraceptives (Davis & Bibace, 1999).

The sexual revolution was fueled in part by "the pill" and other birth control methods. Will the threat of AIDS reverse the tide of changes that occurred in previous decades? Will STD come to mean Sudden Total Disinterest in sex? Will the "germs of endearment" change the terms of endearment? The answers may depend on how quickly people learn to respect HIV and whether its prevention or cure can be achieved.

A Look Ahead Even without STDs to worry about, sexual problems are quite common. In the "Psychology in Action" section we will consider the most common complaints and how they are remedied.

MODULE 14.3 Summary

To what extent do females and males differ in sexual response?

- Sexual response can be divided into four phases: excitement, plateau, orgasm, and resolution.
- There do not appear to be any differences between "vaginal orgasms" and "clitoral orgasms." Fifteen percent of women are consistently multiorgasmic, and at least 50 percent are capable of multiple orgasm.
- Males experience a refractory period after orgasm, and only 5 percent of men are multiorgasmic.
- The similarities between female and male sexual responses far outweigh the differences.

What are the most common sexual disorders?

- Compulsive sexual behaviors (paraphilias) tend to emotionally handicap people.
- The paraphilias include pedophilia, fetishism, voyeurism, exhibitionism, transvestic fetishism, sexual sadism, sexual masochism, and frotteurism.
- Exhibitionists are rarely dangerous and can best be characterized as sexually inhibited and immature.
- The effects of child molestation vary greatly, depending on the severity of the molestation and the child's relationship to the molester.

Have recent changes in attitudes affected sexual behavior?

- In the United States, a liberalization of attitudes toward sex has been paralleled by a gradual increase in sexual behavior over the last 40 years.
- In recent years there has been a greater acceptance of female sexuality and a narrowing of differences in female and male patterns of sexual behavior.
- Forcible rape, acquaintance rape, and rape-supportive attitudes and beliefs are major problems in North America.

What impacts have sexually transmitted diseases had on sexual behavior?

- During the last 20 years the incidence of sexually transmitted diseases has steadily increased.
- STDs and the spread of HIV have had a sizable impact on patterns of sexual behavior, including some curtailment of risk taking.
- Many sexually active people continue to take unnecessary risks with their health by failing to follow safer sex practices.
- The responsibility for practicing safer sex rests with each sexually active individual.

KNOWLEDGE BUILDER

Sexual Response, Attitudes, and Behavior

Recite

1. List the four phases of sexual response identified by Masters and Johnson: _____
2. Males typically experience _____ after ejaculation.
   a. an increased potential for orgasm
   b. a short refractory period
   c. the excitement phase
   d. muscular contractions of the uterus
3. The research of Masters and Johnson suggests that the similarities between female and male sexual responses outweigh the differences. T or F?
4. During lovemaking, 10 to 20 minutes is often required for a woman to go from excitement to orgasm, whereas a male may experience all four stages of sexual response in as little as 4 minutes. T or F?
5. Simultaneous orgasm of the female and male should be the ultimate goal in lovemaking. T or F?
6. Recent research shows that more liberal views regarding sexual behavior have erased the traditional values that link sexual involvement with committed relationships. T or F?
7. Contrary to long-standing belief, it now appears that much female sexual pleasure is focused on
   a. the uterus
   b. the clitoris
   c. the urethra
   d. the cervix
8. One woman in 70 will be raped in her lifetime, and chances are greater than 50 percent that the rapist will be a friend or acquaintance. T or F?
9. The term _____ _____ describes the tendency for the sexual behavior of women and men to be judged differently.
10. Because AIDS is spread by direct contact with body fluids, it can be transmitted by social kissing or contact with food or dishes handled by a person with AIDS. T or F?

Reflect
Critical Thinking

11. Of the following reasons that teenage boys and girls give for engaging in sex—love, curiosity, sexual gratification, peer pressure, and "everyone's doing it"—which do you think they rank first, and which last?

Relate

In what ways are sexual responses of members of the opposite sex similar to your own? In what ways are they different?

Based on your own observations of attitudes toward sex and patterns of sexual behavior, do you think there has been a sexual revolution?

You work in a program that provides counseling to people with AIDS. Should you be worried about contracting the disease? Why or why not?

To what extent do movies, music videos, and video games contribute directly to the perpetuation of rape myths? What about indirectly, by portraying gender role stereotypes?

As a counselor, you are working with a young person who seems to be sexually active. What can you tell this person about STDs and safer sex practices?

Link

Internet addresses frequently change. To find the sites listed here, visit http://www.thomsonedu.com/psychology/coon for an updated list of Internet addresses and direct links to relevant sites.

- **Sexual Response** Explore the sexual response cycle.
- **Paraphilias and Sexual Disorders** Read more about sexual disorders.
- **Child Molestation** Find out more about the prevention of child molestation.

ANSWERS

1. excitement, plateau, orgasm, resolution 2. b 3. T 4. T 5. F 6. F 7. b 8. T 9. F double standard 10. F 11. Peer pressure ranked first (cited by 30 percent of those surveyed) and love ranked last (cited by 8 percent) ("Teen sex," 1989).

MODULE **Psychology in Action**
14.4 Sexual Problems—When Pleasure Fades

SURVEY QUESTION: *What are the most common sexual adjustment problems? How are they treated?*

Sexual dysfunctions are far more common than many people realize. Most people who seek sexual counseling have one or more of the following types of problems (Crooks & Baur, 2008; DSM-IV-TR, 2000; Heiman, 2002):

1. **Desire Disorders:** The person has little or no sexual motivation or desire.
2. **Arousal Disorders:** The person desires sexual activity but does not become sexually aroused.
3. **Orgasm Disorders:** The person does not have orgasms or experiences orgasm too soon or too late.
4. **Sexual Pain Disorders:** The person experiences pain that makes lovemaking uncomfortable or impossible.

There was a time when people suffered such problems in silence. However, in recent years effective treatments have been found for many complaints. Medical treatments or drugs (such as Viagra for men) may be helpful for sexual problems that clearly have physical causes. In other cases, counseling or psychotherapy may be the best approach. Let's briefly investigate the nature, causes, and treatments of sexual dysfunctions.

Desire Disorders

Desire disorders, like most sexual problems, must be defined in relation to a person's age, sex, partner, expectations, and sexual history. It is not at all unusual for a person to briefly lose sexual desire. Typically, erotic feelings return when anger toward a partner fades, or fatigue, illness, and similar temporary problems end. Under what circumstances, then, is loss of desire a dysfunction? First, the loss of desire must be *persistent*. Second, the person must be *troubled by it*. When these two conditions are met, **hypoactive sexual desire** is said to exist. Diminished desire can apply to both sexes. However, it is somewhat more common in women (Heiman, 2002; Segraves & Woodard, 2006).

Some people don't merely lack sexual desire; they are *repelled* by sex and seek to avoid it. A person who suffers from **sexual aversion** feels fear, anxiety, or disgust about engaging in sex. Often, the afflicted person still has some erotic feelings. For example, he or she may still masturbate or have sexual fantasies. Nevertheless, the prospect of having sex with another person causes panic or revulsion (DSM-IV-TR, 2000).

Sexual desire disorders are common. Possible physical causes include illness, fatigue, hormonal difficulties, and the side effects of medicines. Desire disorders are also associated with psychological factors such as depression, fearing loss of control over sexual urges, strict religious beliefs, fear of pregnancy, marital conflict, fear of closeness, and simple loss of attraction to one's partner (King, 2005). It is also not uncommon to find that people with desire disorders were sexually mistreated as children (Bakich, 1995).

Treatment Desire disorders are complex problems. Unless they have a straightforward physical cause, they are difficult to treat. Desire disorders are often deeply rooted in a person's childhood, sexual history, personality, and relationships. In such instances, counseling or psychotherapy is recommended (Crooks & Baur, 2008; King, 2005).

Arousal Disorders

A person suffering from an arousal disorder wants to make love but experiences little or no physical arousal. For women, this means vaginal dryness. For men, it means an inability to maintain an erection. Basically, in arousal disorders the body does not cooperate with the person's desire to make love.

Male Erectile Disorder An inability to maintain an erection for lovemaking is called male **erectile disorder.** This problem, which is also known as erectile dysfunction, was once referred to as *impotence*. However, psychologists now discourage use of the term *impotence* because of its many negative connotations.

Erectile disorders can be primary or secondary. Men suffering from primary erectile dysfunction have never had an erection. Those who previously performed successfully, but then developed a problem, suffer from secondary erectile dysfunction. Either way, persistent erectile difficulties tend to be very disturbing to the man and his sexual partner (Baldo & Eardley, 2005).

How often must a man experience failure for a problem to exist? Ultimately, only the man and his partner can make this judgment. Nevertheless, sex therapists Masters and Johnson (1970) believe that a problem exists when failure occurs on 25 percent or more of a man's lovemaking attempts. Repeated erectile dysfunction should therefore be distinguished from *occasional* erectile problems. Fatigue, anger, anxiety, and drinking too much alcohol can cause temporary erectile difficulties in healthy males. True erectile disorders typically persist for months or years (Rowland, 2007).

It is important to recognize that occasional erectile problems are normal. In fact, "performance demands" or overreaction to the temporary loss of an erection may generate fears and doubts that contribute to a further inhibition of arousal (Abrahamson, Barlow, & Abrahamson, 1989). At such times, it is particularly important for the man's partner to avoid expressing anger, disappointment, or embarrassment. Patient reassurance helps prevent the establishment of a vicious cycle.

What causes erectile disorders? For years, experts held that erectile disorders are rarely caused by physical illness, disease, or damage. Now it is recognized that roughly 40 percent of all cases are organic, or physically caused. The origin of the remaining cases is *psychogenic* (a result of emotional factors). Even when erectile dysfunction is organic, however, it is almost always made worse by anxiety, anger, and dejection. If a man can have an erection at times other than lovemaking (during sleep, for instance), the problem probably is not physical (Baldo & Eardley, 2005).

Organic erectile problems have many causes. Typical sources of trouble include alcohol or drug abuse, diabetes, vascular disease, prostate and urological disorders, neurological problems, and reactions to medication for high blood pressure, heart disease, or stomach ulcers. Erectile problems are also a normal part of aging. As men grow older they typically experience a decline in sexual desire and arousal and an increase in sexual dysfunction (Segraves & Segraves, 1995).

According to Masters and Johnson (1970), primary erectile disorders are often related to harsh religious training, early sexual experiences with a seductive mother, sexual molestation in childhood, or other experiences leading to guilt, fear, and sexual inhibition.

Secondary erectile disorders may be related to anxiety about sex in general, guilt because of an extramarital affair, resentment or hostility toward a sexual partner, fear of inability to perform, concerns about STDs, and similar emotions and conflicts (Shires & Miller, 1998). Often the problem starts with repeated sexual failures caused by drinking too much alcohol or by premature ejaculation. In any event, initial doubts soon become severe fears of failure—which further inhibit sexual response.

Treatment Drugs or surgery may be used in medical treatment of organic erectile disorders. The drug Viagra is successful for about 70 to 80 percent of men with erectile disorders. However, effective treatment should also include counseling to remove fears and psychological blocks (Heiman, 2002). Fixing the "hydraulics" of erectile problems may not be enough to end the problem. It is important for the man to also regain confidence, improve his relationship with his partner, and learn better lovemaking skills. To free him of conflicts, the man and his partner may be assigned a series of exercises to perform. This technique, called **sensate focus,** directs attention to natural sensations of pleasure and builds communication skills (McCabe, 1992).

In sensate focus, the couple is told to take turns caressing various parts of each other's bodies. They are further instructed to carefully avoid any genital contact. Instead, they are to concentrate on giving pleasure and on signaling what feels good to them. This takes the pressure to perform off the man and allows him to learn to give pleasure as a means of receiving it. For many men, sensate focus is a better solution than depending on an expensive drug to perform sexually.

Over a period of days or weeks, the couple proceeds to more intense physical contact involving the breasts and genitals. As inhibitions are reduced and natural arousal begins to replace fear, the successful couple moves on to mutually satisfying lovemaking.

Female Sexual Arousal Disorder Women who suffer from **female sexual arousal disorder** respond with little or no physical arousal to sexual stimulation. The problem thus appears to correspond directly to male erectile difficulties. As in the male, female sexual arousal disorder may be primary or secondary. Also, it is again important to remember that all women occasionally experience inhibited arousal. In some instances the problem may reflect nothing more than a lack of sufficient sexual stimulation before attempting lovemaking (King, 2005).

The causes of inhibited arousal in women are similar to those seen in men. Sometimes the problem is medical, being related to illness or the side effects of medicines or contraceptives. Psychological factors include anxiety, anger or hostility toward one's partner, depression, stress, or distracting worries. Some women can trace their arousal difficulties to frightening childhood experiences, such as molestations (often by older relatives); incestuous relations that produced lasting guilt; a harsh religious background in which sex was considered evil; or cold, unloving childhood relationships. Also common is a need to maintain control over emotions; deep-seated conflicts over being female; and extreme distrust of others, especially males (Read, 1995).

Hypoactive sexual desire A persistent, upsetting loss of sexual desire.
Sexual aversion Persistent feelings of fear, anxiety, or disgust about engaging in sex.
Erectile disorder An inability to maintain an erection for lovemaking.
Sensate focus A form of therapy that directs a couple's attention to natural sensations of sexual pleasure.
Female sexual arousal disorder A lack of physical arousal to sexual stimulation.

Treatment *How does treatment proceed?* Treatment typically includes sensate focus, genital stimulation by the woman's partner, and "nondemanding" intercourse controlled by the woman (Segraves & Althof, 2002). With success in these initial stages, full intercourse is gradually introduced. As sexual training proceeds, psychological conflicts and dynamics typically appear, and as they do, they are treated in separate counseling sessions.

Orgasm Disorders

A person suffering from an orgasm disorder either fails to reach orgasm during sexual activity or reaches orgasm too soon or too late (Regev, Zeiss, & Zeiss, 2006). Notice that such disorders are very much based on expectations. For instance, if a man experiences delayed orgasm, one couple might define it as a problem but another might welcome it. It is also worth noting again that some women rarely or never have orgasm and still find sex pleasurable (King, 2005).

Female Orgasmic Disorder The most prevalent sexual complaint among women is a persistent inability to reach orgasm during lovemaking. It is often clear in **female orgasmic disorder** that the woman is not completely unresponsive. Rather, she is unresponsive in the context of a relationship—she may easily reach orgasm by masturbation but not during lovemaking with her partner.

Then couldn't the woman's partner be at fault? Sex therapists try to avoid finding fault or placing blame. However, it is true that the woman's partner must be committed to ensuring her gratification. Roughly two thirds of all women need direct stimulation of the clitoris to reach orgasm. Therefore, some apparent instances of female orgasmic disorder can be traced to inadequate stimulation or faulty technique on the part of the woman's partner. Even when this is true, sexual adjustment difficulties are best viewed as a problem the couple shares, not just as the "woman's problem," the "man's problem," or her "partner's problem."

Treatment If we focus only on the woman, the most common source of orgasmic difficulties is overcontrol of sexual response. Orgasm requires a degree of abandonment to erotic feelings. It is inhibited by ambivalence or hostility toward the relationship, by guilt, by fears of expressing sexual needs, and by tendencies to control and intellectualize erotic feelings. The woman is unable to let go and enjoy the flow of pleasurable sensations (Segraves & Althof, 2002).

Anorgasmic women (those who do not have orgasms) are first trained to focus on their sexual responsiveness through masturbation or vigorous stimulation by a partner. As the woman becomes consistently orgasmic in these circumstances, her responsiveness is gradually transferred to lovemaking with her partner. Couples also typically learn alternative positions and techniques of lovemaking designed to increase clitoral stimulation. At the same time, communication between partners is stressed, especially with reference to the woman's expectations, motivations, and preferences (Kelly, Strassberg, & Turner, 2006; Regev, Zeiss, & Zeiss, 2006).

Male Orgasmic Disorder Among males, an inability to reach orgasm was once considered a rare problem. But milder forms of **male orgasmic disorder** account for increasing numbers of clients seeking therapy (Rowland, 2007). Typical background factors are strict religious training, fear of impregnating, lack of interest in the sexual partner, symbolic inability to give of oneself, unacknowledged homosexuality, or the recent occurrence of traumatic life events. Power and commitment struggles within relationships may be important added factors.

Treatment Treatment for male orgasmic disorder (also known as retarded ejaculation) consists of sensate focus, manual stimulation by the man's partner (which is designed to orient the male to his partner as a source of pleasure), and stimulation to the point of orgasm followed by immediate intercourse and ejaculation. Work also focuses on resolving personal conflicts and marital difficulties underlying the problem.

Premature Ejaculation Defining premature ejaculation is tricky because of large variations in the time different women take to reach orgasm. Helen Kaplan says that **premature ejaculation** exists when it occurs reflexively or the man cannot tolerate high levels of excitement at the plateau stage of arousal (Kaplan, 1974). Basically, ejaculation is premature if it consistently occurs before the man and his partner want it to occur (Rowland, 2007).

Do many men have difficulties with premature ejaculation? Approximately 50 percent of young adult men have problems with premature ejaculation. Theories advanced to explain it have ranged from the idea that it may represent hostility toward the man's sexual partner (because it deprives the partner of satisfaction) to the suggestion that most early male sexual experiences tend to encourage rapid climax (such as those taking place in the back seat of a car and masturbation). H. S. Kaplan (1974) adds that excessive arousal and anxiety over performance are usually present. Also, some men simply engage in techniques that maximize sensation and make rapid orgasm inevitable.

Ejaculation is a reflex. To control it, a man must learn to recognize the physical signals that it is about to occur. Some men have simply never learned to be aware of these signals.

Whatever the causes, premature ejaculation can be a serious difficulty, especially in the context of long-term relationships (King, 2005).

Treatment Treatment for premature ejaculation is highly successful and relatively simple. The most common treatment is a "stop-start" procedure called the **squeeze technique** (Grenier & Byers, 1995). The man's sexual partner stimulates him manually until he signals that ejaculation is about to occur. The man's partner then firmly squeezes the tip of his penis to inhibit orgasm. When the man feels he has control, stimulation is repeated. Later the squeeze technique is used during lovemaking. Gradually the man acquires the ability to delay orgasm sufficiently for mutually satisfactory lovemaking. During treatment, skills that improve communication between partners are developed, along with a better understanding of the male's sexual response cues (McCarthy & Fucito, 2005).

Sexual Pain Disorders

Pain in the genitals before, during, or after sexual intercourse is called **dyspareunia** (DIS-pah-ROO-nee-ah) (Binik, 2005). Both females and males can experience dyspareunia. However, this problem is actually rare in males. In women, dyspareunia is often related to **vaginismus** (VAJ-ih-NIS-mus), a condition in which muscle spasms of the vagina prevent intercourse (DSM-IV-TR, 2000).

Vaginismus is often accompanied by obvious fears of intercourse, and where fear is absent, high levels of anxiety are present (Reissing et al., 2004). Vaginismus therefore appears to be a phobic response to intercourse. Predictably, its causes include experiences of painful intercourse, rape or other brutal and frightening sexual encounters, fear of men and of penetration, misinformation about sex (belief that it is injurious), fear of pregnancy, and fear of the specific male partner (Read, 1995; Reissing et al., 2003).

Treatment Treatment of vaginismus is similar to what might be done for a nonsexual phobia. It includes extinction of conditioned muscle spasms by progressive relaxation of the vagina, desensitization of fears of intercourse, and masturbation or manual stimulation to associate pleasure with sexual approach by the woman's partner (Bergeron & Lord, 2003). Hypnosis has also been used successfully in some cases.

Summary Solving sexual problems can be difficult. The problems described here are rarely solved without professional help (a possible exception is premature ejaculation). If a serious sexual difficulty is not resolved in a reasonable amount of time, the aid of an appropriately trained psychologist, physician, or counselor should be sought. The longer the problem is ignored, the more difficult it is to solve. But professional help is available.

Relationships and Sexual Adjustment

What can be done to improve sexual adjustment? Often, it is best to view sexual adjustment within the broader context of a relationship (Crooks & Baur, 2008). Conflict and unresolved anger in other areas frequently take their toll in sexual adjustment, and mutually satisfying relationships tend to carry over into sexual relations. Sex is not a performance or a skill to be mastered like playing tennis. It is a form of communication within a relationship. Couples with strong and caring relationships can probably survive most sexual problems. A couple with a satisfactory sex life but a poor relationship rarely lasts. Marriage expert John Gottman believes that a couple must have at least five times as many positive as negative moments in their marriage if it is to survive (Gottman, 1994).

Disagreements about Sex When disagreements arise over issues such as frequency of lovemaking, who initiates lovemaking, or what behavior is appropriate, Masters and Johnson believe that the rule should be, "Each partner must accept the other as the final authority on his or her own feelings." Partners are urged to give feedback about their feelings by following what therapists call the "touch and ask" rule: Touching and caressing should often be followed by questions such as, "Does that feel good?" "Do you like that?" and so forth. Satisfying erotic relationships focus on enhancing sexual pleasure for both partners, not on selfish interest in one's own gratification (Carroll, 2007; Kleinplatz, 1996).

When problems do arise, partners are urged to be *responsive* to each other's needs at an *emotional* level and to recognize that all sexual problems are *mutual*. "Failures" should always be shared without placing blame. Masters and Johnson believe that it is particularly important to avoid the "numbers game." That is, couples should avoid being influ-

---

Female orgasmic disorder A persistent inability to reach orgasm during lovemaking.

Male orgasmic disorder A persistent inability to reach orgasm during lovemaking.

Premature ejaculation Ejaculation that consistently occurs before the man and his partner want it to occur.

Squeeze technique A method for inhibiting ejaculation by compressing the tip of the penis.

Dyspareunia Genital pain before, during, or after sexual intercourse.

Vaginismus Muscle spasms of the vagina.

enced by statistics on the average frequency of lovemaking, by stereotypes about sexual potency, and by the superhuman sexual exploits portrayed in movies and magazines.

Bridges to Sexual Satisfaction According to sex therapist Barry McCarthy, four elements are necessary for a continuing healthy sexual relationship:

1. *Sexual anticipation.* Looking forward to lovemaking is inhibited by routine and poor communication between partners. It is wise for busy couples to set aside time to spend together. Unexpected, spontaneous lovemaking should also be encouraged.
2. *Valuing one's sexuality.* This is most likely to occur when you develop a respectful, trusting, and intimate relationship with your partner. Such relationships allow both partners to deal with negative sexual experiences when they occur.
3. *Feeling that you deserve sexual pleasure.* As previously noted, the essence of satisfying lovemaking is the giving and receiving of pleasure.
4. *Valuing intimacy.* A sense of closeness and intimacy with one's partner helps maintain sexual desire, especially in long-term relationships (McCarthy, 1995; McCarthy & Fucito, 2005).

"Well, if it doesn't matter who's right and who's wrong, why don't I be right and you be wrong?"

Intimacy and Communication

Are there any other guidelines for maintaining a healthy relationship? A study that compared happily married couples with unhappily married couples found that, in almost every regard, the happily married couples showed superior *communication* skills. Three patterns that are almost always related to serious long-term problems in relationships are defensiveness (including whining), stubbornness, and refusal to talk with your partner (the "big freeze") (Gottman & Krokoff, 1989). Many couples find that communication is facilitated by observing the following guidelines.

Avoid "Gunnysacking" Persistent feelings, whether positive or negative, need to be expressed. *Gunnysacking* refers to saving up feelings and complaints. These are then "dumped" during an argument or are used as ammunition in a fight. Gunnysacking is very destructive to a relationship.

Be Open about Feelings Happy couples not only talk more, they convey more personal feelings and show greater sensitivity to their partners' feelings (Driver & Gottman, 2004). As one expert put it, "In a healthy relationship, each partner feels free to express his likes, dislikes, wants, wishes, feelings, impulses, and the other person feels free to react with like honesty to these. In such a relationship, there will be tears, laughter, sensuality, irritation, anger, fear, baby-like behavior, and so on" (Jourard, 1963).

Don't Attack the Other Person's Character Whenever possible, expressions of negative feelings should be given as statements of one's own feelings, not as statements of blame. It is far more constructive to say, "It makes me angry when you leave things around the house" than it is to say, "You're a slob!" Remember, too, that if you use the words "always" or "never," you are probably mounting a character attack.

Don't Try to "Win" a Fight Constructive fights are aimed at resolving shared differences, not at establishing who is right or wrong, superior or inferior.

Recognize That Anger Is Appropriate Constructive and destructive fights are not distinguished by whether or not anger is expressed. A fight is a fight, and anger is appropriate. As is the case with any other emotion in a relationship, anger should be expressed. However, constructive expression of anger requires that couples fight fair by sticking to the real issues and not "hitting below the belt." Resorting to threats, such as announcing, "This relationship is over," is especially damaging.

Try to See Things through Your Partner's Eyes Marital harmony is closely related to the ability to put yourself in another person's place (Long & Andrews, 1990). When a conflict arises, always pause and try to take your partner's perspective. Seeing things through your partner's eyes can be a good reminder that no one is ever totally right or wrong in a personal dispute.

Don't Be a "Mind Reader" The preceding suggestion should not be taken as an invitation to engage in "mind reading." Assuming that you know what your partner is thinking or feeling can muddle or block communication. Hostile or accusatory mind reading, such as in the following examples, can be very disruptive: "You're just looking for an excuse to criticize me, aren't you?" "You don't really want my mother to visit, or you wouldn't say that." Rather than *telling* your partner what she or he thinks, *ask* her or him.

To add to these guidelines, Bryan Strong and Christine DeVault (1994) suggest that if you really want to mess up a relationship, you can almost totally avoid intimacy and communication by doing the following:

Ten Ways to Avoid Intimacy
1. Don't talk about anything meaningful, especially about feelings.
2. Never show your feelings; remain as expressionless as possible.
3. Always be pleasant and pretend everything is okay, even if you are upset or dissatisfied.
4. Always win, never compromise.
5. Always keep busy; that way you can avoid intimacy and make your partner feel unimportant in your life.
6. Always be right; don't let on that you are human.
7. Never argue, or you may have to reveal differences and make changes.
8. Make your partner guess what you want. That way, you can tell your partner that she or he doesn't really understand or love you.
9. Always take care of your own needs first.
10. Keep the television set on. Wouldn't you rather be watching TV than talking with your partner?

Remember, to encourage intimacy, wise couples *avoid* the practices in the preceding list.

As a last point, it is worth restating that sexual adjustment and loving relationships are interdependent. When sex goes well, it's 15 percent of a relationship, and when it goes badly it's 85 percent. As a shared pleasure, a form of intimacy, a means of communication, and a haven from everyday tensions, a positive sexual relationship can do much to enhance a couple's mutual understanding and caring. Likewise, an honest, equitable, and affectionate out-of-bed relationship contributes greatly to sexual satisfaction (Rathus, Nevid, & Fichner-Rathus, 2005).

MODULE 14.4 Psychology in Action Summary

What are the most common sexual adjustment problems? How are they treated?

- Problems with sexual function can involve desire, arousal, orgasm, or pain.
- The most common problems are hypoactive sexual desire, sexual aversion, erectile disorder, female arousal disorder, orgasmic disorder, premature ejaculation, dyspareunia, and vaginismus.
- Behavioral methods, such as sensate focus and the squeeze technique, can be combined with counseling to alleviate many sexual problems.
- Most sexual adjustment problems are closely linked to the general health of a couple's relationship.
- Communication skills that foster and maintain intimacy are the key to successful relationships.

KNOWLEDGE BUILDER

Sexual Problems

Recite

1. Males suffering from primary erectile dysfunction have never been able to have or maintain an erection. T or F?
2. According to the latest figures, most erectile disorders are caused by castration fears. T or F?
3. Sensate focus is the most common treatment for premature ejaculation. T or F?
4. Premature ejaculation is considered the rarest of the male sexual adjustment problems. T or F?
5. As it is for female sexual arousal disorder, the sensate focus technique is a primary treatment mode for male sexual arousal disorder. T or F?
6. Vaginismus, which appears to be a phobic response to sexual intercourse, can also cause dyspareunia. T or F?
7. Masters and Johnson urge sexual partners to recognize that all sexual problems are mutual and not just one partner's problem. T or F?
8. The term *gunnysacking* refers to the constructive practice of hiding anger until it is appropriate to express it. T or F?

Reflect
Critical Thinking

9. Who would you expect to have the most frequent sex and the most satisfying sex, married couples or single persons?

Relate

In plain language, sexual disorders can be summarized this way: The person doesn't want to do it. The person wants to do it but can't get aroused. The person wants to do it, gets aroused, but has problems with orgasm. The person wants to do it and gets aroused, but lovemaking is uncomfortable. What are the formal terms for each of these possibilities?

We all make mistakes in relationships. Using the discussion in the "Psychology in Action" as a guide, which mistakes have you avoided? Which would you like to avoid or correct?

Link

Internet addresses frequently change. To find the sites listed here, visit **http://www.thomsonedu.com/psychology/coon** for an updated list of Internet addresses and direct links to relevant sites.

- **Sexual Arousal Disorder** Explore this discussion of a variety of sexual arousal disorders.
- **Premature Ejaculation** Access helpful information from causes to coping skills.
- **Sexuality and Intimacy** Read a series of articles on the role of intimacy in sexuality.

ANSWERS

1. T 2. F 3. F 4. F 5. T 6. T 7. T 8. F 9. Contrary to mass media portrayals of sexy singles, married couples have the most sex and are most likely to have orgasms when they do. Greater opportunity plus familiarity with a partner's needs and preferences probably account for these findings (Laumann et al., 1994).

Interactive Learning

Psychology: Active Learning Modules Book Companion Website

http://www.thomsonedu.com/psychology/coon

Visit your Book Companion Website, where you will find flash cards, practice quizzes, Internet links, and more to help you study.

ThomsonNOW

Just What You Need to Know NOW!

Spend time on what you need to master rather than on information you already have learned. Take a pre-test for this chapter, and ThomsonNOW will generate a personalized study plan based on your results. The study plan will identify the topics you need to review and direct you to online resources to help you master those topics. You can then take a post-test to help you determine the concepts you have mastered and what you will need to work on. Try it out! Go to www.thomsonedu.com/login to sign in with an access code or to purchase access to this product.

15 Social Behavior

MODULE 15.1 Affiliation, Friendship, and Love
SURVEY QUESTIONS: Why do people affiliate? What factors influence interpersonal attraction?

MODULE 15.2 Groups, Social Influence, and Conformity
SURVEY QUESTION: How does group membership affect our behavior?
SURVEY QUESTION: What have social psychologists learned about conformity?

MODULE 15.3 Compliance, Obedience, and Self-Assertion
SURVEY QUESTION: What have psychologists learned about compliance, obedience, and self-assertion?

MODULE 15.4 Attitudes and Persuasion
SURVEY QUESTION: How are attitudes acquired and changed?
SURVEY QUESTION: Under what conditions is persuasion most effective?

SURVEY QUESTIONS: Is brainwashing actually possible? How are people converted to cult membership?

MODULE 15.5 Prejudice and Intergroup Conflict
SURVEY QUESTION: What causes prejudice and intergroup conflict?

MODULE 15.6 Aggression and Prosocial Behavior
SURVEY QUESTION: How do psychologists explain human aggression?
SURVEY QUESTION: Why are bystanders so often unwilling to help in an emergency?

MODULE 15.7 Psychology in Action: Multiculturalism—Living with Diversity
SURVEY QUESTION: What can be done to avoid prejudice and promote social harmony?

Six Degrees of Separation

"No man is an island, entire of itself." –John Donne

Here's your assignment: You have been given a message and the name, address, and occupation of the person who should receive it. The "target person" lives somewhere else on earth. You can move the message by e-mail, but you may send it only to a first-name acquaintance. That person, in turn, must forward the message to a first-name acquaintance. The message is to be moved in this fashion until it reaches the target person, whom the previous person must know by name.

Sound impossible? Following up on the pioneering work of social psychologist Stanley Milgram (1967), sociologist Duncan Watts asked more than 60,000 senders to use this method to forward e-mails to 18 target recipients in 13 countries. Like Milgram before him, Watts found that the average number of intermediaries was six (Dodds, Muhamad, & Watts, 2003).

How is that possible? Each of us is part of a rich tapestry of social relationships. You probably know at least dozens of people by name. Each of them knows dozens more people, who each know still more people, and so on. Thus, each social relationship connects with many others. By following all the social links, you could reach millions of people just six "layers" out. With the recent explosion in popularity of social networking sites like Blogger, Facebook, Friendster, and MySpace, our social world will undoubtedly expand even more.

Social behavior has been the target of an immense amount of study—too much, in fact, for us to cover in detail. Therefore, this chapter is a social psychology "sampler." Among other things, we will look at what brings people together, what separates them and brings them into conflict, how we influence others, why humans are aggressive, and why we choose to help others. We hope that you will find the topics interesting and thought provoking.

Paul Chesley/Getty Images

MODULE 15.1 Affiliation, Friendship, and Love

ALTHOUGH YOU MAY LIKE BEING ALONE AT TIMES, the fact is, humans are social animals. Imagine if you were deprived of all contact with your family and friends. You would probably find it painfully lonely and disorienting. In this first module, we will explore what brings people together in groups, in friendship, and in love.

Affiliation and Attraction—Come Together

SURVEY QUESTIONS: *Why do people affiliate? What factors influence interpersonal attraction?*

Social psychology is the scientific study of how individuals behave, think, and feel in social situations (that is, in the presence, actual or implied, of others) (Baron, Byrne, & Branscombe, 2007). Each of us is immersed in a complex social world of families, teams, crowds, tribes, companies, parties, troops, bands, sects, gangs, crews, clans, communities, and nations. But what brings us together in the first place? The *need to affiliate* (associate with other people) is based on basic human desires for approval, support, friendship, and information (Baumeister & Bushman, 2008). We also seek the company of others to alleviate fear or anxiety. A classic experiment in which college women were threatened with electric shock illustrates this point.

> **ZILSTEIN'S SHOCK SHOP**
> A man introduced as Dr. Gregor Zilstein ominously explained to arriving participants, "We would like to give each of you a series of electric shocks . . . these shocks will hurt, they will be painful." In the room was a frightening electrical device that seemed to verify Zilstein's plans. While waiting to be shocked, each woman was given a choice of waiting alone or with other participants. Women frightened in this way more often chose to wait with others; those who expected the shock to be "a mild tickle or tingle" were more willing to wait alone. (Schachter, 1959)

Apparently, the frightened women found it comforting to be with others. Should we conclude that "misery loves company"? Actually, that's not entirely correct. In a later experiment, women who expected to be shocked were given the choice of waiting with other future shock recipients, with women waiting to see their college advisers, or alone. Most women chose to wait with other future "victims." In short, misery seems to love miserable company! In general, we prefer to be with people in circumstances similar to our own (Gump & Kulik, 1997).

Is there a reason for that? Yes. Other people provide information that helps us evaluate our own reactions. When a situation is threatening or unfamiliar, or when we are in doubt, *social comparisons* tend to guide our behavior (Kulik, Mahler, & Moore, 2003).

Social Comparison Theory

If you want to know how tall you are, you simply get out a tape measure. But how do you know if you are a good athlete, worker, parent, or friend? How do you know if your views on politics, religion, or hip-hop are unusual or widely shared? When there are no objective standards, the only available yardstick is provided by comparing yourself with others (Miller, 2006).

Social psychologist Leon Festinger (1919–1989) theorized that belonging to groups fills our needs for **social comparison** (comparing your own actions, feelings, opinions, or abilities with those of others). Have you ever "compared notes" with other students after taking an exam? ("How did you do?" "Wasn't that last question hard?") If you have, you were satisfying needs for social comparison (Festinger, 1957).

Typically, we don't make social comparisons randomly or on some absolute scale. Meaningful evaluations are based on

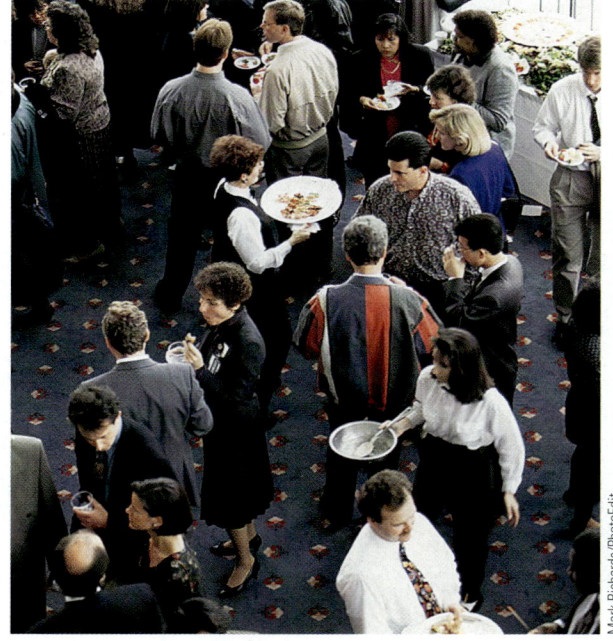

High school class reunions are notorious for the rampant social comparison they often encourage. Apparently it's hard to resist comparing yourself with former classmates to see how you are doing in life.

comparing yourself with people of similar backgrounds, abilities, and circumstances (Stapel & Marx, 2007). To illustrate, let's ask a student named Wendy if she is a good tennis player. If Wendy compares herself with a professional, the answer will be no. But this tells us little about her *relative* ability. Within her tennis group, Wendy is regarded as an excellent player. On a fair scale of comparison, Wendy knows she is good and she takes pride in her tennis skills. In the same way, thinking of yourself as successful, talented, responsible, or fairly paid depends entirely on whom you choose for comparison. Thus, a desire for social comparison provides a motive for associating with others and influences which groups we join (Franzoi & Klaiber, 2007).

Don't people also affiliate out of attraction for one another? They do, of course. Let's see why.

Interpersonal Attraction

"Birds of a feather flock together." "Familiarity breeds contempt." "Opposites attract." "Absence makes the heart grow fonder." Are these statements true? Actually, the folklore about friendship is, at best, a mixture of fact and fiction.

What does attract people to each other? **Interpersonal attraction** (affinity to another person) is the basis for most voluntary social relationships (Berscheid & Regan, 2005). As you might expect, we look for friends and lovers who are kind and understanding, who have attractive personalities, and who like us in return (Sprecher, 1998). Deciding whether you would like to know another person can happen very quickly, sometimes within just minutes of meeting (Sunnafrank, Ramirez, & Metts, 2004). In addition, several less obvious factors influence attraction.

Physical Proximity Our choice of friends (and even lovers) is based more on *physical proximity* (nearness) than we might care to believe. For example, the closer people live to each other, the more likely they are to become friends. Likewise, lovers like to think they have found the "one and only" person in the universe for them. In reality, they have probably found the best match in a 5-mile radius (Buss, 1985)! Marriages are not made in heaven—they are made in local schools, businesses, churches, bars, clubs, and neighborhoods.

Proximity promotes attraction by increasing the *frequency of contact* between people. In general, we are attracted to people we see often. (If you have a reluctant sweetheart, be careful not to send too many love letters—she or he might run off with the letter carrier!) In short, there does seem to be a "boy-next-door" or "girl-next-door" effect in romantic attraction, and a "folks-next-door" effect in friendship. Notice, however, that the Internet is making it increasingly easier to stay in constant "virtual contact," which is leading to more and more long-distance friendships and romances (Lawson & Leck, 2006; Ridings & Gefen, 2004).

What attracts people to each other? Proximity and frequency of contact have a surprisingly large impact.

Physical Attractiveness People who are *physically attractive* are regarded as good looking by others. Beautiful people are generally rated as more appealing than average. This is due, in part, to the *halo effect,* a tendency to generalize a favorable impression to unrelated personal characteristics. Because of it, we assume that beautiful people are also likable, intelligent, warm, witty, mentally healthy, and socially skilled. In reality, physical attractiveness has almost *no* connection to intelligence, talents, or abilities. Perhaps that's why beauty mainly affects our initial interest in getting to know others (Keller & Young, 1996). Later, more meaningful qualities

Social psychology The scientific study of how individuals behave, think, and feel in social situations.
Social comparison Making judgments about ourselves through comparison with others.
Interpersonal attraction Social attraction to another person.

Physical beauty can be socially advantageous because of the widespread belief that "what is beautiful is good." However, physical beauty is generally unrelated to actual personal traits and talents.

gain in importance (Berscheid, 2000; Miller, Perlman, & Brehm, 2007).

Competence People who are *competent* have knowledge, ability, or proficiency. All other things being equal, we are more attracted to people who are talented or competent. However, there's an interesting twist to this. In a revealing classic study, college students listened to audiotapes of candidates for a "college quiz bowl." Two of the candidates seemed to be highly intelligent. The other two were of average ability. In addition, one "intelligent" candidate and one "average" candidate could be heard to clumsily spill coffee on themselves. Later, students rated the intelligent candidate who blundered as *most* attractive. In contrast, the average person who blundered was rated *least* attractive (Aronson, 1969). Thus, the superior but clumsy person was more attractive than the person who was only superior. Apparently, we like people who are competent but imperfect—which makes them more "human."

Similarity Take a moment to make a list of your closest friends. What do they have in common (other than the joy of knowing you)? It is likely that their ages are similar to yours and you are of the same sex and ethnicity. There will be exceptions, of course. But similarity on these three dimensions is the general rule for friendships.

Similarity refers to how alike you are to another person in background, age, interests, attitudes, beliefs, and so forth. In everything from casual acquaintance to marriage, similar people are attracted to each other (Figueredo, Sefcek, & Jones, 2006; Miller, Perlman, & Brehm, 2007). And why not? It's reinforcing to see our beliefs and attitudes shared by others. It shows we are "right" and reveals that they are clever people as well (Alicke, Yurak, & Vredenburg, 1996)!

So similarity also influences mate selection? Yes, in choosing a mate we tend to marry someone who is like us in almost every way, a pattern called *homogamy* (huh-MOG-ah-me) (Blackwell & Lichter, 2004). Studies show that married couples are highly similar in age, education, ethnicity, and religion. To a lesser degree, they are also similar in attitudes and opinions, mental abilities, status, height, weight, and eye color. In case you're wondering, homogamy also applies to unmarried couples who are living together (Blackwell & Lichter, 2004). Homogamy is probably a good thing. The risk of divorce is highest among couples with sizable differences in age and education (Tzeng, 1992).

Self-Disclosure

How do people who are not yet friends learn if they are similar? To get acquainted you must be willing to talk about more than just the weather, sports, or nuclear physics. At some point you must begin to share private thoughts and feelings and reveal yourself to others. This process, which is called **self-disclosure,** is essential for developing close relationships. In general, as friends talk, they gradually deepen the level of liking, trust, and self-disclosure (Levesque, Steciuk, & Ledley, 2002).

We more often reveal ourselves to persons we like than to those we find unattractive. Disclosure also requires a degree of trust. Many people play it safe, or "close to the vest," with people they do not know well. Indeed, self-disclosure is governed by unspoken rules about what's acceptable. Moderate self-disclosure leads to *reciprocity* (a return in kind). In contrast, *overdisclosure* exceeds what is appropriate for a relationship or social situation, giving rise to suspicion and reducing attraction. For example, imagine standing in line at a store and having the stranger in front of you say, "Lately I've been

Excessive self-disclosure is a staple of many television talk shows. Guests frequently reveal intimate details about their personal lives, including private family matters, sex and dating, physical or sexual abuse, major embarrassments, and criminal activities. Viewers probably find such intimate disclosures entertaining, rather than threatening, because they don't have to reciprocate.

thinking about how I really feel about myself. I think I'm pretty well adjusted, but I occasionally have some questions about my sexual adequacy."

When self-disclosure proceeds at a moderate pace, it builds trust, intimacy, reciprocity, and positive feelings. When it is too rapid or inappropriate, we are likely to "back off" and wonder about the person's motives. It's interesting to note that on the Internet (and especially on social networking websites like Facebook and MySpace) people often feel freer to express their true feelings, which can lead to genuine, face-to-face friendships (Bargh, McKenna, & Fitzsimons, 2002). However, it can also lead to some very dramatic overdisclosure (George, 2006).

Loving and Liking—Dating, Rating, Mating

How does romantic attraction differ from interpersonal attraction? **Romantic love** is based on interpersonal attraction, but it also involves high levels of emotional arousal and/or sexual desire (Berscheid & Regan, 2005; Miller, Perlman, & Brehm, 2007). To get another angle on love, psychologist Zick Rubin (1973) chose to think of it as an attitude we hold toward another person. This allowed him to develop "liking" and "love" scales to measure each "attitude" (• Fig. 15.1). Next, he asked dating couples to complete the scales twice, once with their lover in mind and once for a close friend of the same sex.

What were the results? Love for partners and friends differed more than liking did (■ Table 15.1). (**Liking** is affection without passion or deep commitment.) Basically, dating couples like *and* love their partners, but mostly they just like their friends. Women, however, were a little more "loving" of their friends than men were. Does this reflect real differences in the strength of male friendships and female friendships? Maybe not, because it is more acceptable in our culture for women to express love for one another than it is for men. Nevertheless, another study confirmed that dating couples feel a mixture of love and friendship for their partners. In fact, 44 percent of a group of dating persons named their romantic partner as their closest friend (Hendrick & Hendrick, 1993).

Love and friendship differ in another interesting way. Romantic love, in contrast to simple liking, usually involves deep *mutual absorption*. In other words, lovers (unlike friends) attend almost exclusively to one another. It's not surprising, then, that couples who score high on Rubin's love scale spend more time gazing into each other's eyes than do couples who score low on the scale. And what do lovers see when they gaze into each other's eyes? Generally, romantic partners tend to idealize each other, which helps keep relationships going, despite the fact that nobody's perfect (Murray, Holmes, & Griffin, 1996, 2003).

Love Scale

1. I have a few secrets from _____ .

2. _____ has almost no faults.

3. I feel responsible for preventing _____ from feeling bad.

Liking Scale

1. If _____ were seeking work, I would gladly serve as a reference.

2. _____ and I often share the same moods.

3. I admire how well adjusted _____ is.

• **FIGURE 15.1** Sample love-scale and liking-scale items. The items shown here are similar to actual Rubin scale items. Scores on the 13-item Rubin scales correspond to other indications of love and liking.

■ **TABLE 15.1** Average Love and Liking Scores for Date and Same-Sex Close Friend

Attitude toward Dating Partner

	LOVE SCORE	LIKING SCORE
Women	89.5	88.5
Men	89.4	84.7

Attitude toward Close Friend

	LOVE SCORE	LIKING SCORE
Women	65.3	80.5
Men	55.0	79.1

Source: From Zick Rubin, "Measurement of Romantic Love," *Journal of Personality and Social Psychology,* © 1970 American Psychological Association. Reprinted by permission.

Self-disclosure The process of revealing private thoughts, feelings, and one's personal history to others.

Romantic love Love that is associated with high levels of interpersonal attraction, heightened arousal, mutual absorption, and sexual desire.

Liking A relationship based on intimacy, but lacking passion and commitment.

Sex, Evolution, and Mate Selection

Evolutionary psychology is the study of the evolutionary origins of human behavior patterns. Many psychologists believe that evolution left an imprint on men and women that influences everything from sexual attraction and infidelity to jealousy and divorce. According to David Buss, the key to understanding human mating patterns is to understand how evolved behavior patterns guide our choices (Buss, 2004, 2007).

In a study of 37 cultures on six continents, Buss found the following patterns: Compared with women, men are more interested in casual sex; they prefer younger, more physically attractive partners; and they get more jealous over real or imagined sexual infidelities than they do over a loss of emotional commitment. Compared with men, women prefer slightly older partners who appear to be industrious, higher in status, or economically successful; women are more upset by a partner who becomes emotionally involved with someone else, rather than one who is sexually unfaithful (Buss, 2000; Regan et al., 2000) (● Fig. 15.2).

Why do such differences exist? Buss and others believe that mating preferences evolved in response to the differing reproductive challenges faced by men and women. As a rule, women must invest more time and energy in reproduction and nurturing the young than men do. Consequently, women evolved an interest in whether their partners will stay with them and whether their mates have the resources to provide for their children (Buss, 2004, 2007; Regan et al., 2000).

In contrast, the reproductive success of men depends on their mates' fertility. Men, therefore, tend to look for health, youth, and beauty in a prospective mate, as signs of suitability for reproduction (Buss, 2007). This preference, perhaps, is why some older men abandon their first wives in favor of young, beautiful "trophy wives." Evolutionary theory further explains that the male emphasis on their mates' sexual fidelity is based on concerns about the paternity of offspring. From a biological perspective, men do not benefit from investing resources in children they did not sire (Buller, 2005).

Although some evidence supports the evolutionary view of mating, it is important to remember that evolved mating

According to evolutionary psychologists, women tend to be concerned with whether mates will devote time and resources to a relationship. Men place more emphasis on physical attractiveness and sexual fidelity.

tendencies are subtle at best and easily overruled by other factors. Some mating patterns may simply reflect the fact that men still tend to control the power and resources in most societies (Feingold, 1992). Also, early research may be misleading because women tend to give "polite" answers to questions about jealousy. Privately, they may be just as furious about a mate's sexual infidelity as any man would be (Harris, 2004).

Whatever the outcome of the debate about evolution and mate selection, it is important to remember this: Poten-

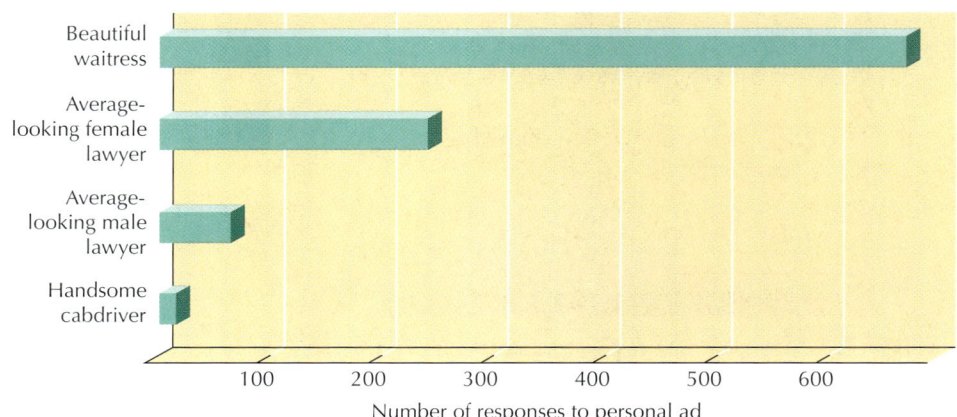

● **FIGURE 15.2** What do people look for when considering potential dating partners? Here are the results of a study in which personal ads were placed in newspapers. As you can see, men were more influenced by looks and women by success (Goode, 1996).

tial mates are rated as most attractive if they are kind, secure, intelligent, and supportive (Klohnen & Luo, 2003; Regan et al., 2000). These qualities are love's greatest allies.

Needs for affiliation and interpersonal attraction inevitably bring people together in groups. In the next section we will explore several interesting aspects of group membership. But first, here's a chance to review what you have learned.

MODULE 15.1 Summary

Why do people affiliate? What factors influence interpersonal attraction?

- Social psychology studies how we behave, think, and feel in social situations.
- We are attracted to other people for reasons that are fairly universal.
- Affiliation is tied to needs for approval, support, friendship, and information. Also, affiliation can reduce anxiety.
- Social comparison theory holds that we affiliate to evaluate our actions, feelings, and abilities.
- Interpersonal attraction is increased by proximity, frequent contact, beauty, and similarity.
- Mate selection is characterized by a large degree of similarity on many dimensions.
- Self-disclosure follows a reciprocity norm: Low levels of self-disclosure are met with low levels in return; moderate self-disclosure elicits more personal replies.
- In comparison with liking, romantic love involves higher levels of emotional arousal and it is accompanied by mutual absorption between lovers.
- Evolutionary psychologists attribute human mating patterns to the reproductive challenges men and women faced during the course of evolution.

KNOWLEDGE BUILDER

Affiliation, Friendship, and Love

Recite

1. Women threatened with electric shock in an experiment generally chose to wait alone or with other women not taking part in the experiment. T or F?
2. Interpersonal attraction is increased by all but one of the following. (Which does not fit?)
   a. physical proximity
   b. physical attractiveness
   c. similarity
   d. overdisclosure
3. High levels of self-disclosure are reciprocated in most social encounters. T or F?
4. Women rate their friends higher on the love scale than do men. T or F?
5. The most striking finding about marriage patterns is that most people choose mates whose personalities are quite unlike their own. T or F?
6. Compared with men, women tend to be more upset by sexual infidelity than by a loss of emotional commitment on the part of their mates. T or F?

Reflect
Critical Thinking

7. How has the Internet altered the effects of proximity on interpersonal attraction?

Relate

How has social comparison affected your behavior? Has it influenced who you associate with?

Think of three close friends. Which of the attraction factors described earlier apply to your friendships?

To what extent do Rubin's findings about love and liking match your own experiences?

Link

Internet addresses frequently change. To find the sites listed here, visit **http://www.thomsonedu.com/psychology/coon** for an updated list of Internet addresses and direct links to relevant sites.

- **Small World Project** Join Duncan Watt's online experiment to see if we are really all connected through six degrees of separation.
- **Social Psychology Network** Explore this massive website devoted to social psychology.

ANSWERS

1. F 2. d 3. F 4. T 5. F 6. F 7. As mentioned earlier, it is now possible to interact with another person through the Internet. This makes actual physical proximity less crucial in interpersonal attraction, because frequent contact is possible even at great distances. Internet romances are a good example of this possibility (Levine, 2000).

Evolutionary psychology Study of the evolutionary origins of human behavior patterns.

MODULE 15.2 Groups, Social Influence, and Conformity

FAMILIES, TEAMS, CROWDS, TRIBES, COMPANIES, parties, troops, bands, sects, gangs, crews, clans, communities, nations. Participation in various groups is a basic fact of social life. How do groups influence our behavior? Because you are member of a group called "psychology class," it would be wise to find out.

Life in Groups—People, People, Everywhere

SURVEY QUESTION: *How does group membership affect our behavior?*

We all belong to many overlapping social groups, and in each we occupy a *position* in the *structure* of the group. **Social roles** are patterns of behavior expected of persons in various social positions (Breckler, Olson, & Wiggins, 2006). For instance, playing the role of mother, boss, or student involves different sets of behaviors and expectations. Some roles are *ascribed* (they are assigned to a person or are not under personal control): male or female, son, adolescent, inmate. *Achieved roles* are voluntarily attained by special effort: spouse, teacher, scientist, bandleader.

What effect does role playing have on behavior? Roles streamline daily interactions by allowing us to anticipate what others will do. When a person is acting as a doctor, mother, clerk, or police officer, we expect certain behaviors. However, roles have a negative side, too. Many people experience **role conflicts,** in which two or more roles make conflicting demands on them. Consider, for example, a teacher who must flunk a close friend's daughter; a mother who has a full-time job; and a soccer coach whose son is on the team but isn't a very good athlete. Likewise, the clashing demands of work, family, and school create role conflicts for many students (Hammer, Grigsby, & Woods, 1998; Senécal, Julien, & Guay, 2003). Role conflicts at work (such as being a good team player versus being a strong manager) lead to job burnout (Jawahar, Stone, & Kisamore, 2007) and negative health outcomes (Pomaki, Supeli, & Verhoeven, 2007).

Group Structure, Cohesion, and Norms

Are there other dimensions of group membership? Two important dimensions of any group are its structure and cohesiveness (Forsyth, 2006). **Group structure** consists of the network of roles, communication pathways, and power in a group. Organized groups such as an army or an athletic team have a high degree of structure. Informal friendship groups may or may not be very structured.

Group cohesiveness refers to the degree of attraction among group members or the strength of their desire to remain in the group. Members of cohesive groups literally stick together: They tend to stand or sit close together, they pay more attention to one another, and they show more signs of mutual affection. Also, their behavior tends to be closely coordinated (Chansler, Swamidass, & Cammann, 2003). Cohesiveness is the basis for much of the power that groups exert over us. Therapy groups, businesses, sports teams, and the like seek to increase cohesion because it helps people work together better (Craig & Kelly, 1999; Marmarosh, Holtz, & Schottenbauer, 2005).

In-groups Cohesiveness is particularly strong for **in-groups** (groups with which a person mainly identifies). Very likely, your own in-groups are defined by a combination of prominent social dimensions, such as nationality, ethnicity, age, education, religion, income, political values, gender, sexual orientation, and so forth. In-group membership helps define who we are socially. Predictably, we tend to attribute positive characteristics to our in-group and negative qualities to **out-groups** (groups with which we do not identify). We also tend to exaggerate differences between members of out-groups and our own groups. This sort of "us-and-them" thinking seems to be a basic fact of social life. It also sets the stage for conflict between groups and for racial and ethnic prejudice—topics we will explore in a later module.

Status In addition to defining roles, a person's social position within groups determines his or her **status,** or level of social power and importance. Higher status bestows special

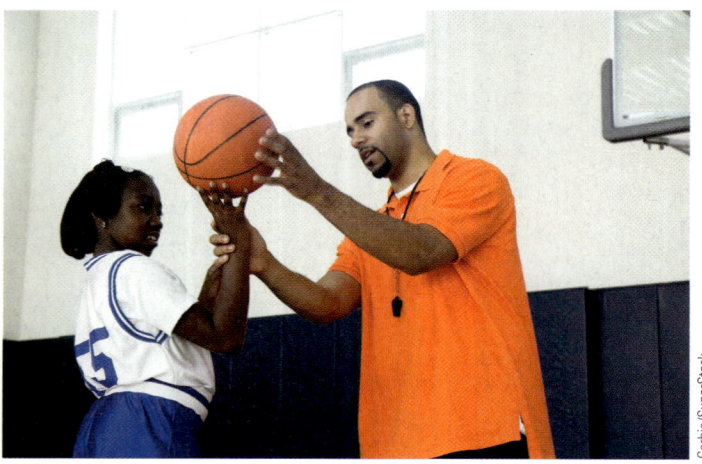

Roles have a powerful impact on social behavior. What kinds of behavior do you expect from your teachers? What behaviors do they expect from you? What happens if either of you fails to match the other's expectations?

privileges and respect. For example, in one experiment, a man walked into a number of bakeries and asked for a croissant while claiming he did not have enough money to pay for it. Half the time he was well dressed and half the time he was poorly dressed. If the man was polite when he asked, he was equally likely to be given a free croissant no matter how he was dressed (95 versus 90 percent). But if he was impolite when he asked, he was much less likely to get a croissant if he was poorly dressed than if he was well dressed (75 versus 20 percent) (Guéguen & Pascual, 2003).

You don't have to be in a bakery for this to work. In most situations, we are more likely to comply with a request made by a high-status (well-dressed) person (Guéguen, 2002). Perhaps the better treatment given "higher status" persons, even when they are impolite, explains some of our society's preoccupation with expensive clothes, cars, and other status symbols.

Norms We are also greatly affected by group norms. A **norm** is a widely accepted (but often unspoken) standard for appropriate behavior. If you have the slightest doubt about the power of norms, try this test: Walk into a crowded supermarket, get in a checkout line, and begin singing loudly in your fullest voice. Are you the 1 person in 100 who could actually carry out these instructions?

The impact of norms is shown by an interesting study of littering. The question was, Does the amount of trash in an area affect littering? To find out, people were given flyers as they walked into a public parking garage. As you can see in • Figure 15.3, the more litter there was on the floor, the more likely people were to add to it by dropping their flyer. Apparently, seeing that others had already littered implied a lax norm about whether littering is acceptable. The moral? The cleaner a public area is kept, the less likely people are to "trash" it (Cialdini, Reno, & Kallgren, 1990).

Making Attributions

Every day we must guess how people will act, often from small shreds of evidence. We do this through a process called **attribution.** As we observe others, we make inferences about them. Why did Vonda insult Sutchai? Why did Nick change his college major? Why does Kirti talk so fast when she's around men? In answering such questions we *attribute* people's behavior to various causes. Whether we are right or wrong about the causes of their behavior, our conclusions affect how *we* act. To learn how we fill in the "person behind the mask," let's explore the making of attributions.

Two people enter a restaurant and order different meals. Nell tastes her food, then salts it. Bert salts his food before he tastes it. How would you explain their behavior? In Nell's case, you might assume that the *food* needed salt. If so, you have attributed her actions to an *external cause* (one that lies outside a person). With Bert, you might be more inclined to conclude that he must really *like* salt. If so, the cause of his behavior is internal. *Internal causes,* such as needs, personality traits, and Bert's taste for salt, lie within the person.

What effects do such interpretations have? It is difficult to fully understand social behavior without considering the attributions that we make. For instance, let's say that at the last five parties you've been to, you've seen a woman named Macy. Based on this, you assume that Macy likes to socialize. You see Macy at yet another gathering and mention that she seems to like parties. She says, "Actually, I hate these parties, but I get invited to play my tuba at them. My music teacher says I need to practice in front of an audience, so I keep attending these dumb events. Want to hear a Sousa march?"

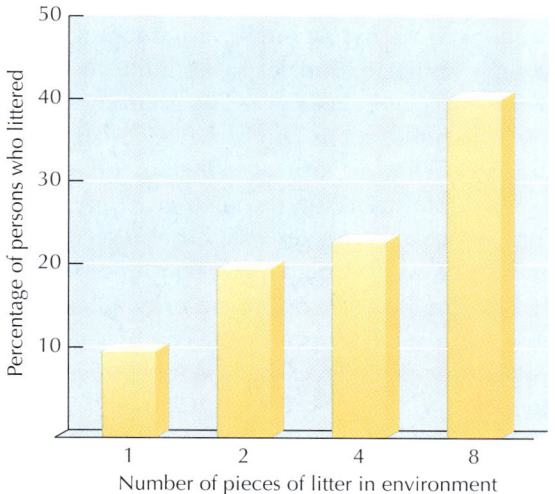

● **FIGURE 15.3** Results of an experiment on norms concerning littering. The prior existence of litter in a public setting implies that littering is acceptable. This encourages others to "trash" the area. (From Cialdini, Reno, & Kallgren, 1990.)

Social role Expected behavior patterns associated with particular social positions (such as daughter, worker, student).
Role conflict Trying to occupy two or more roles that make conflicting demands on behavior.
Group structure The network of roles, communication pathways, and power in a group.
Group cohesiveness The degree of attraction among group members or their commitment to remaining in the group.
In-group A group with which a person identifies.
Out-group A group with which a person does not identify.
Status An individual's position in a social structure, especially with respect to power, privilege, or importance.
Norm A widely accepted standard of conduct for appropriate behavior.
Attribution The process of making inferences about the causes of one's own behavior and that of others.

We seldom know the real reasons for others' actions. That is why we tend to infer causes from *circumstances.* However, in doing so, we often make mistakes like the one with Macy. The most common error is to attribute the actions of others to internal causes (Follett & Hess, 2002; Jones & Nisbett, 1971). This mistake is called the **fundamental attribution error.** We tend to think the actions of others have internal causes even if they are actually caused by external forces or circumstances. One amusing example of this error is the tendency of people to attribute the actions of actors in television programs to the personality of the actor rather than the obvious external cause (that they are playing a character) (Tal-Or & Papirman, 2007).

Where our own behavior is concerned, we are more likely to think that external causes explain our actions. In other words, there is an **actor-observer bias** in how we explain behavior. As *observers,* we attribute the behavior of others to their wants, motives, and personality traits (this is the fundamental attribution error). As *actors,* we tend to find external explanations for our own behavior (Gordon & Kaplar, 2002). No doubt you chose your major in school because of what it has to offer. Other students choose *their* majors because of the kind of people they are. Other people who don't leave tips in restaurants are cheapskates. If you don't leave a tip, it's because the service was bad. And, of course, other people are always late because they are irresponsible. You are late because you were held up by events beyond your control.

Ye Old Double Standard Attributions reveal an interesting double standard regarding the abilities of men and women. In a classic study by Kay Deaux and Tim Emswiller (1974), men and women overheard a male or female perform extremely well on a perception task. Each person was then asked to rate whether the test taker's success was due to ability, luck, or some combination of the two. Both men and women attributed men's success mainly to skill and women's performances mainly to luck! This was true even though male and female performances were identical.

As early as *kindergarten,* boys tend to take credit for successes. Girls tend to discount their own performances ("put themselves down") (Burgner & Hewstone, 1993). In general, there is a strong tendency to assume "He's skilled, she's lucky" when judging men and women (Swim & Sanna, 1996). Throughout life, such attributions no doubt haunt many talented and successful women.

Social Influence—Follow the Leader

SURVEY QUESTION: *What have social psychologists learned about conformity?*

No topic lies nearer the heart of social psychology than **social influence** (changes in behavior induced by the actions of others). When people interact, they almost always affect one another's behavior (Crano, 2000; Kassin, Fein, & Markus, 2008). For example, in a sidewalk experiment, various numbers of people stood on a busy New York City street. On cue they all looked at a sixth-floor window across the street. A camera recorded how many passersby also stopped to stare. The larger the influencing group, the more people were swayed to join in staring at the window (Milgram, Bickman, & Berkowitz, 1969).

Are there different kinds of social influence? Social influence ranges from *mere presence* (changing behavior just because other people are nearby) to intensive indoctrination (brainwashing). Three major forms of social influence are conformity, compliance, and obedience. The gentlest of these three forms of social influence is conformity. We **conform** when we bring our behavior into agreement with the actions, norms, or values of others in the absence of any direct pressure. Compliance is a more directed form of social influence. We *comply* when we change our behavior in response to another person who has little or no authority. Obedience is an even more direct form of social influence. We *obey* when we change our behavior in direct response to the demands of an authority.

Daily behavior is probably most influenced by group pressures for conformity (bringing your behavior into agreement with the actions, norms, or values of others) (Baron, Byrne, & Branscombe, 2007). We all conform to a degree. In fact, some uniformity is a necessity. Imagine being totally unable to anticipate the actions of others. In stores, schools,

Forest Whitaker won an Academy Award for his portrayal of dictator Idi Amin in the film *The Last King of Scotland.* Is Forest Whitaker a ruthless person or did he portray ruthlessness as a part of his role? According to Tal-Or & Papirman (2007), we are prone to attribute actors' screen actions to their personalities rather than to the personalities of the roles they are playing. Why do you think this occurs?

and homes this would be frustrating and disturbing. On the highways it would be lethal.

Conformity

When Fred first started working at the Fleegle Flange Factory, he found it easy to process 300 flanges an hour. Others around him averaged only 200. Fred's co-workers told him to slow down and take it easy. "I get bored," he said and continued to do 300 flanges an hour. At first Fred was welcomed, but now conversations broke up when he approached. Other workers laughed at him or ignored him when he spoke. Although he never made a conscious decision to conform, in another week Fred's output had slowed to 200 flanges an hour. Perhaps the most basic of all group norms is, as Fred discovered, "Thou shalt conform." Like it or not, life is filled with instances of conformity.

The Asch Experiment *How strong are group pressures for conformity?* One of the first experiments on conformity was staged by Solomon Asch (1907–1996). To fully appreciate it, imagine yourself as a subject. Assume that you are seated at a table with six other students. Your task is actually quite simple. On each trial you are shown three lines. Your job is to select the line that matches a "standard" line (● Fig. 15.4).

As the testing begins, each person announces an answer for the first card. When your turn comes, you agree with the others. "This isn't hard at all," you say to yourself. For several more trials your answers agree with those of the group. Then comes a shock. All six people announce that line 1 matches the standard, and you were about to say line 2 matches. Suddenly you feel alone and upset. You nervously look at the lines again. The room falls silent. Everyone seems to be staring at you. The experimenter awaits your answer. Do you yield to the group?

In this study the other "students" were all actors who gave the wrong answer on about a third of the trials to create

Conformity is a subtle dimension of daily life. Notice the similarities in clothing and hairstyles among these couples.

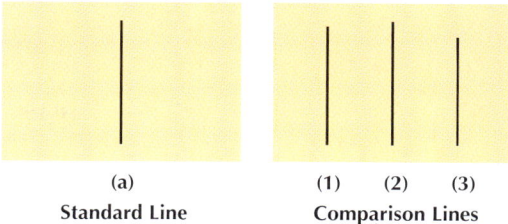

● **FIGURE 15.4** Stimuli used in Solomon Asch's conformity experiments.

group pressure (Asch, 1956). Real students conformed to the group in about one third of the critical trials. Of those tested, 75 percent yielded at least once. People tested alone erred in less than 1 percent of their judgments. Clearly, those who yielded to group pressures were denying what their eyes told them.

Are some people more susceptible to group pressures than others? People with high needs for structure or certainty are more likely to conform. So are people who are anxious, low in self-confidence, or concerned with the approval of others. People who live in cultures that emphasize group cooperation (such as many Asian cultures) are also more likely to conform (Bond & Smith, 1996; Fu et al., 2007).

In addition to personal characteristics, certain situations tend to encourage conformity—sometimes with disastrous results. "Groupthink—Agreement at Any Cost" offers a prime example.

Group Factors in Conformity *How do groups enforce norms?* In most groups, we have been rewarded with acceptance and approval for conformity and threatened with rejection or ridicule for nonconformity. These reactions are called *group sanctions*. Negative sanctions range from laughter, staring, or social disapproval to complete rejection or formal exclusion. If you've ever felt the sudden chill of disapproval by others, you will understand the power of group sanctions.

Wouldn't the effectiveness of group sanctions depend on the importance of the group? Yes. The more important group membership is to a person, the more he or she will be influenced by other group members. The risk of being rejected can be a threat to our sense of personal identity (Crano,

Fundamental attribution error The tendency to attribute the behavior of others to internal causes (personality, likes, and so forth).

Actor-observer bias The tendency to attribute the behavior of others to internal causes while attributing one's own behavior to external causes (situations and circumstances).

Social influence Changes in a person's behavior induced by the presence or actions of others.

Conformity Bringing one's behavior into agreement or harmony with norms or with the behavior of others in a group in the absence of any direct pressure.

CRITICAL THINKING

Groupthink—Agreement at Any Cost

As we write this, debate continues to rage about the Iraq war. Why, for example, were no weapons of mass destruction found in Iraq, even though their existence was the major justification for the war in the first place? Was the decision to invade Iraq made by a small group of policymakers with little tolerance for dissenting views? Already, it has been suggested that this war may have been a result of **groupthink**—an urge by decision makers to maintain each other's approval, even at the cost of critical thinking (Porteus, 2004).

Groupthink has been blamed for many embarrassments, such as the *Columbia* space shuttle disaster in 2003 and the loss, in 1999, of the $165 million *Mars Climate Orbiter*. An analysis of 19 international crises found that groupthink contributed to most (Schafer & Crichlow, 1996). The core of groupthink is misguided loyalty. Group members are hesitant to "rock the boat" or question sloppy thinking. This self-censorship leads people to believe they agree more than they actually do (Henningsen et al., 2006; Whyte, 2000).

To prevent groupthink, group leaders should take the following steps:

- Define each group member's role as a "critical evaluator."
- Avoid revealing any personal preferences in the beginning.
- State the problem factually, without bias.
- Invite a group member or outside person to play devil's advocate.
- Make it clear that group members will be held accountable for decisions.
- Encourage open inquiry and a search for alternate solutions (Baron, 2005; Chen et al., 1996).

In addition, it is advisable to have a "second-chance" meeting to re-evaluate important decisions. That is, each decision should be reached twice.

In fairness to our decision makers, it is worth noting that the presence of too many alternatives can lead to *deadlock*, in which an inability to make a choice can delay taking necessary action (Kowert, 2002). Regardless, in an age clouded by the threat of war, global warming, and terrorism, even stronger solutions to the problem of groupthink would be welcome. Perhaps we should form a group to think about it!

2000). That's why the Asch experiments are impressive. Because these were only temporary groups, sanctions were informal and rejection had no lasting importance. Just the same, the power of the group was evident.

What other factors, besides importance of the group, affect the degree of conformity? In the sidewalk experiment described earlier, we noted that large groups had more influence. In Asch's face-to-face groups the size of the majority also made a difference, but a surprisingly small one. In other studies, the number of people who conformed increased dramatically as the majority grew from two to three people. However, a majority of three produced about as much yielding as a majority of eight. The next time you want to talk someone into (or out of) something, take two friends along and see what a difference it makes! (Sometimes it helps if the two are large and mean looking.)

Even more important than the size of the majority is its *unanimity* (total agreement). Having at least one person in your corner can greatly reduce pressures to conform. When Asch gave subjects an ally (who also opposed the majority by giving the correct answer), conformity was lessened. In terms of numbers, a unanimous majority of three is more powerful than a majority of eight with one dissenting. Perhaps this accounts for the rich diversity of human attitudes, beliefs, opinions, and lifestyles. If you can find at least one other person who sees things as you do (no matter how weird), you can be relatively secure in your opposition to other viewpoints. Incidentally, the Internet now makes it much easier to find that other like-minded person.

MODULE 15.2 Summary

How does group membership affect our behavior?
- To understand social behavior we must know what roles people play, their status, the norms they follow, and the attributions they make.
- Social roles are particular behavior patterns associated with social positions.
- Higher status within groups is associated with special privileges and respect.
- Norms are standards of conduct enforced (formally or informally) by groups.
- We attribute behavior to various causes. These attributions, in turn, affect how we act.
- The fundamental attributional error is to think that internal causes explain the actions of other people. In contrast, we tend to attribute our own behavior to external causes.

What have social psychologists learned about conformity, compliance, obedience, and self-assertion?
- *Social influence* refers to alterations in behavior brought about by the behavior of others.
- The famous Asch experiments demonstrated that people are likely to conform when they face social pressure from other group members.
- *Groupthink* refers to compulsive conformity in group decision making.

KNOWLEDGE BUILDER

Groups, Social Influence, and Conformity

Recite

1. *Status* refers to a set of expected behaviors associated with a social position. T or F?
2. The fundamental attribution error is to attribute the actions of others to internal causes. T or F?
3. The effect one person's behavior has on another is called _____ _____.
4. In Solomon Asch's conformity experiment, participants yielded to group pressure on about _____ of the critical trials.
    a. 1 percent
    b. 10 percent
    c. one third
    d. two thirds
5. Nonconformity is punished by negative group _____.
6. Groupthink is an example of the danger that lies in powerful pressures for group _____.
    a. cohesion
    b. conformity
    c. attribution
    d. reciprocity

Reflect
Critical Thinking

7. Is it possible to be completely nonconforming (that is, to not conform to some group norm)?

Relate

What are the most prominent roles you play? Which are achieved and which are ascribed? How do they affect your behavior? What conflicts do they create?

Do you commit the fundamental attribution error? Try to think of a specific example that illustrates the concept.

Identify a recent time when you conformed in some way. How did norms, group pressure, sanctions, and unanimity contribute to your tendency to conform?

Link

Internet addresses frequently change. To find the sites listed here, visit http://www.thomsonedu.com/psychology/coon for an updated list of Internet addresses and direct links to relevant sites.

- **Stanford Prison Study** Explore Phil Zimbardo's classic study of the power of social roles.
- **Conformity** Find out more about conformity and the Asch experiments.
- **Groupthink** Read about and download a PowerPoint presentation about groupthink.

ANSWERS

1. F 2. T 3. social influence 4. c 5. sanctions 6. b 7. A person who did not follow at least some norms concerning normal social behavior would very likely be perceived as extremely bizarre, disturbed, or psychotic.

MODULE 15.3 Compliance, Obedience, and Self-Assertion

WHAT ARE THE LIMITS of your willingness to comply with the requests of strangers or with the commands of authorities? You've probably seen a bumper sticker that says "Question Authority." Actually, that's not bad advice if it means "Think Critically." However, compliance and obedience are normal parts of social life. When is it appropriate to decline to comply or to resist authority? These are essential questions about how we are affected by social influence.

Compliance—A Foot in the Door

SURVEY QUESTION: *What have psychologists learned about compliance, obedience, and self-assertion?*

Pressures to "fit in" and conform are usually indirect. In contrast, the term **compliance** refers to situations in which one person bends to the requests of another person who has little or no authority. These more direct pressures to comply are quite common. For example, a stranger might ask you to borrow your cell phone so he can make a call; a saleswoman might suggest that you buy a more expensive watch than you had planned on; or a coworker might ask you for the money to buy a cappuccino.

What determines whether a person will comply with a request? Many factors could be listed, but three stand out as especially interesting.

The Foot-in-the-Door Effect People who sell door to door have long recognized that once they get a foot in the door, a sale is almost a sure thing. To state the **foot-in-the-door effect** more formally, a person who first agrees to a small request is later more likely to comply with a larger demand (Pascual & Guéguen, 2005). For instance, if someone asked you to put a large, ugly sign in your front yard to promote safe driving, you would probably refuse. If, however, you had first agreed to put a small sign in your window, you would later be much more likely to allow the big sign in your yard.

Apparently, the foot-in-the-door effect is based on observing one's own behavior. Seeing yourself agree to a small request helps convince you that you didn't mind doing what was asked. After that, you are more likely to comply with a larger request (Pascual & Guéguen, 2005).

The Door-in-the-Face Effect Let's say that a neighbor comes to your door and asks you to feed his dogs, water his plants, and mow his yard while he is out of town for a month. This is quite a major request—one that most people would probably turn down. Feeling only slightly guilty, you tell your neighbor that you're sorry but you can't help him. Now, what if the same neighbor returns the next day and asks if you would at least pick up his mail while he is gone. Chances are very good that you would honor this request, even if you might have originally turned it down, too.

Psychologist Robert Cialdini coined the term **door-in-the-face effect** to describe the tendency for a person who has refused a major request to agree to a smaller request. In other words, after a person has turned down a major request ("slammed the door in your face"), he or she may be more willing to comply with a lesser demand. This strategy works because a person who abandons a large request appears to have given up something. In response, many people feel that they must repay her or him by giving in to the smaller request (Cialdini & Goldstein, 2004). In fact, a good way to get another person to comply with a request is to first do a small favor for the person.

The Lowball Technique Anyone who has purchased an automobile will recognize a third way of inducing compliance. Automobile dealers are notorious for convincing customers to buy cars by offering "lowball" prices that undercut the competition. The dealer first gets the customer to agree to buy at an attractively low price. Then, once the customer is committed, various techniques are used to bump the price up before the sale is concluded.

The **lowball technique** consists of getting a person committed to act and then making the terms of acting less desirable (Guéguen, Pascual, & Dagot, 2002). Here's another example: A fellow student asks to borrow $25 for a day. This seems reasonable and you agree. However, once you have

Calvin and Hobbes © Watterson. Reprinted with permission of Universal Press Syndicate. All rights reserved.

634

DISCOVERING PSYCHOLOGY

How to Drive a Hard Bargain

Your local car lot is a good place to see compliance take place. Automobile salespersons play the compliance game daily and get very good at it. If you understand what they are up to, you will have a far better chance of resisting their tactics.

A Foot in the Door

The salesperson offers you a test drive. If you accept, you will have made a small commitment of time to a particular car and to the salesperson. The salesperson will then ask you to go to an office and fill out some papers "just to see what kind of a price" she or he can offer. If you go along, you will be further committed.

The Lowball Technique

To get things underway the salesperson will offer you a very good price for your trade-in or will ask you to make an offer on the new car, "any offer, no matter how low." The salesperson will then ask if you will buy the car if she or he can sell it for the price you state. If you say yes, you have virtually bought the car. Most people find it very difficult to walk away once bargaining has reached this stage.

The Hook Is Set

Once buyers are "hooked" by a lowball offer, the salesperson goes to the manager to have the sale "approved." On returning, the salesperson will tell you with great disappointment that the dealership would lose money on the deal. "Couldn't you just take a little less for the trade-in or pay a little more for the car?" the salesperson will ask. At this point many people hesitate and grumble, but most give in and accept some "compromise" price or trade-in amount.

Evening the Odds

To combat all of the preceding, you must arm yourself with accurate information. In the past, salespeople had a great advantage in negotiating because they knew exactly how much the dealership paid for each car. Now, you can obtain detailed automobile pricing information on the Internet. With such information in hand, you will find it easier to challenge a salesperson's manipulative tactics.

After you've negotiated a final "best offer," get it in writing. Then walk out. Go to another dealer and see if the salesperson will better the price, in writing. When he or she does, return to the first dealership and negotiate for an even better price. Then decide where to buy. Now that you know some of the rules of the "Car Game," you might even enjoy playing it.

---

given your classmate the money, he explains that it would be easier to repay you after payday, in 2 weeks. If you agree, you've succumbed to the lowball technique. Here's another example: Let's say you ask someone to give you a ride to school in the morning. Only after the person has agreed do you tell her that you have to be there at 6 A.M.

Gaining Compliance To summarize, there are three basic ways to get people to voluntarily comply with a request.

- You can start with a small request that is easy for the person to agree to, and then make a bigger request. (This is the foot-in-the-door strategy.)
- You can make a major request that you know the person will turn down, and then make a smaller request (the one you actually wanted the person to comply with in the first place). (This is the door-in-the-face strategy.)
- You can make a request and get the person to agree to it. Then change the requirements for fulfilling the request to something the person probably wouldn't have otherwise agreed to do. (This is the lowball technique.)

One of the main benefits of knowing these strategies is that you can protect yourself from being manipulated by people using them. For example, "How to Drive a Hard Bargain" explains how car salespersons use compliance techniques on customers.

Obedience—Would You Electrocute a Stranger?

A person who has social power in one situation may have very little in another. In those situations where a person has power, she or he is described as an *authority*. Let's investigate **obedience**, a special type of conformity to the demands of an authority.

Groupthink A compulsion by members of decision-making groups to maintain agreement, even at the cost of critical thinking.

Compliance Bending to the requests of a person who has little or no authority or other form of social power.

Foot-in-the-door effect The tendency for a person who has first complied with a small request to be more likely later to fulfill a larger request.

Door-in-the-face effect The tendency for a person who has refused a major request to subsequently be more likely to comply with a minor request.

Lowball technique A strategy in which commitment is gained first to reasonable or desirable terms, which are then made less reasonable or desirable.

Obedience Conformity to the demands of an authority.

The question is this: If ordered to do so, would you shock a man with a heart condition who is screaming and asking to be released? Certainly, few people would obey. Or would they? In Nazi Germany, obedient soldiers (once average citizens) helped slaughter more than 6 million people in concentration camps. Do such inhumane acts reflect deep character flaws? Are they the acts of heartless psychopaths or crazed killers? Or are they simply the result of obedience to authority? What are the limits of obedience? These are questions that puzzled social psychologist Stanley Milgram (1965) when he began a provocative series of studies on obedience.

How did Milgram study obedience? As was true of the Asch experiments, Milgram's research is best appreciated by imagining yourself as a subject. Place yourself in the following situation.

Milgram's Obedience Studies

Imagine answering a newspaper ad to take part in a "learning" experiment at Yale University. When you arrive, a coin is flipped and a second person, a pleasant-looking man in his 50s, is designated the "learner." By chance you have become the "teacher."

Your task is to read a list of word pairs. The learner's task is to memorize them. You are to punish him with an electric shock each time he makes a mistake. The learner is taken to an adjacent room, and you watch as he is seated in an "electric chair" apparatus. Electrodes are attached to his wrists. You are then escorted to your position in front of a "shock generator." On this device is a row of 30 switches marked from 15 to 450 volts. Corresponding labels range from "Slight Shock" to "Extreme Intensity Shock" and finally "Danger Severe Shock." Your instructions are to shock the learner each time he makes a mistake. You must begin with 15 volts and then move one switch (15 volts) higher for each additional mistake (● Fig. 15.5).

The experiment begins, and the learner soon makes his first error. You flip a switch. More mistakes. Rapidly you reach the 75-volt level. The learner moans after each shock. At 100 volts he complains that he has a heart condition. At 150 volts he says he no longer wants to continue and demands to be released. At 300 volts he screams and says he can no longer give answers.

At some point, you begin to protest to the experimenter. "That man has a heart condition," you say; "I'm not going to kill that man." The experimenter says, "Please continue." Another shock and another scream from the learner and you say, "You mean I've got to keep going up the scale? No, sir. I'm not going to give him 450 volts!" The experimenter says, "The experiment requires that you continue." For a time the learner refuses to answer any more questions and screams with each shock (Milgram, 1965). Then he falls chillingly silent for the rest of the experiment.

It's hard to believe many people would do this. What happened? Milgram also doubted that many people would obey his orders. When he polled a group of psychiatrists before the experiment, they predicted that less than 1 percent of those tested would obey. The astounding fact is that 65 percent obeyed completely by going all the way to the 450-volt level. Virtually no one stopped short of 300 volts ("Severe Shock") (● Fig. 15.6).

Was the learner injured? The time has come to reveal that the "learner" was actually an actor who turned a tape recorder on and off in the shock room. No shocks were ever administered, but the dilemma for the "teacher" was quite real. Subjects protested, sweated, trembled, stuttered, bit their lips, and laughed nervously. Clearly they were disturbed by what they were doing. Nevertheless, most obeyed the experimenter's orders.

Milgram's Follow-Up *Why did so many people obey?* Some have suggested that the prestige of Yale University added to subjects' willingness to obey. Could it be that they assumed the professor running the experiment would not really allow anyone to be hurt? To test this possibility, the study was rerun in a shabby office building in nearby Bridgeport, Connecti-

● **FIGURE 15.5** Scenes from Stanley Milgram's study of obedience: the "shock generator," strapping a "learner" into his chair, and a "teacher" being told to administer a severe shock to the learner. (Scenes from the film *Obedience*, by Stanley Milgram, The Pennsylvania State University, Audio Visual Services. Used by permission.)

DISCOVERING PSYCHOLOGY

Quack Like a Duck

Imagine your response to the following events. On the first day of class, your psychology professor begins to establish the basic rules of behavior for the course. Draw a line under the first instruction you think you would refuse to carry out.

1. Seats are assigned, and you are told to move to a new location.
2. You are told not to talk during class.
3. Your professor tells you that you must have permission to leave early.
4. You are told to bring your textbook to class at all times.
5. Your professor tells you to use only a pencil for taking notes.
6. You are directed to take off your watch.
7. The professor tells you to keep both hands on your desktop at all times.
8. You are instructed to keep both your feet flat on the floor.
9. You are told to stand up and clap your hands three times.
10. Your professor says, "Stick two fingers up your nose and quack like a duck."

At what point would you stop obeying such orders? In reality, you might find yourself obeying a legitimate authority long after that person's demands had become unreasonable (Aronson, Wilson, & Akert, 2007). What would happen, though, if a few students resisted orders early in the sequence? Would that help free others to disobey? For an answer, return to the discussion of Milgram's experiment for some final remarks.

cut. Under these conditions fewer people obeyed (48 percent), but the reduction was minor.

Milgram was disturbed by the willingness of people to knuckle under to authority and senselessly shock someone. In later experiments, he tried to reduce obedience. He found that the distance between the teacher and the learner was important. When subjects were in the *same room* as the learner, only 40 percent fully obeyed. When they were *face to face* with the learner and required to force his hand down on a simulated "shock plate," only 30 percent obeyed (● Fig. 15.7). Distance from the authority also had an effect. When the experimenter gave his orders over the phone, only 22 percent obeyed. You may doubt that Milgram's study of obedience applies to you. If so, take a moment to read "Quack Like a Duck."

Implications Milgram's research raises nagging questions about our willingness to commit antisocial or inhumane acts commanded by a "legitimate authority." The excuse so often

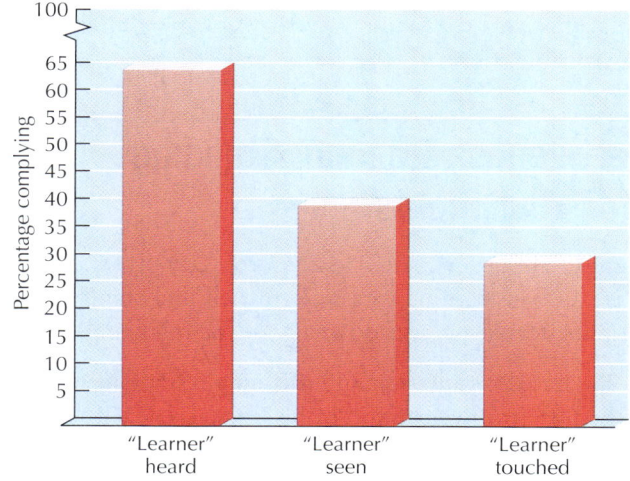

● **FIGURE 15.7** Physical distance from the "learner" had a significant effect on the percentage of subjects obeying orders.

● **FIGURE 15.6** Results of Milgram's obedience experiment. Only a minority of subjects refused to provide shocks, even at the most extreme intensities. The first substantial drop in obedience occurred at the 300-volt level (Milgram, 1963).

given by war criminals—"I was only following orders"—takes on new meaning in this light. Milgram suggested that when directions come from an authority, people rationalize that they are not personally responsible for their actions. In locales as diverse as Vietnam, Rwanda, Bosnia, South Africa, Nicaragua, Sri Lanka, Laos, and Iraq, the tragic result has been "sanctioned massacres" of chilling proportions. Even in everyday life, crimes of obedience are common (Zimbardo, 2007). In order to keep their jobs, many people obey orders to do things that they know are dishonest, unethical, or harmful (Hamilton & Sanders, 1995).

Let us end on a more positive note. In one of his experiments, Milgram found that group support can greatly reduce destructive obedience. When real subjects saw two other "teachers" (both actors) resist orders and walk out of the ex-

Obedience to authority is often necessary and reasonable; however, it can also be destructive.

Associated Press photographer Jeff Widener snapped this timeless photo of a lone protester literally standing up on his own behalf while he halted a column of tanks during the 1989 pro-democracy rallies in Tiananmen Square in Beijing, China. How many of us would find the courage to assert ourselves against such direct expressions of authority?

periment, only 10 percent continued to obey. Thus, a personal assertion of courage or moral fortitude by one or two members of a group may free others to disobey misguided or unjust authority. Let's see how assertive people handle difficult social situations.

Assertiveness Training—Standing Up for Your Rights

Because we all face pressures to conform, comply, and obey, there is value in learning to assert yourself and stand up for your rights. Have you ever done any of the following?

- Hesitated to question an error on a restaurant bill because you were afraid of making a scene?
- Backed out of asking for a raise or a change in working conditions?
- Said yes when you wanted to say no?
- Been afraid to question a grade that seemed unfair?

If you've ever had trouble with similar situations, *assertiveness training* (instruction in how to be self-assertive) may offer a solution. In assertiveness training, people learn assertive behavior through group exercises, videotapes, and staged conflicts. They also learn to practice honesty, disagreeing, questioning authority, and assertive postures and gestures. As their self-confidence improves, nonassertive clients are taken on "field trips" to shops and restaurants where they practice what they have learned.

The first step in assertiveness training is to convince yourself of three basic rights: You have the right to refuse, to request, and to right a wrong. **Self-assertion** involves standing up for these rights by speaking out in your own behalf.

Is self-assertion just getting things your own way? Not at all. A basic distinction can be made between *self-assertion* and *aggressive* behavior. Self-assertion is a direct, honest expression of feelings and desires. It is not exclusively self-serving. People who are nonassertive are usually patient to a fault. Sometimes their pent-up anger explodes with unexpected fury, which can damage relationships. In contrast to assertive behavior, **aggression** involves hurting another person or achieving one's goals at the expense of another. Aggression does not take into account the feelings or rights of others. It is an attempt to get one's own way no matter what. Assertion techniques emphasize firmness, not attack (■ Table 15.2).

The basic idea in assertiveness training is that each assertive action is practiced until it can be repeated even under stress. For example, let's say it really angers you when a store clerk waits on several people who arrived after you did. To improve your assertiveness in this situation, you would begin by *rehearsing* the dialogue, posture, and gestures you would use to confront the clerk or the other customer. Working in front of a mirror can be very helpful. If possible, you should *role play* the scene with a friend. Be sure to have your friend take the part of a really aggressive or irresponsible clerk, as well as a cooperative one. Rehearsal and role playing should also be used when you expect a possible confrontation with someone—for example, if you are going to ask for a raise, challenge a grade, or confront a landlord.

Is that all there is to it? No. Another important principle is *overlearning* (practice that continues after initial mastery of a skill). When you rehearse or role-play assertive behavior, it is essential to continue to practice until your responses become almost automatic. This helps prevent you from getting flustered in the actual situation.

One more technique you may find useful is the *broken record*. This is a self-assertion technique involving repeating a

TABLE 15.2 Comparison of Assertive, Aggressive, and Nonassertive Behavior

	ACTOR	RECEIVER OF BEHAVIOR
Nonassertive behavior	Self-denying, inhibited, hurt, and anxious; lets others make choices; goals not achieved	Feels sympathy, guilt, or contempt for actor; achieves goals at actor's expense
Aggressive behavior	Achieves goals at others' expense; expresses feelings, but hurts others; chooses for others or puts them down	Feels hurt, defensive, humiliated, or taken advantage of; does not meet own needs
Assertive behavior	Self-enhancing; acts in own best interests; expresses feelings; respects rights of others; goals usually achieved; self-respect maintained	Needs respected and feelings expressed; may achieve goal; self-worth maintained

request until it is acknowledged. A good way to prevent assertion from becoming aggression is to simply restate your request as many times and in as many ways as necessary. As an illustration, let's say you are returning a pair of shoes to a store. After two wearings the shoes fell apart, but you bought them 2 months ago and no longer have a receipt. The broken record could sound something like this:

Customer: I would like to have these shoes replaced.

Clerk: Do you have a receipt?

Customer: No, but I bought them here, and since they are defective, I would like to have you replace them.

Clerk: I can't do that without a receipt.

Customer: I understand that, but I want them replaced.

Clerk: Well, if you'll come back this afternoon and talk to the manager . . .

Customer: I've brought these shoes in because they are defective.

Clerk: Well, I'm not authorized to replace them.

Customer: Yes, well, if you'll replace these, I'll be on my way.

Notice that the customer did not attack the clerk or create an angry confrontation. Simple persistence is often all that is necessary for successful self-assertion.

Self-assertion does not supply instant poise, confidence, or self-assurance. However, it is a way of combating anxieties associated with life in an impersonal and sometimes intimidating society. If you are interested in more information, you can consult a book titled *Your Perfect Right* by Alberti and Emmons (2001).

MODULE 15.3 Summary

What have psychologists learned about compliance, obedience, and self-assertion?

- Three strategies for gaining compliance are the foot-in-the-door technique, the door-in-the-face approach, and the lowball technique.
- Most people have a strong tendency to obey legitimate authority. Usually this is desirable, but it can be damaging when social power is used in misguided or unscrupulous ways.
- Obedience to authority in Milgram's studies decreased when the "teacher" and "learner" were close to one another, when the authority was absent, and when others refused to obey.
- Self-assertion helps people meet their needs without resorting to aggressive behavior.

Self-assertion A direct, honest expression of feelings and desires.

Aggression Hurting another person or achieving one's goals at the expense of another person.

KNOWLEDGE BUILDER

Compliance, Obedience, and Self-Assertion

Recite

1. The term *compliance* refers to situations in which a person complies with commands made by a person who has authority. T or F?
2. Which compliance technique involves getting a person committed to act and then making the terms of acting less desirable?
   a. foot in the door
   b. lowball
   c. door in the face
   d. groupthink
3. In Milgram's experiments, the lowest level of obedience occurred when subjects
   a. saw another person refuse to obey
   b. were in the same room with the "learner"
   c. were face to face with the "learner"
   d. received orders over the phone
4. By repeating his obedience experiment in a downtown office building, Milgram demonstrated that the prestige of Yale University was the main reason for subjects' willingness to obey in the original experiment. T or F?
5. "Achieving one's goals without taking into account the rights of others." This statement describes
   a. self-assertion
   b. overdisclosure
   c. cognitive dissonance
   d. aggression

Reflect
Critical Thinking

6. Modern warfare allows killing to take place impersonally and at a distance. How does this relate to Milgram's experiments?

Relate

You would like to persuade people to donate to a deserving charity. How, specifically, could you use compliance techniques to get people to donate?

Are you surprised that so many people obeyed orders in Milgram's experiments? Do you think you would have obeyed? How actively do you question authority?

Pick a specific instance when you could have been more assertive. How would you handle the situation if it occurs again? Think of a specific instance when you were angry and acted aggressively. How could you have handled the situation through self-assertion instead of aggression?

Link

Internet addresses frequently change. To find the sites listed here, visit **http://www.thomsonedu.com/psychology/coon** for an updated list of Internet addresses and direct links to relevant sites.

- **The Two Step** Dig down deeper into the foot-in-the-door and door-in-the-face compliance techniques.
- **Milgram's Study of Obedience** Listen to audio clips of this infamous experiment.
- **Assertiveness** Access a collection of virtual pamphlets on assertiveness.

ANSWERS

1. F 2. b 3. d 4. F 5. d 6. There is a big difference between killing someone in hand-to-hand combat and killing someone by lining up images on a video screen. Milgram's research suggests that it is easier for a person to follow orders to kill another human when the victim is at a distance and removed from personal contact.

MODULE 15.4 Attitudes and Persuasion

WHAT IS YOUR ATTITUDE toward affirmative action, environmental groups, the death penalty, imported automobiles, junk food, psychology? The answers can have far-reaching effects on your behavior. Attitudes are intimately woven into our actions and views of the world. Our tastes, friendships, votes, preferences, and goals are all touched by attitudes. Let's see how attitudes are formed and changed.

Attitudes—Doomsday for the Seekers
HOW ARE ATTITUDES ACQUIRED AND CHANGED?

Hardly a year passes without a doomsday group of one kind or another making the news. In a classic example of such groups, a woman named Mrs. Keech claimed she was receiving messages from alien beings on a planet called Clarion. The aliens told Mrs. Keech that they had detected a fault in the earth's crust that would plunge North America into the ocean, causing an unimaginable disaster. The tragedy would occur on December 21. However, Mrs. Keech and her band of followers, who called themselves the Seekers, had no fear: On December 20 they expected to be met at midnight by a flying saucer and taken to safety in outer space.

The night of December 20 arrived, and the Seekers gathered at Mrs. Keech's house. Many had given up their jobs and possessions to prepare for departure. Expectations were high and commitment was total. But as midnight passed, the world continued to exist. It was a bitter and embarrassing disappointment for the Seekers.

Did the group break up then? Our story now takes an amazing twist—one that intrigued social psychologists. Instead of breaking up, the Seekers became *more* convinced than ever before that they had been right. At about 5 A.M. Mrs. Keech announced she had received a message explaining that the Seekers had saved the world.

Before December 20, the Seekers were uninterested in persuading other people that the world was coming to an end. Now they called newspapers and radio stations to convince others of their accomplishment.

How do we explain this strange turn in behavior? An answer may lie in the concept of *cognitive dissonance,* which also helps explain many aspects of attitude change. We will return to cognitive dissonance in a moment, but first let's answer some basic questions about attitudes.

Belief + Emotion + Action

Our tastes, friendships, votes, preferences, goals, and behavior in many other situations are all touched by attitudes (Baumeister & Bushman, 2008).

What specifically is an attitude? An **attitude** is a mixture of belief and emotion that predisposes a person to respond to other people, objects, or groups in a positive or negative way. Attitudes summarize your *evaluation* of objects (Oskamp & Schultz, 2005). As a result, they predict and direct future actions.

"Your attitude is showing" is sometimes said. Actually, attitudes are expressed through beliefs, emotions, and actions. The *belief component* of an attitude is what you believe about a particular object or issue. The *emotional component* consists of your feelings toward the attitudinal object. The *action component* refers to your actions toward various people, objects, or institutions. Consider, for example, your attitude toward gun control. You will have beliefs about whether gun control would affect rates of crime or violence. You will respond emotionally to guns, finding them either attractive and desirable or threatening and destructive. And you will have a tendency to seek out or avoid gun ownership. The action component of your attitude will probably also include support of organizations that urge or oppose gun control. As you can see, attitudes orient us to the social world. In doing so, they prepare us to act in certain ways (Albarracín, Johnson, & Zanna, 2005). (For another example, see ● Figure 15.8.)

Forming Attitudes

How do people acquire attitudes? Attitudes are acquired in several basic ways. Sometimes, attitudes come from *direct contact* (personal experience) with the object of the attitude—such as opposing pollution when a nearby factory ruins your favorite river (Ajzen, 2005). Some attitudes are simply formed through chance conditioning (learning that takes place by chance or coincidence) (Olson & Zanna, 1993). Let's say, for instance, that you have had three encounters in your lifetime with psychologists. If all three were negative, you might take an unduly dim view of psychology. In the same way, people often develop strong attitudes to-

Attitude A learned tendency to respond to people, objects, or institutions in a positive or negative way.

Issue: Affirmative Action

Belief component
Restores justice
Provides equal opportunity

Emotional component
Optimism

Action component
Vote for affirmative action
Donate to groups that support affirmative action

Belief component
Unfair to majority
Reverse discrimination

Emotional component
Anger

Action component
Vote against affirmative action
Donate to groups that oppose affirmative action

● **FIGURE 15.8** Elements of positive and negative attitudes toward affirmative action.

ward cities, foods, or parts of the country on the basis of one or two unusually good or bad experiences.

Attitudes are also learned through *interaction with others*; that is, through discussion with people holding a particular attitude. For instance, if three of your friends are volunteers at a local recycling center, and you talk with them about their beliefs, you will probably come to favor recycling, too. More generally, there is little doubt that many of our attitudes are influenced by *group membership*. In most groups, pressures to conform shape our attitudes, just as they do our behavior. *Child rearing* (the effects of parental values, beliefs, and practices) also affects attitudes (Bartram, 2006). For example, if both parents belong to the same political party, chances are that their children will belong to that party as adults.

Finally, there can be no doubt that attitudes are influenced by the *mass media* (all media, such as magazines and television, that reach large audiences). Every day we are coaxed, persuaded, and skillfully manipulated by messages in the mass media. Ninety-nine percent of North American homes have a television set, which is on an average of more than 7 hours a day (Steuer & Hustedt, 2002). The information thus channeled into homes has a powerful impact. For instance, frequent viewers mistrust others and overestimate their own chances of being harmed. This suggests that a steady diet of TV violence leads some people to develop a *mean worldview*, in which they regard the world as a dangerous and threatening place (Eschholz, Chiricos, & Gertz, 2003).

Attitudes and Behavior

Why are some attitudes acted on, whereas others are not? To answer this question, let's consider an example. Assume that a woman named Lorraine knows that automobiles add to air pollution, and she hates smog. Why would Lorraine continue to drive to work every day? Probably it is because the *immediate consequences* of our actions weigh heavily on the choices we make. No matter what Lorraine's attitude may be, it is difficult for her to resist the immediate convenience of driving. Our expectations of how *others will evaluate* our actions are also important. Lorraine may resist taking public transit to work for fear that her coworkers will be critical of her environmental stand. Finally, we must not overlook the effects of long-standing *habits* (Oskamp & Schultz, 2005). Let's say that after years of driving to work Lorraine finally vows to shift to public transit. Two months later it would not be unusual for her behavior to show the effects of habit rather than her good intentions.

In short, there are often large differences between attitudes and behavior—particularly between privately held attitudes and public behavior. However, barriers to action typically fall when a person holds an attitude with *conviction*. If you have *conviction* about an issue, it evokes strong feelings, you think about it and discuss it often, and you are knowledgeable about it. Attitudes held with passionate conviction often lead to major changes in personal behavior (Oskamp & Schultz, 2005).

Attitude Change—Why the "Seekers" Went Public

SURVEY QUESTION: *Under what conditions is persuasion most effective?*

Although attitudes are fairly stable, they do change. Some attitude change can be understood in terms of **reference groups** (any group an individual uses as a standard for social comparison). It is not necessary to have face-to-face contact with other people for them to be a reference group. It depends instead on whom you identify with or whose attitudes and values you care about (Ajzen, 2005).

In the 1930s, Theodore Newcomb studied real-life attitude change among students at Bennington College (Alwin, Cohen, & Newcomb, 1991). Most students came from conservative homes, but Bennington was a very liberal school. Newcomb found that most students shifted significantly toward more liberal attitudes during their 4 years at Bennington. Those who didn't change kept their parents and hometown friends as primary reference groups. This is typified by a student who said, "I decided I'd rather stick to my father's ideas." Those who did change identified primarily with the campus community. Notice that all students could count the college and their families as *membership* groups. However, one group or the other tended to become their point of reference.

Persuasion

What about advertising and other direct attempts to change attitudes? Are they effective? **Persuasion** is any deliberate attempt to change attitudes or beliefs through information and arguments (Brock & Green, 2005). Businesses, politicians, and others who seek to persuade us obviously believe that attitudes can be changed. Many billions of dollars are spent yearly on media advertising in the United States and Canada alone.

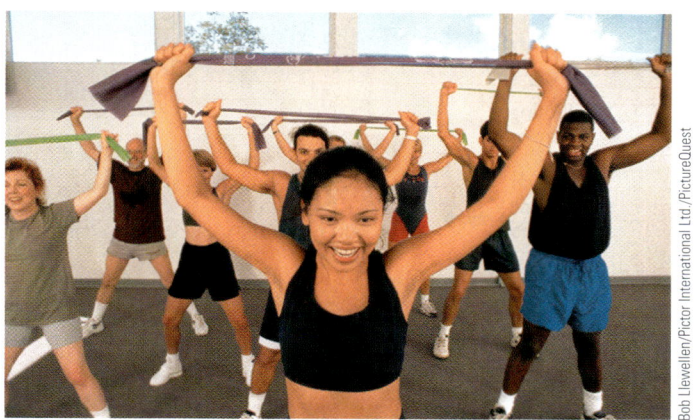

Do you exercise regularly? Like students in the Bennington study, your intentions to exercise are probably influenced by the exercise habits of your reference groups (Terry & Hogg, 1996).

Persuasion. Would you be likely to be swayed by this group's message? Successful persuasion is related to characteristics of the communicator, the message, and the audience.

Persuasion can range from the daily blitz of media commercials to personal discussion among friends. In most cases, the success or failure of persuasion can be understood if we consider the *communicator,* the *message,* and the *audience.*

At a community meeting, let's say you have a chance to promote an issue important to you (for or against building a nuclear power plant nearby, for instance). Whom should you choose to make the presentation, and how should that person present it? Research suggests that attitude change is encouraged when the following conditions are met.

1. The communicator is likable, expressive, trustworthy, an expert on the topic, and similar to the audience in some respect.
2. The message appeals to emotions, particularly to fear or anxiety.
3. The message also provides a clear course of action that will, if followed, reduce fear or produce personally desirable results.
4. The message states clear-cut conclusions.
5. The message is backed up by facts and statistics.
6. Both sides of the argument are presented in the case of a well-informed audience.
7. Only one side of the argument is presented in the case of a poorly informed audience.
8. The persuader appears to have nothing to gain if the audience accepts the message.
9. The message is repeated as frequently as possible (Aronson, 2008; Oskamp & Schultz, 2005).

Reference group Any group that an individual identifies with and uses as a standard for social comparison.

Persuasion A deliberate attempt to change attitudes or beliefs with information and arguments.

You should have little trouble seeing how these principles are applied to sell everything from underarm deodorants to presidents.

Cognitive Dissonance Theory

Cognitions are thoughts. *Dissonance* means clashing. The influential theory of **cognitive dissonance** states that contradicting or clashing thoughts cause discomfort. That is, we have a need for *consistency* in our thoughts, perceptions, and images of ourselves (Cooper, Mirabile, & Scher, 2005; Festinger, 1957).

What happens if people act in ways that are inconsistent with their attitudes or self-images? Typically the contradiction makes them uncomfortable. Such discomfort can motivate people to make their thoughts or attitudes agree with their actions (Tavris & Aronson, 2007). For example, smokers are told on every pack that cigarettes endanger their lives. They light up and smoke anyway. How do they resolve the tension between this information and their actions? They could quit smoking, but it may be easier to convince themselves that smoking is not really so dangerous. To do this, many smokers seek examples of heavy smokers who have lived long lives, they spend their time with other smokers, and they avoid information about the link between smoking and cancer. According to cognitive dissonance theory, we also tend to reject new information that contradicts ideas we already hold. We're all guilty of this "don't bother me with the facts, my mind is made up" strategy at times.

Now recall Mrs. Keech and her doomsday group. Why did their belief in Mrs. Keech's messages *increase* after the world failed to end? Why did the group suddenly become interested in convincing others that they were right? Cognitive dissonance theory explains that after publicly committing themselves to their beliefs, they had a strong need to maintain consistency (Tavris & Aronson, 2007). In effect, convincing others was a way of adding proof that they were correct (■ Table 15.3).

Acting contrary to one's attitudes doesn't always bring about change. How does cognitive dissonance explain that? The amount of justification for acting contrary to your attitudes and beliefs affects how much dissonance you feel. (*Justification* is the degree to which a person's actions are explained by rewards or other circumstances.) In a classic study, college students did an extremely boring task (turning wooden pegs on a board) for a *long* time. Afterward, they were asked to help lure others into the experiment by pretending that the task was interesting and enjoyable. Students paid $20 for lying to others did not change their own negative opinion of the task: "That was *really* boring!" Those who were paid only $1 later rated the task as "pleasant" and "interesting." How can we explain these results? Apparently, students paid $20 experienced no dissonance. These students could reassure themselves that anybody would tell a little white lie for $20. Those paid $1 were faced with the conflicting thoughts: "I lied" and "I had no good reason to do it." Rather than admit to themselves that they had lied, these students changed their attitude toward what they had done (Festinger & Carlsmith, 1959). (See ● Fig. 15.9.)

We are especially likely to experience dissonance after we cause an event to occur that we wish hadn't taken place. Let's

■ **TABLE 15.3** Strategies for Reducing Cognitive Dissonance

Celia, who is a college student, has always thought of herself as an environmental activist. Recently, Celia "inherited" a car from her parents, who were replacing the family "barge." In the past, Celia biked or used public transportation to get around. Her parents' old car is an antiquated gas-guzzler, but she has begun to drive it every day. How might Celia reduce the cognitive dissonance created by the clash between her environmentalism and her use of an inefficient automobile?

STRATEGY	EXAMPLE
Change your attitude	"Cars are not really a major environmental problem."
Add consonant thoughts	"This is an old car, so keeping it on the road makes good use of the resources consumed when it was manufactured."
Change the importance of the dissonant thoughts	"It's more important for me to support the environmental movement politically than it is to worry about how I get to school and work."
Reduce the amount of perceived choice	"My schedule has become too hectic. I really can't afford to bike or take the bus anymore."
Change your behavior	"I'm only going to use the car when it's impossible to bike or take the bus."

Source: Adapted from Franzoi, 2002.

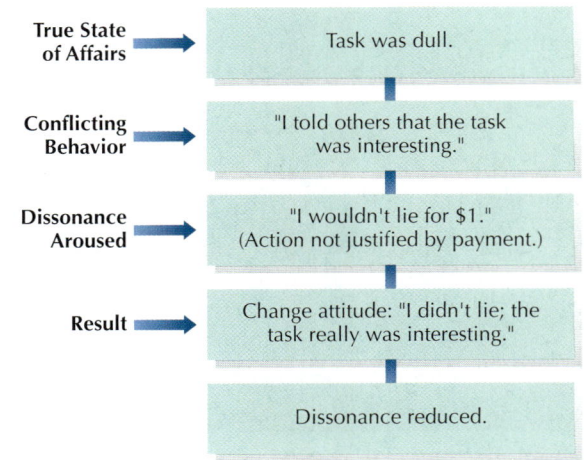

● **FIGURE 15.9** Summary of the Festinger and Carlsmith (1959) study from the viewpoint of a person experiencing cognitive dissonance.

say that you agree to help a friend move to a new apartment. The big day arrives and you feel like staying in bed. Actually, you wish you had never promised to help. To reduce dissonance, you may convince yourself that the work will actually be "good exercise," "sort of fun," or that your friend really deserves the help. We often make such adjustments in attitudes to minimize cognitive dissonance.

Before we leave the topic of attitudes, let's see what psychologists have learned about brainwashing and other high-pressure attempts to change attitudes.

Forced Attitude Change— Brainwashing and Cults

SURVEY QUESTIONS: *Is brainwashing actually possible? How are people converted to cult membership?*

If you're a history enthusiast, you may associate *brainwashing* with techniques used by the Communist Chinese on prisoners during the Korean War (Jowett, 2006). Through various types of "thought reform," the Chinese were able to coerce some of these prisoners to sign false confessions. More recently, the mass murder/suicide at Jonestown, the Branch Davidian tragedy at Waco, the Heaven's Gate group suicide in San Diego, and Osama bin Laden's al-Qaeda movement have heightened public interest in forced attitude change.

How does it differ from other persuasive techniques? Brainwashing, or forced attitude change, requires a captive audience. If you are offended by a television commercial, you can tune it out. Prisoners in POW camps are completely at the mercy of their captors. Complete control over the environment allows a degree of psychological manipulation that would be impossible in a normal setting.

Brainwashing

How does captivity facilitate persuasion? Brainwashing typically begins by making the target person feel completely helpless. Physical and psychological abuse, lack of sleep, humiliation, and isolation serve to *unfreeze*, or loosen, former values and beliefs. When exhaustion, pressure, and fear become unbearable, *change* occurs as the person begins to abandon former beliefs. Prisoners who reach the breaking point may sign a false confession or cooperate to gain relief. When they do, they are suddenly rewarded with praise, privileges, food, or rest. From that point on, a mixture of hope and fear, plus pressures to conform, serves to *refreeze* (solidify) new attitudes (Taylor, 2004).

How permanent are changes caused by brainwashing? In most cases, the dramatic shift in attitudes brought about by brainwashing is temporary. Most "converted" prisoners who returned to the United States after the Korean War eventually reverted to their original beliefs. Nevertheless, brainwashing can be powerful, as shown by the success of cults in recruiting new members.

Cults

Exhorted by their leader, some 900 members of the Reverend Jim Jones's People's Temple picked up paper cups and drank purple Kool-Aid laced with the deadly poison cyanide. Psychologically the mass suicide at Jonestown in 1978 is not so incredible as it might seem (Dein & Littlewood, 2005). The inhabitants of Jonestown were isolated in the jungles of Guyana, intimidated by guards, and lulled with sedatives. They were also cut off from friends and relatives and totally accustomed to obeying rigid rules of conduct, which primed them for Jones's final "loyalty test." Of greater psychological interest is the question of how people reach such a state of commitment and dependency.

Why do people join groups such as the People's Temple? The People's Temple was a classic example of a *cult*. A *cult* is an authoritarian group in which the leader's personality is more important than the beliefs she or he preaches. Cult members give their allegiance to this person, who is regarded as infallible, and they follow his or her dictates without question. Almost always, cult members are victimized by their leaders in one way or another. For example, in April 1993, David Koresh and members of his Branch Davidian group perished in a fire at their Waco, Texas, compound. Like Jim Jones had done years before in Jonestown, Koresh took nearly total control of his followers' lives. He told them what to eat, dictated sexual mores, and had errant followers paddled. Followers were persuaded to surrender money, property, and even their children and wives. Like Jones, Koresh also took mistresses and had children out of wedlock. And like other cult leaders, Jones and Koresh demanded absolute loyalty and obedience to themselves and to their cult, with tragic results (Dein & Littlewood, 2005; Reiterman, 1993).

Psychologist and pioneering brainwashing expert Margaret Singer (1921–2003) studied and aided hundreds of former cult members. Her interviews reveal that in recruiting new members, cults use a powerful blend of guilt, manipulation, isolation, deception, fear, and escalating commitment. In this respect, cults employ high-pressure indoctrination techniques not unlike those used in brainwashing (Singer, 2003; Singer & Addis, 1992). In the United States alone, an estimated 2 to 5 million people have succumbed to the lure of cults (Robinson, Frye, & Bradley, 1997).

Cognitive dissonance An uncomfortable clash between self-image, thoughts, beliefs, attitudes, or perceptions and one's behavior.

In April 1993, David Koresh and members of his Branch Davidian group perished in an inferno at their Waco, Texas, compound. Authorities believe the fire was set by a cult member, under the direction of Koresh. Like Jim Jones had done years before in Jonestown, Koresh took nearly total control of his followers' lives. He told them what to eat, dictated sexual mores, and directed the paddling of errant followers. Followers were persuaded to surrender money, property, and even their children and wives. Like Jones, Koresh also took mistresses and had children out of wedlock. Like other cult leaders, Jones and Koresh demanded absolute loyalty and obedience, with tragic results.

Recruitment Some people studied by Singer were seriously distressed when they joined a cult. Most, however, were simply undergoing a period of mild depression, indecision, or alienation from family and friends (Hunter, 1998). Cult members try to catch potential converts at a time of need—especially when a sense of belonging will be attractive to converts. For instance, many people were approached just after a romance had broken up, or when they were struggling with exams, or were trying to become independent from their families (Sirkin, 1990). At such times, people are easily persuaded that joining the group is all they need to do to be happy again (Hunter, 1998). Adolescents are especially vulnerable to recruitment into cults because they may be seeking a cause to conform to as a replacement for the parental authority they are rebelling against (Richmond, 2004).

Conversion *How is conversion achieved?* Often it begins with intense displays of affection and understanding ("love bombing"). Next comes isolation from non–cult members and drills, discipline, and rituals (all-night meditation or continuous chanting, for instance). These rituals wear down physical and emotional resistance, discourage critical thinking, and generate feelings of commitment (Langone, 2002).

Many cults make clever use of the foot-in-the-door technique described earlier. At first, recruits make small commitments (to stay after a meeting, for example). Then, larger commitments are encouraged (to stay an extra day, to call in sick at work, and so forth). Making a major commitment is usually the final step. The new devotee signs over a bank account or property to the group, moves in with the group, and so forth. Making such major public commitments creates a powerful cognitive dissonance effect. Before long, it becomes virtually impossible for converts to admit they have made a mistake.

Once in the group, members are cut off from family and friends (former reference groups) and the cult can control the flow and interpretation of information to them. Members are isolated from their former value systems and social structures. Conversion is complete when they come to think of themselves more as group members than as individuals. At this point obedience is nearly total (Wexler, 1995).

Implications Behind the "throne" from which Jim Jones ruled Jonestown was a sign bearing these words: "Those who do not remember the past are condemned to repeat it." Sadly, another cult-related tragedy occurred in 2001. The terrorist attacks on the United States were carried out by followers of cult leader Osama bin Laden. At his direction, they learned hatred and contempt for everyone outside their band of true believers. If there is a lesson to be learned from such destructive cults, it is this: All true spiritual leaders have taught love and compassion. They also encourage followers to question their beliefs and to reach their own conclusions about how to live. In contrast, destructive cults show that it is dangerous to trade personal independence and critical thinking for security (Goldberg, 2001).

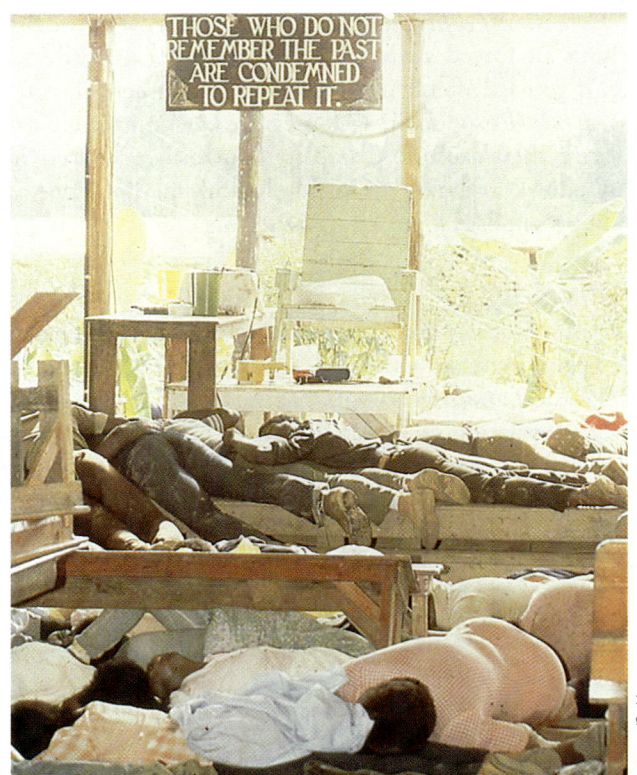

Aftermath of the mass suicide at Jonestown. How do cult-like groups recruit new devotees?

MODULE 15.4 Summary

How are attitudes acquired and changed?
- Attitudes are made up of a belief component, an emotional component, and an action component.
- Attitudes held with conviction are most likely to affect our behavior.
- Attitudes may be formed by direct contact, interaction with others, child-rearing practices, group pressures, peer group influences, reference group membership, the mass media, and chance conditioning.

Under what conditions is persuasion most effective?
- Effective persuasion must take into account characteristics of the communicator, the message, and the audience.
- In general, a likable and believable communicator who repeats a credible message that arouses emotion in the audience and states clear-cut conclusions will be persuasive.
- Cognitive dissonance theory explains many aspects of attitude change.

Is brainwashing actually possible? How are people converted to cult membership?
- Brainwashing is a form of forced attitude change. It depends on control of the target person's environment.
- Three steps in brainwashing are unfreezing, changing, and refreezing attitudes and beliefs.
- Many cults recruit new members with high-pressure indoctrination techniques.

KNOWLEDGE BUILDER

Attitudes and Persuasion

Recite

1. Attitudes have three parts: a _____ component, an _____ component, and an _____ component.

2. Which of the following is associated with attitude formation?
   a. group membership
   b. mass media
   c. chance conditioning
   d. child rearing
   e. all of the preceding
   f. a and d only

3. If you are trying to persuade a well-informed audience, it is usually best to present
   a. one side of the argument
   b. both sides of the argument
   c. the unfreezing, change, refreezing cycle
   d. negative sanctions

4. The amount of cognitive dissonance a person feels is related to how much _____ exists for his or her actions.
   a. reciprocity
   b. justification
   c. chance conditioning
   d. reference

5. Brainwashing differs from other persuasive attempts in that brainwashing requires a _____ _____.

6. Cult members are almost always victimized by their leaders in one way or another. T or F?

Reflect
Critical Thinking

7. Students entering a college gym are asked to sign a banner promoting water conservation. Later, the students shower at the gym. What effect would you expect signing the banner to have on how long students stay in the showers?

8. Cognitive dissonance theory predicts that false confessions obtained during brainwashing are not likely to bring about lasting changes in attitudes. Why?

Relate

Describe an attitude that is important to you. What are its three components?

Which of the various sources of attitudes best explain your own attitudes?

Who belongs to your most important reference group?

Imagine that you would like to persuade voters to support an initiative to preserve a small wilderness area by converting it to a park. Using research on persuasion as a guide, what could you do to be more effective?

How would you explain cognitive dissonance theory to a person who knows nothing about it?

Link

Internet addresses frequently change. To find the sites listed here, visit **http://www.thomsonedu.com/psychology/coon** for an updated list of Internet addresses and direct links to relevant sites.

- **General Persuasion Techniques** Explore a variety of persuasion techniques.
- **Cognitive Dissonance** Read an original article by Festinger and Carlsmith.
- **Heaven's Gate** Read more about the Heaven's Gate cult.

ANSWERS

1. belief, emotional, action 2. e 3. b 4. b 5. captive audience 6. T 7. Cognitive dissonance theory predicts that students who sign the banner will take shorter showers to be consistent with their publicly expressed support of water conservation. This is exactly the result observed in a study done by social psychologist Elliot Aronson. 8. Because there is strong justification for such actions, little cognitive dissonance is created when a prisoner makes statements that contradict his or her beliefs.

MODULE 15.5 Prejudice and Intergroup Conflict

LOVE AND FRIENDSHIP bind people together. Prejudice, which is marked by suspicion, fear, or hatred, has the opposite effect. Prejudice is an all too common part of daily life. What are the origins of prejudice? How can prejudice and hurtful attitudes be reduced?

Prejudice—Attitudes That Injure

SURVEY QUESTION: *What causes prejudice and intergroup conflict?*

Prejudice is a negative emotional attitude held toward members of a specific social group. Prejudices may be reflected in the policies of police departments, schools, or government institutions (Dovidio, Glick, & Rudman, 2005). In such cases, prejudice is referred to as *racism, sexism, ageism,* or *heterosexism,* depending on the group affected. Because it is so prevalent and damaging, let's focus on racism.

Both racial prejudice and racism lead to **discrimination,** or unequal treatment of people who should have the same rights as others. Discrimination prevents people from doing things they should be able to do, such as buying a house, getting a job, voting, or attending a high-quality school. For example, in many cities, African-American drivers have been the target of "racial profiling" in which they are stopped by police without reason. Sometimes they are merely questioned, but many are cited for minor infractions, such as a cracked taillight or an illegal lane change. For many law-abiding citizens, being detained in this manner is a rude awakening (Plous, 2003). It's also one reason why many blacks and other persons of color in America distrust police and the legal system (Dovido et al., 2002).

Becoming Prejudiced

How do prejudices develop? One major theory suggests that prejudice is a form of *scapegoating* (blaming a person or a group for the actions of others or for conditions not of their making). Scapegoating, you may recall, is a type of *displaced aggression* in which hostilities triggered by frustration are redirected at "safer" targets (Nelson, 2006). One interesting classic test of this hypothesis was conducted at a summer camp for young men. The men were given a difficult test they were sure to fail. Additionally, completing the test caused them to miss a trip to the movies, which was normally the high point of their weekly entertainment. Attitudes toward Mexicans and Japanese were measured before the test and after the men had failed the test and missed the movie. Subjects in this study, all European Americans, consistently rated members of the two ethnic groups lower after being frustrated (Miller & Bugelski, 1970). This effect has been easy to observe since the September 11, 2001, terrorist attacks in the United States, when people who looked "foreign" became targets for displaced anger and hostility.

At times, the development of prejudice (like other attitudes) can be traced to direct experiences with members of the rejected group. A child who is repeatedly bullied by members of a particular ethnic group might develop a lifelong dislike for all members of the group. Yet even subtle influences, such as parents' attitudes, the depiction of people in books and on TV, and exposure to children of other races can have an impact. By the time they are 3 years old, many children show signs of race bias (Katz, 2003). Sadly, once prejudices are established, they prevent us from accepting more positive experiences that could reverse the damage (Wilder, Simon, & Faith, 1996).

Distinguished psychologist Gordon Allport (1958) concluded that there are two important sources of prejudice. *Personal prejudice* occurs when members of another ethnic group are perceived as a threat to one's own interests. For example, members of another group may be viewed as competitors for jobs. *Group prejudice* occurs when a person conforms to group norms. Let's say, for instance, that you have no personal reason for disliking out-group members. Nevertheless, your friends, acquaintances, or co-workers expect it of you.

The Prejudiced Personality

Other research suggests that prejudice can be a general personality characteristic. Theodore Adorno and his associates (1950) carefully probed what they called the *authoritarian personality* (ah-thor-ih-TARE-ee-un). These researchers started out by studying anti-Semitism. In the process, they found that people who are prejudiced against one group tend to be prejudiced against *all* out-groups (Perreault & Bourhis, 1999).

What are the characteristics of the prejudice-prone personality? The **authoritarian personality** is marked by rigidity, inhibition, prejudice, and oversimplification (black-and-white thinking). Authoritarians also tend to highly value social conformity (Feldman, 2003) and hence to be very *ethnocentric.* **Ethnocentrism** refers to placing one's own group "at the center," usually by rejecting all other groups. Put more simply, authoritarians consider their own ethnic group superior to others. In fact, authoritarians think they are superior to everyone who is different, not just other ethnic groups (Altemeyer, 2004; Whitley, 1999).

In addition to rejecting out-groups, authoritarians are overwhelmingly concerned with power, authority, and obedience. To measure these qualities, the *F scale* was created (the *F* stands for "fascism"). This scale is made up of statements such as the ones that follow—to which authoritarians readily agree (Adorno et al., 1950).

Authoritarian Beliefs
- Obedience and respect for authority are the most important virtues children should learn.
- People can be divided into two distinct classes: the weak and the strong.
- If people would talk less and work more, everybody would be better off.
- What this country needs most, more than laws and political programs, is a few courageous, tireless, devoted leaders, in whom the people can put their faith.
- Nobody ever learns anything really important except through suffering.
- Every person should have complete faith in some supernatural power whose decisions are obeyed without question.
- Certain religious sects that refuse to salute the flag should be forced to conform to such patriotic action or else be abolished.

As you can see, authoritarians are rather close-minded (Butler, 2000). As children, authoritarians were usually severely punished. Most learned to fear authority (and to covet it) at an early age. Authoritarians are not happy people.

Even if we discount the obvious bigotry of the authoritarian personality, racial prejudice runs deep in many nations. Let's probe deeper into the roots of such prejudiced behavior.

Intergroup Conflict—The Roots of Prejudice

An unfortunate by-product of group membership is that it often limits contact with people in other groups. Additionally, groups themselves may come into conflict. Both events tend to foster hatred and prejudice toward the out-group. The bloody clash of opposing forces in Israel, Ireland, Iraq, Africa, and Hometown, U.S.A., are reminders that intergroup conflict is widespread. Daily, we read of jarring strife between political, religious, or ethnic groups.

Shared beliefs concerning *superiority, injustice, vulnerability,* and *distrust* are common triggers for hostility between groups. Pick almost any group in conflict with others and you will find people thinking along these lines: "We are special people who are superior to other groups, but we have been unjustly exploited, wronged, or humiliated [superiority and injustice]. Other groups are a threat to us [vulnerability]. They are dishonest and have repeatedly betrayed us [distrust]. Naturally, we are hostile toward them. They don't deserve our respect or cooperation" (Eidelson & Eidelson, 2003).

In addition to hostile beliefs about other groups, conflicts are almost always amplified by stereotyped images of out-group members (Bar-Tal & Labin, 2001).

What exactly is a stereotype? **Social stereotypes** are oversimplified images of people in various groups. There is a good chance that you have stereotyped images of some of the following: African Americans, European Americans, Hispanics, Jews, women, Christians, old people, men, Asian Americans, blue-collar workers, rednecks, politicians, business executives, teenagers, and billionaires. In general, the top three categories on which most stereotypes are based are sex, age, and race (Fiske, 1993; Fiske et al., 2002).

Stereotypes tend to simplify people into "us" and "them" categories. Actually, aside from the fact that they always oversimplify, stereotypes often include a mixture of *positive* or

Ethnic pride is gradually replacing stereotypes and discrimination. For example, the African-American festival of Kwanzaa, a holiday celebrated late in December, emphasizes commitment to family, community, and African culture. However, despite affirmations of ethnic heritage, the problem of prejudice is far from solved.

Prejudice A negative emotional attitude held against members of a particular group of people.

Discrimination Treating members of various social groups differently in circumstances where their rights or treatment should be identical.

Authoritarian personality A personality pattern characterized by rigidity, inhibition, prejudice, and an excessive concern with power, authority, and obedience.

Ethnocentrism Placing one's own group or race at the center—that is, tending to reject all other groups but one's own.

Social stereotypes Oversimplified images of the traits of individuals who belong to a particular social group.

● **FIGURE 15.10** Racial stereotypes are common in sports. For example, a study confirmed that many people actually do believe that "white men can't jump." This stereotype implies that black basketball players are naturally superior in athletic ability. White players, in contrast, are falsely perceived as smarter and harder working than black players. Such stereotypes set up expectations that distort the perceptions of fans, coaches, and sportswriters. The resulting misperceptions, in turn, help perpetuate the stereotypes (Stone, Perry, & Darley, 1997).

negative qualities (Fiske et al., 2002) (● Fig. 15.10). ■ Table 15.4 shows stereotyped images of various national and ethnic groups and their changes over a 34-year period. Notice that many of the qualities listed are desirable. Note too, that although the overall trend was a decrease in negative stereotypes, belief in the existence of some negative traits increased.

Even though stereotypes sometimes include positive traits, they are mainly used to control people. When a person is stereotyped, the easiest thing to do is to abide by others' expectations—even if they are demeaning. That's why no one likes to be stereotyped. Being forced into a small, distorted social "box" is limiting and insulting. Stereotypes rob people of their individuality (Maddox, 2004). Without stereotypes there would be far less hate, prejudice, exclusion, and conflict. (For a discussion of extreme stereotyping, see "Terrorists, Enemies, and Infidels.")

When a prejudiced person meets a pleasant or likable member of a rejected group, the out-group member tends to be perceived as "an exception to the rule," not as evidence against the stereotype. This prevents prejudiced persons from changing their stereotyped beliefs (Wilder, Simon, & Faith, 1996). In addition, some elements of prejudice are unconscious, which makes them difficult to change (Dovido et al., 2002).

■ **TABLE 15.4** University Students' Characterization of Ethnic Groups, 1933 and 1967

Trait	PERCENT CHECKING TRAIT 1933	1967	Trait	PERCENT CHECKING TRAIT 1933	1967	Trait	PERCENT CHECKING TRAIT 1933	1967
	Americans			**Italians**			**Jews**	
Industrious	48	23	Artistic	53	30	Shrewd	79	30
Intelligent	47	20	Impulsive	44	28	Mercenary	49	15
Materialistic	33	67	Musical	32	9	Grasping	34	17
Progressive	27	17	Imaginative	30	7	Intelligent	29	37
	Germans			**Irish**			**Blacks**	
Scientific	78	47	Pugnacious	45	13	Superstitious	84	13
Stolid	44	9	Witty	38	7	Lazy	75	26
Methodical	31	21	Honest	32	17	Ignorant	38	11
Efficient	16	46	Nationalistic	21	41	Religious	24	8

Source: M. Karlins, T. L. Coffman, and G. Walters, "On the fading of social stereotypes. Studies in three generations of college students," *Journal of Personality and Social Psychology* 13 (1969):116. Reprinted with permission of the American Psychological Association.

CRITICAL THINKING

Terrorists, Enemies, and Infidels

During times of war, normal people are called upon to kill other humans. How do they turn off their emotions and moral standards? Actually, they don't. Instead, they convince themselves that their actions are just. For example, violence may be seen as necessary to eradicate evil; to serve God; or to protect honor, virtue, justice, or freedom.

Whether it's Catholics and Protestants in Northern Ireland, Israelis and Palestinians, Serbs and Muslims in Bosnia, or al-Qaeda and the United States, each side believes that attack or counterattack is morally justified. And, whether they are right or wrong, both sides use the same psychological mechanisms to justify violence (Wilmot & Hocker, 2007). In violent conflicts between groups, "the enemy" is always portrayed as evil, monstrous, or less than human. Dehumanizing others makes it seem that they *deserve* hatred and even death. Undoubtedly, this provides a degree of emotional insulation that makes it easier for soldiers to harm other humans. However, it also makes terrorism, torture, murder, and genocide possible (Anderson & Bushman, 2002).

A danger in demonizing "the enemy" is that it can lead to misperceptions of the motives and actions of other nations or groups (Silverstein, 1989). Many of the bloodiest conflicts in history have been fueled, in part, by treating "the enemy" as evil and subhuman. Those who actually do hold the moral high ground must be careful not to succumb to the same kind of blind hatred that leads to wanton violence and terrorism. It is also wise to remember that ethnic jokes, racial stereotypes, degrading names, and out-group slurs are small-scale examples of the damage that "enemy" images can do.

Today's racism is often disguised by **symbolic prejudice.** That is, many people realize that crude and obvious racism is socially unacceptable. However, this may not stop them from expressing prejudice in thinly veiled forms when they state their opinions about affirmative action, busing, immigration, crime, and so on. In effect, modern racists find ways to rationalize their prejudice so that it seems to be based on issues other than raw racism. For instance, an African-American candidate and an European-American candidate apply for a job. Both are only moderately qualified for the position. If the person making the hiring decision is European-American, who gets the job? As you might guess, the European-American candidate is much more likely to be hired. In other words, the European-American candidate will be given "the benefit of the doubt" about his or her abilities, whereas the African-American candidate won't. People making such decisions often believe that they aren't being prejudiced, but they unconsciously discriminate against minorities (Dovido et al., 2002).

Two experiments, both in unlikely settings and both using children, offer some additional insights into how stereotypes and intergroup tensions develop.

Experiments in Prejudice

What is it like to be discriminated against? In a unique experiment, elementary school teacher Jane Elliot sought to give her pupils direct experience with prejudice. On the first day of the experiment, Elliot announced that brown-eyed children were to sit in the back of the room and that they could not use the drinking fountain. Blue-eyed children were given extra recess time and got to leave first for lunch. At lunch, brown-eyed children were prevented from taking second helpings because they would "just waste it." Brown-eyed and blue-eyed children were kept from mingling, and the blue-eyed children were told they were "cleaner" and "smarter" (Peters, 1971).

Eye color might seem like a trivial basis for creating prejudices. However, people primarily use skin color to make decisions about the race of another person (Brown, Dane, & Durham, 1998). Surely this is just as superficial a way of judging people as eye color is, especially given recent biological evidence that it does not even make genetic sense to talk about "races" (Bonham, Warshauer-Baker, & Collins, 2005). (See "Understand That Race Is a Social Construction" in Module 15.7.)

At first, Elliot made an effort to constantly criticize and belittle the brown-eyed children. To her surprise, the blue-eyed children rapidly joined in and were soon outdoing her in the viciousness of their attacks. The blue-eyed children began to feel superior, and the brown-eyed children felt just plain awful. Fights broke out. Test scores of the brown-eyed children fell.

How lasting were the effects of this experiment? The effects were short lived, because two days later the children's roles were reversed. Before long, the same destructive effects occurred again, but this time in reverse. The implications of this experiment are unmistakable. In less than one day it was possible to get children to hate each other because of eye color

Symbolic prejudice Prejudice that is expressed in disguised fashion.

CRITICAL THINKING

Is America Purple?

As research shows, it is easy to create prejudice. Pick any simplistic way to divide a group of people into "us" and "them" and popularize it. That's what teacher Jane Elliott did when she divided her class into the brown-eyed kids and the blue-eyed kids. In no time at all, the groups were prejudiced against each other.

But that was just an experiment. It couldn't happen in the real world, right? According to psychologists Conor Seyle and Matthew Newman (2006), we are witnessing just such a real-world example in America today. In order to graphically convey the outcome of the presidential vote in the 2000 election, *USA Today* created a state-by-state map, color coded red and blue to denote states that had voted for the Republican candidate or the Democratic candidate.

Just a few years later, "red" and "blue" have become a national shorthand for dividing Americans into opposing camps. The "reds" are supposed to be Republican, conservative, middle-class, rural, religious, and live in the American heartland. The "blues" are supposed to be Democrat, liberal, upper class, urban, nonreligious, and live on the coasts. The end result is that the complex American social world is reduced to two oversimplified stereotypes, leading to an increase in between-group prejudice (Mundy, 2004).

This oversimplification ignores the fact that, in many states, the presidential votes are very close. Thus, a state that is "red" by 51 percent is nevertheless 49 percent "blue." Besides, many different combinations exist. Former President Bill Clinton is originally from Arkansas (a "red" state), identifies himself as a Southern Baptist, and worships in a Methodist church. Is he "blue"? How do you categorize someone from California (a "blue" state) who is an economic conservative, attends church occasionally, lives in San Francisco, supports gay marriage, and yet votes Republican?

According to Seyle & Newman (2006), a better approach is to recognize that America is made up of a full spectrum of political, social, religious, and economic views and that most Americans are "purple." Thinking this way also highlights the fact that Americans of all political persuasions share more similarities than they do differences when compared with the citizens of other countries. This more tolerant, less polarizing view of America is reflected in the "purple America" map (● Fig. 15.11) (Gastner, Shalizi, & Newman, 2005). Thinking purple just might result in a more productive national discussion about the important issues facing America today.

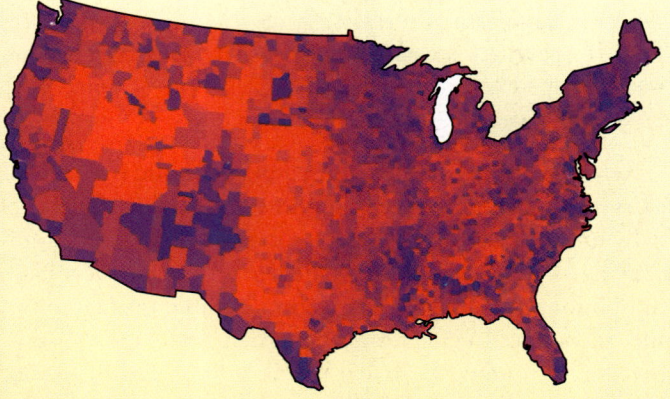

● **FIGURE 15.11** Purple America map. Counties within states voting more than 70 percent Republican appear in red; areas voting more than 70 percent Democratic appear in blue. Shades of purple represent intermediate percentages of voters. (Reprinted by permission of the authors, Michael Gastner, Cosma Shalizi, and Mark Newman, University of Michigan.)

and *status inequalities* (differences in power, prestige, or privileges). Certainly the effects of a lifetime of real racial or ethnic prejudice are infinitely more powerful and destructive (Clark et al., 1999). (See "Is America Purple?")

Equal-Status Contact *What can be done to combat prejudice?* Several lines of thought (including cognitive dissonance theory) suggest that more frequent *equal-status contact* between groups in conflict should reduce prejudice and stereotyping (Olson & Zanna, 1993; Wernet et al., 2003). *Equal-status contact* refers to interacting on an equal footing, without obvious differences in power or status. In various studies, mixed-race groups have been formed at work, in the laboratory, and at schools. The conclusion from such research is that personal contact with a disliked group tends to induce friendly behavior, respect, and liking. However, these benefits occur only when personal contact is cooperative and on an equal footing (Grack & Richman, 1996).

Superordinate Goals Let us now consider a revealing study done with 11-year-old boys. When the boys arrived at a summer camp, they were split into two groups and housed in separate cabins. At first the groups were kept apart to build up separate in-group identities and friendships. Soon each group had a flag and a name (the "Rattlers" and the "Eagles") and each had staked out its territory. At this point the two groups were placed in competition with each other. After a number of clashes, disliking between the groups bordered on hatred: The boys baited each other, started fights, and raided each other's cabins (Sherif et al., 1961).

Were they allowed to go home hating each other? As an experiment in reducing intergroup conflict, and to prevent the boys from remaining enemies, various strategies to reduce tensions were tried. Holding meetings between group leaders did nothing. When the groups were invited to eat together, the event turned into a free-for-all. Finally, emergencies that required *cooperation* among members of both groups were

Module 15.5 • PREJUDICE AND INTERGROUP CONFLICT

Many school districts in the United States have begun requiring students to wear uniforms. Appearance (including gang colors) is one of the major reasons why kids treat each other differently. Uniforms help minimize status inequalities and in-group/out-group distinctions. In Long Beach, California, a switch to uniforms was followed by a 91 percent drop in student assaults, thefts, vandalism, and weapons and drug violations (Ritter, 1998).

staged at the camp. For example, the water supply was damaged so that all the boys had to work together to repair it. Creating this and other *superordinate goals* helped restore peace between the two groups. (A **superordinate goal** exceeds or overrides other lesser goals.)

Cooperation and shared goals seem to help reduce conflict by encouraging people in opposing groups to see themselves as members of a single, larger group (Gaertner et al., 2000). Superordinate goals, in other words, have a "we're all in the same boat" effect on perceptions of group membership (Olson & Zanna, 1993). The power of superordinate goals can be seen in the unity that prevailed in the United States (and throughout much of the rest of the world) for months after the September 11 terrorist attacks. Superordinate goals are also an important factor in helping peacekeepers constructively engage with people from other nationalities (Boniecki & Britt, 2003).

Can such goals exist on a global scale? One example might be a desire to avoid nuclear holocaust. Another that comes to mind is the need to preserve the natural environment on a global scale. Still another is the continuing threat posed by terrorism and religious extremism. Politically, such goals may be far from universal. But their superordinate quality is clearly evident.

"Jigsaw" Classrooms Contrary to the hopes of many, integrating public schools often has little positive effect on racial prejudice. In fact, prejudice may be made worse, and the self-esteem of minority students frequently decreases (Aronson, 2008).

If integrated schools provide equal-status contact, shouldn't prejudice be reduced? Theoretically, yes. But in practice, minority group children often enter schools unprepared to compete on an equal footing. The competitive nature of schools almost guarantees that children will *not* learn to like and understand each other.

With the preceding in mind, social psychologist Elliot Aronson pioneered a way to apply superordinate goals to ordinary classrooms. According to Aronson, such goals are effective because they create **mutual interdependence.** That is, people must depend on one another to meet each person's goals. When individual needs are linked, cooperation is encouraged (Deutsch, 1993).

How has that idea been applied? Aronson has successfully created "jigsaw" classrooms that emphasize cooperation rather than competition. The term *jigsaw* refers to the pieces of a jigsaw puzzle. In a **jigsaw classroom,** each child is given a "piece" of the information needed to complete a project or prepare for a test.

In a typical session, children are divided into groups of five or six and given a topic to study for a later exam. Each child is given his or her "piece" of information and asked to

In a "jigsaw" classroom, children help each other prepare for tests. As they teach each other on what they know, the children learn to cooperate and to respect the unique strengths of each individual.

Superordinate goal A goal that exceeds or overrides all others; a goal that renders other goals relatively less important.
Mutual interdependence A condition in which people must depend on one another to meet each person's needs or goals.
Jigsaw classroom A method of reducing prejudice; each student receives only part of the information needed to complete a project or prepare for a test.

learn it. For example, one child might have information on Thomas Edison's invention of the lightbulb; another, facts about his invention of the long-playing phonograph record; and a third, information about Edison's childhood. After the children have learned their parts, they teach them to others in the group. Even the most competitive children quickly realize that they cannot do well without the aid of everyone in the group. Each child makes a unique and essential contribution, so the children learn to listen to and respect each other.

Does the jigsaw method work? Compared with children in traditional classrooms, children in jigsaw groups are less prejudiced, they like their classmates more, they have more positive attitudes toward school, their grades improve, and their self-esteem increases (Aronson, 2008; Walker & Crogan, 1998). Such results are quite encouraging. As distinguished African-American psychologist Kenneth Clark said, "Racial prejudice . . . debases all human beings—those who are its victims, those who victimize, and in quite subtle ways, those who are merely accessories."

To summarize, prejudice will be reduced when:

- Members of different groups have equal status *within the situation* that brings them together.
- Members of all groups seek a common goal.
- Group members must cooperate to reach the goal.
- Group members spend enough time together for cross-group friendships to develop (Pettigrew, 1998).

Sports teams are an excellent example of a situation in which all these conditions apply. The close contact and interdependent effort required in team sports often create lifelong friendships and break down the walls of prejudice.

MODULE 15.5 Summary

What causes prejudice and intergroup conflict?
- Prejudice is a negative attitude held toward members of various out-groups.
- One theory attributes prejudice to scapegoating.
- Prejudices may be held for personal reasons (personal prejudice) or simply through adherence to group norms (group prejudice).
- Prejudiced individuals tend to have an authoritarian personality.
- Intergroup conflict gives rise to hostility and the formation of social stereotypes.
- Status inequalities tend to build prejudice.
- Equal-status contact, mutual interdependence, and superordinate goals tend to reduce prejudice.
- On a smaller scale, jigsaw classrooms have been shown to combat prejudice.

KNOWLEDGE BUILDER

Prejudice and Intergroup Conflict

Recite

1. Some expressions of prejudice can be thought of as scapegoating or
   a. displaced aggression
   b. empathic arousal
   c. reference group reversal
   d. external attribution

2. The authoritarian personality tends to be prejudiced against all out-groups, a quality referred to as _____.

3. The stereotypes underlying racial and ethnic prejudice tend to evolve from the superordinate goals that often separate groups. T or F?

4. The term *symbolic prejudice* refers to racism or prejudice that is expressed in disguised or hidden form. T or F?

5. One of the reasons that superordinate goals tend to reduce prejudice is that they require cooperation and
   a. social stereotyping
   b. ethnocentrism
   c. unfreezing
   d. equal-status contact

6. Jigsaw classrooms use _____ to create mutual interdependence.
   a. social competition
   b. just-world beliefs
   c. self-fulfilling prophecies
   d. superordinate goals

Reflect
Critical Thinking

7. In court trials, defense lawyers sometimes try to identify and eliminate prospective jurors who have authoritarian personality traits. Can you guess why?

Relate

Mentally scan over the events of the last week. How would they have changed if prejudices of all types ceased to exist?

Think of the most rigid person you know. Does he or she match the profile of the authoritarian personality?

Stereotypes exist for many social categories, even ordinary ones such as "college student" or "unmarried young adult." What stereotypes do you think you face in daily life?

The director of a youth recreation center is concerned about the amount of conflict she is seeing between boys and girls from different racial and ethnic groups. What advice can you give the director?

Link

Internet addresses frequently change. To find the sites listed here, visit **http://www.thomsonedu.com/psychology/coon** for an updated list of Internet addresses and direct links to relevant sites.

- **Understanding Prejudice** Explore different activities that illuminate the causes and consequences of prejudice.
- **Authoritarian Personality** Take the F scale test.
- **Intergroup Conflict** Read an article on intergroup conflict.

ANSWERS

1. a 2. ethnocentrism 3. F 4. T 5. d 6. d 7. Because authoritarians tend to believe that punishment is effective, they are more likely to vote for conviction.

MODULE 15.6 Aggression and Prosocial Behavior

AGGRESSION IS A HUMAN TRAGEDY. Helping others is a source of hope. It might seem that the horrors of war would lead to a worldwide revulsion for killing. In reality, homicide rates have increased in many countries in recent years. What causes aggression? Can violence be reduced? Can we promote prosocial behavior? More than ever, these are pressing questions.

Aggression—The World's Most Dangerous Animal

SURVEY QUESTION: *How do psychologists explain human aggression?*

> *"I know not with what weapons World War III will be fought, but World War IV will be fought with sticks and stones."*—Albert Einstein

For a time, the City Zoo of Los Angeles, California, had on display two examples of the world's most dangerous animal—the only animal capable of destroying the Earth and all other animal species. Perhaps you have already guessed which animal it was. In the cage were two college students, representing the species *Homo sapiens!*

The human capacity for aggression is staggering. It has been estimated that 58 million humans were killed by other humans (an average of nearly one person per minute) during the 125-year period ending with World War II. War, homicide, riots, family violence, assassination, rape, assault, forcible robbery, and other violent acts offer sad testimony to the realities of human aggression.

What causes aggression? **Aggression** refers to any action carried out with the intention of harming another person. Aggression has many potential causes. Brief descriptions of some of the major possibilities follow.

Instincts

Some theorists argue that we are naturally aggressive creatures, having inherited a "killer instinct" from our animal ancestors. Ethologists theorize that aggression is a biologically rooted behavior observed in all animals, including humans (Blanchard & Blanchard, 2003). (An *ethologist* is a person who studies the natural behavior patterns of animals.) Noted ethologist Konrad Lorenz (1966, 1974) also believed that humans lack certain innate patterns that inhibit aggression in animals. For example, in a dispute over territory, two wolves may growl, lunge, bare their teeth, and fiercely threaten each other. In most instances, though, neither is killed or even wounded. One wolf, recognizing the dominance of the other, will typically bare its throat in a gesture of submission. The dominant wolf could kill in an instant, but it is inhibited by the other wolf's submissive gesture. In contrast, human confrontations of equal intensity almost always end in injury or death.

The idea that humans are "naturally" aggressive has an intuitive appeal, but many psychologists question it. Many of Lorenz's "explanations" of aggression are little more than loose comparisons between human and animal behavior. Just labeling a behavior as "instinctive" does little to explain it. More important, we are left with the question of why some individuals or human groups (the Arapesh, the Senoi, the Navajo, the Eskimo, and others) show little hostility or aggression. And, thankfully, the vast majority of humans *do not* kill or harm others.

Biology

Despite problems with the instinctive view, aggression may have biological roots. Physiological studies have shown that some brain areas are capable of triggering or ending aggressive behavior. Also, researchers have found a relationship between aggression and such physical factors as hypoglycemia (low blood sugar), allergy, and specific brain injuries and diseases. For both men and women, higher levels of the hor-

Ritualized human aggression. Violent and aggressive behavior is so commonplace it may be viewed as entertainment. How "natural" is aggressive behavior?

mone testosterone may be associated with more aggressive behavior (Banks & Dabbs, 1996; Harris et al., 1996). Perhaps because of their higher testosterone levels, men are more likely to engage in physical aggression than women (Anderson & Bushman, 2002). However, none of these biological factors can be considered a direct *cause* of aggression (Moore, 2001; Popma et al., 2007). Instead, they probably lower the threshold for aggression, making hostile behavior more likely to occur.

The effects of alcohol and other drugs provide another indication of the role of the brain and biology in violence and aggression. A variety of studies show that alcohol is involved in large percentages of murders and violent crimes. Intoxicating drugs also seem to lower inhibitions to act aggressively—often with tragic results (Anderson & Bushman, 2002; Quigley & Leonard, 2000).

To summarize, the fact that we are biologically *capable* of aggression does not mean that aggression is inevitable or "part of human nature." Twenty eminent scientists who studied the question concluded that "Biology does not condemn humanity to war. . . . Violence is neither in our evolutionary legacy nor in our genes. The same species that invented war is capable of inventing peace" (Scott & Ginsburg, 1994; UNESCO, 1990). Humans are fully capable of learning to inhibit aggression. For example, American Quakers and Amish, who live in this country's increasingly violent culture, adopt nonviolence as a way of life (Bandura, 2001).

Frustration

Step on a cat's tail and you may get nipped. Frustrate a human and you may get insulted. The **frustration-aggression hypothesis** states that frustration tends to lead to aggression.

Does frustration always produce aggression? Although the connection is strong, a moment's thought will show that frustration does not *always* lead to aggression. Frustration, for instance, may lead to stereotyped responding or perhaps to a state of "learned helplessness." (See Modules 11.2 and 11.3.) Also, aggression can occur in the absence of frustration. This possibility is illustrated by sports spectators who start fights, throw bottles, and tear down goal posts after their team has *won*.

Aversive Stimuli Frustration probably encourages aggression because it is uncomfortable. Various *aversive stimuli,* which produce discomfort or displeasure, can heighten hostility and aggression (Anderson, Anderson, & Deuser, 1996; Morgan, 2005). (See • Fig. 15.12.) Examples include insults, high

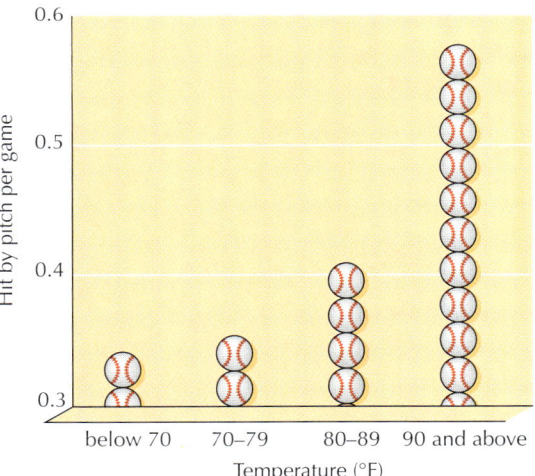

● **FIGURE 15.12** Personal discomfort caused by aversive (unpleasant) stimuli can make aggressive behavior more likely. For example, studies of crime rates show that the incidence of highly aggressive behavior, such as murder, rape, and assault, rises as the air temperature goes from warm to hot to sweltering (Anderson, 1989). The results you see here further confirm the heat-aggression link. The graph shows that there is a strong association between the temperatures at major league baseball games and the number of batters hit by a pitch during those games. When the temperature goes over 90°, watch out for that fastball (Reifman, Larrick, & Fein, 1991)!

Aggression Any action carried out with the intention of harming another person.
Frustration-aggression hypothesis States that frustration tends to lead to aggression.

Road rage and some freeway shootings may be a reaction to the stress and frustration of traffic congestion. The fact that automobiles provide anonymity, or a loss of personal identity, may also encourage aggressive actions that would not otherwise occur.

temperatures, pain, and even disgusting scenes or odors. Such stimuli probably raise overall arousal levels so that we become more sensitive to *aggression cues* (signals that are associated with aggression) (Carlson, Marcus-Newhall, & Miller, 1990). Aversive stimuli also tend to activate ideas, memories, and expressions associated with anger and aggression (Morgan, 2005).

Some cues for aggression are internal (angry thoughts, for instance). Many are external: Certain words, actions, and gestures made by others are strongly associated with aggressive responses. A raised middle finger, for instance, is an almost universal invitation to aggression in North America. Weapons serve as particularly strong cues for aggressive behavior (Morgan, 2005). The implication of this *weapons effect* seems to be that the symbols and trappings of aggression encourage aggression. A prime example is the fact that murders are almost 3 times more likely to occur in homes where guns are kept. Nearly 80 percent of the victims in such homes are killed by a family member or acquaintance (Kellermann et al., 1993).

Social Learning

One of the most widely accepted explanations of aggression is also the simplest. Social learning theory holds that we learn to be aggressive by observing aggression in others (Bandura, 1973). **Social learning theory** combines learning principles with cognitive processes, socialization, and modeling to explain behavior. According to this view, there is no instinctive human programming for fistfighting, pipe bombing, knife wielding, gun loading, 95-mile-an-hour "bean balls," or other violent or aggressive behaviors. Hence, aggression must be learned (● Fig. 15.13). Is it any wonder that people who were the victims of violence during childhood are likely to become violent themselves (Macmillan, 2001)?

Aggressive Models Social learning theorists predict that people growing up in nonaggressive cultures will themselves be nonaggressive. Those raised in a culture with aggressive models and heroes will learn aggressive responses (Bandura, 2001). Considered in such terms, it is no wonder that America has become one of the most violent of all countries. A violent crime occurred every 23 seconds in the United States during 2005 (FBI, 2005). Approximately 40 percent of the population owns firearms. Nationally, 70 percent agree that "When a boy is growing up, it is very important for him to have a few fistfights." Children and adults are treated to an almost nonstop parade of aggressive models, in the media as well as in actual behavior. We are, without a doubt, an aggressive culture.

Media Violence Every day, mainstream media provide an endless stream of bad models, especially concerning violence. TV, movies, computer games, and even music lyrics all contain violence. According to the organization Adults and Children Against Violence Together, young children spend about 35 hours a week in front of TV or computer screens. By the end of elementary school, children will have seen about 8,000 murders and 100,000 other violent acts depicted on TV. Eighty percent of popular video games contain violent content. Many popular toys are also linked to violent media (ACT Against Violence, 2005a). And, of course, teenagers and young people are also chronically exposed to violence in the media.

How much does media violence affect children? As Albert Bandura showed in his studies of imitation (see Module 6.5), children may learn new aggressive actions by watching violent or aggressive behavior, or they may learn that violence is "okay." Either way, they are more likely to act aggressively. Heroes on TV are as violent as the villains, and they usually receive praise for their violence. There is now little doubt that widespread exposure to media violence contributes to aggression (Anderson et al., 2003; DeGaetano, 2005). Boys and girls who watch a lot of violence on TV are much more likely to be aggressive as adults (Huesmann et al., 2003). Violent video games are at least as problematic (Bartholow, Bushman, & Sestir, 2006), and even violent song lyrics increase aggressive tendencies (Anderson, Carnagey, & Eubanks, 2003).

In addition to teaching new antisocial actions, media such as TV and video games may disinhibit dangerous impulses that viewers already have. *Disinhibition* (the removal of inhibition) results in acting out behavior that normally would be restrained. For example, many TV programs give the message that violence is acceptable behavior that leads to success and popularity. For some people, this message can lower inhibitions against acting out hostile feelings (Anderson et al., 2003).

Another effect of media violence is that it tends to lower sensitivity to violent acts (Funk, 2005). As anyone who has seen a street fight or a mugging can tell you, TV violence is sanitized and unrealistic. The real thing is gross, ugly, and gut

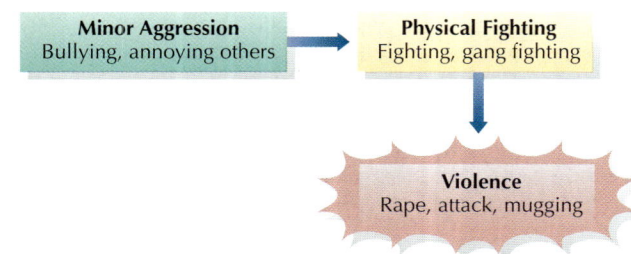

● **FIGURE 15.13** Violent behavior among delinquent boys doesn't appear overnight. Usually, their capacity for violence develops slowly as they move from minor aggression to increasingly brutal acts. Overall aggression increases dramatically in early adolescence as boys gain physical strength and more access to weapons (Loeber & Hay, 1997).

wrenching. Even when media violence is graphic, as it is in many video games, it is experienced in the relaxed and familiar setting of the home. For at least some viewers, this combination diminishes emotional reactions to violent scenes. More than 30 years ago, when Victor Cline and his associates showed a bloody fight film to a group of boys, they found that heavy TV viewers (averaging 42 hours a week) showed much less emotion than those who watched little or no TV (Cline, Croft, & Courrier, 1972). Media, it seems, can cause a *desensitization* (reduced emotional sensitivity) to violence (Huesmann et al., 2003).

Preventing Aggression

What can be done about aggression? Social learning theory implies that "aggression begets aggression." For example, children who are physically abused at home, those who suffer severe physical punishment, and those who merely witness violence in the community are more likely to be involved in fighting, aggressive play, and antisocial behavior at school (Bartholow, Sestir, & Davis, 2005; Margolin & Gordis, 2000).

According to social learning theorists, watching a prizefight, sporting event, or violent TV program may increase aggression, rather than drain off aggressive urges. A case in point is provided by psychologist Leonard Eron, who spent 22 years following more than 600 children into adulthood. Eron (1987) observes, "Among the most influential models for children were those observed on television. One of the best predictors of how aggressive a young man would be at age 19 was the violence of the television programs he preferred when he was 8 years old" (● Fig. 15.14). According to Eron, children learn aggressive strategies and actions from TV violence. Because of this, they are more prone to aggress when they face frustrating situations or cues. Others have found that viewers who experience violent media have more aggressive thoughts. As we have noted, violent thoughts often precede violent actions (Anderson, Carnagey, & Eubanks, 2003). Thus, the spiral of aggression might be broken if we did not so often portray it, reward it, and glorify it (Hughes & Hasbrouck, 1996).

Parents as TV Guides As the preceding studies show, reducing exposure to violent media is one way to lower aggression. However, other than pulling the plug, what can parents do about media's negative effects on children? Actually, quite a lot. Parents can make a big difference if they do the following (ACT Against Violence, 2005b; Frydman, 1999).

1. Start by creating a safe, warm environment at home and school and by modeling positive ways of getting along in the world. Children typically model parents' behavior, including their media viewing habits, and they are guided by parents' reactions to media.
2. Limit total media time so that TV and computer games do not dominate your child's view of the world. If necessary, set schedules for when watching TV or playing video games is allowed. Don't use media as a babysitter.
3. Closely monitor what your child does experience. Change channels or turn off the TV if you object to a program. Be prepared to offer games and activities that stimulate your child's imagination and creativity.
4. Actively seek media your child will enjoy, especially those that model positive behavior and social attitudes.
5. Explore media with your child so that you can counter what is shown. Help your child distinguish between reality and fantasy in media. Reply to distortions and stereotypes as they appear on screen.
6. Discuss the social conflicts and violent solutions shown in media. Ask your child in what ways the situations are unrealistic and why the violence shown would not work in the real world. Encourage the child to propose more mature, realistic, and positive responses to situations.
7. Show by your own disapproval that violent TV and computer game heroes are not the ones to emulate. Remember, children who identify with media characters are more likely to be influenced by media aggression.

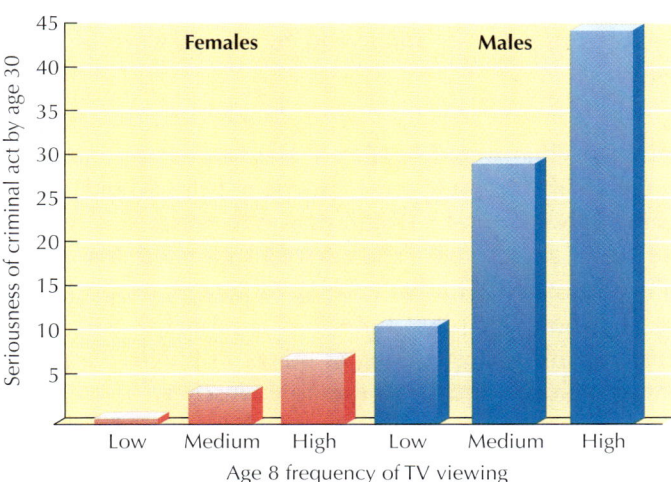

● **FIGURE 15.14** Although TV violence does not cause aggression, it can encourage it. The likelihood of committing criminal acts by age 30 is related to the amount of TV watching a person did when she or he was a child (Eron, 1987). (Graph © 1987 by the American Psychological Association, Inc. Reprinted by permission of the author.)

Social learning theory Combines learning principles with cognitive processes, socialization, and modeling to explain behavior.

By following these guidelines you can help children learn to enjoy television and other media without being overly influenced by programs and advertisers. One study found that elementary school children become less aggressive when they decrease the amount of time they spend watching TV and playing video games (Robinson et al., 2001).

Beyond this, the question remains, how shall we tame the world's most dangerous animal? There is no easy answer, only a challenge of pressing importance (Lench, 2004). For the immediate future, it is clear that we need more people who are willing to engage in helpful, altruistic, **prosocial behavior** (actions that are constructive, altruistic, or helpful to others). In the next section we will examine some of the forces that prevent people from helping others and how prosocial behavior might be promoted.

Prosocial Behavior—Helping Others

SURVEY QUESTION: *Why are bystanders so often unwilling to help in an emergency?*

Late one night in 1964, tenants of a Queens, New York, apartment building watched and listened in horror as a young woman named Kitty Genovese was murdered on the sidewalk outside. From the safety of their rooms, no fewer than 38 people heard the agonized screams as her assailant stabbed her, was frightened off, and returned to stab her again.

Kitty Genovese's murder took more than 30 minutes, but none of her neighbors tried to help. None even called the police until after the attack had ended. Perhaps it is understandable that no one wanted to get involved. After all, it could have been a violent lovers' quarrel. Or helping might have meant risking personal injury. But what prevented these people from at least calling the police?

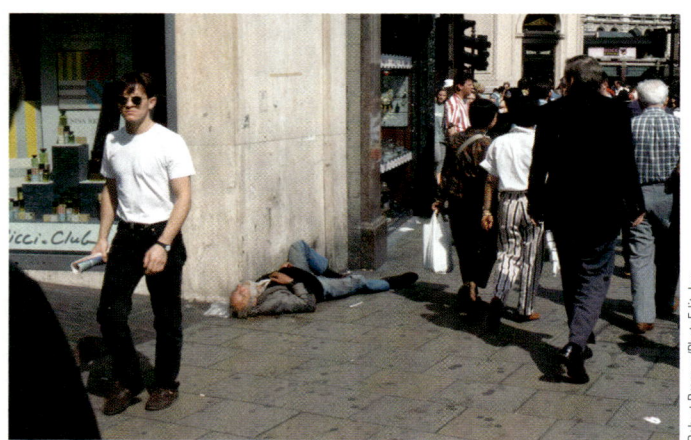
Does the person lying on the ground need help? What factors determine whether a person in trouble will receive help in an emergency? Surprisingly, more potential helpers tend to lower the chances that help will be given.

Isn't this an example of the alienation of city life? News reports treated this incident as evidence of a breakdown in social ties caused by the impersonality of the city. Although it is true that urban living can be dehumanizing, this does not fully explain such *bystander apathy* (the unwillingness of bystanders to offer help during emergencies is also referred to as the *bystander effect*). According to landmark work by psychologists John Darley and Bibb Latané (1968), failure to help is related to the number of people present. Over the years many studies have shown that the *more* potential helpers present, the *less* likely people are to help (Latané, Nida, & Wilson, 1981; Miller, 2006).

Why would people be less willing to help when others are present? In Kitty Genovese's case, the answer is that everyone thought *someone else* would help. The dynamics of this effect are easily illustrated: Suppose that two motorists have stalled at roadside, one on a sparsely traveled country road and the other on a busy freeway. Who gets help first?

On the freeway, where hundreds of cars pass every minute, each driver can assume that someone else will help. Personal responsibility for helping is spread so thin that no one takes action. On the country road, one of the first few people to arrive will probably stop, because the responsibility is clearly theirs. In general, Darley and Latané assume that bystanders are not apathetic or uncaring; they are inhibited by the presence of others.

Bystander Intervention

People must pass through four decision points before giving help. First they must notice that something is happening. Next they must define the event as an emergency. Then they must take responsibility. Finally, they must select a course of action (● Fig. 15.15). Laboratory experiments have shown that each step can be influenced by the presence of other people.

Noticing What would happen if you fainted and collapsed on the sidewalk? Would someone stop to help? Would people think you were drunk? Would they even notice you? Darley and Latané suggest that if the sidewalk is crowded, few people will even see you. This has nothing to do with people blocking one another's vision. Instead, it is related to widely accepted norms against staring at others in public. People in crowds typically "keep their eyes to themselves."

Is there any way to show that this is a factor in bystander apathy? To test this idea, students were asked to fill out a questionnaire either alone or in a room full of people. While the students worked, a thick cloud of smoke was blown into the room through a vent.

Most students left alone in the room noticed the smoke immediately. Few of the people in groups noticed the smoke

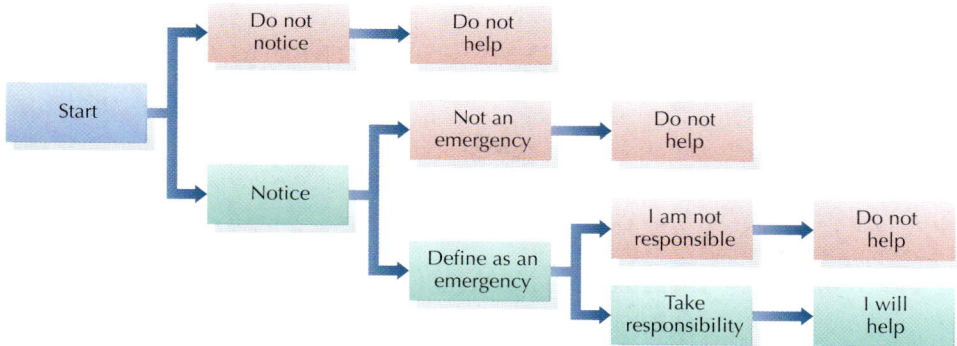

FIGURE 15.15 This decision tree summarizes the steps a person must take before making a commitment to offer help, according to Latané and Darley's model.

until it actually became difficult to see through it. Subjects working in groups politely kept their eyes on their papers and avoided looking at others (or the smoke). In contrast, those who were alone scanned the room from time to time.

Defining an Emergency The smoke-filled room also shows the influence others have on defining a situation as an emergency. When subjects in groups finally noticed the smoke, they cast sidelong glances at others in the room. Apparently, they were searching for clues to help interpret what was happening. No one wanted to overreact or act like a fool if there was no emergency. However, as subjects coolly surveyed the reactions of others, they were themselves being watched. In real emergencies, people sometimes "fake each other out" and underestimate the need for action because each person attempts to appear calm. In short, until someone acts, no one acts.

Taking Responsibility Perhaps the most crucial step in helping is assuming responsibility. In this case, groups limit helping by causing a *diffusion of responsibility* (spreading responsibility among several people).

Is that like the unwillingness of drivers to offer help on a crowded freeway? Exactly. It is the feeling that no one is personally responsible for helping. This problem was demonstrated in an experiment in which students took part in a group discussion over an intercom system. Actually, there was only one real subject in each group; the others were tape-recorded actors. Each subject was placed in a separate room (supposedly to maintain confidentiality), and discussions of college life were begun. During the discussion, one of the "students" simulated an epileptic-like seizure and called out for help. In some cases, subjects thought they were alone with the seizure victim. Others believed they were members of three- or six-person groups.

Subjects who thought they were alone with the "victim" of this staged emergency reported it immediately or tried to help. Some subjects in the three-person groups failed to respond, and those who did were slower. In the six-person groups, more than a third of the subjects took no action at all. People in this experiment were obviously faced with a conflict like that in many real emergencies: Should they be helpful and responsible, or should they mind their own business? Many were influenced toward inaction by the presence of others.

People do help in some emergencies. How are these different? It is not always clear what makes the difference. Helping behavior is complex and influenced by many variables. One naturalistic experiment staged in a New York City subway gives a hint of the kinds of things that may be important. When a "victim" (actor) "passed out" in a subway car, he received more help when carrying a cane than when carrying a liquor bottle. More important, however, was the fact that most people were willing to help in either case (Piliavin, Rodin, & Piliavin, 1969).

To better answer the question, we need to consider some factors not included in Darley and Latané's account of helping.

Who Will Help Whom?

Many studies suggest that when we see a person in trouble, it tends to cause *heightened arousal* (Dovidio et al., 2006). This aroused, keyed-up feeling can motivate us to give aid, but only if the rewards of helping outweigh the costs. Higher costs (such as great effort, personal risk, or possible embarrassment) almost always decrease helping. In addition to general arousal, potential helpers may also feel **empathic arousal.** This means they empathize with the person in need or feel some of the person's pain, fear, or anguish. Helping is much more likely when we are able to take the perspective of others and feel sympathy for their plight (Batson & Powell, 2003).

Empathic arousal is especially likely to motivate helping when the person in need seems to be similar to ourselves

Prosocial behavior Behavior toward others that is helpful, constructive, or altruistic.

Empathic arousal Emotional arousal that occurs when you feel some of another person's pain, fear, or anguish.

(Batson & Powell, 2003). In fact, a feeling of connection to the victim may be one of the most important factors in helping. This, perhaps, is why being in a good mood also increases helping. When we are feeling successful, happy, or fortunate, we may also feel more connected to others (Dovidio & Penner, 2001). In summary, there is a strong **empathy-helping relationship:** We are most likely to help someone in need when we "feel for" that person and experience emotions such as empathy, sympathy, and compassion (Batson, 2006).

Is there anything that can be done to encourage prosocial behavior? People who see others helping are more likely to offer help themselves. Also, persons who give help in one situation tend to perceive themselves as helpful people. This change in self-image encourages them to help in other situations. One more point is that norms of fairness encourage us to help others who have helped us (Dovidio & Penner, 2001). For all these reasons, helping others not only assists them directly, it encourages others to help too.

"De-victimize" Yourself If you should find yourself in need of help during an emergency, what can you do to avoid being a victim of bystander apathy? The work we have reviewed here suggests that you should make sure that you are noticed, that people realize there's an emergency, and that they need to take action. Being noticed can be promoted in some situations by shouting "Fire!" Bystanders who might run away from a robbery or an assault may rush to see where the fire is. At the very least, remember not to just scream. Instead, you should call out "Help" or "I need help right now." Whenever possible, define your situation for bystanders. Say, for instance, "I'm being attacked, call the police." Or, "Stop that man, he has my purse." You can also directly assign responsibility to a bystander by pointing to someone and saying, "You, call the police" or "I'm injured, I need you to call an ambulance" (Cummins, 1995).

Positive Psychology: Everyday Heroes

Every year awards are given to people who risk their lives while saving the lives of others. These heroes are typically honored for saving people from fires, drowning, animal attacks, electrocution, and suffocation. The majority of people who perform such heroic acts are men, perhaps because of the physical dangers involved. However, there are other heroic, prosocial acts that save lives and involve personal risk. Examples are kidney donors, Peace Corp volunteers, and Doctors of the World volunteers. In such endeavors, we find as many women as men, and often more. It is important to remember, perhaps, that sensational and highly visible acts of heroism are only one of many ways in which people engage in selfless, altruistic behavior (Becker & Eagly, 2004). People who serve as community volunteers, tutors, coaches, blood donors, and the like don't just help others. Often, their efforts contribute to personal growth and make them healthier and happier. Thus, it can be said that "We do well by doing good" (Piliavin, 2003).

A Look Ahead The "Psychology in Action" module of this chapter returns to the topic of prejudice for some further thoughts about how to promote tolerance. Don't miss this interesting conclusion to our discussion of social psychology.

MODULE 15.6 Summary

How do psychologists explain human aggression?
- Aggression is a fact of life, but humans are not inevitably aggressive. The same factors that help explain aggression can form the basis for preventing it.
- Ethological explanations of aggression attribute it to inherited instincts.
- Biological explanations of aggression emphasize brain mechanisms and physical factors that lower the threshold for aggression.
- According to the frustration-aggression hypothesis, frustration and aggression are closely linked.
- Frustration is only one of many aversive stimuli that can arouse a person and make aggression more likely.
- Aggression is especially likely to occur when aggression cues are present.
- Social learning theory has focused attention on the role of aggressive models in the development of aggressive behavior.

Why are bystanders so often unwilling to help in an emergency?
- Four decision points must be passed before a person gives help: noticing, defining an emergency, taking responsibility, and selecting a course of action.
- Helping is encouraged by general arousal, empathic arousal, being in a good mood, low effort or risk, and perceived similarity between the victim and the helper.
- Prosocial behavior is most likely to occur when people feel sympathy or empathy for a person in need.
- For several reasons, giving help tends to encourage others to help, too.

KNOWLEDGE BUILDER

Aggression and Prosocial Behavior

Recite

1. The position of ethologists is that there is no biological basis for aggression. T or F?
2. Higher levels of testosterone are associated with more aggressive behavior. T or F?
3. The *weapons effect* refers to the impact that _____ have on behavior.
   a. just-world beliefs
   b. aggression cues
   c. self-fulfilling prophecies
   d. televised models
4. The point of view most at odds with the idea that humans are instinctively aggressive is
   a. social learning theory
   b. the frustration-aggression hypothesis
   c. ethology
   d. the aversive stimuli effect
5. Heavy exposure to media results in lowered emotional sensitivity to violence. T or F?
6. People are more likely to help another who is in trouble if
   a. many other helpers are present
   b. a diffusion of responsibility occurs
   c. they experience empathic arousal
   d. desensitization takes place

Reflect
Critical Thinking

7. If media violence contributes to aggressive behavior in our society, do you think it is possible that media could also promote prosocial behavior?

Relate

Most people have been angry enough at some time to behave aggressively. Which concepts or theories do you think best explain your own aggressive actions?

An elderly woman is at the side of the road, trying to change a flat tire. She obviously needs help. You are approaching her in your car. What must happen before you are likely to stop and help her?

Link

Internet addresses frequently change. To find the sites listed here, visit http://www.thomsonedu.com/psychology/coon for an updated list of Internet addresses and direct links to relevant sites.

- **Anger Management** Read about anger management.
- **The Frustration-Aggression Hypothesis** Read Neal Miller's original paper on the topic.
- **Media Violence** Explore the debate over media violence.

ANSWERS

1. F 2. T 3. b 4. a 5. T 6. c 7. Yes, media could be used to promote helping, cooperation, charity, and brotherhood in the same way that it has encouraged aggression. Numerous studies show, for example, that prosocial behavior on TV increases prosocial behavior by viewers.

Empathy-helping relationship Observation that we are most likely to help someone else when we feel emotions such as empathy and compassion.

MODULE **Psychology in Action**

15.7 Multiculturalism–Living with Diversity

SURVEY QUESTION: *What can be done to avoid prejudice and promote social harmony?*

Today's society is more like a "tossed salad" than a cultural "melting pot." Rather than expecting everyone to be alike, psychologists believe that we must learn to respect and appreciate our differences. **Multiculturalism,** as this is called, gives equal status to different ethnic, racial, and cultural groups. It is a recognition and acceptance of human diversity (Fowers & Richardson, 1996).

Breaking the Prejudice Habit

Most people publicly support policies of equality and fairness. Yet, many still have lingering biases and negative images of African Americans, Latinos, Asian Americans, and other ethnic minorities. How can we make sense of such conflicting attitudes? Patricia Devine, a social psychologist, has shown that a decision to forsake prejudice does not immediately eliminate prejudiced thoughts and feelings. People who are not consciously prejudiced may continue to respond emotionally to members of other ethnic groups (Nosek, Greenwald, & Banaji, 2005). Quite likely this reflects lingering stereotypes and prejudices learned in childhood (Devine et al., 1991; Dion, 2003).

For many people, becoming less prejudiced begins by accepting the value of *openness to the other,* the ability to genuinely appreciate those who differ from us culturally (Fowers & Davidov, 2006). It is important to remember that being open to someone else does not mean that you have to agree with that person or turn your back on your own culture. Openness, in turn, leads to the acceptance of the values of tolerance and equality. People who value tolerance resist intolerant thoughts or feelings, which motivates them to try to alter their own biased reactions (Dovidio & Gaertner, 1999; Zuwerink et al., 1996). But doing so is not easy. Typically, it requires repeated efforts to learn to think, feel, and act differently. Nevertheless, many people have succeeded in overcoming the "prejudice habit" and becoming more open to life experiences in general (Fowers & Davidov, 2006). If you would like to be more open and tolerant, the following points may be helpful to you.

Beware of Stereotyping Stereotypes make the social world more manageable. But placing people in categories almost always causes them to appear more similar than they really are. As a result, we tend to see out-group members as very much alike, even when they are as varied as our friends and family. People who are not prejudiced work hard to actively inhibit stereotyped thoughts and to emphasize fairness and equality. A good way to tear down stereotypes is to get to know individuals from various ethnic and cultural groups (Giliovich, Keltner, & Nisbett, 2005).

Seek Individuating Information When are we most tempted to apply stereotypes? Typically it is when we only have minimal information about a person. Stereotypes help us guess what a person is like and how she or he will act. Unfortunately, these inferences are usually wrong.

One of the best antidotes for stereotypes is **individuating information** (information that helps us see a person as an individual, rather than as a member of a group) (Cameron & Trope, 2004; Click, Zion, & Nelson, 1988). Anything that keeps us from placing a person in a particular social category tends to negate stereotyped thinking. When you meet individuals from various backgrounds, focus on the *person,* not the *label* attached to her or him.

A good example of the effects of individuating information comes from a study in Canada of English-speaking students in a French-language program. Students who were "immersed" (spent most of their waking hours with French Canadians) became more positive toward them. Immersed students were more likely to say they had come to appreciate and like French Canadians; they were more willing to meet and interact with them; and they saw themselves as less different from French Canadians (Lambert, 1987). In fact, with more subtle kinds of symbolic prejudice, such contact may be the best way to reduce intergroup conflict (Dovidio & Gaertner, 1999).

Don't Fall Prey to Just-World Beliefs Do you believe that the world is basically fair? Even if you don't, you may believe that the world is sufficiently just so that people generally get what they deserve. It may not be obvious, but such beliefs can directly increase prejudiced thinking (Hafer & Bègue, 2005).

As a result of discrimination, social conditions, and circumstances (such as recent immigration), minorities may occupy lower socioeconomic positions. **Just-world beliefs** (belief that people generally get what they deserve) can lead us to assume that minority group members wouldn't be in such positions if they weren't inferior in some way. This bit of faulty thinking amounts to blaming people who are *victims* of prejudice and discrimination for their plight. For example, assuming that a poor person is lazy may overlook the fact that discrimination in hiring has made it very difficult for him or her to find a job.

Be Aware of Self-Fulfilling Prophecies You may recall from Chapter 1 that people tend to act in accordance with the behavior expected by others. If you hold strong stereotypes about members of various groups, a vicious cycle can occur. When you meet someone who is different from yourself, you may treat her or him in a way that is consistent with your stereotypes. If the other person is influenced by your behavior, she or he may act in ways that seem to match your stereotype. For example, a person who believes that members of another ethnic group are hostile and unfriendly will probably treat people in that group in ways that provoke hostile and unfriendly response. This creates a self-fulfilling prophecy and reinforces belief in the stereotype. (A **self-fulfilling prophecy** is an expectation that prompts people to act in ways that make the expectation come true.)

Remember, Different Does Not Mean Inferior Some conflicts between groups cannot be avoided. What *can* be avoided is unnecessary **social competition** (rivalry among groups, each of which regards itself as superior to others). The concept of social competition refers to the fact that some individuals seek to enhance their self-esteem by identifying with a group. However, this works only if the group can be seen as superior to others. Because of social competition, groups tend to view themselves as better than their rivals (Baron, Byrne, & Branscombe, 2007). In one survey, every major ethnic group in the United States rated itself as better than any other group (Njeri, 1991).

A person who has high self-esteem does not need to treat others as inferior in order to feel good about himself or herself. Similarly, it is not necessary to degrade other groups in order to feel positive about one's own group identity (Fowers & Davidov, 2006; Messick & Mackie, 1989). In fact, each ethnic group has strengths that members of other groups could benefit from emulating. For instance, African Americans, Asian Americans, and Latinos emphasize family networks that help buffer them from some of the stresses of daily life (Suinn, 1999).

Understand That Race Is a Social Construction From the viewpoint of modern genetics, the concept of race has absolutely no meaning (Bonham, Warshauer-Baker, & Collins, 2005; Sternberg, Grigorenko, & Kidd, 2005). Members of various groups are so varied genetically and human groups have intermixed for so many centuries that it is impossible to tell, biologically, to what "race" any given individual belongs. Thus, race is an illusion based on superficial physical differences and learned ethnic identities. Certainly people *act as if* different races exist. But this is a matter of social labeling, not biological reality. To assume that any human group is biologically superior or inferior is simply wrong. In fact, the best available evidence suggests that all people are descended from the same ancient ancestors. The origins of our species lie in Africa, about 100,000 years ago. Among early human populations, darker skin was a protective adaptation to sun exposure near the equator (Jablonski & Chaplin, 2000). Biologically, we are all brothers and sisters under the skin (Graves, 2001; Smedley & Smedley, 2005).

Look for Commonalities We live in a society that puts a premium on competition and individual effort. One problem with this is that competing with others fosters desires to demean, defeat, and vanquish them. When we cooperate with others we tend to share their joys and suffer when they are in distress (Aronson, 2008; Lanzetta & Englis, 1989). If we don't find ways to cooperate and live in greater harmony, everyone will suffer. That, if nothing else, is one thing that we all have in common. Everyone knows what it feels like to be different. Greater tolerance comes from remembering those times.

Set an Example for Others People who act in a tolerant fashion can serve as models of tolerance for others. An example is the use of newsletters to promote understanding at an ethnically diverse high school in Houston, Texas. Students wrote stories for the newsletter about situations in which cooperation led to better understanding. For instance, a story about a Hispanic-Anglo friendship in a sports team had this headline: "Don't judge somebody until you know them. The color of the skin doesn't matter." Other stories emphasized the willingness of students to get acquainted with people from other ethnic groups and the new perceptions they had of their abilities. After just 5 months of modeling tolerance, hostility between campus ethnic groups was significantly reduced (McAlister et al., 2000).

Tolerance and Cultural Awareness

Living comfortably in a multicultural society means getting to know a little about other groups. Getting acquainted with a person whose cultural background is different from your own can be a wonderful learning experience. No one culture

---

Multiculturalism Giving equal status, recognition, and acceptance to different ethnic and cultural groups.
Individuating information Information that helps define a person as an individual, rather than as a member of a group or social category.
Just-world beliefs Belief that people generally get what they deserve.
Self-fulfilling prophecy An expectation that prompts people to act in ways that make the expectation come true.
Social competition Rivalry among groups, each of which regards itself as superior to others.

has all the answers or the best ways of doing things. Multicultural populations enrich a community's food, music, arts, and philosophy. Likewise, openness toward learning about different racial, cultural, and ethnic groups can be personally rewarding (Fowers & Davidov, 2006).

The importance of cultural awareness often lies in subtleties and details. For example, in large American cities, many small stores are owned by Korean immigrants. Some of these Korean-American merchants have been criticized for being cold and hostile to their customers. Refusing to place change directly in customers' hands, for instance, helped trigger an African-American boycott of Korean grocers in New York City. The core of the problem was a lack of cultural awareness on both sides.

In America, if you walk into a store, you expect the clerk to be courteous to you. One way of showing politeness is by smiling. But in the Confucian-steeped Korean culture, a smile is reserved for family members and close friends. If a Korean or Korean American has no reason to smile, he or she just doesn't smile. There's a Korean saying: "If you smile a lot, you're silly." Expressions such as "thank you" and "excuse me," are also used sparingly, and strangers rarely touch each other—not even to return change.

Here's another example of how ignorance of cultural practices can lead to needless friction and misunderstanding: An African-American woman who wanted to ease racial tensions took a freshly baked pie to her neighbors across the way, who were Orthodox Jews. At the front door the woman extended her hand, not knowing that Orthodox Jews don't shake women's hands unless the woman is a close family member. Once she was inside, she picked up a kitchen knife to cut the pie, not knowing the couple kept a kosher household and used different knives for different foods. The woman's well-intentioned attempt at neighborliness ended in an argument! Knowing a little more about each other's cultures could have prevented both the conflicts just described.

If the Earth's population could be condensed to just 100 people, with all the current human ratios maintained, it would look like this:

- There would be 57 Asians, 21 Europeans, 14 from the Western Hemisphere, including North and South America, and 8 from Africa.
- Seventy would be nonwhite; 30 would be white.
- Sixty-six would be non-Christian and 33 Christian.
- Half of the entire village's wealth would be in the hands of only six people, most of them U.S. citizens.
- Half the people in the village would suffer from malnutrition.
- Within the village are enough nuclear weapons to blow everyone to smithereens many times over.

When you consider the world from such a compressed perspective, the need for tolerance and understanding becomes readily apparent.

MODULE 15.7 Psychology in Action Summary

What can be done to avoid prejudice and promote social harmony?

- Multiculturalism is a recognition and acceptance of human diversity.
- Multicultural harmony can be attained through conscious efforts to be more tolerant of others.
- Greater tolerance can be encouraged by neutralizing stereotypes with individuating information; by looking for commonalities with others; and by avoiding the effects of just-world beliefs, self-fulfilling prophecies, and social competition.
- Cultural awareness is a key element in promoting greater social harmony.

KNOWLEDGE BUILDER

Multiculturalism

Recite

1. *Multiculturalism* refers to the belief that various subcultures and ethnic groups should be blended into a single emergent culture. T or F?
2. Patricia Devine found that many people who hold nonprejudiced beliefs still have prejudiced thoughts and feelings in the presence of minority group individuals. T or F?
3. One of the best antidotes for stereotypes is
   a. accepting just-world beliefs
   b. individuating information
   c. accepting self-fulfilling prophecies
   d. honest social competition
4. Just-world beliefs are the primary cause of social competition. T or F?

Reflect
Critical Thinking

5. Why is it valuable to learn the terms by which members of various groups prefer to be addressed (for example, Mexican-American, Latino/Latina, Hispanic, or Chicano/Chicana)?

Relate

Which strategies for breaking the prejudice habit do you already use? How could you apply the remaining strategies to become more tolerant?

Link

Internet addresses frequently change. To find the sites listed here, visit **http://www.thomsonedu.com/psychology/coon** for an updated list of Internet addresses and direct links to relevant sites.

- **Project Implicit** Test yourself to see if you are unconsciously prejudiced.
- **Multiculturalism Guidelines** Read these guidelines from the American Psychological Association.
- **Diversity in College** Read some relevant research about diversity in college.

ANSWERS

1. F 2. T 3. b 4. F 5. Because labels might have negative meanings that are not apparent to persons outside the group. People who are culturally aware allow others to define their own identities, rather than imposing labels on them.

Interactive Learning

Psychology: Active Learning Modules Book Companion Website

http://www.thomsonedu.com/psychology/coon

Visit your Book Companion Website, where you will find flash cards, practice quizzes, Internet links, and more to help you study.

ThomsonNOW

Just What You Need to Know NOW!

Spend time on what you need to master rather than on information you already have learned. Take a pre-test for this chapter, and ThomsonNOW will generate a personalized study plan based on your results. The study plan will identify the topics you need to review and direct you to online resources to help you master those topics. You can then take a post-test to help you determine the concepts you have mastered and what you will need to work on. Try it out! Go to www.thomsonedu.com/login to sign in with an access code or to purchase access to this product.

16 Applied Psychology

MODULE 16.1 Industrial/Organizational Psychology
SURVEY QUESTION: How is psychology applied in business and industry?
SURVEY QUESTION: What can be done to improve communication at work?

MODULE 16.2 Environmental Psychology
SURVEY QUESTION: What have psychologists learned about the effects of our physical and social environments?

MODULE 16.3 The Psychology of Law and Sports
SURVEY QUESTION: What does psychology reveal about juries and court verdicts?

SURVEY QUESTION: Can psychology enhance athletic performance?

MODULE 16.4 Psychology in Action: Human Factors Psychology—Who's the Boss Here?
SURVEY QUESTION: How are tools designed to better serve human needs?

Insanely Great

By now we're all used to the arrival of yet another insanely great iPod model. But it's not so easy to ignore the impact the iPod has had in its short existence. Consumers have already bought more than 100 million of them, as well as more than 3 billion legal music downloads. The music business will never be the same.

New words like *podcast* and *vodcast* have been invented to describe the downloadable materials available from a growing number of organizations, including schools. Already, more than half of the nation's top 500 schools distribute educational materials through iTunes U, Apple's higher education site. Many more are doing it on their own. For a change, it's not an exaggeration to call a product revolutionary.

Much of the iPod's success hinges on a tiny device called a *click wheel*. This touch-sensitive ring lies at the heart of users' ability to quickly locate that one desired song among thousands. Whether it is the click wheel, the computer mouse, voice-activated computers, or computerized systems that disabled users can control, human factors psychologists depend on understanding human behavior to design better computer tools.

Applied psychology refers to the use of psychological principles and research methods to solve practical problems. Designing computer interfaces is only one way to apply psychology. The largest applied areas are clinical and counseling psychology, but there are many others, such as community psychology, educational psychology, military psychology, health psychology (discussed in Chapter 11), and space psychology. In this chapter we will focus on the application of psychology in five diverse fields, business, the environment, law, sports, and human factors.

MODULE 16.1 Industrial/Organizational Psychology

DO YOU CONSIDER WORK A BLESSING? Or a curse? Or do you simply agree that it is "better to wear out than to rust out"? Whatever your attitude, the simple fact is that most adults work for a living. Whether you are employed now or plan to begin a career after college, it helps to know something about the psychology of work and organizations.

Industrial/Organizational Psychology—Psychology at Work

SURVEY QUESTION: *How is psychology applied in business and industry?*

Industrial/organizational (I/O) psychologists study the behavior of people at work and in organizations (Aamodt, 2007). Very likely, their efforts will affect how you are selected for a job and tested, trained, or evaluated for promotion. Most I/O psychologists are employed by the government, industry, and businesses. Typically, they work in two major areas: (1) studying jobs to identify underlying skills, which can then guide efforts to select people and train them for those jobs (the *industrial* part); and (2) studying organizations to understand how to create structures and company cultures that will improve worker performance (the *organizational* part). To get a better idea of what I/O psychologists do, look at ■ Table 16.1. As you can see, their interests are quite varied.

A key person in any organization is its leader. Family therapist and rabbi Edwin Friedman once remarked, "Leadership can be thought of as a capacity to define oneself to others in a way that clarifies and expands a vision of the future." How do great business leaders inspire their followers?

Theories of Leadership

At 7 A.M. each morning at a major manufacturing plant, more than 400 assembly line workers, supervisors, and top executives begin their day talking, joking, and exercising together, all to the beat of amplified music. To say the least, these are unusual working conditions. To understand the rationale behind them, let's consider two basic theories of leadership.

Theory X and Theory Y Leadership

One of the earliest attempts to improve worker efficiency was made in 1923 by Frederick Taylor, an engineer. To speed up production, Taylor standardized work routines and stressed careful planning, control, and orderliness. Today, versions of Taylor's approach are called *scientific management* (also known as **Theory X leadership,** for reasons explained shortly). **Scientific management** uses time-and-motion studies, task analysis, job specialization, assembly lines, pay schedules, and the like to increase productivity.

It sounds like scientific management treats people as if they were machines. Is that true? To some extent it is. In Taylor's day, many large companies were manufacturers with giant assembly lines. People had to be efficient cogs in the manu-

■ TABLE 16.1 Topics of Special Interest to Industrial/Organizational Psychologists

Absenteeism	Minority workers
Decision making	Pay schedules
Design of organizations	Personnel selection
Employee stress	Personnel training
Employee turnover	Productivity
Interviewing	Promotion
Job enrichment	Task analysis
Job satisfaction	Task design
Labor relations	Work behavior
Leadership	Work environment
Machine design	Work motivation
Management styles	Worker evaluations

Charlie Chaplin captured the worker as machine perfectly in his 1936 film, *Modern Times*. Have you ever worked at a job that made you feel like this?

CRITICAL THINKING

Beyond the Glass Ceiling: Enter the Labyrinth

Aren't women more peopled-oriented than men? And doesn't that imply that women would make better Theory Y leaders? Good thinking. As person-oriented Theory Y leadership styles have become more popular, women are slowly gaining acceptance as leaders (Eagly, 2007). Nearly a quarter of all American organizations have female CEOs (Martin, 2007). Studies have even shown that companies with more women in leadership roles perform better financially (Carter, Simkins, & Simpson, 2003; Krishnan & Park, 2005).

And yet, according to psychologist Alice Eagly, women continue to face unique challenges. Increasingly, cracks are appearing in the *glass ceiling*, the invisible barrier that has prevented women from moving into leadership positions. But the glass ceiling is being replaced by a labyrinth created by a clash between leadership stereotypes and stereotypes of women (Eagly & Karau, 2002). On the one hand, most people expect good leaders to be *agentic*: independent, confident, ambitious, objective, dominant, and forceful. On the other hand, they expect women to be more *communal*: dependent, caring, nurturing, tender, sensitive, and sympathetic. According to traditional gender role stereotypes (see Module 14.1), it is men who are agentic and, therefore, better leaders, despite evidence to the contrary (Eagly, 2007).

What does this mean for a woman who moves into a leadership role? If she practices communal, Theory Y leadership, she is seen as weak. She is "not tough enough" or does not "have the right stuff" to be a leader. Yet if she acts more assertively and confidently, she is scorned for "trying to be a man" (Martin, 2007). This conflict has been perfectly expressed by Carly Fiorina, a former CEO of Hewlett-Packard, who wrote, "In the chat rooms around Silicon Valley . . . I was routinely referred to as either a 'bimbo' or a 'bitch'—too soft or too hard, and presumptuous, besides" (Fiorina, 2006, p. 173).

As traditional gender stereotypes fade, and as Theory Y styles gain wider acceptance, perhaps women will add escaping the leadership labyrinth to their many other successes.

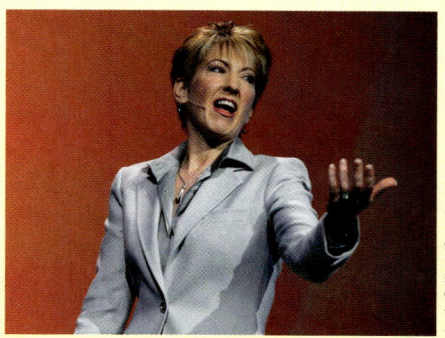

As the CEO of Hewlett-Packard, Carley Fiorina constantly faced the incongruity between leadership stereotypes and stereotypes of women (Fiorina, 2006).

---

facturing machinery. Leaders who follow Theory X have a task orientation rather than a person orientation and tend to assume that workers must be goaded or guided into being productive. Many psychologists working in business, of course, are concerned with improving **work efficiency** (defined as maximum output at lowest cost). As a result, they alter conditions they believe will affect workers (such as time schedules, work quotas, bonuses, and so on). Some might even occasionally wish that people would act like well-oiled machines. However, most recognize that psychological efficiency is just as important as work efficiency. **Psychological efficiency** refers to maintaining good morale, labor relations, employee satisfaction, and similar aspects of work behavior. Leadership styles that ignore or mishandle the human element can be devastatingly costly. Studies have consistently found that happy workers are productive workers (Cote, 1999; Wright & Cropanzano, 2000).

The term *Theory X* was coined by psychologist Douglas McGregor (1960) as a way to distinguish the leadership style associated with scientific management from *Theory Y*, a newer approach, which emphasizes human relations at work.

How is this approach different? **Theory Y leaders** have a person orientation rather than a task orientation and tend to assume that workers enjoy autonomy and are willing to accept responsibility. They also assume that a worker's needs and goals can be meshed with the company's goals, and that people are not naturally passive or lazy. In short, Theory Y assumes that people are industrious, creative, and rewarded by challenging work.

Over the last 85 years, manufacturing has declined in North America while *knowledge companies* have increased greatly (Drucker, 1993). That is, employees are becoming **knowledge workers.** These are people who add value to a

Applied psychology The use of psychological principles and research methods to solve practical problems.
Industrial/organizational (I/O) psychology A field that focuses on the psychology of work and on behavior within organizations.
Theory X leadership (scientific management) An approach to leadership that emphasizes work efficiency.
Work efficiency Maximum output (productivity) at lowest cost.
Psychological efficiency Maintenance of good morale, labor relations, employee satisfaction, and similar aspects of work behavior.
Theory Y leadership A leadership style that emphasizes human relations at work and that views people as industrious, responsible, and interested in challenging work.
Knowledge workers Workers who add value to their company by creating and manipulating information.

company by creating and manipulating information. Some examples are bankers, teachers, lawyers, computer engineers, writers, and scientists. Today in North America, 4 of every 5 persons in the workforce are knowledge workers. It appears that given the proper conditions of freedom and responsibility, many people *will* work hard to gain competence and use their talents. This is especially true for knowledge workers, who usually think of their work as a career rather than as a job.

Consider Rahul, who is a software engineer. He has been working long hours trying to develop a new way to more quickly predict hurricane activity for a satellite weather system. The work efficiency of Rahul's job cannot easily be measured or improved. Instead, his success depends on his own initiative, creativity and commitment to his work. Rahul quit his last job because the leadership of that company made him feel like he was "punching the clock," which is something Rahul does not want to do. The woman who is the chief executive officer of his current company impresses Rahul. In fact, he wonders whether women might not make better business leaders. (See "Beyond the Glass Ceiling.")

A Honda plant at Marysville, Ohio, illustrates many features of Theory Y. As you may already know, the automobile industry has a long history of labor-management clashes and worker discontent. In fact, outright sabotage by assembly line workers is not uncommon. To avoid such problems, Honda initiated a series of simple, seemingly successful measures. They include the following practices.

- Regardless of their position, all employees wear identical white uniforms. This allows workers and supervisors to interact on a more equal footing and builds feelings of teamwork.
- To further minimize status differences, all employees hold the title *associate.*
- Private offices, separate dining halls, and reserved parking spaces for executives were abolished.
- Employees work alongside company executives, to whom they have easy access.
- Every employee has a say in, and responsibility for, quality control and safety.
- Departmental meetings are held daily. At this time, announcements are discussed, decisions are made, and thoughts are freely shared.

Leadership Strategies Two elements that make Theory Y leadership methods effective are *shared leadership* and *management by objectives.* In **shared leadership (participative management),** employees at all levels are directly involved in decision making. By taking part in decisions that affect them, employees like those at the Honda factory come to see work as a cooperative effort—not as something imposed on them by an egotistical leader. The benefits include greater productivity, more involvement in work, greater job satisfaction, and less job-related stress (Kim, 2002; Pearce, Conger, & Locke, 2007).

What does "management by objectives" refer to? In **management by objectives,** workers are given specific goals to meet, so they can tell if they are doing a good job. Typical objectives include reaching a certain sales total, making a certain number of items, or reducing waste by a specific percentage. In any case, workers are free to choose (within limits) how they will achieve their goals. As a result, they feel more independent and take personal responsibility for their work. Workers are especially productive when they receive feedback about their progress toward goals. Clearly, people like to know what the target is and whether they are succeeding (Neubert, 1998).

Many companies also give *groups* of workers even greater freedom and responsibility. This is typically done by creating self-managed teams. A **self-managed team** is a group of employees who work together toward shared goals. Self-managed teams can typically choose their own methods of achieving results, as long as they are effective. Self-managed teams tend to make good use of the strengths and talents of individual employees. They also promote new ideas and improve motivation. Most of all, they encourage cooperation and teamwork within organizations (Lewis, Goodman, & Fandt, 1995). Workers in self-managed teams are much more likely to feel that they are being treated fairly at work (Chansler, Swamidass, & Cammann, 2003) and to develop a positive team atmosphere (Zárraga & Bonache, 2005).

How can workers below the management level be involved more in their work? One answer is the use of **quality circles.** These are voluntary discussion groups that seek ways

Shared leadership techniques encourage employees at all levels to become involved in decision making. Quite often this arrangement leads to greater job satisfaction.

to solve business problems and improve efficiency (Aamodt, 2007). In contrast to self-managed teams, quality circles usually do not have the power to put their suggestions into practice directly. But good ideas speak for themselves and many are adopted by company leaders. Quality circles have many limitations. Nevertheless, studies verify that greater personal involvement can lead to better performance and job satisfaction (Beyer et al., 2003; Geehr, Burke, & Sulzer, 1995).

Job Satisfaction

It often makes perfect sense to apply Theory X methods to work. However, doing so without taking worker needs into account can be a case of winning the battle while losing the war. That is, immediate productivity may be enhanced while job satisfaction is lowered. And when job satisfaction is low, absenteeism skyrockets, morale falls, and there is a high rate of employee turnover, leading to higher training costs and inefficiency (Wright & Bonett, 2007). Understandably, many of the methods used by enlightened Theory Y leaders ultimately improve **job satisfaction,** or the degree to which a person is pleased with his or her work. Job satisfaction is well worth cultivating because positive moods are associated with more cooperation, better performance, a greater willingness to help others, more creative problem solving, and less absenteeism (Brief & Weiss, 2002).

Under what conditions is job satisfaction highest? Basically, job satisfaction comes from a good fit between work and a person's interests, abilities, needs, and expectations (Landy & Conte, 2007). The major factors determining job satisfaction are listed below (adapted from Aamodt, 2007, p. 349). Think of a job you have held. It's likely that the more these factors were present, the higher your job satisfaction was.

1. My job meets my expectations. Y or N?
2. My needs, values, and wants are met by my job. Y or N?
3. The tasks I have to do are enjoyable. Y or N?
4. I enjoy my supervisors and coworkers. Y or N?
5. My coworkers are outwardly happy. Y or N?
6. I am rewarded fairly for doing a good job. Y or N?
7. I have a chance to grow and be challenged. Y or N?

Understandably, the most productive employees are those who are happy at work (Aamodt, 2007; Elovainio et al., 2000). This connection can be seen clearly in the research reported in "Flexible Work."

Job satisfaction is not entirely a matter of work conditions. Anyone who has ever been employed has probably encountered at least one perpetually grumpy co-worker. In other words, workers don't leave their personalities at home.

Happy people are more often happy at work, and they are more likely to focus on what's good about their job, rather than what's bad (Brief & Weiss, 2002).

Making Career Decisions When people become seriously dissatisfied with their work, it may be time to seek a new job. This can be a difficult step to take. One way to improve career decisions is to examine how you approach them. Psychologist Irving Janis and writer Dan Wheeler (1978) have described how people typically deal with work dilemmas, especially those that lead to a major change in jobs or careers. Their analysis suggests that there are four basic coping styles. See if you recognize yourself in any of the following descriptions.

The Vigilant Style This style is the most effective of the four. It describes individuals who evaluate information objectively and make decisions with a clear understanding of the alternatives. Persons using this style make mental "balance sheets" to weigh possible gains and losses before taking action.

The Complacent Style Persons of this type drift along with a nonchalant attitude toward job decisions. They tend to let chance direct their careers and to take whatever comes along without really making plans.

The Defensive-Avoidant Style These people are fully aware of the risks and opportunities presented by career choices and dilemmas. However, they are uncomfortable making decisions. This leads them to procrastinate, rationalize, and make excuses for their inaction and indecision.

The Hypervigilant Style People with this style more or less panic when forced to make career decisions. They may collect hundreds of job announcements and brochures, but they become so frantic that making logical decisions is nearly impossible.

These coping styles may seem exaggerated, but they are easy to observe when people are forced to change jobs or make major alterations in career plans. To relate them to yourself, think about how you have handled vocational deci-

---

Shared leadership (participative management) A leadership approach that allows employees at all levels to participate in decision making.

Management by objectives A management technique in which employees are given specific goals to meet in their work.

Self-managed team A work group that has a high degree of freedom with respect to how it achieves its goals.

Quality circle An employee discussion group that makes suggestions for improving quality and solving business problems.

Job satisfaction The degree to which a person is comfortable with or satisfied with his or her work.

CRITICAL THINKING

Flexible Work

If you've ever worked "9 to 5" in an office, you know that traditional time schedules can be confining. They also doom many workers to a daily battle with rush-hour traffic (Lucas & Heady, 2002). To improve worker morale, I/O psychologists recommend the use of a variety of flexible work arrangements, of which the best known is **flextime,** or flexible working hours. The basic idea of flextime is that starting and quitting times are flexible, as long as employees are present during a core work period (Aamodt, 2007). For example, employees might be allowed to arrive between 7:30 A.M. and 10:30 A.M. and depart between 3:30 P.M. and 6:30 P.M. In a variation called a **compressed workweek,** employees might work fewer days but put in more hours per day.

A different approach to flexible work involves working at home. In knowledge companies, employees are often be able to **telecommute,** by using a computer to remain connected to the office throughout the work day (Golden, Veiga, & Simsek, 2006).

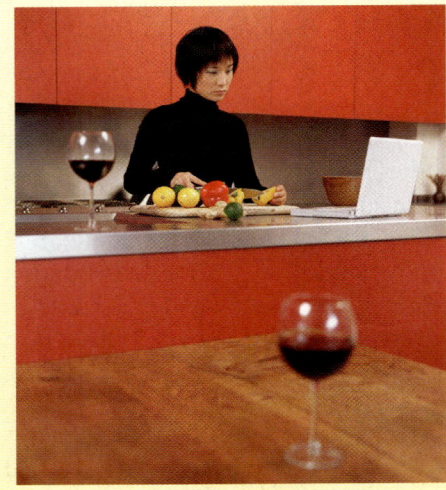

Connecting with work through the Internet makes it possible to telecommute, or work from home (Golden, Veiga, & Simsek, 2006).

Is flexible work really an improvement? Generally speaking, yes. For example, flextime typically has a positive effect on workers' productivity, job satisfaction, absenteeism, and comfort with their work schedules (Baltes et al., 1999). Similarly, telecommuting is especially effective when it allows valued employees to maintain their homes in other cities (Atkin & Lau, 2007). Psychologists theorize that flexible work lowers stress and increases feelings of independence, both of which increase productivity and job satisfaction.

Of course, not everyone wants a compressed workweek or to work from home. Ideally, flexible working arrangements should fit the needs of employees (Rothbard, Phillips, & Dumas, 2005). Regardless, most large organizations now use flexible work arrangements. Perhaps we can conclude that it is better, when possible, to bend working arrangements instead of people.

---

sions to date, or decisions about your college career. Of the four, Janis and Wheeler consider only the vigilant style to be constructive. With this insight, you may be able to improve the quality of your career decisions.

Job Enrichment

For years, the trend in business and industry was to make work more streamlined and efficient and to tie better pay to better work. There is now ample evidence that incentives such as bonuses, earned time off, and profit sharing can increase productivity. However, in recent years far too many jobs have become routine, repetitive, boring, and unfulfilling. To combat the discontent this can breed, many psychologists recommend a strategy called *job enrichment.*

Job enrichment involves making a job more personally rewarding, interesting, or intrinsically motivating. Large corporations such as IBM, Maytag, Western Electric, Chrysler, and Polaroid have used job enrichment with great success. It usually leads to lower production costs, increased job satisfaction, reduced boredom, and less absenteeism (Lewis, Goodman, & Fandt, 1995; Niehoff et al., 2001).

How is job enrichment done? Merely assigning a person more tasks is usually not enriching. Overloaded workers just feel stressed, and they tend to make more errors. Instead, job enrichment applies many of the principles we have discussed. Usually it involves removing some of the controls and restrictions on employees, giving them greater freedom, choice, and authority. In some cases, employees also switch to doing a complete cycle of work. That is, they complete an entire item or project, instead of doing an isolated part of a larger process. Whenever possible, workers are given direct feedback about their work or progress.

True job enrichment increases workers' *knowledge.* That is, workers are encouraged to continuously learn a broad range of skills and information related to their occupations (Campion & McClelland, 1993; Sessa & London, 2006). In short, most people seem to enjoy being good at what they do.

Organizational Culture

Businesses and other organizations, whether they are large or small, develop distinct cultures. Within organizations, **culture** refers to a blend of customs, beliefs, values, attitudes, and rituals. These characteristics give each organization its unique "flavor." Organizational culture includes such things as how people are hired and trained, disciplined, and dismissed. It encompasses how employees dress, communicate, resolve conflicts, share power, identify with organizational goals and values, negotiate contracts, and celebrate special occasions.

People who fit well into a particular organization tend to contribute to its success in ways that are not specifically part

THE CLINICAL FILE

Desk Rage and Healthy Organizations

Like road rage on the highways, "desk rage," or workplace anger, is becoming a frequent occurrence and all too often erupts into workplace violence (Martinko, Douglas, & Harvey, 2006). It's not difficult to understand two common triggers for workplace anger: intense anger is frequently triggered by job-related stresses or feeling that one has been treated unfairly (Spector, 2005). Two other common causes are perceived threats to one's self-esteem and work-related conflicts with others (Glomb, 2002).

What can be done about anger and aggression at work? Most larger companies now offer mental health services to troubled employees and trauma counseling if violence erupts in the workplace. More importantly, healthy organizations actively promote the well-being of people. They do this through trust, by openly confronting problems; empowering employees; and encouraging participation, cooperation, and full use of human potential. Healthy organizations also support well-being in the following ways (Fuqua & Newman, 2002):

- Rather than always complaining and blaming, group members express sincere gratitude for the efforts of others.
- Everyone makes mistakes. The culture in caring organizations includes a capacity to forgive.
- Everyone needs encouragement at times. Encouragement can inspire workers and give them hope, confidence, and courage.
- Showing sensitivity to others can dramatically change the work environment. Sensitivity can take the form of expressing interest in others and in how they are doing. It also includes respecting the privacy of others.
- Compassion for others is a good antidote for destructive competitiveness and petty game playing.
- People have very different needs, values, and experiences. Tolerance and respect for the dignity of others goes a long way toward maintaining individual well-being.

The economic pressures that organizations face can lead to hostile and competitive work environments. However, productivity and quality of life at work are closely intertwined. Effective organizations seek to optimize both (Fuqua & Newman, 2002).

---

of their job description. For example, they are helpful, conscientious, and courteous. They also display good sportsmanship by avoiding pettiness, gossiping, complaining, and making small problems into big ones. (See "Desk Rage and Healthy Organizations.") Like good citizens, the best workers keep themselves informed about organizational issues by attending meetings and taking part in discussions. Workers with these characteristics display what could be called **organizational citizenship.** Understandably, managers and employers highly value workers who are good organizational citizens (Muchinsky, 2006).

Personnel Psychology

Companies can also enhance their chances of success by hiring the right employees in the first place. **Personnel psychology** is concerned with testing, selection, placement, and promotion of employees (Muchinsky, 2006). At present, 9 out of 10 people are or will be employed in business or industry. Thus, nearly everyone who holds a job is sooner or later placed under the "psychological microscope" of personnel selection. Clearly, there is value in knowing how selection for hiring and promotion is done.

Job Analysis

How do personnel psychologists make employee selections? Personnel selection begins with **job analysis,** a detailed description of the skills, knowledge, and activities required by a particular job (Dierdorff & Wilson, 2003; Landy & Conte, 2007). A job analysis may be done by interviewing expert workers or supervisors, giving them questionnaires, directly observing work, or identifying *critical incidents.* **Critical incidents** are situations with which competent employees must be able to cope. The ability to deal calmly with a mechanical emergency, for example, is a critical incident for airline pilots. Once job requirements are known, psychologists can state what skills, aptitudes, and interests are needed (● Fig. 16.1). In addition, some psychologists are now doing

---

Flextime A work schedule that allows flexible starting and quitting times.

Compressed workweek A work schedule that allows an employee to work fewer days per week by putting in more hours per day.

Telecommuting An approach to flexible work that involves working from home but using a computer to stay connected to the office throughout the workday.

Job enrichment Making a job more personally rewarding, interesting, or intrinsically motivating; typically involves increasing worker knowledge.

Organizational culture The social climate within an organization.

Organizational citizenship Making positive contributions to the success of an organization in ways that go beyond one's job description.

Personnel psychology Branch of industrial/organizational psychology concerned with testing, selection, placement, and promotion of employees.

Job analysis A detailed description of the skills, knowledge, and activities required by a particular job.

Critical incidents Situations that arise in a job with which a competent worker must be able to cope.

● **FIGURE 16.1** Analyzing complex skills has also been valuable to the U.S. Air Force. When million-dollar aircraft and the lives of pilots are at stake, it makes good sense to do as much training and research as possible on the ground. Air force psychologists use flight simulators like the one pictured here to analyze the complex skills needed to fly jet fighters. Skills can then be taught without risk on the ground. The General Electric simulator shown here uses a computer to generate full-color images that respond realistically to a pilot's use of the controls. Courtesy of General Electric Company

a broader "work analysis." In this case, they try to identify general characteristics that a person must have to succeed in a variety of work roles, rather than in just a specific job (Hough & Oswald, 2000).

Selection Procedures

After desirable skills and traits are identified, the next step is to learn who has them. Today, the methods most often used for evaluating job candidates include collecting *biodata,* conducting *interviews,* giving *standardized psychological tests,* and employing the *assessment center* approach. Let's see what each entails.

Biodata As simple as it may seem, one good way to predict job success is to collect **biodata** (detailed biographical information) from applicants (Schultz & Schultz, 2006). The idea behind biodata is that looking at past behavior is a good way to predict future behavior. By learning in detail about a person's life, it is often possible to say whether the person is suited for a particular type of work (Hough & Oswald, 2000).

Some of the most useful items of biodata include past athletic interests, academic achievements, scientific interests, extracurricular activities, religious activities, social popularity, conflict with brothers and sisters, attitudes toward school, and parents' socioeconomic status (Muchinsky, 2006). Such facts tell quite a lot about personality, interests, and abilities. In addition to past experiences, a person's recent life activities also help predict job success (Schmidt, Ones, & Hunter, 1992). For instance, you might think that college grades are unimportant, but college grade point average (GPA) predicts success in many types of work (Hough & Oswald, 2000).

Interviews The traditional personal interview is still one of the most popular ways to select people for jobs or promotions. In a **personal interview,** job applicants are questioned about their qualifications. At the same time, interviewers gain an impression of the applicant's personality (Schultz & Schultz, 2006). (Or personalities—but that's another story!)

As discussed in Module 10.6, interviews are subject to the halo effect and similar problems. (Recall that the *halo effect* is the tendency of interviewers to extend favorable or unfavorable impressions to unrelated aspects of an individual's personality.) In addition, interviewees actively engage in *impression management,* seeking to portray a positive image to interviewers (Ellis et al., 2002). It is for reasons like these that psychologists continue to look for ways to improve the accuracy of interviews. (See "Surviving Your Job Interview.") For instance, recent studies suggest that interviews can be improved by giving them more structure (Hough & Oswald, 2000; Tsai, Chen, & Chiu, 2005). For example, each job candidate should be asked the same questions (Campion, Palmer, & Campion, 1998). However, even with their limitations, interviews are a valid and effective way of predicting how people will perform on the job (Landy, Shankster, & Kohler, 1994).

Psychological Testing *What kinds of tests do personnel psychologists use?* General mental ability tests (intelligence tests) tell a great deal about a person's chances of succeeding in various jobs (Schmidt & Hunter, 1998). So do general personality tests and honesty tests (described in Module 10.6) (Hough & Oswald, 2000). In addition, personnel psychologists often use **vocational interest tests.** These paper-and-pencil tests assess people's interests and match them to interests found among successful workers in various occupations (Aamodt, 2007). Tests such as the *Kuder Occupational Interest Survey* and the *Strong-Campbell Interest Inventory* probe interests with items like the following:

I would prefer to
a. visit a museum
b. read a good book
c. take a walk outdoors

Interest inventories typically measure six major themes identified by John Holland (■ Table 16.2). If you take an interest test and your choices match those of people in a given occupation, it is assumed that you, too, would be comfortable doing the work they do (Holland, 1997).

Aptitude tests are another mainstay of personnel psychology. Such tests rate a person's potential to learn tasks or skills used in various occupations. Tests exist for clerical, ver-

DISCOVERING PSYCHOLOGY

Surviving Your Job Interview

Each year, clothing and cosmetics manufacturers spend huge sums to convince us that their products make us more attractive. Actually, such claims are somewhat justified. You might recall from Module 10.6, for instance, that physically attractive people are often given more positive evaluations in interviews–even on traits that have no connection with appearance.

In general, however, indirect efforts to make a good impression, like dressing well, wearing cologne, and flattering the interviewer, are less effective in interviews than direct efforts such as emphasizing your positive traits and past successes (Kristof-Brown, Barrick, & Franke, 2002). However, beware of blatant self-promotion. Excessively "blowing your own horn" tends to lower interviewers' perceptions of competence and suitability for a job (Howard & Ferris, 1996). According to the U. S. Department of Labor (2005), the advice that follows will help you survive your job interview.

Make sure you are prepared for your interview. Know about the company and job for which you are interviewing. Review your job qualifications and your résumé. Think about the kinds of questions you may be asked at the interview and outline broad answers. Consider practicing the interview with a family member or friend.

Be on time for your interview and bring your social security card, résumé, and references. Also, make sure you are well groomed, dressed appropriately, and well mannered. Don't smoke or chew gum. Learn your interviewer's name and shake his or her hand firmly. Relax and answer all questions politely, promptly, and concisely. Cooperate enthusiastically, use positive body language, and remember to avoid slang.

Don't be afraid to ask questions about the potential job and the company you might be working for. Just be sure the answers aren't already easily available on the company website. And avoid questions about salary and benefits unless a job offer is coming.

TABLE 16.2 Vocational Interest Themes

THEMES	SAMPLE COLLEGE MAJORS	SAMPLE OCCUPATIONS
Realistic	Agriculture	Mechanic
Investigative	Physics	Chemist
Artistic	Music	Writer
Social	Education	Counselor
Enterprising	Business	Sales
Conventional	Economics	Clerk

Source: Adapted from Holland, 1997.

bal, mechanical, artistic, legal, and medical aptitudes, plus many others (● Fig. 16.2). For example, tests of clerical aptitude emphasize the capacity to do rapid, precise, and accurate office work. One section of a clerical aptitude test might therefore ask a person to mark all identical numbers and names in a long list of pairs like those shown here.

49837266	49832766
Global Widgets, Inc.	Global Wigets, Inc.
874583725	874583725
Sevanden Corp.	Sevanden Corp.
Wadsworth Publishing	Wadsworth Puhlishing

Paper-and-pencil tests sometimes seem far removed from the day-to-day challenges of work. In recent years, psychologists have tried to make employment testing more interesting

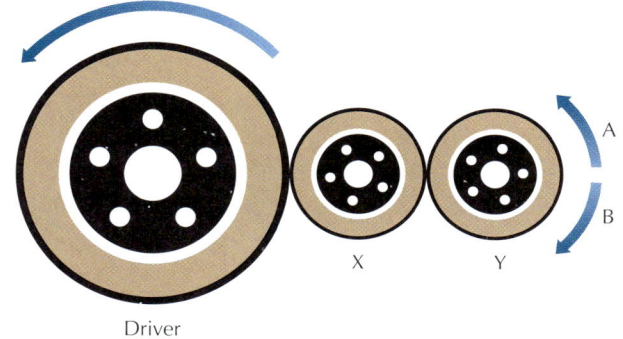

1. If the driver turns in the direction shown, which direction will wheel Y turn?   A   B
2. Which wheel will turn the slowest?   Driver   X   Y

● **FIGURE 16.2** Sample questions like those found on tests of mechanical aptitude. (The answers are A and the Driver.)

Biodata Detailed biographical information about a job applicant.

Personal interview Formal or informal questioning of job applicants to learn their qualifications and to gain an impression of their personalities.

Vocational interest test A paper-and-pencil test that assesses a person's interests and matches them to interests found among successful workers in various occupations.

Aptitude test A test that rates a person's potential to learn skills required by various occupations.

Multimedia computerized test A test that uses a computer to present lifelike situations; test takers react to problems posed by the situations.

Aptitude tests are used to select job candidates and to advise people about what types of work they are likely to be good at.

and relevant. For example, personnel psychologists are developing **multimedia computerized tests,** which rely on computers to present realistic work situations. As potential employees watch typical work scenes unfold, the action freezes on various problems. The applicant is then asked what she or he would do in that situation. In addition to screening job applicants, multimedia presentations can be used to improve the job skills of current employees (Landy, Shankster, & Kohler, 1994; Muchinsky, 2006).

After college, chances are good that you will encounter an *assessment center.* Many large organizations use **assessment centers** to do in-depth evaluations of job candidates. This approach has become so popular that the list of businesses using it—Ford, IBM, Kodak, Exxon, Sears, and thousands of others—reads like a corporate *Who's Who.*

How do assessment centers differ from the selection methods already described? Assessment centers are primarily used to fill management and executive positions. First, applicants are tested and interviewed. Then they are observed and evaluated in simulated work situations. Specifically, **situational judgment tests** are used to present difficult but realistic work situations to applicants (Borman, Hanson, & Hedge, 1997; Lievens & Sackett, 2006). For example, in one exercise applicants are given an **in-basket test** that simulates the decision-making challenges executives face. The test consists of a basket full of memos, requests, and typical business problems. Each applicant is asked to quickly read all the materials and to take appropriate action. In another, more stressful test, applicants take part in a **leaderless group discussion.** This is a test of leadership that simulates group decision making and problem solving. While the group grapples with a realistic business problem, "clerks" bring in price changes, notices about delayed supplies, and so forth. By observing applicants, it is possible to evaluate leadership skills and to see how job candidates cope with stress.

How well does this approach work? Assessment centers have had considerable success in predicting performance in a variety of jobs, careers, and advanced positions (Landy, Shankster, & Kohler, 1994). In the end, perhaps the single most important skill everyone in a corporation must possess is communication, the glue that holds successful organizations together. In the next section we will address some of the basics of good communication at work.

Communication at Work—Getting the Message Across

SURVEY QUESTION: *What can be done to improve communication at work?*

Effective communication is crucial in many work settings. When communication is muddled, important messages may get lost. Feelings can be crushed. Trust may be damaged. Poor decisions are made. Almost always, group effectiveness is impaired. Getting a job, keeping it, and excelling in your work all depend on knowing how to communicate clearly with others (Aamodt, 2007).

Effective Communication

To improve your communication skills, or to keep them sharp, remember the following points (Guffey, 2007; Lehman & DuFrene, 2008).

1. **State your ideas clearly and decisively.** News reporters learn to be precise about the "who, what, when, where, why, and how" of events. At work, the same list is a good guide when you are making a request, giving instructions, or answering a question. Rather than saying, "I need someone to give me a hand sometime with some stuff," it would be better to say, "Blake, would you please meet me in the storeroom in 5 minutes? I need help lifting a box." Notice that the second request answers all of these questions: Who? Blake. What? Could you help me? How? By lifting a box. When? In 5 minutes. Where? In the storeroom. Why? It takes two people.

As you speak, avoid overuse of ambiguous words and phrases ("wiggle words") such as *I guess, I think, kinda, sort of, around, some, about, you know,* and *like*. Here's an example: "Basically, I sort of feel like we should kinda pause. I mean, and, let's see, maybe reconsider, you know, rethink some of this stuff." It would be better to say: "I believe we should revise our plans immediately." Ambiguous messages leave others in doubt as to your true thoughts and wishes.

Also try not to overuse intensifiers (*very, really, absolutely, extra, super, awesome, ultimate, completely,* and so on). Super-extra-frequent use of such awesome words really causes them to completely lose their ultimate effectiveness.

2. **Eschew the meretricious utilization of polysyllabic locutions. (Don't overuse big words.)** Overuse of obscure vocabulary is often a sign of insecurity. Big words may make you sound important, but they can also blur your message. Which of the following two statements is clearer—"Pulchritude possesses solely cutaneous profundity" or "Beauty is only skin deep"?

   Trendy, overused "buzz words" or phrases should also be avoided. Often they are just a way of *sounding like* you are saying something: "Personally, I feel we've got to be more synergistically proactive and start networking in a programmatic fashion if we want to avoid being negatively impacted by future megatrends in the client-purveyor interface." Translation: "I don't have any worthwhile thoughts on the topic."

3. **Avoid excessive use of jargon or slang.** Most professions have their own specialized terminology. Here's an example of some printers' jargon: "TR the last two lines but stet the leading." (Reverse the order of the last two lines but don't change the spacing between them.) Jargon can provide a quick, shorthand way of expressing ideas. However, jargon and technical lingo should be avoided unless you are sure that others are familiar with it. Otherwise, people may misunderstand you or feel left out. Using slang can have the same effect as jargon. Slang that excludes people from a conversation makes them feel belittled.

4. **Avoid loaded words.** Words that have strong emotional meanings (loaded words) can have unintended effects on listeners. For example, the observation "What a stupid-looking tie" implies that anyone who likes the tie is stupid. In the same way, saying "I think the supervisor's new schedule is a *dumb* idea" brands anyone who agrees with the schedule as foolish. Good decision making and problem solving require an atmosphere in which people feel that their ideas are respected, even when they disagree.

5. **Use people's names.** Work relationships go more smoothly when you learn names and use them. An impersonal request such as, "Hey you, could you make five copies of this for me?" is not likely to promote future cooperation. Of course, whether you use a first or last name will depend on how formal your relationship to a person is. In any case, learning names is well worth the effort. (Module 7.6 describes how to improve your memory for names.)

6. **Be polite and respectful.** Being polite is important, but don't be artificially servile or stilted. Overuse of expressions such as *sir, madame, with your permission, if you would be ever so kind,* and so on, can actually be insulting. True politeness puts others at ease. Phony politeness makes people feel they are being made fun of, or manipulated, or that you are faking it to win approval. Being polite can be difficult when tempers flare. If you have a dispute with someone at work, remember to use the techniques of self-assertion described in Module 15.3.

Be aware that your behavior sends messages, too. Actions can parallel, amplify, contradict, or undermine what you are saying. For example, being late for a meeting tells others that they are not very important to you. Likewise, your manner of dress, personal grooming—even the way you decorate your personal workspace—all send messages. Think about the message you want to send and be sensitive to nonverbal channels of information.

Being a Good Listener

Effective communication is a two-way street. In addition to expressing yourself clearly, you must also be a good listener. Here are some pointers that apply to work settings (Guffey, 2007; Lehman & DuFrene, 2008).

1. **Make an honest effort to pay attention.** Stop what you are doing, actively give the speaker your attention, and resist distractions. Communicate your in-

---

Assessment center A program set up within an organization to conduct in-depth evaluations of job candidates.

Situational judgment test Presenting realistic work situations to applicants in order to observe their skills and reactions.

In-basket test A testing procedure that simulates the individual decision-making challenges that executives face.

Leaderless group discussion A test of leadership that simulates group decision making and problem solving.

terest by posture and body position. Make eye contact with the speaker to show your interest.

2. **Try to identify the speaker's purpose.** Is she or he informing, requesting, discussing, persuading, correcting, digressing, or entertaining? Listen for main themes rather than isolated facts. A good listener will be able to answer the question: What is this person's central message? Thus, as you listen, pretend that you will have to summarize the speaker's message for someone else.

3. **Suspend evaluation.** As you listen, try to keep an open mind. Avoid hasty judging, disagreeing, rejecting, or criticizing. There will be time later to think about what was said. After you have heard an entire message, evaluate the information it contains and decide how to use it. Then reply or take action.

4. **Check your understanding.** Let the other person talk, but occasionally acknowledge and confirm what he or she is saying. Restate important parts of the message in your own words to make sure you understand it. Ask questions and clarify points you don't understand. Don't let doubts or ambiguities go unresolved.

5. **Pay attention to nonverbal messages.** Listeners must also be aware of the information provided by gestures, facial expressions, eye contact, touching, body positioning, and voice qualities such as volume, rate, pitch, emphasis, hesitations, and silences. Good listeners are also good observers.

6. **Accept responsibility for effective communication.** As a listener, it is up to you to actively search for meaning and value in what is said. You can facilitate communication as much by being a good listener as you can by being an effective speaker.

The art of effective communication is well worth cultivating. The points made here are basic, but they can go a long way toward ensuring your success at work—like, totally, abso-double-lutely, you know what we mean?

Although we have only scratched the surface of industrial/organizational psychology, it is time to move on for a look at another applied area of great personal relevance. Before we begin, here's a chance to enhance your learning.

MODULE 16.1 Summary

How is psychology applied in business and industry?

- *Applied psychology* refers to the use of psychological principles and research to solve practical problems.
- Industrial/organizational psychologists enhance the quality of work by studying jobs to better match people to them and by studying organizational structures and culture to improve worker performance.
- Two basic leadership styles are Theory X (scientific management) and Theory Y (human relations approaches). Theory X is mostly concerned with work efficiency, whereas Theory Y emphasizes psychological efficiency.
- Theory Y methods include shared leadership (participative management), management by objectives, self-managed teams, and quality circles.
- Job satisfaction influences productivity, absenteeism, morale, employee turnover, and other factors that affect business efficiency.
- Job satisfaction comes from a good fit between work and a person's interests, abilities, needs, and expectations. Job enrichment tends to increase job satisfaction.
- To match people with jobs, personnel psychologists combine job analysis with selection procedures, such as gathering biodata, interviewing, giving standardized psychological tests, and using assessment centers.

What can be done to improve communication at work?

- To improve communication at work, state your message clearly and avoid use of obscure vocabulary, jargon, slang, and loaded words. Learn and use people's names. Be polite but not servile. Be expressive when you speak. Pay attention to nonverbal cues and messages.
- To be a good listener, actively pay attention, identify the speaker's purpose and core message, suspend evaluation while listening, check your understanding, and take note of nonverbal information.

KNOWLEDGE BUILDER

Industrial/Organizational Psychology

Recite

1. Theory X leadership, or scientific management, is concerned primarily with improving _____ _____.

2. Shared leadership management is often a feature of businesses with leaders who adhere to Theory Y. T or F?

3. For the majority of workers, job satisfaction is almost exclusively related to the amount of pay received. T or F?

4. Job enrichment is a direct expression of scientific management principles. T or F?

5. Identifying critical work incidents is sometimes included in a thorough _____ _____.

6. Detailed biographical information about a job applicant is referred to as _____.

7. The Strong-Campbell Inventory is a typical aptitude test. T or F?

8. A leaderless group discussion is most closely associated with which approach to employee selection?
   a. aptitude testing
   b. personal interviews
   c. job analysis
   d. assessment center

9. The sentence "Copy Monica, Steve, and the bean-counters with your input and let's circle the wagons in the A.M." shows the danger of using loaded words. T or F?

Reflect
Critical Thinking

10. In what area of human behavior other than business work would a careful task analysis be helpful?

Relate

If you were leading people in a business setting, which of the leadership concepts discussed in the text do you think you would be most likely to use?

Do you think women can make effective leaders? In business? In politics?

Think of a job you know well (something you have done yourself, or something a person you know does). Could job enrichment be applied to the work? What would you do to increase job satisfaction for people doing similar work?

Which of the various ways of evaluating job applicants do you regard as most valid? Which would you prefer to have applied to yourself?

What changes could you make to improve your effectiveness as a speaker and as a listener? Use the discussion of communication at work as a checklist to identify ways in which you could improve.

Link

Internet addresses frequently change. To find the sites listed here, visit **http://www.thomsonedu.com/psychology/coon** for an updated list of Internet addresses and direct links to relevant sites.

- **Society for Industrial and Organizational Psychology** Visit the website of APA Division 14.
- **Women in Management** Read about how women are cracking the glass ceiling.
- **Job Interview Tips** Explore these tips from the U.S. Department of Labor.

ANSWERS

1. work (or task) efficiency 2. T 3. F 4. F 5. job analysis 6. biodata 7. F 8. d 9. F 10. One such area is sports psychology. As described later in this chapter, sports skills can be broken into subparts, so key elements can be identified and taught. Such methods are an extension of techniques first used for job analyses. To a large extent, attempts to identify the characteristics of effective teaching also rely on task analysis.

MODULE 16.2 Environmental Psychology

WHERE DO YOU THINK IT IS MORE LIKELY THAT A FISTFIGHT WOULD OCCUR: in a church or a country-western bar? If the answer seems obvious, it is because specific environments have a significant impact on behavior. The reverse is also true: People have a significant impact on environments, both natural and constructed. Because of this second possibility, environmental psychologists are concerned with some of the most serious problems facing humanity.

Environmental Psychology—Life in the Big City

SURVEY QUESTION: *What have psychologists learned about the effects of our physical and social environments?*

If cities were drivers, some would get lots of speeding tickets. Others would spend most of their time in the slow lane, watching the scenery go by. Informally, you may have noticed that the pace of life varies from city to city. Psychologist Robert Levine and his students decided to measure the overall tempo of 36 American cities to see how they compare (Levine, 1998).

To rate a city's pace, Levine looked at four indicators: walking speed, working speed, talking speed, and the percentage of men and women wearing watches. The results? The three fastest American cities were Boston, Buffalo, and New York—all in the Northeast. The three slowest cities were in the South and West: Shreveport, Sacramento, and Los Angeles. No surprises here. But Levine's other findings are surprising. Levine and his team also found a correlation between the pace of life and heart disease. Just as there are Type A personalities (heart attack–prone personalities; see Module 11.4), there also seem to be Type A cities. Very likely, Type A people are attracted to fast-paced Type A cities—where they then do their best to keep the pace (Levine, 1998).

The work of Robert Levine, and psychologists like him, falls into an area known as **environmental psychology,** a specialty concerned with the relationship between environments and human behavior (Bell et al., 2006). Environmental psychologists are interested in both **physical environments** (natural or constructed) and **social environments** (defined by groups of people, such as a dance, business meeting, or party). They also give special attention to **behavioral settings** (smaller areas within an environment whose use is well defined, such as an office, locker room, church, casino, or classroom). As you have no doubt noticed, various environments and behavioral settings tend to "demand" certain actions. Consider,

Various behavioral settings place strong demands on people to act in expected ways.

for example, the difference between a library and a campus center lounge. In which would a conversation be more likely to occur?

Other major interests of environmental psychologists are crowding, stressful environments, architectural design, environmental protection, and many related topics (■ Table 16.3). One of the more "personal" topics in environmental psychology concerns the efforts we make to regulate the space around our bodies. Let's see how personal space norms and territoriality affect our behavior.

■ **TABLE 16.3 Topics of Special Interest to Environmental Psychologists**

Architectural design	Noise
Behavioral settings	Personal space
Cognitive maps	Personality and environment
Constructed environments	Pollution
Crowding	Privacy
Energy conservation	Proxemics
Environmental stressors	Resource management
Heat	Territoriality
Human ecology	Urban planning
Littering	Vandalism
Natural environment	

The use of space in public places is governed by unspoken norms, or "rules," about what is appropriate.

Would this technique work with a good friend? Maybe not. Norms governing comfortable or acceptable distances vary according to relationships as well as activities and settings. Hall (1966) identified four basic zones: *intimate, personal, social,* and *public* distance (● Fig. 16.3).

Spatial Norms

Cultural differences also affect spatial norms (Beaulieu, 2004). In many Middle Eastern countries people hold their faces only inches apart while talking. In Western Europe, the English sit closer together when conversing than the French do. The Dutch, on the other hand, sit farther apart than the French (Remland, Jones, & Brinkman, 1991). In many parts of the world, merely crossing a border can dramatically change spatial behavior. The distances listed here apply to face-to-face interactions in North America.

1. **Intimate distance.** For the majority of people, the most private and exclusive space extends about 18 inches out from the skin. Entry within this space (face to face) is reserved for special people or special

Personal Space

Each person has an invisible "spatial envelope" that defines his or her **personal space.** This is an area surrounding the body that is regarded as private and subject to personal control. Basically, personal space extends "I" or "me" boundaries past the skin to the immediate environment.

What effect does personal space have on behavior? Regulating personal space affects many social interactions. Powerful norms define the interpersonal distance we regard as appropriate for formal business, casual conversation, waiting in line with strangers, and other situations or settings.

The systematic study of rules for the use of personal space is called **proxemics** (prok-SEE-miks) (Harrigan, 2005). You can demonstrate personal space and the nature of proxemics by "invading" the space of another person. The next time you are talking with an acquaintance, move closer and watch the reaction. Most people show signs of discomfort and step back to re-establish their original distance. Those who hold their ground will turn to the side, look away, or position an arm in front of themselves as a barrier. If you persistently edge toward your subjects, it should be easy to move them back several feet. Personal space is also illustrated by the fact that many train commuters prefer to stand up if it means they can avoid sitting too close to strangers (Evans & Wener, 2007). Such norms may explain why people who feel offended by another person sometimes say, "Get out of my face."

Intimate (0–1.5)   Personal (1.5–4)   Social (4–12)   Public (12+)

● **FIGURE 16.3** Typical spatial zones (in feet) for face-to-face interactions in North America. Often, we must stand within intimate distance of others in crowds, buses, subways, elevators, and other public places. At such times, privacy is maintained by avoiding eye contact, by standing shoulder to shoulder or back to back, and by positioning a purse, bag, package, or coat as a barrier to spatial intrusions.

Environmental psychology The formal study of how environments affect behavior.
Physical environments Natural settings, such as forests and beaches, as well as environments built by humans, such as buildings, ships, and cities.
Social environment An environment defined by a group of people and their activities or interrelationships (such as a parade, revival meeting, or sports event).
Behavioral setting A smaller area within an environment whose use is well defined, such as a bus depot, waiting room, or lounge.
Personal space An area surrounding the body that is regarded as private and subject to personal control.
Proxemics Systematic study of the human use of space, particularly in social settings.
Intimate distance The most private space immediately surrounding the body (up to about 18 inches from the skin).

circumstances. Lovemaking, comforting others, and cuddling children all take place within this space.

2. **Personal distance.** This is the distance maintained in comfortable interaction with friends. It extends from about 18 inches to 4 feet from the body. Personal distance basically keeps people within "arm's reach" of each other.

3. **Social distance.** Impersonal business and casual social gatherings take place in a range of about 4 to 12 feet. This distance eliminates most touching, and it formalizes conversation by requiring greater voice projection. "Important people" in many business offices use the imposing width of their desks to maintain social distance. A big smelly cigar helps, too.

4. **Public distance.** This is the distance at which formal interactions occur (about 12 feet or more from the body). When people are separated by more than 12 feet, they look "flat" and must raise their voices to speak to one another. Formal speeches, lectures, business meetings, and the like are conducted at public distance.

Because spatial behavior is very consistent, you can learn about your relationship to others by observing the distance you comfortably hold between yourselves. Watch for this dimension in your daily activities. But remember to be aware of cultural differences. Otherwise, you might misread another person's spatial behavior. When two people of different nationalities have different norms for personal space, both are likely to be uncomfortable when talking, as one tries to move closer and the other keeps moving back. This can lead to misunderstandings in which one person feels that the other is being too familiar, whereas that person feels rejected (Beaulieu, 2004).

Territoriality As we move farther from the body, it becomes apparent that personal space also extends to adjacent areas that we claim as our "territory." **Territorial behavior** refers to actions that define a space as one's own or that protect it from intruders. For example, in the library, you might protect your space with a coat, handbag, book, or other personal belonging. "Saving a place" at a theater or a beach also demonstrates the tendency to identify a space as "ours." Even sports teams are territorial, usually showing a home team advantage by playing better on their own home territory than while away and in another team's territory (Neave & Wolfson, 2003).

Respect for the temporary ownership of space is widespread. It is not unusual for a person to "take over" an entire table or study room by looking annoyed when others intrude. Your own personal territory may include your room, specific seats in many of your classes, or a particular table in the campus center or library that "belongs" to you and your friends.

Researchers have found that the more attached you are to an area, the more likely you are to adorn it with obvious **territorial markers** that signal your "ownership." Typical markers include decorations, plants, photographs, or posters. College dorms and business offices are prime places to observe this type of territorial marking. Interestingly, burglars are less likely to break into houses that have lots of obvious territorial markers, such as fences (even if small), parked cars, lawn furniture, exterior lights, and security signs (Brown & Bentley, 1993). "Gated communities" have sprung up in many cities because they mark out a "defensible space" that discourages intrusions (Low, 2001; Tijerino, 1998). (A highly territorial bulldog may help, too.)

Personal space norms define small social environments. As mentioned before, larger physical and social environments also have an impact on us.

Environmental Influences

Much of our behavior is controlled, in part, by specific types of environments. For example, many shopping malls and department stores are designed like mazes. Their twisting pathways encourage shoppers to linger and wander while looking at merchandise. Likewise, many college classrooms

Graffiti, one of the blights of urban life, is an obvious form of territorial marking.

clearly define a speaker-audience relationship. Discussion among students tends to be discouraged by seats that are bolted to the floor, facing an authority at the front of the room (Wong, Sommer, & Cook, 1992). Even public bathrooms influence behavior. Because the seating is limited, few people hold meetings there!

Psychologists have found that a variety of environmental factors influence the amount of vandalism that occurs in public places. On the basis of psychological research, many architects now "harden" and "de-opportunize" public settings to discourage vandalism and graffiti. Some such efforts limit opportunities for vandalism (doorless toilet stalls, tiled walls). Others weaken the lure of likely targets. (Strangely enough, a raised flowerbed around signs helps protect them because people resist trampling the flowers to get to the sign.)

Given the personal impact that environments have, it is important to know how we are affected by stressful or unhealthy environments—a topic we will consider next.

Stressful Environments

Everyone has his or her own list of complaints about large cities. Traffic congestion, pollution, crime, and impersonality are urban problems that immediately come to mind. To this list psychologists have added crowding, noise, and overstimulation as major sources of urban stress. Psychological research has begun to clarify the impact of each of these conditions on human functioning (Marsella, 1998).

Crowding Overpopulation ranks as one of the most serious problems facing the world today. World population has exploded in the last 150 years (● Fig. 16.4). The world's population is now more than 6 billion people and may exceed 10 billion by 2050 (UN, 2004).

Experts estimate that the maximum sustainable population of the Earth is between 5 billion and 20 billion persons. This means the Earth has already entered the lower range of its carrying capacity (Cohen, 1995). Further population increases at the present rate could be disastrous. How many more people can the forests, oceans, croplands, and atmosphere support? The most pessimistic experts believe we have *already* exceeded the number of people the Earth can sustain indefinitely (Global Footprint Network, 2006; Oskamp, 2000).

Nowhere are the effects of overpopulation more evident than in the teeming cities of many underdeveloped nations. Closer to home, the jammed buses, subways, and living quarters of our own large cities are ample testimony to the stresses of crowding.

Is there any way to assess the effect crowding has on people? One approach is to study the effects of overcrowding among animals. Although the results of animal experiments cannot be considered conclusive for humans, they point to some disturbing effects.

For example? In an interesting classic experiment, John Calhoun (1962) let a group of laboratory rats breed without limit in a confined space. Calhoun provided plenty of food, water, and nesting material for the rats. All that the rats lacked was space. At its peak, the colony numbered 80 rats. Yet, it was housed in a cage designed to comfortably hold about 50. Overcrowding in the cage was heightened by the actions of the two most dominant males. These rascals staked out private territory at opposite ends of the cage, gathered harems of 8 to 10 females, and prospered. Their actions forced the remaining rats into a small, severely crowded middle area.

What effect did crowding have on the animals? A high rate of pathological behavior developed in both males and females. Females gave up nest building and caring for their young. Pregnancies decreased, and infant mortality ran extremely high. Many of the animals became indiscriminately aggressive and went on rampaging attacks against others.

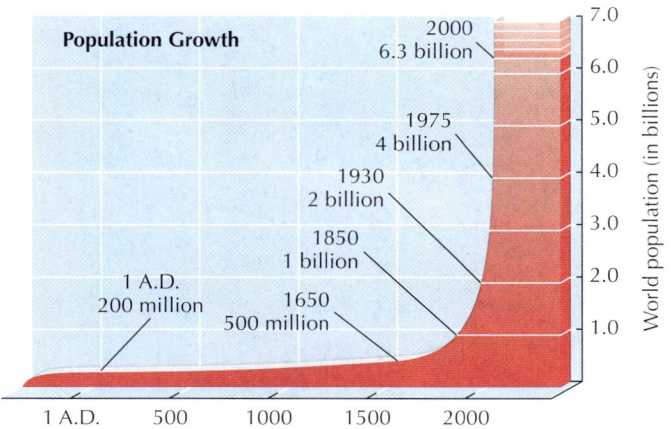

● **FIGURE 16.4** Population growth has exploded since 1850 (graph source: Population Institute, 2006). Overpopulation and rapid population growth are closely connected with environmental damage, international tensions, and rapid depletion of nonrenewable resources. Some demographers predict that if population growth is not limited voluntarily before it reaches 10 billion, it will be limited by widespread food shortages, disease, infant mortality, and early death (Erlich & Erlich, 1990).

Personal distance The distance maintained when interacting with close friends (about 18 inches to 4 feet from the body).

Social distance The distance at which impersonal interaction takes place (about 4 to 12 feet from the body).

Public distance The distance at which formal interactions, such as giving a speech, occur (about 12 feet or more from the body).

Territorial behavior Any behavior that tends to define a space as one's own or that protects it from intruders.

Territorial markers Objects and other signals whose placement indicates to others the "ownership" or control of a particular area.

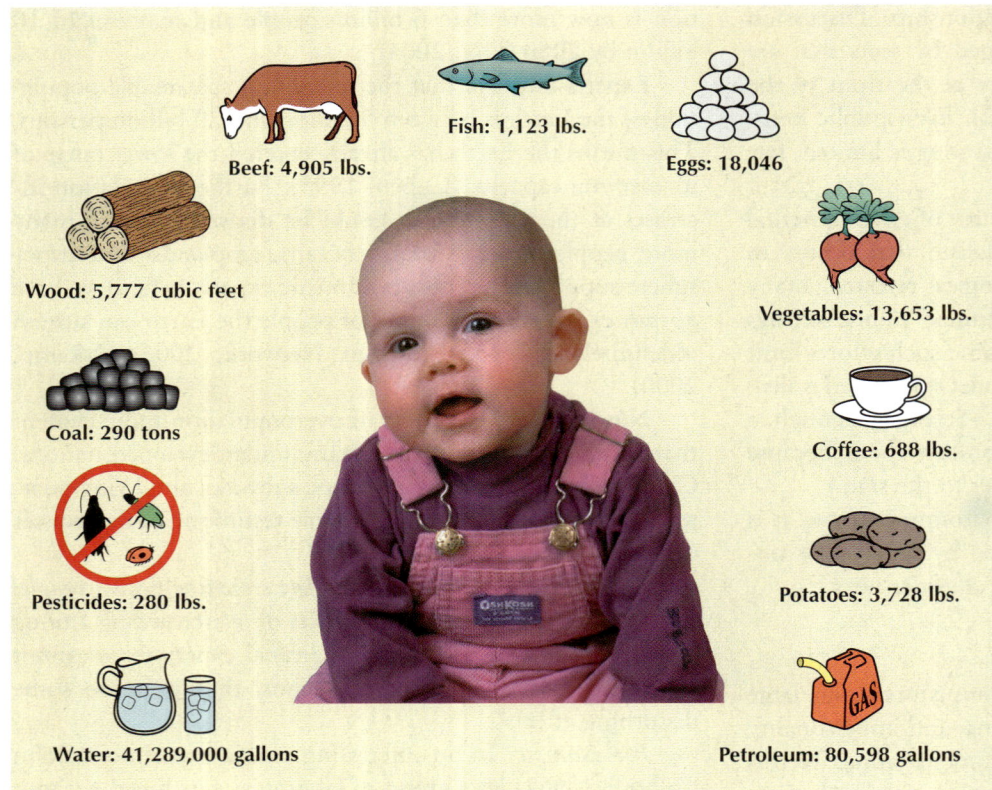

What will it cost the world to provide for a baby born in the year 2000? Without a major conservation effort, a person born in North America will over a lifetime consume, on average, the resources shown here ("Bringing Up Baby," 1999).

effects by crowding people into small places. Most likely, this is because *crowding* is a psychological condition that is separate from **density** (the number of people in a given space).

How does crowding differ from density? Crowding refers to subjective feelings of being overstimulated by social inputs or a loss of privacy. Whether high density is experienced as crowding may depend on relationships among those involved. In an elevator, subway, or prison, high densities may be uncomfortable. In contrast, a musical concert, party, or reunion may be most pleasant at high-density levels. Thus, physical crowding may interact with situations to intensify existing stresses or pleasures (Evans, Lercher, & Kofler, 2002). How-ever, when crowding causes a *loss of control* over one's immediate social environment, stress is likely to result (Pandey, 1999).

Stress probably explains why death rates increase among prison inmates and mental hospital patients who live in

Abnormal sexual behavior was rampant, with some animals displaying hypersexuality and others total sexual passivity. Many of the animals died, apparently from stress-caused diseases. The link between these problems and overcrowding is unmistakable.

But does that apply to humans? Many of the same pathological behaviors can be observed in crowded inner-city ghettos. It is therefore tempting to assume that violence, social disorganization, and declining birthrates as seen in these areas are directly related to crowding. However, the connection has not been so clearly demonstrated with humans. People living in the inner city suffer disadvantages in nutrition, education, income, and health care. These, more than crowding, may deserve the blame. In fact, most laboratory studies using human subjects have failed to produce any serious ill

Times Square in New York, New Year's Eve, 2007. High densities do not automatically produce feelings of crowding. The nature of the situation and the relationships among crowd members are also important.

crowded conditions. Even milder instances of crowding can have a negative impact. People who live in crowded conditions often become more aggressive or guarded and withdrawn from others (Regoeczi, 2003).

Overload One unmistakable result of high densities and crowding is a state that psychologist Stanley Milgram called **attentional overload.** This is a stressful condition that occurs when sensory stimulation, information, and social contacts make excessive demands on attention. Large cities, in particular, tend to bombard residents with continuous input. The resulting sensory and cognitive overload can be quite stressful.

Milgram (1970) believed that city dwellers learn to prevent attentional overload by engaging only in brief, superficial social contacts, by ignoring nonessential events, and by fending off others with cold and unfriendly expressions. In short, many city dwellers find that a degree of callousness is essential for survival.

Kind or Callous? *Is there any evidence that such strategies are actually adopted?* A fascinating study suggests they are. In several large American cities and smaller nearby towns, a young child stood on a busy street corner and asked passing strangers for help, saying, "I'm lost. Can you call my house?" About 72 percent of those approached in small towns offered to help. Only about 46 percent of those who were asked for help in the cities gave aid. In some cities (Boston and Philadelphia) only about one third were willing to help (Takooshian, Haber & Lucido, 1977). An analysis of 65 studies confirmed that country people are more likely to help than city people (Steblay, 1987). The least helpful city tested was New York, where the crime rate is high and people are densely packed together (Levine, 2003). Thus, a blunting of sensitivity to the needs of others may be one of the more serious costs of urban stresses and crowding. As described next, noise also contributes to the sensory assault many people endure in urban environments.

The High Cost of Noise How serious are the effects of daily exposure to noise? A classic study of children attending schools near Los Angeles International Airport suggests that constant noise can be quite damaging. Children from the noisy schools were compared with similar students attending schools farther from the airport (Cohen et al., 1981). The comparison students were from families of comparable social and economic makeup. Testing showed that children attending the noisy schools had higher blood pressure than those from the quieter schools. They were more likely to give up attempts to solve a difficult puzzle. And they were poorer at proofreading a printed paragraph—a task that requires close attention and concentration. Other studies of children living near other airports or in noisy neighborhoods have found similar signs of stress, poor reading skills, and other damag-

As the late Carl Sagan once said, "When you look closely, you find so many things going wrong with the environment, you are forced to reassess the hypothesis of intelligent life on Earth."

ing effects (Evans, 2006; Haines et al., 2001).

The tendency of the noise-battered children to give up or become distracted is a serious handicap. It may even reveal a state of "learned helplessness" (described in Module 11.3) caused by daily, uncontrollable blasts of sound. Even if such damage proves to be temporary, it is clear that **noise pollution** (annoying and intrusive noise) is a major source of environmental stress (Staples, 1996).

Toxic Environments

Human activities drastically change the natural environment. We burn fossil fuels; destroy forests; use chemical products; and strip, clear, and farm the land. In doing so, we alter natural cycles, animal populations, and the very face of the Earth. The long-range impact of such activities is already becoming evident through global warming; the extinction of plants and animals; a hole in the ozone layer; and polluted land, air, water, and oceans (Oskamp, 2002; Winter & Koger, 2004). (See "Planet in Peril?" for more information.)

Density The number of people in a given space or, inversely, the amount of space available to each person.

Crowding A subjective feeling of being over-stimulated by a loss of privacy or by the nearness of others (especially when social contact with them is unavoidable).

Attentional overload A stressful condition caused when sensory stimulation, information, and social contacts make excessive demands on attention.

Noise pollution Stressful and intrusive noise; usually artificially generated by machinery, but also including noises made by animals and humans.

DISCOVERING PSYCHOLOGY

Planet in Peril?

How seriously do human activities impact the environment? See if you can tell which of the following statements are true and which are false.

1. Worldwide, 1 in 6 people suffer from hunger and malnutrition. True or False?
2. By 2025, two thirds of the world's people are likely to be affected by water shortages. True or False?
3. Supplies of oil will begin to decline by 2010. True or False?
4. Continued global warming will lead to increased storms, floods, droughts, and loss of plant and animal species. True or False?
5. Hazardous chemicals are now found in the bodies of all newborn babies. True or False?
6. One in 4 people worldwide are exposed to unhealthy concentrations of air pollutants. True or False?
7. The world is consuming 20 percent more natural resources a year than the planet can produce. True or False?
8. In the last 30 years, the number of plant and animal species fell 30 percent. True or False?
9. Worldwide energy use has risen by 700 percent in the last 40 years. True or False?
10. Fuel economy in American vehicles hit a 22-year low in 2002. True or False?
11. Polar ice and glaciers around the world are melting at a rate not previously seen in human history. True or False?
12. If fully implemented, the Kyoto Treaty will slow global warming, not prevent it. True or False?

As you may have guessed, all the preceding statements are true. Given the scope of threats to the natural environment, only a fundamental change in beliefs may be capable of slowing the damage (Bell et al., 2006). The traditional Western view is that humans are superior to other living things, that natural resources are virtually unlimited, and that we can solve any problem through advances in technology. In contrast, an emerging ecological worldview holds that:

1. Humans are interdependent with all other living creatures. We benefit from their survival.
2. Many of the things we do have unanticipated negative effects on the environment.
3. Natural resources are limited.
4. Humans must respect the Earth's carrying capacity.

Many problems that will become irreversible in 20 or 30 years depend on what we do now. Increasingly, we ignore what Mother Nature is telling us at our own peril.

On a smaller scale there is plenty of evidence that unchecked environmental damage will be costly to our children and descendants. For example, exposure to toxic hazards, such as radiation, pesticides, and industrial chemicals, leads to an elevated risk of physical and mental disease (Evans, 2006).

Sustainable Lifestyles

A worldwide ecological crisis is brewing, and we humans must change course to avoid vast human misery and permanent damage. Of course, corporations and governments do much environmental damage. Thus, many of the solutions will require changes in politics and policies. Ultimately, it will also require changes in individual behavior. Most of the environmental problems we face can be traced back to the human tendency to overuse natural resources (Global Footprint Network, 2006; Oskamp & Schultz, 2006; Winter & Koger, 2004).

Wasted Resources The rapid worldwide consumption of natural resources is a devastating social problem. Resource consumption can be measured as an **ecological footprint,** the amount of land and water area required to replenish the resources that a human population consumes. According to the Global Footprint Network (2006), humans are already consuming more than the Earth can regenerate. Industrialized nations, in particular, are consuming world resources at an alarming rate. North America, for instance, has an ecological footprint about 10 times higher than that of Asia or Africa. In the face of projected shortages and squandered resources, what can be done to encourage conservation on a personal level?

Conservation Try as you might to reduce your use of resources (electricity, for instance), you may find it difficult to do. Environmental psychologists have long known that a lack of prompt *feedback* is a major barrier (Abrahamse et al., 2005). For example, feedback about electricity use (the monthly electricity bill) arrives long after the temptation to turn up the heat or to leave lights on. (See Module 6.2.) Psychologists aware of this problem have shown that lower energy bills result from simply giving families daily feedback about their use of gas or electricity.

Conservation is especially elusive when feedback is entirely unavailable. For example, electricity use in some apartment complexes is "master-metered." In such apartments, families do not receive individual bills for their utilities. Consequently, they consume about 25 percent more energy than they would in an individually metered apartment (McClelland & Cook, 1980). Simply providing individual meters can result in improved conservation and considerable

Shown here are the Skeen family of Pearland, Texas, and the Yadev family of Ahraura, India. Each was photographed by the Material World Project, which documented typical families and their possessions around the world. Developed countries presently have much larger ecological footprints. However, population growth is fastest in developing countries and their hunger for material possessions is rapidly expanding. Achieving sustainable levels of population and consumption are two of the greatest challenges of this century. (From Menzel et al., 1994.)

cost reduction. Savings are magnified further with the addition of programs that give monetary rewards for energy conservation.

Effective resource use feedback is finally becoming widely available as several organizations provide *ecological footprint calculators,* websites that allow individuals to calculate, and therefore track, their individual resource consumption (Global Footprint Network, 2006). With growing public concern over global warming, many people are now calculating their individual **carbon footprint,** the volume of greenhouse gases individual consumption adds to the atmosphere (The Nature Conservancy, 2007).

It is now easier than ever to conserve energy (by installing energy efficient lights, for example) and see an immediate reduction in your carbon footprint. It is also becoming more popular to offset some *carbon debt*—by planting trees, for example. Prompt and accurate information and feedback about energy use is making it possible to aspire to a *carbon-neutral lifestyle,* in which your energy consumption is reduced and the remainder offset so that your overall impact on global warming is zero.

Similar factors can greatly increase recycling, as described in "Reduce, Reuse, Recycle."

Social Dilemmas

Why is it so difficult to get people to take better care of the environment? A pattern of behavior called a *social dilemma* contributes to many environmental problems. A **social dilemma** is any social situation that rewards actions that have undesired

> **Ecological footprint** The amount of land and water area required to replenish the resources that a human population consumes.
> **Carbon footprint** The volume of greenhouse gases individual consumption adds to the atmosphere
> **Social dilemma** A social situation that tends to provide immediate rewards for actions that will have undesired effects in the long run.

DISCOVERING PSYCHOLOGY

Reduce, Reuse, Recycle

What can be done to lighten the environmental impact of our "throw-away" society? As we have discussed, reducing consumption is a start. Personally reusing products and materials that would normally be thrown away is also important. In addition, we can recycle materials such as paper, steel, glass, aluminum, and plastic that can be used to make new products.

What can be done to encourage people to recycle? Psychological research has shown that all of the following strategies promote recycling (Oskamp, 1995; Schmuck & Vlek, 2003; Winter & Koger, 2004).

- **Educate.** Learning about environmental problems and pro-environment values at school has been one of the most effective ways to encourage pro-environmental behavior (Schmuck & Vlek, 2003; Zelezny, 1999).
- **Provide monetary rewards.** As mentioned before, monetary rewards encourage conservation. Requiring refundable deposits on glass bottles is a good example of using incentives to increase recycling.
- **Remove barriers.** Anything that makes recycling more convenient helps. A good example is cities that offer curbside pickup of household recyclables. Some cities even accept unsorted recycling materials, which greatly increases participation in recycling programs. On campus, simply putting marked containers in classrooms is a good way to encourage recycling (Ludwig, Gray, & Rowell, 1998; Winter & Koger, 2004).
- **Use persuasion.** Many recycling programs benefit from media campaigns to persuade people to participate.
- **Obtain public commitment.** People who feel they have committed themselves to recycling are more likely to follow through and actually recycle. Sometimes, people are asked to sign "pledge cards" on which they promise to recycle. Another technique involves having people sign a list committing themselves to recycling. Such lists may or may not be published in a local newspaper. They are just as effective either way.
- **Encourage goal setting.** People who set their own goals for recycling tend to meet them. Goal setting has been used successfully with families, dorms, neighborhoods, offices, factories, and so forth.
- **Give feedback.** To reiterate, feedback proves to be very valuable. Recycling typically increases when families, work groups, dorms, and the like are simply told, on a weekly basis, how much they recycled (Schultz, 1999). Even impersonal feedback can be effective. In one study, signs were placed on recycling containers on a college campus. The signs showed how many aluminum cans had been deposited in the previous week. This simple procedure increased recycling by 65 percent (Larson, Houlihan, & Goernert, 1995).
- **Revise attitudes.** Even people who believe that recycling is worthwhile are likely to regard it as a boring task. Thus, people are most likely to continue recycling if they emphasize the sense of satisfaction they get from contributing to the environment (Werner & Makela, 1998).

People are much more likely to recycle if proper attention is given to psychological factors that promote recycling behavior.

---

effects in the long run (Van Vugt, 2002). In a typical social dilemma, no one individual intentionally acts against the group interest, but if many people act alike, collective harm is done. For example, the rapid transit systems in many large cities are underused. At the same time, the roads are jammed. Why? Because too many people decide that it is convenient to own and drive a separate car (in order to run errands and so on). However, each person's behavior affects the welfare of others. Because everyone wants to drive for "convenience," driving becomes inconvenient: The mass of cars in most cities causes irritating traffic snarls and a lack of parking spaces. Each car owner has been drawn into a dilemma.

The Tragedy of the Commons Social dilemmas are especially damaging when we are enticed into overuse of scarce resources that must be shared by many people. Again, each person acts in his or her self-interest. But collectively, everyone ends up suffering. Ecologist Garrett Hardin (1968, 1985) calls such situations the **tragedy of the commons.** An example we have already discussed is the lack of individual incentives to conserve gasoline, water, or electricity. Whenever personal comfort or convenience is involved, it is highly tempting to "let others worry about it." Yet in the long run everyone stands to lose.

Why does such misguided behavior so often prevail? Again, we see a social dilemma at work: If one person pollutes a river or trashes the roadside, it has little noticeable effect. But as many people do the same, problems that affect everyone quickly mount. Throwing away one plastic bag may seem inconsequential, but across the world 500 billion plastic bags are used every year and it takes hundreds of years for the environment to recycle them. Plastic bags are major polluters of the world's oceans.

As another example, consider the farmer who applies pesticides to a crop to save it from insect damage. The farmer benefits immediately. However, if other farmers follow suit, the local water system may be permanently damaged. In most cases of environmental pollution there are immediate benefits for polluting and major, but delayed, long-term costs. What can we do to avoid such dilemmas?

Escaping Dilemmas Persuasion and education have been used with some success to get individuals and businesses to voluntarily reduce destructive activities. Effective appeals may be based on self-interest (cost savings), the collective good (protecting one's own children and future generations), or simply a personal desire to take better care of the planet (Stern, 1992; Winter & Koger, 2004). It really helps if conservation is seen as a group effort. There is evidence that in most social dilemmas, people are more likely to restrain themselves when they believe others will, too (Messick et al., 1983). Otherwise they are likely to think, "Why should I be a sucker? I don't think anyone else is going to conserve" (fuel, electricity, water, paper, or whatever).

In some cases it is possible to dismantle social dilemmas by rearranging rewards and costs. For example, many companies are tempted to pollute because it saves them money and increases profits. To reverse the situation, a pollution tax could be levied so that it would cost more, not less, for a business to pollute. Likewise, incentives can be offered for responsible behavior. An example is the rebates offered for installing insulation or buying energy-efficient appliances (Dwyer et al., 1993; Schmuck & Vlek, 2003).

Some problems may be harder to solve. What, for instance, can be done about truck drivers who cause dangerous traffic jams because they will not pull over on narrow roads? How can littering be discouraged or prevented? How would you make carpooling or using public transportation the first choice for most people? Or how could people simply be encouraged to stagger their departure times to and from work? All these and more are social dilemmas that need solving. It is important that we not fall into the trap of ignoring them.

Environmental Problem Solving

Although overcrowding, pollution, and overuse of resources rank high on the list of environmental stresses, they are only a few of the many challenges that press for attention. To conclude, let's sample some solutions that psychologists have provided for two more environmental problems.

Problem: Urban Fears The way people think about the environment greatly affects their behavior. Mental "maps" of various areas, for instance, often guide actions and alter decisions. A case in point is a study done in Philadelphia. There researchers found that an existing school bus route contributed to truancy. The problem was that many of its stops were at corners where children were afraid of being attacked and beaten (Conyne & Clack, 1981).

Solution By doing an **environmental assessment,** psychologists develop a picture of environments as they are perceived by the people using them. An assessment often includes such things as charting areas of highest use in buildings, using attitude scales to measure reactions to various settings (such as schools, businesses, and parks), and even having people draw a version of their cognitive map of a building, campus, or city (Coulton, Korbin, & Su, 1996).

In the case of the schoolchildren, residents of the neighborhood were asked to rate how much stress they felt when walking in various areas. The result was a contour map (somewhat like a high- and low-pressure weather map) that showed the areas of highest perceived stress. This "stress map" was then used to reroute school buses to "low-pressure" areas.

Problem: Residential Crowding Anyone who has ever lived in a college dorm knows that at times a dorm hall can be quite a "zoo." Most architects aim to create buildings in which people will be comfortable, happy, and healthy. But sometimes they miss the mark with human behavior. In one well-known experiment, Baum and Valins (1977) found that students housed in long, narrow, corridor-design dormitories often feel crowded and stressed. The crowded students tended to withdraw from others and even made more trips to the campus health center than students living in less-crowded buildings.

Solution **Architectural psychology** is the study of the effects buildings have on behavior. By analyzing buildings, psychologists are often able to suggest design changes that solve or avoid problems (Zeisel, 2006). For example, Baum and Valins (1979) studied two basic dorm arrangements. One dorm had a long corridor with one central bathroom. As a result, residents were constantly forced into contact with one another. The other dorm had rooms clustered in threes. Each of these suites shared a small bathroom. Even though the amount of space available to each student was the same in both dorms, students in the long-corridor dorm reported feeling more

> **Tragedy of the commons** A social dilemma in which individuals, each acting in his or her immediate self-interest, overuse a scarce group resource.
> **Environmental assessment** Measurement and analysis of the effects an environment has on the behavior of people within that environment.
> **Architectural psychology** Study of the effects buildings have on behavior and the design of buildings using behavioral principles.

● **FIGURE 16.5** An architectural solution for crowding. Psychologists divided a dorm hall like that shown in the left diagram (a) into two shorter halls separated by unlocked doors and a lounge area (b). This simple change minimized unwanted social contacts and greatly reduced feelings of crowding among dorm residents. (Adapted from Baum & Davis, 1980.)

crowded. They also made fewer friends in their dorm and showed greater signs of withdrawing from social contact.

What sort of solution does this suggest? A later study showed that small architectural changes can greatly reduce stress in high-density living conditions. Baum and Davis (1980) compared students living in a long-corridor dorm housing 40 students with those living in an altered long-corridor dorm. In the altered dorm, Baum and Davis divided the hallway in half with unlocked doors and made three center bedrooms into a lounge area (● Fig. 16.5). At the end of the term, students living in the divided dorm reported less stress from crowding. They also formed more friendships and were more open to social contacts. In comparison, students in the long-corridor dorm felt more crowded, stressed, and unfriendly, and they kept their doors shut much more frequently—presumably because they "vahnted to be alone."

Similar improvements have been made by altering the interior design of businesses, schools, apartment buildings, mental hospitals, and prisons. In general, the more spaces one must pass through to get from one part of a building to another, the less stressed and crowded people feel (Evans, Lepore, & Schroeder, 1996; Zeisel, 2006).

Conclusion

We have had room here only to hint at the creative and highly useful work being done in environmental psychology. Although many environmental problems remain, it is encouraging to see that behavioral solutions exist for at least some of them. Surely, creating and maintaining healthy environments is one of the major challenges facing coming generations (Gifford, 2002; Oskamp & Schultz, 2006).

We have discussed work and the environment at some length because both have major effects on our lives. To provide a fuller account of the diversity of applied psychology, let's conclude by briefly sampling three additional topics of interest: legal psychology, sports psychology, and media psychology.

MODULE 16.2 Summary

What have psychologists learned about the effects of our physical and social environments?

- Humans affect the environment and environments affect humans. Many problems can be solved by understanding both relationships.
- Environmental psychologists are interested in behavioral settings, physical or social environments, and human territoriality, among other topics.
- Overpopulation is a major world problem, often reflected at an individual level in crowding.
- Animal experiments indicate that excessive crowding can be unhealthy. However, human research shows that psychological feelings of crowding do not always correspond to density.
- One major consequence of crowding is attentional overload.
- Environmental psychologists have offered solutions to many practical problems—from noise pollution to architectural design. Their work often begins with a careful environmental assessment.
- Providing feedback about resource use is an effective way to promote conservation.
- Various psychological strategies can promote recycling.
- The origins of many environmental disasters lie in overpopulation and overconsumption (the tragedy of the commons).
- Environmental problems such as crowding, pollution, and wasted resources are based on human behavior; they can only be solved by changing individual behavior patterns.

KNOWLEDGE BUILDER

Environmental Psychology

Recite

1. If two people position themselves 5 feet apart while conversing, they are separated by a gap referred to as _____ distance.

2. Although male rats in Calhoun's crowded animal colony became quite pathological, female rats continued to behave in a relatively normal fashion. T or F?

3. To clearly understand behavior, it is necessary to make a distinction between crowding and _____ (the number of people in a given space).

4. Milgram believed that many city dwellers prevent attentional overload by limiting themselves to superficial social contacts. T or F?

5. Using ecological footprint calculators to provide feedback is one effective approach for bringing about energy conservation. T or F?

6. Performing an environmental _____ might be a good prelude to redesigning college classrooms to make them more comfortable and conducive to learning.

Reflect
Critical Thinking

7. Many of the most damaging changes to the environment being caused by humans will not be felt until sometime in the future. How does this complicate the problem of preserving environmental quality?

Relate

What is the nature of the natural environment, constructed environment, social environment, and behavioral setting you are in right now?

What forms of territorial behavior are you aware of in your own actions?

Have you ever experienced a stressful level of crowding? Was density or control the key factor?

Have you ever calculated your carbon footprint? Why not try it? You might be surprised by what you find.

Link

Internet addresses frequently change. To find the sites listed here, visit **http://www.thomsonedu.com/psychology/coon** for an updated list of Internet addresses and direct links to relevant sites.

- **Ecological Footprint Quiz** Determine your ecological footprint with this quiz.
- **Carbon Calculator** Determine your own carbon footprint.
- **Human Impact** Read more about human influences on the biosphere.

ANSWERS

1. social 2. F 3. density 4. T 5. T 6. assessment 7. A delay of consequences (rewards, benefits, costs, and punishments) tends to reduce their impact on immediate behavior.

MODULE 16.3 The Psychology of Law and Sports

TWO OF THE BEST PLACES TO SEE PSYCHOLOGY IN ACTION are at the local courthouse and at sporting events. Courtroom hearings and sports are both "contests" that bring out some of the best and worst of human behavior. Although the focus of attention might seem to be legal matters or athletic performance, the law and sports are prime arenas for applying psychology.

Psychology and Law—Judging Juries

SURVEY QUESTION: *What does psychology reveal about juries and court verdicts?*

Jury trials are often fascinating studies in human behavior. Does the defendant's appearance affect the jury's decision? Do the personality characteristics or attitudes of jurors influence how they vote? These and many more questions have been investigated by psychologists interested in law. Specifically, the **psychology of law** is the study of the behavioral dimensions of the legal system (■ Table 16.4).

Jury Behavior

When a case goes to trial, jurors must listen to days or weeks of testimony and then decide guilt or innocence. How do they reach their decision? Psychologists use **mock juries** (simulated juries) to probe such questions. In some mock juries volunteers are simply given written evidence and arguments to read before making a decision. Others watch videotaped trials staged by actors. Either way, studying the behavior of mock juries helps us understand what determines how real jurors vote (Kerr & Bray, 2005).

Some of the findings of jury research are unsettling (Levett et al., 2005). Studies show that jurors are rarely able to put aside their biases, attitudes, and values while making a decision (Devine et al., 2001). For example, jurors are less likely to find attractive defendants guilty (on the basis of the same evidence) than unattractive defendants (Perlman & Cozby, 1983). There is an interesting twist, however. If good looks helped a person commit a crime, it can work against her or him in court (Tedeschi, Lindskold, & Rosenfeld, 1985). An example would be a handsome man accused of swindling money from an unmarried middle-aged woman.

A second major problem is that jurors are not very good at separating evidence from other information, such as their perceptions of the defendant, attorneys, witnesses, and what they think the judge wants. For example, if complex scientific evidence is presented, jurors tend to be swayed more by the expertise of the witness than by the evidence itself (Cooper, Bennett, & Sukel, 1996). Similarly, today's jurors place too much confidence in DNA evidence because crime-solving programs like *CSI* and *Forensic Files* make it seem simple (Myers, 2007). Further, jurors who have been exposed to pretrial publicity tend to inappropriately incorporate that information into their jury deliberations, often without being aware it has happened (Ruva, McEvoy, & Bryant, 2007).

Often the jurors' final verdict is influenced by inadmissible evidence, such as mention of a defendant's prior conviction. When jurors are told to ignore information that slips out in court, they find it very hard to do so. A related problem occurs when jurors take into account the severity of the punishment a defendant faces (Sales & Hafemeister, 1985). Jurors are not supposed to let this affect their verdict, but many do.

A fourth area of difficulty arises because jurors usually cannot suspend judgment until all the evidence is in. Typically, they form an opinion early in the trial. It then becomes hard for them to fairly judge evidence that contradicts their opinion.

Problems like these are troubling in a legal system that prides itself on fairness. However, all is not lost. The more severe the crime and the more clear-cut the evidence, the less a jury's quirks affect the verdict (Tedeschi, Lindskold, & Rosenfeld, 1985). Although it is far from perfect, the jury system works reasonably well in most cases.

■ TABLE 16.4	Topics of Special Interest in the Psychology of Law
Arbitration	Juror attitudes
Attitudes toward law	Jury decisions
Bail setting	Jury selection
Capital punishment	Mediation
Conflict resolution	Memory
Criminal personality	Parole board decisions
Diversion programs	Police selection
Effects of parole	Police stress
Expert testimony	Police training
Eyewitness testimony	Polygraph accuracy
Forensic hypnosis	Sentencing decisions
Insanity plea	White-collar crime

CRITICAL THINKING

Death-Qualified Juries

People in a **death-qualified jury** must favor the death penalty or at least be indifferent to it. That way, jurors are capable of voting for the death penalty if they think it is justified.

In order for the death penalty to have meaning, death-qualified juries may be a necessity. However, psychologists have discovered that the makeup of such juries tends to be biased. Specifically, death-qualified juries are likely to contain a disproportionate number of people who are male, white, high income, conservative, and authoritarian. Given the same facts, jurors who favor the death penalty are more likely to read criminal intent into a defendant's actions (Goodman-Delahunty, Greene, & Hsiao, 1998) and are much more likely than average to convict a defendant (Allen, Mabry, & McKelton, 1998; Butler, 2007).

Could death-qualified juries be too willing to convict? It is nearly impossible to say how often the bias inherent in death-qualified juries results in bad verdicts. However, the possibility that some innocent persons have been executed may be one of the inevitable costs of using death as the ultimate punishment.

Jury Selection

Before a trial begins, opposing attorneys are allowed to disqualify potential jurors who may be biased. For example, a person who knows anyone connected with the trial can be excluded. Beyond this, attorneys try to use jury selection to remove people who may cause trouble for them. For instance, juries composed of women are more likely to vote for conviction in child sexual assault trials (Golding et al., 2007). In many cases, the composition of a jury has a major effect on the verdict of a trial (Devine et al., 2001).

Only a limited number of potential jurors can be excused. As a result, many attorneys ask psychologists for help in identifying people who will favor or harm their efforts. In **scientific jury selection,** social science principles are applied to the process of choosing a jury (Seltzer, 2006). Several techniques are typically used. As a first step, *demographic information* may be collected for each juror. Much can be guessed by knowing a juror's age, sex, race, occupation, education, political affiliation, religion, and socioeconomic status. Most of this information is available from public records.

To supplement demographic information, a *community survey* may be done to find out how local citizens feel about the case. The assumption is that jurors probably have attitudes similar to people with backgrounds like their own. Although talking with potential jurors outside the courtroom is not permitted, other information networks are available. For instance, a psychologist may interview relatives, acquaintances, neighbors, and co-workers of potential jurors.

Back in court, psychologists also often watch for *authoritarian personality* traits in potential jurors. Authoritarians tend to believe that punishment is effective, and they are more likely to vote for conviction (Devine et al., 2001). At the same time, the psychologist typically observes potential jurors' *nonverbal behavior*. The idea is to try to learn from body language which side the person favors (Sales & Hafemeister, 1985).

In the United States, murder trials require a special jury—one made up of people who are not opposed to the death penalty. "Death-Qualified Juries" examines the implications of this practice.

In the well-publicized case of O. J. Simpson, who was accused of brutally killing his wife, a majority of African Americans thought Simpson was innocent during the early stages of the trial. In contrast, the majority of European Americans thought he was guilty. The opinions of both groups changed little over the course of the yearlong trial. (Simpson was eventually acquitted, but he later lost a lawsuit brought by his wife's family.) The fact that emerging evidence and arguments had little effect on what people believed shows why jury makeup can sometimes decide the outcome of a trial (Brigham & Wasserman, 1999; ForsterLee et al., 2006).

Cases like O. J. Simpson's and those of other wealthy individuals raise troubling ethical questions. In each case, wealthy clients had the advantage of psychological jury selection—something most people cannot afford. Attorneys,

Psychology of law Study of the psychological and behavioral dimensions of the legal system.
Mock jury A group that realistically simulates a courtroom jury.
Scientific jury selection Using social science principles to choose members of a jury.
Death-qualified jury A jury composed of people who favor the death penalty or at least are indifferent to it.

The behavior of juries and jurors has been extensively studied. The findings of such studies are applied by psychologists who act as advisers to attorneys during the jury selection process. Jury selection in the O. J. Simpson murder trial took 2 months, as defense and prosecution lawyers struggled for the advantage in jury makeup.

of course, can't be blamed for trying to improve their odds of winning a case. And because both sides help select jurors, the net effect in most instances is probably a more balanced jury. At its worst, jury analysis leads to unjust verdicts. At its best, it helps to identify and remove only people who would be highly biased (Strier, 1999).

Jury research is perhaps the most direct link between psychology and law, but there are others. Psychologists evaluate people for sanity hearings, do counseling in prisons, profile criminals, advise lawmakers on public policy, help select and train police cadets, and more (Brewer & Williams, 2005; Wrightsman & Fulero, 2005). In the future, it is quite likely that psychology will have a growing impact on law and the courts.

Sports Psychology—The Athletic Mind

SURVEY QUESTION: *Can psychology enhance athletic performance?*

Sports psychology is the study of the behavioral dimensions of sports performance (Cox, 2007). As almost all serious athletes soon learn, peak performance requires more than physical training. Mental and emotional "conditioning" are also important. Recognizing this fact, many teams, both professional and amateur, now include psychologists on their staffs. On any given day, a sports psychologist might teach an athlete how to relax, how to ignore distractions, or how to cope with emotions. The sports psychologist might also provide personal counseling for performance-lowering stresses and conflicts (LeUnes & Nation, 2002). Other psychologists are interested in studying factors that affect athletic achievement, such as skill learning, the personality profiles of champion athletes, the effects of spectators, and related topics (■ Table 16.5). In short, sports psychologists seek to understand and improve sports performance and to enhance the benefits of participating in sports (Cox, 2007).

Sports often provide valuable information on human behavior in general. For example, one study of adolescents found a link between sports participation and physical self-esteem that was, in turn, linked with overall self-esteem (Bowker, 2006). In other work, psychologists have learned that such benefits are most likely to occur when competition, rejection, criticism, and the "one-winner mentality" are minimized. When working with children in sports, it is also important to emphasize fair play, intrinsic rewards, self-control of emotions, independence, and self-reliance. Adults, of course, may also benefit from sports. For many, the payoffs are stress reduction, a better self-image, and improved general health.

Before the advent of sports psychology, it was debatable whether athletes improved because of "homespun" coaching methods or in spite of them. For example, in early studies of volleyball and gymnastics, it became clear that people teaching these sports had very little knowledge of crucial, underlying skills (Salmela, 1974, 1975).

■ TABLE 16.5 Topics of Special Interest to Sports Psychologists

Achievement motivation	Hypnosis
Athletic personality	Mental practice
Athletic task analysis	Motor learning
Coaching styles	Peak performance
Competition	Positive visualization
Control of attention	Self-regulation
Coping strategies	Skill acquisition
Emotions and performance	Social facilitation
Exercise and mental health	Stress reduction
Goal setting	Team cooperation
Group (team) dynamics	Training procedures

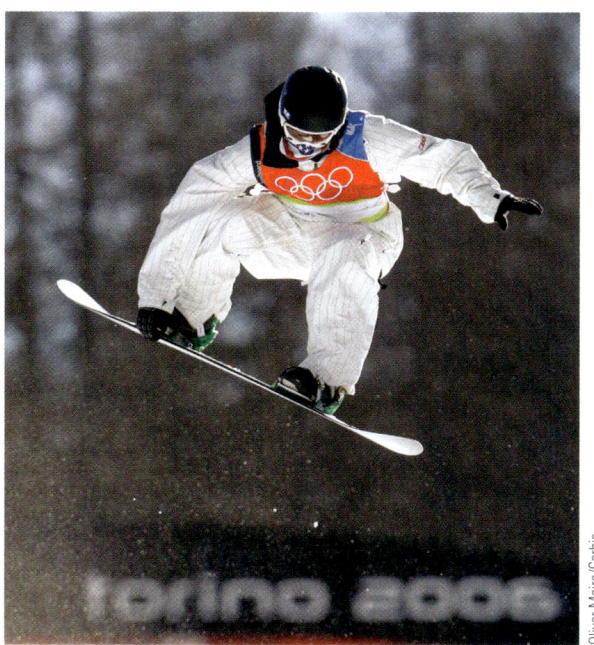

Sports psychologists have played a significant role in helping prepare athletes for peak performance in the Olympic Games. Stress management, attention regulation, mental imagery, motivation, self-confidence, and many other psychological factors greatly affect athletic performance.

Testing by psychologists has shown that umpires can call balls and strikes more accurately if they stand behind the outside corner of home plate. This position supplies better height and distance information because umpires are able to see pitches pass in front of the batter (Ford et al., 1999).

How has psychology helped? An ability to do detailed studies of complex skills has been one of the major contributions. In a **task analysis,** sports skills are broken into subparts, so that key elements can be identified and taught. Such methods are an extension of techniques first used for job analyses, as described earlier. For example, it doesn't take much to be off target in the Olympic sport of marksmanship. The object is to hit a bull's-eye the size of a dime at the end of a 165-foot-long shooting range. Nevertheless, an average of 50 bull's-eyes out of 60 shots is not unusual in international competition (prone position).

What does it take—beyond keen eyes and steady hands—to achieve such accuracy? The answer is surprising. Sports psychologists have found that top marksmen consistently squeeze the trigger *between* heartbeats (● Fig. 16.6). Apparently the tiny tremor induced by a heartbeat is enough to send the shot astray (Pelton, 1983). Without careful psychological study, it is doubtful that this element of marksmanship would have been identified. Now that its importance is known, competitors have begun to use various techniques—from relaxation training to biofeedback—to steady and control their heartbeat. In the future, the best marksmen may be those who set their sights on mastering their hearts.

Motor Skills Sports psychologists are very interested in how we learn motor skills. A **motor skill** is a series of actions molded into a smooth and efficient performance. Typing, walking, pole-vaulting, shooting baskets, playing golf, driving a car, writing, and skiing are all motor skills.

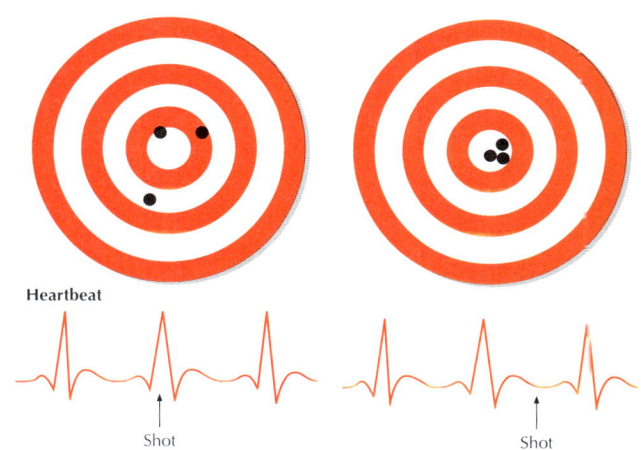

● **FIGURE 16.6** The target on the left shows what happens when a marksman fires during the heart's contraction. Higher scores, as shown by the three shots on the right, are more likely when shots are made between heartbeats. (Adapted from Pelton, 1983.)

Sports psychology Study of the psychological and behavioral dimensions of sports performance.

Task analysis Breaking complex skills into their subparts.

Motor skill A series of actions molded into a smooth and efficient performance.

A basketball player may never make exactly the same shot twice in a game. This makes it almost impossible to practice every shot that might occur. How, then, do athletes become skillful? Typically, athletic performances involve learning *motor programs.* A **motor program** is a mental plan or model of what a skilled movement should be like. Motor programs allow an athlete—or a person simply walking across a room—to perform complex movements that fit changing conditions. If, for example, you have learned a "bike-riding" motor program, you can easily ride bicycles of different sizes and types on a large variety of surfaces.

Throughout life you will face the challenge of learning new motor skills. How can psychology make your learning more effective? Studies of sports skills suggest that you should keep the following points in mind for optimal skill learning:

1. Begin by observing and imitating a *skilled model.* Modeling provides a good mental picture of the skill. At this point, try simply to grasp a visual image of the skilled movement.
2. Learn *verbal rules* to back up motor learning. Such rules are usually most helpful in the early phases of skill learning. When first learning cross-country skiing, for example, it is helpful to say, "left arm, right foot, right arm, left foot." Later, as a skill becomes more automated, internal speech may actually get in the way.
3. Practice should be as *lifelike* as possible so that artificial cues and responses do not become a part of the skill. A competitive diver should practice on the board, not on a trampoline. If you want to learn to ski, try to practice on snow, not straw.
4. Get *feedback* from a mirror, videotape, coach, or observer. Whenever possible, get someone experienced in the skill to direct attention to *correct responses* when they occur.
5. When possible, it is better to practice *natural units* rather than breaking the task into artificial parts. When learning to type, it is better to start with real words rather than nonsense syllables.
6. Learn to *evaluate* and *analyze* your own performance. Remember, you are trying to learn a motor program, not just train your muscles. Motor skills are actually very mental.

The last point leads to one more suggestion. Research has shown that **mental practice,** or merely imagining a skilled performance, can aid learning (Short, Ross-Stewart, & Monsma, 2006). This technique seems to help by refining motor programs. Of course, mental practice is not superior to actual practice. Mental practice tends to be most valuable after you have mastered a task at a basic level (Tenenbaum, Bar-Eli, & Eyal, 1996). When you begin to get really good at a skill, give mental practice a try. You may be surprised at how effective it can be (Morris, Spittle, & Watt, 2005).

Positive Psychology: Peak Performance

One of the most interesting topics in sports psychology is the phenomenon of *peak performance.* During **peak performance,** physical, mental, and emotional states are harmonious and optimal. Many athletes report episodes during which they felt almost as if they were in a trance. The experience has also been called "flow" because the athlete becomes one with his or her performance and flows with it. At such times, athletes experience intense concentration, detachment, a lack of fatigue and pain, a subjective slowing of time, and feelings of unusual power and control (Csikszmentmihalyi, 1999). It is at just such times that "personal bests" tend to occur.

A curious aspect of flow is that it cannot be forced to happen. In fact, if a person stops to think about it, the flow state goes away. Psychologists are now seeking to identify conditions that facilitate peak performance and the unusual mental state that usually accompanies it (Csikszmentmihalyi, 1999).

Even though flow may be an elusive state, there is much that athletes can do mentally to improve performance (Porter, 2003). A starting point is to make sure that their *arousal level is appropriate for the task* at hand. For a sprinter at a track meet, that may mean elevating arousal to a very high level. The sprinter could, for example, try to become angry by picturing a rival cheating. For a golfer or a gymnast, lowering arousal may be crucial, in order to avoid "choking" during a big event. One way of controlling arousal is to go through a *fixed routine* before each game or event. Athletes also learn to use *imagery and relaxation techniques* to adjust their degree of arousal (Gould & Udry, 1994).

Imaging techniques can be used to *focus attention* on the athlete's task and to *mentally rehearse* it beforehand. For example, golf great Jack Nicklaus "watches a movie" in his head before each shot. During events, athletes learn to *use cognitive-behavioral strategies to guide their efforts* in a supportive, positive way (Beauchamp et al., 1996). For instance, instead of berating herself for being behind in a match, a tennis player could use the time between points to savor a good shot or put an error out of mind. In general, athletes benefit from avoiding negative, self-critical thoughts that distract them and undermine their confidence (Cox, 2007). Finally, top athletes tend to use more *self-regulation strategies,* in which they evaluate their performance and make adjustments to keep it at optimum levels (Anshel, 1995; Kim, Singer, & Radlo, 1996).

The psychological dimension of sport is illustrated by the existence of a small but well-documented "home court advantage" in most sports. That is, sports teams are more likely to win at home than they are when they compete "on the road." To some extent, this is based on familiarity with the home court, support from the home crowd, and a lack of travel demands. But most of the advantage occurs because athletes approach home games with greater confidence and optimal arousal levels (Bray & Widmeyer, 2000). When athletes are well matched in skill, small psychological advantages can make a difference between winning and losing. On some occasions, the home court advantage may also be related to body rhythms. When sports teams travel eastward over one or more time zones, they perform more poorly than they do when they travel westward. This is exactly what we would expect from people whose circadian rhythms are disrupted. It provides "real-world" support for other observations about body rhythms (Worthen & Wade, 1999).

At present, sports psychology is a very young field and still much more an art than a science. Nevertheless, interest in the field is rapidly expanding (Petrie & Diehl, 1995).

A Look Ahead Although we have sampled several major areas of applied psychology, they are by no means the only applied specialties. The upcoming "Psychology in Action" module explores the applied topic of human factors psychology.

MODULE 16.3 Summary

What does psychology reveal about juries and court verdicts?

- The legal system is concerned almost as much with human behavior as it is with the law.

- Optimal performance in sports is strongly influenced by mental and emotional factors.
- The psychology of law includes studies of courtroom behavior and other topics that pertain to the legal system. Psychologists also serve various consulting and counseling roles in legal, law enforcement, and criminal justice settings.
- Studies of mock juries show that jury decisions are often far from objective.
- Scientific jury selection is used in attempts to choose jurors who have particular characteristics. In some instances, this may result in juries that have a particular bias or that do not represent the community as a whole.
- A bias toward convicting defendants is characteristic of many death-qualified juries.

Can psychology enhance athletic performance?

- Sports psychologists seek to enhance sports performance and the benefits of sports participation. A careful task analysis of sports skills is one of the major tools for improving coaching and performance.
- A motor skill is a nonverbal response chain assembled into a smooth performance. Motor skills are guided by internal mental models called motor programs.
- Motor skills are refined through direct practice, but mental practice can also contribute to improvement.
- During moments of peak performance, physical, mental, and emotional states are optimal.
- Top performers in sports often use a variety of self-regulation strategies to focus their attention and maintain optimal levels of arousal.

Motor program A mental plan or model that guides skilled movement.
Mental practice Imagining a skilled performance to aid learning.
Peak performance A performance during which physical, mental, and emotional states are harmonious and optimal.

KNOWLEDGE BUILDER

The Psychology of Law and Sports

Recite

1. Despite their many limitations, one thing that jurors are good at is setting aside inadmissible evidence. T or F?
2. Which of the following is *not* commonly used by psychologists to aid jury selection?
   a. mock testimony
   b. information networks
   c. community surveys
   d. demographic data
3. Members of death-qualified juries are more likely to have authoritarian personality traits. T or F?
4. Mental models, called _____ _____, appear to underlie well-learned motor skills.
5. Learning verbal rules to back up motor learning is usually most helpful in the early stages of acquiring a skill. T or F?
6. The flow experience is closely linked with instances of _____ performance.

Reflect
Critical Thinking

7. When an athlete follows a set routine before an event, what source of stress has she or he eliminated?

Relate

What advice would you give a person who is about to serve on a jury if he or she wants to make an impartial judgment? How could you apply the concepts of task analysis, mental practice, and peak performance to a sport you are interested in?

Link

Internet addresses frequently change. To find the sites listed here, visit **http://www.thomsonedu.com/psychology/coon** for an updated list of Internet addresses and direct links to relevant sites.

- **The Innocence Project** Read case studies of people wrongly convicted, often because of faulty eyewitness testimony.
- **Careers in Psychology and Law** Find out about career opportunities in forensic psychology.
- **Sports Psychology** Read sports training articles.

ANSWERS

1. F 2. a 3. T 4. motor programs 5. T 6. peak 7. As discussed in Module 11.2, stress is reduced when a person feels in control of a situation. Following a routine helps athletes maintain a sense of order and control so that they are not over-aroused when the time comes to perform.

MODULE *Psychology in Action*

16.4 Human Factors Psychology— Who's the Boss Here?

SURVEY QUESTION: *How are tools designed to better serve human needs?*

Should we serve machines or should they serve us? The demands that machines can make will be all too familiar if you have ever struggled with a new cell phone or failed to put together that "easy to assemble" home gym. Despite all they do for us, machines are of little value unless we humans can operate them effectively. An awkward pocket calculator might just as well be a paperweight. An automobile design that blocks large areas of the driver's vision could be deadly.

Designing for Human Use

The goal of **human factors psychology** (also known as **ergonomics**) is to design machines and work environments so they are *compatible* with our sensory and motor capacities (Gamache, 2004). For example, displays must be easy to perceive, controls must be easy to use, and the tendency to make errors must be minimized (● Fig. 16.7). (A *display* is any dial, screen, light, or other device used to provide information about a machine's activity to a human user. A *control* is any knob, handle, button, lever, or other device used to alter the activity of a machine.)

Psychologist Donald Norman (1994) refers to successful human factors engineering as **natural design,** because it is based on perceptual signals that people understand naturally, without needing to learn them. An example is the row of vertical buttons in elevators that mimic the layout of the floors. This is simple, natural, and clear. One way to create more natural designs is to use *metaphors* to create resemblances between different subjects. One famous example is the *desktop metaphor*. The design of all current personal computers presents a visual "desktop" with images of "files," "folders," and even a "trashcan." That way, you can use your knowledge of real desktops to immediately begin to use the virtual "desktop" on your computer. Earlier personal computer interfaces, which required you to type in coded instructions, were much harder to use. Similarly, digital cameras are designed to look a lot like film cameras. That way you can use your knowledge of how a mechanical camera works to start using a digital camera.

Effective design also provides *feedback* (information about the effect of making a response). The audible click designed into many computer keyboards is a good example. As Norman points out, the cause of many accidents is not just "human error." The real culprit is poor design. Human factors psychologists helped design many of the tools we rely on each day, such as "user-friendly" computers, home appliances, cameras, personal digital assistants (PDAs), airplane controls, and traffic signals.

Usability Testing To design useful tools, human factors psychologists do **usability testing.** That is, they directly measure the ease with which people can learn to use a machine (Norman & Panizzi, 2006). Health and safety are also important targets of usability testing. For example, construction

"The directions were easy to understand...until you got past step 2."

> **Human factors psychology (ergonomics)** A specialty concerned with making machines and work environments compatible with human perceptual and physical capacities.
>
> **Natural design** Human factors engineering that makes use of naturally understood perceptual signals.
>
> **Usability testing** The empirical investigation of the ease with which users can learn to use a machine.

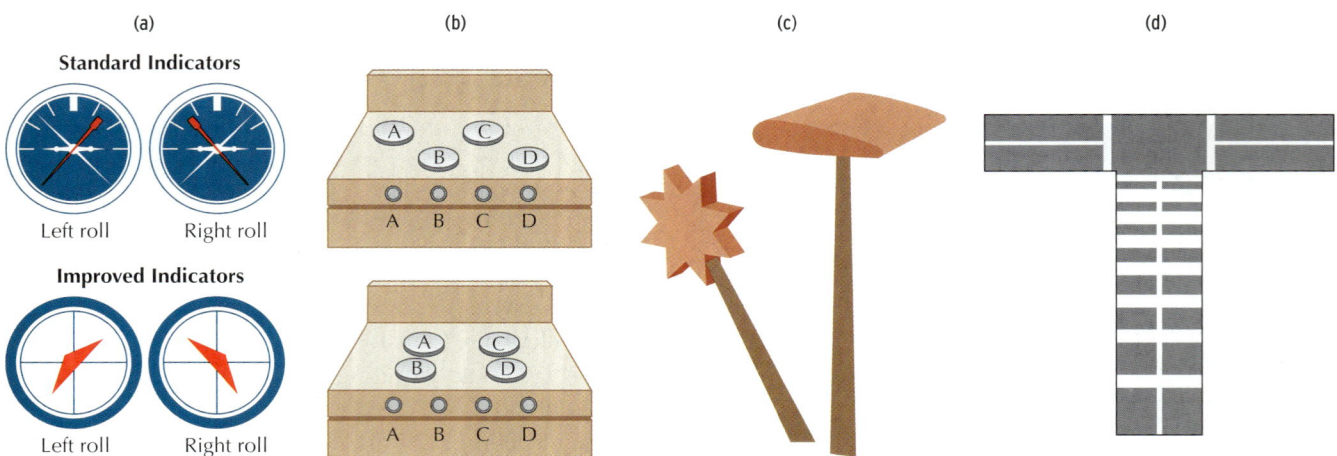

● **FIGURE 16.7** Human factors engineering. *(a)* Early roll indicators in airplanes were perceptually confusing and difficult to read (top). Improved displays are clear even to nonpilots. Which would you prefer if you were flying an airplane in heavy fog? *(b)* Even on a stove, the placement of controls is important. During simulated emergencies, people made no errors in reaching for the controls on the top stove. In contrast, they erred 38 percent of the time with the bottom arrangement (Chapanis & Lindenbaum, 1959). *(c)* Sometimes the shape of a control is used to indicate its function, to discourage errors. For example, the left control might be used to engage and disengage the gears of an industrial machine, whereas the right control might operate the landing flaps on an airplane. *(d)* This design depicts a street intersection viewed from above. Psychologists have found that painting white lines across the road makes drivers feel like they are traveling faster. This effect is even stronger if the lines get progressively closer together. Placing lines near dangerous intersections or sections of highway has dramatically lowered accident rates.

workers who install steel rods in the floors of large buildings spend most of their work days awkwardly bent over. To avoid injuries and to minimize fatigue, machines have been designed that allow workers to do the job while standing upright. People using these machines are faster, and they spend less time in backbreaking positions (Vi, 2006).

One interesting form of usability testing is the *thinking aloud protocol*. In this case, people are asked to say everything they are thinking as they use a machine. By comparing their actual performance with what they were thinking, it is often possible to fine-tune the details of a design (Norman & Panizzi, 2006).

Human–Computer Interaction

Using human factors methods to design computers and software is referred to as **human–computer interaction (HCI)**. Traditionally, machines were designed to make us stronger (such as the automobile, which moves us faster and farther than we could go on our own). In contrast, computers are meant to make us smarter (such as software that can balance a checkbook more quickly and accurately than you could on your own) (Norman, 1994). In the world of HCI, controls are also called input devices and displays are called output devices. Humans communicate with computers through the *interface,* or set of input and output devices a computer provides.

The typical laptop computer today relies on a keyboard, touch pad, and perhaps voice recognition for input. Output is

Human-computer interaction designers are actively seeking new ways to interface people with computers. The Nintendo Wii controller, which allows you to use body and hand movements for control, is one example.

handled by a display screen and audio speakers. Many experts believe that current computer interfaces are too limited when compared with the richness of human communication. Accordingly, the search is on for ways to open up new channels of communication between humans and computers. As mentioned at the beginning of this chapter, the click wheel interface is a key to the success of the iPod. The Nintendo Wii game console is another example. The Wii wand allows players to interface with the game through hand and body movements.

This is no small advance, as any Wii enthusiast can tell you. It allows computer games to incorporate much more physical activity than is possible with traditional game controllers.

In addition to projecting a person's actions into a virtual world, computer interfaces can create a sense of being present in a remote location. *Telepresence,* as this is called, was illustrated in 2001 when a surgeon in New York used *telesurgery* to remove the diseased gallbladder of a patient an ocean away in France. In this instance, the surgeon controlled robotic hands to perform the surgery. Because a good surgeon relies on the sense of touch, it will be important to improve telepresence systems so they provide touch feedback to users (Lederman et al., 2004; Lederman & Klatsky, 2004).

Using Tools Effectively

Even the best designed tools, whether for the body or the mind, can be misused or underused. Do you feel like you are in control of the tools in your life or do you sometimes worry that they control you? Here are a few tips for making sure you get the most out of the tools you use.

Understand Your Task Using a tool like a digital camera, a cell phone, or a PDA can be challenging, especially if you are not sure what it can do. Begin by finding out more about what specific tasks your new tool is designed to help you accomplish. For example, if you are buying photo editing software for your digital camera, find out what tools it offers to adjust, improve, and transform photographs. In our hectic modern world, it is often tempting to **satisfice** or just get by, rather than doing things really well. Satisficing is not just a matter of being lazy. Getting by can be a survival skill, but it does not always take full advantage of the tools available to us. For example, if you know a little about photography and jump into using your new digital camera, you may be satisfied with just being able to take a basic photo. However, if you stop there, you will have used about 10 percent of what your camera is capable of doing.

Understand Your Tools As tempting as it may be to just dive in and use your new tool, do take a peek at the instruction manual. Many modern tools, especially electronic devices, have valuable capacities hidden several layers down in menus. Without reading a manual, you might never find some of them, no matter how user friendly the device's interface may be.

Space Habitats

Let us conclude on a high note: Nowhere are the demands on human factors psychology greater than in space flight. Every machine, tool, and environment in a spacecraft must be carefully adapted for human use. Already, we are discovering that life in a space station isn't easy, physically or mentally. For months at a time, space station residents are restricted to tiny living quarters with little privacy. These conditions and other sources of stress, make it clear that the design of space habitats must take many human needs into account. For instance, researchers have learned that astronauts prefer rooms with clearly defined "up" and "down"—even in the weightlessness of space. This can be done by color-coding walls, floors, and ceilings, and by orienting furniture and controls so they all face the "ceiling" (Suedfeld & Steel, 2000).

Ideally there should be some flexibility in the use of living and work areas inside a space station. Behavior patterns change over time, and being able to control one's environment helps lower stress. At the same time, people need stability. Psychologists have found, for instance, that eating becomes an important high point in monotonous environments. Eating at least one meal together each day can help keep crew members working as a social unit.

Sleep cycles must be carefully controlled in space to avoid disrupting body rhythms (Suedfeld & Steel, 2000). In past space missions some astronauts found they couldn't sleep while other crew members continued to work and talk. Problems with sleep can be worsened by the constant noise on a space station. At first, such noise is annoying. After weeks or

Assembly of the International Space Station by space shuttle crews began in 1998. The space station now provides a habitat in which men and women can live and work in space for extended periods. Solving the behavioral problems of living in space will be an important step toward human exploration of the solar system. (Art courtesy of NASA.)

Human-computer interaction (HCI) The application of human factors to the design of computers and computer software.

Satisficing Engaging in behavior that achieves a minimum result, rather than maximizing the outcome of that behavior.

months, it can become a serious stressor. Researchers are experimenting with various earmuffs, eyeshades, and sleeping arrangements to alleviate such difficulties.

Privacy Psychologists are helping engineers design space habitats so they meet human needs for privacy. However, privacy must be based mainly on temporarily blocking out visual and auditory contact with others. In its current configuration, the International Space Station has too little room for separate quarters.

Forced togetherness is stressful mainly because temporary retreat from others is difficult or impossible. Thus, control over the amount of group contact is more important than actually having a private room. Designers do recognize, however, the need to define private territories. It is important to identify small areas that can be personalized and "owned" by each individual. Desks, lockers, sleep stations, and the like can fill this need if they are not shared with others.

Sensory Restriction Sensory monotony can be a problem in space, even with the magnificent vistas of Earth below. (How many times would you have to see the North American continent before you lost interest?)

Researchers are developing stimulus environments that will use music, movies, and other diversions to combat monotony and boredom. Again, they are trying to provide choice and control for space crews. Studies of confined living in the Arctic and elsewhere make it clear that one person's symphony is another's grating noise. Where music is concerned, individual earphones may be all that is required to avoid problems.

Most people in restricted environments find that they prefer solitary pastimes such as reading, listening to music, looking out windows, writing, and watching films or television. As much as anything, this preference may show again the need for privacy. Reading or listening to music is a good way to psychologically withdraw from the group. Experiences with confining environments on Earth (such as Biosphere 2) suggest that including live animals and plants in space habitats could reduce stress and boredom (Suedfeld & Steel, 2000).

Life on Spaceship Earth Why is the idea of living in space so fascinating? Perhaps it is because human strengths and weaknesses are magnified in the miniature world of a space station. As psychologist Yvonne Clearwater (1985) says:

> The space station represents the first glimmerings of recognition that some of the toughest challenges in space—as on Earth—concern human behavior, not technology. . . . Ironically, the farther we go

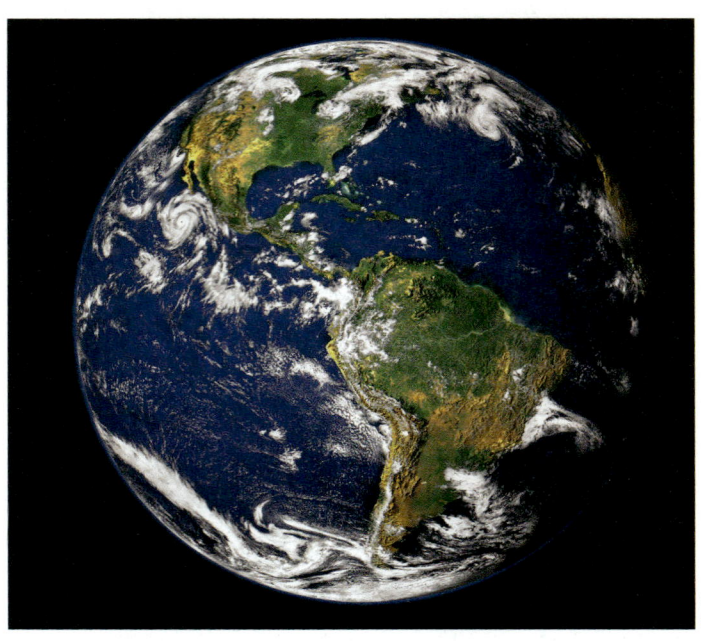

from Earth and the longer we stay away, the more we will need to know about ourselves. Scientists working on the space effort believe that psychological factors will become increasingly important for the success or failure of future space missions.

It is curiously fitting that the dazzling technology of space travel has highlighted the inevitable importance of human behavior. Here on Earth, as in space, we cannot count on cleverly designed machines or technology alone to solve problems. The threat of nuclear war, social conflict, crime, prejudice, infectious disease, overpopulation, environmental damage, famine, homicide, economic disaster—these and most other major problems facing us are behavioral.

Will spaceship Earth endure? It's a psychological question.

MODULE 16.4 Psychology in Action Summary

How are tools designed to better serve human needs?
- Human factors psychologist (also known as ergonomists) design tools to be compatible with our sensory and motor capacities.
- Successful human factors engineering uses natural design, which makes use of perceptual signals that people understand naturally.

- Human factors psychologists rely on usability testing to empirically confirm that machines are easy to learn and use.
- Human–computer interaction (HCI) is the application of human factors to the design of computers and computer software.
- To use tools effectively it is useful to know something about the tool and the task you are using it to complete. Be aware of satisficing.
- Space habitats must be designed with special attention to the numerous human factors issues raised by space flight.

KNOWLEDGE BUILDER

Human Factors Psychology

Recite

1. Human factors psychologists are interested in finding ways to help people adapt to working with machines. T or F?
2. According to Donald Norman, successful human factors engineering makes use of perceptual signals that people understand naturally. T or F?
3. Usability testing is used to empirically investigate machine designs. T or F?
4. To use tools effectively it is worth
    a. understanding your tool
    b. satisficing
    c. understanding your task
    d. overcoming writer's block
5. Researchers have learned that astronauts don't really care if living quarters have clearly defined "up" and "down" orientations. T or F?
6. Research shows that needs for privacy can be met by providing ways to temporarily withdraw from social contact with a group, even when physical withdrawal is impossible. T or F?

Reflect
Critical Thinking

7. Check out this photo of a men's urinal in Amsterdam's Schiphol Airport. Is that fly real? If not, why is it there?

This fly is not real; it is painted onto this urinal from Amsterdam's Schiphol Airport. Why?

Relate

Is there a machine whose design you admire? Can you express why the design works for you?

Have you thought about how you write? How does your approach differ from the one in this module? Are you using your word processor to your best advantage? What could you be improving?

Link

Internet addresses frequently change. To find the sites listed here, visit **http://www.thomsonedu.com/psychology/coon** for an updated list of Internet addresses and direct links to relevant sites.

- **Bad Human Factors Designs** Explore these examples of poor human factors design.
- **Human–Computer Interaction** Read about training in human-computer interaction design.
- **International Space Station** Visit the NASA home page for the International Space Station.

ANSWERS

1. F 2. T 3. T 4. a and c 5. F 6. T 7. Men tend to aim at the "fly" and hence are more accurate when they urinate. The result is much cleaner men's washrooms.

Interactive Learning

 Psychology: Active Learning Modules Book Companion Website

http://www.thomsonedu.com/psychology/coon

Visit your Book Companion Website, where you will find flash cards, practice quizzes, Internet links, and more to help you study.

ThomsonNOW
Just what you need to know NOW!

Spend time on what you need to master rather than on information you already have learned. Take a pre-test for this chapter, and ThomsonNOW will generate a personalized study plan based on your results. The study plan will identify the topics you need to review and direct you to online resources to help you master those topics. You can then take a post-test to help you determine the concepts you have mastered and what you will need to work on. Try it out! Go to **www.thomsonedu.com/login** to sign in with an access code or to purchase access to this product.

The Journey Continues: Psychology and You

At the beginning of this book we described psychology as a journey of self-discovery. It is our sincere hope that you have found enough relevance and value here to spark a lifelong interest in psychology. As your personal journey continues, one thing is certain: Many of your greatest challenges and most treasured moments will involve other people. You would be wise to continue adding to your understanding of human behavior. Psychology's future looks exciting. What role will it play in your life, real or virtual?

Appendix: Behavioral Statistics

MODULE A.1 Descriptive Statistics
SURVEY QUESTION: What are descriptive statistics?
SURVEY QUESTION: How are statistics used to identify an average score?
SURVEY QUESTION: What statistics do psychologists use to measure how much scores differ from one another?

MODULE A.2 Inferential Statistics
SURVEY QUESTION: What are inferential statistics?
SURVEY QUESTION: How are correlations used in psychology?

Statistics from "Heads" to "Tails"

Let's say a friend of yours invites you to try your hand at a "game of chance." He offers to flip a coin and pay you a dollar if the coin comes up heads. If the coin shows tails, you must pay him a dollar. He flips the coin: tails—you pay him a dollar. He flips it again: tails. Again: tails. And again: tails. And again: tails.

At this point you are faced with a choice. Should you continue the game in an attempt to recoup your losses? Or should you assume that the coin is biased and quit before you really get "skinned"? Taking out your trusty pocket calculator (and, of course, the statistics book you carry with you at all times), you compute the odds of obtaining 5 tails in a row from an unbiased coin. The probability is 0.031 (roughly 3 times out of 100).

If the coin really is honest, 5 consecutive tails is a rare event. Wisely, you decide that the coin is probably biased and refuse to play again. (Unless, of course, your "friend" is willing to take "tails" for the next 5 tosses!)

Perhaps a decision could have been made in this hypothetical example without using statistics. But notice how much clearer the situation becomes when it is expressed statistically.

Psychologists try to extract and summarize useful information from the observations they make. To do so, they use two major types of statistics. **Descriptive statistics** summarize or "boil down" numbers so they become more meaningful and easier to communicate to others. In comparison, **inferential statistics** are used for decision making, for generalizing from small samples, and for drawing conclusions. As was the case in the coin-flipping example, psychologists must often base decisions on limited data. Such decisions are much easier to make with the help of inferential statistics. Let's see how statistics are used in psychology.

MODULE A.1 Descriptive Statistics

LET'S SAY YOU HAVE COMPLETED A STUDY ON HUMAN BEHAVIOR. The results seem interesting, but can you really tell what your data reveal just by looking at a jumble of numbers? To get a clear picture of how people behaved, you will probably turn to descriptive statistics. By summarizing the results of your study, statistics will help you draw valid conclusions about what you observed.

Descriptive Statistics—Psychology by the Numbers

SURVEY QUESTION: *What are descriptive statistics?*

Statistics bring greater clarity and precision to psychological thought and research (Gravetter & Wallnau, 2007). To see how, let's begin by considering three basic types of descriptive statistics: *graphical statistics,* measures of *central tendency,* and measures of *variability*. Let's start with **graphical statistics,** which present numbers pictorially, so they are easier to visualize.

Graphical Statistics

■ Table A.1 shows simulated scores on a test of hypnotic susceptibility given to 100 college students. With such disorganized data, it is hard to form an overall "picture" of the differences in hypnotic susceptibility. But by using a *frequency distribution,* large amounts of information can be neatly organized and summarized. A **frequency distribution** is made by breaking down the entire range of possible scores into classes of equal size. Next, the number of scores falling into each class is recorded. In ■ Table A.2, the raw data from Table A.1 have been condensed into a frequency distribution. Notice how much clearer the pattern of scores for the entire group becomes.

Frequency distributions are often shown *graphically* to make them more "visual." A **histogram,** or graph of a frequency distribution, is made by labeling class intervals on the *abscissa* (X axis or horizontal line) and frequencies (the number of scores in each class) on the *ordinate* (Y axis or vertical line). Next, bars are drawn for each class interval; the height of each bar is determined by the number of scores in each class (● Fig. A.1). An alternate way of graphing scores is the more familiar **frequency polygon** (● Fig. A.2). Here, points are placed at the center of each class interval to indicate the number of scores. Then the dots are connected by straight lines.

■ **TABLE A.2** Frequency Distribution of Hypnotic Susceptibility Scores

CLASS INTERVAL	NUMBER OF PERSONS IN CLASS
0–19	10
20–39	20
40–59	40
60–79	20
80–99	10

■ **TABLE A.1** RAW SCORES OF HYPNOTIC SUSCEPTIBILITY

55	86	52	17	61	57	84	51	16	64
22	56	25	38	35	24	54	26	37	38
52	42	59	26	21	55	40	59	25	57
91	27	38	53	19	93	25	39	52	56
66	14	18	63	59	68	12	19	62	45
47	98	88	72	50	49	96	89	71	66
50	44	71	57	90	53	41	72	56	93
57	38	55	49	87	59	36	56	48	70
33	69	50	50	60	35	67	51	50	52
11	73	46	16	67	13	71	47	25	77

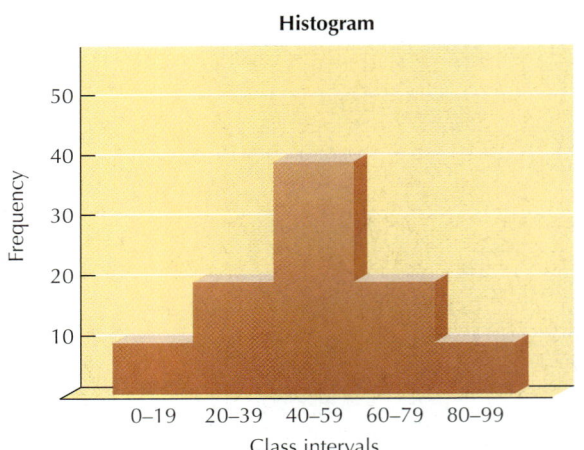

● **FIGURE A.1** Frequency histogram of hypnotic susceptibility scores contained in Table A.2.

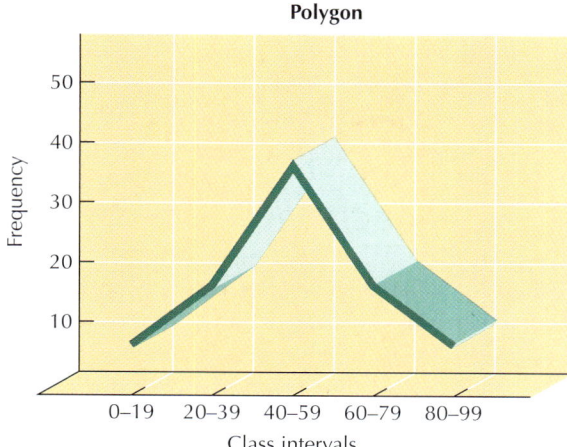

● **FIGURE A.2** Frequency polygon of hypnotic susceptibility scores contained in Table A.2.

Measures of Central Tendency

SURVEY QUESTION: *How are statistics used to identify an average score?*

Notice in Table A.2 that more scores fall in the range 40–59 than elsewhere. How can we show this fact? A measure of **central tendency** is simply a number describing a "typical score" around which other scores fall. A familiar measure of central tendency is the mean, or "average." But as we shall see in a moment, other types of "averages" can be used. To illustrate each we need an example: Table A.3 shows the raw data for an imaginary experiment in which two groups of subjects were given a test of memory. Assume that one group was given a drug that might improve memory (let's call the drug Rememberine). The second group received a placebo. Is there a difference in memory scores between the two groups? It's difficult to tell without computing an average.

The Mean As one type of "average," the **mean** is calculated by adding all the scores for each group and then dividing by the total number of scores. Notice in ■ Table A.3 that the means reveal a difference between the two groups.

The mean is sensitive to extremely high or low scores in a distribution. For this reason it is not always the best

■ **TABLE A.3** Raw Scores on a Memory Test for Subjects Taking Rememberine or a Placebo

SUBJECT	GROUP 1 REMEMBERINE	GROUP 2 PLACEBO
1	65	54
2	67	60
3	73	63
4	65	33
5	58	56
6	55	60
7	70	60
8	69	31
9	60	62
10	68	61
Sum	650	540
Mean	65	54
Median	66	60

$$\text{Mean} = \frac{\Sigma X}{N} \text{ or } \frac{\text{Sum of all scores, X}}{\text{number of scores}}$$

$$\text{Mean Group 1} = \frac{65 + 67 + 73 + 65 + 58 + 55 + 70 + 69 + 60 + 68}{10}$$
$$= \frac{650}{10} = 65$$

$$\text{Mean Group 2} = \frac{54 + 60 + 63 + 33 + 56 + 60 + 60 + 31 + 62 + 61}{10}$$
$$= \frac{540}{10} = 54$$

Median = the middle score or the mean of the two middle scores*

Median Group 1 = 55 58 60 65 ⎡65 67⎤ 68 69 70 73
$$= \frac{65 + 67}{2} = 66$$

Median Group 2 = 31 33 54 56 ⎡60 60⎤ 60 61 62 63
$$= \frac{60 + 60}{2} = 60$$

*indicates middle score(s).

Descriptive statistics Mathematical tools used to describe and summarize numeric data.

Inferential statistics Mathematical tools used for decision making, for generalizing from small samples, and for drawing conclusions.

Graphical statistics Techniques for presenting numbers pictorially, often by plotting them on a graph.

Frequency distribution A table that divides an entire range of scores into a series of classes and then records the number of scores that fall into each class.

Histogram A graph of a frequency distribution in which the number of scores falling in each class is represented by vertical bars.

Frequency polygon A graph of a frequency distribution in which the number of scores falling in each class is represented by points on a line.

Central tendency The tendency for a majority of scores to fall in the midrange of possible values.

Mean A measure of central tendency calculated by adding a group of scores and then dividing by the total number of scores.

measure of central tendency. (Imagine how distorted it would be to calculate average yearly incomes from a small sample of people that happened to include a multimillionaire.) In such cases the middle score in a group of scores—called the *median*—is used instead.

The Median The **median** is found by arranging scores from the highest to the lowest and selecting the score that falls in the middle. In other words, half the values in a group of scores fall below the median and half fall above. Consider, for example, the following weights obtained from a small class of college students: 105, 111, 123, 126, 148, 151, 154, 162, 182. The median for the group is 148, the middle score. Of course, if there is an even number of scores, there will be no "middle score." This problem is handled by averaging the two scores that "share" the middle spot. This procedure yields a single number to serve as the median. (See the bottom panel of Table A.3.)

The Mode A final measure of central tendency is the *mode*. The **mode** is simply the most frequently occurring score in a group of scores. If you were to take the time to count the scores in Table A.3, you would find that the mode of Group 1 is 65 and the mode of Group 2 is 60. The mode is usually easy to obtain. However, the mode can be an unreliable measure, especially in a small group of scores. The mode's advantage is that it gives the score actually obtained by the greatest number of people.

Measures of Variability

SURVEY QUESTION: *What statistics do psychologists use to measure how much scores differ from one another?*

Let's say a researcher discovers two drugs that lower anxiety in agitated patients. However, let's also assume that one drug consistently lowers anxiety by moderate amounts, whereas the second sometimes lowers it by large amounts, sometimes has no effect, or may even increase anxiety in some patients. Overall, there is no difference in the *average* (mean) amount of anxiety reduction. Even so, an important difference exists between the two drugs. As this example shows, it is not enough to simply know the average score in a distribution. Usually, we would also like to know if scores are grouped closely together or scattered widely.

Measures of **variability** provide a single number that tells how "spread out" scores are. When the scores are widely spread, this number gets larger. When they are close together, it gets smaller. If you look again at the example in Table A.3, you will notice that the scores within each group vary widely. How can we show this fact?

The Range The simplest way would be to use the **range,** which is the difference between the highest and lowest scores. In Group 1 of our experiment the highest score is 73, and the lowest is 55; thus, the range is 18 (73 − 55 = 18). In Group 2 the highest score is 63, and the lowest is 31; this makes the range 32. Scores in Group 2 are more spread out (are more variable) than those in Group 1.

The Standard Deviation A better measure of variability is the **standard deviation** (an index of how much a typical score differs from the mean of a group of scores). To obtain the standard deviation, we find the deviation (or difference) of each score from the mean and then square it (multiply it by itself). These squared deviations are then added and averaged (the total is divided by the number of deviations). Taking the square root of this average yields the standard deviation (■ Table A.4). Notice again that the variability for Group 1 (5.4) is smaller than that for Group 2 (where the standard deviation is 11.3).

■ **TABLE A.4 Computation of the Standard Deviation**

GROUP 1 MEAN = 65

SCORE − MEAN	DEVIATION (d)	DEVIATION SQUARED (d^2)
65 − 65 =	0	0
67 − 65 =	2	4
73 − 65 =	8	64
65 − 65 =	0	0
58 − 65 =	−7	49
55 − 65 =	−10	100
70 − 65 =	5	25
69 − 65 =	4	16
60 − 65 =	−5	25
68 − 65 =	3	9
		292

$$SD = \sqrt{\frac{\text{sum of } d^2}{n}} = \sqrt{\frac{292}{10}} = \sqrt{29.2} = 5.4$$

GROUP 2 MEAN = 54

SCORE − MEAN	DEVIATION (d)	DEVIATION SQUARED (d^2)
54 − 54 =	0	0
60 − 54 =	6	36
63 − 54 =	9	81
33 − 54 =	−21	441
56 − 54 =	2	4
60 − 54 =	6	36
60 − 54 =	6	36
31 − 54 =	−23	529
62 − 54 =	8	64
61 − 54 =	7	49
		1276

$$SD = \sqrt{\frac{\text{sum of } d^2}{n}} = \sqrt{\frac{1276}{10}} = \sqrt{127.6} = 5.4$$

Standard Scores

A particular advantage of the standard deviation is that it can be used to "standardize" scores in a way that gives them greater meaning. For example, John and Heather both took psychology midterms, but in different classes. John earned a score of 118, and Heather scored 110. Who did better? It is impossible to tell without knowing what the average score was on each test, and whether John and Heather scored at the top, middle, or bottom of their classes. We would like to have one number that gives all this information. A number that does this is the *z-score*.

To convert an original score to a **z-score,** we subtract the mean from the score. The resulting number is then divided by the standard deviation for that group of scores. To illustrate, Heather had a score of 110 in a class with a mean of 100 and a standard deviation of 10. Therefore, her z-score is +1.0 (Table A.5). John's score of 118 came from a class having a mean of 100 and a standard deviation of 18; thus, his z-score is also +1.0. (See ■ Table A.5.) Originally it looked as if John did better on his midterm than Heather did. But we now see that relatively speaking, their scores were equivalent. Compared with other students, each was an equal distance above average.

The Normal Curve

When chance events are recorded, we find that some outcomes have a high probability and occur very often; others have a lower probability and occur infrequently; still others have little probability and occur rarely. As a result, the distribution (or tally) of chance events typically resembles a *normal curve* (● Fig. A.3). A **normal curve** is bell shaped, with a large number of scores in the middle, tapering to very few extremely high and low scores. Most psychological traits or events are determined by the action of a large number of factors. Therefore, like chance events, measures of psychological

■ **TABLE A.5 Computation of a z-score**

$$z = \frac{X - \bar{X}}{SD} = \text{or } \frac{\text{score} - \text{mean}}{\text{standard deviation}}$$

Susan: $z = \frac{110 - 100}{10} = \frac{+10}{10} = +1.0$

John: $z = \frac{118 - 100}{18} = \frac{+18}{18} = +1.0$

● **FIGURE A.3** The normal curve. The normal curve is an idealized mathematical model. However, many measurements in psychology closely approximate a normal curve. The scales you see here show the relationship of standard deviations, z-scores, and other measures to the curve.

variables tend to roughly match a normal curve. For example, direct measurement has shown such characteristics as height, memory span, and intelligence to be distributed approximately along a normal curve. In other words, many people have average height, memory ability, and intelligence. However, as we move above or below average, fewer and fewer people are found.

Median A measure of central tendency found by arranging scores from the highest to the lowest and selecting the score that falls in the middle. That is, half the values in a group of scores fall above the median and half fall below.

Mode A measure of central tendency found by identifying the most frequently occurring score in a group of scores.

Variability The tendency for a group of scores to differ in value. Measures of variability indicate the degree to which a group of scores differ from one another.

Range The difference between the highest and lowest scores in a group of scores.

Standard deviation An index of how much a typical score differs from the mean of a group of scores.

z-score A number that tells how many standard deviations above or below the mean a score is.

Normal curve A bell-shaped distribution, with a large number of scores in the middle, tapering to very few extremely high and low scores.

It is very fortunate that so many psychological variables tend to form a normal curve, because much is known about the curve. One valuable property concerns the relationship between the standard deviation and the normal curve. Specifically, the standard deviation measures off set proportions of the curve above and below the mean. For example, in ● Figure A.4, notice that roughly 68 percent of all cases (IQ scores, memory scores, heights, or whatever) fall between one standard deviation above and below the mean (± 1 SD); 95 percent of all cases fall between ± 2 SD; and 99 percent of the cases can be found between ± 3 SD from the mean.

■ Table A.6 gives a more complete account of the relationship between z-scores and the percentage of cases found in a particular area of the normal curve. Notice, for example, that 93.3 percent of all cases fall below a z-score of +1.5. A z-score of 1.5 on a test (no matter what the original, or "raw," score was) would be a good performance, because roughly 93 percent of all scores fall below this mark. Relationships between the standard deviation (or z-scores) and the normal curve do not change. This makes it possible to compare various tests or groups of scores if they come from distributions that are approximately normal.

■ TABLE A.6 Computation of a z-score

Z-SCORE	PERCENTAGE OF AREA TO THE LEFT OF THIS VALUE	PERCENTAGE OF AREA TO THE RIGHT OF THIS VALUE
−3.0 SD	00.1	99.9
−2.5 SD	00.6	99.4
−2.0 SD	02.3	97.7
−1.5 SD	06.7	93.3
−1.0 SD	15.9	84.1
−0.5 SD	30.9	69.1
0.0 SD	50.0	50.0
+0.5 SD	69.1	30.9
+1.0 SD	84.1	15.9
+1.5 SD	93.3	06.7
+2.0 SD	97.7	02.3
+2.5 SD	99.4	00.6
+3.0 SD	99.9	00.1

MODULE A.1 Summary

What are descriptive statistics?

- The results of psychological studies are often expressed as numbers, which must be summarized and interpreted before they have any meaning.
- Summarizing numbers visually, by using various types of graphs, makes it easier to see trends and patterns in the results of psychological investigations.
- Two basic questions about a group of numbers are: What is the average (central tendency)? How much do the numbers vary (variability)?
- Descriptive statistics organize and summarize numbers.
- Graphical statistics, such as histograms and frequency polygons, are used to represent numbers pictorially.

How are statistics used to identify an average score?

- Measures of central tendency define the "typical score" in a group of scores.
- The mean is found by adding all the scores in a group and then dividing by the total number of scores.
- The median is found by arranging a group of scores from the highest to the lowest and selecting the middle score.
- The mode is the score that occurs most frequently in a group of scores.

What statistics do psychologists use to measure how much scores differ from one another?

- Measures of variability provide a number that shows how how much scores vary.
- The range is the difference between the highest score and the lowest score in a group of scores.
- The standard deviation shows how much, on average, all the scores in a group differ from the mean.
- To change an original score into a standard score (or z-score), you must subtract the mean from the score and then divide the result by the standard deviation.
- Standard scores (z-scores) tell, in standard deviation units, how far above or below the mean a score is. This allows meaningful comparisons between scores from different groups.
- Scores that form a normal curve are easy to interpret because the properties of the normal curve are well known.

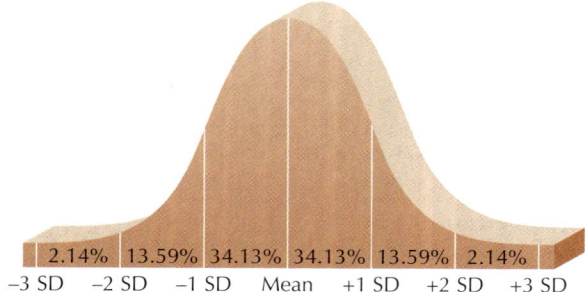

● **FIGURE A.4** Relationship between the standard deviation and the normal curve.

KNOWLEDGE BUILDER

Descriptive Statistics

Recite

1. _____ statistics summarize numbers so they become more meaningful or easier to communicate; _____ statistics are used for decision making, generalizing, or drawing conclusions.
2. Histograms and frequency polygons are graphs of frequency distributions. T or F?
3. Three measures of central tendency are the mean, the median, and the _____.
4. If scores are placed in order, from the smallest to the largest, the median is defined as the middle score. T or F?
5. As a measure of variability, the standard deviation is defined as the difference between the highest and lowest scores. T or F?
6. A z-score of −1 tells us that a score fell one standard deviation below the mean in a group of scores. T or F?
7. In a normal curve, 99 percent of all scores can be found between +1 and −1 standard deviations from the mean. T or F?

Reflect

Critical Thinking

8. You are asked to calculate the mean income of the following annual salaries: $2,000,000, $33,000, $27,000, $22,000, $21,000. Why might you refuse? What statistic might you propose to calculate instead?

Relate

Let's say you ask 100 people how long they sleep each night and record their answers. How could you show these scores graphically?

To find the average amount of sleep for your subjects, would you prefer to know the most frequent score (the mode), the middle score (the median), or the arithmetic average (the mean)?

How could you determine how much sleep times vary? That is, would you prefer to know the highest and lowest scores (the range) or the average amount of variation (the standard deviation)?

How would you feel about receiving your scores on classroom tests in the form of z-scores?

Do you think the distribution of scores in your study of sleep would form a normal curve? Why or why not?

Link

Internet addresses frequently change. To find the sites listed here, visit **http://www.thomsonedu.com/psychology/coon** for an updated list of Internet addresses and direct links to relevant sites.

- **Frequency Distribution of Tossing Coins and Dice** Automatically calculate frequency distributions for tossing coins or dice and plot the results as a frequency polygon.
- **Measures of Central Tendency** Work through another example of measures of central tendency.
- **Descriptive Statistics** Further explore descriptive statistics.

ANSWERS

1. Descriptive, inferential 2. T 3. mode 4. T 5. F 6. T 7. F 8. The single large salary in this small group will distort the mean. In cases like this, the median is a better measure of central tendency.

MODULE A.2 Inferential Statistics

YOU WOULD LIKE TO KNOW if boys are more aggressive than girls. You observe a group of 5-year-old boys and girls on a playground. After collecting data for a week you find that the boys committed more aggressive acts than the girls. Could this difference just be a meaningless fluctuation in aggression? Or does it show conclusively that boys are more aggressive than girls? Inferential statistics were created to answer just such questions (Sprinthall, 2007).

Inferential Statistics—Significant Numbers

SURVEY QUESTION: *What are inferential statistics?*

Let's say that a researcher studies the effects of a new therapy on a small group of depressed individuals. Is she or he interested only in these particular individuals? Usually not, because except in rare instances, psychologists seek to discover general laws of behavior that apply widely to humans and animals. Undoubtedly the researcher would like to know if the therapy holds any promise for all depressed people. As stated earlier, **inferential statistics** are techniques that allow us to make inferences. That is, they allow us to generalize from the behavior of small groups of subjects to that of the larger groups they represent.

Samples and Populations

In any scientific study, we would like to observe the entire set, or **population,** of subjects, objects, or events of interest. However, this is usually impossible or impractical. Observing all terrorists, all cancer patients, or all mothers-in-law could be both impractical (because all are large populations) and impossible (because people change political views, may be unaware of having cancer, and change their status as relatives). In such cases, **samples** (smaller cross sections of a population) are selected, and observations of the sample are used to draw conclusions about the entire population.

For any sample to be meaningful, it must be **representative.** That is, the sample group must truly reflect the membership and characteristics of the larger population. In our earlier hypothetical study of a memory drug, it would be essential for the sample of 20 people to be representative of the general population. A very important aspect of representative samples is that their members are chosen at **random.** In other words, each member of the population must have an equal chance of being included in the sample.

Significant Differences

In our imaginary drug experiment, we found that the average memory score was higher for the group given the drug than it was for persons who didn't take the drug (the placebo group). Certainly this result is interesting, but could it have occurred by chance? If two groups were repeatedly tested (with neither receiving any drug), their average memory scores would sometimes differ. How much must two means differ before we can consider the difference "real" (not due to chance)?

Notice that the question is similar to one discussed earlier: How many tails in a row must we obtain when flipping a coin before we can conclude that the coin is biased? In the case of the coin, we noted that obtaining 5 tails in a row is a rare event. Thus, it became reasonable to assume that the coin was biased. Of course, it is possible to get 5 tails in a row when flipping an honest coin. But becaues this outcome is unlikely, we have good reason to suspect that something other than chance (a loaded coin, for instance) caused the results. Similar reasoning is used in tests of statistical significance.

Tests of **statistical significance** provide an estimate of how often experimental results could have occurred by chance alone. The results of a significance test are stated as a probability. This probability gives the odds that the observed difference was due to chance. In psychology, any experimental result that could have occurred by chance 5 times (or less) out of 100 (in other words, a probability of .05 or less) is considered *significant.* In our memory experiment, the probability is .025 ($p = .025$) that the group means would differ as much as they do by chance alone. This allows us to conclude with reasonable certainty that the drug actually did improve memory scores.

Correlation—Rating Relationships

SURVEY QUESTION: *How are correlations used in psychology?*

As we noted in Module 1.6, many of the statements that psychologists make about behavior do not result from the use of experimental methods. Rather, they come from keen observations and measures of existing phenomena. A psychologist might note, for example, that the higher a couple's socioeconomic and educational status, the smaller the number of children they are likely to have. Or that grades in high school are related to how well a person is likely to do in college. Or even that as rainfall levels increase within a given metropolitan area, crime rates decline. In these instances, we are dealing with the fact that two variables are **correlating** (varying together in some orderly fashion).

Relationships

Psychologists are very interested in detecting relationships between events: Are children from single-parent families more likely to misbehave at school? Is wealth related to happiness? Is there a relationship between childhood exposure to the Internet and IQ at age 20? Is the chance of having a heart attack related to having a hostile personality? All of these are questions about correlation (Howell, 2008).

The simplest way of visualizing a correlation is to construct a **scatter diagram.** In a scatter diagram, two measures (grades in high school and grades in college, for instance) are obtained. One measure is indicated by the X axis and the second by the Y axis. The scatter diagram plots the intersection (crossing) of each pair of measurements as a single point. Many such measurement pairs give pictures like those shown in ● Figure A.5.

Figure A.5 also shows scatter diagrams of three basic kinds of relationships between variables (or measures). Graphs A, B, and C show *positive relationships* of varying strength. As you can see, in a **positive relationship,** increases in the X measure (or score) are matched by increases on the Y measure (or score). An example would be finding that higher IQ scores (X) are associated with higher college grades (Y). A **zero correlation** suggests that no relationship exists between two measures. (See graph D.) This might be the result of comparing subjects' hat sizes (X) to their college grades (Y). Graphs E and F both show a **negative relationship** (or correlation). Notice that as values of one measure increase, those of the second become smaller. An example might be the relationship between amount of alcohol consumed and scores on a test of coordination: Higher alcohol levels are correlated with lower coordination scores.

The Correlation Coefficient

The strength of a correlation can also be expressed as a **coefficient of correlation.** This coefficient is simply a number falling somewhere between +1.00 and –1.00. If the number is zero or close to zero, it indicates a weak or nonexistent relationship. If the correlation is +1.00, a **perfect positive relationship** exists; if the correlation is –1.00, a **perfect negative relationship** has been discovered. The most commonly used correlation coefficient is called the Pearson *r*.

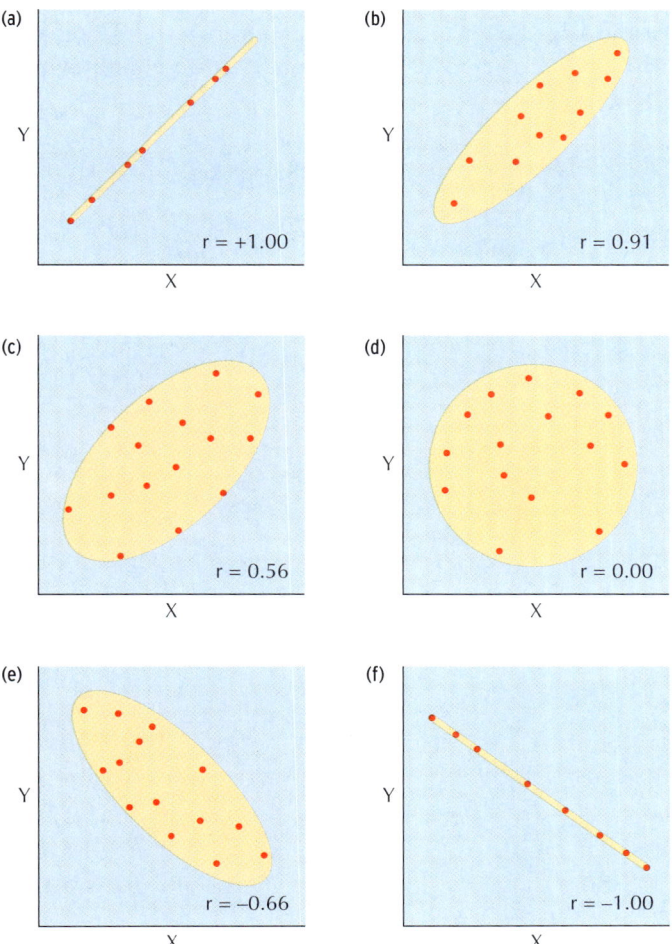

● **FIGURE A.5** Scatter diagrams showing various degrees of relationship for a positive, zero, and negative correlation.

Population An entire group of animals, people, or objects belonging to a particular category (for example, all college students or all married women).

Sample A smaller subpart of a population.

Representative sample A small, randomly selected part of a larger population that accurately reflects characteristics of the whole population.

Random selection Choosing a sample so that each member of the population has an equal chance of being included in the sample.

Statistical significance The degree to which an event (such as the results of an experiment) is unlikely to have occurred by chance alone.

Correlation The existence of a consistent, systematic relationship between two events, measures, or variables.

Scatter diagram A graph that plots the intersection of paired measures; that is, the points at which paired X and Y measures cross.

Positive relationship A mathematical relationship in which increases in one measure are matched by increases in the other (or decreases correspond with decreases).

Zero correlation The absence of a (linear) mathematical relationship between two measures.

Negative relationship A mathematical relationship in which increases in one measure are matched by decreases in the other.

Coefficient of correlation A statistical index ranging from –1.00 to +1.00 that indicates the direction and degree of correlation.

Perfect positive relationship A mathematical relationship in which the correlation between two measures is +1.00.

Perfect negative relationship A mathematical relationship in which the correlation between two measures is –1.00.

Calculation of the Pearson r is relatively simple, as shown in ■ Table A.7. (The numbers shown are hypothetical.)

As stated in Module 1.6, correlations in psychology are rarely perfect. Most fall somewhere between zero and plus or minus 1. The closer the correlation coefficient is to +1.00 or −1.00, the stronger the relationship. An interesting example of some typical correlations is provided by a study that compared the IQs of adopted children with the IQs of their biological mothers. At age 4, the children's IQs correlated .28 with their biological mothers' IQs. By age 7 the correlation was .35. And by age 13 it had grown to .38. Over time, the IQs of adopted children become more similar to the IQs of their biological mothers.

Prediction Correlations often provide highly useful information. For instance, it is valuable to know that there is a correlation between cigarette smoking and lung cancer rates. Another example is the fact that higher consumption of alcohol during pregnancy is correlated with lower birth weight and a higher rate of birth defects. There is a correlation between the number of recent life stresses experienced and the likelihood of emotional disturbance. Many more examples could be cited, but the point is, correlations help us to identify relationships that are worth knowing.

Correlations are particularly valuable for making *predictions*. If we know that two measures are correlated, and we know a person's score on one measure, we can predict his or her score on the other. For example, most colleges have formulas that use multiple correlations to decide which applicants have the best chances for success. Usually the formula includes such predictors as high school GPA, teacher ratings, extracurricular activities, and scores on the *Scholastic Assessment Test* (SAT) or some similar test. Although no single predictor is perfectly correlated with success in college, together the various predictors correlate highly and provide a useful technique for screening applicants.

There is an interesting "trick" you can do with correlations that you may find useful. It works like this: If you *square* the correlation coefficient (multiply r by itself), you will get a number telling the **percent of variance** (amount of variation in scores) accounted for by the correlation. For example, the correlation between IQ scores and college grade point average is .5. Multiplying .5 times .5 gives .25, or 25 percent. This means that 25 percent of the variation in college grades is accounted for by knowing IQ scores. In other words, with a correlation of .5, college grades are "squeezed" into an oval like the one shown in graph C, Figure A.5. IQ scores take away some of the possible variation in corresponding grade

■ **TABLE A.7 IQ and Grade Point Average for Computing Pearson r**

STUDENT NO.	IQ (X)	GRADE POINT AVERAGE (Y)	X SCORE SQUARED (X^2)	Y SCORE SQUARED (Y^2)	X TIMES Y (XY)
1	110	1.0	12,100	1.00	110.0
2	112	1.6	12,544	2.56	179.2
3	118	1.2	13,924	1.44	141.6
4	119	2.1	14,161	4.41	249.9
5	122	2.6	14,884	6.76	317.2
6	125	1.8	15,625	3.24	225.0
7	127	2.6	16,124	6.76	330.2
8	130	2.0	16,900	4.00	260.0
9	132	3.2	17,424	10.24	422.4
10	134	2.6	17,956	6.76	348.4
11	136	3.0	18,496	9.00	408.0
12	138	3.6	19,044	12.96	496.8
Total	1503	27.3	189,187	69.13	3488.7

$$r = \frac{\Sigma XY - \frac{(\Sigma X)(\Sigma Y)}{N}}{\sqrt{\left[\Sigma X^2 - \frac{(\Sigma X)^2}{N}\right]\left[\Sigma Y^2 - \frac{(\Sigma Y)^2}{N}\right]}}$$

$$= \frac{3488.7 - \frac{1503(27.3)}{12}}{\sqrt{\left[189{,}187 - \frac{(1503)^2}{12}\right]\left[69.13 - \frac{(27.3)^2}{12}\right]}}$$

$$= \frac{69.375}{81.088} = 0.856 = 0.86$$

point averages. If there were no correlation between IQ and grades, grades would be completely free to vary, as shown in Figure A.5, graph D.

Along the same line, a correlation of +1.00 or −1.00 means that 100 percent of the variation in the Y measure is accounted for by knowing the X measure: If you know a person's X score, you can tell exactly what the Y score is. An example that comes close to this state of affairs is the high correlation (.86) between the IQs of identical twins. In any group of identical twins, 74 percent of the variation in the "Y" twins' IQs is accounted for by knowing the IQs of their siblings (the "X's").

Squaring correlations to obtain the *percent variance* accounted for is a useful tool for interpreting the correlations encountered in the media and the psychological literature. For example, sweeping pronouncements about relationships are occasionally made on the basis of correlations in the .25 to .30 range even though the values mean that only 6 to 9 percent of the variance is accounted for by the observed correlation. Such correlations may document relationships worth noting, but they are rarely something to get excited about.

Correlation and Causation It is very important to reiterate that finding a correlation between two measures does not automatically mean that one causes the other: Correlation does not demonstrate **causation.** When a correlation exists, the best we can say is that two variables are related. Of course, this does not mean that it is impossible for two correlated variables to have a cause-and-effect relationship. Rather, it means that we cannot *conclude,* solely on the basis of correlation, that a causal link exists. To gain greater confidence that a cause-and-effect relationship exists, an experiment must be performed. (See Module 1.5.)

Often, two correlated measures are related as a result of the influence of a third variable. For example, we might observe that the more hours students devote to studying, the better their grades. Although it is tempting to conclude that more studying produces (causes) better grades, it is possible (indeed, it is probable) that grades and the amount of study time are both related to the amount of motivation or interest a student has.

The difference between cause-and-effect data and data that reveal a relationship of unknown origin is one that should not be forgotten. Because we rarely run experiments in daily life, the information on which we act is largely correlational. This should make us more humble and more tentative in the confidence with which we make pronouncements about human behavior.

MODULE A.2 Summary

What are inferential statistics?
- Inferential statistics are used to make decisions, to generalize from samples, and to draw conclusions from data.
- Most studies in psychology are based on samples. Findings from representative samples are assumed to also apply to entire populations.
- In psychology experiments, differences in the average performance of groups could occur purely by chance. Tests of statistical significance tell us if the observed differences between groups are common or rare. If a difference is large enough to be improbable, it suggests that the results did not occur by chance alone.

How are correlations used in psychology?
- Pairs of scores that vary together in an orderly fashion are said to be correlated.
- Correlation is used to identify relationships between events or measures and to make predictions.
- The relationship between two variables or measures can be positive or negative.
- Correlation coefficients tell how strongly two groups of scores are related.
- Correlation alone does not demonstrate cause-and-effect links between variables or measures.

Percent of variance A portion of the total amount of variation in a group of scores.
Causation The act of causing some effect.

KNOWLEDGE BUILDER

Inferential Statistics

Recite

1. In inferential statistics, observations of a _____ are used to make inferences and draw conclusions about an entire _____.
2. A representative sample can be obtained by selecting members of the sample at _____.
3. If the results of an experiment could have occurred by chance alone less than 25 times out of 100, the result is considered statistically significant. T or F?
4. A scatter diagram can be used to plot and visualize a _____ between two groups of scores.
5. In a negative relationship, increases in X scores correspond to decreases in Y scores. T or F?
6. A perfect positive correlation exists when the correlation coefficient is 0.00. T or F?
7. It is important to remember that correlation does not demonstrate _____.

Reflect

Critical Thinking

8. Suppose it was found that sleeping with your clothes on is correlated with waking up with a headache. Could you conclude that sleeping with your clothes on causes headaches?

Relate

Informally, you have probably inferred something about a population of people based on the small sample you have observed directly. How could statistics improve the accuracy of your inferences?

If you were trying to test whether a drug causes birth defects, what level of statistical significance would you use? If you were doing a psychology experiment, what level would you be comfortable with?

See if you can identify at least one positive relationship and one negative relationship involving human behavior that you have observed. How strong do you think the correlation would be in each case? What correlation coefficient would you expect to see?

A woman you know drinks more coffee in the winter than she does in the summer. She also has more colds in the winter. She decides to reduce the amount of coffee she drinks to help prevent colds. What can you tell her about correlation and causation?

Link

Internet addresses frequently change. To find the sites listed here, visit **http://www.thomsonedu.com/psychology/coon** for an updated list of Internet addresses and direct links to relevant sites.

- **Concepts and Applications of Inferential Statistics** Browse this full online statistics textbook.
- **Scatter Diagram** Explore correlation by better understanding scatter diagrams.
- **Correlations** Vary the correlations and view the corresponding scatter diagram.

ANSWERS

1. sample, population 2. random 3. F 4. correlation 5. T 6. F 7. Causation 8. No. To reiterate, correlation does not prove causality. It is more likely here that a third factor is causing *both* the sleeping with the clothes on at night *and* the headaches (too much alcohol, anyone?).

Interactive Learning

Psychology: Active Learning Modules Book Companion Website

http://www.thomsonedu.com/psychology/coon
Visit your Book Companion Website, where you will find flash cards, practice quizzes, Internet links, and more to help you study.

ThomsonNOW

Just what you need to know NOW!

Spend time on what you need to master rather than on information you already have learned. Take a pre-test for this chapter, and ThomsonNOW will generate a personalized study plan based on your results. The study plan will identify the topics you need to review and direct you to online resources to help you master those topics. You can then take a post-test to help you determine the concepts you have mastered and what you will need to work on. Try it out! Go to **www.thomsonedu.com/login** to sign in with an access code or to purchase access to this product.

Glossary

Ablation (ab-LAY-shun) Surgical removal of tissue.

Absolute threshold The minimum amount of physical energy necessary to produce a sensation.

Abstract principles Concepts and ideas removed from specific examples and concrete situations.

Accommodation In vision, changes in the shape of the lens of the eye.

Accommodation In Piaget's theory, the modification of existing mental patterns to fit new demands (that is, mental schemes are changed to accommodate new information or experiences).

Acculturative stress Stress caused by the many changes and adaptations required when a person moves to a foreign culture.

Acetylcholine The neurotransmitter released by neurons to activate muscles.

Acquaintance (date) rape Forced intercourse that occurs in the context of a date or other voluntary encounter.

Acquisition The period in conditioning during which a response is reinforced.

Action component How one tends to act toward the object of an attitude.

Action potential The nerve impulse.

Activation-synthesis hypothesis An attempt to explain how dream content is affected by motor commands in the brain that occur during sleep but are not carried out.

Active listener A person who knows how to maintain attention, avoid distractions, and actively gather information from lectures.

Activity theory Theory stating that the best adjustment to aging occurs when people remain active mentally, socially, and physically.

Actor-observer bias The tendency to attribute the behavior of others to internal causes while attributing one's own behavior to external causes (situations and circumstances).

Acute stress disorder A psychological disturbance lasting up to 1 month following stresses that would produce anxiety in anyone who experienced them.

Adaptation level An internal or mental "average" or "medium" point that is used to judge amounts.

Adaptive behaviors Actions that aid attempts to survive and adapt to changing conditions.

Adjustment disorder An emotional disturbance caused by ongoing stressors within the range of common experience.

Adolescence The culturally defined period between childhood and adulthood.

Adrenal glands Endocrine glands that arouse the body, regulate salt balance, adjust the body to stress, and affect sexual functioning.

Affectional needs Emotional needs for love and affection.

Ageism An institutionalized tendency to discriminate on the basis of age; prejudice based on age.

Aggression Any response made with the intent of causing harm or achieving one's goals at the expense of another person.

Aggression cues Stimuli or signals that are associated with aggression and that tend to elicit it.

Aggressive pornography Media depictions of sexual violence or of forced participation in sexual activity.

Agnosia An inability to grasp the meaning of stimuli, such as words, objects, or pictures.

Agoraphobia (ah-go-rah-FOBE-ee-ah) **(without panic)** The fear that something extremely embarrassing will happen if one leaves the house or enters unfamiliar situations.

Alarm reaction First stage of the GAS, during which bodily resources are mobilized to cope with a stressor.

Alcohol myopia Shortsighted thinking and perception that occurs during alcohol intoxication.

Algorithm A learned set of rules that always leads to the correct solution of a problem.

All-or-nothing thinking Classifying objects or events as absolutely right or wrong, good or bad, acceptable or unacceptable, and so forth.

Alpha waves Large, slow brain waves associated with relaxation and falling asleep.

Altered state of consciousness (ASC) A condition of awareness distinctly different in quality or pattern from waking consciousness.

Alzheimer's disease An age-related disease characterized by memory loss, mental confusion, and, in its later stages, a nearly total loss of mental abilities.

Ambivalence Mixed positive and negative feelings or simultaneous attraction and repulsion.

Amphetamine psychosis A loss of contact with reality due to repeated amphetamine use.

Ambivalent attachment An emotional bond marked by conflicting feelings of affection, anger, and emotional turmoil.

Amygdala (ah-MIG-dah-luh) A part of the limbic system associated with fear responses.

Anal stage The psychosexual stage corresponding roughly to the period of toilet training (ages 1 to 3).

Anal-expulsive personality A disorderly, destructive, cruel, or messy person.

Anal-retentive personality A person who is obstinate, stingy, or compulsive, and who generally has difficulty "letting go."

Androgen Any of a number of male sex hormones, especially testosterone.

Androgyny (an-DROJ-ih-nee) The presence of both "masculine" and "feminine" traits in a single person (as masculinity and femininity are defined within one's culture).

Andropause A gradual decline in testosterone levels in older men.

Anger control Personal strategies for reducing or curbing anger.

Anhedonia (an-he-DAWN-ee-ah) An inability to feel pleasure.

Anima An archetype representing the female principle.

Animal model In research, an animal whose behavior is used to derive principles that may apply to human behavior.

Animus An archetype representing the male principle.

Anorexia nervosa (AN-uh-REK-see-yah ner-VOH-sah) Active self-starvation or a sustained loss of appetite that has psychological origins.

Anosmia Loss or impairment of the sense of smell.

Antecedents Events that precede a response.

Anterograde amnesia Loss of the ability to form or retrieve memories for events that occur after an injury or trauma.

Anthropomorphic (AN-thro-po-MORE-fik) **error** The error of attributing human thoughts, feelings, or motives to animals, especially as a way of explaining their behavior.

Antidepressants Mood-elevating drugs.

Antipsychotics Drugs that, in addition to having tranquilizing effects, also tend to reduce hallucinations and delusional thinking. (Also called **major tranquilizers.**)

Antisocial personality A person who lacks a conscience; who is emotionally shallow, impulsive, selfish, and tends to manipulate others.

Anxiety Apprehension, dread, or uneasiness similar to fear but based on an unclear threat.

Anxiety disorder Disruptive feelings of fear, apprehension, or anxiety, or distortions in behavior that are anxiety related.

Anxiety reduction hypothesis Explains the self-defeating nature of avoidance responses as a result of the reinforcing effects of relief from anxiety.

Anxiolytics Drugs (such as Valium) that produce relaxation or reduce anxiety.

Aphasia (ah-FAZE-yah) A speech disturbance resulting from brain damage.

Apparent-distance hypothesis An explanation of the moon illusion stating that the horizon seems more distant than the night sky.

Applied psychology The use of psychological principles and research methods to solve practical problems.

Approach-approach conflict Choosing between two positive, or desirable, alternatives.

Approach-avoidance conflict Being attracted to and repelled by the same goal or activity.

Aptitude A capacity for learning certain abilities.

Aptitude test A test that rates a person's potential to learn skills required by various occupations.

Archetype A universal idea, image, or pattern, found in the collective unconscious.

Architectural psychology Study of the effects buildings have on behavior and the design of buildings using behavioral principles.

Arousal theory Assumes that people prefer to maintain ideal, or comfortable, levels of arousal.

Artificial intelligence Any artificial system (often a computer program) that is capable of human-like problem solving or intelligent responding.

Assertiveness training Instruction in how to be self-assertive.

Assessment center A program set up within an organization to conduct in-depth evaluations of job candidates.

Assimilation In Piaget's theory, the application of existing mental patterns to new situations (that is, the new situation is assimilated to existing mental schemes).

Association area (or cortex) All areas of the cerebral cortex that are not primarily sensory or motor in function.

Astigmatism (ah-STIG-mah-tiz-em) Defects in the cornea, lens, or eye that cause some areas of vision to be out of focus.

Attention Voluntarily focusing on a specific sensory input.

Attentional overload A stressful condition caused when sensory stimulation, information, and social contacts make excessive demands on attention.

Attention-deficit hyperactivity disorder (ADHD) A behavioral problem characterized by short attention span, restless movement, and impaired learning capacity.

Attitude A learned tendency to respond to people, objects, or institutions in a positive or negative way.

Attitude scale A collection of attitudinal statements with which respondents indicate agreement or disagreement.

Attribution The mental process of making inferences about the causes of events, one's own behavior, and that of others. In emotion, the process of attributing arousal to a particular source.

Authenticity In Carl Rogers's terms, the ability of a therapist to be genuine and honest about his or her own feelings.

Authoritarian parents Parents who enforce rigid rules and demand strict obedience to authority.

Authoritarian (ah-thor-ih-TARE-ee-un) **personality** A personality pattern characterized by rigidity, inhibition, prejudice, and an excessive concern with power, authority, and obedience.

Authoritative parents Parents who supply firm and consistent guidance combined with love and affection.

Autism A severe disorder involving mutism, sensory spin-outs, sensory blocking, tantrums, unresponsiveness to others, and other difficulties.

Autokinetic effect The apparent movement of a stationary pinpoint of light displayed in a darkened room.

Autonomic nervous system (ANS) The system of nerves carrying information to and from the internal organs and glands.

Autonomy versus shame and doubt A conflict created when growing self-control (autonomy) is pitted against feelings of shame or doubt.

Aversion therapy Suppressing an undesirable response by associating it with aversive (painful or uncomfortable) stimuli.

Aversive stimulus A stimulus that is painful or uncomfortable.

Avoidance learning Learning to make a response in order to postpone or prevent discomfort.

Avoidance-avoidance conflict Choosing between two negative, undesirable alternatives.

Avoidant attachment An emotional bond marked by a tendency to resist commitment to others.

Axon (AK-sahn) Fiber that carries information away from the cell body of a neuron.

Axon terminals Branching fibers at the ends of axons.

Babbling The repetition by infants of meaningless language sounds (including both vowel and consonant sounds).

Bait shyness An unwillingness or hesitation on the part of animals to eat a particular food.

Barnum effect The tendency to consider a personal description accurate if it is stated in very general terms.

Base rate The basic rate at which an event occurs over time; the basic probability of an event.

Basic anxiety A primary form of anxiety that arises from living in a hostile world.

Basic emotions The first distinct emotions to emerge in infancy.

Basic needs The first four levels of needs in Maslow's hierarchy; lower needs tend to be more potent than higher needs.

Basic suggestion effect The tendency of hypnotized persons to carry out suggested actions as if they were involuntary.

Behavior modification The application of learning principles to change human behavior, especially maladaptive behavior.

Behavior therapy Any therapy designed to actively change behavior.

Behavioral assessment Recording the frequency of various behaviors.

Behavioral contract A formal agreement stating behaviors to be changed and consequences that apply.

Behavioral dieting Weight reduction based on changing exercise and eating habits, rather than temporary self-starvation.

Behavioral genetics The study of inherited behavioral traits and tendencies.

Behavioral medicine The study of behavioral factors in medicine, physical illness, and medical treatment.

Behavioral personality theory Any model of personality that emphasizes learning and observable behavior.

Behavioral risk factors Behaviors that increase the chances of disease, injury, or premature death.

Behavioral setting A smaller area within an environment whose use is well defined, such as a bus depot, waiting room, or lounge.

Behaviorism The school of psychology that emphasizes the study of overt, observable behavior.

Belief component What a person thinks or believes about the object of an attitude.

Bereavement Period of emotional adjustment that follows the death of a loved one.

Beta waves Small, fast brain waves associated with being awake and alert.

Beta-endorphin A natural, painkilling brain chemical similar to morphine.

Biased sample A subpart of a larger population that does not accurately reflect characteristics of the whole population.

Bilingualism An ability to speak two languages.

Binge drinking Consuming five or more drinks in a short time.

Binocular depth cues Perceptual features that require two eyes and impart information about distance and three-dimensional space.

Biodata Detailed biographical information about a job applicant.

Biofeedback Information given to a person about his or her ongoing body activities; aids voluntary regulation of body states.

Biological aging Physiological changes that accompany growing older.

Biological biasing effect Hypothesized effect that prenatal exposure to sex hormones has on development of the body, nervous system, and later behavior patterns.

Biological perspective The attempt to explain behavior in terms of underlying biological principles.

Biological predisposition The presumed hereditary readiness of humans to learn certain skills, such as how to use language, or a readiness to behave in particular ways.

Biological rhythm Any repeating cycle of biological activity, such as sleep and waking cycles or changes in body temperature.

Bipolar disorders Emotional disorders involving both depression and mania or hypomania.

Bipolar I disorder A mood disorder in which a person has episodes of mania (excited, hyperactive, energetic, grandiose behavior) and also periods of deep depression.

Bipolar II disorder A mood disorder in which a person is mostly depressed (sad, despondent, guilt ridden) but has also had one or more episodes of mild mania (hypomania).

Bisexual A person romantically and erotically attracted to both men and women.

Blind spot An area of the retina lacking visual receptors.

Bottom-up processing Organizing perceptions by beginning with low-level features.

Brainstem The lowest portions of the brain, including the cerebellum, medulla, pons, and reticular formation.

Brainstorming Method of creative thinking that separates the production and evaluation of ideas.

Brainwashing Engineered or forced attitude change involving a captive audience.

Brief psychodynamic therapy A modern therapy based on psychoanalytic theory but designed to produce insights more quickly.

Brightness constancy The apparent (or relative) brightness of objects remains the same as long as they are illuminated by the same amount of light.

Broca's (BRO-cahs) **area** A language area related to grammar and pronunciation.

Broken record A self-assertion technique involving repeating a request until it is acknowledged.

Browser Software that facilitates access to text, images, sounds, video, and other information stored in formats used on the Internet.

Bulimia (bue-LIHM-ee-yah) **nervosa** Excessive eating (gorging) usually followed by self-induced vomiting and/or taking laxatives.

Burnout A job-related condition of mental, physical, and emotional exhaustion.

Bystander apathy Unwillingness of bystanders to offer help during emergencies or to become involved in others' problems.

Caffeinism Excessive consumption of caffeine, leading to dependence and a variety of physical and psychological complaints.

Cannon-Bard theory States that activity in the thalamus causes emotional feelings and body arousal to occur simultaneously.

Carbon footprint The volume of greenhouse gases individual consumption adds to the atmosphere.

Cardinal trait A personality trait so basic that all of a person's activities relate to it.

Caregiving styles Identifiable patterns of parental caretaking and interaction with children.

Case study An in-depth focus on all aspects of a single person.

Castration Surgical removal of the testicles or ovaries.

Cataplexy (CAT-uh-plex-see) A sudden temporary paralysis of the muscles.

Catatonic schizophrenia Schizophrenia marked by stupor; rigidity; unresponsiveness; posturing; mutism; and, sometimes, agitated, purposeless behavior.

Causation The act of causing some effect.

Central nervous system (CNS) The brain and spinal cord.

Central tendency The tendency for a majority of scores to fall in the midrange of possible values.

Central traits The core traits that characterize an individual personality.

Cerebellum (ser-ah-BEL-uhm) A brain structure that controls posture and coordination.

Cerebral cortex (seh-REE-brel or ser-EH-brel) The outer layer of the cerebrum.

Cervix (SER-vix) The lower end of the uterus that projects into the vagina.

Character Personal characteristics that have been judged or evaluated; a person's desirable or undesirable qualities.

Chromosomes Thread-like "colored bodies" in the nucleus of each cell that are made up of DNA.

Chronological age A person's age in years.

Circadian (SUR-kay-dee-AN) **rhythms** Cyclical changes in body functions and arousal levels that vary on a schedule approximating a 24-hour day.

Clairvoyance The purported ability to perceive events at a distance or through physical barriers.

Classical conditioning A form of learning in which reflex responses are associated with new stimuli.

Client-centered (or person-centered) therapy A nondirective therapy based on insights gained from conscious thoughts and feelings; emphasizes accepting one's true self.

Climacteric A point during late middle age when males experience a significant change in health, vigor, or appearance.

Clinical case study A detailed investigation of a single person, especially one suffering from some injury or disease.

Clinical method Studying psychological problems and therapies in clinical settings.

Clinical psychologist A psychologist who specializes in the treatment of psychological and behavioral disturbances or who does research on such disturbances.

Clinical study A detailed investigation of a single person, especially one suffering from some injury or disease.

Clitoris (KLIT-er-iss) Small, sensitive organ made up of erectile tissue; located above the vaginal opening.

Coefficient of correlation A statistical index ranging from -1.00 to $+1.00$ that indicates the direction and degree of correlation.

Coercive power Social power based on the ability to punish others.

Cognition The process of thinking or mentally processing information (images, concepts, words, rules, and symbols).

Cognitive behaviorism An approach that combines behavioral principles with cognition (perception, thinking, anticipation) to explain behavior.

Cognitive dissonance An uncomfortable clash between self-image, thoughts, beliefs, attitudes, or perceptions and one's behavior.

Cognitive interview Use of various cues and strategies to improve the memory of eyewitnesses.

Cognitive learning Higher-level learning involving thinking, knowing, understanding, and anticipation.

Cognitive map Internal images or other mental representations of an area (maze, city, campus, and so forth) that underlie an ability to choose alternative paths to the same goal.

Cognitive therapy A therapy directed at changing the maladaptive thoughts, beliefs, and feelings that underlie emotional and behavioral problems.

Collective unconscious A mental storehouse for unconscious ideas and images shared by all humans.

Color blindness A total inability to perceive colors.

Color weakness An inability to distinguish some colors.

Common traits Personality traits that are shared by most members of a particular culture.

Community health campaign A community-wide education program that provides information about how to lessen risk factors and promote health.

Community mental health center A facility offering a wide range of mental health services, such as prevention, counseling, consultation, and crisis intervention.

Comparison level A personal standard used to evaluate rewards and costs in a social exchange.

Compensation Counteracting a real or imagined weakness by emphasizing desirable traits or seeking to excel in the area of weakness or in other areas.

Compliance Bending to the requests of a person who has little or no authority or other form of social power.

Computer simulations Computer programs that mimic some aspect of human thinking, decision making, or problem solving.

Compressed workweek A work schedule that allows an employee to work fewer days per week by putting in more hours per day.

Concentrative meditation Mental exercise based on attending to a single object or thought.

Concept A generalized idea representing a category of related objects or events.

Concept formation The process of classifying information into meaningful categories.

Conceptual rule A formal rule for deciding if an object or event is an example of a particular concept.

Concrete operational stage Period of intellectual development during which children become able to use the concepts of time, space, volume, and number, but in ways that remain simplified and concrete, rather than abstract.

Condensation Combining several people, objects, or events into a single dream image.

Conditioned emotional response (CER) An emotional response that has been linked to a previously non-emotional stimulus by classical conditioning.

Conditioned response (CR) A learned response elicited by a conditioned stimulus.

Conditioned stimulus (CS) A stimulus that evokes a response because it has been repeatedly paired with an unconditioned stimulus.

Conditioning chamber (Skinner box) An apparatus designed to study operant conditioning in animals.

Conditions of worth Internal standards used to judge the value of one's thoughts, actions, feelings, or experiences.

Conduct disorder A pattern in which children consistently violate rules and behave aggressively and destructively.

Conductive hearing loss Poor transfer of sounds from the eardrum to the inner ear.

Cones Visual receptors for colors and daylight visual acuity.

Conflict A stressful condition that occurs when a person must choose between incompatible or contradictory alternatives.

Conformity Bringing one's behavior into agreement or harmony with norms or with the behavior of others in a group in the absence of any direct pressure.

Congenital problems Problems or defects that originate during prenatal development in the womb.

Conjunctive concept A class of objects that have two or more features in common. (For example, to qualify as an example of the concept an object must be both red *and* triangular.)

Connotative meaning The subjective, personal, or emotional meaning of a word or concept.

Conscience The part of the superego that causes guilt when its standards are not met.

Conscious The region of the mind that includes all mental contents a person is aware of at any given moment.

Consciousness Mental awareness of sensations, perceptions, memories, and feelings.

Consequences Effects that follow a response.

Conservation In Piaget's theory, mastery of the concept that the weight, mass, and volume of matter remain unchanged (are conserved) even when the shape or appearance of objects changes.

Consistency With respect to child discipline, the maintenance of stable rules of conduct.

Consolidation Process by which relatively permanent memories are formed in the brain.

Constructive processing Reorganizing or updating memories on the basis of logic, reasoning, or the addition of new information.

Contact comfort A pleasant and reassuring feeling human and animal infants get from touching or clinging to something soft and warm, usually their mother.

Context Information surrounding a stimulus.

Continuous reinforcement A schedule in which every correct response is followed by a reinforcer.

Control Altering conditions that influence behavior.

Control Where pain is concerned, refers to an ability to regulate the pain stimulus.

Control group In a controlled experiment, the group of subjects exposed to all experimental conditions or variables *except* the independent variable.

Control questions In a polygraph exam, questions that almost always provoke anxiety.

Conventional moral reasoning Moral thinking based on a desire to please others or to follow accepted rules and values.

Convergent thinking Thinking directed toward discovery of a single established correct answer; conventional thinking.

Conversion disorder A body symptom that mimics a physical disability but is actually caused by anxiety or emotional distress.

Conviction Beliefs that are important to a person and that evoke strong emotion.

Cooing Spontaneous repetition of vowel sounds by infants.

Cooperative play Play in which two or more children must coordinate their actions; if children don't cooperate, the game ends.

Coping statements Reassuring, self-enhancing statements that are used to stop self-critical thinking.

Correlation The existence of a consistent, systematic relationship between two events, measures, or variables.

Correlational method Making measurements to discover relationships between events.

Correlational study A nonexperimental study designed to measure the degree of relationship (if any) between two or more events, measures, or variables.

Corticalization (KORE-tih-kal-ih-ZAY-shun) An increase in the relative size of the cerebral cortex.

Counseling psychologist A psychologist who specializes in the treatment of milder emotional and behavioral disturbances.

Counselor A mental health professional who specializes in helping people with problems not involving serious mental disorder; for example, marriage counselors, career counselors, or school counselors.

Counterirritation Using mild pain to block more intense or long-lasting pain.

Covert reinforcement Using positive imagery to reinforce desired behavior.

Covert sensitization Use of aversive imagery to reduce the occurrence of an undesired response.

Cowper's glands Two small glands that secrete a clear fluid into the urethra during sexual excitement.

Cranial nerves Major nerves that leave the brain without passing through the spinal cord.

Creative self The "artist" in each of us that creates a unique identity and style of life.

Cretinism Stunted growth and intellectual disability caused by an insufficient supply of thyroid hormone.

Crisis intervention Skilled management of a psychological emergency.

Critical incidents Situations that arise in a job, with which a competent worker must be able to cope.

Critical situations Situations during childhood that are capable of leaving a lasting imprint on personality.

Critical thinking An ability to evaluate, compare, analyze, critique, synthesize, and reflect on information.

Cross-stimulation effect In group problem solving, the tendency of one person's ideas to trigger ideas from others.

Crowding A subjective feeling of being over-stimulated by a loss of privacy or by the nearness of others (especially when social contact with them is unavoidable).

Crystallized abilities Abilities that a person has intentionally learned; accumulated knowledge and skills.

CT scan Computed tomography scan; a computer-enhanced X-ray image of the brain or body.

Cue External stimuli that guide responses, especially by signaling the presence or absence of reinforcement.

Cult A group that professes great devotion to some person and follows that person almost without question; cult members are typically victimized by their leaders in various ways.

Cultural relativity The idea that behavior must be judged relative to the values of the culture in which it occurs.

Culture An ongoing pattern of life, characterizing a society at a given point in history.

Culturally skilled therapist A therapist who has the awareness, knowledge, and skills necessary to treat clients from diverse cultural backgrounds.

Culture-fair test A test (such as an intelligence test) designed to minimize the importance of skills and knowledge that may be more common in some cultures than in others.

Curve of forgetting A graph that shows the amount of memorized information remembered after varying lengths of time.

Curvilinear relationship A relationship that forms a curved line when graphed.

Cyclothymic (SIKE-lo-THY-mik) **disorder** Moderate manic and depressive behavior that persists for 2 years or more.

Dark adaptation Increased retinal sensitivity to light.

Daydream A vivid waking fantasy.

Death-qualified jury A jury composed of people who favor the death penalty or at least are indifferent to it.

Decay When referring to memory, the fading or weakening of memories assumed to occur when memory traces become weaker.

Declarative memory That part of long-term memory containing specific factual information.

Deductive thought Thought that applies a general set of rules to specific situations; for example, using the laws of gravity to predict the behavior of a single falling object.

Deep lesioning (LEE-zhun-ing) Removal of tissue within the brain by use of an electrode.

Deep sleep Stage 4 sleep; the deepest form of normal sleep.

Defense mechanism A habitual and often unconscious psychological process used to reduce anxiety.

Deinstitutionalization Reduced use of full-time commitment to mental institutions to treat mental disorders.

Delayed speech Speech that begins well after the normal age for language development has passed.

Delta waves Large, slow brainwaves that occur in deeper sleep (stages 3 and 4).

Delusion A false belief held against all contrary evidence.

Delusional disorder A psychosis marked by severe delusions of grandeur, jealousy, persecution, or similar preoccupations.

Dementia A serious mental impairment in old age caused by deterioration of the brain.

Demonology In medieval Europe, the study of demons and the treatment of persons "possessed" by demons.

Dendrites (DEN-drytes) Neuron fibers that receive incoming messages.

Denial Protecting oneself from an unpleasant reality by refusing to perceive it.

Denotative meaning The exact, dictionary definition of a word or concept; its objective meaning.

Density The number of people in a given space or, inversely, the amount of space available to each person.

Dependent variable In an experiment, the condition (usually a behavior) that is affected by the independent variable.

Depressant A substance that decreases activity in the body and nervous system.

Depression A state of despondency marked by feelings of powerlessness and hopelessness.

Depressive disorders Emotional disorders primarily involving sadness, despondency, and depression.

Deprivation In development, the loss or withholding of normal stimulation, nutrition, comfort, love, and so forth; a condition of lacking.

Depth cues Features of the environment and messages from the body that supply information about distance and space.

Depth perception The ability to see three-dimensional space and to accurately judge distances.

Description In scientific research, the process of naming and classifying.

Descriptive statistics Mathematical tools used to describe and summarize numeric data.

Desensitization A reduction in emotional sensitivity to a stimulus. Can be used to deliberately reduce fear or anxiety by repeatedly exposing a person to emotional stimuli while the person is deeply relaxed.

Determinism The idea that all behavior has prior causes that would completely explain one's choices and actions if all such causes were known.

Detoxification In the treatment of alcoholism, the withdrawal of the patient from alcohol.

Developmental level An individual's current state of physical, emotional, and intellectual development.

Developmental milestone A significant turning point or marker in personal development.

Developmental psychology The study of progressive changes in behavior and abilities from conception to death.

Developmental task Any skill that must be mastered, or personal change that must take place, for optimal development.

Deviation IQ An IQ obtained statistically from a person's relative standing in his or her age group; that is, how far above or below average the person's score was relative to other scores.

Diagnostic interview An interview used to find out how a person is feeling and what complaints or symptoms he or she has.

Difference threshold The minimum difference between two that is detectable to an observer.

Diffusion of responsibility Spreading the responsibility to act among several people; reduces the likelihood that help will be given to a person in need.

Direct instruction Presentation of factual information by lecture, demonstration, and rote practice.

Direct observation Assessing behavior through direct surveillance.

Discovery learning Learning based on insight and understanding.

Discrimination Treating members of various social groups differently in circumstances where their rights or treatment should be identical.

Discriminative stimuli Stimuli that precede rewarded and nonrewarded responses in operant conditioning.

Disease-prone personality A personality type associated with poor health; marked by persistent negative emotions, including anxiety, depression, and hostility.

Disengagement theory of aging Theory stating that it is normal for older people to withdraw from society and from roles they held earlier.

Dishabituation A reversal of habituation.

Disinhibition The removal of inhibition; results in acting out behavior that normally would be restrained.

Disjunctive concept A concept defined by the presence of at least one of several possible features. (For example, to qualify an object must be either blue *or* circular.)

Disorganized schizophrenia Schizophrenia marked by incoherence, grossly disorganized behavior, bizarre thinking, and flat or grossly inappropriate emotions.

Displaced aggression Redirecting aggression to a target other than the actual source of one's frustration.

Displacement Directing emotions or actions toward safe or unimportant dream images.

Dissociative amnesia Loss of memory (partial or complete) for important information related to personal identity.

Dissociative disorder Temporary amnesia, multiple personality, or depersonalization.

Dissociative fugue Sudden travel away from home, plus confusion about one's personal identity.

Dissociative identity disorder The presence of two or more distinct personalities (multiple personality).

Disuse The theory that memory traces weaken when memories are not periodically used or retrieved.

Divergent thinking Thinking that produces many ideas or alternatives; a major element in original or creative thought.

Divided attention Allotting mental space or effort to various tasks or parts of a task.

DNA Deoxyribonucleic acid, a molecular structure that contains coded genetic information.

Dogmatism An unwarranted positiveness or certainty in matters of belief or opinion.

Dominant gene A gene whose influence will be expressed each time the gene is present.

Dominant hemisphere A term usually applied to the side of a person's brain that produces language.

Door-in-the-face effect The tendency for a person who has refused a major request to subsequently be more likely to comply with a minor request.

Double approach-avoidance conflict Being simultaneously attracted to and repelled by each of two alternatives.

Double standard Applying different standards for judging the appropriateness of male and female sexual behavior.

Double-blind experiment An arrangement in which both participants and experimenters are unaware of whether participants are in the experimental group or the control group.

Down syndrome A genetic disorder caused by the presence of an extra chromosome; results in intellectual disability.

Downward comparison Comparing yourself with a person who ranks lower than you on some dimension.

Dream processes Mental filters that hide the true meanings of dreams.

Dream symbols Images in dreams that serve as visible signs of hidden ideas, desires, impulses, emotions, relationships, and so forth.

Dream symbols Images in dreams whose personal or emotional meanings differ from their literal meanings.

Drive The psychological expression of internal needs or valued goals strong enough to goad a person to action—for example, hunger, thirst, or a drive for success.

Drug interaction A combined effect of two drugs that exceeds the addition of one drug's effects to the other.

Drug tolerance A reduction in the body's response to a drug.

Dynamic touch Touch experienced when the body is in motion; a combination of sensations from skin receptors, muscles, and joints.

Dyslexia An inability to read with understanding, often caused by a tendency to misread letters (by seeing their mirror images, for instance).

Dyspareunia (DIS-pah-ROO-nee-ah) Genital pain before, during, or after sexual intercourse.

Dysthymic (dis-THY-mik) **disorder** Moderate depression that persists for 2 years or more.

Early childhood education program Programs that provide stimulating intellectual experiences, typically for disadvantaged preschoolers.

Echoic memory A brief continuation of sensory activity in the auditory system after a sound is heard.

Echolalia A compulsion, sometimes observed in autistic children, to repeat everything that is said.

Educational psychology The field that seeks to understand how people learn and how teachers instruct.

Ecological footprint The amount of land and water area required to replenish the resources that a human population consumes.

Ego The executive part of personality that directs rational behavior.

Ego ideal The part of the superego representing ideal behavior; a source of pride when its standards are met.

Egocentric thought Thought that is self-centered and fails to consider the viewpoints of others.

Eidetic (eye-DET-ik) **imagery** The ability to retain a "projected" mental image long enough to use it as a source of information.

Ejaculation The release of sperm and seminal fluid by the male at the time of orgasm.

Elaborative rehearsal Rehearsal that links new information with existing memories and knowledge.

Electra conflict A girl's sexual attraction to her father and feelings of rivalry with her mother.

Electrical stimulation of the brain (ESB) Direct electrical stimulation and activation of brain tissue.

Electroconvulsive shock (ECS) An electric current passed directly through the brain, producing a convulsion.

Electroconvulsive therapy (ECT) A treatment for severe depression, consisting of an electric shock passed directly through the brain, which induces a convulsion.

Electrode Any device (such as a wire, needle, or metal plate) used to electrically stimulate nerve tissue or to record its activity.

Electroencephalograph (ee-LEK-tro-in-SEF-ah-LOG-ruh-fee) **(EEG)** A device that detects, amplifies, and records electrical activity in the brain.

Emblems Gestures that have widely understood meanings within a particular culture.

Emotion A state characterized by physiological arousal, changes in facial expression, gestures, posture, and subjective feelings.

Emotional appraisal Evaluating the personal meaning of a stimulus or situation.

Emotional attachment An especially close emotional bond that infants form with their parents, caregivers, or others.

Emotional component One's feelings toward the object of an attitude.

Emotional expression Outward signs that an emotion is occurring.

Emotional feelings The private, subjective experience of having an emotion.

Emotional intelligence Emotional competence, including empathy, self-control, self-awareness, and other skills.

Emotion-focused coping Managing or controlling one's emotional reaction to a stressful or threatening situation.

Empathic arousal Emotional arousal that occurs when you feel some of another person's pain, fear, or anguish.

Empathy A capacity for taking another's point of view; the ability to feel what another is feeling.

Empathy-helping relationship Observation that we are most likely to help someone else when we feel emotions such as empathy and compassion.

Empty nest syndrome Psychological disturbance experienced by some women after their last child leaves home.

Encoding Converting information into a form in which it will be retained in memory.

Encoding failure Failure to store sufficient information to form a useful memory.

Encopresis A lack of bowel control; "soiling."

Encounter group A group experience that emphasizes intensely honest interchanges among participants regarding feelings and reactions to one another.

Endocrine (EN-duh-krin) **system** Glands whose secretions pass directly into the bloodstream or lymph system.

Endogenous (en-DODGE-eh-nus) **depression** Depression that appears to be produced from within (perhaps by chemical imbalances in the brain), rather than as a reaction to life events.

Engineering psychology (human factors engineering) A specialty concerned with making machines and work environments compatible with human perceptual and physical capacities.

Engram A "memory trace" in the brain.

Enrichment Deliberately making an environment more novel, complex, and perceptually or intellectually stimulating.

Enuresis An inability to control urination, particularly with regard to bed-wetting.

Enrichment In development, deliberately making an environment more stimulating, nutritional, comforting, loving, and so forth.

Environment ("nurture") The sum of all external conditions affecting development, including especially the effects of learning.

Environmental assessment Measurement and analysis of the effects an environment has on the behavior of people within that environment.

Environmental psychology The formal study of how environments affect behavior.

Epididymis (ep-ih-DID-ih-mus) A coiled structure at the top of the testes in which sperm are stored.

Epinephrine (ep-eh-NEF-rin) An adrenal hormone that tends to arouse the body; epinephrine is associated with fear. (Also known as adrenaline.)

Episodic (ep-ih-SOD-ik) **drive** A drive that occurs in distinct episodes.

Episodic (ep-ih-SOD-ik) **memory** A subpart of declarative memory that records personal experiences that are linked with specific times and places.

Equal-status contact Social interaction that occurs on an equal footing, without obvious differences in power or status.

Erectile disorder An inability to maintain an erection for lovemaking.

Erogenous (eh-ROJ-eh-nus) **zones** Areas of the body that produce pleasure and/or provoke erotic desire.

Erogenous zone Any body area that produces pleasurable sensations.

Eros Freud's name for the "life instincts."

Escape Reducing discomfort by leaving frustrating situations or by psychologically withdrawing from them.

Escape learning Learning to make a response in order to end an aversive stimulus.

Estrogen Any of a number of female sex hormones.

Estrus Changes in the sexual drives of animals that create a desire for mating; particularly used to refer to females in heat.

Ethnocentrism Placing one's own group or race at the center—that is, tending to reject all other groups but one's own.

Ethologist A person who studies the natural behavior patterns of animals.

Eugenics Selective breeding for desirable characteristics.

Evaluation fears Fears of being inadequate, embarrassed, ridiculed, or rejected.

Evolutionary psychology Study of the evolutionary origins of human behavior patterns.

Excitement phase The first phase of sexual response, indicated by initial signs of sexual arousal.

Existential therapy An insight therapy that focuses on the elemental problems of existence, such as death, meaning, choice, and responsibility; emphasizes making courageous life choices.

Expectancy An anticipation concerning future events or relationships, including anticipation about the effect a response will have, especially regarding reinforcement.

Experiential intelligence Specialized knowledge and skills acquired through learning and experience.

Experiment A formal trial undertaken to confirm or disconfirm a hypothesis about cause and effect.

Experimental group In a controlled experiment, the group of subjects exposed to the independent variable or experimental condition.

Experimental method Investigating causes of behavior through controlled experimentation.

Experimental subjects Humans (also referred to as **subjects** or **participants**) or animals whose behavior is investigated in an experiment.

Experimenter effect Changes in subjects' behavior caused by the unintended influence of an experimenter's actions.

Expert power Social power derived from possession of knowledge or expertise.

Expert systems Computer programs designed to respond as a human expert would; programs based on the knowledge and rules that underlie human expertise in specific topics.

Explicit memory A memory that a person is aware of having; a memory that is consciously retrieved.

Expressive behaviors Behaviors that express or communicate emotion or personal feelings.

External cause A cause of behavior that is assumed to lie outside a person.

External urethral orifice (yoo-REE-thral OR-ih-fis) The opening at the tip of the penis through which urine and semen pass.

Extinction The weakening of a conditioned response through removal of reinforcement.

Extracellular thirst Thirst caused by a reduction in the volume of fluids found between body cells.

Extraneous variables Conditions or factors excluded from influencing the outcome of an experiment.

Extrasensory perception (ESP) The purported ability to perceive events in ways that cannot be explained by known capacities of the sensory organs.

Extrinsic motivation Motivation based on obvious external rewards, obligations, or similar factors.

Extrovert A person whose attention is directed outward; a bold, outgoing person.

Eye movement desensitization and reprocessing (EMDR) A technique for reducing fear or anxiety; based on holding upsetting thoughts in mind while rapidly moving the eyes from side to side.

Facial agnosia (ag-KNOW-zyah) Inability to perceive familiar faces.

Facial feedback hypothesis States that sensations from facial expressions help define what emotion a person feels.

Factor analysis A statistical technique used to correlate multiple measurements and identify general underlying factors.

Fallacy of positive instances The tendency to remember or notice information that fits one's expectations, while forgetting discrepancies.

Fallopian tube (feh-LOPE-ee-en) One of two tubes that carry eggs from the ovaries to the uterus.

Familial intellectual disability Mild intellectual disability associated with homes that are intellectually, nutritionally, and emotionally impoverished.

Family therapy Technique in which all family members participate, both individually and as a group, to change destructive relationships and communication patterns.

Fantasy Fulfilling unmet desires in imagined achievements or activities.

Feedback Information returned to a person about the effects a response has had; also known as knowledge of results.

Feeling of knowing The ability to predict beforehand whether one will be able to remember something.

Female orgasmic disorder A persistent inability to reach orgasm during lovemaking.

Female sexual arousal disorder A lack of physical arousal to sexual stimulation.

Figure-ground organization Part of a stimulus appears to stand out as an object (figure) against a less prominent background (ground).

Five-factor model Proposes that there are five universal dimensions of personality.

Fixation A lasting conflict developed as a result of frustration or overindulgence.

Fixation In problem solving, a tendency to repeat wrong solutions or faulty responses, especially as a result of becoming blind to alternatives.

Fixed interval (FI) schedule A reinforcer is given only when a correct response is made after a set amount of time has passed since the last reinforced response. Responses made during the time interval are not reinforced.

Fixed ratio (FR) schedule A set number of correct responses must be made to get a reinforcer. For example, a reinforcer is given for every four correct responses.

Flashbulb memories Memories created at times of high emotion that seem especially vivid.

Flexibility In tests of creativity, flexibility is indicated by the number of different types of solutions produced.

Flextime A work schedule that allows flexible starting and quitting times.

Fluency In tests of creativity, fluency refers to the total number of solutions produced.

Fluid abilities Innate, nonlearned abilities based on perceptual, motor, or intellectual speed and flexibility.

fMRI scan Magnetic resonance imaging that records brain activity.

Foot-in-the-door effect The tendency for a person who has first complied with a small request to be more likely later to fulfill a larger request.

Forcible rape Sexual intercourse carried out against the victim's will, under the threat of violence or bodily injury.

Foreclosed identity The result of shutting down personal growth.

Formal operations stage Period of intellectual development characterized by thinking that includes abstract, theoretical, and hypothetical ideas.

Fovea An area at the center of the retina containing only cones.

Frame of reference An internal perspective relative to which events are perceived and evaluated.

Fragile X syndrome A genetic form of intellectual disability caused by a defect in the X chromosome.

Framing In thought, the terms in which a problem is stated or the way that it is structured.

Fraternal twins Twins conceived from two separate eggs.

Free association In psychoanalysis, the technique of having a client say anything that comes to mind, regardless of how embarrassing or unimportant it may seem.

Free choice The ability to freely make choices that are not controlled by genetics, learning, or unconscious forces.

Free will The idea that human beings are capable of freely making choices or decisions.

Frequency distribution A table that divides an entire range of scores into a series of classes and then records the number of scores that fall into each class.

Frequency polygon A graph of a frequency distribution in which the number of scores falling in each class is represented by points on a line.

Frequency theory Holds that tones up to 4,000 hertz are converted to nerve impulses that match the frequency of each tone.

Frontal lobes A brain area associated with movement, the sense of self, and higher mental functions.

Frustration A negative emotional state that occurs when one is prevented from reaching a goal.

Frustration-aggression hypothesis States that frustration tends to lead to aggression.

Fully functioning person A person living in harmony with her or his deepest feelings, impulses, and intuitions.

Functional fixedness A rigidity in problem solving caused by an inability to see new uses for familiar objects.

Functional MRI (fMRI) Functional magnetic resonance imaging that records brain activity.

Functional solution A detailed, practical, and workable solution.

Functionalism The school of psychology concerned with how behavior and mental abilities help people adapt to their environments.

Fundamental attribution error The tendency to attribute the behavior of others to internal causes (personality, likes, and so forth).

Galvanic skin response (GSR) A change in the electrical resistance (or inversely, the conductance) of the skin, due to sweating.

Gate control theory Proposes that pain messages pass through neural "gates" in the spinal cord.

Gender Psychological and social characteristics associated with being male or female; defined especially by one's gender identity and learned gender roles.

Gender bias (in research) A tendency for females and female issues to be under-represented in research, psychological or otherwise.

Gender identity One's personal, private sense of maleness or femaleness.

Gender role The pattern of behaviors that are regarded as "male" or "female"

by one's culture; sometimes also referred to as a sex role.
Gender role socialization The process of learning gender behaviors considered appropriate for one's sex in a given culture.
Gender role stereotypes Oversimplified and widely held beliefs about the basic characteristics of men and women.
General adaptation syndrome (GAS) A series of bodily reactions to prolonged stress; occurs in three stages: alarm, resistance, and exhaustion.
General intelligence test A test that measures a wide variety of mental abilities.
General solution A solution that correctly states the requirements for success but not in enough detail for further action.
Generalized anxiety disorder A chronic state of tension and worry about work, relationships, ability, or impending disaster.
Generativity versus stagnation A conflict of middle adulthood in which self-interest is countered by an interest in guiding the next generation.
Genes Specific areas on a strand of DNA that carry hereditary information.
Genetic disorders Problems caused by defects in the genes or by inherited characteristics.
Genetic sex Sex as indicated by the presence of *XX* (female) or *XY* (male) chromosomes.
Genital sex Sex as indicated by the presence of male or female genitals.
Genital stage Period of full psychosexual development, marked by the attainment of mature adult sexuality.
Gerontologist One who scientifically studies aging and its effects.
Gestalt psychology A school of psychology emphasizing the study of thinking, learning, and perception in whole units, not by analysis into parts.
Gestalt therapy An approach that focuses on immediate experience and awareness to help clients rebuild thinking, feeling, and acting into connected wholes; emphasizes the integration of fragmented experiences.
g-factor A general ability factor or core of general intellectual ability that involves reasoning, problem-solving ability, knowledge, memory, and successful adaptation to one's surroundings.
Giftedness The possession of a high IQ or special talents or aptitudes.
Glans penis (glanz PEA-nis) The tip of the penis.
Goal The target or objective of motivated behavior.
Gonadal sex Sex as indicated by the presence of ovaries (female) or testes (male).

Gonads The primary sex glands—the testes in males and ovaries in females.
Grammar A set of rules for combining language units into meaningful speech or writing.
Graphical statistics Techniques for presenting numbers pictorially, often by plotting them on a graph.
Grief An intense emotional state that follows the death of a lover, friend, or relative.
Group cohesiveness The degree of attraction among group members or their commitment to remaining in the group.
In-group A group with which a person identifies.
Group intelligence test Any intelligence test that can be administered to a group of people with minimal supervision.
Group prejudice Prejudice held out of conformity to group views.
Group sanctions Rewards and punishments (such as approval or disapproval) administered by groups to enforce conformity among members.
Group structure The network of roles, communication pathways, and power in a group.
Group therapy Psychotherapy conducted in a group setting to make therapeutic use of group dynamics.
Groupthink A compulsion by members of decision-making groups to maintain agreement, even at the cost of critical thinking.
Growth hormone A hormone, secreted by the pituitary gland, that promotes body growth.
Growth needs In Maslow's hierarchy, the higher-level needs associated with self-actualization.
Growth spurt An often dramatic acceleration in physical growth that coincides with puberty.
Guided imagery Intentional visualization of images that are calming, relaxing, or beneficial in other ways.
Gustation The sense of taste.
Habit A deeply ingrained, learned pattern of behavior.
Habituation A decrease in perceptual response to a repeated stimulus.
Hair cells Receptor cells within the cochlea that transduce vibrations into nerve impulses.
Half-way house A community-based facility for individuals making the transition from an institution (mental hospital, prison, and so forth) to independent living.
Hallucination An imaginary sensation, such as seeing, hearing, or smelling things that don't exist in the real world.
Hallucinogen (hal-LU-sin-oh-jin) A substance that alters or distorts sensory impressions.

Halo effect The tendency to generalize a favorable or unfavorable first impression to unrelated details of personality.
Handedness A preference for the right or left hand in most activities.
Hardy personality A personality style associated with superior stress resistance.
Hassle (microstressor) Any distressing, day-to-day annoyance.
Health psychology Study of the ways in which behavioral principles can be used to prevent illness and promote health.
Heredity ("nature") The transmission of physical and psychological characteristics from parents to offspring through genes.
Heterosexism The belief that heterosexuality is better or more natural than homosexuality.
Heterosexual A person romantically and erotically attracted to members of the opposite sex.
Heuristic (hew-RIS-tik) Any strategy or technique that aids problem solving, especially by limiting the number of possible solutions to be tried.
Hidden observer A detached part of the hypnotized person's awareness that silently observes events.
Hierarchy A rank-ordered series of higher and lower amounts, levels, degrees, or steps.
Hierarchy of human needs Abraham Maslow's ordering of needs, based on their presumed strength or potency.
Higher-order conditioning Classical conditioning in which a conditioned stimulus is used to reinforce further learning; that is, a CS is used as if it were a US.
Hippocampus (HIP-oh-CAMP-us) A part of the limbic system associated with emotion and the transfer of information from short-term memory to long-term memory.
Histogram A graph of a frequency distribution in which the number of scores falling in each class is represented by vertical bars.
Homeostasis (HOE-me-oh-STAY-sis) A steady state of body equilibrium.
Homogamy Marriage of two people who are similar to one another.
Homosexual A person romantically and erotically attracted to same-sex persons.
Honesty test A paper-and-pencil test designed to detect attitudes, beliefs, and behavior patterns that predispose a person to dishonest behavior.
Hormonal sex Sex as indicated by a preponderance of estrogens (female) or androgens (male) in the body.
Hormone A glandular secretion that affects bodily functions or behavior.
Human factors psychology (ergonomics) A specialty concerned with making machines and work environments compatible with human perceptual and physical capacities.
Human growth sequence The pattern of physical development from conception to death.
Human nature Those traits, qualities, potentials, and behavior patterns most characteristic of the human species.
Human–computer interaction (HCI) The application of human factors to the design of computers and computer software.
Humanism An approach to psychology that focuses on human experience, problems, potentials, and ideas.
Hydrocephaly A buildup of cerebrospinal fluid within brain cavities.
Hyperopia (HI-per-OPE-ee-ah) Difficulty focusing on nearby objects (farsightedness).
Hypersomnia (hi-per-SOM-nee-ah) Excessive daytime sleepiness. This can result from depression, insomnia, narcolepsy, sleep apnea, sleep drunkenness (a very slow transition to waking), periodic limb movements, drug abuse, and other problems.
Hypnagogic images Vivid mental images that may occur just as one enters stage 1 sleep.
Hypnosis An altered state of consciousness characterized by narrowed attention and increased suggestibility.
Hypnotic susceptibility One's capacity for becoming hypnotized.
Hypoactive sexual desire A persistent, upsetting loss of sexual desire.
Hypochondriac (HI-po-KON-dreeak) A person who complains about illnesses that appear to be imaginary.
Hypochondriasis (HI-po-kon-DRYuh-sis) A preoccupation with fears of having a serious disease. Ordinary physical signs are interpreted as proof that the person has a disease, but no physical disorder can be found.
Hypothalamus (HI-po-THAL-ahmus) A small area at the base of the brain that regulates many aspects of motivation and emotion, especially hunger, thirst, and sexual behavior.
Hypothesis (hi-POTH-eh-sis) The predicted outcome of an experiment or an educated guess about the relationship between variables.
Hypothetical possibilities Suppositions, guesses, or projections.
Iconic (EYE-kon-ick) **memory** A mental image or visual representation.
Id The primitive part of personality that remains unconscious, supplies energy, and demands pleasure.
Ideal self An idealized image of oneself (the person one would like to be).
Identical twins Twins who develop from a single egg and have identical genes.
Identification Feeling emotionally connected to a person and seeing oneself as like him or her. Taking on some of the characteristics of an admired

person, usually as a way of compensating for perceived personal weaknesses or faults.

Identity versus role confusion A conflict of adolescence, involving the need to establish a personal identity.

Illogical thought Thought that is intuitive, haphazard, or irrational.

Illusion A misleading or distorted perception.

Illustrators Gestures people use to illustrate what they are saying.

Image Most often, a mental representation that has picture-like qualities; an icon.

Imagery rehearsal Mentally rehearsing and changing a nightmare in an attempt to prevent it from reoccurring.

Imaginary audience The group of people a person imagines is watching (or will watch) his or her actions.

I-message A message that states the effect someone else's behavior has on you.

Imitation An attempt to match one's own behavior to another person's behavior.

Immune system System that mobilizes the body's defenses (such as white blood cells) against invading microbes and other disease agents.

Implicit memory A memory that a person does not know exists; a memory that is retrieved unconsciously.

Imprinting A rapid and relatively permanent type of learning that occurs during a limited period early in life.

Inattentional blindness Failure to perceive a stimulus that is in plain view but not the focus of attention.

In-basket test A testing procedure that simulates the individual decision-making challenges that executives face.

Incentive value The value of a goal above and beyond its ability to fill a need.

Incongruence State that exists when there is a discrepancy between one's experiences and self-image or between one's self-image and ideal self.

Incongruent person A person who has an inaccurate self-image or whose self-image differs greatly from the ideal self.

Incremental problem solving Thinking marked by a series of small steps that lead to an original solution.

Independent variable In an experiment, the condition being investigated as a possible cause of some change in behavior. The values that this variable takes are chosen by the experimenter.

Individual intelligence test A test of intelligence designed to be given to a single individual by a trained specialist.

Individual traits Personality traits that define a person's unique individual qualities.

Individuating information Information that helps define a person as an individual, rather than as a member of a group or social category.

Inductive thought Thinking in which a general rule or principle is gathered from a series of specific examples; for instance, inferring the laws of gravity by observing many falling objects.

Industrial/organizational (I/O) psychology A field that focuses on the psychology of work and on behavior within organizations.

Industry versus inferiority A conflict in middle childhood centered around lack of support for industrious behavior, which can result in feelings of inferiority.

Inferential statistics Mathematical tools used for decision making, for generalizing from small samples, and for drawing conclusions.

Information bits Meaningful units of information, such as numbers, letters, words, or phrases.

Information chunks Information bits grouped into larger units.

In-group A group with which a person identifies.

Informational view Perspective that explains learning in terms of information imparted by events in the environment.

Initiative versus guilt A conflict between learning to take initiative and overcoming feelings of guilt about doing so.

Insanity A legal term that refers to a mental inability to manage one's affairs or to be aware of the consequences of one's actions.

Insecure-ambivalent attachment An anxious emotional bond marked by both a desire to be with a parent or caregiver and some resistance to being reunited.

Insecure-avoidant attachment An anxious emotional bond marked by a tendency to avoid reunion with a parent or caregiver.

Insight A sudden mental reorganization of a problem that makes the solution obvious.

Insomnia Difficulty in getting to sleep or staying asleep.

Inspection time The amount of time a person must look at a stimulus to make a correct judgment about it.

Instrumental behaviors Behaviors directed toward the achievement of some goal; behaviors that are instrumental in producing some effect.

Integrity versus despair A conflict in old age between feelings of integrity and the despair of viewing previous life events with regret.

Intellectual disability (formerly **mental retardation**) The presence of a developmental disability, a formal IQ score below 70, or a significant impairment of adaptive behavior.

Intellectualization Separating emotion from a threatening or anxiety-provoking situation by talking or thinking about it in impersonal "intellectual" terms.

Intelligence An overall capacity to think rationally, act purposefully, and deal effectively with the environment.

Intelligence quotient (IQ) An index of intelligence defined as a person's mental age divided by his or her chronological age and multiplied by 100.

Interference The tendency for new memories to impair retrieval of older memories, and the reverse.

Internal cause A cause of behavior assumed to lie within a person—for instance, a need, preference, or personality trait.

Internal images Mental images or visual depictions used in memory and thinking.

Internet An electronic network of interlinked computers.

Interpersonal attraction Social attraction to another person.

Interpretation Where pain is concerned, the meaning given to a stimulus.

Intersexual person A person who has genitals suggestive of both sexes.

Interview (personality) A face-to-face meeting held for the purpose of gaining information about an individual's personal history, personality traits, current psychological state, and so forth.

Intimacy versus isolation The challenge of overcoming a sense of isolation by establishing intimacy with others.

Intimate distance The most private space immediately surrounding the body (up to about 18 inches from the skin).

Intracellular thirst Thirst triggered when fluid is drawn out of cells due to an increased concentration of salts and minerals outside the cell.

Intrinsic motivation Motivation that comes from within, rather than from external rewards; motivation based on personal enjoyment of a task or activity.

Introspection To look within; to examine one's own thoughts, feelings, or sensations.

Introvert A person whose attention is focused inward; a shy, reserved, self-centered person.

Intuition Quick, impulsive thought that does not make use of formal logic or clear reasoning.

Intuitive thought Thinking that makes little or no use of reasoning and logic.

Ion (EYE-on) channels Tiny openings through the axon membrane.

Iris Circular muscle that controls the amount of light entering the eye.

Isolation Separating contradictory thoughts or feelings into "logic-tight" mental compartments so that they do not come into conflict.

James-Lange theory States that emotional feelings follow bodily arousal and come from awareness of such arousal.

Jigsaw classroom A method of reducing prejudice; each student receives only part of the information needed to complete a project or prepare for a test.

Job analysis A detailed description of the skills, knowledge, and activities required by a particular job.

Job enrichment Making a job more personally rewarding, interesting, or intrinsically motivating; typically involves increasing worker knowledge.

Job satisfaction The degree to which a person is comfortable with or satisfied with his or her work.

Just noticeable difference (JND) Any noticeable difference in a stimulus.

Just-world beliefs Belief that people generally get what they deserve.

Keyword method As an aid to memory, using a familiar word or image to link two items.

Kinesics (kih-NEEZ-iks) Study of the meaning of body movements, posture, hand gestures, and facial expressions; commonly called body language.

Kinesthetic senses The senses of body movement and positioning.

Knowledge of results (KR) Informational feedback.

Knowledge workers Workers who add value to their company by creating and manipulating information.

Labia majora (LAY-bee-ah mah-JOR-ah) The larger outer lips of the vulva.

Labia minora (LAY-bee-ah mih-NOR-ah) Inner lips of the vulva, surrounding the vaginal opening.

Language Words or symbols, and rules for combining them, that are used for thinking and communication.

Large-group awareness training Any of a number of programs (many of them commercialized) that claim to increase self-awareness and facilitate constructive personal change.

Latency According to Freud, a period in childhood when psychosexual development is more or less interrupted.

Latent dream content The hidden or symbolic meaning of a dream, as revealed by dream interpretation and analysis.

Latent learning Learning that occurs without obvious reinforcement and that remains unexpressed until reinforcement is provided.

Lateralization Differences between the two sides of the body; especially, differences in the abilities of the brain hemispheres.

Law of effect Responses that lead to desirable effects are repeated; those that produce undesirable results are not.

Leaderless group discussion A test of leadership that simulates group decision-making and problem solving.

Learned helplessness A learned inability to overcome obstacles or to avoid punishment; learned passivity and inaction to aversive stimuli.

Learning Any relatively permanent change in behavior that can be attributed to experience.

Learning disorder Any problem with thinking, perception, language, attention, or activity levels that tends to impair learning ability.

Learning theorist A psychologist interested in the ways that learning shapes behavior and explains personality.

Legitimate power Social power based on a person's position as an agent of an accepted social order.

Lexigram A geometric shape used as a symbol for a word.

Libido (lih-BEE-doe) In Freudian theory, the force, primarily pleasure oriented, that energizes the personality.

Life change units (LCUs) Numerical values assigned to each life event on the SRRS.

Life expectancy The average number of years a person of a given sex, race, and nationality can expect to live.

Life skills training A program that teaches stress reduction, self-protection, decision making, self-control, and social skills.

Life stages Widely recognized periods of life corresponding to broad phases of development.

Life-span perspective The study of continuity and change in behavior over a lifetime.

Lifestyle disease A disease related to health-damaging personal habits.

Light sleep Stage 1 sleep, marked by small, irregular brainwaves and some alpha waves.

Liking A relationship based on intimacy, but lacking passion and commitment.

Limbic system A system in the forebrain that is closely linked with emotional response.

Linear relationship A relationship that forms a straight line when graphed.

Links Connections built into Internet sites that let you "jump" from one site to the next.

Lobes of the cerebral cortex Areas on the cortex bordered by major fissures or defined by their functions.

Localization of function The research strategy of linking specific structures in the brain with specific psychological or behavioral functions.

Lock and key theory Holds that odors are related to the shapes of chemical molecules.

Logical consequences Reasonable consequences that are defined by parents.

Logical thought Drawing conclusions on the basis of formal principles of reasoning.

Logotherapy A form of existential therapy that emphasizes the need to find and maintain meaning in one's life.

Long sleeper A person averaging 9 hours of sleep or more per night.

Long-term memory (LTM) The memory system used for relatively permanent storage of meaningful information.

Lowball technique A strategy in which commitment is gained first to reasonable or desirable terms, which are then made less reasonable or desirable.

Lucid dream A dream in which the dreamer feels awake and capable of normal thought and action.

Magnetic resonance imaging (MRI) Magnetic resonance imaging; a three-dimensional image of the brain or body, based on its response to a magnetic field.

Maintenance rehearsal Silently repeating or mentally reviewing information to hold it in short-term memory.

Major depressive disorder A mood disorder in which the person has suffered one or more intense episodes of depression.

Major mood disorders Disorders marked by lasting extremes of mood or emotion and sometimes accompanied by psychotic symptoms.

Maladaptive behavior Behavior that makes it difficult to adapt to the environment and meet the demands of day-to-day life.

Male orgasmic disorder A persistent inability to reach orgasm during lovemaking.

Management by objectives A management technique in which employees are given specific goals to meet in their work.

Management techniques Combining praise, recognition, approval, rules, and reasoning to enforce child discipline.

Mandala A circular design representing balance, unity, and completion.

Manifest dream content The surface, "visible" content of a dream; dream images as they are remembered by the dreamer.

Massed practice A practice schedule in which studying continues for long periods, without interruption.

Mastery training Reinforcement of responses that lead to mastery of a threat or control over one's environment.

Masturbation Producing sexual pleasure or orgasm by directly stimulating the genitals.

Maternal influences The aggregate of all psychological effects mothers have on their children.

Maternity blues A brief and relatively mild state of depression often experienced by mothers 2 or 3 days after giving birth.

Maturation The physical growth and development of the body and nervous system.

Maximum life span The biologically defined maximum number of years humans can live under optimal conditions.

Mean A measure of central tendency calculated by adding a group of scores and then dividing by the total number of scores.

Means-ends analysis An analysis of how to reduce the difference between the present state of affairs and a desired goal.

Mechanical solution A problem solution achieved by trial and error or by a fixed procedure based on learned rules.

Median A central tendency found by arranging scores from the highest to the lowest and selecting the score that falls in the middle. That is, half the values in a group of scores fall above the median and half fall below.

Medicated birth The common practice in Western medicine of giving painkilling drugs during labor and birth.

Meditation A mental exercise for producing relaxation or heightened awareness.

Medulla (meh-DUL-ah) The structure that connects the brain with the spinal cord and controls vital life functions.

Melatonin (mel-ah-TONE-in) A hormone released by the pineal gland in response to daily cycles of light and dark.

Memory The mental system for receiving, encoding, storing, organizing, altering, and retrieving information.

Memory cue Any stimulus associated with a particular memory. Memory cues usually enhance retrieval.

Memory decay The fading or weakening of memories assumed to occur when memory traces become weaker.

Memory task Any task designed to test or assess memory.

Memory traces Physical changes in nerve cells or brain activity that take place when memories are stored.

Menopause The female "change of life" signaled by the end of regular monthly menstrual periods.

Mental age The average mental ability people display at a given age.

Mental disorder A significant impairment in psychological functioning.

Mental hospitalization Placing a person in a protected, therapeutic environment staffed by mental health professionals.

Mental images Mental pictures or visual depictions used in memory and thinking.

Mental practice Imagining a skilled performance to aid learning.

Mental set A predisposition to perceive or respond in a particular way.

Meta-analysis A statistical technique for combining the results of many studies on the same subject.

Meta-needs In Maslow's hierarchy, needs associated with impulses for self-actualization.

Metacognitive skills An ability to manage one's own thinking and problem-solving efforts.

Microcephaly A disorder in which the head and brain are abnormally small.

Microsleep A brief shift in brainwave patterns to those of sleep.

Mindfulness A state of open, nonjudgmental, awareness of current experience.

Mindfulness meditation Mental exercise based on widening attention to become aware of everything experienced at any given moment.

Minnesota Multiphasic Personality Inventory-2 (MMPI-2) One of the best-known and most widely used objective personality questionnaires.

Mirror neuron A neuron that becomes active when a motor action is carried out *and* when another organism is observed carrying out the same action.

Mirror technique Observing another person reenact one's own behavior, like a character in a play; designed to help persons see themselves more clearly.

MMPI-2 profile A graphic representation of an individual's scores on each of the primary scales of the MMPI-2.

Mnemonic (nee-MON-ik) Any kind of memory system or aid.

Mock jury A group that realistically simulates a courtroom jury.

Mode A measure of central tendency found by identifying the most frequently occurring score in a group of scores.

Model A person who serves as an example in observational learning.

Monocular depth cues Perceptual features that require just one eye and impart information about distance and three-dimensional space.

Mood A low-intensity, long-lasting emotional state.

Mood disorder A major disturbance in mood or emotion, such as depression or mania.

Moon illusion The apparent change in size that occurs as the moon moves from the horizon (large moon) to overhead (small moon).

Moral anxiety Apprehension felt when thoughts, impulses, or actions conflict with the superego's standards.

Moral development The development of values, beliefs, and thinking abilities that act as a guide regarding what is acceptable behavior.

Morphemes (MOR-feems) The smallest meaningful units in a language, such as syllables or words.

Motherese (parentese) A pattern of speech used when talking to infants, marked by a higher-pitched voice; short, simple sentences; repetition; slower speech; and exaggerated voice inflections.

Motivation Internal processes that initiate, sustain, and direct activities.

Motor cortex A brain area associated with control of movement.

Motor program A mental plan or model that guides skilled movement.

Motor skill A series of actions molded into a smooth and efficient performance.

MRI scan Magnetic resonance imaging; a computer-enhanced three-dimensional representation of the brain or body based on the body's response to a magnetic field.

Müller-Lyer (MEOO-ler-LIE-er) **illusion** Two equal-length lines tipped with inward or outward pointing V's appear to be of different lengths.

Multiculturalism Giving equal status, recognition, and acceptance to different ethnic and cultural groups.

Multimedia computerized test A test that uses a computer to present lifelike situations; test takers react to problems posed by the situations.

Multiple approach-avoidance conflict Being simultaneously attracted to and repelled by each of several alternatives.

Multiple aptitude test Test that measures two or more aptitudes.

Multiple intelligences Howard Gardner's theory that there are several specialized types of intellectual ability.

Mutual absorption With regard to romantic love, the nearly exclusive attention lovers give to each other.

Munchausen by proxy An affected person fakes the medical problems of someone in his or her care in order to gain attention.

Munchausen syndrome An affected person fakes his or her own medical problems in order to gain attention.

Mutual interdependence A condition in which two or more persons must depend on each other to meet each person's needs or goals.

Myelin (MY-eh-lin) A fatty layer coating some axons.

Myopia (my-OPE-ee-ah) Difficulty focusing on distant objects (nearsightedness).

Narcolepsy (NAR-koe-lep-see) Sudden, irresistible, daytime sleep attacks that may last anywhere from a few minutes to a half hour. Victims may fall asleep while standing, talking, or even driving.

Natural clinical test An accident or other natural event that allows the gathering of data on a psychological phenomenon of interest.

Natural consequences The effects that naturally tend to follow a particular behavior.

Natural design Human factors engineering that makes use of naturally understood perceptual signals.

Natural selection Darwin's theory that evolution favors those plants and animals best suited to their living conditions.

Naturalistic observation Observing behavior as it unfolds in natural settings.

Near-death experience (NDE) A pattern of subjective experiences that may occur when a person is clinically dead and then resuscitated.

Need An internal deficiency that may energize behavior.

Need for achievement (nAch) The desire to excel or meet some internalized standard of excellence.

Need for power The desire to have social impact and control over others.

Need to affiliate The desire to associate with other people.

Negative after-potential A drop in electrical charge below the resting potential.

Negative correlation A statistical relationship in which increases in one measure are matched by decreases in the other.

Negative instance In concept learning, an object or event that does not belong to the concept class.

Negative reinforcement Occurs when a response is followed by an end to discomfort or by the removal of an unpleasant event.

Negative relationship A mathematical relationship in which increases in one measure are matched by decreases in the other.

Negative self-statements Self-critical thoughts that increase anxiety and lower performance.

Negative transfer Mastery of one task conflicts with learning or performing another.

Neo-Freudian A psychologist who accepts the broad features of Freud's theory but has revised the theory to fit his or her own concepts.

Nerve A bundle of neuron fibers.

Network model A model of memory that views it as an organized system of linked information.

Neural intelligence The innate speed and efficiency of a person's brain and nervous system.

Neurilemma (NOOR-rih-LEM-ah) A layer of cells that encases many axons.

Neurological soft signs Subtle behavioral signs of brain dysfunction, including clumsiness, an awkward gait, poor hand-eye coordination, and other perceptual and motor problems.

Neurogenesis (noor-oh-JEN-uh-sis) The production of new brain cells.

Neuron (NOOR-on) An individual nerve cell.

Neuropeptides (NOOR-oh-PEP-tides) Brain chemicals, such as enkephalins and endorphins, that regulate the activity of neurons.

Neurosis An outdated term once used to refer, as a group, to anxiety disorders, somatoform disorders, dissociative disorders, and some forms of depression.

Neurotic anxiety Apprehension felt when the ego struggles to control id impulses.

Neurotransmitter (NOOR-oh-TRANS-mit-ers) Any chemical released by a neuron that alters activity in other neurons.

Neutral stimulus (NS) A stimulus that does not evoke a response.

Night blindness Blindness under conditions of low illumination.

Night terror A state of panic during NREM sleep.

Nightmare A bad dream that occurs during REM sleep.

Nightmare disorder Vivid, recurrent nightmares that significantly disturb sleep.

Noise pollution Stressful and intrusive noise; usually artificially generated by machinery, but also including noises made by animals and humans.

Noise-induced hearing loss Damage caused by exposing the hair cells to excessively loud sounds.

Nonhomeostatic drive A drive that is relatively independent of physical deprivation cycles or bodily need states.

Non-REM (NREM) sleep Non–rapid eye movement sleep characteristic of stages 1, 2, 3, and 4.

Norepinephrine An adrenal hormone that tends to arouse the body; norepinephrine is associated with anger. (Also known as noradrenaline.)

Norm (social) A widely accepted (but often unspoken) standard of conduct for appropriate behavior.

Norm (testing) An average score for a designated group of people.

Normal curve A bell-shaped curve characterized by a large number of scores in a middle area, tapering to very few extremely high and low scores.

Obedience Conformity to the demands of an authority.

Object permanence Concept, gained in infancy, that objects continue to exist even when they are hidden from view.

Objective test A test that gives the same score when different people correct it.

Observational learning Learning achieved by watching and imitating the actions of another or noting the consequences of those actions.

Observational record A detailed summary of observed events or a videotape of observed behavior.

Observer bias The tendency of an observer to distort observations or perceptions to match his or her expectations.

Observer effect Changes in a person's behavior brought about by an awareness of being observed.

Obsessive-compulsive disorder An extreme preoccupation with certain thoughts and compulsive performance of certain behaviors.

Occipital (awk-SIP-ih-tal) **lobes** Portion of the cerebral cortex where vision registers in the brain.

Oedipus conflict A boy's sexual attraction to his mother and feelings of rivalry with his father.

Olfaction The sense of smell.

Open teaching Instruction based on active teacher-student discussion.

Open-ended interview An interview in which persons are allowed to freely state their views.

Operant conditioning (instrumental learning) Learning based on the consequences of responding.

Operant extinction The weakening or disappearance of a nonreinforced operant response.

Operant reinforcer Any event that reliably increases the probability or frequency of responses it follows.

Operant stimulus discrimination The tendency to make an operant response when stimuli previously associated with reward are present and to withhold the response when stimuli associated with nonreward are present.

Operant stimulus generalization The tendency to respond to stimuli similar to those that preceded operant reinforcement.

Operational definition Defining a scientific concept by stating the specific actions or procedures used to measure it. For example, "hunger" might be defined as "the number of hours of food deprivation."

Opponent-process theory With respect to emotions, a theory that states that strong emotions tend to be followed by an opposite emotional state; also, the strength of both emotional states changes over time.

Opponent-process theory Theory of color vision based on three coding systems (red or green, yellow or blue, black or white).

Oral stage The period when infants are preoccupied with the mouth as a source of pleasure and means of expression.

Oral-aggressive personality A person who uses the mouth to express hostility by shouting, cursing, biting, and so forth. Also, one who actively exploits others.

Oral-dependent personality A person who wants to passively receive attention, gifts, love, and so forth.

Organ of Corti (KOR-tee) Center part of the cochlea, containing hair cells, canals, and membranes.

Organic mental disorder A mental or emotional problem caused by brain diseases or injuries.

Organismic valuing A natural, undistorted, full-body reaction to an experience.

Organizational citizenship Making positive contributions to the success of an organization in ways that go beyond one's job description.

Organizational culture The social climate within an organization.

Orgasm A climax and release of sexual excitement.

Orientation response Bodily changes that prepare an organism to receive information from a particular stimulus.

Originality In tests of creativity, originality refers to how novel or unusual solutions are.

Out-group A group with which a person does not identify.

Ovary (OH-vah-ree) One of the two female reproductive glands; ovaries are the source of hormones and eggs.

Overgeneralization Blowing a single event out of proportion by extending it to a large number of unrelated situations.

Overlearning Continuing to study and learn after you think you've mastered a topic.

Overly permissive parents Parents who give little guidance, allow too much freedom, or do not require the child to take responsibility.

Pain disorder Pain that has no identifiable physical cause and appears to be of psychological origin.

Panic disorder (with agoraphobia) A chronic state of anxiety and brief moments of sudden panic. The person fears that these panic attacks will occur in public places or unfamiliar situations.

Panic disorder (without agoraphobia) A chronic state of anxiety and also brief moments of sudden, intense, unexpected panic.

Paranoid psychosis A delusional disorder centered especially on delusions of persecution.

Paranoid schizophrenia Schizophrenia marked by a preoccupation with delusions or by frequent auditory hallucinations related to a single theme, especially grandeur or persecution.

Paraphilias (PAIR-eh-FIL-ih-ahs) Compulsive or destructive deviations in sexual preferences or behavior.

Paraprofessional An individual who works in a near-professional capacity under the supervision of a more highly trained person.

Parapsychology The study of extranormal psychological events, such as extrasensory perception.

Parasympathetic branch A part of the autonomic system that quiets the body and conserves energy.

Parasympathetic rebound Excess activity in the parasympathetic nervous system following a period of intense emotion.

Parasympathetic system A branch of the ANS that quiets the body.

Parental styles Identifiable patterns of parental caretaking and interaction with children.

Parentese A pattern of speech used when talking to infants, marked by a higher-pitched voice; short, simple sentences; repetition; slower speech; and exaggerated voice inflections.

Parietal (puh-RYE-ih-tal) **lobes** Area of the brain where body sensations register.

Partial hospitalization An approach in which patients receive treatment at a hospital during the day but return home at night.

Partial reinforcement A pattern in which only a portion of all responses are reinforced.

Partial reinforcement effect Responses acquired with partial reinforcement are more resistant to extinction.

Participants Humans (also referred to as **experimental subjects**) whose behavior is investigated in an experiment.

Participative management An approach to management that allows employees at all levels to participate in decision making.

Passive compliance Passively bending to unreasonable demands or circumstances.

Paternal influences The aggregate of all psychological effects fathers have on their children.

Peak experiences Temporary moments of self-actualization.

Peak performance A performance during which physical, mental, and emotional states are harmonious and optimal.

Peer counselor A nonprofessional person who has learned basic counseling skills.

Peer group A group of people who share similar social status.

Percent of variance A portion of the total amount of variation in a group of scores.

Pelvic bone One of the bones at the front of the pelvis (the pelvis connects the spine with the legs).

Perception The mental process of organizing sensations into meaningful patterns.

Perceptual construction A mental model of external events.

Perceptual defense Resistance to perceiving threatening or disturbing stimuli.

Perceptual expectancy (or **set**) A readiness to perceive in a particular manner, induced by strong expectations.

Perceptual features Important elements of a stimulus pattern, such as lines, shapes, edges, spots, and colors.

Perceptual hypothesis An initial guess regarding how to organize (perceive) a stimulus pattern.

Perceptual learning Changes in perception that can be attributed to prior experience; a result of changes in how the brain processes sensory information.

Perceptual reconstruction A mental model of external events.

Perfect negative relationship A mathematical relationship in which the correlation between two measures is -1.00.

Perfect positive relationship A mathematical relationship in which the correlation between two measures is $+1.00$.

Performance intelligence Intelligence measured by solving puzzles, assembling objects, completing pictures, and other nonverbal tasks.

Periodic limb movement syndrome Muscle twitches (primarily affecting the legs) that occur every 20 to 40 seconds and severely disturb sleep.

Peripheral nervous system (PNS) All parts of the nervous system outside the brain and spinal cord.

Peripheral vision Vision at the edges of the visual field.

Persona The "mask" or public self presented to others.

Personal distance The distance maintained when interacting with close friends (about 18 inches to 4 feet from the body).

Personal interview Formal or informal questioning of job applicants to learn their qualifications and to gain an impression of their personalities.

Personal prejudice Prejudicial attitudes held toward persons who are perceived as a direct threat to one's own interests.

Personal space An area surrounding the body that is regarded as private and subject to personal control.

Personal unconscious A mental storehouse for a single individual's unconscious thoughts.

Personality A person's unique and relatively stable behavior patterns.

Personality disorder A maladaptive personality pattern.

Personality questionnaire A paper-and-pencil test consisting of questions that reveal aspects of personality.

Personality theory A system of concepts, assumptions, ideas, and principles used to understand and explain personality.

Personality trait A stable, enduring quality that a person shows in most situations.

Personality type A style of personality defined by a group of related traits.

Personnel psychology Branch of industrial/organizational psychology concerned with testing, selection, placement, and promotion of employees.

Persuasion A deliberate attempt to change attitudes or beliefs with information and arguments.

PET scan Positron emission tomography; a computer-generated image of brain activity, based on glucose consumption in the brain.

Phallic personality A person who is vain, exhibitionistic, sensitive, and narcissistic.

Phallic stage The psychosexual stage (roughly ages 3 to 6), when a child is preoccupied with the genitals.

Phantom limb The illusory sensation that a limb still exists after it is lost through accident or amputation.

Pharmacotherapy (FAR-meh-koe-THER-eh-pea) The use of drugs to alleviate the symptoms of emotional disturbance.

Phenylketonuria (FEN-ul-KEET-uh-NUREee-ah) A genetic disease that allows phenylpyruvic acid to accumulate in the body.

Pheromone An airborne chemical signal.

Phonemes (FOE-neems) The basic speech sounds of a language.

Phototherapy A treatment for seasonal affective disorder that involves exposure to bright, full-spectrum light.

Physical dependence Physical addiction, as indicated by the presence of drug tolerance and withdrawal symptoms.

Physical environments Natural settings, such as forests and beaches, as well as environments built by humans, such as buildings, ships, and cities.

Physiological changes (in emotion) Alterations in heart rate, blood pressure, perspiration, and other involuntary responses.

Pica Eating or chewing on inedible objects or substances such as chalk, ashes, and the like.

Pictorial depth cues Monocular depth cues found in paintings, drawings, and photographs that impart information about space, depth, and distance.

Pineal (pin-EE-ul) **gland** A gland in the brain that helps regulate body rhythms and sleep cycles.

Pituitary gland The "master gland" whose hormones influence other endocrine glands.

Place theory A theory that higher and lower tones excite specific areas of the cochlea.

Placebo (plah-SEE-bo) An inactive substance given in the place of a drug in psychological research or by physicians who wish to treat a complaint by suggestion.

Placebo effect Changes in behavior due to expectations that a drug (or other treatment) will have some effect.

Plasticity The capacity of our brains to change in response to experience.

Plateau phase The second phase of sexual response, during which physical arousal is further heightened.

Pleasure principle A desire for immediate satisfaction of wishes, desires, or needs.

Polygenic (pol-ih-JEN-ik) **characteristics** Personal traits or physical properties that are influenced by many genes working in combination.

Polygraph A device for recording heart rate, blood pressure, respiration, and galvanic skin response; commonly called a "lie detector."

Pons An area on the brainstem that acts as a bridge between the medulla and other structures.

Population An entire group of animals or people belonging to a particular category (for example, all college students or all married women).

Positive correlation A statistical relationship in which increases in one measure are matched by increases in the other (or decreases correspond with decreases).

Positive instance In concept learning, an object or event that belongs to the concept class.

Positive psychology The study of human strengths, virtues, and effective functioning.

Positive reinforcement Occurs when a response is followed by a reward or other positive event.

Positive relationship A mathematical relationship in which increases in one measure are matched by increases in the other (or decreases correspond with decreases).

Positive self-regard Thinking of oneself as a good, lovable, worthwhile person.

Positive transfer Mastery of one task aids learning or performing another.

Possible self A collection of thoughts, beliefs, feelings, and images concerning the person one could become.

Postconventional moral reasoning Moral thinking based on carefully examined and self-chosen moral principles.

Postpartum depression A mild to moderately severe depression that begins within 3 months following childbirth.

Posttraumatic stress disorder (PTSD) A psychological disturbance lasting more than 1 month following stresses that would produce anxiety in anyone who experienced them.

Power assertion The use of physical punishment or coercion to enforce child discipline.

Precognition The purported ability to accurately predict future events.

Preconscious An area of the mind containing information that can be voluntarily brought to awareness.

Preconventional moral reasoning Moral thinking based on the consequences of one's choices or actions (punishment, reward, or an exchange of favors).

Prediction An ability to accurately forecast behavior.

Prefrontal area (cortex) The very front of the frontal lobes; involved in sense of self, reasoning, and planning.

Prejudice A negative emotional attitude held against members of a particular group of people.

Premack principle Any high-frequency response can be used to reinforce a low-frequency response.

Premature ejaculation Ejaculation that consistently occurs before the man and his partner want it to occur.

Preoperational stage A period of intellectual development during which children begin to use language and think symbolically, yet remain intuitive and egocentric in their thought.

Prepared childbirth A collection of techniques designed to manage discomfort and facilitate birth so that the use of painkilling drugs can be avoided or minimized.

Presbyopia (prez-bee-OPE-ee-ah) Farsightedness caused by aging.

Pressure A stressful condition that occurs when a person must meet urgent external demands or expectations.

Primary appraisal Deciding if a situation is relevant to oneself and if it is a threat.

Primary auditory area Part of the temporal lobe where auditory information is first registered.

Primary emotions According to Robert Plutchik's theory, the most basic emotions are fear, surprise, sadness, disgust, anger, anticipation, joy, and acceptance.

Primary motives Innate motives based on biological needs.

Primary motor area (or cortex) A brain area associated with control of movement.

Primary reinforcers Nonlearned reinforcers; usually those that satisfy physiological needs.

Primary sexual characteristics Sex as defined by the genitals and internal reproductive organs.

Primary somatosensory (SO-mat-oh-SEN-so-ree) **area (cortex)** A receiving area for body sensations.

Primary visual area The part of occipital lobe that first receives input from the eyes.

Priming Facilitating the retrieval of an implicit memory by using cues to activate hidden memories.

Private self-consciousness Preoccupation with inner feelings, thoughts, and fantasies.

Proactive (pro-AK-tiv) **interference** The tendency for old memories to interfere with the retrieval of newer memories.

Problem finding The active discovery of problems to be solved.

Problem-focused coping Directly managing or remedying a stressful or threatening situation.

Procedural memory Long-term memories of conditioned responses and learned skills.

Programmed instruction Any learning format that presents information in small amounts, gives immediate practice, and provides continuous feedback to learners.

Progressive relaxation A method for producing deep relaxation of all parts of the body.

Projection Attributing one's own feelings, shortcomings, or unacceptable impulses to others.

Projective tests Psychological tests making use of ambiguous or unstructured stimuli.

Prosocial behavior Behavior toward others that is helpful, constructive, or altruistic.

Prostate (PROSS-tate) A gland located at the base of the urinary bladder that supplies most of the fluid that makes up semen.

Prototype An ideal model used as a prime example of a particular concept.

Proxemics (prok-SEE-miks) Systematic study of the human use of space, particularly in social settings.

Pseudopsychology (SUE-doe-psychology) Any false and unscientific system of beliefs and practices that is offered as an explanation of behavior.

Psi (sigh) **phenomena** Events that seem to lie outside the realm of accepted scientific laws.

Psyche The mind, mental life, and personality as a whole.

Psychiatric social worker A mental health professional trained to apply social science principles to help patients in clinics and hospitals.

Psychiatrist A medical doctor with additional training in the diagnosis and treatment of mental and emotional disorders.

Psychoactive drug A substance capable of altering attention, memory, judgment, time sense, self-control, mood, or perception.

Psychoanalysis A Freudian therapy that emphasizes the use of free association, dream interpretation, resistances, and transference to uncover unconscious conflicts.

Psychoanalyst A mental health professional (usually a medical doctor) trained to practice psychoanalysis.

Psychoanalytic theory Freudian theory of personality that emphasizes unconscious forces and conflicts.

Psychodrama A therapy in which clients act out personal conflicts and feelings in the presence of others who play supporting roles.

Psychodynamic theory Any theory of behavior that emphasizes internal conflicts, motives, and unconscious forces.

Psychogenic Having psychological origins, rather than physical causes.

Psychokinesis The purported ability to mentally alter or influence objects or events.

Psychological dependence Drug dependence that is based primarily on emotional or psychological needs.

Psychological efficiency Maintenance of good morale, labor relations, employee satisfaction, and similar aspects of work behavior.

Psychological perspective The traditional view that behavior is shaped by psychological processes occurring at the level of the individual.

Psychological situation A situation as it is perceived and interpreted by an individual, not as it exists objectively.

Psychological trauma A psychological injury or shock, such as that caused by violence, abuse, neglect, separation, and so forth.

Psychologist A person highly trained in the methods, factual knowledge, and theories of psychology.

Psychology The scientific study of behavior and mental processes.

Psychology of law Study of the psychological and behavioral dimensions of the legal system.

Psychoneuroimmunology Study of the links among behavior, stress, disease, and the immune system.

Psychopathology The scientific study of mental, emotional, and behavioral disorders; also, abnormal or maladaptive behavior.

Psychophysics Study of the relationship between physical stimuli and the sensations they evoke in a human observer.

Psychosexual stages The oral, anal, phallic, and genital stages, during which various personality traits are formed.

Psychosis A withdrawal from reality marked by hallucinations and delusions, disturbed thought and emotions, and personality disorganization.

Psychosocial dilemma A conflict between personal impulses and the social world that affects development.

Psychosomatic (SIKE-oh-so-MAT-ik) **disorders** Illnesses in which psychological factors contribute to bodily damage or to damaging changes in bodily functioning.

Psychosurgery Any surgical alteration of the brain designed to bring about desirable behavioral or emotional changes.

Psychotherapy Any psychological technique used to facilitate positive changes in a person's personality, behavior, or adjustment.

Psychotic disorder A severe mental disorder characterized by a retreat from reality, by hallucinations and delusions, and by social withdrawal.

PsycINFO A searchable, online database that provides brief summaries of the scientific and scholarly literature in psychology.

Puberty The biologically defined period during which a person matures sexually and becomes capable of reproduction.

Public distance Distance at which formal interactions, such as giving a speech, occur (about 12 feet or more from the body).

Public self-consciousness Intense awareness of oneself as a social object.

Punisher Any consequence that reduces the frequency of a target behavior.

Punishment Any event that follows a response and *decreases* its likelihood of occurring again.

Pupil The opening at the front of the eye through which light passes.

Quality circle An employee discussion group that makes suggestions for improving quality and solving business problems.

Racism Racial prejudice that has become institutionalized (that is, it is reflected in government policy, schools, and so forth) and that is enforced by the existing social power structure.

Random assignment The use of chance (for example, flipping a coin) to assign subjects to experimental and control groups.

Random search strategy Trying possible solutions to a problem in a more or less random order.

Random selection Choosing a sample so that each member of the population has an equal chance of being included in the sample.

Range The difference between the highest and lowest scores in a group of scores.

Rape myths False beliefs about rape that tend to blame the victim and increase the likelihood that some men will think that rape is justified.

Rapid eye movements (REMs) Swift eye movements during sleep.

Rating scale A list of personality traits or aspects of behavior on which a person is rated.

Rational-emotive behavior therapy (REBT) An approach that states that irrational beliefs cause many emotional problems and that such beliefs must be changed or abandoned.

Rationalization Justifying your behavior by giving reasonable and "rational," but false, reasons for it.

Reaction formation Preventing dangerous impulses from being expressed in behavior by exaggerating opposite behavior.

Reaction range The limits environment places on the effects of heredity.

Readiness A condition that exists when maturation has advanced enough to allow the rapid acquisition of a particular skill.

Reality principle Delaying action (or pleasure) until it is appropriate.

Reality testing Obtaining additional information to check on the accuracy of perceptions.

Recall To supply or reproduce memorized information with a minimum of external cues.

Receptor sites Areas on the surface of neurons and other cells that are sensitive to neurotransmitters or hormones.

Recessive gene A gene whose influence will be expressed only when it is paired with a second recessive gene.

Reciprocal inhibition The presence of one emotional state can inhibit the occurrence of another, such as joy preventing fear or anxiety inhibiting pleasure.

Recoding Reorganizing or modifying information to assist storage in memory.

Recognition memory An ability to correctly identify previously learned information.

Rectum The lowest section of the large intestine.

Redintegrative memories Memories that are reconstructed or expanded by starting with one memory and then following chains of association to other, related memories.

Reference group Any group that an individual identifies with and uses as a standard for social comparison.

Referent power Social power gained when one is used as a point of reference by others.

Referred pain Pain that is felt in one part of the body but comes from another.

Reflection In client-centered therapy, the process of rephrasing or repeating thoughts and feelings expressed by clients so they can become aware of what they are saying.

Reflex An innate, automatic response to a stimulus; for example, an eye blink.

Reflective intelligence An ability to become aware of one's own thinking habits.

Reflex arc The simplest behavior, in which a stimulus provokes an automatic response.

Refractory period A short period after orgasm during which males are unable to again reach orgasm.

Refusal skills training Program that teaches youths how to resist pressures to begin smoking (can also be applied to other drugs and health risks).

Regression Retreating to an earlier level of development or to earlier, less demanding habits or situations.

Reinforcement Any event that increases the probability that a particular response will occur.

Reinforcement value The subjective value a person attaches to a particular activity or reinforcer.

Relational concept A concept defined by the relationship between features of an object or between an object and its surroundings (for example, "greater than," "lopsided").

Relaxation response The pattern of internal bodily changes that occurs at times of relaxation.

Relearning Learning again something that was previously learned. Used to measure memory of prior learning.

Reliability The ability of a test to yield the same score, or nearly the same score, each time it is given to the same person.

REM behavior disorder A failure of normal muscle paralysis, leading to violent actions during REM sleep.

REM rebound The occurrence of extra rapid eye movement sleep following REM sleep deprivation.

REM sleep Sleep marked by rapid eye movements and a return to stage 1 EEG patterns.

Reminding system Pain based on small nerve fibers; reminds the brain that the body has been injured.

Replicate To reproduce or repeat.

Representative sample A small, randomly selected part of a larger population that accurately reflects characteristics of the whole population.

Representativeness heuristic A tendency to select wrong answers because they seem to match pre-existing mental categories.

Repression The unconscious process by which memories, thoughts, or impulses are held out of awareness. Also referred to as motivated forgetting.

Research method A systematic approach to answering scientific questions.

Resistance A blockage in the flow of free association; topics the client resists thinking or talking about.

Resolution The fourth phase of sexual response, involving a return to lower levels of sexual tension and arousal.

Respondent reinforcement Reinforcement that occurs when an unconditioned stimulus closely follows a conditioned stimulus.

Response Any muscular action, glandular activity, or other identifiable aspect of behavior.

Response chaining The assembly of separate responses into a series of actions that lead to reinforcement.

Response cost Removal of a positive reinforcer after a response is made.

REST Restricted environmental stimulation therapy.

Resting potential The electrical charge of a neuron at rest.

Restless legs syndrome An irresistible urge to move the legs in order to relieve sensations of creeping, tingling, prickling, aching, or tension.

Restricted Environmental Stimulation Therapy (**REST**) A form of sensory deprivation that results in a variety of psychological benefits.

Reticular (reh-TICK-you-ler) **formation** A network within the medulla and brainstem; associated with attention, alertness, and some reflexes.

Reticular activating system (**RAS**) A part of the reticular formation that activates the cerebral cortex.

Retina The light-sensitive layer of cells at the back of the eye.

Retrieval Recovering information from storage in memory.

Retroactive (RET-ro-AK-tiv) **interference** The tendency for new memories to interfere with the retrieval of old memories.

Retrograde amnesia Loss of memory for events that preceded a head injury or other amnesia-causing event.

Reversibility of thought Recognition that relationships involving equality or identity can be reversed (for example, if A = B, then B = A).

Reward Anything that produces pleasure or satisfaction; a positive reinforcer.

Reward power Social power based on the capacity to reward a person for acting as desired.

Rhodopsin The light-sensitive pigment in the rods.

Rods Visual receptors for dim light that produce only black and white sensations.

Role conflict Trying to occupy two or more roles that make conflicting demands on behavior.

Role reversal Taking the role of another person to learn how one's own behavior appears from the other person's perspective.

Romantic love Love that is associated with high levels of interpersonal attraction, heightened arousal, mutual absorption, and sexual desire.

Rorschach Technique A projective test comprised of 10 standardized inkblots.

Rote learning Learning that takes place mechanically, through repetition and memorization, or by learning rules.

Run of luck A statistically unusual outcome (as in getting five heads in a row when flipping a coin) that could still occur by chance alone.

Sample A smaller subpart of a population.

Satisficing Engaging in behavior that achieves a minimum result, rather than maximizing the outcome of that behavior.

Scaffolding The process of adjusting instruction so that it is responsive to a beginner's behavior and supports the beginner's efforts to understand a problem or gain a mental skill.

Scapegoating Blaming a person or a group of people for conditions not of their making.

Scatter diagram A graph that plots the intersection of paired measures; that is, the points at which paired X and Y measures cross.

Schachter's cognitive theory States that emotions occur when physical arousal is labeled or interpreted on the basis of experience and situational cues.

Schedule of reinforcement A rule or plan for determining which responses will be reinforced.

Schizophrenia (SKIT-soh-FREN-ee-uh) A psychosis characterized by delusions, hallucinations, apathy, and a "split" between thought and emotion.

Scientific jury selection Using social science principles to choose members of a jury.

Scientific management (Theory X) An approach to managing employees that emphasizes work efficiency.

Scientific method A form of critical thinking based on careful measurement and controlled observation.

Scientific observation An empirical investigation that is structured so that it answers questions about the world.

Scrotum (SKROE-tehm) The sac-like pouch that holds the testes.

Seasonal affective disorder (SAD) Depression that occurs only during fall and winter; presumably related to decreased exposure to sunlight.

Secondary appraisal Deciding how to cope with a threat or challenge.

Secondary elaboration Making a dream more logical and complete while remembering it.

Secondary motives Motives based on learned needs, drives, and goals.

Secondary reinforcer A learned reinforcer; often one that gains reinforcing properties by association with a primary reinforcer.

Secondary sexual characteristics Sexual features other than the genitals and reproductive organs—breasts, body shape, facial hair, and so forth.

Secondary traits Traits that are inconsistent or relatively superficial.

Secure attachment A stable and positive emotional bond.

Selective attention Giving priority, usually voluntarily, to a particular incoming sensory message.

Selective perception Perceiving only certain stimuli among a larger array of possibilities.

Self A continuously evolving conception of one's personal identity.

Self archetype An unconscious image representing, unity, wholeness, completion, and balance.

Self-actualization The ongoing process of fully developing one's personal potential.

Self-actualizer One who is living creatively and making full use of his or her potentials.

Self-assertion A direct, honest expression of feelings and desires.

Self-concept A person's perception of his or her own personality traits.

Self-defeating bias A distortion of thinking that impairs behavior.

Self-disclosure The process of revealing private thoughts, feelings, and one's personal history to others.

Self-efficacy (EF-uh-keh-see) Belief in your capacity to produce a desired result.

Self-esteem Regarding oneself as a worthwhile person; a positive evaluation of oneself.

Self-fulfilling prophecy An expectation that prompts people to act in ways that make the expectation come true.

Self-handicapping Arranging to perform under conditions that usually impair performance, so as to have an excuse for a poor showing.

Self-help group A group of people who share a particular type of problem and provide mutual support to one another.

Self-image Total subjective perception of one's body and personality (another term for self-concept).

Self-managed team A work group that has a high degree of freedom with respect to how it achieves its goals.

Self-recording Self-management based on keeping records of response frequencies.

Self-regulated learning Deliberately reflective and active self-guided study.

Self-reinforcement Praising or rewarding oneself for having made a particular response (such as completing a school assignment).

Self-testing Evaluating learning by posing questions to yourself.

Semantic memory A subpart of declarative memory that records impersonal knowledge about the world.

Semantics The study of meanings in words and language.

Seminal vesicles (SEM-in-uhl VES-ih-kuhlz) These two small organs (one on each side of the prostate) supply fluid that becomes part of semen.

Sensate focus A form of therapy that directs a couple's attention to natural sensations of sexual pleasure.

Sensation The immediate response in the brain caused by excitation of a sensory organ; also, the process of detecting physical energies with the sensory organs.

Sensitive period During development, a period of increased sensitivity to environmental influences. Also, a time during which certain events must take place for normal development to occur.

Sensitivity group A group experience consisting of exercises designed to increase self-awareness and sensitivity to others.

Sensorimotor stage Stage of intellectual development during which sensory input and motor responses become coordinated.

Sensorineural hearing loss Loss of hearing caused by damage to the inner ear hair cells or auditory nerve.

Sensory adaptation A decrease in sensory response to an unchanging stimulus.

Sensory analysis Separation of sensory information into important elements.

Sensory coding Codes used by the sense organs to transmit information to the brain.

Sensory conflict theory Explains motion sickness as the result of a mismatch among information from vision, the vestibular system, and kinesthesis.

Sensory deprivation (SD) Any major reduction in the amount or variety of sensory stimulation.

Sensory gating Alteration of sensory messages in the spinal cord.

Sensory memory The first, normally unconscious, stage of memory, which holds an exact record of incoming information for a few seconds or less.

Sensory neuron A nerve cell that carries information from the senses toward the CNS.

Separation anxiety disorder Severe and prolonged distress displayed by children when they are separated from their parents or caregivers.

Serial position effect The tendency to make the most errors in remembering the middle items of an ordered list.

Set point The proportion of body fat that tends to be maintained by changes in hunger and eating.

Sex One's biological classification as female or male.

Sex drive The strength of one's motivation to engage in sexual behavior.

Sexism Institutionalized prejudice against members of either sex, based solely on their gender.

Sex-linked trait Traits other than sex that are influenced by genes carried on an X chromosome (or, rarely, on a Y chromosome).

Sexual and gender identity disorders Any of a wide range of difficulties with sexual identity, deviant sexual behavior, or sexual adjustment.

Sexual aversion Persistent feelings of fear, anxiety, or disgust about engaging in sex.

Sexual orientation One's degree of emotional and erotic attraction to members of the same sex, opposite sex, or both sexes.

Sexual script An unspoken mental plan that defines a plot, dialogue, and actions expected to take place in a sexual encounter.

Sexually transmitted disease (STD) A disease that is typically passed from one person to the next by intimate physical contact; a venereal disease.

Shape constancy The perceived shape of an object is unaffected by changes in its retinal image.

Shaping Gradually molding responses to a final desired pattern.

Shared leadership (participative management) A leadership approach that allows employees at all levels to participate in decision making.

Short sleeper A person averaging 5 hours of sleep or less per night.

Short-term memory (STM) The memory system used to hold small amounts of information in our conscious awareness for about a dozen seconds.

Shyness A tendency to avoid others, plus uneasiness and strain when socializing.

Sidedness A combination of preference for hand, foot, eye, and ear.

Signal In early language development, any behavior, such as touching, vocalizing, gazing, or smiling, that allows nonverbal interaction and turn-taking between parent and child.

Simultaneous color contrast Changes in perceived hue that occur when a colored stimulus is displayed on backgrounds of various colors.

Single-blind experiment An arrangement in which participants remain unaware of whether they are in the experimental group or the control group.

Situational demands Unstated expectations that define desirable or appropriate behavior in various settings and social situations.

Situational determinants External conditions that strongly influence behavior.

Situational judgment test Presenting realistic work situations to applicants in order to observe their skills and reactions.

Situational test Simulating real-life conditions so that a person's reactions may be directly observed.

Size constancy The perceived size of an object remains constant, despite changes in its retinal image.

Size-distance invariance The strict relationship between the distance an object lies from the eyes and the size of its image.

Skin receptors Sensory organs for touch, pressure, pain, cold, and warmth.

Skin senses The senses of touch, pressure, pain, heat, and cold.

Sleep apnea (AP-nee-ah) During sleep, breathing stops for 20 seconds or more until the person wakes a little, gulps in air, and settles back to sleep; this cycle may be repeated hundreds of times per night.

Sleep deprivation Being prevented from getting desired or needed amounts of sleep.

Sleep drunkenness A slow transition to clear consciousness after awakening; sometimes associated with irritable or aggressive behavior.

Sleep hormone A sleep-promoting substance found in the brain and spinal cord.

Sleep patterns The order and timing of daily sleep and waking periods.

Sleep spindles Distinctive bursts of brainwave activity that indicate a person is asleep.

Sleep stages Levels of sleep identified by brainwave patterns and behavioral changes.

Sleep terror disorder The repeated occurrence of night terrors that significantly disturb sleep.

Sleep-deprivation psychosis A major disruption of mental and emotional functioning brought about by sleep loss.

Sleeptalking Speaking that occurs during NREM sleep.

Sleep-wake schedule disorder A mismatch between the sleep-wake schedule demanded by a person's body rhythm and that demanded by the environment.

Sleepwalking disorder Repeated incidents of leaving bed and walking about while asleep.

Social anxiety A feeling of apprehension in the presence of others.

Social comparison Making judgments about ourselves through comparison with others.

Social competition Rivalry among groups, each of which regards itself as superior to others.

Social development The development of self-awareness, attachment to parents or caregivers, and relationships with other children and adults.

Social dilemma A social situation that tends to provide immediate rewards for actions that will have undesired effects in the long run.

Social distance Distance at which impersonal interaction takes place (about 4 to 12 feet from the body).

Social distance scale A rating of the degree to which a person would be willing to have contact with a member of another group.

Social environment An environment defined by a group of people and their activities or interrelationships (such as a parade, revival meeting, or sports event).

Social exchange Any exchange between two people of attention, information, affection, favors, or the like.

Social exchange theory A theory stating that rewards must exceed costs for relationships to endure.

Social influence Changes in a person's behavior induced by the presence or actions of others.

Social learning theory An explanation of personality that combines learning principles, cognition, and the effects of social relationships.

Social markers Visible or tangible signs that indicate a person's social status or role.

Social motives Learned motives acquired as part of growing up in a particular society or culture.

Social nonconformity Failure to conform to societal norms or the usual minimum standards for social conduct.

Social norms Unspoken rules that define acceptable and expected behavior for members of a group.

Social phobia An intense, irrational fear of being observed, evaluated, embarrassed, or humiliated by others in social situations.

Social power The capacity to control, alter, or influence the behavior of another person.

Social psychology The scientific study of how individuals behave, think, and feel in social situations.

Social Readjustment Rating Scale (SRRS) A scale that rates the impact of various life events on the likelihood of illness.

Social referencing Observing others in social situations to obtain information or guidance.

Social reinforcement Praise, attention, approval, and/or affection from others.

Social reinforcer Reinforcement based on receiving attention, approval, or affection from another person.

Social role Expected behavior patterns associated with particular social positions (such as daughter, worker, student).

Social skills Proficiency at interacting with others.

Social smile Smiling elicited by social stimuli, such as seeing a parent's face.

Social stereotypes Oversimplified images of the traits of individuals who belong to a particular social group.

Social support Close, positive relationships with other people.

Solitary play Playing alone.

Sociocultural perspective The focus on the importance of social and cultural contexts in influencing the behavior of individuals.

Soma (SOH-mah) The main body of a neuron or other cell.

Somatic nervous system The system of nerves linking the spinal cord with the body and sense organs.

Somatic therapy Any bodily therapy, such as drug therapy, electroconvulsive therapy, or psychosurgery.

Somatization (som-ah-tuh-ZAY-shun) **disorder** Afflicted persons have numerous physical complaints. Typically, they have consulted many doctors, but no organic cause for their distress can be identified.

Somatoform (so-MAT-oh-form) **disorder** Physical symptoms that mimic disease or injury for which there is no identifiable physical cause.

Somatosensory area A receiving area for bodily sensations.

Somesthetic sense Sensations produced by the skin, muscles, joints, viscera, and organs of balance.

Somnambulism (som-NAM-bue-liz-im) Sleepwalking; occurs during NREM sleep.

Source traits Basic underlying traits, or dimensions, of personality; each source trait is reflected in a number of surface traits.

Spaced practice Practice spread over many relatively short study sessions.

Special aptitude test A test to predict a person's likelihood of succeeding in a particular area of work or skill.

Specific goal A goal with a clearly defined and measurable outcome.

Specific phobia An intense, irrational fear of specific objects, activities, or situations.

Speed of processing The speed with which a person can mentally process information.

Spinal nerves Major nerves that carry sensory and motor messages in and out of the spinal cord.

Split-brain operation Cutting the corpus callosum.

Spontaneous recovery The reappearance of a learned response after its apparent extinction.

Sports psychology Study of the psychological and behavioral dimensions of sports performance.

SQ4R method An active study-reading technique based on these steps: survey, question, read, recite, reflect, and review.

Squeeze technique A method for inhibiting ejaculation by compressing the tip of the penis.

Stage ESP The simulation of ESP for the purpose of entertainment.

Stage hypnosis Use of hypnosis to entertain; often, merely a simulation of hypnosis for that purpose.

Stage of exhaustion The third stage of the GAS, at which time the body's resources are exhausted and serious health consequences occur.

Stage of resistance The second stage of the GAS, during which bodily adjustments to stress stabilize, but at a high physical cost.

Standard deviation An index of how much a typical score differs from the mean of a group of scores.

State-dependent learning Memory influenced by one's bodily state at the time of learning and at the time of retrieval. Improved memory occurs when the bodily states match.

Statistical abnormality Abnormality defined on the basis of an extreme score on some dimension, such as IQ or anxiety.

Statistical significance The degree to which an event (such as the results of an experiment) is unlikely to have occurred by chance alone.

Status An individual's position in a social structure, especially with respect to power, privilege, or importance.

Status inequalities Differences in the power, prestige, or privileges of two or more persons or groups.

Stereoscopic vision Perception of space and depth caused chiefly by the fact that the eyes receive different images.

Sterilization Medical procedures such as vasectomy or tubal ligation that make a man or a woman infertile.

Stimulant A substance that increases activity in the body and nervous system.

Stimulation hearing loss Damage caused by exposing the hair cells to excessively loud sounds.

Stimulus Any physical energy sensed by an organism.

Stimulus control Stimuli present when an operant response is acquired tend to control when and where the response is made.

Stimulus discrimination The learned ability to respond differently to similar stimuli.

Stimulus drives Drives based on needs for exploration, manipulation, curiosity, and stimulation.

Stimulus generalization The tendency to respond to stimuli similar to, but not identical to, a conditioned stimulus.

Stimulus motives Innate needs for stimulation and information.

Storage Holding information in memory for later use.

Stress The mental and physical condition that occurs when a person must adjust or adapt to the environment.

Stress disorder A significant emotional disturbance caused by stresses outside the range of normal human experience.

Stress inoculation Use of positive coping statements to control fear and anxiety.

Stress management The application of behavioral strategies to reduce stress and improve coping skills.

Stress reaction The physical response to stress, consisting mainly of bodily changes related to autonomic nervous system arousal.

Stressor A specific condition or event in the environment that challenges or threatens a person.

Stress-vulnerability model Attributes psychosis to a combination of environmental stress and inherited susceptibility.

Striving for superiority According to Adler, this basic drive propels us toward perfection.

Stroboscopic movement An illusion of movement in which an object is shown in rapidly changing series of positions.

Structuralism The school of thought concerned with analyzing sensations and personal experience into basic elements.

Structured interview An interview that follows a prearranged plan, usually a series of planned questions.

Stuttering Chronic hesitation or stumbling in speech.

Style of life The pattern of personality and behavior that defines the pathway each person takes through life.

Subcortex All brain structures below the cerebral cortex.

Subjective experience Reality as it is perceived and interpreted, not as it exists objectively.

Subjective well-being General life satisfaction combined with frequent positive emotions and relatively few negative emotions.

Sublimation Working off unmet desires, or unacceptable impulses, in activities that are constructive.

Subliminal perception Perception of a stimulus below the threshold for conscious recognition.

Substance-related disorder Abuse of or dependence on a mood- or behavior-altering drug.

Sudden infant death syndrome (SIDS) The sudden, unexplained death of an apparently healthy infant.

Superego A judge or censor for thoughts and actions.

Superordinate goal A goal that exceeds or overrides all others; a goal that renders other goals relatively less important.

Superstitious behavior A behavior repeated because it seems to produce reinforcement, even though it is actually unnecessary.

Suppression A conscious effort to put something out of mind or to keep it from awareness.

Surface traits The visible or observable traits of one's personality.

Surrogate mother A substitute mother (often an inanimate dummy in animal research).

Survey method Using questionnaires and surveys to poll large groups of people.

Syllogism A format for analyzing logical arguments.

Symbolic prejudice Prejudice that is expressed in disguised fashion.

Symbolization The nonliteral expression of dream content.

Sympathetic branch A part of the ANS that activates the body at times of stress.

Sympathetic system A branch of the ANS that arouses the body.

Synapse (SIN-aps) The microscopic space between two neurons, over which messages pass.

Synesthesia Experiencing one sense in terms normally associated with another sense; for example, "seeing" colors when a sound is heard.

Syntax Rules for ordering words when forming sentences.

Systematic desensitization (dee-SEN-sih-tih-ZAY-shun) A reduction in fear, anxiety, or aversion brought about by planned exposure to aversive stimuli.

Task analysis Breaking complex skills into their subparts.

Taste aversion An active dislike for a particular food.

Taste bud The receptor organ for taste.

Teaching strategy A plan for effective teaching.

Telecommuting An approach to flexible work that involves working from home but using a computer to stay connected to the office throughout the workday.

Telepathy The purported ability to directly know another person's thoughts.

Temperament The hereditary physical core of personality, including emotional and perceptual sensitivity, activity levels, prevailing mood, irritability, and adaptability.

Temporal lobes Areas that include the sites on each side of the brain where hearing registers in the brain.

Tension-release method A procedure for systematically achieving deep relaxation of the body.

Teratogen (teh-RAT-uh-jen) Radiation, a drug, or other substance capable of altering fetal development in nonheritable ways that cause birth defects.

Term schedule A written plan that lists the dates of all major assignments for each of your classes for an entire semester or quarter.

Terminal decline An abrupt decline in measured intelligence about 5 years before death.

Territorial behavior Any behavior that tends to define a space as one's own or that protects it from intruders.

Territorial markers Objects and other signals whose placement indicates to others the "ownership" or control of a particular area.

Test anxiety High levels of arousal and worry that seriously impair test performance.

Test battery A group of tests and interviews given to the same individual.

Test standardization Establishing standards for administering a test and interpreting scores.

Testis (TES-tis, singular; testes, plural) One of the two male reproductive glands; the testes are a source of hormones and sperm.

Testosterone (tes-TOSS-teh-rone) A male sex hormone, secreted mainly by the testes and responsible for the development of many male sexual characteristics.

Thalamus (THAL-uh-mus) A brain structure that relays sensory information to the cerebral cortex.

Thanatologist (THAN-ah-TOL-oh-jist) A specialist who studies emotional and behavioral reactions to death and dying.

Thanatos The death instinct postulated by Freud.

Thematic Apperception Test (TAT) A projective test consisting of 20 different scenes and life situations about which respondents make up stories.

Theory A system of ideas designed to interrelate concepts and facts in a way that summarizes existing data and predicts future observations.

Theory of mind A child's current understanding of the mind, including the desires, beliefs, intentions, and feelings of others.

Theory X leadership (scientific management) An approach to leadership that emphasizes work efficiency.

Theory Y leadership A leadership style that emphasizes human relations at work and that views people as industrious, responsible, and interested in challenging work.

Therapeutic alliance A caring relationship that unites a therapist and a client in working to solve the client's problems.

Therapy placebo effect Improvement caused not by the actual process of therapy but by a client's expectation that therapy will help.

Thought stopping Use of aversive stimuli to interrupt or prevent upsetting thoughts.

Threshold The point at which a nerve impulse is triggered.

Thyroid gland Endocrine gland that helps regulate the rate of metabolism.

Tip-of-the-tongue (TOT) state The feeling that a memory is available but not quite retrievable.

Token economy A therapeutic program in which desirable behaviors are reinforced with tokens that can be exchanged for goods, services, activities, and privileges.

Token reinforcer A tangible secondary reinforcer such as money, gold stars, poker chips, and the like.

Top-down processing Applying higher-level knowledge to rapidly organize sensory information into a meaningful perception.

Tragedy of the commons A social dilemma in which individuals, each acting in his or her immediate self-interest, overuse a scarce group resource.

Trait profile A graph of the scores obtained on several personality traits.

Trait theorist A psychologist interested in classifying, analyzing, and interrelating traits to understand personality.

Trait-situation interaction The influence that external settings or circumstances have on the expression of personality traits.

Tranquilizer A drug that lowers anxiety and reduces tension.

Transference The tendency of patients to transfer feelings to a therapist that correspond to those the patient had for important persons in his or her past.

Transformation The mental ability to change the shape or form of a substance (such as clay or water) and to perceive that its volume remains the same.

Transformation rules Rules by which a simple declarative sentence may be changed to other voices or forms (past tense, passive voice, and so forth).

Transition period Time span during which a person leaves an existing life pattern behind and moves into a new pattern.

Transsexual A person with a deep conflict between his or her biological sex and preferred psychological and social gender roles.

Traumatic stresses Extreme events that cause psychological injury or intense emotional pain.

Trichromatic (TRY-kro-MAT-ik) **theory** A theory of color vision based on three cone types: red, green, and blue.

Trust versus mistrust A conflict early in life about learning to trust others and the world.

Twin study A comparison of the characteristics of twins who were raised together or separated at birth; used to identify the relative impact of heredity and environment.

Two-way bilingual education A program in which English-speaking children and children with limited English proficiency are taught half the day in English and half in a second language.

Type A personality A personality type with an elevated risk of heart disease; characterized by time urgency, anger, and hostility.

Type B personality All personality types other than Type A; a low-cardiac-risk personality.

Unconditional positive regard An unqualified, unshakable acceptance of another person.

Unconditioned response (UR) An innate, unlearned, reflex response elicited by an unconditioned stimulus.

Unconditioned stimulus (US) A stimulus innately capable of eliciting a response.

Unconscious The region of the mind that is beyond awareness, especially impulses and desires not directly known to a person.

Uncritical acceptance The tendency to believe generally positive or flattering descriptions of oneself.

Understanding In problem solving, a deeper comprehension of the nature of the problem.

Understanding In psychology, understanding is achieved when the causes of a behavior can be stated.

Undifferentiated schizophrenia Schizophrenia lacking the specific features of catatonic, disorganized, or paranoid types.

Upward comparison Comparing yourself with a person who ranks higher than you on some dimension.

Unstructured interview An interview in which conversation is informal and topics are taken up freely as they arise.

Urethra (yoo-REE-thra) The tube through which urine drains as it leaves the body. In males, semen also passes through the urethra.

Urinary bladder The sac that collects urine before it is eliminated from the body.

Usability testing The empirical investigation of the ease with which users can learn and use a machine.

Uterus (YOO-ter-us) The pear-shaped muscular organ in which the fetus develops during pregnancy; also known as the womb.

Vagina (vah-JINE-ah) Tube-like structure connecting the external female genitalia with the uterus.

Vaginismus (VAJ-ih-NIS-mus) Muscle spasms of the vagina.

Validity The ability of a test to measure what it purports to measure.

Validity scales Scales that tell whether test scores should be invalidated for lying, inconsistency, or "faking good."

Variable Any condition that changes or can be made to change; a measure, event, or state that may vary.

Variable interval (VI) schedule A reinforcer is given for the first correct response made after a varied amount of time has passed since the last reinforced response. Responses made during the time interval are not reinforced.

Variable ratio (VR) schedule A varied number of correct responses must be made to get a reinforcer. For example, a reinforcer is given after three to seven correct responses; the actual number changes randomly.

Vas deferens (vaz DEH-fur-enz) The duct that carries sperm from the testes to the urethra.

Verbal intelligence Intelligence measured by answering questions involving vocabulary, general information, arithmetic, and other language- or symbol-oriented tasks.

Vestibular senses The senses of balance, position in space, and acceleration.

Vicarious classical conditioning Classical conditioning brought about by observing another person react to a particular stimulus.

Vicarious desensitization (dee-SEN-sih-tih-ZAY-shun) A reduction in fear or anxiety that takes place vicariously ("secondhand") when a client watches models perform the feared behavior.

Virtual reality exposure Use of computer-generated images to present fear stimuli. The virtual environment responds to a viewer's head movements and other inputs.

Visceral pain Pain originating in the internal organs.

Visible spectrum That part of the electromagnetic spectrum to which the eyes are sensitive.

Visual acuity The sharpness of visual perception.

Visual agnosia (ag-KNOW-zyah) Inability to identify seen objects.

Vocational interest test A paper-and-pencil test that assesses a person's interests and matches them to interests found among successful workers in various occupations.

Waking consciousness A state of normal, alert awareness.

Warning system Pain based on large nerve fibers; warns that bodily damage may be occurring.

Weapons effect The observation that weapons serve as strong cues for aggressive behavior.

Weber's law The just noticeable difference is a constant proportion of the original stimulus intensity.

Weekly time schedule A written plan that allocates time for study, work, and leisure activities during a 1-week period.

Wellness A positive state of good health; more than the absence of disease.

Wernicke's (VER-nick-ees) **area** A temporal lobe brain area related to language comprehension.

Wish fulfillment Freudian belief that many dreams express unconscious desires.

Withdrawal of love Withholding affection to enforce child discipline.

Withdrawal symptoms Physical illness and discomfort following the withdrawal of a drug.

Work efficiency Maximum output (productivity) at lowest cost.

Working memory Another name for short-term memory, especially as it is used for thinking and problem solving.

World Wide Web (WWW) A system of information "sites" accessible through the Internet.

X chromosome The female chromosome contributed by the mother; produces a female when paired with another X chromosome and a male when paired with a Y chromosome.

Y chromosome The male chromosome contributed by the father; produces a male when paired with an X chromosome. Fathers may give either an X or a Y chromosome to their offspring.

Yerkes-Dodson law A summary of the relationships among arousal, task complexity, and performance.

You-message A message that threatens, accuses, bosses, lectures, or criticizes another person.

Zener cards A deck of 25 cards bearing various symbols and used in early parapsychological research.

Zero correlation The absence of a (linear) mathematical relationship between two measures.

Zone of proximal development Refers to the range of tasks a child cannot yet master alone, but that she or he can accomplish with the guidance of a more capable partner.

z-score A number that tells how many standard deviations above or below the mean a score is.

References

AAIDD (2004). *Montreal declaration on intellectual disabilities.* Washington, DC: American Association on Mental Retardation. Retrieved June 25, 2007, from http://www.aaidd.org/pdf/DeclarationMTL.pdf.

Aamodt, M. G. (2007). *Industrial/organizational psychology: An applied approach* (5th ed.). Belmont, CA: Cengage Learning/Wadsworth.

Abel, G. G., & Harlow, N. (2001). *The stop child molestation book.* La Vergne, TN: Lightning Source.

Abel, G. G., Wiegel, M., & Osborn, C. A. (2007). Pedophilia and other paraphilias. In L. VandeCreek, F. L. Peterson. Jr., et al. (Eds.), *Innovations in clinical practice: Focus on sexual health. Innovations in clinical practice.* Sarasota: Professional Resource Press.

Abel, T., & Lattal, K. M. (2001). Molecular mechanisms of memory acquisition, consolidation and retrieval. *Current Opinion in Neurobiology, 11*(2), 180–187.

Abrahamse, W., Steg, L., Vlek, C., & Rothengatter, T. (2005). A review of intervention studies aimed at household energy conservation. *Journal of Environmental Psychology, 25*(3), 273–291.

Abrahamson, D. J., Barlow, D. H., & Abrahamson, L. S. (1989). Differential effects of performance demand and distraction on sexually functional and dysfunctional males. *Journal of Abnormal Psychology, 98*(3), 241–247.

Abrams, D. B., Brown, R., Niaura, R. S., Emmons, K., et al. (2003). *The tobacco dependence treatment handbook: A guide to best practices.* New York: Guilford.

Accordino, D. B., Accordino, M. P., & Slaney, R. B. (2000). An investigation of perfectionism, mental health, achievement, and achievement motivation in adolescents. *Psychology in the Schools, 37*(6), 535–545.

ACT Against Violence (2005a). *Facts related to media violence.* Washington, DC: Adults and Children Against Violence Together. Retrieved October 18, 2006, from http://www.actagainstviolence.com/materials/handouts/FamilyMV1.pdf.

ACT Against Violence (2005b). *Early violence prevention.* Washington, DC: Adults and Children Against Violence Together. Retrieved October 18, 2006, from http://www.actagainstviolence.com/violprevent/index.html.

Adams, J. (1988). *Conceptual blockbusting.* New York: Norton.

Adamson, K. (2004). *Kate's journey: Triumph over adversity.* Redondo Beach, CA: Nosmada Press.

Addis, K. M., & Kahana, M. J. (2004). Decomposing serial learning: What is missing from the learning curve? *Psychonomic Bulletin & Review, 11*(1), 118–174.

Adler, S. A., & Orprecio, J. (2006). The eyes have it: Visual pop-out in infants and adults. *Developmental Science, 9,* 189–206.

Adorno, T. W., Frenkel-Brunswik, E., Levinson, D. J., & Sanford, R. N. (1950). *The authoritarian personality.* New York: Harper.

Afifi, T. O., Brownridge, D. A., Cox, B. J., & Sareen, J. (2006). Physical punishment, childhood abuse and psychiatric disorders. *Child Abuse & Neglect, 30*(10), 1093–1103.

Ahima. R. S., & Osei, S. Y. (2004). Leptin signaling. *Physiology & Behavior, 81,* 223–241.

Ajzen, I. (2005). *Attitudes, personality and behaviour* (2nd ed.). New York: McGraw-Hill.

Akerstedt, T., Hume, K., Minors, D., & Waterhouse, J. (1993). Regulation of sleep and naps on an irregular schedule. *Sleep, 16*(8), 736–743.

Albarracín, D., Johnson, B. T., & Zanna, M. P. (Eds.) (2005). *The handbook of attitudes.* Mahwah, NJ: Erlbaum.

Alberti, R., & Emmons, M. (2001). *Your perfect right* (8th ed.). San Luis Obispo, CA: Impact.

Alberto, P. A., & Troutman, A. C. (2006). *Applied behavior analysis for teachers* (7th ed.). Englewood Cliffs, NJ: Prentice Hall.

Alcock, J. E. (2003). Give the null hypothesis a chance: Reasons to remain doubtful about the existence of psi. *Journal of Consciousness Studies, 10*(6–7), 29–50.

Alcock, J. E., Burns, J., & Freeman, A. (2003). *Psi wars: Getting to grips with the paranormal.* Exeter, UK: Imprint Academic Press.

Alicke, M. D., Yurak, T. J., & Vredenburg, D. S. (1996). Using personal attitudes to judge others. *Journal of Research in Personality, 30*(1), 103–119.

Allen, D., Carlson, D., & Ham, C. (2007). Well-being: New paradigms of wellness-inspiring positive health outcomes and renewing hope. *American Journal of Health Promotion, 21*(3), 1–9.

Allen, K., Blascovich, J., & Mendes, W. B. (2002). Cardiovascular reactivity in the presence of pets, friends, and spouses: The truth about cats and dogs. *Psychosomatic Medicine, 64*(5), 727–739.

Allen, M., Mabry, E., & McKelton, D. (1998). Impact of juror attitudes about the death penalty on juror evaluations of guilt and punishment: A meta-analysis. *Law & Human Behavior, 22*(6), 715–731.

Allgower, A., Wardle, J., & Steptoe, A. (2001). Depressive symptoms, social support, and personal health behaviors in young men and women. *Health Psychology, 20*(3), 223–227.

Allik, J. (2000). Available and accessible information in memory and vision. In E. Tulving (Ed.), *Memory, consciousness, and the brain: The Tallinn Conference.* Hove, UK: Psychology Press.

Allport, G. W. (1958). *The nature of prejudice.* Garden City, NY: Anchor Books, Doubleday.

Allport, G. W. (1961). *Pattern and growth in personality.* New York: Holt, Rinehart, & Winston.

Alsaker, F. D. (1992). Pubertal timing, overweight, and psychological adjustment. *Journal of Early Adolescence, 12*(4), 396–419.

Alsaker, F. D. (1995). Is puberty a critical period for socialization? *Journal of Adolescence, 18*(4), 427–444.

Altemeyer, B. (2004). Highly dominating, highly authoritarian personalities. *Journal of Social Psychology, 144*(4), 421–447.

Altman, L. K. (2002). AIDS threatens to claim 65M more lives by '20. *Arizona Daily Star,* July 3, A7.

Altschuler, G. C. (2001). Battling the cheats. *The New York Times: Education,* Jan. 7, 15.

Alvarado, N. (1994). Empirical validity of the Thematic Apperception Test. *Journal of Personality Assessment, 63*(1), 59–79.

Alvino, J., & the Editors of Gifted Children Monthly (1996). *Parents' guide to raising a gifted child.* New York: Ballantine.

Alwin, D. F., Cohen, R. L., & Newcomb, T. M. (1991). *Political attitudes over the life span: The Bennington women after fifty years.* Madison, WI: University of Wisconsin Press.

Amabile, T., Hadley, C. N., & Kramer, S. J. (2002). Creativity under the gun. *Harvard Business Review, 80*(8), 52–61.

Amato, P. R., & Fowler, F. (2002). Parenting practices, child adjustment, and family diversity. *Journal of Marriage & Family, 64*(3), 703–716.

Ambady, N., & Rosenthal, R. (1993). Half a minute: Predicting teacher evaluations from thin slices of nonverbal behavior and physical attractiveness. *Journal of Personality & Social Psychology, 64,* 431–441.

American Lung Association (2006). *Smokeless tobacco fact sheet.* Retrieved June 6, 2007, from http://www.lungusa.org/site/pp.asp?c=dvLUK9O0E&b=1694879.

Ancis, J. R., Chen, Y., & Schultz, D. (2004). Diagnostic challenges and the so-called culture-bound syndromes. In J. R. Ancis (Ed.), *Culturally responsive interventions: Innovative approaches to working with diverse populations.* New York: Brunner-Routledge.

Anderson, C. A. (1989). Temperature and aggression. *Psychological Bulletin, 106,* 74–96.

Anderson, C. A. (2004). An update on the effects of violent video games. *Journal of Adolescence, 27,* 113–122.

Anderson, C. A., & Bushman, B. J. (2001). Effects of violent video games on aggressive behavior, aggressive cognition, aggressive affect, physiological arousal, and prosocial behavior: A meta-analytic review of the scientific literature. *Psychological Science, 12*(5), 353–359.

Anderson, C. A., & Bushman, B. J. (2002). Human aggression. *Annual Review of Psychology, 53,* 27–51.

Anderson, C. A., Anderson, K. B., & Deuser, W. E. (1996). Examining an affective aggression framework. *Personality & Social Psychology Bulletin, 22*(4), 366–376.

Anderson, C. A., Berkowitz, L., Donnerstein, E., Huesmann, L. R., et al. (2003). The influence of media violence on youth. *Psychological Science in the Public Interest, 4,* 1–30.

Anderson, C. A., Carnagey, N. L., & Eubanks, J. (2003). Exposure to violent media: The effects of songs with violent lyrics on aggressive thoughts and feelings. *Journal of Personality & Social Psychology, 84*(5), 960–971.

Anderson, J. R. (2005). *Cognitive psychology and its implications* (6th ed.). New York: Worth.

Anderson, M. C. (2001). Active forgetting: Evidence for functional inhibition as a source of memory failure. *Journal of Aggression, Maltreatment & Trauma, 4*(2), 185–210.

Anderson, M. C., & Bell, T. (2001). Forgetting our facts: The role of inhibitory processes in the loss of propositional knowledge. *Journal of Experimental Psychology: General, 130*(3), 544–570.

Anderson, M. C., & Green, C. (2001). Suppressing unwanted memories by executive control. *Nature, 410*(6826), 366–369.

Anderson, M. C., Ochsner, K. N., Kuhl, B., Cooper, J., et al. (2004). Neural systems underlying the suppression of unwanted memories. *Science, 303*, 232–235.

Andrasik, F. (2003). Behavioral treatment approaches to chronic headache. *Neurological Sciences, 24*(Suppl 2), S80–S85.

André, C., Jaber-Filho, J. A., Carvalho, M., Jullien, C., et al. (2003). Predictors of recovery following involuntary hospitalization of violent substance abuse patients. *The American Journal on Addictions, 12*(1), 84–89.

Andresen, J. (2000). Meditation meets behavioural medicine: The story of experimental research on meditation. *Journal of Consciousness Studies, 7*(11–12), 17–73.

Annett, M. (2002). *Handedness and brain asymmetry: The right shift theory.* Hove, UK: Psychology Press.

Annett, M., & Manning, M. (1990). Arithmetic and laterality. *Neuropsychologia, 28*(1), 61–69.

Anshel, M. H. (1995). An examination of self-regulatory cognitive-behavioural strategies of Australian elite and non-elite competitive male swimmers. *Australian Psychologist, 30*(2), 78–83.

Antle, M. C., & Mistlberger, R. E. (2005). Circadian rhythms. In I. Q. Whishaw & B. Kolb (Eds.), *The behavior of the laboratory rat: A handbook with tests.* New York: Oxford University Press.

Antony, M. M. (2004). *10 simple solutions to shyness: How to overcome shyness, social anxiety & fear of public speaking.* Oakland, CA: New Harbinger.

APA. (2000). *2000 APA directory survey.* Washington, DC: American Psychological Association. Retrieved May 18, 2007, from http://research.apa.org/2000membershipt4.pdf.

APA. (2002). Ethical principles of psychologists and code of conduct. *American Psychologist, 57,* 1060–1073. Retrieved May 18, 2007, from http://www.apa.org/ethics/homepage.html.

APA. (2003). Guidelines on multicultural education, training, research, practice, and organizational change for psychologists. *American Psychologist, 58*(5), 377–402.

APA. (2004). *Sexual orientation and homosexuality.* Washington, DC: American Psychological Association. Retrieved July 29, 2007, from http://www.apahelpcenter.org/articles/article.php?id=31.

APA. (2005). *2005 APA directory survey.* Washington, DC: American Psychological Association. Retrieved May 18, 2007, from http://research.apa.org/profile2005t3.pdf.

APA. (2007). *Report of the APA Task Force on the sexualization of girls.* Washington, DC: American Psychological Association. Retrieved July 26, 2007, from http://www.apa.org/pi/wpo/sexualization.html.

Arbona, C. B., Osma, J., Garcia-Palacios, A., Quero, S., et al. (2004). Treatment of flying phobia using virtual reality: Data from a 1-year follow-up using a multiple baseline design. *Clinical Psychology & Psychotherapy, 11*(5), 311–323.

Ariely, D., & Wertenbroch, K. (2002). Procrastination, deadlines, and performance: Self-control by precommitment. *Psychological Science, 13*(3), 219–224.

Armeli, S., Gunthert, K. C., & Cohen, L. H. (2001). Stressor appraisals, coping, and post-event outcomes: The dimensionality and antecedents of stress-related growth. *Journal of Social & Clinical Psychology, 20*(3), 366–395.

Arnett, J. J. (2000). Emerging adulthood. *American Psychologist, 55*(5), 469–480.

Arnett, J. J. (2001). Conceptions of the transition to adulthood. *Journal of Adult Development, 8*(2), 133–143.

Arnett, J. J. (2004). *Emerging adulthood: The winding road from late teens through the twenties.* New York: Oxford University Press.

Arnett, J. J., & Galambos, N. L. (Eds.). (2003). *New directions for child and adolescent development: Exploring cultural conceptions of the transition to adulthood.* San Francisco: Jossey-Bass.

Arnett, J. J., & Tanner, J. L. (Eds.). (2006). *Emerging adults in America: Coming of age in the 21st century.* Washington, DC: American Psychological Association.

Aronoff, J., Barclay, A. M., & Stevenson, L. A. (1988). The recognition of threatening facial stimuli. *Journal of Personality & Social Psychology, 54*(4), 647–655.

Aronow, E., Altman Weiss, K., & Reznikoff, M. (2001). *A practical guide to the Thematic Apperception Test: The TAT in clinical practice.* New York: Brunner-Routledge.

Aronson, E. (1969). Some antecedents of interpersonal attraction. In W. J. Arnold & D. Levine (Eds.), *Nebraska Symposium on Motivation.* Lincoln: University of Nebraska Press.

Aronson, E. (2008). *The social animal* (10th ed.). New York: Worth.

Aronson, E., Wilson, T. D., & Akert, R. M. (2007). *Social psychology* (6th ed.). Englewood Cliffs, NJ: Prentice Hall.

Arthur, W., & Doverspike, D. (2001). Predicting motor vehicle crash involvement from a personality measure and a driving knowledge test. *Journal of Prevention & Intervention in the Community, 22*(1), 35–42.

Artz, S. (2005). To die for: Violent adolescent girls' search for male attention. In D. J. Pepler, K. C. Madsen, et al. (Eds.), *The development and treatment of girlhood aggression.* Mahwah, NJ: Erlbaum.

Ary, D. V., Duncan, T. E., Biglan, A., Metzler, C. W., et al. (1999). Development of adolescent problem behavior. *Journal of Abnormal Child Psychology, 27*(2), 141–150.

Asch, S. E. (1956). Studies of independence and conformity: A minority of one against a unanimous majority. *Psychological Monographs, 70*(416).

Ash, D. W., & Holding, D. H. (1990). Backward versus forward chaining in the acquisition of a keyboard skill. *Human Factors, 32*(2), 139–146.

Ashby, F. G., & Maddox, W. T. (2005). Human category learning. *Annual Review of Psychology, 56,* 149–178.

Aslin, R. N., & Smith, L. B. (1988). Perceptual development. *Annual Review of Psychology, 39,* 435–473.

Asmundson, G. J. G., & Taylor, S. (2005). *It's not all in your head.* London: Psychology Press.

Assanand, S., Pinel, J. P. J., & Lehman, D. R. (1998). Personal theories of hunger and eating. *Journal of Applied Social Psychology, 28*(11), 998–1015.

Athenasiou, R., Shaver, P., & Tavris, C. (1970). Sex. *Psychology Today, 4*(2), 37–52.

Atkin, D. J., & Lau, T. Y. (2007). Information technology and organizational telework. In C. A. Lin & D. J Atkin (Eds.), *Communication technology and social change: Theory and implications.* Mahwah, NJ: Erlbaum.

Atkinson, R.C., & Schiffrin, R.M. (1968). Human memory: a proposed system and its control processes. In K. W. Spence & J. T. Spence (Eds.), *The psychology of learning and motivation* (Vol. 2). London: Academic Press.

Atwood, J. D. (2006). Mommy's little angel, daddy's little girl: Do you know what your pre-teens are doing? *American Journal of Family Therapy, 34*(5), 447–467.

Aucoin, K. J., Frick, P. J., & Bodin, S. D. (2006). Corporal punishment and child adjustment. *Journal of Applied Developmental Psychology, 27*(6), 527–541.

Avery, D. H., Eder, D. N., Bolte, M. A., Hellekson, C. J., et al. (200_). Dawn simulation and bright light in the treatment of SAD. *Biological Psychiatry, 50*(3), 205–216.

Awadallah, N., Vaughan, A., Franco, K., Munir, F., et al. (2005). Munchausen by proxy: A case, chart series, and literature review of older victims. *Child Abuse & Neglect, 29*(8), 931–941.

Ayers, L., Beaton, S., & Hunt, H. (1999). The significance of transpersonal experiences, emotional conflict, and cognitive abilities in creativity. *Empirical Studies of the Arts, 17*(1), 73–82.

Ayllon, T. (1963). Intensive treatment of psychotic behavior by stimulus satiation and food reinforcement. *Behavior Research & Therapy, 1,* 53–61.

Ayllon, T., & Azrin, N. H. (1965). The measurement and reinforcement of behavior of psychotics. *Journal of the Experimental Analysis of Behavior, 8,* 357–383.

Baard, P. P., Deci, E. L., & Ryan, R. M. (2004). Intrinsic need satisfaction: A motivational basis of performance and well-being in two work settings. *Journal of Applied Social Psychology, 34*(10), 2045–2068.

Bachman, J. G., & Johnson, L. D. (1979). The freshmen. *Psychology Today, 13,* 78–87.

Baddeley, A. D. (2003). Working memory: Looking back and looking forward. *Nature Reviews Neuroscience, 4*(10), 829–839.

Baer, J. M. (1993). *Creativity and divergent thinking.* Mahwah, NJ: Erlbaum.

Bagley, C., & Tremblay, P. (1998). On the prevalence of homosexuality and bisexuality, in a random community survey of 750 men aged 18 to 27. *Journal of Homosexuality, 36*(2), 1–18.

Bailey, C. H., & Kandel, E. R. (2004). Synaptic growth and the persistence of long-term memory: A molecular perspective. In M. S. Gazzaniga (Ed.), *The cognitive neurosciences* (3rd ed.). Cambridge, MA: MIT Press.

Bailey, L. M., & McKeever, W. F. (2004). A large-scale study of handedness and pregnancy/birth risk events: Implications for genetic theories of handedness. *Laterality: Asymmetries of Body, Brain & Cognition, 9*(2), 175–188.

Baillargeon, R. (1991). Reasoning about the height and location of a hidden object in 4.5- and 6.5-month-old infants. *Cognition, 38*(1), 13–42.

Baillargeon, R. (2004). Infants' reasoning about hidden objects: Evidence for event-general and event-specific expectations. *Developmental Science, 7*(4), 391–424.

Baillargeon, R., De Vos, J., & Graber, M. (1989). Location memory in 8-month-old infants in a non-search AB task. *Cognitive Development, 4,* 345–367.

Bain, S. K., & Allin, J. D. (2005). Stanford-Binet Intelligence Scales, Fifth Edition. *Journal of Psychoeducational Assessment, 23*(1), 87–95.

Bajracharya, S. M., Sarvela, P. D., & Isberner, F. R. (1995). A retrospective study of first sexual intercourse experiences among undergraduates. *Journal of American College Health, 43*(4), 169–177.

Baker, T. B., Brandon, T. H., & Chassin, L. (2004). Motivational influences on cigarette smoking. *Annual Review of Psychology, 55,* 463–491.

Bakich, I. (1995). Hypnosis in the treatment of sexual desire disorders. *Australian Journal of Clinical & Experimental Hypnosis, 23*(1), 70–77.

Baldo, O., & Eardley, I. (2005). Diagnosis and investigation of men with erectile dysfunction. *Journal of Men's Health & Gender, 2*(1), 79–86.

Balk, D. E., Lampe, S., Sharpe, B., Schwinn, S., et al. (1998). TAT results in a longitudinal study of bereaved college students. *Death Studies, 22*(1), 3–21.

Balsam, K. F., & Mohr, J. J. (2007). Adaptation to sexual orientation stigma: A comparison of bisexual and lesbian/gay adults. *Journal of Counseling Psychology, 54*(3), 306–319.

Baltes, B. B., Briggs, T. E., Huff, J. W., Wright, J. A., et al. (1999). Flexible and compressed workweek schedules. *Journal of Applied Psychology, 84*(4), 496–513.

Bandura, A. (1971). *Social learning theory.* New York: General Learning Press.

Bandura, A. (1973). *Aggression: A social learning analysis.* Englewood Cliffs, NJ: Prentice-Hall.

Bandura, A. (2001). Social cognitive theory: An agentic perspective. *Annual Review of Psychology, 52,* 1–26.

Bandura, A., & Walters, R. (1959). *Adolescent aggression.* New York: Ronald.

Bandura, A., Blanchard, E. B., & Ritter, B. (1969). Relative efficacy of desensitization and modeling approaches for inducing behavioral, affective, and attitudinal changes. *Journal of Personality & Social Psychology, 13*(3), 173–199.

Bandura, A., Ross, D., & Ross, S. A. (1963). Vicarious reinforcement and imitative learning. *Journal of Abnormal and Social Psychology, 67,* 601–607.

Banich, M. T. (2004). *Cognitive neuroscience and neuropsychology* (2nd ed.). Boston: Houghton Mifflin.

Banks, A., & Gartrell, N. K. (1995). Hormones and sexual orientation: A questionable link. *Journal of Homosexuality, 28*(3–4), 247–268.

Banks, T., & Dabbs, Jr., J. M. (1996). Salivary testosterone and cortisol in delinquent and violent urban subculture. *Journal of Social Psychology, 136*(1), 49–56.

Barabasz, A. (2000). EEG markers of alert hypnosis. *Sleep & Hypnosis, 2*(4), 164–169.

Barber, T. X. (2000). A deeper understanding of hypnosis: Its secrets, its nature, its essence. *American Journal of Clinical Hypnosis, 42*(3–4), 208–272.

Bard, C., Fleury, M., & Goulet, C. (1994). Relationship between perceptual strategies and response adequacy in sport situations. *International Journal of Sport Psychology, 25*(3), 266–281.

Bargh, J. A., McKenna, K. Y. A., & Fitzsimons, G. M. (2002). Can you see the real me? Activation and expression of the "true self" on the Internet. *Journal of Social Issues, 58*(1), 33–48.

Barkataki, I., Kumari, V., Das, M., Taylor, P. et al. (2006). Volumetric structural brain abnormalities in men with schizophrenia or antisocial personality disorder. *Behavioural Brain Research, 169*(2), 239–247.

Barlow, D. H. (2000). Unraveling the mysteries of anxiety and its disorders from the perspective of emotion theory. *American Psychologist, 55,* 1247–1263.

Barlow, D. H. (2002). *Anxiety and its disorders* (2nd ed.). New York: Guilford.

Barlow, D. H. (2004). Psychological treatments. *American Psychologist, 59*(9), 869–878.

Barnett, J., Behnke, S. H., Rosenthal, S., & Koocher, G. (2007). In case of ethical dilemma, break glass: Commentary on ethical decision making in practice. *Professional Psychology: Research & Practice, 38*(1), 7–12.

Barnier, A. J., McConkey, K. M., & Wright, J. (2004). Posthypnotic amnesia for autobiographical episodes: Influencing memory accessibility and quality. *International Journal of Clinical and Experimental Hypnosis, 52*(3), 260–279.

Baron, R. A., Byrne, D., & Branscombe, N. R. (2007). *Mastering social psychology.* Boston, MA: Pearson/Allyn and Bacon.

Baron, R. S. (2005). So right it's wrong: Groupthink and the ubiquitous nature of polarized group decision making. In M. P. Zanna, (Ed.), *Advances in experimental social psychology* (Vol. 37). San Diego: Elsevier.

Baron, R. S. (2005). So right it's wrong: Groupthink and the ubiquitous nature of polarized group decision making. In M. P. Zanna (Ed.), *Advances in experimental social psychology* (Vol. 37). San Diego: Elsevier.

Barrett, D. (1993). The "committee of sleep": A study of dream incubation for problem solving. *Dreaming, 3*(2), 115–122.

Barrett, D., Greenwood, J. G., & McCullagh, J. F. (2006). Kissing laterality and handedness. *Laterality: Asymmetries of Body, Brain & Cognition, 11*(6), 573–579.

Barrick, M. R., Moun, M. K., & Judge, T. A. (2001). Personality and performance at the beginning of the new millennium. *International Journal of Selection & Assessment, 9*(1–2), 9–30.

Barron, F. (1958). The psychology of imagination. *Scientific American, 199*(3), 150–170.

Barrowcliff, A. L., & Haddock, G. (2006). The relationship between command hallucinations and factors of compliance: A critical review of the literature. *Journal of Forensic Psychiatry & Psychology, 17*(2), 266–298.

Bar-Tal, D., & Labin, D. (2001). The effect of a major event on stereotyping: Terrorist attacks in Israel and Israeli adolescents' perceptions of Palestinians, Jordanians and Arabs. *European Journal of Social Psychology, 31*(3), 265–280.

Bartholow, B. D., & Anderson, C. A. (2002). Effects of violent video games on aggressive behavior. *Journal of Experimental Social Psychology, 38*(3), 283–290.

Bartholow, B. D., Bushman, B. J., & Sestir, M. A. (2006). Chronic violent video game exposure and desensitization to violence: Behavioral and event-related brain potential data. *Journal of Experimental Social Psychology, 42*(4), 532–539.

Bartholow, B. D., Sestir, M. A., & Davis, E. B. (2005). Correlates and consequences of exposure to video game violence: Hostile personality, empathy, and aggressive behavior. *Personality and Social Psychology Bulletin, 31*(11), 1573–1586.

Bartlett, J. C., & Searcy, J. (1993). Inversion and configuration of faces. *Cognitive Psychology, 25*(3), 281–316.

Bartram, B. (2006). An examination of perceptions of parental influence on attitudes to language learning. *Educational Research, 48*(2), 211–222.

Basson, R., Brotto, L. A., Laan, E., Redmond, G., et al. (2005). Assessment and management of women's sexual dysfunctions: Problematic desire and arousal. *Journal of Sexual Medicine, 2*(3), 291–300.

Bastian, B., & Haslam, N. (2006). Psychological essentialism and stereotype endorsement. *Journal of Experimental Social Psychology, 42*(2), 228–235.

Bath, H. (1996). Everyday discipline or control with care. *Journal of Child & Youth Care, 10*(2), 23–32.

Batson, C. D. (2006). "Not all self-interest after all": Economics of empathy-induced altruism. In D. De Cremer, M. Zeelenberg, et al. (Eds.), *Social psychology and economics.* Mahwah, NJ: Erlbaum.

Batson, C. D., & Powell, A. A. (2003). Altruism and prosocial behavior. In T. Millon & M. J. Lerner (Eds.), *Handbook of psychology: Personality and social psychology* (Vol. 5). New York: Wiley.

Batterham, R. L., Cohen, M. A., Ellis, S. M., Le Roux, C. E., et al. (2003). Inhibition of food intake in obese subjects by peptide YY3–36. *New England Journal of Medicine, 349*(Sept. 4), 941–948.

Baum, A., & Davis, G. E. (1980). Reducing the stress of high-density living: An architectural intervention. *Journal of Personality & Social Psychology, 38,* 471–481.

Baum, A., & Posluszny, D. M. (1999). Health psychology. *Annual Review of Psychology, 50,* 137–163.

Baum, A., & Valins, S. (1979). Architectural mediation of residential density and control: Crowding and the regulation of social contact. *Advances in Experimental & Social Psychology, 12,* 131–175.

Baum, A., & Valins, S. (Eds.). (1977). *Human response to crowding: Studies of the effects of residential group size.* Mahwah, NJ: Erlbaum.

Bauman, L. J., Karasz, A., & Hamilton, A. (2007). Understanding failure of condom use intention among adolescents: Completing an intensive preventive intervention. *Journal of Adolescent Research, 22*(3), 248–274.

Baumeister, R. F., & Bushman, B. (2008). *Social psychology and human nature.* Belmont, CA: Cengage Learning/Wadsworth.

Baumeister, R. F., Campbell, J. D., Krueger, J. I., & Vohs, K. D. (2003). Does high self-esteem cause better performance, interpersonal success, happiness, or healthier lifestyles? *Psychological Science in the Public Interest, 4*(1), 1–44.

Baumrind, D. (1991). The influence of parenting style on adolescent competence and substance use. *Journal of Early Adolescence, 11*(1), 56–95.

Baumrind, D. (2005). Patterns of parental authority and adolescent autonomy. In J. Smetana (Ed.), *New directions for child development: Changes in parental authority dur-*

ing adolescence. San Francisco: Jossey-Bass.

Baumrind, D., Larzelere, R. E., & Cowan, P. A. (2002). Ordinary physical punishment: Is it harmful? *Psychological Bulletin, 128*(4), 580–589.

Beach, F. A. (Ed.). (1965). *Sex and behavior.* New York: Wiley.

Bearman, P. S., Moody, J., & Stovel, K. (2004). Chains of affection: The structure of adolescent romantic and sexual networks. *American Journal of Sociology, 110*(1), 44–91.

Beauchamp, P. H., Halliwell, W. R., Fournier, J. F., & Koestner, R. (1996). Effects of cognitive-behavioral psychological skills training on the motivation, preparation, and putting performance of novice golfers. *Sport Psychologist, 10*(2), 157–170.

Beaulieu, C. M. J. (2004). Intercultural study of personal space: A case study. *Journal of Applied Social Psychology, 34*(4), 794–805.

Beck, A. T. (1991). Cognitive therapy. *American Psychologist, 46*(4), 368–375.

Beck, A. T. (2004). Cognitive patterns in dreams and daydreams. In R. I. Rosner & W. J. Lyddon (Eds.), *Cognitive therapy and dreams.* New York: Springer.

Beck, A. T., & Greenberg, R. L. (1974). *Coping with depression.* Institute For Rational Living.

Beck, A. T., Brown, C., Berchick, R. J., Stewart, B. L., et al. (1990). Relationship between hopelessness and ultimate suicide. *American Journal of Psychiatry, 147*(2), 190–195.

Beck, B. L., Koons, S. R., & Milgrim, D. L. (2000). Correlates and consequences of behavioral procrastination. *Journal of Social Behavior & Personality, 15*(5), 3–13.

Beck, J. S. (2002). Beck therapy approach. In M. Hersen & W. H. Sledge (Eds.), *Encyclopedia of psychotherapy.* San Diego: Academic Press.

Beck, R. C. (2004). *Motivation: Theories and principles* (5th ed.). Englewood Cliffs, NJ: Prentice Hall.

Becker, S. W., & Eagly, A. H. (2004). The heroism of women and men. *American Psychologist, 59*(3), 163–178.

Beebe, B., Gerstman, L., Carson, B., Dolins, M., et al. (1982). Rhythmic communication in the mother–infant dyad. In M. Davis (Ed.), *Interaction rhythms, periodicity in communicative behavior.* New York: Human Sciences Press.

Beeber, L. S., Chazan-Cohen, R., Squires, J., Harden, B. J., et al. (2007). The Early Promotion and Intervention Research Consortium (E-PIRC): Five approaches to improving infant/toddler mental health in Early Head Start. *Infant Mental Health Journal, 28*(2), 130–150.

Beeman, M. J., & Chiarello, C. (1998). Complementary right- and left-hemisphere language comprehension. *Current Directions in Psychological Science, 7*(1), 2–8.

Beersma, D. G. M., & Gordijn, M. C. M. (2007). Circadian control of the sleep-wake cycle. *Physiology & Behavior, 90*(2–3), 190–195.

Behrend, D. A., Beike, D. R., & Lampinen, J. M. (2004). *The self and memory.* Hove, UK: Psychology Press.

Beirne-Smith, M., Patton, J., & Shannon, K. (2006). *Mental retardation: An introduction to intellectual disability* (7th ed.). Englewood Cliffs, NJ: Prentice Hall.

Belenky, G., Wesensten, N. J., Thorne, D. R., Thomas, M. L., et al. (2003). Patterns of performance degradation and restoration during sleep restriction and subsequent recovery: A sleep dose-response study. *Journal of Sleep Research, 12*(1), 1–12.

Beljan, J. R., Rosenblatt, L. S., Hetherington, N. W., Layman, J., et al. (1972). Human performance in the aviation environment. *NASA Contract no 2-6657, Pt. Ia,* 253–259.

Bell, P. A., Greene, T., Fisher, J., & Baum, A. S. (2006). *Environmental psychology* (5th ed.). Mahwah, NJ: Erlbaum.

Bellezza, F. S., Six, L. S., & Phillips, D. S. (1992). A mnemonic for remembering long strings of digits. *Bulletin of the Psychonomic Society, 30*(4), 271–274.

Belsky, J. (1996). Parent, infant, and social-contextual antecedents of father–son attachment security. *Developmental Psychology, 32*(5), 905–913.

Bem, S. L. (1974). The measurement of psychological androgyny. *Journal of Consulting & Clinical Psychology, 42*(2), 155–162.

Bem, S. L. (1975). Androgyny vs. the tight little lives of fluffy women and chesty men. *Psychology Today,* Sept., 58–62.

Bem, S. L. (1981). Gender schema theory. A cognitive account of sex typing. *Psychological Review, 88,* 354–364.

Benbow, C. P. (1986). Physiological correlates of extreme intellectual precocity. *Neuropsychologia, 24*(5), 719–725.

Benjafield, J. G. (2004). *A history of psychology* (2nd ed.). Boston: Allyn & Bacon.

Benloucif, S., Bennett, E. L., & Rosenzweig, M. R. (1995). Norepinephrine and neural plasticity: The effects of xylamine on experience-induced changes in brain weight, memory, and behavior. *Neurobiology of Learning & Memory, 63*(1), 33–42.

Bensafi, M., Zelano, C., Johnson, B., Mainland, J., et al. (2004). Olfaction: From sniff to percept. In M. S. Gazzaniga (Ed.), *The cognitive neurosciences* (3rd ed.). Cambridge, MA: MIT Press.

Ben-Shakhar, G., & Dolev, K. (1996). Psychophysiological detection through the guilty knowledge technique: Effect of mental countermeasures. *Journal of Applied Psychology, 81*(3), 273–281.

Benski, C. (1998). Testing new claims of dermo-optical perception. *Skeptical Inquirer, 22*(1), 21–26.

Bensley, L., & Van Eenwyk, J. (2001). Video games and real-life aggression. *Journal of Adolescent Health, 29*(4), 244–257.

Benson, H. (1977). Systematic hypertension and the relaxation response. *The New England Journal of Medicine, 296,* 1152–1156.

Benson, J., Greaves, W., O'Donnell, M., & Taglialatela, J. (2002). Evidence for symbolic language processing in a Bonobo (Pan paniscus). *Journal of Consciousness Studies, 9*(12), 33–56.

Bergeron, S., & Lord, M. J. (2003). The integration of pelvi-perineal reeducation and cognitive-behavioral therapy in the multidisciplinary treatment of the sexual pain disorders. *Sexual & Relationship Therapy, 18,* 135–141.

Bergin, A. E. (1991). Values and religious issues in psychotherapy and mental health. *American Psychologist, 46*(4), 394–403.

Bernat, J. A., Calhoun, K. S., & Stolp, S. (1998). Sexually aggressive men's responses to a date rape analogue. *Journal of Sex Research, 35*(4), 41–348.

Berne, E. (1964). *Games people play.* New York: Grove.

Bernstein, H. J., Beale M. D., Burns C., & Kellner C. H. (1998). Patient attitudes about ECT after treatment. *Psychiatric Annals, 28*(9), 524–527.

Bernthal, M. J. (2003). The effects of professional wrestling viewership on children. *The Sport Journal, 6*(3). Retrieved June 6, 2007, from http://www.thesportjournal.org/2003Journal/Vol6-No3/wrestling.htm.

Berntsen, D., & Thomsen, D. K. (2005). Personal memories for remote historical events: Accuracy and clarity of flashbulb memories related to World War II. *Journal of Experimental Psychology: General, 134*(2), 242–257.

Berry, J. W. (1990). The psychology of acculturation. In R. A. Dienstbier & J. J. Berman (Eds.), *Nebraska Symposium on Motivation 1989: Cross-cultural perspectives, 37.* Lincoln: University of Nebraska Press.

Berry, J. W., Phinney, J. S, Sam, D. L., & Vedder, P. (2005). *Immigrant youth in cultural transition.* Mahwah, NJ: Erlbaum.

Berscheid, E. (2000). Attraction. In A. Kazdin (Ed.), *Encyclopedia of psychology.* Washington, DC: American Psychological Association.

Berscheid, E., & Regan, P. (2005). *The psychology of interpersonal relationships.* Englewood Cliffs, NJ: Prentice Hall.

Bersoff, D. M. (1999). Why good people sometimes do bad things: Motivated reasoning and unethical behavior. *Personality & Social Psychology Bulletin, 25*(1), 28–39.

Bertsch, G. J. (1976). Punishment of consummatory and instrumental behavior: A review. *Psychological Record, 26,* 13–31.

Besnard, D., & Cacitti, L. (2005). Interface changes causing accidents: An empirical study of negative transfer. *International Journal of Human-Computer Studies, 62*(1), 105–125.

Best, D. (2002). Cross-cultural gender roles. In J. Worell (Ed.), *Encyclopedia of women and gender.* New York: Oxford University Press.

Betancur, C., Velez, A., Cabanieu, G., le Moal, M., et al. (1990). Association between left-handedness and allergy: A reappraisal. *Neuropsychologia, 28*(2), 223–227.

Beyer, M., Gerlach, F. M., Flies, U., Grol, R., et al. (2003). The development of quality circles/peer review groups as a tool for quality improvement in Europe: Results of a survey in 26 European countries. *Family Practice, 20,* 443–451.

Bhushan, B., & Khan, S. M. (2006). Laterality and accident proneness: A study of locomotive drivers. *Laterality: Asymmetries of Body, Brain & Cognition, 11*(5), 395–404.

Bialystok, E. (2001). *Bilingualism in development: Language, literacy, and cognition.* New York: Cambridge.

Binder, J. L. (2004). *Key competencies in brief dynamic psychotherapy: Clinical practice beyond the manual.* New York: Guilford.

Binik, Y. M. (2005). Should dyspareunia be retained as a sexual dysfunction in DSM-V? A painful classification decision. *Archives of Sexual Behavior, 34*(1), 11–21.

Birch, J., & McKeever, L. M. (1993). Survey of the accuracy of new pseudoisochromatic plates. *Ophthalmic & Physiological Optics, 13*(1), 35–40.

Birnbaum, M. H. (2004). Human research and data collection via the Internet. *Annual Review of Psychology, 55,* 803–832.

Bisson, J. I., Ehlers, A., Matthews, R., Pilling, S., et al. (2007). Psychological treatments for chronic post-traumatic stress disorder: Systematic review and meta-analysis. *British Journal of Psychiatry, 190*(2), 97–104.

Blackmore, S. (2001). What can the paranormal teach us about consciousness? *Skeptical Inquirer, 25*, 22–27.

Blackmore, S. (2004). *Consciousness: An introduction*. New York: Oxford University Press.

Blackwell, D. L., & Lichter, D. T. (2004). Homogamy among dating, cohabiting, and married couples. *Sociological Quarterly, 45*(4), 719–737.

Blair, K. S., Richell, R. A., Mitchell, D. G. V., Leonard, A., et al. (2006). They know the words, but not the music: Affective and semantic priming in individuals with psychopathy. *Biological Psychology, 73*(2), 114–123.

Blakemore, C., & Cooper, G., (1970). Development of the brain depends on the visual environment. *Nature, 228*, 477–478.

Blanchard, D. C., & Blanchard, R. J. (2003). What can animal aggression research tell us about human aggression? *Hormones & Behavior, 44*(3), 171–177.

Blanchard, E. B., Kuhn, E., Rowell, D. L., Hickling, E. J., et al. (2004). Studies of the vicarious traumatization of college students by the September 11th attacks: Effects of proximity, exposure and connectedness. *Behaviour Research & Therapy, 42*(2), 191–205.

Blatner, A. (2006). Current trends in psychodrama. *International Journal of Psychotherapy, 10*(3), 43–53.

Bloch, M., Daly, R. C., & Rubinow, D. R. (2003). Endocrine factors in the etiology of postpartum depression. *Comprehensive Psychiatry, 44*(3), 234–246.

Bloch, S. (2006). *Introduction to the psychotherapies* (4th ed.). New York: Oxford University Press.

Blood, A. J., & Zatorre, R. J. (2001). Intensely pleasurable responses to music correlate with activity in brain regions implicated in reward and emotion. *Proceedings National Academy of Sciences, 98*(20) 11818–11823.

Bloom, B. (1985). *Developing talent in young people*. New York: Ballantine.

Bloom, C. M., & Lamkin, D. M. (2006). The Olympian struggle to remember the cranial nerves: Mnemonics and student success. *Teaching of Psychology, 33*(2), 128–129.

Bloom, J. W. (1998). The ethical practice of WebCounseling. *British Journal of Guidance & Counselling, 26*(1), 53–59.

Blunt, A., & Pychyl, T. A. (2005). Project systems of procrastinators: A personal project-analytic and action control perspective. *Personality & Individual Differences, 38*(8), 1771–1780.

Bockting, W. O., & Coleman, E. (Eds.). (2003). *Masturbation as a means of achieving sexual health*. New York: Haworth Press.

Boergers, J., Spirito, A., & Donaldson, D. (1998). Reasons for adolescent suicide attempts. *Journal of the American Academy of Child & Adolescent Psychiatry, 37*(12), 1287–1293.

Bohannon, J. N., & Stanowicz, L. B. (1988). The issue of negative evidence: Adult responses to children's language errors. *Developmental Psychology, 24*(5), 684–689.

Boivin, D. B., Czeisler, C. A., & Waterhouse, J. W. (1997). Complex interaction of the sleep-wake cycle and circadian phase modulates mood in healthy subjects. *Archives of General Psychiatry, 54*(2), 145–152.

Boldero, J. M., Moretti, M. M., Bell, R. C., & Francis, J. J. (2005). Self-discrepancies and negative affect: A primer on when to look for specificity, and how to find it. *Australian Journal of Psychology, 57*(3), 139–147.

Bonanno, G. A., Papa, A., Lalande, K., Westphal, M., et al. (2004). The importance of being flexible. *Psychological Science, 15*(7), 482–487.

Bond, R., & Smith, P. B. (1996). Culture and conformity: A meta-analysis of studies using Asch's (1952, 1956) line judgment task. *Psychological Bulletin, 119*(1), 111–137.

Bond, T., & Wooten, V. (1996). The etiology and management of insomnia. *Virginia Medical Quarterly, 123*(4), 254–255.

Bongard, S., al'Absi, M., & Lovallo, W. R. (1998). Interactive effects of trait hostility and anger expression on cardiovascular reactivity in young men. *International Journal of Psychophysiology, 28*(2), 181–191.

Bonham, V., Warshauer-Baker, E., & Collins, F. S. (2005). Race and ethnicity in the genome era: The complexity of the constructs. *American Psychologist, 60*(1), 9–15.

Boniecki, K. A., & Britt, T. W. (2003). Prejudice and the peacekeeper. In T. W. Britt & A. B Adler (Eds.), *The psychology of the peacekeeper: Lessons from the field*. Westport, CT: Praeger.

Bood, S., Sundequist, U., Kjellgren, A., Norlander, T., et al. (2006). Eliciting the relaxation response with the help of floatation-REST (Restricted Environmental Stimulation Technique) in patients with stress-related ailments. *International Journal of Stress Management, 13*(2), 154–175.

Booker, J. M., & Hellekson, C. J. (1992). Prevalence of seasonal affective disorder in Alaska. *American Journal of Psychiatry, 149*(9), 1176–1182.

Bootzin, R. R., & Epstein, D. R. (2000). Stimulus control. In K. L. Lichstein & C. M. Morin (Eds.), *Treatment of late life insomnia*. Thousand Oaks, CA: Sage.

Borlongan, C. V., Sanberg, P. R., & Freeman, T. B. (1999). Neural transplantation for neurodegenerative disorders. *Lancet, 353*(Suppl 1), S29–30.

Borman, W. C., Hanson, M. A., & Hedge, J. W. (1997). Personnel psychology. *Annual Review of Psychology, 48*, 299–337.

Bornstein, M. H., & Tamis-LeMonda, C. S. (2001). Mother–infant interaction. In A. Fogel & G. Bremmer (Eds.), *Blackwell handbook of infant development*. London: Blackwell.

Bornstein, R. F. (1996). Sex differences in dependent personality disorder prevalence rates. *Clinical Psychology: Science & Practice, 3*(1), 1–12.

Borod, J. C., Bloom, R. L., Brickman, A. M., Nakhutina, L., et al. (2002). Emotional processing deficits in individuals with unilateral brain damage. *Applied Neuropsychology, 9*(1), 23–36.

Botes, A. (2000). A comparison between the ethics of justice and the ethics of care. *Journal of Advanced Nursing, 32*(5), 1071–1075.

Bouchard, T. J., Jr. (1983). Twins—Nature's twice-told tale. In *Yearbook of science and the future*. Chicago: Encyclopedia Britannica.

Bouchard, T. J., Jr. (2004). Genetic influence on human psychological traits: A survey. *Current Directions in Psychological Science, 13*(4), 148–151.

Bouchard, T. J., Jr., Lykken, D. T., McGue, M., Segal, N. L., et al. (1990). Sources of human psychological differences: The Minnesota study of twins reared apart. *Science, 250*, 223–228.

Bourne, E. J. (2005). *The anxiety & phobia workbook* (4th ed.). Oakland, CA: New Harbinger.

Bovbjerg, D. H., Redd, W. H., Jacobsen, P. B., Manne, S. L., et al. (1992). An experimental analysis of classically conditioned nausea during cancer chemotherapy. *Psychosomatic Medicine, 54*(6), 623–637.

Bower, G. H. (1981). Mood and memory. *American Psychologist, 36*, 129–148.

Bower, G. H., & Springston, F. (1970). Pauses as recoding points in letter series. *Journal of Experimental Psychology, 83*, 421–430.

Bowker, A. (2006). The relationship between sports participation and self-esteem during early adolescence. *Canadian Journal of Behavioural Science, 38*(3), 214–229.

Boyle, S. H., Williams, R. B., Mark, D., Brummett, B. H., et al. (2004). Hostility as a predictor of survival in patients with coronary artery disease. *Psychosomatic Medicine, 66*(5), 629–632.

Brach, T. (2003). *Radical acceptance*. New York: Bantam Books.

Bradley, R. H., & Corwyn, R. F. (2002). Socioeconomic status and child development. *Annual Review of Psychology, 53*, 377–399.

Bradley, R., Greene, J., Russ, E., Dutra, L., et al. (2005). A multidimensional meta-analysis of psychotherapy for PTSD. *American Journal of Psychiatry, 162*(2), 214–227.

Bradshaw, S. D. (2006). Shyness and difficult relationships: Formation is just the beginning. In D. C. Kirkpatrick, D. S. Duck, et al. (Eds.), *Relating difficulty: The processes of constructing and managing difficult interaction*. Mahwah, NJ: Erlbaum.

Brainerd, C. J. (2003). Jean Piaget, learning research, and American education. In B. J. Zimmerman & D. H. Schunk (Eds.), *Educational psychology: A century of contributions*. Mahwah, NJ: Erlbaum.

Brannon, L. (1996). *Gender*. Boston: Allyn & Bacon.

Brannon, L., & Feist, J. (2007). *Health psychology: An introduction to behavior and health* (6th ed.). Belmont, CA: Cengage Learning/Wadsworth.

Bransford, J. D., & McCarrell, N. S. (1977). A sketch of cognitive approach to comprehension: Some thoughts about understanding what it means to comprehend. In P. N. Johnson-Laird & P. C. Wason (Eds.), *Thinking: Readings in cognitive science*. Cambridge, UK: Cambridge University Press.

Braun, A. R., Balkin, T. J., & Herscovitch, P. (1998). Dissociated pattern of activity in visual cortices and their projections during human rapid eye movement sleep. *Science, 279*(5347), 91–95.

Braun, K. A., Ellis, R., & Loftus, E. F. (2002). Make my memory: How advertising can change memories of the past. *Psychology and Marketing, 19*, 1–23.

Braun, S. (2001). Seeking insight by prescription. *Cerebrum, 3*(2), 10–21.

Braun-LaTour, K. A., & LaTour, M. S. (2004). Assessing the long-term impact of a consistent advertising campaign on consumer memory. *Journal of Advertising, 33*(2), 49–61.

Bray, S. R., & Widmeyer, W. N. (2000). Athletes' perceptions of the home advantage. *Journal of Sport Behavior, 23*(1), 1–10.

Breckler, S. J., Olson, J., & Wiggins, E. (2006). *Social psychology alive*. Belmont, CA: Cengage Learning/Wadsworth.

Breedlove, S. M., Cooke, B. M., & Jordan, C. L. (1999). The orthodox view of brain sexual differentiation. *Brain, Behavior & Evolution, 54*(1), 8–14.

Brennan, F. X., Beck, K. D., & Servatius, R. J. (2003). Lever press escape/avoidance conditioning in rats: Safety signal length and avoidance performance. *Integrative Physiological & Behavioral Science, 38*(1), 36–44.

Breslau, N., Johnson, E. O., Hiripi, E., & Kessler, R. (2001). Nicotine dependence in the United States. *Archives of General Psychiatry, 58*(9), 810–816.

Bressi, C., Albonetti, S., & Razzoli, E. (1998). "Communication deviance" and schizophrenia. *New Trends in Experimental & Clinical Psychiatry, 14*(1), 33–39.

Bretherton, R., & Orner, R. J. (2004). Positive psychology and psychotherapy: An existential approach. In P. A. Linley & S. Joseph (Eds.), *Positive psychology in practice.* New York: Wiley.

Brewer, J. S. (1981). Duration of intromission and female orgasm rates. *Medical Aspects of Human Sexuality, 15*(4), 70–71.

Brewer, K. R., & Wann, D. L. (1998). Observational learning effectiveness as a function of model characteristics. *Social Behavior & Personality, 26*(1), 1–10.

Brewer, N., & Wells, G. L. (2006). The confidence-accuracy relationship in eyewitness identification: Effects of lineup instructions, foil similarity, and target-absent base rates. *Journal of Experimental Psychology: Applied, 12*(1), 11–30.

Brewer, N., & Williams, K. D. (Eds.). (2005). *Psychology and law: An empirical perspective.* New York: Guilford.

Bridges, K. M. B. (1932). Emotional development in early infancy. *Child Development, 3*, 324–334.

Bridges, L. J. (2003). Trust, attachment, and relatedness. In M. H. Bornstein, L. Davidson, et al. (Eds.), *Well-being: Positive development across the life course.* Mahwah, NJ: Erlbaum.

Brief, A. P., & Weiss, H. M. (2002). Organizational behavior. *Annual Review of Psychology, 53*, 279–307.

Brigham, J. C., & Wasserman, A. W. (1999). The impact of race, racial attitude, and gender on reactions to the criminal trial of O. J. Simpson. *Journal of Applied Social Psychology, 29*(7), 1333–1370.

Bringing up baby. (1999). *Sierra,* Jan–Feb, 17.

Brinton, R. D., & Wang, J. M. (2006). Therapeutic potential of neurogenesis for prevention and recovery from Alzheimer's disease: Allopregnanolone as a proof of concept neurogenic agent. *Current Alzheimer Research, 3*(3), 185–190.

Brock, T. C., & Green, M. C. (Eds.). (2005). *Persuasion: Psychological insights and perspectives* (2nd ed.). Thousand Oaks, CA: Sage.

Brodley, B. T. (2006). Non-directivity in client-centered therapy. *Person-Centered & Experiential Psychotherapies, 5*(1), 36–52.

Brooks-Gunn, J., & Warren, M. P. (1988). The psychological significance of secondary sexual characteristics in nine- to eleven-year-old girls. *Child Development, 59*(4), 1061–1069.

Brothen, T., & Wambach, C. (2001). Effective student use of computerized quizzes. *Teaching of Psychology, 28*(4), 292–294.

Brown, A. E., Jeffcott, Jr., H. A. (1970). *Absolutely mad inventions.* New York: Dover Publications.

Brown, A. M. (1990). Development of visual sensitivity to light and color vision in human infants: A critical review. *Vision Research, 30*(8), 1159–1188.

Brown, A. S. (2004). *The déjà vu experience.* New York: Psychology Press.

Brown, A. S., Cohen, P., Harkavy-Friedman, J., Babulas, V., et al. (2001). Prenatal rubella, premorbid abnormalities, and adult schizophrenia. *Biological Psychiatry, 49*(6), 473–486.

Brown, B. B., & Bentley, D. L. (1993). Residential burglars judge risk. *Journal of Environmental Psychology, 13*(1), 51–61.

Brown, K. W. & Ryan, R. M. (2003). The benefits of being present. *Journal of Personality and Social Psychology, 84*(4), 822–848.

Brown, L. M. (2005). *Girlfighting: Betrayal and rejection among girls.* New York: New York University Press.

Brown, R. L., Leonard, T., Saunders, L. A., & Papasouliotis, O. (1997). A two-item screening test for alcohol and other drug problems. *Journal of Family Practice, 44*(2), 151–160.

Brown, R., & McNeill, D. (1966). The "tip of the tongue" phenomenon. *Journal of Verbal Learning and Verbal Behavior, 5,* 325–337.

Brown, S. A., Tapert, S. F., Granholm, E., & Delis, D. C. (2000). Neurocognitive functioning of adolescents: Effects of protracted alcohol use. *Alcoholism: Clinical & Experimental Research, 24*(2), 164–171.

Brown, S. G., Roy, E., Rohr, L., & Bryden, P. (2006). Using hand performance measures to predict handedness. *Laterality: Asymmetries of Body, Brain & Cognition, 11*(1), 1–14.

Brown, T. A., & Barlow, D. H. (2007). *Casebook in abnormal psychology* (3rd ed.). Belmont, CA: Cengage Learning/Wadsworth.

Brown, T. D., Dane, F. C., & Durham, M. D. (1998). Perception of race and ethnicity. *Journal of Social Behavior & Personality, 13*(2), 295–306.

Browne, B. A. (1998). Gender stereotypes in advertising on children's television in the 1990s. *Journal of Advertising, 27*(1), 83–96.

Browne, N., & Keeley, S. (2007). *Asking the right questions: A guide to critical thinking* (8th ed.). Englewood Cliffs, NJ: Prentice Hall.

Brownell, K. D. (2003). *Food fight.* New York: McGraw-Hill.

Bruch, M. A. (2001). Shyness and social interaction. In R. Crozier & L. Alden (Eds.), *International handbook of social anxiety.* Sussex, UK: Wiley.

Bruer, J. T. (2001). A critical and sensitive period primer. In D. B. Bailey, Jr., J. T. Bruer, et al. (Eds.), *Critical thinking about critical periods.* Baltimore, MD: Paul H. Brookes.

Bruner, J. (1973). *Going beyond the information given.* New York: Norton.

Bruner, J. (1983). *Child's talk.* New York: Norton.

Bryden, P. J., Bruyn, J., & Fletcher, P. (2005). Handedness and health: An examination of the association between different handedness classifications and health disorders. *Laterality: Asymmetries of Body, Brain & Cognition, 10*(5), 429–440.

Buchwald, A. (1965). Psyching out. *Washington Post,* June 20.

Buddie, A. M. (2004). Alternatives to twelvestep programs. *Journal of Forensic Psychology Practice, 4*(3), 61–70.

Budney, A. J., & Hughes, J. R. (2006). The cannabis withdrawal syndrome. *Current Opinion in Psychiatry, 19*(3), 233–238.

Buehner, M. J., & May, J. (2003). Rethinking temporal contiguity and the judgement of causality: Effects of prior knowledge, experience, and reinforcement procedure. *Quarterly Journal of Experimental Psychology: Human Experimental Psychology, 56A*(5), 865–890.

Buller, D. J. (2005). *Adapting minds: Evolutionary psychology and the persistent quest for human nature.* Cambridge, MA: MIT Press.

Bunde, J., & Suls, J. (2006). A quantitative analysis of the relationship between the cook-medley hostility scale and traditional coronary artery disease risk factors. *Health Psychology, 25*(4), 493–500.

Bunn, G. C. (2007). Spectacular science: The lie detector's ambivalent powers. *History of Psychology, 10*(2), 156–178.

Burchinal, M. R., Roberts, J. E., Riggins, R., Zeisel, S. A., et al. (2000). Relating quality of center-based child care to early cognitive and language development longitudinally. *Child Development, 71*(2), 339–357.

Burger, J. M. (2008). *Personality* (7th ed.). Belmont, CA: Cengage Learning/Wadsworth.

Burger, J. M., & Lynn, A. L. (2005). Superstitious behavior among American and Japanese professional baseball players. *Basic & Applied Social Psychology, 27*(1), 71–76.

Burgess, C. A., & Kirsch, I. (1999). Expectancy information as a moderator of the effects of hypnosis on memory. *Contemporary Hypnosis, 16*(1), 22–31.

Burgess, M. C. R., & Weaver, G. E. (2003). Interest and attention in facial recognition. *Perceptual & Motor Skills, 96*(2), 467–480.

Burgner, D., & Hewstone, M. (1993). Young children's causal attributions for success and failure. *British Journal of Developmental Psychology, 11*(2), 125–129.

Burlingame, G. M., & Davies, R. (2002). Self-help groups. In M. Hersen & W. H. Sledge (Eds.), *Encyclopedia of psychotherapy.* San Diego: Academic Press.

Burlingame, G. M., Fuhriman, A., & Mosier, J. (2003). The differential effectiveness of group psychotherapy: A meta-analytic perspective. *Group Dynamics: Theory, Research, & Practice, 7*(1), 3–12.

Burnett, R. C., Medin, D. L., Ross, N. O., & Blok, S. V. (2005). Ideal is typical. *Canadian Journal of Experimental Psychology, 59*(1), 3–10.

Burns, D. D., & Persons, J. (1982). Hope and hopelessness: A cognitive approach. In L. E. Abt & I. R. Stuart (Eds.), *The newer therapies: A sourcebook.* New York: Van Nostrand Reinhold.

Burns, T. (2004). *Community mental health teams: A guide to current practices.* New York: Oxford University Press.

Burt, S. A., McGue, M., Carter, L. A., & Iacono, W. G. (2007). The different origins of stability and change in antisocial personality disorder symptoms. *Psychological Medicine, 37*(1), 27–38.

Burton, C. M., & King, L. A. (2004). The health benefits of writing about intensely positive experiences. *Journal of Research in Personality, 38*(2), 150–163.

Burtt, H. E. (1941). An experimental study of early childhood memory: Final report. *Journal of General Psychology, 58,* 435–439.

Bushman, B. J., & Anderson, C. A. (2001). Media violence and the American public. *American Psychologist, 56*(6/7), 477–489.

Bushnell, L. W., Sai, F., & Mullin, L. T. (1989). Neonatal recognition of the mother's face. *British Journal of Developmental Psychology, 7*(1), 3–15.

Bushnell, M. C., Villemure, C., & Duncan, G. H. (2004). Psychophysical and neurophysiological studies of pain modulation by attention. In D. D. Price & M. C. Bushnell (Eds.), *Psychological methods of pain control: Basic science and clinical perspectives*. Seattle: IASP Press.

Buss, D. M. (1985). Human mate selection. *American Scientist, 73*, 47–51.

Buss, D. M. (2000). *The dangerous passion*. New York: Free Press.

Buss, D. M. (2004). *Evolutionary psychology: The new science of the mind* (2nd ed.). Boston: Allyn & Bacon.

Buss, D. M. (2007). The evolution of human mating. *Acta Psychologica Sinica, 39*(3), 502–512.

Butcher, J. N. (2005). *A beginner's guide to the MMPI-2* (2nd ed.). Washington, DC: American Psychological Association.

Butcher, J. N., Mineka, S., & Hooley, J. (2007). *Abnormal psychology and modern life* (13th ed.). Boston: Allyn & Bacon.

Butkovic, A., & Bratko, D. (2003). Generation and sex differences in sensation seeking: Results of the family study. *Perceptual and Motor Skills, 97*(3, Pt. 1), 965–970.

Butler, B. (2007). The role of death qualification in capital trials involving juvenile defendants. *Journal of Applied Social Psychology, 37*(3), 549–560.

Butler, J. C. (2000). Personality and emotional correlates of right-wing authoritarianism. *Social Behavior & Personality, 28*(1), 1–14.

Butler, M. G. (2001). *Overcoming social anxiety and shyness: A self-help guide using cognitive behavioral techniques*. New York: New York University Press.

Butler, R. (1954). Curiosity in monkeys. *Scientific American, 190*(18), 70–75.

Byrne, S. M., & McLean, N. J. (2002). The cognitive-behavioral model of bulimia nervosa: A direct evaluation. *International Journal of Eating Disorders, 31*, 17–31.

Cahill, S. P., Carrigan, M. H., & Frueh, B. C. (1999). Does EMDR work? and if so, why? *Journal of Anxiety Disorders, 13*(1–2), 5–33.

Cahn, B. R., & Polich, J. (2006). Meditation states and traits: EEG, ERP, and neuroimaging studies. *Psychological Bulletin, 132*(2), 180–211.

Calhoun, J. B. (1962). A "behavioral sink." In E. L. Bliss (Ed.), *Roots of behavior*. New York: Harper & Row.

Callahan, C. M. (2006). Giftedness. In G. G. Bear & K. M. Minke (Eds.), *Children's needs III: Development, prevention, and intervention*. Washington, DC: National Association of School Psychologists.

Camara, W. J., & Schneider, D. L. (1994). Integrity tests. *American Psychologist, 49*(2), 112–119.

Cameron, J. A., & Trope, Y. (2004). Stereotype-biased search and processing of information about group members. *Social Cognition, 22*(6), 650–672.

Cameron, J., & Pierce, W. D. (2002). *Rewards and intrinsic motivation: Resolving the controversy*. Westport, CO: Bergin & Garvey.

Campbell, L., Campbell, B., & Dickinson, D. (2003). *Teaching and learning through multiple intelligences* (3rd ed.). Boston: Allyn & Bacon.

Campion, M. A., & McClelland, C. L. (1993). Follow-up and extension of interdisciplinary costs and benefits of enlarged jobs. *Journal of Applied Psychology, 78*(3), 339–351.

Campion, M. A., Palmer, D. K., & Campion, J. E. (1998). Structuring employment interviews to improve reliability, validity and users' reactions. *Current Directions in Psychological Science, 7*(3), 77–82.

Canli, T., Desmond, J. E., Zhao, Z., Glover, G., et al. (1998). Hemispheric asymmetry for emotional stimuli detected with fMRI. *Neuroreport, 9*(14) 3233–3239.

Cannon, W. B. (1932). *The wisdom of the body*. New York: Norton.

Cannon, W. B. (1934). Hunger and thirst. In C. Murchinson (Ed.), *Handbook of general experimental psychology*. Worcester, MA: Clark University Press.

Cannon, W. B., & Washburn, A. L. (1912). An exploration of hunger. *American Journal of Physiology, 29*, 441–454.

Caplan, P. J. (1995). *They say you're crazy*. Reading, MA: Addison-Wesley.

Capuzzi, D. (2003). *Approaches to group counseling*. Englewood Cliffs, NJ: Prentice Hall.

Cardoso, S. H. (2000). Our ancient laughing brain. *Cerebrum, 2*(4), 15–30.

Carducci, B. J., & Fields, T. H. (2007). *The shyness workbook for teens*. Champaign, IL: Research Press.

Carlbring, P., Gunnarsdóttir, M., Hedensjö, L., Andersson, G., et al. (2007). Treatment of social phobia: Randomised trial of internet-delivered cognitive-behavioural therapy with telephone support. *British Journal of Psychiatry, 190*(2), 123–128.

Carlson, M., Marcus-Hewhall, A., & Miller, N. (1990). Effects of situational aggression cues: A quantitative review. *Journal of Personality & Social Psychology, 58*(4), 622–633.

Carlson, N. R. (2005). *Physiology of behavior* (8th ed.). Boston: Allyn & Bacon.

Carlson, N. R. (2007). *Physiology of behavior* (9th ed.). Boston: Allyn & Bacon.

Carnagey, N. L., & Anderson, C. A. (2004). Violent video game exposure and aggression: A literature review. *Minerva Psichiatrica, 45*(1), 1–18.

Carney, R. N., & Levin, J. R. (2001). Remembering the names of unfamiliar animals: Keywords as keys to their kingdom. *Applied Cognitive Psychology, 15*(2), 133–143.

Carney, R. N., & Levin, J. R. (2003). Promoting higher-order learning benefits by building lower-order mnemonic connections. *Applied Cognitive Psychology, 17*(5), 563–575.

Carroll, D. W. (2008). *Psychology of language* (5th ed.). Belmont, CA: Cengage Learning/Wadsworth.

Carroll, J. L. (2007). *Sexuality now: Embracing diversity* (2nd ed.). Belmont, CA: Cengage Learning/Wadsworth.

Carroll, J. M., & Russell, J. A. (1996). Do facial expressions signal specific emotions? Judging emotion from the face in context. *Journal of Personality & Social Psychology, 70*(2), 205–218.

Carskadon, M. A., Acebo, C., & Jenni, O. C. (2004). Regulation of adolescent sleep: Implications for behavior. *Annals of the New York Academy of Science, 1021*, 276–291.

Carter, D. A., Simkins, B. J., & Simpson, W. G. (2003). Corporate governance, board diversity, and firm value. *Financial Review, 38*, 33–53.

Cartwright, D. (2002a). *Psychoanalysis, violence and rage-type murder: Murdering minds*. New York: Brunner-Routledge.

Cartwright, D. (2002b). The narcissistic exoskeleton: The defensive organization of the rage-type murderer. *Bulletin of the Menninger Clinic, 66*(1), 1–18.

Cartwright, R., & Lamberg, L. (1992). *Crisis dreaming*. New York: HarperCollins.

Casey, P. (2001). Multiple personality disorder. *Primary Care Psychiatry, 7*(1), 7–11.

Caspi, A. Sugden, K., Moffitt, T. E., Taylor, A., et al. (2003). Influence of life stress on depression: Moderation by a polymorphism in the 5-HTT gene. *Science, 301*(5631), 386–389.

Caspi, A., Roberts, B. W., & Shiner, R. L. (2005). Personality development: Stability and change. *Annual Review of Psychology, 56*, 453–484.

Cassady, J. C. (2004). The influence of cognitive test anxiety across the learning-testing cycle. *Learning & Instruction, 14*(6), 569–592.

Castro, J. R., & Rice, K. G. (2003). Perfectionism and ethnicity: Implications for depressive symptoms and self-reported academic achievement. *Cultural Diversity & Ethnic Minority Psychology, 9*(1), 64–78.

Castro, J., Gila, A., Gual, P., Lahortiga, F., et al. (2004). Perfectionism dimensions in children and adolescents with anorexia nervosa. *Journal of Adolescent Health, 35*(5), 392–398.

Catalano, R., Novaco, R., & McConnell, W. (1997). A model of the net effect of job loss on violence. *Journal of Personality & Social Psychology, 72*(6), 1440–1447.

Cattell, R. B. (1949). *Culture Free Intelligence Test, Scale 1, Handbook*. Champaign, IL: Institute of Personality and Ability.

Cattell, R. B. (1965). *The scientific analysis of personality*. Baltimore: Penguin.

Cattell, R. B. (1973). Personality pinned down. *Psychology Today*, July, 40–46.

Cautela, J. R., & Kearney, A. J. (1986). *The covert conditioning handbook*. New York: Springer.

Cavaco, S., Anderson, S. W., Allen, J. S., Castro-Caldas, A., et al. (2004). The scope of preserved procedural memory in amnesia. *Brain: A Journal of Neurology, 127*(8), 1853–1867.

CDC. (2002). *Teenagers in the United States: sexual activity, contraceptive use, and childbearing, 2002*. Atlanta, GA: Centers for Disease Control and National Center for Health Statistics, National Vital Statistics System. Retrieved July 30, 2007, from http://0-www.cdc.gov.mill1.sjlibrary.org:80/nchs/data/series/sr_23/sr23_024.pdf.

CDC. (2002). *Overweight, obesity, and healthy weight among persons 20 years of age and over, according to sex, age, race, and Hispanic origin: United States, 1960–62, 1971–74, 1976–80, 1988–94, and 1999–2000*. Atlanta: Centers for Disease Control and Prevention. Retrieved July 8, 2007, from http://www.cdc.gov/nchs/data/hus/tables/2002/02hus070.pdf.

CDC. (2003). *Deaths, percent of total deaths, and death rates for 15 leading causes of death in 5-year age groups, by race and sex: United State, 2000*. Atlanta: Centers for Disease Control and National Center for Health Statistics, National Vital Statistics System. Retrieved July 25, 2007, from http://www.cdc.gov/nchs/datawh/statab/unpubd/mortabs/lcwk1_10.htm.

CDC. (2005). Annual smoking–attributable mortality, years of potential life lost, and productivity losses: United States, 1997–2001. *Centers for Disease Control and Prevention Morbidity and Mortality Weekly Report, 54*(25), 625–628.

CDC. (2007). *Sexual violence: Fact sheet*. Atlanta: National Center for Injury Prevention and Control.

Retrieved July 29, 2007, from http://www.cdc.gov/ncipc/factsheets/svfacts.htm.

Chabas, D., Taheri, S., Renier, C., & Mignot, E. (2003). The genetics of narcolepsy. *Annual Review of Genomics and Human Genetics, 4,* 459–483.

Chakos, M. H., Alvir, J. M. J., Woerner, M., & Koreen, A. (1996). Incidence and correlates of tardive dyskinesia in first episode of schizophrenia. *Archives of General Psychiatry, 53*(4), 313–319.

Chamberlin, J. (2004). Survey says: More Americans are seeking mental health treatment. *Monitor on Psychology,* July/Aug., 17.

Chamberlin, J., & Rogers, J. A. (1990). Planning a community-based mental health system. *American Psychologist, 45*(11), 1241–1244.

Chambers, R. A., Taylor, J. R., & Potenza, M. N. (2003). Developmental neurocircuitry of motivation in adolescence: A critical period of addiction vulnerability. *American Journal of Psychiatry, 160*(6), 1041–1052.

Chambless, D. L., & Ollendick, T. H. (2001). Empirically supported psychological interventions. *Annual Review of Psychology, 52,* 685–716.

Chamorro-Premuzic, T., & Furnham, A. (2003). Personality predicts academic performance. *Journal of Research in Personality, 37*(4), 319–338.

Chan, G. C.-K., Hinds, T. R., Impey, S., & Storm, D. R. (1998). Hippocampal neurotoxicity of _-sup-9-tetrahydrocannabinol. *Journal of Neuroscience, 18*(14), 5322–5332.

Chance, P. (2006). *Learning and behavior* (5th ed.). Belmont, CA: Cengage Learning/Wadsworth.

Chansler, P. A., Swamidass, P. M., & Cammann, C. (2003). Self-managing work teams: An empirical study of group cohesiveness in "natural work groups" at a Harley-Davidson Motor Company plant. *Small Group Research, 34*(1), 101–120.

Chao, R., & Tseng, V. (2002). Parenting of Asians. In M. H. Bornstein (Ed.), *Handbook of parenting* (Vol. 4): *Social conditions and applied parenting* (2nd ed.). Mahwah, NJ: Erlbaum.

Chapanis, A., & Lindenbaum, L. E. (1959). A reaction time study of four control-display linkages. *Human Factors, 1,* 1–7.

Chapman, R. A. (Ed.). (2006). *The clinical use of hypnosis in cognitive behavior therapy: A practitioner's casebook.* New York: Springer Publishing.

Chassin, L., Presson, C. C., Sherman, S. J., & Kim, K. (2003). Historical changes in cigarette smoking and smoking-related beliefs after 2 decades in a midwestern community. *Health Psychology, 22*(4), 347–353.

Chaves, J. F. (2000). Hypnosis. In A. Kazdin (Ed.), *Encyclopedia of psychology.* Washington, DC: American Psychological Association.

Check, J. V. P., & Malamuth, N. M. (1983). Sex role stereotyping and reactions to depictions of stranger versus acquaintance rape. *Journal of Personality & Social Psychology, 45,* 344–356.

Cheek, J., & Buss, A. H. (1979). *Scales of shyness, sociability and self-esteem and correlations among them.* Unpublished research, University of Texas. (Cited by Buss, 1980.)

Chen, K., & Kandel, D. B. (1995). The natural history of drug use from adolescence to the mid-thirties in a general population sample. *American Journal of Public Health, 85*(1), 41–47.

Chen, Z., Lawson, R. B., Gordon, L. R., & McIntosh, B. (1996). Groupthink: Deciding with the leader and the devil. *Psychological Record, 46*(4), 581–590.

Chen, Z., Mo, L., & Honomichl, R. (2004). Having the memory of an elephant. *Journal of Experimental Psychology: General, 133*(3), 415–433.

Cheng, H., Cao, Y., & Olson, L. (1996). Spinal cord repair in adult paraplegic rats: Partial restoration of hind limb function. *Science, 273*(5274), 510.

Chess, S., & Thomas, A. (1986). *Know your child.* New York: Basic.

Chesson, A. L., Anderson, W. M., Littner, M., Davila. D, et al. (1999). Practice parameters for the nonpharmacologic treatment of chronic insomnia. *Sleep, 22,* 1128–1133.

Chester, A., & Glass, C. A. (2006). Online counselling: A descriptive analysis of therapy services on the internet. *British Journal of Guidance & Counselling, 34*(2), 145–160.

Cheyne, J. A. (2005). Sleep paralysis episode frequency and number, types, and structure of associated hallucinations. *Journal of Sleep Research, 14*(3), 319–324.

Cheyne, J. A., Rueffer, S. D., & Newby-Clark, I. R. (1999). Hypnagogic and hypnopompic hallucinations during sleep paralysis: Neurological and cultural construction of the nightmare. *Consciousness & Cognition, 8,* 319–337.

Chisolm, T. H., Willott, J. F., & Lister, J. J. (2003). The aging auditory system: Anatomic and physiologic changes and implications for rehabilitation. *International Journal of Audiology, 42*(Suppl 2), 2S3–2S10.

Chomsky, N. (1975). *Reflections on language.* New York: Pantheon.

Chomsky, N. (1986). *Knowledge of language.* New York: Praeger.

Christensen, A., & Jacobson, N. S. (1994). Who (or what) can do psychotherapy. *Psychological Science, 5*(1), 8–14.

Christian, K. M., & Thompson, R. F. (2005). Long-term storage of an associative memory trace in the cerebellum. *Behavioral Neuroscience, 119*(2), 526–537.

Christophersen, E. R., & Mortweet, S. L. (2003). *Parenting that works: Building skills that last a lifetime.* Washington, DC: American Psychological Association.

Chua, P., & Fujino, D. C. (1999). Negotiating new Asian-American masculinities: Attitudes and gender expectations. *Journal of Men's Studies, 7*(3), 391–413.

Cialdini, R. B., & Goldstein, N. J. (2004). Social influence: Compliance and conformity. *Annual Review of Psychology, 55,* 591–621.

Cialdini, R. B., Eisenberg, N., Green, B. L., Rhoads, K., et al. (1998). Undermining the undermining effect of reward on sustained interest. *Journal of Applied Social Psychology, 28*(3), 249–263.

Cialdini, R. B., Reno, R. R., & Kallgren, C. A. (1990). A focus theory of normative conduct: Recycling the concept of norms to reduce littering in public places. *Journal of Personality & Social Psychology, 58*(6), 1015–1026.

Ciarrochi, J., Dean, F. P., & Anderson, S. (2002). Emotional intelligence moderates the relationship between stress and mental health. *Personality & Individual Differences, 32*(2), 197–209.

Cinciripini, P. M., Wetter, D. W., & McClure, J. B. (1997). Scheduled reduced smoking. *Addictive Behaviors, 22*(6), 759–767.

Clark, D., Boutros, N., & Mendez, M. (2005). *The brain and behavior* (2nd ed.). Cambridge, UK: Cambridge University Press.

Clark, R., Anderson, N. B., Clark, V. R., & Williams, D. R. (1999). Racism as a stressor for African Americans. *American Psychologist, 54*(10), 805–816.

Clayton, N. S., Yu, K. S., & Dickinson, A. (2001). Scrub jays (Aphelocoma coerulescens) form integrated memories of the multiple features of caching episodes. *Journal of Experimental Psychology: Animal Behavior Processes, 27,* 17–29.

Clearfield, M. W., & Nelson, N. M. (2006). Sex differences in mothers' speech and play behavior with 6-, 9-, and 14-month-old infants. *Sex Roles, 54*(1–2), 127–137.

Clearwater, Y. (1985). A human place in outer space. *Psychology Today,* July, 34–43.

Clements, A. M., Rimrodt, S. L., Abel, J. R., Blankner, J. G. et al. (2006). Sex differences in cerebral laterality of language and visuospatial processing. *Brain & Language, 98*(2), 150–158.

Click, P., Zion, C., & Nelson, C. (1988). What mediates sex discrimination in hiring decisions? *Journal of Personality & Social Psychology, 55*(2), 178–186.

Cline, V. B., Croft, R. G., & Courrier, S. (1972). Desensitization of children to television violence. *Journal of Personality & Social Psychology, 27,* 360–365.

Cnattingius, S., Signorello, L. B., Ammerén, G., Clausson, B., et al. (2000). Caffeine intake and the risk of first-trimester spontaneous abortion. *New England Journal of Medicine, 343*(25), 1839–1845.

Cochran, S. D. (2001). Emerging issues in research on lesbians' and gay men's mental health. *American Psychologist, 56*(11), 931–947.

Cohen, J. E. (1995). *How many people can the earth support?* New York: Norton.

Cohen, P., Cohen, J., Kasen, S., Velez, C. N., et al. (1993). An epidemiological study of disorders in late adolescence: I. Age- and gender-specific prevalence. *Journal of Child Psychology & Psychiatry, 6,* 851–867.

Cohen, S., Evans, G. W., Krantz, D S., & Stokols, D. (1981). Cardiovascular and behavioral effects of community noise. *American Scientist, 69,* 528–535.

Colapinto, J. (2000). *As nature made him: The boy who was raised as a girl.* New York: HarperCollins.

Cole, J. (1995). *Pride and a daily marathon.* Cambridge, MA: MIT Press.

Coles, C. D., & Black, M. M. (2006). Introduction to the special issue. *Journal of Pediatric Psychology. Special Issue: Prenatal Substance Exposure: Impact on Children's Health, Development, School Performance, and Risk Behavior, 31*(1), 1–4.

Colin, A. K., Moore, K., & West, A. N. (1996). Creativity, oversensitivity, and rate of habituation. *EDRA: Environmental Design Research Association, 20*(4), 423–427.

Collins, A. M., & Quillian, M. R. (1969). Retrieval time from semantic memory. *Journal of Verbal Learning & Verbal Behavior, 8,* 240–247.

Collins, N. L., Cooper, M. L., Albino, A., & Allard, L. (2002). Psychosocial vulnerability from adolescence to adulthood: A prospective study of attachment style differences in relationship functioning and partner choice. *Journal of Personality, 70*(6), 965–1008.

Collins, W. A., & Gunnar, M. R. (1990). Social and personality development. *Annual Review of Psychology,* 41, 387–416.

Collop, N. A. (2005). Obstructive sleep apnea: treatment overview and controversies. In P. R. Carney, J. D. Geyer, & R. B. Berry (Eds.), *Clinical sleep disorders*. Philadelphia: Lippincott Williams & Wilkins.

Comer, R. J. (2005). *Fundamentals of abnormal psychology* (4th ed.). New York: Worth.

Compton, W. C. (2005). *An introduction to positive psychology*. Belmont, CA: Cengage Learning/Wadsworth.

Conway, A. R. A., Cowan, N., & Bunting, M. F. (2001). The cocktail party phenomenon revisited. *Psychonomic Bulletin & Review, 8*(2), 331–335.

Conway, M. A., Cohen, G., & Stanhope, N. (1992). Very long-term memory for knowledge acquired at school and university. *Applied Cognitive Psychology, 6*(6), 467–482.

Conyne, R. K., & Clack, R. J. (1981). *Environmental assessment and design*. New York: Praeger.

Cooper, J., Bennett, E. A., & Sukel, H. L. (1996). Complex scientific testimony: How do jurors make decisions? *Law & Human Behavior, 20*(4), 379–394.

Cooper, J., Mirabile, R., & Scher, S. J. (2005). Actions and attitudes: The theory of cognitive dissonance. In T. C. Brock & M. C. Green (Eds.), *Persuasion: Psychological insights and perspectives* (2nd ed). Thousand Oaks, CA: Sage.

Cooper, M. J. (2005). Cognitive theory in anorexia nervosa and bulimia nervosa: Progress, development and future directions. *Clinical Psychology Review, 25*(4), 511–531.

Cooper, P. J., & Murray, L. (2001). The treatment and prevention of postpartum depression and associated disturbances in child development. *Archives of Women's Mental Health, 3*(Suppl 2), 5.

Cooper, R. P., Abraham, J., Berman, S., & Staska, M. (1997). The development of infants' preference for motherese. *Infant Behavior & Development, 20*(4), 477–488.

Corballis, M. C. (2002). *From hand to mouth: The origins of language*. Princeton, NJ: Princeton University Press.

Corbin, W. R., & Fromme, K. (2002). Alcohol use and serial monogamy as risks for sexually transmitted diseases in young adults. *Health Psychology, 21*(3), 229–236.

Coren, S. (1992). *The left-hander syndrome*. New York: Free Press.

Coren, S. (1996). *Sleep thieves*. New York: Free Press.

Coren, S., Ward, L. M., & Enns, J. T. (2004). *Sensation and perception* (6th ed.). New York: Wiley.

Corey, G. (2008). *Theory and practice of group counseling* (7th ed.). Belmont, CA: Cengage Learning/Wadsworth.

Corkin, S. (2002). What's new with the amnesic patient H.M.? *Nature Reviews Neuroscience, 3*, 153–160.

Cormier, J. F., & Thelen, M. H. (1998). Professional skepticism of multiple personality disorder. *Professional Psychology: Research and Practice, 29*(2), 163–167.

Correa-Chávez, M., Rogoff, B., & Arauz, R. M. (2005). Cultural patterns in attending to two events at once. *Child Development, 76*(3), 664–678.

Corrigan, P. W., & Penn, D. L. (1999). Lessons from social psychology on discrediting psychiatric stigma. *American Psychologist, 54*(9), 765–776.

Corrigan, P. W., & Watson, A. C. (2005). Findings from the National Comorbidity Survey on the frequency of violent behavior in individuals with psychiatric disorders. *Psychiatry Research, 136*(2–3), 153–162.

Corrigan, P. W., Watson, A. C., Gracia, G., Slopen, N., et al. (2005). Newspaper stories as measures of structural stigma. *Psychiatric Services, 56*(5), 551–556.

Corsini, R. J. (2001). *Handbook of innovative therapy* (2nd ed.). New York: Wiley.

Costa, Jr., P. T., & McCrae, R. R. (2006). Trait and factor theories. In J. C. Thomas, D. L. Segal, et al. (Eds.), *Comprehensive handbook of personality & psychopathology* (Vol. 1): *Personality and everyday functioning*. New York: Wiley.

Côté, J. E. (2006). Emerging adulthood as an institutionalized moratorium: Risks and benefits to identity formation. In J. J. Arnett & J. L. Tanner (Eds.), *Emerging adults in America: Coming of age in the 21st century*. Washington, DC: American Psychological Association.

Côté, J. E., & Levine, C. (2002). *Identity formation, agency, and culture*. Mahwah, NJ: Erlbaum.

Cote, S. (1999). Affect and performance in organizational settings. *Current Directions in Psychological Science, 8*(2), 65–68.

Coulton, C. J., Korbin, J. E., & Su, M. (1996). Measuring neighborhood context for young children in an urban area. *American Journal of Community Psychology, 24*(1), 5–32.

Coursey, R. D., Ward-Alexander, L., & Katz, B. (1990). Cost-effectiveness of providing insurance benefits for posthospital psychiatric halfway house stays. *American Psychologist, 45*(10), 1118–1126.

Court, J. H., & Court, P. C. (2001). Repression: R. I. P. *Australian Journal of Clinical & Experimental Hypnosis, 29*(1), 8–16.

Cowan, G., Heiple, B., Marquez, C., Khatchadourian, D., et al. (2005). Heterosexuals' attitudes toward hate crimes and hate speech against gays and lesbians: Old-fashioned and modern heterosexism. *Journal of Homosexuality, 49*(2), 67–82.

Cowan, N. (2001). The magical number 4 in short-term memory. *Behavioral & Brain Sciences, 24*(1), 87–185.

Cowan, N. (2005). *Working memory capacity*. Hove, UK: Psychology Press.

Cowden, C. R. (2005). Worry and its relationship to shyness. *North American Journal of Psychology, 7*(1), 59–69.

Cowles, J. T. (1937). Food tokens as incentives for learning by chimpanzees. *Comparative Psychology, Monograph, 14*(5, Whole no. 71).

Cox, R. H. (2007). *Sport psychology: Concepts and applications* (6th ed.). New York: McGraw-Hill.

Craig, L. (2006). Does father care mean fathers share?: A comparison of how mothers and fathers in intact families spend time with children. *Gender & Society, 20*(2), 259–281.

Craig, T. Y., & Kelly, J. R. (1999). Group cohesiveness and creative performance. *Group Dynamics, 3*(4), 243–256.

Craik, F. I. M. (1970). The fate of primary items in free recall. *Journal of Verbal Learning & Verbal Behavior, 9*, 143–148.

Craik, F. I. M., & Bialystok, E. (2005). Intelligence and executive control: Evidence from aging and bilingualism. *Cortex, 41*(2), 222–224.

Crano, W. D. (2000). Milestones in the psychological analysis of social influence. *Group Dynamics: Theory, Research, & Practice, 4*(1), 68–80.

Cravatt, B. F., Prospero-Garcia O., Siuzdak G., Gilula, N. B., et al. (1995). Chemical characterization of a family of brain lipids that induce sleep. *Science, 268*(5216), 1506–1509.

Crawley, S. B., & Sherrod, K. B. (1984). Parent–infant play during the first year of life. *Infant Behavior & Development, 7*, 65–75.

Crencavage, L. M., & Norcross, J. C. (1990). Where are the commonalities among the therapeutic common factors? *Professional Psychology: Research & Practice, 21*(5), 372–378.

Crisp, A., Gowers, S., Joughin, N., McClelland, L., et al. (2006). The enduring nature of anorexia nervosa. *European Eating Disorders Review, 14*(3), 147–152.

Cromdal, J. (1999). Childhood bilingualism and metalinguistic skills. *Applied Psycholinguistics, 20*(1), 1–20.

Crooks, R., & Baur, K. (2008). *Our sexuality* (10th ed.). Belmont, CA: Cengage Learning/Wadsworth.

Cropley, A. (2006). In praise of convergent thinking. *Creativity Research Journal, 18*, 391–404.

Crosby, R. A., & Yarber, W. L. (2001). Perceived versus actual knowledge about correct condom use among U.S. adolescents: results from a national study. *Journal of Adolescent Health, 28*(5), 415–420.

Crown, C. L., Feldstein, S., Jasnow, M. D., Beebe, B., et al. (2002). The cross-modal coordination of interpersonal timing. *Journal of Psycholinguistic Research, 31*(1), 1–23.

Crowther, J. H., Sanftner, J., Bonifazi, D. Z., & Shepherd, K. L. (2001). The role of daily hassles in binge eating. *International Journal of Eating Disorders, 29*, 449–454.

Csikszentmihalyi, M. (1997). *Creativity*. New York: HarperCollins.

Csikszentmihalyi, M. (1999). If we are so rich, why aren't we happy? *American Psychologist, 54*(10), 821–827.

Csikszentmihalyi, M., Abuhamdeh, S., Nakamura, J. (2005). Flow. In A. J. Elliot & C. S. Dweck (Eds.), *Handbook of competence and motivation*. New York: Guilford.

Cull, M. (2002). Treatment of intersex needs open discussion. *British Medical Journal, 324*(7342), 919.

Cull, W. L., Shaughnessy, J. J., & Zechmeister, E. B. (1996). Expanding understanding of the expanding-pattern-of-retrieval mnemonic. *Journal of Experimental Psychology: Applied, 2*(4) 365–378.

Cummings, M. R. (2006). *Human heredity: Principles and issues* (7th ed.). Belmont, CA: Cengage Learning/Wadsworth.

Cummins, D. D. (1995). *The other side of psychology*. New York: St. Martins.

Curci, A., & Luminet, O. (2006). Follow-up of a cross-national comparison on flashbulb and event memory for the September 11th attacks. *Memory, 14*(3), 329–344.

Czeisler, C. A., Duffy, J. F., Shanahan, T. L., Brown, E. N., et al. (1999). Stability, precision, and near-24-hour period of the human circadian pacemaker. *Science, 284*(5423), 2177–2181.

Czeisler, C. A., Richardson, G. S., Zimmerman, J. C., Moore-Ede, M. C., et al. (1981). Entrainment of human circadian rhythms by light-dark cycles: A reassessment. *Photochemistry, Photobiology, 34*, 239–247.

Dane, S., & Erzurumluoglu, A. (2003). Sex and handedness differences in eye-hand visual reaction times in handball players. *International Journal of Neuroscience, 113*(7), 923–929.

Daniels, H. (2005). Vygotsky and educational psychology: Some preliminary remarks. *Educational & Child Psychology, 22*(1), 6–17.

Danziger, N., Prkachin, K. M., & Willer, J.-C. (2006). Is pain the price of empathy? The perception of others' pain in patients with congenital insensitivity to pain. *Brain: A Journal of Neurology, 129*(9), 2494–2507.

Darley, J. M. (2000). Bystander phenomenon. In A. E. Kazdin (Ed.), *Encyclopedia of psychology* (Vol. 1). Washington, DC: American Psychological Association.

Darley, J. M., & Latané, B. (1968). Bystander intervention in emergencies: Diffusion of responsibility. *Journal of Personality & Social Psychology, 8,* 377–383.

Darling, C. A., Davidson, J. K., & Passarello, L. C. (1992). The mystique of first intercourse among college youth: The role of partners, contraceptive practices, and psychological reactions. *Journal of Youth & Adolescence, 21*(1), 97–117.

Darou, W. S. (1992). Native Canadians and intelligence testing. *Canadian Journal of Counselling, 26*(2), 96–99.

Daruna, J. H. (2004). *Introduction to psychoneuroimmunology.* Amsterdam: Elsevier.

Darwin, C. (1872). *The expression of emotion in man and animals.* Chicago: University of Chicago Press.

Das, J. P. (2000). Mental retardation. In A. Kazdin (Ed.), *Encyclopedia of psychology.* Washington, DC: American Psychological Association.

Dauvilliers, Y., Cervena, K, Carlander, B., Espa, F., et al. (2004). Dissociation in circadian rhythms in a pseudohypersomnia form of fatal familial insomnia. *Neurology, 63*(12), 2416–2418.

Davanloo, H. (1995). Intensive short-term dynamic psychotherapy. *International Journal of Short-Term Psychotherapy, 10*(3–4), 121–155.

Davidovitch, N., & Milgram, R. M. (2006). Creative thinking as a predictor of teacher effectiveness in higher education. *Creativity Research Journal, 18,* 385–390.

Davidson, P. R., & Parker, K. C. H. (2001). Eye movement desensitization and reprocessing (EMDR): A meta-analysis. *Journal of Consulting & Clinical Psychology, 69*(2), 305–316.

Davidson, R. J., Kabat-Zinn, J., Schumacher, J., Rosenkranz, M., et al. (2003). Alternations in brain and immune function produced by mindfulness meditation. *Psychosomatic Medicine, 65*(4), 564–570.

Davidson, T. L. (2000). Latent learning. In A. E. Kazdin (Ed.), *Encyclopedia of psychology* (Vol. 4). Washington, DC: American Psychological Association.

Davies, M., & McCartney, S. (2003). Effects of gender and sexuality on judgements of victim blame and rape myth acceptance in a depicted male rape. *Journal of Community & Applied Social Psychology, 13*(5), 391–398.

Davis, D., & Follette, W. C. (2002). Rethinking the probative value of evidence. *Law & Human Behavior, 26*(2), 133–158.

Davis, M. J., & Bibace, R. (1999). Dating couples and their relationships: Intimacy and contraceptive use. *Adolescence, 34*(133), 1–7.

Davis, M. R., McMahon, M., & Greenwood, K. M. (2005). The efficacy of mnemonic components of the cognitive interview: Towards a shortened variant for time-critical investigations. *Applied Cognitive Psychology, 19*(1), 75–93.

Davison, G. C., & Neale, J. M. (2006). *Abnormal psychology* (10th ed.). San Francisco: Jossey-Bass.

Dawson, G., & Toth, K. (2006). Autism spectrum disorders. In D. Cicchetti & D. J. Cohen (Eds.), *Developmental psychopathology* (Vol. 3): *Risk, disorder, and adaptation* (2nd ed.). Hoboken, NJ: Wiley.

de Jong, P. J., & Muris, P. (2002). Spider phobia. *Journal of Anxiety Disorders, 16*(1), 51–65.

de las Fuentes, C., & Vasquez, M. J. T. (1999). Immigrant adolescent girls of color. In N. G. Johnson, M. C. Roberts, et al. (Eds.), *Beyond appearance.* Washington, DC: American Psychological Association.

de Leon, C. F. M. (2005). Social engagement and successful aging. *European Journal of Ageing, 2*(1), 64–66.

de Mello, M. F., de Jesus Mari, J., Bacaltchuk, J., Verdeli, H., et al. (2005). A systematic review of research findings on the efficacy of interpersonal therapy for depressive disorders. *European Archives of Psychiatry & Clinical Neuroscience, 255*(2), 75–82.

de Rios, M. D., & Grob, C. S. (2005). Editors' introduction: Ayahuasca use in cross-cultural perspective. *Journal of Psychoactive Drugs, 37*(2), 119–121.

DeArmond, S., Tye, M., Chen, P. Y., Krauss, A., et al. (2006). Age and gender stereotypes: New challenges in a changing workplace and workforce. *Journal of Applied Social Psychology, 36*(9), 2184–2214.

Deaux, K., & Emswiller, T. (1974). Explanation of successful performance on sex-linked tasks: What is skill for the male is luck for the female. *Journal of Personality & Social Psychology, 29,* 80–85.

Deckers, L. (2005). *Motivation: Biological, psychological, and environmental* (2nd ed.). Boston: Allyn & Bacon.

Deckro, G. R., Ballinger, K. M., Hoyt, M., Wilcher, M., et al. (2002). The evaluation of a mind/body intervention to reduce psychological distress and perceived stress in college students. *Journal of American College Health, 50*(6), 281–287.

Deeb, S. S. (2004). Molecular genetics of color-vision deficiencies. *Visual Neuroscience, 21*(3), 191–196.

DeGaetano, G. (2005). The impact of media violence on developing minds and hearts. In S. Olfman (Ed.), *Childhood lost: How American culture is failing our kids.* Westport, CT: Praeger Publishers.

Dein, S., & Littlewood, R. (2005). Apocalyptic suicide: From a pathological to an eschatological interpretation. *International Journal of Social Psychiatry, 51*(3), 198–210.

Deinzer, R., Kleineidam, C., Stiller-Winkler, R., Idel, H., et al. (2000). Prolonged reduction of salivary immunoglobulin A (sIgA) after a major academic exam. *International Journal of Psychophysiology, 37,* 219–232.

Delgado, B. M., & Ford, L. (1998). Parental perceptions of child development among low-income Mexican American families. *Journal of Child & Family Studies, 7*(4), 469–481.

Delpero, W. T., O'Neill, H., Casson, E., & Hovis, J. (2005). Aviation-relevent epidemiology of color vision deficiency. *Aviation, Space, & Environmental Medicine, 76*(2), 127–133.

Demos, J. N. (2005). *Getting started with neurofeedback.* New York: Norton.

Denmark, F. L., Rabinowitz, V. C., & Sechzer, J. A. (2005). *Engendering psychology: Women and gender revisited* (2nd ed.). Boston: Allyn & Bacon.

Denollet, J., & Van Heck, G. L. (2001). Psychological risk factors in heart disease. *Journal of Psychosomatic Research, 51*(3), 465–468.

Derlega, V. J., Winstead, B. A., & Jones, W. H. (2005). *Personality: Contemporary theory and research* (3rd ed.). Belmont, CA: Cengage Learning/Wadsworth.

Deutsch, M. (1993). Educating for a peaceful world. *American Psychologist, 48*(5), 510–517.

Devine, D. J., Clayton, L. D., Dunford, B.B., Seying, R., et al. (2001). Jury decision making: 45 years of empirical research on deliberating groups. *Psychology, Public Policy, & Law, 7*(3), 622–727.

Devine, P. G., Monteith, M. J., Zuerink, J. R., & Elliot, A. J. (1991). Prejudice with and without compunction. *Journal of Personality & Social Psychology, 60*(6), 817–830.

Devlin, B., Daniels, M., & Roeder, K. (1997). The heritability of IQ. *Nature, 388*(6641), 468–471.

Devoto, A., Lucidi, F., Violani, C., & Bertini, M. (1999). Effects of different sleep reductions on daytime sleepiness. *Sleep, 22*(3), 336–343.

Di Forti, M., Lappin, J. M., & Murray, R. M. (2007). Risk factors for schizophrenia: All roads lead to dopamine. *European Neuropsychopharmacology, 17*(Suppl 2), S101–S107.

Di Marzo, V., Goparaju, S. K., Wang, L., Liu, J., et al. (2001). Leptin-regulated endocannabinoids are involved in maintaining food intake. *Nature, 410*(6830), 822–825.

Diamond, L. M. (1998). Development of sexual orientation among adolescent and young adult women. *Developmental Psychology, 34*(5), 1085–1095.

Diano, S., Farr, S. A., Benoit, S. C., McNay, E. C., et al. (2006). Ghrelin controls hippocampal spine synapse density and memory performance. *Nature Neuroscience, 9,* 381–388.

Dickens, W. T., & Flynn, J. R. (2001). Heritability estimates versus large environmental effects: The IQ paradox resolved. *Psychological Review, 108,* 346–369.

Dickerson, F. B., Tenhula, W. N., & Green-Paden, L. D. (2005). The token economy for schizophrenia: Review of the literature and recommendations for future research. *Schizophrenia Research, 75*(2–3), 405–416.

Dickinson, D. K., & Tabors, P. O. (Eds.). (2001). *Beginning literacy with language.* Baltimore: Paul H. Brookes.

Dick-Niederhauser, A., & Silverman, W. K. (2006). Separation anxiety disorder. In J. E. Fisher & W. T. O'Donohue (Eds.), *Practitioner's guide to evidence-based psychotherapy.* New York: Springer.

Dierdorff, E. C., & Wilson, M. A. (2003). A meta-analysis of job analysis reliability. *Journal of Applied Psychology, 88*(4), 635–646.

Dieterich, S. E., Assel, M. A., Swank, P., Smith, K. E., et al. (2006). The impact of early maternal verbal scaffolding and child language abilities on later decoding and reading comprehension skills. *Journal of School Psychology, 43*(6), 481–494.

Dinan, T. G. (2001). Stress, depression and cardiovascular disease. *Stress & Health: Journal of the International Society for the Investigation of Stress, 17*(2), 65–66.

Dingus, T. A., Klauer, S. G., Neale, V. L., Petersen, A., et al. (2006). The 100-Car Naturalistic Driving Study, Phase II—results of the 100-car field experiment. *National Highway Traffic Safety Administration Report No. DOT HS 810 593.* Retrieved May 18, 2007, from http://www-nrd.nhtsa.dot.gov/departments/nrd-13/driver-distraction/PDF/100CarMain.pdf.

Dinkmeyer, D., Sr., McKay, G. D., & Dinkmeyer, D., Jr. (1997). *The parent's handbook.* Circle Pines, MN: American Guidance Service.

Dion, K. L. (2003). Prejudice, racism, and discrimination. In T. Millon & M. J. Lerner (Eds.), *Personality and social psychology: The comprehensive handbook of psychology* (Vol. 5). New York: Wiley.

Dirkzwager, A. J. E., Bramsen, I., & Van Der Ploeg, H. M. (2001). The longitudinal course of post-traumatic stress disorder symptoms among aging military veterans. *Journal of Nervous & Mental Disease, 189*(12), 846–853.

Distin, K. (2006). *Gifted children: A guide for parents and professionals.* London: Jessica Kingsley Publishers.

Dixon, M. J., Smilek, D., & Merikle, P. M. (2004). Not all synaesthetes are created equal: Projector versus associator synaesthetes. *Cognitive, Affective, & Behavioral Neuroscience, 4*(3), 335–343.

Dobelle, W. H. (2000). Artificial vision for the blind by connecting a television camera to the visual cortex. *American Society of Artificial Internal Organs, 46,* 3–9.

Dobson, K. S., Backs-Dermott, G. J., & Dozois, D. J. A. (2000). Cognitive and cognitive-behavioral therapies. In C. R. Snyder & R. E. Ingram (Eds.), *Handbook of psychological change: Psychotherapy processes and practices for the 21st century.* New York: Wiley.

Dodds, P. S., Muhamad, R., & Watts, D. J. (2003). An experimental study of search in global social networks. *Science, 301*(5634), 827–829.

Doidge, N. (1997). Empirical evidence for the efficacy of psychoanalytic psychotherapies and psychoanalysis. *Psychoanalytic Inquiry,* (Suppl.), 102–150.

Dollard, J., & Miller, N. E. (1950). *Personality and psychotherapy: An analysis in terms of learning, thinking and culture.* New York: McGraw-Hill.

Domhoff, W. (2003). *The scientific study of dreams: Neural networks, cognitive development, and content analysis.* Washington, DC: American Psychological Association.

Domingo, R. A., & Goldstein-Alpern, N. (1999). "What dis?" and other toddler-initiated, expressive language-learning strategies. *Infant-Toddler Intervention, 9*(1), 39–60.

Domjan, M. (2006). *The principles of learning and behavior* (5th ed.). Belmont, CA: Cengage Learning/Wadsworth.

Donate-Bartfield, E., & Passman, R. H. (2004). Relations between children's attachments to their mothers and to security blankets. *Journal of Family Psychology, 18*(3), 453–458.

Dooling, D. J., & Lachman, R. (1971). Effects of comprehension on retention of prose. *Journal of Experimental Psychology, 88,* 216–222.

Doran, S. M., Van Dongen, H. P., & Dinges, D. F. (2001). Sustained attention performance during sleep deprivation. *Archives of Italian Biology, 139,* 253–267.

Dorman, M. F., & Wilson, B. S. (2004). The design and function of cochlear implants. *American Scientist, 92*(Sept.–Oct.), 436–445.

Dosher, B. A., & Ma, J. (1998). Output loss or rehearsal loop? *Journal of Experimental Psychology: Learning, Memory, & Cognition, 24*(2), 316–335.

Dougall, A. L., & Baum, A. (2003). Stress, coping, and immune function. In M. Gallagher & R. J. Nelson (Eds.), *Handbook of psychology: Biological psychology* (Vol. 3). New York: John Wiley.

Dougherty, D. D., Baer, L., Cosgrove, G. R., Cassem, E. H., et al. (2002). Prospective long-term follow-up of 44 patients who received cingulotomy for treatment-refractory obsessive-compulsive disorder. *American Journal of Psychiatry, 159*(2), 269–275.

Douvan, E. (1997). Erik Erikson: Critical times, critical theory. *Child Psychiatry & Human Development, 28*(1), 15–21.

Dovidio, J. F., & Gaertner, S. L. (1999). Reducing prejudice: Combating intergroup biases. *Current Directions in Psychological Science, 8*(4), 101–105.

Dovidio, J. F., & Penner, L. A. (2001). Helping and altruism. In M. Hewstone & M. Brewer (Eds.), *Handbook of social psychology.* London: Blackwell.

Dovidio, J. F., Gaertner, S. L., Kawakami, K., & Hodson, G. (2002). Why can't we just get along? *Cultural Diversity and Ethnic Minority Psychology, 8*(2), 88–102.

Dovidio, J. F., Glick, P., & Rudman, L. A. (Eds.). (2005). *On the nature of prejudice: Fifty years after Allport.* Malden, MA: Blackwell.

Dovidio, J. F., Piliavin, J. A., Schroeder, D. A., & Penner, L. A. (2006). *The social psychology of prosocial behavior.* Mahwah, NJ: Erlbaum.

Dowling, K. W. (2005). The effect of lunar phases on domestic violence incident rates. *Forensic Examiner, 14*(4), 13–18.

Dozois, D. J. A., & Dobson, K. S. (2002). Depression. In M. M. Antony & D. H. Barlow (Eds.), *Handbook of assessment and treatment planning for psychological disorders.* New York: Guilford.

Dozois, D. J. A., & Dobson, K. S. (Eds.). (2004). *The prevention of anxiety and depression: Theory, research, and practice.* Washington, DC: American Psychological Association.

Draguns, J. G., Gielen, U. P., & Fish, J. M. (2004). Approaches to culture, healing, and psychotherapy. In U. P. Gielen, J. M. Fish, et al. (Eds.), *Handbook of culture, therapy, and healing.* Mahwah, NJ: Erlbaum.

Drigotas, S. M., Rusbult, C. E., Wieselquist, J., & Whitton, S. W. (1999). Close partner as sculptor of the ideal self: Behavioral affirmation and the Michelangelo phenomenon. *Journal of Personality & Social Psychology, 77*(2), 293–323.

Driver, J. L., & Gottman, J. M. (2004). Daily marital interactions and positive affect during marital conflict among newlywed couples. *Family Process, 43*(3), 301–314.

Drolet, G., Dumont, E. C., Gosselin, I., Kinkead, R., et al. (2001). Role of endogenous opioid system in the regulation of the stress response. *Progress in Neuro-Psychopharmacology & Biological Psychiatry, 25*(4), 729–741.

Drucker, P. (1993). *Post-capitalist society.* New York: HarperCollins.

Druckman, D., & Bjork, R. A. (1994). *Learning, remembering, believing: Enhancing human performance.* Washington, DC: National Academy Press.

DSM-IV-TR: Diagnostic and statistical manual of mental disorders (5th ed.). (2000). Washington, DC: American Psychiatric Association.

Duclos, S. E., & Laird, J. D. (2001). The deliberate control of emotional experience through control of expressions. *Cognition & Emotion, 15,* 27–56.

Duffy, J. F., & Wright, Jr., K. P. (2005). Entrainment of the human circadian system by light. *Journal of Biological Rhythms, 20*(4), 326–338.

Dulewicz, V., & Higgs, M. (2000). Emotional intelligence. *Journal of Managerial Psychology, 15*(4), 341–372.

Duncan, J. (2005). Frontal lobe function and general intelligence: Why it matters. *Cortex, 41*(2), 215–217.

Duncker, K. (1945). On problem solving. *Psychological Monographs, 58*(270).

Durand, V. M., & Barlow, D. H. (2006). *Essentials of abnormal psychology* (4th ed.). Belmont, CA: Cengage Learning/Wadsworth.

Durham, M. D., & Dane, F. C. (1999). Juror knowledge of eyewitness behavior. *Journal of Social Behavior & Personality, 14*(2), 299–308.

Durrant, J. E., & Janson, S. (2005). Legal reform, corporal punishment and child abuse: The case of Sweden. *International Review of Victimology, 12,* 139–158.

Dutta, T., & Mandal, M. K. (2005). The relationship of handedness and accidents: A meta-analytical review of findings. *Psychological Studies, 50*(4), 309–316.

Dutton, D. G., & Aron, A. P. (1974). Some evidence for heightened sexual attraction under conditions of high anxiety. *Journal of Personality & Social Psychology, 30,* 510–517.

Dwyer, W. O., Leeming, F. C., Cobern, M. K., Porter, B. E., et al. (1993). Critical review of behavioral interventions to preserve the environment. *Environment and Behavior, 25*(3), 275–321.

Dyer, K. A. (2001). Dealing with death and dying in medical education and practice. Retrieved May 24, 2007, from http://dying.about.com/gi/dynamic/offsite.htm?zi=1/XJ&sdn=dying&cdn=health&tm=176&f=10&su=p247.2.140.ip_p726.2.152.ip_p284.8.150.ip_&tt=2&bt=0&bts=0&zu=http%3A//www.journeyofhearts.org/jofh/kirstimd/AMSA/mywish.htm.

Dywan, J., & Bowers, K. S. (1983). The use of hypnosis to enhance recall. *Science, 222,* 184–185.

Dzokoto, V. A., & Adams, G. (2005). Understanding genital-shrinking epidemics in West Africa: Koro, juju, or mass psychogenic illness? *Culture, Medicine & Psychiatry, 29*(1), 53–78.

Eagly, A. H. (2000). Gender roles. In A. Kazdin (Ed.), *Encyclopedia of psychology.* Washington, DC: American Psychological Association.

Eagly, A. H. (2001). Social role theory of sex differences and similarities. In J. Worell (Ed.), *Encyclopedia of women and gender.* San Diego: Academic Press.

Eagly, A. H. (2007). Female leadership advantage and disadvantage: Resolving the contradictions. *Psychology of Women Quarterly, 31*(1), 1–12.

Eagly, A. H., & Karau, S. J. (2002). Role congruity theory of prejudice toward female leaders. *Psychological Review, 109*(3), 573–598.

Ebbinghaus, H. (1885). *Memory: A contribution to experimental psychology.* Translated by H. A. Ruger & C. E. Bussenius, 1913. New York: New York Teacher's College, Columbia University.

Eckerman, D. A. (1999). Scheduling reinforcement about once a day. *Behavioural Processes, 45*(1–3), 101–114.

Eddy, K. T., Dutra, L., Bradley, R., & Westen, D. (2004). A multidimensional meta-analysis of psychotherapy and pharmacotherapy for obsessive-compulsive disorder. *Clinical Psychology Review, 24*(8), 1011–1030.

Eichenbaum, H., & Fortin, N. J. (2005). Bridging the gap between brain and behavior: Cognitive and neural mechanisms of episodic memory. *Journal of the Experimental Analysis of Behavior, 84*(3), 619–629.

Eidelson, R. J., & Eidelson, J. I. (2003). Dangerous ideas. *American Psychologist, 58*(3), 182–192.

Eifert, G. H., & Lejuez, C. W. (2000). Aversion therapy. In A. E. Kazdin (Ed.), *Encyclopedia of psychology*. Washington, DC: American Psychological Association.

Eimas, P. D., Quinn, P. C., & Cowan, P. (1994). Development of exclusivity in perceptually based categories of young infants. *Journal of Experimental Child Psychology, 58*(3), 418–431.

Eisenberg, N., Valiente, C., Fabes, R. A., Smith, C. L., et al. (2003). The relations of effortful control and ego control to children's resiliency and social functioning. *Developmental Psychology, 39*(4), 761–776.

Eisler, I., Simic, M., Russell, G. F. M., & Dare, C. (2007). A randomised controlled treatment trial of two forms of family therapy in adolescent anorexia nervosa: A five-year follow-up. *Journal of Child Psychology & Psychiatry, 48*(6), 552–560.

Eisler, J. A., Justice, Jr., J. B., & Neill, D. B. (2004). Individual differences in reward sensitivity: Implications for psychostimulant abuse vulnerability. *North American Journal of Psychology, 6*(3), 527–544.

Ekman, P. (1993). Facial expression and emotion. *American Psychologist, 48*(4), 384–392.

Ekman, P., Levenson, R. W., & Friesen, W. V. (1983). Autonomic nervous system activity distinguishes among emotions. *Science, 223,* 1208–1210.

Elder, P. (2006). *Critical thinking: Learn the tools the best thinkers use.* Englewood Cliffs, NJ: Prentice-Hall.

Eliot, L. (1999). *What's going on in there?* New York: Bantam.

Elli, K. A., & Nathan, P. J. (2001). The pharmacology of human working memory. *International Journal of Neuropsychopharmacology, 4*(3), 299–313.

Ellickson, P. L., Martino, S. C., & Collins, R. L. (2004). Marijuana use from adolescence to young adulthood. *Health Psychology, 23*(3), 299–307.

Elliott, M., & Williams, D. (2003). The client experience of counselling and psychotherapy. *Counselling Psychology Review, 18*(1), 34–38.

Elliott, M., Browne, K., & Kilcoyne, J. (1995). Child sexual abuse prevention: What offenders tell us. *Child Abuse & Neglect, 19*(5), 579–594.

Ellis, A. (1979). The practice of rational-emotive therapy. In A. Ellis & J. Whiteley (Eds.), *Theoretical and empirical foundations of rational-emotive therapy.* Monterey, CA: Brooks/Cole.

Ellis, A. (1995). Changing rational-emotive therapy (RET) to rational emotive behavior therapy (REBT). *Journal of Rational-Emotive & Cognitive Behavior Therapy, 13*(2), 85–89.

Ellis, A. (2004). Why rational emotive behavior therapy is the most comprehensive and effective form of behavior therapy. *Journal of Rational-Emotive & Cognitive Behavior Therapy, 22*(2), 85–92.

Ellis, P. J., West, B. J., Ryan, A. M., & Deshon, R. P. (2002). The use of impression management tactics in structured interviews: A function of question type. *Journal of Applied Psychology, 87,* 1200–1208.

Elovainio, M., Kivimaeki, M., Steen, N., & Kalliomaeki-Levanto, T. (2000). Organizational and individual factors affecting mental health and job satisfaction. *Journal of Occupational Health Psychology, 5*(2) 269–277.

Emmorey, K., Grabowski, T., McCullough, S., Damasio, H., et al. (2003). Neural systems underlying lexical retrieval for sign language. *Neuropsychologia, 41*(1), 85–95.

Emurian, H. H. (2005). Web-based programmed instruction: Evidence of rule-governed learning. *Computers in Human Behavior, 21*(6), 893–915.

Engle, D. E., & Arkowitz, H. (2006). *Ambivalence in psychotherapy: Facilitating readiness to change.* New York: Guilford.

Enns, J. T., & Coren, S. (1995). The box alignment illusion. *Perception & Psychophysics, 57*(8), 1163–1174.

Enns, M. W., Cox, B. J., & Clara, I. P. (2005). Perfectionism and neuroticism: A longitudinal study of specific vulnerability and diathesis-stress models. *Cognitive Therapy & Research, 29*(4), 463–478.

Erickson, C. D., & Al-Timimi, N. R. (2001). Providing mental health services to Arab Americans. *Cultural Diversity & Ethnic Minority Psychology, 7*(4), 308–327.

Ericsson, K. A. (2000). How experts attain and maintain superior performance. *Journal of Aging & Physical Activity, 8*(4), 366–372.

Ericsson, K. A., & Charness, N. (1994). Expert performance. *American Psychologist, 49*(8), 725–747.

Ericsson, K. A., & Chase, W. G. (1982). Exceptional memory. *American Scientist, 70,* 607–615.

Ericsson, K. A., Delaney, P. F., Weaver, G., & Mahadevan, R. (2004). Uncovering the structure of a memorist's superior "basic" memory capacity. *Cognitive Psychology, 49*(3), 191–237.

Erikson, E. H. (1963). *Childhood and society.* New York: Norton.

Erlacher, D., & Schredl, M. (2004). Dreams reflecting waking sport activities: A comparison of sport and psychology students. *International Journal of Sport Psychology, 35*(4), 301–308.

Erlich, P. R., & Erlich, A. H. (1990). The population explosion. *The Amicus Journal,* Winter, 18–29.

Ernst, E. (1994). Is acupuncture effective for pain control? *Journal of Pain & Symptom Management, 9*(2), 72–74.

Eron, L. D. (1987). The development of aggressive behavior from the perspective of a developing behaviorism. *American Psychologist, 42,* 435–442.

Eschholz, S., Chiricos, T., & Gertz, M. (2003). Television and fear of crime: Program types, audience traits, and the mediating effect of perceived neighborhood racial composition. *Social Problems, 50*(3), 395–415.

Espie, C. A. (2002). Insomnia. *Annual Review of Psychology, 53,* 215–243.

Esterling, B. A., L'Abate, L., Murray, E. J., & Pennebaker, J. W. (1999). Empirical foundations for writing in prevention and psychotherapy: Mental and physical health outcomes. *Clinical Psychology Review, 19*(1), 79–96.

Ethier, K. A., Kershaw, T., Niccolai, L., Lewis, J. B., et al. (2003). Adolescent women underestimate their susceptibility to sexually transmitted infections. *Sexually Transmitted Infections, 79,* 408–411.

Evans, G. W. (2006). Child development and the physical environment. *Annual Review of Psychology, 57,* 423–451.

Evans, G. W., Lercher, P., & Kofler, W. W. (2002). Crowding and children's mental health: the role of house type. *Journal of Environmental Psychology, 22,* 221–231.

Evans, G.W., Lepore, S. J., & Schroeder, A. (1996). The role of interior design elements in human responses to crowding. *Journal of Personality & Social Psychology, 70*(1), 41–46.

Evans, G. W., & Wener, R. E. (2007). Crowding and personal space invasion on the train: Please don't make me sit in the middle. *Journal of Environmental Psychology, 27*(1), 90–94.

Everly, G. S. (2002). Thoughts on peer (paraprofessional) support in the provision of mental health services. *International Journal of Emergency Mental Health, 4*(2), 89–92.

Ewen, R. B. (2003). *An introduction to theories of personality* (6th ed.). Mahwah, NJ: Erlbaum.

Ewing, G. (2001). Altruistic, egoistic, and normative effects on curbside recycling. *Environment & Behavior, 33*(6), 733–764.

Eysenck, H. J. (1994). The outcome problem in psychotherapy: What have we learned? *Behaviour Research & Therapy, 32*(5), 477–495.

Eysenck, H. J. (Ed.). (1981). *A model for personality.* New York: Springer-Verlag.

Fabrega, H., Jr. (2004). Culture and the origins of psychopathology. In U. P. Gielen, J. M., Fish, et al. (Eds.), *Handbook of culture, therapy, and healing.* Mahwah, NJ: Erlbaum.

Fagan, J. F., & Holland, C. R. (2007). Racial equality in intelligence: Predictions from a theory of intelligence as processing. *Intelligence, 35*(4), 319–334.

Fahim, C., Stip, E., Mancini-Marïe, A., Mensour, B., et al. (2005). Brain activity during emotionally negative pictures in schizophrenia with and without flat affect: An fMRI study. *Psychiatry Research: Neuroimaging, 140*(1), 1–15.

Fahle, M., & Poggio, T. (Eds.). (2002). *Perceptual learning.* Cambridge, MA: MIT Press.

Fain, G. L. (2003). *Sensory transduction.* Sunderland, MA: Sinauer.

Faith, M. S., Wong, F. Y., & Carpenter, K. M. (1995). Group sensitivity training: Update, meta-analysis, and recommendations. *Journal of Counseling Psychology, 42*(3), 390–399.

Falkowski, C. (2000). *Dangerous drugs.* Center City, MN: Hazelden Information Education.

Farah, M. J. (2004). *Visual agnosia* (2nd ed.). Cambridge, MA: MIT Press.

Farah, M. J. (2006). Prosopagnosia. In M. J. Farah & T. E. Feinberg (Eds.), *Patient-based approaches to cognitive neuroscience* (2nd ed.). Cambridge, MA: MIT Press.

Farrimond, T. (1990). Effect of alcohol on visual constancy values and possible relation to driving performance. *Perceptual & Motor Skills, 70*(1), 291–295.

Farroni, T., Massaccesi, S., Pividori, D., & Johnson, M. H. (2004). Gaze following in newborns. *Infancy, 5*(1), 39–60.

FBI (2005). *Crime in the United States, 2005.* Washington, DC: Federal Bureau of Investigation. Retrieved September 3, 2007, from http://www.fbi.gov/ucr/05cius/.

Feingold, A. (1992). Gender differences in mate selection preferences. *Psychological Bulletin, 111,* 304–341.

Feldhusen, J. F., & Goh, B. E. (1995). Assessing and accessing creativity: An integrative review of theory, research, and development. *Creativity Research Journal, 8*(3), 231–247.

Feldman, D. H. (2004). Piaget's stages: The unfinished symphony of cognitive development. *New*

Ideas in Psychology, 22(3), 175–231.
Feldman, S. (2003). Enforcing social conformity: A theory of authoritarianism. *Political Psychology, 24*(1), 41–47.
Fellous, J.-M., & Ledoux, J. E. (2005). Toward basic principles for emotional processing: What the fearful brain tells the robot. In J.-M. Fellous & M. A. Arbib (Eds.), *Who needs emotions? The brain meets the robot.* New York: Oxford University Press.
Fenn, K. M., Nusbaum, H. C., & Margoliash, D. (2003). Consolidation during sleep of perceptual learning of spoken language. *Nature, 425*(6958), 614–616.
Fenton, G. W. (1998). Neurosurgery for mental disorder. *Irish Journal of Psychological Medicine, 15*(2), 45–48.
Fernald, A. (1989). Intonation and communicative intent in mothers' speech to infants: Is the melody the message? *Child Development, 60*(6), 1497–1510.
Fernald, A., Perfors, A., & Marchman, V. A. (2006). Picking up speed in understanding: Speech processing efficiency and vocabulary growth across the 2nd year. *Developmental Psychology, 42*(1), 98–116.
Féron, F., Perry, C., Cochrane, J., Licina, P., et al. (2005). Autologous olfactory ensheathing cell transplantation in human spinal cord injury. *Brain: A Journal of Neurology, 128*(12), 2951–2960.
Ferrari, J. R., & Scher, S. J. (2000). Toward an understanding of academic and nonacademic tasks procrastinated by students: The use of daily logs. *Psychology in the Schools, 37*(4), 359–366.
Festinger, L. (1957). *A theory of cognitive dissonance.* Stanford, CA: Stanford University Press.
Festinger, L., & Carlsmith, J. M. (1959). Cognitive consequences of forced compliance. *Journal of Abnormal & Social Psychology, 58,* 203–210.
Field, C. E., Nash, H. M., Handwerk, M. L., & Friman, P. C. (2004). A modification of the token economy for nonresponsive youth in family-style residential care. *Behavior Modification, 28*(3), 438–457.
Fields, R. M., & Margolin, J. (2001). *Coping with trauma.* Washington, DC: American Psychological Association.
Figueredo, A. J., Sefcek, J. A., & Jones, D. N. (2006). The ideal romantic partner personality. *Personality & Individual Differences, 41*(3), 431–441.
Fink, M. (2000). Electroshock revisited. *American Scientist, 88*(March–April), 162–167.
Fink, M., & Taylor, M. A. (2003). *Catatonia: A clinician's guide to diagnosis and treatment.* London: Cambridge University Press.
Fiorina, C. (2006). *Tough choices: A memoir.* New York: Penguin.
First, M. B., & Pincus, H. A. (2002). The DSM-IV text revision: Rationale and potential impact on clinical practice. *Psychiatric Services, 53,* 288–292.
Fischer, A. H., Manstead, A. S. R., Rodriquez Mosquera, P. M., & van Vianen, A. E. M. (2004). Gender and culture differences in emotion. *Emotion, 4*(1), 87–94.
Fisher, B. S., Cullen, F. T., & Daigle, L. E. (2005). The discovery of acquaintance rape: The salience of methodological innovation and rigor. *Journal of Interpersonal Violence, 20*(4), 493–500.
Fisher, R. P., & Geiselman, R. E. (1987). Enhancing eyewitness memory with the cognitive interview. In M. M. Gruneberg, P. E. Morris, et al. (Eds.), *Practical aspects of memory: Current research and issues.* Chinchester, UK: Wiley.
Fisher, S. (1973). *The female orgasm.* New York: Basic.
Fisher, S., & Greenberg, R. P. (1996). *Freud scientifically reappraised.* New York: Wiley.
Fiske, S. T. (1993). Social cognition and social perception. *Annual Review of Psychology, 44,* 155–194.
Fiske, S. T., Cuddy, A. J. C., Glick, P., & Xu, J. (2002). A model of (often mixed) stereotype content. *Journal of Personality & Social Psychology, 82*(6), 878–902.
Flanagan, M. B., May, J. G., & Dobie, T. G. (2004). The role of vection, eye movement, and postural instability in the etiology of motion sickness. *Journal of Vestibular Research: Equilibrium & Orientation, 14*(4), 335–346.
Flannery, D. J., Rowe, D. C., & Gulley, B. L. (1993). Impact of pubertal status, timing, and age on adolescent sexual experience and delinquency. *Journal of Adolescent Research, 8*(1), 21–40.
Flavell, J. H. (1992). Cognitive development: Past, present, and future. *Developmental Psychology, 28*(6), 998–1005.
Fleming, J. (1974). Field report: The state of the apes. *Psychology Today,* Jan., 46.
Flowe, H. D., & Ebbese, E. B. (2007). The effect of lineup member similarity on recognition accuracy in simultaneous and sequential lineups. *Law & Human Behavior, 31*(1), 33–52.
Fobair, P. (1997). Cancer support groups and group therapies. *Journal of Psychosocial Oncology, 15*(3–4), 123–147.
Fochtmann, L. J. (1995). Intractable sneezing as a conversion symptom. *Psychosomatics, 36*(2), 103–112.
Fogel, S. M., Nader, R., Cote, K. A., & Smith, C. T. (2007). Sleep spindles and learning potential. *Behavioral Neuroscience, 121*(1), 1–10.
Folkman, S., & Moskowitz, J. T. (2004). Coping. *Annual Review of Psychology, 55,* 745–774.
Follett, K., & Hess, T. M. (2002). Aging, cognitive complexity, and the fundamental attribution error. *Journals of Gerontology: Series B: Psychological Sciences and Social Sciences, 57B*(4), 312–323.
Fontaine, K. R., Redden, D. T., Wang, C., Westfall, A. O., et al. (2003). Years of life lost due to obesity. *Journal of the American Medical Association, 289,* 187–193.
Fontenelle, D. H. (1989). *How to live with your children.* Tucson, AZ: Fisher Books.
Foo, P., Warren, W. H., Duchon, A., & Tarr, M. J. (2005). Do humans integrate routes into a cognitive map? Map- versus landmark-based navigation of novel shortcuts. *Journal of Experimental Psychology: Learning, Memory, & Cognition, 31*(2), 195–215.
Foot, M., & Koszycki, D. (2004). Gender differences in anxiety-related traits in patients with panic disorder. *Depression & Anxiety, 20*(3), 123–130.
Forbes, G. B., Adams-Curtis, L. E., & White, K. B. (2004). First- and second-generation measures of sexism, rape myths and related beliefs, and hostility toward women: Their interrelationships and association with college students' experiences with dating aggression and sexual coercion. *Violence Against Women, 10*(3), 236–261.
Ford, D. Y., & Moore, J. L. (2006). Being gifted and adolescent: Issues and needs of students of color. In F. A. Dixon & S. M. Moon (Eds.), *The handbook of secondary gifted education.* Waco, TX: Prufrock Press.
Ford, G. G., Gallagher, S. H., Lacy, B. A., Bridwell, A. M., et al. (1999). Repositioning the home plate umpire to provide enhanced perceptual cues and more accurate ball-strike judgments. *Journal of Sport Behavior, 22*(1), 28–44.
Forney, W. S., Forney, J. C., & Crutsinger, C. (2005). Developmental stages of age and moral reasoning as predictors of juvenile delinquents' behavioral intention to steal clothing. *Family & Consumer Sciences Research Journal, 34*(2), 110–126.
ForsterLee, R., ForsterLee, L., Horowitz, I. A., & King, E. (2006). The effects of defendant race, victim race, and juror gender on evidence processing in a murder trial. *Behavioral Sciences & the Law, 24*(2), 179–198.
Forsyth, D. R. (2006). *Group dynamics* (4th ed.). Belmont, CA: Cengage Learning/Wadsworth.
Forsyth, J. P., & Savsevitz, J. (2002). Behavior therapy: Historical perspective and overview. In M. Hersen & W. H. Sledge (Eds.), *Encyclopedia of psychotherapy.* San Diego: Academic Press.
Fosse, R., Stickgold, R., & Hobson, J. A. (2001). The mind in REM sleep: Reports of emotional experience. *Sleep: Journal of Sleep & Sleep Disorders Research, 24*(8), 947–955.
Foster, C. A., Witcher, B. S., Campbell, W. K., & Green, J. D. (1998). Arousal and attraction. *Journal of Personality & Social Psychology, 74*(1), 86–101.
Foster, G., & Ysseldyke, J. (1976). Expectancy and halo effects as a result of artificially induced teacher bias. *Contemporary Educational Psychology, 1,* 37–45.
Fowers, B. J., & Davidov, B. J. (2006). The virtue of multiculturalism: Personal transformation, character, and openness to the other. *American Psychologist, 61*(6), 581–594.
Fowers, B. J., & Davidov, B. J. (2006). The virtue of multiculturalism: Personal transformation, character, and openness to the other. *American Psychologist, 61*(6), 581–594.
Fowers, B. J., & Richardson, F. C. (1996). Why is multiculturalism good? *American Psychologist, 51*(6), 609–621.
Foxhall, K. (2000). Suddenly, a big impact on criminal justice. *APA Monitor, Jan.,* 36–37.
Frank, J. D., & Frank, J. (2004). Therapeutic components shared by all psychotherapies. In A. Freeman, M. J. Mahoney, et al. (Eds.), *Cognition and psychotherapy* (2nd ed.). New York: Springer.
Franken, R. E. (2007). *Human motivation* (6th ed.). Belmont, CA: Cengage Learning/Wadsworth.
Frankl, V. (1955). *The doctor and the soul.* New York: Knopf.
Franzoi, S. L. (2002). *Social psychology.* New York: McGraw-Hill.
Franzoi, S. L., & Klaiber, J. R. (2007). Body use and reference group impact: With whom do we compare our bodies? *Sex Roles, 56*(3–4), 205–214.
Fraser, C. (2002). Fact and fiction: A clarification of phantom limb phenomena. *British Journal of Occupational Therapy, 65*(6), 256–260.
Frederick, C. J. (1987) Psychic trauma in victims of crime and terrorism. In G. R. VandenBos & B. K. Bryant (Eds.), *Cataclysms, crises, and catastrophes: Psychology in action.* Washington, DC: American Psychological Association.
Fredrickson, B. L. (2003). The value of positive emotions. *American Scientist, 91,* 330–335.
Fredrickson, B. L., & Branigan, C. (2005). Positive emotions broaden the scope of attention and

thought-action repertoires. *Cognition & Emotion, 19*(3), 313–332.

Freeman, D., & Garety, P. A. (2004). *Paranoia: The psychology of persecutory delusions.* New York: Routledge.

Freiwald, W. A., & Kanwisher, N. G. (2004). Visual selective attention: Insights from brain imaging and neurophysiology. In M. S. Gazzaniga (Ed.), *The cognitive neurosciences* (3rd ed.). Cambridge, MA: MIT Press.

Freize, I. H. (1987). The female victim. In G. R. VandenBos & B. K. Bryant (Eds.), *Cataclysms, crises, and catastrophes: Psychology in action.* Washington, DC: American Psychological Association.

French, C. C., Fowler, M., McCarthy, K., & Peers, D. (1991). A test of the Barnum effect. *Skeptical Inquirer, 15*(4), 66–72.

French, S. E., Kim, T. E., & Pillado, O. (2006). Ethnic identity, social group membership, and youth violence. In N. G. Guerra & E. P. Smith (Eds.), *Preventing youth violence in a multicultural society.* Washington, DC: American Psychological Association.

Freud, S. (1900). *The interpretation of dreams.* London: Hogarth.

Freud, S. (1949). *An outline of psychoanalysis.* New York: Norton.

Frey, M. C., & Detterman, D. K. (2004). Scholastic assessment or g? The relationship between the scholastic assessment test and general cognitive ability. *Psychological Science, 15*(6), 373–378.

Fried, P. A., & Smith, A. M. (2001). A literature review of the consequences of prenatal marihuana exposure. *Neurotoxicology and Teratology, 23*(1), 1–11.

Friedman, H. S. (2002). *Health psychology* (2nd ed.). Englewood Cliffs, NJ: Prentice-Hall.

Friedman, L. (2006). What is psychoanalysis? *Psychoanalytic Quarterly, 75*(3), 689–713.

Friedman, L. J. (2004). Erik Erikson on generativity: A biographer's perspective. In E. de St. Aubin, D. P. McAdams, et al. (Eds.), *The generative society: Caring for future generations.* Washington, DC: American Psychological Association.

Friedman, M., & Rosenman, R. H. (1983). *Type A behavior and your heart.* New York: Knopf.

Friedman, R. C., Bucci, W., Christian, C., Drucker, P., et al. (1998). Private psychotherapy patients of psychiatrist psychoanalysts. *American Journal of Psychiatry, 155,* 1772–1774.

Fritz, C. O., Morris, P. E., Acton, M., Voelkel, A. R., et al. (2007). Comparing and combining retrieval practice and the keyword mnemonic for foreign vocabulary learning. *Applied Cognitive Psychology, 21*(4), 499–526.

Froufe, M., & Schwartz, C. (2001). Subliminal messages for increasing self-esteem: Placebo effect. *Spanish Journal of Psychology, 4*(1), 19–25.

Frydman, M. (1999). Television, aggressiveness and violence. *International Journal of Adolescent Medicine & Health, 11*(3–4), 335–344.

Fu, J. H., Morris, M. W., Lee, S., Chao, M., et al. (2007). Epistemic motives and cultural conformity: Need for closure, culture, and context as determinants of conflict judgments. *Journal of Personality & Social Psychology, 92*(2), 191–207.

Fukuda, K., & Ishihara, K. (2001). Age-related changes of sleeping pattern during adolescence. *Psychiatry & Clinical Neurosciences, 55*(3), 231–232.

Funder, D. C. (2006). *The personality puzzle* (4th ed.). New York: Norton.

Funk, J. B. (2005). Children's exposure to violent video games and desensitization to violence. *Child and Adolescent Psychiatric Clinics of North America, 14*(3), 387–404.

Fuqua, D. R., & Newman, J. L. (2002). Creating caring organizations. *Consulting Psychology Journal: Practice & Research, 54*(2), 131–140.

Furnham, A., Chamorro-Premuzic, T., & Callahan, I. (2003). Does graphology predict personality and intelligence? *Individual Differences Research, 1*(2), 78–94.

FVPF. (2007). Domestic violence is a serious, widespread social problem in America: The facts. Family Violence Prevention Fund. Retrieved July 29, 2007, from http://www.endabuse.org/resources/facts/.

Gable, S. L., Reis, H. T., Impett, E. A., & Asher, E. R. (2004). What do you do when things go right? *Journal of Personality & Social Psychology, 87*(2), 228–245.

Gable, S. L., Reis, H. T., Impett, E., & Asher, E. R. (2004). What do you do when things go right? The intrapersonal and interpersonal benefits of sharing positive events. *Journal of Personality & Social Psychology, 87,* 228–245.

Gaertner, S. L., Dovidio, J. F., Banker, B. S., Houlette, M., et al. (2000). Reducing intergroup conflict: From superordinate goals to decategorization, recategorization, and mutual differentiation. *Group Dynamics, 4*(1), 98–114.

Galambos, N. L., Barker, E. T., & Tilton-Weaver, L. C. (2003). Who gets caught at maturity gap? A study of pseudomature, immature and mature adolescents. *International Journal of Behavioral Development, 27*(3), 253–263.

Galanter, M., Hayden, F., Castañeda, R, & Franco, H. (2005). Group therapy, self-help groups, and network therapy. In R. J. Frances, S. I. Miller, et al. (Eds.), *Clinical textbook of addictive disorders* (3rd ed.). New York: Guilford.

Galati, D., Scherer, K. R., & Ricci-Bitti, P. E. (1997). Voluntary facial expression of emotion: Comparing congenitally blind with normally sighted encoders. *Journal of Personality & Social Psychology, 73*(6), 1363–1379.

Galea, S., & Resnick, H. (2005). Posttraumatic stress disorder in the general population after mass terrorist incidents: Considerations about the nature of exposure. *CNS Spectrums, 10*(2), 107–115.

Galea, S., Ahern, J., Resnick, H., Kilpatrick, D., et al. (2002). Psychological sequelae of the September 11 terrorist attacks in New York City. *New England Journal of Medicine, 346*(13), 982–987.

Gamache, G. (2004). *Essentials in human factors.* San Mateo, CA: Usernomics.

Ganis, G., Thompson, W. L., & Kosslyn, S. M. (2004). Brain areas underlying visual mental imagery and visual perception: An fMRI study. *Cognitive Brain Research, 20*(2), 226–241.

Ganster, D. C., Fox, M. L., & Dwyer, D. J. (2001). Explaining employees' health care costs: A prospective examination of stressful job demands, personal control, and physiological reactivity. *Journal of Applied Psychology, 86,* 954–964.

Garbarino, S., Beelke, M., Costa, G., Violani, C., et al. (2002). Brain function and effects of shift work: Implications for clinical neuropharmacology. *Neuropsychobiology, 45,* 50–56.

Garbarino, S., Mascialino, B., Penco, M. A., Squarcia, S., et al. (2004). Professional shift-work drivers who adopt prophylactic naps can reduce the risk of car accidents during night work. *Sleep: Journal of Sleep & Sleep Disorders Research, 27*(7), 1295–1302.

García-Junco-Clemente, P., Linares-Clemente, P., & Fernández-Chacón, R. (2005). Active zones for presynaptic plasticity in the brain. *Molecular Psychiatry, 10*(2), 185–200.

Gardner, H. (2003). *Multiple intelligences after twenty years.* Invited Address, American Educational Research Association, April. Retrieved July 3, 2007, from http://www.pz.harvard.edu/PIs/HG_MI_after_20_years.pdf.

Gardner, H. (2004). *Frames of mind* (Tenth-anniversary ed.). New York: Basic.

Gardner, R. A., & Gardner, B. T. (1989). *Teaching sign language to chimpanzees.* Albany, NY: State University of New York Press.

Garland, A. F., & Zigler, E. (1993). Adolescent suicide prevention. *American Psychologist, 48*(2), 169–182.

Garlow, S. J., Purselle, D. C., & Heninger, M. (2007). Cocaine and alcohol use preceding suicide in African American and White adolescents. *Journal of Psychiatric Research, 41*(6), 530–536.

Garnets, L. D. (2002). Sexual orientation in perspective. *Cultural Diversity & Ethnic Minority Psychology, 8*(2), 115–129.

Garnets, L. D., & Kimmel, D. (1991). Lesbian and gay male dimensions in the psychological study of human diversity. *Psychological perspectives on human diversity in America.* Washington, DC: American Psychological Association.

Gastner, M. T., Shalizi, C. R., & Newman, M. E. J. (2005). Maps and cartograms of the 2004 US presidential election results. *Advances in Complex Systems, 8*(1), 117–123.

Gates, A. I. (1958). Recitation as a factor in memorizing. In J. Deese (Ed.), *The psychology of learning.* New York: McGraw-Hill.

Gatchel, R. J., & Oordt, M. S. (2003). Insomnia. In R. J. Gatchel & M. S. Oordt (Eds.), *Clinical health psychology and primary care: Practical advice and clinical guidance for successful collaboration.* Washington, DC: American Psychological Association.

Gayle, H. (2000). An overview of the global HIV/AIDS epidemic, with a focus on the United States. *AIDS, 14*(Suppl 2), S8–S17.

Gazzaniga, M. S. (1970). *The bisected brain.* New York: Plenum.

Gazzaniga, M. S. (2005). Forty-five years of split-brain research and still going strong. *Nature Reviews Neuroscience, 6*(8), 653–659.

Geary, N. (2004). Endocrine controls of eating: CCK, leptin, and ghrelin. *Physiology & Behavior, 81*(5), 719–733.

Gedo, J. E. (2002). The enduring scientific contributions of Sigmund Freud. *Perspectives in Biology & Medicine, 45,* 200–211.

Geehr, J. L., Burke, M. J., & Sulzer, J. L. (1995). Quality circles: The effects of varying degrees of voluntary participation on employee attitudes and program efficacy. *Educational & Psychological Measurement, 55*(1), 124–134.

Gegenfurtner, K. R., & Kiper, D. C. (2003). Color vision. *Annual Review of Neuroscience, 26,* 181–206.

Geiselman, R. E., Fisher, R. P., MacKinnon, D. P., & Holland, H. L. (1986). Eyewitness memory enhancement with the cognitive interview. *American Journal of Psychology, 99,* 385–401.

Geliebter, A., & Aversa, A. (2003). Emotional eating in overweight, normal weight, and underweight individuals. *Eating Behaviors, 3*(4), 341–347.

Genesee, F., Paradis., J., & Crago, M. (2004). *Dual language development and disorders: A handbook on bilingualism and second language learning.* Baltimore: Paul H. Brookes.

George, A. (2006). Living online: The end of privacy? *New Scientist, 2659* (Sept. 18), 50–51.

Georgiades, A., Serwood, A., Gullette, E. C., Babyak, M. A., et al. (2000). Effects of exercise and weight loss on mental stress-induced cardiovascular responses in individuals with high blood pressure. *Hypertension, 36,* 171–176.

Germain, A., Krakow, B., Faucher, B., Zadra, A., et al. (2004). Increased mastery elements associated with imagery rehearsal treatment for nightmares in sexual assault survivors with PTSD. *Dreaming, 14*(4), 195–206.

German, T. P., & Barrett, H. C. (2005). Functional fixedness in a technologically sparse culture. *Psychological Science, 16*(1), 1–5.

German, T. P., & Defeyter, M. A. (2000). Immunity to functional fixedness in young children. *Psychonomic Bulletin & Review, 7*(4), 707–712.

Gersh, R. D. (1982). Learning when not to shoot. *Santa Barbara News Press,* June 20.

Gershoff, E. T. (2002). Corporal punishment by parents and associated child behaviors and experiences: A meta-analytic and theoretical review. *Psychological Bulletin, 128*(4), 539–579.

Gerwood, J. B. (1998). The legacy of Viktor Frankl. *Psychological Reports, 82*(2), 673–674.

Geschwind, N. (1979). Specializations of the human brain. *Scientific American, 241,* 180–199.

Gewirtz, J. C., & Davis, M. (1998). Application of Pavlovian higher-order conditioning to the analysis of the neural substrates of fear conditioning. *Neuropharmacology, 37*(4–5), 453–459.

Giarratano, J. C., & Riley, G. (2005). *Expert systems, principles and programming* (4th ed.). Belmont, CA: Cengage Learning/Wadsworth.

Gibson, E. J., & Walk, R. D. (1960). The "visual cliff." *Scientific American, 202*(4), 67–71.

Gibson, K. R. (2002). Evolution of human intelligence: The roles of brain size and mental construction. *Brain, Behavior & Evolution, 59*(1–2), 10–20.

Gifford, R. (2002). *Environmental psychology: Principles and practice* (3rd ed.). Colville, WA: Optimal Books.

Gilbert, P. (2001). *Overcoming depression.* New York: Oxford University Press.

Giliovich, T., Keltner, D., & Nisbett, R. (2005). *Social psychology.* New York: Norton.

Gillespie, C. F., & Nemeroff, C. B. (2007). Corticotropin-releasing factor and the psychobiology of early-life stress. *Current Directions in Psychological Science, 16*(2), 85–89.

Gilligan, C. (1982). *In a different voice.* Cambridge, MA: Harvard University Press.

Gilligan, C., & Attanucci, J. (1988). Two moral orientations: Gender differences and similarities. *Merrill-Palmer Quarterly, 34*(3), 223–237.

Gilman, S. E., Cochran, S. D., Mays, V. M., Hughes, M., et al. (2001). Risk of psychiatric disorders among individuals reporting same-sex sexual partners in the National Comorbidity Survey. *American Journal of Public Health, 91*(6), 933–939.

Ginet, M., & Py, J. (2001). A technique for enhancing memory in eyewitness testimonies for use by police officers and judicial officials: The cognitive interview. *Travail Humain, 64*(2), 173–191.

Ginott, H. G. (1965). *Between parent and child: New solutions to old problems.* New York: Macmillan.

Ginsberg, D. L. (2006). Fatal agranulocytosis four years after clozapine discontinuation. *Primary Psychiatry, 13*(2), 32–33.

Giuseppe, R. (2005). Virtual reality in psychotherapy: Review. *CyberPsychology & Behavior. Special Use of Virtual Environments in Training and Rehabilitation: International Perspectives, 8*(3), 220–230.

Gladwell, M. (2005). *Blink: The power of thinking without thinking.* New York: Little, Brown.

Gleason, J. B. (2005). *The development of language* (6th ed.). Boston: Allyn & Bacon.

Glisky, M. L., Williams, J. M., & Kihlstrom, J. F. (1996). Internal and external mental imagery perspectives and performance on two tasks. *Journal of Sport Behavior, 19*(1), 3–18.

Global Footprint Network (2006). *Ecological footprint: Overview.* Retrieved August 9, 2007, from http://www.footprintnetwork.org/gfn_sub.php?content=footprint_overview.

Glomb, T. M. (2002). Workplace anger and aggression. *Journal of Occupational Health Psychology, 7*(1), 20–36.

Glover, R. J. (2001). Discriminators of moral orientation: Gender role or personality? *Journal of Adult Development, 8*(1), 1–7.

Gobet, F. (2005). Chunking models of expertise: Implications for education. *Applied Cognitive Psychology, 19*(2), 183–204.

Gobet, F., & Simon, H. A. (1996). Recall of random and distorted chess positions: Implications for the theory of expertise. *Memory & Cognition, 24*(4), 493–503.

Goel, V., & Dolan, R. J. (2004). Differential involvement of left prefrontal cortex in inductive and deductive reasoning. *Cognition, 93*(3), 109–121.

Goel, V., & Grafman, J. (1995). Are the frontal lobes implicated in "planning" functions? Interpreting data from the Tower of Hanoi. *Neuropsychologia, 33*(5), 623–642.

Gogate, L. J., Bahrick, L. E., & Watson, J. D. (2000). A study of multimodal motherese: The role of temporal synchrony between verbal labels and gestures. *Child Development, 71*(4), 878–894.

Goldberg, C. (2001). Of prophets, true believers, and terrorists. *The Dana Forum on Brain Science, 3*(3), 21–24.

Goldberg, R. (2006). *Drugs across the spectrum* (5th ed.). Belmont, CA: Cengage Learning/Wadsworth.

Golden, J. (2005). *Message in a bottle: The making of fetal alcohol syndrome.* Cambridge, MA: Harvard University Press.

Golden, T. D., Veiga, J. F., & Simsek, Z. (2006). Telecommuting's differential impact on work-family conflict: Is there no place like home? *Journal of Applied Psychology, 91*(6), 1340–1350.

Goldenberg, H., & Goldenberg, I. (2004). *Family therapy: An overview* (6th ed.). Pacific Grove, CA: Brooks/Cole.

Goldfried, M. R. (2001). Integrating gay, lesbian, and bisexual issues into mainstream psychology. *American Psychologist, 56*(11), 977–987.

Golding, J. M., Bradshaw, G. S., Dunlap, E. E., & Hodell, E. C. (2007). The impact of mock jury gender composition on deliberations and conviction rates in a child sexual assault trial. *Child Maltreatment, 12*(2), 182–190.

Goldman, H. H. (1998). Deinstitutionalization and community care. *Harvard Review of Psychiatry, 6*(4), 219–222.

Goldstein, E. B. (2007). *Sensation and perception* (7th ed.). Belmont, CA: Cengage Learning/Wadsworth.

Goldstein, E. B. (2008). *Cognitive psychology: Connecting mind, research and everyday experience* (2nd ed.). Belmont, CA: Cengage Learning/Wadsworth.

Goleman, D. (1995). *Emotional intelligence.* New York: Bantam.

Goodall, J. (1990). *Through a window: My thirty years with the chimpanzees of the Gombe.* Boston: Houghton Mifflin.

Goode, E. (1996). Gender and courtship entitlement: Responses to personal ads. *Sex Roles, 34*(3–4), 141–169.

Goodman-Delahunty, J. Greene, E., & Hsiao, W. (1998). Construing motive in videotaped killings: The role of jurors' attitudes toward the death penalty. *Law & Human Behavior, 22*(3), 257–271.

Goodwin, R. D., Fergusson, D. M., & Horwood, L. J. (2005). Childhood abuse and familial violence and the risk of panic attacks and panic disorder in young adulthood. *Psychological Medicine, 35*(6), 881–890.

Goodwin, S. A., & Fiske, S. T. (2001). Power and gender. In R. K. Unger (Ed.), *Handbook of the psychology of women and gender.* New York: Wiley.

Gopnik, A., Meltzoff, A. N., & Kuhl, P. K. (2000). *The scientist in the crib: What early learning tells us about the mind.* New York: HarperCollins.

Gordon, A. K., & Kaplar, M. E. (2002). A new technique for demonstrating the actor-observer bias. *Teaching of Psychology, 29*(4), 301–303.

Gordon, T. (2000). *Parent effectiveness training: The proven program for raising responsible children.* New York: Three Rivers Press.

Gorman, J. M. (1996). *The essential guide to mental health.* New York: St. Martin's Griffin.

Gottlieb, G. (1998). Normally occurring environmental and behavioral influences on gene activity: From central dogma to probabilistic epigenesis. *Psychological Review, 105*(4), 792–802.

Gottman, J. M. (1994). *Why marriages succeed or fail.* New York: Simon & Schuster.

Gottman, J. M., & Krokoff, L. J. (1989). Marital interaction and satisfaction: A longitudinal view. *Journal of Consulting & Clinical Psychology, 57*(1), 47–52.

Gould, D., & Udry, E. (1994). Psychological skills for enhancing performance: Arousal regulation strategies. *Medicine & Science in Sports & Exercise, 26*(4), 478–485.

Gould, E., & Gross, C. G. (2002). Neurogenesis in adult mammals: Some progress and problems. *Journal of Neuroscience, 22*(3), 619–623.

Gould, R. (1975). Growth toward self-tolerance. *Psychology Today,* Feb., 74–78.

Grabe, M. (2006). *Integrating technology for meaningful learning.* Boston: Houghton Mifflin.

Grack, C., & Richman, C. L. (1996). Reducing general and specific heterosexism through cooperative contact. *Journal of Psychology & Human Sexuality, 8*(4), 59–68.

Grande, T., Rudolf, G., Oberbracht, C., & Pauli-Magnus, C. (2003). Progressive changes in patients' lives after psychotherapy. *Psychotherapy Research, 13*(1), 43–58.

Grandner, M. A., & Kripke, D. F. (2004). Self-reported sleep complaints with long and short sleep: A nationally representative sample. *Psychosomatic Medicine, 66,* 239–241.

Granrud, C. E. (2004). Visual metacognition and the development of size constancy. In D. T. Levin (Ed.), *Thinking and seeing: Visual metacognition in adults and children*. Cambridge, MA: MIT Press.

Grant, B. F., & Dawson, D. A. (1997). Age at onset of alcohol use and its association with DSM-IV alcohol abuse and dependence. *Journal of Substance Abuse, 9,* 103.

Grant, B. F., Hasin, D. S., Stinson, F. S., Dawson, D. A., et al. (2006). The epidemiology of DSM-IV panic disorder and agoraphobia in the United States: Results from the National Epidemiologic Survey on Alcohol and Related Conditions. *Journal of Clinical Psychiatry, 67*(3), 363–374.

Grant, I., Gonzalez, R., Carey, C., & Natarajan, L. (2001). Long-term neurocognitive fconsequences of marijuana. In *National Institute on Drug Abuse Workshop on Clinical Consequences of Marijuana,* August 13, Rockville, MD.

Graves, J. L. (2001). *The emperor's new clothes*. Piscataway, NJ: Rutgers University Press.

Gravetter, F. J., & Wallnau, L. B. (2007). *Statistics for the behavioral sciences* (7th ed.). Belmont, CA: Cengage Learning/Wadsworth.

Gray, J. M., & Wilson, M. A. (2007). A detailed analysis of the reliability and validity of the sensation seeking scale in a UK sample. *Personality & Individual Differences, 42*(4), 641–651.

Graziottin, A. (1998). The biological basis of female sexuality. *International Clinical Psychopharmacology, 13*(Suppl 6), S15–S22.

Greenberg, D. L. (2004). President Bush's false "flashbulb" memory of 9/11/01. *Applied Cognitive Psychology, 18*(3), 363–370.

Greene, D., & Lepper, M. R. (1974). How to turn play into work. *Psychology Today,* Sept., 49.

Greenfield, P. M. (1997). You can't take it with you: Why abilities assessments don't cross cultures. *American Psychologist, 52,* 1115–1124.

Greenglass, E. R., Burke, R. J., & Konarski, R. (1998). Components of burnout, resources, and gender-related differences. *Journal of Applied Social Psychology, 28*(12), 1088–1106.

Greenglass, E. R., Burke, R. J., & Moore, K. A. (2003). Reactions to increased workload: Effects on professional efficacy of nurses. *Applied Psychology: An International Review, 52*(4), 580–597.

Greenwald, R. (2006). Eye movement desensitization and reprocessing with traumatized youth. In N. B. Webb (Ed.), *Working with traumatized youth in child welfare: Social work practice with children and families*. New York: Guilford.

Greenwood, J. G., Greenwood, J. J. D., McCullagh, J. F., Beggs, J., et al. (2006). A survey of sidedness in Northern Irish schoolchildren: The interaction of sex, age, and task. *Laterality: Asymmetries of Body, Brain & Cognition, 12*(1), 1–18.

Gregory, R. L. (1990). *Eye and brain: The psychology of seeing*. Princeton, NJ: Princeton University Press.

Gregory, R. L. (2003). Seeing after blindness. *Nature Neuroscience, 6*(9), 909–910.

Grenier, G., & Byers, E. S. (1995). Rapid ejaculation: A review of conceptual, etiological, and treatment issues. *Archives of Sexual Behavior, 24*(4), 447–472.

Griffin, D. R. (1992). *Animal minds*. Chicago: University of Chicago Press.

Griffin, W. A. (2002). Family therapy. In M. Hersen & W. H. Sledge (Eds.), *Encyclopedia of psychotherapy*. San Diego: Academic Press.

Griffin-Fennell, F., & Williams, M. (2006). Examining the complexities of suicidal behavior in the African American community. *Journal of Black Psychology, 32*(3), 303–319.

Grigorenko, E. L. (2005). The inherent complexities of gene-environment interactions. *Journals of Gerontology: Series B: Psychological Sciences & Social Sciences, 60B*(1, Spec. Issue), 53–64.

Grigorenko, E. L., & Sternberg, R. J. (2003). The nature-nurture issue. In A. Slater & G. Bremner (Eds.), *An introduction to developmental psychology*. Malden, MA: Blackwell.

Grobstein, P., & Chow, K. L. (1975). Perceptive field development and individual experience. *Science, 190,* 352–358.

Gross, J. J. (2001). Emotion regulation in adulthood: Timing is everything. *Current Directions in Psychological Science, 10*(6), 214–219.

Grubin, D., & Madsen, L. (2005). Lie detection and the polygraph: A historical review. *Journal of Forensic Psychiatry & Psychology, 16*(2), 357–369.

Grunbaum, J. A., Kann, L., Kinchen, S., & Ross, J., et al. (2004). Youth Risk Behavior Surveillance: United States, 2003. *Centers for Disease Control and Prevention Morbidity and Mortality Weekly Report Surveillance Summary, 53*(SS02), 1–96.

Gruner, C. R., & Tighe, M. R. (1995). Semantic differential measurements of connotations of verbal terms and their doublespeak facsimiles in sentence contexts. *Psychological Reports, 77*(3, Pt. 1), 778.

Grzegorek, J. L., Slaney, R. B., Franze, S., & Rice, K. G. (2004). Self-criticism, dependency, self-esteem, and grade point average satisfaction among clusters of perfectionists and nonperfectionists. *Journal of Counseling Psychology, 51*(2), 192–200.

Guastello, D. D., & Guastello, S. J. (2003). Androgyny, gender role behavior, and emotional intelligence among college students and their parents. *Sex Roles, 49*(11-12), 663–673.

Guéguen, N. (2002). Status, apparel and touch: Their joint effects on compliance to a request. *North American Journal of Psychology, 4*(2), 279–286.

Guéguen, N., & Pascual, A. (2003). Status and people's tolerance towards an ill-mannered person: A field study. *Journal of Mundane Behavior, 4*(1). Retrieved August 4, 2007 from http://www.mundanebehavior.org/issues/v4n1/gueguenpascual.htm.

Guéguen, N., Pascual, A., & Dagot, L. (2002). Low-ball and compliance to a request: An application in a field setting. *Psychological Reports, 91*(1), 81–84.

Guffey, M. E. (2007). Essentials of business communication (7th ed.). Belmont, CA: Cengage Learning/South-western.

Gullette, D. L., & Lyons, M. A. (2005). Sexual sensation seeking, compulsivity, and HIV risk behaviors in college students. *Journal of Community Health Nursing, 22*(1), 47–60.

Gump, B. B., & Kulik, J. A. (1997). Stress, affiliation, and emotional contagion. *Journal of Personality & Social Psychology, 72*(2), 305–319.

Gündogan, N. Ü., Durmazlar, N., Gümüs, K., Özdemir, P. G., et al. (2005). Projected color slides as a method for mass screening test for color vision deficiency (a preliminary study). *International Journal of Neuroscience, 115*(8), 1105–1117.

Gur, R. E., Cowell, P., Turetsky, B. I., Gallacher, F., et al. (1998). A follow-up magnetic resonance imaging study of schizophrenia. *Archives of General Psychiatry, 55*(2), 145–152.

Gurung, R. (2006). *Health psychology: A cultural approach*. Belmont, CA: Cengage Learning/Wadsworth.

Gustavsson, J. P., Weinryb, R. M., Göransson, S., Pedersen, N. L., et al. (1997). Stability and predictive ability of personality traits across 9 years. *Personality & Individual Differences, 22*(6), 783–791.

Haas, B. W., Omura, K., Constable, R. T., & Canli, T. (2007). Is automatic emotion regulation associated with agreeableness? A perspective using a social neuroscience approach. *Psychological Science, 18*(2), 130–132.

Haas, L. J., Benedict, J. G., & Kobos, J. C. (1996). Psychotherapy by telephone: Risks and benefits for psychologists and consumers. *Professional Psychology: Research & Practice, 27*(2), 154–160.

Haber, R. N. (1969). Eidetic images; with biographical sketches. *Scientific American, 220*(12), 36–44.

Haber, R. N. (1970). How we remember what we see. *Scientific American, 222*(5), 104–112.

Haber, R. N., & Haber, L. (2000). Eidetic imagery. In A. E. Kazdin, (Ed.), *Encyclopedia of psychology* (Vol. 3). Washington, DC: American Psychological Association.

Haddad, S. (2003). Islam and attitudes toward U.S. policy in the Middle East: Evidence from survey research in Lebanon. *Studies in Conflict & Terrorism, 26*(2), 135–154.

Hadwin, A. F., Kirby, J. R., & Woodhouse, R. A. (1999). Individual differences in notetaking, summarization and learning from lectures. *Alberta Journal of Educational Research, 45*(1), 1–17.

Haenschel, C., Vernon, D. J., Dwivedi, P., Gruzelier, J. H., et al. (2005). Event-related brain potential correlates of human auditory sensory memory-trace formation. *Journal of Neuroscience, 25*(45), 10494–10501.

Hafer, C. L., & Bègue, L. (2005). Experimental research on just-world theory: Problems, developments, and future challenges. *Psychological Bulletin, 131*(1), 128–167.

Haier, R. J., Jung, R. E., Yeo, R. A., Head, K., et al. (2004). Structural brain variation and general intelligence. *NeuroImage, 23,* 425–433.

Haier, R. J., Siegel, B. V., Nuechterlein, K. H., Hazlett, E., et al. (1988). Cortical glucose metabolic rate correlates of abstract reasoning and attention studied with positron emission tomography. *Intelligence, 12,* 199–217.

Haier, R. J., White, N. S., & Alkire, M. T. (2003). Individual differences in general intelligence correlate with brain function during nonreasoning tasks. *Intelligence, 31*(5), 429–441.

Haines, M. M., Stansfeld, S. A., Job R. F. S., Berglund, B., et al. (2001). Chronic aircraft noise exposure, stress responses, mental health and cognitive performance in school children. *Psychological Medicine, 31*(2), 265–277.

Halbert, J., Crotty, M., & Cameron, I. D. (2002). Evidence for the optimal management of acute and chronic phantom pain. *Clinical Journal of Pain, 18*(2), 84–92.

Hall, C. (1966). *The meaning of dreams.* New York: McGraw-Hill.

Hall, C. (1974). What people dream about. In R. L. Woods & H. B. Greenhouse (Eds.), *The new world of dreams: An anthology.* New York: Macmillan.

Hall, E. T. (1966). *The hidden dimension.* Garden City, NY: Doubleday.

Hall, J. (2006). *What is clinical psychology?* (4th ed.). New York: Oxford University Press.

Hallahan, D. P., & Kauffman, J. M. (2006). *Exceptional learners* (10th ed.). Boston: Allyn & Bacon.

Halpern, D. F. (2001). Sex difference research: Cognitive abilities. In J. Worell (Ed.), *Encyclopedia of women and gender.* New York: Oxford University Press.

Hamilton, V. L., & Sanders, J. (1995). Crimes of obedience and conformity in the workplace. *Journal of Social Issues, 51*(3), 67–88.

Hammer, J. C., Fisher, J. D., Fitzgerald, P., & Fisher, W. A. (1996). When two heads aren't better than one: AIDS risk behavior in college-age couples. *Journal of Applied Social Psychology, 26*(5), 375–397.

Hammer, L. B., Grigsby, T. D., & Woods, S. (1998). The conflicting demands of work, family, and school among students at an urban university. *Journal of Psychology, 132*(2), 220–226.

Hancock, P. A., & Ganey, H. C. N. (2003). From the inverted-U to the extended-U: The evolution of a law of psychology. *Journal of Human Performance in Extreme Environments, 7*(1), 5–14.

Handsfield, H. H. (2001). Resurgent sexually transmitted diseases among men who have sex with men. *Medscape Infectious Disease,* Medscape.com.

Hanley, S. J., & Abell, S. C. (2002). Maslow and relatedness: Creating an interpersonal model of self-actualization. *Journal of Humanistic Psychology, 42*(4), 37–56.

Hansell, J. H. (2007). *Abnormal psychology: The enduring issues* (2nd ed.). New York: Wiley.

Hansen, C. J., Stevens, L. C., & Coast, J. R. (2001). Exercise duration and mood state. *Health Psychology, 20*(4), 267–275.

Hansen, N. B., Lambert, M. J., & Forman, E. M. (2002). The psychotherapy dose-response effect and its implications for treatment delivery services. *Clinical Psychology: Science & Practice, 9*(3), 329–334.

Hanton, S., Mellalieu, S. D., & Hall, R. (2004). Self-confidence and anxiety interpretation: A qualitative investigation. *Psychology of Sport & Exercise, 5*(4), 477–495.

Hardaway, C. A., & Gregory, K. B. (2005). Fatigue and sleep debt in an operational navy squadron. *International Journal of Aviation Psychology, 15*(2), 157–171.

Hardin, G. (1968). The tragedy of the commons. *Science, 162,* 1243–1248.

Hardin, G. (1985). *Filters against folly.* New York: Viking.

Harding, D. J., Fox, C., & Mehta, J. D. (2002). Studying rare events through qualitative case studies. *Sociological Methods & Research, 31*(2), 174–217.

Harding, R. W., Morgan, F. H., Indermaur, D., Ferrante, A. M., et al. (1998). Road rage and the epidemiology of violence. *Studies on Crime & Crime Prevention, 7*(2), 221–238.

Hare, R. D. (2006). Psychopathy: A clinical and forensic overview. *Psychiatric Clinics of North America, 29*(3), 709–724.

Harker, L., & Keltner, D. (2001). Expressions of positive emotion in women's college yearbook pictures and their relationship to personality and life outcomes across adulthood. *Journal of Personality & Social Psychology, 80*(1), 112–124.

Harlow, H. F., & Harlow, M. K. (1962). Social deprivation in monkeys. *Scientific American, 207,* 136–146.

Harlow, J. M. (1868). Recovery from the passage of an iron bar through the head. *Publications of the Massachusetts Medical Society, 2,* 327–347.

Harrigan, J. A. (2005). Proxemics, kinesics, and gaze. In J. A. Harrigan, R. Rosenthal, et al. (Eds.), *The new handbook of methods in nonverbal behavior research.* New York: Oxford University Press.

Harris, C. (2004). The evolution of jealousy. *American Scientist, 92,* 62–71.

Harris, J. A., Rushton, J. P., Hampson, E., & Jackson, D. N. (1996). Salivary testosterone and self-report aggressive and pro-social personality characteristics in men and women. *Aggressive Behavior, 22*(5), 321–331.

Harris, J. C. (2003). Pinel delivering the insane. *Archives of General Psychiatry, 60*(6), 552.

Harris, J. R., & Liebert, R. M. (1991). *The child.* Englewood Cliffs, NJ: Prentice Hall.

Harrison, P. J., & Weinberger, D. R. (2005). Schizophrenia genes, gene expression, and neuropathology: On the matter of their convergence. *Molecular Psychiatry, 10*(1), 40–68.

Hart, B., & Risley, T. R. (1999). *The social world of children learning to talk.* Baltimore: Paul H. Brookes.

Hart, D., & Carlo, G. (2005). Moral development in adolescence. *Journal of Research on Adolescence, 15*(3), 223–233.

Hartgens, F., & Kuipers, H. (2004). Effects of androgenic–anabolic steroids in athletes. *Sports Medicine, 34*(8), 513–554.

Hartlep, K. L., & Forsyth, G. A. (2000). The effect of self-reference on learning and retention. *Teaching of Psychology, 27*(4), 269–271.

Hartmann, P., Reuter, M., & Nyborg, H. (2006). The relationship between date of birth and individual differences in personality and general intelligence: A largescale study. *Personality & Individual Differences, 40*(7), 1349–1362.

Harvey, C. A., Curson, D. A., Pantelis, C., & Taylor, J. (1996). Four behavioural syndromes of schizophrenia. *British Journal of Psychiatry, 168*(5), 562–570.

Harway, M. (Ed.). (2004). *Handbook of couples therapy.* San Francisco: Jossey-Bass.

Hashibe, M., Straif, K., Tashkin, D. P., Morgenstern, H., et al. (2005). Epidemiologic review of marijuana use and cancer risk. *Alcohol, 35*(3), 265–275.

Hashimoto, I., Suzuki, A., Kimura, T., Iguchi Y., et al. (2004). Is there training-dependent reorganization of digit representations in area 3b of string players? *Clinical Neurophysiology, 115*(2), 435–447.

Hauck, F. R., Moore, C. M., Herman, S. M., Donovan, M., et al. (2002). The contribution of prone sleeping position to the racial disparity in sudden infant death syndrome. *Pediatrics, 110,* 772–780.

Hauri, P., & Linde, S. (1990). *No more sleepless nights.* New York: Wiley.

Hayes, C. (1951). *The ape in our house.* New York: Harper & Row.

Hayne, H., & Rovee-Collier, C. (1995). The organization of reactivated memory in infancy. *Child Development, 66*(3), 893–906.

Heath, R. G. (1963). Electrical self-stimulation of the brain in man. *American Journal of Psychiatry, 120,* 571–577.

Hebl, M. R., King, E. G., & Lin, J. (2004). The swimsuit becomes us all: Ethnicity, gender, and vulnerability to self-objectification. *Personality & Social Psychology Bulletin, 30,* 1322–1331.

Hecht, J. (2007). *The happiness myth: Why what we think is right is wrong.* New York: HarperCollins.

Heiby, E. M. (1983). Assessment of frequency of self-reinforcement. *Journal of Personality & Social Psychology, 44,* 1304–1307.

Heilman, M. E., Wallen, A. S., Fuchs, D., & Tamkins, M. M. (2004). Penalties for success: Reactions to women who succeed at male gender-typed tasks. *Journal of Applied Psychology, 89*(3), 416–427.

Heiman, J. R. (2002). Sexual dysfunction: Overview of prevalence, etiological factors, and treatments. *Journal of Sex Research, 39*(1), 73–78.

Heimann, M., & Meltzoff, A. N. (1996). Deferred imitation in 9- and 14-month-old infants. *British Journal of Developmental Psychology, 14*(March), 55–64.

Heinrichs, R. W. (2001). *In search of madness: Schizophrenia and neuroscience.* New York: Oxford University Press.

Heisel, M. J., Flett, G. L., & Hewitt, P. L. (2003). Social hopelessness and college student suicide ideation. *Archives of Suicide Research, 7*(3), 221–235.

Helgeson, V. S. (2005). *The psychology of gender* (2nd ed.). Englewood Cliffs, NJ: Prentice Hall.

Hellerstein, D. J., Rosenthal, R. N., Pinsker, H., Samstag, L. W., et al. (1998). A randomized prospective study comparing supportive and dynamic therapies. *Journal of Psychotherapy Practice & Research, 7*(4), 261–271.

Hellige, J. B. (1993). *Hemispheric asymmetry.* Cambridge, MA: Harvard University Press.

Helson, R., & Srivastava, S. (2002). Creative and wise people. *Personality & Social Psychology Bulletin, 28*(10), 1430–1440.

Helwig, A. A. (1998). Gender-role stereotyping: Testing theory with a longitudinal sample. *Sex Roles, 38*(5–6), 403–423.

Henderson, N. D. (1982). Human behavior genetics. *Annual Review of Psychology, 33,* 403–440.

Hendrick, S. S., & Hendrick, C. (1993). Lovers as friends. *Journal of Social & Personal Relationships, 10*(3), 459–466.

Henman, L. D. (2001). Humor as a coping mechanism. *Humor: International Journal of Humor Research, 14*(1), 83–94.

Henningsen, D. D., Henningsen, M. L. M., Eden, J., & Cruz, M. G. (2006). Examining the symptoms of groupthink and retrospective sensemaking. *Small Group Research, 37*(1), 36–64.

Hepper, P. G., Wells, D. L., & Lynch, C. (2005). Prenatal thumb sucking is related to postnatal handedness. *Neuropsychologia, 43*(3), 313–315.

Hepper, P.G., McCartney, G. R., & Shannon, E. A. (1998). Lateralised behaviour in first trimester human foetuses. *Neuropsychologia, 36*(6), 531–534.

Hergenhahn, B. R. (2005). *An introduction to the history of psychology* (5th ed.). Belmont, CA: Cengage Learning/Wadsworth.

Hergenhahn, B. R., & Olson, M. (2007). *An introduction to theories of personality* (7th ed.). Englewood Cliffs, NJ: Prentice Hall.

Hergenhahn, B. R., & Olson, M. (2005). *Introduction to the theories* *of learning* (6th ed.). Englewood Cliffs, NJ: Prentice Hall.

Heriot, S. A., & Pritchard, M. (2004). "Reciprocal Inhibition as the Main Basis of Psychotherapeutic Effects" by Joseph Wolpe (1954). *Clinical Child Psychology & Psychiatry, 9*(2), 297–307.

Hermann, B., Seidenberg, M., Sears, L., Hansen, R., et al. (2004). Cerebellar atrophy in temporal lobe epilepsy affects procedural memory. *Neurology, 63*(11), 2129–2131.

Hernstein, R., & Murray, C. (1994). *The bell curve.* New York: Free Press.

Herrmann, D. J., Yoder, C. Y., Gruneberg, M., & Payne, D. G. (2006). *Applied cognitive psychology: A textbook.* Mahwah, NJ: Erlbaum.

Herxheimer, A., & Waterhouse, J. (2003). The prevention and treatment of jet lag. *British Medical Journal, 326*(7384), 296–297.

Herz, R. S. (2001). Ah sweet skunk! *Cerebrum, 3*(4), 31–47.

Hettich, P. I. (2005). *Connect college to career: Student guide to work and life transition.* Belmont, CA: Cengage Learning/Wadsworth.

Higbee, K. L. (1997). Novices, apprentices, and mnemonists: Acquiring expertise with the phonetic mnemonic. *Applied Cognitive Psychology, 11*(2), 147–161.

Higbee, K. L., Clawson, C., DeLano, L., & Campbell, S. (1990). Using the link mnemonic to remember errands. *Psychological Record, 40*(3), 429–436.

Higgins, S. T., Heil, S. H., & Lussier, J. P. (2004). Clinical implications of reinforcement as a determinant of substance use disorders. *Annual Review of Psychology, 55,* 431–461.

Higham, P. A., & Gerrard, C. (2005). Not all errors are created equal: Metacognition and changing answers on multiple-choice tests. *Canadian Journal of Experimental Psychology, 59*(1), 28–34.

Hilgard, E. R. (1968). *The experience of hypnosis.* New York: Harcourt Brace Jovanovich.

Hilgard, E. R. (1977). *Divided consciousness.* New York: Wiley.

Hilgard, E. R. (1994) Neodissociation theory. In S. J. Lynn & J. W. Rhue (Eds.), *Dissociation: Clinical, theoretical and research perspectives.* New York: Guilford.

Hilsenroth, M. J. (2000). Rorschach test. In A. Kazdin (Ed.), *Encyclopedia of psychology.* Washington, DC: American Psychological Association.

Hinkel, E. (Ed.). (2005). *Handbook of research in second language teaching and learning.* Mahwah, NJ: Erlbaum.

Hinterberger, T., Kübler, A., Kaiser, J., Neumann, N., et al. (2003). A brain-computer interface (BCI) for the locked-in: Comparison of different EEG classifications for the thought translation device. *Clinical Neurophysiology, 114*(3), 416–425.

Hintzman, D. L. (2005). Memory strength and recency judgments. *Psychonomic Bulletin & Review, 12*(5), 858–864.

Hirstein, W. (2005). *Brain fiction: Self-deception and the riddle of confabulation.* Cambridge, MA: MIT Press.

Hiscock, M., Perachio, N., & Inch, R. (2001). Is there a sex difference in human laterality? *Journal of Clinical & Experimental Neuropsychology, 23*(2), 137–148.

Hite, S. (1976). *The Hite report.* New York: Macmillan.

Hobson, J. A. (2000). Dreams: Physiology. In A. Kazdin (Ed.), *Encyclopedia of psychology.* Washington, DC: American Psychological Association.

Hobson, J. A. (2001). *Consciousness.* New York: Freeman.

Hobson, J. A. (2005). Sleep is of the brain, by the brain and for the brain. *Nature, 437*(7063), 1254–1256.

Hobson, J. A., Pace–Schott, E. F., & Stickgold, R. (2000). Dream science 2000. *Behavioral & Brain Sciences, 23*(6), 1019–1035, 1083–1121.

Hochstenbach, J., Mulder, T., van Limbeek, J., Donders, R., et al. (1998). Cognitive decline following stroke: A comprehensive study of cognitive decline following stroke. *Journal of Clinical & Experimental Neuropsychology, 20*(4), 503–517.

Hodapp, R. M. (1994). Mental retardation. *Encyclopedia of human behavior* (Vol. 3). San Diego: Academic Press.

Hodgson, R., & Miller, P. (1982). *Selfwatching.* New York: Facts on File.

Hofer, B. K., & Yu, S. L. (2003). Teaching self-regulated learning through a "Learning to Learn" course. *Teaching of Psychology, 30*(1), 30–33.

Hoff, E. (2006). How social contexts support and shape language development. *Developmental Review, 26*(1), 55–88.

Hoff, E., & Tian, C. (2005). Socioeconomic status and cultural influences on language. *Journal of Communication Disorders, 38*(4), 271–278.

Hoffart, A. (2005). Interpersonal therapy for social phobia: Theoretical model and review of the evidence. In M. E. Abelian (Ed.), *Focus on psychotherapy research.* Hauppauge, NY: Nova Science Publishers.

Hoffer, A., & Youngren, V. R. (2004). Is free association still at the core of psychoanalysis? *International Journal of Psychoanalysis, 85*(6), 1489–1492.

Hoffman, H. G., Garcia-Palacios, A., Carlin, A., Furness, T. A., et al. (2003). Interfaces that heal: Coupling real and virtual objects to treat spider phobia. *International Journal of Human–Computer Interaction, 16*(2), 283–300.

Hogan, E. H., Hornick, B. A., & Bouchoux, A. (2002). Focus on communications: Communicating the message: Clarifying the controversies about caffeine. *Nutrition Today, 37,* 28–35.

Hogben, D., & Lawson, M. J. (1992). Superiority of the keyword method for backward recall in vocabulary acquisition. *Psychological Reports, 71*(3, Pt. 1), 880–882.

Hoge, C. W., Castro, C. A., Messer, S. C., McGurk, D., et al. (2004). Combat duty in Iraq and Afghanistan, mental health problems, and barriers to care. *New England Journal of Medicine, 351*(1), 13–22.

Hohwy, J., & Rosenberg, R. (2005). Unusual experiences, reality testing and delusions of alien control. *Mind & Language, 20*(2), 141–162.

Holden, C. (1980). Twins reunited. *Science 80,* Nov., 55–59.

Holland, J. L. (1997). *Making vocational choices.* Odessa, FL: Psychological Assessment Resources.

Holmes, J., & Adams, J. W. (2006). Working memory and children's mathematical skills: Implications for mathematical development and mathematics curricula. *Educational Psychology, 26*(3), 339–366.

Holmes, M. (2002). Rethinking the meaning and management of intersexuality. *Sexualities, 5*(2), 159–180.

Holmes, P. S., & Collins, D. J. (2001). The PETTLEP approach to motor imagery: A functional equivalence model for sport psychologists. *Journal of Applied Sport Psychology, 13*(1), 60–83.

Holmes, T. H., & Rahe, R. H. (1967). The social readjustment rating scale. *Journal of Psychosomatic Research, 11*(2), 213–218.

Holstein, M. (1997). Reflections on death and dying. *Academic Medicine, 72*(10), 848–855.

Holtzen, D. W. (2000). Handedness and professional tennis. *International Journal of Neuroscience, 105*(1–4), 101–111.

Holzinger, B., LaBerge, S., & Levitan, L. (2006). Psychophysiological correlates of lucid dreaming. *Dreaming, 16*(2), 88–95.

Horgan, J. (2005). The forgotten era of brain chips. *Scientific American, 293*(4), 66–73.

Horn, J., Nelson, C. E., & Brannick, M. T. (2004). Integrity, conscientiousness, and honesty. *Psychological Reports, 95*(1), 27–38.

Horn, R. R., Williams, A. M., Scott, M. A., & Hodges, N. J. (2005). Visual search and coordination changes in response to video and point-light demonstrations without KR. *Journal of Motor Behavior, 37*(4), 265–274.

Horne, R. S. C., Andrew, S., Mitchell, K., Sly, D. J., et al. (2001). Apnoea of prematurity and arousal from sleep. *Early Human Development, 61*(2), 119–133.

Hortman, G. (2003). What do facial expressions convey? *Emotion, 3*(2), 150–166.

Horvath, L. S., Milich, R., Lynam, D., Leukefeld, C., et al. (2004). Sensation seeking and substance use: A cross-lagged panel design. *Individual Differences Research, 2*(3), 175–183.

Hosch, H. M., & Cooper, D. S. (1982). Victimization as a determinant of eyewitness accuracy. *Journal of Applied Psychology, 67,* 649–652.

Hough, L. M., & Oswald, F. L. (2000). Personnel selection. *Annual Review of Psychology, 51,* 631–664.

Howard, A., Pion, G. M., Gottfredson, G. D., Flattau, P. E., et al. (1986). The changing face of American psychology. *American Psychologist, 41,* 1311–1327.

Howard, I. P., & Rogers, B. J. (2001a). *Seeing in depth* (Vol. 1): *Basic mechanisms.* Toronto: Porteous.

Howard, I. P., & Rogers, B. J. (2001b) *Seeing in depth* (Vol. 2): *Depth perception.* Toronto: Porteous.

Howard, J. L., & Ferris, G. R. (1996). The employment interview context. *Journal of Applied Social Psychology, 26*(2), 112–136.

Howell, D. C. (2008). *Fundamental statistics for the behavioral sciences* (6th ed.). Belmont, CA: Cengage Learning/Wadsworth.

Howes, C. (1997). Children's experiences in center-based child care as a function of teacher background and adult:child ratio. *Merrill–Palmer Quarterly, 43*(3), 404–425.

Hsia, Y., & Graham, C. H. (1997). Color blindness. In A. Byrne, D. R. Hilbert, et al. (Eds.), *Readings on color* (Vol. 2): *The science of color.* Cambridge, MA: MIT Press.

Hu, S., Pattatucci, A. M., Patterson, C., Li, L., et al. (1995). Linkage between sexual orientation and chromosome Xq28 in males but not in females. *Nature Genetics 11*(3), 248–256.

Hubble, M.A., Duncan, B. L., & Miller, S. D. (Eds.) (1999). *The heart and soul of change: What works in therapy.* Washington, DC: American Psychological Association.

Hubel D. H., & Wiesel, W. N. (2005). *Brain & visual perception:*

The story of a 25-year collaboration. New York: Oxford University Press.

Hübner, R., & Volberg, G. (2005). The integration of object levels and their content: A theory of global/local processing and related hemispheric differences. *Journal of Experimental Psychology: Human Perception & Performance, 31*(3), 520–541.

Huesmann, L. R., Moise-Titus, J., Podolski, C., & Eron, L. D. (2003). Longitudinal relations between children's exposure to TV violence and their aggressive and violent behavior in young adulthood: 1977–1992. *Developmental Psychology, 39*(2), 201–221.

Hughes, J. N., & Hasbrouck, J. E. (1996). Television violence: Implications for violence prevention. *School Psychology Review, 25*(2), 134–151.

Hughes, J. R., Oliveto, A. H., Liguori, A., Carpenter, J., et al. (1998). Endorsement of DSM-IV dependence criteria among caffeine users. *Drug & Alcohol Dependence, 52*(2), 99–107.

Huijbregts, S. C., Séguin, J. R., Zelazo, P. D., Parent, S., et al. (2006). Interrelations between maternal smoking during pregnancy, birth weight and sociodemographic factors in the prediction of early cognitive abilities. *Infant & Child Development, 15*(6), 593–607.

Human Rights Watch. (2003). *Ill-equipped: U.S. prisons and offenders with mental illness*. New York: Human Rights Watch.

Hunt, R. R., & Ellis, H. C. (2004). *Fundamentals of cognitive psychology* (7th ed.). New York: McGraw-Hill.

Hunter, E. (1998). Adolescent attraction to cults. *Adolescence, 33*(131), 709–714.

Hunter, J. P., Katz, J., & Davis, K. D. (2003). The effect of tactile and visual sensory inputs on phantom limb awareness. *Brain, 126*(3), 579–589.

Hutchinson, S. R. (2004). Survey research. In K. deMarrais & S. D. Lapan (Eds.), *Foundations for research: Methods of inquiry in education and the social sciences. Inquiry and pedagogy across diverse contexts*. Mahwah, NJ: Erlbaum.

Hutchinson, S., Lee, L. H. L., Gaab, N., & Schlaug, G. (2003). Cerebellar volume of musicians. *Cerebral Cortex, 13*(9), 943–949.

Hyde, J. S. (2004). *Half the human experience: The psychology of women* (6th ed.). Boston: Houghton Mifflin.

Hyde, J. S., & DeLamater, J. D. (2006). *Understanding human sexuality* (9th ed.). New York: McGraw-Hill.

Hyman, R. (1996a). Evaluation of the military's twenty-year program on psychic spying. *Skeptical Inquirer, 20*(2), 21–23.

Hyman, R. (1996b). The evidence for psychic functioning: Claims vs. reality. *Skeptical Inquirer, 20*(2), 24–26.

Hysenbegasi, A., Hass, S. L., & Rowland, C. R. (2005). The impact of depression on the academic productivity of university students. *Journal of Mental Health Policy & Economics, 8*(3), 145–151.

Ida, Y., & Mandal, M. K. (2003). Cultural differences in side bias: Evidence from Japan and India. *Laterality: Asymmetries of Body, Brain & Cognition, 8*(2), 121–133.

Ingram, V. (2003). Alzheimer's disease. *American Scientist, 91,* 312–321.

Iosif, A., & Ballon, B. (2005). Bad moon rising: The persistent belief in lunar connections to madness. *Canadian Medical Association Journal, 173*(12), 1498–1500.

Ivanco, T. L., & Racine, R. J. (2000). Long-term potentiation in the pathways between the hippocampus and neocortex in the chronically implanted, freely moving, rat. *Hippocampus, 10,* 143–152.

Iversen, L. (2006). *Speed, ecstasy, ritalin: The science of amphetamines*. New York: Oxford University Press.

Izard, C. E. (1977). *Human emotions*. New York: Plenum.

Izard, C. E. (1990). Facial expressions and the regulation of emotions. *Journal of Personality & Social Psychology, 58*(3), 487–498.

Izard, C. E., Fantauzzo, C. A., Castle, J. M., Haynes, O. M., et al. (1995). The ontogeny and significance of infants' facial expressions in the first 9 months of life. *Developmental Psychology, 31*(6), 997–1013.

Jablonski, N.G., & Chaplin, G. (2000). The evolution of human skin coloration. *Journal of Human Evolution, 39*(1), 57–106.

Jackson, S. L. (2008). *Research methods: A modular approach*. Belmont, CA: Cengage Learning/Wadsworth.

Jackson, T., Fritch, A., Nagasaka, T., & Gunderson, J. (2002). Towards explaining the association between shyness and loneliness. *Social Behavior & Personality, 30*(3), 263–270.

Jackson, T., Towson, S., & Narduzzi, K. (1997). Predictors of shyness. *Social Behavior & Personality, 25*(2), 149–154.

Jacob, A., Prasad, S., Boggild, M., & Chandratre, S. (2004). Charles Bonnet syndrome: Elderly people and visual hallucinations. *British Medical Journal, 328*(7455), 1552–1554.

Jacobs, M. (2003). *Sigmund Freud*. Thousand Oaks, CA: Sage.

Jacobs, M. K., Christensen, A., Snibbe, J. R., Dolezal-Wood, S., et al. (2001). A comparison of computer-based versus traditional individual psychotherapy. *Professional Psychology: Research & Practice, 32*(1), 92–96.

Jacobs, S. R., & Dodd, D. K. (2003). Student burnout as a function of personality, social support, and workload. *Journal of College Student Development, 44*(3), 291–303.

Jacobsen, P. B., Bovbjerg, D. H., Schwartz, M. D., Andrykowski, M. A., et al. (1993). Formation of food aversions in cancer patients receiving repeated infusions of chemotherapy. *Behavior Research & Therapy, 31*(8), 739–748.

Jaffe, J., Beatrice, B., Feldstein, S., Crown, C. L., et al. (2001). Rhythms of dialogue in infancy. *Monographs of the Society for Research in Child Development, 66*(2), vi–131.

Jamison, K. R. (2001). Suicide in the young: An essay. *Cerebrum, 3*(3), 39–42.

Janis, I. L., & Wheeler, D. (1978). Thinking clearly about career choices. *Psychology Today, 11,* 66–78.

Janssen, S. A., & Arntz, A. (2001). Real-life stress and opioid-mediated analgesia in novice parachute jumpers. *Journal of Psychophysiology, 15*(2), 106–113.

Janus, S. S., & Janus, C. L. (1993). *The Janus report*. New York: Wiley.

Jarvin, L., & Sternberg, R. J. (2003). Alfred Binet's contributions to educational psychology. In B. J. Zimmerman & D. H. Schunk (Eds.), *Educational psychology: A century of contributions*. Mahwah, NJ: Erlbaum.

Jawahar, I. M., Stone, T. H., & Kisamore, J. L. (2007). Role conflict and burnout: The direct and moderating effects of political skill and perceived organizational support on burnout dimensions. *International Journal of Stress Management, 14*(2), 142–159.

Jay, T. B. (2003). *Psychology of language*. Englewood Cliffs, NJ: Prentice Hall.

Jeffery, R. W., & Wing R. R. (2001). The effects of an enhanced exercise program on long-term weight loss. *Obesity Research, 9*(3), O193.

Jenkins, J. G., & Dallenbach, K. M. (1924). Oblivescence during sleep and waking. *American Journal of Psychology, 35,* 605–612.

Jerabek, I., & Standing, L. (1992). Imagined test situations produce contextual memory enhancement. *Perceptual & Motor Skills, 75*(2), 400.

Johnson, K. E., & Mervis, C. B. (1997). Effects of varying levels of expertise on the basic level of categorization. *Journal of Experimental Psychology: General, 126*(3), 248–277.

Johnson, K. J., & Fredrickson, B. L. (2005). "We all look the same to me": Positive emotions eliminate the own-race bias in face recognition. *Psychological Science, 16*(11), 875–881.

Johnson, S. (2005). *Everything bad is good for you: How today's popular culture is actually making us smarter*. New York: Riverhead.

Johnson, S. M., & White, G. (1971). Self-observation as an agent of behavioral change. *Behavior Therapy, 2,* 488–497.

Johnson, T. J. (2002). College students' self-reported reasons for why drinking games end. *Addictive Behaviors, 27*(1), 145–153.

Jones, E. E., & Nisbett, R. E. (1971). The actor and observer: Divergent perceptions of the causes of behavior. In E. E. Jones, D. E. Kanouse, et al. (Eds.), *Attribution: Perceiving the causes of behavior*. Morristown, NJ: General Learning Press.

Jones, G. V., & Martin, M. (2001). Confirming the X-linked handedness gene as recessive, not additive. *Psychological Review, 108*(4), 811–813.

Jones, L., & Petruzzi, D. C. (1995). Test anxiety: A review of theory and current treatment. *Journal of College Student Psychotherapy, 10*(1), 3–15.

Jones, M. E., Russell, R. L., & Bryant, F. B. (1998). The structure of rape attitudes for men and women. *Journal of Research in Personality, 32*(3), 331–350.

Jones, M. K., & Menzies, R. G. (1998). Danger ideation reduction therapy (DIRT) for obsessive-compulsive washers. *Behaviour Research & Therapy, 36*(10), 959–970.

Jones, R. N. (2003). Racial bias in the assessment of cognitive functioning of older adults. *Aging & Mental Health, 7*(2), 83–102.

Jones, S. S., & Hong, H.-W. (2001). Onset of voluntary communication: Smiling looks to mother. *Infancy, 2*(3), 353–370.

Jorm, A. F., Korten, A. E., Rodgers, B., Jacomb, P. A., et al. (2002). Sexual orientation and mental health. *British Journal of Psychiatry, 180*(5), 423–427.

Jourard, S. M. (1963). *Personal adjustment*. New York: Macmillan.

Jouvet, M. (1999). *The paradox of sleep*. Cambridge, MA: MIT Press.

Jowett, G. S. (2006). Brainwashing: The Korean POW controversy and the origins of a myth. In G. S. Jowett & V. O'Donnell (Eds.), *Readings in propaganda and persuasion: New and classic essays*. Thousand Oaks, CA, Sage.

Joyce, P., & Sills, C. (2001). *Skills in Gestalt counseling & psychotherapy.* Newbury Park: Sage.

Juliano, L. M., & Griffiths, R. R. (2004). A critical review of caffeine withdrawal: Empirical validation of symptoms and signs, incidence, severity, and associated features. *Psychopharmacology, 176*(1), 1–29.

Julien, R. M. (2005). *A primer of drug action: A comprehensive guide to the actions, uses, and side effects* (10th ed.). New York: Worth.

Jussim, L., & Harber, K. D. (2005). Teacher expectations and self-fulfilling prophecies: Knowns and unknowns, resolved and unresolved controversies. *Personality & Social Psychology Review, 9*(2), 131–155.

Kagan, J. (1971). *Change and continuity in infancy.* New York: Wiley.

Kagan, J. (2004). New insights into temperament. *Cerebrum, 6*(1), 51–66.

Kagan, J. (2005). Personality and temperament: Historical perspectives. In M. Rosenbluth, S. H. Kennedy, et al. (Eds.), *Depression and personality: Conceptual and clinical challenges.* Washington, DC: American Psychiatric Publishing.

Kahneman, D. (2003). A perspective on judgment and choice. *American Psychologist, 58*(9), 697–720.

Kahneman, D., & Tversky, A. (1972). Subjective probability: A judgment of representativeness. *Cognitive Psychology, 3,* 430–454.

Kahneman, D., & Tversky, A. (1973). On the psychology of prediction. *Psychological Review, 80,* 237–251.

Kahneman, D., Krueger, A. B., Schkade, D., Schwarz, N., et al. (2004). A survey method for characterizing daily life experience: The day reconstruction method. *Science, 306*(5702), 1776–1780.

Kahneman, D., Slovic, P., & Tversky, A. (1982). *Judgment under uncertainty: Heuristics and biases.* Cambridge, MA: Cambridge University Press.

Kalat, J. W. (2007). *Biological psychology* (8th ed.). Belmont, CA: Cengage Learning/Wadsworth.

Kalat, J. W., & Shiota, M. N. (2007). *Emotion.* Belmont, CA: Cengage Learning/Wadsworth.

Kallio, S., & Revonsuo, A. (2003). Hypnotic phenomena and altered states of consciousness: A multilevel framework of description and explanation. *Contemporary Hypnosis, 20*(3), 111–164.

Kamimori, G. H., Johnson, D., Thorne, D., & Belenky, G. (2005). Multiple caffeine doses maintain vigilance during early morning operations. *Aviation, Space, & Environmental Medicine, 76*(11), 1046–1050.

Kamin, L. J. (1981). *The intelligence controversy.* New York: Wiley.

Kandel, E. R., Schwartz, J. H., & Jessell, T. M. (2003). *Principles of neuroscience* (5th ed.). New York: McGraw-Hill.

Kaplan, H. S. (1974). *The new sex therapy.* New York: Brunner/Mazel.

Kaplan, P. S. (1998). *The human odyssey.* Pacific Grove, CA: Brooks/Cole.

Kapleau, P. (1966). *The three pillars of Zen.* New York: Harper & Row.

Kapur, S., & Lecrubier, Y. (Eds.). (2003). *Dopamine in the pathophysiology and treatment of schizophrenia: New findings.* Washington, DC: Taylor & Francis.

Karim, A. A., Hinterberger, T., Richter, J, Mellinger, J., et al. (2006). Neural internet: Web surfing with brain potentials for the completely paralyzed. *Neurorehabilitation & Neural Repair, 20*(4), 508–515.

Karon, B. P., & Widener, A. J. (1997). Repressed memories and World War II: Lest we forget! *Professional Psychology: Research & Practice, 28*(4), 338–340.

Kasser, T., & Ryan, R. M. (1993). A dark side of the American dream: Correlates of financial success as a central life aspiration. *Journal of Personality & Social Psychology, 65*(2), 410–422.

Kasser, T., & Ryan, R. M. (1996). Further examining the American dream: Differential correlates of intrinsic and extrinsic goals. *Personality & Social Psychology Bulletin, 22*(3), 280–287.

Kassin, S. M. (2005). On the psychology of confessions: Does innocence put innocents at risk? *American Psychologist, 60*(3), 215–228.

Kassin, S. M., Fein, S., & Markus, H. R. (2008). *Social psychology* (7th ed.). Boston: Houghton Mifflin.

Kassin, S. M., Tubb, V. A., Hosch, H. M., & Memon, A. (2001). On the "general acceptance" of eyewitness testimony research. *American Psychologist, 56*(5), 405–416.

Kataria, S. (2004). A clinical guide to pediatric sleep: Diagnosis and management of sleep problems. *Journal of Developmental & Behavioral Pediatrics, 25*(2), 132–133.

Katz, P. A. (2003). Racists or tolerant multiculturalists? *American Psychologist, 58*(11), 897–909.

Kaufman, A. S. (2000). Intelligence tests and school psychology: Predicting the future by studying the past. *Psychology in the Schools, 37*(1), 7–16.

Kaufman, L., & Kaufman, J. H. (2000). Explaining the moon illusion. *Proceedings of the National Academy of Sciences, 97*(1), 500–505.

Kaufmann, J. (2007). Transfiguration: A narrative analysis of male-to-female transsexual. *International Journal of Qualitative Studies in Education, 20*(1), 1–13.

Kawai, K., Sugimoto, K., Nakashima, K., Miura, H., et al. (2000). Leptin as a modulator of sweet taste sensitivities in mice. *Proceedings: National Academy of Sciences, 97*(20), 11044–11049.

Kawasaki, H., Adolphs, R., Oya, H., Kovach, C. et al. (2005). Analysis of single-unit responses to emotional scenes in human ventromedial prefrontal cortex. *Journal of Cognitive Neuroscience, 17*(10), 1509–1518.

Kearney, C. A., Sims, K. E., Pursell, C. R., & Tillotson, C. A. (2003). Separation anxiety disorder in young children: A longitudinal and family analysis. *Journal of Clinical Child & Adolescent Psychology, 32*(4), 593–598.

Kebbell, M. R., & Wagstaff, G. F. (1998). Hypnotic interviewing: The best way to interview eyewitnesses? *Behavioral Sciences & the Law, 16*(1), 115–129.

Keefe, F. J., Abernethy, A. P., & Campbell, L. C. (2005). Psychological approaches to understanding and treating disease-related pain. *Annual Review of Psychology, 56,* 601–630.

Keel, P. K., & Klump, K. L. (2003). Are eating disorders culture-bound syndromes? Implications for conceptualizing their etiology. *Psychological Bulletin, 129*(5), 747–769.

Keller, M. C., & Young, R. K. (1996). Mate assortment in dating and married couples. *Personality & Individual Differences, 21*(2), 217–221.

Kellermann, A. L., Rivara, F. P., Rushforth, N. B., Banton, J. G., et al. (1993). Gun ownership as a risk factor for homicide in the home. *New England Journal of Medicine, 329*(15), 1084–1091.

Kelley, H. H. (1950). The warm–cold variable in first impressions of persons. *Journal of Personality, 18,* 431–439.

Kelly, I. W. (1999). "Debunking the debunkers": A response to an astrologer's debunking of skeptics. *Skeptical Inquirer,* Nov.-Dec., 37–43.

Kelly, M. P., Strassberg, D. S., & Turner, C. M. (2006). Behavioral assessment of couples' communication in female orgasmic disorder. *Journal of Sex & Marital Therapy, 32*(2), 81–95.

Kempermann, G. (2005). *Adult neurogenesis: Stem cells and neuronal development in the adult brain.* New York: Oxford University Press.

Kendler, K. S., Thornton, L. M., & Prescott, C. A. (2001). Gender differences in the rates of exposure to stressful life events and sensitivity to their depressogenic effects. *American Journal of Psychiatry, 158*(4), 587–593.

Kennaway, D. J., & Wright, H. (2002). Melatonin and circadian rhythms. *Current Topics in Medicinal Chemistry, 2,* 199–209.

Kenneth, M., Carpenter, K. M., & Hasin, D. S. (1998). Reasons for drinking alcohol. *Psychology of Addictive Behaviors, 12*(3), 168–184.

Kenny, P. J., & Markou, A. (2006). Nicotine self-administration acutely activates brain reward systems and induces a long-lasting increase in reward sensitivity. *Neuropsychopharmacology, 31*(6), 1203–1211.

Kerr, N. L., & Bray, R. M. (2005). Simulation, realism, and the study of the jury. In N. Brewer & K. D. Williams, (Eds.), *Psychology and law: An empirical perspective.* New York: Guilford.

Kety, S. S. (1979). Disorders of the human brain. *Scientific American, 241,* 202–214.

Keyes, C. L. M., & Haidt, J. (2003). Introduction: Human flourishing. In C. L. M. Keyes & J. Haidt (Eds.), *Flourishing.* Washington, DC: American Psychological Association.

Keysers, C., Xiao, D.-K., Földiák, P., & Perrett, D. I. (2005). Out of sight but not out of mind: The neurophysiology of iconic memory in the superior temporal sulcus. *Cognitive Neuropsychology, 22*(3–4), 316–332.

Kida, T. E. (2006). *Don't believe everything you think.* Buffalo, NY: Prometheus.

Kiecolt-Glaser, J. K., McGuire, L., Robles, T. F., & Glaser, R. (2002). Emotions, morbidity, and mortality. *Annual Review of Psychology, 53,* 83–107.

Killen, J. D., & Fortmann, S. P. (1997). Craving is associated with smoking relapse. *Experimental and Clinical Psychopharmacology, 5*(2), 137–142.

Kim, J., Singer, R. N., & Radlo, S. J. (1996). Degree of cognitive demands in psychomotor tasks and the effects of the five-step strategy on achievement. *Human Performance, 9*(2), 155–169.

Kim, S. (2000). Bogglers. *Discover,* Dec., 98.

Kim, S. (2002). Participative management and job satisfaction: Lessons for management leadership. *Public Administration Review, 62*(2), 231–241.

Kim-Cohen, J., Moffitt, T. E., Caspi, A., & Taylor, A. (2004). Genetic and environmental processes in young children's resilience and vulnerability to socioeconomic deprivation. *Child Development, 75*(3), 651–668.

King, B. E. (2005). *Human sexuality today* (5th ed.). Englewood Cliffs, NJ: Prentice Hall.

King, H. E. (1961). Psychological effects of excitation in the limbic system. In D. E. Sheer (Ed.), *Electrical stimulation of the brain*. Austin: University of Texas Press.

King, N. J., Muris, P., & Ollendick, T. H. (2005). Childhood fears and phobias: Assessment and treatment. *Child & Adolescent Mental Health, 10*(2), 50–56.

Kingsley, C. H. & Lambert, K. G. (2006). The maternal brain. *Scientific American, 294*(1), 72–79.

Kinnunen, L. H., Moltz, H., Metz, J., & Cooper, M. (2004). Differential brain activation in exclusively homosexual and heterosexual men produced by the selective serotonin reuptake inhibitor, fluoxetine. *Brain Research, 1024*(1–2), 251–254.

Kinsey, A., Pomeroy, W., & Martin, C. (1948). *Sexual behavior in the human male*. Philadelphia: Saunders.

Kinsey, A., Pomeroy, W., & Martin, C. (1953). *Sexual behavior in the human female*. Philadelphia: Saunders.

Kirsch, I., & Lynn, S. J. (1995). The altered state of hypnosis. *American Psychologist, 50*(10), 846–858.

Kirsch, I., & Sapirstein, G. (1998). Listening to Prozac but hearing placebo: A meta-analysis of antidepressant medication. *Prevention & Treatment, 1*, art. 0002a. Retrieved May 18, 2007, from http://journals.apa.org/prevention/volume1/pre0010002a.html.

Kirsch, I., (2005). The flexible observer and neodissociation theory. *Contemporary Hypnosis, 22*(3), 121–122.

Kirsh, S. J. (2005). *Children, adolescents, and media violence: A critical look at the research*. Newbury Park: Sage.

Kirveskari, E., Salmelin, R., & Hari, R. (2006). Neuromagnetic responses to vowels vs. tones reveal hemispheric lateralization. *Clinical Neurophysiology, 117*(3), 643–648.

Kiser, L. J., Heston, J. D., & Paavola, M. (2006). Day treatment centers/Partial hospitalization settings. In T. A. Petti & C. Salguero (Eds.), *Community child & adolescent psychiatry: A manual of clinical practice and consultation*. Washington, DC: American Psychiatric Publishing.

Kisilevsky, B. S., Hains, S. M. J., Jacquet, A.-Y., Granier-Deferre, C., et al. (2004). Maturation of fetal responses to music. *Developmental Science, 7*(5), 550–559.

Kitayama, S., Markus, H. R., & Kurokawa, M. (2000). Culture, emotion, and well-being: Good feelings in Japan and the United States. *Cognition & Emotion, 14,* 93–124.

Kite, M. E., Russo, N. F., Brehm, S. S., Fouad, N. A., et al. (2001). Women psychologists in academe. *American Psychologist, 56*(12), 1080–1098.

Klein, B., Richards, J. C., & Austin, D. W. (2006). Efficacy of internet therapy for panic disorder. *Journal of Behavior Therapy & Experimental Psychiatry, 37*(3), 213–238.

Klein, K., & Boals, A. (2001a). The relationship of life event stress and working memory capacity. *Applied Cognitive Psychology, 15*(5), 565–579.

Klein, K., & Boals, A. (2001b). Expressive writing can increase working memory capacity. *Journal of Experimental Psychology: General, 130*(3), 520–533.

Kleinke, C. L., Peterson, T. R., & Rutledge, T. R. (1998). Effects of self-generated facial expressions on mood. *Journal of Personality and Social Psychology, 74*(1), 272–279.

Kleinplatz, P. J. (1996). The erotic encounter. *Journal of Humanistic Psychology, 36*(3), 105–123.

Klohnen, E. C., & Luo, S. (2003). Interpersonal attraction and personality: What is attractive—self similarity, ideal similarity, complementarity or attachment security? *Journal of Personality & Social Psychology, 85*(4), 709–722.

Knaus, W. J., & Ellis, A. (2002). *The procrastination workbook: Your personalized program for breaking free from the patterns that hold you back*. Oakland, CA: New Harbinger Press.

Knight, J. (2005). The truth about lying. *Nature, 428*, 692–694.

Knoops, K. T. B., de Groot, L. C., Kromhout, D., Perrin, A., et al. (2004). Mediterranean diet, lifestyle factors, and 10-year mortality in elderly European men and women. *Journal of the American Medical Association, 292*(12), 1433–1439.

Koch, C. (2004). *The quest for consciousness: A neurobiological approach*. Englewood, CO: Roberts.

Koch, W. H., & Pratarelli, M. E. (2004). Effects of intro/extraversion and sex on social internet use. *North American Journal of Psychology, 6*(3), 371–382.

Kohlberg, L. (1969). The cognitive-developmental approach to socialization. In A. Goslin (Ed.), *Handbook of socialization theory and research*. Chicago: Rand McNally.

Kohlberg, L. (1981). *Essays on moral development* (Vol. 1): *The philosophy of moral development*. San Francisco: Harper.

Kohn, C. S., & Antonuccio, D. O. (2002). Treatment of kleptomania using cognitive and behavioral strategies. *Clinical Case Studies, 1*(1), 25–38.

Köke, A., Schouten J. S., Lamerichs-Geelen. M. J. H., Lipsch J. S. M., et al. (2004). Pain reducing effect of three types of transcutaneous electrical nerve stimulation in patients with chronic pain: A randomized crossover trial. *Pain, 108*(1–2), 36–42.

Kolb, B. (1990). Recovery from occipital stroke: A self-report and an inquiry into visual processes. *Canadian Journal of Psychology, 44*(2), 130–147.

Kolb, B., & Whishaw, I.Q. (2006). *Introduction to brain and behavior* (2nd ed.). New York: Freeman-Worth.

Kolb, B., Gibb, R., & Gorny, G. (2003). Experience-dependent changes in dendritic arbor and spine density in neocortex vary with age and sex. *Neurobiology of Learning & Memory, 79*(1), 1–10.

Kornhaber, M. L., & Gardner, H. (2006). Multiple intelligences: Developments in implementation and theory. In M. A. Constas & R. J. Sternberg (Eds.), *Translating theory and research into educational practice: Developments in content domains, large-scale reform, and intellectual capacity*. Mahwah, NJ: Erlbaum.

Korol, C., Craig, K. D., & Firestone, P. (2003). Dissociative and somatoform disorders. In P. Firestone & W. L. Marshall (Eds.), *Abnormal psychology: Perspectives* (2nd ed.). Toronto: Prentice Hall.

Koss, M. P. (1993). Rape. *American Psychologist, 48*(10), 1062–1069.

Koss, M. P. (2000). Blame, shame, and community: Justice responses to violence against women. *American Psychologist, 55*(11), 1332–1343.

Kosslyn, S. M. (1983). *Ghosts in the mind's machine*. New York: Norton.

Kosslyn, S. M. (1985). Stalking the mental image. *Psychology Today,* May, 23–28.

Kosslyn, S. M. (2005). Mental images and the brain. *Cognitive Neuropsychology, 22*(3–4), 333–347.

Kosslyn, S. M., Ball, T. M., & Reiser, B. J. (1978). Visual images preserve metric spatial information: Evidence from studies of image scanning. *Journal of Experimental Psychology: Human Perception and Performance, 4,* 47–60.

Kosslyn, S. M., Thompson, W. L., Costantini-Ferrando, M. F., Alpert, N. M., et al. (2000). Hypnotic visual illusion alters color processing in the brain. *American Journal of Psychiatry, 157*(8), 1279–1284.

Kosson, D. S., Suchy, Y., Mayer, A. R., & Libby, J. (2002). Facial affect recognition in criminal psychopaths. *Emotion, 2*(4), 398–411.

Kotkin, M., Daviet, C., & Gurin, J. (1996). The Consumer Reports mental health survey. *American Psychologist, 51*(10), 1080–1082.

Kottler, J. A. (2004). *Introduction to therapeutic counseling*. Belmont, CA: Cengage Learning/Wadsworth.

Kowert, P. A. (2002). *Groupthink or deadlock: When do leaders learn from their advisors? SUNY series on the presidency*. Albany, NY: State University of New York Press.

Kozart, M. F. (2002). Understanding efficacy in psychotherapy. *American Journal of Orthopsychiatry, 72*(2), 217–231.

Krakow, B., & Krakow, J. K. (2002). *Turning nightmares into dreams*. Albuquerque, NM: New Sleepy-Times.

Krakow, B., & Zadra, A. (2006). Clinical management of chronic nightmares: Imagery rehearsal therapy. *Behavioral Sleep Medicine, 4*(1), 45–70.

Krall, E. A., Garvey, A. J., & Garcia, R. I. (2002). Smoking relapse after 2 years of abstinence: Findings from the VA Normative Aging Study. *Nicotine & Tobacco Research, 4*(1), 95–100.

Krantz, D. S., & McCeney, M. K. (2002). Effects of psychological and social factors on organic disease. *Annual Review of Psychology, 53,* 341–369.

Krishnan, H. A., & Park, D. (2005). A few good women—on top management teams. *Journal of Business Research, 58,* 1712–1720.

Kristof-Brown, A. L., Barrick, M. R., & Franke, M. (2002). Applicant impression management: Dispositional influences and consequences for recruiter perceptions of fit and similarity. *Journal of Management, 28,* 27–46.

Ksir, C. J., Hart, C. L., & Ray, O. S. (2006). *Drugs, society, and human behavior* (11th ed.). New York: McGraw-Hill.

Kübler-Ross, E. (1975). *Death: The final stage of growth*. Englewood Cliffs, NJ: Prentice Hall.

Kubovy, M., & Gepshtein, S. (2003). Grouping in space and in space-time: An exercise in phenomenological psychophysics. In R. Kimchi, M. Behrmann, et al. (Eds.), *Perceptual organization in vision: Behavioral and neural perspectives*. Mahwah, NJ: Erlbaum.

Kuehner, C. (2003). Gender differences in unipolar depression: an update of epidemiological findings and possible explanations. *Acta Psychiatrica Scandinavica, 108*(3), 163–174.

Kuhl, P. K. (2004). Early language acquisition: Cracking the speech code. *Nature Reviews Neuroscience, 5*(11), 831–841.

Kuhn, C. M., & Wilson, W. A. (2001). Our dangerous love affair with Ecstasy. *Cerebrum, 3*(2), 22–33.

Kulik, J., Mahler, H. I. M., & Moore, P. J. (2003). Social comparison affiliation under threat: Effects on recovery from major surgery. In P. Salovey & A. J. Rothman (Eds.), *Social psychology of health: Key readings in social psychology.* New York: Psychology Press.

Kumaran, D., & Maguire, E. A. (2005). The human hippocampus: Cognitive maps or relational memory? *Journal of Neuroscience, 25*(31), 7254–7259.

Kunkel, M. A. (1993). A teaching demonstration involving perceived lunar size. *Teaching of Psychology, 20*(3), 178–180.

Kusseling, F. S., Shapiro, M. F., Greenberg, J. M., & Wenger, N. S. (1996). Understanding why heterosexual adults do not practice safer sex: A comparison of two samples. *AIDS Education & Prevention, 8*(3), 247–257.

Laan, E., Everaerd, W., van Bellen, G., & Hanewald, G. J. F. P. (1994). Women's sexual and emotional responses to male- and female-produced erotica. *Archives of Sexual Behavior, 23*(2), 153–169.

LaBar, K. S., & LeDoux, J. E. (2002). Emotional learning circuits in animals and man. In R. J. Davidson, K. R. Scherer, et al. (Eds.), *Handbook of affective sciences.* New York: Oxford University Press.

Laberge, L., Petit, D., Simard, C., Vitaro, F., et al. (2001). Development of sleep patterns in early adolescence. *Journal of Sleep Research, 10*(1), 59–67.

LaBerge, S. (2000). Lucid dreaming: Evidence and methodology. In F. E. Pace-Schott, M. Solms, et al. (Eds.), *Sleep and dreaming: Scientific advances and reconsiderations.* Cambridge, UK: Cambridge University Press.

Labov, W. (1973). The boundaries of words and their meanings. In C. J. N. Bailey & R. W. Shuy (Eds.), *New ways of analyzing variation in English.* Washington, DC: Georgetown University Press.

LaBrie, R. A., & Shaffer, H. J. (2007). Gambling with adolescent health. *Journal of Adolescent Health, 40*(5), 387–389.

Lacayo, A. (1995). Neurologic and psychiatric complications of cocaine abuse. *Neuropsychiatry, Neuropsychology, & Behavioral Neurology, 8*(1), 53–60.

Lachman, M. E. (2004). Development in midlife. *Annual Review of Psychology, 55,* 305–331.

Lackner, J. R., & DiZio, P. (2005). Vestibular, proprioceptive, and haptic contributions to spatial orientation. *Annual Review of Psychology, 56,* 115–147.

Lamb, M. R., & Yund, E. W. (1996). Spatial frequency and attention. *Perception & Psychophysics, 58*(3), 363–373.

Lambert, M. J. (1999). Are differential treatment effects inflated by researcher therapy allegiance? *Clinical Psychology: Science & Practice, 6*(1), 127–130.

Lambert, M. J., & Cattani-Thompson, K. (1996). Current findings regarding the effectiveness of counseling. *Journal of Counseling & Development, 74*(6), 601–608.

Lambert, M. J., & Ogles, B. M. (2002). The efficacy and effectiveness of psychotherapy. In M. J. Lambert (Ed.), *Handbook of psychotherapy and behavior change* (5th ed.). New York: Wiley.

Lambert, W. E. (1987). The effects of bilingual and bicultural experiences on children's attitudes and social perspectives. In P. Homel, M. Palij, et al. (Eds.), *Childhood bilingualism.* Mahwah, NJ: Erlbaum.

Lance, C. E., LaPointe, J. A., & Stewart, A. M. (1994). A test of the context dependency of three causal models of halo rater error. *Journal of Applied Psychology, 79*(3), 332–340.

Landau, J. D., & Bavaria A. J. (2003). Does deliberate source monitoring reduce students's misconceptions about psychology? *Teaching of Psychology, 30,* 311–314.

Landy, F. J., & Conte, J. M. (2007). *Work in the 21st century: An introduction to industrial and organizational psychology* (2nd ed.). London: Blackwell.

Landy, F. J., Shankster, L. J., & Kohler, S. S. (1994). Personnel selection and placement. *Annual Review of Psychology, 45,* 261–296.

Langer, E. J. (2000). Mindful learning. *Current Directions in Psychological Science, 9*(6), 220–223.

Langleben, D. D., Dattilio, F. M., & Gutheil, T. G. (2006). True lies: Delusions and lie-detection technology. *Journal of Psychiatry & Law, 34*(3), 351–370.

Langleben, D. D., Loughead, J. W., Bilker, W. B., Ruparel, K., et al. (2005). Telling truth from lie in individual subjects with fast event-related fMRI. *Human Brain Mapping, 26*(4), 262–272.

Langleben, D. D., Schroeder, L, Maldjian, J. A., Gur, R. C., et al. (2002). Brain activity during simulated deception: An event-related functional magnetic resonance study. *NeuroImage, 15,* 727–732.

Langone, M. D. (2002). Cults, conversion, science, and harm. *Cultic Studies Review, 1*(2), 178–186.

Lanzetta, J. T., & Englis, B. G. (1989). Expectations of cooperation and competition and their effects on observers' vicarious emotional responses. *Journal of Personality & Social Psychology, 56*(4), 543–554.

Larner, A. J., Moss, J., Rossi, M. L., & Anderson, M. (1994). Congenital insensitivity to pain. *Journal of Neurology, Neurosurgery & Psychiatry, 57*(8), 973–974.

Larsen, R. J., & Buss, D. M. (2005). *Personality psychology* (2nd ed.). New York: McGraw-Hill.

Larsen, R. J., & Kasimatis, M. (1990). Individual differences in entrainment of mood to the weekly calendar. *Journal of Personality & Social Psychology, 58*(1), 164–171.

Larsen, R.J., & Prizmic, Z. (2004). Affect regulation. In R. Baumeister & K. D. Voohs (Eds.), *Handbook of self-regulation: Research, theory, and applications.* New York: Guilford.

Larson, M. E., Houlihan, D., & Goernert, P. N. (1995). Effects of informational feedback on aluminum can recycling. *Behavioral Interventions, 10*(2), 111–117.

Larsson, B., Carlsson, J., Fichtel, Å., & Melin, L. (2005). Relaxation treatment of adolescent headache sufferers: Results from a school-based replication series. *Headache: The Journal of Head & Face Pain, 45*(6), 692–704.

Larsson, J.-O., Larsson, H., & Lichtenstein, P. (2004). Genetic and environmental contributions to stability and change of ADHD symptoms between 8 and 13 years of age: A longitudinal twin study. *Journal of the American Academy of Child & Adolescent Psychiatry, 43*(10), 1267–1275.

Latané, B., Nida, S. A., & Wilson, D. W. (1981). The effects of group size on helping behavior. In J. P. Rushton & R. M. Sorrentino (Eds.), *Altruism and helping behavior: Social, personality and developmental perspectives.* Mahwah, NJ: Erlbaum.

Lattal, K. A., Reilly, M. P., & Kohn, J. P. (1998). Response persistence under ratio and interval reinforcement schedules. *Journal of the Experimental Analysis of Behavior, 70*(2), 165–183.

Laub, J. H., & Sampson, R. J. (2003). *Shared beginnings, divergent lives: Delinquent boys to age 70.* Cambridge, MA: Harvard University Press.

Laumann, E., Michael, R., Michaels, S., & Gagnon, J. (1994). *The social organization of sexuality.* Chicago: University of Chicago Press.

Laurent, G., Stopfer, M., Friedrich, R. W., Rabinovich, M. I., et al. (2001). Odor encoding as an active, dynamical process. *Annual Review of Neuroscience, 24,* 263–297.

Lavie, P. (2001). Sleep-wake as a biological rhythm. *Annual Review of Psychology, 52,* 277–303.

Lawson, H. M., & Leck, K. (2006). Dynamics of Internet dating. *Social Science Computer Review, 24*(2), 189–208.

Lay, C., & Verkuyten, M. (1999). Ethnic identity and its relation to personal self-esteem. *Journal of Social Psychology, 139*(3), 288–299.

Lazar, S. W. (2005). Mindfulness research. In C. K. Germer, R. D. Siegel, et al. (Eds.), *Mindfulness and psychotherapy.* New York: Guilford.

Lazar, S. W., Bush, G., Gollub, R. L., Fricchione, G. L., et al. (2000). Functional brain mapping of the relaxation response and meditation. *Neuroreport, 11*(7), 1581–1585.

Lazarus, R. S. (1991a). Progress on a cognitive–motivational–relational theory of emotion. *American Psychologist, 46*(8), 819–834.

Lazarus, R. S. (1991b). Cognition and motivation in emotion. *American Psychologist, 46*(4), 352–367.

Lazev, A. B., Herzog, T. A., & Brandon, T. H. (1999). Classical conditioning of environmental cues to cigarette smoking. *Experimental and Clinical Psychopharmacology, 7*(1), 56–63.

Leal, M. C., Shin, Y. J., Laborde, M.-L., Calmels, M.-N., et al. (2003). Music perception in adult cochlear implant recipients. *Acta Oto-Laryngologica, 123*(7), 826–835.

Leavens, D. A., & Hopkins, W. D. (1998). Intentional communication by chimpanzees. *Developmental Psychology, 34*(5), 813–822.

LeBlanc, G., & Bearison, D. J. (2004). Teaching and learning as a bi-directional activity: Investigating dyadic interactions between child teachers and child learners. *Cognitive Development, 19*(4), 499–515.

Lederman, S. J., & Klatzky, R. L. (2004). Haptic identification of common objects: Effects of constraining the manual exploration process. *Perception & Psychophysics, 66*(4), 618–628.

Lederman, S. J., Howe, R. D., Klatzky, R. L., & Hamilton, C. (2004). Force variability during surface contact with bare finger or rigid probe. *12th International Symposium on Haptic Interfaces for Virtual Environment and Teleoperator Systems,* 154–160.

LeDoux, J. (1996). *The emotional brain: The mysterious underpinnings of emotional life.* New York: Simon & Schuster.

LeDoux, J. (1999). The power of emotions. In R. Conlan (Ed.), *States of mind.* New York: Wiley.

LeDoux, J. E., & Gorman, J. M. (2001). A call to action: Overcoming anxiety through active coping. *American Journal of Psychiatry, 158*(12), 1953–1955.

Lee, J. M., Ku, J. H., Jang, D. P., Kim, D., et al. (2002). Virtual reality system for treatment of the fear of public speaking using image-based rendering and moving pictures. *CyberPsychology & Behavior, 5*(3), 191–195.

Lee, M., Zimbardo, P. G., & Bertholf, M. (1977). Shy murderers. *Psychology Today,* Nov., 69.

Leenaars, A. A., Lester, D., & Wenckstern, S. (2005). Coping with: The art and the research. In R. I. Yufit & D. Lester (Eds.), *Assessment, treatment, and prevention of suicidal behavior.* New York: Wiley.

Leeper, R. W. (1935). A study of a neglected portion of the field of learning: The development of sensory organization. *Pedagogical Seminary & Journal of Genetic Psychology, 46,* 41–75.

Lefcourt, H. M. (2003). Humor as a moderator of life stress in adults. In C. E. Schaefer (Ed.), *Play therapy with adults.* New York: Wiley.

Lefkowitz, E. S., & Zeldow, P. B. (2006). Masculinity and femininity predict optimal mental health: A belated test of the androgyny hypothesis. *Journal of Personality Assessment, 87*(1), 95–101.

Lefrançois, G. R. (2006). *Theories of human learning: What the old woman said* (5th ed.). Belmont, CA: Cengage Learning/Wadsworth.

Lehman, C. M., & DuFrene, D. D. (2008). *Business communication* (15th ed.). Belmont, CA: Cengage Learning/South-western.

Lehman, D. R., Chiu, C., & Schaller, M. (2004). Psychology and culture. *Annual Review of Psychology, 55,* 689–714.

Leichtman, M. (2004). Projective tests: The nature of the task. In M. J. Hilsenroth & D. L. Segal (Eds.), *Comprehensive handbook of psychological assessment* (Vol. 2): *Personality assessment.* New York: Wiley.

Leiter, M. P., & Maslach, C. (2005). *Banishing burnout: Six strategies for improving your relationship with work.* San Francisco: Jossey-Bass.

Lejuez, C. W., Eifert, G. H., Zvolensky, M. J., & Richards, J. B. (2000). Preference between onset predictable and unpredictable administrations of 20% carbon-dioxide-enriched air: Implications for better understanding the etiology and treatment of panic disorder. *Journal of Experimental Psychology: Applied, 6*(4), 349–358.

Lench, H. C. (2004). Anger management: Diagnostic differences and treatment implications. *Journal of Social & Clinical Psychology, 23*(4), 512–531.

Lenton, A. P., & Bryan, A. (2005). An affair to remember: The role of sexual scripts in perceptions of sexual intent. *Personal Relationships, 12*(4), 483–498.

Lenzenweger, M. F., & Gottesman, I. I. (1994). Schizophrenia. In V. S. Ramachandran (Ed.), *Encyclopedia of human behavior.* San Diego: Academic Press.

Leor, J., Poole, W. K., & Kloner, R. A. (1996). Sudden cardiac death triggered by earthquake. *The New England Journal of Medicine, 334*(7), 413.

Lepore, F. E. (2002). When seeing is not believing. *Cerebrum, 4*(2), 23–38.

Leslie, K., & Ogilvie, R. (1996). Vestibular dreams: The effect of rocking on dream mentation. *Dreaming: Journal of the Association for the Study of Dreams, 6*(1), 1–16.

Lessow-Hurley, J. (2005). *Foundations of dual language instruction* (4th ed.). Boston: Allyn & Bacon.

Lester, D. (2006). Sexual orientation and suicidal behavior. *Psychological Reports, 99*(3), 923–924.

Lester, D., & Yang, B. (2005). Regional and time-series studies of suicide in nations of the world. *Archives of Suicide Research, 9*(2), 123–133.

Lettvin, J. Y. (1961). Two remarks on the visual system of the frog. In W. Rosenblith (Ed.), *Sensory communication.* Cambridge, MA: MIT Press.

LeUnes, J., & Nation, J. R. (2002). *Sport psychology* (3rd ed.). Belmont, CA: Cengage Learning/Wadsworth.

Levant, R. F. (1996). The new psychology of men. *Professional Psychology: Research & Practice, 27*(3), 259–265.

Levant, R. F. (2001). Men and masculinity. In J. Worell (Ed.), *Encyclopedia of women and gender.* San Diego: Academic Press.

Levant, R. F. (2003). Treating male alexithymia. In L. B. Silverstein & T. J. Goodrich (Eds.), *Feminist family therapy: Empowerment in social context.* Washington, DC: American Psychological Association.

Levant, R. F., Good, G. E., Cook, S. W., O'Neil, J. M., et al. (2006). The Normative Male Alexithymia Scale: Measurement of a gender-linked syndrome. *Psychology of Men & Masculinity, 7*(4), 212–224.

LeVay, S. (1993). *The sexual brain.* Cambridge, MA: MIT Press.

LeVay, S. (2006). *The biology of sexual orientation.* Retrieved July 30, 2007, from http://members.aol.com/slevay/page22.html.

LeVay, S., & Valente, S. M. (2006). *Human sexuality* (2nd ed.). Sunderland, MA: Sinauer Associates.

Levenston, G. K., Patrick, C. J., Bradley, M. M., & Lange, P. J. (2000). The psychopathic observer. *Journal of Abnormal Psychology, 109,* 373–385.

Levesque, M. J., Steciuk, M., & Ledley, C. (2002). Self-disclosure patterns among well-acquainted individuals. *Social Behavior & Personality, 30*(6), 579–592.

Levett, L. M., Danielsen, E. M., Kovera, M. B., & Cutler, B. L. (2005). The psychology of jury and juror decision making. In N. Brewer & K. D. Williams (Eds.), *Psychology and law: An empirical perspective.* New York: Guilford.

Levi, A. M. (1998). Are defendants guilty if they were chosen in a lineup? *Law & Human Behavior, 22*(4), 389–407.

Levin, B. E. (2006). Metabolic sensing neurons and the control of energy homeostasis. *Physiology & Behavior, 89*(4), 486–489.

Levin, R., & Fireman, G. (2002). Nightmare prevalence, nightmare distress, and self-reported psychological disturbance. *Sleep: Journal of Sleep & Sleep Disorders Research, 25*(2), 205–212.

Levine, D. (2000). Virtual attraction: What rocks your boat. *CyberPsychology & Behavior, 3*(4), 565–573.

Levine, M., & Harrison, K. (2004). Media's role in the perpetuation and prevention of negative body image and disordered eating. In J. K. Thompson (Ed.), *Handbook of eating disorders and obesity.* New York: Wiley.

Levine, R. V. (1998). *A geography of time.* New York: Basic.

Levine, R. V. (2003). The kindness of strangers. *American Scientist, 91*(May-June), 226–233.

Levinson, D. J. (1986). A conception of adult development. *American Psychologist, 41*(1), 3–13.

Levinson, D. J., & Levinson, J. D. (1996). *The seasons of a woman's life.* New York: Knopf.

Levitsky, D. A., Nussbaum, M., Halbmaier, C.A., & Mrdjenovic, G. (2003). The Freshman 15: A model for the study of techniques to curb the "epidemic" of obesity. *Society for the Study of Ingestive Behavior: Annual Meeting,* July 15–19, University of Groningen, Haren, The Netherlands.

Levy, D. A. (2003). *Tools of critical thinking: Metathoughts for psychology.* Long Grove, IL: Waveland Press.

Levy, J., & Reid, M. (1976). Cerebral organization. *Science, 194,* 337–339.

Lewchanin, S., & Zubrod, L. A. (2001). Choices in life: A clinical tool for facilitating midlife review. *Journal of Adult Development, 8*(3), 193–196.

Lewis, M. (1995). Self-conscious emotions. *American Scientist, 83*(Jan-Feb.), 68–78.

Lewis, P. S., Goodman, S. H., & Fandt, P. M. (1995). *Management.* St Paul, MN: West.

Lewy, A. J., Bauer V. K., Cutler, N. L., Sack, R. L., et al. (1998). Morning vs. evening light treatment of patients with winter depression. *Archives of General Psychiatry, 55*(10), 890–896.

Leyendecker, B., Harwood, R. L., Comparini, L., & Yalçinkaya, A. (2005). Socioeconomic status, ethnicity, and parenting. In T. Luster & L. Okagaki (Eds.), *Parenting: An ecological perspective* (2nd ed.). Mahwah, NJ: Erlbaum.

Lichtman, A. H., & Martin, B. R. (2006). Understanding the pharmacology and physiology of cannabis dependence. In R. Roffman & R. S. Stephens (Eds.), *Cannabis dependence. Its nature, consequences and treatment.* New York: Cambridge University Press.

Liddell, S. K. (2003). *Grammar, gesture and meaning in American Sign Language.* Cambridge, UK: Cambridge University Press.

Lidz, C. W., Banks, S., Simon, L., Schubert, C., et al. (2007). Violence and mental illness: A new analytic approach. *Law & Human Behavior, 31*(1), 23–31.

Lieberman, D. A. (2004). *Learning and memory: An integrative approach.* Belmont, CA: Cengage Learning/Wadsworth.

Lievens, F., & Sackett, P. R. (2006). Video-based versus written situational judgment tests: A comparison in terms of predictive validity. *Journal of Applied Psychology, 91*(5), 1181–1188.

Lilienfeld, S. O. (1999). Projective measures of personality and psychopathology. *Skeptical Inquirer,* Sept.-Oct., 32–39.

Lilienfeld, S. O. (2005). Pseudoscience, nonscience, and nonsense in clinical psychology: Dangers and remedies. In K. A. Fowler, J. M. Lohr, et al. (Eds.), *Destructive trends in mental health: The well-intentioned path to harm.* New York: Routledge.

Lilienfeld, S. O., Fowler, K. A., Lohr, J. M., & Lynn, S. (2005). Pseudoscience, nonscience & nonsense in clinical psychology: Dangers and remedies. In R. H. Wright & N. A. Cummings (Eds.), *Destructive trends in mental health: The well-intentioned path to harm.* New York: Routledge.

Lindemann, B. (2000). A taste for umami. *Nature Neuroscience, 3,* 99–100.

Lindemann, B. (2001). Receptors and transduction in taste. *Nature, 413,* 219–225.

Linden, W. (2005). *Stress management: From basic science to better practice.* Thousand Oaks, CA: Sage.

Linderoth, B., & Foreman, R. D. (2006). Mechanisms of spinal cord stimulation in painful syndromes: Role of animal models. *Pain Medicine, 7*(Suppl 1), S14–S26.

Lindsay, E. W., Mize, J., & Pettit, G. S. (1997). Differential pay patterns of mothers and fathers of sons and daughters. *Sex Roles, 37*(9–10), 643–661.

Lipsey, M. W., & Wilson, D. B. (1993). The efficacy of psychological, educational, and behavioral treatment: Confirmation from meta-analysis. *American Psychologist, 48,* 1181–1209.

Liu, X., Matochik, J. A., Cadet, J., & London, E. D. (1998). Smaller volume of prefrontal lobe in polysubstance abusers. *Neuropsychopharmacology, 18*(4), 243–252.

Liu, Y., Gao, J., Liu, H., & Fox, P. T. (2000). The temporal response of the brain after eating revealed by functional MRI. *Nature, 405,* 1058–1062.

Locke, B. D., & Mahalik, J. R. (2005). Examining masculinity norms, problem drinking, and athletic involvement as predictors of sexual aggression in college men. *Journal of Counseling Psychology, 52*(3), 279–283.

Loeber, R., & Hay, D. (1997). Key issues in the development of aggression and violence from childhood to early adulthood. *Annual Review of Psychology, 48,* 371–410.

Loehlin, J. C., McCrae, R. R., Costa, P. T., & John, O. (1998). Heritabilities of common and measure-specific components of the Big Five personality factors. *Journal of Research in Personality, 32*(4), 431–453.

Loftus, E., & Loftus, G. (1980). On the permanence of stored information in the human brain. *American Psychologist, 35,* 409–420.

Loftus, E. F. (2003a). Make-believe memories. *American Psychologist, 58*(11), 867–873.

Loftus, E. F. (2003b). Memory in Canadian courts of law. *Canadian Psychology, 44*(3), 207–212.

Loftus, E. F., & Bernstein, D. M. (2005). Rich false memories: The royal road to success. In A. F. Healy (Ed.), *Experimental cognitive psychology and its applications.* Washington, DC: American Psychological Association.

Loftus, E. F., & Ketcham, K. (1994). *The myth of repressed memory: False memories and allegations of abuse.* New York: St. Martin's Press.

Loftus, E. F., & Palmer, J. C. (1974). Reconstruction of automobile destruction: An example of interaction between language and memory. *Journal of Verbal Learning & Verbal Behavior, 13,* 585–589.

Loftus, G. R., & Mackworth, N. H. (1978). Cognitive determinants of fixation location during picture viewing. *Journal of Experimental Psychology: Human Perception & Performance, 4,* 565–572.

LoLordo, V. M. (2001). Learned helplessness and depression. In M. E. Carroll & J. B. Overmier (Eds.), *Animal research and human health: Advancing human welfare through behavioral science.* Washington, DC: American Psychological Association.

Long, E. C., & Andrews, D. W. (1990). Perspective taking as a predictor of marital adjustment. *Journal of Personality & Social Psychology, 59*(1), 126–131.

Long, V. O. (1989). Relation of masculinity to self-esteem and self-acceptance in male professionals, college students, and clients. *Journal of Counseling Psychology, 36*(1), 84–87.

López, S. R., & Guarnaccia, P. J. J. (2000). Cultural psychopathology. *Annual Review of Psychology, 51,* 571–598.

Lorenz, K. (1966). *On aggression.* Translated by M. Kerr-Wilson. New York: Harcourt Brace Jovanovich.

Lorenz, K. (1974). *The eight deadly sins of civilized man.* Translated by M. Kerr-Wilson. New York: Harcourt Brace Jovanovich.

Lovaas, O., & Simmons, J. (1969). Manipulation of self-destruction in three retarded children. *Journal of Applied Behavior Analysis, 2,* 143–157.

Low, K. G., & Feissner, J. M. (1998). Seasonal affective disorder in college students: Prevalence and latitude. *Journal of American College Health, 47*(3), 135–137.

Low, S. M. (2001). The edge and the center: Gated communities and the discourse of urban fear. *American Anthropologist, 103*(1), 45–58.

Lucas, F., & Sclafani, A. (1990). Hyperphagia in rats produced by a mixture of fat and sugar. *Physiology & Behavior, 47*(1), 51–55.

Lucas, J. L., & Heady, R. B. (2002). Flextime commuters and their driver stress, feelings of time urgency, and commute satisfaction. *Journal of Business & Psychology, 16*(4), 565–572.

Luce, G. G. (1965). *Current research on sleep and dreams.* Health Service Publication no. 1389. Washington, DC: U.S. Department of Health, Education, and Welfare.

Luchins, D. J., Cooper, A. E., Hanrahan, P., & Rasinski, K. (2004). Psychiatrists' attitudes toward involuntary hospitalization. *Psychiatric Services, 55*(9), 1058–1060.

Ludwig, T. D., Gray, T. W., & Rowell, A. (1998). Increasing recycling in academic buildings. *Journal of Applied Behavior Analysis, 31*(4), 683–686.

Lumley, M. A. (2004). Alexithymia, emotional disclosure, and health: A program of research. *Journal of Personality, 72*(6), 1271–1300.

Lundh, L., Berg, B., Johansson, H., Nilsson, L., et al. (2002). Social anxiety is associated with a negatively distorted perception of one's own voice. *Cognitive Behaviour Therapy, 31*(1), 25–30.

Luppa, M., Heinrich, S., Angermeyer, M. C., König, H.-H., et al. (2007). Cost-of-illness studies of depression: A systematic review. *Journal of Affective Disorders, 98*(1–2), 29–43.

Luria, A. R. (1968). *The mind of a mnemonist.* New York: Basic Books.

Lustig, C., May, C. P., Hasher, L. (2001). Working memory span and the role of proactive interference. *Journal of Experimental Psychology: General, 130*(2), 199–207.

Luyben, P. D., Hipworth, K., & Pappas, T. (2003). Effects of CAI on the academic performance and attitudes of college students. *Teaching of Psychology, 30*(2), 154–158.

Lykken, D. T. (1998). *A tremor in the blood: Uses and abuses of the lie detector.* New York: Plenum.

Lykken, D. T. (2001). Lie detection. In W. E. Craighead & C. B. Nemeroff (Eds.), *The Corsini encyclopedia of psychology and behavioral science* (3rd ed.). New York: Wiley.

Lynch, K. B., Geller, S. R., & Schmidt, M. G. (2004). Multiyear evaluation of the effectiveness of a resilience-based prevention program for young children. *Journal of Primary Prevention, 24*(3), 335–353.

Lynch, T. R., Robins, C. J., Morse, J. Q., & Krause, E. D. (2001). A mediational model relating affect intensity, emotion inhibition, and psychological distress. *Behavior Therapy, 32*(3), 519–536.

Lynn, S. J., & Kirsch, I. (2006). Introduction: Definitions and early history. In S. J. Lynn & I. Kirsch (Eds.), *Essentials of clinical hypnosis: An evidence-based approach.* Washington, DC: American Psychological Association.

Lyons, A. C., & Chamberlain, K. (2006). *Health psychology.* Cambridge, MA: Cambridge University Press.

Lyubomirsky, S., & Tucker, K. L. (1998). Implications of individual differences in subjective happiness for perceiving, interpreting, and thinking about life events. *Motivation & Emotion, 22*(2), 155–186.

Maas, J. (1999). *Power Sleep.* New York: HarperCollins.

Maccoby, E. E. (1990). Gender and relationships: A developmental account. *American Psychologist, 45*(4), 513–520.

Maccoby, E. E., & Jacklin, C. N. (1974). *The psychology of sex differences.* Stanford, CA: Stanford University Press.

Mack, A. (2002). Is the visual world a grand illusion? *Journal of Consciousness Studies, 9*(5–6), 102–110.

Mackintosh, N. J. (2003). Pavlov and associationism. *Spanish Journal of Psychology, 6*(2), 177–184.

Macklin, C. B., & McDaniel, M. A. (2005). The bizarreness effect: Dissociation between item and source memory. *Memory, 13*(7), 682–689.

MacLeod, C. M. (2005). The Stroop task in cognitive research. In A. Wenzel & D. C. Rubin (Eds.), *Cognitive methods and their application to clinical research.* Washington, DC: American Psychological Association.

Macmillan, R. (2001). Violence and the life course. *Annual Review of Sociology, 27,* 1–22.

Maddi, S. R. (2006). Hardiness: The courage to grow from stresses. *Journal of Positive Psychology, 1*(3), 160–168.

Maddock, J. E., Laforge, R. G., Rossi, J. S., & O'Hare, T. (2001). The College Alcohol Problems Scale. *Addictive Behaviors, 26,* 385–398.

Maddock, J., & Glanz, K. (2005). The relationship of proximal normative beliefs and global subjective norms to college students' alcohol consumption. *Addictive Behaviors, 30*(2), 315–323.

Maddox, K. B. (2004). Perspectives on racial phenotypicality bias. *Personality & Social Psychology Review, 8*(4), 383–401.

Maguire, E. A., Frackowiak, R. S. J., & Frith, C. D. (1997). Recalling routes around London: Activation of the hippocampus in taxi drivers. *Journal of Neuroscience, 17*(8), 7103.

Maguire, E. A., Valentine, E. R., Wilding, J. M., & Kapur, N. (2003). Routes to remembering: The brains behind superior memory. *Nature Neuroscience, 6*(1), 90–95.

Mah, K., & Binik, Y. M. (2001). The nature of human orgasm: A critical review of major trends. *Clinical Psychology Review, 21*(6), 823–856.

Mahay, J., & Laumann, E. O. (2004). Meeting and mating over the life course. In E. O. Laumann & R. Michael (Eds.), *The sexual organization of the city.* Chicago: University of Chicago Press.

Maheu, M. M., Pulier, M. L., Wilhelm, F. H., McMenamin, J. P., et al. (2004). *The mental health professional and the new technologies: A handbook for practice today.* Mahwah, NJ: Erlbaum.

Maier, N. R. F. (1949). *Frustration.* New York: McGraw-Hill.

Maier, S. F. (2001). Exposure to the stressor environment prevents the temporal dissipation of behavioral depression/learned helplessness. *Biological Psychiatry, 49*(9), 763–773.

Mailis-Gagnon, A., & Israelson, D. (2005). *Beyond pain: Making the mind-body connection.* Ann Arbor, MI: University of Michigan Press.

Malaspina, D., Reichenberg, A., Weiser, M., Fennig, S., et al.

(2005). Paternal age and intelligence: Implications for age-related genomic changes in male germ cells. *Psychiatric Genetics, 15*(2), 117–125.

Manalo, E. (2002). Uses of mnemonics in educational settings: A brief review of selected research. *Psychologia: An International Journal of Psychology in the Orient, 45*(2), 69–79.

Mandler, J. M., & McDonough, L. (1998). On developing a knowledge base in infancy. *Developmental Psychology, 34*(6), 1274–1288.

Mangan, M. A. (2004). A phenomenology of problematic sexual behavior occurring in sleep. *Archives of Sexual Behavior, 33*(3), 287–293.

Mangels, J. A., Picton, T. W., & Craik, F. I. M. (2001). Attention and successful episodic encoding: An event-related potential study. *Brain Research, 11,* 77–95.

Manschreck, T. C. (1996). Delusional disorder: The recognition and management of paranoia. *Journal of Clinical Psychiatry, 57*(3, Suppl), 32–38.

Mansouri, A., & Adityanjee. (1995). Delusion of pregnancy in males: A case report and literature review. *Psychopathology, 28*(6), 307–311.

Mantyla, T. (1986). Optimizing cue effectiveness: Recall of 600 incidentally learned words. *Journal of Experimental Psychology: Learning, Memory, and Cognition, 12*(1), 66–71.

Marcus, E. (2002). Psychoanalytic psychotherapy and psychoanalysis: An overview. In M. Hersen & W. H. Sledge (Eds.), *Encyclopedia of psychotherapy.* San Diego: Academic Press.

Margolin, G., & Gordis, E. B. (2000). The effects of family and community violence on children. *Annual Review of Psychology, 51,* 445–479.

Markowitz, J. C. (2005). Interpersonal therapy. In J. M. Oldham, A. E. Skodol et al. (Eds.), *The American Psychiatric Publishing textbook of personality disorders.* Washington, DC: American Psychiatric Publishing.

Marks, D. F. (2000). *The psychology of the psychic.* Buffalo, NY: Prometheus.

Markus, H. R., Uchida, Y., Omoregie, H., Townsend, S. S. M., et al. (2006). Going for the gold: Models of agency in Japanese and American contexts. *Psychological Science, 17*(2), 103–112.

Markus, H., & Nurius, P. (1986). Possible selves. *American Psychologist, 41,* 954–969.

Marmarosh, C., Holtz, A., & Schottenbauer, M. (2005). Group cohesiveness, group-derived collective self-esteem, group-derived hope, and the well-being of group therapy members. *Group Dynamics: Theory, Research, & Practice, 9*(1), 32–44.

Marsella, A. J. (1998). Urbanization, mental health, and social deviancy. *American Psychologist, 53*(6), 624–634.

Marshall, R. D., Bryant, R. A., Amsel, L., Suh, E. J., et al. (2007). The psychology of ongoing threat: Relative risk appraisal, the September 11 attacks, and terrorism-related fears. *American Psychologist, 62*(4), 304–316.

Marsiglia, F. F., Kulis, S., Hecht, M. L., & Sills, S. (2004). Ethnicity and ethnic identity as predictors of drug norms and drug use among preadolescents in the US southwest. *Substance Use & Misuse, 39*(7), 1061–1094.

Martens, R., & Trachet, T. (1998). *Making sense of astrology.* Amherst, MA: Prometheus.

Martin, A. J., & Marsh, H. W. (2003). Fear of failure: Friend or foe? *Australian Psychologist, 38*(1), 31–38.

Martin, C. L., & Fabes, R. A. (2001). The stability and consequences of young children's same-sex peer interactions. *Developmental Psychology, 37*(3), 431–446.

Martin, E. K., Taft, C. T., & Resick, P. A. (2007). A review of marital rape. *Aggression & Violent Behavior, 12*(3), 329–347.

Martin, G., & Pear, J. (2003). *Behavior modification* (7th ed.). Englewood Cliffs, NJ: Prentice Hall.

Martin, L. R., Friedman, H. S., & Schwartz, J. E. (2007). Personality and mortality risk across the life span: The importance of conscientiousness as a biopsychosocial attribute. *Health Psychology, 26*(4), 428–436.

Martin, S. (2007). The labyrinth of leadership. *Monitor on Psychology,* July-Aug., 90–91.

Martin, W. L. B., & Freitas, M. B. (2002). Mean mortality among Brazilian left- and right-handers: Modification or selective elimination. *Laterality, 7*(1), 31–44.

Martinez-Gonzalez, M. A., Gual, P., Lahortiga, F., Alonso, Y., et al. (2003). Parental factors, mass media influences, and the onset of eating disorders in a prospective population-based cohort. *Pediatrics, 111,* 315–320.

Martinko, M. J., Douglas, S. C., & Harvey, P. (2006). Understanding and managing workplace aggression. *Organizational Dynamics, 35*(2), 117–130.

Martino, G., & Marks, L. E. (2001). Synesthesia: Strong and weak. *Current Directions in Psychological Science, 10*(2), 61–65

Marx, B. P., Gross, A. M., & Adams, H. E. (1999). The effect of alcohol on the responses of sexually coercive and noncoercive men to an experimental rape analogue. *Sexual Abuse: Journal of Research & Treatment, 11*(2), 131–145.

Mashour, G. A., Walker, E. E., & Martuza, R. L. (2005). Psychosurgery: Past, present, and future. *Brain Research Reviews, 48*(3), 409–419.

Masi, G., Mucci, M., & Millepiedi, S. (2001). Separation anxiety disorder in children and adolescents. *CNS Drugs, 15*(2), 93–104.

Maslach, C., Schaufeli, W. B., & Leiter, M. P. (2001). Job burnout. *Annual Review of Psychology, 52,* 397–422.

Maslow, A. H. (1954). *Motivation and personality.* New York: Harper.

Maslow, A. H. (1967). Self-actualization and beyond. In J. F. T. Bugental (Ed.), *Challenges of humanistic psychology.* New York: McGraw-Hill.

Maslow, A. H. (1969). *The psychology of science.* Chicago: Henry Regnery.

Maslow, A. H. (1970). *Motivation and personality.* New York: Harper & Row.

Maslow, A. H. (1971). *The farther reaches of human nature.* New York: Viking.

Masse, L. C., & Tremblay, R. E. (1997). Behavior of boys in kindergarten and the onset of substance use during adolescence. *Archives of General Psychiatry, 54*(1), 62.

Masten, A. S. (2001). Ordinary magic: Resilience processes in development. *American Psychologist, 56*(3), 227–238.

Masters, W. H., & Johnson, V. E. (1966). *Human sexual response.* Boston: Little, Brown.

Masters, W. H., & Johnson, V. E. (1970). *The pleasure bond: A new look at sexuality and commitment.* Boston: Little, Brown.

Matheny, K. B., Brack, G. L., McCarthy, C. J., Penick, J. M. (1996). The effectiveness of cognitively-based approaches in treating stress-related symptoms. *Psychotherapy, 33*(2), 305–320.

Matossian, M. K. (1982). Ergot and the Salem witchcraft affair. *American Scientist, 70,* 355–357.

Matson, J. L., Sevin, J. A., Fridley D., & Love, S. R. (1990). Increasing spontaneous language in three autistic children. *Journal of Applied Behavior Analysis, 23*(2), 223–227.

Matthews, G., Deary, I. J., & Whiteman, M. C. (2003). *Personality traits* (2nd ed.). New York: Cambridge University Press.

Matthews, P. H., & Matthews, M. S. (2004). Heritage language instruction and giftedness in language minority students: Pathways toward success. *Journal of Secondary Gifted Education, 15*(2), 50–55.

Mayer, J. D. (2005). A tale of two visions: Can a new view of personality help integrate psychology? *American Psychologist, 60*(4), 294–307.

Mayer, J. D., Salovey, P., Caruso, D. R., & Sitarenios, G. (2001). Emotional intelligence as standard intelligence. *Emotion, 1*(3), 232–242.

Mayer, R. E. (1995). *Thinking, problem solving, and cognition.* New York: Freeman.

Mayer, R. E. (2004). Should there be a three-strikes rule against pure discovery learning? *American Psychologist, 59*(1), 14–19.

Mays, V. M., & Cochran, S. D. (2001). Mental health correlates of perceived discrimination among lesbian, gay, and bisexual adults in the United States. *American Journal of Public Health, 91*(11), 1869–1876.

Mazur, J. E. (2006). *Learning and behavior* (6th ed.). Englewood Cliffs, NJ: Prentice Hall.

McAdams, D. P., & Pals, J. L. (2006). A new Big Five: Fundamental principles for an integrative science of personality. *American Psychologist, 61*(3), 204–217.

McAlister, A. L., Ama, E., Barroso, C., Peters, R. J., et al. (2000). Promoting tolerance and moral engagement through peer modeling. *Cultural Diversity & Ethnic Minority Psychology, 6*(4), 363–373.

McBride, W. J., Murphy, J. M., & Ikemoto, S. (1999). Localization of brain reinforcement mechanisms. *Behavioural Brain Research, 101*(2), 129–152.

McCabe, M. P. (1992). A program for the treatment of inhibited sexual desire in males. *Psychotherapy, 29*(2), 288–296.

McCabe, M. P., & Ricciardelli, L. A. (2004). Weight and shape concerns of boys and men. In Thompson, J. K. (Ed.), *Handbook of eating disorders and obesity.* New York: Wiley.

McCall, W. V., Prudic, J., Olfson, M., & Sackeim, H. (2006). Health-related quality of life following ECT in a large community sample. *Journal of Affective Disorders, 90*(2–3), 269–274.

McCarley, R. W. (1998). Dreams: Disguise of forbidden wishes or transparent reflections of a distinct brain state? In R. M. Bilder, F. F. LeFever, et al. (Eds.), *Neuroscience of the mind on the centennial of Freud's Project for a Scientific Psychology.* New York: New York Academy of Sciences.

McCarthy, B. W. (1995). Bridges to sexual desire. *Journal of Sex Education & Therapy, 21*(2), 132–141.

McCarthy, B. W., & Fucito, L. M. (2005). Integrating medication, realistic expectations, and therapeutic interventions in the treatment of male sexual dysfunction. *Journal of Sex & Marital Therapy, 31*(4), 319–328.

McClelland, D. C. (1961). *The achieving society.* New York: Van Nostrand.

McClelland, D. C. (1965). Achievement and entrepreneurship. *Journal of Personality & Social Psychology, 1,* 389–393.

McClelland, D. C. (1975). *Power: The inner experience.* New York: Irvington.

McClelland, D. C. (1994). The knowledge-testing–educational complex strikes back. *American Psychologist, 49*(1), 66–69.

McClelland, D. C., & Cheriff, A. D. (1997). The immunoenhancing effects of humor on secretory IgA and resistance to respiratory infections. *Psychology & Health, 12*(3), 329–344.

McClelland, D. C., & Pilon, D. A. (1983). Sources of adult motives in patterns of parent behavior in early childhood. *Journal of Personality & Social Psychology, 44,* 564–574.

McClelland, J. L., & Rogers, T. T. (2003). The parallel distributed processing approach to semantic cognition. *Nature Reviews Neuroscience, 4*(4), 310–322.

McClelland, L., & Cook, S. W. (1980). Promoting energy conservation in master-metered apartments through group financial incentives. *Journal of Applied & Social Psychology, 10,* 20–31.

McCluskey, U. (2002). The dynamics of attachment and systems-centered group psychotherapy. *Group Dynamics, 6*(2), 131–142.

McCrae, R. R., & Costa, P. T. (2001). A five-factor theory of personality. In L. A. Pervin & O. P. John (Eds.), *Handbook of personality.* New York: Guilford.

McCrae, R. R., & Terracciano, A. (2005). Universal features of personality traits from the observer's perspective: Data from 50 cultures. *Journal of Personality & Social Psychology, 88*(3), 547–561.

McDonald, J. K., Yanchar, S. C., & Osguthorpe, R. (2005). Learning from programmed instruction: Examining implications for modern instructional technology. *Educational Technology Research & Development, 53*(2), 84–98.

McGaugh, J. L. (2004). The amygdala modulates the consolidation of memories of emotionally arousing experiences. *Annual Review of Neuroscience, 27,* 1–28.

McGregor, D. (1960). *The human side of enterprise.* New York: McGraw-Hill.

McGregor, I., McAdams, D. P., & Little, B. R. (2006). Personal projects, life stories, and happiness: On being true to traits. *Journal of Research in Personality, 40*(5), 551–572.

McGuffin, P., Rijsdijk, F., Andrew, M., Sham, P., et al. (2003). The heritability of bipolar affective disorder and the genetic relationship to unipolar depression. *Archives of General Psychiatry, 60*(5), 497–502.

McIntosh, W. D., Harlow, T. F., & Martin, L. L. (1995). Linkers and nonlinkers: Goal beliefs as a moderator of the effects of everyday hassles on rumination, depression, and physical complaints. *Journal of Applied Social Psychology, 25*(14), 1231–1244.

McKay, A. (2005). Sexuality and substance use: The impact of tobacco, alcohol, and selected recreational drugs on sexual function. *Canadian Journal of Human Sexuality, 14*(1–2), 47–56.

McKeever, L. (2006). Online plagiarism detection services: Saviour or scourge?. *Assessment & Evaluation in Higher Education, 31*(2), 155–165.

McKeever, W. F. (2000). A new family handedness sample with findings consistent with X-linked transmission. *British Journal of Psychology, 91*(1), 21–39.

McKeever, W. F., Cerone, L. J., Suter, P. J., & Wu, S. M. (2000). Family size, miscarriage-proneness, and handedness. *Laterality, 5*(2), 111–120.

McKenna, M. W., & Ossoff, E. P. (1998). Age differences in children's comprehension of a popular television program. *Child Study Journal, 28*(1), 52–68.

McKenzie, K., Serfaty, M., & Crawford, M. (2003). Suicide in ethnic minority groups. *British Journal of Psychiatry, 183*(2), 100–101.

McKim, W. A. (2003). *Drugs and behavior* (5th ed.). Englewood Cliffs, NJ: Prentice Hall.

McKone, E., Brewer, J. L., MacPherson, S., Rhodes, G., et al. (2007). Familiar other-race faces show normal holistic processing and are robust to perceptual stress. *Perception, 36*(2), 244–248.

McLewin, L. A., & Muller, R. T. (2006). Childhood trauma, imaginary companions, and the development of pathological dissociation. *Aggression & Violent Behavior, 11*(5), 531–545.

McLoyd, V. C., & Smith, J. (2002). Physical discipline and behavior problems in African American, European American, and Hispanic children: Emotional support as a moderator. *Journal of Marriage & Family, 64*(1), 40–53.

McMahon, S., & Koltzenburg, M. (2005). *Wall & Melzacks textbook of pain* (5th ed.). London: Churchill Livingstone.

McNally, R. J., & Clancy, S. A. (2005). Sleep paralysis, sexual abuse, and space alien abduction. *Transcultural Psychiatry, 42*(1), 113–122.

McNally, R. J., Clancy, S. A., & Barrett, H. M. (2004). Forgetting trauma? In D. Reisberg & P. Hertel (Eds.), *Memory & emotion.* New York: Oxford University Press.

McNamara, D. S., & Scott, J. L. (2001). Working memory capacity and strategy use. *Memory & Cognition, 29*(1), 10–17.

McRobbie, H., & Hajek, P. (2007). Effects of rapid smoking on postcessation urges to smoke. *Addiction, 102*(3), 483–489.

Mead, M. (1935). *Sex and temperament in three primitive societies.* New York: Morrow.

Medhus, E. (2001). *Child rearing challenges.* Retrieved May 25, 2007, from http://www.drmedhus.com/childchallenges.htm

Mehrabian, A. (2000). Beyond IQ. *Genetic Social, and General Psychology Monographs, 126,* 133–239.

Meier, P. S., Donmall, M. C., McElduff, P., Barrowclough, C., et al. (2006). The role of the early therapeutic alliance in predicting drug treatment dropout. *Drug & Alcohol Dependence, 83*(1), 57–64.

Meltzoff, A. N. (2005). Imitation and other minds: The "Like Me" Hypothesis. In S. Hurley & N. Chater (Eds.), *Perspectives on imitation: From neuroscience to social science* (Vol. 2): *Imitation, human development, and culture.* Cambridge, MA: MIT Press.

Meltzoff, A. N., & Prinz, W. (2002). *The imitative mind: Development, evolution, and brain bases.* Cambridge, MA: Cambridge University Press.

Melzack, R. (1999). From the gate to the neuromatrix. *Pain* (Suppl. 6), S121–S126.

Melzack, R., & Katz, J. (2004). The gate control theory: Reaching for the brain. In T. Hadjistavropoulos & K. D. Craig (Eds.), *Pain: Psychological perspectives.* Mahwah, NJ: Erlbaum.

Melzack, R., & Katz, J. (2006). Pain in the 21st century: The neuromatrix and beyond. In G. Young, A. W. Kane, et al. (Eds.), *Psychological knowledge in court: PTSD, pain, and TBI.* New York: Springer.

Melzack, R., & Wall, P. D. (1996). *The challenge of pain.* Harmondsworth, UK: Penguin.

Mendolia, M. (2002). An index of self-regulation of emotion and the study of repression in social contexts that threaten or do not threaten self-concept. *Emotion, 2*(3), 215–232.

Meneses, G. D., & Beerlipalacio, A. (2005). Recycling behavior: A multidimensional approach. *Environment & Behavior, 37*(6), 837–860.

Menzel, P., Eisert, S., Mann, C. C., & Kennedy, P. (1994). *Material world: A global family portrait.* San Francisco: Sierra Club Books.

Mercer, J. (2006). *Understanding attachment: Parenting, child care, and emotional development.* Westport, CT: Praeger.

Merritt, J. M., Stickgold, R., Pace-Schott, E., Williams, J., et al. (1994). Emotion profiles in the dreams of men and women. *Consciousness & Cognition, 3*(1), 46–60.

Mesquita, B., & Markus, H. R. (2004). Culture and emotion: Models of agency as sources of cultural variation in emotion. In A. S. R. Manstead, S. R. Antony, et al. (Eds.), *Feelings and emotions: The Amsterdam symposium.* New York: Cambridge University Press.

Messer, S. B., & Kaplan, A. H. (2004). Outcomes and factors related to efficacy of brief psychodynamic therapy. In D. P. Charman (Ed.), *Core processes in brief psychodynamic psychotherapy: Advancing effective practice.* Mahwah, NJ: Erlbaum.

Messick, D. M., & Mackie, D. M. (1989). Intergroup relations. *Annual Review of Psychology, 40,* 45–81.

Messick, D. M., Wilke, H., Brewer, M., Kramer, R. M., et al. (1983). Individual adaptations and structural change as solutions to social dilemmas. *Journal of Personality & Social Psychology, 44,* 294–309.

Meyer, G. J., Finn, S. E., Eyde, L. D., Kay, G. G., et al. (2001). Psychological testing and psychological assessment. *American Psychologist, 56*(2), 128–165.

Meyers, L. (2006). Behind the scenes of the "Dr. Phil" show. *Monitor on Psychology, 37*(9), 63.

Michael, D., & Chen, S. (2006). *Serious games: Games that educate, train, and inform.* Boston, MA: Cengage Learning/Course Technology.

Michalak, E. E., & Lam, R. W. (2002). Seasonal affective disorder: The latitude hypothesis revisited. *Canadian Journal of Psychiatry, 47*(8), 787–788.

Michalko, M. (1998). *Cracking creativity.* Berkeley, CA: Ten Speed Press.

Michel, C., Caldara, R., & Rossion, B. (2006). Same-race faces are perceived more holistically than other-race faces. *Visual Cognition, 14*(1), 55–73.

Michelangelo, I., Stefania, B., Donatella, P., Maria, C. Z., et al. (2006). Electrocortical effects of MDMA are potentiated by acoustic stimulation in rats. *BMC Neuroscience,* DOI :10.1186/1471-2202-7-13. Retrieved May 25, 2007, from http://www.biomedcentral.com/content/pdf/1471-2202-7-13.pdf.

Middaugh, S. J., & Pawlick, K. (2002). Biofeedback and behavioral treatment of persistent pain in the older adult: A review and a study. *Applied Psychophysiology & Biofeedback, 27*(3), 185–202.

Mielke, H. W. (1999). Lead in the inner cities. *American Scientist, 87*(Jan.–Feb.), 62–73.

Mignot, E. (2001). A hundred years of narcolepsy research. *Archives of Italian Biology, 139,* 207–220.

Milgram, S. (1963). Behavioral study of obedience. *Journal of Abnormal and Social Psychology, 67,* 371–378.

Milgram, S. (1965). Some conditions of obedience and disobedience to authority. *Human Relations, 18,* 57–76.

Milgram, S. (1967). The small-world problem. *Psychology Today,* May, 61–67.

Milgram, S. (1970). The experience of living in the cities: A psychological analysis. *Science, 167,* 1461–1468.

Milgram, S. (1974). *Obedience to authority: An experimental view.* New York: Harper & Row.

Milgram, S., Bickman, L., & Berkowitz, L. (1969). Note on the drawing power of crowds of different size. *Journal of Personality & Social Psychology, 13,* 79–82.

Miller, D. T. (2006). *An invitation to social psychology.* Belmont, CA: Cengage Learning/Wadsworth.

Miller, E. K., & Cohen, J. D. (2001). An integrative theory of prefrontal cortex function. *Annual Review of Neuroscience, 24,* 167–202.

Miller, G. A. (1956). The magical number seven, plus or minus two: Some limits on our capacity for processing information. *Psychological Review, 63,* 81–87.

Miller, G. A. (1999). On knowing a word. *Annual Review of Psychology, 50,* 1–19.

Miller, G. E., Cohen, S., & Ritchey, A. K. (2002). Chronic psychological stress and the regulation of pro-inflammatory cytokines. *Health Psychology, 21*(6), 531–541.

Miller, N. E. (1944). Experimental studies of conflict. In J. McV. Hunt (Ed.), *Personality and the behavior disorders* (Vol. 1). New York: Ronald Press.

Miller, N. E., & Bugelski. R. (1970). The influence of frustration imposed by the in-group on attitudes expressed toward out-groups. In R. I. Evans & R. M. Rozelle (Eds.), *Social psychology in life.* Boston: Allyn & Bacon.

Miller, N., Pedersen, W. C., Earleywine, M., & Pollock, V. E. (2003). A theoretical model of triggered displaced aggression. *Personality & Social Psychology Review, 7*(1), 75–97.

Miller, R., Perlman, D., & Brehm, S. S. (2007). *Intimate relationships* (4th ed.). New York: McGraw-Hill.

Miller, W. R., & Munoz, R. F. (2005). *Controlling your drinking: Tools to make moderation work for you.* New York: Guilford.

Millman, R. B., & Ross, E. J. (2003). Steroid and nutritional supplement use in professional athletes. *American Journal on Addictions, 12*(Suppl 2), S48–S54.

Millon, T. (1981) *Disorders of personality: DSM-III: Axis II.* New York: Wiley.

Milne, R., & Bull, R. (2002). Back to basics: A componential analysis of the original cognitive interview mnemonics with three age groups. *Applied Cognitive Psychology, 16*(7), 743–753.

Milner, B. (1965). Memory disturbance after bilateral hippocampal lesions. In P. Milner & S. Glickman (Eds.), *Cognitive processes and the brain.* Princeton, NJ: Van Nostrand.

Miltenberger, R. G. (2008). *Behavior modification: Principles and procedures* (4th ed.). Belmont, CA: Cengage Learning/Wadsworth.

Miltner, W. H. R., Krieschel, S., Hecht, H., Trippe, R., et al. (2004). Eye movements and behavioral responses to threatening and nonthreatening stimuli during visual search in phobic and nonphobic subjects. *Emotion, 4*(4), 323–339.

Milton, J., & Wiseman, R. (1997). *Guidelines for extrasensory perception research.* Hertfordshire, UK: University of Hertfordshire Press.

Milton, J., & Wiseman, R. (1999b). A meta-analysis of mass-media tests of extrasensory perception. *British Journal of Psychology, 90*(2), 235–240.

Minda, J. P., & Smith, J. D. (2001). Prototypes in category learning. *Journal of Experimental Psychology: Learning, Memory, & Cognition, 27*(3), 775–799.

Minton, H. L. (2000). Psychology and gender at the turn of the century. *American Psychologist, 55*(6), 613–615.

Miotto, K., Darakjian, J., Basch, J., Murray, S., et al. (2001). Gamma-hydroxybutyric acid: Patterns of use, effects and withdrawal. *American Journal on Addictions, 10*(3), 232–241.

Miranda, R., & Kihlstrom, J. F. (2005). Mood congruence in childhood and recent autobiographical memory. *Cognition & Emotion, 19*(7), 981–998.

Mirsky, A. F., & Duncan, C. C. (2005). Pathophysiology of mental illness: A view from the fourth ventricle. *International Journal of Psychophysiology, 58*(2–3), 162–178.

Mirsky, A. F., Bieliauskas, L. M., Van Kammen, D. P., Jonsson, E., et al. (2000). A 39-year followup of the Genain quadruplets. *Schizophrenia Bulletin, 3,* 5–18.

Mischel, W. (2004). Toward an integrative science of the person. *Annual Review of Psychology, 55,* 1–22.

Mischel, W., & Shoda, Y. (1998). Reconciling processing dynamics and personality dispositions. *Annual Review of Psychology, 49,* 229–258.

Mischel, W., Shoda, Y., & Smith, R. E. (2004). *Introduction to personality: Toward an integration* (7th ed.). Hoboken, NJ: Wiley.

Mistlberger, R. E. (2005). Circadian regulation of sleep in mammals: Role of the suprachiasmatic nucleus. *Brain Research Reviews, 49*(3), 429–454.

Mitchell, D. (1987). Firewalking cults: Nothing but hot air. *Laser,* Feb., 7–8.

Mitru, G., Millrood, D.L., & Mateika, J. H. (2002). The impact of sleep on learning and behavior in adolescents. *Teachers College Record, 104*(4), 704–726.

Miyake, A. (2001). Individual differences in working memory. *Journal of Experimental Psychology: General, 130*(2), 163–168.

Moerman, D. E. (2002). The meaning response and the ethics of avoiding placebos. *Evaluation & the Health Professions. Special Recent Advances in Placebo Research, 25*(4), 399–409.

Mogg, K., Bradley, B. P., Hyare, H., & Lee, S. (1998). Selective attention to food-related stimuli in hunger. *Behaviour Research & Therapy, 36*(2), 227–237.

Moghaddam, B. (2002). Stress activation of glutamate neurotransmission in the prefrontal cortex. *Biological Psychiatry, 51*(10), 775–787.

Mohr, D. C., Hart, S. L., Julian, L., Catledge, C., et al. (2005). Telephone-administered psychotherapy for depression. *Archives of General Psychiatry, 62*(9), 1007–1014.

Mokdad, A. H., Marks, J. S., Stroup, D. F., & Gerberding, J. L. (2004). Actual causes of death in the United States, 2000. *Journal of the American Medical Association, 291*(March 10), 1238–1245.

Monahan, J., Steadman, H. J., Silver, E., Appelbaum, P. S., et al. (2001). *Rethinking risk assessment: The MacArthur Study of Mental Disorder and Violence.* New York: Oxford University Press.

Montgomery, P., & Dennis, J. (2004). A systematic review of non-pharmacological therapies for sleep problems in later life. *Sleep Medicine Reviews, 8*(1), 47–62.

Moor, J. (Ed.). (2003). *The Turing test: The elusive standard of artificial intelligence.* London: Kluwer Academic Publishers.

Moore, S. A., & Zoellner, L. A. (2007). Overgeneral autobiographical memory and traumatic events: An evaluative review. *Psychological Bulletin, 133*(3), 419–437.

Moore, T. O. (2001). Testosterone and male behavior: Empirical research with hamsters does not support the use of castration to deter human sexual aggression. *North American Journal of Psychology, 3*(3), 503–520.

Moore-Ede, M. C., Sulzman, F. M., & Fuller, C. A. (1982). *The clocks that time us.* Cambridge, MA: Harvard University Press.

Moran, J. M., Macrae, C. N., Heatherton, T. F., Wyland, C. L. et al. (2006). Neuroanatomical evidence for distinct cognitive and affective components of self. *Journal of Cognitive Neuroscience, 18*(9), 1586–1594.

Moras, K. (2002). Research on psychotherapy. In M. Hersen & W. H. Sledge (Eds.), *Encyclopedia of psychotherapy.* San Diego: Academic Press.

Moreno, J. L. (1953). *Who shall survive?* New York: Beacon.

Morgan, J. P. (Ed.). (2005). *Psychology of aggression.* Hauppauge, NY: Nova Science Publishers.

Morgenstern, J., Labouvie, E., McCrady, B. S., Kahler, C. W., et al. (1997). Affiliation with Alcoholics Anonymous after treatment. *Journal of Consulting & Clinical Psychology, 65*(5), 768–777.

Morisse, D., Batra, L., Hess, L., & Silverman, R. (1996). A demonstration of a token economy for the real world. *Applied & Preventive Psychology, 5*(1), 41–46.

Moritz, A. P., & Zamchech, N. (1946). Sudden and unexpected deaths of young soldiers. *American Medical Association Archives of Pathology, 42,* 459–494.

Morris, T., Spittle, M., & Watt, T. (2005). *Imagery in sport.* Champaign, IL: Human Kinetics.

Morrison, R. G., & Wallace, B. (2001). Imagery vividness, creativity and the visual arts. *Journal of Mental Imagery, 25*(3–4), 135–152.

Morsella, E., & Krauss, R. M. (2004). The role of gestures in spatial working memory and speech. *American Journal of Psychology, 117*(3), 411–424.

Mosher, W. D., Chandra, C., & Jones, J. (2005). Sexual behavior and selected health measures: Men and women 15–44 years of age, United States, 2002. Atlanta: Centers for Disease Control. Retrieved August 25, 2006, from http://www.cdc.gov/nchs/data/ad/ad362.pdf.

Most, S. B., Scholl, B. J., Clifford, E. R., & Simons, D. J. (2005). What you see is what you set: Sustained inattentional blindness and the capture of awareness. *Psychological Review, 112*(1), 217–242.

Motivala, S. J., & Irwin, M. R. (2007). Sleep and immunity: Cytokine pathways linking sleep and health outcomes. *Current Directions in Psychological Science, 16*(1), 21–25.

Muchinsky, P. M. (2006). *Psychology applied to work* (8th ed.). Belmont,

CA: Cengage Learning/ Wadsworth.

Mundy, A. (2004). Divided we stand. *American Demographics, 26*(5), 26–31.

Munsey, C. (2006). RxP legislation made historic progress in Hawaii. *APA Monitor*, June, 42.

Murray, B. (2001). A daunting unbelievable experience. *Monitor on Psychology*, Nov., 18.

Murray, J. B. (1995). Evidence for acupuncture's analgesic effectiveness and proposals for the physiological mechanisms involved. *Journal of Psychology, 129*(4), 443–461.

Murray, J. B. (2002). Phencyclidine (PCP): A dangerous drug, but useful in schizophrenia research. *Journal of Psychology, 136*(3), 319–327.

Murray, S. L., Holmes, J. G., & Griffin, D. W. (1996). The self-fulfilling nature of positive illusions in romantic relationships. *Journal of Personality & Social Psychology, 71*(6), 1155–1180.

Murray, S., Holmes, J. G., & Griffin, D. W. (2003). Reflections on the self-fulfilling effects of positive illusions. *Psychological Inquiry, 14*(3–4), 2003, 289–295.

Mussen, P. H., Conger, J. J., Kagan, J., & Geiwitz, J. (1979). *Psychological development: A life span approach*. New York: Harper & Row.

Musso, M., Weiller, C., Kiebel, S., Muller, S. P., et al. (1999). Training-induced brain plasticity in aphasia. *Brain, 122*, 1781–1790.

Mustanski, B. S., Chivers, M. L., & Bailey, J. M. (2002). A critical review of recent biological research on human sexual orientation. *Annual Review of Sex Research, 13*, 89–140.

Myers, H. F., Lesser, I., Rodriguez, N., Mira, C. B., et al. (2002). Ethnic differences in clinical presentation of depression in adult women. *Cultural Diversity & Ethnic Minority Psychology, 8*(2), 138–156.

Myers, L. (2007). The problem with DNA. *Monitor on Psychology*, June, 52–53.

NAFE (2004). Salary survey. *National Association for Female Executives Magazine, 27*(4), 20–21.

Nagel, T. (1974). What is it like to be a bat? *The Philosophical Review, 83*, 435–450.

Nairne, J. S. (2002). Remembering over the short-term. *Annual Review of Psychology, 53*, 53–81.

Naitoh, P., Kelly, T. L., & Englund, C. E. (1989). *Health effects of sleep deprivation*. U.S. Naval Health Research Center Report no. 89-46.

Nakamichi, M. (2004). Tool-use and toolmaking by captive, group-living orangutans (Pongo pygmaeus abelii) at an artificial termite mound. *Behavioural Processes, 65*(1), 87–93.

Nakamura, J., & Csikszentmihalyi, M. (2003). The motivational sources of creativity as viewed from the paradigm of positive psychology. In L. G. Aspinwall & U. M. Staudinger (Eds.), *A psychology of human strengths: Fundamental questions and future directions for a positive psychology*. Washington, DC: American Psychological Association.

National Academy of Sciences. (2002). *The polygraph and lie detection*. Washington, DC: National Academy of Sciences.

National Institute of Child Health and Human Development. (1999). The NICHD Study of Early Child Care: Child outcomes when child care center classes meet recommended standards for quality. *American Journal of Public Health, 89*, 1072–1077.

Nau, S. D., & Lichstein, K. L. (2005). Insomnia: Causes and treatments. In P. R. Carney, J. D. Geyer, et al. (Eds.), *Clinical sleep disorders*. Philadelphia: Lippincott Williams & Wilkins.

Naveh-Benjamin, M., Guez, J., & Sorek, S. (2007). The effects of divided attention on encoding processes in memory: Mapping the locus of interference. *Canadian Journal of Experimental Psychology, 61*(1), 1–12.

NCCDPHP (National Center for Chronic Disease Prevention and Health Promotion). (2004). *Health effects of cigarette smoking*. Retrieved July 19, 2006, from http://www.cdc.gov/Tobacco/factsheets/HealthEffectsofCigaretteSmoking_Factsheet.htm\

Neath, I., & Surprenant, A. (2003). *Human memory* (2nd ed.). Belmont, CA: Cengage Learning/ Wadsworth.

Neave, N., & Wolfson, S. (2003). Testosterone, territoriality, and the "home advantage." *Physiology & Behavior, 78*(2), 269–275.

Needles, D. J., & Abramson, L. Y. (1990). Positive life events, attributional style, and hopefulness: Testing a model of recovery from depression. *Journal of Abnormal Psychology, 99*(2), 156–165.

Nehlig, A. (Ed.). (2004). *Coffee, tea, chocolate, and the brain*. Boca Raton, FL: CRC Press.

Neisser, U., Boodoo, G., Bouchard, T. J., Boykin, A. W., et al. (1996). Intelligence: Knowns and unknowns. *American Psychologist, 51*(2), 77–101.

Nelson, C. A. (1999). How important are the first 3 years of life? *Applied Developmental Science, 3*(4), 235–238.

Nelson, G., & Prilleltensky, I. (Eds.). (2005). *Community psychology: In pursuit of liberation and well-being*. New York: Palgrave MacMillan.

Nelson, T. D. (2005). Ageism: Prejudice against our feared future self. *Journal of Social Issues, 61*(2), 207–221.

Nelson, T. D. (2006). *The psychology of prejudice* (2nd ed.). Needham Heights, MA: Allyn and Bacon.

Nemeroff, C. B., Bremner, J. D., Foa, E. B., Mayberg, H. S., et al. (2006). Posttraumatic stress disorder: A state-of-the-science review. *Journal of Psychiatric Research, 40*(1), 1–21.

Neter, E., & Ben-Shakhar, G. (1989). The predictive validity of graphological inferences: A meta-analytic approach. *Personality & Individual Differences, 10*(7), 737–745.

Neubert, M. J. (1998). The value of feedback and goal setting over goal setting alone and potential moderators of this effect: A meta-analysis. *Human Performance, 11*(4), 321–335.

Neufeld, R. W. J., Carter, J. R., Nicholson, I. R., & Vollick, D. N. (2003). Schizophrenia. In P. Firestone & W. L. Marshall (Eds.), *Abnormal psychology: Perspectives* (2nd ed.). Toronto: Prentice Hall.

Neuman, G. A., & Baydoun, R. (1998). An empirical examination of overt and covert integrity tests. *Journal of Business & Psychology, 13*(1), 65–79.

Neumeister, A. (2004). Neurotransmitter depletion and seasonal affective disorder: Relevance for the biologic effects of light therapy. *Primary Psychiatry. Special Neurotransmitter Depletion, 11*(6), 44–48.

Nevid, J. S., & Greene, B. (2005). *Abnormal psychology in a changing world, media and research update* (5th ed.). Englewood Cliffs, NJ: Prentice Hall.

Newman, A. W., & Thompson, J. W. (2001). The rise and fall of forensic hypnosis in criminal investigation. *Journal of the American Academy of Psychiatry & the Law, 29*(1), 75–84.

Ng, S. H. (2002). Will families support their elders? Answers from across cultures. In T. Nelson (Ed.), *Ageism: Stereotyping and prejudice against older persons*. Cambridge, MA: MIT Press.

Niaura, R., Todaro, J. F., Stroud, L., Spiro, A., et al. (2002). Hostility, the metabolic syndrome, and incident coronary heart disease. *Health Psychology, 21*(6), 588–593.

Nickell, J. (2001). John Edward: Hustling the bereaved. *Skeptical Inquirer*, Nov.-Dec., 19–22.

Nickerson, R. S., & Adams, M. J. (1979). Long-term memory for a common object. *Cognitive Psychology, 11*, 287–307.

NIDA. (2006). *Tobacco addiction*. National Institute on Drug Abuse, NIH Publication Number 06-4342. Retrieved July 24, 2006, from http://www.nida.nih.gov/PDF/RRTobacco.pdf.

Niedzwienska, A. (2004). Metamemory knowledge and the accuracy of flashbulb memories. *Memory, 12*(5), 603–613.

Niehaus, D. J. H., Stein, D. J., Koen, L., Lochner, C., et al. (2005). A case of "Ifufunyane": A Xhosa culture-bound syndrome. *Journal of Psychiatric Practice, 11*(6), 411–413.

Niehoff, B. P., Moorman, R. H., Blakely, G., & Fuller, J. (2001). The influence of empowerment and job enrichment on employee loyalty in a downsizing environment. *Group & Organization Management, 26*(1), 93–113.

Nielsen, D. M., & Metha, A. (1994). Parental behavior and adolescent self-esteem in clinical and nonclinical samples. *Adolescence, 29*(115), 525–542.

Nielsen, M., & Dissanayake, C. (2004). Pretend play, mirror self-recognition and imitation: A longitudinal investigation through the second year. *Infant Behavior & Development, 27*(3), 342–365.

NIMH (2003). *In harm's way: Suicide in America*. Bethesda, MD: National Institute of Mental Health. Retrieved July 25, 2007, from http://www.nimh.nih.gov/publicat/harmsway.cfm.

NIMH (2005). *Getting help: Locate services*. Bethesda, MD: National Institute of Mental Health. Retrieved August 20, 2007, from http://www.nimh.nih.gov/tools/contactus.cfm.

NIMH. (2006a). *Facts about anxiety disorders*. Bethesda, MD: National Institute of Mental Health. Retrieved July 25, 2007, from http://www.nimh.nih.gov/publicat/anxiety.cfm

NIMH. (2006b). *The numbers count: Mental disorders in America*. Bethesda, MD: National Institute of Mental Health. Retrieved July 25, 2007, from http://www.nimh.nih.gov/publicat/numbers.cfm.

Nisbett, R. E. (2005). Heredity, environment, and race differences in IQ: A commentary on Rushton and Jensen (2005). *Psychology, Public Policy, & Law, 11*(2), 302–310.

Njeri, I. (1991). Beyond the melting pot. *Los Angeles Times*, Jan. 13, E1, E8.

Noble, P. (1997). Violence in psychiatric in-patients. *International Review of Psychiatry, 9*(2–3), 207–216.

Noice, H., & Noice, T. (1999). Long-term retention of theatrical roles. *Memory, 7*(3), 357–382.

Noland, J. S., Singer, L. T., Short, E. J., Minnes, S., et al. (2005). Prenatal drug exposure and selective attention in preschoolers.

Neurotoxicology & Teratology, 27(3), 429–438.

Nolen-Hoeksema, S. (2007). *Abnormal psychology* (4th ed.). New York: McGraw-Hill.

Norcross, J. C., Hedges, M., & Prochaska, J. O. (2002). The face of 2010: A Delphi poll on the future of psychotherapy. *Professional Psychology: Research & Practice, 33*(3), 316–322.

Norem, J. K. (2002). *The positive power of negative thinking: Using defensive pessimism to harness anxiety and perform at your peak.* New York: Basic Books.

Nori, G. (1998). Glucagon and the control of meal size. In G. P. Smith (Ed.), *Satiation: From gut to brain.* New York: Oxford University Press.

Norlander, T., Bergman, H., & Archer, T. (1998). Effects of flotation rest on creative problem solving and originality. *Journal of Environmental Psychology, 18*(4), 399–408.

Norlander, T., Bergman, H., & Archer, T. (1999). Primary process in competitive archery performance: Effects of floatation REST. *Journal of Applied Sport Psychology, 11*(2), 194–209.

Norman, D. A. (1994) *Things that make us smart.* Menlo Park, CA: Addison-Wesley.

Norman, K. L., & Panizzi, E. (2006). Levels of automation and user participation in usability testing. *Interacting with Computers, 18*(2), 246–264.

Norris, R. M., & Weinman, J. A. (1996). Psychological change following a long sail training voyage. *Personality & Individual Differences, 21*(2), 189–194.

North, C. S. (1987). *Welcome silence.* New York: Simon & Schuster.

North, C. S., Kienstra, D. M., Osborne, V. A., Dokucu, M. E., et al. (2006). Interrater reliability and coding guide for nonpsychotic formal thought disorder. *Perceptual & Motor Skills, 103*(2), 395–411.

Northcutt, R. G. (2004). Taste buds: Development and evolution. *Brain, Behavior & Evolution, 64*(3), 198–206.

Norton, P. (2003). *Teaching with technology: Designing opportunities to learn.* Belmont, CA: Cengage Learning/Wadsworth.

Nosek, B. A., Greenwald, A. G., & Banaji, M. R. (2005). Understanding and using the implicit association test: II. Method variables and construct validity. *Personality & Social Psychology Bulletin, 31*(2), 166–180.

Nurnberger, J. I., & Zimmerman, J. (1970). Applied analysis of human behaviors: An alternative to conventional motivational inferences and unconscious determination in therapeutic programming. *Behavior Therapy, 1,* 59–69.

Oakley R. (2004). How the mind hurts and heals the body. *American Psychologist, 59*(1), 29–40.

Oakley, D. A., Whitman, L. G., & Halligan, P. W. (2002). Hypnotic imagery as a treatment for phantom limb pain. *Clinical Rehabilitation, 16*(4), 368–377.

Oberauer, K., & Göthe, K. (2006). Dual-task effects in working memory: Interference between two processing tasks, between two memory demands, and between storage and processing. *European Journal of Cognitive Psychology, 18*(4), 493–519.

Obhi, S. S., & Haggard, P. (2004). Free will and free won't. *American Scientist, 92*(July–Aug.), 358–365.

Ochoa, J. G., & Pulido, M. (2005). Parasomnias. In P. R. Carney, J. D. Geyer, et al. (Eds.), *Clinical sleep disorders.* Philadelphia: Lippincott Williams & Wilkins.

O'Conner, T. G., Marvin, R. S., Rutter, M., Olrick, J. T., et al. (2003). Child–parent attachment following early institutional deprivation. *Development & Psychopathology, 15*(1), 19–38.

O'Connor, M. G., Sieggreen, M. A., Bachna, K., Kaplan, B., et al. (2000). Long-term retention of transient news events. *Journal of the International Neuropsychological Society, 6*(1), 44–51.

O'Craven, K. M., & Kanwisher, N. (2000). Mental imagery of faces and places activates corresponding stimulus-specific brain regions. *Journal of Cognitive Neuroscience, 12*(6), 1013–1023.

Ogloff, J. R. P. (2006). Psychopathy/antisocial personality disorder conundrum. *Australian & New Zealand Journal of Psychiatry, 40*(6), 519–528.

Ohayon, M. M., Guilleminault, C., & Priest, R. G. (1999). Night terrors, sleepwalking, and confusional arousals in the general population. *Journal of Clinical Psychiatry, 60*(4), 268–276.

O'Keeffe, C., & Wiseman, R. (2005). Testing alleged mediumship: Methods and results. *British Journal of Psychology, 96*(2), 165–179.

Okiishi, J., Lambert, M. J., Nielsen, S. L., & Ogles, B. M. (2003). Waiting for supershrink: An empirical analysis of therapist effects. *Clinical Psychology & Psychotherapy, 10*(6), 361–373.

Olds, M. E., & Fobes, J. L. (1981). The central basis of motivation: Intracranial self-stimulation studies. *Annual Review of Psychology, 32,* 523–574.

O'Leary, E. (2006). Person-centred gestalt therapy. In E. O'Leary & M. Murphy (Eds.), *New approaches to integration in psychotherapy.* New York: Routledge.

Olio, K. A. (2004). The truth about "false memory syndrome." In P. J. Caplan & L. Cosgrove (Eds.), *Bias in psychiatric diagnosis. A project of the association for women in psychology.* Northvale, NJ: Jason Aronson.

Olson, J. M., & Zanna, M. P. (1993). Attitudes and attitude change. *Annual Review of Psychology, 44,* 117–154.

Olson-Buchanan, J. B., & Drasgow, F. (2006). Multimedia situational judgment tests: The medium creates the message. In J. A. Weekley & R. E. Ployhart (Eds.), *Situational judgment tests: Theory, measurement, and application.* Mahwah, NJ: Erlbaum.

Olszewski, P. K., Li, D., Grace, M. K., Billington, C. J., et al. (2003). Neural basis of orexigenic effects of ghrelin acting within lateral hypothalamus. *Peptides, 24*(4), 597–602.

O'Neill, B. (2003). *Don't believe everything you read online.* BBC News. Retrieved May 18, 2007, from http://newswww.bbc.net.uk/1/hi/magazine/3151595.stm.

O'Neill, P. (2005). The ethics of problem definition. *Canadian Psychology, 46,* 13–20.

Ones, D. S., & Viswesvaran, C. (2001). Integrity tests and other criterion-focused occupational personality scales (COPS) used in personnel selection. *International Journal of Selection & Assessment, 9*(1–2), 31–39.

Ones, D. S., Viswesvaran, C., & Schmidt, F. L. (2003). Personality and absenteeism: A meta-analysis of integrity tests. *European Journal of Personality, 17*(Suppl. 1), S19–S38.

Onwuegbuzie, A. J. (2000). Academic procrastinators and perfectionistic tendencies among graduate students. *Journal of Social Behavior & Personality, 15*(5), 103–109.

Ooki, S. (2005). Genetic and environmental influences on the handedness and footedness in Japanese twin children. *Twin Research & Human Genetics, 8*(6), 649–656.

Oppliger, P. A. (2007). Effects of gender stereotyping on socialization. In R. W. Preiss, B. M. Gayle, et al. (Eds.), *Mass media effects research: Advances through meta-analysis.* Mahwah, NJ: Erlbaum.

Ord, T. J., Martins E. P., Thakur S., Mane K. K., et al. (2005). Trends in animal behaviour research (1968–2002): Ethoinformatics and the mining of library databases. *Animal Behaviour, 69*(6), 1399–1413.

Orleans, C. T. (2000). Promoting the maintenance of health behavior change. *Health Psychology, 19*(Suppl. 1), 76–83.

Orleans, C. T., Gruman, J., & Hollendonner, J. K. (1999). Rating our progress in population health promotion: Report card on six behaviors. *American Journal of Health Promotion, 14*(2), 75–82.

Ormay, T. (2006). Cybertherapy: Psychotherapy on the Internet. *International Journal of Psychotherapy, 10*(2), 51–60.

Ornstein, R., & Ehrlich, P. (1989). *New world new mind.* New York: Simon & Schuster.

Ornstein, S., & Isabella, L. (1990). Age vs. stage models of career attitudes of women: A partial replication and extension. *Journal of Vocational Behavior, 36,* 1–19.

O'Roark, A. M. (2001). Personality assessment, projective methods and a triptych perspective. *Journal of Projective Psychology & Mental Health, 8*(2), 116–126.

Osgood, C. E. (1952). The nature and measurement of meaning. *Psychological Bulletin, 49,* 197–237.

Oskamp, S. (1995). Resource conservation and recycling: Behavior and policy. *Journal of Social Issues, 51*(4), 157–177.

Oskamp, S. (2000). A sustainable future for humanity? *American Psychologist, 55*(5), 496–508.

Oskamp, S. (2002). Summarizing sustainability issues and research approaches. In P. Schmuck & W. P. Schultz (Eds.), *Psychology of sustainable development.* Dordrecht, Netherlands: Kluwer.

Oskamp, S., & Schultz, P. W. (2005). *Attitudes and opinions* (3rd ed.). Mahwah, NJ: Erlbaum.

Oskamp, S., & Schultz, P. W. (2006). Using psychological science to achieve ecological sustainability. In S. I. Donaldson, D. E. Berger, et al. (Eds.), *Applied psychology: New frontiers and rewarding careers.* Mahwah, NJ: Erlbaum.

Oster, H. (2005). The repertoire of infant facial expressions: a ontogenetic perspective. In J. Nadel & D. Muir (Eds.), *Emotional development: Recent research advances.* New York: Oxford University Press.

Overmier, J. B., & LoLordo, V. M. (1998). Learned helplessness. In O'Donohue, W. T. (Ed.), *Learning and behavior therapy.* Boston: Allyn & Bacon.

Oyserman, D., Bybee, D., Terry, K., & Hart-Johnson, T. (2004). Possible selves as roadmaps. *Journal of Research in Personality, 38*(2), 130–149.

Page, K. (1999). The graduate. *Washington Post Magazine, 152*(May 16), 18–20.

Page, M. P. A., Madge, A., Cumming, N., & Norris, D. G. (2007). Speech errors and the phonological similarity effect in short-term memory: Evidence suggesting a common locus. *Journal of Memory & Language, 56*(1), 49–64.

Pagnin, D., de Queiroz, V., Pini, S., & Cassano, G. B. (2004). Efficacy of ECT in depression: A meta-analytic review. *Journal of ECT, 20*(1), 13–20.

Palm, K., & Gibson, P. (1998). Recovered memories of childhood sexual abuse: Clinicians' practices and beliefs. *Professional Psychology: Research & Practice, 29*(3), 257–261.

Palmer, S. E. (1992). Common region: A new principle of perceptual grouping. *Cognitive Psychology, 24*(3), 436–447.

Pals, J. L. (2006). Narrative identity processing of difficult life experiences: Pathways of personality development and positive self-transformation in adulthood. *Journal of Personality, 74*(4), 1079–1110.

Pandey, S. (1999). Role of perceived control in coping with crowding. *Psychological Studies, 44*(3), 86–91.

Panksepp, J., & Pasqualini, M. S. (2005). The search for the fundamental brain/mind sources of affective experience. In J. Nadel & D. Muir (Eds.), *Emotional development: Recent research advances*. New York: Oxford University Press.

Papa, F. J., Aldrich, D., & Schumacker, R. E. (1999). The effects of immediate online feedback upon diagnostic performance. *Academic Medicine, 74*(Suppl. 10), S16–S18.

Papanicolaou, A. C. (Ed.). (2006). *The amnesias: A clinical textbook of memory disorders*. New York: Oxford University Press.

Paquette, D., Carbonneau, R., Dubeau, D., Bigras, M., et al. (2003). Prevalence of father-child rough-and-tumble play and physical aggression in preschool children. *European Journal of Psychology of Education, 18*(2), 171–189.

Paquette, V., Lévesque, J., Mensour, B., Leroux, J.-M., et al. (2003). "Change the mind and you change the brain": Effects of cognitive-behavioral therapy on the neural correlates of spider phobia. *NeuroImage, 18*, 401–409.

Paradis, C. M., Solomon, L. Z., Florer, F., & Thompson, T. (2004). Flashbulb memories of personal events of 9/11 and the day after for a sample of New York City residents. *Psychological Reports, 95*(1), 304–310.

Park, D. C., Smith, A. D., & Cavanaugh, J. C. (1990). Metamemories of memory researchers. *Memory & Cognition, 18*(3), 321–327.

Park, N., Peterson, C., & Seligman, M.E. P. (2004). Strengths of character and well-being. *Journal of Social & Clinical Psychology, 23*(5), 603–619.

Parke, R. D. (2004). Development in the family. *Annual Review of Psychology, 55*, 365–399.

Parker, A., Ngu, H., & Cassaday, H. J. (2001). Odour and Proustian memory. *Applied Cognitive Psychology, 15*(2), 159–171.

Parker, J. D. A. (2005). The relevance of emotional intelligence for clinical psychology. In R. Schulze & R. D. Roberts (Eds.), *Emotional intelligence: An international handbook* (pp. 271–287). Ashland, OH: Hogrefe & Huber.

Pascual, A., & Guéguen, N. (2005). Foot-in-the-door and door-in-the-face: A comparative meta-analytic study. *Psychological Reports, 96*(1), 122–128.

Pasupathi, M., & Staudinger, U. M. (2001). Do advanced moral reasoners also show wisdom? *International Journal of Behavioral Development, 25*(5), 401–415.

Patterson, C. J. (2002). Lesbian and gay parenthood. In M. Bornstein (Ed.), *Handbook of Parenting, 3, 4, 5*. Mahwah, NJ: Erlbaum.

Paulhus, D. L. (1998). Interpersonal and intrapsychic adaptiveness of trait self-enhancement. *Journal of Personality and Social Psychology, 74*(5), 1197–1208.

Paulsson, T., & Parker, A. (2006). The effects of a two-week reflection-intention training program on lucid dream recall. *Dreaming, 16*(1), 22–35.

Pavlidis, I., Eberhardt, N. L., & Levine, J. A. (2002). Seeing through the face of deception. *Nature, 415*(6867), 35.

Pavlov, I. P. (1927). *Conditioned reflexes*. Translated by G. V. Anrep. New York: Dover.

Pearce, C. L., Conger, J. A., & Locke, E. A. (2007). Shared leadership theory. *Leadership Quarterly, 18*(3), 281–288.

Pelton, T. (1983). The shootists. *Science 83, 4*(4), 84–86.

Penfield, W. (1957). Brain's record of past a continuous movie film. *Science News Letter*, April 27, 265.

Penfield, W. (1958). *The excitable cortex in conscious man*. Springfield, IL: Charles C. Thomas.

Pennebaker, J. W. (2004). *Writing to heal: A guided journal for recovering from trauma and emotional upheaval*. Oakland, CA: New Harbinger Press.

Pennebaker, J. W., & Chung, C. K. (2007). Expressive writing, emotional upheavals, and health. In H. S. Friedman & R. C. Silver (Eds.), *Foundations of health psychology*. New York: Oxford University Press.

Peplau, L. A. (2003). Human sexuality: How do men and women differ? *Current Directions in Psychological Science, 12*(2), 37–40.

Perin, C. T. (1943). A quantitative investigation of the delay of reinforcement gradient. *Journal of Experimental Psychology, 32*, 37–51.

Perlman, D., & Cozby, P. C. (1983). *Social psychology*. New York: Holt, Rinehart & Winston.

Perls, F. (1969). *Gestalt therapy verbatim*. Lafayette, CA: Real People.

Perreault, S., & Bourhis, R. Y. (1999). Ethnocentrism, social identification, and discrimination. *Personality & Social Psychology Bulletin, 25*(1), 92–103.

Perry, R. P. (2003). Perceived (academic) control and causal thinking in achievement settings. *Canadian Psychology, 44*(4), 312–331.

Perry, R. P., Hladkyj, S., Pekrun, R. H., & Pelletier, S. T. (2001). Academic control and action control in the achievement of college students: A longitudinal field study. *Journal of Educational Psychology, 93*(4), 776–789.

Pervin, L. A., Cervone, D., & John, O. P. (2005). *Personality: Theory and research* (9th ed.). New York: Wiley.

Pesant, N., & Zadra, A. (2006). Dream content and psychological well-being: A longitudinal study of the continuity hypothesis. *Journal of Clinical Psychology, 62*(1), 111–121.

Pescatello, L. S. (2001). Exercising for health. *Western Journal of Medicine, 174*(2), 114–118.

Peters, W. A. (1971). *A class divided*. Garden City, NY: Doubleday.

Peterson, C., & Chang, E. C. (2003). Optimism and flourishing. In C. L. M. Keyes & J. Haidt (Eds.), *Flourishing*. Washington, DC: American Psychological Association.

Peterson, C., & Seligman, M. E. P. (2004). *Character strengths and virtues*. Washington, DC: American Psychological Association.

Peterson, C., & Vaidya, R. S. (2001). Explanatory style, expectations, and depressive symptoms. *Personality & Individual Differences, 31*(7), 1217–1223.

Peterson, L. R., & Peterson, M. J. (1959). Short-term retention of individual verbal items. *Journal of Experimental Psychology, 58*, 193–198.

Peterson, S. E. (1992). The cognitive functions of underlining as a study technique. *Reading Research & Instruction, 31*(2), 49–56.

Petrie, T. A., & Diehl, N. S. (1995). Sport psychology in the profession of psychology. *Professional Psychology: Research & Practice, 26*(3), 288–291.

Pett, M. A., & Johnson, M. J. M. (2005). Development and psychometric evaluation of the Revised University Student Hassles Scale. *Educational & Psychological Measurement, 65*(6), 984–1010.

Pettigrew, T. F. (1998). Intergroup contact theory. *Annual Review of Psychology, 49*, 65–85.

Peverly, S. T., Brobst, K. E., Graham, M., & Shaw, R. (2003). College adults are not good at self-regulation. *Journal of Educational Psychology, 95*(2), 335–346.

Phillips, D. P., Liu, G. C., Kwok, K., Jarvinen, J., et al. (2001). The *Hound of the Baskervilles* effect: Natural experiment on the influence of psychological stress on timing of death. *British Medical Journal, 323*(7327), 1443–1446

Piaget, J. (1951, original French, 1945). *The psychology of intelligence*. New York: Norton.

Piaget, J. (1952). *The origins of intelligence in children*. New York: International University Press.

Pickel, K. L., French, T. A., & Betts, J. M. (2003). A cross-modal weapon focus effect: The influence of a weapon's presence on memory for auditory information. *Memory, 11*(3), 277–292.

Piek, J. P. (2006). *Infant motor development*. Champaign, Il: Human Kinetics Publishers.

Pierce, W. D., & Cheney, C. D. (2004). *Behavior analysis and learning* (3rd ed.). Mahwah, NJ: Erlbaum.

Pierrehumbert, B., Ramstein, T., Karmaniola, A., Miljkovitch, R., et al. (2002). Quality of child care in the preschool years. *International Journal of Behavioral Development, 26*(5), 385–396.

Pierrel, R., & Sherman, J. G. (1963). Train your pet the Barnabus way. *Brown Alumni Monthly*, Feb., 8–14.

Piliavin, I. M., Rodin, J., & Piliavin, J. A. (1969). Good samaritanism: An underground phenomenon? *Journal of Personality & Social Psychology, 13*, 289–299.

Piliavin, J. A. (2003). Doing well by doing good: Benefits to the benefactor. In C. L. M. Keyes & J. Haidt (Eds.), *Flourishing*. Washington, DC: American Psychological Association.

Pillow, D. R., Zautra, A. J., & Sandler, I. (1996). Major life events and minor stressors: Identifying mediational links in the stress process. *Journal of Personality & Social Psychology, 70*(2), 381–394.

Pinel, J. P. J., Assanand, S., & Lehman, D. R. (2000). Hunger, eating, and ill health. *American Psychologist, 55*(10), 1105–1116.

Pines, A. M., Ben-Ari, A., Utasi, A., & Larson, D. (2002). A cross-cultural investigation of social support and burnout. *European Psychologist, 7*(4), 256–264.

Pinker, S., & Jackendoff, R. (2005). The faculty of language: What's special about it? *Cognition, 95*(2), 201–236.

Pizam, A., Jeong, G.-H., Reichel, A., Van Boemmel, H., et al. (2004). The relationship between risk-taking, sensation-seeking, and the tourist behavior of young adults: A cross-cultural study. *Journal of Travel Research, 42*, 251–260.

Plazzi, G., Vetrugno, R., Provini, F., Montagna, P. (2005). Sleepwalking and other ambulatory behaviours during sleep. *Neurological Sciences, 26*(Suppl 3), S193–S198.

Pliner, P., & Mann, N. (2004). Influence of social norms and palatability on amount consumed and food choice. *Appetite, 42*(2), 227–237.

Plous, S. (2003). *Understanding prejudice and discrimination*. New York: McGraw-Hill.

Plutchik, R. (2003). *Emotions and life*. Washington, DC: American Psychological Assocation.

Poland, J., & Caplan, P. J. (2004). The deep structure of bias in psychiatric diagnosis. In P. J. Caplan & L. Cosgrove (Eds.), *Bias in psychiatric diagnosis. A project of the association for women in psychology*. Lanham, MD: Jason Aronson.

Polemikos, N., & Papaeliou, C. (2000). Sidedness preference as an index of organization of laterality. *Perceptual & Motor Skills, 91*(3, Pt 2), 1083–1090.

Polivy, J., & Herman, C. P. (2002). Causes of eating disorders. *Annual Review of Psychology, 53*, 187–213.

Pollner, M. (1998). The effects of interviewer gender in mental health interviews. *Journal of Nervous & Mental Disease, 186*(6), 369–373.

Pollock, V. E., Briere, J., Schneider, L., Knop, J., et al. (1990). Childhood antecedents of antisocial behavior. *American Journal of Psychiatry, 147*(10), 1290–1293.

Pomaki, G., Supeli, A., & Verhoeven, C. (2007). Role conflict and health behaviors: Moderating effects on psychological distress and somatic complaints. *Psychology & Health, 22*(3), 317–335.

Pope, H. G., Gruber, A. J., & Yurgelun-Todd, D. (1995). The residual neuropsychological effects of cannabis. *Drug & Alcohol Dependence, 38*(1), 25–34.

Popma, A., Vermeiren, R., Geluk, C., Rinne, T., et al. (2007). Cortisol moderates the relationship between testosterone and aggression in delinquent male adolescents. *Biological Psychiatry, 61*(3), 405–411.

Population Institute (2006). *Population issues*. Washington, DC: Population Institute. Retrieved August 14, 2007, from http://www.populationinstitute.org/population-issues/.

Porter, K. (2003). *The mental athlete: Inner training for peak performance in all sports*. Champaign, IL: Human Kinetics.

Porter, S., Campbell, M. A., Birt, A. R., & Woodworth, M. T. (2003). "He said, she said": A psychological perspective on historical memory evidence in the courtroom. *Canadian Psychology, 44*(3), 190–206.

Porteus, L. (2004). "Group Think" Led to Iraq WMD Assessment. *Fox News*, July 11. Retrieved August 4, 2007, from http://www.foxnews.com/story/0,2933,125123,00.html.

Posada, G., Jacobs, A., Richmond, M. K., Carbonell, O. A., et al. (2002). Maternal caregiving and infant security in two cultures. *Developmental Psychology, 38*(1), 67–78.

Poulton, R. G., & Andrews, G. (1996). Change in danger cognitions in agoraphobia and social phobia during treatment. *Behaviour Research & Therapy, 34*(5–6), 413–421.

Powell, A. L., & Thelen, M. H. (1996). Emotions and cognitions associated with bingeing and weight control behavior in bulimia. *Journal of Psychosomatic Research, 40*(3), 317–328.

Powell, R. A., Symbaluk, D. G., & Macdonald, S. E. (2005). *Introduction to learning and behavior*. Belmont, CA: Cengage Learning/Wadsworth.

Preckel, F., Holling, H., & Wiese, M. (2006). Relationship of intelligence and creativity in gifted and non-gifted students: An investigation of threshold theory. *Personality & Individual Differences, 40*(1), 159–170.

Premack, A. J., & Premack, D. (1972). Teaching language to an ape. *Scientific American,* Oct., 92–99.

Premack, D., & Premack, A. J. (1983). *The mind of an ape*. New York: Norton.

Pressley, M. (1987). Are key-word method effects limited to slow presentation rates? An empirically based reply to Hall and Fuson (1986). *Journal of Educational Psychology, 79*(3), 333–335.

Prigerson, H. G., Maciejewski, P. K., & Rosenheck, R. A. (2002). Population attributable fractions of psychiatric disorders and behavioral outcomes associated with combat exposure among US men. *American Journal of Public Health, 92*, 59–63.

Priluck, R., & Till, B. D. (2004). The role of contingency awareness, involvement, and need for cognition in attitude formation. *Journal of the Academy of Marketing Science, 32*(3), 329–344.

Prinstein, M. J., Meade, C. S. & Cohen, G. L. (2003). Adolescent oral sex, peer popularity, and perceptions of best friends' sexual behavior. *Journal of Pediatric Psychology, 28*(4), 243–249.

Prochaska, J. O., & Norcross, J. C. (2007). *Systems of psychotherapy: A transtheoretical analysis* (6th ed.). Belmont, CA: Cengage Learning/Wadsworth.

Provencher, M. D., Dugas, M. J., & Ladouceur, R. (2004). Efficacy of problem-solving training and cognitive exposure in the treatment of generalized anxiety disorder: A case replication series. *Cognitive & Behavioral Practice, 11*(4), 404–414.

Puca, R. M., & Schmalt, H. (1999). Task enjoyment: A mediator between achievement motives and performance. *Motivation & Emotion, 23*(1), 15–29.

Pychyl, T. A., Lee, J. M., Thibodeau, R., & Blunt, A. (2000). Five days of emotion: An experience sampling study of undergraduate student procrastination. *Journal of Social Behavior & Personality, 15*(5), 239–254.

Quednow, B. B., Jessen, F., Kühn, K.-W., Maier, W., et al. (2006). Memory deficits in abstinent MDMA (ecstasy) users: Neuropsychological evidence of frontal dysfunction. *Journal of Psychopharmacology, 20*(3), 373–384.

Quigley, B. M., & Leonard, K. E. (2000). Alcohol, stress, and violence. In V. B. Van Hasselt & M. Hersen (Eds.), *Aggression and violence: An introductory text*. Boston: Allyn & Bacon.

Quinn, P. C., & Bhatt, R. S. (1998). Visual pop-out in young infants. *Infant Behavior & Development, 21*(2), 273–288.

Raag, T., & Rackliff, C. L. (1998). Preschoolers' awareness of social expectations of gender: Relationships to toy choices. *Sex Roles, 38*(9–10), 685–700.

Rabius, V., McAlister, A. L., Geiger, A., Huang, P., et al. (2004). Telephone counseling increases cessation rates among young adult smokers. *Health Psychology, 23*(5), 539–541.

Rachman, S. (2004). *Anxiety* (2nd ed.). New York: Routledge.

Rahman, Q., & Wilson, G. D. (2003). Born gay? The psychobiology of human sexual orientation. *Personality & Individual Differences, 34*(8), 1337–1382.

Rainville, P. (2004). Pain & emotions. In D. D. Price & M. C. Bushnell (Eds.), *Psychological methods of pain control: Basic science and clinical perspectives*. Seattle: IASP Press.

Ramachandran, V. S. (1995). 2-D or not 2-D—that is the question. In R. Gregory, J. Harris, et al. (Eds.), *The artful eye*. New York: Oxford University Press.

Ramanaiah, N. V., Detwiler, F. R. J., & Byravan, A. (1995). Sex-role orientation and satisfaction with life. *Psychological Reports, 77*(3, Dec., Pt 2), 1260–1262.

Ramsay, M. C., Reynolds, C. R., & Kamphaus, R. W. (2002). *Essentials of behavioral assessment*. New York: Wiley.

Randi, J. (1983). Science and the chimera. In G. O. Abell & B. Singer (Eds.), *Science and the paranormal*. New York: Scribner's.

Randi, J. (1997). *An encyclopedia of claims, frauds, and hoaxes of the occult and supernatural*. New York: St. Martin's Press.

Rathus, R., Nevid, J., & Fichner-Rathus, L. (2005). *Human sexuality in a world of diversity* (6th ed.). Boston: Allyn & Bacon.

Rau, H., Bührer, M., & Weitkunat, R. (2003). Biofeedback of R-wave-to-pulse interval normalizes blood pressure. *Applied Psychophysiology and Biofeedback, 28*(1), 37–46.

Rau, P. R. (2005). *Drowsy driver detection and warning system for commercial vehicle drivers: Field operational test design, data analyses, and progress*. National Highway Traffic Safety Administration Paper Number 05-0192. Retrieved July 24, 2006, from http://www-nrd.nhtsa.dot.gov/pdf/nrd-01/esv/esv19/05-0192-W.pdf.

Rau, W., & Durand, A. (2000). The academic ethic and college grades: Does hard work help students to "make the grade"? *Sociology of Education, 73*(1), 19–38.

Read, J. (1995). Female sexual dysfunction. *International Review of Psychiatry, 7*(2), 175–182.

Reed, J. D., & Bruce, D. (1982). Longitudinal tracking of difficult memory retrievals. *Cognitive Psychology, 14*, 280–300.

Reed, S. K. (2007). *Cognition: Theory and applications* (7th ed.). Belmont, CA: Cengage Learning/Wadsworth.

Reevy, G. M., & Maslach, C. (2001). Use of social support: Gender and personality differences. *Sex Roles, 44*(7–8), 437–459.

Regan, P. C., Levin, L., Sprecher, S., Christopher, F. S., et al. (2000). Partner preferences: What characteristics do men and women desire in their short-term sexual and long-term romantic partners? *Journal of Psychology & Human Sexuality, 12*(3), 1–21.

Regev, L. G., Zeiss, A., & Zeiss, R. (2006). Orgasmic disorders. In J. E. Fisher & W. T. O'Donohue (Eds.), *Practitioner's guide to evidence-based psychotherapy*. New York: Springer Science.

Regoeczi, W. C. (2003). When context matters: A multilevel analysis of household and neighbourhood crowding on aggression and withdrawal. *Journal of Environmental Psychology, 23*(4), 457–470.

Reid, M. R., Mackinnon, L. T., & Drummond, P. D. (2001). The effects of stress management on symptoms of upper respiratory tract infection, secretory immunoglobulin A, and mood in young adults. *Journal of Psychosomatic Research, 51*(6), 721–728.

Reid, P. T. (2002). Multicultural psychology. *Cultural Diversity & Ethnic Minority Psychology, 8*(2), 103–114.

Reiff, S., Katkin, E. S., & Friedman, R. (1999). Classical conditioning of the human blood pressure response. *International Journal of Psychophysiology, 34*(2), 135–145.

Reifman, A. S., Larrick, R. P., & Fein, S. (1991). Temper and temperature on the diamond: The heat-aggression relationship in major league baseball. *Personality & Social Psychology Bulletin, 17*(5), 580–585.

Reisner, A. D. (2006). A case of Munchausen Syndrome by proxy with subsequent stalking behavior. *International Journal of Offender Therapy & Comparative Criminology, 50*(3), 245–254.

Reiss, M., Tymnik, G., Koegler, P., Koegler, W., et al. (1999). Laterality of hand, foot, eye, and ear in twins. *Laterality, 4*(3), 287–297.

Reiss, S., & Havercamp, S. M. (2005). Motivation in developmental context: A new method for studying self-actualization. *Journal of Humanistic Psychology, 45*(1), 41–53.

Reissing, E. D., Binik, Y. M., Khalifé, S., Cohen, D., et al. (2004). Vaginal spasm, pain, and behavior: An empirical investigation of the diagnosis of vaginismus. *Archives of Sexual Behavior, 33*(1), 5–17.

Reissing, E. D., Binik, Y. M., Khalifé, S., Cohen, D., et al. (2003). Etiological correlates of vaginismus: Sexual and physical abuse, sexual knowledge sexual self-schema and relationship adjustment. *Journal of Sex & Marital Therapy, 29*(1), 47–59.

Reiterman, T. (1993). Parallel roads led to Jonestown, Waco. *The Los Angeles Times*, April 23, A24.

Reitman, D., Murphy, M. A., Hupp, S. D. A., & O'Callaghan, P. M. (2004). Behavior change and perceptions of change: Evaluating the effectiveness of a token economy. *Child & Family Behavior Therapy, 26*(2), 17–36.

Remland, M. S., Jones, T. S., & Brinkman, H. (1991). Proxemic and haptic behavior in three European countries. *Journal of Nonverbal Behavior, 15*(4), 215–232.

Renner, M. J., & Mackin, R. S. (1998). A life stress instrument for classroom use. *Teaching of Psychology, 25*(1), 46–48.

Rentfrow, P. J., & Gosling, S. D. (2003). The do re mi's of everyday life: The structure and personality correlates of music preferences. *Journal of Personality & Social Psychology, 84*(6), 1236–1256.

Reppucci, N. D., Woolard, J. L., & Fried, C. S. (1999). Social, community, and preventive interventions. *Annual Review of Psychology, 50,* 387–418.

Rescorla, R. A. (1987). A Pavlovian analysis of goal-directed behavior. *American Psychologist, 42,* 119–126.

Rescorla, R. A. (2004). Spontaneous recovery. *Learning & Memory, 11*(5), 501–509.

Restak, R. M. (2001). *The secret life of the brain*. New York: Dana Press.

Rhine, J. B. (1953). *New world of the mind*. New York: Sloane.

Rice, M. E. (1997). Violent offender research and implications for the criminal justice system. *American Psychologist, 52*(4), 414–423.

Richards, J. M., & Gross, J. J. (2000). Emotion regulation and memory: The cognitive costs of keeping one's cool. *Journal of Personality & Social Psychology, 79*(3), 410–424.

Richardson, D. R., Green, L. R. (1999). Social sanction and threat explanations on gender effects in direct and indirect aggression. *Aggressive Behavior, 25,* 425–434.

Richmond, L. J. (2004). When spirituality goes awry: Students in cults. *Professional School Counseling, 7*(5), 367–375.

Ricketts, M. S., & Galloway, R. E. (1984). Effects of three different one-hour single-session treatments for test anxiety. *Psychological Reports, 54,* 113–119.

Ridenour, T. A., Maldonado-Molina M., Compton, W. M., Spitznagel, E. L., et al. (2005). Factors associated with the transition from abuse to dependence among substance abusers: Implications for a measure of addictive liability. *Drug & Alcohol Dependence, 80*(1), 1–14.

Ridings, C. M., & Gefen, D. (2004). Virtual community attraction: Why people hang out online. *Journal of Computer-Mediated Communication, 10*(1).

Riefer, D. M., Keveri, M. K., & Kramer, D. L. (1995). Name that tune: Eliciting the tip-of-the-tongue experience using auditory stimuli. *Psychological Reports, 77*(3, Pt. 2), 1379–1390.

Rieke, M. L., & Guastello, S. J. (1995). Unresolved issues in honesty and integrity testing. *American Psychologist,* June, 458–459.

Riley, W., Jerome, A., Behar, A., & Zack, S. (2002). Feasibility of computerized scheduled gradual reduction for adolescent smoking cessation. *Substance Use & Misuse, 37*(2), 255–263.

Riquelme, H. (2002). Can people creative in imagery interpret ambiguous figures faster than people less creative in imagery? *Journal of Creative Behavior, 36*(2), 105–116.

Ritter, J. (1998). Uniforms changing the culture of the nation's classrooms. *USA Today,* Oct. 15, 1A, 2A.

Riva, G., & Wiederhold, B. K. (2006). Emerging trends in cybertherapy: Introduction to the special issue. *PsychNology Journal, 4*(2), 121–128.

Rizzolatti, G., & Craighero, L. (2004). The mirror-neuron system. *Annual Review of Neuroscience, 27,* 169–192.

Roberti, J. W. (2004). A review of behavioral and biological correlates of sensation seeking. *Journal of Research in Personality, 38,* 256–279.

Roberts, B. W., Walton, K. E., & Viechtbauer, W. (2006). Patterns of mean-level change in personality traits across the life course: a meta-analysis of longitudinal studies. *Psychological Bulletin, 132,* 1–25.

Roberts, D. F., Foehr, U. G., & Rideout, V. (2005). *Generation M: Media in the lives of 8-18 year-olds.* Kaiser Family Foundation. Retrieved June 6, 2007, from http://www.kff.org/entmedia/7251.cfm.

Roberts, R. E., Phinney, J. S., Masse, L. C., Chen, Y. R., et al. (1999). The structure of ethnic identity of young adolescents from diverse ethnocultural groups. *Journal of Early Adolescence, 19*(3), 301–322.

Roberts, W. A. & Roberts, S. (2002). Two tests of the stuck-in-time hypothesis. *Journal of General Psychology, 129*(4), 415–429.

Roberts, W. A. (2002). Are animals stuck in time? *Psychological Bulletin, 128*(3), 473–489.

Robertson, I. S. (2001). *Problem solving*. Hove, UK: Psychology Press.

Robertson, L. C., & Sagiv, N. (2005). *Synesthesia: Perspectives from cognitive neuroscience*. New York: Oxford University Press.

Robins, R. W., Gosling, S. D., & Craik, K. H. (1998). Psychological science at the crossroads. *American Scientist, 86,* (July–Aug.), 310–313.

Robinson, A., & Clinkenbeard, P. R. (1998). Giftedness. *Annual Review of Psychology, 49,* 117–139.

Robinson, B., Frye, E. M., & Bradley, L. J. (1997). Cult affiliation and disaffiliation. *Counseling & Values, 41*(2), 166–173.

Robinson, T. E., & Berridge, K. C. (2003). Addiction. *Annual Review of Psychology, 54,* 25–53.

Robinson, T. N., Wilde, M. L., Navracruz, L. C., Haydel, K. F., et al. (2001). Effects of reducing children's television and video game use on aggressive behavior. *Archives of Pediatrics & Adolescent Medicine, 155*(1), 17–23.

Robinson-Riegler, B., & McDaniel, M. (1994). Further constraints on the bizarreness effect: Elaboration at encoding. *Memory & Cognition, 22*(6), 702–712.

Rock, A. (2004). *The mind at night: The new science of how and why we dream*. New York: Basic Books.

Rodd, Z. A., Bell, R. L., McQueen, V. K., Davids, M. R., et al. (2005). Chronic ethanol drinking by alcohol-preferring rats increases the sensitivity of the posterior ventral tegmental area to the reinforcing effects of ethanol. *Alcoholism: Clinical & Experimental Research 29*(3), 358–366.

Roeckelein, J. E. (2004). *Imagery in psychology: A reference guide*. Westport, CT: Praeger.

Roediger, III, H. L., & McDermott, K. B. (1995). Creating false memories: Remembering words not presented on lists. *Journal of Experimental Psychology: Learning, Memory, and Cognition, 21*(4), 803–814.

Roediger, III, H. L., & Amir, N., (2005). Implicit memory tasks: Retention without conscious recollection. In A. Wenzel & D. C. Rubin (Eds.), *Cognitive methods and their application to clinical research*. Washington, DC: American Psychological Association.

Rogers, C. R. (1959). A theory of therapy, personality, and interpersonal relationships, as developed in the client-centered framework. In S. Koch (Ed.), *Psychology: A study of a science* (Vol. 3). New York: McGraw-Hill.

Rogers, C. R. (1961). *On becoming a person: A therapist's view of psychotherapy*. Boston: Houghton Mifflin.

Rogers, S., & Silver, S. M. (2002). Is EMDR an exposure therapy? A review of trauma protocols. *Journal of Clinical Psychology, 58*(1), 43–59.

Rohsenow, D. J., & Smith R. E. (1982). Irrational beliefs as predictors of negative affective states. *Motivation and Emotion, 6,* 299–301.

Roid, G. (2003). *Technical manual: Stanford-Binet Intelligence Scales* (5th ed.). Itasca, IL: Riverside.

Roney, J. R. (2003). Effects of visual exposure to the opposite sex: Cognitive aspects of mate attraction in human males. *Personality & Social Psychology Bulletin, 29,* 393–404.

Roos, P. E., & Cohen, L. H. (1987). Sex roles and social support as moderators of life stress adjustment. *Journal of Personality & Social Psychology, 52,* 576–585.

Rosch, E. (1977). Classification of real-world objects: Origins and representations in cognition. In P. N. Johnson-Laird & P. C. Wason (Eds.), *Thinking: Reading in cognitive science*. Cambridge, UK: Cambridge University Press.

Rosen, G., Hugdahl, K., Ersland, L., Lundervold, A., et al. (2001). Different brain areas activated during imagery of painful and non-painful "finger movements" in a subject with an amputated arm. *Neurocase, 7*(3), 255–260.

Rosenberg, L. B. (1994). The effect of interocular distance upon depth perception when using stereoscopic displays to perform work within virtual and telepresent environments. *USAF AMRL Technical Report (Wright-Patterson)*, July, AL/CF-TR-1994-0052.

Rosenberg, S. S., & Lynch, J. E. (2002). Fritz Perls revisited: A micro-assessment of a live clinical session. *Gestalt Review, 6*(3), 184–202.

Rosenhan, D. L. (1973). On being sane in insane places. *Science, 179,* 250–258.

Rosenkranz, M.A., Jackson, D. C., Dalton, K. M., Dolski, I., et al. (2003). Affective style and in vivo immune response: Neurobehavioral mechanisms. *Proceedings of the National Academy of Sciences, 100,* 11148–11152.

Rosenman, R. H., Brand, R. J., Jenkins, C. D., Friedman, M., et al. (1975). Coronary heart disease in the Western Collaborative Group Study: Final follow-up experience of 8 1/2 years. *Journal of the American Medical Association, 233,* 872–877.

Rosenthal, D., & Quinn, O. W. (1977). Quadruplet hallucinations: Phenotypic variations of a schizophrenic genotype. *Archives of General Psychiatry, 34*(7), 817–827.

Rosenthal, R. (1965). *Clever Hans: A case study of scientific method. Introduction to Clever Hans: (The horse of Mr. Von Osten),* by O. Pfungst. New York: Holt, Rinehart & Winston.

Rosenthal, R. (1973). The Pygmalion effect lives. *Psychology Today,* Sept., 56–63.

Rosenthal, R. (1994). Science and ethics in conducting, analyzing, and reporting psychological research. *Psychological Science, 5,* 127–134.

Rosenthal, S. L., Von Ranson, K. M., Cotton, S., Biro, F. M., et al. (2001). Sexual initiation: Predictors and developmental trends. *Sexually Transmitted Diseases, 28*(9), 527–532.

Rosenthal, T. L. (1993). To soothe the savage breast. *Behavior Research & Therapy, 31*(5), 439–462.

Rosenthal, T. L., & Rosenthal, R. (1980). *The vicious cycle of stress reaction.* Renate & Ted Rosenthal, Stress Management Clinic, Department of Psychiatry, University of Tennessee College of Medicine, Memphis, Tennessee.

Rosenzweig, M. R., Breedlove, S. M., & Watson, N. V. (2004). Biological psychology: *An introduction to behavioral and cognitive neuroscience* (4th ed.). Sunderland, MA: Sinauer Associates.

Rosnow, R. L. (2006). *Writing papers in psychology: A student guide to research papers, essays, proposals, posters, and handouts* (7th ed.). Belmont, CA: Cengage Learning/Wadsworth.

Ross, H. E., & Plug, C. (2002). *The mystery of the moon illusion.* New York: Oxford University Press.

Ross, M., Heine, S. J., Wilson, A. E., & Sugimori, S. (2005). Cross-cultural discrepancies in self-appraisals. *Personality & Social Psychology Bulletin, 31*(9), 1175–1188.

Ross, P. E. (2006). The expert mind. *Scientific American, 294*(7), 64–71.

Rothbard, N. P., Phillips, K. W., & Dumas, T. L. (2005). Managing multiple roles: Work-family policies and individuals' desires for segmentation. *Organization Science, 16*(3), 243–258.

Rothschild, B., & Rand, M. (2006). *Help for the helper: The psychophysiology of compassion fatigue and vicarious trauma.* New York: Norton.

Rotter, J. B., & Hochreich, D. J. (1975). *Personality.* Glenview, IL: Scott, Foresman.

Rowe, B. (2007). *College awareness guide: What students need to know to succeed in college.* Englewood Cliffs, NJ: Prentice Hall.

Rowland, D. L. (2007). Sexual health and problems: Erectile dysfunction, premature ejaculation, and male orgasmic disorder. In J. E. Grant & M. N. Potenza (Eds.), *Textbook of men's mental health.* Washington, DC: American Psychiatric Publishing.

Rozin, P., Kabnick, K., Pete, E., Fischler, C., et al. (2003). The ecology of eating: Smaller portion sizes in France than in the United States help explain the French paradox. *Psychological Science, 14*(5), 450–454.

Rubenstein, C. (1983). The modern art of courtly love. *Psychology Today, 17*(7), 43–49.

Rubenstein, C. (2002). What turns you on? *My Generation,* July–Aug., 55–58.

Rubenstein, C., & Tavris, C. (1987). Special survey results: 2600 women reveal the secrets of intimacy. *Redbook, 159,* 147–149.

Rubin, D. C. (1985). The subtle deceiver: Recalling our past. *Psychology Today,* Sept., 38–46.

Rubin, Z. (1973). *Liking and loving: An invitation to social psychology.* New York: Holt.

Rudd, M. D., Joiner, T. E., Jr., & Rajab, M. H. (2001). *Treating suicidal behavior.* New York: Guilford.

Rueckl, J. G., & Galantucci, B. (2005). The locus and time course of long-term morphological priming. *Language & Cognitive Processes, 20*(1), 115–138.

Rummens, J., Beiser, M., & Noh, S. (Eds.). (2003). *Immigration, ethnicity and health.* Toronto: University of Toronto Press.

Runco, M. A. (2003). *Critical creative processes.* Cresskill, NJ: Hampton Press.

Runco, M. A. (2004). Creativity. *Annual Review of Psychology, 55,* 657–687.

Rushton, J. P., & Jensen, A. R. (2005). Thirty years of research on race differences in cognitive ability. *Psychology, Public Policy, & Law, 11,* 235–294.

Russell, S., & Norvig, P. (2003). *Artificial intelligence: A modern approach* (2nd ed.). Englewood Cliffs, NJ: Prentice Hall.

Russo, M. B., Brooks, F. R., Fontenot, J., Dopler, D. M., et al. (1998). Conversion disorder presenting as multiple sclerosis. *Military Medicine, 163*(10), 709–710.

Rutledge, T., & Linden, W. (1998). To eat or not to eat: Affective and physiological mechanisms in the stress–eating relationship. *Journal of Behavioral Medicine, 21*(3), 221–240.

Ruva, C., McEvoy, C., & Bryant, J. B. (2007). Effects of pre-trial publicity and jury deliberation on juror bias and source memory errors. *Applied Cognitive Psychology, 21*(1), 45–67.

Ryan, M. P. (2001). Conceptual models of lecture learning. *Reading Psychology, 22*(4), 289–312.

Ryan, R. M., & Deci, E. L. (2000). Self-determination theory and the facilitation of intrinsic motivation, social development, and well-being. *American Psychologist, 55,* 68–78.

Ryckman, R. M. (2008). *Theories of personality* (9th ed.). Belmont, CA: Cengage Learning/Wadsworth.

Ryff, C. D. (1995). Psychological well-being in adult life. *Current Directions in Psychological Science, 4*(4), 99–104.

Ryff, C. D., & Keyes, C. L. (1995). The structure of psychological well-being revisited. *Journal of Personality & Social Psychology, 69*(4), 719–727.

Ryff, C. D., & Singer, B. (2000). Interpersonal flourishing. *Personality & Social Psychology Review, 4,* 30–44.

Ryff, C. D., Singer, B. H., & Palmersheim, K. A. (2004). Social inequalities in health and well-being: The role of relational and religious protective factors. In O. G. Brim, C. D. Ryff, et al. (Eds.), *How healthy are we? A national study of wellbeing at midlife.* Chicago, IL: University of Chicago Press.

Saadeh, W., Rizzo, C. P., & Roberts, D. G. (2002). Spanking. *Clinical Pediatrics, 41*(2), 87–88.

Sackeim, H. A., Haskett, R. F., Mulsant, B. H., Thase, M. E., et al. (2001). Continuation pharmacotherapy in the prevention of relapse following electroconvulsive therapy. *Journal of the American Medical Association, 285,* 1299–1307.

Sahelian, R. (1998). *5-HTP.* Wakefield, RI: Moyer Bell.

Saksida, L. M., & Wilkie, D. M. (1994). Time-of-day discrimination by pigeons. *Animal Learning & Behavior, 22,* 143–154.

Sales, B. D., & Hafemeister, T. L. (1985). Law and psychology. In E. M. Altmeir & M. E. Meyer (Eds.), *Applied specialties in psychology.* New York: Random House.

Salmela, J. H. (1974). An information processing approach to volleyball. *C.V.A. Technical Journal, 1,* 49–62.

Salmela, J. H. (1975). Psycho-motor task demands of artistic gymnastics. In J. H. Salmela (Ed.), *The advanced study of gymnastics: A textbook.* Springfield, IL: Charles C Thomas.

Salmon, P. (2001). Effects of physical exercise on anxiety, depression, and sensitivity to stress: A unifying theory. *Clinical Psychology Review, 21*(1), 33–61.

Salovey, P., & Mayer, J. (1997). *Emotional development and emotional intelligence.* New York: Basic Books.

Salthouse, T. A. (2004). What and when of cognitive aging. *Current Directions in Psychological Science, 13*(4), 140–144.

SAMHAS (Substance Abuse and Mental Health Services Administration). (2005). *Overview of Findings from the 2004 National Survey on Drug Use and Health.* Rockville, MD: Office of Applied Studies, NSDUH Series H-27, DHHS Publication No. SMA 05-4061. Retrieved June 6, 2007, from http://www.oas.samhsa.gov/nsduh/2k4nsduh/2k4overview/2k4overview.pdf.

Sankofa, B. M., Hurley, E. A., Allen, B. A., & Boykin, A. W. (2005). Cultural expression and black students' attitudes toward high achievers. *Journal of Psychology: Interdisciplinary & Applied, 139*(3), 247–259.

Santrock, J. W. (2007). *Child development* (11th ed.). New York: McGraw-Hill.

Santrock, J. W., & Halonen, J. S. (2007). *Connections to college success.* Belmont, CA: Cengage Learning/Wadsworth.

Sarason, I. G., & Sarason, B. R. (2005). *Abnormal psychology* (11th ed.). Englewood Cliffs, NJ: Prentice Hall.

Sateia, M. J., & Nowell, P. D. (2004). Insomnia. *Lancet, 364*(9449), 1959–1973.

Saunders, T., Driskell, J. E., Johnston, J. H., Salas, E. (1996). The effect of stress inoculation training on anxiety and performance. *Journal of Occupational Health Psychology, 1*(2), 170–186.

Savage-Rumbaugh, S., & Lewin, R. (1996). *Kanzi.* New York: Wiley.

Savage-Rumbaugh, S., Murphy, J., Sevcik, R. A., Brakke, K. E., et al. (1993). Language comprehension in ape and child. *Monographs of the Society for Research in Child Development, Serial No. 233* (Vol. 58, Nos. 3–4).

Savage-Rumbaugh, S., Sevcik, R. A., Brakke, K. E., Rumbaugh, D. M., et al. (1990). Symbols: Their communicative use, comprehension, and combination by bonobos (Pan paniscus). *Advances in Infancy Research, 6,* 221–278.

Savage-Rumbaugh, S., Shanker, S., & Taylor, T. (1998). *Apes, language, and mind.* New York: Oxford University Press.

Sawyer, R. G., & Smith, N. G. (1996). A survey of situational factors at first intercourse among college students. *American Journal of Health Behavior, 20*(4), 208–217.

Saxton, M., Houston-Price, C., & Dawson, N. (2005). The prompt hypothesis: Clarification requests as corrective input for grammatical errors. *Applied Psycholinguistics, 26*(3), 393–414.

Saywitz, K. J., Mannarino, A. P., Berliner, L., & Cohen, J. A. (2000). Treatment for sexually abused children and adolescents. *American Psychologist, 55*(9), 1040–1049.

Schachter, S. (1959). *Psychology of affiliation.* Stanford, CA: Stanford University Press.

Schachter, S., & Wheeler, L. (1962). Epinephrine, chlorpromazine and amusement. *Journal of Abnormal & Social Psychology, 65,* 121–128.

Schacter, D. L. (1996). *Searching for memory: The brain, the mind, and the past.* New York: Basic Books.

Schacter, D. L. (2000). Memory: Memory systems. In A. Kazdin (Ed.), *Encyclopedia of psychology.* Washington, DC: American Psychological Association.

Schacter, D. L. (2001). *The seven sins of memory.* Boston: Houghton Mifflin.

Schacter, D. L., Norman, K. A., & Koutstaal, W. (1998). The cognitive neuroscience of constructive memory. *Annual Review of Psychology, 49,* 289–318.

Schafer, M., & Crichlow, S. (1996). Antecedents of groupthink: A quantitative study. *Journal of Conflict Resolution, 40*(3), 415–435.

Schaie, K. W. (1994). The course of adult intellectual development. *American Psychologist, 49*(4), 304–313.

Schaie, K. W. (2005). *Developmental influences on adult intelligence: The Seattle longitudinal study.* New York: Oxford University Press.

Scheck, B., Neufeld, P., & Dwyer, J. (2000). *Actual innocence.* New York: Doubleday.

Schenck, C. H., & Mahowald, M. W. (2005). Rapid eye movement and non-REM sleep parasomnias. *Primary Psychiatry, 12*(8), 67–74.

Schick, T., & Vaughn, L. (2004). *How to think about weird things: Critical thinking for a new age* (4th ed.). New York: McGraw-Hill.

Schilling, M. A. (2005). A "Small-World" network model of cognitive insight. *Creativity Research Journal, 17*(2–3), 131–154.

Schiraldi, G. R., & Brown, S. L. (2001). Primary prevention for mental health: Results of an exploratory cognitive-behavioral college course. *Journal of Primary Prevention, 22*(1), 55–67.

Schleicher, S. S., & Gilbert, L. A. (2005). Heterosexual dating discourses among college students: Is there still a double standard? *Journal of College Student Psychotherapy, 19*(3), 7–23.

Schlosberg, H. (1954). Three dimensions of emotion. *Psychological Review, 61,* 81–88.

Schmidt, F. L., & Hunter, J. E. (1998). The validity and utility of selection methods in personnel psychology. *Psychological Bulletin, 124*(2), 262–274.

Schmidt, F. L., Ones, D. S., & Hunter, J. E. (1992). Personnel selection. *Annual Review of Psychology, 43,* 627–670.

Schmitt, D. P., & Allik, J. (2005). Simultaneous administration of the Rosenberg Self-Esteem Scale in 53 nations: Exploring the universal and culture-specific features of global self-esteem. *Journal of Personality & Social Psychology, 89*(4), 623–642.

Schmitt, E. (2001). U.S. now more diverse, ethnically and racially. *New York Times,* Apr. 1, A18.

Schmolck, H., Buffalo, E. A., & Squire, L. R. (2000). Memory distortions develop over time. *Psychological Science, 11*(1), 39–45.

Schmuck, P., & Vlek, C. (2003). Psychologists can do much to support sustainable development. *European Psychologist, 8*(2), 66–76.

Schneider, K. J. (2002). Humanistic psychotherapy. In M. Hersen & W. H. Sledge (Eds.), *Encyclopedia of psychotherapy.* San Diego: Academic Press.

Schneider, K. J., Bugental, J. F. T., & Pierson, J. F. (2001). Introduction. *The Handbook of Humanistic Psychology.* Thousand Oaks, CA: Sage.

Schneiderman, N., Antoni, M. H., Saab, P. G., & Ironson, G. (2001). Health psychology: Psychological and biobehavioral aspects of chronic disease management. *Annual Review of Psychology, 52,* 555–580.

Schooler, C. (1998). Environmental complexity and the Flynn effect. In U. Neisser (Ed.), *The rising curve: Long-term gains in IQ and related measures.* Washington, DC: American Psychological Association.

Schopp, L. H., Demiris, G., & Glueckauf, R. L. (2006). Rural backwaters or front-runners? Rural telehealth in the vanguard of psychology practice. *Professional Psychology: Research & Practice, 37*(2), 165–173.

Schouten, S. A. (1994). An overview of quantitatively evaluated studies with mediums and psychics. *Journal of the American Society for Psychical Research, 88*(3), 221–254.

Schreiber, E. H., & Schreiber, D. E. (1999). Use of hypnosis with witnesses of vehicular homicide. *Contemporary Hypnosis, 16*(1), 40–44.

Schreiber, F. R. (1973). *Sybil.* Chicago: Regency.

Schroeder, J. E. (1995). Self-concept, social anxiety, and interpersonal perception skills. *Personality & Individual Differences, 19*(6), 955–958.

Schuel, H., Chang, M. C., Burkman, L. J., Picone, R. P., et al. (1999). Cannabinoid receptors in sperm. In G. Nahas, K. M. Sutin, et al. (Eds.), *Marihuana and medicine.* Totowa, NJ: Humana Press.

Schuetze, P., & Eiden, R. D. (2006). The association between maternal cocaine use during pregnancy and physiological regulation in 4- to 8-week-old infants: An examination of possible mediators and moderators. *Journal of Pediatric Psychology, 31*(1), 15–26.

Schuiling, G. A. (2004). Death in Venice: The homosexuality enigma. *Journal of Psychosomatic Obstetrics & Gynecology, 25*(1), 67–76.

Schultheiss, O. C., Wirth, M. M., & Stanton, S. J. (2004). Effects of affiliation and power motivation arousal on salivary progesterone and testosterone. *Hormones and Behavior, 46*(5), 592–599.

Schultz, D. P., & Schultz, S. E. (2005). *Theories of personality* (8th ed.). Belmont, CA: Cengage Learning/Wadsworth.

Schultz, D. P., & Schultz, S. E. (2006). *Psychology and work today* (9th ed.). Englewood Cliffs, NJ: Prentice Hall.

Schultz, D. P., & Schultz, S. E. (2008). *A history of modern psychology* (9th ed.). Belmont, CA: Cengage Learning/Wadsworth.

Schultz, H. T. (2004). Good and bad movie therapy with good and bad outcomes. *The Amplifier: Official Newsletter of APA Division 46, Media Psychology,* Fall/Winter. Retrieved May 18, 2007, from http://www.apa.org/divisions/div46/Amp%20Winter%2005/for%20Website/ampwinter05.html#therapy.

Schultz, P. W. (1999). Changing behavior with normative feedback interventions. *Basic & Applied Social Psychology, 21*(1), 25–36.

Schum T. R., Kolb, T. M., McAuliffe T. L., Simms, M., et al. (2002). Sequential acquisition of toilet-training skills: A descriptive study of gender and age differences in normal children. *Pediatrics, 3,* e48. Retrieved May 25, 2007, from http://pediatrics.aappublications.org/cgi/content/abstract/109/3/e48.

Schum, T. R., McAuliffe, T. L., Simms, M. D., Walter, J. A., et al. (2001). Factors associated with toilet training in the 1990s. *Ambulatory Pediatrics, 1*(2), 79–86.

Schuster, M. A., Stein, B. D., Jaycox, L. H., Collins, R. L., et al. (2001). A national survey of stress reactions after the September 11, 2001, terrorist attacks. *New England Journal of Medicine, 345*(20) 1507–1512.

Schwartz, B. L. (2002). *Tip-of-the-tongue states: Phenomenology, mechanism, and lexical retrieval.* Mahwah, NJ: Erlbaum.

Schwartz, M. S., & Andrasik, F. (Eds.). (2003). *Biofeedback: A practitioner's guide* (3rd ed.). New York: Guilford.

Sclafani, A., & Springer, D. (1976). Dietary obesity in adult rats: Similarities to hypothalamic and human obesity syndromes. *Psychology & Behavior, 17,* 461–471.

Scoboria, A., Mazzoni, G., Kirsch, I., & Milling, L. S. (2002). Immediate and persisting effects of misleading questions and hypnosis on memory reports. *Journal of Experimental Psychology: Applied, 8*(1), 26–32.

Scott, J. P., & Ginsburg, B. E. (1994). The Seville statement on violence revisited. *American Psychologist, 49*(10), 849–850.

Scott, L., & O'Hara, M. W. (1993). Self-discrepancies in clinically anxious and depressed university students. *Journal of Abnormal Psychology, 102*(2), 282–287.

Scurfield, R. M. (2002). Commentary about the terrorist acts of September 11, 2001: Posttraumatic reactions and related social and policy issues. *Trauma Violence & Abuse, 3*(1), 3–14.

Searcy, W. A., & Nowicki, S. (2005) *The evolution of animal communication: Reliability and deception in signaling systems.* Princeton, NJ: Princeton University Press.

Seckel, A. (2000). *The art of optical illusions.* London: Carlton Books.

Segerdahl, P., Fields, W., & Savage-Rumbaugh, S. (2005). *Kanzi's primal language: The cultural initiation of primates into language.* New York: Palgrave MacMillan.

Segerstrom, S., & Miller, G. E. (2004). Psychological stress and the human immune system: A meta-analytic study of 30 years of inquiry. *Psychological Bulletin, 130*(4), 601–630.

Segraves, R. T., & Segraves, K. B. (1995). Human sexuality and aging. *Journal of Sex Education & Therapy, 21*(2), 88–102.

Segraves, R., & Woodard, T. (2006). Female hypoactive sexual desire disorder: History and current status. *Journal of Sexual Medicine, 3*(3), 408–418.

Segraves, T., & Althof, S. (2002). Psychotherapy and pharmacotherapy for sexual dysfunctions. In P. E. Nathan & J. M. Gorman (Eds.), *A guide to treatments that work* (2nd ed.). New York: Oxford University Press.

Seidler, G. H., & Wagner, F. E. (2006). Comparing the efficacy of EMDR and trauma-focused cognitive-behavioral therapy in the treatment of PTSD: A meta-analytic study. *Psychological Medicine, 36*(11), 1515–1522.

Seidman, B. F. (2001). Medicine wars. *Skeptical Inquirer,* Jan.–Feb., 28–35.

Seitz, A., & Watanabe, T. (2005). A unified model for perceptual learning. *Trends in Cognitive Sciences, 9*(7), 329–334.

Sekuler, R., & Blake, R. (2006). *Perception* (5th ed.). New York: McGraw-Hill.

Seligman, M. E. P. (1972). For helplessness: Can we immunize the weak? In *Readings in psychology today* (2nd ed.). Del Mar, CA: CRM.

Seligman, M. E. P. (1989). *Helplessness.* New York: Freeman.

Seligman, M. E. P. (1989). Research in clinical psychology: Why is there so much depression today? In I. S. Cohen (Ed.), *The G. Stanley Hall lecture series* (Vol. 9). Washington, DC: American Psychological Association.

Seligman, M. E. P. (1994). *What you can change and what you can't.* New York: Knopf.

Seligman, M. E. P. (1995). The effectiveness of psychotherapy. *American Psychologist, 50*(12), 965–974.

Seligman, M. E. P. (1998). Why therapy works. *APA Monitor, 29*(12), 2.

Seligman, M. E. P. (2002). *Authentic happiness.* New York: Free Press.

Seligman, M. E. P. (2003). Positive psychology: Fundamental assumptions. *Source Psychologist, 16*(3), 126–127.

Seligman, M. E. P., & Csikszentmihalyi, M. (2000). Positive psychology: An introduction. *American Psychologist, 55,* 5–14.

Seltzer, R. (2006). Scientific jury selection: Does it work?. *Journal of Applied Social Psychology, 36*(10), 2417–2435.

Selye, H. (1976). *The stress of life.* New York: Knopf.

Senécal, C., Julien, E., & Guay, F. (2003). Role conflict and academic procrastination: A self-determination perspective.

European Journal of Social Psychology, 33(1), 135–145.

Service, R. F. (1994). Will a new type of drug make memory-making easier? *Science, 266,* 218–219.

Sessa, V. I., & London, M. (2006). *Continuous learning in organizations: Individual, group, and organizational perspectives.* Mahwah, NJ: Erlbaum.

Seybolt, D. C., & Wagner, M. K. (1997). Self-reinforcement, gender-role, and sex of participant in prediction of life satisfaction. *Psychological Reports, 81*(2), 519–522.

Seyle, D. C., & Newman, M. L. (2006). A house divided? The psychology of red and blue America. *American Psychologist, 61*(6), 571–580.

Shaffer, D. R. (2002). *Developmental psychology.* Belmont, CA: Cengage Learning/Wadsworth.

Shaffer, J. B., & Galinsky, M. D. (1989). *Models of group therapy.* Englewood Cliffs, NJ: Prentice Hall.

Shafir, E. (1993). Choosing versus rejecting: Why some options are both better and worse than others. *Memory and Cognition, 21,* 546–556.

Shafton, A. (1995). *Dream reader.* Albany, NY: State University of New York Press.

Shakesby, A. C., Anwyl, R., & Rowan, M. J. (2002). Overcoming the effects of stress on synaptic plasticity in the intact hippocampus: Rapid actions of serotonergic and antidepressant agents. *Journal of Neuroscience, 22,* 3638–3644.

Shapiro, C. M., Trajanovic, N. N., & Fedoroff, J. P. (2003). Sexsomnia: A new parasomnia? *Canadian Journal of Psychiatry, 48*(5), 311–317.

Shapiro, D. A., Barkham, M., Stiles, W. B., Hardy, G. E., et al. (2003). Time is of the essence: A selective review of the fall and rise of brief therapy research. *Psychology & Psychotherapy: Theory, Research & Practice, 76*(3), 211–235.

Shapiro, F. (2001). *Eye movement desensitization and reprocessing: Basic principles, protocols and procedures* (2nd ed.). New York: Guilford.

Shapiro, F., & Forrest, M. S. (2004). *EMDR: The breakthrough therapy for overcoming anxiety, stress, and trauma.* New York: Basic Books.

Shapiro, J. M. (2006). A "memory-jamming" theory of advertising. *Social Science Research Network.* Retrieved June 20, 2007, from http://ssrn.com/abstract=903474.

Shapiro, S. L., & Walsh, R. (2006). The meeting of meditative disciplines and Western psychology: A mutually enriching dialogue. *American Psychologist, 61*(3), 227–239.

Sharf, R. S. (2008). *Theories of psychotherapy & counseling: Concepts and cases* (4th ed.). Belmont, CA: Cengage Learning/Wadsworth.

Shaywitz, B. A, Shaywitz, S. E., Pugh, K. R., Constable, R. T., et al. (1995). Sex differences in the functional organization of the brain for language. *Nature, 373*(6515), 607–609.

Shaywitz, S. E., & Gore, J. C. (1995). Sex differences in functional organization of the brain for language. *Nature, 373*(6515), 607.

Sheehy, M., & Cournos, F. (1992). What is mental illness? In F. I. Kass, J. M. Oldham, et al. (Eds.), *The Columbia University College of Physicians and Surgeons complete home guide to mental health.* New York: Sharpe Communications/Henry Holt.

Sheldon, K. M., Ryan, R. M., Rawsthorne, L. J., & Ilardi, B. (1997). Trait self and true self: Cross-role variation in the Big-Five personality traits and its relations with psychological authenticity and subjective well-being. *Journal of Personality & Social Psychology, 73*(6), 1380–1393.

Shen, J., Botly, L. C. P., Chung, S. A., Gibbs, A. L., et al. (2006). Fatigue and shift work. *Journal of Sleep Research, 15*(1), 1–5.

Shepard, R. N. (1975). Form, formation, and transformation of internal representations. In R. L. Solso (Ed.), *Information processing and cognition: The Loyola Symposium.* Mahwah, NJ: Erlbaum.

Sherif, M., Harvey, O. J., White, B. J., Hood, W. R., et al. (1961). *Intergroup conflict and cooperation: The Robbers Cave experiment.* University of Oklahoma, Institute of Group Relations.

Shiffman, S., Scharf, D. M., Shadel, W. G., Gwaltney, C. J., et al. (2006). Analyzing milestones in smoking cessation: Illustration in a nicotine patch trial in adult smokers. *Journal of Consulting & Clinical Psychology, 74*(2), 276–285.

Shires, A., & Miller, D. (1998). A preliminary study comparing psychological factors associated with erectile dysfunction in heterosexual and homosexual men. *Sexual & Marital Therapy, 13*(1), 37–49.

Shneerson, J. M. (2005). *Sleep medicine: A guide to sleep and its disorders* (2nd ed.). London: Blackwell.

Shneidman, E. S. (1987a). At the point of no return. *Psychology Today,* March, 54–58.

Shneidman, E. S. (1987b). Psychological approaches to suicide. In G. R. VandenBos & B. K. Bryant (Eds.), *Cataclysms, crises, and catastrophes: Psychology in action.* Washington, DC: American Psychological Association.

Shore, H. (2003). Personal communication.

Short, S. E., Ross-Stewart, L., & Monsma, E. V. (2006). Onwards with the evolution of imagery research in sport psychology. *Athletic Insight: Online Journal of Sport Psychology, 8*(3), 1–15.

Shurkin, J. N. (1992). *Terman's kids.* Boston: Little, Brown.

Siegel, R. K. (2005). *Intoxication: The universal drive for mind-altering substances.* Rochester, VT: Park Street Press.

Siegler, R. S. (2004). *Children's thinking* (4th ed.). Mahwah, NJ: Erlbaum.

Siegler, R. S., DeLoache, J. S., & Eisenberg, N. (2006). *How children develop* (2nd ed.). New York: Worth.

Siever, L. J., & Koenigsberg, H. W. (2000). The frustrating no-man's-land of borderline personality disorder. *Cerebrum, 2*(4), 85–99.

Sigelman, C. K., & Rider, E. A. (2006). *Life-span human development* (5th ed.). Belmont, CA: Cengage Learning/Wadsworth.

Silver, S. M., Rogers, S., Knipe, J., & Colelli, G. (2005). EMDR therapy following the 9/11 terrorist attacks: A community-based intervention project in New York City. *International Journal of Stress Management, 12*(1), 29–42.

Silverstein, B. (1989). Enemy images. *American Psychologist, 44*(6), 903–913.

Simeon, D., Guralnik, O., Knutelska, M., & Schmeidler, J. (2002). Personality factors associated with dissociation: Temperament, defenses, and cognitive schemata. *American Journal of Psychiatry, 159,* 489–491.

Simister, J., & Cooper, C. (2005). Thermal stress in the U.S.A.: Effects on violence and on employee behaviour. *Stress & Health, 21,* 3–15.

Simner, M. L., & Goffin, R. D. (2003). A position statement by the international graphonomics society on the use of graphology in personnel selection testing. *International Journal of Testing, 3*(4), 353–364.

Simon, G. E, Ludman, E. J., Tutty, S., Operskalski, B., et al. (2004). Telephone psychotherapy and telephone care management for primary care patients starting antidepressant treatment. *Journal of the American Medical Association, 292,* 935–942.

Simons, D. J., & Chabris, C. F. (1999). Gorillas in our midst: Sustained inattentional blindness for dynamic events. *Perception, 28,* 1059–1074.

Simons, D. J., & Levin, D. T. (1998). Failure to detect changes to people during a real-world interaction. *Psychonomic Bulletin & Review, 5*(4), 644–649.

Simons, J. S., Dodson, C. S., Bell, D., & Schacter, D. L. (2004). Specific- and partial-source memory: Effects of aging. *Psychology & Aging, 19*(4), 689–694.

Simonton, D. K., & Baumeister, R. F. (2005). Positive psychology at the summit. *Review of General Psychology, 9*(2), 99–102.

Simpson, D. D., Joe, G. W., Fletcher, B. W., Hubbard, R. L., et al. (1999). A national evaluation of treatment outcomes for cocaine dependence. *Archives of General Psychiatry, 57*(6), 507–514.

Singer, M. T. (2003). *Cults in our midst: The continuing fight against their hidden menace* (rev. ed.). San Francisco: Jossey-Bass.

Singer, M. T., & Addis, M. E. (1992). Cults, coercion, and contumely. *Cultic Studies Journal, 9*(2), 163–189.

Singleton, J. L., & Newport, E. L. (2004). When learners surpass their models: The acquisition of American Sign Language from inconsistent input. *Cognitive Psychology, 49*(4), 370–407.

Sinha, R., Garcia, M., Paliwal, P., Kreek, M. J., et al. (2006). Stress-induced cocaine craving and hypothalamic-pituitary-adrenal responses are predictive of cocaine relapse outcomes. *Archives of General Psychiatry, 63*(3), 324–331.

Sipos, A., Rasmussen, F., Harrison, G., Tynelius, P., et al. (2004). Paternal age and schizophrenia: A population based cohort study. *British Medical Journal, 329*(7474), 1070.

Sirkin, M. I. (1990). Cult involvement: A systems approach to assessment and treatment. *Psychotherapy, 27*(1), 116–123.

Skeels, H. M. (1966). Adult status of children with contrasting early life experiences. *Monograph of the Society for Research in Child Development, 31*(3), 105.

Skillsoft (2006). *IT pros more likely to suffer from stress, says new survey.* Retrieved July 17, 2007, from http://www.skillsoft.com/EMEA/news/19-May-06.asp.

Skinner, B. F. (1938). *The behavior of organisms: An experimental analysis.* New York: Appleton-Century-Crofts.

Skipton, L. H. (1997). The many faces of character. *Consulting Psychology Journal: Practice & Research, 49*(4), 235–245.

Skoog, I. (1996). Sex and Swedish 85-year-olds. *British Journal of Clinical Psychology, 334*(17), 1140–1141.

Slaby, A. E., Garfinkel, B. D., & Garfinkel, L. F. (1994). *No one say my pain.* New York: Norton.

Slater, A., Mattock, A., & Brown, E. (1990). Size constancy at birth: Newborn infants' responses to retinal and real size. *Journal of Experimental Child Psychology, 49*(2), 314–322.

Slater, A., Mattock, A., Brown, E., & Bremner, J. G. (1991). Form perception at birth: Cohen and Younger (1984) revisited. *Journal of Experimental Child Psychology, 51*(3), 395–406.

Slijper, F. M. E., Drop, S. L. S., Molenaar, J. C.; de Muinck, K., et al. (2000). "Long-term psychological evaluation of intersex children": Reply. *Archives of Sexual Behavior, 29*(1), 119–121.

Slot, L. A. B., & Colpaert, F. C. (1999). Recall rendered dependent on an opiate state. *Behavioral Neuroscience, 113*(2), 337–344.

Smedley, A., & Smedley, B. D. (2005). Race as biology is fiction, racism as a social problem is real. *American Psychologist, 60*(1), 16–26.

Smith, A. P. (2005). Caffeine at work. *Human Psychopharmacology: Clinical & Experimental, 20*(6), 441–445.

Smith, A. P., Clark, R., & Gallagher, J. (1999). Breakfast cereal and caffeinated coffee: Effects on working memory, attention, mood and cardiovascular function. *Physiology & Behavior, 67*(1), 9–17.

Smith, C., Carey, S., & Wiser, M. (1985). On differentiation: A case study of the development of the concepts of size, weight, and density. *Cognition, 21*(3), 177–237.

Smith, E., & Delargy, M (2005). Locked-in syndrome. *British Medical Journal, 330,* 406–409.

Smith, J. L., & Cahusac, P. M. B. (2001). Right-sided asymmetry in sensitivity to tickle. *Laterality, 6*(3), 233–238.

Smith, L. F. (2002). The effects of confidence and perception of test-taking skills on performance. *North American Journal of Psychology, 4*(1), 37–50.

Smith, M. L., Cottrell, G. W., Gosselin, F., & Schyns, P. G. (2005). Transmitting and decoding facial expressions. *Psychological Science, 16*(3), 184–189.

Smith, T. W. (1990). *Adult sexual behavior in 1989: Number of partners, frequency, and risk.* Paper presented to the American Association for the Advancement of Science, February 1990, New Orleans.

Smith, T. W., Glazer, K., Ruiz, J. M., & Gallo, L. C. (2004). Hostility, anger, aggressiveness, and coronary heart disease: An interpersonal perspective on personality, emotion, and health. *Journal of Personality, 72*(6), 1217–1270.

Smith, T. W., Ruiz, J. M., & Uchino, B. N. (2004). Mental activation of supportive ties, hostility, and cardiovascular reactivity to laboratory stress in young men and women. *Health Psychology, 23*(5), 476–485.

Smyth, M. M., & Waller, A. (1998). Movement imagery in rock climbing. *Applied Cognitive Psychology, 12*(2), 145–157.

Sobel, E., Shine, D., DiPietro, D., & Rabinowitz, M. (1996). Condom use among HIV/infected patients in South Bronx, New York. *AIDS, 10*(2), 235–236.

Sobolewski, J. M., & Amato, P. R. (2005). Economic hardship in the family of origin and children's psychological well-being in adulthood. *Journal of Marriage & Family, 67*(1), 141–156.

Solomon, J. L., Marshall, P., & Gardner, H. (2005). Crossing boundaries to generative wisdom: An analysis of professional work. In R. J. Sternberg & J. Jordan (Eds.), *A handbook of wisdom: Psychological perspectives.* New York: Cambridge University Press.

Solowij, N., Stephens, R. S., Roffman, R. A., & the Marijuana Treatment Project Research Group. (2002). Cognitive functioning of long-term heavy cannabis users seeking treatment. *Journal of the American Medical Association, 287,* 1123–1131.

Solso, R. L., MacLin, M. K., & MacLin, O. H. (2005). *Cognitive psychology* (7th ed). Boston: Allyn and Bacon.

Somberg, D. R., Stone, G., & Claiborn, C. D. (1993). Informed consent: Therapist's beliefs and practices. *Professional Psychology: Research & Practice, 24*(2), 153–159.

Sommers-Flanagan, J., & Sommers-Flanagan, R. (2002). *Clinical interviewing* (3rd ed.). New York: Wiley.

Soussignan, R. (2002). Duchenne smile, emotional experience, and autonomic reactivity. *Emotion, 2*(1), 52–74.

Soyez, V., & Broekaert, E. (2003). How do substance abusers and their significant others experience the re-entry phase of therapeutic community treatment: a qualitative study. *International Journal of Social Welfare, 12*(3), 211–220.

Spangenberg, J. J., & Lategan, T. P. (1993). Coping, androgyny, and attributional style. *South African Journal of Psychology, 23*(4), 195–203.

Spector, P. E. (2005). *Industrial and organizational psychology: Research and practice* (4th ed.). New York: Wiley.

Spence, S., & David, A. (Eds.). (2004). *Voices in the brain: The cognitive neuropsychiatry of auditory verbal hallucinations.* London: Psychology Press.

Sperry, R. W. (1968). Hemisphere deconnection and unity in conscious awareness. *American Psychologist, 23,* 723–733.

Spiegler, M. D., & Guevremont, D. C. (2003). *Contemporary behavior therapy.* Belmont, CA: Cengage Learning/Wadsworth

Spinella, M. (2005). Compulsive behavior in tobacco users. *Addictive Behaviors, 30*(1), 183–186.

Spiro Wagner, P., & Spiro, C. S. (2005). *Divided minds: Twin sisters and their journey through schizophrenia.* New York, St. Martin's Press, 2005

Sporer, S. L. (2001). Recognizing faces of other ethnic groups. *Psychology, Public Policy, & Law, 7*(1), 36–97.

Sprecher, S. (1998). Insiders' perspectives on reasons for attraction to a close other. *Social Psychology Quarterly, 61*(4), 287–300.

Sprecher, S., & Hatfield, E. (1996) Premarital sexual standards among U.S. college students. *Archives of Sexual Behavior, 25*(3), 261–288.

Springer, S. P., & Deutsch, G. (1998). *Left brain, right brain.* New York: Freeman.

Sprinthall, R. C. (2007). *Basic statistical analysis* (8th ed.). Boston: Allyn & Bacon.

Squire, L. R. (2004). Memory systems of the brain: A brief history and current perspective. *Neurobiology of Learning & Memory, 82,* 171–177.

Squire, L. R., & Kandel, E. R. (2000). *Memory: From mind to molecule.* New York: Worth.

Squire, L. R., & Zola-Morgan, S. (1988). Memory: Brain systems and behavior. *Trends in Neurosciences, 11*(4), 170–175.

Srivastava, S., John, O. P., Gosling, S. D., & Potter, J. (2003). Development of personality in early and middle adulthood: Set like plaster or persistent change? *Journal of Personality & Social Psychology, 84*(5), 1041–1053.

Sroufe, L. A., Egeland, B., Carlson, E., & Collins, W. A. (2005). Placing early attachment experiences in developmental context: The Minnesota Longitudinal Study. In K. E. Grossmann, K. Grossmann, et al. (Eds.), *Attachment from infancy to adulthood: The major longitudinal studies.* New York: Guilford.

Staemmler, F.-M. (2004). Dialogue and interpretation in Gestalt therapy: Making sense together. *International Gestalt Journal, 27*(2), 33–57.

Stanovich, K. E. (2007). *How to think straight about psychology* (8th ed.). Boston: Allyn & Bacon.

Stapel, D. A., & Marx, D. M. (2007). Distinctiveness is key: How different types of self-other similarity moderate social comparison effects. *Personality & Social Psychology Bulletin, 33*(3), 439–448.

Staples, S. L. (1996). Human response to environmental noise. *American Psychologist, 51*(2), 143–150.

Steblay, N. M. (1987). Helping behavior in rural and urban environments: A meta-analysis. *Psychological Bulletin, 102*(3), 346–356.

Stein, L. M., & Memon, A. (2006). Testing the efficacy of the cognitive interview in a developing country. *Applied Cognitive Psychology, 20*(5), 597–605.

Stein, M. D., & Friedmann, P. D. (2005). Disturbed sleep and its relationship to alcohol use. *Substance Abuse, 26*(1), 1–13.

Stein, M. T., & Ferber, R. (2001). Recent onset of sleepwalking in early adolescence. *Journal of Development, Behavior, and Pediatrics, 22,* S33–S35.

Steinberg, L. (2001). Adolescent development. *Annual Review of Psychology, 52,* 83–110.

Stemler, S. E., & Sternberg, R. J. (2006). Using situational judgment tests to measure practical intelligence. In J. A. Weekley & R. E. Ployhart (Eds.), *Situational judgment tests: Theory, measurement, and application.* Mahwah, NJ: Erlbaum.

Stephan, W., Berscheid, E., & Walster, E. (1971). Sexual arousal and heterosexual perception. *Journal of Personality & Social Psychology, 20*(1), 93–101.

Stephens, K., Kiger, L., Karnes, F. A., & Whorton, J. E. (1999). Use of nonverbal measures of intelligence in identification of culturally diverse gifted students in rural areas. *Perceptual & Motor Skills, 88*(3, Pt. 1), 793–796.

Stern, P. C. (1992). Psychological dimensions of global environmental change. In M. R. Rosenzweig & L. W. Porter (Eds.), *Annual Review of Psychology, 43,* 269–302.

Stern, S. L., Dhanda, R., & Hazuda, H. P. (2001). Hopelessness predicts mortality in older Mexican and European Americans. *Psychosomatic Medicine, 63*(3), 344–351.

Sternberg, E. M. (2000). *The balance within: The science of connecting health with emotions.* New York: Freeman.

Sternberg, R. J. (2001). What is the common thread of creativity? *American Psychologist, 56*(4), 360–362.

Sternberg, R. J. (2004). Culture and intelligence. *American Psychologist, 59*(5), 325–338.

Sternberg, R. J., & Davidson, J. D. (1982). The mind of the puzzler. *Psychology Today,* June, 37–44.

Sternberg, R. J., & Grigorenko, E. L. (2005). Cultural explorations of the nature of intelligence. In A. F. Healy (Ed.), *Experimental cognitive psychology and its applications.* Washington, DC: American Psychological Association.

Sternberg, R. J., & Grigorenko, E. L. (2006). Cultural intelligence and successful intelligence. *Group & Organization Management, 31*(1), 27–39.

Sternberg, R. J., & Lubart, T. I. (1995). *Defying the crowd.* New York: Free Press.

Sternberg, R. J., Grigorenko, E. L., & Kidd, K. K. (2005). Intelligence, race, and genetics. *American Psychologist, 60*(1), 46–59.

Steuer, F. B., & Hustedt, J. T. (2002). *TV or No TV? A primer on the psychology of television.* Lanham, MD: University Press of America.

Stewart, A. J. & McDermott, C. (2004). Gender in psychology. *Annual Review of Psychology, 55,* 519–544.

Stewart, A. J., & Ostrove, J. M. (1998). Women's personality in middle age. *American Psychologist, 53*(11), 1185–1194.

Stewart, A. J., & Vandewater, E. A. (1999). "If I had it to do over again . . .": Midlife review, midcourse corrections, and women's well-being in midlife. *Journal of Personality & Social Psychology, 76*(2), 270–283.

Stewart-Williams, S. (2004). The placebo puzzle: Putting together the pieces. *Health Psychology, 23*(2), 198–206.

Stickgold, R., & Walker, M. (2004). To sleep, perchance to gain creative insight? *Trends in Cognitive Sciences, 8*(5), 191–192.

Stipek, D. (2001). *Motivation to learn* (4th ed.). Boston: Allyn & Bacon.

Stöber, J. (2004). Dimensions of test anxiety: Relations to ways of coping with pre-exam anxiety and uncertainty. *Anxiety, Stress & Coping: An International Journal, 17*(3), 213–226.

Stockhorst, U., Klosterhalfen, S., & Steingrueber, H. (1998). Conditioned nausea and further side-effects in cancer chemotherapy. *Journal of Psychophysiology, 12*(Supp. 1), 14–33.

Stokes, D. M. (2001). The shrinking filedrawer. *Skeptical Inquirer,* May–June, 22–25.

Stokoe, W. C. (2001). *Language in hand: Why sign came before speech.* Washington, DC: Gallaudet University Press.

Stolerman, I. P., & Jarvis, M. J. (1995). The scientific case that nicotine is addictive. *Psychopharmacology, 117*(1), 2–10.

Stone, J., Perry, Z. W., & Darley, J. M. (1997). "White men can't jump." *Basic and Applied Social Psychology, 19*(3), 291–306.

Stoppard, J. M., & McMullen, L. M. (Eds.). (2003). *Situating sadness: Women and depression in social context.* New York: New York University Press.

Strack. F., Martin, L. L., & Stepper, S. (1988). Inhibiting and facilitating conditions of facial expressions: A non-obtrusive test of the facial feedback hypothesis. *Journal of Personality & Social Psychology, 54,* 768–777.

Straneva, P. A., Maixner, W., Light, K. C., Pedersen, C. A., et al. (2002). Menstrual cycle, beta-endorphins, and pain sensitivity in premenstrual dysphoric disorder. *Health Psychology, 21*(4), 358–367.

Strange, J. R. (1965). *Abnormal psychology.* New York: McGraw-Hill.

Straub, R. (2006). *Health psychology* (2nd ed.) New York: Worth.

Strayer, D. L., Drews, F. A., & Johnston, W. A. (2003). Cell phone–induced failures of visual attention during simulated driving. *Journal of Experimental Psychology: Applied, 9*(1), 23–32.

Strickler, E. M., & Verbalis, J. G. (1988). Hormones and behavior: The biology of thirst and sodium appetite. *American Scientist,* May–June, 261–267.

Strier, F. (1999). Whither trial consulting? Issues and projections. *Law & Human Behavior, 23*(1), 93–115.

Stroeher, S. K. (1994). Sixteen kindergartners' gender-related views of careers. *Elementary School Journal, 95*(1), 95–103.

Strong, B., & DeVault, C. (1994). *Understanding our sexuality.* St. Paul, MN: West.

Strongman, K. T. (2003). *The psychology of emotion: From everyday life to theory* (5th Ed.). New York: Wiley.

Strote, J., Lee, J. E., & Wechsler, H. (2002). Increasing MDMA use among college students: Results of a national survey. *Journal of Adolescent Health, 30*(1), 64–72.

Sturges, J. W., & Sturges, L. V. (1998). In vivo *systematic desensitization* in a single-session treatment of an 11-year old girl's elevator phobia. *Child & Family Behavior Therapy, 20*(4), 55–62.

Stuss, D. T., & Alexander, M. P. (2000). The anatomical basis of affective behavior, emotion and self-awareness: A specific role of the right frontal lobe. In G. Hatano, N. Okada, et al. (Eds.), *Affective minds: The 13th Toyota conference.* Amsterdam: Elsevier.

Stuss, D. T., & Knight, R. T. (2002). *Principles of frontal lobe function.* New York: Oxford University Press.

Stuss, D. T., & Levine, B. (2002). Adult clinical neuropsychology. *Annual Review of Psychology, 53,* 401–433.

Sue, D., Sue, D. W., & Sue, S. (1996). *Understanding abnormal behavior.* Boston: Houghton Mifflin.

Suedfeld, P., & Steel, G. D. (2000). The environmental psychology of capsule habitats. *Annual Review of Psychology, 51,* 227–253.

Suedfeld, P., & Borrie, R. A. (1999). Health and therapeutic applications of chamber and floatation restricted environmental stimulation therapy (REST). *Psychology & Health, 14*(3), 545–566.

Sugihara, Y., & Warner, J. A. (1999). Endorsements by Mexican-Americans of the Bem Sex-Role Inventory: Cross-ethnic comparison. *Psychological Reports, 85*(1), 201–211.

Sugimoto, K., & Ninomiya, Y. (2005). Introductory remarks on umami research: Candidate receptors and signal transduction mechanisms on umami. *Chemical Senses, 30*(Suppl. 1), i21–i22, 2005.

Suinn, R. M. (1975). *Fundamentals of behavior pathology* (2nd ed.). New York: Wiley.

Suinn, R. M. (1999). Scaling the summit: Valuing ethnicity. *APA Monitor,* March, 2.

Suinn, R. M. (2001). The terrible twos—Anger and anxiety. *American Psychologist, 56*(1), 27–36.

Suls, J. (1989). Self-awareness and self-identity in adolescence. In J. Worell & F. Danner (Eds.), *The adolescent as decision-maker.* New York: Academic Press.

Sumathipala, A., Siribaddana, S. H., & Bhugra, D. (2004). Culture-bound syndromes: The story of dhat syndrome. *British Journal of Psychiatry, 184*(3), 200–209.

Sumerlin, J. R., & Bundrick, C. M. (1996). Brief Index of Self-Actualization: A measure of Maslow's model. *Journal of Social Behavior & Personality, 11*(2), 253–271.

Sumi, K., & Kanda, K. (2002). Relationship between neurotic perfectionism, depression, anxiety, and psychosomatic symptoms. *Personality & Individual Differences, 32*(5), 817–826.

Sunnafrank, M., Ramirez, A., & Metts, S. (2004). At first sight: Persistent relational effects of get-acquainted conversations. *Journal of Social & Personal Relationships, 21*(3), 361–379.

Sutherland, R. J., Lehmann, H., Spanswick, S. C., Sparks, F. T., et al. (2006). Growth points in research on memory and hippocampus. *Canadian Journal of Experimental Psychology, 60*(2), 166–174.

Suzuki, L., & Aronson, J. (2005). The cultural malleability of intelligence and its impact on the racial/ethnic hierarchy. *Psychology, Public Policy, & Law, 11,* 320–327.

Svartdal, F. (2003). Extinction after partial reinforcement: Predicted vs. judged persistence. *Scandinavian Journal of Psychology, 44*(1), 55–64.

Swaak, J., de Jong, T., & van Joolingen, W. R. (2004). The effects of discovery learning and expository instruction on the acquisition of definitional and intuitive knowledge. *Journal of Computer Assisted Learning, 20*(4), 225–234.

Swann, W. B., Jr., Chang-Schneider, C., & Larsen McClarty, K. (2007). Do people's self-views matter? Self-concept and self-esteem in everyday life. *American Psychologist, 62*(2), 84–94.

Swim, J. K., & Sanna, L. J. (1996). He's skilled, she's lucky: A meta-analysis of observers' attributions for women's and men's successes and failures. *Personality & Social Psychology Bulletin, 22*(5), 507–519.

Synhorst, L. L., Buckley, J. A., Reid, R., Epstein, M. H., et al. (2005). Cross informant agreement of the Behavioral and Emotional Rating Scale–2nd Edition (BERS-2) parent and youth rating scales. *Child & Family Behavior Therapy, 27*(3), 1–11.

Szabo, A. (2003). The acute effects of humor and exercise on mood and anxiety. *Journal of Leisure Research, 35*(2), 152–162.

Takooshian, H., Haber, S., & Lucido, D. J. (1977). Who wouldn't help a lost child? You, maybe. *Psychology Today,* Feb., 67.

Talbott, J. A. (2004). Deinstitutionalization: Avoiding the disasters of the past. *Psychiatric Services, 55*(10), 1112–1115.

Talley, P. F., Strupp, H. H., & Morey, L. C. (1990). Matchmaking in psychotherapy: Patient–therapist dimensions and their impact on outcome. *Journal of Consulting & Clinical Psychology, 58*(2), 182–188.

Tal-Or, N., & Papirman, Y. (2007). The fundamental attribution error in attributing fictional figures' characteristics to the actors. *Media Psychology, 9*(2), 331–345.

Tamis-LeMonda, C. S., Bornstein, M. H., & Baumwell, L. (2001). Maternal responsiveness and children's achievement of language milestones. *Child Development, 72,* 748–767.

Tamis-LeMonda, C. S., Shannon, J. D., Cabrera, N. J., & Lamb, M. E. (2004). Fathers and mothers at play with their 2- and 3-year-olds: Contributions to language and cognitive development. *Child Development, 75*(6), 1806–1820.

Tanner, J. M. (1973). Growing up. *Scientific American,* Sept., 34–43.

Taraban, R., Rynearson, K., & Kerr, M. (2000). College students' academic performance and self-reports of comprehension strategy use. *Reading Psychology, 21*(4), 283–308.

Tardif, T. Z., & Sternberg, R. J. (1988). What do we know about creativity? In R. J. Sternberg (Ed.), *The nature of creativity.* New York: Cambridge University Press.

Taris, T. W., Bakker, A. B., Schaufeli, W. B., Stoffelsen, J., et al. (2005). Job control and burnout across occupations. *Psychological Reports, 97*(3), 955–961.

Taub, E. (2004). Harnessing brain plasticity through behavioral techniques to produce new treatments in neurorehabilitation *American Psychologist, 59*(8), 692–704.

Tausig, M., Michello, J., & Subedi, S. (2004). *A sociology of mental illness* (2nd ed.). Englewood Cliffs, NJ: Prentice Hall.

Tavris, C., & Aronson, E. (2007). *Mistakes were made (but not by me): Why we justify foolish beliefs, bad decisions, and hurtful acts.* New York: Harcourt.

Taylor, G. J., & Taylor-Allan, H. L. (2007). Applying emotional intelligence in understanding and treating physical and psychological disorders: What we have learned from alexithymia. In R. Bar-On, M. J. G. Reuven, et al. (Eds.), *Educating people to be emotionally intelligent.* Westport, CT: Praeger.

Taylor, K. (2004). *Brainwashing: The science of thought control.* New York: Oxford University Press.

Taylor, S. E. (2002). Classical conditioning. In M. Hersen & W. H. Sledge (Eds.), *Encyclopedia of psychotherapy.* San Diego: Academic Press.

Taylor, S. E. (2006). *Health psychology* (6th ed.). New York: McGraw-Hill.

Taylor, S. E., Kemeny, M. E., Reed, G. M., Bower, J. E., et al. (2000). Psychological resources, positive illusions, and health. *American Psychologist, 55*(1), 99–109.

Taylor, S. E., Lerner, J. S., Sherman, D. K., Sage, R. M., & McDowell, N. K. (2003). Are self-enhancing cognitions associated with healthy or unhealthy biological profiles? *Journal of Personality & Social Psychology, 85*(4), 605–615.

Taylor-Seehafer, M., & Rew, L. (2000). Risky sexual behavior among adolescent women. *Journal of Social Pediatric Nursing, 5*(1), 15–25.

Tedeschi, J. T., Lindskold, S., & Rosenfeld, P. (1985). *Introduction to social psychology.* St. Paul: West Publishing.

Teen sex: Not for love. (1989). *Psychology Today,* May, 10. They'd kill for $1 million. (1991). *Los Angeles Times,* July 1, A8.

Tenenbaum, G., Bar-Eli, M., & Eyal, N. (1996). Imagery orientation and vividness: Their effect on a motor skill performance. *Journal of Sport Behavior, 19*(1), 32–49.

Terman, L. M., & Merrill, M. A. (1937, revised 1960). *Stanford–Binet Intelligence Scale.* Boston: Houghton Mifflin.

Terman, L. M., & Oden, M. (1959). *The gifted group in mid-life* (Vol. 5): *Genetic studies of genius.* Stanford, CA: Stanford University Press.

Terry, D. J., & Hogg, M. A. (1996). Group norms and the attitude-behavior relationship. *Personality & Social Psychology Bulletin, 22*(8), 776–793.

Thase, M. E. (2006). Major depressive disorder. In F. Andrasik (Ed.), *Comprehensive handbook of personality and psychopathology* (Vol. 2): *Adult psychopathology.* New York: Wiley.

The Nature Conservancy (2007). *Carbon calculator.* The Nature Conservancy. Retrieved August 10, 2007, from http://www.nature.org/initiatives/climatechange/calculator/.

Thelen, E. (2000). Infancy: Perception and motor development. In A. Kazdin (Ed.), *Encyclopedia of psychology.* Washington, DC: American Psychological Association.

Thiessen, E. D., Hill, E. A., & Saffran, J. R. (2005). Infant-directed speech facilitates word segmentation. *Infancy, 7*(1), 53–71.

Thomas, E. M. (2004). *Aggressive behaviour outcomes for young children: Change in parenting environment predicts change in behaviour.* Ottawa, ON: Statistics Canada. Retrieved June 6, 2007, from http://www.statcan.ca/cgi-bin/downpub/listpub.cgi?catno=89-599-MIE2004001.

Thompson, C. P., Cowan, T. M., & Frieman, J. (1993). *Memory search by a menorist.* Mahwah, NJ: Erlbaum.

Thompson, R. A., & Nelson, C. A. (2001). Developmental science and the media. *American Psychologist, 56*(1), 5–15.

Thompson, R. F. (2005). In search of memory traces. *Annual Review of Psychology, 56,* 1–23.

Thorpy, M. J. (2006). Cataplexy associated with narcolepsy: Epidemiology, pathophysiology and management. *CNS Drugs, 20*(1), 43–50.

Thorson, J. A., & Powell, F. C. (1990). Meanings of death and intrinsic religiosity. *Journal of Clinical Psychology, 46*(4), 379–391.

Thyen, U., Richter-Appelt, H., Wiesemann, C., Holterhus, P. M., et al. (2005). Deciding on gender in children with intersex conditions: Considerations and controversies. *Treatments in Endocrinology, 4*(1), 1–8.

Tidwell, M. O., Reis, H. T., & Shaver, P. R. (1996). Attachment, attractiveness, and social interaction. *Journal of Personality & Social Psychology, 71*(4), 729–745.

Tierny, J. (1987). Stitches: Good news; Better health linked to sin, sloth. *Hippocrates,* Sept.–Oct., 30–35.

Tijerino, R. (1998). Civil spaces: A critical perspective of defensible space. *Journal of Architectural & Planning Research, 15*(4), 321–337.

Till, B. D., & Priluck, R. L. (2000). Stimulus generalization in classical conditioning: An initial investigation and extension. *Psychology & Marketing, 17*(1), 55–72.

Timmerman, C. K., & Kruepke, K. A. (2006). Computer-assisted instruction, media richness, and college student performance. *Communication Education, 55*(1), 73–104.

Timmerman, I. G. H., Emmelkamp, P. M. G., & Sanderman, R. (1998). The effects of a stress-management training program in individuals at risk in the community at large. *Behaviour Research & Therapy, 36*(9), 863–875.

Tipples, J., Atkinson, A. P., & Young, A. W. (2002). The eyebrow frown: A salient social signal. *Emotion, 2*(3), 288–296.

Tobler, N. S., Roona, M. R., Ochshorn, P., Marshall, D. G., et al. (2000). School-based adolescent drug prevention programs: 1998 meta-analysis. *Journal of Primary Prevention, 20,* 275–337.

Tolman, E. C., & Honzik, C. H. (1930). Introduction and removal of reward and maze performance in rats. *University of California Publications in Psychology, 4,* 257–275.

Tolman, E. C., Ritchie, B. F., & Kalish, D. (1946). Studies in spatial learning: II. Place learning versus response learning. *Journal of Experimental Psychology, 36,* 221–229.

Tomasello, M. (2003). *Constructing a language: A usage-based theory of language acquisition.* Cambridge MA: Harvard University Press.

Toneatto, T. (2002). Cognitive therapy for problem gambling. *Cognitive & Behavioral Practice, 9*(3), 191–199.

Toneatto, T., Sobell, L. C., Sobell, M. B., & Rubel, E. (1999). Natural recovery from cocaine dependence. *Psychology of Addictive Behaviors, 13*(4), 259–268.

Toro, C. T., & Deakin, J. F. W. (2007). Adult neurogenesis and schizophrenia: A window on abnormal early brain development? *Schizophrenia Research, 90*(1–3), 1–14.

Torrey, E. F. (1996). *Out of the shadows.* New York: John Wiley & Sons.

Tourangeau, R. (2004). Survey research and societal change. *Annual Review of Psychology, 55,* 775–801.

Toyota, H., & Kikuchi, Y. (2005) Encoding richness of self-generated elaboration and spacing effects on incidental memory. *Perceptual & Motor Skills, 101*(2), 621–627.

Trainor, L. J., & Desjardins, R. N. (2002). Pitch characteristics of infant-directed speech affect infants' ability to discriminate vowels. *Psychonomic Bulletin & Review, 9*(2), 335–340.

Travis, F., Arenander, A., & DuBois, D. (2004). Psychological and physiological characteristics of a proposed object-referral/self-referral continuum of self-awareness. *Consciousness & Cognition, 13,* 401–420.

Treffert, D. A., & Christensen, C. D. (2005). Inside the mind of a savant. *Scientific American, 293*(6), 108–113.

Trehub, S. E., Unyk, A. M., & Trainor, L. J. (1993a). Adults identify infant-directed music across cultures. *Infant Behavior & Development, 16*(2), 193–211.

Trehub, S. E., Unyk, A. M., & Trainor, L. J. (1993b). Maternal singing in cross-cultural perspective. *Infant Behavior & Development, 16*(3), 285–295.

Trepel, C., & Racine, R. J. (1999). Blockade and disruption of neocortical long-term potentiation following electroconvulsive shock in the adult, freely moving rat. *Cerebral Cortex, 9*(3), 300–305.

Triandis, H. C., & Suh, E. M. (2002). Cultural influences on personality. *Annual Review of Psychology, 53,* 133–160.

Troll, L. E., & Skaff, M. M. (1997). Perceived continuity of self in very old age. *Psychology & Aging, 12*(1), 162–169.

Truax, S. R. (1983). Active search, mediation, and the manipulation of cue dimensions: Emotion attribution in the false feedback paradigm. *Motivation & Emotion, 7,* 41–60.

Trull, T. (2005). *Clinical psychology* (7th ed.). Belmont, CA: Cengage Learning/Wadsworth.

Tsai, G., & Coyle, J. T. (2002). Glutamatergic mechanisms in schizophrenia. *Annual Review of Pharmacology & Toxicology, 42,* 165–179.

Tsai, W.-C., Chen, C.-C., & Chiu, S-F. (2005). Exploring boundaries of the effects of applicant impression management tactics in job interviews. *Journal of Management, 31*(1), 108–125.

Tse, L. (1999). Finding a place to be: Ethnic identity exploration of Asian Americans. *Adolescence, 34*(133), 121–138.

Tugade, M. M., Fredrickson, B. L., & Barrett, L. F. (2004). Psychological resilience and positive emotional granularity: Examining the benefits of positive emotions on coping and health. *Journal of Personality, 72*(6), 1161–1190.

Tulving, E. (1989). Remembering and knowing the past. *American Scientist, 77*(4), 361–367.

Tulving, E. (2002). Episodic memory. *Annual Review of Psychology, 53,* 1–25.

Turiel, E. (2006).Thought, emotions, and social interactional processes in moral development. In M. Killen & J. G. Smetana (Eds.), *Handbook of moral development.* Mahwah, NJ: Erlbaum.

Turkheimer, E., Haley, A., Waldron, M., D'Onofrio, B. M., et al. (2003). Socioeconomic status modifies heritability of IQ in young children. *Psychological Science, 14,* 623–628.

Turner, S. J. M. (1997). The use of the reflective team in a psychodrama therapy group. *International Journal of Action Methods, 50*(1), 17–26.

Tversky, A., & Kahneman, D. (1981). The framing of decisions and the psychology of choice. *Science, 211,* 453–458.

Tversky, A., & Kahneman, D. (1982). Judgments of and by representativeness. In D. Kahneman, P. Slovic, et al (Eds.), *Judgment under uncertainty: Heuristics and biases.* Cambridge, UK: Cambridge University Press.

Twenge, J. M., & Campbell, W. K. (2001). Age and birth cohort differences in self-esteem. *Personality & Social Psychology Review, 5*(4), 321–344.

Tye-Murray, N., Spencer, L., & Woodworth, G. G. (1995). Acquisition of speech by children who have prolonged cochlear implant experience. *Journal of Speech & Hearing Research, 38*(2), 327–337.

Tzeng, M. (1992). The effects of socioeconomic heterogamy and changes on marital dissolution for first marriages. *Journal of Marriage & Family, 54,* 609–619.

U.S. Department of Energy Human Office of Science. (2005). *About the Human Genome Project.* Washington, DC: U.S. Department of Energy. Retrieved May 25, 2007, from http://www.ornl.gov/sci/ techresources/Human_Genome/ project/about.shtml.

U.S. Department of Labor (2005). *Occupational outlook handbook job interview tips.* Washington, DC: U. S. Department of Labor. Retrieved August 9, 2007, from http://www. bls.gov/oco/oco20045.htm.

UN (2004). *World population to 2300.* New York: United Nations. Retrieved August 9, 2007, from http://www.un.org/esa/population/ publications/longrange2/ WorldPop2300final.pdf.

UNAIDS (2006). *UNAIDS/ WHOAIDS Epidemic Update: December 2006.* New York: United Nations. Retrieved July 27, 2007, from http://www.unaids.org/en/ HIV_data/epi2006/default.asp.

Underwood, B. J. (1957). Interference and forgetting. *Psychological Review, 64,* 49–60.

UNESCO. (1990). The Seville statement on violence. *American Psychologist, 45*(10), 1167–1168.

Unsworth, G., & Ward, T. (2001). Video games and aggressive behaviour. *Australian Psychologist, 36*(3), 184–192.

Urbina, S. (2004). *Essentials of psychological testing.* New York: Wiley.

USDHHS (U.S. Department of Health and Human Services). (2004). *The health consequences of smoking: A report of the Surgeon General, executive summary.* Washington, DC: Department of Health and Human Services. Retrieved June 6, 2007, from http:// www.cdc.gov/tobacco/data_ statistics/sgr/sgr_2004/00_pdfs/ executivesummary.pdf.

Uwe P. Gielen, U. P., Fish, J. M., & Draguns, J. G. (Eds.). (2006). *Handbook of culture, therapy, and healing.* Mahwah, NJ: Erlbaum.

Vaillant, G. E. (2002). *Aging well.* Boston: Little, Brown.

Vaillant, G. E. (2005). Alcoholics Anonymous: Cult or cure? *Australian & New Zealand Journal of Psychiatry, 39*(6), 431–436.

Vaillant, G. E., & Mukamal, K. (2001). Successful aging. *American Journal of Psychiatry, 158*(6), 839–847.

Valins, S. (1966). Cognitive effects of false heart-rate feedback. *Journal of Personality & Social Psychology, 4,* 400–408.

Valins, S. (1967). Emotionality and information concerning internal reactions. *Journal of Personality & Social Psychology, 6,* 458–463.

van der Hart, O., Lierens, R., & Goodwin, J. (1996). Jeanne Fery: A sixteenth-century case of dissociative identity disorder. *Journal of Psychohistory, 24*(1), 18–35.

van Deurzen, E., & Kenward, R. (2005). *Dictionary of existential psychotherapy and counselling.* Thousand Oaks, CA: Sage.

van Dierendonck, D., & Te Nijenhuis, J. (2005). Flotation restricted environmental stimulation therapy (REST) as a stress-management tool: A meta-analysis. *Psychology & Health, 20*(3), 405–412.

van Elst, L. T., Valerius, G., Büchert, M., Thiel, T., et al. (2005). Increased prefrontal and hippocampal glutamate concentration in schizophrenia: Evidence from a magnetic resonance spectroscopy study. *Biological Psychiatry, 58*(9), 724–730.

Van Goozen, S. H. M., Cohen-Kettenis, P. T., Gooren, L. J. G., & Frijda, N. H. (1995). Gender differences in behaviour: Activating effects of cross-sex hormones. *Psychoneuroendocrinology, 20*(4), 343–363.

Van Lawick-Goodall, J. (1971). *In the shadow of man.* New York: Houghton Mifflin.

Van Rooij, J. J. F. (1994). Introversion–extraversion: Astrology versus psychology. *Personality & Individual Differences, 16*(6), 985–988.

Van Vugt, M. (2002). Central, individual, or collective control? Social dilemma strategies for natural resource management. *American Behavioral Scientist, 45*(5), 783–800.

Vandell, D. L. (2004). Early child care: The known and the unknown. *Merrill–Palmer Quarterly. 50*(3), 387–414.

Vasa, R. A., Carlino, A. R., & Pine, D. S. (2006). Pharmacotherapy of depressed children and adolescents: Current issues and potential directions. *Biological Psychiatry, 59*(11), 1021–1028.

Velakoulis, D., & Pantelis, C. (1996). What have we learned from functional imaging studies in schizophrenia? *Australian & New Zealand Journal of Psychiatry, 30*(2), 195–209.

Venezia, M., Messinger, D. S., Thorp, D., & Mundy, P. (2004). The development of anticipatory smiling. *Infancy, 6*(3), 397–406.

Vi, P. (2006). A field study investigating the effects of a rebar-tying machine on trunk flexion, tool usability and productivity. *Ergonomics, 49*(14), 1437–1455.

Videon, T. M. (2005). Parent–child relations and children's psychological well-being: Do dads matter? *Journal of Family Issues, 26*(1), 55–78.

Viegener, B. J., Perri, M. G., Nezu, A. M., Renjilian, D. A., et al. (1990). Effects of an intermittent, low-fat, low-calorie diet in the behavioral treatment of obesity. *Behavior Therapy, 21*(4), 499–509.

Viveros, M. P., Llorente, R., Moreno, E., & Marco, E. M. (2005). Behavioural and neuroendocrine effects of cannabinoids in critical developmental periods. *Behavioural Pharmacology, 16*(5–6), 353–362.

Vogel, E. K., Woodman, G. F., & Luck, S. J. (2006). The time course of consolidation in visual working memory. *Journal of Experimental Psychology: Human Perception and Performance, 32*(6), 1436–1451.

Vogler, R. E., & Bartz, W. R. (1992). *Teenagers and alcohol.* Philadelphia: Charles Press.

Vogler, R. E., Weissbach, T. A., Compton, J. V., & Martin, G. T. (1977). Integrated behavior change techniques for problem drinkers in the community. *Journal of Consulting and Clinical Psychology, 45,* 267–279.

Volkow, N. D., Gillespie, H., Mullani, N., & Tancredi, L. (1996). Brain glucose metabolism in chronic marijuana users at baseline and during marijuana intoxication. *Psychiatry Research: Neuroimaging, 67*(1), 29–38.

Volpicelli, J. R., Ulm, R. R., Altenor, A., & Seligman, M. E. P. (1983). Learned mastery in the rat. *Learning and Motivation, 14,* 204–222.

Vygotsky, L. S. (1962). *Thought and language.* Cambridge, MA: MIT Press.

Vygotsky, L. S. (1978). *Mind in society.* Cambridge, MA: Harvard University Press.

Wager, T. D., Rilling, J. K., Smith, E. E., Sokolik, A., et al. (2004). Placebo-induced changes in fMRI in the anticipation and experience of pain. *Science, 303*(Feb. 20), 1162–1166.

Wagstaff, G., Brunas-Wagstaff, J., Cole, J., & Wheatcroft, J. (2004). New directions in forensic hypnosis: Facilitating memory with a focused meditation technique. *Contemporary Hypnosis, 21*(1), 14–27.

Waid, W. M., & Orne, M. T. (1982). The physiological detection of deception. *American Scientist, 70*(July–Aug.), 402–409.

Wainright, J. L., Russell, S. T., & Patterson, C. J. (2004). Psychosocial adjustment, school outcomes, and romantic relationships of adolescents with same-sex parents. *Child Development, 75*(6), 1886–1898.

Wakefield, J. C. (1992). The concept of mental disorder. *American Psychologist, 47*(3), 373–388.

Wald, J., & Taylor, S. (2000). Efficacy of virtual reality exposure therapy to treat driving phobia. *Journal of Behavior Therapy & Experimental Psychiatry, 31*(3–4), 249–257.

Walker, E., Kestler, L. Bollini, A., & Hochman, K. M. (2004). Schizophrenia: Etiology and course. *Annual Review of Psychology, 55*, 401–430.

Walker, I., & Crogan, M. (1998). Academic performance, prejudice, and the Jigsaw classroom. *Journal of Community & Applied Social Psychology, 8*(6), 381–393.

Walker, M. P., & Stickgold, R. (2006). Sleep, memory, and plasticity. *Annual Review of Psychology, 57*, 139–166.

Wallach, M. A., & Kogan, N. (1965). *Modes of thinking in young children.* New York: Holt.

Walster, E. (1971). Passionate love. In B. I. Murstein (Ed.), *Theories of attraction and love.* New York: Springer.

Walton, C. E., Bower, M. L., & Bower, T. G. (1992). Recognition of familiar faces by newborns. *Infant Behavior & Development, 15*(2), 265–269.

Wampold, B. E., Minami T., Tierney, S. C., Baskin, T. W., et al. (2005). The placebo is powerful: Estimating placebo effects in medicine and psychotherapy from randomized clinical trials. *Journal of Clinical Psychology, 61*(7), 835–854.

Wampold, B. E., Mondin, G. W., Moody, M., Stich, E., et al. (1997). A meta-analysis of outcome studies comparing bona fide psychotherapies. *Psychological Bulletin, 122*(3), 203–215.

Wandersman, A., & Florin, P. (2003). Community interventions and effective prevention. *American Psychologist, 58*(6–7), 441–448.

Wang, Q., & Conway, M. A. (2004). The stories we keep: Autobiographical memory in American and Chinese middle-aged adults. *Journal of Personality, 72*(5), 911–938.

Wang, S. S., & Brownell, K. D. (2005). Public policy and obesity: The need to marry science with advocacy. *Psychiatric Clinics of North America, 28*(1), 235–252.

Ward, C., & Rana-Deuba, A. (1999). Acculturation and adaptation revisited. *Journal of Cross-Cultural Psychology, 30*(4), 422–442.

Ward, J. (2006). *The student's guide to cognitive neuroscience.* Hove, UK: Psychology Press.

Ward, L. M. (2004). Wading through the stereotypes: Positive and negative associations between media use and Black adolescents' conceptions of self. *Developmental Psychology, 40*, 284–294.

Wark, G. R., & Krebs, D. L. (1996). Gender and dilemma differences in real-life moral judgment. *Developmental Psychology, 32*(2), 220–230.

Warren, D. J., & Normann, R. A. (2005). Functional reorganization of primary visual cortex induced by electrical stimulation in the cat. *Vision Research, 45*, 551–565.

Waterfield, R. (2002). *Hidden depths: The story of hypnosis.* London: Macmillan.

Watson, D. L., & Tharp, R. G. (2007). *Self-directed behavior* (9th ed.). Belmont, CA: Cengage Learning/Wadsworth.

Watson, J. B. (1913/1994). Psychology as the behaviorist views it. *Psychological Review, 101*(2), 248–253.

Way, I., vanDeusen, K. M., Martin, G., Applegate, B., et al. (2004). Vicarious trauma: A comparison of clinicians who treat survivors of sexual abuse and sexual offenders. *Journal of Interpersonal Violence, 19*(1), 49–71.

Wechsler, H., & Wuethrich, B. (2002). *Dying to drink.* Emmaus, PA: Rodale Books.

Wechsler, H., Lee, J. E., Kuo, M., Seibring, M., et al. (2002). Trends in college binge drinking during a period of increased prevention efforts. *Journal of American College Health, 50*(5), 203–217.

Wedding, D., & Corsini, R. J. (2005). *Case studies in psychotherapy* (4th ed.). Belmont, CA: Cengage Learning/Wadsworth.

Weekley, J. A., & Jones, C. (1997). Video-based situational testing. *Personnel Psychology, 50*(1), 25–49.

Weems, C. F. (1998). The evaluation of heart rate biofeedback using a multi-element design. *Journal of Behavior Therapy & Experimental Psychiatry, 29*(2), 157–162.

Wehr, T. A., Duncan, W. C., Sher, L., Aeschbach, D., et al. (2001). A circadian signal of change of season in patients with seasonal affective disorder. *Archives of General Psychiatry, 58*(12), 1108–1114.

Weinberg, R. A. (1989). Intelligence and IQ. *American Psychologist, 44*(2), 98–104.

Weintraub, M. I. (1983). *Hysterical conversion reactions.* New York: SP Medical & Scientific Books.

Weishaar, M. E. (2006). A cognitive-behavioral approach to suicide risk reduction in crisis intervention. In A. R. Roberts & K. R. Yeager, (Eds.), *Foundations of evidence-based social work practice.* New York: Oxford University Press.

Weisskirch, R. S. (2005). Ethnicity and perceptions relationship to ethnic identity development. *International Journal of Intercultural Relations, 29*(3), 355–366.

Weissman, A. M., Jogerst, G. J., & Dawson, J. D. (2003). Community characteristics associated with child abuse in Iowa. *Child Abuse & Neglect, 27*(10), 1145–1159.

Weiten, W. (1998). Pressure, major life events, and psychological symptoms. *Journal of Social Behavior & Personality, 13*(1), 51–68.

Weitzman, E. R. (2004). Poor mental health, depression, and associations with alcohol consumption, harm, and abuse in a national sample of young adults in college. *Journal of Nervous & Mental Disease, 192*(4), 269–277.

Wells, B. E., & Twenge, J. M. (2005). Changes in young people's sexual behavior and attitudes, 1943–1999: A cross-temporal meta-analysis. *Review of General Psychology, 9*(3), 249–261.

Wells, G. L. (2001). Police lineups: Data, theory, and policy. *Psychology, Public Policy, & Law, 7*(4), 791–801.

Wells, G. L., & Olsen, E. A. (2003). Eyewitness testimony. *Annual Review of Psychology, 54*, 277–295.

Wells, G. L., Memon, A., & Penrod, S. D. (2006). Eyewitness evidence: Improving its probative value. *Psychological Science in the Public Interest, 7*(2), 45–75.

Weltzin, T. E., Weisensel, N., Franczyk, D., Burnett, K., et al. (2005). Eating disorders in men: Update. *Journal of Men's Health & Gender, 2*(2), 186–193.

Werner, C. M., & Makela, E. (1998). Motivations and behaviors that support recycling. *Journal of Environmental Psychology, 18*(4), 373–386.

Wernet, S. P., Follman, C., Magueja, C., & Moore-Chambers, R. (2003). Building bridges and improving racial harmony: An evaluation of the Bridges Across Racial Polarization Program. In J. J. Stretch, E. M. Burkemper, et al. (Eds.), *Practicing social justice.* New York: Haworth Press.

Wertheimer, M. (1959). *Productive thinking.* New York: Harper & Row.

Wesensten, N. J., Belenky, G., Kautz, M. A., Thorne, D. R., et al. (2002). Maintaining alertness and performance during sleep deprivation: Modafinil versus caffeine. *Psychopharmacology, 159*(2), 238–247.

Wessel, I., & Wright, D. B. (Eds.) (2004). *Emotional memory failures.* Hove, UK: Psychology Press.

West, R., & Sohal, T. (2006). "Catastrophic" pathways to smoking cessation: Findings from national survey. *British Medical Journal, 332*(7539), 458–460.

West, T. G. (1991). *In the mind's eye.* Buffalo, NY: Prometheus.

Wethington, E. (2000). Expecting stress: Americans and the "midlife crisis." *Motivation & Emotion, 24*(2), 85–103.

Wethington, E. (2003). Turning points as opportunities for psychological growth. In C. L. M. Keyes & J. Haidt (Eds.), *Flourishing.* Washington, DC: American Psychological Association.

Wethington, E., Kessler, R. C., & Pixley, J. E. (2004). Turning points in adulthood. In O. G. Brim, C. D. Ryff, et al. (Eds.), *How healthy are we?: A national study of well-being at midlife.* Chicago: University of Chicago Press.

Wexler, M. N. (1995). Expanding the groupthink explanation to the study of contemporary cults. *Cultic Studies Journal, 12*(1), 49–71.

Whipple, B. (2000). Beyond the G spot. *Scandinavian Journal of Sexology, 3*(2), 35–42.

Whitaker, B. G. (2007). Internet-based attitude assessment: Does gender affect measurement equivalence? *Computers in Human Behavior, 23*(3), 1183–1194.

White, G. L., & Taytroe, L. (2003). Personal problem-solving using dream incubation: Dreaming, relaxation, or waking cognition? *Dreaming, 13*(4), 193–209.

White, J. (2006). *Intelligence, destiny and education: The ideological roots of intelligence testing.* New York: Brunner-Routledge.

Whitehouse, A. J. O., Maybery, M. T., & Durkin, K. (2006). The development of the picture-superiority effect. *British Journal of Developmental Psychology, 24*(4), 767–773.

Whitley, B. E. (1999). Right-wing authoritarianism, social dominance orientation, and prejudice. *Journal of Personality & Social Psychology, 77*(1), 126–134.

Whitton, E. (2003). *Humanistic approach to psychotherapy.* New York: Wiley.

Whyte, G. (2000). Groupthink. In A. E. Kazdin (Ed.), *Encyclopedia of psychology* (Vol. 4). Washington, DC: American Psychological Association.

Wickett, J. C., Vernon, P. A., & Lee, D. H. (2000). Relationships between factors of intelligence and brain volume. *Personality & Individual Differences, 29*(6), 1095–1122.

Widiger, T. A. (2005). Classification and diagnosis: Historical development and contemporary issues. In J. E. Maddux & B. A. Winstead (Eds.), *Psychopathology: Foundations for a contemporary understanding.* Mahwah, NJ: Erlbaum.

Widner, Jr., R. L., Otani, H., & Winkelman, S. E. (2005). Tip-of-the-tongue experiences are not merely strong feeling-of-knowing experiences. *Journal of General Psychology, 132*(4), 392–407.

Wiederhold, B. K., & Wiederhold, M. D. (2005). Acrophobia. In B. K. Wiederhold & M. D. Wiederhold, *Virtual reality therapy for anxiety disorders: Advances in evaluation and treatment.* Washington: American Psychological Association.

Wiederman, M. W. (2001). Gender differences in sexuality: Perceptions, myths, and realities. *Family Journal-Counseling & Therapy for Couples & Families, 9*(4), 468–471.

Wigfield, A., & Eccles, J. (Eds.). (2002). *Development of achievement motivation.* San Diego: Academic Press.

Wilber, M. K., & Potenza, M. N. (2006). Adolescent gambling: Research and clinical implications. *Psychiatry, 3*(10), 40–46.

Wilder, D. A., Simon, A. F., & Faith, M. (1996). Enhancing the impact of counterstereotypic information. *Journal of Personality & Social Psychology, 71*(2), 276–287.

Wilding, J., & Valentine, E. (1994). Memory champions. *British Journal of Psychology, 85*(2), 231–244.

Wilkinson, D., & Abraham, C. (2004). Constructing an integrated model of the antecedents of adolescent smoking. *British Journal of Health Psychology, 9*(3), 315–333.

Wilkinson, M. (2006). The dreaming mindbrain: A Jungian perspective. *Journal of Analytical Psychology, 51*(1), 43–59.

Williams, G., Cai, X. J., Elliott, J. C., & Harrold, J. A. (2004). Anabolic neuropeptides. *Physiology & Behavior, 81*(2), 211–222.

Williams, N. (2002). The imposition of gender: Psychoanalytic encounters with genital atypicality. *Psychoanalytic Psychology, 19*(3), 455–474.

Williams, R. (1989). *The trusting heart: Great news about Type A behavior.* New York: Random House.

Williams, R. B., Barefoot, J. C., & Schneiderman, N. (2003). Psychosocial risk factors for cardiovascular disease: More than one culprit at work. *JAMA: Journal of the American Medical Association, 290*(16), 2190–2192.

Williams, R. L., & Eggert, A. (2002). Notetaking predictors of test performance. *Teaching of Psychology, 29*(3), 234–236.

Williams, R. L., & Long, J. D. (1991). *Toward a self-managed life style.* Boston: Houghton Mifflin.

Williams, R. L., Agnew, H. W., & Webb, W. B. (1964). Sleep patterns in young adults: An EEG study. *Electroencephalography & Clinical Neurophysiology, 17,* 376–381.

Williamson, D. A., Ravussin, E., Wong, M.-L., Wagner, A., et al. (2005). Microanalysis of eating behavior of three leptin deficient adults treated with leptin therapy. *Appetite, 45,* 75–80.

Willoughby, T., Wood, E., Desmarais, S., Sims, S., et al. (1997). Mechanisms that facilitate the effectiveness of elaboration strategies. *Journal of Educational Psychology, 89*(4), 682–685.

Wilmot, W. W., & Hocker, J. L. (2007). *Interpersonal conflict* (7th ed.). Boston: McGraw-Hill.

Wilson, F. L. (1995). The effects of age, gender, and ethnic/cultural background on moral reasoning. *Journal of Social Behavior & Personality, 10*(1), 67–78.

Wilson, T. D. (2002). *Strangers to ourselves: Discovering the adaptive unconscious.* Cambridge, MA: Harvard University Press.

Winger, G., Woods, J. H., Galuska, C. M., & Wade-Galuska, T. (2005). Behavioral perspectives on the neuroscience of drug addiction. *Journal of the Experimental Analysis of Behavior, 84*(3), 667–681.

Wingood, G. M., DiClemente, R.J., Bernhardt, J. M., Harrington, K., et al. (2003). A prospective study of exposure to rap music videos and African American female adolescents' health. *American Journal of Public Health, 93,* 437–439.

Winner, E. (2003). Creativity and talent. In M. H. Bornstein, L. Davidson, et al. (Eds.), *Well-being: Positive development across the life course.* Mahwah, NJ: Erlbaum.

Winstead, B. A., & Sanchez, J. (2005). Gender and psychopathology. In J. E. Maddux & B. A. Winstead (Eds.), *Psychopathology: Foundations for a contemporary understanding.* Mahwah, NJ: Erlbaum.

Winter, D. D. N., & Koger, S. M. (2004). *The psychology of environmental problems* (2nd ed.). Mahwah, NJ: Erlbaum.

Wise, R. A., & Safer, M. A. (2004). What US judges know and believe about eyewitness testimony. *Applied Cognitive Psychology, 18*(4), 427–443.

Wiseman, R., & Watt, C. (2006). Belief in psychic ability and the misattribution hypothesis: A qualitative review. *British Journal of Psychology, 97*(3), 323–338.

Witelson, S. F. (1991). Neural sexual mosaicism: Sexual differentiation of the human temporo-parietal region for functional asymmetry. *Psychoneuroendocrinology, 16*(1–3), 131–153.

Witelson, S. F., Beresh, H., & Kigar, D. L. (2006). Intelligence and brain size in 100 postmortem brains: Sex, lateralization and age factors. *Brain: A Journal of Neurology, 129*(2), 386–398.

Witherington, D. C., Campos, J. J., Anderson, D. I., Lejeune, L., et al. (2005). Avoidance of heights on the visual cliff in newly walking infants. *Infancy, 7*(3), 285–298.

Withers, N. W., Pulvirenti, L., Koob, G. F., & Gillin, J. C. (1995). Cocaine abuse and dependence. *Journal of Clinical Psychopharmacology, 15*(1), 63–78.

Witt, S. D. (1997). Parental influences on children's socialization to gender roles. *Adolescence, 32*(126), 253–259.

Wixted, J. T. (2004). The psychology and neuroscience of forgetting. *Annual Review of Psychology, 55,* 235–269.

Wixted, J. T. (2005). A theory about why we forget what we once knew. *Current Directions in Psychological Science, 14*(1), 6–9.

Wolfe, J. B. (1936). Effectiveness of token rewards for chimpanzees. *Comparative Psychology Monographs, 12*(5), Whole no. 60.

Wolfe, J. M., Kluender, K. R., Levi, D. M., Bartoshuk, L. M., et al. (2005). *Sensation and perception.* Sunderland, MA: Sinauer Associates.

Wolpe, J. (1974). *The practice of behavior therapy* (2nd ed.). New York: Pergamon.

Wolpin, M., Marston, A., Randolph, C., & Clothier, A. (1992). Individual difference correlates of reported lucid dreaming frequency and control. *Journal of Mental Imagery, 16*(3–4), 231–236.

Wong, C. Y., Sommer, R., & Cook, E. J. (1992). The soft classroom 17 years later. *Journal of Environmental Psychology, 12*(4), 337–343.

Wood, E., & Willoughby, T. (1995). Cognitive strategies for test-taking. In E. Wood, V. Woloshyn, et al. (Eds.), *Cognitive strategy instruction for middle and high schools.* Cambridge, MA: Brookline Books.

Wood, J. M., Nezworski, M. T., Lilienfeld, S. O., & Garb, H. N. (2003). The Rorschach Inkblot test, fortune tellers, and cold reading. *Skeptical Inquirer, 27*(4), 29–33.

Woods, S. C., Schwartz, M. W, Baskin, D. G., & Seeley, R J. (2000). Food intake and the regulation of body weight. *Annual Review of Psychology, 51,* 255–277.

Worthen, J. B., & Marshall, P. H. (1996). Intralist and extralist sources of distinctiveness and the bizarreness effect. *American Journal of Psychology, 109*(2), 239–263.

Worthen, J. B., & Wade, C. E. (1999). Direction of travel and visiting team athletic performance: Support for a circadian dysrhythmia hypothesis. *Journal of Sport Behavior, 22*(2), 279–287.

Wraga, M., Shephard, J. M., Church, J. A., Inati, S., et al. (2005). Imagined rotations of self versus objects: An fMRI study. *Neuropsychologia, 43*(9), 1351–1361.

Wright, T. A., & Bonett, D. G. (2007). Job satisfaction and psychological well-being as nonadditive predictors of workplace turnover. *Journal of Management, 33*(2), 141–160.

Wright, T. A., & Cropanzano, R. (2000). Psychological well-being and job satisfaction as predictors of job performance. *Journal of Occupational Health Psychology, 5*(1), 84–94.

Wrightsman, L. S., & Fulero, S. M. (2005). *Forensic psychology* (2nd ed.). Belmont, CA: Cengage Learning/Wadsworth.

Wu, C. W. H., & Kaas, J. H. (2002). The effects of long-standing limb loss on anatomical reorganization of the somatosensory afferents in the brainstem and spinal cord. *Somatosensory & Motor Research, 19*(2), 153–163.

Wulf, G., McConnel, N., Gärtner, M., & Schwarz, A. (2002). Enhancing the learning of sport skills through external-focus feedback. *Journal of Motor Behavior, 34*(2), 171–182.

Wyatt, J. W., Posey, A., Welker, W., & Seamonds, C. (1984). Natural levels of similarities between identical twins and between unrelated people. *Skeptical Inquirer, 9,* 62–66.

Wynne, C. D. L. (2004). The perils of anthropomorphism. *Nature, 428*(6983), 606.

X Day, S., & Schneider, P. L. (2002). Psychotherapy using distance technology. *Journal of Counseling Psychology, 49*(4), 499–503.

Yahnke, B. H., Sheikh, A. A., & Beckman, H. T. (2003). Imagery and the treatment of phobic disorders. In A. A. Sheikh (Ed.), *Healing images: The role of imagination in health.* Amityville, NY: Baywood Publishing.

Yarmey, A. D. (2003). Eyewitness identification: Guidelines and recommendations for identification procedures in the United States and in Canada. *Canadian Psychology, 44*(3), 181–189.

Yedidia, M. J., & MacGregor, B. (2001). Confronting the prospect of dying. *Journal of Pain & Symptom Management, 22*(4), 807–819.

Yeh, C. J. (2003). Age, acculturation, cultural adjustment, and mental health symptoms of Chinese, Korean, and Japanese immigrant youths. *Cultural Diversity & Ethnic Minority Psychology, 9*(1), 34–48.

Yip, P. S. F., & Thorburn, J. (2004). Marital status and the risk of suicide: Experience from England and Wales, 1982–1996. *Psychological Reports, 94*(2), 401–407.

Yokota, F., & Thompson, K. M. (2000). Violence in G-rated animated films. *Journal of the American Medical Association, 283*(20), 2716.

Yonas, A., Elieff, C. A., & Arterberry, M. E. (2002). Emergence of sensitivity to pictorial depth cues: Charting development in individual infants. *Infant Behavior & Development, 25*(4), 495–514.

Yoshida, M. (1993). Three-dimensional electrophysiological atlas created by computer mapping of clinical responses elicited on stimulation of human subcortical structures. *Stereotactic & Functional Neurosurgery, 60*(1–3), 127–134.

Yost, W. A. (2007). *Fundamentals of hearing: An introduction* (5th ed.). San Diego: Elsevier.

Young, S. M., & Pinsky, D. (2006). Narcissism and celebrity. *Journal of Research in Personality, 40*(5), 463–471.

Zarcadoolas, C., Pleasant, A., & Greer, D. S. (2006). *Advancing health literacy: A framework for understanding and action.* San Francisco: Jossey-Bass.

Zarraga, C., & Bonache, J. (2005). The impact of team atmosphere on knowledge outcomes in self-managed teams. *Organization Studies, 26*(5), 661–681.

Zeisel, J. (2006). *Inquiry by design: Environment/behavior/neuroscience in architecture, interiors, landscape, and planning.* New York: Norton.

Zelezny, L. C. (1999). Educational interventions that improve environmental behaviors: A meta-analysis. *Journal of Environmental Education, 31*(1), 5–14.

Zellner, D. A., Harner, D. E., & Adler, R. L. (1989). Effects of eating abnormalities and gender on perceptions of desirable body shape. *Journal of Abnormal Psychology, 98*(1), 93–96.

Zemishlany, Z., Aizenberg, D., & Weizman, A. (2001). Subjective effects of MDMA ("Ecstasy") on human sexual function. *European Psychiatry, 16*(2), 127–130.

Zentall, T. R. (2002). A cognitive behaviorist approach to the study of animal behavior. *Journal of General Psychology. Special Issue: Animal Behavior, 129*(4), 328–363.

Zentall, T. R. (2005). Animals may not be stuck in time. *Learning and Motivation, 36*(2), 208–225.

Zhang R. L., Zhang Z. G., & Chopp, M. (2005). Neurogenesis in the adult ischemic brain: generation, migration, survival, and restorative therapy. *Neuroscientist, 11*(5), 408–416.

Zimbardo, P. (2007). *The Lucifer Effect: Understanding how good people turn evil.* New York: Random House.

Zimbardo, P. G., Pilkonis, P. A., & Norwood, R. M. (1978). The social disease called shyness. In *Annual editions, personality and adjustment 78/79.* Guilford, CT: Dushkin.

Zohar, D. (1998). An additive model of test anxiety: Role of exam-specific expectations. *Journal of Educational Psychology, 90*, 330–340.

Zola, S. M., & Squire, L. R. (2001). Relationship between magnitude of damage to the hippocampus and impaired recognition in monkeys. *Hippocampus, 11*, 92–98.

Zuckerman, M. (1990). The psychophysiology of sensation seeking. *Journal of Personality, 58*(1), 313–345.

Zuckerman, M. (1996). Item revisions in the Sensation Seeking Scale Form V (SSS-V). *EDRA: Environmental Design Research Association, 20*(4), 515.

Zuckerman, M. (2000). Sensation seeking. In A. Kazdin (Ed.), *Encyclopedia of psychology.* Washington, DC: American Psychological Association.

Zuckerman, M. (2002). Genetics of sensation seeking. In J. Benjamin, R. P. Ebstein, et al. (Eds.), *Molecular genetics and the human personality.* Washington, DC: American Psychiatric Publishing.

Zuwerink, J. R., Devine, P. G., Monteith, M. J., & Cook, D. A. (1996). Prejudice toward Blacks: With and without compunction. *Basic & Applied Social Psychology, 18*(2), 131–150.

Credits

This page constitutes an extension of the copyright page. We have made every effort to trace the ownership of all copyrighted material and to secure permission from copyright holders. In the event of any question arising as to the use of any material, we will be pleased to make the necessary corrections in future printings. Thanks are due to the following authors, publishers, and agents for permission to use the material indicated.

Chapter 1. 13: Corbis Images/Jupiterimages **14:** Jeff Greenberg/PhotoEdit **17:** Mireille Vauier/Woodfin Camp/Jupiterimages **17:** Warren Morgan/Corbis **17:** Anne-Marie Weber/Getty Images **17:** Greg Johnston/Lonely Planet Images **16:** Ron Cohn/The Gorilla Foundation **18:** Charles Gupton/Stock Boston **21:** Bettmann/Corbis **21:** Dennis Coon **24:** Dan McCoy/Rainbow **27:** Archives of the History of American Psychology, University of Akron **28:** Archives of the History of American Psychology, University of Akron **28:** Archives of the History of American Psychology, University of Akron **28:** Neena Leen/Life Magazine/Timepix/Getty Images **29:** Archives of the History of American Psychology, University of Akron **30:** Archives of the History of American Psychology, University of Akron **30:** Bettmann/Corbis **31, all:** Archives of the History of American Psychology, University of Akron **33:** Patrick Giardino/Corbis **36:** Universal Studios/The Kobal Collection **44:** Royalty-Free/Corbis **47:** Baron Hugo van Lawick/National Geographic Society **54:** John Nordell/The Image Works

Chapter 2. 53: Arthur Toga, UCLA/Photo Researchers, Inc. **60:** Blend Images/Jupiterimages **64:** CNRI/Photo Researchers, Inc. **66, top:** AJPhoto/Photo Researchers, Inc. **66, bottom:** WDCN/Univ. College London/Photo Researchers, Inc. **67:** Courtesy of Richard Haier, University of California, Irvine **67:** Langleben et al., Human Brain Mapping (2005). Courtesy of Daniel Langleben, University of Pennsylvania **72:** Ronald C. James **75:** Shaywitz et al., 1995 NMR Research/Yale Medical School **83:** Rod Planch/Photo Researchers, Inc. **82:** Getty Images **82:** Amanda Edwards/Getty Images **84:** Brad Mangin/Getty Images **88:** Custom Medical Stock Photo **89:** Bob Daemmrich/The Image Works **83:** Tom McCarthy/PhotoEdit

Chapter 3. 97: Paul Kuroda/Superstock **99:** Biophoto Associates/Photo Researchers, Inc. **100:** Myrleen Ferguson/PhotoEdit **101:** Reprinted by permission of the publisher from *The Postnatal Development of the Human Cerebral Cortex, Vols. I–III* by Jesse LeRoy Conel, Cambridge, Mass.: Harvard University Press, Copyright © 1935, 1975 by the President and Fellows of Harvard College. **101, left:** Petit Format/Photo Researchers, Inc. **101, right:** Ted Wood **102:** Anna Kaufman Moon/Stock Boston **105:** Margaret Miller/Photo Researchers, Inc. **106:** From A.N. Meltzoff & M. K. Moore, "Imitation of facial and manual gestures by human neonates," *Science,* 1977,198, 75–78 **106:** Robert L. Fantz, Copyright © 1961 by Scientific American, Inc. All Rights Reserved **106:** Rubberball Productions/Getty Images **108:** Michael Newman/PhotoEdit **111, left:** Chris Lowe/Index Stock Imagery **111, right:** Michael Newman/PhotoEdit **114:** BananaStock/SuperStock **116:** Jeff Greenberg/PhotoEdit **120:** Gary Conner/Index Stock Imagery **122:** Tony Freeman/PhotoEdit **122:** Farrell Grehan/Corbis **123:** FogStock LLC/Index Stock Imagery **135:** Sarah Putnum/Index Stock Imagery **136:** Jeff Greenberg/PhotoEdit **139:** Tony Ranze/AFP/Getty Image **140:** Michael Newman/PhotoEdit **143:** image100/SuperStock

Chapter 4. 149: © 2007 "Pintos" by Bev Doolittle®, courtesy of The Greenwich Workshop, Inc. www.greenwichworkshop.com **157:** Omnikron/Photo Researchers, Inc. **159:** Michael Newman/PhotoEdit **161:** Jon L. Barken/Index Stock Imagery **165:** Dr. G. Oran Bredberg/SPL/Photo Researchers, Inc. **167, top:** Richard Costana, *Discover Magazine*, 1993 **167, bottom:** Omikron/Photo Researchers, Inc. **169:** Herve Donnezan/Photo Researchers, Inc. **171:** Roger Ressmeyer/Corbis **173, left:** Yvaral, © 1990, Marilyn Numerisee #420, Courtesy of Circle Gallery **173, right:** Mark Richards/PhotoEdit **176:** E. R. Degginger/Animals Animals **177:** © Shigeo Fukuda, 1985 **179:** Mark Richards/PhotoEdit **180, top:** Bob Western **180, bottom:** © 2008 Magic Eye Inc., www.magiceye.com **182:** Dennis Coon **183:** M. C. Escher's "Convex and Concave" © 2002 Cordon Art B. V. Baarn—Holland. All rights reserved. **184:** Dennis Coon **187:** Art © Estate of Al Held/Licensed by VAGA, NY, NY **189, top:** Superstock, Inc./SuperStock **189, center:** Bob Daemmrich/The Image Works **189, bottom:** Mark McKenna **194:** Susan Van Etten/PhotoEdit **196:** Dennis Coon **198:** AP/Wide World Photo

Chapter 5. 203: Iconica/Getty Images **205:** Joel Gordon **206:** Timothy Ross/The Image Works **208:** Yale Joel/TimePix/Getty Images **210:** Detroit Institute of the Arts/SuperStock **216:** Michael Newman/PhotoEdit **217:** Kactus Foto/SuperStock **221, all:** Dennis Coon **223:** Dennis Coon **231:** National Library of Medicine **233:** The Everett Collection **237:** Creasource Series/Jupiterimages **238:** Reprinted with permission from SCIENCE NEWS, the weekly newsmagazine of science, copyright 1993 **239:** Courtesy of Dr. Lester Grinspoon/Harvard Medical School **240:** Courtesy of the Brant County Health Unit **242:** Courtesy of Maryanne Mott

Chapter 6. 247: David R. Frazier/PhotoEdit **252:** Dennis Coon **259:** Yale Joel/Life Magazine/TimePix/Getty Images **262:** Chimp-O-Mat, Yukes Regional Primate Research Center, Emory University **266:** Christoph Wilhelm/Getty Images **268:** George McCarthy/NPL/Minden Pictures **269:** Carleton Ray/Photo Researchers, Inc. **272:** Jiang Jin/SuperStock **276:** Peter Cade/Getty Images **278:** Bambu Productions/Getty Images **279:** Courtesy of Albert Bandura/Stanford University **280:** Erik S. Lesser/AP/Wide World Photo **282:** Rubberball/SuperStock

Chapter 7. 287: Richard Heinzen/SuperStock **290:** Malcolm Linton/Liaison/Getty Images **293:** From Wilder Penfield, The Excitable Cortex in Conscious Man, 1958. Courtesy of the author and Charles C. Thomas Publisher, Springfield, Illinois **294:** William Fritsch/Jupiterimages **296:** A. Ramey/PhotoEdit **301:** SW Production/Index Stock Imagery **306:** Paul Conklin/PhotoEdit **308:** Andy Reynolds/Getty Images **309:** AP/Wide World Photo **310:** AP/Wide World Photo **312, left:** © Tulving, E. (1989). Remembering and knowing the past. *American Scientist,* 77,(4), 361–367 **312, right:** Jeffrey L. Rotman/Corbis **319:** Gregg Segal/Getty Image **323:** Ulrike Welsch

Chapter 8. 327: Richard Green **328, top:** James D. Wilson/Getty Images **328, bottom:** David Young-Wolff/PhotoEdit **331:** AP/Wide World Photo **333, top:** Dan McCoy/Rainbow **333, right:** Christiana Dittmann/Rainbow **334:** Stan Godlweski/Getty Images **335, left:** Getty Images **335, center:** Archiv/Photo Researchers, Inc. **335, right:** Courtesy of Cray Computer **342:** Dennis Coon **342:** Brian Bailey/Getty Images **345:** Billy Hustace/Getty Images **345:** Guy Edwards/Getty Images **347:** Myrleen Ferguson Cate/PhotoEdit **348:** The Great Ape Trust of Iowa **357:** Time Life Pictures/Getty Images **359:** Hulton Archive/Getty Images **359:** Rainbow **359:** Image Bank/Getty Images

Chapter 9. 371: Camay Sungu/AP/Wide World Photo **373:** David Austen/Woodfin Camp and Associates, Inc. **377:** Coutesy of Neal Miller **378:** Charron Smith Amgen, Inc. John Sholtis, The Rockerfeller University **380, top:** Royalty-Free/Corbis **380,left:** Frederick M. Brown/Getty Images **380, right:** Frazier Harrison/Getty Images **382:** AP/Wide World Photo **383:** Alain Evrard/Photo Researchers, Inc. **386:** Courtesy of Harry F. Harlow, University of Wisconsin Primate Laboratory **387:** Jeffrey L. Rotman/Corbis **389:** Kevin Lamarque/Reuters/Corbis **391:** Reuters/Corbis **392:** Rick Friedman/Corbis **392:** Gregory A. Beaumont/® The Great Arcata to Ferndale World Championship Cross Country Kinetic Sculpture Race **397:** Bob Daemmrich/The Image Works **400:** Gary Conner/PhotoEdit **401, top:** Sergei Karpukhgin/Reuters/Corbis **401, bottom:** Amy Etra/PhotoEdit **403:** Chad Slattery/Getty Images **404:** Dennis Coon **408:** Peter Beavis/Getty Images

Chapter 10. 413: Andre Forget/AP/Wide World Photo **414, left:** Matthew Mendelsohn/Corbis **414, right:** Bill Bachman/PhotoEdit **415:** Courtesy of Pam Wagner **417:** O'Brien Productions/Corbis **424:** Eleanor Bentall/Corbis **428:** "All is Vanity" by Allen Gilbert **429:** Bettmann/Corbis **432:** fotostock/SuperStock **433:** Joel Gordon **434:** David Young-Wolff/PhotoEdit **435:** Laura Dwight/PhotoEdit **440:** Photolibrary/Jupiterimages **444:** Zia Soleil/Getty Image **446:** David McNew/Newsmakers/Getty Images **452:** Digital Vision/Getty Images

Chapter 11. 457: Greg Epperson/Index Stock Imagery **459, left:** Darren Robb/Getty Images **459, right:** Jeffery Allan Salter/Corbis SABA **461:** Reuters/Corbis **464:** Tom Stewart/Corbis **465:** Daniel G. Lavoie/Corbis **466:** Rubberball/Getty Images **467:** Ken Cedeno/Corbis **470, top:** Tony Anderson/Getty Images **470, bottom:**

Credits

Royalty-Free/Corbis **477:** Scott Cunningham/Getty Images **478:** Stephen Rose/Rainbow **479:** Barbara Stitzer/PhotoEdit **482:** Purestock/SuperStock **484:** Morton Beebe/Corbis **485:** Dan McCoy/Rainbow **486:** Hisham Ibrahim/Getty Images **489:** Tim Pannell/Corbis

Chapter 12. 497: Rubberball/Getty Images **499:** Rick Friedman/Corbis **500:** American Psychiatric Association **502:** Scott Camazine/Photo Researchers, Inc. **503:** Courtesy of Ulrike Kantor Gallery **508, top:** Cary Wolinsky/Stock Boston **508, bottom:** Courtesy of Robert Hare **511, left:** Brent Stirton/The Image Bank/Getty Images **511, center:** Bettmann/Corbis **511, right:** Dennis Coon **512:** Paula Bronstein/Getty Images **514:** Bruce Ayres/Getty Images **518:** Benelux Press/Getty Images **519:** Bettmann/Corbis **519:** Joe Sohm/The Image Works **520:** Alan Oddie/PhotoEdit, Inc. **522:** Peter Granser/Laif/Aurora Photos **522:** Grunnitis/Photo Researchers, Inc. **523, left:** Bruce Ely **523, right:** Curt Borgwardt/Corbis Sygma **525:** Derik Bayes/Courtesy Guttman-Maclay Life Picture Service **526:** Dennis Brack/Black Star **526:** The Brookhaven National Library

Chapter 13. 541: Zigy Kaluzny/Getty Images **543:** Daniele Pellegrini/Photo Researchers, Inc. **543:** CIMMYT **544, top left:** Mary Evans Picture Library/Photo Researchers, Inc. **544, top right:** Bettmann/Corbis **544, bottom:** Peter Aprahamian/Corbis **550:** Getty Images **554:** Christopher A. Record/AP/Wide World Photo **555:** Courtesy of Albert Bandura **556:** Courtesy of Larry Hodges, Thomas and Rob Kooper **556:** Georgia Tech Telephoto **564:** Jon Bradley/Getty Images **568:** Gilles Mingasson/Getty Images **570:** Courtesy of Rodger Casier **571:** Will & Deni McIntyre/Photo Researchers, Inc. **572, left:** Peter Southwick/Stock Boston **572, right:** Bruce Ayers/Getty Images **575:** Sheila Terry/Photo Researchers, Inc.

Chapter 14. 583: David Lo Tai Wai/Getty Images **589:** Robert Caputo/Stock Boston **590:** Alex Mares-Manton/Getty Images **591, left:** Kevin Fitzgerald/Getty Images **591, right:** Vario Press/Imapress/The Image Works **604:** ABC-TV/The Kobal Collection/Brakha, Moshe **605:** Karen Kasmauski/Corbis **609:** Leonard Lessin/Photo Researchers, Inc.

Chapter 15. 621: Paul Chesley/Getty Images **622:** Mark Richards/PhotoEdit **623:** Jeff Greenberg/PhotoEdit **624, top:** John W. Gertz/zefa/Corbis **624, bottom:** Ralf-Finn Hestoft/Corbis **626:** Bill Bachmann/PhotoEdit **628:** Corbis/SuperStock **630:** Fox Searchlight/The Kobal Collection/Davidson, Neil **631:** Roy Morsch/Corbis **636:** Scenes from the film "Obedience," by Stanley Milgram, The Pennsylvania State University, Audio Visual Services. Used by permission **638, left:** Rubberball/Jupiterimages **638, right:** Jeff Widener/AP/Wide World Photo **643, left:** Bob Llewellen/Pictor International Ltd./Jupiterimages **643, right:** AFP/Getty Images **646, top:** Greg Smith/Corbis **646, bottom:** Bettmann/Corbis **649:** David Young-Wolff/ PhotoEdit **650:** NBAE/Getty Images **653, top:** Mary Kate Denny/PhotoEdit **653, bottom:** Jonathan Nourok/PhotoEdit **656:** GDT/Getty Images **657:** Jon Love/Getty Images **660:** Robert Brenner/PhotoEdit

Chapter 16. 669: SuperStock Inc. **670:** Chaplin/Unlimited Artists/The Kobal Collection **671:** Justin Sullivan/Getty Images **672:** Yellow Dog Productions/Getty Images **674:** Image Source/Jupiterimages **676:** Courtesy of the General Electric Company **678:** Bill Aron/PhotoEdit, Inc. **682:** F. Fedrick/The Image Works **683:** Stockbyte/Getty Images **684:** Amanda Morris/The Image Works **686, top:** Laura Dwight/Corbis **686, bottom:** Spencer Platt/Getty Images **687:** Jeff Greenberg/PhotoEdit **689, all:** Peter Ginter/Material World World **690:** Cleo/PhotoEdit **695:** Tony Savion/The Image Works **696:** AFP/Getty Images **697, left:** Oliver Maire/Corbis **697, right:** Richard Pasley/Stock Boston **702:** AFP/Getty Images **703:** NASA **704:** NASA **706:** Maarten Udema Fotografie

Appendix. 709: Comstock Images/Jupiterimages

Name Index

Aamodt, M. G., 670, 673–674, 676, 678
Abel, G. G., 603
Abel, J. R., 587
Abel, T., 312
Abell, S. C., 439
Abraham, J., 120, 278
Abrahamse, W., 688
Abrahamson, D. J., 613
Abrahamson, L. S., 613
Abrams, D. B., 234
Abramson, L. Y., 480
Abuhamdeh, S., 386
Accordino, D. B., 424
Accordino, M. P., 424
Acebo, C., 207
Acton, M., 322
Adams, G., 503
Adams, H. E., 606
Adams, J. W., 289, 355
Adams, M., 304
Adams-Curtis, L. E., 606
Adamson, K., 68
Addis, K. M., 300
Addis, M. E., 645
Adler, A., 30
Adler, R. L., 382
Adler, S. A., 151
Adorno, T. W., 648–649
Aeschbach, D., 532
Afifi, T. O., 274
Ahern, J., 467
Ahima, R. S., 378
Ainsworth, M., 112
Aizenberg, D., 232
Ajzen, I., 641, 643
Akerstedti, T., 208
Akert, R. M., 637
al'Absi, M., 487
Albarracín, D., 641
Alberti, R., 639
Alberto, P. A., 273–274
Alcock, J. E., 195–196
Aldrich, D., 263
Alexander. M. P., 76
Alicke, M. D., 624
Alkire, M. T., 70
Allen, D., 461
Allen, J. S., 297
Allen, K., 489, 493
Allen, M., 695
Allgower, A., 458
Allik, J., 418
Allin, J. D., 330
Allport, G. W., 422, 648
Alonso, Y., 382
Alsaker, F. D., 129
Altemeyer, B., 648
Altenor, A., 478
Althof, S., 614
Altman Weiss, K., 449
Altman, L. K., 609
Alvarado, N., 449
Alvino, J., 124, 333
Alvir, J. M. J., 570

Alwin, D. F., 643
Ama, E., 665
Amabile, T., 392
Amato, P. R., 102, 144
Ambady, N., 361
Amir, N., 302
Ammerén, G., 233
Amsel, L., 467
Ancis, J. R., 503
Anderson, C. A., 279–280, 469, 651, 657, 658–659
Anderson, D. I., 179
Anderson, J. R., 4, 318, 352
Anderson, K. B., 657
Anderson, M. C., 168, 308, 310
Anderson, N. B., 468, 652
Anderson, S. W., 297
Anderson, W. M., 214
Andersson, G., 551
Andrasik, F., 485–486
André, C., 572
Andresen, J., 223
Andrew, M., 531
Andrew, S., 215, 263
Andrews, D. W., 616
Andrykowski, M. A., 379
Annett, M., 43
Anshel, M. H., 698
Antle, M. C., 374
Antoni, M. H., 464
Antonuccio, D. O., 553
Antony, M. M., 453
Anwyl, R., 313
Appelbaum, P. S., 523
Applegate, B., 254
Arauz, R. M., 329
Arbona, C. B., 556
Archer, T., 224
Arenander, A., 224
Ariely, D., 6
Arkowitz, H., 545
Armeli, S., 488
Arnett, J. J., 129, 130–131
Arntz, A., 62
Aron, 404
Aronow, E., 449
Aronson, E., 624, 637, 643–644, 653–654, 665
Aronson, J., 366
Arterberry, M. E., 179
Arthur, W., 424
Ary, D. V., 240
Asch, S., 631–632
Ash, D. W., 318
Ashby, F. G., 342
Asher, E. R., 407, 489
Aslin, R. N., 179
Asmundson, G. J. G., 484
Assanand, S., 379–381
Athenasiou, R., 604
Atkin, D. J., 674
Atkinson, A. P., 400
Atkinson, R. C., 288
Attanucci, J., 133
Aucoin, K. J., 274

Austin, D. W., 551
Aversa, A., 379
Avery, D. H., 532
Awadallah, N., 513
Ayers, L., 360
Ayllon, T., 558

Baard, P. P., 391
Babulas, V., 524
Babyak, M. A., 459
Bacaltchuk, J., 545
Bachman, J. G., 136
Backs-Dermott, 561
Baddeley, A. D., 289
Baer, D., 554
Baer, J. M., 357, 360
Baer, L., 571
Bagley, C., 598
Bahrick, L. E., 120
Bailey, J. M., 597
Bailey, L. M., 91, 312
Baillargeon, R., 125, 126
Bain, S. K., 330
Bajracharya, S. M., 606
Baker, T. B., 233
Bakker, A. B., 465
Baldo, O., 612
Balk, D. E., 449
Balkin, T. J., 210
Ball, T., 315
Ballinger, K. M., 224, 493
Ballon, B., 54
Balsam, K. F., 598
Baltes, B. B., 674
Banaji, M. R., 664
Bandon, T. H., 283
Bandura, A., 273, 278, 434, 467, 555, 657–658
Banich, M. T., 75
Banker, B. S., 653
Banks, S., 523
Banks, T., 597, 657
Banton, J. G., 658
Bar-Eli, M., 698
Bar-Tal, D., 649
Barabasz, A., 220
Barber, T. X., 220
Bard, C., 402
Barefoot, J. C., 487
Bargh, J. A., 625
Barkataki, I., 526
Barker, E. T., 131
Barkham, M., 566
Barlow, D. H., 500, 502–503, 509, 511, 512, 514, 516, 518, 525, 535, 545, 565, 613, 688
Baron, R. A., 622, 630–631, 665
Barrett, D., 244, 310
Barrett, H. C., 354–355
Barrett, L. F., 461
Barrick, M. R., 424, 677
Barroso, C., 665
Barrowcliff, A. L., 518
Barrowclough, C., 579
Bartholow, B. D., 280, 658–659

Bartlett, J. C., 189
Bartoshuk, L. M., 166
Bartram, B., 642
Bartz, W. R., 237
Basch, J., 235
Baskin, D. G., 379
Baskin, T. W., 43, 579
Basson, R., 594
Bastian, B., 343
Batra, L., 559
Batson, C. D., 661–662
Batterham, R. L., 378
Baum, A., 464, 691–692
Baum, S., 458
Bauman, L. J., 609
Baumeister, R. F., 33, 417, 622, 641
Baumrind, D., 113, 144, 274
Baumwell, L., 119
Baur, K., 384, 584, 591, 595–596, 603, 605, 612, 615
Bavaria, A. J., 15
Baydoun, R., 448
Beale, M. D., 571
Bearison, D. J., 126–127
Bearman, P. S., 607
Beaton, S., 360
Beatrice, B., 119
Beauchamp, P. H., 698
Beaulieu, C. M. J., 683–684
Bechman, H. T., 555
Beck, A. T., 390, 479, 536, 560–561
Beck, B. L., 6
Beck, K. D., 273
Beck, R. C., 370
Becker, S. W., 662
Beebe, B., 119, 483
Beeber, L. S., 102
Beeman, M. J., 76
Beerlinpalaci, A., 263
Beersma, D. G. M., 374
Beggs, J., 90
Bègue, L., 664
Behar, A., 234, 283
Behrend, D. A., 286, 311
Beike, D. R., 286, 311
Beirne-Smith, M., 334
Belenky, G., 206
Bell, D., 295
Bell, R. C., 441
Bell, R. L., 261
Bell, T., 308
Bellezza, F. S., 316
Belsky, J., 112
Bem, S., 590–591
Ben-Ari, A., 466
Ben-Shakhar, G., 21, 398
Benbow, C. P., 92
Benedict, J. G., 550
Benjafield, J. G., 28
Benloucif, S., 102
Bennett, E., 694
Bennett, E. L., 102
Benoit, S. C., 377
Bensafi, M., 166
Benski, C., 53

Name Index

Bensley, L., 280
Benson, H., 224
Benson, J., 348
Bentley, D. L., 684
Berchick, R. J., 536
Beresh, H., 73
Berg, B., 452
Bergeron, S., 615
Berglund, B., 687
Bergman, H., 224
Berkowitz, L., 630, 658
Berliner, L., 603
Berman, S., 120
Bernat, J. A., 606
Berne, E., 568
Bernhardt, J. M., 280
Bernstein, H. J., 571
Bernsten, D. M., 304, 309
Bernthal, M. J., 279
Berridge, K. C., 229–230
Berscheid, E., 188, 623–625
Bersoff, D. M., 432
Bertholf, M., 450
Bertini, M., 216
Bertsch, G. J., 273
Besnard, D., 304
Best, D., 589
Betancur, C., 92
Betts, J. M., 198
Beyer, M., 673
Bhugra, D., 503
Bhushan, B., 92
Bialystok, E., 346
Biascovich, J., 489
Bibace, R., 610
Bickman, L., 630
Bieliauskas, L. M., 49, 524
Biglan, A., 240
Bigras, M., 85, 114
Bilker, W. B., 70–71
Billington, C. J., 377
Binder, J. L., 545
Binet, A., 328–329, 365
Binik, Y. M., 600–601, 615
Birch, J., 160
Birnbaum, M. H., 50
Bisson, J. I., 467
Bjork, R. A., 54, 204, 224, 390
Black, M. M., 101
Blackmore, C., 204–205, 223
Blackmore, S., 20
Blackwell, D. L., 624
Blair, K. S., 508
Blake, R., 155, 165
Blake, W., 199
Blakemore, C., 151
Blanchard, D. C., 656
Blanchard, E. B., 254, 555
Blanchard, R. J., 656
Blankner, J. G., 587
Blascovich, J., 493
Bloch, M., 531
Bloch, S., 542
Blok, S. V., 343
Blood, A. J., 84
Bloom, B., 389–390
Bloom, C. M., 322
Bloom, J. W., 551
Bloom, R. L., 75–76
Blunt, A., 6, 7
Boals, A., 493
Bockting, W. O., 596
Bodin, S. D., 274
Boergers, J., 536
Boggild, M., 191

Bohannon, J. N., 119
Boivin, D. B., 395
Boldero, J. M., 441
Bollini, A., 524, 525–527, 570
Bolte, M. A., 532
Bonache, J., 672
Bonanno, G. A., 407
Bond, R., 631
Bond, T., 100
Bonett, D. G., 673
Bongard, S., 487
Bonham, V., 651, 665
Boniecki, K. A., 653
Bood, S., 224
Boodoo, G., 365, 367
Booker, J. M., 532
Bootzin, R. R., 214
Borlongan, C. V., 63
Borman, W. C., 678
Bornham, V., 367
Bornstein, M. H., 101, 119, 500
Borod, J. C., 75–76
Borrie, R. A., 224
Botes, A., 133
Botly, L. C. P., 374
Bouchard, T. J., Jr., 365, 367, 416
Bouchoux, A., 512
Bouchoux, Z., 232
Bourhis, R. Y., 648
Bourne, E. J., 555
Boutros, N., 76
Bovbjerg, D. H., 251, 379
Bower, G. H., 292, 307
Bower, J. E., 479
Bower, M. L., 106
Bower, T. G., 106
Bowers, K. S., 295
Boykin, A. W., 365, 367
Boyle, S. H., 487
Brach, T., 549
Brack, G. L., 494
Bradley, B. P., 188
Bradley, L. J., 645
Bradley, M. M., 508
Bradley, R. H., 102, 566
Bradshaw, G. S., 695
Bradshaw, S. D., 452
Braid, J., 220
Brainerd, C. J., 124
Brakke, K. E., 348
Bramsen, I., 512
Brandon, T. H., 233
Branigan, C., 188, 409
Brannick, M. T., 448
Brannon, L., 430, 458, 482
Branscombe, N. R., 622, 630, 665
Bratko, D., 387
Braun, A. R., 210
Braun, K. A., 232, 295
Braun-LaTour, K. A., 294
Bray, R. M., 694
Bray, S. R., 699
Breckler, S. J., 628
Breedlove, S. M., 59, 587
Brehm, S. S., 588, 624–625
Bremmer, J. G., 106
Bremner, J. D., 512
Brennan, F. X., 273
Breslau, N., 233
Bretherton, R., 549
Brewer, J. L., 306
Brewer, J. S., 601
Brewer, K. R., 198, 278
Brewer, M., 691
Brewer, N., 696

Brickman, A. M., 75–76
Bridges, L. J., 108
Bridwell, A. M., 697
Brief, A. P., 673
Briere, J., 508
Briggs, T. E., 674
Brigham, J. C., 695
Brinkman, H., 683
Brinton, R. D., 63
Britt, T. W., 653
Brock, T. C., 643
Brodley, B. T., 548
Broekaett, E., 572
Brooks, F. R., 514
Brooks-Gunn, J., 129
Brothen, T., 5
Brotto, L. A., 594
Brown, A. E., 359
Brown, A. M., 500
Brown, A. S., 524
Brown, B. B., 684
Brown, C., 536
Brown, E., 106, 174
Brown, K. W., 225
Brown, L. M., 436
Brown, R. L., 228, 234, 300
Brown, S. A., 235
Brown, S. G., 90
Brown, S. L., 494
Brown, T. A., 509, 512, 516, 545
Brown, T. D., 651
Brown. A. M., 106
Browne, B. A., 590
Browne, K., 603
Browne, N., 20
Brownell, K. D., 379–381
Brownridge, D. A., 274
Bruce, D., 319
Bruch, M. A., 452
Bruer, J. T., 102
Bruner, J., 1, 105
Bruyn, J., 92
Bryan, A., 594
Bryant, F. B., 606
Bryant, J. B., 295, 694
Bryant, R. A., 467
Bryden, P. J., 92
Brydne, P., 90
Bucci, W., 545
Büchert, M., 525
Buchwald, A., 446–447
Buckley, J. A., 445
Buddie, A. M., 235
Budney, A. J., 238
Buehner, M. J., 175
Buffalo, E. A., 310
Bugelski, R., 648
Bugental, J. F. T., 30
Buller, D. J., 626
Bummett, B. H., 487
Bunde, J., 487
Bundrick, C. M., 439
Bunn, G. C., 397
Bunting, M. F., 152
Burchinal, M. R., 112
Burger, J. M., 258, 414, 444
Burgess, C. A., 221, 295
Burgess, M. C. A., 306
Burgner, D., 630
Burke, M. J., 673
Burke, R. J., 466
Burkman, L. J., 239
Burlingame, G. M., 564, 578
Burnett, K., 382
Burnett, R. C., 343

Burns, C., 571
Burns, D. D., 560
Burns, J., 195–196
Burns, T., 573
Burt, S. A., 508
Burton, 493
Burtt, H. E., 302
Bush, G., 224
Bushman, B. J., 279–280, 469, 622, 641, 651, 657–658
Bushnell, M. C., 170
Buss, D. M., 416, 417, 452, 623, 626
Butcher, J. N., 446–447, 498
Butkovic, A., 387
Butler, B., 695
Butler, J. C., 649
Butler, M. G., 453
Butler, R., 386
Bybee, D., 442
Byers, E. S., 615
Byravan, A., 591
Byrne, D., 622, 630, 665
Byrne, S. M, 382

Cabanieu, G., 92
Cabrera, N. J., 115
Cacitti, L., 304
Cadet, J., 77
Cahill, S. P., 556
Cahn, B. R., 223
Cahusac, P. M. B., 395
Cai, X. J., 377–378
Caldara, R., 306
Calhoun, J., 685
Calhoun, K. S., 606
Calkins, M., 31
Callahan, C. M., 333
Callahan, I., 21
Calmels, M.-N., 166
Cameron, J., 392
Cameron, J. A., 664
Cameron, J. D., 170
Cammann, C., 628, 672
Campbell, B., 334
Campbell, J. D., 417
Campbell, L. E., 334
Campbell, S., 324
Campbell, W. K., 403, 417
Campion, L. E., 676
Campion, M. A., 674, 676
Campos, J. J., 179
Canli, T., 395, 407
Cannon, W. B., 373, 376, 402, 405
Cao, Y., 64
Caplan, P. J., 500
Capuzzi, D., 564
Carbonell, O. A., 112
Carbonneau, R., 85, 114
Cardoso, S. H., 84
Carducci, B. J., 453
Carey, C., 239
Carlander, B., 206
Carlbring, P., 551
Carlin, A, 556
Carlino, A. R., 570
Carlo, G., 132
Carlsmith, J. M., 644
Carlson, D., 461
Carlson, M., 658
Carlson, N. R., 60, 79, 83, 87, 168
Carlsson, J., 485
Carnagey, N. L., 279–280, 658–659
Carney, R. N., 322
Carpenter, J., 233
Carpenter, K. M., 235, 565

Carrigan, M. H., 556
Carroll, D. W., 118, 119, 344
Carroll, J. L., 585, 589, 598, 615
Carroll, J. M., 400
Carskodon, M. A., 207
Carter, D. A., 671
Carter, J. R., 521
Carter, M., 508
Cartwright, D., 450
Cartwright, R, 242–243
Carvalho, M., 572
Casey, P., 512
Caspi, A., 114, 415–416, 531
Cassaday, H. J., 306
Cassady, J. C., 388
Cassem, E. H., 571
Casson, E., 159
Castañeda, R., 578
Castro, J. R., 382, 424
Castro-Caldas, A., 297
Catalano, R., 469
Catledge, C., 550
Cattani-Thompson, K., 565
Cattell, R. B., 422–423
Cautela, J. R., 575–576
Cavaco, S., 297
Cavanaugh, J. C., 304
Cerone, L. J., 91
Cervena, K., 206
Cervone, D., 418, 435
Chabas, D., 215
Chabris, C., 152
Chakos, M. H., 570
Chamberlain, K., 456, 463–464
Chamberlin, J., 572, 577
Chambers, R. A., 230
Chambless, D. L., 560
Chamorro-Premuzic, T., 21, 424
Chan, G. C.-K., 239
Chance, P., 250–251, 268, 270, 379
Chandra, C., 595, 598, 604
Chandratre, S., 191
Chang, E. C., 488
Chang, M. C., 239
Chang-Schneider, C., 417
Chansler, P. A., 628, 672
Chao, M., 631
Chao, R., 115
Chapanis, A., 702
Chaplin, G., 665
Chapman, R. A., 223
Chase, W. G., 316
Chassin, L., 233
Chassin, P., 460
Chaves, J. F., 221
Chazan-Cohen, R., 102
Check, J., 606
Cheek, J., 452
Chen, C.-C., 676
Chen, K., 240
Chen, P. Y., 588–589
Chen, S., 263
Chen, Y. R., 130, 503
Chen, Z., 354, 632
Cheney, C. D., 257
Cheng, H., 64
Cheriff, A. D., 494
Chess, S., 103
Chesson, A. L., 214
Chester, A., 551
Cheyne, J. A., 210
Chiarello, C., 76
Chiricos, T., 642
Chisolm, T. H., 165
Chiu, C., 34

Chiu, S.-F., 676
Chivers, M. L., 597
Chomsky, N., 118, 346, 348–349
Chopp, M., 63
Chow, K. L., 151
Christensen, A., 567, 578
Christensen, C. D., 326
Christian, C., 545
Christian, K. M., 83
Christopher, F. S., 626
Christophersen, E. R., 435
Chua, P., 592
Chung, S. A., 374, 493
Church, J. A., 340
Cialdini, R. B., 392, 629, 634
Cinciripini, P. M., 234
Clack, R. J., 691
Claiborn, C. D., 579
Clancy, S. A., 210, 310
Clara, J. P., 424
Clark, D., 76
Clark, K., 654
Clark, R., 319, 468, 652
Clark, V. R., 468, 652
Claussen, B., 233
Clawson, C., 324
Clayton, N. S., 268
Clearfield, M. W., 590
Clearwater, Y., 704
Clements, A. M., 587
Click, P., 664
Clifford, E. R., 152, 175
Cline, V. B., 659
Clinkenbeard, P. R., 333
Clothier, A., 244
Cnattingius, S., 233
Coast, J. R., 492
Cobern, M. K., 691
Cochran, S. D., 598
Coffman, T. L., 650
Cohen, G., 304
Cohen, J., 482
Cohen, J. A., 603
Cohen, J. E., 685
Cohen, L. H., 488, 592
Cohen, M. A., 378
Cohen, P., 482, 524
Cohen, R. L., 643
Cohen, S., 464, 687
Cohen-Kettenis, P. T., 384
Colapinto, J., 587
Cole, J., 168
Coleman, E., 596
Coles, C. D., 101
Colin, A. K., 199
Collins, A. M., 296
Collins, D. J., 342
Collins, F. S., 367, 651, 665
Collins, R. L., 239, 296, 467
Collins, W. A., 112
Collop, N. A., 215
Colpaert, F. C., 307
Comer, R. J., 498
Comier, J. F., 512
Comparini, L., 115
Compton, J. V., 554
Compton, W. C., 33, 395, 542
Compton, W. M., 230
Conger, J. J., 118
Constable, R. T., 79, 407
Conte, J. M., 673, 675
Conway, M., 304
Conway, M. A., 152, 290
Conyne, R. K., 691
Cook, D. A., 664

Cook, E. J., 685
Cook, S. W., 401, 688
Cooke, B. M., 587
Cooper, A. E., 503
Cooper, C., 14–15
Cooper, D. S., 198
Cooper, G., 151, 204
Cooper, J., 310, 644, 694
Cooper, M. J., 380, 382, 597
Cooper, P. J., 531
Cooper, R. P., 120
Corballis, M. C., 347
Corbin, W. R., 609
Coreea-Chávez, M., 329
Coren, S., 90, 92, 160, 177, 192, 206
Corey, G., 564–565
Corkin, S., 312
Corrigan, P. W., 523, 532
Corsini, R. J., 49, 553
Corwyn, R. F., 102
Cosgrove, G. R., 571
Costa, P. T., Jr., 416, 421, 423
Costantini-Ferrando, M. F., 220
Côté, J., 130, 136
Cote, S., 671
Cottrell, G. W., 400
Coulton, C. J., 691
Cournos, F., 519
Courrier, S., 659
Coursey, R. D., 572
Court, J. H., 310
Court, P. C., 310
Cowan, G., 598
Cowan, N., 152, 292
Cowan, P. A., 126, 144, 274
Cowan, T. M., 317
Cowden, C. R., 452
Cowell, P., 526
Cowles, J. T., 261
Cox, B. J., 274, 424
Cox, R. H., 696, 698
Coyle, J. T., 525
Cozby, P. C., 694
Crago, M., 346
Craig, K. D., 513
Craig, L., 114
Craig, T. Y., 628
Craighero, L., 77
Craik, F. I. M., 305, 346
Craik, K. H., 33
Crano, W. D., 630, 631–632
Cravatt, B. F., 208
Crawford, M., 535
Crawley, S. B., 114
Crencavage, L. M., 567
Crichlow, S., 632
Crisp, A., 382
Croft, R. G., 659
Crogan, M., 654
Crooks, R., 384, 584, 591, 595–596, 603, 605, 612, 615
Cropanzano, R., 671
Cropley, A., 357
Crosby, R. A., 609
Crotty, M., 170
Crown, C. L., 119
Crowther, J. H., 483
Crutsinger, C., 132
Cruz, M. G., 632
Csikszentmihalyi, M., 33, 360, 386, 392, 698
Cuddy, A. J. C., 649–650
Cull, W. L., 319, 587
Cumming, N., 289

Cummings, M. R., 99
Cummins, D. D., 662
Curci, A., 310
Cutler, B. L., 694
Czeisler, C. A., 207, 395

D'Onofrio, B. M., 337
Dabb, J. M., Jr., 657
Dagot, L., 634
Daigle, L. E., 606
Dalton, K. M., 464
Daly, R. C., 531
Damasio, H., 347
Dane, F. C., 198, 651
Dane, S., 92
Daniels, H., 126
Daniels, M., 337
Danielsen, E. M., 694
Danziger, N., 168
Darakjian, J., 235
Darley, C. A., 18
Darley, J. M., 18, 650, 660–661
Darling, C. A., 602
Daruna, J. H., 464
Darwin, C., 28, 400, 404
Das, J. P., 334
Das, M., 526
Dattilio, F. M., 70
Dauvilliers, Y., 206
Davaloo, H., 545
David, A., 191
Davidov, B. J., 569, 664–666
Davidovitch, N., 357
Davids, M. R., 261
Davidson, J., 353
Davidson, J. K., 602
Davidson, J. R., 224
Davidson, P. R., 556
Davidson, T. L., 276
Davies, M., 607
Davies, R., 578
Daviet, C., 565
Davila, D., 214
Davis, D., 362
Davis, E. B., 659
Davis, G. E., 692
Davis, K. D., 170
Davis, M. J., 610
Davis, M. R., 295
Davison, G. C., 524
Dawson, D. A., 510
Dawson, G., 326
Dawson, J. D., 469
Dawson, N., 119
de Groot, L. C., 459–460
de Jesus Mari, J., 545
de Jong, P. J., 253
de Jong, T., 277
de Leon, C. F. M., 139
de Mello, M. F., 545
de Muinck, K., 587
de Rios, M. D., 205
Deakin, B., 63
Deakin, J. F. W., 526
DeArmond, S., 588–589
Deary, I. J., 415, 421
Deaux, K., 630
Deci, E. L., 391–392
Deckers, L., 373
Deckro, G. R., 224, 493
Deeb, S. S., 159
DeGaetano, G., 658
Dein, S., 645
Deinzer, R., 464
DeLamater, J. D., 384, 582, 584, 602

Delancy, P. F., 316–317
DeLano, L., 324
Delargy, M., 85
Delgado, B. M., 115
Delis, D. C., 235
Delpero, W. T., 159
Dement, W., 216
Demiris, G., 551
Denmark, F. L., 34, 435
Dennis, J., 214
Denollet, J., 487
Derlega, V. J., 452
Deshon, R. P., 676
Desjardins, R. N., 120
Desmarais, S., 293, 323
Desmond, J. E., 395
Detterman, D. K., 331
Detwiler, F. R. J., 591
Deuser, W. E., 657
Deutsch, G., 76, 92
Deutsch, M., 653
DeVault, C., 604, 617
Devine, P. G., 664, 694–695
Devlin, B., 337
Devot, A., 216
Dewey, J., 31
Dhanda, R., 477
Di Forti, M., 62
Di Marzo, V., 377
Diano, S., 377
Dick-Niederhauser, A., 111
Dickens, W. T., 337
Dickerson, F. B., 559
Dickinson, A., 268
Dickinson, D. K., 119, 334
DiClemente, R. J., 280
Diehl, N. S., 699
Dierdorff, E. C., 675
Dieterich, 127
Dinan, T. G., 487
Dingers, D. F., 206
Dingus, T. A., 46
Dinkmeyer, D., Jr., 143, 145
Dinkmeyer, D., Sr., 143, 145
Dion, K. L., 664
DiPietro, D., 610
Dirkczwagner, A. J. E., 512
Dissanayake, C., 111
Distin, K., 333
DiZio, P., 171
Dobelle, W. H., 151
Dobie, T. G., 171
Dobson, K. S., 530, 560–561
Dockucu, M. E., 496
Dodd, D. K., 466
Dodds, P. S., 620
Dodson, C. S., 295
Doidge, N., 546
Dolan, R. J., 77
Dolev, K., 398
Dolezal-Wood, S., 567
Dollard, J., 433–435
Dolski, I., 464
Domhoff, W., 217, 243
Domingo, R. A., 119
Domjan, M., 248, 266
Donaldson, D., 536
Donate-Bartfield, E., 111
Donatella, P., 232
Donders, R., 79
Donmall, M. C., 579
Donnerstein, E., 658
Donovan, M., 216
Dooling, D. J., 289
Dopler, D. M.

Doran, S. M., 206
Dorman, M. F., 166
Dosher, B. A., 306
Dougall, A. L., 464
Dougherty, D. D., 571
Douglas, S. C., 675
Douvan, E., 129
Dove, A., 365
Doverspike, D., 424
Dovidio, J. F., 648, 650–651, 653, 662, 664
Dowling, K. W., 54
Dozois, D. J. A., 530, 560–561
Draguns, J. G., 34, 569
Dragsow, F., 446
Drews, F. A., 152
Drigotas, S. M., 442
Driver, J. L., 616
Drolet, G., 62
Drop, S. L. S., 587
Drucker, P., 545, 671
Druckman, D., 54, 204, 221, 224, 390, 518
Drummond, P. D., 464
Dubeau, D., 85, 114
DuBois, D., 224
Duchon, A., 276
Duclos, S. E., 404
Duffy, J. F., 207, 374
DuFrene, D. D., 678–679
Dulewicz, V., 407
Dumas, T. L., 674
Dumont, E. C., 62
Duncan, B. L., 579
Duncan, C. C., 542
Duncan, G. H., 170
Duncan, J., 77
Duncan, T. E., 240
Duncan, W. C., 532
Duncker, K., 351, 354
Dunlap, E. E., 695
Durand, A., 6
Durand, V. M., 500, 502–503, 514, 525, 535
Durham, M. D., 198, 651
Durkin, K., 301
Durmazlar, N., 160
Dutra, L., 566
Dutta, T., 92
Dwivedi, P., 288
Dwyer, D. J., 465
Dwyer, J., 198
Dwyer, W. O., 691
Dyer, K., 141
Dywan, J., 295
Dzokoto, V. A., 503

Eagly, A. H., 586, 590, 662, 671
Eardley, I., 612
Earleywine, M., 469
Ebbese, E. B., 301
Ebbinghaus, H., 304
Eberhardt, N. L., 398
Eckerman, D. A., 267
Eddy, K. T., 566
Eden, J., 632
Eder, D. N., 532
Eggert, A., 4
Ehlers, A., 467
Ehrlich, P., 187
Eichenbaum, H., 311
Eidelson, J. I., 649
Eidelson, R. J., 649
Eiden, R. D., 101
Eifert, G. H., 465, 553, 555

Eilser, J. A., 261
Eimas, P. D., 126
Einstein, A., 656
Eisenberg, N., 114
Eisert, S., 689
Eisler, I., 564–565
Ekman, P., 400, 404
Elder, P., 20, 48
Elieff, C. A., 179
Eliot, L., 120
Elli, K. A., 312
Ellickson, P. L., 239
Elliot, A. J., 694–695
Elliott, J. C., 377–378
Elliott, M., 579, 603
Ellis, A., 4, 5, 6, 561–562
Ellis, H. C., 352
Ellis, P. J., 676
Ellis, R., 294
Ellis, S. M., 378
Elovainio, M., 673
Emmons, K., 234
Emmons, M., 639
Emmorey, K., 347
Emswiller, T., 630
Emurian, H. H., 263
Engle, D. E., 545
Englis, B. G., 665
Englund, C. E., 206
Enns, J. T., 160, 177, 192
Enns, M. W., 424
Epstein, D. R., 214
Epstein, M. H., 445
Ericsson, K. A., 138–139, 316–317, 390
Erikson, E. H., 30, 115, 135–136, 430
Erlacher, D., 216
Erlich, A., 685
Erlich, P., 685
Ernst, E., 169
Eron, L. D., 279–280, 658–659
Erzurumluoglu, A., 92
Eschholz, S., 642
Espa, F., 206
Espie, C. A., 213–214
Esterling, B. A., 493
Ethier, K. A., 607
Eubanks, J., 279, 658–659
Evans, G. W., 683, 686–688, 692
Everaerd, W., 595
Everly, G. S., 573
Ewen, 438
Ewing, G., 263
Eyal, N., 698
Eyde, L. D., 445
Eysenck, H., 418, 545

Fabes, R. A., 114, 436, 590
Fabrega, H., Jr., 499
Fagan, J. F., 366
Fahim, C., 518
Fahle, M., 188
Fahortiga, F., 382
Fain, G. L., 150
Faith, M. S., 565, 648, 650
Falkowski, C., 235
Fandt, P. M., 672, 674
Farah, M. J., 79–80
Farr, S. A., 377
Farrimond, T., 174
Farroni, T., 106
Fedoroff, J. P., 214
Fein, S., 630, 657
Feingold, A., 626

Feissner, J. M., 531
Feist, J., 458, 482
Feldhusen, J. F., 358
Feldman, D. H., 123–124
Feldstein, S., 119
Fellous, J.-M., 84
Fenn, K. M., 204
Fenning, S., 525
Fenton, G. W., 571
Ferber, R., 214
Fergusson, D. M., 101
Fernald, A., 118, 120
Fernández-Chacón, R., 313
Ferrante, A. M., 468
Ferrari, J. R., 7
Ferris, G. R., 677
Festinger, L., 622, 644
Fichner-Rathus, L., 587, 597–598, 617
Fichtel, A., 485
Field, C. E., 559
Fields, R. M., 467
Fields, T. H., 453
Fields, W., 348
Figueredo, A. J., 624
Fink, M., 571
Finn, S. E., 445
Fiorina, C., 671
Fireman, G., 215
Firestone, P., 513
First, M. B., 500
Fischer, A. H., 401
Fischler, C., 379
Fish, J. M., 34, 569
Fisher, 601
Fisher, B. S., 606
Fisher, J. D., 610
Fisher, R. P., 295
Fisher, S., 217
Fisher, W. A., 610
Fiske, S. T., 588, 649–650
Fitzgerald, P., 610
Fitzsimons, G. M., 625
Flanagan, M. B., 171
Flannery, D. J., 129
Flavell, J. H., 122
Fleming, J., 347
Fletcher, B. W., 232
Fletcher, P., 92
Flett, G. L., 536
Flies, U., 673
Florer, F., 310
Florin, P., 460
Flowe, H. D., 301
Flynn, J. R., 337
Foa, E. B., 512
Fobair, P., 578
Fobes, J. L., 261
Fochtmann, L. J., 514
Foehr, U. G., 279
Földiák, P., 288
Folkman, S., 465, 468
Follerre, W. C., 362
Follett, K., 630
Fontaine, K. R., 458
Fontenelle, D. H., 144
Fontenot, J., 514
Foo, P., 276
Foot, M., 510
Forbes, G. B., 606
Ford, D. Y., 333
Ford, G. G., 697
Ford, L., 115
Foreman, R. D., 169
Forman, E. M., 566

Forney, J. C., 132
Forney, W. S., 132
Forrest, M. S., 556
Forsyth, D. R., 628
Forsyth, G. A., 293
Forsyth, J. P., 553
Fortin, N. J., 311
Fortmann, S. P., 233
Foster, C. A., 403
Foster, G., 46
FosterLee, L., 695
FosterLee, R., 695
Fouad, N. A., 588
Fournier, J. F., 698
Fouts, R, 348
Fowers, B. J., 569, 664–666
Fowler, F., 144
Fowler, K. A., 23
Fowler, M., 22
Fox, C., 49
Fox, M. L., 465
Fox, P. T., 378
Foxhall, K., 198
Frackowiak, R. S. J., 84
Francis, J. J., 441
Franco, H., 578
Franco, K., 513
Franczyk, D., 382
Franke, M., 677
Franken, R. E., 372, 383, 388
Frankl, V., 549
Frantz, R., 105
Franze, S., 424
Franzoi, S. L., 623
Fraser, C., 170, 190
Frederick, C. J., 603
Frederickon, B. L., 461
Frederickson, B. L., 188, 409, 461, 488
Freeman, A., 195–196
Freeman, D., 522
Freeman, T. B., 63
Freidman, E., 670
Freidman, H. S., 464
Freitas, M. B., 92
Freiwald, W. A., 152
French, C. C., 22
French, S. E., 130
French, T. A., 198
Frenkel-Brunswik, E., 648–649
Freud, A., 30
Freud, S., 30, 31, 217, 427, 429–430, 515, 544, 548, 600
Frey, M. C., 331
Fricchinone, G. L., 224
Frick, P. J., 274
Fridley, D., 257
Fried, C. S., 606
Fried, P. A., 239
Friedman, H. S., 424
Friedman, L. J., 137, 544–545
Friedman, M., 486
Friedman, R. C., 253, 545
Friedmanm, P. D., 216
Friedrich, R. W., 166
Frieman, J., 317
Friesen, W. V., 404
Frijda, N. H., 384
Friman, P. C., 559
Frith, C. D., 84
Fritz, C. O., 322
Fromme, K., 609
Froufe, M., 204
Frueh, B. C., 556
Frydman, M., 659

Frye, E. M., 645
Fu, J. H., 631
Fuchs, D., 589
Fucito, L. M., 615–616
Fuhriman, A., 564
Fujino, D. C., 592
Fukuda, K., 207
Fukuda, S., 177
Fulero, S. M., 696
Funder, D. C., 416, 425
Funk, J. B., 658
Fuqua, D. R., 675
Furness, T. A., 556
Furnham, A., 21, 424

Gaab, N., 83
Gable, S. L., 407, 489
Gaertner, S. L., 650–651, 653
Gagnon, J., 596
Galambos, N. L., 131
Galanter, M., 578
Galantucci, B., 302
Galati, D., 400
Galea, S., 467
Galinsky, M. D., 565
Gallacher, F., 526
Gallagher, J., 319
Gallagher, S. H., 697
Gallo, L. C., 487
Galloway, R. E., 388
Galuska, C. M., 227
Ganey, H. C. N., 386–387
Ganis, G., 341
Ganster, D. C., 465
Gao, J., 378
Garb, H. N., 195, 376, 449
Garbarino, S., 207, 374
Garcia, M., 232
Garcia, R. I., 233
Garcia-Junco-Clemente, P., 313
Garcia-Palacios, A., 556
Gardner, B. T., 347
Gardner, H., 334–335, 363, 367
Gardner, R. A., 347
Garety, P. A., 522
Garfinkel, B. D., 536
Garfinkel, L. F., 536
Garland, A. F., 535
Garlow, S. J., 535
Garnets, L. D., 597–598, 600
Gärtner, M., 263
Gartrell, J. M., Jr., 597
Garvey, A. J., 233
Gastner, M. T., 652
Gatchel, R. J., 486
Gates, A. I., 318
Gayle, H., 607–608
Gazzaniga, M. S., 75
Geary, N., 378
Gedo, J. E., 30
Geehr, J. L., 673
Gefen, D., 623
Gegenfurtner, K. R., 159
Geiger, A., 550
Geiselman, E., 295
Geiselman, R. E., 295
Geiwitz, J., 118
Geliebter, A., 379
Geller, S. R., 114
Genesee, F., 346
Georgiades, A., 459
Gepshtein, S., 175
Gerberding, J. L., 458–459
Gerlach, F. M., 673
German, T. P., 244, 354–355

Gerrard, C., 7
Gersh, R. D., 446
Gershoff, E. T., 20, 144, 274
Gertz, M., 642
Gerwood, J. B., 549
Geschwind, N., 77, 93
Giarratano, J. G., 336
Gibb, R, 63
Gibbs, A. L., 374
Gibson, E. J., 179
Gibson, K. R., 73
Gibson, P., 309
Gielen, U. P., 34, 569
Gifford, R., 692
Gila, A., 382
Gilbert, L. A., 605
Gilbert, P., 560
Giliovich, T., 664
Gillespie, C. F., 467
Gillespie, M., 239
Gilligan, C., 132–133
Gillin, J. C., 230
Gilman, S. E., 598
Gilula, N. B., 208
Ginet, M., 295
Ginott, H., 145
Ginsberg, D. L., 570
Ginsburg, P. E., 657
Giuseppe, R., 556
Gladwell, M., 361
Glanz, K., 235
Glaser, R., 464, 488
Glass, C. A., 551
Glazer, K., 487
Gleason, J. B., 118
Glick, P., 648, 649–650
Glisky, M. L., 342
Glomb, T. M., 675
Glover, G., 395
Glover, R. J., 133
Glueckauf, R. L., 551
Gobert, F., 316, 352
Gobet, F., 292
Goel, V., 77
Goernert, P. N., 690
Goffin, R. D., 21
Gogate, L. J., 120
Goh, B. E., 358
Goldberg, C., 646
Goldberg, R., 235
Golden, J., 101
Golden, T. D., 674
Goldenberg, C., 564
Goldenberg, R., 564
Goldfried, M. R., 598
Golding, J. M., 695
Goldman, H. H., 572
Goldstein, E. B., 156, 159, 288–289, 292–293
Goldstein, N. J., 634
Goldstein-Alpern, N., 119
Golelli, G., 556
Goleman, H. H., 84
Gollub, R. L., 224
Gonzalez, R., 239
Good, G. E., 401
Goodall, J., 46, 47
Goode, E., 626
Goodman, S. H., 672, 674
Goodman-Delahunty, J., 695
Goodwin, J., 542
Goodwin, R. D., 101
Goodwin, S. A., 588
Gooren, L. J. G., 384
Goparaju, S. K., 377

Gopnik, A., 106–108, 118, 127
Göransson, S., 414
Gordijn, M. C. M., 374
Gordis, E. B., 659
Gordon, A. K., 630
Gordon, L. R., 632
Gordon, T., 145
Gore, J. C., 79
Gorman, J. M., 467, 572
Gorny, G., 63
Gosling, S., 422
Gosling, S. D., 33, 415
Gosselin, F., 400
Gosselin, I., 62
Göthe, K., 289
Gottesman, I. I., 524
Gottman, J. M., 615–616
Gould, D., 698
Gould, E., 63
Gould, K., 137
Gowers, S., 382
Grabe, M., 264
Grabowski, T., 347
Grace, M. K., 377
Gracia, G., 523
Grack, C., 652
Grafman, J., 77
Graham, C. H., 159
Grainer-Deferre, C., 100
Grande, T., 567
Grandner, M. A., 207
Granholm, E., 235
Granrud, C. E., 174
Grant, B. F., 510
Grant, I., 239
Graves, J. L., 665
Gravetter, F. J., 710
Gray, J. M., 386
Gray, T. W., 690
Graziottin, A., 595
Greaves, W., 348
Green, C., 310
Green, J. D., 403
Green, L. R., 436
Green, M. C., 643
Green-Paden, L. D., 559
Greenberg, D. L., 310
Greenberg, J. M., 609
Greenberg, R. P., 217, 479
Greene, B., 529
Greene, D., 392
Greene, E., 695
Greene, J., 566
Greenfield, P. M., 329, 366
Greenglass, E. R., 465
Greenwald, A. G., 664
Greenwald, R., 556
Greenwood, J. G., 90
Greenwood, J. J. D., 90
Greenwood, K. M., 295
Greer, D. S., 459–460
Gregory, R., 191–192
Gregory, R. L., 173
Grenier, G., 615
Griffin, D. W., 625
Griffin, W. A., 565
Griffin-Fennell, F., 535
Griffiths, R. R., 233
Grigorenko, E. L., 328, 334, 336–337, 365–366, 665
Grigsby, T. D., 628
Grob, C. S., 205
Grobstein, P., 151
Grol, R., 673
Gross, A. M., 606

Gross, C. G., 63
Gross, J. J., 405–406
Gruber, A. J., 239
Grubin, D., 397
Gruman, J., 458
Grunbaum, J. A., 459–460
Gruneberg, M., 319
Gruner, C. R., 344
Gruzelier, J. H., 288
Grzegorek, J. L., 424
Gual, P., 382
Guarnaccia, P. J. J., 503
Guastello, J. L., 448, 591
Guay, F., 628
Guéguen, N., 629, 634
Guevremont, D. C., 261, 553–544, 559
Guez, J., 305
Guffey, M. E., 678–679
Guilleminault, C., 215
Gullette, D. L., 387
Gullette, E. C., 459
Gully, B. L., 129
Gump, B. B., 622
Gümüs, K., 160
Gunderson, J., 452
Gündogan, N., 160
Gunnar, M. R., 112
Gunnarsdóttir, M., 551
Gunthert, K. C., 488
Gur, R. E., 526
Guralnik, O., 512
Gurin, J., 565
Gurung, R., 458, 468, 484
Gustavsson, J. P., 414
Gutheil, T. G., 70
Gwaltney, C. J., 234

Haas, B. W., 407
Haas, L. J., 550
Haber, L., 315–316
Haber, R. N., 315–316
Haber, S., 687
Haddad, S., 50
Haddock, G., 518
Hadley, C. N., 392
Hadwin, A. F., 318
Haenshel, C., 288
Hafemeister, T. L., 694, 695
Hafer, C. L., 664
Haggard, P., 61
Haidt, J., 440
Haier, R. J., 70, 79
Haines, M. M., 687
Hains, S. M. J., 100
Hajek, P., 554
Halbert, J., 170
Haley, A., 337
Hall, C., 242
Hall, E. T., 216, 683
Hall, J., 560
Hall, R., 390
Hallahan, D. P., 332, 334
Halliwell, W. R., 698
Halonen, J. S., 4, 318
Halpren, D. F., 587
Ham, C., 461
Hamilton, A., 609
Hamilton, C., 703
Hamilton, V. L., 637
Hammer, J. C., 610, 628
Hampson, E., 657
Hancock, P. A., 386–387
Handsfield, H. H., 609
Handwerk, M. L., 559

Hanewald, G. J. F. P., 595
Hanley, J. S., 439
Hanrahan, P., 503
Hansen, C. J., 492
Hansen, R., 297
Hanson, M. A., 678
Hanton, S., 390
Harber, K. D., 44
Harden, B. J., 102
Hardin, G., 690
Harding, D. J., 49
Harding, R. W., 468
Hardy, G. E., 566
Hare, R., 508
Hari, R., 91
Harkavy-Fredman, J., 524
Harker, L., 415
Harlow, H. F., 277
Harlow, J. M., 48
Harlow, M. K., 277
Harlow, N., 603
Harlow, T. F., 479
Harner, D. E., 382
Harrigan, J. A., 402, 683
Harrington, K., 280
Harris, C., 626
Harris, J. A., 657
Harris, J. C., 544
Harris, J. R., 107
Harrison, K., 382
Harrison, P. J., 524
Harrold, J. A., 377–378
Hart, C. L., 238, 240
Hart, D., 132
Hart, S. L., 550
Hart-Johnson, T., 442
Hartgens, F., 88
Hartlep, K. L., 293
Hartman, P., 22
Harvey, P., 675
Harway, M., 565
Harwood, R. L., 115
Hasbrouck, J. E., 659
Hasen, N. B., 566
Hasher, L., 307
Hashibe, M., 239
Hashimoto, I., 77
Hasin, D. S., 235, 510
Haslam, M., 343
Hass, S. L., 479
Hatfield, E., 605
Hauck, F. R., 216
Havercamp, S. M., 390, 438
Hay, D., 658
Haydel, K. F., 660
Hayden, F., 578
Hayes, C., 347
Hazlett, E., 70–71
Hazuda, H. P., 477
Head, K., 79
Hebb, D. O., 98
Hebl, M. R., 605
Hecht, H., 510
Hecht, M. L., 130, 405
Hedensjö, L., 551
Hedge, J. W., 678
Hedges, M., 567
Heiby, E. M., 434
Heil, S. H., 240
Heilman, M. E., 589
Heiman, J. R., 612–613
Heine, S. J., 418
Heinrichs, R. W., 521
Heiple, B., 598
Heisel, M. J., 536

Helgeson, V. S., 587, 591
Hellekson, C. J., 532
Hellerstein, D. J., 542
Hellige, J. B., 91
Helson, R., 363
Hendrick, C., 625
Hendrick, S. S., 625
Heninger, M., 535
Henman, L. D., 494
Henningsen, D. D., 632
Henningsen, M. L. M., 632
Hepper, P. G., 91
Hergenhahn, B. R., 27, 257, 414
Heriot, S. A., 554
Herman, C. P., 380, 382
Herman, S. M., 216
Hermann, B., 297, 312
Hernstein, R., 366
Herrmann, D. J., 319
Herscovitch, P., 210
Herxheimer, A., 374
Herzog, T. A., 283
Hess, L., 559
Hess, T. M., 630
Heston, J. D., 572
Hettich, P. I., 318
Hewitt, P. L., 536
Hewstone, M., 630
Hickling, E. J., 254
Higbee, K. L., 324
Higgins, M., 407
Higgins, S. T., 240
Higham, P. A., 7
Hilgard, E., 220
Hill, E. A., 120
Hilsenroth, M. J., 448–449
Hinds, T. R., 239
Hinkel, E., 346
Hinterberger, T., 85
Hintzman, D. L., 304
Hipworth, K., 263
Hiripi, E., 233
Hirstein, W., 70, 74
Hiscock, M., 587
Hite, S., 601
Hladkyi, S., 4
Hobson, J. A., 210, 217–218, 244
Hochman, K. M., 524, 525–527, 570
Hochreich, D. J., 433
Hochstenbach, J., 79
Hocker, J. L., 651
Hodell, E. C., 695
Hodgson, R., 511
Hodson, G., 650–651
Hofer, B. K., 5
Hoff, C., 119
Hoffart, E., 545
Hoffman, H. G., 556
Hogan, E. H., 232
Hogben, D., 323
Hoge, E. H., 512
Hogg, M. A., 643
Hohwy, J., 191
Holding, D. H., 318
Holland, C. R., 366
Holland, H. L., 295
Holland, J., 676
Hollendonner, J. K., 458
Holling, H., 333, 358, 360
Holmes, J. G., 289, 625
Holmes, M., 587
Holmes, P. S., 342
Holmes, T., 482
Holstein, M., 141
Holterhus, P. M., 587

Holtz, A., 628
Holzinger, B., 244
Hong, H.-W., 108
Honomichl, R., 354
Honzik, C. H., 276
Hooley, J., 498
Hopkins, W. D., 348
Horgan, J., 61
Horn, J., 448
Horn, R. R., 263
Horne, R. S. C., 215
Horney, K., 30
Hornick, B. A., 232, 512
Horowitz, I. A., 695
Hortman, G., 394
Horwood, L. J., 101
Hosch, H. M., 198
Hough, L. M., 676
Houlette, M., 653
Houlihan, D., 690
Houston-Price, C., 119
Hovath, L. S., 387
Hovis, J., 159
Howard, I. P., 179, 180
Howard, J. L., 677
Howe, R. D., 703
Hoyte, M., 224, 493
Hsia, Y., 159
Hsiao, W., 695
Huang, P., 550
Hubbard, R. L., 232
Hubble, M. A., 579
Hubel, D. H., 150
Hübner, R., 76
Huesmann, L. R., 279, 658–659
Huff, J. W., 674
Hughes, J. N., 659
Hughes, J. R., 233, 238
Hughes, M., 598
Huijbregts, S. C., 101
Hume, K., 208
Hunt, H., 360
Hunt, R. R., 352
Hunter, E., 646
Hunter, J. E., 676
Hunter, J. P., 170
Hupp, S. D., 559
Hustedt, J. T., 642
Hutchinson, S. R., 50, 83
Hyare, H., 188
Hyde, J. S., 31, 384, 582, 584, 602
Hyman, R., 195–196
Hysenbegasi, A., 479

Iacono, W. G., 508
Ida, Y., 92
Idel, H., 464
Iguchi, Y., 77
Ikemoto, S., 261
Ilardi, B., 440
Impett, E. A., 407, 489
Impey, S., 239
Inati, S., 340
Inch, R., 587
Indermaur, D., 468
Iosif, A., 54
Ironson, G., 464
Irwin, M. R., 464
Isberner, F. R., 606
Ishihara, K., 207
Israelson, D., 170
Ivanco, T. L., 313
Iversen, L., 230, 232
Izard, C., 108, 404

Jaber-Filho, J. A., 572
Jablonski, N. G., 665
Jackendoff, R., 347
Jacklin, C. N., 589
Jackson, D. C., 464
Jackson, D. N., 657
Jackson, P., 297
Jackson, S. L., 14, 23, 25, 46
Jackson, T., 452
Jacob, A, 112, 191
Jacobs, M., 427, 431, 477, 544
Jacobs, M. K., 30, 567
Jacobs, S. R., 466
Jacobsen, P. B., 251, 379
Jacobson, N. S., 578
Jacomb, P. A., 598
Jacquet, A.-Y., 100
Jaffe, J., 119
James, W., 27, 31, 402
Jamison, K. R., 535–536
Jang, D. P., 556
Janis, J., 673
Janssen, S. A., 62
Janus, C. L., 595–596, 601, 604–605
Janus, S. S., 595–596, 601, 604–605
Jarvin, L, 328
Jarvinen, J., 397
Jarvis, M. J., 233
Jasnow, M. D., 119, 483
Jawahar, I. M., 628
Jay, T. B., 345
Jaycox, L. H., 467
Jefcott, H. A., Jr., 359
Jeffery, R. W., 381
Jenni, O. C., 207
Jensen, A. R., 366
Jeong, G.-H., 387
Jerabek, I., 306
Jerome, A., 234, 283
Jessell, T. M., 84
Jessen, F., 232
Job, R. F. S., 687
Joe, G. W., 232
Jogerst, G. J., 469
Johansson, H., 452
John, O. P., 415, 416, 418, 435
Johnson, B. T., 166, 641
Johnson, D., 206
Johnson, E. O., 233
Johnson, K. E., 342
Johnson, K. J., 188
Johnson, L. D., 136
Johnson, M. H., 106
Johnson, M. J. M., 483
Johnson, S. M., 283, 337
Johnson, T. J., 235
Johnson, V., 600, 602, 612–613, 615
Johnson, W. A., 152
Joiner, T. E., Jr., 536
Jones, C., 446
Jones, D. N., 624
Jones, E. E., 630
Jones, G. V., 91
Jones, J., 595, 598, 604
Jones, L., 388
Jones, M. E., 606
Jones, M. K., 560
Jones, S. S., 108
Jones, T. S., 683
Jones, W. H., 452
Jonsson, E., 49, 524
Jordan, C. L., 587
Jorm, A. F., 598
Joughin, N., 382
Jourard, S. M., 616

Jouvet, M., 206
Jowett, G. S., 645
Joyce, P., 549
Judge, T. A., 424
Julian, L., 550
Juliano, L. M., 233
Julien, E., 628
Julien, R. M., 227, 230–233, 238, 240, 569
Jullien, C., 572
Jung, C., 30, 416
Jung, R. E., 79
Jussim, L., 44
Justice, J. B., Jr., 261, 564–565

Kaas, J. H., 170
Kabat-Zinn, J., 224
Kabnick, K., 379
Kagan, J., 103, 107, 118, 365, 414
Kahana, M. J., 300
Kahler, C. W., 235
Kahneman, D., 50, 361–362
Kalat, J. W., 58, 69, 83, 98, 230, 394, 396, 400, 416
Kalish, D., 276
Kallgren, C. A., 392, 629
Kallio, S., 220–221
Kalliomaeki-Levanto, T., 673
Kaman, D., 392
Kamimori, G. H., 206
Kamin, L. J., 337, 366
Kamphaus, R. W., 445
Kan, S. M., 92
Kanda, K., 424
Kandel, D. B., 240
Kandel, E. R., 84, 312–313
Kann, L., 459–460
Kanwisher, N. G., 152, 341
Kaplan, A. H., 545
Kaplan, H. S., 614
Kaplan, P. S., 115, 118
Kaplar, M. E., 630
Kapleau, P., 199
Kapur, N., 317
Kapur, S., 525
Karasz, A., 609
Karim, A. A., 85
Karlins, M., 650
Karmaniola, A., 112
Karnes, F. A., 366
Kasen, S., 482
Kasimatis, M., 395
Kasser, T., 389, 391
Kassin, S. M., 198, 397, 630
Kataria, S., 215
Katkin, E. S., 253
Katz, B., 572
Katz, J., 169–170
Katz, P. A., 648
Kauffman, J. M., 332, 334
Kaufman, A. S., 328
Kaufman, J. H., 183–184
Kaufman, L., 183–184
Kaufmann, J., 582
Kawai, K., 379
Kawakami, K., 650–651
Kay, G. G., 445
Kearney, A. J., 575–576
Kearney, C. A., 112
Kebbell, M. R., 295
Keel, P., 503
Keeley, S., 20
Keller, M. C., 623
Kellerman, A. L., 658
Kelley, H. H., 187

Kellner, C. H., 571
Kelly, I. W., 22
Kelly, J. R., 628
Kelly, M. P., 445, 614
Kelly, T. L., 206
Keltner, D., 415, 664
Kemeny, M. E., 479
Kempermann, G., 63
Kennaway, D. J., 87
Kennedy, P., 689
Kenneth, M., 235
Kenny, P. J., 261
Kenward, R., 548
Kerr, M., 2
Kerr, N. L., 694
Kershaw, P., 607
Kessler, R., 233
Kessler, R. C., 137
Kestler, L., 524, 525–527, 570
Ketcham, K., 295
Kety, S. S., 519
Keveri, M. K., 300
Keyes, C. L. M., 440
Keysers, C., 288
Khatchadourian, D, 598
Kida, T. E., 20, 23, 54
Kidd, K. K., 328, 366, 665
Kiebel, S., 85
Kiecolt-Glaser, J. K., 464
Kiecolt-Glaser, K. K., 488
Kienstra, D. M., 496
Kigar, D. L., 73
Kiger, L., 366
Kihlstrom, J. F., 342
Kikuchi, Y., 293
Kilcoyne, J., 603
Killen, J. D., 233
Kilpatrick, D., 467
Kim, C., 556
Kim, J., 698
Kim, K., 460
Kim, T. E., 130
Kim-Cohen, J., 114
Kimmel, D., 600
Kimura, T., 77
Kinchen, S., 459–460
King, B. E., 606, 612–615
King, E. G., 605, 695
King, H. E., 84
King, L. A., 493
King, N. J., 253–254
Kingsley, C. H., 85
Kinkead, R., 62
Kinnunen, L. H., 597
Kinsey, A., 594
Kiper, D. C., 159
Kirby, J. R., 318
Kirsch, I., 44, 220–221, 280, 295
Kirveskari, E., 91
Kisamore, J. L., 628
Kiser, L. J., 572
Kisilevsky, B. S., 100
Kitayama, S., 401
Kite, M. E., 588
Kivimaeki, M., 673
Kjellgren, A., 224
Klaiber, J. R., 623
Klatsky, R. L., 703
Klauer, S. G., 46
Klein, B., 551
Klein, K., 493
Kleineidam, C., 464
Kleinke, C. L., 404
Kleinplatz, P. J., 615
Klohnen, E. C., 627

Kloner, R. A., 396
Klosterhalfen, S., 379
Kluender, K. R., 166
Klump, K., 503
Knaus, W. J., 4, 5, 6
Knight, J., 398
Knight, R. T., 77
Knipe, J., 556
Knoops, K. T. B., 459–460
Knop, J., 508
Knutelska, M., 512
Kobos, J. C., 550
Koch, C., 204–205
Koch, W. H., 421
Koegler, P., 91
Koegler, W., 91
Koen, L., 569, 674
Koenigsberg, H. W., 507
Koestner, R., 698
Kofler, W. W., 686
Koger, S. M., 687–688, 690–691
Kohlberg, L., 132
Kohler, S. S., 676, 678
Kohn, C. S., 553
Kohn, J. P., 268
Köke, A., 169
Kolb, B., 63, 79, 85
Kolb, T. M., 108
Koltzenburg, M., 168–169, 383
Koob, G. F., 230
Koons, S. R., 6
Korbin, J. E., 691
Koreen, A., 570
Kornhaber, M. L., 334
Korol, C., 513
Korten, A. E., 598
Koss, M. P., 606–607
Kosslyn, S. M., 220, 315, 340–341
Kosson, D. S., 507
Koszycki, D., 510
Kotkin, M., 565
Kottler, J. A., 561–562, 567
Koutstaal, W., 294
Kovera, M. B., 694
Kowert, P. A., 632
Krakow, B., 215, 244
Krakow, J. K., 215
Krall, E. A., 233
Kramer, D. L., 300
Kramer, R. M., 691
Kramer, S. J., 392
Krantz, D. S., 487, 687
Krause, E. D., 405
Krauss, A., 588–589
Krauss, R. M., 347
Krebs, D. L., 133
Kreek, M. J., 232
Krieschel, S., 510
Kripke, D. F., 207
Krishnan, H. A., 671
Kristof-Brown, A. L., 677
Kromhout, D., 459–460
Krueger, A. B., 50
Krueger, J. I., 417
Kruepke, K. A., 263
Ksir, C. J., 238, 240
Ku, J. H., 556
Kübler-Ross, E., 140
Kubovy, M., 175
Kuehner, C., 530
Kuhl, B., 310
Kuhl, P. K., 106–107, 118, 127
Kuhn, C. M., 232
Kuhn, E., 254
Kühn, K.-W., 232

Kuipers, H., 88
Kulik, J. A., 622
Kulis, S., 130
Kumaran, D., 84
Kumari, V., 526
Kuo, M., 235
Kurokawa, M., 401
Kusseling, F. S., 609
Kwok, K., 397

L'Abate, L., 493
Laan, E., 594–595
LaBar, K. S., 84
LaBerge, L., 207
Labin, D., 649
Laborde, M.-L., 166
Labouvie, E., 235
LaBrie, R. A., 562
Lacayo, A., 230
Lachman, R., 289
Lackner, J. R., 171
Lacy, B. A., 697
Ladd-Franklin, C., 31
Laforge, R. G., 235
Lahortiga, F., 382
Laird, J. D., 404
Lalande, K., 407
Lam, R. W., 531
Lamb, M. E., 115
Lamberg, L., 242–243
Lambert, K. G., 85
Lambert, M. J., 566, 579
Lambert, W. E., 46, 565, 664
Lamerichs-Geelen, M. J. H., 169
Lamkin, D. M., 322
Lampe, S., 449
Lampinen, J. M., 286, 311
Lance, C. E., 444
Landau, J. D., 15
Landy, F. J., 673, 675, 676, 678
Lang, C., 402, 405
Lange, P. J., 508
Langleben, D. D., 70–71, 398
Langone, M. D., 646
Lanzetta, J. T., 665
LaPointe, J. A., 444
Lappin, J. M., 62
Larner, A. J., 168
Larrick, R. P., 657
Larsen McClarty, K., 417
Larsen, R. J., 395, 407, 416, 452
Larson, D., 466
Larson, M. E., 690
Larsson, B., 485
Larsson, H., 100
Larsson, J.-O., 100
Larzelere, R. E., 144, 274
Latané, B., 18, 660–661
Lategan, T. P., 591
LaTour, M. S., 294
Lattal, K. A., 268
Lattal, K. M., 312
Lau, T. Y., 674
Laub, J. H., 508
Laumann, E. O., 596, 604
Laurent, G., 166
Lavie, P., 205, 209
Lawson, H. M., 623
Lawson, M. J., 323
Lawson, R. B., 632
Lay, C., 418
Lazar, S. W., 223–224
Lazarus, R. S., 404, 405, 465–466, 475
Lazev, A. B., 283

le Moal, M., 92
Le Roux, C., 378
Leal, M. C., 166
Leavens, D. A., 348
LeBerge, S., 244
LeBlanc, G., 126–127
Leck, K., 623
Lecrubier, Y., 525
Lederman, S. J., 703
Ledley, C., 624
LeDoux, J. E., 84, 429, 467
Lee, D. H., 73
Lee, J. E., 232, 235
Lee, J. M., 7, 556
Lee, L. H. L., 83
Lee, M., 450
Lee, S., 188, 631
Leeming, F. C., 691
Leenaars, A. A., 536
Leeper, M. R., 392
Lefkowitz, E. S., 591
Lefrançois, G. R., 262, 276, 278
Lehman, C. M., 678–679
Lehman, D. R., 34, 379–381
Lehmann, H., 311
Leichtman, M., 448
Leikind, B., 54
Leiter, M. P., 466
Lejeune, L., 179
Lejuez, C. W., 465, 553, 555
Lench, H. C., 660
Lenton, A. P., 594
Lenzenweger, M. F., 524
Leonard, A., 508
Leonard, K. E., 657
Leonard, T., 228
Leor, J., 396
Lepore, F. E., 190
Lepore, S. J., 692
Lercher, P., 686
Lerner, J. S., 458, 479, 488
Leslie, K., 244
Lesser, I., 530, 694
Lessow-Hurley, J., 346
Lester, D., 535, 536, 598
Lettvin, J. Y., 151
Leukefeld, C., 387
Levant, R. F., 401, 590–591
LeVay, S., 585–587, 597
Levenson, R. W., 404
Levenston, G. K., 508
Levesque, M. J., 624
Levett, L. M., 694
Levi, D. M., 166, 198
Levin, B. E., 373
Levin, D. T., 305
Levin, J. R., 322
Levin, L., 626
Levin, R., 215
Levine, B. E., 75, 687
Levine, C., 136
Levine, J. A., 398
Levine, M., 382
Levine, R. V., 682
Levinson, D. J., 138, 648–649
Levinson, J. D., 138
Levitan, L., 244
Levy, J., 91
Lewin, R., 348
Lewis, J. B., 607
Lewis, M., 111
Lewis, P. S., 672, 674
Leyendecker, B., 115
Li, D., 377
Libby, J., 507

Liberman, R. P., 560
Lichstein, K. L., 213–214
Lichtenstein, P., 100
Lichter, D. T., 624
Lichtman, A. H., 238
Liddell, S. K., 346
Lidz, C. W., 523
Lieberman, D. A., 288, 294, 296, 298, 311, 322
Liebert, R. M., 107
Lierens, R., 542
Lievens, F., 678
Light, K. C., 62
Liguori, A., 233
Lilienfeld, S. O., 23, 53, 195, 376
Lin, J., 605
Linares-Clemente, P., 313
Lindemann, B., 167–168
Linden, W., 379, 492
Lindenbaum, L. E., 702
Linderoth, B., 169
Lindsay, E. W., 115
Lindskold, S., 694
Lipsch, J. S. M., 169
Lipsey, M. W., 566
Lister, J. J., 165
Little, B. R., 441
Littlewood, R., 645
Littner, M., 214
Liu, G., 397
Liu, H., 378
Liu, J., 377
Liu, X., 77
Liu, Y., 378
Llorente, R., 101
Lochner, C., 569, 674
Locke, B. D., 606
Loeber, R., 658
Loehlin, J. C., 416
Loftus, E. F., 286, 294–295, 309
Loftus, G., 153, 286
Lohr, J. M., 23
LoLordo, V. M., 477–478, 530
London, E. D., 77
London, M., 674
Long, E. C., 616
Long, J. D., 576
Long, V. O., 591
López, S. R., 503
Lord, M. J., 615
Lorenz, K., 656
Loughead, J. W., 70–71
Lovaas, O., 559
Lovallo, W. R., 487
Love, S. R., 257
Low, K G., 531
Low, S. M., 684
Lucas, F., 379
Luce, G. G., 206
Luchins, D. J., 503
Lucidi, F., 216
Lucido, D. J., 687
Luck, S. J., 311
Ludmann, E. J., 550
Ludwig, T. D., 690
Luminet, O., 310
Lumley, M. A., 370, 405
Lundh, L., 452
Luo, S., 627
Luria, A., 316
Lussier, J. P., 240
Lustig, C., 307
Luyben, P. D., 263
Lykken, D. T., 397–398, 416
Lynam, D., 387

Lynch, C., 91
Lynch, J. E., 549
Lynch, K. B., 114
Lynch, T. R., 405
Lynn, A. L., 258
Lynn, S. J., 23, 220–221
Lyons, A. C., 456, 463–464
Lyons, M. A., 387
Lyubomirsky, S., 488

Ma, J., 306
Maas, J., 206, 214
Mabry, E., 695
Maccoby, E. E., 589
Macdonald, S. E., 269
MacGregor, B., 140
Maciejewski, P. K., 512
Mack, A., 152
Mackie, D. M., 664–665
Mackin, R. S., 491
MacKinnon, D. P., 295
Mackinnon, L. T., 464
Mackintosh, N. J., 249
Macklin, C. B., 4
MacLeod, C. M., 345
MacLin, M. K., 340, 352
MacLin, O. H., 340, 352
Macmillan, R., 658
MacPherson, S., 306
Maddi, S. R., 488
Maddock, J. E., 235–236
Maddox, W. T., 342, 650
Madge, A., 289
Madsen, L., 397
Maguire, E. A., 84, 317
Mah, K., 600–601
Mahadevan, R., 316–317
Mahalik, J. R., 606
Mahay, J., 604
Maheu, M. M., 550
Mahler, H. I. M., 622
Mahowald, M. W., 214
Maier, N. R. F., 470, 530
Maier, W., 232
Mailis-Gagnon, A., 170
Mainland, J., 166
Maixner, W., 62
Makela, E., 690
Malamuth, N., 606
Malaspina, D., 525
Maldonado-Molina, M., 230
Manalo, E., 322
Mancini-Marïe, A., 518
Mandal, M. K., 92
Mandler, J. M., 106
Mane, K. K., 17
Mangan, M. A., 214
Mangels, J. A., 305
Mann, C. C., 689
Mann, N., 379
Mannarino, A. P., 603
Manne, S. L., 251
Manning, M., 43
Manschreck, T. C., 520
Mansouri, A., 518
Manstead, A. S. R., 401
Mantryla, T., 318
Marchman, V. A., 118
Marco, E. M., 101
Marcus, E., 544–545
Marcus-Newhall, A., 658
Margoliash, D., 204
Margolin, G., 659
Margolin, J., 467

Maria, C. Z., 232
Marin, M., 91
Mark, D., 487
Markou, A., 261
Markowitz, J. C., 545
Marks, D. F., 194–195
Marks, J. S., 458–459
Marks, L. E., 340
Markus, H., 441
Markus, H. R., 401, 630
Marmarosh, C., 628
Marqeuz, C., 598
Marsella, A. J., 685
Marsh, H. W., 479
Marshall, D. G., 460
Marshall, P. H., 322, 363
Marshall, R. D., 467
Marsiglia, F. F., 130
Marston, A., 244
Marston, W., 397
Martens, R., 22
Martin, A. J., 479
Martin, B. R., 238
Martin, C. L., 436, 590, 594
Martin, E. K., 606
Martin, G. T., 254, 282, 554
Martin, L. L., 404, 479
Martin, L. R., 424
Martin, S., 671
Martin, W. L. B., 92
Martinez-Gonzalez, M. A., 382
Martinko, M. J., 675
Martino, G., 340
Martino, S. C., 239
Martins, E. P., 17
Martuza, R. L., 571
Marvin, R. S., 112, 304
Marx, B. P., 606
Marx, D. M., 623
Mascialino, B., 207
Mashour, G. A., 571
Masi, G., 112
Maslach, C., 591
Maslow, A., 30, 31, 198, 390–391, 438–439
Massaccesi, S., 106
Masse, L. C., 130, 240
Mastach, C., 466
Masten, A. S., 114
Masters, W., 600, 602, 612–613, 615
Mateika, J. H., 207
Matheny, K. B., 494
Matochik, J. A., 77
Matossian, M. K., 542
Matson, J. L., 257
Matthews, G., 415, 421
Matthews, M. S., 346
Matthews, P. H., 346
Matthews, R., 467
Mattock, A., 106, 174
May, C. P., 307
May, J. G., 171, 175
Mayberg, H. S., 512
Maybery, M. T., 301
Mayer, A. R., 507
Mayer, J., 407
Mayer, J. D., 419
Mazur, J. E., 256, 258
Mazzoni, G., 295
McAdams, D. P., 415, 419, 441
McAlister, A. L., 550, 665
McAuliffe, T. L., 108
McBride, W. J., 261
McCabe, M. P., 382
McCall, W. V., 571

McCarley, R., 217–218
McCarthy, B. W., 615–616
McCarthy, C. J., 494
McCarthy, K., 22
McCartney, G. R., 91
McCartney, S., 607
McCeney, M. K., 487
McClelland, C. L., 674
McClelland, D. C., 389, 435, 494
McClelland, J. L., 336, 366
McClelland, L., 382, 687–688
McClure, J. B., 234
McCluskey, U., 564
McConnel, N., 263
McConnell, W., 469
McCrady, B. S., 235
McCrae, R. R., 416, 421, 423
McCullagh, J. F., 90
McCullough, S., 347
McDaniel, M. A., 4, 322
McDermott, C., 588
McDermott, K. B., 295
McDonald, J. K., 263
McDonough, L., 106
McDowell, N. K., 458, 479, 488
McElduff, P., 579
McEvoy, C., 295, 694
McGaugh, J. L., 311
McGregor, D., 671
McGregor, I., 441
McGue, M., 416, 508
McGuffin, P., 531
McGuire, L., 464, 488
McIntosh, B., 632
McIntosh, W. D., 479
McKay, A., 384
McKay, G. D., 143, 145
McKeever, L. M., 160
McKeever, W. F., 91
McKelton, D., 695
McKenna, K. Y. A., 625
McKenna, M. W., 280
McKenzie, K., 535
McKim, W. A., 234–235
McKone, E., 306
McLaren, W., 233
McLean, N. J., 382
McLewin, L. A., 512
McLoyd, V. C., 274
McMahon, M., 295
McMahon, S., 168–169, 383
McMenamin, J. P., 550
McMullen, L. M., 530
McNally, R. J., 210, 310
McNamara, D. C., 324
McNay, E. C., 377
McNeill, D., 300
McQueen, V. K., 261
McRobbie, H., 554
Mead, M., 589
Medhus, E., 115
Medin, D. L., 343
Mehrabian, A., 407
Mehta, J. D., 49
Meichenbaum, D., 494
Meier, P. S., 579
Melin, L., 485
Mellalieu, S. D., 390
Mellinger, J., 85
Melnick, M., 49
Meltzoff, A. N., 105–107, 118, 127
Melzack, R., 169–170
Memon, A., 198, 301
Memon, R., 295
Mendes, W. B., 489, 493

Mendez, M., 76
Mendolia, M., 476
Meneses, G. D., 263
Mensour, B., 518
Menzel, P., 689
Menzies, R. G., 560
Mercer, J., 112
Merritt, J. M., 217
Mervis, C. B., 342
Mesmer, F., 220
Mesquita, B., 401
Messer, S. B., 545
Messick, D. M., 664–665, 691
Messinger, D. S., 108
Metha, A., 144
Metts, S., 623
Metz, J., 597
Metzler, C. W., 240
Meyer, G. J., 445
Meyers, L., 550
Michael, D., 263
Michael, R., 596
Michaels, S., 596
Michalak, E. E., 531
Michalko, M., 333
Michel, C., 306
Michelangelo, I., 232
Michello, J., 573
Mielke, H. W., 519
Mignot, E., 215
Milgram, D. L., 6, 43
Milgram, R. M., 357
Milgram, S., 620, 630, 636–637, 687
Milich, R., 387
Miljkovitch, R., 112
Millepiedi, S., 112
Miller, D. T., 613, 622, 660
Miller, G. A., 292, 344
Miller, G. E., 464
Miller, N. E., 433–435, 469, 471–472, 648, 658
Miller, P., 511
Miller, R., 624–625
Miller, S. D., 579
Miller, W. R., 237
Milling, L. S., 295
Millman, R. B., 88
Millrood, D. L., 207
Milner, B., 312
Miltenberger, R. E., 553, 559
Miltner, W. H. R., 510
Milton, J., 195–196
Minami, T., 43, 579
Minda, J. P., 343
Mineka, S., 498
Minnes, S., 239
Minors, D., 208
Minton, H. L., 31
Miotto, K., 235
Mira, C. B., 530, 694
Mirabile, R., 644
Mirsky, A. F., 49, 524, 542
Mischel, W., 414, 425, 432–433
Mistlberger, R. E., 374
Mitchell, D. G. V., 54, 508
Mitchell, K., 215, 263
Mitru, G., 207
Miura, H., 379
Miyake, A., 289
Mize, J., 115
Mo, L., 354
Moerman, D. E., 44
Moffitt, T. E., 114, 531
Mogg, K., 188
Moghaddam, B., 525

Mohr, D. C., 550
Mohr, J. J., 598
Moise-Titus, J., 279–280, 658–659
Mokdad, A. H., 458–459
Molenaar, J. C., 587
Moltz, H., 597
Monahan, J., 523
Monsma, E. V., 698
Montagna, P., 214
Monteith, M. J., 664, 694–695
Montgomery, P., 214
Moody, J., 607
Moor, J., 335
Moore, C. M., 216
Moore, J. L., 333
Moore, K., 199
Moore, K. A., 466
Moore, P. J., 622
Moore, S. A., 310
Moore-Ede, M. C., 207
Moras, K., 565
Moreno, E., 101
Moreno, J. L., 564
Moretti, M. M., 441
Morey, L. C., 579
Morgan, F. H., 468
Morgan, J. P., 657–658
Morgenstern, H., 239
Morgenstern, J., 235
Morisse, D., 559
Moritz, A. P., 396
Morris, M. W., 631
Morris, P. E., 322
Morris, T., 698
Morrison, R. G., 341
Morse, J. Q., 405
Morsella, E., 347
Mortweet, S. L., 435
Mosher, W. D., 595, 598, 604
Mosier, J., 564
Moskowitz, J. T., 465, 468
Moss, J., 168
Most, S. B., 152, 175
Motivala, S. J., 464
Moun, M. K., 424
Mucci, M., 112
Muchinsky, P. M., 675–676
Muhamad, R., 620
Mukamal, K., 458
Mulder, T., 79
Mullani, N., 239
Muller, R. T., 512
Muller, S. P., 85
Mundy, A., 652
Mundy, P., 108
Munir, F., 513
Munoz, R. F., 237
Munsey, C., 36, 578
Muris, P., 253–254
Murphy, J. M., 261, 348
Murphy, M. A., 559
Murray, B., 378, 381, 550
Murray, C., 366
Murray, E. J., 493
Murray, H., 448
Murray, J. B., 169, 525
Murray, L., 531
Murray, R. M., 62
Murray, S., 235, 625
Mussen, P. H., 118
Musso, M., 85
Mustanski, B. S., 597
Myers, H. F., 530, 694

Nagasaka, T., 452
Nagel, T, 205
Nairne, J. S., 292, 306–307
Naitoh, P., 206
Nakamichi, M., 46, 75–76
Nakamura, J., 386, 392
Nakashima, K., 379
Nash, H. M., 559
Natarajan, L., 239
Nathan, P. J., 312
Nau, S. D., 213–214
Naveh-Benjamin, M., 305
Navracruz, L. C., 660
Neale, J. M., 524
Neale, V. L., 46
Neath, I., 288, 292–293, 302, 307, 316, 319, 322, 324
Neave, N., 684
Needles, D. J., 480
Nehlig, A., 232
Neill, D. B., 261, 564–565
Neisser, U., 365, 367
Nelson, C., 664
Nelson, C. A., 102
Nelson, C. E., 448
Nelson, N. M., 590
Nelson, T. D., 139, 648
Nemeroff, C. B., 467, 512
Neter, E., 21
Neubert, M. J., 672
Neufeld, P., 198
Neufeld, R. W. J., 521
Neuman, G. A., 448
Neumeister, A., 532
Nevid, J. S., 529, 587, 597–598, 617
Newby-Clark, I. R., 210
Newcomb, T. M., 643
Newman, A. W., 295
Newman, J. L., 675
Newman, M. E. J., 652
Newport, E. L., 347
Nezu, A. M., 381
Nezworski, M. T., 195, 376, 449
Ng, S. H., 139
Ngu, H., 306
Niaura, R. S., 234, 487
Niccolai, L., 607
Nicholson, I. R., 521
Nickell, J., 23, 53
Nickerson, R., 304
Nida, S. A., 660
Niedzwienska, A., 310
Niehaus, D. J. H., 569
Niehoff, D. J. H., 674
Nielsen, M., 111
Nielsen, S. L., 579
Nielson, D. M., 144
Nilsson, L, 452
Ninomiya, Y., 167
Nisbett, R., 664
Nisbett, R. E., 366–367, 630
Njeri, I., 33, 665
Noble, P., 523
Noland, J. S., 239
Nolen-Hoeksema, S., 502, 530
Norcross, J. C., 549, 567, 579
Nori, G., 378
Norlander, T., 224
Norman, D. A., 1, 701–702
Norman, K. A., 294
Norman, K. L., 701–702
Normann, R. A., 151
Norris, D. G., 289
North, C. S., 496, 498
Norvig, P., 336

Norwood, R. M., 453
Nosek, B. A., 664
Novaco, R., 469
Nowell, P. D., 213
Nowicki, S., 347
Nuechterlein, K. H., 70–71
Nurius, P., 441
Nurnberger, J. I., 284
Nusbaum, H. C., 204
Nyborg, H., 22

Oberauer, K., 289
Oberbracht, C., 567
Obhi, S. S., 61
O'Callaghan, P. M., 559
Ochsner, K. N., 310
O'Conner, M. G., 112
O'Connor, T. G., 304
O'Craven, K. M., 341
Ocshorn, P., 460
Oden, M., 332
O'Donnell, M., 348
Ogilvie, R., 244
Ogles, B. M., 566, 579
Ogloff, J. R. P., 507–508
O'Hara, M. W., 479
O'Hare, T., 235
Ohayon, M. M., 215
O'Keeffe, C., 195–196
Okiishi, J., 579
O'Leary, E., 549
Olds, M. E., 261
Olfson, M., 571
Oliveto, A. H., 233
Ollendick, T. H., 253–254, 560
Olrick, J. T., 112, 304
Olsen, E. A., 301
Olson, E. A., 198
Olson, J. M., 628, 641, 652–653
Olson, L., 64
Olson, M., 257, 414
Olson-Buchanan, J. B., 446
Olszewski, P. K., 377
Omura, K., 407
O'Neil, J. M., 401
O'Neill, H., 159
O'Neill, P., 53
Ones, D. S., 448, 676
Ooki, S., 91
Oordt, M. S., 486
Operskalski, B., 550
Oppliger, P. A., 590
Ord, T. J., 17
Orleans, C. T., 458, 461
Ormay, T., 550
Orne, M. T., 398
Orner, R. J., 549
Ornstein, R., 187
O'Roark, A. M., 450
Orprecio, J., 151
Osborne, V. A., 496
Osei, S. Y., 378
Osguthorpe, R., 263
Oskamp, S., 641–643, 685, 687–688, 690, 692
Osma, J., 556
Ossoff, E. P., 280
Oster, H., 108
Oswald, F. L., 676
Otani, H., 300
Overmeir, J. B., 477
Oyserman, D., 442
Özdemir, P. G., 160

Paavola, M., 572
Pace-Schott, E. F., 210, 217
Page, K., 131
Page, M. P., 289
Paliwal, P., 232
Palm, K., 309
Palmer, D. K., 676
Palmer, J., 294
Palmer, S. E., 175
Palmersheim, K. A., 137
Pals, J. L., 415, 419, 441
Pandey, S., 686
Panizzi, E., 701–702
Pantelis, C., 526
Papa, A., 407
Papa, F. J., 263
Papaeliou, C., 92
Papanicolaou, A. C., 311
Papasouiotis, O., 228
Papirman, Y., 630
Pappas, T., 263
Paquette, V., 85, 114
Paradis, C. M., 310
Paradis, J., 346
Parent, S., 101
Park, D. C., 304, 440, 671
Parke, R. D., 103, 115
Parker, A., 244, 306
Parker, J. D. A., 407
Parker, K. C. H., 556
Pascual, A., 629, 634
Passarello, L. C., 602
Passman, R. H., 111
Pasupathi, M., 133
Patrick, C. J., 508
Patterson, C. J., 597
Patton, J., 334
Paulhus, D. L., 417
Pauli-Magnus, C., 567
Paulsson, T., 244
Pavlidis, I., 398
Pavlov, I., 31, 249
Payne, D., 319
Pear, J., 282
Pedersen, C. A., 62
Pedersen, N. L., 414
Pedersen, W. C., 469
Peers, D., 22
Pefors, A., 118
Pelletier, R. S. T., 4
Pelton, T., 697
Pemack, D., 282
Penco, M. A., 207
Penfield, W., 293
Penick, J. M., 494
Penn, D. L., 532
Pennebaker, J. W., 405, 493
Penner, L. A., 662
Penrod, S. D., 301
Peplau, L. A., 594
Peracio, N., 587
Perkrun, R. H., 4
Perlman, D., 624–625, 694
Perls, F., 243, 549
Perreault, S., 648
Perrett, D. I., 288
Perri, M. G., 381
Perrin, A., 459–460
Perry, R. P., 4, 477
Perry, Z. W., 650
Persons, J., 560
Pervin, L. A., 418, 435
Pesant, N., 216
Pescatello, L. S., 460
Pete, E., 379

Peters, R. J., 665
Peters, W. A., 651
Petersen, A., 46
Peterson, C., 440, 478, 488
Peterson, L. R., 292
Peterson, M. J., 292
Peterson, S. E., 318
Peterson, T. R., 404
Petit, D., 207
Petrie, T. A., 699
Petruzzi, D. C., 388
Pett, M. A., 483
Pettit, G. S., 115
Phillips, D. P., 397
Phillips, D. S., 316
Phillips, K. W., 674
Phinney, J. S., 130
Piaget, J., 122–125
Pickel, K. L., 198
Picone, R. P., 239
Picton, T. W., 305
Piek, J. P., 107–108
Pierce, W. D., 257, 392
Pierrehumbert, B., 112
Pierrel, R., 258
Pierson, J. F., 30
Piliavin, I. M., 661
Piliavin, J. A., 661–662
Pilkonis. P. A., 453
Pillado, O., 130
Pilling, S., 467
Pillow, D. R., 483
Pilon, D. A., 435
Pincus, H. A., 500
Pine, D. S., 570
Pinel, J. P. J., 379–381
Pines, A. M., 466
Pinker, S., 347
Pinsker, H., 542
Pinsky, D., 507
Pividori, D., 106
Pixley, J. E., 137
Pizam, A., 387
Plazzi, G., 214
Pleasant, A., 459–460
Pliner, P., 379
Plous, S., 648
Plug, C., 183–184
Plutchik, R., 394, 409
Podolski, C., 279–280, 658–659
Poggio, T., 188
Poland, J., 500
Polemikos, N., 92
Polich, J., 223
Polivy, J., 380, 382
Pollner, M., 444
Pollock, V. E., 469, 508
Pomaki, G., 628
Pomeroy, W., 594
Poole, W. K., 396
Pope, H. G., 239
Porter, B. E., 691
Porteus, J., 632
Posda, G., 112
Posey, A., 415
Posluszny, S., 458
Potenza, M. N., 230, 562
Potter, J., 415
Powell, A. A., 661–662
Powell, A. L., 269, 382
Powell, F. C., 140
Prasad, S., 191
Pratarelli, M. E., 421
Preckel, F., 333, 358, 360
Premack, A. J., 347–348

Prenick, D., 347–348
Preson, C. C., 460
Prest, R. G., 215
Prigerson, H. G., 512
Priluck, R., 251–252
Prinz, W., 105
Pritchard, M., 554
Prizmic, Z., 407
Prkachin, K. M., 168
Prochaska, J. O., 549, 567, 579
Prospero-Garcia, O., 208
Provini, F., 214
Prudic, J., 571
Puca, R. M., 389
Pugh, K. R., 79
Pulier, M. L., 550
Pulvirenti, L., 230
Pursell, C. R., 112
Purselle, D. C., 535
Py, J., 295
Pychyl, T. A., 6, 7

Quednow, B. M., 232
Quero, S., 556
Quigley, B. M., 657
Quillian, M. R., 296
Quinn, O. W., 49
Quinn, P. C., 126

Raag, T., 590
Rabinovich, M. I., 166
Rabinowitz, M., 610
Rabinowitz, V. C., 34, 435
Rabius, V., 550
Rache, R., 482
Rachman, S., 509
Racine, R. J., 313
Rackliff, C. L., 590
Radlo, S. J., 698
Rahman, Q., 597
Rainville, P., 170
Rajab, M. H., 536
Ramanaiah, N. V., 591
Ramirez, J., 623
Ramsay, M. C., 445
Ramstein, T., 112
Rana-Deuba, A., 484
Rand, M., 254
Randi, J., 194, 196–197
Randolph, C., 244
Rank, O., 30
Rasinski, K., 503
Rathus, R., 587, 597–598, 617
Rau, P. R., 206
Rau, W., 6
Ravussin, E., 378
Rawsthrone, L. J., 440
Ray, O. S., 238, 240
Read, S. K., 613, 615
Redd, W. H., 251
Redden, D. T., 458
Redmond, G., 594
Reed, G. M., 479
Reed, J. D., 319
Reed, S. K., 345
Reevy, G. M., 591
Regan, P. C., 623, 625, 626
Regev, L. G., 614
Regoeczi, W. C., 687
Reichel, A., 387
Reichenberg, A., 525
Reid, M. R., 91, 464
Reid, P. T., 34
Reid, R., 445
Reiff, S., 253

Reifman, A. S., 657
Reilly, M. P., 268
Reis, H. T., 113, 407, 489
Reiser, B., 315
Reisner, A. D., 513
Reiss, M., 91
Reiss, S., 390, 438
Reiterman, T., 645–646
Reitman, D., 559
Remland, M. S., 683
Renier, C., 215
Renjilian, D. A., 381
Renner, M. J., 491
Reno, R. R., 392, 629
Rentfrow, P., 422
Reppucci, N. D., 606
Rescorla, R. A., 251–252
Resick, P. A., 606
Resnick, H., 467
Restak, R. M., 230
Reuter, M., 22
Revonsuo, A., 220–221
Rew, L., 607
Reynolds, C. R., 445
Reznikoff, M., 449
Rhine, J. B., 194–195
Rhodes, G., 306
Ricci-Bitti, P. E., 400
Ricciardelli, L. A., 382
Rice, K. G., 424
Rice, M. E., 523
Richards, J. B., 465
Richards, J. C., 551
Richards, J. M., 405
Richardson, D. R., 436
Richardson, F. C., 664
Richardson, G. S., 207
Richell, R. A., 508
Richman, C. L., 652
Richmond, L. J., 646
Richmond, M. K., 112
Richter, J., 85
Richter-Appelt, H., 587
Ricketts, M. S., 388
Ridenour, T. A., 230
Rideout, V., 279
Rider, E. A., 111
Riding, C. M., 623
Riefer, D. M., 300
Rieke, M. L., 448
Riggins, R., 112
Rijsdijk, F., 531
Riley, G., 336
Riley, W., 234, 283
Rilling, J. K., 44
Rimrodt, S. L., 587
Riquelme, H., 360
Ritchey, A. K., 464
Ritchie, B. F., 276
Ritter, B., 555
Riva, G., 551
Rivara, F. P., 658
Rizzo, C. P., 274
Rizzolatti, G., 77
Roberti, J. W., 387
Roberts, B. W., 415–416, 441
Roberts, D. F., 279
Roberts, D. G., 274
Roberts, J. E., 112
Roberts, R. E., 130
Roberts, W. A., 268
Robertson, I. S., 352
Robertson, L. C., 340
Robins, C. J., 405
Robins, R. W., 33

Robinson, A., 333
Robinson, B., 645
Robinson, T. E., 229–230
Robinson, T. N., 660
Robinson-Riegler, B., 322
Robles, T. F., 464, 488
Rock, A., 210, 242, 544
Rodd, Z. A., 261
Rodgers, B., 598
Rodin, J., 661
Rodriguez, N., 530, 694
Rodriquez Mosquera, P. M., 401
Roeckelein, J. E., 315
Roeder, K., 337
Roediger, H. L., 295, 302
Roffman, R. A., 239
Rogers, B. J., 179, 180
Rogers, C. R., 30, 31, 438, 440, 442, 515, 548, 572
Rogers, S., 556
Rogers, T. T., 336
Rogoff, B., 329
Rohr, L., 90
Roid, G., 329
Roney, J. R., 595
Roona, M. R., 460
Roos, P. E., 592
Rorschach, H., 448
Rosch, E., 343
Rosenberg, L. B., 181
Rosenberg, R., 191
Rosenberg, S. S., 549
Rosenfeld, P., 694
Rosenheck, R. A., 512
Rosenkranz, M., 224
Rosenkranz, M. A., 464
Rosenman, R., 486
Rosenthal, D., 49
Rosenthal, R. N., 24, 44, 361, 542
Rosenthal, T. L., 493, 531
Rosenzweig, M. R., 59, 102
Ross, D., 278
Ross, E. J., 88
Ross, H. E., 183–184
Ross, J., 459–460
Ross, M., 418
Ross, N. O., 343, 390
Ross, P. E., 352
Ross, S. A., 278
Ross-Stewart, L., 698
Rossi, J. S., 235
Rossi, M. L., 168
Rossion, B., 306
Rothbard, N. P., 674
Rothschild, B., 254
Rotter, J. B., 433
Rowan, M. J., 313
Rowe, B., 4, 7
Rowe, D. C., 129
Rowell, A., 690
Rowell, D., 254
Rowland, R. C., 479
Rowland, D. L., 612, 614
Roy, E., 90
Rozin, P., 379
Rubel, E., 240
Rubenstein, C., 137, 604
Rubin, Z., 625
Rubinow, D. R., 531
Rudd, M. D., 536
Rudman, L. A., 648
Rudolf, G., 567
Rueckl, J. G., 302
Rueffer, S. D., 210
Ruiz, J. M., 487, 489, 493

Rumbaugh, D. M., 348
Runco, M. A., 357–358, 360
Ruparel, K., 70–71
Rusbult, C. E., 442
Rushforth, N. B., 658
Rushton, J. P., 366, 657
Russ, E., 566
Russell, J. A, 400
Russell, R. L., 606
Russell, S. T., 336, 597
Russo, M. B., 514
Russo, N. F., 588
Rutledge, T., 379
Rutledge, T. R., 404
Rutter, M., 112, 304
Ruva, C., 295, 694
Ryan, A. M., 676
Ryan, M. P., 4
Ryan, R. M., 225, 389, 391–392, 440
Ryckman, R. M., 417
Ryff, C. C., 137
Rynearson, K., 2

Saab, P. G., 464
Saadeh, W., 274
Sackeim, H., 571
Sackett, P. R., 678
Safer, M. A., 198
Saffran, J. R., 120
Sagan, C., 20
Sage, R. M., 458, 479, 488
Sagiv, N., 340
Sahelian, R., 214
Saksida, L. M., 268
Sales, B. D., 694, 695
Salmela, J. H., 696
Salmelin, R., 91
Salmon, P., 492
Salovey, P., 407
Salthouse, T. A., 138
Sampson, R. J., 508
Samstag, L. W., 542
Sanberg, P. R., 63
Sanchez, J., 530
Sanders, J., 637
Sandler, I., 483
Sanford, R. N., 648–649
Sanftner, J., 483
Sanna, L. J., 630
Santrock, J. W., 4, 114, 318
Sapirstein, G., 44
Sarason, B. R., 533
Sarason, I. G., 533
Sareen, J., 274
Sarvela, P. D., 606
Sateia, M. J., 213
Saunders, L. A., 228
Savage-Rumbaugh, S., 348
Savsevitz, J., 553
Sawyer, R. G., 604
Saxton, M., 119
Saywitz, K. J., 603
Schachter, S., 622
Schacter, D. L., 294, 295–296, 304, 306, 313, 318
Schacter, S., 403
Schafer, M., 632
Schaie, W., 138–139
Schaller, M., 34
Scharf, D. M., 234
Schaufeli, W. B., 465, 466
Scheck, B., 198
Schenck, C. H., 214
Scher, S. J., 7, 644
Scherer, K. R., 400

Schick, T., 21, 196–197
Schiffrin, R. M., 288
Schilling, M. A., 352
Schiraldi, G. R., 494
Schkade, D., 50
Schlaug, G., 83
Schleicher, S. S., 605
Schlosberg, H., 401
Schmalt, H., 389
Schmeidler, J., 512
Schmidt, F. L., 448, 676
Schmidt, M. G., 114
Schmitt, D. P., 418
Schmitt, E., 33
Schmolck, H., 310
Schmuck, P., 690, 691
Schneider, K. J., 30, 548
Schneider, L., 508, 550
Schneiderman, N., 464, 487
Scholl, B. J., 152, 175
Schooler, C., 337
Schopp, L. H., 551
Schottenbauer, M., 628
Schouten, J. S., 169
Schredl, M., 216
Schreiber, D. E., 295
Schreiber, E. H., 295
Schreiber, F. G., 512
Schroeder, A., 692
Schroeder, J. E., 452
Schubert, C., 523
Schuel, H., 239
Schuiling, G. A., 597
Schultheiss, O. C., 85
Schultz, D. P., 29, 249, 256, 427, 434, 503, 676
Schultz, H. T., 36
Schultz, P. W., 641–643, 688, 690, 692
Schultz, S. E., 29, 249, 256, 427, 434, 676
Schum, T. R., 108
Schumacher, J., 224
Schumacker, R. E., 263
Schuster, M. A., 467
Schutetz, P., 101
Schwartz, C., 204
Schwartz, D. P., 300
Schwartz, J. E., 424
Schwartz, J. H., 84
Schwartz, M. D., 379
Schwartz, M. S., 486
Schwartz, M. W., 379
Schwarz, A., 263
Schwarz, N., 50
Schwinn, S., 449
Schyns, P. G., 400
Sclafani, A., 379
Scoboria, A., 295
Scott, J. L., 324
Scott, J. P., 657
Scott, L., 479
Scurfield, P., 467
Seamonds, C., 415
Searcy, J., 189
Searcy, W. A., 347
Sears, L., 297
Sechzer, J. A., 34, 435
Seeley, R. J., 379
Sefcek, J. A., 624
Segal, N. L., 416
Segerdahl, P., 348
Segerstrom, S., 464
Segraves, R., 612
Segraves, T., 614

Séguin, J. R., 101
Seibering, M., 235
Seidenberg, M., 297
Seidler, G. H., 556
Seidman, B. F., 44
Seitz, A., 188
Sekuler, R., 155, 165
Seligman, M. E. P., 33, 440, 477, 530, 578, 597
Seltzer, R., 695
Selye, H., 461
Senécal, C., 628
Serfaty, M., 535
Servatius, R. J., 273
Service, R. F., 313
Serwood, A., 459
Sessa, V. I., 674
Sestir, M. A., 280, 658–659
Sevcik, R. A., 348
Sevin, J. A., 257
Seybolt, D. C., 434
Seyle, C., 652
Shadel, W. G., 234
Shaffer, D., 126
Shaffer, H. J., 562
Shaffer, J. B., 565
Shafir, E., 361–362
Shafir, R. S, 542
Shafton, A., 210, 211
Shakesby, A. C., 313
Shalizi, C. R., 652
Sham, P., 531
Shanker, S., 348
Shankster, L. J., 676, 678
Shannon, E. A., 91
Shannon, J. D., 115
Shannon, K., 334
Shapiro, C. M., 214
Shapiro, D. A., 566
Shapiro, F., 556
Shapiro, J., 294
Shapiro, M. F., 609
Shapiro, S., 224
Shaughnessy, J. J., 319
Shaver, P., 604
Shaver, P. R., 113
Shaywitz, B. A., 79
Shaywitz, S. E., 79
Sheehy, M., 519
Sheikh, A. A., 555
Sheldon, K. M., 440
Shen, J., 374
Shephard, J. M., 340
Sher, L. A., 532
Sherman, D. K., 458, 479, 488
Sherman, J. G., 258
Sherman, S. J., 460
Sherrod, K. B., 114
Shiffman, S., 234
Shin, Y. J., 166
Shine, D., 610
Shiner, R. L., 415–416
Shiota, M. N., 394, 396, 400
Shires, A., 613
Shneerson, J. M., 213
Shneidman, E., 536
Shoda, Y., 425, 432–433
Shore, H., 550
Short, E. J., 239
Short, S. E., 698
Shurkin, J. N., 333
Siegel, B. V., 70
Siegel, R. K., 204–205
Siegler, R. S., 124
Siever, L. J., 507

Sigelman, C. K., 111
Signorello, L. B., 233
Sills, C., 549
Sills, S., 130
Silver, E., 523
Silver, S. M., 556
Silverman, R., 559
Silverman, W. K., 111
Silverstein, B., 651
Simard, C., 207
Simeon, D., 512
Simister, N. J., 14–15
Simkins, B. J., 671
Simmon, J., 559
Simms, M., 108
Simner, M. L., 21
Simon, A. F., 648, 650
Simon, G. E., 550
Simon, H. A., 352
Simon, L., 523
Simons, D. J., 152, 175, 305
Simons, J. S., 295
Simonton, D. K., 33
Simpson, D. D., 232
Simpson, W. G., 671
Sims, K. E., 112
Sims, S., 293, 323
Simsek, Z., 674
Singer, B. H., 137
Singer, L. T., 239
Singer, M. T., 645
Singer, R. N., 698
Singleton, J. L., 347
Sinha, R., 232
Siribadana, S. H., 503
Sirkin, M. I., 646
Siuzdak, G., 208
Six, L. S., 316
Skeels, H. M., 337
Skinner, B. F., 28–29, 257
Skipton, L. H., 414
Skoog, I., 596
Slaby, A. E., 536
Slaney, R. B., 424
Slater, A., 106, 174
Slijper, F. M. E., 587
Slopen, N., 523
Slot, L. A. B., 307
Slovic, P., 361
Sly, D. J., 215, 263
Smedley, A., 665
Smedley, B. D., 665
Smith, A. D., 304
Smith, A. M., 239
Smith, A. P., 319
Smith, C. L., 114
Smith, E. E., 44, 85
Smith, J., 277
Smith, J. D., 343
Smith, J. L., 395
Smith, L. B., 179
Smith, L. F., 388
Smith, M. L., 400
Smith, N. G., 604
Smith, P. B., 631
Smith, R. E., 432–433
Smith, T. W., 487, 489, 493
Snibbe, J. R., 567
Sobel, E., 610
Sobell, L. C., 240
Sobell, M. B., 240
Sobolewski, J. M., 102
Sohal, T., 234
Sokolik, A., 44
Solomon, J. L., 363

Solomon, L. Z., 310
Solowij, N., 239
Solso, R. L., 340, 352
Somberg, D. R., 579
Somers-Flanagan, J., 444
Somers-Flanagan, R., 444
Sommer, R., 685
Sorek, S., 305
Soussignan, R., 404
Soyez, V., 572
Spangenberg, J. J., 591
Spanswick, S. C., 311
Sparks, F. T., 311
Spector, P. E., 448, 675
Spence, S., 191
Spencer, L., 166
Sperry, R., 74–75
Spiegler, M. D., 261, 553–544, 559
Spinella, M., 233
Spirito, A., 536
Spiro Wagner, P., 415
Spiro, A., 487
Spiro, C. S., 415
Spittle, M., 698
Spitznagel, E. L., 230
Sporer, S. L., 188
Sprecher, S., 605, 623, 626
Springer, D., 379
Springer, S. P., 76, 92
Springston, F., 292
Squarcia, S., 207
Squire, L. R., 310, 311–313
Squires, J., 102
Srivastava, S., 363, 415
Staemmler, F.-M., 549
Standing, L., 306
Stanhope, N., 304
Stanovich, K. E., 14, 15, 23, 25, 54
Stanowicz, L. B., 119
Stansfeld, S. A., 687
Stanton, S. J., 85
Stapel, D. A., 623
Staples, S. W., 687
Staska, M., 120
Staudinger, U. M., 133
Steadman, H. J., 523
Steblay, N. M., 687
Steciuk, M., 624
Steel, G. D., 703–704
Steen, N., 673
Stefania, B., 232
Stein, B. D., 467
Stein, D. J., 569, 674
Stein, M. D., 216
Stein, M. T., 214, 295
Steinberg, L., 129, 334, 336–337
Steingrueber, H., 379
Stemler, S. E., 366
Stephan, W., 188
Stephens, K., 366
Stephens, R. S., 239
Stepper, S., 404
Steptoe, A., 458
Stern, P. C., 691
Stern, S. L., 477
Sternberg, E. M., 461, 482
Sternberg, R. J., 328, 353, 360, 355–366, 665
Steuer, F. B., 642
Stevens, L. C., 492
Stewart, A. J., 138, 588
Stewart, A. M., 444
Stewart, B. L., 536
Stewart-Williams, S., 43, 62
Stickgold, R., 210, 216, 217, 244

Stiles, W. B., 566
Stiller-Winkler, R., 464
Stinson, F. S., 510
Stip, E., 518
Stipek, D., 388
Stöber, J., 388
Stockhorst, U., 379
Stoffelsen, J., 465
Stokes, D. M., 195
Stokoe, W. C., 347
Stokols, D., 687
Stolerman, I. P., 233
Stolp, S., 606
Stone, G., 579
Stone, J., 650
Stone, T. H., 628
Stopfer, M., 166
Stoppard, J. M., 530
Storm, D. R., 239
Stovel, K., 607
Strack, F., 404
Straif, K., 239
Straneva, P. A., 62
Strassberg, D. S., 445, 614
Straub, R., 459
Strayer, D. L., 152
Strickler, E. M., 383
Strier, F., 696
Stroecher, S. K., 590
Strong, B., 604, 617
Strongman, K. T., 405–406, 466
Strote, J., 232
Stroud, L., 487
Stroup, D. F., 458–459
Strupp, H. H., 579
Sturges, J. W., 555
Sturges, L. V., 555
Stuss, D. T., 75–76, 77
Su, M., 691
Subedi, S., 573
Suchy, Y., 507
Sue, D., 603
Sue, S., 603
Suedfeld, P., 224, 703–704
Sugden, K., 531
Sugihara, Y., 591
Sugimori, S., 418
Sugimoto, K., 167, 379
Suh, E. J., 467
Suh, E. M., 436
Suinn, R. M., 461, 522, 665
Sukel, H. L., 694
Suls, J., 130, 487
Sulzer, J. L., 673
Sumathipala, A., 503
Sumerlin, J. R., 439
Sumi, K., 424
Sundequist, U., 224
Sunnafrank, M., 623
Supeli, A., 628
Surprenant, A., 288, 292–293, 302, 307, 316, 319, 322, 324
Suter, P. J., 91
Sutherland, R. J., 311
Suzuki, A., 77
Suzuki, L., 366
Svartdal, F., 266
Swaak, J., 277
Swamidass, P. M., 628, 672
Swann, W. B., Jr., 417
Swim, J. K., 630
Symbaluk, D. G., 269
Synhorst, L. L., 445
Szabo, A., 494

Tabors, P. O., 119
Taft, C. T., 606
Taglialatela, J., 348
Taheri, S., 215
Takooshian, H., 687
Tal-Or, N., 630
Talbott, J. A., 572
Talley, P. F., 579
Tamis-LeMonda, C. S., 101, 115, 119
Tamkins, M. M., 589
Tancredi, L., 239
Tanner, J. L., 130–131
Tapert, S. F., 235
Taraban, R., 2
Tardif, T. Z., 360
Taris, T. W., 465
Tarr, M. J., 276
Tashkin, D. P., 239
Taub, E., 63
Tausig, M., 573
Tavris, C., 604, 644
Taylor, A., 114, 531
Taylor, F., 670
Taylor, G. J., 407
Taylor, J. R., 230
Taylor, K., 645
Taylor, S. E., 251, 458, 468, 479, 484–485, 488, 556
Taylor, T., 348
Taylor-Allan, H. L., 407
Taylor-Seehafer, M., 607
Taytroe, L., 218
Te Nijenhuis, J., 224
Tedeschi, J. T., 694
Tenenbaum, G., 698
Tenhula, W. N., 559
Terman, L., 329
Terman, L. M., 332
Terry, D. J., 643
Terry, K., 442
Thakur, S., 17
Tharp, R. G., 250, 282–283, 388, 575–577
Thase, M. E., 542
Thelen, E., 108
Thelen, M. H., 382, 512
Thibodeau, R., 7
Thiel, T., 525
Thiessen, E. D., 120
Thomas, A., 103
Thomas, C. C., 293
Thomas, E. M., 273
Thomas, M. L., 206
Thompson, C. P., 317
Thompson, J. W., 295
Thompson, K. M., 279
Thompson, R. A., 102, 312
Thompson, R. F., 43, 83
Thompson, T., 310
Thompson, W. L., 220, 341
Thomsen, D. K., 304
Thomson, D., 295
Thorburn, J., 536
Thorndike, E. L., 256
Thorne, D. R., 206
Thorp, D., 108
Thorson, J. A., 140
Thropy, M. J., 215
Thyen, U., 587
Tian, C., 119
Tidwell, M. O., 113
Tierney, S. C., 43, 579
Tighe, M. R., 344
Tijerino, R., 684
Till, B. D., 251–252

Tillotson, C. A., 112
Tilton-Weaver, L. C., 131
Timmerman, C. K., 263
Tipples, J., 400
Titchener, E., 27, 31
Tobler, N. S., 460
Todaro, J. F., 487
Tolman, E. C., 276
Tomasello, M., 119
Toneatto, T., 240
Toro, C. T., 63, 526
Torrey, E. F., 572
Toth, K., 326
Townson, S., 452
Toyota, H., 293
Trachet, T., 22
Trainor, L. J., 120
Trajanovic, N. N., 214
Travis, F., 224
Treffert, D. A., 326
Trehub, S. E., 120
Tremblay, P., 598
Tremblay, R. E., 240
Trepel, C., 313
Triandis, H. C., 436
Trippe, R., 510
Trope, Y., 664
Troutman, A. C., 273–274
Truax, S. R., 403
Trull, T., 542, 545
Tsai, G., 525
Tsai, W.-C., 676
Tse, L., 130
Tseng, V., 115
Tubb, V. A., 198
Tucker, K. L., 488
Tugade, M. M., 461
Tulving, E., 297, 312
Turetsky, B. I., 526
Turiel, E., 132
Turkheimer, E., 337
Turner, C. M., 445, 614
Turner, S. J. M., 564
Tutty, S., 550
Tversky, A., 361–362
Twenge, J. M., 417, 604
Tye, M., 588–589
Tye-Murray, N., 166
Tymnik, G., 91
Tzeng, M., 624

Uchino, B. N., 489, 493
Udry, E., 698
Ulm, R. R., 478
Unsworth, G., 280
Unyk, A. M., 120
Utasi, A., 466
Uwe, P., 569

Vaidya, R. S., 478
Vaillant, G. E., 139, 235, 458
Valente, S. M., 585–587, 597
Valentine, E. R., 317
Valerius, G., 525
Valiente, C., 114
Valins, S., 403, 691
van Bellen, G., 595
Van Boemmel, H., 387
Van Dammen, D. P., 524
van der Hart, O., 542
Van Der Ploeg, H. M., 512
van Deurzen, E., 548
van Dierendonck, D., 224
Van Dongen, H. P., 206
Van Eenwyk, J., 280

van Elst, L. T., 525
Van Goozen, S. H. M., 384
Van Heck, G. L., 487
van Joolingen, W. R., 277
Van Kammen, D. P., 49
Van Lawick-Goodall, J., 46
van Limbeek, J., 79
van Vianen, A. E. M., 401
Van Vugt, M., 690
Vandell, D. L., 112
vanDeusen, K. M., 254
Vandewater, E. A., 138
Vasa, R. A., 570
Vaughan, A., 513
Vaughn, L., 21, 196–197
Veiga, J. F., 674
Velakoulis, D., 526
Velez, A., 92
Velez, C. N., 482
Venezia, M., 108
Verbalis, J. G., 383
Verdeli, H., 545
Verhoeven, C., 628
Verkuyten, M., 418
Vernon, D. J., 288
Vernon, P. A., 73
Vetrugno, R., 214
Vi, P., 702
Videon, T. M., 115
Viechtbauer, W., 415, 441
Viegener, B. J., 381
Viek, C., 690
Villemure, C., 170
Violani, C., 216
Viswesvaran, C., 448
Viveros, M. P., 101
Vlek, C., 691
Voelkel, A. R., 322
Vogel, E. K., 311
Vogler, R. E., 237, 554
Vohs, K. D., 417
Volberg, G., 76
Volkow, N. D., 239
Vollick, D. N., 521
Volpicelli, J. R., 478
Vredenburg, D. S., 624
Vygotsky, L., 126–127

Wade, C. E., 699
Wade-Galuska, T., 227
Wagner, F. E., 556
Wagner, M. K., 434
Wagner, T. D., 44
Wagstaff, G. F., 295
Waid, W. M., 398
Wainwright, J. L., 597
Wakefield, J. C., 500
Wald, J., 556
Waldron, M., 337
Walk, R. D., 179
Walker, E. E., 524, 525–527, 570
Walker, I., 654
Walker, M., 244
Walker, M. P., 216
Wall, P., 169
Wallace, B., 341
Wallen, A. S., 589
Wallnau, L. B., 710
Walsh, R., 224
Walster, E., 188
Walter, J. A., 108
Walters, G., 650
Walters, R., 273
Walton, C. E., 106
Walton, K. E., 415, 441

Wambach, C., 5
Wampold, B. E., 43, 579
Wandersman, A., 460
Wang, C., 458
Wang, J. M., 63
Wang, L., 377
Wang, Q., 290
Wang, S. S., 380
Wanger, A., 378
Wann, D. W., 278
Ward, C., 484
Ward, J., 75, 77–78
Ward, L. M., 160, 177
Ward, T., 280
Ward-Alexander, L., 572
Wardle, J., 458
Wark, G. R., 133
Warner, J. A., 591
Warren, D. J., 151
Warren, M. P., 129
Warren, W. H., 276
Warshauer-Baker, E., 367, 651, 665
Washburn, A. L., 376
Washburn, M., 31
Wasserman, A. W., 695
Watanabe, T., 188
Waterhouse, J. W., 208, 374, 395
Waterman, I., 168
Watson, A. C., 523
Watson, D. L., 250, 282–283, 388, 575–577
Watson, J. B., 28, 31
Watson, J. D., 120
Watson, N. V., 59
Watt, C., 194
Watt, T., 698
Watts, D. J., 620
Way, L., 254
Weaver, G., 316–317
Weaver, G. E., 306
Wechsler, H., 232, 235–236, 365
Wedding, D., 49
Weekley, J. A., 446
Wehr, T. A., 532
Weiller, C., 85
Weinberg, R. A., 337
Weinberger, D. R., 524
Weinryb, R. M., 414
Weisbach, T. A., 554
Weisensel, N., 382
Weiser, M., 525
Weishaar, M. E., 537
Weiss, H. M., 673
Weisskirch, R. S., 130
Weissman, A. M., 469
Weiten, W., 465
Weitzman, E. R., 479
Weizman, A., 232
Welker, W., 415
Wells, B. E., 604
Wells, D. L., 91
Wells, G. L., 198, 301
Weltzin, T. E., 382

Wenckstern, S., 536
Wener, R. E., 683
Wenger, N. S., 609
Werner, C. M., 690
Wertenbroch, K., 6
Wertheimer, M., 29, 31, 277
Wesensten, N. J., 206, 232
Wessel, I., 307
West, A. N., 199
West, B. J., 676
West, R., 234
West, T. G., 341
Westen, D., 566
Westfall, A. O., 458
Westphal, M., 407
Wethington, E., 137–138
Wetter, D. W., 234
Wexler, M. N., 646
Wheeler, D., 673
Wheeler, L., 403
Whipple, B., 600
Whishaw, I. Q., 85
Whitaker, B. G., 50
White, G. L., 218, 283
White, J., 337, 365, 367
White, K. B., 606
White, N. S., 70
Whitehouse, A. J. O., 301
Whiteman, M. C., 415, 421
Whitley, B. E., 648
Whitton, E., 548
Whitton, S. W., 442
Whorton, J. E., 366
Whyte, G., 632
Wickett, J. C., 73
Widmeyer, W. N., 699
Widner, R. L., Jr., 300
Wiederhold, B. K., 253, 551, 556
Wiederhold, M. D., 253, 556
Wiederman, M. W., 595
Wiese, M., 333, 358, 360
Wiesel, W. N., 150
Wieselquist, J., 442
Wiesemann, C., 587
Wigfield, A. J., 388
Wiggins, E., 628
Wilber, M. K., 562
Wilcher, M., 224, 493
Wilde, M. L., 660
Wilder, D. A., 648, 650
Wilding, J. M., 317
Wilhelm, F. H., 550
Wilke, H., 691
Wilkie, D. M., 268
Wilkinson, M., 218, 278
Willamson, D. A., 378
Willer, J.-C., 168
Williams, D. R., 579, 652
Williams, G., 377–378
Williams, J. M., 217, 342
Williams, K. D., 696
Williams, M., 535
Williams, N., 587

Williams, R. B., 487
Williams, R. L., 4, 576
Willott, J. F., 165
Willoughby, T., 7, 293, 323
Wilmot, W. W., 651
Wilson, A. E., 418
Wilson, B. S., 166
Wilson, D. B., 566
Wilson, D. W., 660
Wilson, F. L., 133
Wilson, G. D., 597
Wilson, M. A., 386, 675
Wilson, T. D., 361, 637
Wilson, W. A., 232
Wing, R. R., 381
Winger, G., 227
Wingood, G. M., 280
Winkelman, S. E., 300
Winner, E., 333, 350
Winstead, B. A., 452, 530
Winter, D. D. N., 687–688, 690–691
Wirth, M. M., 85
Wise, R. A., 198
Wiseman, R., 194–196
Witcher, B. S., 403
Witelson, S. F., 73
Witherington, D. C., 179
Withers, N. W., 230
Witt, S. D., 586
Wixted, J. T., 308, 311
Woerner, M., 570
Wolfe, J. B., 261
Wolfe, J. M., 166
Wolfson, S., 684
Wolpe, J., 577
Wolpin, M., 244
Wong, C. Y., 685
Wong, F. Y., 565
Wong, M.-L., 378
Wood, E., 7, 293, 323
Wood, J. M., 195, 449
Woodard, T., 612
Woodhouse, R. A., 318
Woodman, G. F., 311
Woods, J. H., 227
Woods, J. M., 376
Woods, S. C., 379, 628
Woodworth, G. G., 166
Woolard, J. L., 606
Worthen, J. B., 322, 699
Wraga, M., 340
Wright, D. B., 307
Wright, H., 87
Wright, J. A., 674
Wright, K. P., Jr., 207, 374
Wright, T. A., 671, 673
Wrightsman, L. S., 696
Wu, C. W. H., 170
Wu, S. M., 91
Wuethrich, B., 235
Wulf, G., 263
Wundt, W., 27, 31

Wyatt, J. W., 415
Wynne, C. D. L., 47

Xiao, D.-K., 288
Xu, J., 649–650

Yahnke, B. H., 555
Yalcinkaya, A., 115
Yanchar, S. C., 263
Yang, B., 535
Yarber, W. L., 609
Yarmey, A. D., 198
Yedidia, M. J., 140
Yeh, C. J., 484
Yeo, R. A., 79
Yip, P. S. F., 536
Yoder, C. Y., 319
Yokota, F., 279
Yonas, A., 179
Yoshida, M., 69
Young, A. W., 400
Young, R. K., 623
Young, S. M., 507
Ysseldyke, J., 46
Yu, K. S., 268
Yu, S. L., 5
Yurak, T. J., 624
Yurgelum-Todd, D., 239

Zack, S., 234, 283
Zadra, A., 215, 216, 244
Zamchech, N., 396
Zanna, M. P., 641, 652–653
Zarcadoolas, C., 459–460
Zárraga, C., 672
Zatorre, R. J., 84
Zautra, D. R., 483
Zechmeister, E. B., 319
Zedlow, P. B., 591
Zeisel, J., 691–692
Zeisel, S. A., 112
Zeiss, A., 614
Zeiss, R., 614
Zelano, C., 166
Zelazo, P. D., 101
Zellner, D. A., 382
Zemishlany, Z., 232
Zentall, T. R., 29, 268
Zhang, R. L., 63
Zhang, Z. G., 63
Zhao, Z., 395
Zigler, E., 535
Zimbardo, P. G., 450, 453, 637
Zimmerman, J. C., 207, 284
Zion, C., 664
Zoellner, L. A., 310
Zohar, D., 388
Zola, S. M., 311–312
Zuckerman, M., 386–387
Zuerink, J. R., 694–695
Zuwerink, J. R., 664
Zvolensky, M. J., 465

Subject Index

Ablation, 69
Abnormality, 498
Absolute threshold, 150
Acceptance
　death and, 140
　self, 438
　uncritical, 22–23
Accommodation, 122–123
Acculturative stress, 484
Achievement, 388–390
Achievers, characteristics of, 389
Acquaintance rape, 606
Acquisition, 250
Acromegaly, 86
Action component, 641
Action potential, 59
Action therapy, 542
Activation-synthesis hypothesis, 217–218
Active learning, 2–3
Active listening, 3–4, 567
Acuity, 156
Adaptability, 591
Adaptation, dim light, 159, 161
Adaptation, sensory, 150
Adaptive behaviors, 394
Adjustment disorders, 509
Adler, Alfred, 30
Adolescence
　defined, 129
　psychosocial dilemmas in, 136
　sleep patterns, 207
Adrenal glands, 87
Adulthood. *See also* Elderly
　development states, 133–139
　transition to, 130
　young, 136
Advertising, 294
Aerial perspective, 182
Affectional needs, 112
Affiliation, 622–623
Afterimages, 158
Age
　IQ and, 329
　regression, 223
　suicide risks and, 535
Ageism, 139
Aggression
　assertiveness *versus*, 638
　cues, 658
　defined, 469, 656
　displaced, 469, 648
　frustration and, 657–658
　instinctive view of, 656–657
　media violence and, 658–659
　preventing, 659–660
　punishment and, 273
　social learning theory, 658–659
　television and, 279–280
　weapons effect, 658
Aging, 139
Agnosia, facial, 80
Agnosia, visual, 79
Agoraphobia, 510
Agreeableness, 423

Alarm reaction, 463
Alcohol abuse
　aversion therapy for, 554
　binge drinking, 235–236
　health and, 460
　incidents, 235
　positive reinforcement and, 236
　recognizing, 236
　sex drive and, 384
　treatment, 237, 554
Alcoholics Anonymous (AA), 237
Alda, Alan, 309
Alexithymia, 370
Algorithm, 351
All-or-nothing thinking, 560
Alpha waves, 209
Alternate response, 283
Alzheimer's disease, 520
Ambiguous stimuli, 175
Ambivalence, 472
Ambivalent attachment style, 113
Ames room, 189
Amnesia, 221–222, 512
Amok, 504
Amphetamine psychosis, 231
Amphetamines, 230–231, 525
Amygdala, 84
Anagrams Test, 358
Anal stage, 427, 429–430
Anal-expulsive personality, 427, 430
Anal-retentive personality, 427, 430
Analytic intelligence, 366
Analyze This, 36
Anarcia, 500
Androgens, 584
Androgyny, 590–592
Anger, 140, 616
Anger Management, 36
Anhedonia, 231
Animal language, 347–349
Animal Mind, The (Washburn), 31
Animal models
　conditioning studies, 268
　function, 16–17
　sleep, 205
Anorexia nervosa, 380
Anosmia, 166
ANS (autonomic nervous system)
　branches, 396–397
　characterization, 64–65
　emotions and, 395–396
　fight or flight syndrome, 396
　hormone regulation by, 87
　sudden death and, 396–397
Antecedents, 248, 283
Anthropomorphic error, 47
Antisocial personality disorders, 507–509
Anxiety
　defined, 475
　moral, 429
　neurotic, 429
　separation, 111
　social, 452
　test, 388

Anxiety disorders
　drug therapy, 570
　origins, 509
　perspectives on, 514–516
　symptoms, 502
　types of, 509–512
Anxiolytics, 570
Aphasia, 77
Aphrodisiacs, 384
Apparent-distance hypothesis, 184
Applied psychology
　defined, 668
　environmental, 682–693
　human factors, 701–704
　industrial/organizational, 670–678
　jury selection, 694–696
　sports, 696–699
Appraisal, emotional, 404–405
Appraisal, stressors, 465–467
Approach-approach conflicts, 471
Approach-avoidance conflicts, 471–472
Aptitude tests, 676–677
Arab Americans, 116
Archimedes, 359–360
Architectural psychology, 691–692
Arousal
　complexity, 594
　disorders, 612–614
　emotions and, 402–404
　gender differences, 594–595
　heightened, 661–663
　levels, 387–388
　theory, 386–387
Artificial hearing, 166
Artificial intelligence, 335–336
ASC (altered states of consciousness)
　changes during, 204
　dreams, 211, 216–218, 242–244
　drug-induced, 227
　hypnosis, 220–223
　meditation, 223–225
　sleep, 204–210, 204–216
　sleep deprivation, 224–225
Asch experiment, 631
Asian Americans, 116
ASL (American Sign Language), 346–347
Assertiveness training, 638–639
Assessment centers, 677–678
Assimilation, 122
Association areas, 77
Astigmatism, 156
Astrology, 22
Atkinson-Schiffrin model, 288
Attachment, 111–112
Attention. *See* Selective attention
Attentional overload, 687
Attitudes
　behavior and, 642
　components, 641
　defined, 641
　forced changes, 645–646
　forming, 641–642
　persuasion, 643–645

Attraction. *See* Interpersonal attraction
Attribution theory, 403–404
Attributions, 629–630
Auditory area, 78
Auditory ossicles, 163
Authoritarian parents, 113
Authoritarian personality, 648, 695
Authoritative parents, 113–114, 143
Autism, 326
Autonomy, 136, 438
Aversion therapy
　alcohol abuse treatment, 554
　characterization, 553
　desensitization, 554–556
　smoking cessation by, 554
Aversion, taste, 379
Aversive stimuli, 657
Avoidance learning, 273
Avoidance-avoidance conflicts, 471
Avoidant attachment style, 113
Awareness
　levels of, 429
　perceptual, 198–199
　value of, 199
Axon terminals, 58–59
Axons, 58

Baillargeon, Renee, 125
Bandura, Albert, 278
Barbiturates, 234
Bargaining, 140
Barnum effect, 23
Barnum, P. T., 23
Base rate, 362
Basic suggestion effect, 221
Beautiful Mind, A, 191
Behavior
　androgynous, 590–592
　attitudes and, 642
　expressive, 590
　instrumental, 590
　jury, 694–695
　sexual, 594–597
　social (*See* Social behavior)
　territorial, 684
Behavior modification, 493, 553
Behavior therapy
　aversion approach, 553–556
　characterization, 553
　cognitive approach, 560–562
　critical thinking, 20–21
　defined, 14
　disease-promoting, 458–459
　disordered, 499–500
　expressive, 436
　health-promoting, 459–460
　instrumental, 436
　operant approach, 558–559
　personality and, 433
　punishment's effects on, 272
　self-managed, 282–283, 575–580
　superstitious, 258
　traits and, 421
　types of, 14
Behavioral assessment, 445

Subject Index I-15

Behavioral genetics, 416
Behavioral medicine, 458
Behavioral personality theories, 432
Behavioral risk factors, 458–459
Behavioral settings, 682
Behaviorism. *See also* Cognitive behaviorism
  anxiety disorder approach, 515
  history, 28–29
  insomnia, 214
  personality theory of, 418
  perspective, 33
Beliefs
  common sense, 15
  component, 641
  irrational, 561
  shy, 453
Bell curve. *See* Normal curve
Beta waves, 209
Bias
  courtesy, 50
  observer, 46
  sampling, 50
  self-defeating, 452
Bilingualism, 346
bin Laden, Osama, 646
Binet, Alfred, 329
Binge drinking, 235
Binocular depth cues, 179–181
Biodata, 678
Biofeedback training, 485–486
Biological biasing effect, 587
Biological perspective, 32–33
Biological predisposition, 119
Biological rhythm, 205
Bipolar disorders, 529–530
Birth defects. *See* Congenital problems
Bisexuality, 597
Blind spot, 156
Blindness, color, 159–160
Blindness, inattentional, 152
Blink (Gladwell), 361
Body language, 401–402
Boiled frog syndrome, 187
Borderline personality disorder, 507
Bottom-up processing, 186
Brain. *See also* specific regions
  addictive drugs effects, 230
  chemistry, schizophrenia and, 525
  complexity of, 84–85
  dominance, 90–91
  effects of alcohol, 236
  emotions and, 395
  function, 84
  gender differences, 79
  lateralization, 92–93
  mapping, 68–71
  memory and, 311–313
  nerves in, 56–60
  neural networks, 62–63
  neural regulators, 62
  neurotransmitters, 60–62
  plasticity, 63
  repair, 63
  size, 56
  synapses, 60–62
  thinking process and, 85
Brainwashing, 645
Brainwave boxes, 170
Brand memory, 294
Brightness, 155
Brightness constancy, 174
Broca's area, 77
Browser, 8

BSRI (Bem sex role inventory), 590–592
Bulimia nervosa, 381
Burnout, 466
Bystander intervention, 660–661

Caffeine, 232–233
Caffeinism, 232
CAI (computer-assisted instruction), 263–264
Calkins, Mary, 31
Cannon-Bard theory, 402
Carbon footprint, 689
Cardiac personality, 486–488
Cardinal traits, 422
Career decisions, 673
Caring, 132–133
Case study, 48
Castration, 595–596
Cataplexy, 215
Catatonic schizophrenia, 521–522
Causation, 48
Central tendency measure, 711–712
Central traits, 422
Cephalocaudal maturation pattern, 107
Cerebellum, 82
Cerebral cortex
  characterization, 73
  hemispheres, 73–76
  lobes, 76–81
CERs (conditioned emotional responses), 253
Cervix, 585
Character, 414
Chemical senses, 166–168
Chemotherapy, 251
Child molestation, 602–603
Child's Guide to Life on Earth, A (Vygotsky), 126
Childhood and Society (Erikson), 135
Children
  cognitive development, 122–128
  communicating with, 145–146
  disciplining, 143–145
  gifted, 332–333
  intersexaul, 586–587
  media violence and, 658–659
  psychosocial dilemmas in, 136
Chimpanzees, 347–348
Chomsky, Noam, 118–119, 346
Chromosomes, 99
Chronological age, 329
Chunking, 292
Cigarette smoking, 234
Circadian rhythms, 374
Clairvoyance, 194
Classical conditioning
  defined, 248
  in humans, 253–254
  Pavlov's experiment, 249–250
  principles, 250–253
Clever Hans, 24
Client-centered therapy, 548
Clinical case studies, 68
Clinical method, 48–49
Clinical psychologists, 36
Clinton, Hillary, 588
Clitoral organism, 600–601
Clitoris, 585
Closure, 175
CNS (central nervous system), 64
Cocaine, 231–232
Cochlea, 163
Cocktail party effect, 152

Coefficient of correlation, 47–48
Cognition, 1
Cognitive behaviorism
  approach, 560–562
  history, 29
  perspective, 33
Cognitive development
  Piaget's theory, 122–126
  Vygotsky's theory, 126–127
Cognitive dissonance theory, 641, 644–645
Cognitive learning, 276–278
Cognitive maps, 276
Cognitive psychology
  anxiety disorder approach, 516
  area of study, 16
  interview, 295, 319–320
Cognitive science, 33
Cold readings, 195
College Life Stress Inventory, 490
Color blindness, 159–160
Color vision, 158–159
Color weakness, 159
Common region, 175
Common traits, 421
Communication
  effective, 145
  infants, 119–120
  language development and, 119–120
  sexual, 616–617
  workplace, 678–670
Community health, 460–461
Comparative psychologists, 16
Compensation, 475–476
Complacent style, 673
Compliance, 634–635
Concentrative meditation, 223–224
Concept formation, 342–343
Concepts, 340, 342–344
Conceptual rule, 343
Concrete operational stage, 123–124
Condensation, 242
Conditioned response, 28, 249
Conditioned stimulus, 249, 379
Conditioning. *See* Classical conditioning; Operant conditioning
Conditions of worth, 442
Conductive hearing, 165
Cones, 156–158
Confidentiality, 569
Conflicts
  managing, 472
  occurrence, 470
  types of, 471–472
Conformity, 630–632
Congenital pain insensitivity, 168
Congenital problems, 100
Connector neurons, 65
Connotative meaning, 344
Conscience, 132, 427
Conscientious, 423–424
Conscious, 427, 429
Consciousness. *See also* ASC (altered states of consciousness)
  components, 204
  defined, 205
Consequences, 248
Consequences Test, 357–359
Conservation
  conditioning and, 263
  environmental, 688–689
  mastery of, 123
Consistency, 144, 425
Consolidation, 311–312

Constructions, 186
Constructive processing, 294
Contiguity, 175
Contingency, 257
Continuity, 175
Contracting, 283–284
Control
  defined, 18
  groups, 41
  perceived lack of, 466
  questions, 397
Conventional level reasoning, 132
Convergence, 180–181
Convergent thinking, 357
Conversation, 123–124, 453–454
Conversion, 646
Conversion disorder, 514
Convictions, 642
Coping statements, 494
Corpus callosum, 73
Correlation coefficient, 717–719
Correlation-rating relationships
  causation, 719
  correlation coefficient, 717–719
  prediction, 718–719
  relationships, 717
  use of, 716–717
Correlational studies, 47–48
Corticalization, 73
Counseling psychologists, 36
Counselors, 39
Counterirritation, 169
Courtesy bias, 50
Covert behavior, 14
Covert reinforcement, 576
Covert sensitization, 575–576
Cowper's glands, 585
Cranial nerves, 65
Creativity
  dreams and, 244
  intrinsic motivation and, 392
  personality and, 360
  tests, 357–359
  thinking and, 357–360
Critical incidents, 675
Critical situations, 435
Critical thinking, 20–21, 26
Crowding, 685–686, 691
Crystal methamphetamine, 231
Crystal, Billy, 36
Crystallized abilities, 139
CT (computed tomographic) scan, 68
Cue-dependent forgetting, 306–307
Cues
  binocular depth, 179–181
  eating, 378–379, 381
  habit breaking and, 283
  memory, 306, 318
  monocular depth, 181–184
  personality, 433
Cults, 645–646
Cultural psychologists, 16, 569
Cultural relativity, 34
Culture
  eating habits and, 379
  emotional expression and, 401
  gender roles and, 589
  IQ and, 365–367
  normalcy and, 499
  politics of, 366–367
  problem solving and, 354–355
  workplace, 674
Culture-fair testing, 365–366

I-16 Subject Index

Curve of forgetting, 304
Cyclothymic disorders
    characterization, 529

da Vinci, Leonardo, 92
Dahmer, Jeffrey, 523
Dark adaptation, 159, 161
Darwin, Charles, 28
Date reduction system, 150
Day care, 112
Death
    reactions to, 140–141
    statistics, 140
    sudden, 396–397
Death instinct, 427–428
Deep lesioning, 69
Deep sleep, 209
Defense mechanisms, 475–476
Defensive-avoidant style, 673
Deinstitutionalization, 572
Delgado, José, 61
Delta waves, 209
Delusional disorders, 520–521
Delusions, 518
Dementia, 138–139, 519–520
Dendrites, 58
Denial, 140, 475
Denotative meaning, 344
Density, 686
Dependence, 227–230
Dependent personality disorder, 500
Dependent variables, 41–42
Depressants, 227
Depression
    biology and, 531
    characterization, 529
    classification, 502
    coping with, 479–480
    death and, 140
    drug therapy, 570
    helplessness and, 478–479
    major, 529
    mastery training, 478
    postpartum, 531
    recognizing, 479
    students and, 479
Deprivation, environmental, 102
Depth cues, 179
Depth perception, 185
Description, 17
Descriptive statistics
    central tendency measure, 711–712
    defined, 708
    graphical, 710–711
    normal curve, 713–714
    standard scores, 713
    variability measure, 712–714
Desensitization, 576–577
Desire disorders, 612
Desk rage, 675
Desktop metaphor, 701
Determinism, 30
Development
    adult stages, 135–137
    cognitive, 122–128
    environmental factors, 99–102
    genetic factors, 98–99
    growth sequence, 100
    language, 118–122
    lifespan challenges, 135–142
    moral, 129–134
    neonates, 105–107
    parenting and, 143–146
    personality, 429–430, 434–436
    psychosocial theory, 135–137
    social, 111–117

Developmental level, 103
Developmental psychology, 16, 98
Developmental tasks, 135
Devi, Shakuntala, 340
Deviation IQs, 331
Dewey, John, 31
Dhat, 504
Dieting
    behavioral, 381
    function of, 379
    yo-yo, 379–380
Difference thresholds, 151
Digital media, 8
Direct observation, 445–446
Directive therapy, 542
Discipline. *See also* Punishment
    approaches, 143–144
    consistent, 144
    constructive, 144–145
Discovery learning, 277–278
Discrimination
    defined, 252
    prejudice and, 648
    stimulus, 253
    stimulus control, 269–270
Discriminative stimuli, 269
Disease-prone personality, 458
Dishabituation, 199
Disinhibition, 658
Disjunctive concepts, 343
Disordered behavior, 499–500
Disorganized schizophrenia, 521–522
Displaced aggression, 648
Displacement, 242
Dissociative amnesia, 512
Dissociative disorders, 502, 512–513
Dissociative identity disorder, 512
Disuse, 306
Divergent thinking, 357
Diversity, 664–667
Dixon, Jeanne, 54
DNA
    characterization, 98
    organization, 99
    police use, 198
Dominant genes, 99
Door-in-the-face effect, 634
Dopamine, 525
Double approach-avoidance conflict, 472
Double standard, 605, 630
Double-blind experiment, 44
Doubt, 136
Dove, Adrian, 365
Drapetomania, 500
Dreams
    creativity, 244
    everyday events in, 216–217
    Freudian analysis, 217, 242, 544–545
    lucid, 244
    processes, 242
    REM sleep and, 211, 216
    symbols, 217, 544–545
    theories, 217–218, 242–243
    using, 243–244
Drives, 372, 433
Drug interaction, 235
Drug tolerance, 227
Drug-dependency insomnia, 213
Drugs
    abuse potential, 228–230
    antidepressant, 570
    antipsychotic, 570
    brain function and, 230

    dependence, 227–230
    depressants, 234–238
    hallucinogens, 238–239
    psychoactive, 227, 230
    schizophrenia mimicking, 525
    stimulants, 230–234
DSM-IV-TR (Statistical Manual of Mental Disorders), 500
Dual memory, 290
Dwarfism, 86
Dyspareunia, 615
Dysthymic disorders, 529

Ear, 163
Eating. *See also* Hunger
    cues, 378–379, 381
    dieting and, 379–380
    disorders, 380–382, 382
    emotional, 379
Ebbinghaus curve, 304
Ebbinghaus, Herman, 304
Echoic memory, 288
Echolocation, 150
Ecological footprint, 688
Ecstasy. *See* MDMA (methylenedioxymethamphetamine)
ECT (electroconvulsive therapy), 570–571
Educational psychology, 28
EEG (electroencephalograph)
    function, 69
    invention, 15
    sleep studies, 209
Effector cells, 65
Efficiency, 671
Ego, 427–428
Ego ideal, 427
Egocentric thought, 123
Eidetic imagery, 315–316
Elaborative rehearsal, 293
Elderly, 138–139
Electra conflict, 427, 430
EMDR (eye movement desensitization and reprocessing), 556
Emergencies, 661
Emotional appraisal, 404–405
Emotional component, 641
Emotional expressions, 394
Emotional feelings, 394–395
Emotional intelligence, 407–410
Emotions
    accepted, 145
    ANS and, 395–398
    brain and, 395
    characterization, 394
    conditioned responses, 253
    contemporary model, 405–407
    cultural differences, 401
    development, 108–109
    expressing, 401–402, 404
    flexibility, 409
    focusing on, 568
    gender differences, 401
    intuition and, 362
    lie detectors and, 397–398
    managing, 408
    negative, 131
    pain and, 170
    perceptual, 188
    physiological changes, 394
    positive, 409
    problem solving and, 355
    reflecting, 568–569
    sexual, 616
    suppressing, 405

    theories of, 402–407
    types of, 394–395
    understanding, 408
    using, 408
    writing about, 493
Empathic arousal, 661
Empathy, 408
Empathy-helping relationship, 662
Empiricism, 14–15
Encoding, 288
Encoding failures, 304–306
Encounter groups, 565
Endocrine system, 85–89
Endogenous, 530
Endorphins, 62
Enkephalins, 62
Enrichment, environmental, 102
Environment
    assessing, 691
    deprivation, 102
    development and, 99–102
    enrichment, 102
    ergonomics, 701–702
    influences, 684–685
    intelligence and, 336–337
    personal space, 683
    physical, 682
    prenatal influences, 100–101
    problem solving, 691–692
    reaction range, 102–103
    as schizophrenia risk, 524
    sensitive periods, 101–102
    social dilemma over, 682, 689–691
    spatial norms, 683–684
    stressful, 685–687
    sustainability, 688–689
    toxic, 687–688
    tragedy of commons, 690–691
Environmental psychology, 682
Epididymis, 585
Epinephrine, 87
Episodic drive, 383
Episodic memory, 297–298
Equal-status contact, 652
Erectile disorder, 612–613
Ergonomics
    defined, 701
    human-computer interaction, 702–703
    space habitats, 703–704
    tool use, 703
    usability testing, 701–702
Ergotism, 543
Erikson, Erik, 30, 135–137
Erogenous zone, 427, 429, 594
Eros, 427–428
Erotomanic type delusions, 520
ESB (electrical stimulation of brain), 69
Escape, 469–470
Escape learning, 273
Escher, M. C., 92
ESP (extrasensory perception)
    appraisal, 194–197
    fraud in, 195
    stages, 196–197
    study of, 194
Essay tests, 7–8
Estrogens, 384, 584
Estrus, 384
Ethics, 43
Ethnic differences
    adolescence, 129
    identity and, 130
    parenting styles, 115
    suicide risks and, 535

Ethnocentrism, 648
Evaluation fears, 452
Evolutionary psychologists, 16
Excitement phase, 600
Exercise
    sleep and, 214
    stress reduction and, 492
    weight control and, 381
Exhaustion, stages of, 464
Exhibitionism, 602
Existentialism, 515, 548–549
Expectancies, 251–252
Expectancy, 433
Experiential cognition, 1
Experimental group, 41
Experimenter effect, 44
Experiments. *See also* specific
        experiments
    control, 42
    ethics, 43
    experimenter effect, 44
    participants, 41–42
    placebo effect, 42–44
    variables, 41–42
Explicit memories, 302
Expressive behavior, 436, 590
External frustrations, 468
External urethral orifice, 585
Extinction
    habit breaking and, 283
    nonreinforcement and, 558–559
    spontaneous recovery and, 252
Extracellular thirst, 383
Extraneous variables, 41
Extrinsic motivation, 391–392
Extroverts, 416–417, 423
Eye movement desensitization, 556
Eye structure, 155–158
Eyewitnesses, 198–200

Facial agnosia, 80
Facial expression, 400–401, 404
Facial feedback hypothesis, 404
Factor analysis, 422
Facts declarative memory, 297
Fallacy of positive instances, 22
Fallopian tube, 585
Familial intellectual disability, 334
Family-based therapy, 564–565
Fantasy, 475
Faulty concepts, 343
Fears. *See* Phobias
Feedback, 262–263
Feeling of knowing, 300
Feelings. *See* Emotions
Fellowship, 439
Female arousal disorder, 613–614
Female organism disorder, 614
Fetishism, 602
Feyman, Richard, 333
Fight or flight syndrome, 396
Figure-ground organization, 174
Fiorina, Carly, 671
Five-factor model, 423–425
Fixations, 354–355, 427
Fixed interval (FI) schedule, 267–268
Fixed ratio (FR) schedule, 267
Flashbulb memories, 310–311
Flavors, 166–167
Fluid abilities, 139
Fluid reasoning, 329
fMRI (functional magnetic resonance
        imaging), 70
Food intake, 214
Foot-in-the door effect, 634

Forebrain, 83–84
Forensic memory, 295
Forensic psychologists, 16
Forgetting. *See also* Memory
    cue-dependent, 306–307
    curve of, 304
    encoding failures, 304–306
    flashbulb memories, 310–311
    interference, 307–310
    memory decay, 306
    repressed memories, 310
Formal operations stage, 124
Fovea, 157
Frame of reference, 30, 568
Framing, 362–363
Fraser's spiral, 190
Free association, 544
Free choice, 438
Free will, 30
Frequency distribution, 710
Frequency polygon, 710
Frequency theory, 164
Freud, Anna, 30
Freud, Sigmund
    dream theory, 217, 242, 544
    psychosexual stage theory, 429–430
    unconsciousness theory, 30–31
Frontal loves, 76–78
Frotteurism, 602
Frustration-aggression hypothesis,
        657–658
Frustrations
    coping with, 470
    defined, 468
    reactions of, 469–470
    types of, 468
Fully functioning person, 440
Functional fixedness, 354
Functional solutions, 351
Functionalism, 27–28
Fundamental attribution error, 630
Furtado, Nelly, 56

G-factor, 328
Gallup polls, 50
Galvanic skin response (GSR), 397
Gambler's fallacy, 562
Gardner, Howard, 334–335, 367
GAS (general adaptation syndrome),
        463–464
Gate control theory, 169
Geller, Uri, 194, 196
Gender. *See also* Sex
    assigning, 587
    characteristics, 584
    defined, 584
Gender differences. *See also* Men;
        Women
    adolescence and, 129
    arousal, 594–595
    brain specialization, 79
    depression risk, 530–531
    emotional expression, 401
    normalcy and, 500
    origins, 587–590
    personality, 435
    sexual behavior, 600–602
    suicide risks and, 535
Gender identity, 585–587
Gender psychologists, 16
Gender roles
    androgynous, 590–592
    behavior, 590
    BSRI, 590–592
    cultural influence, 589

    influences, 588
    socialization, 586, 589–590
    stereotyping, 588
General solution, 351
Generalizations, 252, 269
Generalized anxiety disorder, 509–510
Generativity, 136–137
Genes, 99
Genetic disorders, 100–109
Genetic sex, 585
Genital sex, 585
Genital stage, 427, 429, 430
Genovese, Kitty, 660
Gestalt therapy
    approach, 549–550
    basis, 549
    history, 29–30
Gestural language, 346–347
GHB (gamma-hydroxybutyrate),
        234–235
Ghost sickness, 504
Giftedness, 332–333
Gilligan, Carol, 132–133
Ginott, Haim, 145
Glans penis, 585
Glenn, John, 139
Glove anesthesia, 514
GLP-1 (glucagon-like peptide), 377–378
Goals
    motivation and, 372
    psychology, 17–18
    setting, 6
    superordinate, 652–653
Gonadal sex, 585
Gonads, 584
Grammar, 345–346
Grandiose type delusions, 520
Graphical statistics, 710–711
Graphology, 21
Grasping reflex, 105
Group awareness training, 565
Group prejudice, 648
Group therapy
    advantages, 564
    characterization, 542
    family-based, 564–565
    locating, 578
    psychodrama, 564
Groups
    attributions, 629–630
    cohesiveness, 628
    conformity, 631–632
    double standards, 630
    in- and out-, 628
    influences, 630–632
    IQ tests, 331–332
    membership, 642
    norms, 629
    social influence, 630–632
    social roles, 628
    status, 628–629
    structure, 628
Groupthink, 632
Growth hormone, 86
Growth needs, 390
Guided discovery, 277–278
Guided imagery, 493
Guilt, 136
Gunnysacking, 616
Gustation, 166

Habits, 189, 433
Habituate, 199
Hair cells, 163

Halfway houses, 572
Hallucinations
    defined, 190, 518
    explanations for, 190–191
    UFO abductions, 210
Hallucinogens, 238–239
Halo effect
    attraction and, 623
    hiring and, 676
    personality assessment, 444
Handedness, 90–94
Hardiness, 488
Hardy personality, 488
Harris polls, 50
Hassles, 483–484
Hawking, Stephen W., 328
Health psychology
    behavior and, 458–460
    community campaigns, 460–461
    defense mechanisms, 475–481
    defined, 458
    early prevention and, 460
    learned helplessness, 477–480
    stress (*See* Stress)
    wellness, 461
Hearing
    artificial, 166
    loss, 165
    process, 163–165
    stimulus for, 163
Hearing aids, 165
Height in picture plane, 181
Hemispheres, cerebral
    connection, 73
    damage to, 74
    dominance and, 90–91
    function, 73–74
    lateralization, 92–93
    specialization, 74–76
    stroke and, 75
Heredity
    defined, 98
    genetics of, 98–99
    intelligence and, 336–337
    personality and, 416
    as schizophrenia risk, 524–525
    sexual orientation and, 597
Heterosexuals, 597
Heuristics, 352, 361–362
Hidden observer, 220
Hierarchy
    desensitization, 554
    of needs, 390–391
    self-management and, 577
Higher order conditioning, 250–251
Hilgard, Ernest, 220
Hindbrain, 82–83
Hippocampus, 84, 311
Hispanic Americans, 116
Histogram, 710
History
    behaviorism, 28–29
    biological perspective, 32–33
    functionalism, 27–28
    Gestalt, 29
    humanism, 30–31
    mental illness treatments, 543–544
    notable events, 31
    psychoanalysis, 30
    psychological perspective, 33
    sexual revolution, 603–604
    sociocultural perspective, 33–34
    structuralism, 27
    women pioneers, 31

HIV/AIDS, 607–608
Hoffman, Dustin, 326
Homeostasis, 372–373
Homosexuality, 597–599
Honesty tests, 448
Hope, 478
Hormones
 defined, 85
 sex, 384, 584–585
 sleep, 208
Horney, Karen, 30
Hospitalization, 571–572
Hostility reduction, 487–488
Hue, 155
Human Genome Project, 98
Human growth sequence, 100
Human-computer interaction, 702–703
Humanistic psychology
 anxiety disorder approach, 515
 client-centered, 548
 existential, 548–549
 focus, 438
 history, 30–31
 personality development, 442
 personality theory of, 418, 438–443
 positive personalities, 440
 self theory, 440–442
 self-actualization, 438–439
Humor, sense of, 439
Hunger. *See also* Eating
 brain mechanisms, 376–378
 external factors, 378–379
 internal factors, 376
 memory and, 319
Hyperopia, 155
Hypersomnia, 207, 213
Hyperthyroidism, 87
Hypervigilant style, 673
Hypnic jerk, 209
Hypnosis, 220–223
Hypnotic susceptibility, 221
Hypoactive sexual desire, 612
Hypochondriasis, 484, 513
Hypopituitary, 86
Hypothalamus, 83, 376–378
Hypothesis testing, 24
Hypothyroidism, 87

I-message, 145
Iconic memory, 288
ICS (intracranial self-stimulation), 260–261
Id, 427
Ideal self, 440
Identification, 435, 475
Identity, 129–130, 136
Identity disorder, 512
Ifufunyane, 569
Illogical thought, 357
Illusions, 189–191
Imagery, 315–316, 340
Imitating models, 278–279
Imitation, 435
Immediate consequence, 642
Immune system, 464
Implicit memories, 302
In-basket test, 677–678
In-groups, 628
Inattentional blindness, 152
Incentive value, 372
Incongruence, 440
Incongruent person, 440
Incus, 163

Independent variables, 41
Individual therapy, 542
Individual traits, 426
Individuating information, 664
Inductive thought, 357
Industrial psychology, 28
Industrial/organizational psychology
 communication, 678–670
 function, 670
 job analysis, 675–676
 job enrichment, 674
 job satisfaction, 673–674
 organizational culture, 674–675
 personnel, 675
 selection procedures, 676–678
 theories, 670–673
Industry, 136
Infants. *See also* Neonates
 cognition, 124–126
 communication by, 119–120
 emotional development, 108–109
 maturation, 107–110
 motor development, 107–108
 social development, 111–117
Inferential statistics
 correlation-rating relationships, 716–719
 defined, 708
 populations, 716
 samples, 716
Inferiority, 136
Information
 bits, 292
 chunks, 292
 individuating, 664
 operant conditioning and, 257
 recall, 300
 recognizing, 300–301
 relearning, 301–302
Informational view, 251
Initiative, 136
Insanity, 504–505
Insecure-ambivalent attachment, 112
Insecure-avoidant attachment, 112
Insight therapy, 542
Insightful solutions, 352–355
Insomnia, 213–214
Instances, positive, 22
Instrumental behavior, 436, 590
Intellectual disability, 333–334
Intellectualization, 475
Intelligence
 defining, 328–329
 emotional, 407–410
 nature v. nurture, 336–337
 neonate's, 105–107
 observing, 328
 variations in, 332–334
Intelligence tests
 factors, 329–330
 types, 329–331, 334–336
 value of, 329
Interference, 307–310
Intergroup conflict, 649–650
Internet therapy, 550–551
Interpersonal attraction
 competence, 624
 defined, 623
 physical attractiveness, 623–624
 physical proximity, 623
 romantic love, 625–627
 self-disclosure, 624–625
 similarity and, 624
Interpersonal psychotherapy (IPT), 545

Interpersonal relationships, 439
Interposition. *See* Overlap
Interpretation of Dreams, The (Freud), 217
Intersexual children, 586–587
Intersexual person, 586
Interviews
 cognitive, 295, 319–320
 personal, 678–679
 personality assessment, 444–445
Intimacy, 136, 616–617
Intimate distance, 683–684
Intracellular thirst, 383
Intrinsic motivation, 391–392
Introspection, 27
Introverts, 416–417
Intuition, 360–363
Intuitive thought, 123
Ion channels, 59–60
Ions, 59
IQ (intelligence quotient)
 culture and, 365–367
 deviation, 331
 factors influencing, 336–337
 measures, 329–330
Irrational beliefs, 561
Isolation
 thought, 475
 death and, 140
 defined, 136

Jackson, Peter, 297
James, William, 27–28, 31
James-Lange theory, 402
Jealous type delusions, 520
Jet lag, 374
Jigsaw classrooms, 653–654
Job analysis, 675–676
Job satisfaction, 673–674
Jones, Jim, 646
Judgment, errors in, 361–362
Jung, Carl, 30
Juries
 behavior, 694–695
 death-qualified, 695
 mock, 694
 selecting, 695–696
Just-world beliefs, 664
Justice, 132–133

Kaczynski, Theodore, 523
Keyword method, 322–323
Kinesics, 401–402
Kinesthetic images, 342
Kinesthetic senses, 168
Knowledge
 intelligence and, 329
 of results, 263
 workers, 671
Koro, 504
Kübler-Ross, Elisabeth, 140
Kuder Occupational Interest Survey, 676

Labia majora, 585
Labia minora, 585
Ladd-Franklin, Christine, 31
Language
 body, 401–402
 development, 118–120
 structure of, 345–347
 thinking and, 340
 thought and, 344–349
 types, 346–349
Large-group awareness training, 565

Latency, 427, 430
Latent content, 544
Latent learning, 276–278
Lateral hypothalamus, 377
Lateralization, 92–93
Law of effect, 256
Law, psychology of, 694
LDS, 525
Leaderless group discussion, 677–678
Leadership, 670–673
Learned helplessness
 defined, 477
 depression and, 478–479
 examples, 477–478
 hope and, 478
Learning. *See also* Active learning; Overlearning
 aids, 263–265
 antecedents, 248
 classical conditioning, 248–254
 cognitive, 276–278
 consequences, 248
 defined, 248
 digital media, 8–11
 modeling, 278–281
 operant conditioning, 248–249, 256–270
 perceptual, 188–192
 personality, 432–437
 problem solving and, 354–355
 procrastination, 6–7
 punishment and, 272–275
 reinforcement, 248
 self-regulated, 5–6
 state-dependent, 306–307
 strategies, 4–5
 theorists, 16
 whole vs. part, 318
Lectures, LISAN method, 3–4
Left brain, 75–76
Left handiness, 92
Leikind, Bernard, 54
Lesioning, 69
Levinson, Daniel, 138
Lexigrams, 348–349
Libido, 428
Lie detectors, 397–398
Life shills training, 460
Lifestyles, 458–459, 688–689
Light, 155, 181
Light sleep, 209
Liking, 625
Limbic system, 83–84
Linear perspective, 181
LISAN method, 3–4
Listening skills, 679–680
Lobes
 frontal, 76–78
 occipital, 78–80
 parietal, 77–78
 prefontal, 77
 temporal, 78
Localization, 151
Localize function, 68
Lock and key theory, 166
Loftus, Elizabeth, 309
Logical consequences, 145–146
Logical thought, 357
Long sleepers, 207
Looking chamber, 105–107
Love, 143, 625–627
Lowball technique, 634–635
LSD (lysergic acid diethylamide), 238
LTM (long-term memory)
 brain and, 312

constructing, 293–296
organizing, 296–297
permanence, 293
types of, 297–298
Lucid dreams, 244

Ma, Yo Yo, 56, 60
Maasai, 290
Maintenance rehearsal, 292–293
Maladaptive, 499
Maladaptive personality patterns, 507
Male orgasmic disorder, 614
Malleus, 163
Management by objectives, 672
Management techniques, 143
Manic depression. *See* Bipolar disorders
Manifest content, 544
Marijuana, 238–239
Marriage
   mate selection, 625–627
   sexual adjustment, 615–616
   suicide risks and, 535–536
Maslow, Abraham, 30–31, 198, 438
Massed practice, 319
Mastery training, 478
Masturbation, 596
Mate selection
   evolution and, 626–627
   romantic love and, 625
   sex and, 626–627
Material World Project, 689
Maternal influences, 114–115
Matrix, 170
Maturation
   adolescence, 129
   defined, 107
   language development and, 118
   motor development, 107–108
   rate, 107
McGraw, Dr. Phil, 550
McLaren, Wayne, 233
MDMA (methylenedioxymethamphetamine), 232
Mean, defined, 711–712
Mechanical solution, 351
Media. *See also* Television
   attitude formation and, 642
   digital, 8
   modeling, 279–280
   psychologist image in, 36
   psychology on, 53–55, 550
   violence, 658–659
Median, defined, 712
Meditation, 223–225, 492–493
Medulla, 82
Melatonin, 87
Memory. *See also* Forgetting; Working memory
   brain and, 311–313
   cues, 306
   decay, 306
   defined, 288
   exceptional, 315–321
   flashbulb, 310–311
   forensic, 295
   hunger and, 319
   hypnosis and, 221
   improving, 315–321
   long-term, 289–290, 293–298, 312
   measuring, 300–303
   recovered, 308
   repressed, 310
   short-term, 289, 292–293
   sleep and, 319
   stages, 288–290
   strategies for, 316–317, 319–320
   traces, 306
Memory pill, 313
Men
   career stereotypes, 589
   eating disorders, 382
   erectile disorder, 612–613
   orgasmic disorder, 614–615
   reproductive structures, 585
   sexual response, 601
   suicide risks and, 535
Menarche, 584
Menopause, 584
Mental adaptations, 122–123
Mental age, 329
Mental disorders. *See also* specific disorders
   behavior-associated, 499–500
   community treatment programs, 573
   defined, 500
   drug therapy, 570
   DSM-IV-TR classification, 500–505
   ECT, 570–571
   folk names, 504
   general risk factors, 504
   hospitalization for, 571–572
   insanity and, 504–505
   overview of, 502–504
   psychiatric labeling, 532–534
   psychosurgery, 571
   social stigma, 532–533
   treatment, 533, 543
Mental imagery, 315, 340–341
Mental practice, 698
Mentally gifted, 332–333
Mentally retardation. *See* Intellectual disability
Meta-needs, 390
Metabolic disorder, 334
Michelangelo, 92
Microsleep, 207
Microstressors, 483–484
Midcourse corrections, 138
Midlife crisis, 137–138
Milgram's obedience studies, 636–638
Mindfulness meditation, 223, 225
Mirror neurons, 77
Miss Cleo, 195
Mistrust, 136
Mitchell, Edgar, 196
MMPI-2 (Minnesota Multiphasic Personality Inventory-2), 446
Mnemonics
   defined, 317
   examples, 322–325
   learning and, 4
Mock juries, 694
Mode, defined, 712
Modeling, 278–281
Monocular depth cues, 181–184
Mood disorders, 502. *See also specific disorders*
   causes, 530
   characterization, 529
   major, 529
Moods, 395
Moon illusion, 183–184
Moral anxiety, 427, 429
Moral development
   conscience and, 132
   identity search and, 129–130
   levels, 132–133
   puberty and, 129
   transition to adulthood, 130
   twixters, 131
Moro reflex, 105
Morphemes, 345
Mother Teresa, 438
Motherese, 120
Motivation
   defined, 372
   extrinsic, 391–392
   intrinsic, 391–392
   model, 372–374
Motives. *See also* Primary motives; Social motives
   perceptual, 188
   in perspective, 390–393
   social, 388–390
   types, 372–373
Motor development, 107–108
Motor neurons, 65
Motor programs, 698
Motor skills, 697
MRI (magnetic resonance imaging)
   characterization, 68
   functional, 70
   schizophrenic brains, 526
Müller-Lyer illusion, 190–192
Multiculturalism, 664–665
Multimedia computerized tests, 677–678
Multiple approach-avoidance conflict, 472
Multiple intelligences, 334–335
Multiple sclerosis, 63–64
Munchausen syndrome, 513
Munchausen syndrome by proxy, 513
Murray, Henry, 448
Mutism, 522
Mutual interdependence, 653
Myelin, 63
Myopia, 155

Narcolepsy, 213, 215
Native Americans, 205
Natural clinical tests, 48
Natural consequences, 145–146
Natural design, 701
Natural selection, 28
Naturalistic observation
   characterization, 46
   limitations, 46–47
   recordings, 47
Nature. *See* Heredity
Nearness, 175
Needs. *See also* Motives
   achievement, 388–389
   hierarchy of, 390–391
Negative after-potential, 60
Negative correlation, 48
Negative reinforcement, 259
Negative relationship, 717
Negative self-statements, 494
Negative transfer, 308
Neo-Freudians, 30
Neonates
   defined, 105
   development, 105–107
   temperament, 103
Nerves
   characterization, 63–64
   components, 58–59
   function, 58
   impulses, 59–60
   pain carrying, 168–169
   types, 65
Nervous system. *See also* specific branches
   nerves, 63–64
   neurons, 63–64
   subparts, 64–66
Network model, 296
Neural regulators, 62
Neurilemma, 64
Neurogenesis, 63
Neurons
   characterization, 63–64
   mirror, 77
   types, 65
Neuropeptides, 62
Neurosis, 503
Neurotic anxiety, 427, 429
Neuroticism, 423
Neutral stimulus, 249
Nicholson, Jack, 36
Nicotine, 233–234
Night terrors, 215
Nightmare disorder, 213
Nightmares, 215
Noise pollution, 687
Noise-induced hearing loss, 165
Nonconformity, 498
Nondirective therapy, 542
Nonexperimental research, 46–47
Nonreinforcement, 558–559
Noradrenaline, 231
Norepinephrine, 87
Normal curve, 332, 713–714
Normality, 498
Norms. *See* Social norms
Notes, 4
NPY (neuropeptide Y), 377
NREM (non-rapid eye movements) sleep, 210–211
Nurture. *See* Environment

Obedience, 635–639
Obesity, 378–379
Obsessive-compulsive disorder, 511–512
Object permanence, 123
Objective test, 446
Objective tests, 7
Objectivity, 186–193
Observational learning, 278–279
Observational record, 47
Observer bias, 46
Observer effect, 46
Occipital lobes, 78–80
Oedipus conflict, 427, 430
Olfaction, 166
Openness, 423
Operant conditioning
   approaches, 558–559
   defined, 248–249
   history, 29
   occurrence, 256–260
   reinforcers, 260–265
Operant extinction, 259
Operant reinforcer, 256
Operant stimulus generalizations, 269
Operational definitions, 24
Opponent-process theory, 158
Oral stage, 427, 429–430
Oral-aggressive personality, 427, 430
Oral-dependent personality, 427, 430
Order effects, 308
Organ of Corti, 163
Organismic valuing, 442

I-20 Subject Index

Organization
  memory and, 318
  perceptions, 174–178
  sensations, 174–178
Orgasms, 600, 614–615
Originality, 357
Other-race effect, 187
Otolith organs, 170–171
Out-groups, 628
Oval window, 163
Ovary, 585
Overgeneralization, 560
Overlap, 181
Overlearning
  assertiveness training, 638
  defined, 5
  studies, 318
Overload, 687
Overly permissive parents, 113
Overt behavior, 14
Ovulation, 584

Pain
  avoidance, 383
  control, 169–170
  emotions and, 170
  function, 168
  gate, 169
  hypnosis and, 223
  insensitivity, 168
  receptors, 168
  sexual, 615
Pain disorder, 513
Palmistry, 21
Panic disorders, 510
Paradoxical intention, 214
Paranoid psychosis, 520–521
Paranoid schizophrenia, 521–523
Paraphilias, 602
Parapsychology, 194
Parasympathetic rebound, 396
Paraventricular nucleus, 377
Parentese, 120
Parenting
  developmental impact, 115
  effective, 143–146
  ethnic differences, 115
  media violence prevention, 659–660
  styles, 113–114
Parents
  exaggerated speaking patterns, 120
  Piaget's guide for, 125
  Vygotsky's view of, 127
Parietal lobes, 77–78
Partial hospitalization, 572
Partial reinforcement effect, 266–268
Participants, 41–42
Participative management, 672
Paternal influences, 114–115
Pavlov's experiment, 249–250
Pavlov, Ivan, 28, 31, 249–250
Peak experiences, 439
Peak performance, 698–699
Pedophilia, 602
Peek, Kim, 326, 334
Peer counselors, 578
Pelvic bone, 585
People's Temple, 645
Percent of variance, 718
Perception psychologists, 16
Perceptions
  constancies, 173–174
  creation, 152
  depth, 179–185
  emotions, 188
  expectancies, 186–187
  extrasensory, 194–197
  eyewitness, 198–200
  motives, 188
  objectivity and, 186–193
  organization, 174–178
  problem solving and, 355
  of reality, 438
Perceptual awareness, 198–199
Perceptual constructions, 186
Perceptual features, 150–151
Perceptual habits, 189
Perceptual hypothesis, 175
Perceptual sets, 186–187
Perfect negative relationship, 717
Perfect positive relationship, 717
Performance intelligence, 331
Periodic limb movement syndrome, 213
Peripheral vision, 157–158
Permissive parents. *See* Overly permissive parents
Persecutory type delusions, 520
Personal distance, 684
Personal frustrations, 468
Personal interviews, 678–679
Personal prejudice, 648
Personal space, 683
Personality
  authoritarian, 648, 695
  behavior and, 433
  cardiac, 486–488
  creative, 360
  defined, 414
  disease-prone, 458
  dynamics of, 428–429
  gender and, 435
  genetics, 416
  hardy, 488
  humanistic theories, 438–443
  learning theories, 432–437
  musical taste and, 422
  positive traits, 440
  prejudice, 648–649
  psychoanalytic theory of, 427–431
  psychology of, 414–420
  self theory, 440–442
  self-concept and, 417
  self-esteem and, 417–418
  shyness, 452–454
  social learning theory, 433–434
  structure of, 427–428
  theories, 417–419
  traits, 414–415
  twin studies, 415–416
  types, 416–417
Personality assessment
  direct observation, 445–446
  honesty tests, 448
  interviews, 444–445
  projective tests of, 448–450
  questionnaires, 446–448
  rating scale, 445–446
  research example, 450
  situational testing, 446
Personality development
  behavioral theory, 434–436
  Freudian theory, 429–430
  humanistic theory, 442
Personality disorders. *See also* specific disorders
  antisocial, 507–509
  anxiety-based, 509–514
  dissociative, 512
  maladaptive patterns, 507
  stress-based, 512
  symptoms, 502–503
Personnel psychology, 675
Persuasion, 643–644
PET (positron emission tomography), 70, 526
Phallic stage, 427, 429–430
Pharmacotherapy, 570
Phobias, 452, 510–511
Phonemes, 345
Phosphenes, 151
Photographic memory, 315–316
Physical dependence, 227
Physical energy, 150
Physical environments, 682
Physical proximity, 623
Physical strength, 221
Physiological changes, 394
Piaget, Jean, 122–125
Picasso, Pablo, 92
Pictorial depth, 181
Pineal gland, 87
Pinel, Philippe, 543–544
Pinna, 163
Pituitary gland, 86–87
Place theory, 164
Placebos, 42–44
Plasticity, 63
Plateau phase, 600
Pleasure principle, 427–4428
PNS (parasympathetic nervous system), 64–65, 396–397
Politics
  IQ testing, 366–367
  prejudice and, 652
  racial, 366–367
Polygenic characteristics, 99
Polygraphs, 397
Pons, 82
Ponzo illusion, 184
Pop-out, 151
Populations, 49–50, 716
Positive correlation, 48
Positive instances, 22
Positive psychology, 33
Positive reinforcement, 256–257, 558
Positive relationship, 717
Positive self-regard, 442
Positive therapy, 542
Positive transfer, 308
Possible selves, 441
Postconventional-level reasoning, 132
Postpartum depression, 531
Poverty, 102
Power assertion, 143
Power, need for, 389
Practical intelligence, 366
Precognition, 194
Preconscious, 427, 429
Preconventional-level reasoning, 132
Prediction, 18
Prefrontal area, 77
Prefrontal lobotomy, 571
Prejudice
  becoming, 648
  combating, 652–654
  defined, 648
  experiments in, 651–654
  overcoming, 664–665
  personality, 648–649
  politics and, 652
  stereotyping and, 649–650
  symbolic, 651
  terrorism and, 651
Premack, David, 347
Premature ejaculation, 614–615
Prenatal influences, development, 100–101
Prenatal sexual development, 585–586
Preoperational stage, 123
Preparation, 388
Presbyopia, 156
Pressure, 464
Prevention
  disease, 460
  early, 460
  suicide, 536
  terrorism, 398
  violence, 659–660
Primary appraisal, 466
Primary motives
  bases, 372
  homeostasis and, 373
  hunger, 376–382
  pain, 383
  sex drive, 383–384
  thirst, 383
Primary motor area, 77
Primary sexual characteristics, 585
Primary somatosensory area, 78
Prime, 36
Primed hidden memories, 302
Principles of Psychology (James), 27
Privacy, 704
Private self-consciousness, 452
Proactive interference, 308
Problem clarification, 567–568
Problem solving
  barriers to, 355
  culture and, 354
  framing and, 362–363
  intuition and, 360–361
  solution approaches, 351–355
Procrastination, 6–7
Professional help guidelines, 577–579
Progressive relaxation, 493
Projection, 475–476
Projective tests, 448–450
Prosocial behavior, 660–662
Prostate, 585
Prototypes, 343
Proxemics, 683
Proximodistal maturation pattern, 107
Pseudomemories, 295, 301, 309
Pseudopsychology, 21–23
Psi phenomena, 194
Psyche, 427–428
Psychiatric care
  approaches, 569
  community programs, 573
  hospitalization, 571–572
  therapies, 570–571
Psychiatric social workers, 38
Psychiatrists, 36
Psychoactive drugs, 227, 230
Psychoanalysis
  characterization, 544
  dream analysis, 544–545
  effectiveness, 545–546
  history, 30
  main goal, 544
  modern approaches, 545
  resistance analysis, 545
  theory, 427–431
  transference, 545
Psychoanalysts, 36, 567–568
Psychodynamic theory
  anxiety disorder approach, 515
  dreams, 217

focus, 417
tenants, 33
Psychokinesis, 194
Psychological dependence, 227–228
Psychological efficiency, 671
Psychological perspective, 33
Psychological situation, 433
Psychological testing, 676–678
Psychological trauma, 524
Psychologists
 degrees required, 36
 evaluating, 578–579
 locating, 577–579
 media, 550
 portrayal of, 36
 qualifications, 578–579
Psychology. See also specific branches
 benefits of, 12
 career in, 38
 defined, 14
 developmental, 98
 ethics, 38
 goals, 17–18
 media image, 53–55
 profession, 38
 specialties, 38–39
Psychoneuroimmunology, 464
Psychopathology, 498
Psychophysics, 150
Psychosexual stages, 427, 429
Psychosis
 amphetamine, 231
 nature of, 518–520
 organic, 519–520
 paranoid, 520–521
Psychosocial dilemma, 135
Psychosocial theory, 135–137
Psychosomatic disorders, 484–485
Psychotherapy
 core features, 566–567
 counseling skills, 567–569
 dimensions of, 542
 effectiveness, 565–566
 future of, 567
 myths, 542
 origins, 542–544
 time involved, 566
Psychotic disorders, 502
PsycINFO, 9, 11
PTSD (posttraumatic stress disorder), 512
Puberty, 87, 129
Public distance, 684
Public self-consciousness, 452
Publications, 25
Punishers, 272
Punishment. See also Discipline
 effects of, 260, 272
 operant therapy and, 558
 variables affecting, 272–275

Quality circles, 672
Quantitative reasoning, 329
Questionnaires, 422, 446–448
Questions
 active learning, 2
 closed, 569
 control, 397
 text, 1

Race, 366–367, 665
Racial profiling, 648
Randi, James, 53, 197
Random assignment, 42
Random search strategy, 352

Random, defined, 716
Range, defined, 712
Rank, Otto, 30
Rape
 acquaintance, 606
 forcible, 606
 gender role stereotyping and, 606
 myths, 606
RAS (reticular activating system), 83
Rating scale, 445–446
Rationalization, 475–476
Reaction formation, 475–476
Reaction range, development, 102–103
Readiness, 108
Reading, 1–2
Reality
 perceptions of, 438
 principle, 427, 428
 testing, 190
Reasoning, quantitative, 329
REBT (rational-emotive behavior therapy), 561–562
Receptor sites, 61
Recessive genes, 99
Reciprocal influences, development, 103
Reciprocal inhibition, 554
Recitation
 active learning, 2–3
 memory and, 317–318
 text, 2
Recognition memory, 301
Recovered memory, 309
Recovery, spontaneous, 252
Recruitment, 646
Rectum, 585
Recycling, 263
Redintegrative memories, 296–297
Reeves, Keanu, 170
Reflection, 2–3
Reflective cognition, 1
Reflex arc, 65
Reflexes, 105–107, 248
Refractory period, 601
Refusal skills training, 460
Regression, 475–476
Rehearsal
 advantages of, 318
 information, 292–293
 test taking and, 388
Reinforcement
 defined, 248
 negative, 259
 partial, 266–268
 positive, 256–257
 respondent, 250
 shaping, 258–259
 timing, 258
Reinforcement values, 434
Reinforcers, 260–262
Relational concepts, 343
Relative motion, 182
Relative size, 181
Relaxation, 214, 388
Relaxation response, 224
Relearning, 301–302
REM (rapid eye movements) sleep, 209–211, 216
REM behavior disorder, 213
Remembering. See Memory
Reminding system, 169
Repeated frustrations, 468
Representative samples, 49
Representative, defined, 716

Representativeness, 361–362
Repressed memories, 310
Repressed thoughts, 30
Repression, 475–476
Research
 animal use, 16–17
 clinical, 48–49
 correlational studies, 47–48
 defined, 15
 empirical, 14–15
 ESP, 195–196
 experimental, 41–44
 nonexperimental, 46–47
 reports, 25
 scientific, 23–25
 specialties, 16
 survey, 49–51
Resistance analysis, 545
Resolution, 600
Respondent reinforcement, 250
Response
 chains, 258, 283
 conditioned, 28
 costs, 260
 personality and, 433
Responsibility, diffusion of, 661
REST (restricted environmental stimulation therapy), 224
Resting potential, 59
Restructuring thoughts, 388
Reticular formation (RF), 83
Retina, 157
Retinal disparity, 180
Retrieval, 288
Retroactive interference, 308
Reversible figures, 174
Reviews, 2
Rewards, 433
Rhine, J. B., 194–195
Right brain, 75–76
Right handiness, 92
Robinson, Cheri, 151
Rods, 156–158
Rogers, Carl, 30–31, 438, 440–442, 515
Role confusion, 136
Role reversal, 564
Romantic love, 625–627
Rooting reflex, 105
Rorschach, Hermann, 448
Rorschach inkblock test, 448
Rote learning, 277
Run of luck, 195

Samples, 716
Sane hallucinations, 191
Santana, Carlos, 56
SAT (scholastic assessment test), 331
Satiety system, 377
Savant, 326
Scaffolding, 126
Scapegoating, 469, 648
Scatter diagram, 717
Schachter's cognitive theory, 402–405
Schedules, 6, 266–268
Schizophrenia
 brain and, 526
 causes, 524–525
 characterization, 521
 types, 521–524
Schweitzer, Albert, 438
Scientific jury selection, 695
Scientific management, 670
Scientific method, 23–26
Scientific observation, 15

Scripts, 594
Scrotum, 585
Seasonal affective disorder (SAD), 531–532
Seat-of-the-pants phenomenon, 152
Secondary appraisal, 466
Secondary elaboration, 242
Secondary motives, 372–373
Secondary sexual characteristics, 584
Secondary traits, 422
Secondhand conditioning, 253–254
Secret, The, 54
Secure attachment style, 113
Securely attached, 112
Selection, 318
Selective attention, 152–154
Selective perception, 560
Self, 438, 440
Self-actualization, 30–31, 438–439
Self-assertion, 638
Self-awareness, 408
Self-concept, 417
Self-confidence, 390
Self-consciousness, 452
Self-defeating bias, 452
Self-directed desensitization, 576–577
Self-disclosure, 624–625
Self-efficacy, 434
Self-esteem, 144, 417–418
Self-evaluation, 30
Self-fulfilling prophecies, 44, 665
Self-help groups, 578
Self-image, 30, 440
Self-management
 behavior and, 282–283
 covert reinforcement, 576
 covert sensitization, 575–576
 hierarchy use, 577
 self-directed desensitization, 576–577
 teams, 672
 thought stopping, 576
 use of, 575
Self-recording, 283–284
Self-regard, positive, 442
Self-regulated learning, 5–6
Self-reinforcement, 434
Self-testing, 5
Semantic memory, 297
Semantics, 344
Seminal vesicles, 585
Sensate focus, 613
Sensation psychologists, 16
Sensations
 creation, 152
 organization, 174–178
 seeking, 386
Senses. See also specific sense
 chemical, 166–168
 somesthetic, 168–170
Sensitive periods, development, 101–102
Sensitivity groups, 565
Sensitization, 575–576
Sensorimotor stage, 123
Sensorineural hearing loss, 165
Sensory systems
 adaptation, 150
 analysis, 150–151
 change, 223
 coding, 151–152
 memory, 288
 neurons, 65
 restriction, 704
 selection, 150

Separation anxiety, 111
Serial position effect, 300, 318
Serious games. *See* CAI (computer-assisted instruction)
Set point, 378
Sex. *See also* Gender
 characteristics, 584
 dimensions, 585
 drive, 383–384, 595–596
 hormones, 384, 584–585
Sexsomnia, 214
Sexual and gender identity disorders, 502–503
Sexual aversion, 612
Sexual behavior
 arousal, 594–597
 attitudes toward, 603–607
 atypical, 602–603
 behavioral risks, 608–610
 criminal, 606–607
 double standard, 605
 intimacy, 616–617
 relational adjustments, 615–616
 safe practices, 609
 satisfaction with, 616
 STD risk, 607–608
Sexual development
 biology, 584
 gender characteristics, 584–585
 prenatal, 585–586
Sexual disagreements, 615–616
Sexual disorders
 arousal, 612–614
 desire, 612
 orgasm, 614–615
 pain related, 615
Sexual masochism, 602
Sexual orientation, 597–598
Sexual response, 600–602
Sexual revolution
 attitudes, 604
 history, 603–604
 reaction against, 604–605
 young girls and, 605
Sexual sadism, 602
Sexual scripts, 594
Shadows, 181
Shame, 136
Shape constancy, 174
Shaping, 258–259, 558
Shared leadership, 672
Shift work, 374
Short sleepers, 207
Shyness
 beliefs and, 453
 dynamics of, 452–453
 elements, 452
 situational causes, 452
 social skills and, 453–454
Sidedness, 90
SIDS (sudden infant death syndrome), 215–216
Sign language, 346–347
Signal words, 3
Silence, 569
Similarity, 175, 624
Simpson, O. J., 695–696
Simultaneous orgasm, 601
Single-blind experiment, 44
Single-word stage, 118
Singles, 119
Sioux Indians, 205
Situational determinants, 432
Situational judgment tests, 677–678
Situational testing, 446

Sixteen Personality Factor Questionnaire (16 PF), 422
Size constancy, 173–174
Size-distance invariance, 192
Skills procedural memory, 297
Skin senses, 168
Skinner, B. F., 28–29
Skinner box, 28
Sleep
 basic types, 209–211
 disturbances, 213–219
 dreams, 216–218
 drunkenness, 213
 hormone, 208
 memory and, 319
 need for, 205–206
 patterns, 206–208
 quiz, 204
 restriction, 214
 spindles, 209
 stages, 209
Sleep apnea, 213, 215
Sleep terror disorder, 213
Sleep-deprivation psychosis, 206
Sleep-wake schedule disorder, 213
Sleepwalking disorder, 213
Smell, sense of, 166
Smiles, infants, 108
Smoking, 234
Smoking cessation, 554
SNS (somatic nervous system), 64–65
Social anxiety, 452
Social behavior
 affiliation, 622–623
 aggression, 656–660
 assertiveness, 638–639
 attitudes, 641–648
 attraction, 623–627
 compliance, 634–635
 diversity and, 664–667
 groups, 628–633
 intergroup conflict, 649–651
 obedience, 635–638
 prejudice, 648–654
 prosocial, 660–662
Social comparison theory, 622–623
Social competition, 665
Social desirability, 50
Social development
 affectional needs, 112
 attachment and, 111–112
 day car, 112
 defined, 111
 maternal influences, 114–115
 parenting styles, 113–114
 paternal influences, 114–115
Social dilemmas, 689–691
Social distance, 684
Social environments, 682
Social learning theory, 433–434, 658–659
Social motives, 388–389
Social nonconformity, 498
Social norms, 34
Social phobia, 511
Social psychologists, 16
Social psychology, 622
Social reinforcement, 435
Social reinforcers, 262
Social roles, 628
Social skills, 452, 453–454
Social smile, 108
Social stereotypes, 343
Social stigma, 532–533
Social support, 488–489

Social workers, 38
Social-recreational drugs, 229
Sociocultural perspective, 33–34
Sociopaths. *See* Antisocial personality disorder
Solitude, 439
Somas, 58
Somatic type delusions, 520
Somatization disorder, 513
Somatoform disorders
 diagnosis, 513
 forms of, 514
 symptoms, 502–503
Somatosensory area, 78
Somesthetic senses, 168–170
Somnambulists, 214
Sound waves, 163
Source traits, 422–423
Space habitats, 703–704
Spaced practice, 318–319
Spatial norms, 683–684
Specialties, 38–39
Specific phobia, 510–511
Spinal nerves, 65
Split-brain operation, 74–75
Spontaneity, 438
Spontaneous recovery, 252
Spontaneous remission, 545–546
Sports psychology, 696–699
SQ4R method, 1–3
SSRS (Social Readjustment Rating Scale), 482–483
Stage hypnosis, 220–221
Standard deviation, 712
Standard scores, 713
Stanford-Binet scales, 329–330
Stapes, 163
State-dependent learning, 306–307
Statistical abnormality, 498
Statistical significance, 716
Statistics. *See* Descriptive statistics; Inferential statistics
Status, 628–629
STD (sexual transmitted disease), 607
Stereocilia, 163
Stereoscopic vision, 180
Stereotypes
 avoiding, 664
 characteristics, 649–650
 defined, 649
 gender roles, 588
 social, 343
Sterilization, 596
Stimulants, 214, 227
Stimulus, 27, 249
Stimulus control
 conditioning and, 268–270, 558
 as insomnia treatment, 214
 self-management and, 575–576
Stimulus discrimination, 253
Stimulus drives, 386–387
Stimulus generalization, 252
Stimulus motives, 372
STM (short-term memory)
 chunking, 292
 defined, 289
 rehearsing information, 292–293
Storage, 288
Streep, Meryl, 36
Stress
 acculturative, 484
 cardiac personality, 486–488
 conflict and, 470–473
 disorders, 512
 effects of, 463

elements of, 464
 environmental factors, 685–687
 frustration and, 468–470
 GAS and, 463–464
 hardy personality, 488
 health and, 464, 482–490
 inoculation, 494
 life events and, 482–484
 psychosomatic disorders and, 484–485
 reaction, 463
 signs of, 464
 traumatic, 467
 upsetting thoughts and, 494
Stress Game, 490
Stress management
 behavior modification, 493
 biofeedback training, 485–486
 bodily reactions, 490–493
 defined, 490
 social support, 488–489
Stressors, 464–467
Strokes, 79
Strong-Campbell Interest Inventory, 676
Structuralism, 27
Structured interview, 444
Studying. *See* Learning
Subcortex, 82–85
Subjective experience, 438
Subjects, 41–42
Sublimation, 475, 477
Substance-related disorders, 502–503
Success. *See* Achievement
Sucking reflex, 105
Sudden death, 396–397
Suicide
 age and, 535
 common thoughts and feelings, 536–537
 crisis intervention, 537
 ethnicity and, 535
 gender and, 535
 immediate causes, 536
 marital status and, 535–536
 prevention, 536
Superego, 427
Superordinate goals, 652–653
Superstitious behaviors, 258
Supportive therapy, 542
Surface traits, 422–423
Survey
 active learning, 2
 methods, 49–50
 text, 1
Susceptibility, hypnotic, 221
Susto, 504
Sweat lodge ceremony, 205
Sybil (Schreiber), 512
Symbolic prejudice, 651
Symbolization, 242
Sympathetic branch, 65
Synaesthesia, 340
Synapses, 60–62
Syntax, 345

Task analysis, 697
Task centering, 438
Taste, 379
Taste aversion, 379
Taste buds, 167–168
Taste, sense of, 166–168
TAT (thematic apperception test), 448–449
Telegraphic speech, 118

Telepathy, 194
Telephone therapy, 550
Television, 279–280, 658–660
Temperament, 103, 414
Temporal lobes, 78
Temporary insomnia, 213
Tension-relax method, 555
Teratogens, 101
Term schedule, 7
Terman, Lewis, 332
Territorial behavior, 684
Territorial markers, 684
Terrorism, 398, 651
Testis, 585
Testosterone, 585
Tests
  anxiety, 388
  battery, 449
  common sense beliefs, 15
  hypothesis, 24
  situational, 446
  taking skills, 7–8
Text reading, 1–2
Texture gradients, 181
Thalamus, 83
Thanatologist, 140
Thanatos, 427–428
Theory X leadership, 670–673
Theory Y leadership, 670–673
Therapy placebo effect, 565
Thirst, 383
Thomson, Donald, 295
ThomsonNow, 9
Thoughts
  basic units, 340
  brain and, 85
  concepts, 342–344
  creative, 357–360
  intuitive, 360–363
  language and, 344–349
  mental imagery, 340–341
  preoperational stage, 123
  problem solving, 351–356
  reflecting, 568–569
  restructuring, 388
  stopping, 576
  upsetting, 494
Threats, coping with, 468
Thyroid gland, 87
Time management, 6
Time out, 558
Time-limited therapy, 542
Tip-of-the-tongue (TOT) state, 300

Titchener, Edward, 27, 31
Token economies, 559
Token reinforcers, 261–262
Tomlin, Lily, 233
Top-down processing, 186
Toxic environments, 687–688
Tragedy of commons, 690–691
Training, transfer, 308–310
Trait-situation interaction, 425
Traits
  behavior prediction and, 421
  classifying, 421–423
  consistency, 425
  five-factor model, 423–425
  identifying, 421
  personality, 414–415
  positive, 440
  profiles, 422
  theories, 418, 421–426
Tranquilizers, 235
Transfer of training, 308–310
Transference, 545
Transformation, 122
Transformation rules, 346
Transvestic fetishism, 602
Traumatic stress, 467
Trepanning, 543
Trichromatic theory, 158
Trust, 136
Turn-taking, 119
Twin studies
  depression, 531
  intelligence, 336–337
  personality, 415–416
Twixters, 131
Tympanic membrane, 163
Type A personalities, 486
Type B personalities, 486

UFO abduction, 210
Umami, 166–167
Unconditional positive regard, 442
Unconditioned response, 249
Unconditioned stimulus, 249, 379
Unconscious
  awareness and, 429
  defined, 427
  psychoanalytic theory, 30
Uncritical acceptance, 22–23
Understanding, 17–18, 351
Undifferentiated schizophrenia, 521, 524
Unstructured interview, 444

Unusual Uses Test, 357
Urethra, 585
Urinary bladder, 585
Usability testing, 701–702
Uterus, 585

Vagina, 585
Vaginismus, 615
Validity scales, 447
Values reinforcement, 434
Van Gogh, Vincent, 323
Variability measure, 712–714
Variable interval (VI) schedule, 268
Variable ratio (VR) schedule, 267
Variables
  defined, 41
  in experiments, 41–42
  types of, 41–42
Vas deferens, 585
Ventromedial hypothalamus, 377
Verbal intelligence, 331
Vestibular senses, 168
Vestibular system, 170–172
Vicarious classical conditioning, 254
Vicarious desensitization, 555
Video games, 280, 337
Vigilant style, 673
Violence. *See also* Aggression
  against women, 660
  media, 658–660
  workplace, 675
Virtual reality exposure, 556
Visible spectrum, 155
Vision
  color, 158–159
  dim light adaptation, 159, 161
  dimensions, 155
  eye structure and, 155–158
  neonate's, 106
  peripheral, 157–158
  primary area, 78–79
  problems with, 155–156
  stereoscopic, 180
Visual acuity, 156
Visual agnosia, 79
Visual perception, 173–174
Visual-spatial processing, 329
Vocational interest testing, 676–678
Vos Savant, Marilyn, 331, 333
Voyeurism, 602
Vygotsky's, Lev, 126–127

Waking consciousness, 205
Warning system, 168
Washburn, Margaret, 31
Waterman, Ian, 168
Watson, John B., 28
Weapons effect, 658
Wechsler tests, 331
Weekly time schedule, 6
Wellness, 461
Wernicke's area, 78
Wertheimer, Max, 29, 31
White matter, 65
Withdrawal of love, 143
Withdrawal symptoms, 227
Women
  arousal disorder, 613–614
  orgasmic disorder, 614
  reproductive structures, 585
  sexual response, 600–601
  social support needs, 488–489
  suicide risks and, 535
  Theory Y leaders, 671
Word signals, 3
Work efficiency, 671
Workable solutions, 351
Working memory, 289, 329
Workplace
  communication, 678–670
  job analysis, 675–676
  job enrichment, 674
  job satisfaction, 673–674
  organizational culture, 674–675
  personnel, 675
  schedule changes, 374
  selection procedures, 676–678
  styles, 673–674
World Wide Web, 8
Worth, 442
Wundt, Wihelm, 27, 31

X chromosome, 585

Y chromosome, 585–586
Yerkes-Dodson law, 387
Yo-yo dieting, 379–380
You-messages, 145

Zar, 504
Zener cards, 195
Zero correlation, 717
Zone proximal development, 126
Zulus, 192

TO THE OWNER OF THIS BOOK:

I hope that you have found *Psychology: Modules for Active Learning,* Eleventh Edition, useful. So that this book can be improved in a future edition, would you take the time to complete this sheet and return it? Thank you.

School and address: _____

_____

Department: _____

Instructor's name: _____

1. What I like most about this book is: _____

_____

_____

2. What I like least about this book is: _____

_____

_____

3. My general reaction to this book is: _____

_____

_____

4. The name of the course in which I used this book is: _____

_____

5. Were all of the chapters of the book assigned for you to read? _____

   If not, which ones weren't? _____

6. In the space below, or on a separate sheet of paper, please write specific suggestions for improving this book and anything else you'd care to share about your experience in using this book.

_____

_____

_____

_____

_____

FOLD HERE

BUSINESS REPLY MAIL
FIRST-CLASS MAIL   PERMIT NO. 34   BELMONT CA

POSTAGE WILL BE PAID BY ADDRESSEE

Attn: Jaime Perkins, Psychology Editor

Thomson Wadsworth
10 Davis Dr
Belmont CA 94002-9801

NO POSTAGE
NECESSARY
IF MAILED
IN THE
UNITED STATES

FOLD HERE

OPTIONAL:

Your name: _____   Date: _____

May we quote you, either in promotion for *Psychology: Modules for Active Learning*, Eleventh Edition, or in future publishing ventures?

Yes: _____   No: _____

Sincerely yours,

Dennis Coon and John Mitterer